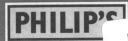

STRE

County Durham and Teesside

First published in 1996 as 'Durham' by

Philip's, a division of
Octopus Publishing Group Ltd
2-4 Heron Quays, London E14 4JP

Third colour edition 2004
Second impression with revisions 2005
DURCB

ISBN-10 0-540-08673-8 (pocket)
ISBN-13 978-0-540-08673-3 (pocket)

© Philip's 2005

This product includes mapping data licensed from
Ordnance Survey® with the permission of the
Controller of Her Majesty's Stationery Office.
© Crown copyright 2005. All rights reserved.
Licence number 100011710.

Printed and bound in Spain
by Cayfosa-Quebecor

Contents

II **Administrative and Postcode boundaries**

III **Key to map symbols**

IV **Key to map pages**

VI **Route planning**

1 **Street maps** at 2⅔ inches to 1 mile

174 **Street maps** at 1⅓ inches to 1 mile

206 **Street maps** at 2⅔ inches to 1 mile

210 **Street maps of Durham, Stockton-on-Tees and Middlesbrough city centres** at 5⅓ inches to 1 mile

216 **Index** of towns and villages

218 **Index** of streets, hospitals, industrial estates, railway stations, schools, shopping centres, universities and places of interest

Digital Data

The exceptionally high-quality mapping found in this atlas is available as digital data in TIFF format, which is easily convertible to other bitmapped (raster) image formats.

The index is also available in digital form as a standard database table. It contains all the details found in the printed index together with the National Grid reference for the map square in which each entry is named.

For further information and to discuss your requirements, please contact Philip's on 020 7644 6932 or james.mann@philips-maps.co.uk

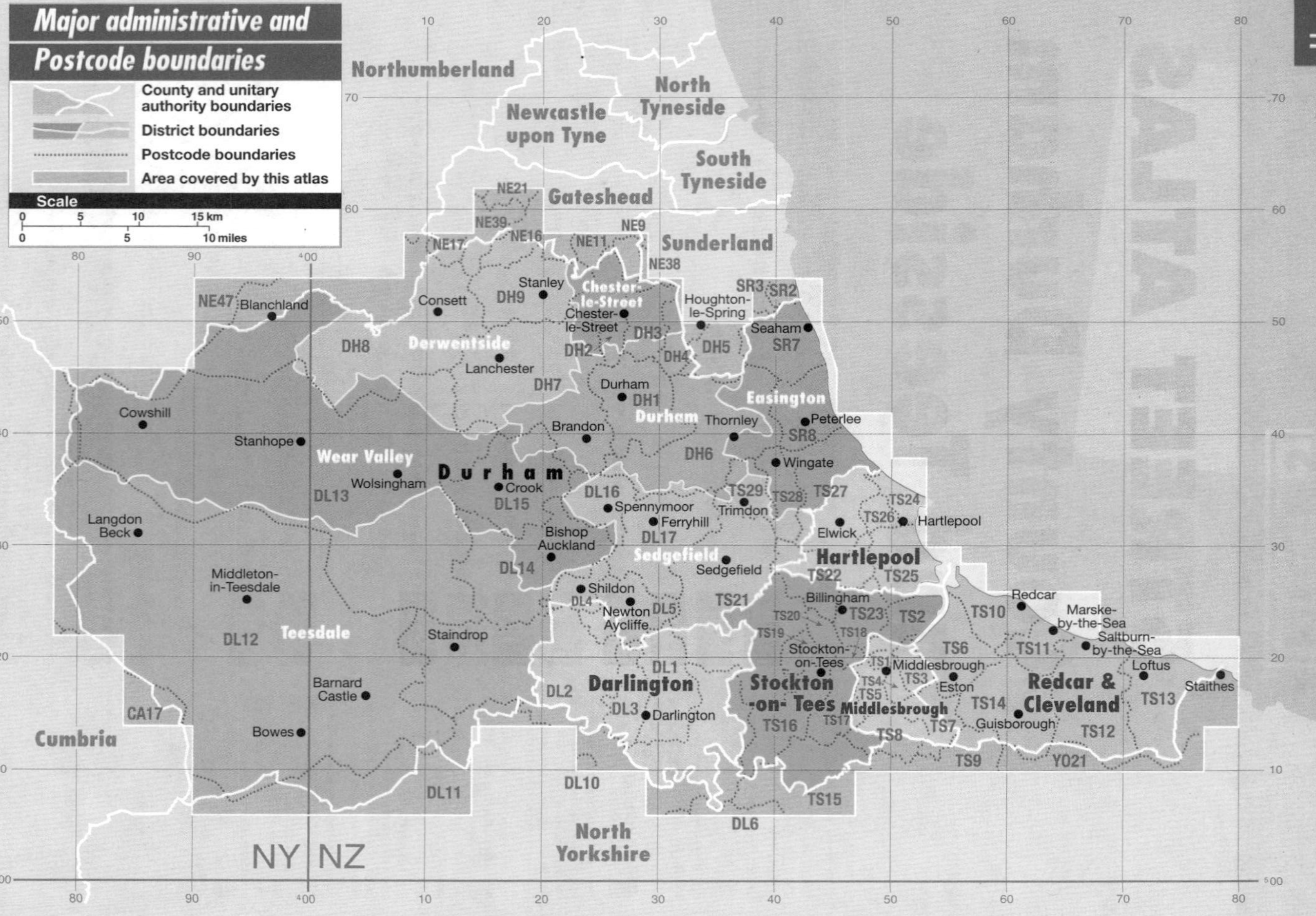

Major administrative and
Postcode boundaries

County and unitary
authority boundaries
District boundaries
Postcode boundaries
Area covered by this atlas

Scale

0   5   10   15 km
0   5   10 miles

Key to map symbols

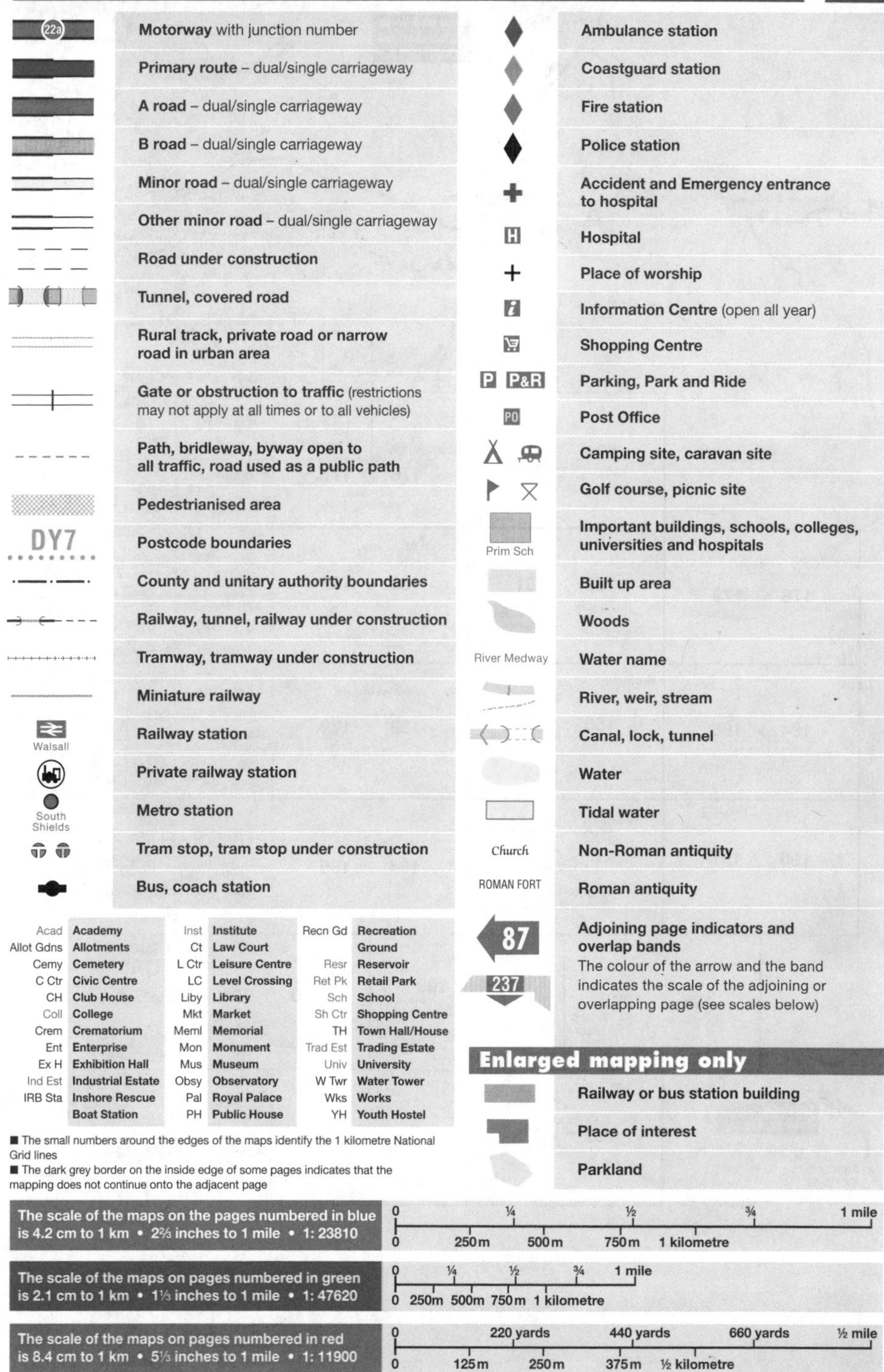

III

Symbol	Description		Symbol	Description
	Motorway with junction number (22a)		◆	Ambulance station
	Primary route – dual/single carriageway		◆	Coastguard station
	A road – dual/single carriageway		◆	Fire station
	B road – dual/single carriageway		◆	Police station
	Minor road – dual/single carriageway		✚	Accident and Emergency entrance to hospital
	Other minor road – dual/single carriageway		H	Hospital
	Road under construction		+	Place of worship
	Tunnel, covered road		i	Information Centre (open all year)
	Rural track, private road or narrow road in urban area		🛒	Shopping Centre
	Gate or obstruction to traffic (restrictions may not apply at all times or to all vehicles)		P P&R	Parking, Park and Ride
	Path, bridleway, byway open to all traffic, road used as a public path		PO	Post Office
	Pedestrianised area		⚑ ✕	Golf course, picnic site
DY7	Postcode boundaries		Prim Sch	Important buildings, schools, colleges, universities and hospitals
	County and unitary authority boundaries			Built up area
	Railway, tunnel, railway under construction			Woods
	Tramway, tramway under construction		River Medway	Water name
	Miniature railway			River, weir, stream
Walsall	Railway station			Canal, lock, tunnel
	Private railway station			Water
South Shields	Metro station			Tidal water
	Tram stop, tram stop under construction		Church	Non-Roman antiquity
	Bus, coach station		ROMAN FORT	Roman antiquity

Acad	Academy	Inst	Institute	Recn Gd	Recreation Ground		
Allot Gdns	Allotments	Ct	Law Court				
Cemy	Cemetery	L Ctr	Leisure Centre	Resr	Reservoir		
C Ctr	Civic Centre	LC	Level Crossing	Ret Pk	Retail Park		
CH	Club House	Liby	Library	Sch	School		
Coll	College	Mkt	Market	Sh Ctr	Shopping Centre		
Crem	Crematorium	Meml	Memorial	TH	Town Hall/House		
Ent	Enterprise	Mon	Monument	Trad Est	Trading Estate		
Ex H	Exhibition Hall	Mus	Museum	Univ	University		
Ind Est	Industrial Estate	Obsy	Observatory	W Twr	Water Tower		
IRB Sta	Inshore Rescue Boat Station	Pal	Royal Palace	Wks	Works		
		PH	Public House	YH	Youth Hostel		

Adjoining page indicators and overlap bands
The colour of the arrow and the band indicates the scale of the adjoining or overlapping page (see scales below)

Enlarged mapping only

Railway or bus station building
Place of interest
Parkland

■ The small numbers around the edges of the maps identify the 1 kilometre National Grid lines
■ The dark grey border on the inside edge of some pages indicates that the mapping does not continue onto the adjacent page

The scale of the maps on the pages numbered in blue is 4.2 cm to 1 km • 2⅔ inches to 1 mile • 1: 23810

The scale of the maps on pages numbered in green is 2.1 cm to 1 km • 1⅓ inches to 1 mile • 1: 47620

The scale of the maps on pages numbered in red is 8.4 cm to 1 km • 5⅓ inches to 1 mile • 1: 11900

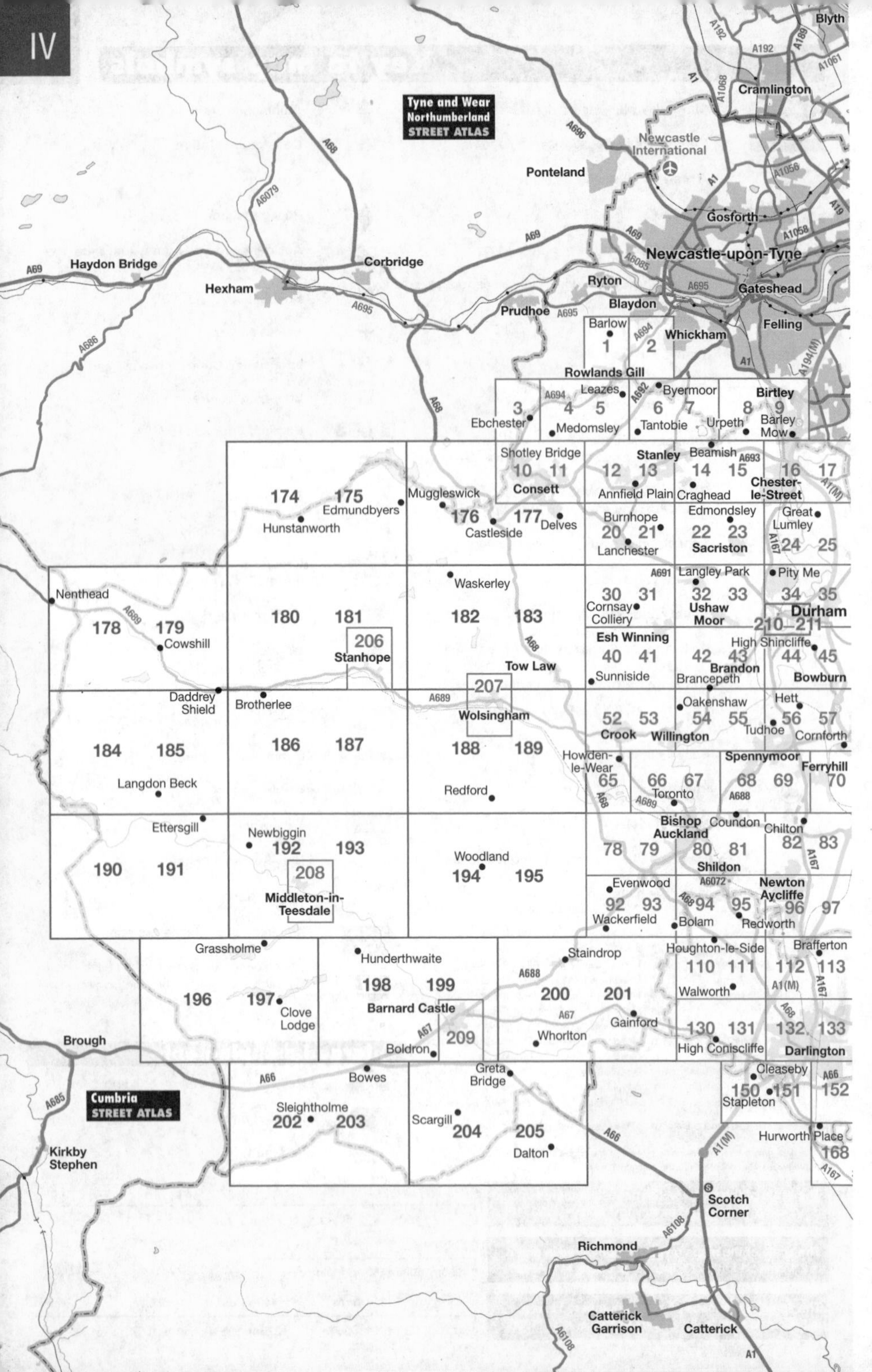
Tyne and Wear
Northumberland
STREET ATLAS
Cumbria
STREET ATLAS
Blyth
Cramlington
Newcastle International
Ponteland
Gosforth
Newcastle-upon-Tyne
Gateshead
Felling
Haydon Bridge
Hexham
Corbridge
Ryton
Blaydon
Prudhoe
Whickham
Barlow
Rowlands Gill
Leazes
Byermoor
Birtley
Ebchester
Medomsley
Tantobie
Urpeth
Barley Mow
Shotley Bridge
Consett
Stanley
Beamish
Annfield Plain
Craghead
Chester-le-Street
Muggleswick
Edmundbyers
Hunstanworth
Castleside
Delves
Burnhope
Lanchester
Edmondsley
Sacriston
Great Lumley
Waskerley
Langley Park
Pity Me
Nenthead
Cornsay Colliery
Ushaw Moor
Durham
Cowshill
Stanhope
Tow Law
Esh Winning
High Shincliffe
Sunniside
Brandon
Brancepeth
Bowburn
Daddrey Shield
Brotherlee
Wolsingham
Oakenshaw
Hett
Crook
Willington
Tudhoe
Cornforth
Howden-le-Wear
Spennymoor
Ferryhill
Langdon Beck
Redford
Toronto
Ettersgill
Newbiggin
Bishop Auckland
Coundon
Chilton
Woodland
Shildon
Evenwood
Newton Aycliffe
Middleton-in-Teesdale
Wackerfield
Bolam
Redworth
Grassholme
Hunderthwaite
Staindrop
Houghton-le-Side
Brafferton
Walworth
Clove Lodge
Barnard Castle
Gainford
Whorlton
High Coniscliffe
Darlington
Brough
Boldron
Bowes
Greta Bridge
Cleasby
Stapleton
Sleightholme
Scargill
Dalton
Hurworth Place
Kirkby Stephen
Scotch Corner
Richmond
Catterick Garrison
Catterick
1 2 3 4 5 6 7 8 9 10 11 12 13 14 15 16 17
20 21 22 23 24 25 30 31 32 33 34 35
40 41 42 43 44 45 52 53 54 55 56 57
65 66 67 68 69 70 78 79 80 81 82 83
92 93 94 95 96 97 110 111 112 113
130 131 132 133 150 151 152 168
174 175 176 177 178 179 180 181 182 183
184 185 186 187 188 189 190 191 192 193 194 195
196 197 198 199 200 201 202 203 204 205
206 207 208 209 210 211
A69 A68 A6079 A695 A686 A696 A1 A192 A189 A1068 A1061 A1056 A19 A1058 A6085 A694 A692 A693 A1(M) A167 A691 A689 A688 A6072 A67 A66 A685 A6108 A194(M)

V

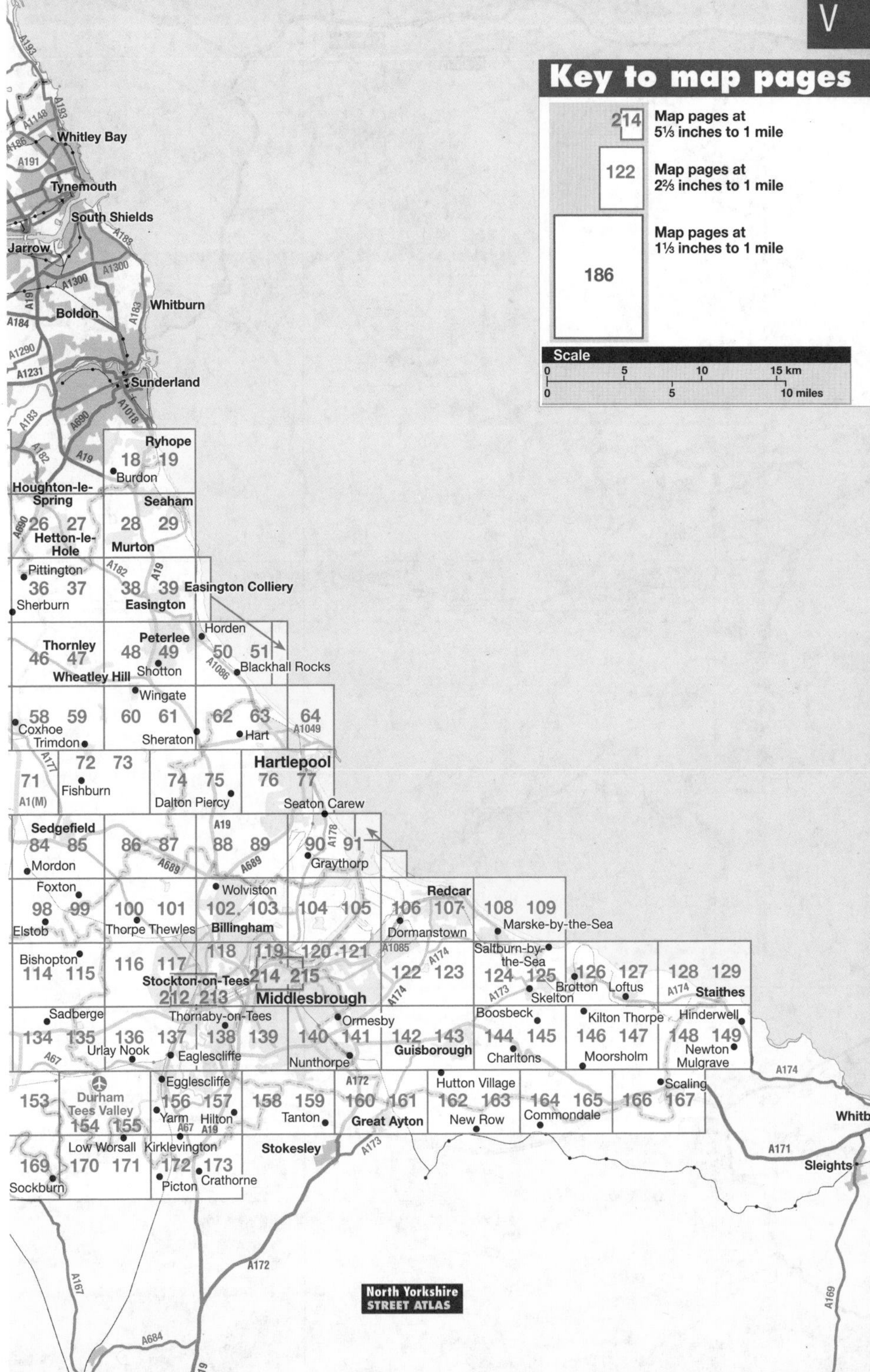

Key to map pages

214	Map pages at 5⅓ inches to 1 mile
122	Map pages at 2⅔ inches to 1 mile
186	Map pages at 1⅓ inches to 1 mile

Scale

0   5   10   15 km

0   5   10 miles

Whitley Bay

Tynemouth

South Shields

Jarrow

Boldon

Whitburn

Sunderland

Houghton-le-Spring

Ryhope

18 19

Burdon

26 27

Hetton-le-Hole

Seaham

28 29

Murton

Pittington

36 37

Sherburn

38 39 Easington Colliery

Easington

Thornley

46 47

Wheatley Hill

Peterlee

48 49

Shotton

Horden

50 51

Blackhall Rocks

58 59

Coxhoe

Trimdon

60 61

Wingate

Sheraton

62 63

Hart

64

71

Fishburn

72 73

74 75

Dalton Piercy

Hartlepool

76 77

Seaton Carew

Sedgefield

84 85

Mordon

86 87

88 89

90 91

Graythorp

Foxton

98 99

Elstob

100 101

Thorpe Thewles

Wolviston

102 103

Billingham

104 105

Redcar

106 107

Dormanstown

108 109

Marske-by-the-Sea

Bishopton

114 115

116 117

118

Stockton-on-Tees

119 120 121

214 215

212 213

Middlesbrough

Saltburn-by-the-Sea

122 123

124 125

Skelton

126 127

Brotton Loftus

128 129

Staithes

Sadberge

134 135

Urlay Nook

Thornaby-on-Tees

136 137

Eaglescliffe

138 139

Ormesby

140 141

Nunthorpe

142 143

Guisborough

Boosbeck

144 145

Charltons

Kilton Thorpe

146 147

Moorsholm

Hinderwell

148 149

Newton Mulgrave

153

Durham Tees Valley

154 155

Low Worsall

Egglescliffe

156 157

Yarm Hilton

Kirklevington

172 173

Picton Crathorne

158 159

Tanton

Hutton Village

160 161

Great Ayton

162 163

New Row

164 165

Commondale

166 167

Scaling

Whitby

169 170 171

Sockburn

Stokesley

Northallerton

North Yorkshire STREET ATLAS

Sleights

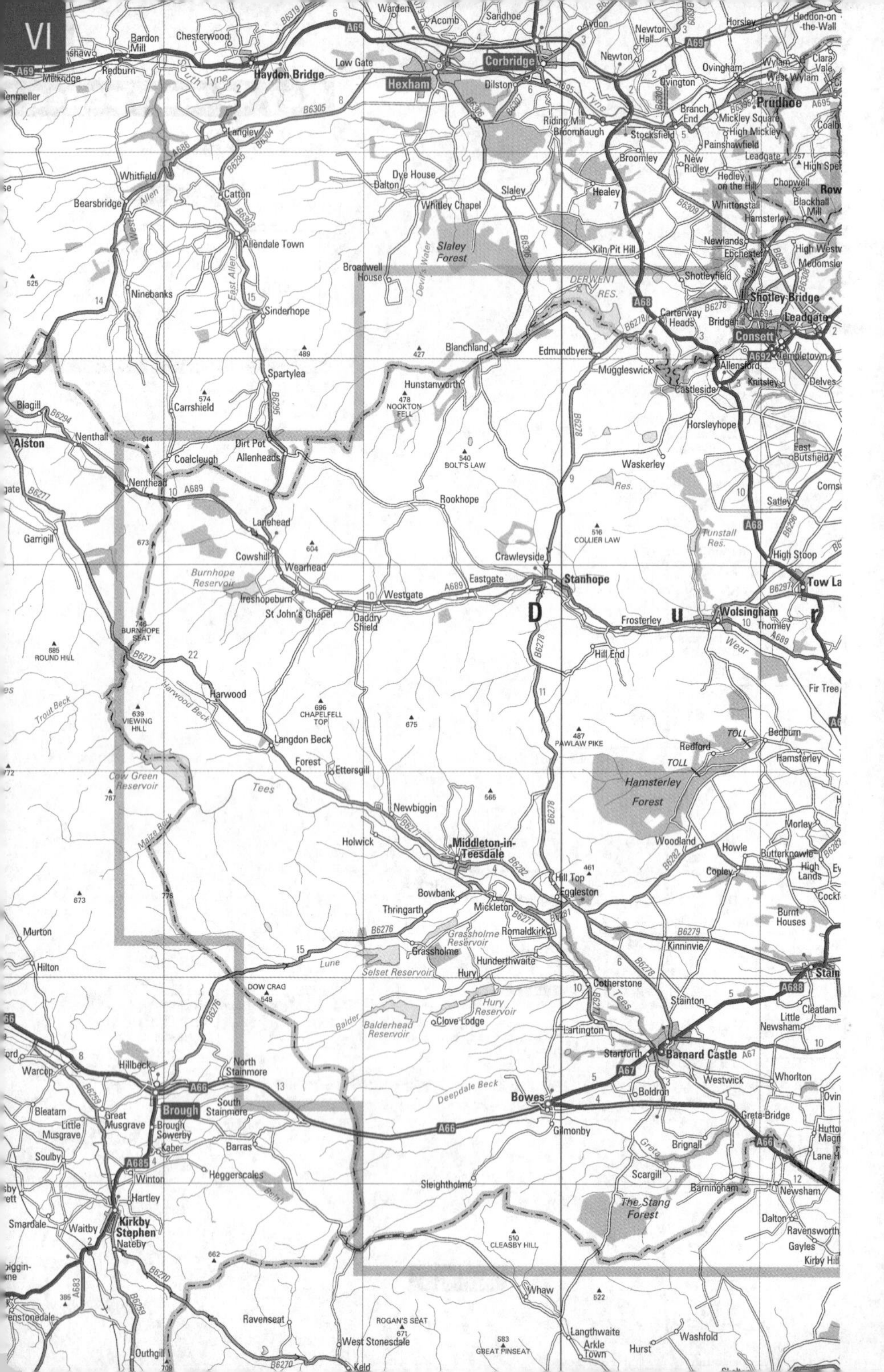
Warden
Acomb
Sandhoe
Aydon
Newton Hall
Horsley
Heddon-on-the-Wall
Bardon Mill
Chesterwood
A69
Corbridge
Newton
Ovingham
Wylam
Clara Vale
West Wylam
Redburn
Melkridge
Haydon Bridge
Low Gate
Hexham
Dilston
Ovington
Prudhoe
South Tyne
Tyne
B6305
Branch End
Mickley Square
High Mickley
Riding Mill
Broomhaugh
Stocksfield
Painshawfield
Langley
Broomley
Leadgate
High Spen
New Ridley
Whitfield
A686
B6295
B6304
Dye House
Dalton
Slaley
Healey
Hedley on the Hill
Chopwell
Bearsbridge
Catton
Whitley Chapel
Whittonstall
Blackhall Mill
Hamsterley
West Allen
B6309
B6306
Allendale Town
Slaley Forest
Kiln Pit Hill
Newlands
Ebchester
High Westwood
Medomsley
Devil's Water
Broadwell House
Shotleyfield
525
Ninebanks
East Allen
DERWENT RES.
A68
Shotley Bridge
Leadgate
Sinderhope
Carterway Heads
Bridgehill
B6278
A694
Consett
489
427
Blanchland
Edmundbyers
Muggleswick
A692
Allensford
Templetown
Spartylea
Hunstanworth
478 NOOKTON FELL
Castleside
Knitsley
Delves
574
Carrshield
Blagill
B6294
Horsleyhope
Alston
Nenthall
614
Dirt Pot
Allenheads
540 BOLT'S LAW
East Butsfield
Coalcleugh
Waskerley
Nenthead
A689
Res.
Cornsay
B6277
Rookhope
Satley
Garrigill
Lanehead
673
604
516 COLLIER LAW
Tunstall Res.
Cowshill
Crawleyside
High Stoop
Burnhope Reservoir
Wearhead
Eastgate
Stanhope
Tow Law
Ireshopeburn
Westgate
B6297
St John's Chapel
Daddry Shield
Frosterley
Wolsingham
Thornley
746 BURNHOPE SEAT
Wear
685 ROUND HILL
Hill End
Harwood
Fir Tree
Trout Beck
Harwood Beck
639 VIEWING HILL
696 CHAPELFELL TOP
675
487 PAWLAW PIKE
Langdon Beck
Bedburn
Redford
TOLL
Hamsterley
Forest
Ettersgill
Cow Green Reservoir
Tees
767
565
Hamsterley Forest
Newbiggin
Maize Beck
B6277
Holwick
Middleton-in-Teesdale
Woodland
Howle
Butterknowle
Morley
B6282
High Lands
Hill Top
461
Eggleston
Copley
776
873
Bowbank
Thringarth
Mickleton
Cockfield
Romaldkirk
Grassholme Reservoir
B6279
B6281
Burnt Houses
Murton
B6276
Grassholme
Kinninvie
Hilton
Lune
Hunderthwaite
Selset Reservoir
Hury
DOW CRAG 549
Cotherstone
Stainton
A688
Staindrop
Hury Reservoir
Balder
Balderhead Reservoir
Clove Lodge
Lartington
Cleatlam
Little Newsham
Warcop
Hillbeck
North Stainmore
Startforth
Barnard Castle
A67
Brough
South Stainmore
Deepdale Beck
Bowes
Westwick
Whorlton
Bleatarn
Great Musgrave
Little Musgrave
Brough Sowerby
Kaber
Barras
Boldron
A66
Gilmonby
Greta Bridge
Soulby
A685
Winton
Heggerscales
Greta
Brignall
Scargill
Hartley
Belah
Sleightholme
Barningham
Newsham
The Stang Forest
Smardale
Waitby
Kirkby Stephen
Nateby
510 CLEASBY HILL
Dalton
Ravensworth
Gayles
Kirby Hill
662
B6270
A683
385
Whaw
522
Ravenstonedale
B6259
Ravenseat
ROGAN'S SEAT 671
Langthwaite
Arkle Town
Washfold
583 GREAT PINSEAT
West Stonesdale
Hurst
Outhgill
Keld

Route Planning

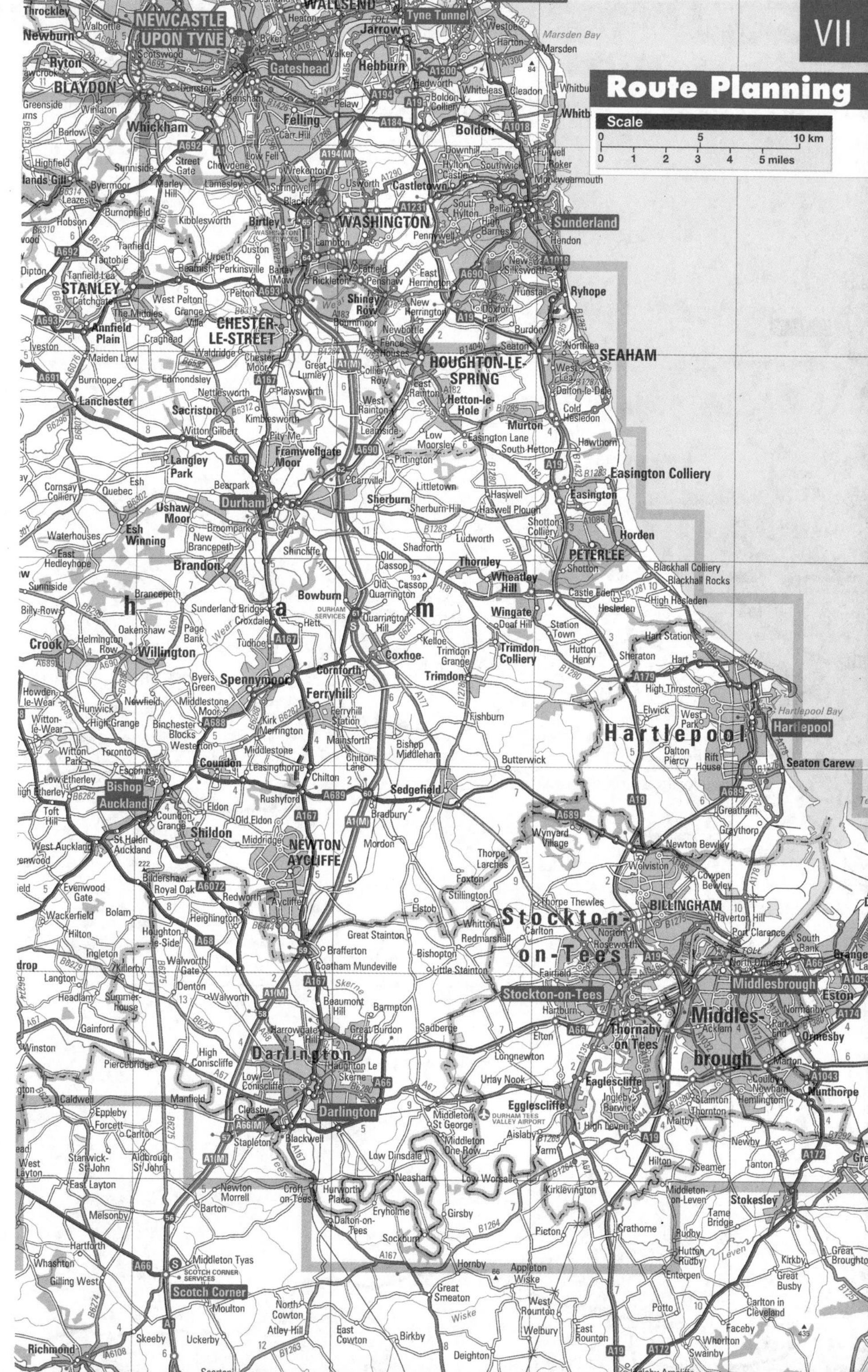
Scale
0
5
10 km
0
1
2
3
4
5 miles
NEWCASTLE UPON TYNE
Gateshead
WALLSEND
Tyne Tunnel
Jarrow
Hebburn
BLAYDON
Whickham
Felling
Boldon
Sunderland
WASHINGTON
Castletown
STANLEY
CHESTER-LE-STREET
HOUGHTON-LE-SPRING
SEAHAM
Ryhope
Lanchester
Sacriston
Durham
Easington Colliery
Easington
Horden
PETERLEE
Brandon
Bowburn
Crook
Willington
Spennymoor
Ferryhill
Hartlepool
Hartlepool Bay
Seaton Carew
Bishop Auckland
Shildon
NEWTON AYCLIFFE
Sedgefield
BILLINGHAM
Stockton-on-Tees
Middlesbrough
Thornaby on Tees
Eaglescliffe
Darlington
DURHAM TEES VALLEY AIRPORT
Yarm
Stokesley
Scotch Corner
SCOTCH CORNER SERVICES
Richmond
Nunthorpe
Marsden Bay

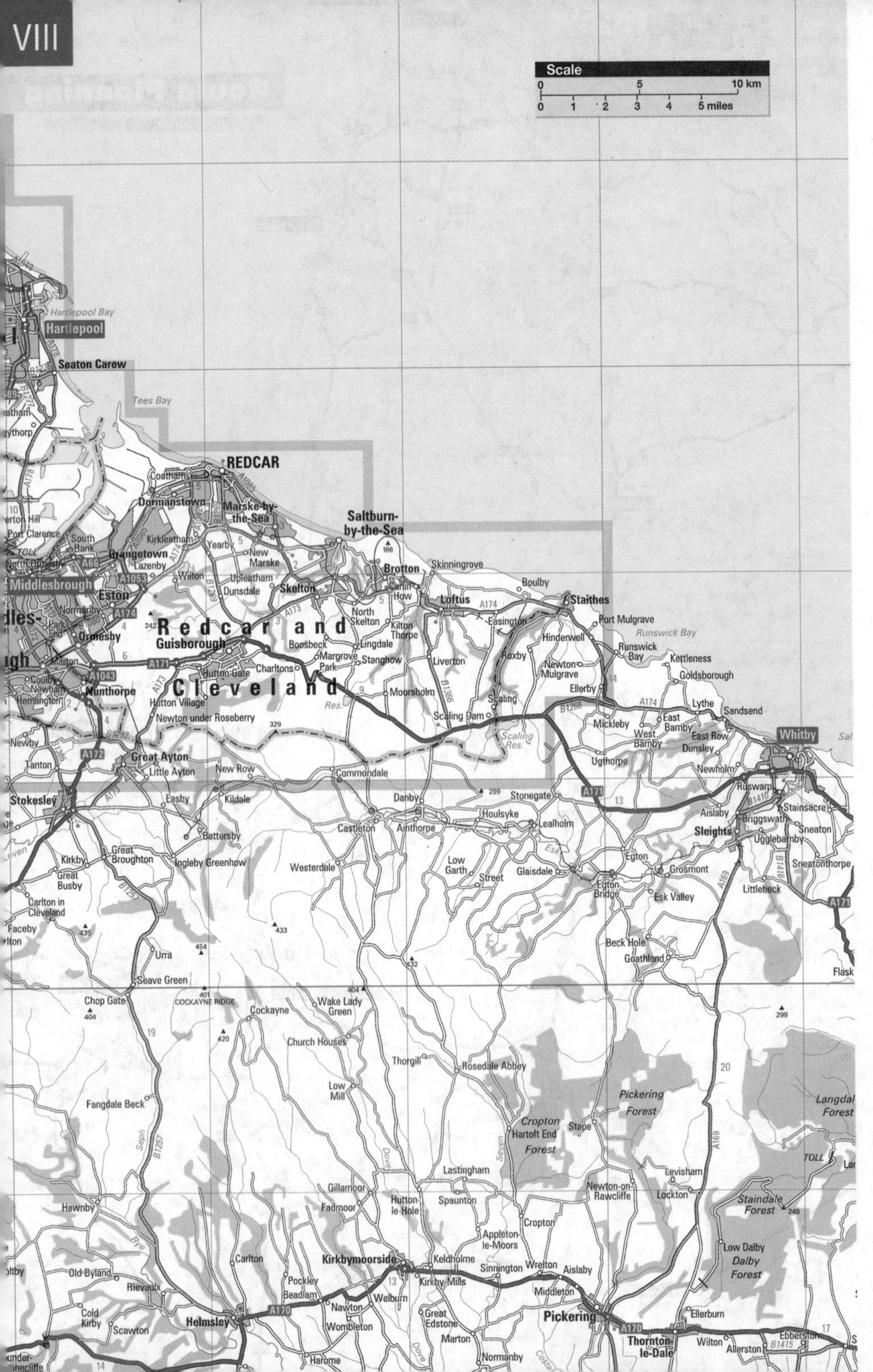
Scale
0
5
10 km
0
1
2
3
4
5 miles
Hartlepool Bay
Hartlepool
Seaton Carew
Tees Bay
REDCAR
Coatham
Dormanstown
Marske-by-the-Sea
Saltburn-by-the-Sea
Port Clarence
South Bank
Grangetown
Kirkleatham
Yearby
New Marske
Lazenby
TOLL
North Ormesby
A66
A1053
Middlesbrough
Eston
Wilton
Upleatham
Dunsdale
Skelton
Brotton
Skinningrove
Carlin How
Boulby
Loftus
Staithes
A174
Easington
Port Mulgrave
Runswick Bay
Normanby
A174
242
Redcar and Cleveland
North Skelton
Kilton Thorpe
Park End
Ormesby
Guisborough
Boosbeck
Lingdale
Hinderwell
Runswick Bay
Kettleness
Goldsborough
Marton
A171
A1043
Hutton Gate
Charltons
Margrove Park
Stanghow
Liverton
Roxby
Newton Mulgrave
Coulby Newham
Hemlington
Nunthorpe
A173
Hutton Village
Moorsholm
B1366
Scaling
Ellerby
Res.
Scaling Dam
B1266
A174
Lythe
Sandsend
Newton under Roseberry
329
Mickleby
East Barnby
West Barnby
East Row
Dunsley
Whitby
Newby
A172
Great Ayton
Scaling Res.
Tanton
Little Ayton
New Row
Commondale
Ugthorpe
Newholm
Stokesley
Easby
Kildale
299
Danby
Stonegate
A171
Ruswarp
Stainsacre
Houlsyke
Lealholm
Aislaby
Briggswath
B1410
Castleton
Ainthorpe
Sleights
Sneaton
Battersby
Ugglebarnby
Esk
Leven
Kirkby
Great Broughton
Ingleby Greenhow
Westerdale
Low Garth
Egton
Grosmont
Sneatonthorpe
Great Busby
Street
Glaisdale
Egton Bridge
B1416
Littlebeck
Esk Valley
A171
Carlton in Cleveland
B1125
A169
Faceby
435
433
Beck Hole
454
Goathland
Urra
432
Flask
Seave Green
Chop Gate
404
401
COCKAYNE RIDGE
Wake Lady Green
299
404
Cockayne
19
420
Church Houses
Thorgill
Rosedale Abbey
20
Low Mill
Pickering Forest
Langdale Forest
Fangdale Beck
Cropton
Hartoft End
Forest
Stape
Seph
B1257
Seven
Dove
A169
TOLL
Lastingham
Levisham
Gillamoor
Newton-on-Rawcliffe
Lockton
Fadmoor
Hutton-le-Hole
Spaunton
Staindale Forest
248
Hawnby
Cropton
Appleton-le-Moors
Rye
Low Dalby
Dalby Forest
Carlton
Kirkbymoorside
Keldholme
Old Byland
Pockley
Sinnington
Wrelton
Aislaby
Rievaulx
Beadlam
13
Kirkby Mills
Middleton
Nawton
Welburn
A170
Cold Kirby
Scawton
Helmsley
Wombleton
Great Edstone
Pickering
A170
Ellerburn
Marton
Thornton-le-Dale
Wilton
Allerston
B1415
Ebberston
17
14
Harome
Normanby
Dove
Costa

2

Tyne & Wear STREET ATLAS
A B C D E F
8 7 61 6 5 60 4 3 59 2 1 58
14 15 16
Greenside
Reeley Mires Farm
NE40
Reeley Mires West Wood
Reeley Mires Wood
Barlow Burn
Chicken's Wood
Brockwell
Little Brockwell
SELBY'S GRAVE
SILVERDALE DR 1
WAVERLEY CL 2
HARTSIDE CRES 3
WEST LA 4
Barlow Letch
BARLOW LA
NE21
North Farm
South Farm
Norman's Riding Wood
Water Gate Sewage Works
Huntley Gill
Barlow Gill Wood
The Black Horse (PH)
Barlow
Ricklees Farm
Spenside Farm
Martin's Wood
BARLOW RD
GARESFIELD LA
Winlaton Care Village
BARLOW CRES
BARLOW FELL RD
Barlow Fell
Pawston Birks
PAWSTON RD
1 FRONT RD
2 STROTHERS RD
Lillycrook Hill
High Thornley
B6315 ROGUES LA
RAMSAY ST
WATSON ST
AGED MINERS' HOMES
ASHTREE LA
Resr
COLLINGDON RD
COLLINGDON GN
WISHART TERR
HIGH SPEN CT
ASHFIELD CT
Spen Banks
Sherburn Tower Farm
HOLLINHILL LA
WEST HIGH HORSE CL
SPEN BURN
GREENLEA CL
FELL VIEW
DENE VIEW
STOKER TERR
SCHOOL LA
Hookergate Sch
High Spen
SPEN LA
Spen Burn
Sherburn Green Wood
NE39
HUGAR RD
B6315
WOODLANDS CL
ERRWOOD CRES
Low Spen
BURNOP TERR
ROBSON TERR
BEECHWOOD
WOOD TERR
CHOPWELL WOODS RD
HOOKERGATE LA
Hooker Gate
Low Spen Farm
Low Spen Burn
WILLIAM MORRIS AVE
WOODLEA RD
NORTH VIEW W
NORTH VIEW
A J COOK'S COTTS
ENGEL ST
KEIR HARDIE ST
SOUTH VIEW W
SOUTH VIEW E
COWELL GR
DENE VIEW
THE GREEN
EAST VIEW
PONTOP VIEW
HOLLINSIDE TERR
BARKWOOD RD
LEAZES VIEW
VALLEY VIEW
PARK RD
WHINFIELD TERR
SMAILES LA
Cemy
St Joseph's RC Prim Sch
Highfield Com Prim Sch
HILLCROFT
Highfield
WELLFIELD RD
MARGARET TERR
NELL TERR
OLGA TERR
ALLOY TERR
GLENCOE RISE
GLENCOE TERR
VICTORIA TERR
WOODSIDE WLK
WHINFIELD WAY
LINTZFORD LA
ALBERT ST
ALEXANDRA ST
Pallis Burn
Beda Hills
Whinfield Ind Est
LOW WEST AVE
WEST AVE
CROSS TERR
ORCHARD AVE
ORCHARD DENE
ORCHARD RD
DENE AVE
DENE RD
WINGROVE
BURNSIDE RD
WOODLANDS RD
REDSTART CT
STEWARTSFIELD
SOUTH SHERBURN
KELL'S WAY
MIDDLETON AVE
Liby
NORMAN RD
Rowlands Gill
STRATHMORE AVE
STRATHMORE RD B6315
A694 DIPWOOD RD
RIVERSIDE WAY
DERWENT AVE
STIRLING AVE
STIRLING LA
DERWENT VALLEY COTTS
Derwent Bridge
THE GROVE
TAYLOR AVE
THE AVENUE
THE CRESCENT
TOWNLEY FIELDS
HOLLYDENE
WINDSOR CT
STATION RD
BURNOPFIELD RD B6314
River Derwent
BUSTY BANK
B6314
A694 LOCKHAUGH RD
COWEN TERR
NORWOOD CRES
THORNLEY VIEW
THORNFIELD PL
CHAPEL VIEW
GLEN CL
ASHTREE CL
SHERBURN PARK DR
SHERBURN GN
POWTHAUGH
AVON CL
Sch
DOMINIES CL
HILLSIDE CL
CARNFORTH GDNS
SNIPES DENE
GILL RD
BROCKWELL DR
ROOKSWOOD GDNS
GARESFIELD GDNS
LILLYCROFT
SOUTHWOOD CRES
LILLEY TERR
ROWLAND BURN WAY
FARNDALE CL
GLENDALE CL
MELDON WAY
BEVERLEY DR
DENHAM
KNOBBYENDS LA
REDESDALE AVE

5
2

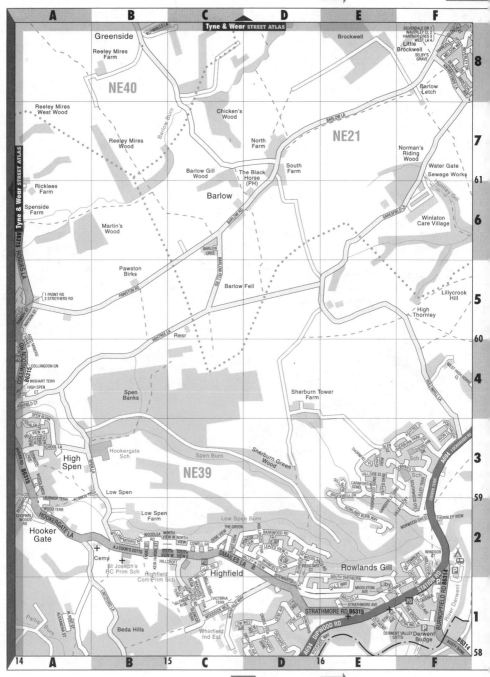

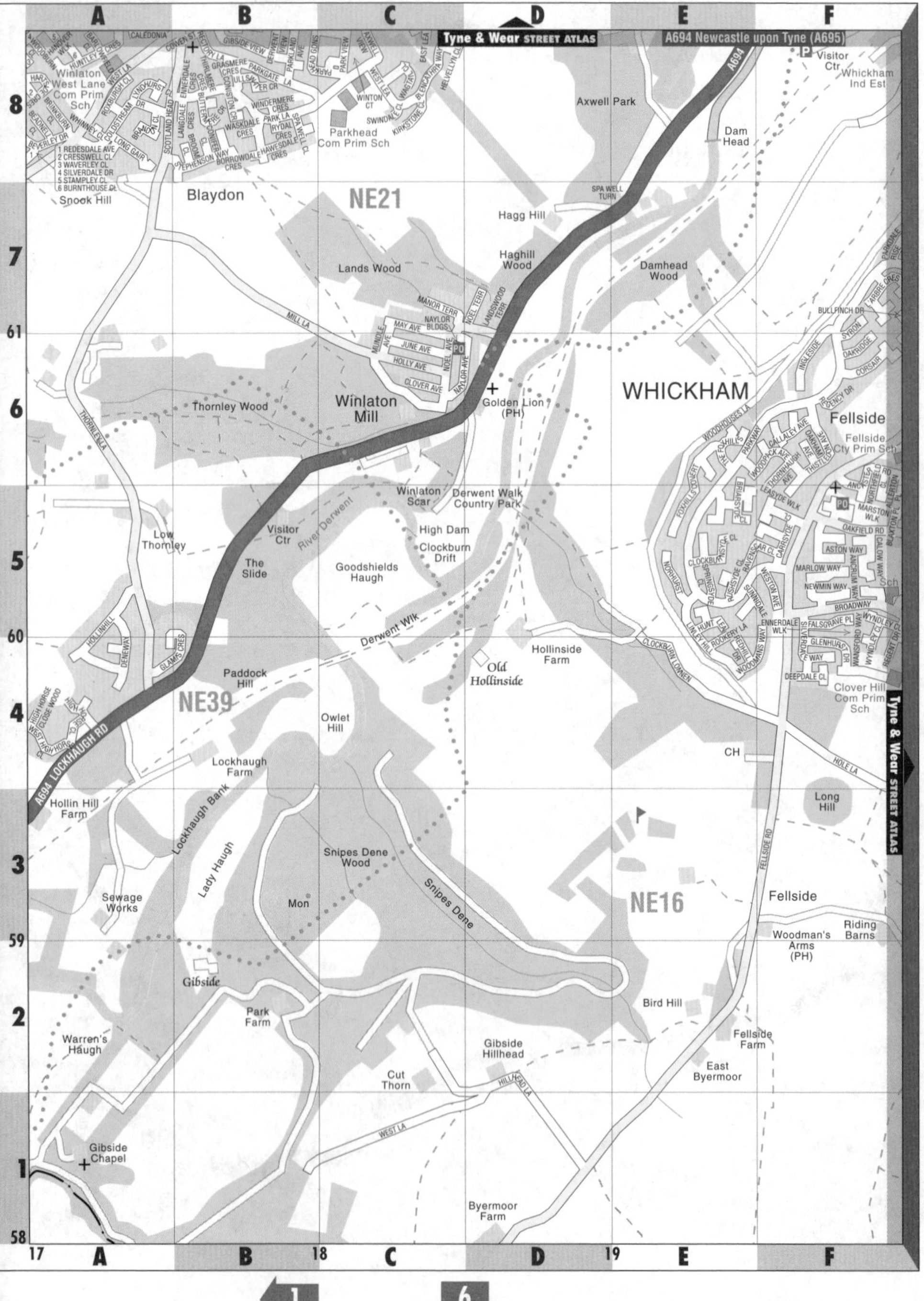

A **B** **C** **D** **E** **F**

Visitor Ctr
Whickham Ind Est

8

Winlaton
West Lane
Com Prim
Sch

1 REDESDALE AVE
2 CRESSWELL CL
3 WAVERLEY CL
4 SILVERDALE DR
5 STAMPLEY CL
6 BURNTHOUSE CL

Parkhead
Com Prim Sch

Axwell Park

Dam
Head

Blaydon

NE21

Hagg Hill

7

Lands Wood

Haghill
Wood

Damhead
Wood

BULLFINCH DR

61

MANOR TERR

MAY AVE
NAYLOR
BLDGS

HOLLY AVE

CLOVER AVE

6

Thornley Wood

Winlaton
Mill

Golden Lion
(PH)

WHICKHAM

Fellside

Fellside,
Cty Prim Sch

PO

Winlaton
Scar

Derwent Walk
Country Park

5

Low
Thornley

Visitor
Ctr

The
Slide

River Derwent

Goodshields
Haugh

High Dam
Clockburn
Drift

ASTON WAY

MARLOW WAY

NEWMIN WAY

BROADWAY

60

Derwent Wlk

Hollinside
Farm

Clover Hill
Com Prim
Sch

Paddock
Hill

Old
Hollinside

4

NE39

Owlet
Hill

CH

HOLE LA

Hollin Hill
Farm

Lockhaugh
Farm

Long
Hill

3

Sewage
Works

Lockhaugh
Bank

Lady Haugh

Snipes Dene
Wood

Mon

Snipes Dene

NE16

Fellside

Woodman's
Arms
(PH)

Riding
Barns

59

Gibside

Park
Farm

Bird Hill

Fellside
Farm

2

Warren's
Haugh

Gibside
Hillhead

East
Byermoor

Cut
Thorn

HILLSIDE LA

WEST LA

1

Gibside
Chapel

Byermoor
Farm

58

17 **A** **B** 18 **C** **D** 19 **E** **F**

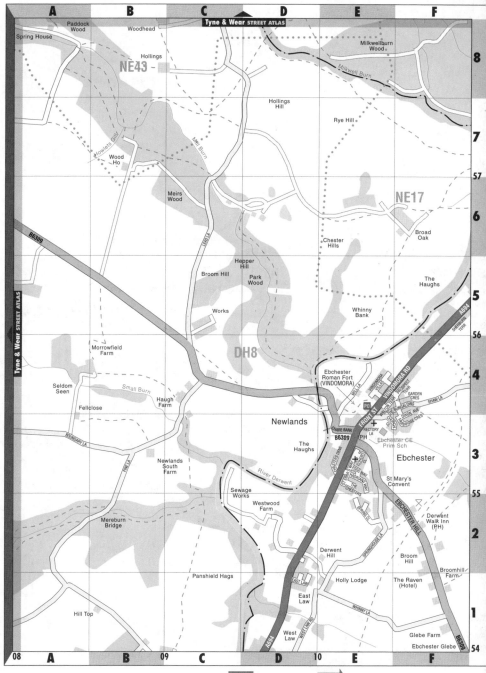

4
A
B
C
D
E
F
Tyne & Wear STREET ATLAS
Paddock Wood
Spring House
Woodhead
Hollings
NE43
Milkwellburn Wood
Milkwell Burn
Hollings Hill
Rye Hill
Howlets Gill
Mill Burn
Wood Ho
Meirs Wood
NE17
Broad Oak
Chester Hills
B6309
LEAD LA
Hepper Hill
Broom Hill
Park Wood
The Haughs
Whinny Bank
Works
A694
SHERBURN TERR
Morrowfield Farm
DH8
Ebchester Roman Fort (VINDOMORA)
VINDOMORA VILLAS
VINDOMORA RD
PROSPECT TERR
GARDEN CRES
SHAW LA
MILL LA
Seldom Seen
Small Burn
Haugh Farm
PO
FRONT ST
WALTON TERR
THE BUNGALOWS
DIXON AVE
FAIRBRIDGE CRES
CHURCH CL
Fellclose
Newlands
CHARE BANK
RECTORY LA
BOUNDARY LA
B6309
PH
Ebchester CE Prim Sch
The Haughs
Ebchester
FINE LA
Newlands South Farm
CHESTERS DENE
COHORT CL
FOSS WAY
ST EBBA'S WAY
HADRIANS WAY
THE CHESTERS
River Derwent
St Mary's Convent
Sewage Works
Westwood Farm
SPRING CL
EBCHESTER HILL
Derwent Walk Inn (PH)
Mereburn Bridge
SPRINGHOUSE LA
Derwent Hill
Broom Hill
Broomhill Farm
Panshield Hags
EAST LAW
Holly Lodge
The Raven (Hotel)
East Law
WHINNY LA
Hill Top
West Law
WEST LAW RD
A694
Glebe Farm
Ebchester Glebe
B6309
8
7
57
6
5
56
4
3
55
2
1
54
08
09
10
10
4

3

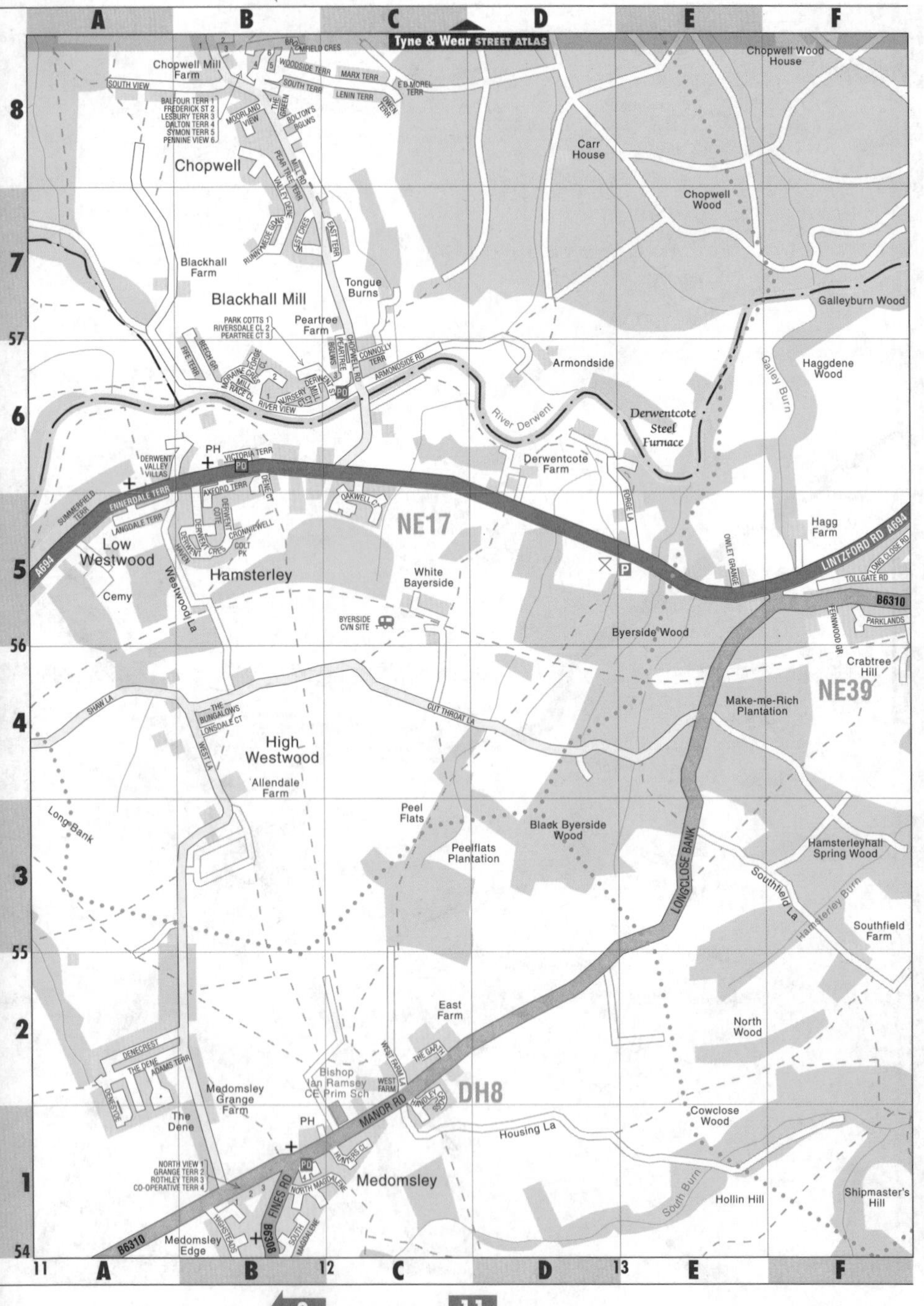

Tyne & Wear STREET ATLAS
Chopwell Mill Farm
Chopwell
Blackhall Farm
Blackhall Mill
Tongue Burns
Peartree Farm
Carr House
Chopwell Wood
Chopwell Wood House
Galleyburn Wood
Haggdene Wood
Armondside
River Derwent
Derwentcote Steel Furnace
Derwentcote Farm
NE17
Low Westwood
Hamsterley
Cemy
Westwood La
White Bayerside
Byerside Wood
Hagg Farm
LINTZFORD RD A694
B6310
Crabtree Hill
NE39
Make-me-Rich Plantation
High Westwood
Allendale Farm
Long Bank
Peel Flats
Peelflats Plantation
Black Byerside Wood
LONGCLOSE BANK
Hamsterleyhall Spring Wood
Southfield La
Southfield Farm
East Farm
North Wood
Bishop Ian Ramsey CE Prim Sch
DH8
Medomsley Grange Farm
The Dene
MANOR RD
Cowclose Wood
Housing La
Medomsley
Hollin Hill
Shipmaster's Hill
Medomsley Edge
A694
A B C D E F

3
11

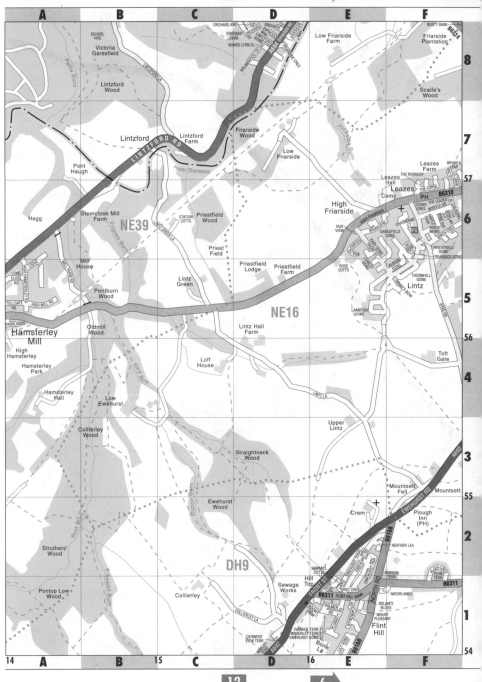

1
6

A
B
C
D
E
F
Victoria Garesfield
Lintzford Wood
Low Friarside Farm
Friarside Plantation
Scaife's Wood
Lintzford
Lintzford Farm
Friarside Wood
Low Friarside
LINTZFORD RD
River Derwent
Pont Haugh
Hagg
Steelclose Mill Farm
NE39
Priestfield Wood
Priest Field
Mill House
Pontburn Wood
Lintz Green
Priestfield Lodge
Priestfield Farm
High Friarside
Leazes Farm
Leazes Hall
Leazes
Cemy
Lintz
NE16
Hamsterley Mill
High Hamsterley
Hamsterley Park
Oldmill Wood
Lintz Hall Farm
Loft House
Toft Gate
Hamsterley Hall
Low Ewehurst
Upper Lintz
Collierley Wood
Straightneck Wood
Mountsett Fell
Mountsett
Ewehurst Wood
Crem
Plough Inn (PH)
Struthers' Wood
DH9
Hill Top
Sewage Works
Pontop Low Wood
Collierley
Flint Hill
Bone La
EWEHURST RD
FRONT ST
NORTH RD
COLLIERLEY LA
LINTZ LA
LINTZ GREEN LA
SYKE RD
HIGH FRIARSIDE
A694
A692
B6310
B6311
B6168
B6314
Red Burn
Fogoes Burn
Pont Burn
Pikewell Burn
Dipton Burn
Pallis Burn
Jockside Burn
8
7
6
5
4
3
2
1
57
56
55
54
14
15
16

12
6

5 2

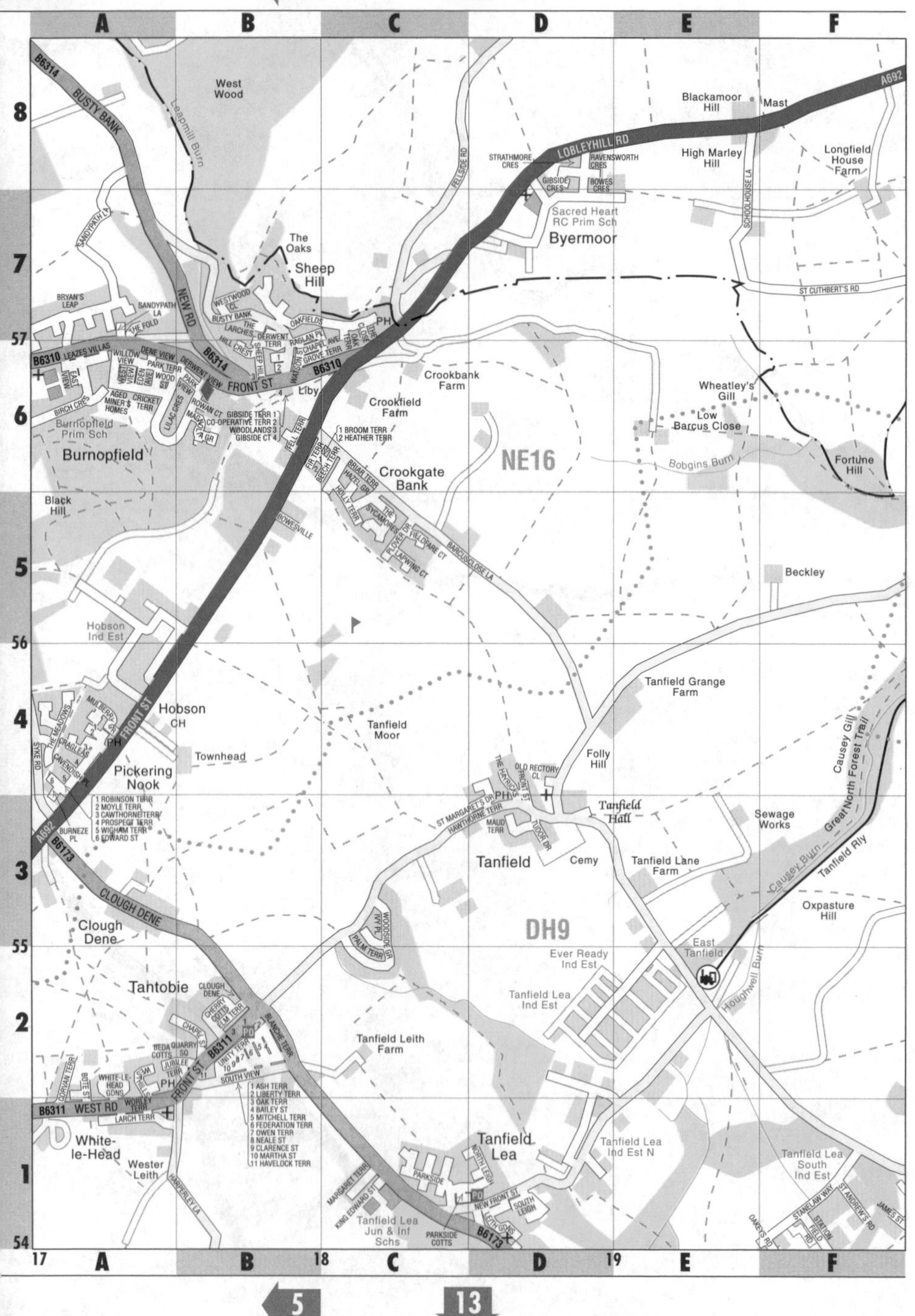
A B C D E F
8
7
57
6
5
56
4
3
55
2
1
54
17 18 19
West Wood
Leapmill Burn
BUSTY BANK
B6314
NEW RD
The Oaks
Sheep Hill
SANDYPATH LA
BRYAN'S LEAP
SANDYPATH LA
THE FOLD
WESTWOOD CL
BUSTY BANK
OAKFIELDS
RAGLAN PL
CHAPEL AVE
GROVE TERR
OAK TERR
THE CLOSE
PH
B6310
LEAZES VILLAS
DENE VIEW
DERWENT VIEW
PARK TERR
FRONT ST
Liby
BIRCH CRES
AGED MINER'S HOMES
CRICKET TERR
LILAC GRS
ROWAN CT
1 BROOM TERR
2 HEATHER TERR
FELL TERR
Burnopfield Prim Sch
Burnopfield
Crookgate Bank
Crookfield Farm
Crookbank Farm
BRIAR TERR
HAZEL GR
HOLLY TERR
THE SYCAMORES
PLOVER DR
FIELDFARE CT
LAPWING CT
BARCUSCLOSE LA
BOWESVILLE
Black Hill
FELLSIDE RD
STRATHMORE CRES
LOBLEYHILL RD
RAVENSWORTH CRES
GIBSIDE CRES
BOWES CRES
Sacred Heart RC Prim Sch
Byermoor
Blackamoor Hill
Mast
A692
High Marley Hill
SCHOOLHOUSE LA
Longfield House Farm
ST CUTHBERT'S RD
Wheatley's Gill
Low Barcus Close
Bobgins Burn
NE16
Fortune Hill
Beckley
Hobson Ind Est
Hobson
CH
Townhead
Tanfield Moor
Tanfield Grange Farm
Folly Hill
MULBERRY
THE MEADOWS
CRAGLEAS
CAVENDISH PL
STYLE RD
Pickering Nook
1 ROBINSON TERR
2 MOYLE TERR
3 CAWTHORNE TERR
4 PROSPECT TERR
5 WIGHAM TERR
6 EDWARD ST
BURNEZE PL
A692
B6173
CLOUGH DENE
Clough Dene
OLD RECTORY CL
FRONT ST
THE HAYRICKS
ST MARGARET'S DR
HAWTHORNE TERR
MAUD TERR
TUDOR DR
Tanfield Hall
Tanfield
Cemy
Tanfield Lane Farm
Sewage Works
Causey Gill
Great North Forest Trail
Tanfield Rly
Causey Burn
Oxpasture Hill
BRIAR TERR
IVY PL
WOODSIDE GR
PALM TERR
DH9
Ever Ready Ind Est
East Tanfield
Houghwell Burn
Tanfield Lea Ind Est
Tantobie
CLOUGH DENE
CHERRY COTTS
ELM TERR
BLANCHE TERR
CHAPEL ST
BEDA COTTS
QUARRY SQ
JUBILEE TERR
B6311
UNITY TERR
SOUTH VIEW
Tanfield Leith Farm
CORVAN TERR
BOTE ST
WHITE-LE-HEAD GDNS
WEST RD
WORLEY TERR
LARCH TERR
1 ASH TERR
2 LIBERTY TERR
3 OAK TERR
4 BAILEY ST
5 MITCHELL TERR
6 FEDERATION TERR
7 OWEN TERR
8 NEALE ST
9 CLARENCE ST
10 MARTHA ST
11 HAVELOCK TERR
White-le-Head
Wester Leith
HARPERLEY LA
Tanfield Lea
NORTH LEIGH
PARKSIDE
MARGARET TERR
KING EDWARD ST
NEW FRONT ST
SOUTH LEIGH
LEITH GDNS
PARKSIDE COTTS
Tanfield Lea Jun & Inf Schs
B6173
Tanfield Lea Ind Est N
Tanfield Lea South Ind Est
STANELAW WAY
STATION FIELD RD
ST ANDREW'S RD
JAMES ST
OAKEYS RD

5 13

8

A B C D E F

A692 Gateshead (A1, A184)
A6076 to A692
Tyne & Wear STREET ATLAS

8 7 57 6 5 56 4 3 55 2 1 54

Sunniside
Marley Hill Com Prim Sch
Marley Hill
CHURCH ST
LOBLEYHILL RD
A692
ST CUTHBERTS PK
ST CUTHBERT'S RD
Marley Hill
Andrews House
BURDON PLAIN
A6076
High Park Wood
Ravensworth Grange
Great North Forest Trial
BIRKLAND LA
BIRKHEADS LA
BIRKHEAD COTTS
NE16
NE11
Tanfield Rly
Andrew's House
Hedley West House Farm
HEDLEY LA
Whinnel Hill
Bobgins Burn
Hedley Fell
PH
Hotel
Hedley Hall Farm
Causey Arch
Causey Arch
Causey
Park Head
Causey Burn
Ridley Gill
Redburn Banks
Causey Gill
COPPY LA
Ridley Hill
Beamish Red Row
PH
Coppy Wood
Mill Wood
Red Burn
Beamish East Moor
Causey Hall Farm
BEAMISHBURN RD
Coppy
Beamish Burn
CAUSEY RD
Planetree House
Starling Bridge
Pockerley Hills
Beamish Burn
Beamish Hall
DH9
Great North Forest Trial
Beamish The North of England Open Air Mus
Pockerley
South Causey Farm
Carrickshill Wood
CH
Flint Mill
Beamish Park
FRANCIS ST
Park House
Home Farm
Birch Wood
High Forge
PH
1 CAUSEY WAY
2 JAMES ST
Kip Hill
Phelp's Bridge
MAHOGANY ROW
Hammer Square
HAMMER SQUARE BANK
Ousbrough Hill
A6076
ARGYLE CT
BADGER'S WOOD

20 A B 21 C D 22 E F

14
8

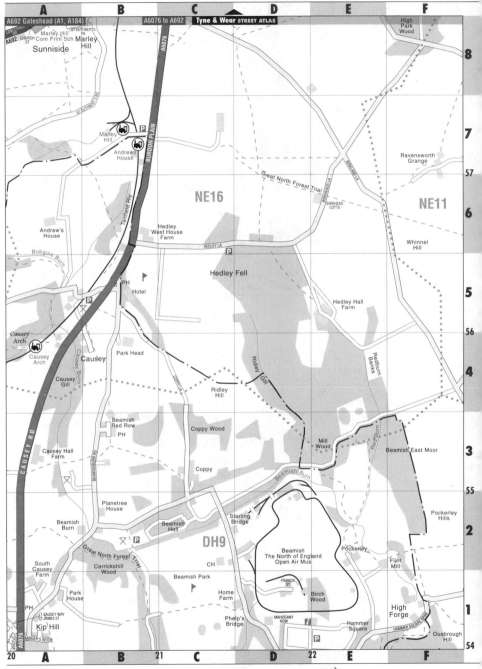

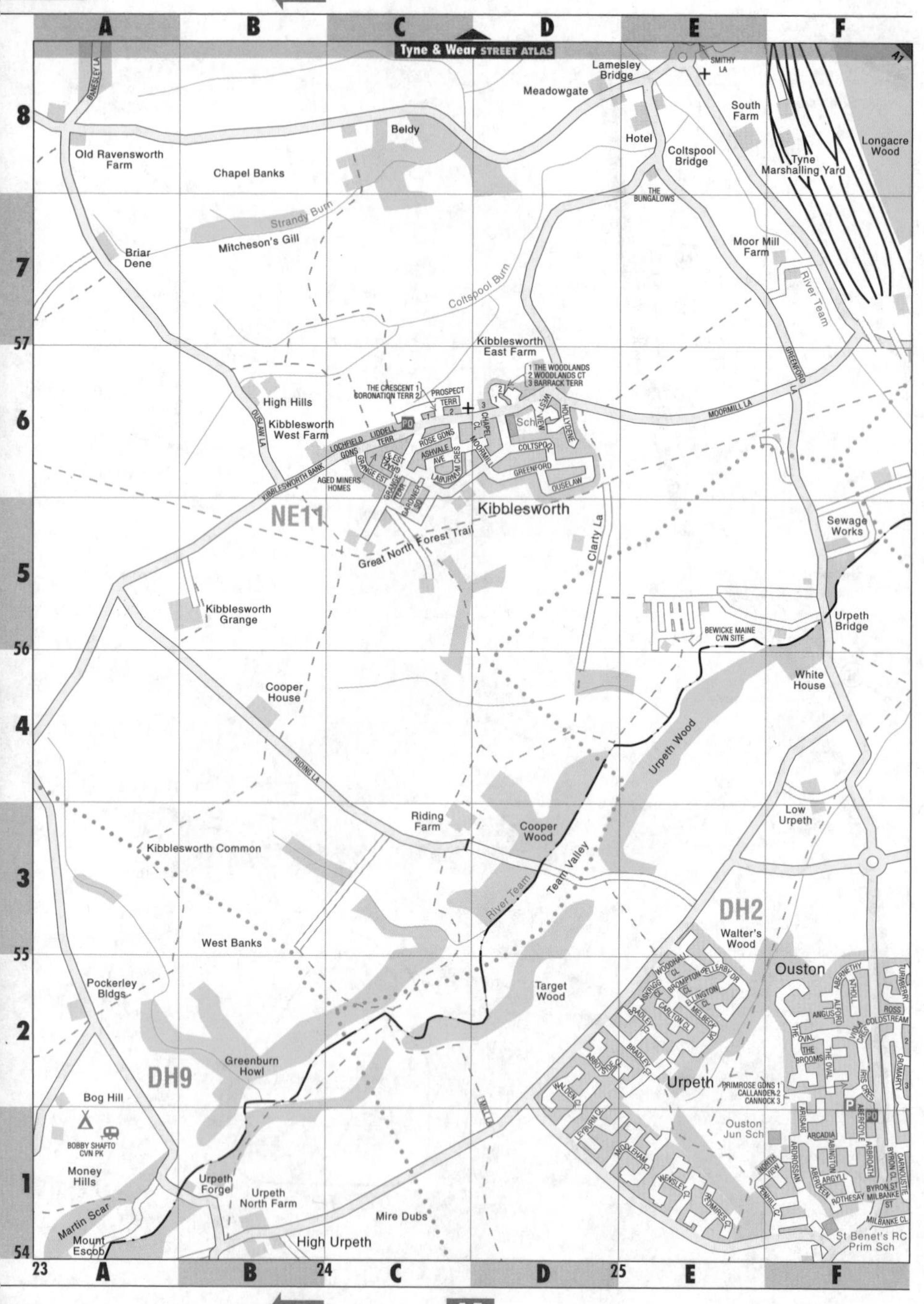

A B C D E F

8

Old Ravensworth Farm

Chapel Banks

Beldy

Meadowgate

Lamesley Bridge

SMITHY LA

South Farm

Hotel

Coltspool Bridge

Tyne Marshalling Yard

Longacre Wood

A1

PINE CT/LA

7

Briar Dene

Mitcheson's Gill

Strandy Burn

Coltspool Burn

THE BUNGALOWS

Moor Mill Farm

River Team

GREENWOOD

57

Kibblesworth East Farm

High Hills

Kibblesworth West Farm

THE CRESCENT 1
CORONATION TERR 2

PROSPECT TERR

1 THE WOODLANDS
2 WOODLANDS CT
3 BARRACK TERR

Sch

MOORMILL LA

HOLLY TERR

6

AVENUE RD

LOCKHEID BANK

ROSE GDNS

LIDDELL TERR

ASHDALE

AVENUE EST

AGED MINERS' HOMES

KIBBLESWORTH BANK

ASHDALE AVE

MURRAY

GREENFORD

COLTSPOOL

OUSELAW

NE11

Kibblesworth

Great North Forest Trail

Clarty La

5

Kibblesworth Grange

Cooper House

BEWICKE MAINE CVN SITE

Urpeth Bridge

Sewage Works

White House

56

RIDING LA

4

Riding Farm

Cooper Wood

Urpeth Wood

Low Urpeth

3

Kibblesworth Common

West Banks

River Team

Team Valley

DH2

Walter's Wood

Ouston

55

Pockerley Bldgs

Target Wood

MACDONALD CL

BROMPTON CL

CELLSFIELD CL

INGSTON

METCALF

Urpeth

PRIMROSE GDNS 1
CALLANDER 2
CANNOCK 3

Ouston Jun Sch

ALEXANDER

MACDUFF

COLDSTREAM

ANGUS

THE BROOMS

ROSS

THE OVAL

CANMORE

DALE

2

DH9

Greenburn Howl

Bog Hill

BOBBY SHAFTO CVN PK

Money Hills

LINACRE

WHITTLE

MOSS TERRACE

MOSSDALE

BRANDLING

DUNECHT

ARCADIA

BYRON ST
MILBANKE ST

ROSS

RUTHESAY

ARGYLL

LAMMARY

DANSDALE

DRUMBURGH CL

1

Martin Scar

Mount Escob

Urpeth Forge

Urpeth North Farm

High Urpeth

Mire Dubs

LIMEA

Ouston

St Benet's RC Prim Sch

54

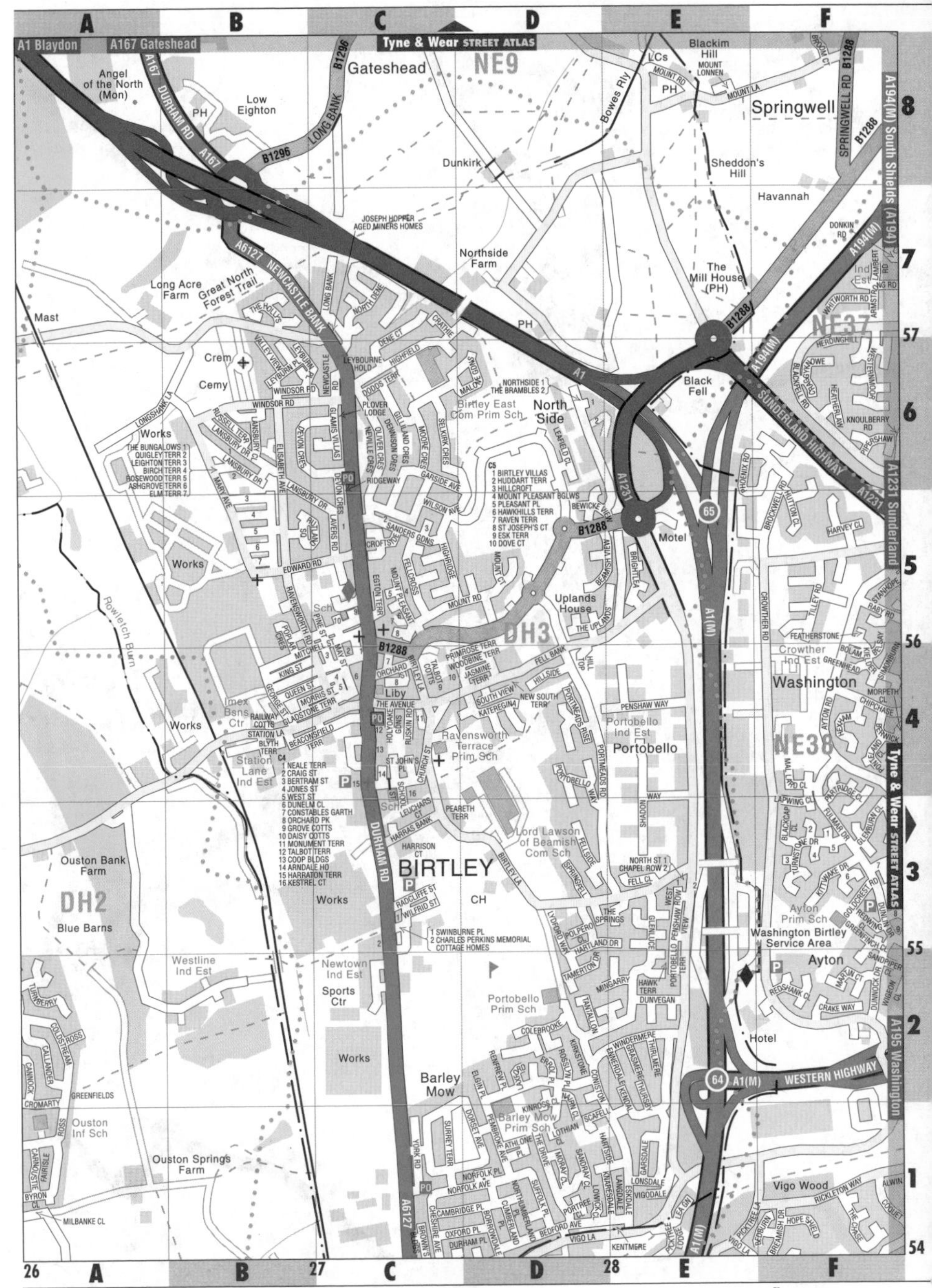

Tyne & Wear STREET ATLAS

Gateshead NE9

A1 Blaydon A167 Gateshead

Springwell

Angel of the North (Mon)

Low Eighton

Dunkirk

Blackim Hill

Sheddon's Hill

Havannah

Northside Farm

The Mill House (PH)

NE37

Long Acre Farm

Great North Forest Trail

JOSEPH HOPPER AGED MINERS HOMES

57

Mast

Black Fell

Northside Com Prim Sch

North Side

Crem

Cemy

Birtley East Com Prim Sch

Knoulberry Rd

6

Works

THE BUNGALOWS 1
QUIGLEY TERR 2
LEIGHTON TERR 3
BIRCHTERR 4
BOREWOOD TERR 5
ASHGROVE TERR 6
ELM TERR 7

CS
1 BIRTLEY VILLAS
2 HUDDART TERR
3 HILLCROFT
4 MOUNT PLEASANT BGLWS
5 PLEASANT PL
6 HAWKHILLS TERR
7 RAVEN TERR
8 ST JOSEPH'S CT
9 ESK TERR
10 DOVE CT

65

Works

B1288

Motel

5

Uplands House

DH3

56

Crowther Ind Est Greenwell

Washington

B1288

NE38

Ravensworth Terrace Prim Sch

Portobello Ind Est

Portobello

4

Ouston Bank Farm

DH2

Blue Barns

Station Lane Ind Est

1 NEALE TERR
2 CRAIG ST
3 BERTRAM ST
4 JONES ST
5 WEST ST
6 DUNELM CL
7 CONSTABLES GARTH
8 ORCHARD PK
9 GROVE COTTS
10 DAISY COTTS
11 MONUMENT TERR
12 TALBOT TERR
13 COOP BLDGS
14 ARNDALE HO
15 HARRATON TERR
16 KESTREL CT

Pearth Terr

Lord Lawson of Beamish Com Sch

Washington Birtley Service Area

Ayton Prim Sch

3

Ayton

BIRTLEY

CH

55

Westline Ind Est

Newtown Ind Est

Sports Ctr

1 SWINBURNE PL
2 CHARLES PERKINS MEMORIAL COTTAGE HOMES

The Springs

Hotel

A1(M) WESTERN HIGHWAY

2

Greenfields

Ouston Inf Sch

Works

Portobello Prim Sch

Barley Mow

Barley Mow Prim Sch

64

Vigo Wood

1

Ouston Springs Farm

MILBANKE CL

Vigo La

54

F3
1 WHEATEAR CL
2 FIELDFARE CL
3 STONECHAT CL
4 CORMORANT CL
5 PLOVER CL
6 WHITETHROAT CL
7 GLENHOLME CL
8 TEAL CL
9 WREN CL

176

3

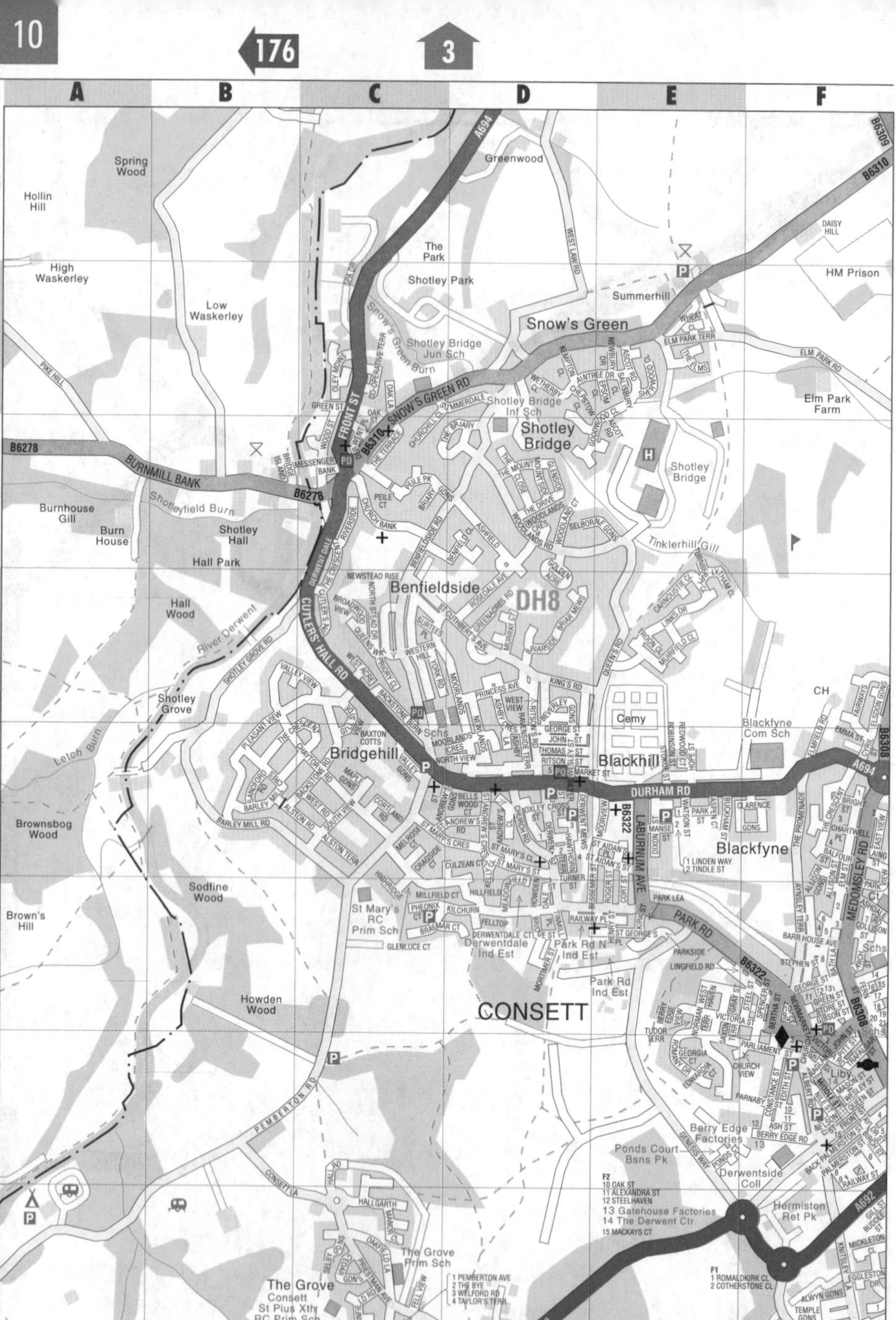

176

177

D4	F2	F3	10 PROSPECT ST	20 HARTINGTON ST
1 TEMPLAR ST	1 JOHN STREET SQ	1 JAMESON ST	11 GARDEN CL	21 HERBERT ST
2 HAWTHORN ST	2 THOMAS ST	2 AVONDALE RD	12 GARDEN PL	
3 ST OSWIN'S PL	3 VICTORIA CT	3 HUTCHINSON AVE	13 CLARENDON ST	F4
4 HAWTHORN COTTS	4 ANN ST	4 BEVERLEY GDNS	14 STANLEY ST	1 STRATFORD GDNS
5 KELLEHER CT	5 SEYMOUR ST	5 BEVERLEY TERR	15 STANLEY GDNS	2 BEACONSFIELD ST
	6 ROSEBERY TERR	6 BARR HILLS	16 PALM ST	3 MORLEY GDNS
	7 KELVIN GDNS	7 BELLE VUE GDNS	17 LIVINGSTONE ST	4 BALFOUR GDNS
	8 UNSWORTH ST	8 CLEADON ST	18 MAPLE ST	
	9 UNSWORTH GDNS	9 PROSPECT PL	19 SHERBURN VILLAS	

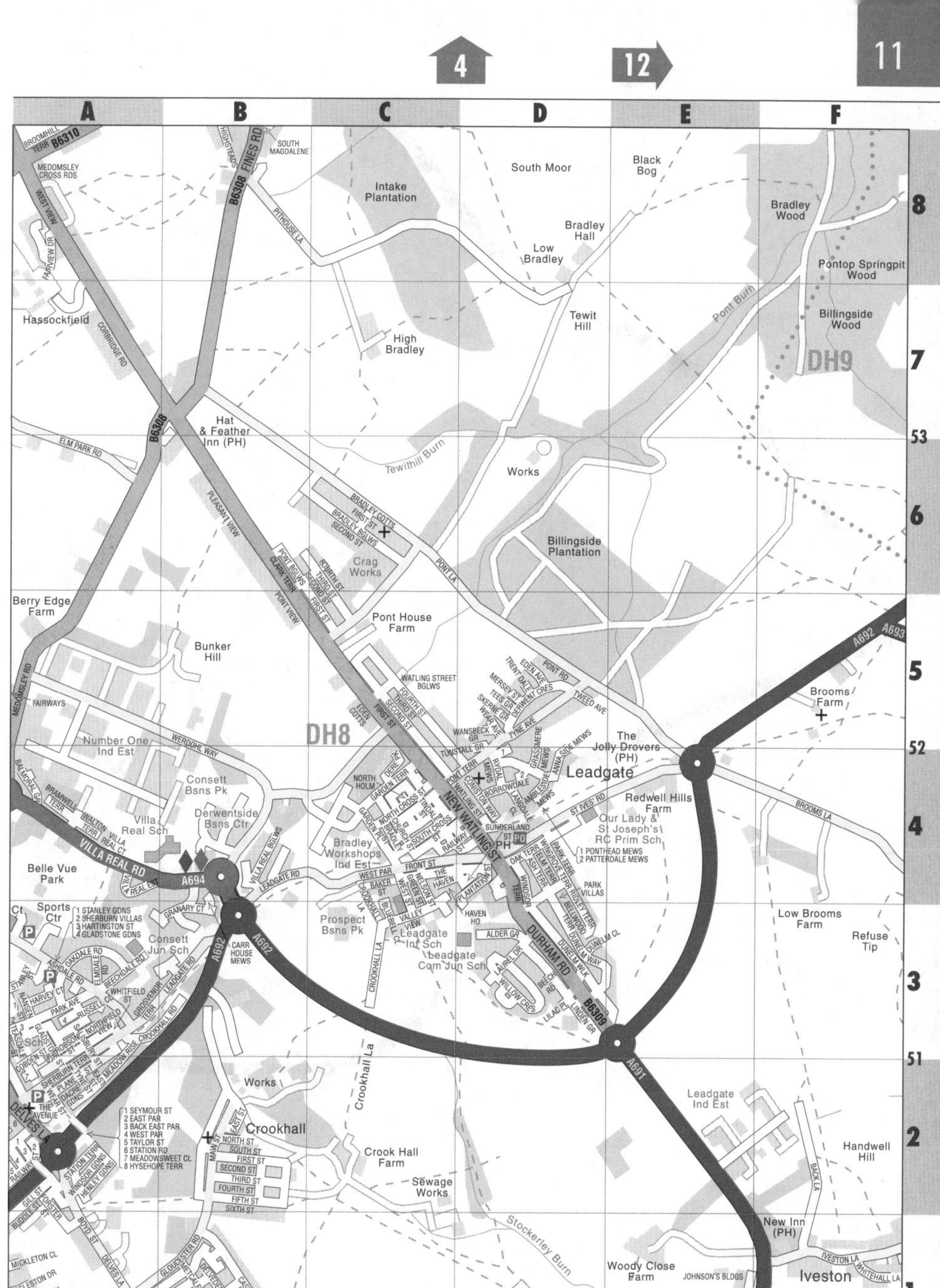
South Moor
Black Bog
Intake Plantation
Bradley Hall
Low Bradley
Bradley Wood
Pontop Springpit Wood
Billingside Wood
Tewit Hill
High Bradley
Hassockfield
DH9
Hat & Feather Inn (PH)
Tewithill Burn
Works
Billingside Plantation
Crag Works
Berry Edge Farm
Pont House Farm
Bunker Hill
Brooms Farm
DH8
Number One Ind Est
The Jolly Drovers (PH)
Consett Bsns Pk
Leadgate
Redwell Hills Farm
Derwentside Bsns Ctr
Villa Real Sch
Our Lady & St Joseph's RC Prim Sch
Bradley Workshops Ind Est
Belle Vue Park
Sports Ctr
Prospect Bsns Pk
Low Brooms Farm
Consett Jun Sch
Leadgate Inf Sch
Leadgate Com Jun Sch
Refuse Tip
Works
Crookhall
Leadgate Ind Est
Crook Hall Farm
Handwell Hill
Sewage Works
Stockerley Burn
New Inn (PH)
Woody Close Farm
Iveston
Works
A694
A692
A691
A693
B6308
B6310
B6309
VILLA REAL RD
NEW WATLING ST
DURHAM RD
PONT LA
BROOMS LA
CROOKHALL RD
DELVES LA
IVESTON LA
1 STANLEY GDNS
2 SHERBURN VILLAS
3 HARTINGTON ST
4 GLADSTONE GDNS
1 SEYMOUR ST
2 EAST PAR
3 BACK EAST PAR
4 WEST PAR
5 TAYLOR ST
6 STATION RD
7 MEADOWSWEET CL
8 HYSEHOPE TERR
1 PONTHEAD MEWS
2 PATTERDALE MEWS
1 ROMALDKIRK CL
2 COTHERSTONE CL
JOHNSON'S BLDGS
PARKER'S BLDGS
A B C D E F
8 7 53 6 5 52 4 3 51 2 1 50
11 12 13

4
12
177
12

11
5

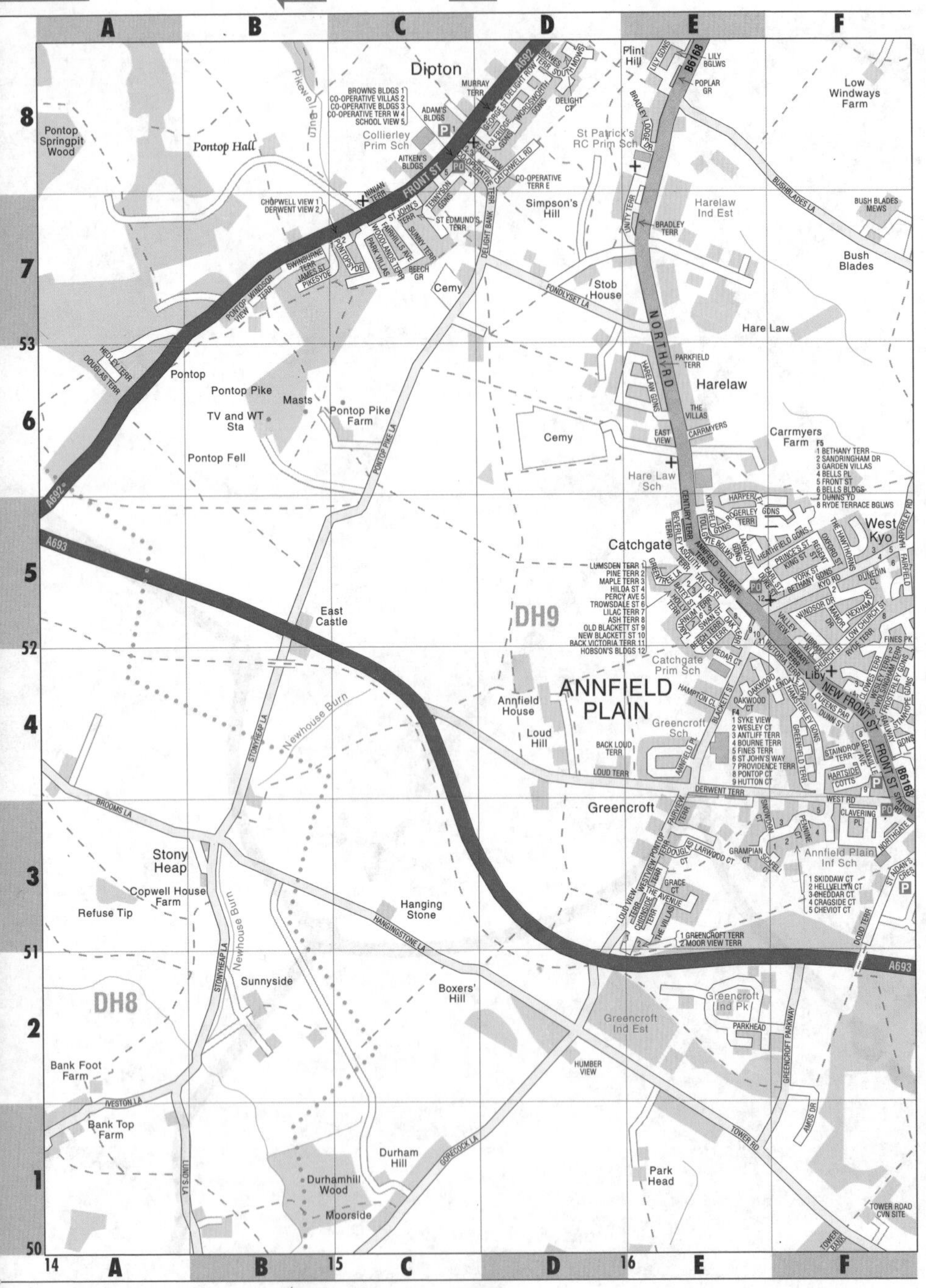
A
B
C
D
E
F
8
7
53
6
5
52
4
3
51
2
1
50
14
15
16
Dipton
Plint Hill
B6168
LILY BGLWS
POPLAR GR
Low Windways Farm
Pontop Springpit Wood
Pontop Hall
Pikewell Burn
BROWNS BLDGS 1
CO-OPERATIVE VILLAS 2
CO-OPERATIVE BLDGS 3
CO-OPERATIVE TERR W 4
SCHOOL VIEW 5
MURRAY TERR
BOWES TERR
DELIGHT ROW
SOUTH MDWS
DELIGHT CT
ADAM'S BLDGS
Collierley Prim Sch
St Patrick's RC Prim Sch
BRADLEY LODGE DR
AITKEN'S BLDGS
FRONT ST
CATCHWELL RD
CO-OPERATIVE TERR E
NINIAN TERR
CHOPWELL VIEW 1
DERWENT VIEW 2
ST JOHN'S TERR
TENNYSON GDNS
ST EDMUND'S TERR
Simpson's Hill
Harelaw Ind Est
UNITY TERR
BRADLEY TERR
BUSHBLADES LA
BUSH BLADES MEWS
Bush Blades
SWINBURNE TERR
JAMES ST
PIKESYDE
PONTOPS DE
WOODLANDS TERR
FAIRHILLS AVE
PARK VILLAS
SUNNY TERR
BEECH GR
DELIGHT BANK
Cemy
Stob House
FONDLYSET LA
A692
PONTOP VIEW
WINDSOR TERR
NORTH RD
Hare Law
HEDLEY TERR
DOUGLAS TERR
Pontop
Pontop Pike
Masts
TV and WT Sta
Pontop Pike Farm
PARKFIELD TERR
HARELAW GDNS
Harelaw
THE VILLAS
CARRMYERS
EAST VIEW
Cemy
PONTOP PIKE LA
Pontop Fell
Carrmyers Farm
F5
1 BETHANY TERR
2 SANDRINGHAM DR
3 GARDEN VILLAS
4 BELLS PL
5 FRONT ST
6 BELLS BLDGS
7 DUNNS YD
8 RYDE TERRACE BGLWS
Hare Law Sch
A692
A693
Catchgate
West Kyo
LUMSDEN TERR 1
PINE TERR 2
MAPLE TERR 3
HILDA ST 4
PERCY AVE 5
TROWSDALE ST 6
LILAC TERR 7
ASH TERR 8
OLD BLACKETT ST 9
NEW BLACKETT ST 10
BACK VICTORIA TERR 11
HOBSON'S BLDGS 12
East Castle
DH9
TOLLGATE TERR
VICTORIA TERR
LIBRARY TERR
NEW FRONT ST
Liby
Catchgate Prim Sch
ANNFIELD PLAIN
Annfield House
Loud Hill
Newhouse Burn
HAMPTON CL
BLACKETT ST
OAKWOOD CT
F4
1 SYKE VIEW
2 WESLEY CT
3 ANTLIFF TERR
4 BOURNE TERR
5 FINES TERR
6 ST JOHN'S WAY
7 PROVIDENCE TERR
8 PONTOP CT
9 HUTTON CT
Greencroft Sch
BACK LOUD TERR
LOUD TERR
ANNFIELD PL
FRONT ST
B6168
STONYHEAP LA
BROOMS LA
DERWENT TERR
WEST RD
Greencroft
CLAVERING PL
NORTHGATE
HARTSIDE COTTS
STAINDROP TERR
Stony Heap
LARWOOD CT
GRAMPIAN CT
Annfield Plain Inf Sch
1 SKIDDAW CT
2 HELLVELLYN CT
3 CHEDDAR CT
4 CRASSIDE CT
5 CHEVIOT CT
Copwell House Farm
Refuse Tip
Hanging Stone
GRACE CT
THE AVENUE
THE VILLAS
HANGINGSTONE LA
1 GREENCROFT TERR
2 MOOR VIEW TERR
DODD TERR
A693
Sunnyside
Boxers' Hill
DH8
Greencroft Ind Pk
PARKHEAD
Greencroft Ind Est
GREENCROFT PARKWAY
Bank Foot Farm
HUMBER VIEW
IVESTON LA
Bank Top Farm
AMOS DR
TOWER RD
LUND'S LA
Durham Hill
GORECOCK LA
Park Head
Durhamhill Wood
Moorside
TOWER ROAD CVN SITE

11
20

A B C D E F

1 MEMORIAL HOMES
2 JOICEY TERR
3 WEST LEIGH

Tanfield Lea South Ind Est

STATION FIELD RD
CLARK TERR 1
RODHAM TERR 2
GORDON TERR 3
SOUTH THORN 4
WATSON ST 5
SHAFTO TERR 6
CATHERINE TERR 7
ERNEST TERR 8

Rogerley Hill
Broom Hill
Woodside
Harperley Hall Farm
Harperley Hall
Harperley Hotel
Harperley
Tanfield Comp Sch
Broomhill
Cockshot Hill
Kyo Burn
Pea Farm
Barley Hill
East Kyo
East Kyo Farm
Linn's Hill
Oxhill
Derwent Walk
The Ox Inn (PH)
Oxhill Farm

WEST SHIELD ROW VILLAS
OSBORNE VILLAS
SHIELD ROW GDNS

NORTH THORN 9
PARK AVE 10
MANOR RD 11
BREWERY SQ 12
ELITE BLDGS 13
BENTON TERR 14
MONA ST 15
BEACONSFIELD ST 16

STANLEY
Derwentside Coll
L Ctr
Liby
ST JOSEPHS CT

South Stanley
Stanley Sch of Tech
Schs
Liby

UNITY TERR 1
EDWARD TERR 2
CORONATION TERR 3
WINDSOR TERR 4
JUBILEE TERR 5
SABIN TERR 6
MULBERRY TERR 7
DUDLEY TERR 8
WOODBINE TERR 9
SYCAMORE TERR 10
CATHERINE TERR 11
HAWTHORN TERR 12
PERCY TERR 13
PROSPECT TERR 14

DH9
New Kyo
South Moor
St Marys RC Prim Sch
South Moor

1 HEDLEY HO
2 HOLYOAKE TERR
3 BEECH TERR
4 EAST VIEW

HUSTLEDOWN RD
MIDDLES RD B6313

Morrison Road North Ind Est

1 JOHNSON TERR
2 MORDUE TERR
3 VINCENT TERR
4 NEW DURHAM RD

Stanleyburn Farm
Stanley Burn
PH
Langley Moor Plantation
Quaking Houses
Mast
New Acres
DH7
Langley Moor
LANCHESTER RD
A6076
WAGTAIL LA
NEWACRES RD

8 7 53 6 5 52 4 3 51 2 1 50

17 A B 18 C D 19 E F

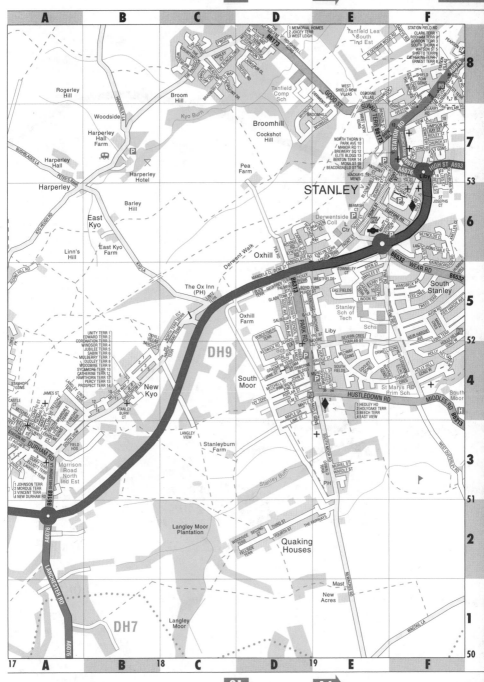

13
7

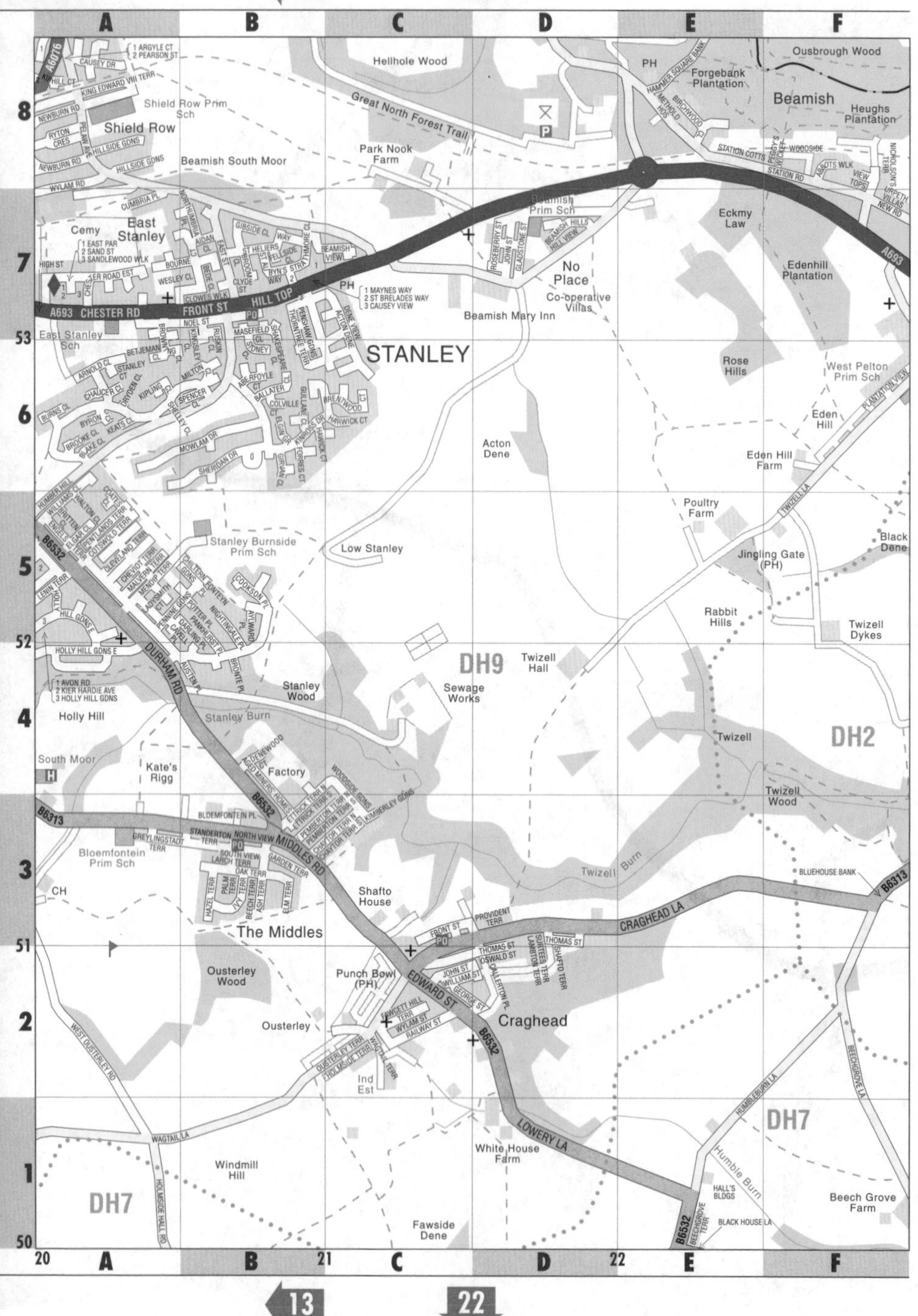
A
B
C
D
E
F
8
7
53
6
5
52
4
3
51
2
1
50
20
21
22
Hellhole Wood
Great North Forest Trail
Ousbrough Wood
Forgebank Plantation
Beamish
Heughs Plantation
PH
Shield Row Prim Sch
Shield Row
Beamish South Moor
Park Nook Farm
Cemy
East Stanley
Beamish Prim Sch
Eckmy Law
Edenhill Plantation
No Place
Co-operative Villas
Beamish Mary Inn
A693
A693 CHESTER RD
FRONT ST
HILL TOP
East Stanley Sch
STANLEY
Rose Hills
West Pelton Prim Sch
Eden Hill
Acton Dene
Eden Hill Farm
Poultry Farm
Black Dene
Stanley Burnside Prim Sch
Low Stanley
Jingling Gate (PH)
Rabbit Hills
Twizell Dykes
B6532
DH9
Twizell Hall
Sewage Works
Stanley Wood
Stanley Burn
Holly Hill
DURHAM RD
Twizell
DH2
South Moor
Kate's Rigg
Factory
Twizell Wood
B6313
BLOEMFONTEIN PL
MIDDLES RD
Bloemfontein Prim Sch
Twizell Burn
BLUEHOUSE BANK
CH
Shafto House
CRAGHEAD LA
The Middles
Ousterley Wood
Punch Bowl (PH)
EDWARD ST
Craghead
Ousterley
WEST OUSTERLEY RD
Ind Est
HUMBLEBURN LA
BEECHGROVE LA
DH7
WAGTAIL LA
LOWERY LA
White House Farm
Humble Burn
Windmill Hill
HOLMSIDE HALL RD
HALL'S BLDGS
Beech Grove Farm
BLACK HOUSE LA
Fawside Dene

13
22

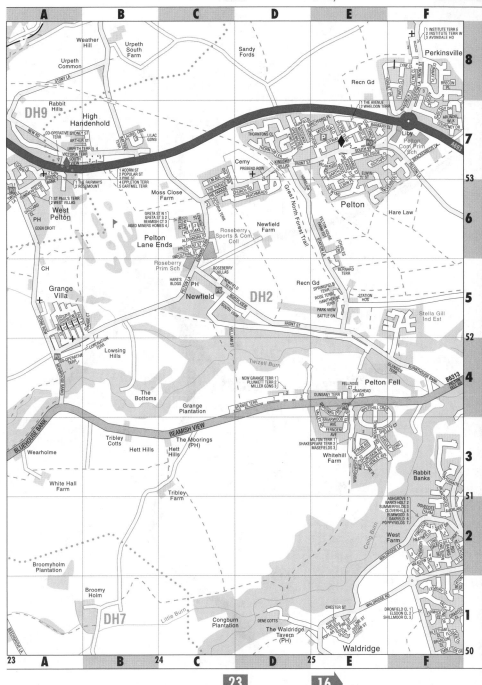

A B C D E F

8

Weather Hill
Urpeth South Farm
Sandy Fords
Urpeth Common
STONY LA
Recn Gd
1 INSTITUTE TERR E
2 INSTITUTE TERR W
3 AVONDALE HO
Perkinsville
LYNE CL
COQUET DR
TWEED CL
WANSBECK CL
OUSTON LA
FRONT ST
CONWAY PL
BRECON PL
ASCOT PL
GAIRLOCH DR
ARUNDEL WLK
COURTNEY DR

7

Rabbit Hills
DH9
High Handenhold
NEW RD
CO-OPERATIVE TERR
SYDNEY ST
ARTHUR ST
URPETH TERR
VICTORIA TERR
SOUTH VIEW
LAUREL CRES
LILAC GDNS
BAYTREE TERR
1 ACORN ST
2 POPULAR ST
3 PINE ST
4 EPPLETON TERR
5 CARTMEL TERR
1 THE AVENUE
2 WHELDON TERR
THORNTONS CL
THORNTON LEA
KING'S LA
GREENACRES
MOSSWAY
FAIRFIELD
SANDYFORD PL
SANDYFORD
MIDDLEFIELD
IVYWAY
HYLTON TERR
ERNEST ST
CONSTANCE ST
BARBARY CL
SOUTH VIEW
FIELDSIDE
Liby
Pelton Com Prim Sch
BRACKENBEDS LA
A693
KINGSWAY VILLAS
FRONT ST
Cemy
PREBEND ROW

53

EDENFIELD
GREENS BANK
1 THE FAIRWAYS
2 ROSEMOUNT
TWIZELL LA
SUMMERFIELD
1 ST PAUL'S TERR
2 WEST VILLAS
ORCHARD CL
West Pelton
PH
EDEN CROFT
ELM AVE
OAK TERR
THE PARADE
VICTORIA TERR
CHURCH RD
HEATHMEADS
Moss Close Farm
VICARAGE CL
THE GARTH
WOOD ST
ORCHARD ST
GRANGE ST
ELWIN ST
ELWIN PL
THE WYND
SOUTHFIELD
BRACKENBEDS CL
PELTON LA
HARELAW
Pelton
Hare Law

6

GRETA ST N 1
GRETA ST S 2
BEAMISH CT 3
AGED MINERS HOMES 4
PELTON MEWS
LOVAINE ST
HOLYOAKE ST
ALEXANDRA ST
PROVIDENT ST
INDUSTRIAL ST
EDWARD TERR
Pelton Lane Ends
Roseberry Sports & Com Coll
Newfield Farm
Great North Forest Trail
PELTON HOUSE FARM EST
STATION LA
CHARLES TERR
BERNARD TERR
CH
Roseberry Prim Sch
ROSEBERRY VILLAS

5

Grange Villa
HARE'S BLDGS
PH
PELTON LA
Newfield
NEWFIELD TERR
NORTH VIEW
SOUTH VIEW
DH2
Recn Gd
SPRINGFIELD TERR
ROSE TERR
HAWTHORNE TERR
PARK VIEW
BATTLE GN
STATION HOS
Stella Gill Ind Est
STONE ROW
ALBERT ST
QUEEN ST
WEST ST
EAST ST
PINE ST
GRANGE CT
WILLIAM ST
FRONT ST

52

CORONATION TERR
Lowsing Hills
CO-OPERATIVE TERR
NEWBRIDGE BANKS
Twizell Burn
GLENSIDE TERR
BURNHOUSE BANK

4

NEW GRANGE TERR 1
PLUNKETT TERR 2
MILLER GDNS 3
Pelton Fell
B6313
PELTON FELL RD
FELLROSE CT
CRAGHEAD RD
DUNSANY TERR
The Bottoms
Grange Plantation
GRANGE TERR
GARDINER CRES
VALLEY RD
FELL RD
WHITEHILL CRES
BRIARWOOD AVE
FERNDENE AVE
TENNYSON RD
SHELLEY CT
SHELLEY GDNS
BLUEHOUSE BANK
BEAMISH VIEW
Tribley Cotts
The Moorings (PH)
Hett Hills
Hett Hills
MILTON TERR 1
SHAKESPEARE TERR 2
MASEFIELDS 3
BYRON AVE
RUSKIN AVE
HENLEY AVE
COLERIDGE PL
WORDSWORTH AVE

3

Wearholme
Whitehill Farm
White Hall Farm
Tribley Farm
Rabbit Banks
GRAYTHWAITE
BRANTWOOD

51

ASHGROVE 1
BANKS HOLT 2
SUMMERFIELDS 3
CLOVERHILL 4
ELMWOOD 5
OAKFIELD 6
POPPYFIELDS 7
DOVECOTE FARM
AUCKLAND

2

Cong Burn
West Farm
FOXGLOVE
HEATHFIELD
WEST DR
LONG DALE
GILL CROFT
RED BANKS
LONG BURN DR
WALDRIDGE LA
MOORMOOR
MEADOW DR
Broomyholm Plantation
Broomy Holm
LESBURY CL
NORTON CL

1

DH7
Little Burn
Congburn Plantation
DENE COTTS
The Waldridge Tavern (PH)
CHESTER ST
OAK ST
PINE ST
LIME ST
POPLAR ST
OLIVE ST
CEDAR ST
WALDRIDGE RD
Waldridge
DRONFIELD CL 1
ELSDON CL 2
SHILLMOOR CL 3
FENWICK CL
FALSTONE DR
CRASTER CL
FLEETHAM CL
FLODDEN CL
BRANDON CL
EMBLETON DR
BEECHGROVE LA

50

23 A B 24 C D 25 E F

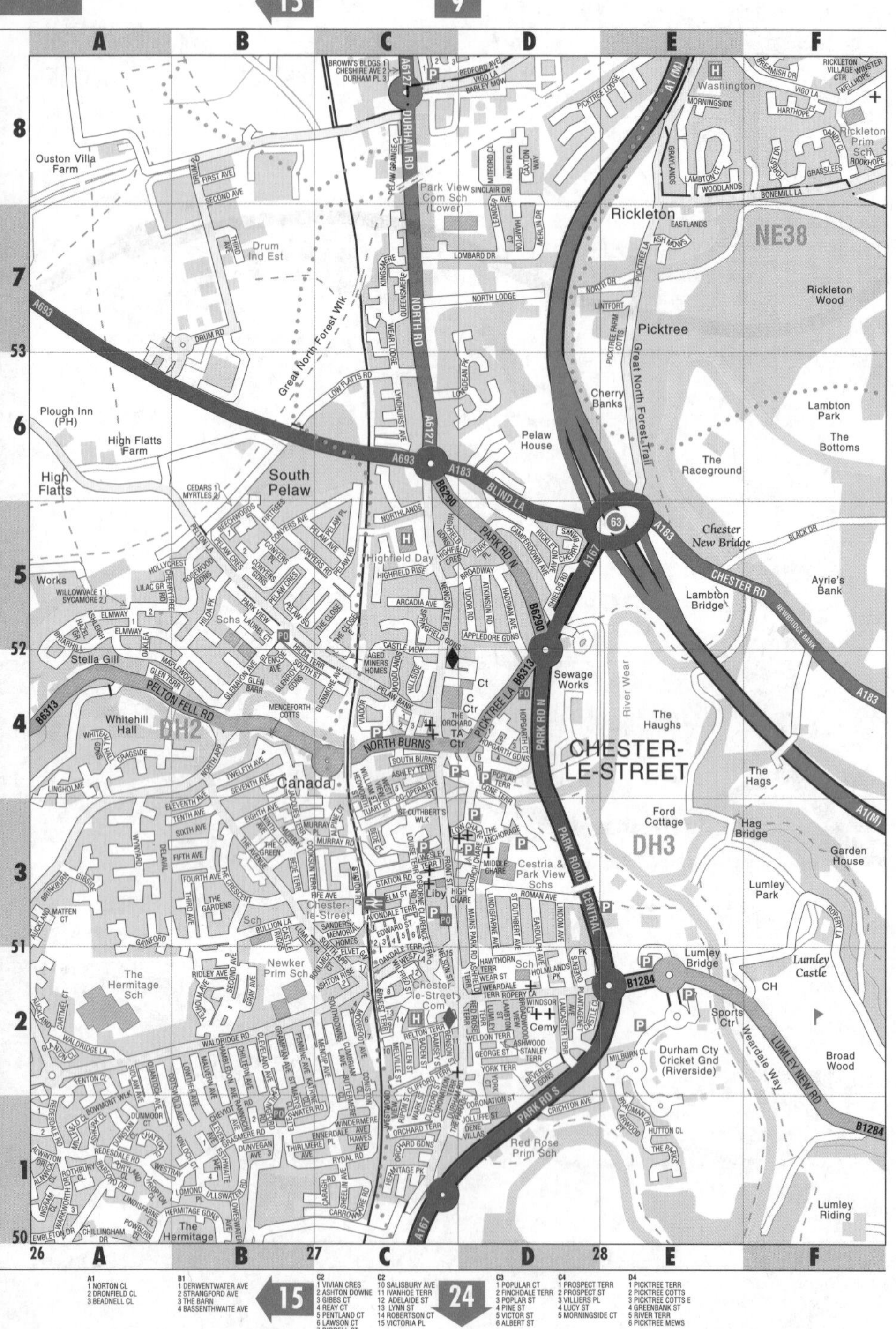

A1
1 NORTON CL
2 DRONFIELD CL
3 BEADNELL CL

B1
1 DERWENTWATER AVE
2 STRANGFORD AVE
3 THE BARN
4 BASSENTHWAITE AVE

C2
1 VIVIAN CRES
2 ASHTON DOWNE
3 GIBBS CT
4 REAY CT
5 PENTLAND CT
6 LAWSON CT
7 RIDDELL CT
8 HEMEL ST
9 THOMAS ST

C2
10 SALISBURY AVE
11 IVANHOE TERR
12 ADELAIDE ST
13 LYNN ST
14 ROBERTSON CT
15 VICTORIA PL

C3
1 POPULAR CT
2 FINCHDALE TERR
3 POPLAR ST
4 PINE ST
5 VICTOR ST
6 ALBERT ST

C4
1 PROSPECT TERR
2 PROSPECT ST
3 VILLIERS PL
4 LUCY ST
5 MORNINGSIDE CT

D4
1 PICKTREE TERR
2 PICKTREE COTTS
3 PICKTREE COTTS E
4 GREENBANK ST
5 RIVER TERR
6 PICKTREE MEWS

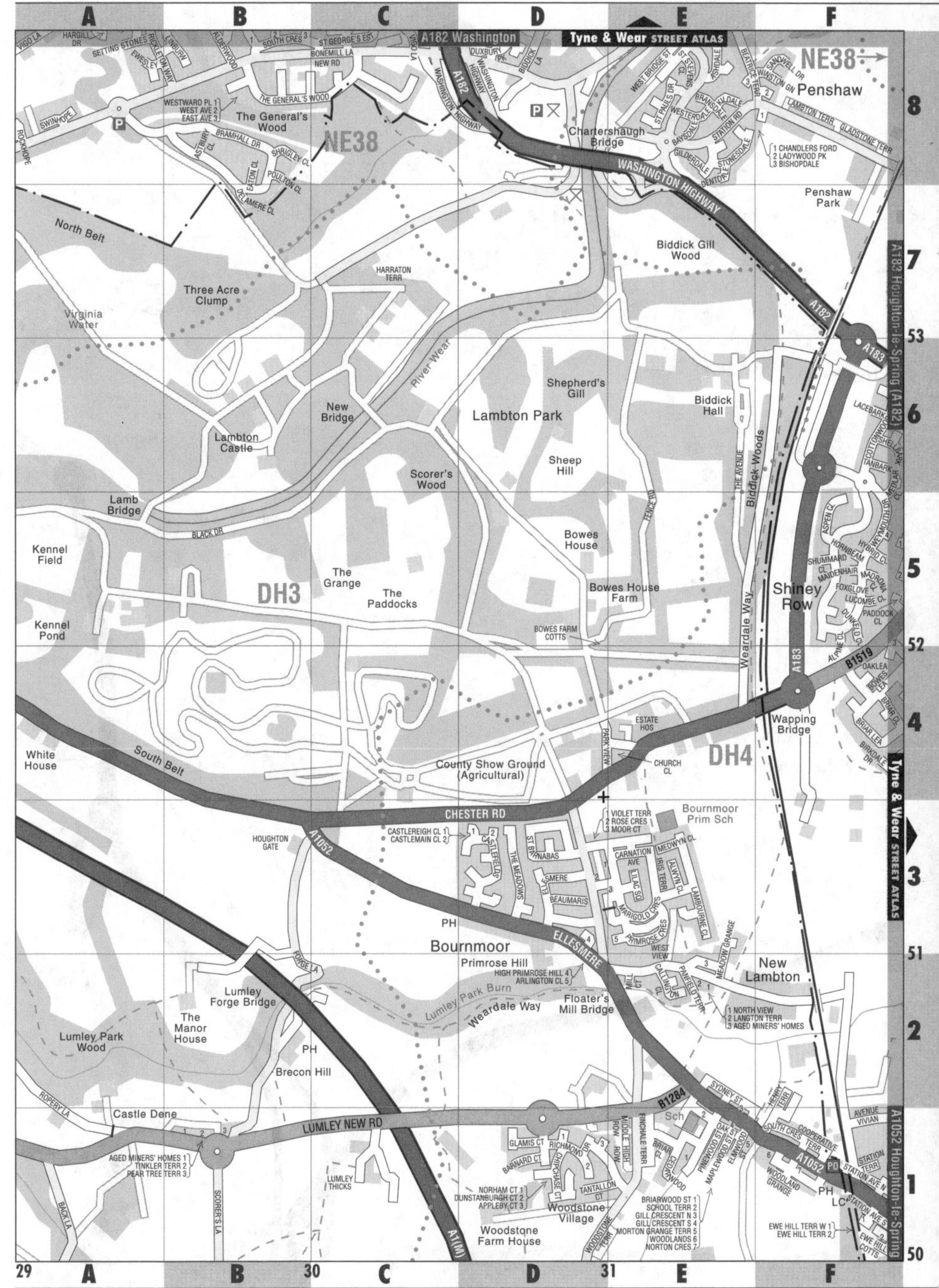

NE38

A182 Washington

Penshaw

1 CHANDLERS FORD
2 LADYWOOD PK
3 BISHOPDALE

Penshaw Park

North Belt

Virginia Water

Three Acre Clump

HARRATON TERR.

River Wear

Shepherd's Gill

Lambton Park

Biddick Gill Wood

Biddick Hall

Biddick Woods

New Bridge

Lambton Castle

Scorer's Wood

Sheep Hill

The Avenue

Shiney Row

Lamb Bridge

BLACK DR

DH3

The Grange

The Paddocks

Bowes House

Bowes House Farm

BOWES FARM COTTS

Weardale Way

Kennel Field

Kennel Pond

White House

South Belt

ESTATE HOS

County Show Ground (Agricultural)

CHURCH CL

DH4

Wapping Bridge

CHESTER RD

HOUGHTON GATE

CASTLEREIGH CL 1
CASTLEMAIN CL 2

VIOLET TERR
ROSE CRES
MOOR CT

Bournmoor Prim Sch

CARNATION AVE

Bournmoor

PH

ELLESMERE

BEAUMARIS

Primrose Hill

HIGH PRIMROSE HILL 4
ARLINGTON CL 5

New Lambton

1 NORTH VIEW
2 LANGTON TERR
3 AGED MINERS' HOMES

Lumley Forge Bridge

The Manor House

Lumley Park Burn

Weardale Way

Floater's Mill Bridge

Lumley Park Wood

PH

Brecon Hill

Castle Dene

LUMLEY NEW RD

AGED MINERS' HOMES 1
TINKLER TERR 2
PEAR TREE TERR 3

GLAMIS CT

LUMLEY THICKS

B1284

Sch

A1052

PH

LC

NORHAM CT 1
DUNSTANBURGH CT 2
APPLEBY CT 3

Woodstone Village

Woodstone Farm House

BRIARWOOD ST 1
SCHOOL TERR 2
GILL CRESCENT N 3
GILL CRESCENT S 4
MORTON GRANGE TERR 5
WOODLANDS 6
NORTON CRES 7

EWE HILL TERR W 1
EWE HILL TERR 2

F5
1 GAINSBOROUGH CRES
2 BURNDEN GR
3 GOLF COURSE RD
4 MORINDA CL

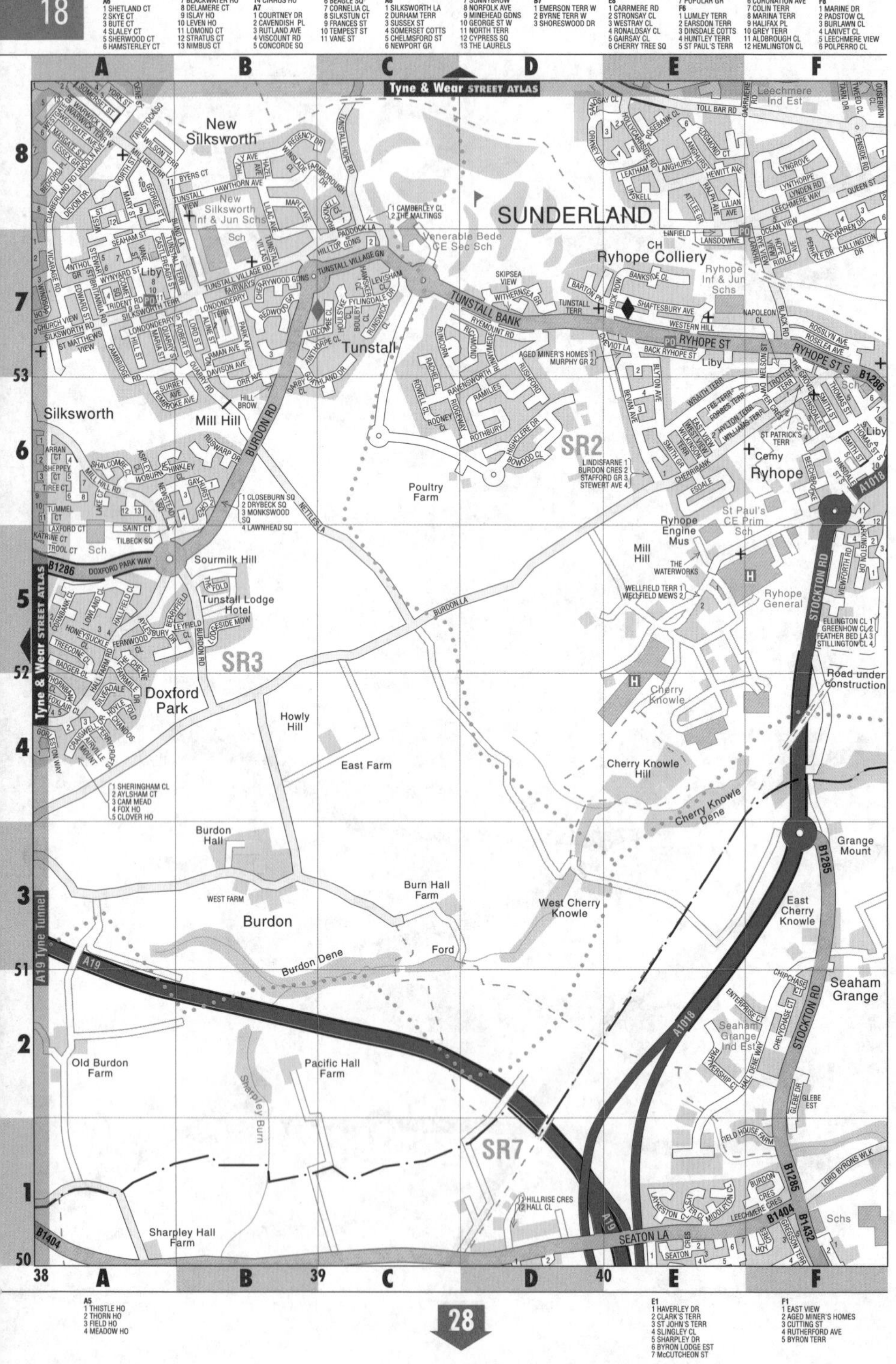
A6
1 SHETLAND CT
2 SKYE CT
3 BUTE CT
4 SLALEY CT
5 SHERWOOD CT
6 HAMSTERLEY CT
7 BLACKWATER HO
8 DELAMERE CT
9 ISLAY HO
10 LEVEN HO
11 LOMOND CT
12 STRATUS CT
13 NIMBUS CT
14 CIRRUS HO
A7
1 COURTNEY DR
2 CAVENDISH PL
3 RUTLAND AVE
4 VISCOUNT RD
5 CONCORDE SQ
6 BEAGLE SQ
7 CORNELIA CL
8 SILKSTUN CT
9 FRANCES ST
10 TEMPEST ST
11 VANE ST
A8
1 SILKSWORTH LA
2 DURHAM TERR
3 SUSSEX ST
4 SOMERSET COTTS
5 CHELMSFORD ST
6 NEWPORT GR
7 SUNNYBROW
8 NORFOLK AVE
9 MINEHEAD GDNS
10 GEORGE ST W
11 NORTH TERR
12 CYPRESS SQ
13 THE LAURELS
B7
1 EMERSON TERR W
2 BYRNE TERR W
3 SHORESWOOD DR
E8
1 CARRMERE RD
2 STRONSAY CL
3 WESTRAY CL
4 RONALDSAY CL
5 GAIRSAY CL
6 CHERRY TREE SQ
7 POPULAR GR
F6
1 LUMLEY TERR
2 EARSDON TERR
3 DINSDALE COTTS
4 HUNTLEY TERR
5 ST PAUL'S TERR
6 CORONATION AVE
7 COLIN TERR
8 MARINA TERR
9 HALIFAX PL
10 GREY TERR
11 ALDBROUGH CL
12 HEMLINGTON CL
F8
1 MARINE DR
2 PADSTOW CL
3 BURLAWN CL
4 LANIVET CL
5 LEECHMERE VIEW
6 POLPERRO CL
Tyne & Wear STREET ATLAS
New Silksworth
SUNDERLAND
Ryhope Colliery
Tunstall
Silksworth
Mill Hill
Ryhope
Poultry Farm
Sourmilk Hill
Tunstall Lodge Hotel
SR2
SR3
Doxford Park
Howly Hill
East Farm
Cherry Knowle Hill
Cherry Knowle Dene
Burdon Hall
Burn Hall Farm
West Cherry Knowle
East Cherry Knowle
Grange Mount
Burdon
Burdon Dene
Ford
Seaham Grange
Seaham Grange Ind Est
Old Burdon Farm
Pacific Hall Farm
Sharpley Burn
SR7
Sharpley Hall Farm
A19 Tyne Tunnel
A19
A1018
B1285
B1286
B1404
B1432
Road under construction
A5
1 THISTLE HO
2 THORN HO
3 FIELD HO
4 MEADOW HO
E1
1 HAVERLEY DR
2 CLARK'S TERR
3 ST JOHN'S TERR
4 SLINGLEY CL
5 SHARPLEY DR
6 BYRON LODGE EST
7 McCUTCHEON ST
F1
1 EAST VIEW
2 AGED MINER'S HOMES
3 CUTTING ST
4 RUTHERFORD AVE
5 BYRON TERR

28

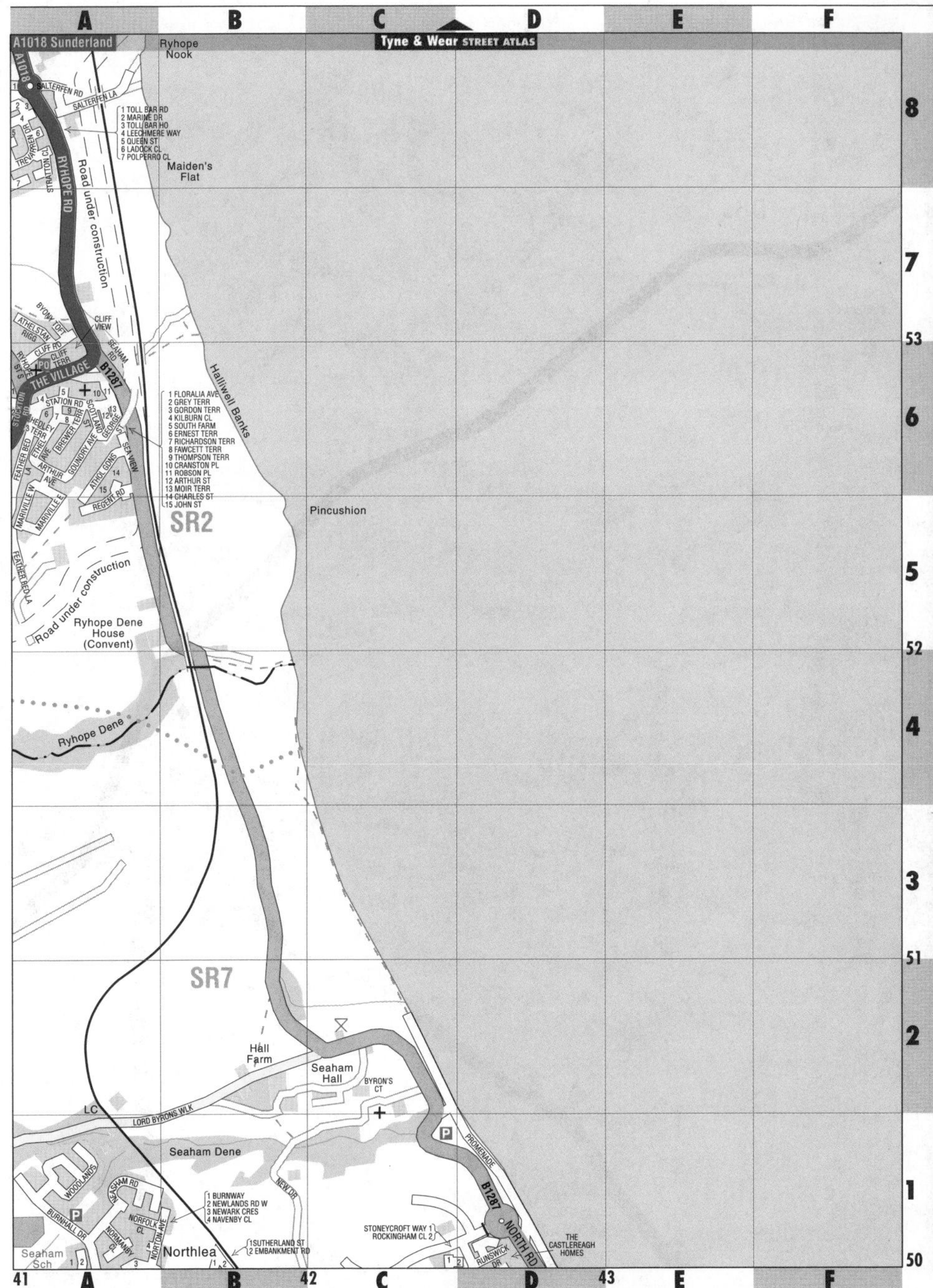

A B C D E F

A1018 Sunderland

Ryhope
Nook

8

1 TOLL BAR RD
2 MARINE DR
3 TOLL BAR HO
4 LEECHMERE WAY
5 QUEEN ST
6 LADDOCK CL
7 POLPERRO CL

Maiden's
Flat

SALTERFEN RD
SALTERFEN LA

Road under construction

RYHOPE RD

7

BYOM CL
CLIFF
VIEW

CLIFF TERR

53

ATHELSTAN
RIGG

B1287

THE VILLAGE

STATION RD

Hallwell Banks

1 FLORALIA AVE
2 GREY TERR
3 GORDON TERR
4 KILBURN CL
5 SOUTH FARM
6 ERNEST TERR
7 RICHARDSON TERR
8 FAWCETT TERR
9 THOMPSON TERR
10 CRANSTON PL
11 ROBSON PL
12 ARTHUR ST
13 MOIR TERR
14 CHARLES ST
15 JOHN ST

6

FEATHER RD

MARLBORO

SR2

Pincushion

AXLE GDNS

REGISTER RD

5

FEATHER RD A4

Road under construction

Ryhope Dene
House
(Convent)

52

Ryhope Dene

4

3

SR7

51

Hall
Farm

Seaham
Hall

BYRON'S
CT

2

LC

LORD BYRONS WLK

P

PROMENADE

Seaham Dene

NEW DR

P

B1287

1 BURNWAY
2 NEWLANDS RD W
3 NEWARK CRES
4 NAVENBY CL

WOODLANDS

SEAHAM RD

NORFOLK ST

NORTH RD

RUNSWICK DR

1

P

BURNHILL RD

Seaham
Sch

Northlea

1 SUTHERLAND ST
2 EMBANKMENT RD

STONEYCROFT WAY 1
ROCKINGHAM CL 2

THE
CASTLEREAGH
HOMES

50

41   A   B   42   C   D   43   E   F

177 12

A B C D E F

8 7 49 6 5 48 4 3 47 2 1 46

DH8 DH9 DH7

Low Woodside
Woodside Bank A691
Stockerley La
Esp Green
Stockerley Plantation
Ladywell Banks
Lund's La
Gorecock La
Stockerley Burn
Newhouse Burn
Shoulder of Mutton
Greencroft Park
Park Gill
Spring Wood
High Crow Wood
Greencroft Park House
Fence Banks
Tower Bank
Tower Rd
Maiden Hall Farm
Mawsfield
A6076 Howden Bank
Howden Burn
Back La
Newhouses Farm
Newhouse Bridge
Ornsby Hill
Ornsby Hill
St Bede's RC Comp Sch
Consett Rd
St Bede's Ct
A6076
Crow Hall
Lanchester
Low Meadows
Lizards
Kitswell Rd
Smallhope Burn
Cemy
Victoria Terr 1
Victoria St 2
Croft Ct 3
Kitswell Rd
Sunnybanks
Elmfield
Southway
Burnside
Fenhall Pk
Millfield
Thornlea
Ridgeway
Mount Park Dr
Alderside Cres
The Close
Croft View
Front St
Ashleigh Gr
Mount View
Mount Pleasant
Woodham
Sch
Sch
Liby
PO
P
1 Church View
2 The Square
3 The Garths
4 Percy Cres
5 Greta Pl
6 Hallgarth Terr
Derwentside Coll
Deanery View
Peth Bank
Holmside Ave
Deneside
West View
Durham Rd A691
Woodlands
Valley Gr
Greenwell Pk
Newbiggin La
Newbiggin
Branch Villa
Margery Flatts
Fox Hills Cres
Alderdene
Broadoak Dr
Brook View
Lee Hill Ct
Prospect Terr
Station Rd
B6296
PH
Cecil Cres
Meadow Way
Woodlea
Railway St
Ford St
Briardene
Alderdene Burn
Fox Hills
Yeckhouse La
Cadger Bank
Humberhill Dr
Watling
West Dr
West Dr
B6301
Smallhope Dr
Middlewood Rd
Colepike Rd
The Paddock
Ford Cres
Ford Rd
Longovicium Roman Fort
Humberhill La
Upper Houses Farm
Mast
Humber Hill
Hollinside Hall
Hollinside Farm
Middlewood Farm
Hollinside
Sewage Works
Greenwell Ford
Ford Bridge
Bargate Bank B6301
The Rookery
River Browney
Colepike Home Farm
Colepike Hall
B6296
Bargate

14 15 16

177 30

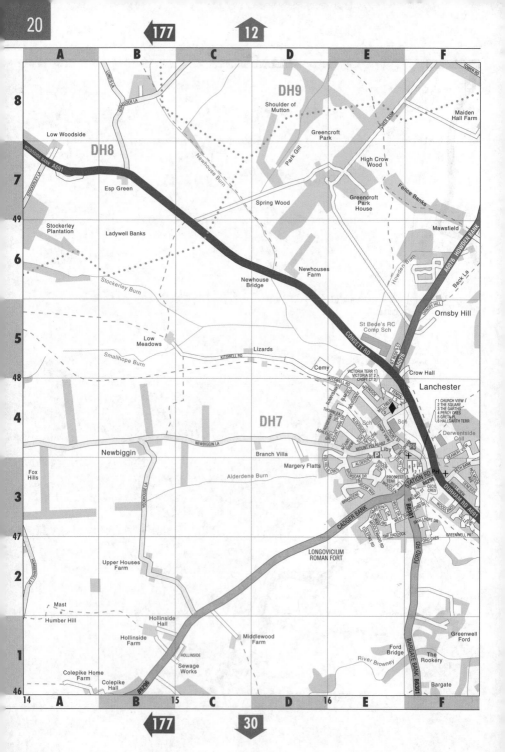

13
22

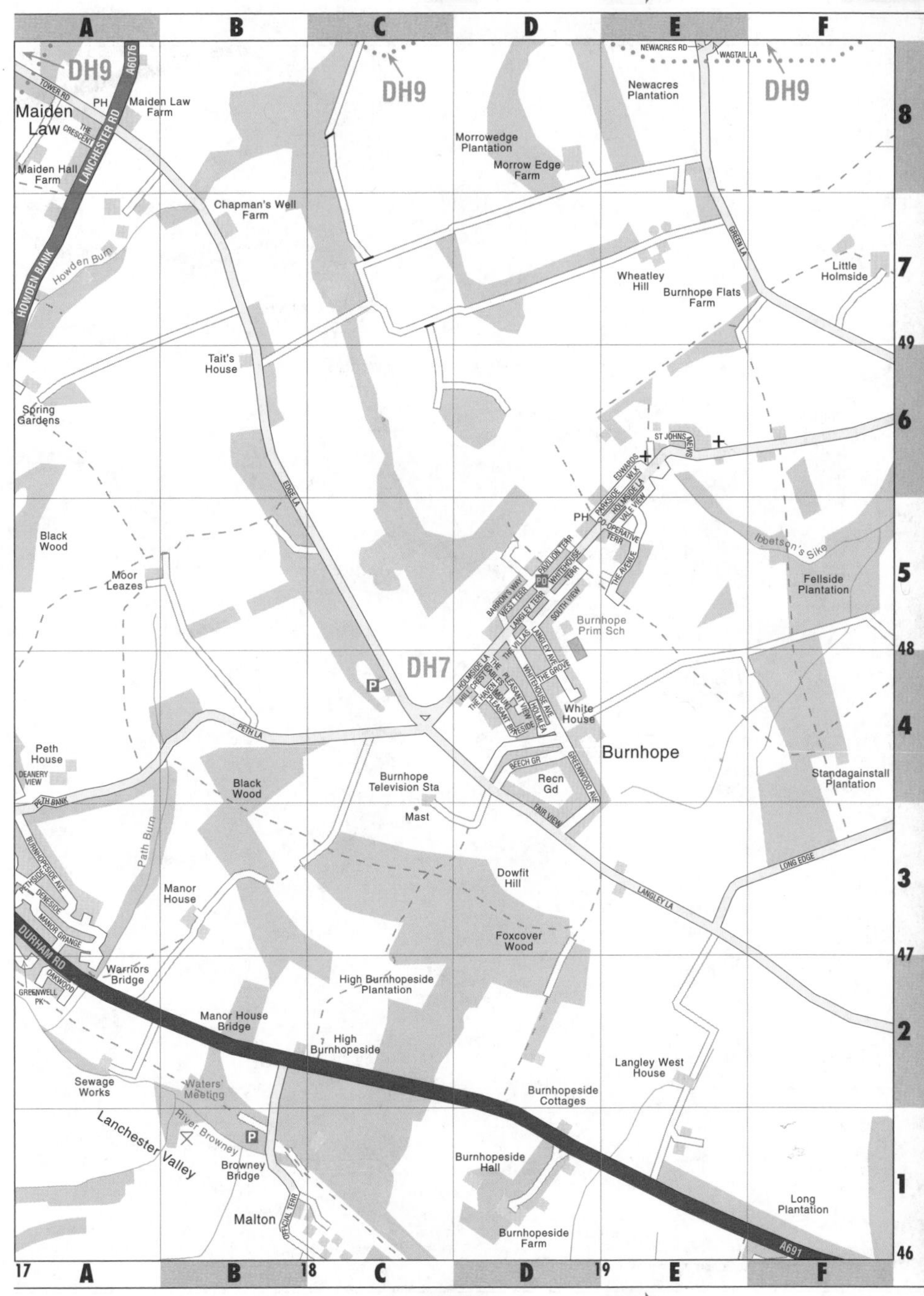
A
B
C
D
E
F
8
7
49
6
5
48
4
3
47
2
1
46
17
18
19
DH9
DH9
DH9
DH7
A6076
TOWER RD
PH
Maiden Law Farm
Maiden Law
THE CRESCENT
LANCHESTER RD
Maiden Hall Farm
HOWDEN BANK
Howden Burn
Chapman's Well Farm
Morrowedge Plantation
Morrow Edge Farm
NEWACRES RD
WAGTAIL LA
Newacres Plantation
GREEN LA
Wheatley Hill
Burnhope Flats Farm
Little Holmside
Tait's House
Spring Gardens
ST JOHNS MEWS
EDWARDS WLK
PARKSIDE
HOLMSIDE LA
VALE VIEW
PH
CO-OPERATIVE TERR
PAVILION TERR
WHITEHOUSE TERR
THE AVENUE
Ibbetson's Sike
Fellside Plantation
EDGE LA
Black Wood
Moor Leazes
BARRON'S WAY
WEST TERR
PO
LANGLEY TERR
SOUTH VIEW
Burnhope Prim Sch
THE VILLAS
LANGLEY AVE
HOLMSIDE LA
THE GABLES
PLEASANT VIEW
HILL CREST
THE HAVEN
MOUNT PLEASANT
WHITEHOUSE AVE
THE GROVE
HOLMLEA
BRAESIDE
White House
P
PETH LA
Peth House
DEANERY VIEW
Burnhope
BEECH GR
GREENWOOD AVE
Recn Gd
Standagainstall Plantation
PETH BANK
Black Wood
Burnhope Television Sta
Mast
FAIR VIEW
BURNHOPESIDE AVE
Path Burn
PETHSIDE
DENESIDE
Manor House
Dowfit Hill
LONG EDGE
LANGLEY LA
MANOR GRANGE
DURHAM RD
Foxcover Wood
Warriors Bridge
OAKWOOD
GREENWELL PK
High Burnhopeside Plantation
Manor House Bridge
High Burnhopeside
Langley West House
Sewage Works
Waters' Meeting
Burnhopeside Cottages
Lanchester Valley
River Browney
P
Browney Bridge
Burnhopeside Hall
Malton
OFFICIAL TERR
Long Plantation
Burnhopeside Farm
A691

31
22

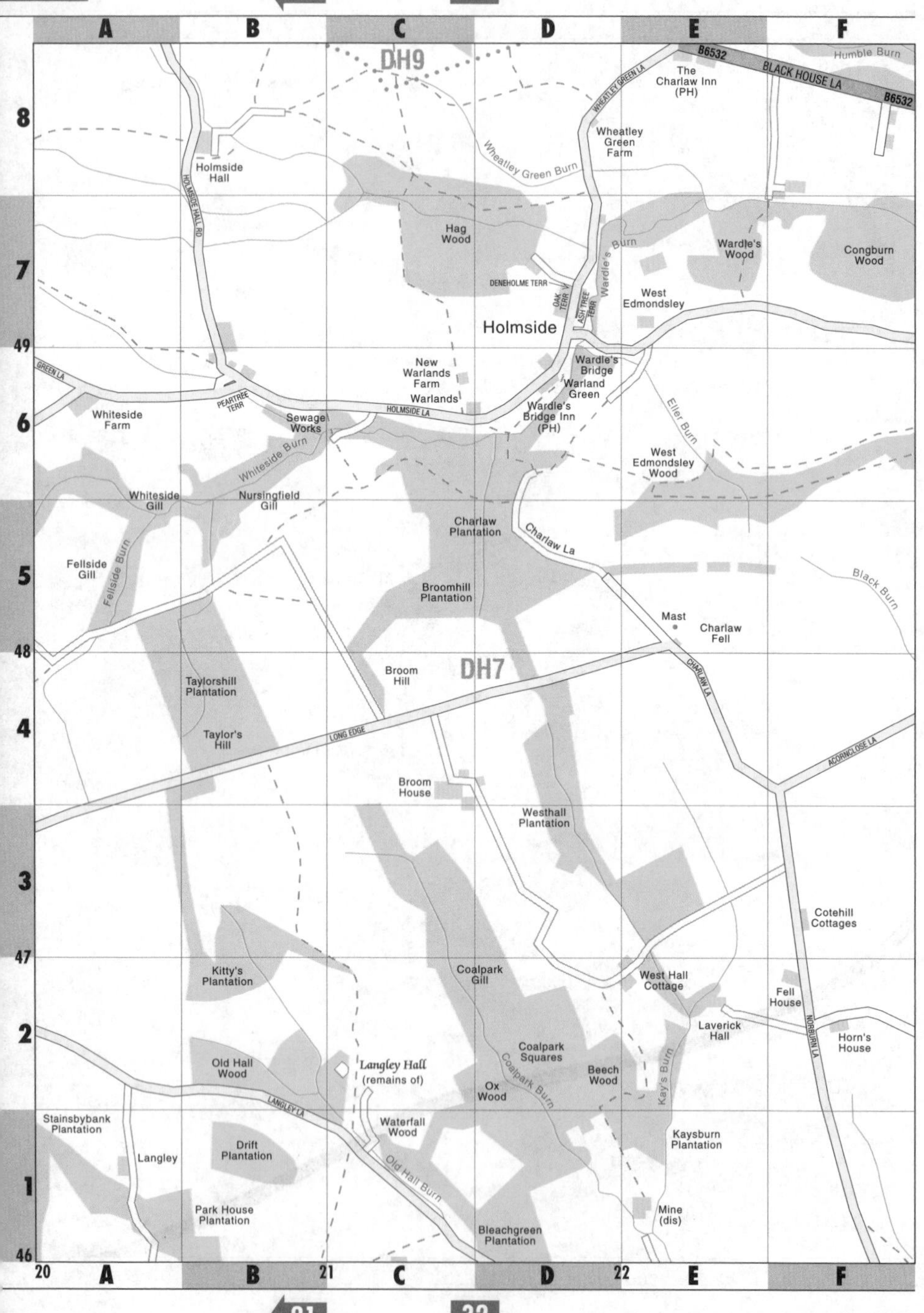

A B C D E F

8

7

49

6

5

48

4

3

47

2

1

46

20 A B 21 C D 22 E F

DH9

B6532 BLACK HOUSE LA B6532
Humble Burn

The Charlaw Inn (PH)

WHEATLEY GREEN LA

Wheatley Green Burn

Wheatley Green Farm

HOLMSIDE HALL RD

Holmside Hall

Hag Wood

Wardle's Burn

Wardle's Wood

Congburn Wood

DENEHOLME TERR

OAK TERR

ASH TREE TERR

West Edmondsley

Holmside

GREEN LA

Whiteside Farm

PEARTREE TERR

New Warlands Farm

Warlands

HOLMSIDE LA

Wardle's Bridge
Warland Green

Wardle's Bridge Inn (PH)

West Edmondsley Wood

Eller Burn

Black Burn

Sewage Works

Whiteside Burn

Whiteside Gill

Nursingfield Gill

Fellside Gill

Fellside Burn

Charlaw Plantation

Charlaw La

Broomhill Plantation

Mast

Charlaw Fell

DH7

Taylorshill Plantation

Broom Hill

Taylor's Hill

LONG EDGE

CHARLAW LA

AGORING EDGE LA

Broom House

Westhall Plantation

Cotehill Cottages

Kitty's Plantation

Coalpark Gill

West Hall Cottage

Fell House

Horn's House

NORDEN LA

Stainsbybank Plantation

Old Hall Wood

LANGLEY LA

Langley Hall (remains of)

Coalpark Squares

Coalpark Burn

Ox Wood

Beech Wood

Kay's Burn

Laverick Hall

Langley

Drift Plantation

Waterfall Wood

Old Hall Burn

Kaysburn Plantation

Park House Plantation

Bleachgreen Plantation

Mine (dis)

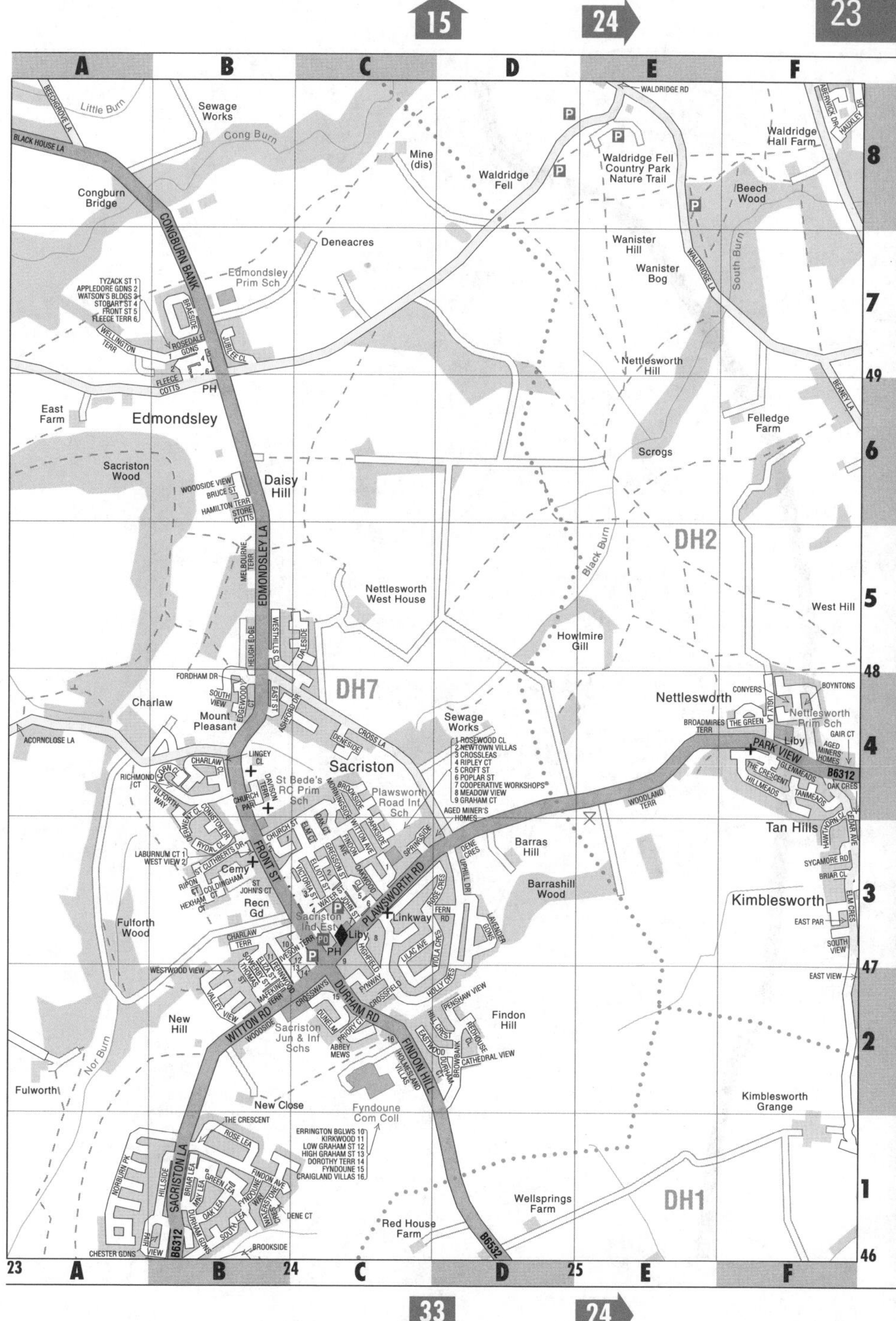
15
24
Sewage Works
Little Burn
Cong Burn
BLACK HOUSE LA
Congburn Bridge
Mine (dis)
Waldridge Fell
Waldridge Fell Country Park Nature Trail
WALDRIDGE RD
Waldridge Hall Farm
Beech Wood
Deneacres
Edmondsley Prim Sch
CONGBURN BANK
Wanister Hill
Wanister Bog
WALDRIDGE LA
South Burn
TYZACK ST 1
APPLEDORE GDNS 2
WATSON'S BLDGS 3
STOBART ST 4
FRONT ST 5
FLEECE TERR 6
WELLINGTON TERR
ROSEDALE GDNS
JUBILEE CL
FLEECE COTTS
PH
Nettlesworth Hill
East Farm
Edmondsley
Felledge Farm
BEANEY LA
Sacriston Wood
Daisy Hill
Scrogs
WOODSIDE VIEW
BRUCE ST
HAMILTON TERR
STORE COTTS
DH2
EDMONDSLEY LA
MELBOURNE TERR
Black Burn
Nettlesworth West House
West Hill
Howlmire Gill
HEUGH EDGE
WESTHILLS CL
DALESIDE
FORDHAM DR
SOUTH VIEW
EDGEWOOD CT
EAST ST
ASHFORD DR
DH7
Charlaw
Mount Pleasant
Nettlesworth
CONYERS
BOYNTONS
Nettlesworth Prim Sch
BROADMIRES TERR
THE GREEN
UGLY LA
GAIR CT
ACORNCLOSE LA
Sewage Works
CROSS LA
DENESIDE
Sacriston
1 ROSEWOOD CL
2 NEWTOWN VILLAS
3 CROSSLEAS
4 RIPLEY CT
5 CROFT ST
6 POPLAR ST
7 COOPERATIVE WORKSHOPS
8 MEADOW VIEW
9 GRAHAM CT
PARK VIEW
Liby
AGED MINERS' HOMES
B6312
GLENMEADS
OAK CRES
CHARLAW CL
LINGEY CL
RICHMOND CT
ACORN CL
St Bede's RC Prim Sch
Plawsworth Road Inf Sch
THE CRESCENT
HILLMEADS
TANMEADS
WOODLAND TERR
FULFORTH WAY
DERWENT CL
CONISTON DR
CHURCH PAR
DAVISON TERR
MORNINGSIDE
BROOKSIDE
PARKSIDE
AGED MINER'S HOMES
Tan Hills
HAWTHORN CL
CEDAR AVE
RYDAL CL
CHURCH ST
ELM CT
OAK CT
WITTON AVE
FINDON AVE
SPRINGSIDE
DENE CRES
Barras Hill
LABURNUM CT 1
WEST VIEW 2
ST CUTHBERTS DR
Cemy
FRONT ST
GREGSON ST
OAKWOOD
UPHILL DR
SYCAMORE RD
RIPON CT
COLDINGHAM CT
HEXHAM CT
ST JOHN'S CT
VICTORIA ST
ELLIOT ST
CLIVE ST
PLAWSWORTH RD
ROSE CRES
Barrashill Wood
BRIAR CL
ELM CRES
Recn Gd
WATER ST
JOHN ST
Linkway
FERN RD
Kimblesworth
Fulforth Wood
Sacriston Ind Est
PO
Liby
PH
CHARLAW TERR
IVESON TERR
HIGHFIELD
LILAC AVE
VIOLA CRES
LAVENDER GDNS
EAST PAR
SOUTH VIEW
WESTWOOD VIEW
SOMERBY ST
ELIZA ST
THOMAS ST
FERNWOOD
FYNWAY
HOLLY CRES
EAST VIEW
VALLEY VIEW
MAFEKING TERR
CROSSWAYS
DURHAM RD
CROSSFIELD
PENSHAW VIEW
New Hill
WITTON RD
Findon Hill
Nor Burn
WOODSIDE
Sacriston Jun & Inf Schs
DUNELM
PRIORY CT
ABBEY MEWS
HILL CREST
EASTWOOD
REDHOUSE CL
BROWBANK
DURHAM CT
CATHEDRAL VIEW
FINDON HILL
HOLMESLAND VILLAS
Fulworth
New Close
Fyndoune Com Coll
Kimblesworth Grange
THE CRESCENT
ROSE LEA
ERRINGTON BGLWS 10
KIRKWOOD 11
LOW GRAHAM ST 12
HIGH GRAHAM ST 13
DOROTHY TERR 14
FYNDOUNE 15
CRAIGLAND VILLAS 16
NORBURN PK
HILLSIDE
SACRISTON LA
BRIAR LEA
MAY LEA
GREEN LEA
FINDON AVE
OAK LEA
FYNDOUNE WAY
WATERSTONE CRES
DENE CT
Wellsprings Farm
DH1
SOUTH LEA
DURHAM GDNS
Red House Farm
B6532
CHESTER GDNS
FAIR VIEW
B6312
BROOKSIDE
A B C D E F
8 7 49 6 5 48 4 3 47 2 1 46
23 24 25
33
24

23
16

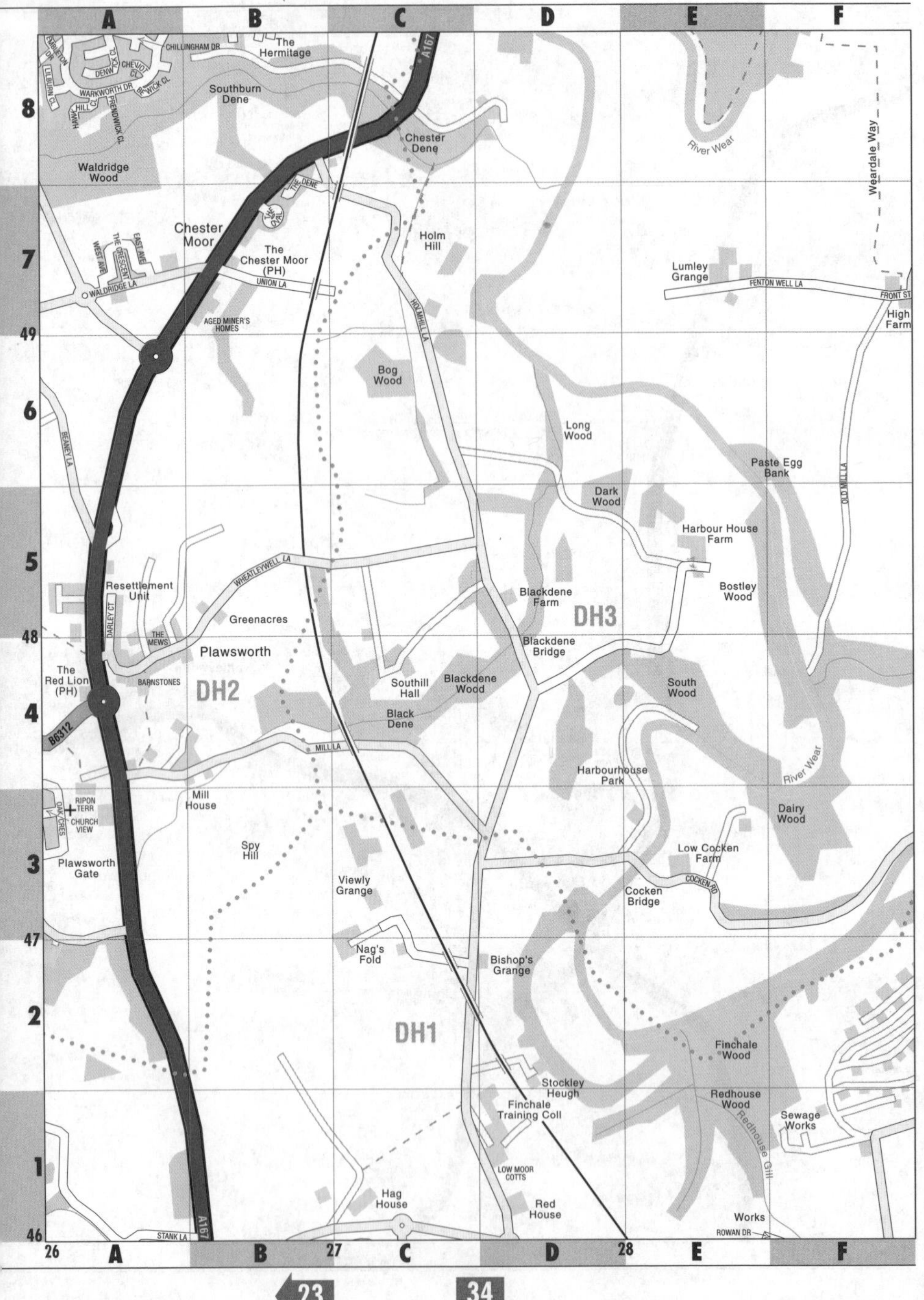
The Hermitage
CHILLINGHAM DR
Southburn Dene
Waldridge Wood
WARKWORTH DR
PRENDWICK CL
CHEVIOT CL
Chester Dene
River Wear
Weardale Way
Chester Moor
The Chester Moor (PH)
UNION LA
WALDRIDGE LA
WEST AVE
THE CRESCENT
EAST AVE
AGED MINER'S HOMES
Holm Hill
HOLMHILL LA
Lumley Grange
FENTON WELL LA
FRONT ST
High Farm
Bog Wood
BEANEY LA
Long Wood
Paste Egg Bank
OLD MILL LA
Dark Wood
Harbour House Farm
WHEATLEYWELL LA
Resettlement Unit
Greenacres
Blackdene Farm
Bostley Wood
DH3
DARLEY CT
THE MEWS
Plawsworth
Blackdene Bridge
The Red Lion (PH)
BARNSTONES
DH2
Southill Hall
Blackdene Wood
South Wood
B6312
Black Dene
MILL LA
River Wear
Harbourhouse Park
Mill House
RIPON TERR
OAK CRES
CHURCH VIEW
Dairy Wood
Spy Hill
Low Cocken Farm
Plawsworth Gate
Viewly Grange
COCKEN RD
Cocken Bridge
Nag's Fold
Bishop's Grange
DH1
Finchale Wood
Stockley Heugh
Finchale Training Coll
Redhouse Wood
Redhouse Gill
Sewage Works
LOW MOOR COTTS
Hag House
Red House
Works
ROWAN DR
STANK LA
A167

23
34

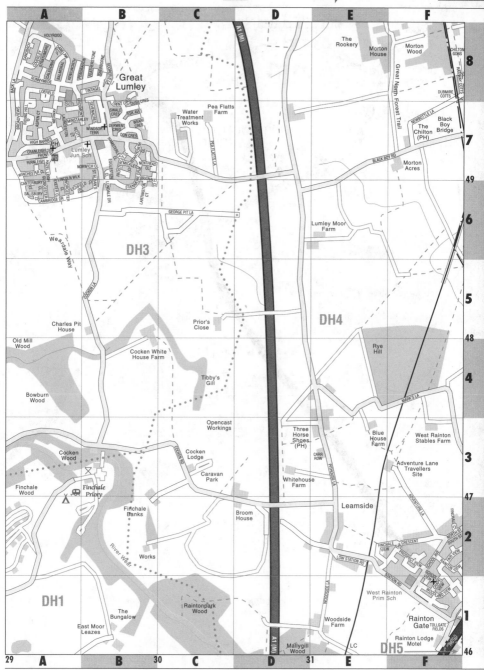

17
26

A B C D E F

Great Lumley
Water Treatment Works
Pea Flatts Farm
The Rookery
Morton House
Morton Wood
Great North Forest Trail
The Chilton (PH)
Black Boy Bridge
Morton Acres
Lumley Jun Sch
DH3
Weardale Way
Lumley Moor Farm
Prior's Close
DH4
Charles Pit House
Old Mill Wood
Cocken White House Farm
Rye Hill
Tibby's Gill
Bowburn Wood
Opencast Workings
Three Horse Shoes (PH)
Blue House Farm
West Rainton Stables Farm
Cocken Wood
Cocken Lodge
Adventure Lane Travellers Site
Caravan Park
Whitehouse Farm
Finchale Wood
Finchale Priory
Finchale Banks
Broom House
Leamside
River Wear
Works
West Rainton Prim Sch
DH1
Raintonpark Wood
The Bungalow
East Moor Leazes
Woodside Farm
Rainton Gate
Rainton Lodge Motel
Mallygill Wood
DH5

29 A B 30 C D 31 E F

35
26

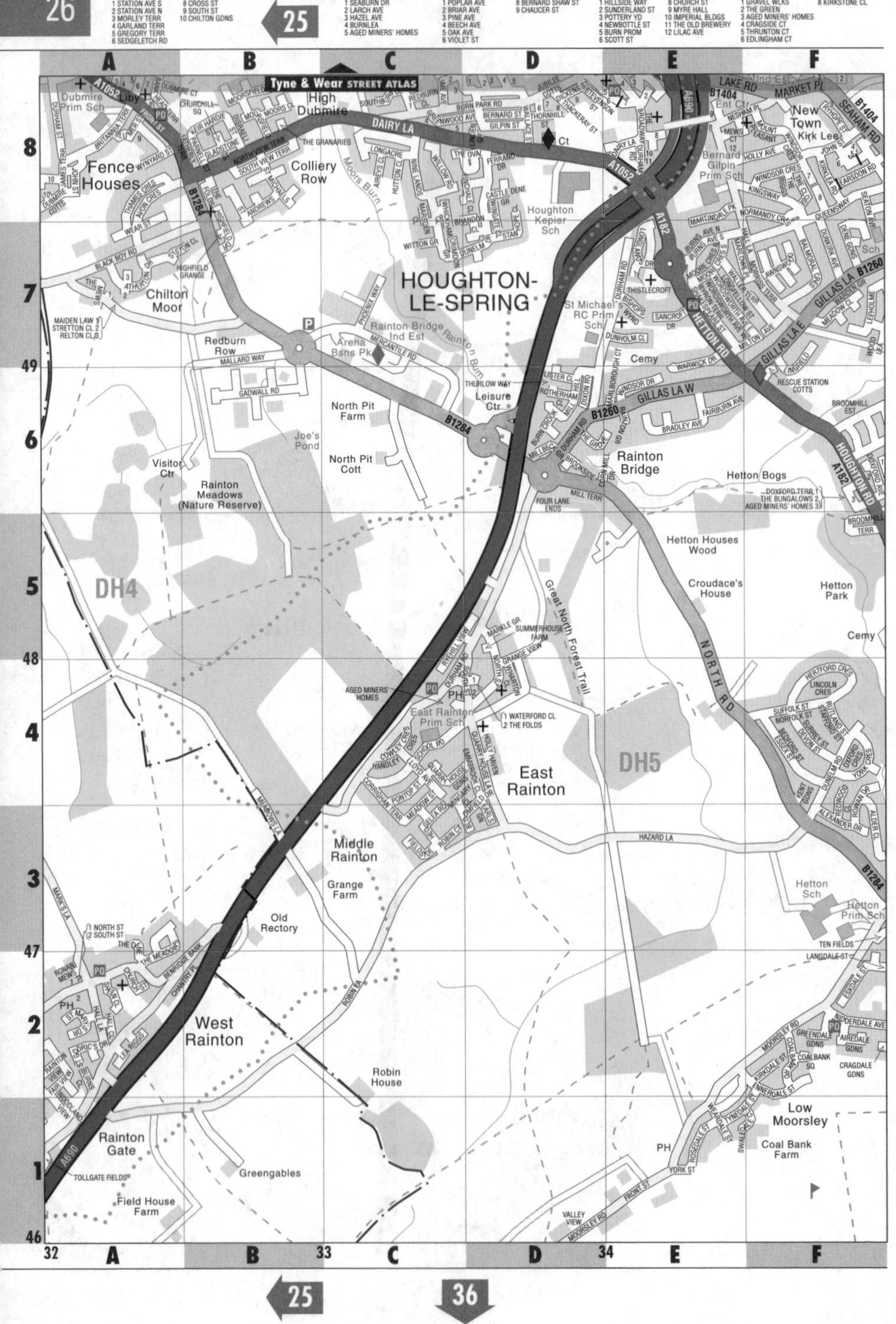

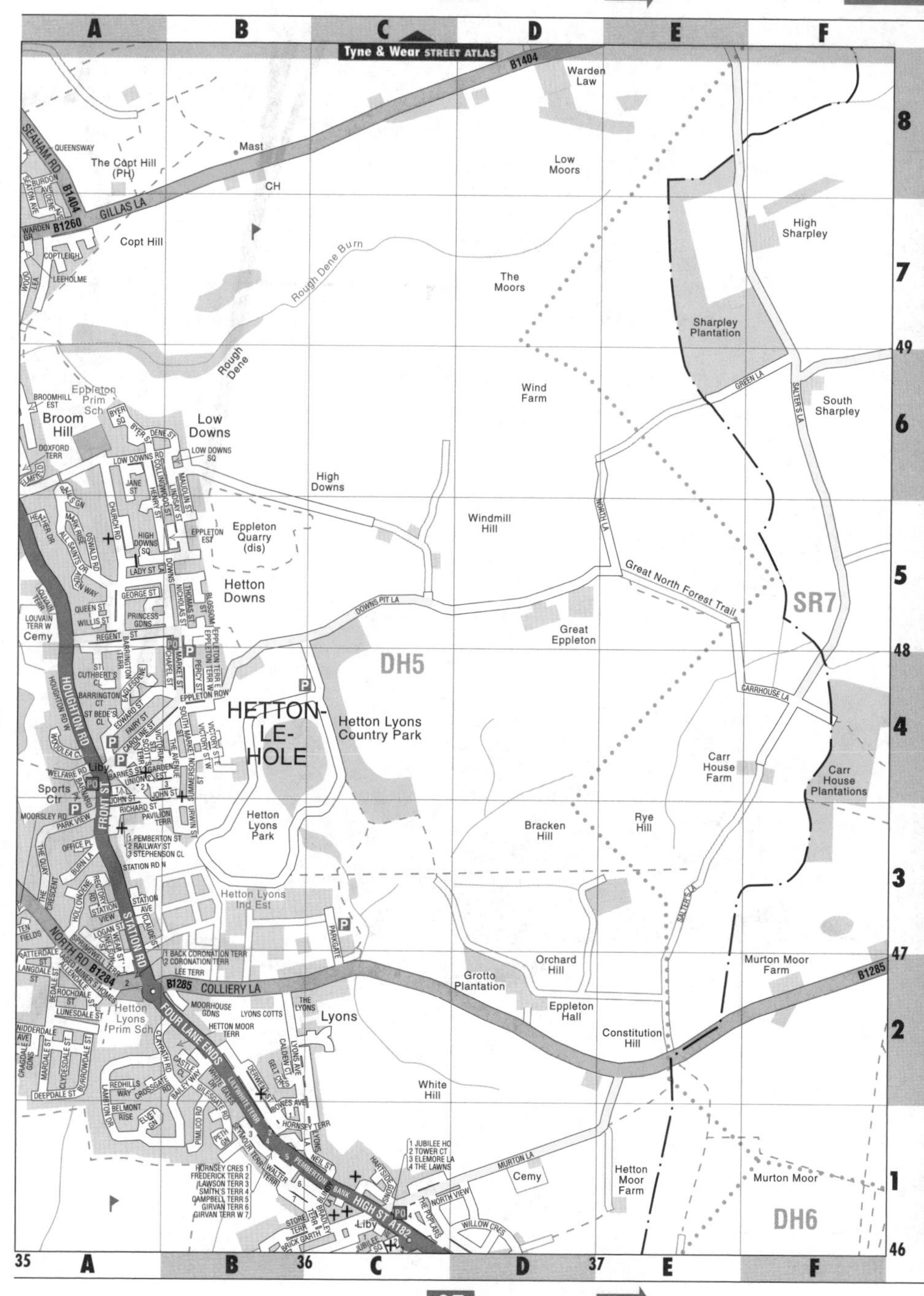

Tyne & Wear STREET ATLAS

Warden Law

B1404

8

Queensway

The Copt Hill
(PH)

Mast

Low
Moors

CH

GILLAS LA

B1260

Copt Hill

High
Sharpley

7

COPTLEIGH
LEEHOLME

Rough Dene Burn

The
Moors

49

Rough
Dene

Sharpley
Plantation

Eppleton
Prim Sch

BROOMHILL
EST

Broom
Hill

Low
Downs

Wind
Farm

South
Sharpley

6

DOXFORD
TERR

LOW DOWNS
SQ

GREEN LA
SALTER LA

LOW DOWNS RD

High
Downs

Windmill
Hill

Eppleton
Quarry
(dis)

Hetton
Downs

Great North Forest Trail

SR7

5

DOWNS PIT LA

NORTH LA

Great
Eppleton

48

DH5

CUTHBERT

ST BEDE'S

P

CARRHOUSE LA

4

HETTON-
LE-
HOLE

Hetton Lyons
Country Park

Carr
House
Farm

Carr
House
Plantations

Lib

P

P

Sports
Ctr

MOORSLEY RD
PARK VIEW

Hetton
Lyons
Park

Rye
Hill

3

P

Bracken
Hill

SALTER LA

OFFICE ROW

STATION RD N

1 PEMBERTON ST
2 RAILWAY ST
3 STEPHENSON CL

Hetton Lyons
Ind Est

NORTH RD B1284

STATION RD

Hetton
Lyons
Prim Sch

1 BACK CORONATION TERR
2 CORONATION TERR
LEE TERR

Orchard
Hill

Murton Moor
Farm

47

B1285

B1285

COLLIERY LA

MOORHOUSE
GDNS

LYONS COTTS

Lyons

Grotto
Plantation

Eppleton
Hall

2

HETTON MOOR
TERR

CALROYD TER

Constitution
Hill

REDHILLS
WAY

White
Hill

Hetton
Moor
Farm

Murton Moor

CROFTDALE

BELMONT
RISE

HIGH ST A182

1 JUBILEE HO
2 TOWER CT
3 ELEMORE LA
4 THE LAWNS

Cemy

DH6

1

1 HORNSEY CRES
FREDERICK TERR 2
LAWSON TERR 3
SMITH'S TERR 4
CAMPBELL TERR 5
GIRVAN TERR 6
GIRVAN TERR W 7

MURTON LA

NORTH VIEW

WILLOW CRES

BANK

Lib

27 18

A B C D E F

8

Sharpley Burn B1404

Seaton Gr

PH

Seaton Burn

Seaton

St Cuthbert's RC Prim Sch

Westlea Prim Sch

Eastlea

Westlea

7

Seaton Bank Top

Seaton Moor House

49

6

Haverley House

Stotfold Farm

Mast

West Farm

St Cuthbert's Terr

Slingley Hill West

Slingley Hill East

SR7

5

Dalton Moor

48

Dalton Dene

Dunelm Terr

4

Water Gate

Sandy Hill

Burnside

Dalton Dene

D'Arcy Sq

Truro Ave

Murton Bridge

Murton Jubilee Prim Sch

Liby

Murton Prim Sch

3

Aged Miners Homes

1 Henry St N
2 James St N
3 Wood's Terr E
4 Wood's Terr N
5 Glenhurst Terr
6 Western Terr E
7 Western Terr N
8 West Coronation St
9 North Coronation St
10 Windsor Terr

Briar Glen

STATION RD

47

B1285

Jedburgh St

Murton

Church St

Dalton Pk

2

St Joseph's RC Prim Sch

Cemy

Church St

11 Victoria Terr
12 South View
13 William Johnson St
14 Brooklyn St
15 Brooklyn Terr N
16 West Ellen St
17 East Ellen St
18 Cookson Terr
19 Ada St W
20 Ada St E

Hesledon Moor East

Hesledon Bank

Murton Recn Gd

Croup Hill

1

Long Run

Batter Law Hill

46

DH6

38 A 39 B C 40 D E F

19

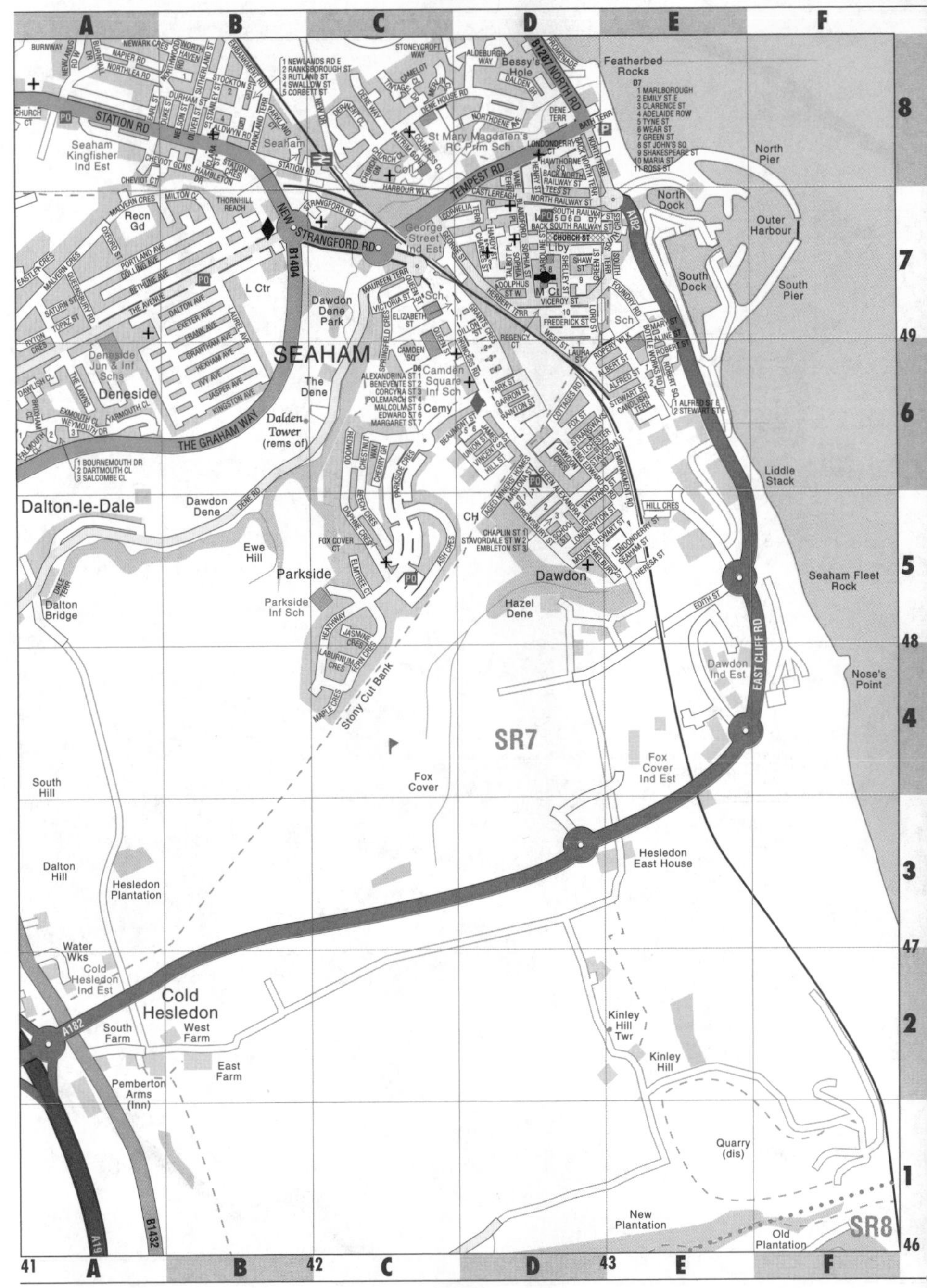

A B C D E F
8 7 6 5 4 3 2 1
49 48 47 46
41 42 43
SEAHAM
Seaham Kingfisher Ind Est
STATION RD
Seaham
Recn Gd
L Ctr
Dawdon Dene Park
Deneside Jun & Inf Schs
Deneside
THE GRAHAM WAY
Dalden Tower (rems of)
The Dene
Camden Square Inf Sch
Cemy
George Street Ind Est
St Mary Magdalen's RC Prim Sch
Bessy's Hole
Featherbed Rocks
North Pier
North Dock
Outer Harbour
South Dock
South Pier
Liby
Sch
Liddle Stack
Dalton-le-Dale
Dawdon Dene
Ewe Hill
Parkside
Parkside Inf Sch
Dawdon
Hazel Dene
Dalton Bridge
Seaham Fleet Rock
Dawdon Ind Est
Nose's Point
EAST CLIFF RD
Stony Cut Bank
SR7
Fox Cover
Fox Cover Ind Est
South Hill
Dalton Hill
Hesledon Plantation
Hesledon East House
Water Wks
Cold Hesledon Ind Est
Cold Hesledon
West Farm
South Farm
East Farm
Pemberton Arms (Inn)
Kinley Hill Twr
Kinley Hill
Quarry (dis)
New Plantation
Old Plantation
SR8
A182
A19
B1432
B1404
B1287 NORTH RD
TEMPEST RD
NEW STRANGFORD RD

39

183
20

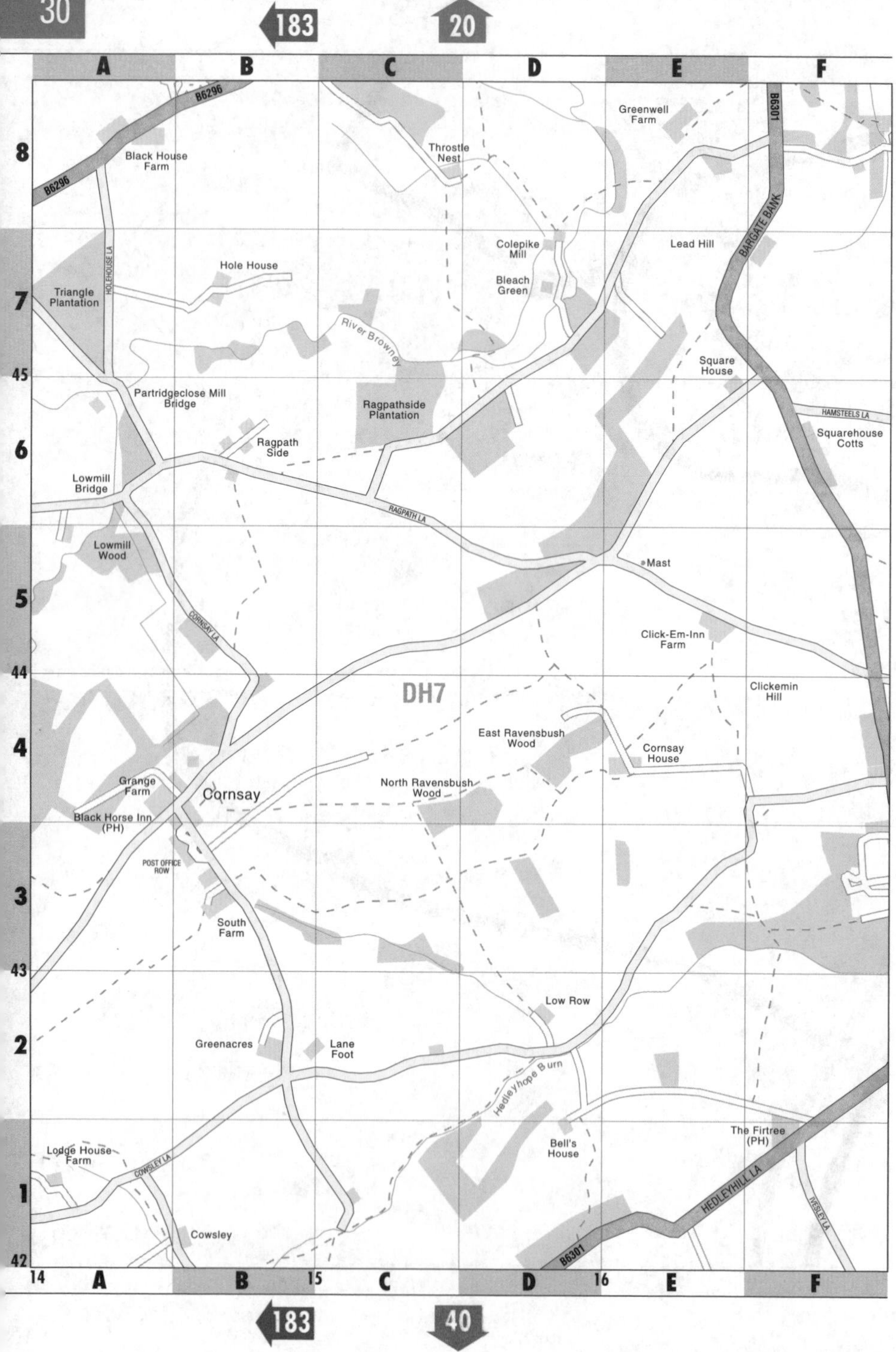
A
B
C
D
E
F
8
7
45
6
5
44
4
3
43
2
1
42
14
15
16
B6296
Black House Farm
Throstle Nest
Greenwell Farm
B6301
Hole House
HOLEHOUSE LA
Triangle Plantation
Colepike Mill
Bleach Green
Lead Hill
BARGATE BANK
River Browney
Square House
Partridgeclose Mill Bridge
Ragpathside Plantation
HAMSTEELS LA
Squarehouse Cotts
Ragpath Side
Lowmill Bridge
RAGPATH LA
Lowmill Wood
Mast
CORNSAY LA
Click-Em-Inn Farm
DH7
Clickemin Hill
East Ravensbush Wood
Cornsay House
Grange Farm
Cornsay
North Ravensbush Wood
Black Horse Inn (PH)
POST OFFICE ROW
South Farm
Low Row
Greenacres
Lane Foot
Hedleyhope Burn
Lodge House Farm
COWSLEY LA
Bell's House
The Firtree (PH)
HEDLEYHILL LA
IVESLEY LA
Cowsley
B6301

183
40

21
32

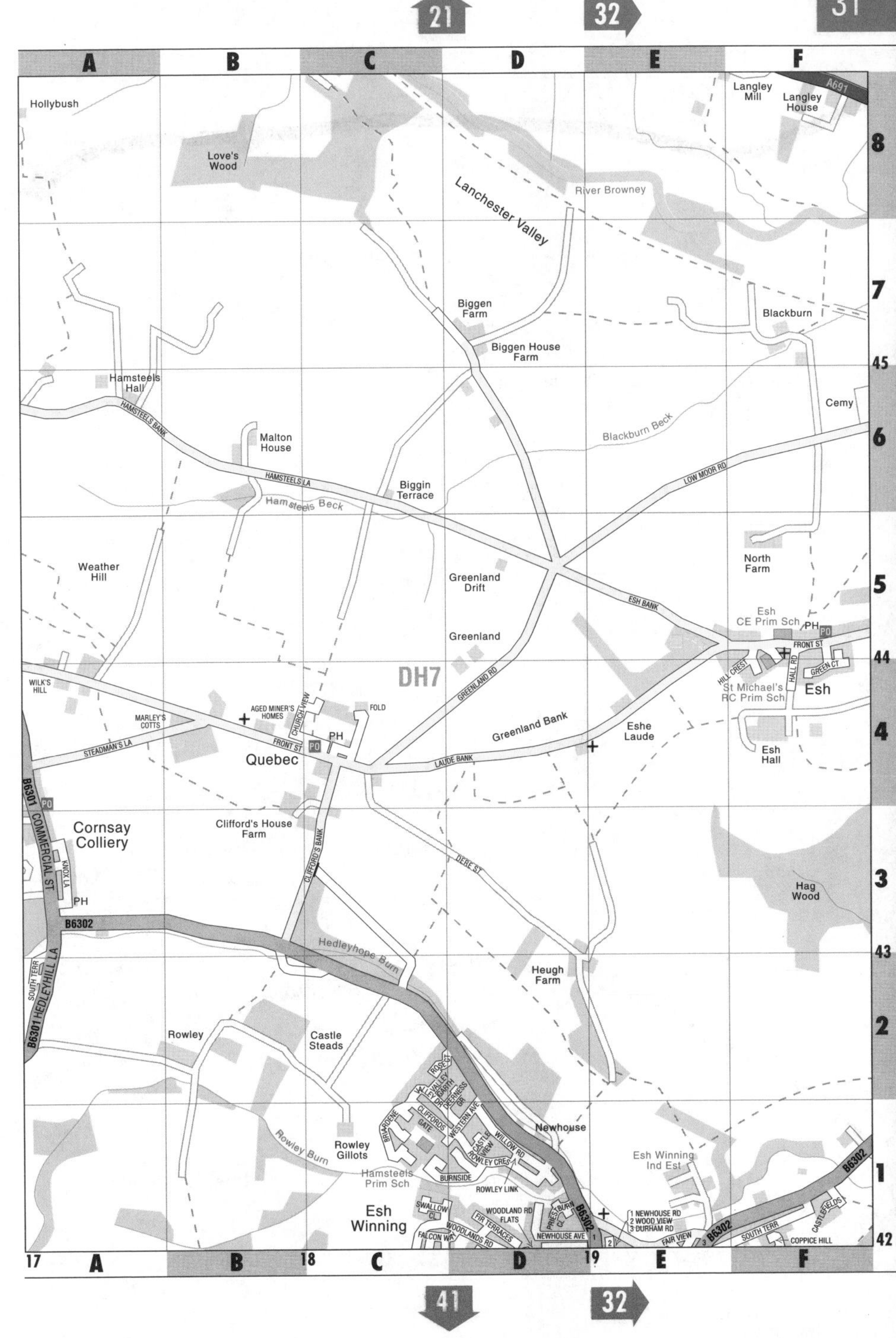
A
B
C
D
E
F
8
7
45
6
5
44
4
3
43
2
1
42
17
18
19
Hollybush
Love's Wood
Lanchester Valley
River Browney
Langley Mill
Langley House
A691
Biggen Farm
Biggen House Farm
Blackburn
Hamsteels Hall
HAMSTEELS BANK
Malton House
HAMSTEELS LA
Hamsteels Beck
Biggin Terrace
Blackburn Beck
LOW MOOR RD
Cemy
North Farm
Weather Hill
Greenland Drift
Greenland
ESH BANK
Esh CE Prim Sch
PH
PO
FRONT ST
HILL CREST
HALL RD
GREEN CT
St Michael's RC Prim Sch
Esh
DH7
WILK'S HILL
MARLEY'S COTTS
AGED MINER'S HOMES
CHURCH VIEW
FOLD
GREENLAND RD
Greenland Bank
Eshe Laude
STEADMAN'S LA
FRONT ST
PO
PH
Quebec
LAUDE BANK
Esh Hall
B6301
COMMERCIAL ST
Cornsay Colliery
Clifford's House Farm
KNOX LA
PH
CLIFFORD'S BANK
DERE ST
Hag Wood
B6302
Hedleyhope Burn
Heugh Farm
SOUTH TERR
B6301 HEDLEYHILL LA
Rowley
Castle Steads
ROSE CT
VALLEY GARTH
VALLEY DR
DEERNESS GR
CLIFFORDS GATE
WESTERN AVE
BRIARDENE
CASTLE VIEW
WILLOW RD
Newhouse
Rowley Burn
Rowley Gillots
ROWLEY CRES
BURNSIDE
Hamsteels Prim Sch
ROWLEY LINK
Esh Winning Ind Est
B6302
Esh Winning
SWALLOW CL
WOODLAND RD FLATS
FIR TERRACES
PRIESTBURN CL
B6302
1 NEWHOUSE RD
2 WOOD VIEW
3 DURHAM RD
CASTLEFIELDS
FALCON WAY
WOODLANDS RD
NEWHOUSE AVE
FAIR VIEW
B6302
SOUTH TERR
COPPICE HILL

41
32

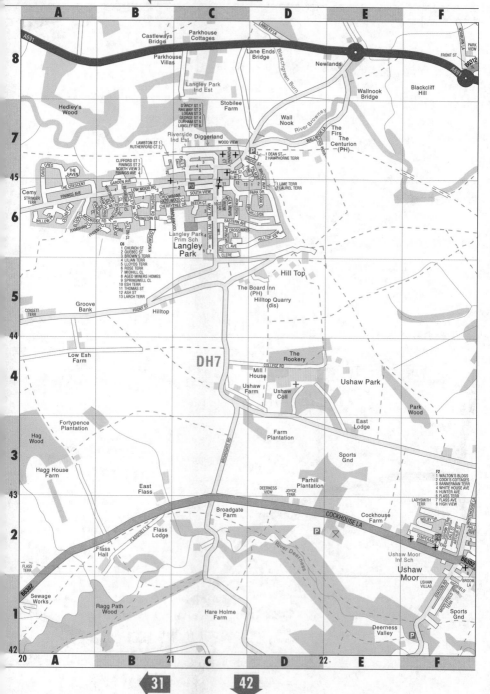

31
22

A B C D E F

8

A691

Castleways Bridge
Parkhouse Cottages
Parkhouse Villas
LANGLEY LA
Lane Ends Bridge
Bleachgreen Burn
Newlands
Wallnook Bridge
MORRISON LA
PARK VIEW
FRONT ST
B6312
Blackcliff Hill

Langley Park Ind Est
Hedley's Wood
D'ARCY ST 1
RAILWAY ST 2
LOGAN ST 3
GEORGE ST 4
DURHAM ST 5
LANGLEY ST 6
Stobilee Farm
Wall Nook
River Browney
WALLNOOK LA
The Firs
The Centurion (PH)

7

LAMBTON ST 1
RUTHERFORD CT 2
Riverside Ind Est
Diggerland
WOOD VIEW
BROWNEY CT
P
1 DEAN ST
2 HAWTHORNE TERR

45

CLIFFORD ST 1
FININGS ST 2
NORTH VIEW 3
FININGS AVE 4
DALE
CAES
THE HAVEN
THE CRESCENT
GARDEN AVE
LOW MOOR RD
BROWNEY
OAK ST
ELM ST
BRICK ROW
1 LIME TERR
2 LAUREL TERR

Cemy
STRINGER TERR
FININGS AVE
PARK DR
HILLSIDE

6

WILLOW
ESPLEY CT
RAMSHAW CL
PHOENIX
ELDORNE CL
ELMORE
WHINFIELD
HOSPITAL RD
WITTON CL
HARRINGTON CL
HAZELWOOD
CHERRYTREE DR
SOUTH VIEW
BEECH CT
HAZEL MEWS
LINZEL MEWS
BYRNE TERR
PARK DR
EASTERN AVE

Langley Park Prim Sch
HILLTOP VIEW
CROSSWAYS
LILAC AVE
FAST
HILLTOP VIEW

Langley Park

C6
1 CHURCH ST
2 QUEBEC ST
3 BROWN'S TERR
4 LILIAN TERR
5 LLOYDS TERR
6 ROSE TERR
7 MICHILL CL
8 AGED MINERS HOMES
9 SPRINGWELL CL
10 ESH TERR
11 THOMAS ST
12 ASH ST
13 LARCH TERR

CLERE

5

Groove Bank
CONSETT TERR
FRONT ST
Hilltop
Hill Top
The Board Inn (PH)
Hilltop Quarry (dis)

44

Low Esh Farm

DH7

The Rookery

4

Mill House
College RD
Ushaw Farm
Ushaw Coll
Ushaw Park

Fortypence Plantation
Hag Wood

East Lodge
Park Wood

3

Hagg House Farm
East Flass
Farm Plantation
Sports Gnd

43

DEERNESS VIEW
JOYCE TERR
Farhill Plantation

F2
1 WALTON'S BLDGS
2 COCK'S COTTAGES
3 BANNERMAN TERR
4 WHITE HOUSE AVE
5 HUNTER AVE
6 FLASS TERR
7 FLASS AVE
8 HIGH VIEW
LADYSMITH TERR

2

FLASHALL LA
Flass Lodge
Broadgate Farm
BROADGATE RD
COCKHOUSE LA
Cockhouse Farm
WELBY DR
TEMPERANCE
LANN TERR
HALL AVE

Flass Hall
River Deerness
Ushaw Moor Inf Sch
USHAW VILLAS
B6302
BROOM LA
LADYSMITH TERR
HIGHFIELD

FLASS TERR
Sewage Works
B6302

1

Ragg Path Wood
Hare Holme Farm
Ushaw Moor
Sports Gnd

Deerness Valley
P

42

20 A B 21 C D 22 E F

31
42

A B C D E F
Witton Gilbert
Witton Gilbert Prim Sch
Fyndoune
Little Gill
Potter House
Bog Wood
Sewage Works
Sleight's House
Trout's Lane Sch
Hartside Farm
Half-Way Houses
Earl's House
Lodge Hill
Bear Park
Sniperley Hall
Sniperley Farm
Lodge Farm
DH7
DH1
Sniperley Park
Bearpark Hall Farm
Bearpark (remains of)
Aden Cottage
Stotgate Farm
Bearpark Prim Sch
Bearpark
Lanchester Valley Wlk
River Browney
Whitesmocks
Moorsley Banks
Fernhill
Deerness Valley Comp Sch
Works
Sewage Works
Aldin Grange Farm
Old Arbour House
Arbour House
Durham Johnston Comp Sch
Broom Hall
St Joseph's RC Prim Sch
Ushaw Moor Jun Sch
Cemy
Sports Ctr
Quarry House
Baxter Wood
Recn Gd
DENE BANK
FRONT ST
SACRISTON LA
B6312
B6532
A167
A691
B6302
DURHAM RD
BROOM LA
POTTERHOUSE LA
ALDIN GRANGE TERR
TOLL HOUSE RD
QUARRY HOUSE LA
8 7 6 5 4 3 2 1
45 44 43 42
23 24 25

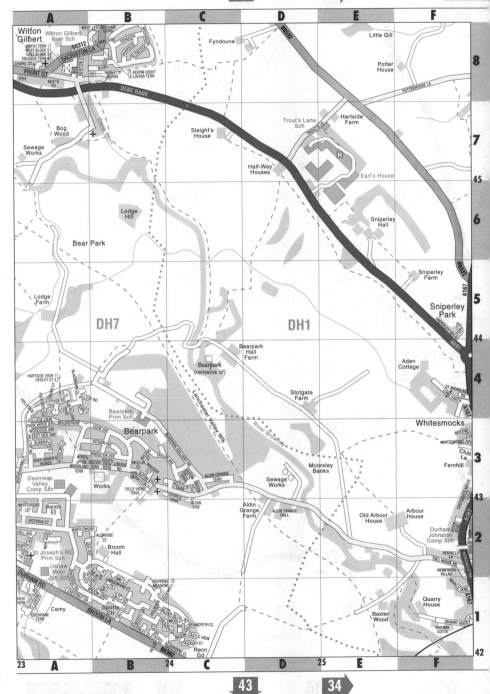

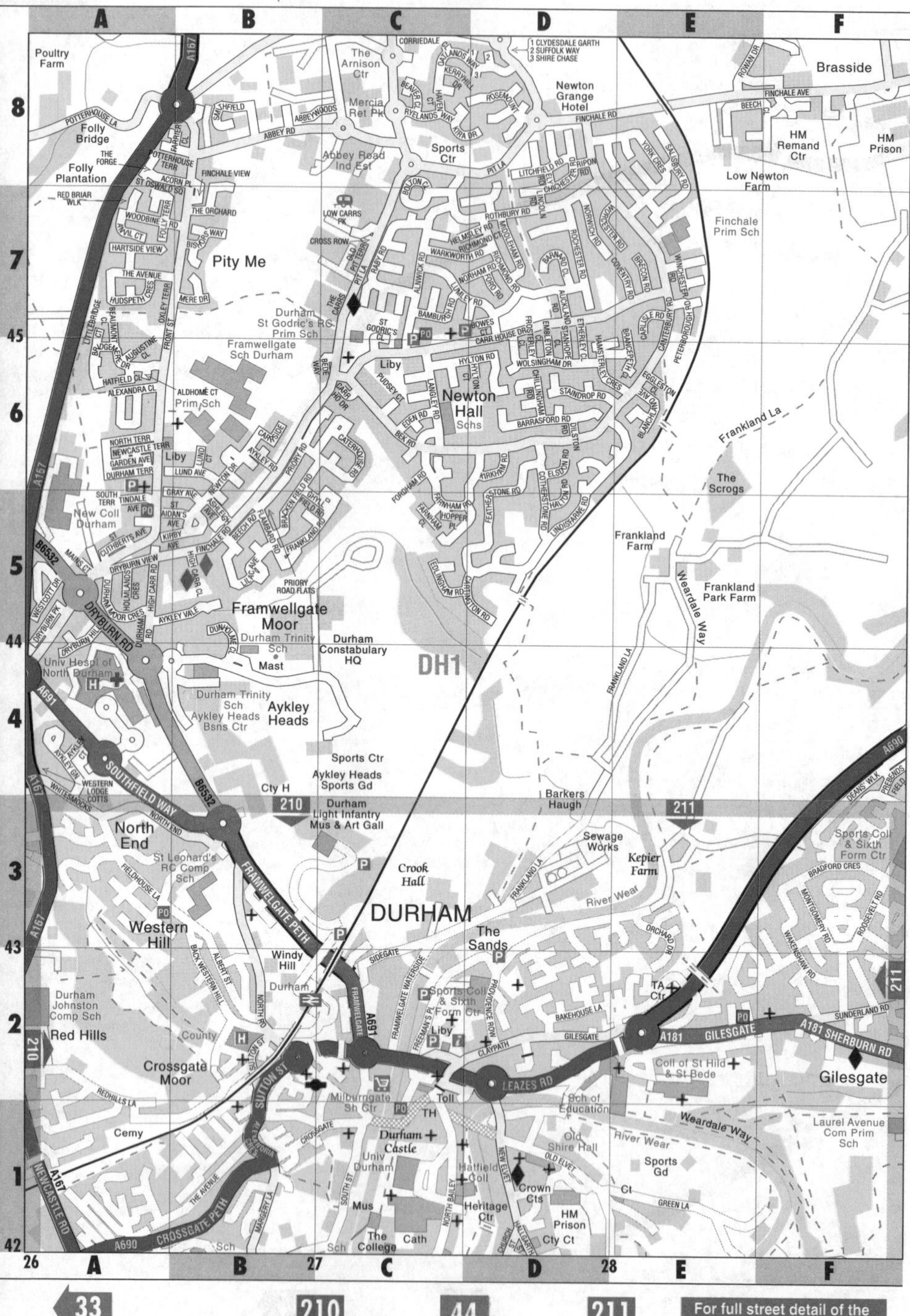

For full street detail of the highlighted area see pages 210 and 211.

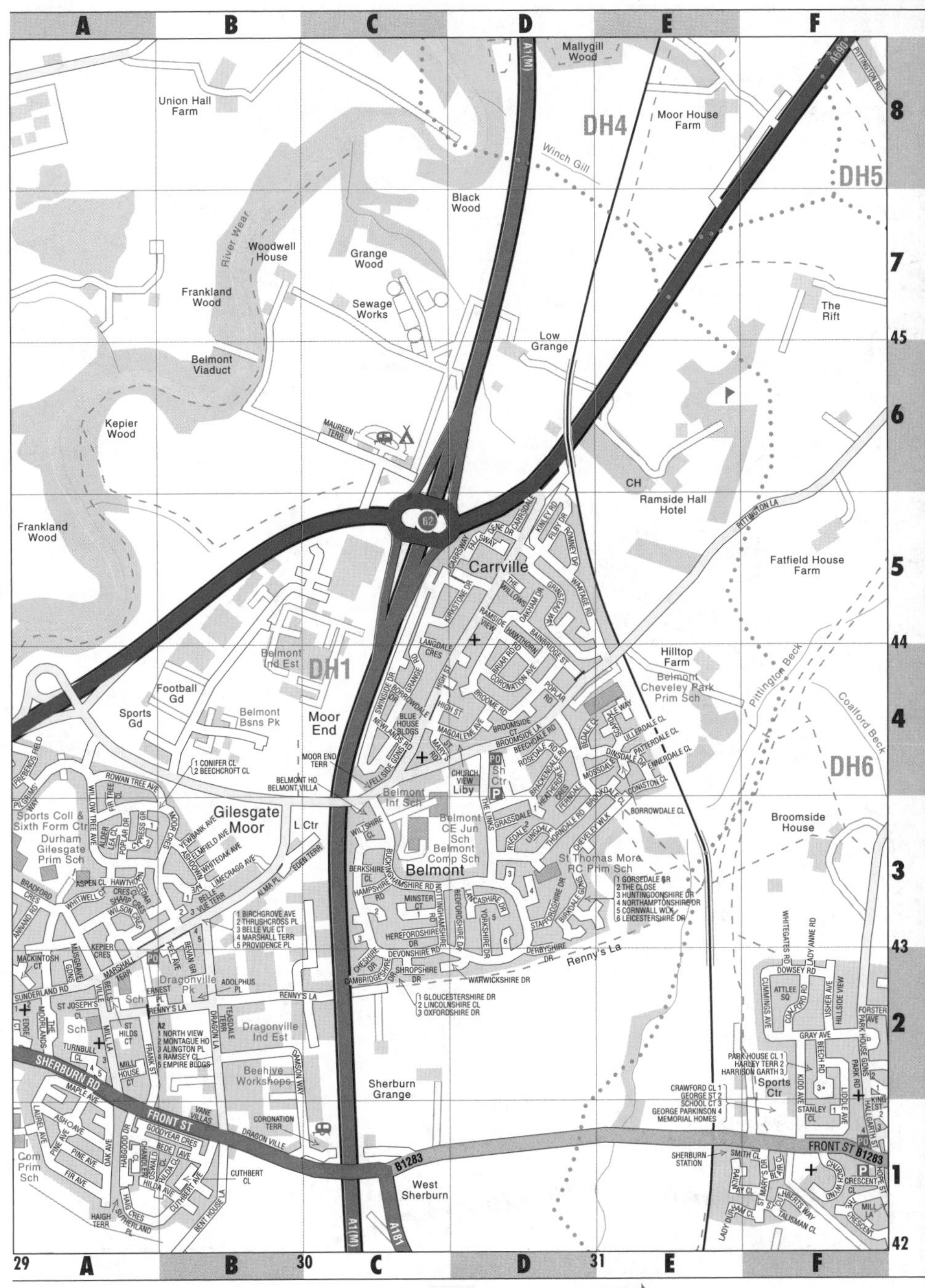
25
36
45
DH4
DH5
DH1
DH6
Mallygill Wood
Union Hall Farm
Moor House Farm
Winch Gill
Black Wood
River Wear
Woodwell House
Grange Wood
Frankland Wood
Sewage Works
The Rift
Low Grange
Belmont Viaduct
Kepier Wood
Maureen Terr
CH
Ramside Hall Hotel
Pittington La
Frankland Wood
Carrville
Fatfield House Farm
Belmont Ind Est
Hilltop Farm
Football Gd
Belmont Cheveley Park Prim Sch
Sports Gd
Belmont Bsns Pk
Moor End
Pittington Beck
Coalford Beck
Gilesgate Moor
Belmont Inf Sch
Liby
Broomside House
Sports Coll & Sixth Form Ctr
Durham Gilesgate Prim Sch
L Ctr
Belmont CE Jun Sch
Belmont Comp Sch
Belmont
St Thomas More RC Prim Sch
Renny's La
Dragonville Pk
Dragonville Ind Est
Beehive Workshops
Sherburn Grange
Sports Ctr
Sherburn Rd
Front St
B1283
West Sherburn
Com Prim Sch
A1(M)
A181
A690
Sherburn Station
Front St B1283

35
26

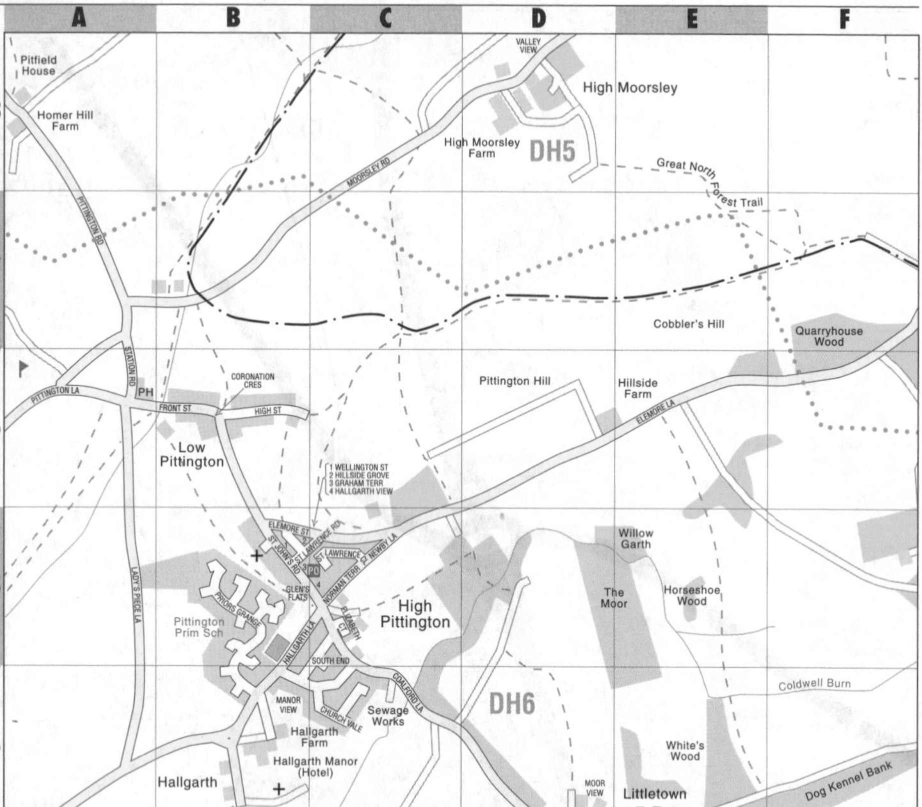

A B C D E F

8

Pitfield House

Homer Hill Farm

High Moorsley

High Moorsley Farm

DH5

VALLEY VIEW

Great North Forest Trail

MOORSLEY RD

PITTERS RD

7

Cobbler's Hill

Quarryhouse Wood

45

Pittington Hill

Hillside Farm

STATION RD

PITTINGTON LA

PH

FRONT ST

HIGH ST

CORONATION CRES

6

Low Pittington

ELEMORE LA

1 WELLINGTON ST
2 HILLSIDE GROVE
3 GRAHAM TERR
4 HALLGARTH VIEW

ELEMORE ST

ST JOHN'S RD

LAWRENCE

PO

NEWRY LA

QUARRY MASTERS RD

NORMANTON RD

Willow Garth

GLEN'S FLATS

5

High Pittington

The Moor

Horseshoe Wood

Pittington Prim Sch

LADY'S PIECE LA

PIKE'S GRANGE

HALLGARTH LA

SOUTH END

44

COALFORD LA

Coldwell Burn

MANOR VIEW

CHURCH VALE

Sewage Works

DH6

4

Hallgarth Farm

Hallgarth Manor (Hotel)

White's Wood

MOOR VIEW

Littletown

PLANTATION AVE

Dog Kennel Bank

Hallgarth

3

Pittington Bridge

Coalford Beck

Littletown Farm

Littletown House

Duke of York (PH)

Hastings House

LITTLETOWN WAY

Stand Bridge

43

2

FORSTER AVE

PARK CL

PASSIE RISE

Sherburn Village Prim Sch

COCKSHOLA LA

Cook's Hold Farm

Saw Mill

Black Banks

1

WHALTON CL

Sherburn

1 CHASE CT
2 KINNOCK CL
3 HALLGARTH VILLAS
4 BROADVIEW VILLAS

ALSTON WLK

B1283

PEART CL

CHAPEL CT

SOUTH ST

FRONT ST

Sherburn Hill

WEST TERR

WESLEY TERR

GAINSFORD TERR

LOCAL AVE

LOCAL AVE

AGED MINERS HOMES

PALATINE VIEW

PH

Sherburn Hill Prim Sch

NORTH VIEW

SOUTH VIEW

JUBILEE CRES

THE CROFT

KELL CRES

PINDERS WAY

High House Farm

1 CO-OPERATIVE VILLAS
2 BRIGHTON TERR
3 DURHAM LA

FRONT ST

B1283

42

32 A B 33 C D 34 E F

35
46

38

A B C D E F

8
7
45
6
5
44
4
3
43
2
1
42

Brick Garth
Dorset St
Elemore La
Prospect Cres
Thames St
Tees St
High St A182
The Elms
Willow Cres
Frosterley Cl
Easington Lane
Ullswater Ave
Rydal Ave
Coniston
Grasmere Ave
Loweswater Ave
Buttermere Ave
Tamar St
Tay St
Easington Lane Prim Sch
South Hetton Rd
Works
The Vale (PH)
Vale St
James Terr
Lorne St
Elemore Vale
White Hill Rd
Sheriff's Ave
Eden Ave
School View
Sheriff's Moor
Coronation Gv
Queen Elizabeth Ave
South View
Wordsworth
Ruskin Av
CH
Elemore La
Hetton le Hill
DH5
White Hill
Sheriff's Moor
Whitegates Equestrian Centre
Salter's La
Buttermere Cres
Patrick Cres
Conishead Terr
Ullswater Terr
Keswick Terr
Derwent Terr
Donald Ave
Windsor Dr
Argyle Pl
Ravensworth Ct
Logan Terr
Coldwell Cl
Front St
South Hetton Ind Est
Sycamore Cl
Hedley Terr
Elemore View
Dinsdale Dr
Plantation Walk
Bessemer Rd
Pasteur Rd
A182
Jubilee Sq
Cedar Ct
B1280
Cockhill Plantation
South Hetton Prim Sch
Carters Cres
Frederick Terr
Hetton le Hill Wood
Elemore
Cherry Garth
East Wood
Coldwell Burn
Pig Hill
Salter's La
High Fallowfield
Elemore Hall Sch
Low Haswell
Low Haswell Banks
Chapel Garth
High Haswell
Coldwell Burn Farm
Elemore Grange
Lily Hill
Green La
Brown's Plantation
Lily Hill Plantation
Sycamore Terr 1
Allendale Terr 2
Maplewood Dr 3
Cherry Dr 4
East Villas
Dabble Hill
Green La
DH6
Station St
Front St East
George St
Pesspool La
Alexandra Terr
Kestrel Way
Acer Dr
Almond Cl
Blossomfield Way
Dene Terr
Howarth Terr
Burt Cl
Phillips Cl
PO
PH
Chapel La
Field House Terr
Haswell Lodge
Church St
Church View
Haswell
Haswell Prim Sch
Faraday Terr
Richmond Terr
Pesspool Ave
Pesspool Terr
Hall La
Kingston Cres
Windsor Terr
Pesspool Bglws
Watson's Hill
Barnett Sq
Salter's La
Hospital Farm
Mazine Terr
Haswell Moor Farm
The Bottoms
Durham La
Hesewell Cres
Gloucester Terr
B1280
Greenacres
Haswell Plough
Kent Terr
Rutland Terr
McAteer Ct
Limekiln Hill
Prospect Hill
Front St
Attlee Cres
B1283
Plough Farm
North View
The Gables (PH)
Durham La
B1283

35 A B 36 C D 37 E F

47
38

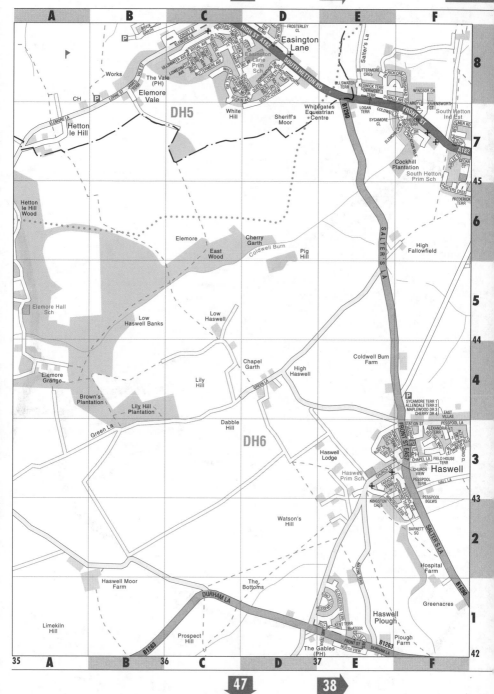

A B C D E F

8

Little Coop House Farm

East Batter Law Farm

SR7

Coop House Wood

West Batter Law Farm

South Hetton Ind Est

BESSEMER RD

1 FREDERICK TERR
2 ROSE COTTS
3 FALLOWFIELD TERR

7

KINGSMERE RD

A182 FRONT ST

PH

South Hetton

HEATHDALE

Coop Hill

WEST LA

45

QUIN RD

SIMPSON TERR

CHARTERS CRES

CORONATION SQ

GRASMERE TERR

PARKLANDS GR

THE AVENUE

BEVIN GR

MILBURN

PINDER CRES

BRYDON CRES

ASHBROOKE

Carr's Farm

Great Coop House Farm

Round Hill

6

ASHCROFT

MATTHEW

FORSTER CRES

DRESSER TERR

Hallfield

MATTHEWS CRES

VICARAGE CL

Milestone Hill

Low Fallowfield

5

North Hill

West Moor House Farm

Milestone House

44

Duncombe Moor

DH6

4

Holy Cross Farm

Junction House Farm

A182 HALL WLKS

PESSPOOL LA

B1283

CHESTNUT DR

Cove Holes

Rymer's Moor

SR8

Bridge Hills

A19

KIPPERING BANKS

DURHAM LA

3

Pesspool Hall

HALL LA

Low Ling Close

Cow Close Farm

Holmlea

43

Mawson's Hill

Loaning BURN

Calf Close Farm

2

High Ling Close

Moor House Farm

Mast

Pesspool Wood

Quarry (dis)

Pesspool Dene

DURHAM LA

KITCHING RD

1

B1280 SALTER'S LA

Tuthill House

Sandy Carrs

Westmoor Farm

North West Ind Est

HACKWORTH RD

MILL HILL

42

B1283

Tuthill Bridge

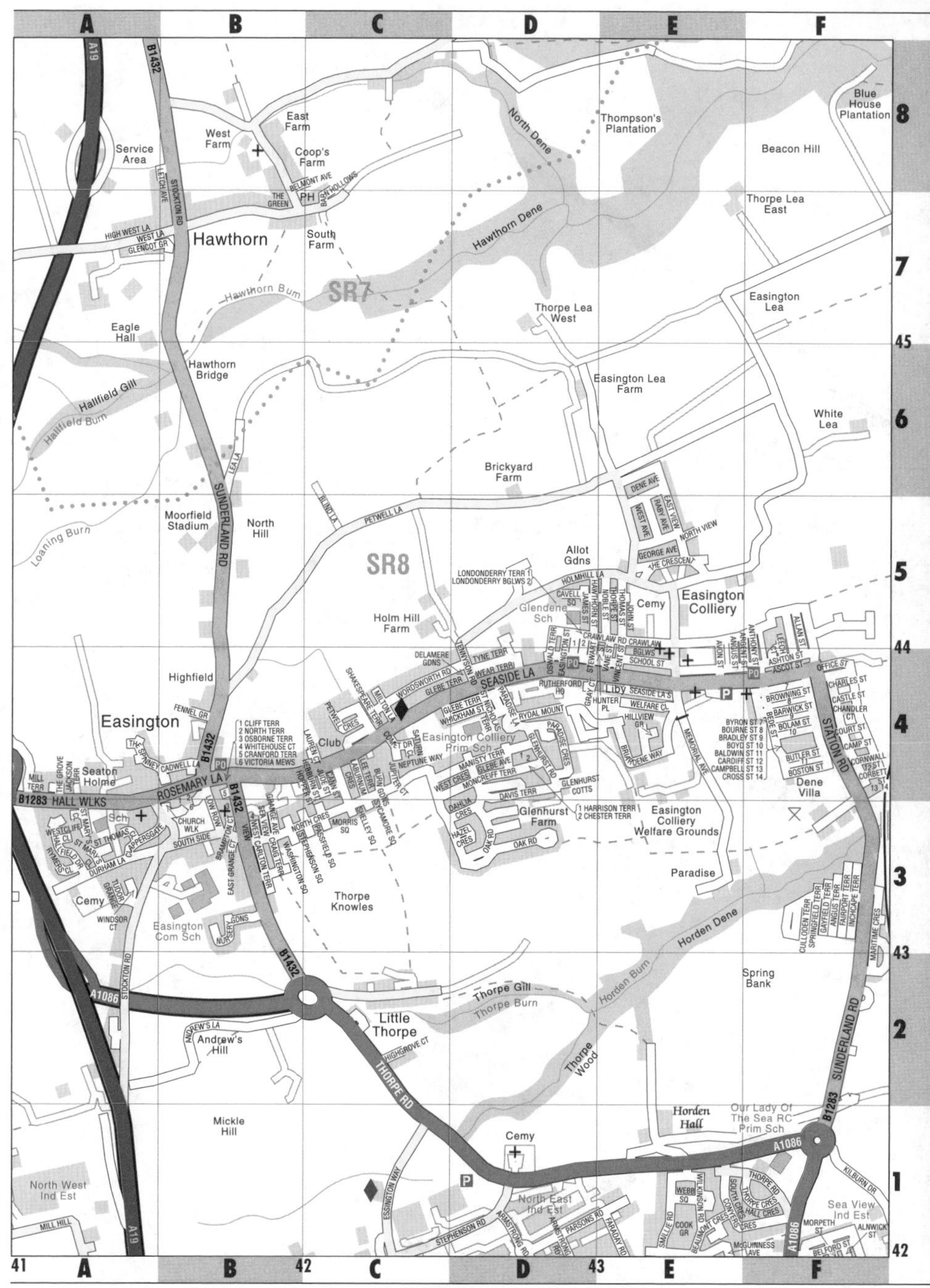
A
B
C
D
E
F
8
7
6
5
4
3
2
1
45
44
43
42
41
Hawthorn
West Farm
East Farm
Coop's Farm
South Farm
Service Area
Thompson's Plantation
North Dene
Hawthorn Dene
Blue House Plantation
Beacon Hill
Thorpe Lea East
Thorpe Lea West
Easington Lea
SR7
Hawthorn Burn
Eagle Hall
Hawthorn Bridge
Hallfield Gill
Easington Lea Farm
White Lea
Brickyard Farm
Moorfield Stadium
North Hill
Loaning Burn
SR8
Allot Gdns
Easington Colliery
Cemy
Holm Hill Farm
Glendene Sch
Highfield
Easington
Seaton Holme
Club
Easington Colliery Prim Sch
Glenhurst Farm
Easington Colliery Welfare Grounds
Dene Villa
Paradise
Thorpe Knowles
Easington Com Sch
Horden Dene
Spring Bank
Thorpe Gill
Thorpe Burn
Little Thorpe
Andrew's Hill
Thorpe Wood
Mickle Hill
Horden Hall
Our Lady Of The Sea RC Prim Sch
North West Ind Est
North East Ind Est
Sea View Ind Est
SUNDERLAND RD
STOCKTON RD
ROSEMARY LA
SEASIDE LA
HALL WLKS
THORPE RD
STATION RD
PETWELL LA
A19
A1086
B1432
B1283

183
30

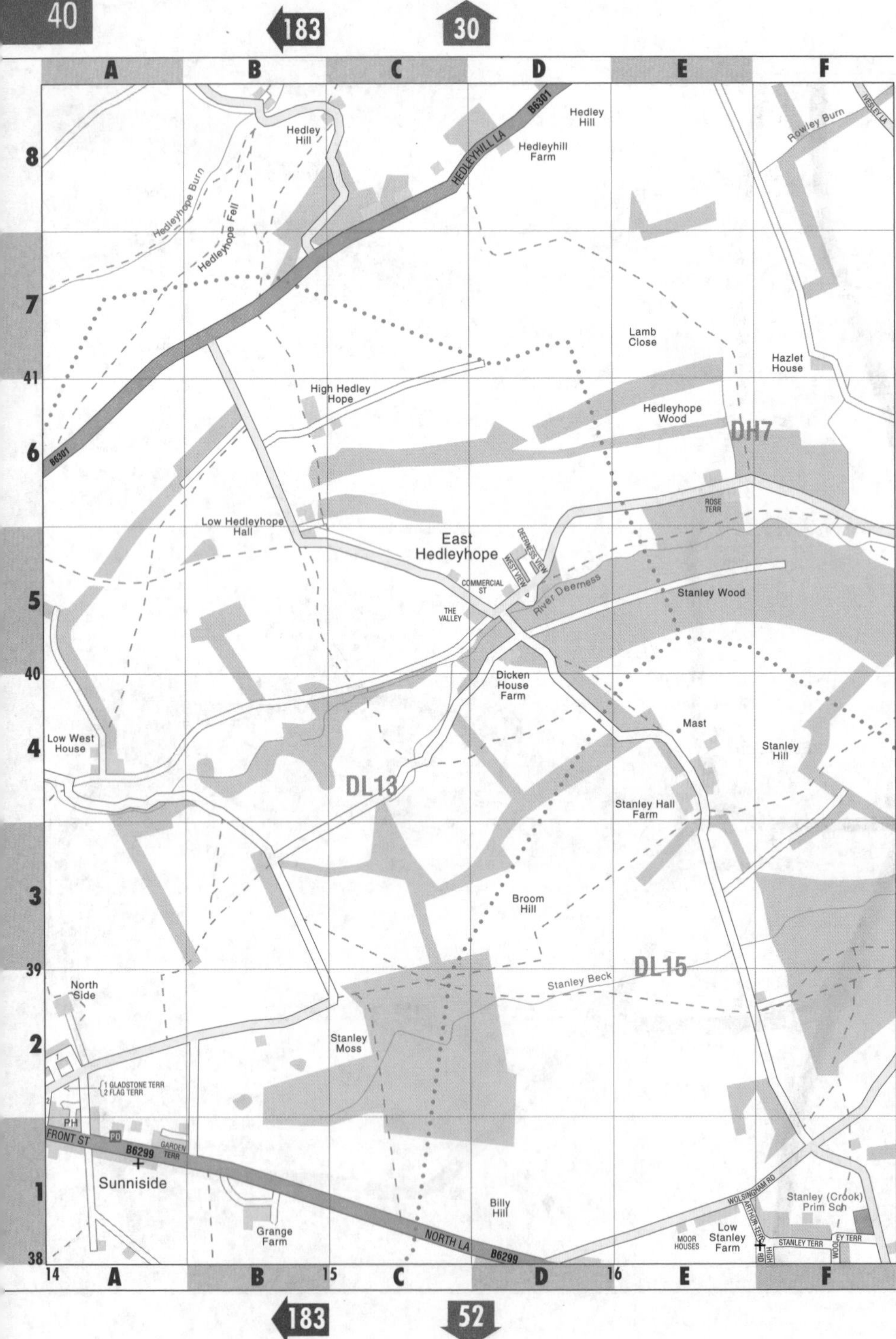
A
B
C
D
E
F
Hedley Hill
Hedley Hill
Hedleyhill Farm
HEDLEYHILL LA
B6301
Rowley Burn
WESLEY LA
Hedleyhope Burn
Hedleyhope Fell
Lamb Close
Hazlet House
High Hedley Hope
Hedleyhope Wood
DH7
B6301
ROSE TERR
Low Hedleyhope Hall
East Hedleyhope
DEERNESS VIEW
WEST VIEW
COMMERCIAL ST
River Deerness
Stanley Wood
THE VALLEY
Dicken House Farm
Mast
Low West House
Stanley Hill
DL13
Stanley Hall Farm
Broom Hill
DL15
Stanley Beck
North Side
Stanley Moss
1 GLADSTONE TERR
2 FLAG TERR
PH
PO
FRONT ST
B6299
GARDEN TERR
Sunniside
Billy Hill
WOLSINGHAM RD
ARTHUR TERR
Stanley (Crook) Prim Sch
Grange Farm
NORTH LA
B6299
MOOR HOUSES
Low Stanley Farm
HIGH RD
STANLEY TERR
WOOD
8
7
41
6
5
40
4
3
39
2
1
38
14
15
16

183
52

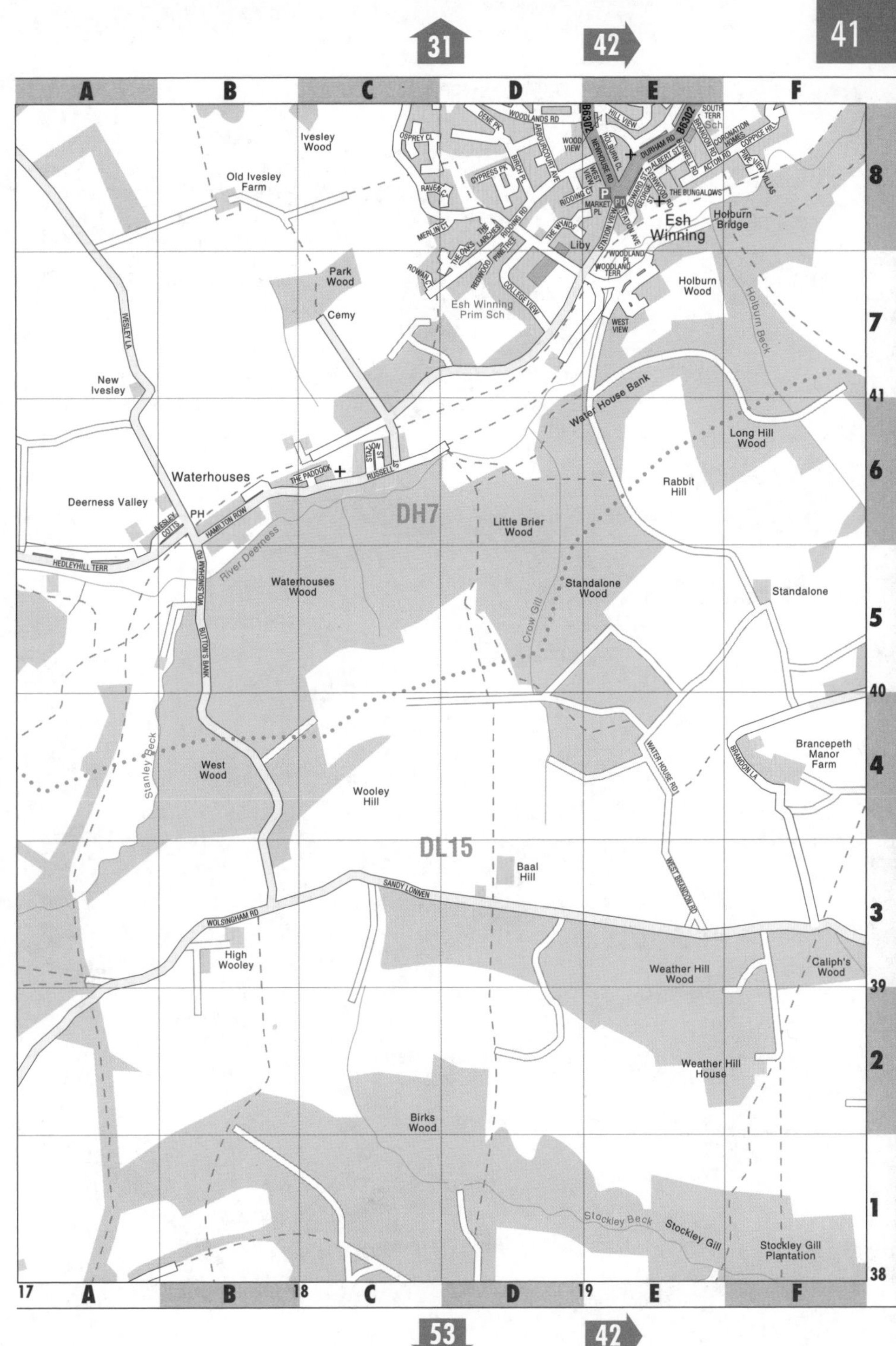

A B C D E F

8

7

41

6

5

40

4

3

39

2

1

38

Ivesley Wood

Old Ivesley Farm

Park Wood

Cemy

New Ivesley

Waterhouses

Deerness Valley

PH

HEDLEYHILL TERR

Waterhouses Wood

West Wood

Stanley Beck

High Wooley

WOLSINGHAM RD

DL15

Wooley Hill

Birks Wood

SANDY LONNEN

Baal Hill

River Deerness

HAMILTON ROW

BUTTON'S BANK

MESLEY LA

BESLEY COTTS

ON PRIMROSE PLAN

THE PADDOCK

RUSSELL'S

DH7

Little Brier Wood

Crow Gill

Standalone Wood

Standalone

Brancepeth Manor Farm

BRANCEPETH LA

WEST BRANDON RD

WATER HOUSE RD

Water House Bank

Long Hill Wood

Rabbit Hill

Weather Hill Wood

Weather Hill House

Caliph's Wood

Stockley Beck Stockley Gill

Stockley Gill Plantation

WOODLANDS RD

HILL VIEW

DURHAM RD

NEWHOUSE RD

BB302

SOUTH TERR

CORONATION

ACTON RD

COPPICE HILL

VILLAS

Esh Winning

Holburn Bridge

Holburn Wood

Holburn Beck

WEST VIEW

Esh Winning Prim Sch

COLLEGE VIEW

WOODLAND TERR

Liby

The Bungalows

MARKET PL

WOODLAND

OSPREY CL

CYPRESS PK

RAVEN CL

MERLIN CT

THE LARCHES

THE WYNDS

ROWAN

DENE CT

ARCHDEACON LANE

WOOD VIEW

41
32

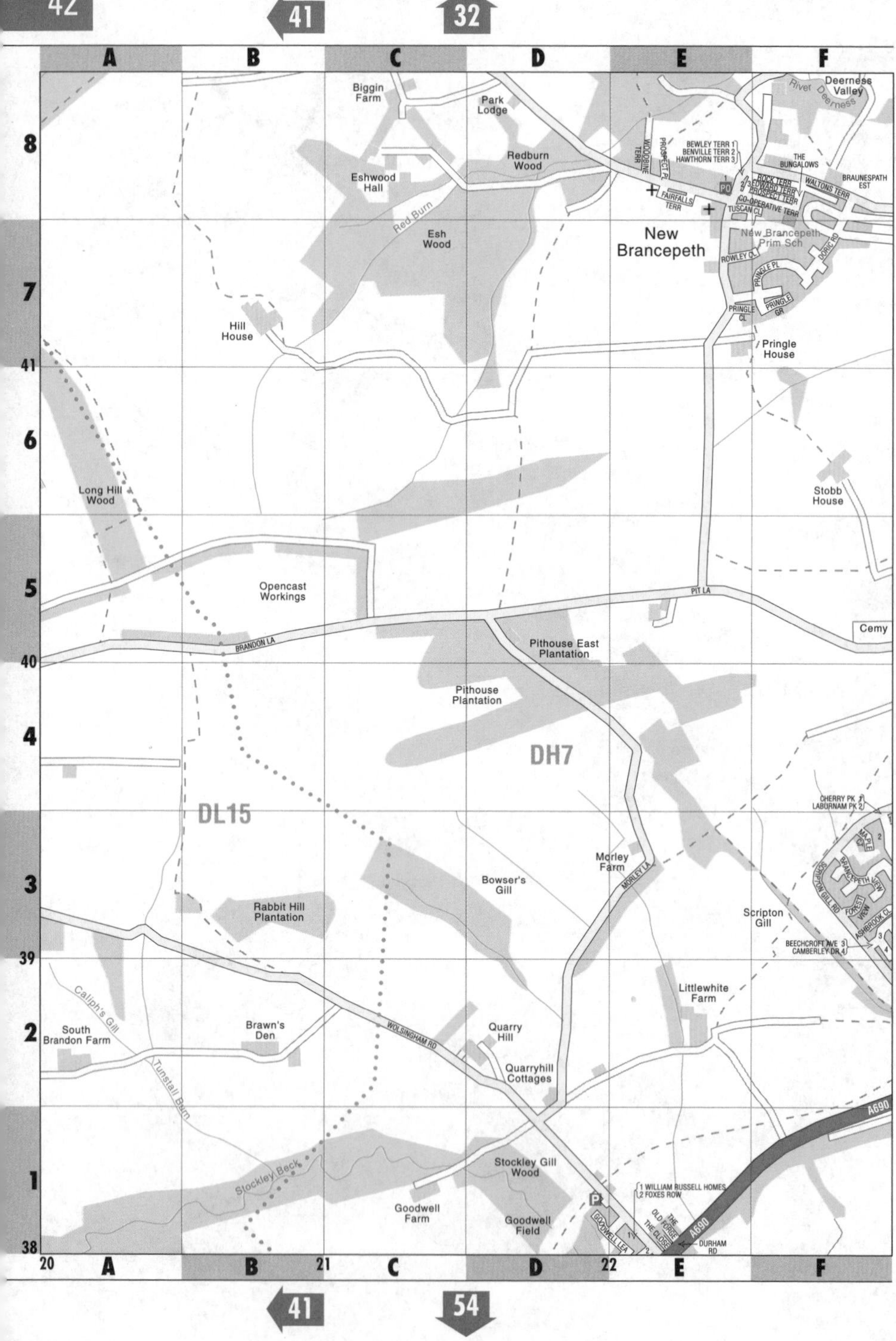
A
B
C
D
E
F
Biggin Farm
Park Lodge
Deerness Valley
River Deerness
Redburn Wood
Eshwood Hall
Red Burn
Esh Wood
WOODBINE TERR
PROSPECT PL
BEWLEY TERR 1
BENVILLE TERR 2
HAWTHORN TERR 3
THE BUNGALOWS
ROCK TERR
EDWARD TERR
PROSPECT TERR
WALTONS TERR
BRAUNESPATH EST
FAIRFALLS TERR
CO-OPERATIVE TERR
TUSCAN CL
PO
New Brancepeth
New Brancepeth Prim Sch
ROWLEY CL
PRINGLE PL
DORIC RD
PRINGLE CL
PRINGLE GR
Hill House
Pringle House
Long Hill Wood
Stobb House
Opencast Workings
PIT LA
Cemy
BRANDON LA
Pithouse East Plantation
Pithouse Plantation
DH7
DL15
CHERRY PK 1
LABURNAM PK 2
MAPLE CT
BRANCEPETH VIEW
SCRIPTON GILL RD
FOREST VIEW
ASHBROOK CL
BEECHCROFT AVE 3
CAMBERLEY DR 4
Morley Farm
MORLEY LA
Bowser's Gill
Scripton Gill
Rabbit Hill Plantation
Littlewhite Farm
Caliph's Gill
South Brandon Farm
Brawn's Den
WOLSINGHAM RD
Quarry Hill
Quarryhill Cottages
Tunstall Burn
A690
Stockley Beck
Stockley Gill Wood
1 WILLIAM RUSSELL HOMES
2 FOXES ROW
Goodwell Farm
Goodwell Field
GOODWELL LEA
THE OLD FORGE
THE CLOSE
DURHAM RD
8
7
41
6
5
40
4
3
39
2
1
38
20
21
22

41
54

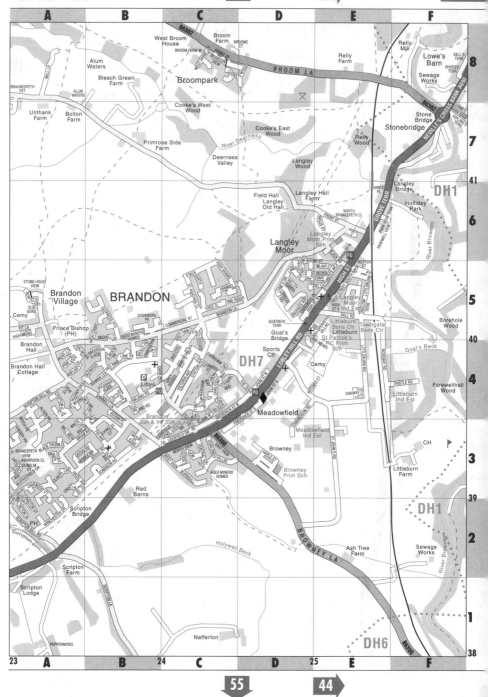

44

A B C D E F

8 7 6 5 4 3 2 1

41 40 39 38

23 24 25

West Broom House
Broom Farm
BROOME CT
BROOM FARM W
FRONT ST
BRANDON VIEW
WEST FARM CT
COOKE'S WOOD
B6302
BROOM LA
Broompark
Alum Waters
Bleach Green Farm
ALUM WATERS
MILL LA
BRAUNESPETH EST
Unthank Farm
Bolton Farm
Cooke's West Wood
Cooke's East Wood
Primrose Side Farm
River Deerness
Deerness Valley
Relly Farm
Relly Mill
Lowe's Barn
KELL'S TERR
RHODES' TERR
Sewage Works
NEVILLE'S CROSS BANK A690
LOWE'S BARN BANK
KIPLING'S TER
Stone Bridge
Stonebridge
Relly Wood
Langley Wood
ANN'S PL
Langley Bridge
DH1
Holliday Park
Field Hall
Langley Old Hall
Langley Hall Farm
NORTH BRANCEPETH CL
FRONT ST
ANGUS ST
GROVE TERR
PARK VIEW TERR
FAREWELL VIEW
River Browney
Langley Moor
Langley Moor Prim Sch
BLACK RD
HIGH ST N
PO
BOYNE CT
BLAIR CT
RUTTER ST
HIGH ST
HIGH STREET SOUTH BACK
ST CUTHBERTS WLK
ST BEDES WAY
LITTLEBURN LA
ONSLOW TERR
Langley Moor Ind Est
MILL RD
STOBB HOUSE VIEW
NORTH END
OLD GDNS
Cemy
Brandon Village
BRANDON
STACK GARTH
HIGH SHAWS
HEMMEL CT
ST AGATHAS CL
TIREE CL
THE RIGGS
BRANDON LA
COMMERCIAL ST
SYCAMORE PK
DEERNESS HTS
PIT LA
HIGH MDWS
Prince Bishop (PH)
HIGH CROFT
MIDHILL CL
AGED MINERS' HOMES
Brandon Hall
Brandon Hall Cottage
GOATBECK TERR
Goat's Bridge
LOBLEY HILL RD
CO-OPERATIVE VILLAS
CHURCH MDWS
Littleburn Bsns Ctr
Littleburn
Towngate Bsns Ctr
St Patrick's RC Prim Sch
LITTLEBURN RD
ROSEBAY RD
Borehole Wood
Goat's Beck
Sports Ctr
DH7
Cemy
FRENSHAM WAY
ARTEMIS CT
THISTLE RD
Farewellhall Wood
Littleburn Ind Est
OAKWAY CT
Liby
P
PO
CARR AVE
VICTORIA AVE
STATION AVE
JOHN ST N
JOHN ST S
THE TERR
LOWLAND RD
Meadowfield
FREDERICK ST N
FREDERICK ST S
EDWARDSON RD
Brandon Jun & Inf Sch
LEESFIELD DR
SCRIPTON GILL RD
ALDER PK
BEECH PK
CHERRY PK
BELL MDW
BRIAR AVE
FIR AVE
CYPRESS CT
MOOR EDGE
Meadowfield Ind Est
ST JOHN'S RD
B6300
NORTH VIEW
SOUTH VIEW
CENTRAL AVE
DORLONCO VILLAS
EAST VIEW
WEST VIEW
BURNIGILL
AGED MINERS' HOMES
Browney
HARLE ST
Browney Prim Sch
CH
Littleburn Farm
BRANCEPETH VIEW
ASHBROOK CL
DUNELM CT
MURRAYFIELD DR
BLACK THORN CL
GROVE RD
MIDDLE GR
DOMINION RD
CLOVER LAID
HAZEL AVE
CROFT RIGG
CAVENDISH CT
LEXINGTON CT
WINCHESTER DR
Red Barns
Scripton Bridge
PH
SCRIPTON GILL RD
Scripton Gill
DH1
BROWNEY LA
Holywell Beck
Ash Tree Farm
Sewage Works
River Browney
Scripton Farm
Scripton Lodge
SCRIPTON LA
Nafferton
PEPPERMIRES
DH6
B6300

55

44

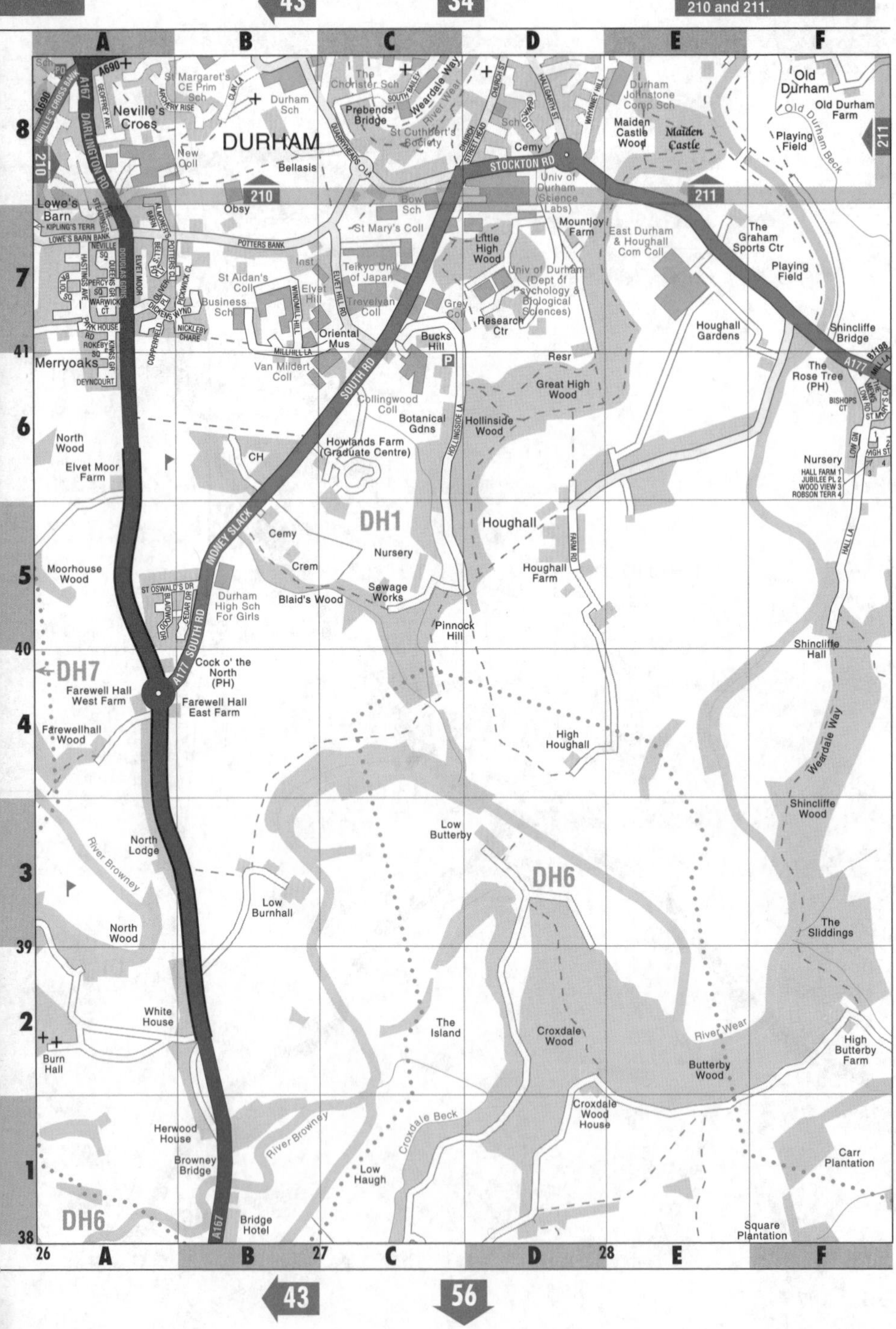

35
46

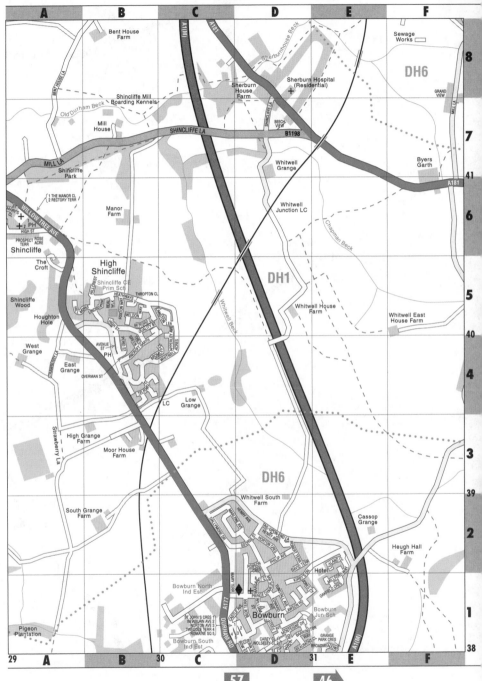

A
B
C
D
E
F
Bent House Farm
Sewage Works
DH6
Sherburn House Farm
Sherburn Hospital (Residential)
Shincliffe Mill Boarding Kennels
Mill House
SHINCLIFFE LA
B1198
MILL LA
Shincliffe Park
Whitwell Grange
Byers Garth
A181
Manor Farm
Whitwell Junction LC
Shincliffe
The Croft
High Shincliffe
Shincliffe CE Prim Sch
DH1
Shincliffe Wood
Houghton Hole
Whitwell House Farm
Whitwell East House Farm
West Grange
East Grange
Low Grange
High Grange Farm
Moor House Farm
Strawberry La
DH6
Whitwell South Farm
South Grange Farm
Cassop Grange
Heugh Hall Farm
Bowburn North Ind Est
Hotel
Bowburn
Bowburn Jun Sch
Pigeon Plantation
Bowburn South Ind Est
DURHAM RD
A177
A1(M)
1 THE MANOR CL
2 RECTORY TERR
ST JOHN'S CRES 1
NEWBURN AVE 2
NORTON AVE 3
TWEDDLE TERR 4
ROMAINE SQ 5
8
7
41
6
5
40
4
3
39
2
1
38
29
30
31

57
46

45
36

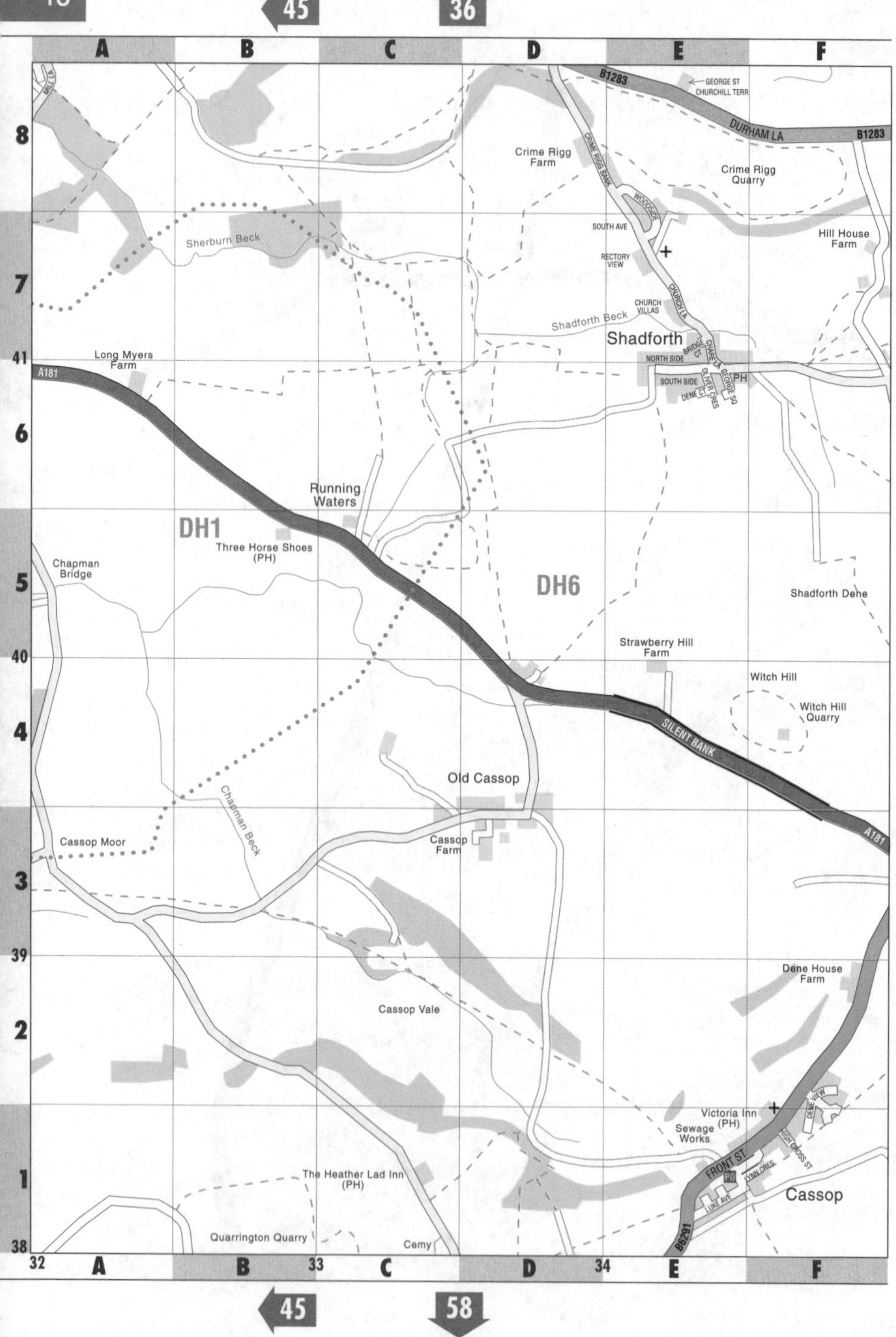
A
B
C
D
E
F
8
7
41
6
5
40
4
3
39
2
1
38
32
33
34
B1283
GEORGE ST
CHURCHILL TERR
DURHAM LA
B1283
MILL LA
Crime Rigg
Farm
Crime Rigg
Quarry
CRIME RIGG BANK
WOODSIDE
SOUTH AVE
RECTORY
VIEW
CHURCH LA
Hill House
Farm
Sherburn Beck
CHURCH
VILLAS
Shadforth Beck
Shadforth
BRIDGE
CT
CHARE LA
NORTH SIDE
SOUTH SIDE
OLIVER CRES
GEORGE SQ
DENE CT
PH
Long Myers
Farm
A181
Running
Waters
DH1
Three Horse Shoes
(PH)
Chapman
Bridge
DH6
Shadforth Dene
Strawberry Hill
Farm
Witch Hill
Witch Hill
Quarry
SILENT BANK
Old Cassop
Chapman Beck
Cassop Moor
Cassop
Farm
A181
Dene House
Farm
Cassop Vale
Victoria Inn
(PH)
DENE VIEW
Sewage
Works
HIGH CROSS ST
FRONT ST
PO
LYNN CRES
The Heather Lad Inn
(PH)
LUKE AVE
Cassop
B6291
Quarrington Quarry
Cemy

45
58

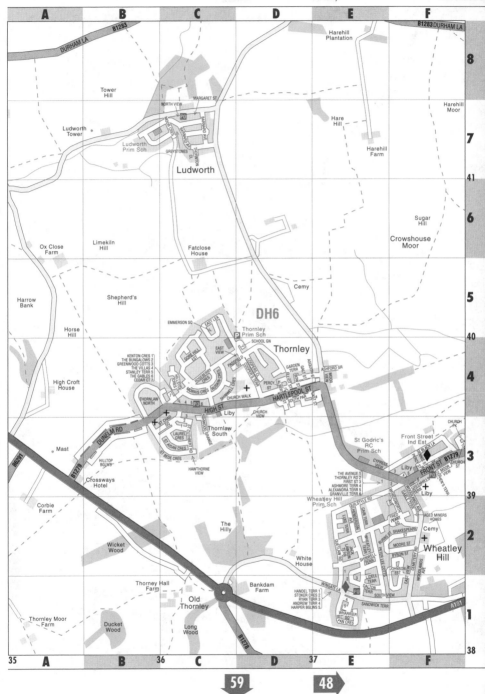
37

48

A B C D E F
8 7 6 5 4 3 2 1
41 40 39 38
35 36 37
B1283 DURHAM LA
Harehill Plantation
Tower Hill
Harehill Moor
NORTH VIEW
MARGARET ST
Hare Hill
Ludworth Tower
MOOR CRES
BARNARD AVE
Ludworth Prim Sch
GREYSTONES
THORNTON CL
Harehill Farm
Ludworth
Sugar Hill
Crowshouse Moor
Ox Close Farm
Limekiln Hill
Fatclose House
Cemy
Harrow Bank
Shepherd's Hill
DH6
EMMERSON SQ
EAST LEA
Thornley Prim Sch
SCHOOL GN
Horse Hill
Thornley
GORE HILL EST
EAST VIEW
PASSFIELD SQ
COOPERS CL
COOPER'S TERR
KENTON CRES 1
THE BUNGALOWS 2
GREENWOOD COTTS 3
THE VILLAS 4
STANLEY TERR 5
THE GABLES 6
CEDAR CT 7
GARDEN TERR
GALT ST
BOW ST
ASQUITH ST
ASHFORD GR
MOOR VIEW
HILLSYDE CRES
ROSEBERRY CRES
RUSKIN CRES
High Croft House
MORRIS CRES
SHINWELL CRES
ELLIOT ST
ALBERT ST
PERCY ST
CHURCH WALK
HARTLEPOOL ST
SOUTH PAR
EAST ST
THORNLAW NORTH
HIGH ST
Liby
CHURCH VIEW
ST CHAD SQ
ST CUTHBERT RD
ASHWOOD GRANGE
Thornlaw South
DUNELM RD
LAUREL CRES
ST AIDAN CRES
ST BEDE CRES
Mast
HAWTHORNE VIEW
St Godric's RC Prim Sch
CHURCH PK
Front Street Ind Est
BLACK LA
BENNIS ST
PERCY ST
FRONT ST B1279
CHURCH ST
CYPRESS VIEW
MOOR VIEW
STEPHEN'S TERR
HILLTOP BGLWS
B6291
B1279
Crossways Hotel
THE AVENUE 1
THORNLEY RD 2
FIRST ST 3
ASHMORE TERR 4
ALEXANDRA TERR 5
GRANVILLE TERR 6
GREENHILLS TERR
Wheatley Hill Prim Sch
QUILSTYLE RD
WORDSWORTH AVE
GABLE TERR
WOODLANDS AVE
Corbie Farm
HENDERSON AVE
LUKE TERR
CAIN TERR
FRED PEART SQ
AGED MINERS HOMES
The Hilly
BURNS ST
SHAKESPEARE ST
Cemy
MOORE ST
QUETLAW RD
JACK LAWSON TERR
WHEATLEY TERR
Wicket Wood
SHINWELL TERR
PETER LEE COTTS
CEMETERY RD
BYRON ST
Wheatley Hill
White House
JOHNSON EST
EAST VIEW
WOODLANDS AVE
LIDELL TERR
Thorney Hall Farm
Bankdam Farm
WINGATE LA
DALTON TERR
SOUTH VIEW
HANDEL TERR 1
STOKER CRES 2
RYAN TERR 3
ANDREW TERR 4
HARPER BGLWS 5
Old Thornley
SANDWICK TERR
A181
Thornley Moor Farm
WHARRIER SQ
BEVAN CRES
Ducket Wood
Long Wood
B1278

59
48

B1283
DURHAM LA
B1283
B1290
Pemberton Arms (PH)
North Moor Farm
Haswell Moor
Recn Gd
Thorpe Moor

1 CROSSFIELD CRES
2 MARCIA AVE
3 CHURCH VIEW
4 GRANGE TERR

Landing Strip

Shotton Prim Sch

Our Lady of Lourdes RC Prim Sch
FLEMING CT
AGED MINERS HOMES
WAVERLEY CL
BURN
BELVEDERE GDNS

Harehill Moor

Fleming Field

STATION RD

Shotton Colliery Ind Est

8

7

41

6

5

40

4

3

39

2

1

38

North West Ind Est

Thorpe Moor

MILL HILL
DAVY DR
PEMBE RD

FIENNES RD
BURDON DR

WHITEHOUSE CRES

South West Ind Est
SR8

THAYNER WAY

Flemingfield Farm

SUTHERLAND LGR
JUBILEE
ARDEN ST
ASHBROOKE EST
COWLEY ST
DUNELM
ELDON
THE TERRACE
FRONT ST
SHOTTON RD
ROSE COTTS

COOPERATIVE TERR
BEVAN GROVE
HAMILTON
Libry
VICTORIA ST
BANK TERR
CORONATION COTTS
BRIDGE RD
MOORE ST
BYRON TERR
BURN'S TERR

GEORGE
EAST TER
KING ST
NEW EDEN
MILTON GR
EDEN

Whitehouse Ind Pk

Whitehouse Ind Pk

WHITWORTH RD
BRACKEN HILL
Bracken Hill
WINCHESTER

SHOTTON LA
Shotton Colliery
DH6

1 WILLIAM MORRIS TERR
2 KEIR HARDIE TERR

Brackenhill Farm No 1

Brackenhill

High Crow's House

A COOK TERR

Low Crow's House

SALTERS LA

DIXON ESTATE BGLWS

Swan Castle Farm

Gore Burn

Calfpasture Dene

Bracken Hill Ind Pk

Wapping Burn

Haswell Plantation

LYNN TERR

Edder Acres

Edderacres Dene

B1279

Thornley Station Ind Est

Round Hill

Office St

Green Hills

Thornley Crossings

WATSON'S CL
DODD'S CL
B1279
PATTON WLK
WEARDALE PK

Edderacres Burn

Edderacres Plantation

Winning Plantation

Warden Lodge

Burn Plantation

Nanny's Plantation

Green Hills Moor
TS28

TS27
New Winning

A19

A181

Foxhole Wood

DURHAM RD
TAYLOR DR
B1280
WINGROVE GREEN
WELLFIELD RD N
WELLFIELD RD
WELLFIELD RD S
OSBOROUGH
MARTINDALE WLK
STEWART DR

THE MALTINGS

1 RAILWAY COTTS
2 WELLFIELD TERR
3 HIGH WINNING COTTS

Catchgate Farm

MOORE SQ 1
LAING SQ 2
SALTER'S LA 3
DODD'S TERR
DOBSON TERR
INGRAM WAY
THE CLOISTERS

Wellfield

A181

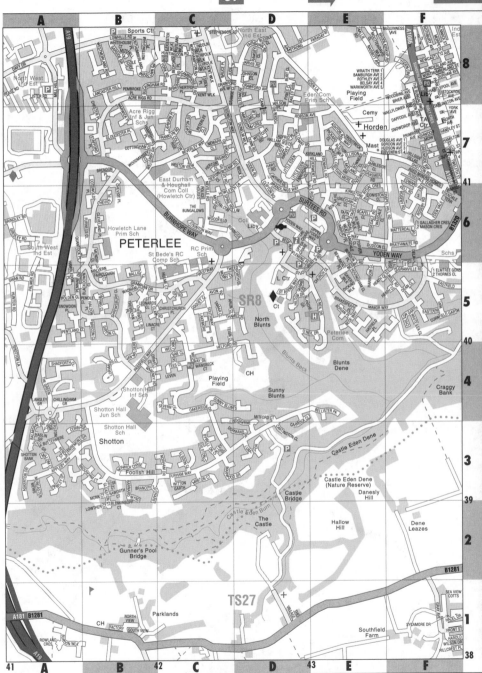

A B C D E F

PETERLEE

Horden

Shotton

SR8

TS27

North West Ind Est

South West Ind Est

North East Ind Est

Acre Rigg Inf & Jun Schs

East Durham & Houghall Com Coll (Howletch Ctr)

Howletch Lane Prim Sch

St Bede's RC Comp Sch

RC Prim Sch

Eden Com Prim Sch

Shotton Hall Inf Sch

Shotton Hall Jun Sch

Shotton Hall Sch

North Blunts

Sunny Blunts

Blunts Dene

Blunts Beck

Peterlee Com

Playing Field

Craggy Bank

Castle Eden Dene

Castle Eden Dene (Nature Reserve)

Castle Eden Burn

Castle Bridge

The Castle

Danesly Hill

Hallow Hill

Dene Leazes

Gunner's Pool Bridge

Parklands

Southfield Farm

Foolish Hill

Burnhope Way

Surtees Rd

Yoden Way

A19 A181 A1086 B1281 B1320

8 7 6 5 4 3 2 1

41 40 39 38

41 A B 42 C D 43 E F

49

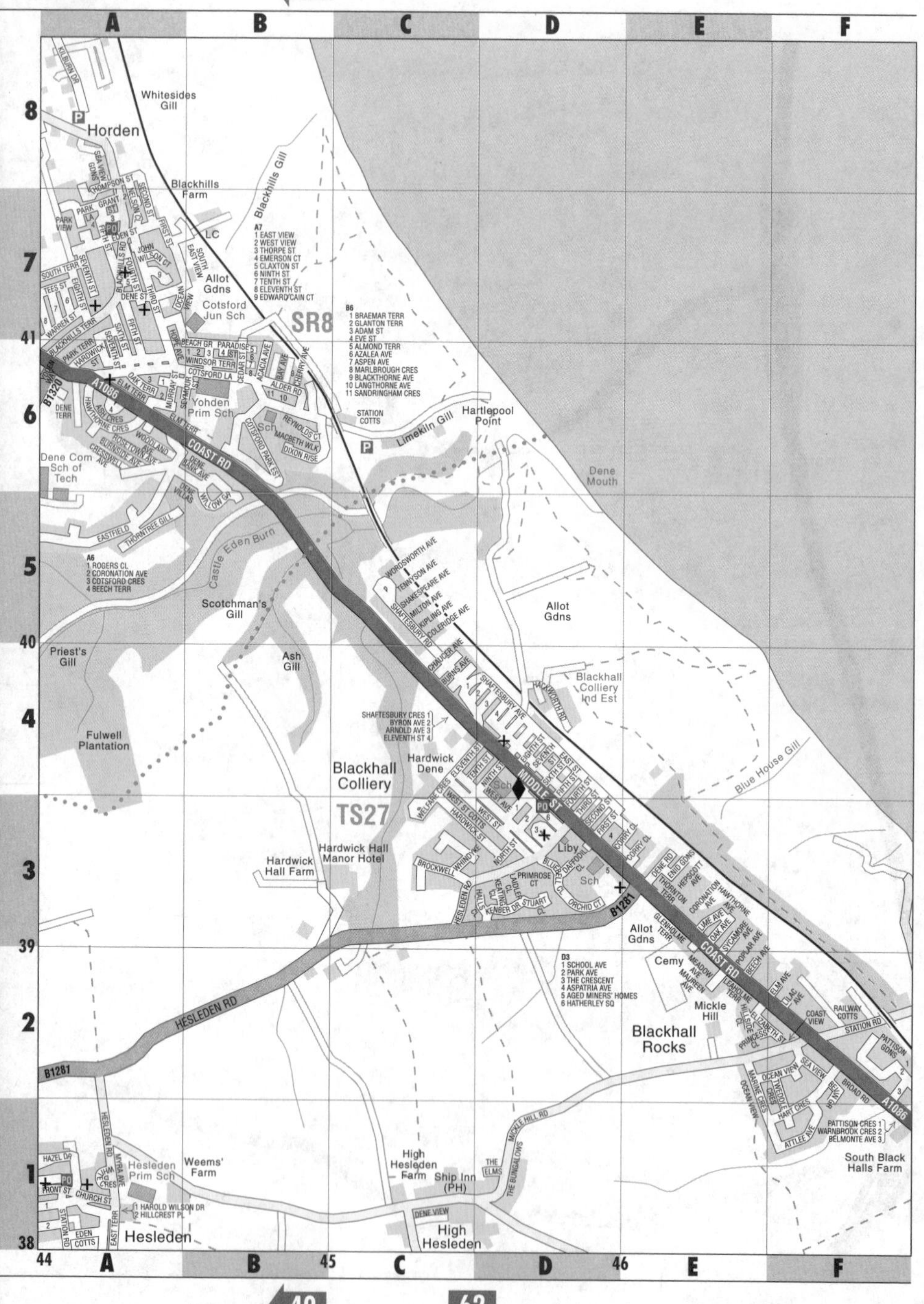

Horden
Whitesides Gill
Blackhills Farm
Blackhills Gill
Allot Gdns
Cotsford Jun Sch
SR8
Yohden Prim Sch
Dene Com Sch of Tech
Station Cotts
Limekiln Gill
Hartlepool Point
Dene Mouth
Castle Eden Burn
Scotchman's Gill
Priest's Gill
Ash Gill
Fulwell Plantation
Blackhall Colliery
TS27
Hardwick Dene
Hardwick Hall Manor Hotel
Hardwick Hall Farm
Blackhall Colliery Ind Est
Blue House Gill
Cemy
Mickle Hill
Blackhall Rocks
South Black Halls Farm
High Hesleden Farm
Ship Inn (PH)
High Hesleden
Hesleden
Hesleden Prim Sch
Weems' Farm
COAST RD
A1086
B1281
HESLEDEN RD
MIDDLE ST
A7
1 EAST VIEW
2 WEST VIEW
3 THORPE ST
4 EMERSON CT
5 CLAXTON ST
6 NINTH ST
7 TENTH ST
8 ELEVENTH ST
9 EDWARD CAIN CT
B6
1 BRAEMAR TERR
2 GLANTON TERR
3 ADAM ST
4 EVE ST
5 ALMOND TERR
6 AZALEA AVE
7 ASPEN AVE
8 MARLBROUGH CRES
9 BLACKTHORNE AVE
10 LANGTHORNE AVE
11 SANDRINGHAM CRES
A6
1 ROGERS CL
2 CORONATION AVE
3 COTSFORD CRES
4 BEECH TERR
SHAFTESBURY CRES 1
BYRON AVE 2
ARNOLD AVE 3
ELEVENTH ST 4
D3
1 SCHOOL AVE
2 PARK AVE
3 THE CRESCENT
4 ASPATRIA AVE
5 AGED MINERS' HOMES
6 HATHERLEY SQ
PATTISON CRES 1
WARNBROOK CRES 2
BELMONTE AVE 3
1 HAROLD WILSON DR
2 HILLCREST PL

49
62

50

50
63

39

C D E

Blue House Plantation
Hive Point

8

Beacon Point
Beacon Hill
Shippersea Bay

7

Shippersea Point

45

Shot Rock

6

Loom

5

SR8

44

Busiers Holes
Bed Slide
Fox Holes

4

Fox Holes Dene
Horden Burn
Horden Dene

3

Horden Point

43

2

Warren House Gill
Ash Gill

1

TIMBER RD
KILBURN DR
Sea View Ind Est

42

44 C D 45 E

39
50

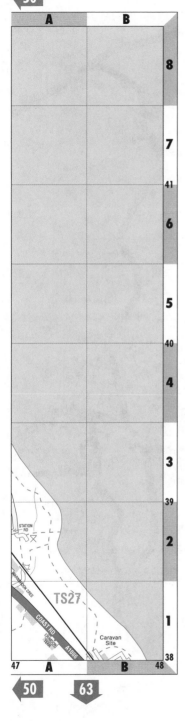

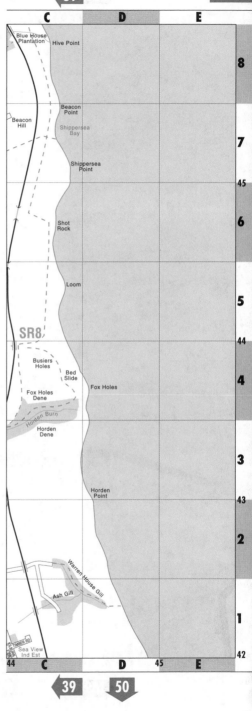

8

Recn Gd

Jobson Terr

Stanley Crook

Mount Pleasant

World's End

B6299

Alma Terr

NORTH LA

Heights of Alma

Billy Hill

Wilson St

Francis Terr

HILL TERR

WEST TERR

WELL BANK B6298

Co-Operative Terr

Black Rd

Reservoir Terr 1
Railway Terr 2

B6299

White Lea Farm

WHITE LEA RD

Old White Lea Farm

DL13

Old White Lea Cottage

ARTHUR PIT COTTS

WHITE LEA RD

Pease's West Prim Sch

Stanley Way

Low Albert Terr

Institute Terr

Billy Row

North Roddymoor Farm

7

Dun Cow Inn (PH)

CRAIG LEA RD

IVY CRES
CHESTNUT GR 2

PEASE'S WEST

Billy Row Gr

37

Roddymoor

Myrtle Gr

Oak Gdns

East Terr

Billy Hall Farm

6

Craig Lea

Red House Farm

Roddymoor Farm

Fire And Rescue Station Cotts

TEMPERANCE AVE

West Roddymoor

RODDYMOOR RD

Farrers Arms (PH)

Pease's West Sports Ctr

Crook Beck

5

Comrie House

STEELS HOS

PEASEHOLM BANK

Hartside Prim Sch

Percy St

PARK AVE

Allot Gdns

Church Hill

GARDEN PL

36

DL15

HIGH WHITWELL TERR

HIGH WHITWELL TERR

ACACIA GDNS

CEDAR GDNS

CALDWELL AVE

St Mary's Ave

Milburn St

St Cuthbert's RC Prim Sch

4

LABURNUM AVE 1
WILLOW AVE 2

LILAC GDNS

West Villas

CHURCH ST

B6298

P

Crook Prim Sch

3

MOWN MEADOWS RD

Cold Knot

FIVE HOS

Middle Mown Meadows

Low Mown Meadows

PINE TREE GDNS

LOVAIN TERR

HIGH WEST RD

WEST RD

WEST RD

A689

ORCHARD

P

Crook
Cross
Ctr

Worthington Cl

PENHOLME CL

Emerson St

P

35

A689

High Woodfield West

High Woodfield East

Woodfield Hill

KINGSLEY DR

BROWNING PL

WESTFIELD DR

HAMSTER LN

BATLEY

BURN DENE

Grasmere Gr

Beechburn Pk

WEST BRIDGE ST 1
EAST BRIDGE ST 2
GREENFIELD COTTS 3
STANHOPE TERR 4
KING ALBERT PL 5
WINDSOR TERR 6
ALEXANDRA TERR 7
VICTORIA AVE 8
BELLE VUE 9
HOWE TERR 10

L Ctr

Macdonald Ind Est

Castle Close Ind Est

CASTLE CL

CROOK

WIDDOWFIELD TERR

CROFT

2

PROSPECT RD

PROSPECT RD

B6298

NEW RD

Brookside Cotts

High Farm

Crook (Beechburn) Ind Est

PENNINE CT

1

INSTITUTE TERR

CORONATION TERR

PLANTATION TERR

WAVERLEY

THE GROVE

A68

The Greenhead (Hotel)

GREEN HEAD

High Beechburn

Greenhead

High Farm

Fold House Farm

Low Beechburn

A689

THE VICTORIA

RUMBY HILL

RUMBY HILL LA

LIMEKILN AVE

Watergate Lane Farm

34

A68

Fir Tree

Redmires Farm

Fox Covert Plantation

White House Farm

14   **15**   **16**

E4
1 WATERLOO CL
2 FLANDERS WAY
3 NELSON ST
4 CALVERT ST
5 MORAVIAN ST
6 WHITFIELD ST
7 VICTORIA ST
8 ROSEMOUNT TERR

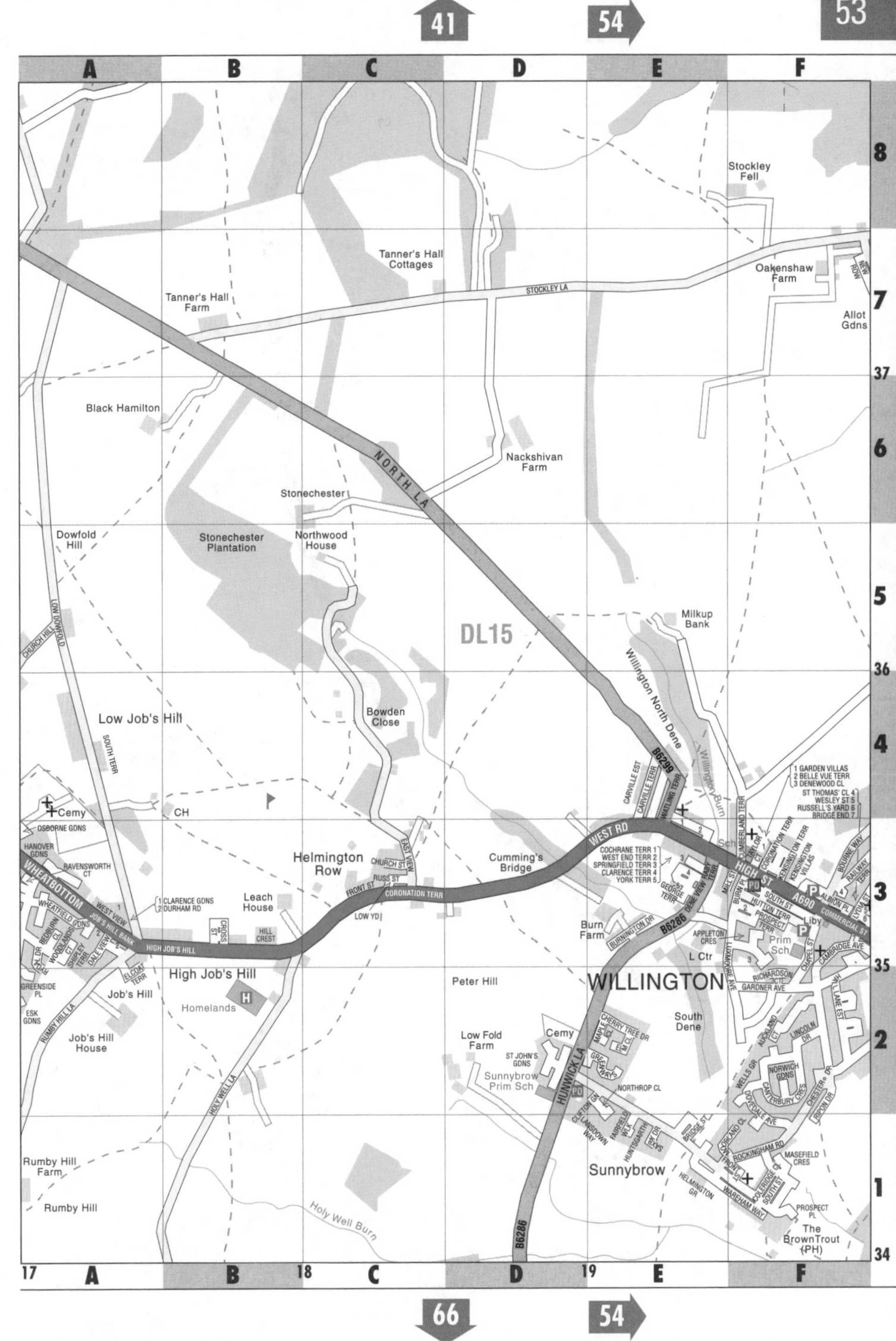
41
54
A
B
C
D
E
F
8
7
37
6
5
36
4
3
35
2
1
34
17
18
19
66
54
Stockley Fell
Tanner's Hall Cottages
Oakenshaw Farm
STOCKLEY LA
NEW ROW
Tanner's Hall Farm
Allot Gdns
Black Hamilton
NORTH LA
Nackshivan Farm
Stonechester
Dowfold Hill
Stonechester Plantation
Northwood House
Milkup Bank
DL15
CHURCH HILL
LOW DOWFOLD
Willington North Dene
Bowden Close
Low Job's Hill
SOUTH TERR
B6299
Willington Burn
CARVILLE EST
CARVILLE TERR
WATLING TERR
1 GARDEN VILLAS
2 BELLE VUE TERR
3 DENEWOOD CL
ST THOMAS' CL 4
WESLEY ST 5
RUSSELL'S YARD 6
BRIDGE END 7
Cemy
CH
OSBORNE GDNS
HANOVER GDNS
RAVENSWORTH CT
Helmington Row
EAST VIEW
CHURCH ST
RUSS ST
FRONT ST
CORONATION TERR
Cumming's Bridge
WEST RD
COCHRANE TERR 1
WEST END TERR 2
SPRINGFIELD TERR 3
CLARENCE TERR 4
YORK TERR 5
HIGH ST
A690
COMMERCIAL ST
1 CLARENCE GDNS
2 DURHAM RD
WHEATBOTTOM
JOB'S HILL BANK
WEST VIEW
Leach House
LOW YD
CROSS ST
HILL CREST
HIGH JOB'S HILL
Burn Farm
BURNINGTON DR
B6286
DENE VIEW
APPLETON CRES
PROSPECT TERR
Liby
Prim Sch
CAMBRIDGE AVE
L Ctr
High Job's Hill
Job's Hill
Homelands
Peter Hill
WILLINGTON
RICHARDSON CT
GARDNER AVE
GREENSIDE PL
ESK GDNS
RUMBY HILL LA
Job's Hill House
Low Fold Farm
Cemy
CHERRY TREE DR
ELM CL
ST JOHN'S GDNS
South Dene
LINCOLN DR
NORWICH GDNS
Sunnybrow Prim Sch
HUNWICK LA
NORTHROP CL
HOLY WELL LA
WELLS GR
CANTERBURY CRES
CHESTER DR
RIPON DR
DOVEDALE AVE
BRIDGE ST
ROCKINGHAM RD
MASEFIELD CRES
Rumby Hill Farm
Sunnybrow
HELMINGTON GR
COLERIDGE CL
SOUTH ST
WAREHAM WAY
Rumby Hill
Holy Well Burn
PROSPECT PL
The BrownTrout (PH)
BOURNE WAY
RAILWAY TERR
ALBION PL
LYON ST
MILL ST
BURN PL
CUMBERLAND TERR
TAYLOR CT
HUTTON TERR

53
42

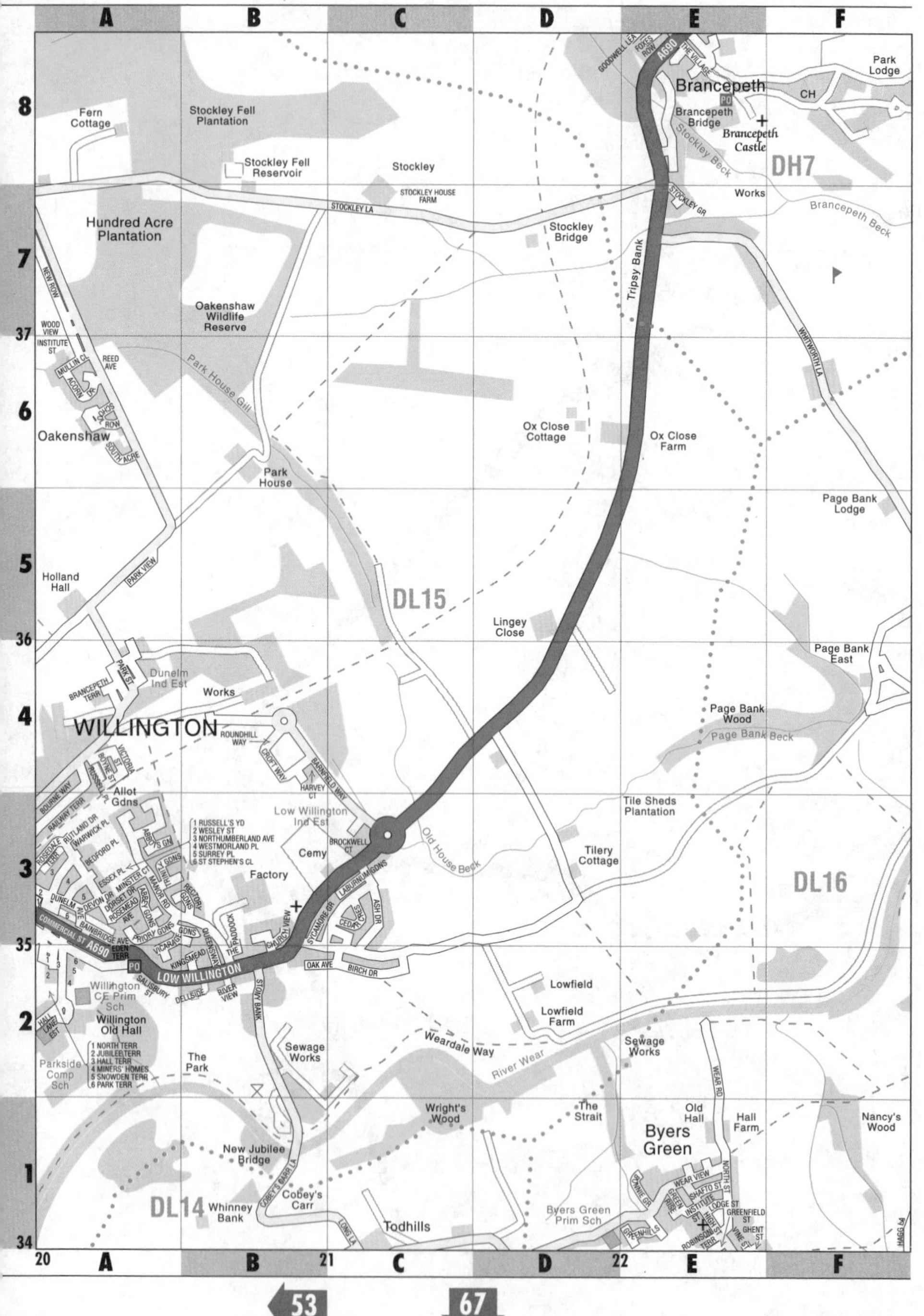
A B C D E F
8
7
37
6
5
36
4
3
35
2
1
34
20 21 22
Fern Cottage
Stockley Fell Plantation
Stockley Fell Reservoir
Stockley
Stockley House Farm
Stockley La
Brancepeth
Brancepeth Bridge
Brancepeth Castle
Park Lodge
CH
PO
DH7
Stockley Beck
Works
Brancepeth Beck
Stockley Gr
Goodwell Lea
Foxes Row
The Village
A690
Hundred Acre Plantation
Stockley Bridge
Tripsy Bank
New Row
Wood View
Institute St
Mullin Cl
Reed Ave
Acorn Dr
Oakenshaw Wildlife Reserve
Park House Gill
Oakenshaw
South Acre
Ox Close Cottage
Ox Close Farm
Whitworth La
Park House
Page Bank Lodge
Holland Hall
Park View
DL15
Lingey Close
Page Bank East
Brancepeth Terr
Park St
Dunelm Ind Est
Works
WILLINGTON
Roundhill Way
Croft Way
Barnfield Way
Harvey Ct
Page Bank Wood
Page Bank Beck
Victoria St
Bothe St
Russell Pl
Allot Gdns
Bourne Way
Railway Terr
Rutland Dr
Warwick Pl
Rosedale Terr
Bedford Pl
Low Willington Ind Est
1 Russell's Yd
2 Wesley St
3 Northumberland Ave
4 Westmorland Pl
5 Surrey Pl
6 St Stephen's Cl
Tile Sheds Plantation
Brockwell Ct
Cemy
Old House Beck
Tilery Cottage
Essex Pl
Minster Ct
Trinity Gdns
Factory
DL16
Dunelm Ave
Devon Dr
Dorset Dr
Rosemead Ave
Abbey Gdns
Manor Rd
Rectory Gdns
Priory Gdns
The Paddock
Church View
Sycamore Gr
Laburnum Gdns
Cedar Cres
Ash Dr
Commercial St A690
Bainbridge Ave
Eden Terr
Vicarage
Kingsmead
Queensway
Oak Ave
Birch Dr
Salisbury St
Low Willington
Dellside
River View
Stony Bank
Lowfield
Lowfield Farm
Willington CE Prim Sch
Willington Old Hall
Hall Lane Est
1 North Terr
2 Jubilee Terr
3 Hall Terr
4 Miners' Homes
5 Snowden Terr
6 Park Terr
Parkside Comp Sch
The Park
Sewage Works
Weardale Way
River Wear
Sewage Works
Wear Rd
Wright's Wood
The Strait
Old Hall
Hall Farm
Byers Green
Nancy's Wood
New Jubilee Bridge
Cobey's Carr La
Cobey's Carr
DL14
Whinney Bank
Long La
Todhills
Byers Green Prim Sch
Bonnie Gr
Green Ridge
Wear View
Shafto St
Institute St
North St
Lodge St
Greenfield St
High St
Greenhills
Robinson Terr
Vine St
Ghent St
Hagg La

53
67

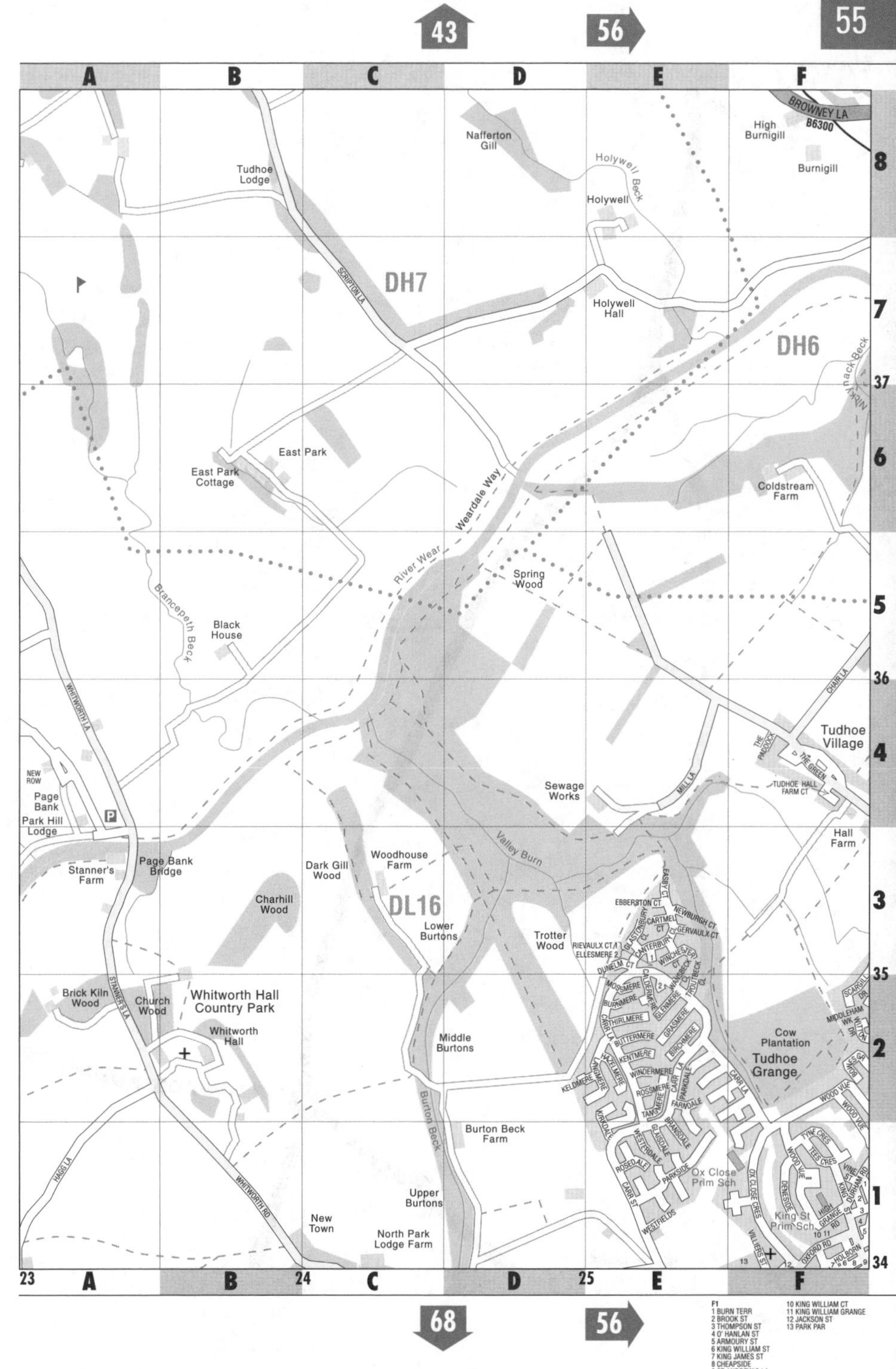

55
44

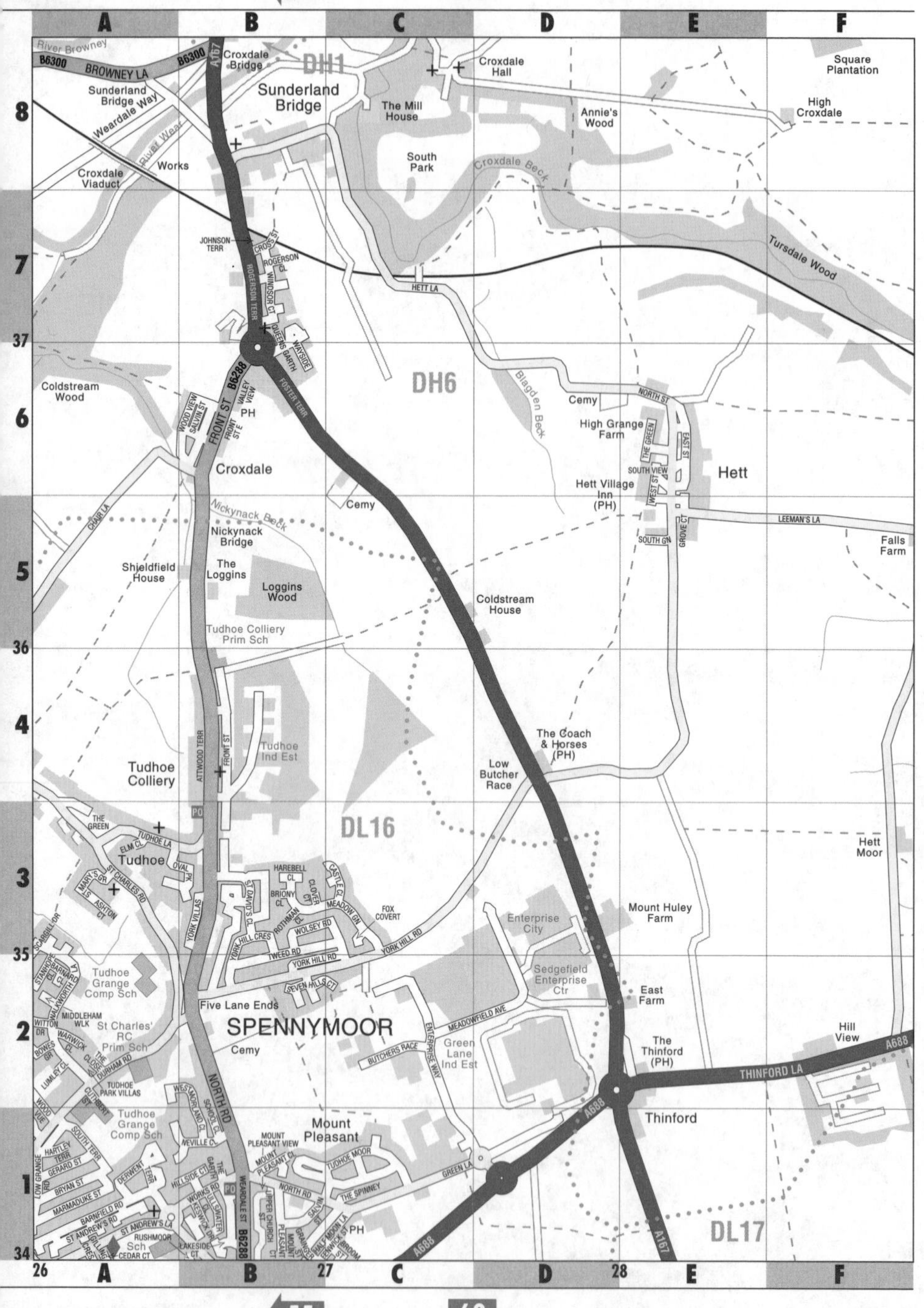
A
B
C
D
E
F
8
7
37
6
5
36
4
3
35
2
1
34
26
27
28
River Browney
B6300
BROWNEY LA
A167
Croxdale Bridge
DH1
Sunderland Bridge
Weardale Way
River Wear
Croxdale Viaduct
Works
Croxdale Hall
The Mill House
South Park
Croxdale Beck
Annie's Wood
Square Plantation
High Croxdale
Tursdale Wood
JOHNSON TERR
CROSS ST
ROGERSON CL
ROGERSON TERR
WINDSOR CT
QUEENS GARTH
WAYSIDE
HETT LA
DH6
Blagden Beck
Coldstream Wood
B6288
FRONT ST
VALLEY VIEW
FOSTER TERR
WOOD VIEW
SALVIN ST
PH
Cemy
NORTH ST
High Grange Farm
THE GREEN
EAST ST
SOUTH VIEW
WEST ST
Hett
Hett Village Inn (PH)
Croxdale
Nickynack Beck
CHAIR LA
Nickynack Bridge
SOUTH GN
GROVE CT
LEEMAN'S LA
Falls Farm
Shieldfield House
The Loggins
Loggins Wood
Coldstream House
Tudhoe Colliery Prim Sch
ATTWOOD TERR
FRONT ST
Tudhoe Ind Est
The Coach & Horses (PH)
Low Butcher Race
Tudhoe Colliery
PO
THE GREEN
TUDHOE LA
ELM CL
Tudhoe
OVAL PK
DL16
Hett Moor
HAREBELL CL
CASTLE CL
ST MARY'S GR
ST CHARLES RD
ASHTON CT
YORK VILLAS
ST DAVID'S CL
BRIONY CL
CLOVER CT
ROTHMAN CL
MEADOW GN
FOX COVERT
WOLSEY RD
YORK HILL CRES
YORK HILL RD
TWEED RD
Enterprise City
Mount Huley Farm
SCARGILL DR
STANHOPE CL
BARNARD CL
WALKWORTH
Tudhoe Grange Comp Sch
SEVEN HILLS CT
Sedgefield Enterprise Ctr
East Farm
MIDDLEHAM WLK
Five Lane Ends
WITTON DR
St Charles' RC Prim Sch
SPENNYMOOR
MEADOWFIELD AVE
ENTERPRISE WAY
Hill View
A688
BOWES GR
WARWICK CL
THE CLOSE
DURHAM RD
Cemy
BUTCHERS RACE
Green Lane Ind Est
The Thinford (PH)
THINFORD LA
LUMLEY CL
TUDHOE PARK VILLAS
NORTH RD
CUTHBERT
WESTMORLAND CL
SCHOOL CL
WOOD VUE
Tudhoe Grange Comp Sch
Thinford
Mount Pleasant
SOUTH TERR
NEVILLE CL
MOUNT PLEASANT VIEW
HARTLEY TERR
GERARD ST
DERWENT TERR
MOUNT PLEASANT CL
TUDHOE MOOR
LOW GRANGE RD
BRYAN ST
HILLSIDE CL
THE GARTH
PO
NORTH RD
SALVIN ST
THE SPINNEY
GREEN LA
MARMADUKE ST
WORKS RD
ULLSWATER
KESWICK DR
WEARDALE ST
UPPER CHURCH ST
MOUNT PLEASANT CT
GRAINGER ST
HALF MOON LA
BARNFIELD RD
ST ANDREW'S RD
ST ANDREW'S LA
RUSHMOOR
Sch
GILLING CRES
CEDAR CT
LAKESIDE CT
FENWICK ST
BROOM
PH
A167
DL17

55
69

45
58

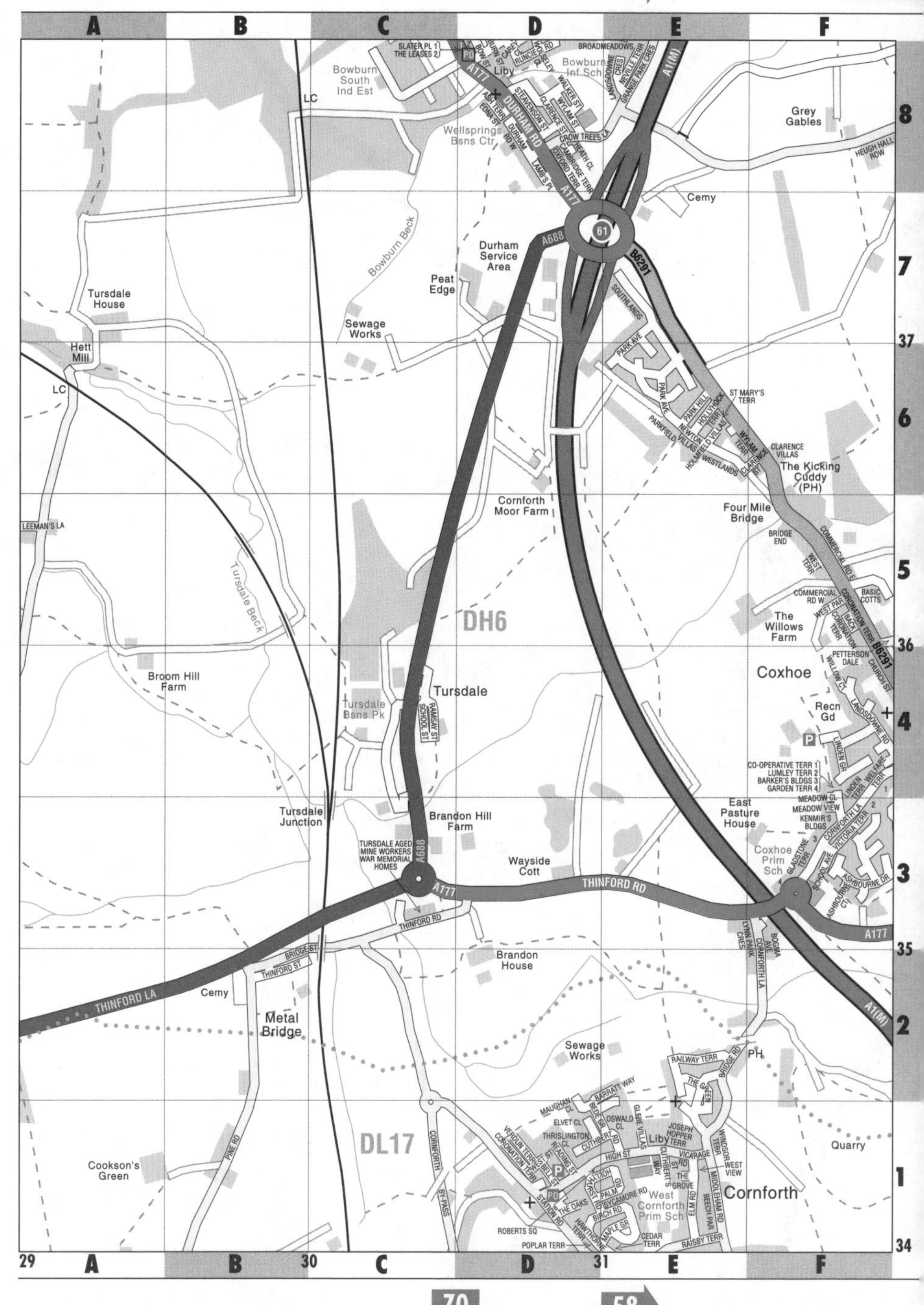
Bowburn South Ind Est
Liby
Wellsprings Bsns Ctr
DURHAM RD
A177
A1(M)
Bowburn Inf Sch
Grey Gables
HEUGH HALL ROW
Cemy
Bowburn Beck
Durham Service Area
A688
B6291
61
Peat Edge
Tursdale House
Hett Mill
LC
Sewage Works
SOUTHLANDS
PARK AVE
PARK HILL
HOLLYHOCK TERR
ST MARY'S TERR
NEWTON
PARKFIELD VILLAS
HOLMEFIELD VILLAS
WESTLANDS
WYLAM TERR
CLARENCE ST
CLARENCE VILLAS
The Kicking Cuddy (PH)
Four Mile Bridge
BRIDGE END
WEST TERR
COMMERCIAL RD E
Cornforth Moor Farm
LEEMAN'S LA
Tursdale Beck
DH6
COMMERCIAL RD W
CORONATION TERR
BASIC COTTS
The Willows Farm
WEST PAR
BACK CORONATION TERR
PETTERSON DALE
CHURCH ST
Coxhoe
Broom Hill Farm
Tursdale
Tursdale Bsns Pk
RAMSAY ST
SCHOOL ST
Recn Gd
LANDSDOWNE RD
WILLOW CT
LINDEN GR
CO-OPERATIVE TERR 1
LUMLEY TERR 2
BARKER'S BLDGS 3
GARDEN TERR 4
MEADOW CL
MEADOW VIEW
KENMIR'S BLDGS
East Pasture House
Tursdale Junction
Brandon Hill Farm
TURSDALE AGED MINE WORKERS WAR MEMORIAL HOMES
Wayside Cott
THINFORD RD
Coxhoe Prim Sch
GLADSTONE TERR
SCHOOL AVE
CORNFORTH LA
VICTORIA TERR
ASHBOURNE DR
ASHBOURNE CT
LYNN PARK CRES
BOGMA AVE
BRIDGE ST
THINFORD ST
Brandon House
THINFORD LA
Cemy
Metal Bridge
Sewage Works
RAILWAY TERR
THE GREEN
BRIDGE RD
PH
BARRATT WAY
MAUGHAN CL
BEDE GR
OSWALD CL
GLEBE VILLAS
JOSEPH HOPPER TERR
ELVET CL
THRISLINGTON CL
CUTHBERT RD
Liby
VICARAGE
WINDSOR TERR
WEST VIEW
Quarry
DL17
PINE RD
CORNFORTH BY-PASS
VERDUN TERR
CORONATION TERR
READING ST
HIGH ST
ST CUTHBERTS WAY
THE GROVE
MIDDLEHAM RD
Cornforth
Cookson's Green
STATION RD
THE OAKS
PALM
SYCAMORE RD
West Cornforth Prim Sch
ELM RD
BEECH PAR
BIRCH RD
MAPLE GR
HAWTHORNE TERR
ROBERTS SQ
POPLAR TERR
CEDAR TERR
RAISBY TERR
A B C D E F
8 7 6 5 4 3 2 1
37 36 35 34
29 30 31

70
58

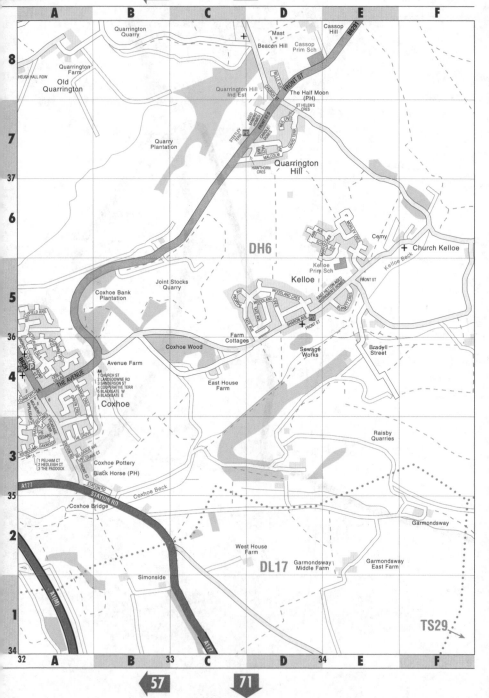

A B C D E F

8

HEUGH HALL ROW

Quarrington
Quarry

Quarrington
Farm

Old
Quarrington

Mast
Beacon Hill

Cassop
Hill

B6291

Cassop
Prim Sch

7

37

Quarry
Plantation

Quarrington Hill
Ind Est

FRONT ST

The Half Moon
(PH)

St Helen's
Cres

STEETLEY TERR

RD

Quarrington
Hill

HAWTHORN
CRES

MALCOLM

6

Coxhoe Bank
Plantation

Joint Stocks
Quarry

DH6

AV

SCHOOL RD

MIDDLE CRES

Cemy

Church Kelloe

Kelloe
Prim Sch

Kelloe

Kelloe Beck

FRONT ST

5

36

Avenue Farm

Coxhoe Wood

WOODLAND

WOODLAND CRES

SHARON AVE

RD

FRONT ST

EAST HETTON AGED
MINEWORKERS HOMES

PLANTE CRES

Farm
Cottages

Sewage
Works

Bradyll
Street

4

THE AVENUE

A4
1 CHURCH ST
2 LANSDOWNE RD
3 SANDERSON ST
4 COOPERATIVE TERR
5 BLACKGATE W
6 BLACKGATE E

East House
Farm

Coxhoe

3

1 PELHAM CT
2 HEDLEIGH CT
3 THE PADDOCK

Coxhoe Pottery

Black Horse (PH)

Raisby
Quarries

35

A177

STATION RD

Coxhoe Beck

Coxhoe Bridge

Garmondsway

2

West House
Farm

DL17

Garmondsway
Middle Farm

Garmondsway
East Farm

Simonside

A177

1

A1(M)

TS29

34

32 A 33 B C 34 D E F

47
60

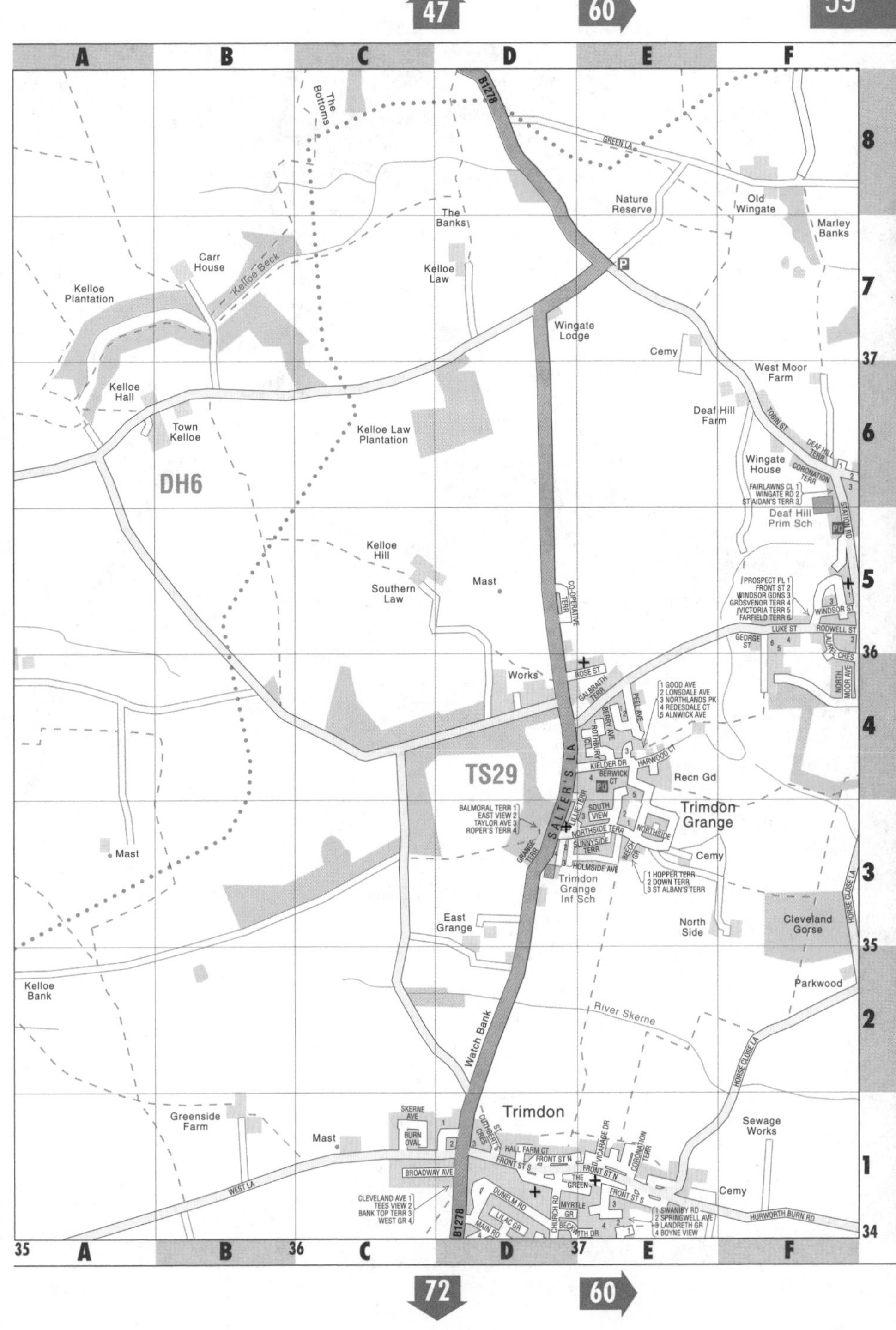
The Bottoms
B1278
GREEN LA
Nature Reserve
Old Wingate
Marley Banks
The Banks
Carr House
Kelloe Beck
Kelloe Law
Kelloe Plantation
Wingate Lodge
Cemy
West Moor Farm
Kelloe Hall
Town Kelloe
Kelloe Law Plantation
Deaf Hill Farm
TOBIN ST
DEAF HILL TERR
Wingate House
CORONATION TERR
DH6
FAIRLAWNS CL 1
WINGATE RD 2
ST AIDAN'S TERR 3
Deaf Hill Prim Sch
STATION RD
Kelloe Hill
Southern Law
Mast
CO-OPERATIVE TERR
PROSPECT PL 1
FRONT ST 2
WINDSOR GDNS 3
GROSVENOR TERR 4
VICTORIA TERR 5
FARFIELD TERR 6
WINDSOR ST
LUKE ST
RODWELL ST
GEORGE ST
LAURA CRES
NORTH MOOR AVE
Works
ROSE ST
GALBRAITH TERR
PEEL AVE
BERRY AVE
ROTHBURY CL
1 GOOD AVE
2 LONSDALE AVE
3 NORTHLANDS PK
4 REDESDALE CT
5 ALNWICK AVE
KIELDER DR
HARWOOD CT
BERWICK CT
Recn Gd
TS29
SALTER'S LA
BALMORAL TERR 1
EAST VIEW 2
TAYLOR AVE 3
ROPER'S TERR 4
LILLIE TERR
SOUTH VIEW
NORTHSIDE TERR
NORTHSIDE
SUNNYSIDE TERR
Trimdon Grange
GRANGE TERR
BEECH GR
HOLMSIDE AVE
Cemy
Trimdon Grange Inf Sch
1 HOPPER TERR
2 DOWN TERR
3 ST ALBAN'S TERR
Mast
East Grange
North Side
Cleveland Gorse
HORSE CLOSE LA
Kelloe Bank
Parkwood
River Skerne
Watch Bank
HORSE CLOSE LA
Greenside Farm
SKERNE AVE
Trimdon
Sewage Works
BURN OVAL
CUTHBERT'S CRES
ST
Mast
HALL FARM CT
VICARAGE DR
CORONATION TERR
FRONT ST S
FRONT ST N
BROADWAY AVE
THE GREEN
WEST LA
DUNELM RD
CHURCH RD
MYRTLE GR
FRONT ST S
Cemy
CLEVELAND AVE 1
TEES VIEW 2
BANK TOP TERR 3
WEST GR 4
LILAC GR
MAIN RD
BECKWITH DR
1 SWANBY RD
2 SPRINGWELL AVE
3 LANDRETH GR
4 BOYNE VIEW
HURWORTH BURN RD
B1278
A B C D E F
8 7 6 5 4 3 2 1
37 36 35 34
35 36 37

72
60

59
48

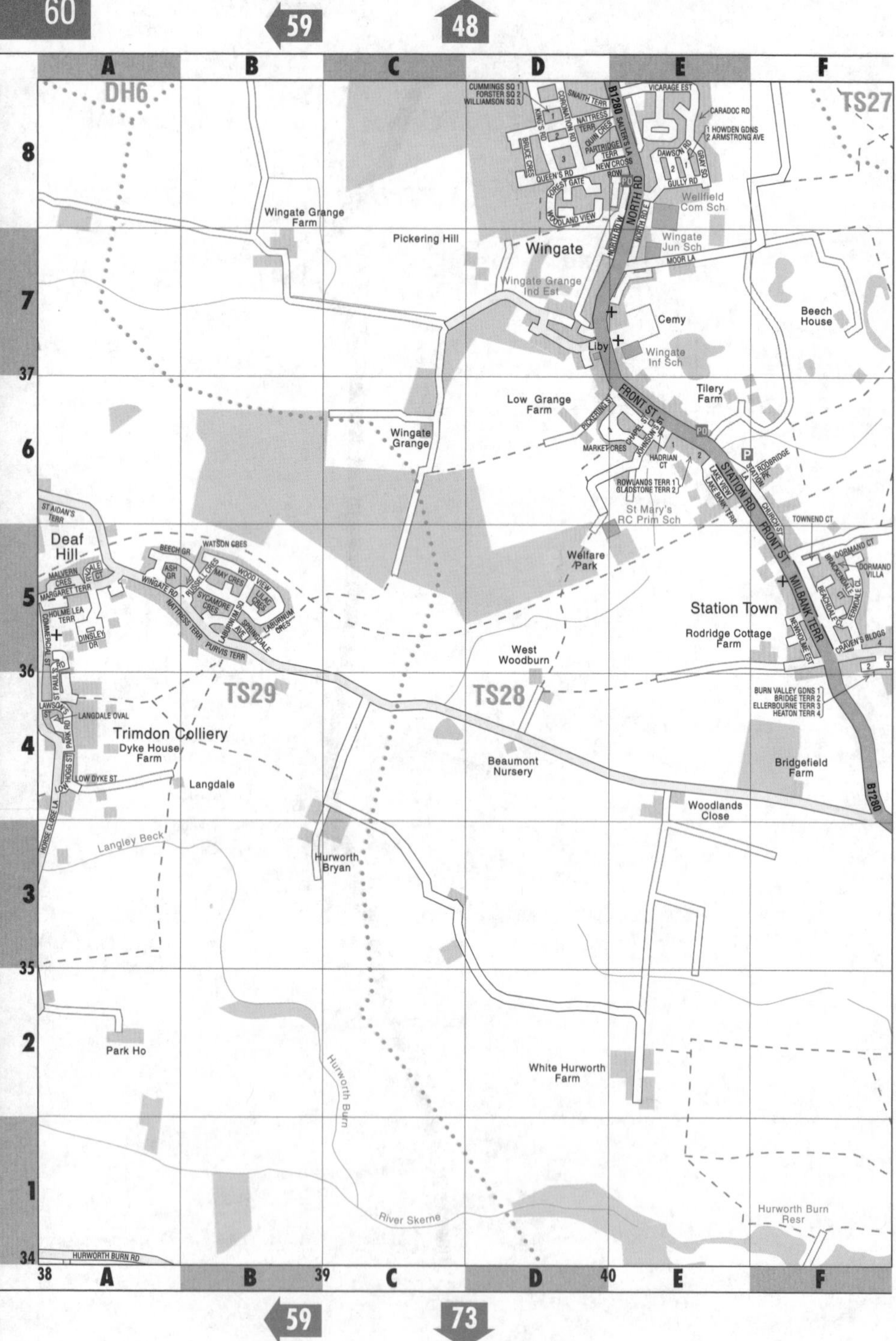
A
B
C
D
E
F
8
7
37
6
5
36
4
3
35
2
1
34
38
39
40
DH6
TS27
TS29
TS28
CUMMINGS SQ 1
FORSTER SQ 2
WILLIAMSON SQ 3
SNAITH TERR
VICARAGE EST
CARADOC RD
1 HOWDEN GDNS
2 ARMSTRONG AVE
CORONATION RD
KING'S RD
BRUCE CRES
NATTRESS TERR
QUIN CRES
PARTRIDGE TERR
NEW CROSS ROW
QUEEN'S RD
FOREST GATE
WOODLAND VIEW
B1280
SALTERS LA
NORTH RD
NORTH RD W
NORTH RD E
DAWSON RD
GRAY SQ
GULLY RD
Wellfield Com Sch
Wingate Grange Farm
Pickering Hill
Wingate
Wingate Jun Sch
MOOR LA
Wingate Grange Ind Est
Cemy
Beech House
Liby
Wingate Inf Sch
Low Grange Farm
Tilery Farm
PICKERING ST
FRONT ST
CHAPEL ST
JOHNSON'S ST
Wingate Grange
MARKET CRES
HADRIAN CT
ROWLANDS TERR 1
GLADSTONE TERR 2
STATION RD
STATION LA
RODBRIDGE PK
LAKE VIEW
LAKE BANK TERR
CHURCH ST
St Mary's RC Prim Sch
TOWNEND CT
DORMAND CT
DORMAND VILLA
BRACKENDALE CT
FERNDALE CL
BEACHDALE CL
MILBANK TERR
Deaf Hill
ST AIDAN'S TERR
MALVERN CRES
RYDALE CT
MARGARET TERR
HOLME LEA TERR
COMMERCIAL ST
DINSLEY DR
BEECH GR
WATSON CRES
ASH GR
RUSSELL CRES
MAY CRES
WOOD VIEW
WINGATE RD
SYCAMORE CRES
LILAC CRES
NATTRESS TERR
LABURNUM SQ
LABURNUM CRES
AVE
SPRINGDALE
PURVIS TERR
Welfare Park
Station Town
Rodridge Cottage Farm
NEWHOLME EST
CRAVEN'S BLDGS
West Woodburn
BURN VALLEY GDNS 1
BRIDGE TERR 2
ELLERBOURNE TERR 3
HEATON TERR 4
ST PAUL'S RD
LAWSON ST
LANGDALE OVAL
PARK RD
Trimdon Colliery
Dyke House Farm
HOGG ST
LOW DYKE ST
Langdale
Beaumont Nursery
Bridgefield Farm
Woodlands Close
HORSE CLOSE LA
Langley Beck
Hurworth Bryan
Park Ho
Hurworth Burn
White Hurworth Farm
River Skerne
Hurworth Burn Resr
HURWORTH BURN RD

59
73

49
62

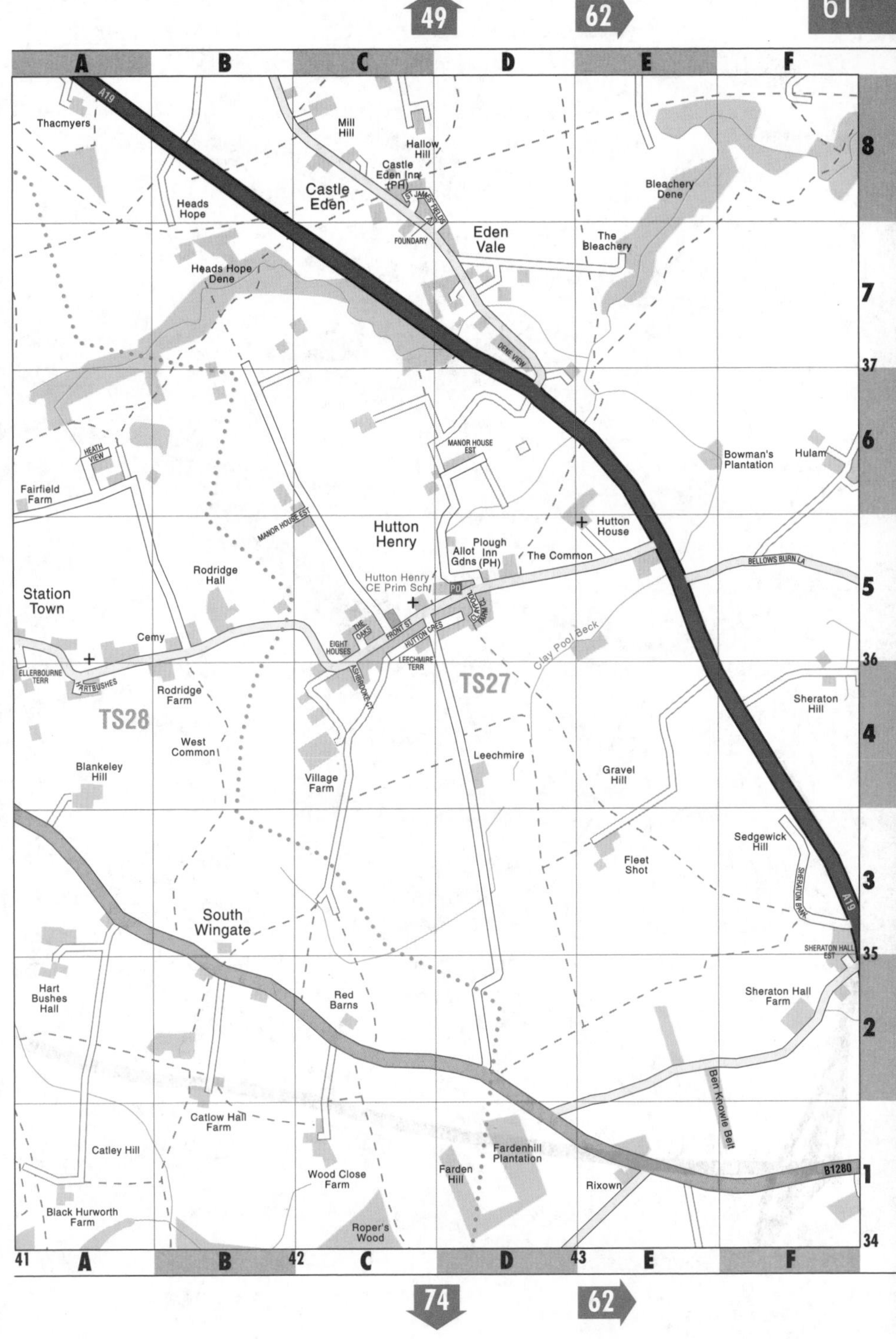
A
B
C
D
E
F
A19
Thacmyers
Mill Hill
Hallow Hill
Castle Eden Inn (PH)
Castle Eden
ST JAMES FIELDS
Heads Hope
Bleachery Dene
8
FOUNDARY
Eden Vale
The Bleachery
Heads Hope Dene
7
DENE VIEW
37
HEATH VIEW
MANOR HOUSE EST
6
Bowman's Plantation
Hulam
Fairfield Farm
MANOR HOUSE EST
Hutton Henry
Hutton House
Allot Gdns
Plough Inn (PH)
The Common
BELLOWS BURN LA
Rodridge Hall
Hutton Henry CE Prim Sch
PO
5
Station Town
CLAYPOOL FARM CL
Clay Pool Beck
Cemy
THE OAKS
FRONT ST
HUTTON CRES
EIGHT HOUSES
LEECHMIRE TERR
36
ELLERBOURNE TERR
HARTBUSHES
ASHBROOKE CT
TS27
Rodridge Farm
Sheraton Hill
TS28
4
West Common
Leechmire
Blankeley Hill
Gravel Hill
Village Farm
Sedgewick Hill
Fleet Shot
3
SHERATON BANK
A19
South Wingate
SHERATON HALL EST
35
Hart Bushes Hall
Red Barns
Sheraton Hall Farm
2
Ben Knowle Belt
Catlow Hall Farm
Catley Hill
Fardenhill Plantation
Farden Hill
B1280
1
Wood Close Farm
Rixown
Black Hurworth Farm
Roper's Wood
34
41
A
B
42
C
D
43
E
F

74
62

61
50

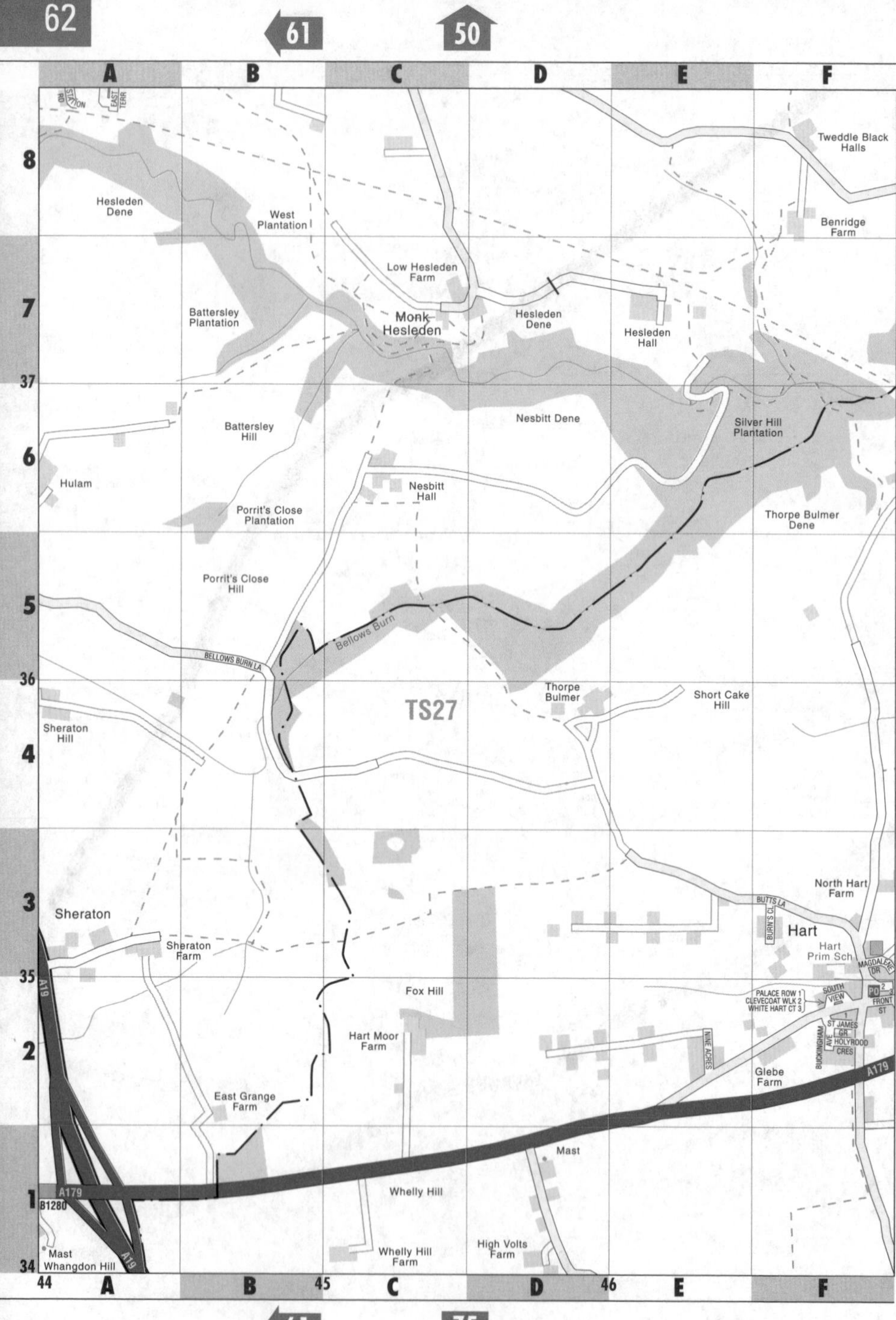
A
B
C
D
E
F
STATION RD
EAST TERR
Tweddle Black Halls
Hesleden Dene
West Plantation
Benridge Farm
Low Hesleden Farm
Battersley Plantation
Monk Hesleden
Hesleden Dene
Hesleden Hall
Battersley Hill
Nesbitt Dene
Silver Hill Plantation
Hulam
Nesbitt Hall
Porrit's Close Plantation
Thorpe Bulmer Dene
Porrit's Close Hill
Bellows Burn
BELLOWS BURN LA
Thorpe Bulmer
Short Cake Hill
TS27
Sheraton Hill
North Hart Farm
BUTTS LA
BURN'S CL
Sheraton
Hart
Sheraton Farm
Hart Prim Sch
MAGDALENE DR
Fox Hill
PALACE ROW 1
CLEVECOAT WLK 2
WHITE HART CT 3
SOUTH VIEW
PO
FRONT ST
Hart Moor Farm
NINE ACRES
ST JAMES GR
BUCKINGHAM AVE
HOLYROOD CRES
Glebe Farm
A179
East Grange Farm
A19
Mast
A179
Whelly Hill
B1280
Whelly Hill Farm
High Volts Farm
Mast
Whangdon Hill
8
7
37
6
5
36
4
3
35
2
1
34
44
45
46

61
75

51
64

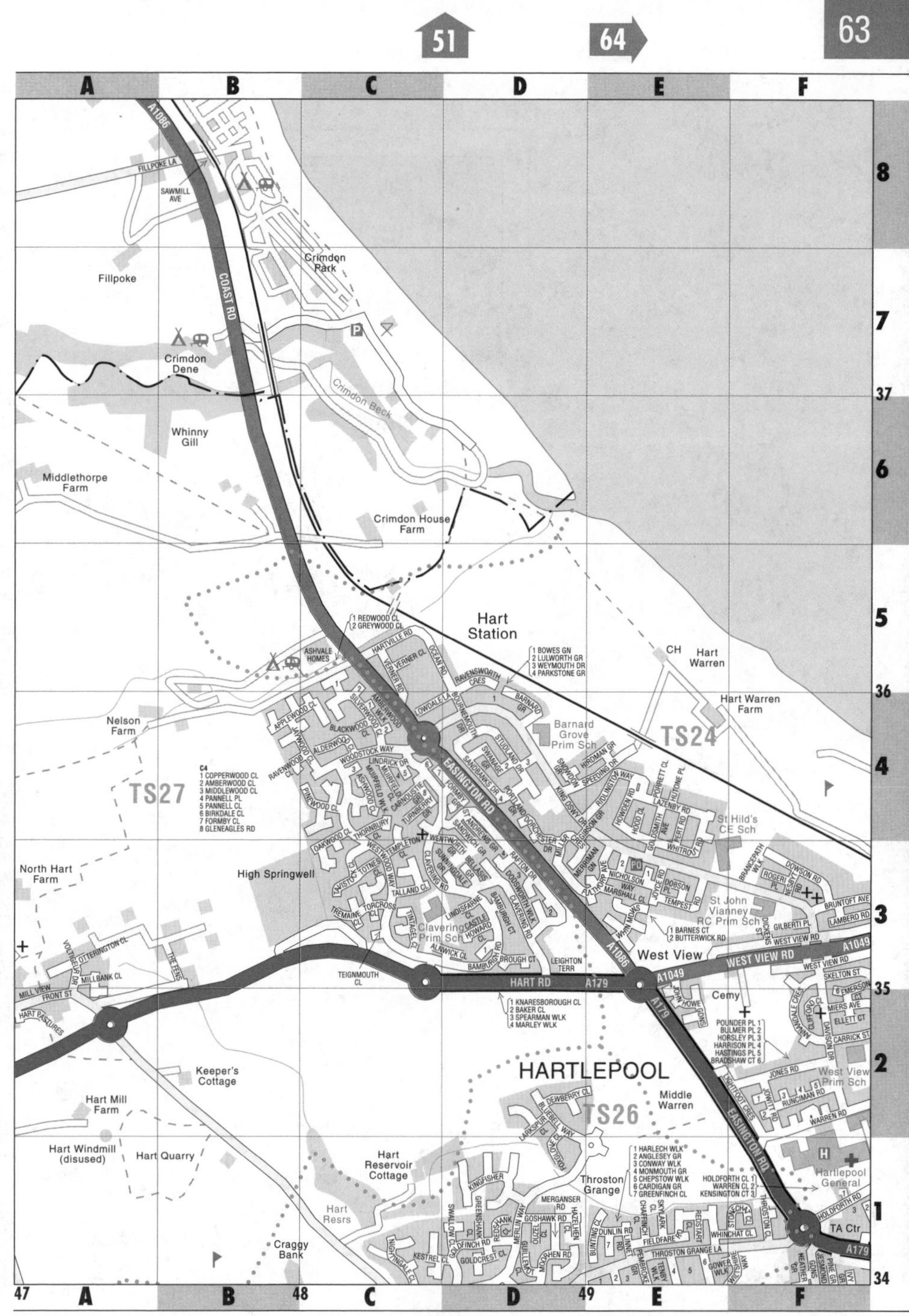
A
B
C
D
E
F
8
7
37
6
5
36
4
3
35
2
1
34
47
48
49
A1086
FILLPOKE LA
SAWMILL AVE
COAST RD
Fillpoke
Crimdon Park
Crimdon Dene
Crimdon Beck
Whinny Gill
Middlethorpe Farm
Crimdon House Farm
Hart Station
1 REDWOOD CL
2 GREYWOOD CL
ASHVALE HOMES
1 BOWES GN
2 LULWORTH GR
3 WEYMOUTH DR
4 PARKSTONE GR
CH
Hart Warren
Hart Warren Farm
Nelson Farm
Barnard Grove Prim Sch
TS24
TS27
C4
1 COPPERWOOD CL
2 AMBERWOOD CL
3 MIDDLEWOOD CL
4 PANNELL PL
5 PANNELL CL
6 BIRKDALE CL
7 FORMBY CL
8 GLENEAGLES RD
EASINGTON RD
St Hild's CE Sch
North Hart Farm
High Springwell
St John Vianney RC Prim Sch
Clavering Prim Sch
1 BARNES CT
2 BUTTERWICK RD
West View
WEST VIEW RD
A1049
TEIGNMOUTH CL
HART RD
A179
LEIGHTON TERR
1 KNARESBOROUGH CL
2 BAKER CL
3 SPEARMAN WLK
4 MARLEY WLK
Cemy
POUNDER PL 1
BULMER PL 2
HORSLEY PL 3
HARRISON PL 4
HASTINGS PL 5
BRADSHAW CT 6
MILL VIEW
FRONT ST
HART PASTURES
Keeper's Cottage
HARTLEPOOL
West View Prim Sch
Hart Mill Farm
TS26
Middle Warren
Hart Windmill (disused)
Hart Quarry
Hart Reservoir Cottage
1 HARLECH WLK
2 ANGLESEY GR
3 CONWAY WLK
4 MONMOUTH GR
5 CHEPSTOW WLK
6 CARDIGAN GR
7 GREENFINCH CL
Throston Grange
HOLDFORTH CL 1
WARREN CL 2
KENSINGTON CT 3
Hartlepool General
Hart Resrs
TA Ctr
Craggy Bank
THROSTON GRANGE LA
HOLDFORTH RD

76
64

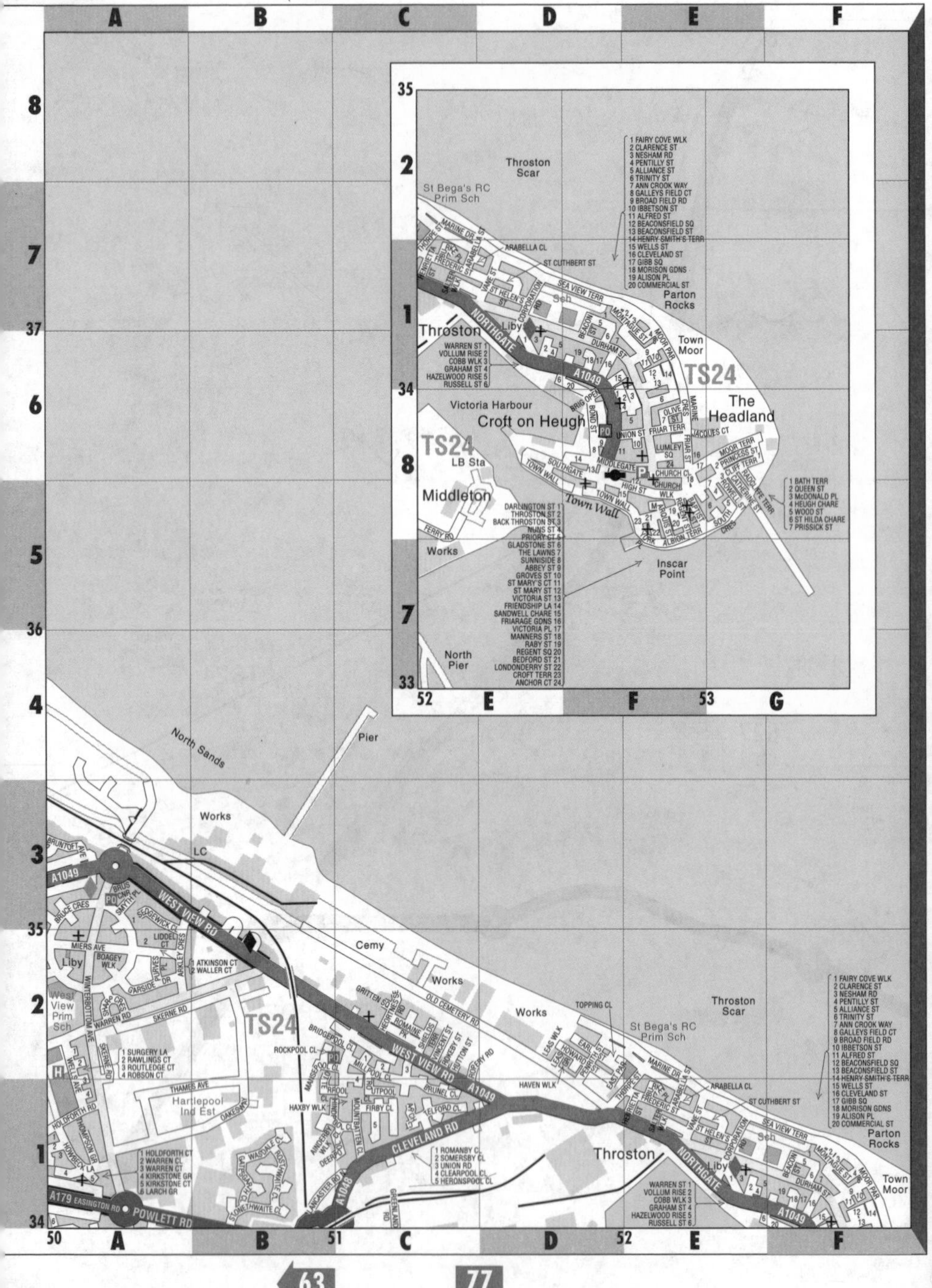

A **B** **C** **D** **E** **F**

8

7

37

34

6

5

36

4

3

35

2

34

50 **A** 51 **B** **C** 52 **D** **E** **F**

35
2
1
34
8
7
33
52 **E** **F** 53 **G**

Throston Scar
St Bega's RC Prim Sch
Throston
NORTHGATE
ARABELLA CL
ST CLUTHBERT ST
SEA VIEW TERR
Liby
WARREN ST 1
VOLLUM RISE 2
COBB WLK 3
GRAHAM ST 4
HAZELWOOD RISE 5
RUSSELL ST 6
A1049
Victoria Harbour
Croft on Heugh
TS24
LB Sta
Middleton
Works
Ferry Rd
North Pier
Town Wall
Town Moor
The Headland
TS24
Parton Rocks
Inscar Point

1 FAIRY COVE WLK
2 CLARENCE ST
3 NESHAM RD
4 PENTILLY ST
5 ALLIANCE ST
6 TRINITY ST
7 ANN CROOK WAY
8 GALLEYS FIELD CT
9 BROAD FIELD RD
10 IBBETSON ST
11 ALFRED ST
12 BEACONSFIELD SQ
13 BEACONSFIELD ST
14 HENRY SMITH'S TERR
15 WELLS ST
16 CLEVELAND ST
17 GIBB SQ
18 MORISON GDNS
19 ALISON PL
20 COMMERCIAL ST

DARLINGTON ST 1
THROSTON ST 2
BACK THROSTON ST 3
MARS ST 4
PRIORY ST 5
GLADSTONE ST 6
THE LAWNS 7
SUNNISIDE 8
ABBEY ST 9
GROVES ST 10
ST MARY'S CT 11
ST MARY ST 12
VICTORIA ST 13
FRIENDSHIP LA 14
SANDWELL CHARE 15
FRIARAGE GDNS 16
VICTORIA PL 17
MANNERS ST 18
RABY ST 19
REGENT SQ 20
BEDFORD ST 21
LONDONDERRY ST 22
CROFT TERR 23
ANCHOR CT 24

1 BATH TERR
2 QUEEN ST
3 McDONALD PL
4 HEUGH CHARE
5 WOOD ST
6 ST HILDA CHARE
7 PRISSICK ST

North Sands
Pier
Works
LC
WEST VIEW RD
A1049
BRUCE CRES
JOHN POUNTY CT
MIERS AVE
BOAGEY WLK
Liby
West View Prim Sch
WARREN RD
CARRER
ATKINSON CT
WALLER CT
LIDDEL CT
OKERNE RD
PARSIDE
Cemy
OLD CEMETERY RD
GRITTEN CL
Works
Works
TOPPING CL
St Bega's RC Prim Sch
Throston Scar
TS24
ROCKPOOL CL
THAMES AVE
HAXBY WLK
Hartlepool Ind Est
BRUNEL CL
FIRBY CL
HAVEN WLK
Throston
NORTHGATE
ARABELLA CL
ST CUTHBERT ST
SEA VIEW TERR
Liby
Town Moor
A1049
CLEVELAND RD
A1048
A179 EASINGTON RD
POWLETT RD

1 SURGERY LA
2 RAWLINGS CT
3 ROUTLEDGE CT
4 ROBSON CT

1 HOLDFORTH CT
2 WARREN CL
3 UNION RD
4 KIRKSTONE GR
5 KIRKSTONE CT
6 LARCH GR

1 ROMANBY CL
2 SOMERSBY CL
3 UNION RD
4 CLEARPOOL CL
5 HERONSPOOL CL

1 FAIRY COVE WLK
2 CLARENCE ST
3 NESHAM RD
4 PENTILLY ST
5 ALLIANCE ST
6 TRINITY ST
7 ANN CROOK WAY
8 GALLEYS FIELD CT
9 BROAD FIELD RD
10 IBBETSON ST
11 ALFRED ST
12 BEACONSFIELD SQ
13 BEACONSFIELD ST
14 HENRY SMITH'S TERR
15 WELLS ST
16 CLEVELAND ST
17 GIBB SQ
18 MORISON GDNS
19 ALISON PL
20 COMMERCIAL ST

WARREN ST 1
VOLLUM RISE 2
COBB WLK 3
GRAHAM ST 4
HAZELWOOD RISE 5
RUSSELL ST 6

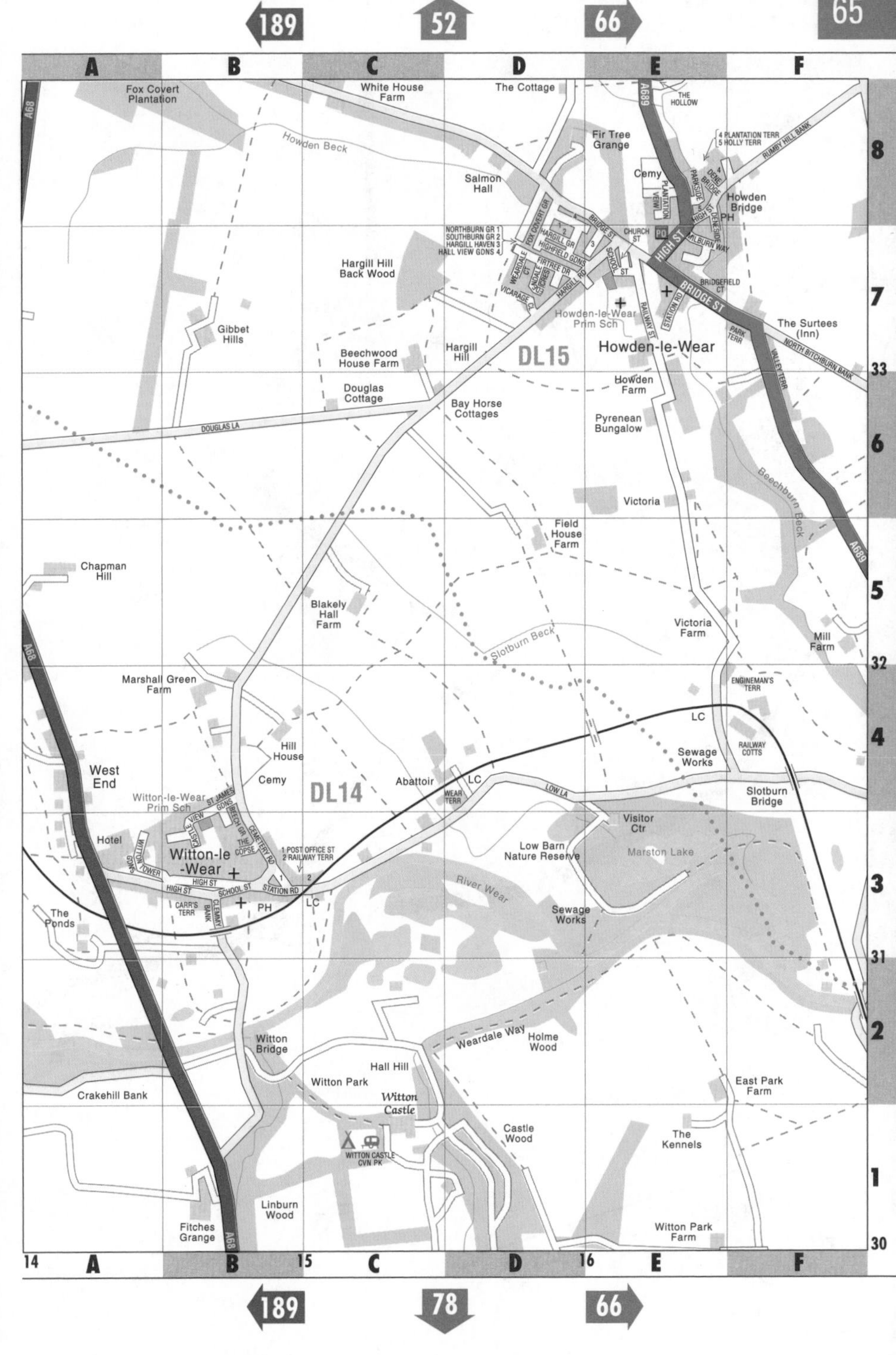
189
52
66
A
B
C
D
E
F
Fox Covert Plantation
White House Farm
The Cottage
THE HOLLOW
A689
A68
Howden Beck
Fir Tree Grange
4 PLANTATION TERR
5 HOLLY TERR
RUMBY HILL BANK
Cemy
PLANTATION VIEW
PARKSIDE
DENE BRIDGE
Howden Bridge
Salmon Hall
HIGH ST
DENESIDE
PH
NORTHBURN GR 1
SOUTHBURN GR 2
HARGILL HAVEN 3
HALL VIEW GDNS 4
FOX COVERT GR
HARGILL GR
HIGHFIELD GDNS
BRIDGE ST
CHURCH ST
MILBURN WAY
FIRTREE DR
WEARDALE CT
LINDALE CRES
HARGILL RD
SCHOOL ST
VICARAGE CL
Hargill Hill Back Wood
BRIDGEFIELD CT
STATION RD
RAILWAY ST
Howden-le-Wear Prim Sch
Howden-le-Wear
The Surtees (Inn)
PARK TERR
NORTH BITCHBURN BANK
VALLEY TERR
Gibbet Hills
Beechwood House Farm
Hargill Hill
DL15
Howden Farm
Douglas Cottage
Bay Horse Cottages
Pyrenean Bungalow
DOUGLAS LA
Beechburn Beck
Victoria
Field House Farm
Chapman Hill
Blakely Hall Farm
Victoria Farm
Slotburn Beck
Mill Farm
Marshall Green Farm
ENGINEMAN'S TERR
LC
Hill House
Sewage Works
RAILWAY COTTS
West End
Cemy
DL14
Abattoir
WEAR TERR
LOW LA
Slotburn Bridge
Witton-le-Wear Prim Sch
ST JAMES GDNS
CASTLE VIEW
BEECH GR
CEMETERY RD
THE COPSE
Visitor Ctr
Hotel
WITTON TOWER GDNS
1 POST OFFICE ST
2 RAILWAY TERR
Low Barn Nature Reserve
Marston Lake
Witton-le-Wear
HIGH ST
SCHOOL ST
STATION RD
River Wear
The Ponds
CARR'S TERR
CLEMMY BANK
PH
Sewage Works
Weardale Way
Holme Wood
Witton Bridge
Hall Hill
Witton Park
East Park Farm
Crakehill Bank
Witton Castle
Castle Wood
The Kennels
WITTON CASTLE CVN PK
Linburn Wood
Fitches Grange
Witton Park Farm
8
7
33
6
5
32
4
3
31
2
1
30
14
15
16
78

65 53

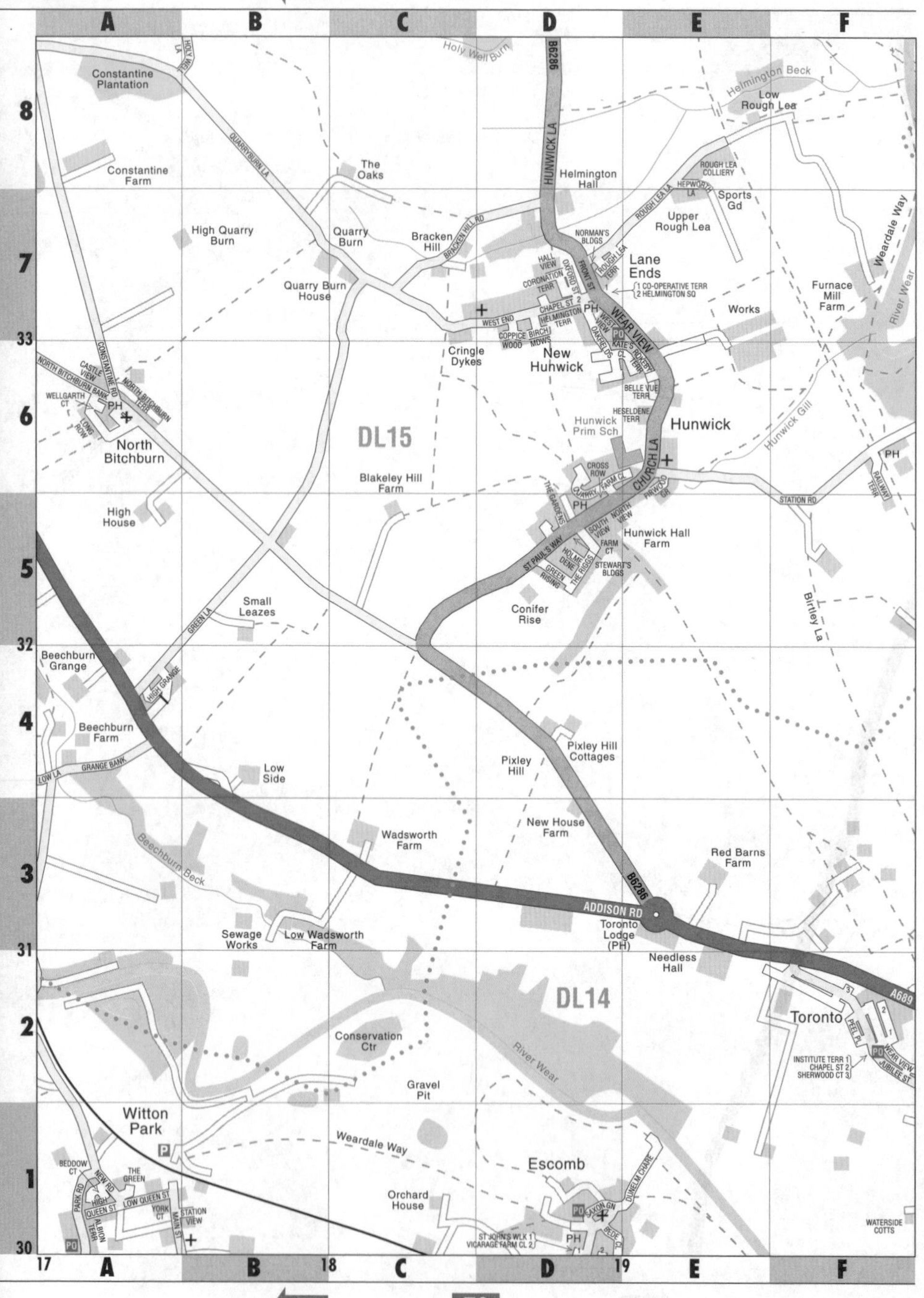
A
B
C
D
E
F
8
7
33
6
5
32
4
3
31
2
1
30
17
18
19
Holy Well Burn
B6286
Helmington Beck
Low Rough Lea
Constantine Plantation
Constantine Farm
Quarryburn La
Holy Well La
The Oaks
Hunwick La
Helmington Hall
Rough Lea Colliery
Hepworth La
Sports Gd
Upper Rough Lea
Rough Lea La
High Quarry Burn
Quarry Burn
Bracken Hill
Bracken Hill Rd
Norman's Bldgs
Lane Ends
Quarry Burn House
Hall View
Coronation Terr
Oxford St
Front St
1 Co-operative Terr
2 Helmington Sq
Furnace Mill Farm
Weardale Way
River Wear
Works
Chapel St
Helmington Terr
West End
Coppice Wood
Birch Mdws
PH
PO
Wear View
Cringle Dykes
New Hunwick
Oakfields
Kate's Cl
Rokeby Terr
Belle Vue Terr
Castle View
North Bitchburn Bank
North Bitchburn Terr
Constantine Rd
Wellgarth Ct
Long Row
North Bitchburn
DL15
Hunwick Prim Sch
Heseldene Terr
Hunwick
Hunwick Gill
Church La
Cross Row
Farm Cl
Quarry
Parwood Gr
Station Rd
Railway Terr
Blakeley Hill Farm
High House
The Gardens
North View
South View
Hunwick Hall Farm
St Paul's Way
Holme Dene
The Riggs
Farm Ct
Stewart's Bldgs
Green Rising
Conifer Rise
Birtley La
Small Leazes
Green La
Beechburn Grange
High Grange
Beechburn Farm
Grange Bank
Low La
Pixley Hill Cottages
Pixley Hill
Low Side
New House Farm
Wadsworth Farm
Red Barns Farm
Beechburn Beck
Addison Rd
Toronto Lodge (PH)
Sewage Works
Low Wadsworth Farm
Needless Hall
DL14
A689
Toronto
Peel Pl
Institute Terr 1
Chapel St 2
Sherwood Ct 3
Wear View
Jubilee St
Conservation Ctr
River Wear
Gravel Pit
Witton Park
P
Weardale Way
Escomb
Dunelm Chare
Beddow Ct
The Green
New Rd
Park Rd
High Queen St
Low Queen St
York Ct
Station View
Main St
Albion Terr
Orchard House
Saxon Gn
Bede Cl
St John's Wlk 1
Vicarage Farm Cl 2
Waterside Cotts

65 79

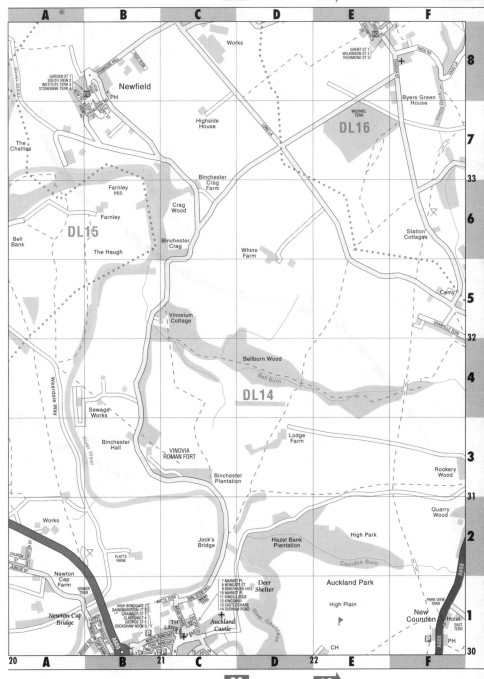

54
68

A
B
C
D
E
F
Works
GREENFIELD ST
HIGH ST
GHENT ST 1
WILKINSON ST 2
RICHMOND ST 3
HAGG RD
HAGG LA
CHURCH ST
PRIMROSE HILL
HIGH ROW
GARDEN ST 1
SOUTH VIEW 2
INSTITUTE TERR 3
STONEBANK TERR 4
Newfield
PH
SPRINGBANK RD
GREY ST
NEW PK VIEW
WEST TERR
LYDIA TERR
PO
River Wear
Byers Green House
Hagg Beck
MICHAEL TERR
DL16
Highside House
LONG LA
The Challies
Binchester Crag Farm
Farnley Hill
Crag Wood
Farnley
DL15
Bell Bank
Station Cottages
Binchester Crag
The Haugh
Whins Farm
Cemy
Vinovium Cottage
GRANVILLE TERR
Bellburn Wood
Bell Burn
DL14
Weardale Way
Sewage Works
Lodge Farm
Binchester Hall
River Wear
VINOVIA ROMAN FORT
Rookery Wood
Binchester Plantation
Quarry Wood
Works
High Park
Jock's Bridge
Hazel Bank Plantation
CHURCH ST
BARRINGTON ST
JUBILEE ST
FLATTS FARM
Coundon Burn
Newton Cap Farm
GOMER TERR
7 MARKET PL
8 NEWGATE ST
9 BAKEHOUSE HILL
10 MARKET PL
11 KINGS LODGE
12 KINGSWAY
13 CASTLE CHARE
14 DURHAM ROAD
Deer Shelter
Auckland Park
A688
DIAL STOB HILL
BATTS TERR
WEAR TERR
HIGH BONDGATE 1
GAINSBOROUGH CT 2
GRAINGER ST 3
CLAYTON CT 4
GEORGE ST 5
COCKSHAW NOOK 6
WEAR CHARE
SILVER ST
High Plain
PARK VIEW TERR
Newton Cap Bridge
LOWER BRIDGE ST
BRIDGE ST
NEWTON CAP BANK
BRIDGE RD
A689
TH
Liby
Auckland Castle
River Gaunless
NORTH BONDGATE
FORE BONDGATE
FINKLE ST
New Coundon
Hotel
EAST TERR
PH
A688
CH
8
7
33
6
5
32
4
3
31
2
1
30
20
21
22

80
68

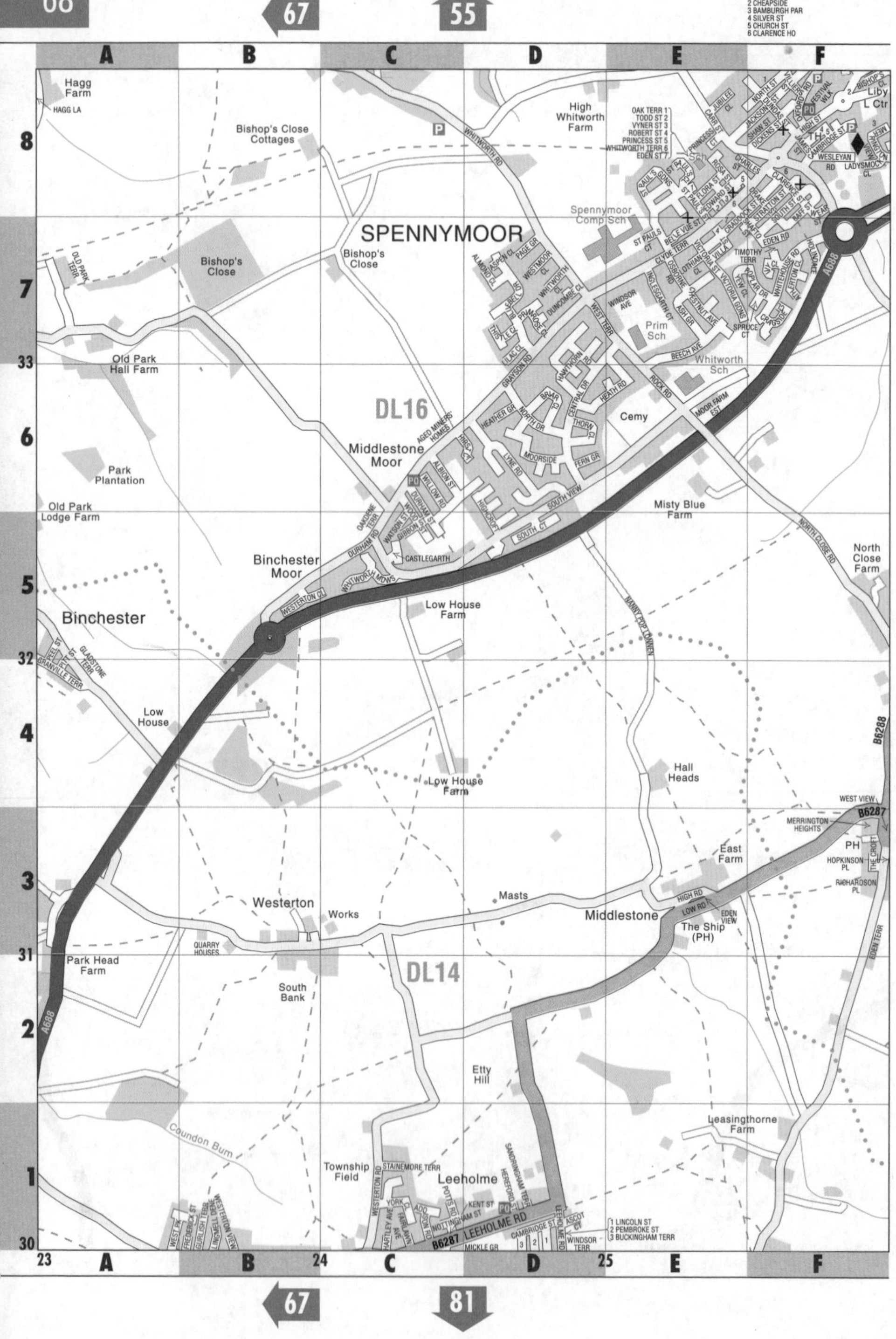

56
70

Low Spennymoor
Skibbereen
Red Hall Farm
Merrington Lane
Merrington Lane Ind Est
Sewage Works
Mary Lands
Dean & Chapter Ind Est
Liby
High Hill House
Low Hill House
Oaklea
VYNERS CL
Ferryhill Windmill (dis)
Dean Bank
Fox Covert
Mast
Allot Gdns
North Close
Ferryhill Bus Ent Coll
MERRINGTON RD
DL16
DL17
East Roughlea
Bridge House Farm
West Roughlea Farm
Kirk Merrington
Kirk Merrington Prim Sch
WEST CL
Chilton Ind Est
Blue House
Mast
Cemy
Dene Bridge
Merrington Grange
DENE VILLAS
DL14
Blue House Farm
West Chilton Farm
A167
A688
B6288
B6287
1 CATHERINE CL
2 SYCAMORE CT
3 CEDAR CT
1 ST ANDREW'S LA
2 UPPER CHURCH ST
3 GRAINGER ST
1 WEST ST
2 PARKER TERR
3 KENSINGTON GDNS
4 GLEBE HOUSES
5 MANOR CT
6 CHESTNUT AVE
7 WILLOW RD
1 THE VILLAS
2 WESTCOTT TERR
3 LIGHTFOOT TERR
4 HAIG TERR
5 HACKWORTH ST
6 BARRINGTON TERR
7 ST CUTHBERT'S TERR
8 DEAN BANK GRANGE
9 HOLYOAKE ST
1 COULTON TERR
2 BEDE PL
3 ROCKCLIFFE TERR
4 HOPKINSON PL
5 RICHARDSON PL
6 MISSION PL
7 CHAPEL ST
8 RAMSHAW TERR
9 CORONATION TERR
10 JOWSEY PL
THE JOSEPH PATTERSON CRES
THE WILLIAM KEERS CRES
DENE BRIDGE ROW
AVENUE 1
AVENUE 3
AVENUE 4
CHILTON WAY
WINDLESTONE LA
DURHAM RD
DARLINGTON RD
BRIDGE HOUSE EST
MAIN ST
SOUTH SIDE (DEAN RD)
DEAN RD
33
32
31
30
26
27
28

82
70

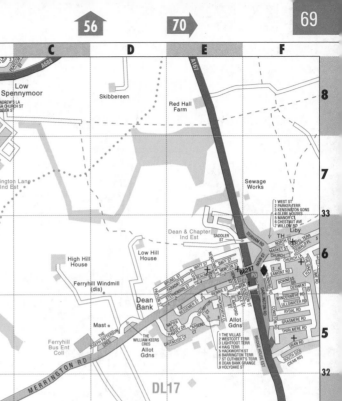

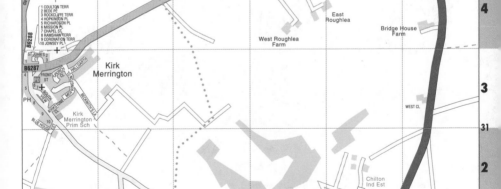

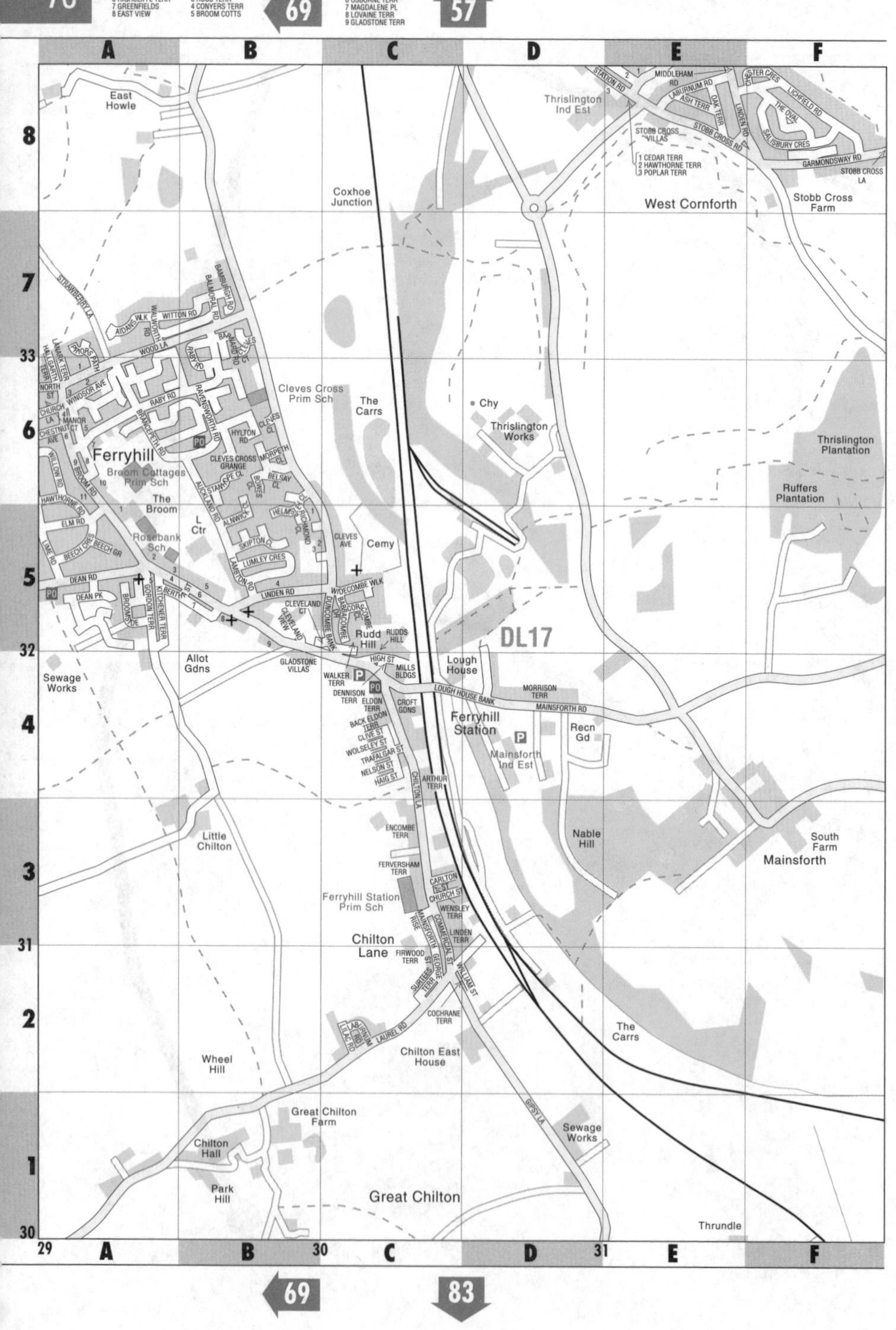

58
72

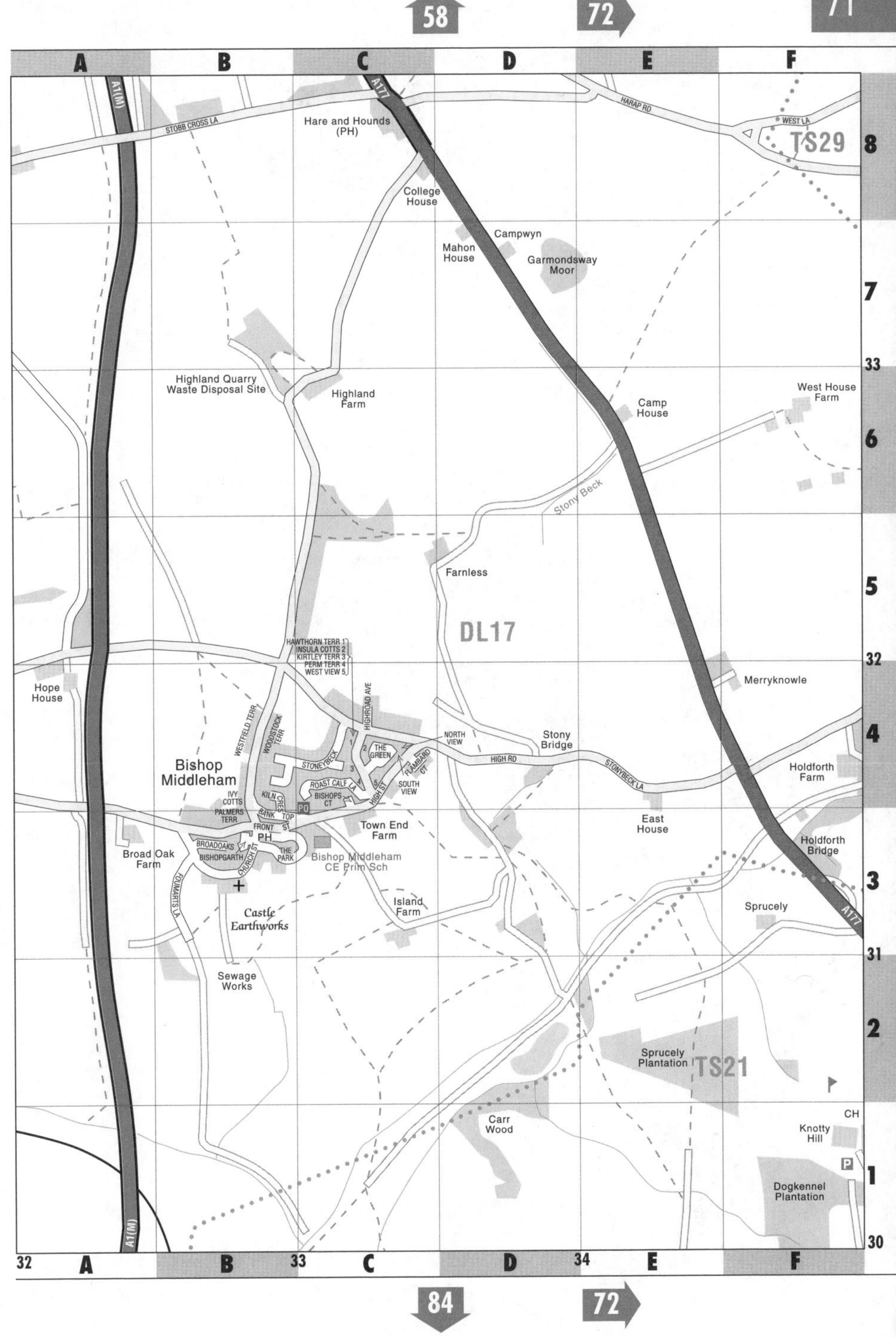
A
B
C
D
E
F
A1(M)
A177
STOBB CROSS LA
Hare and Hounds
(PH)
HARAP RD
WEST LA
TS29
8
College
House
Campwyn
Mahon
House
Garmondsway
Moor
7
33
Highland Quarry
Waste Disposal Site
Highland
Farm
Camp
House
West House
Farm
6
Stony Beck
Farnless
5
DL17
HAWTHORN TERR 1
INSULA COTTS 2
KIRTLEY TERR 3
PERM TERR 4
WEST VIEW 5
32
Hope
House
Merryknowle
WESTFIELD TERR
WOODSTOCK TERR
HIGHROAD AVE
THE GREEN
NORTH VIEW
Stony
Bridge
4
Bishop
Middleham
STONEYBECK
FLAMBARD CT
HIGH RD
STONYBECK LA
Holdforth
Farm
IVY
COTTS
ROAST CALF LA
BISHOPS CT
SOUTH VIEW
HIGH ST
PALMERS
TERR
KILN CRES
PO
BANK TOP
FRONT ST
East
House
Town End
Farm
PH
BROADOAKS
BISHOPGARTH
CHURCH ST
THE PARK
Holdforth
Bridge
Broad Oak
Farm
Bishop Middleham
CE Prim Sch
FOUMARTS LA
Castle
Earthworks
Island
Farm
Sprucely
3
31
Sewage
Works
2
Sprucely
Plantation
TS21
CH
Carr
Wood
Knotty
Hill
P
1
Dogkennel
Plantation
30
32
33
34

84
72

A B C D E F

8

7

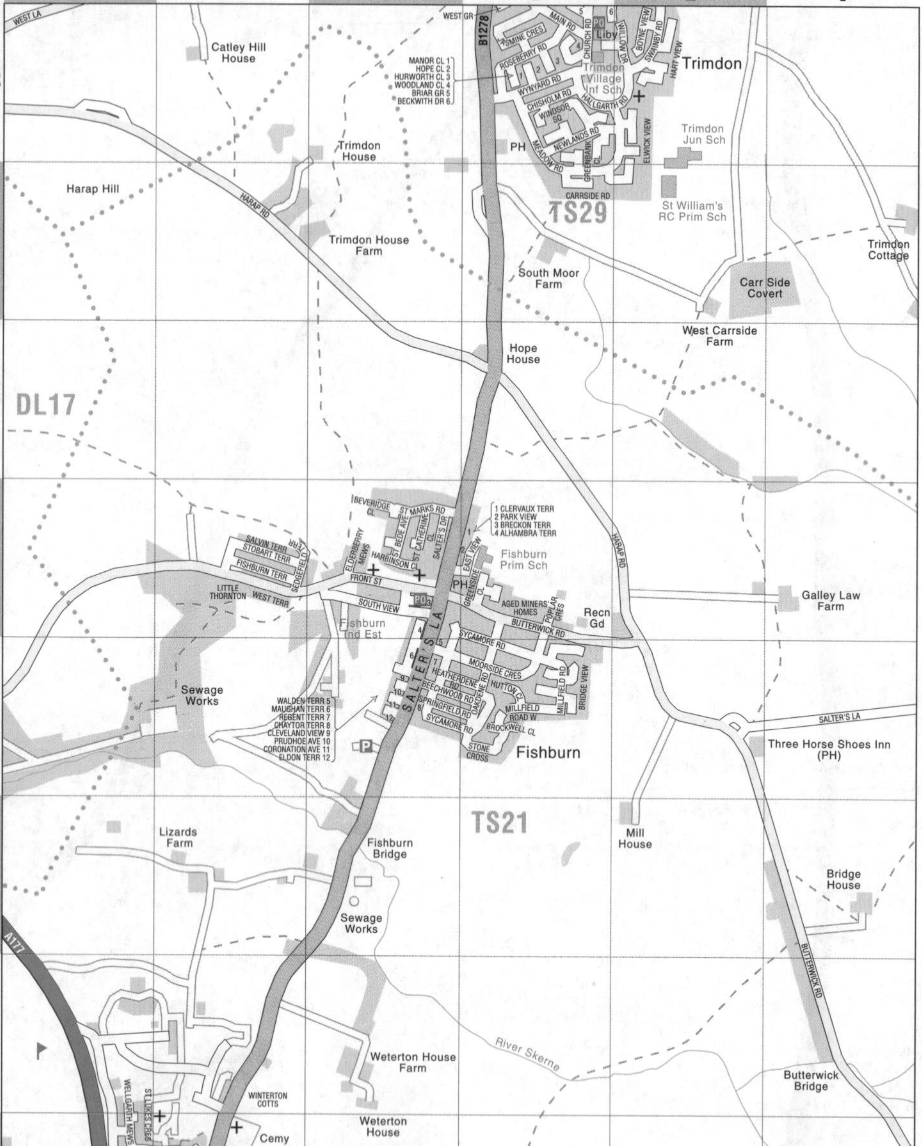

33

6 DL17

5

32

4

3

31

2

1

30

35 A B 36 C D 37 E F

WEST LA

Catley Hill House

Trimdon House

Harap Hill

HARAP RD

Trimdon House Farm

WEST GR
B1278
MAIN RD
PRIMROSE CRES
ROSEBURY RD
CHURCH RD
BYRNE VIEW
STANLEY RD
Liby
MANOR CL 1
HOPE CL 2
HURWORTH CL 3
WOODLAND CL 4
BRIAR GR 5
BECKWITH DR 6
WYNYARD RD
HART VIEW
Trimdon Village Inf Sch
BELLGARTH RD
Trimdon
CHISHOLM RD
WINDSOR SQ
NEWLANDS RD
GREENBANK RD
ELWICK VIEW
Trimdon Jun Sch
PH
CARRSIDE RD
TS29
St William's RC Prim Sch
Trimdon Cottage

South Moor Farm

Carr Side Covert

West Carside Farm

Hope House

1 CLERVAUX TERR
2 PARK VIEW
3 BRECKON TERR
4 ALHAMBRA TERR

BEVERIDGE CL
ST MARKS RD
ST CATHERINE
SALVIN TERR
STOBART TERR
FISHBURN TERR
ELLENBOROUGH
CRESCENT
HARRISON TERR
FRONT ST
DALTON ST
PARK VIEW
Fishburn Prim Sch

LITTLE THORNTON
WEST TERR
SOUTH VIEW
PH
AGED MINERS HOMES
BUTTERWICK RD
Recn Gd

Galley Law Farm

Fishburn Ind Est

SALTER'S LA
SYCAMORE RD
MOORSIDE CRES
HEATHERDENE
BEECHWOOD RD
SPRINGFIELD RD
HUTTON
MILLFIELD RD
BRIDGE VIEW
MILLFIELD ROAD W
BROCKNELL CL

WALDEN TERR 5
MAUGHAN TERR 6
REGENT TERR 7
GRAYTOR TERR 8
CLEVELAND VIEW 9
PRUDHOE AVE 10
CORONATION AVE 11
ELDON TERR 12
SYCAMORE RD
STONE CROSS

Fishburn

Three Horse Shoes Inn (PH)

SALTER'S LA

Sewage Works

Lizards Farm

Fishburn Bridge

Sewage Works

TS21

Mill House

Bridge House

A177

B1278

WELLGARTH MEWS
SALTERS CRES
WINTERTON COTTS

Weterton House Farm

River Skerne

Butterwick Bridge

BUTTERWICK RD

Cemy

Weterton House

Redcar Beck

TWINPIKE WLK
MILCLONE WLK
HOMESTALL CL
FAIRFIELD
MANOR HILL
MEADOW HILL
PASTURE FIELD
WINTERTON COTTS

Howle Hope

Works

Firtree Hill

The Brocks

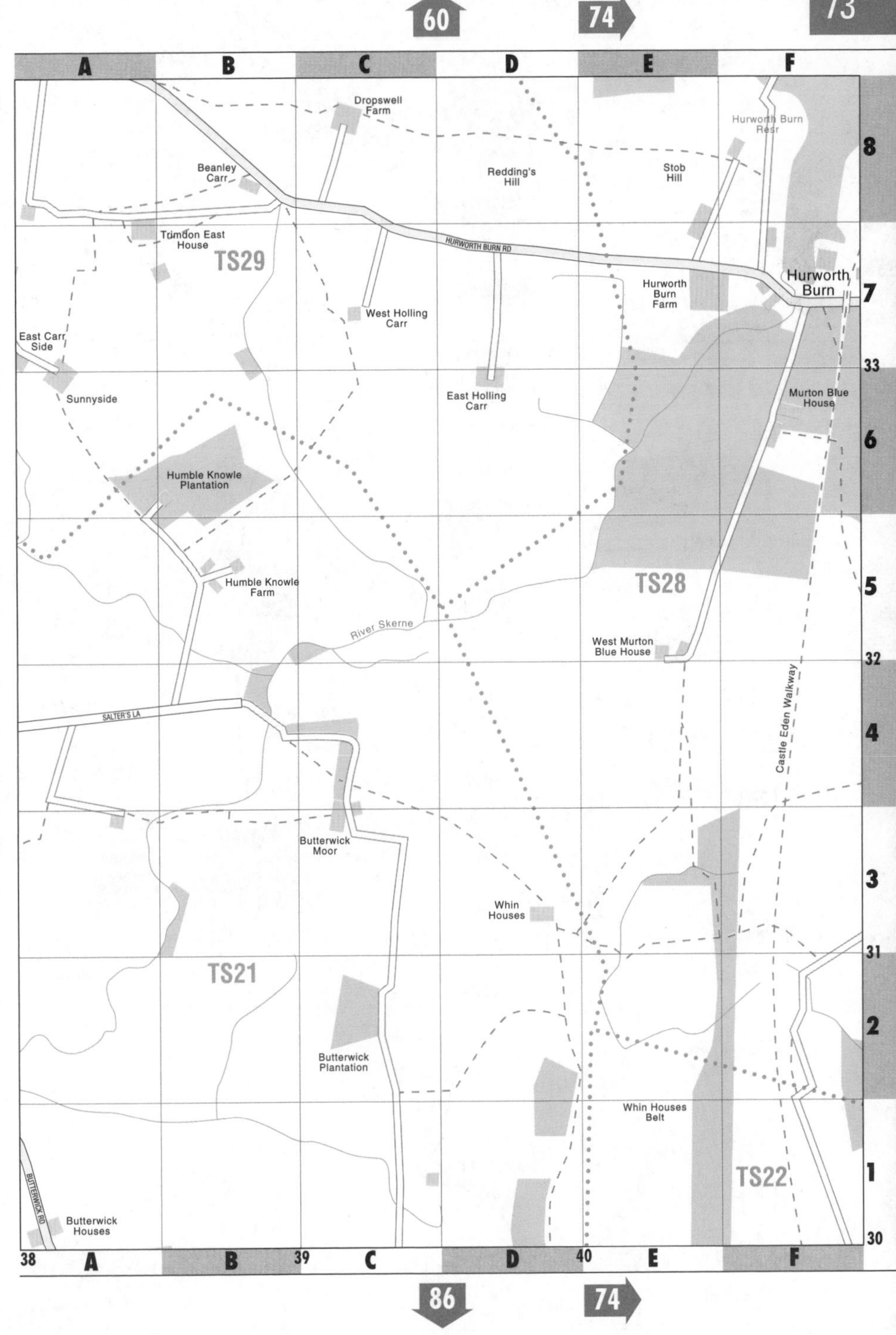

8

Hurworth Burn
Resr

Dropswell
Farm

Beanley
Carr

Redding's
Hill

Stob
Hill

Trimdon East
House

TS29

HURWORTH BURN RD

7

West Holling
Carr

Hurworth
Burn Farm

Hurworth
Burn

East Carr
Side

33

Sunnyside

East Holling
Carr

Murton Blue
House

6

Humble Knowle
Plantation

5

Humble Knowle
Farm

TS28

River Skerne

West Murton
Blue House

32

SALTER'S LA

Castle Eden Walkway

4

Butterwick
Moor

3

Whin
Houses

31

TS21

2

Butterwick
Plantation

Whin Houses
Belt

TS22

1

30

BUTTERWICK RD

Butterwick
Houses

73
61

A
B
C
D
E
F
8
7
33
6
5
32
4
3
31
2
1
30
41
42
43
Roper's Wood
Kirsup's Plantation
Pike Whin Moor
Sheraton Grange Farm
Sheraton West Grange
Middle Moor Plantation
HURWORTH BURN RD
Pudding Poke Farm
Murton Blue House Plantations
Black Wood
Cotsfold Close Farm
Tilery Plantation
COAL LA
Murton East Farm
Birches Plantation
Amerston Beck
Beacon Hill Farm
Pawton Hill Farm
Scotland Wood
TS28
Cole Hill Farm
High Wood
Murton Hall Farm
TS27
Quaker Gill
Stotfold Moor
East Murton Farm
Cow Pasture Wood
Crookfoot Reservoir
Embleton Old Hall
Winterley Hill Plantation
Cobbler's Plantation
Crookfoot Cottage
Tinkers Gill
Embleton Moor
Amerston Hill
Amerston Beck
Amerston Gill
TS22
Amerston Hall

73
87

62
76

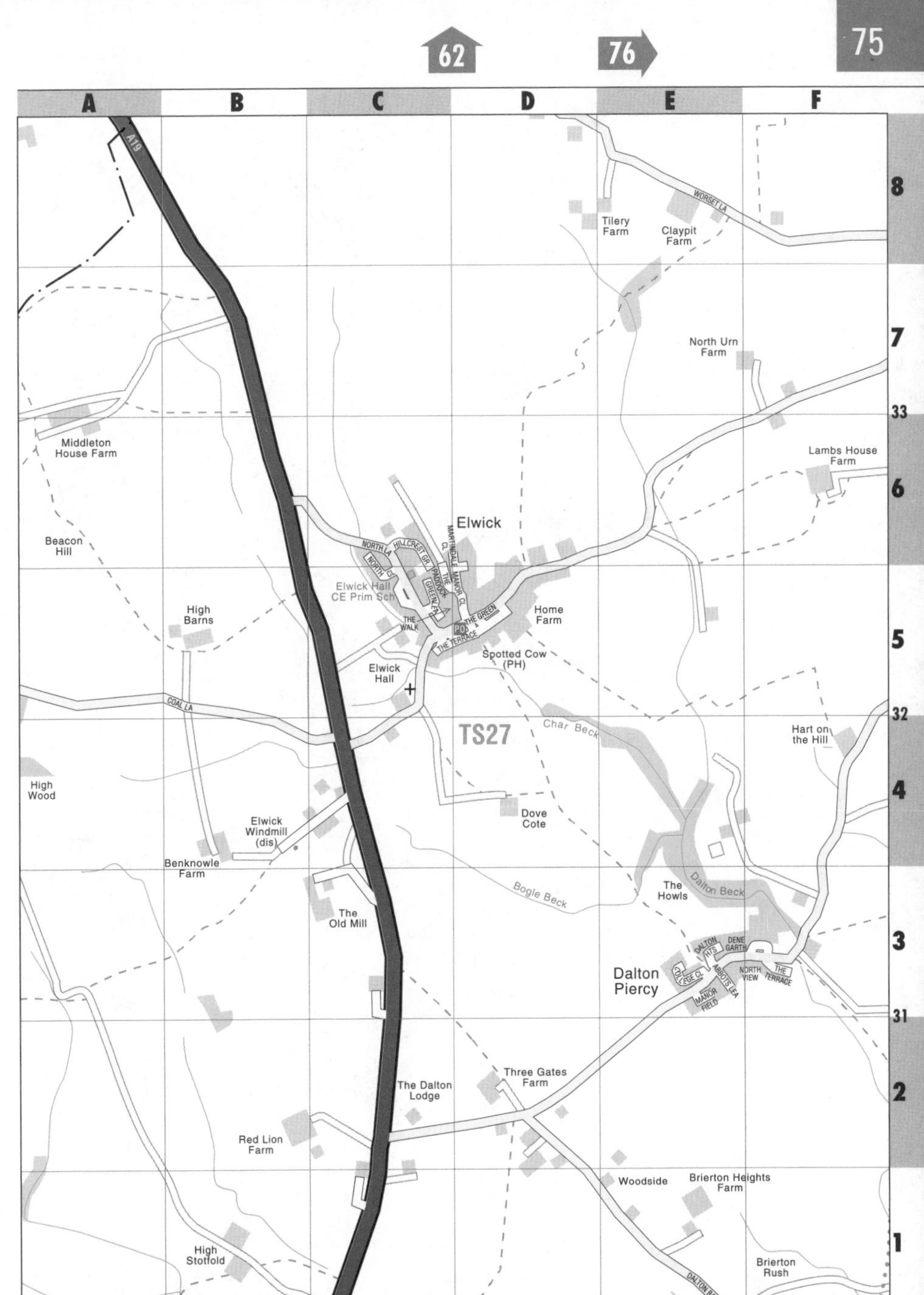
A
B
C
D
E
F
A19
WORSET LA
Tilery Farm
Claypit Farm
North Urn Farm
Middleton House Farm
Lambs House Farm
Beacon Hill
Elwick
NORTH LA
HILLCREST GR
MARTINDALE CL
MANOR CL
THE PADDOCK
GREEN LA
THE GREEN
THE TERRACE
THE WALK
Elwick Hall CE Prim Sch
High Barns
Home Farm
Spotted Cow (PH)
Elwick Hall
COAL LA
TS27
Char Beck
Hart on the Hill
High Wood
Dove Cote
Elwick Windmill (dis)
Benknowle Farm
Bogle Beck
The Howls
Dalton Beck
The Old Mill
DALTON HTS
DENE GARTH
Dalton Piercy
COLLEGE CL
ABBOTS LEA
NORTH VIEW
THE TERRACE
MANOR FIELD
Three Gates Farm
The Dalton Lodge
Red Lion Farm
Woodside
Brierton Heights Farm
High Stotfold
Brierton Rush
DALTON BACK LA
8
7
33
6
5
32
4
3
31
2
1
30
44
45
46

88
76

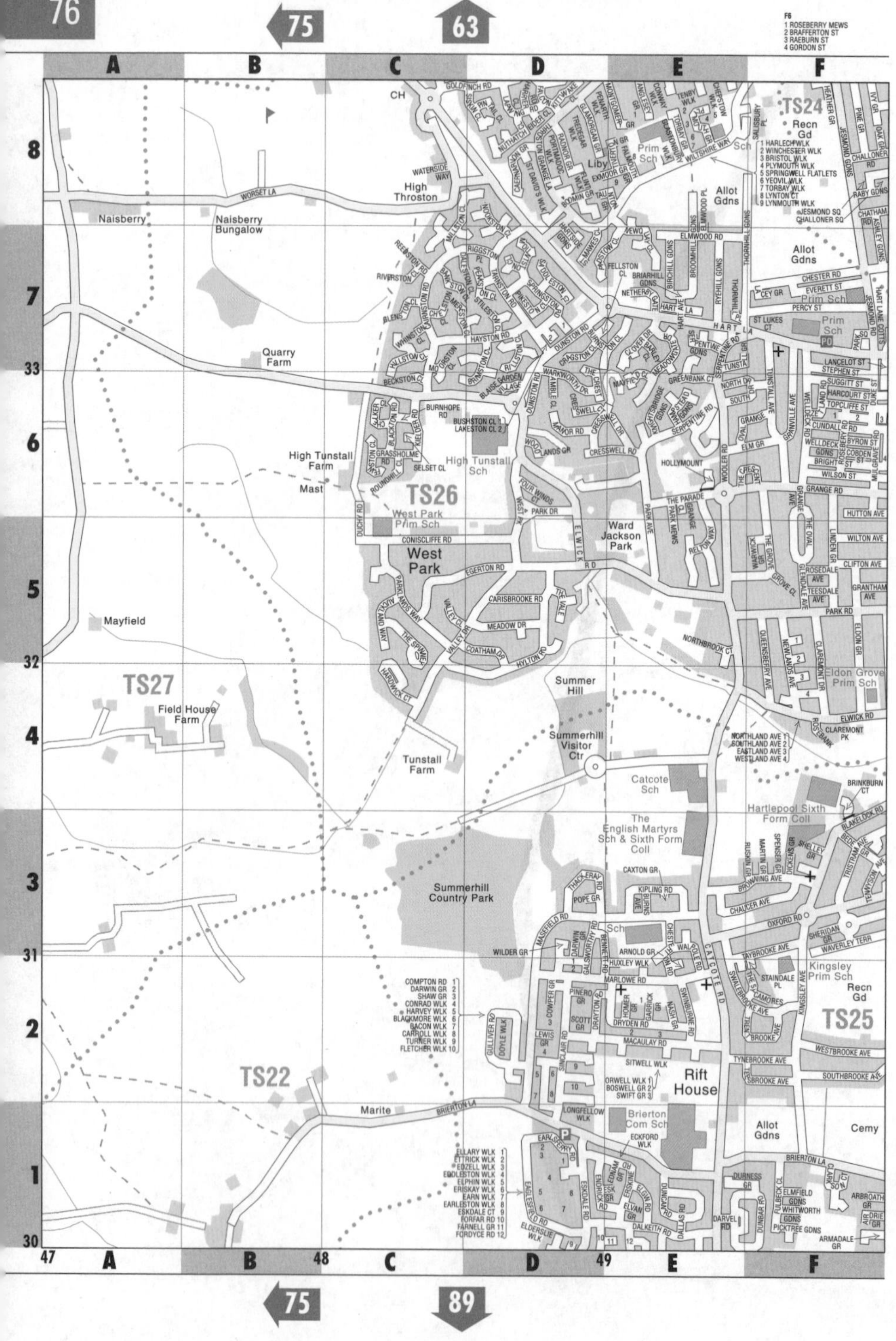

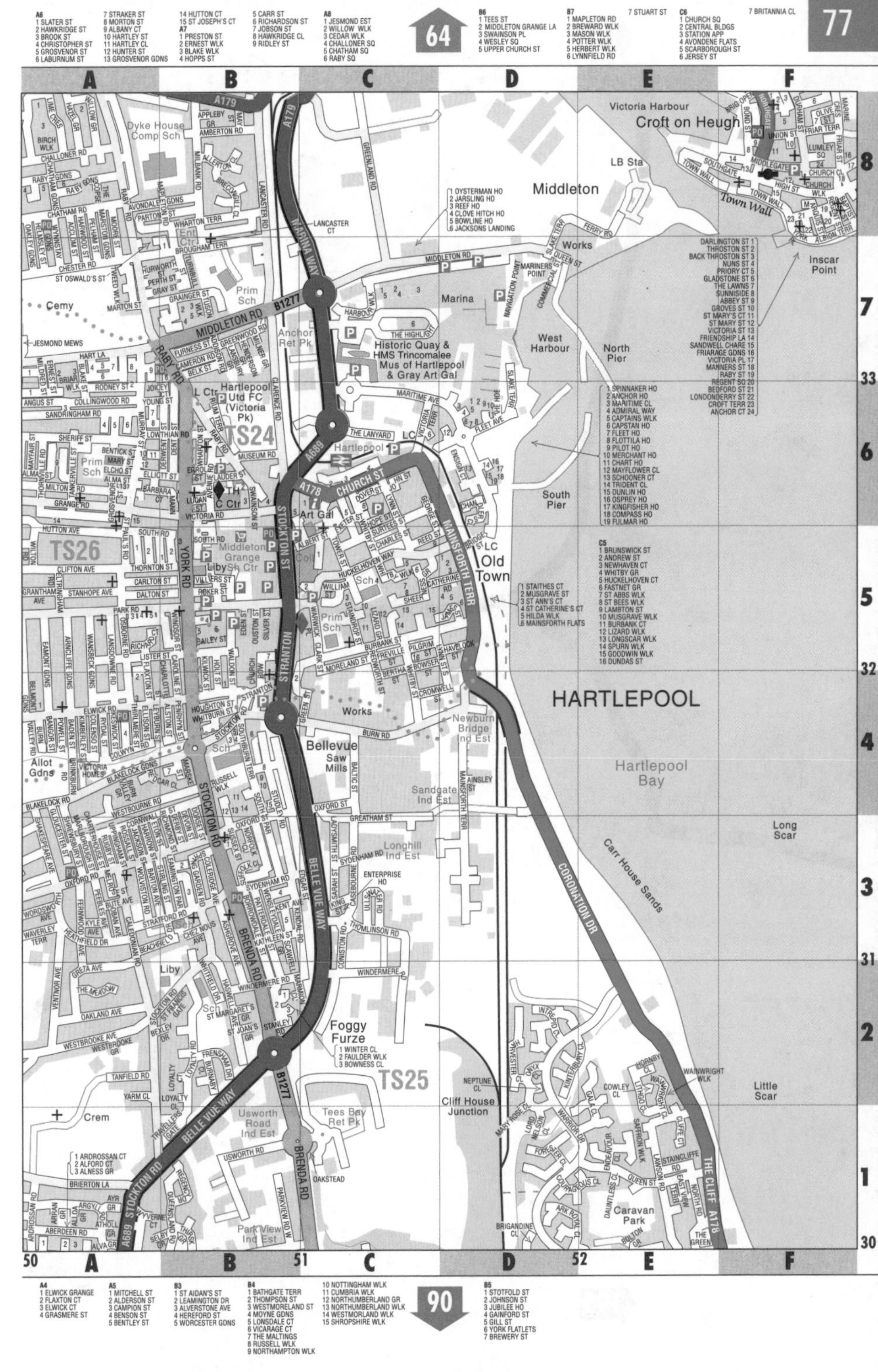

64

A8			A8	B6	B7		C6	
1 SLATER ST	7 STRAKER ST	14 HUTTON CT	1 JESMOND EST	1 TEES ST	1 MAPLETON RD	7 STUART ST	1 CHURCH SQ	7 BRITANNIA CL
2 HAWKRIDGE ST	8 MORTON ST	15 ST JOSEPH'S CT	2 WILLOW WLK	2 MIDDLETON GRANGE LA	2 BREWARD WLK		2 CENTRAL BLDGS	
3 BROOK ST	9 ALBANY CT	A7	3 CEDAR WLK	3 SWAINSON PL	3 MASON WLK		3 STATION APP	
4 CHRISTOPHER ST	10 HARTLEY ST	2 PRESTON ST	4 CHALLONER SQ	4 WESLEY SQ	4 POTTER WLK		4 AVONDENE FLATS	
5 GROSVENOR ST	11 HARTLEY CL	2 ERNEST WLK	5 CHATHAM SQ	5 UPPER CHURCH ST	5 HERBERT WLK		5 SCARBOROUGH CT	
6 LABURNUM ST	12 HUNTER ST	3 BLAKE WLK	6 RABY SQ		6 LYNNFIELD ST		6 JERSEY ST	
	13 GROSVENOR GDNS	4 HOPPS ST						
		5 CARR ST						
		6 RICHARDSON ST						
		7 JOBSON ST						
		8 HAWKRIDGE CL						
		9 RIDLEY ST						

90

A4	A5	B3	B4		B5
1 ELWICK GRANGE	1 MITCHELL ST	1 ST AIDAN'S ST	1 BATHGATE TERR	10 NOTTINGHAM WLK	1 STOTFOLD ST
2 FLAXTON CT	2 ALDERSON ST	2 LEAMINGTON DR	2 THOMPSON ST	11 CUMBRIA WLK	2 JOHNSON ST
3 ELWICK CT	3 CAMPION ST	3 ALVERSTONE AVE	3 WESTMORELAND ST	12 NORTHUMBERLAND GR	3 JUBILEE RD
4 GRASMERE ST	4 BENSON ST	4 HEREFORD ST	4 MOYNE GDNS	13 NORTHUMBERLAND WLK	4 GAINFORD ST
	5 BENTLEY ST	5 WORCESTER GDNS	5 LONSDALE CT	14 WESTMORLAND WLK	5 GILL ST
			6 VICARAGE CT	15 SHROPSHIRE WLK	6 YORK FLATLETS
			7 THE MALTINGS		7 BREWERY ST
			8 RUSSELL WLK		
			9 NORTHAMPTON WLK		

195
65

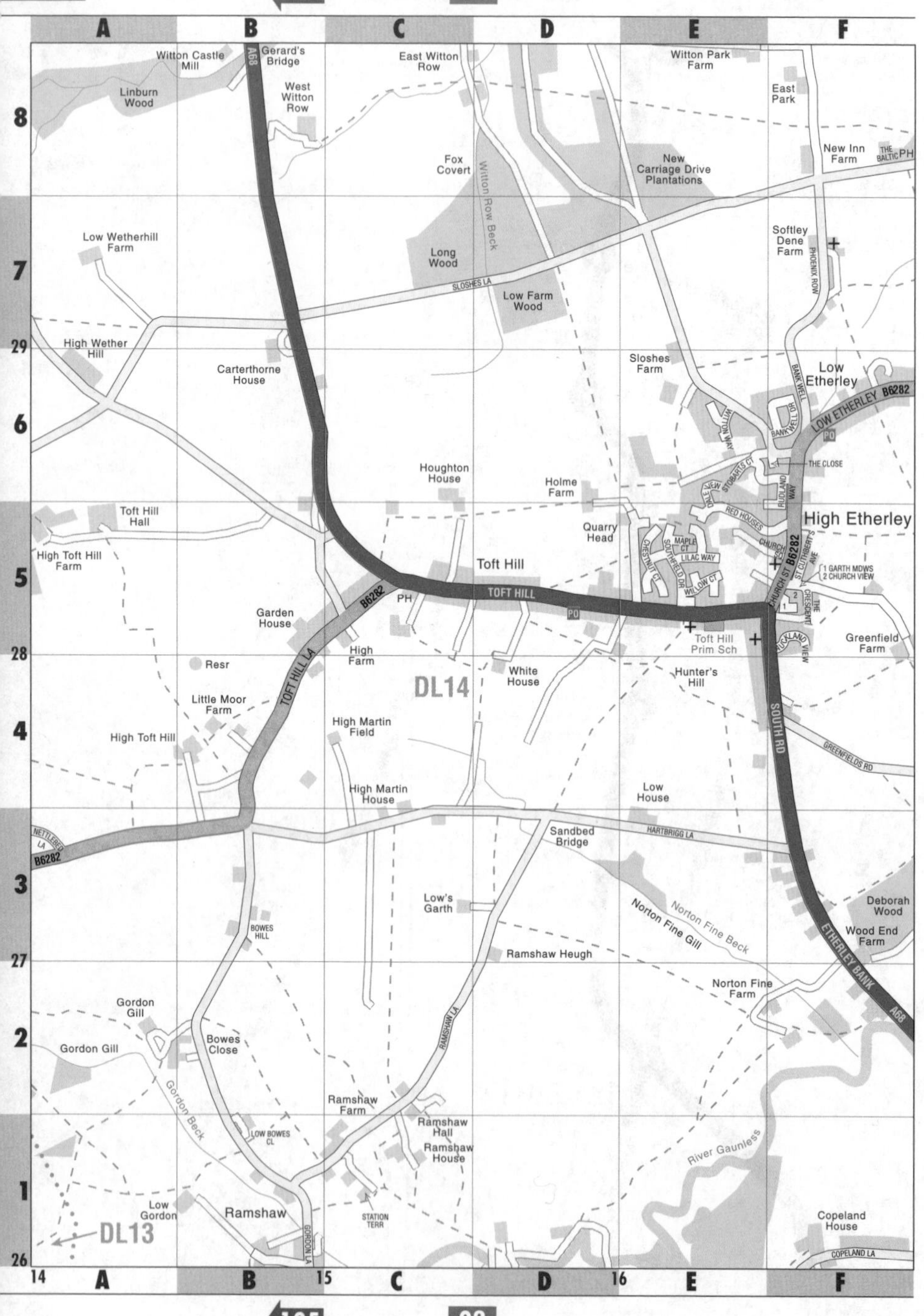
A
B
C
D
E
F
8
7
29
6
5
28
4
3
27
2
1
26
14
15
16
Witton Castle Mill
Gerard's Bridge
A68
East Witton Row
Witton Park Farm
East Park
Linburn Wood
West Witton Row
New Inn Farm
THE BALTIC PH
Fox Covert
Witton Row Beck
New Carriage Drive Plantations
Low Wetherhill Farm
Softley Dene Farm
PHOENIX ROW
Long Wood
SLOSHES LA
Low Farm Wood
High Wether Hill
Carterthorne House
Sloshes Farm
Low Etherley
BANK WELL
LOW ETHERLEY
B6282
BANKWELL DR
WITTON WAY
PO
THE CLOSE
STOBARTS CT
Houghton House
Holme Farm
DALE VIEW
RUDLAND WAY
RED HOUSES
Toft Hill Hall
Quarry Head
High Etherley
High Toft Hill Farm
MAPLE CT
CHESTNUT CT
SOUTHFIELD DR
LILAC WAY
CHURCH
ST CUTHBERT'S AVE
Toft Hill
WILLOW CT
1 GARTH MDWS
2 CHURCH VIEW
CHURCH ST
B6282
PH
TOFT HILL
THE CRESCENT
Garden House
PO
Toft Hill Prim Sch
BUCKLAND VIEW
Greenfield Farm
Resr
High Farm
White House
Hunter's Hill
TOFT HILL LA
DL14
Little Moor Farm
SOUTH RD
High Martin Field
High Toft Hill
GREENFIELDS RD
High Martin House
Low House
NETTLEBED LA
B6282
Sandbed Bridge
HARTBRIGG LA
Low's Garth
Norton Fine Beck
Norton Fine Gill
Deborah Wood
BOWES HILL
Wood End Farm
Ramshaw Heugh
ETHERLEY BANK
A68
Norton Fine Farm
Gordon Gill
RAMSHAW LA
Bowes Close
Gordon Gill
Gordon Beck
Ramshaw Farm
Ramshaw Hall
LOW BOWES CL
Ramshaw House
River Gaunless
STATION TERR
Low Gordon
Ramshaw
GORDON LA
DL13
Copeland House
COPELAND LA

195
92

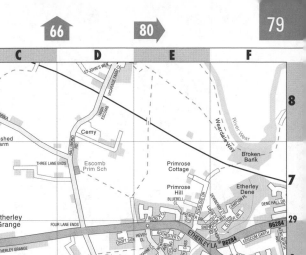

A B C D E F

8 7 6 5 4 3 2 1

Woodside Farm
Woodside
Carwood Farm
Cemy
St Chad's RC Prim Sch
Woodlands House Farm
Hecklewood Neuk Farm
Tileshed Farm
Cemy
Hecklewood
Escomb Prim Sch
Primrose Cottage
Broken Bank
River Wear
Weardale Way
Primrose Hill
Etherley Dene
Etherley Grange
Sundown Farm
PH
ETHERLEY RD
FOUR LANE ENDS
ETHERLEY LA
B6284
Greencroft Farm
Etherley Moor
Etherley Dene
Playing Fields
WOODHOUSE LA
B6282
Coal Burn
Greenfield Manor Farm
Bishop Auckland Coll
Wigdan Walls
St John's RC Comp Sch
Woodhouses Farm
Bay Horse (PH)
GREENFIELDS RD
Woodhouses
DL14
BISHOP AUCKLAND
Woodhouse Lodge
Woodhouse Farm
North Leazes
Greenfields Ind Est
Tindale Crescent
Abraham Ind Est
Leazes Farm
A688
Pickwick Ind Est
Spring Gardens Bridge
West Auckland
MANOR RD
St Helens Ind Est
Motel
St Helen Auckland
ETHERLEY BANK
River Gaunless
TOADPOOL
A68
STAINDROP RD
STATION RD
DARLINGTON RD
Oakley Cross Beck
Aptec Enterprise Pk
Oakley Cross Prim Sch
Broom Mill
Cemy
COPELAND LA
BURNSHOUSE LA

29 28 27 26

17 A B 18 C D 19 E F

93
80

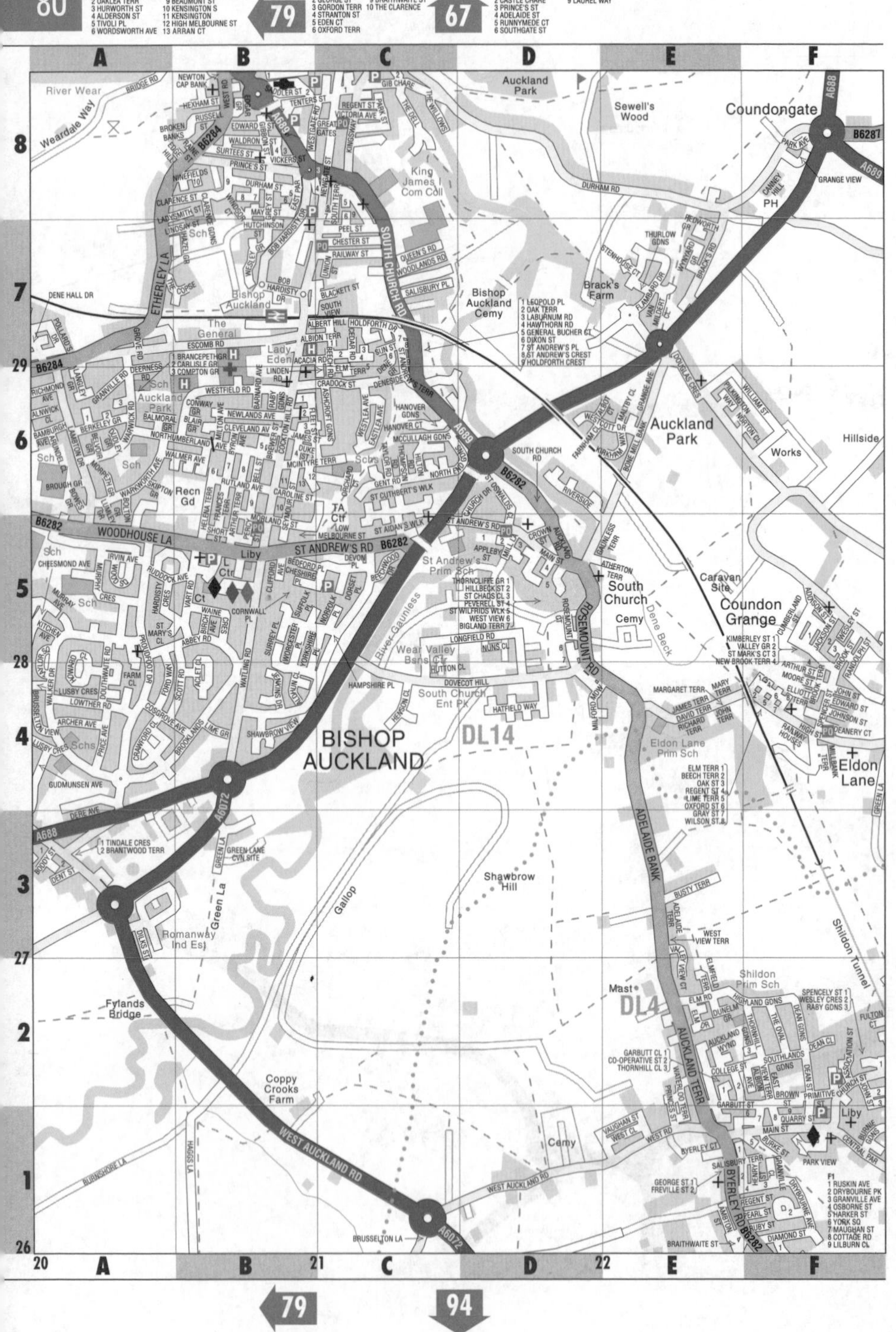
B6
1 WADDINGTON ST
2 OAKLEA TERR
3 HURWORTH ST
4 ALDERSON ST
5 TIVOLI PL
6 WORDSWORTH AVE
7 CHATSWORTH AVE
8 RAVENSWORTH AVE
9 BEAUMONT ST
10 KENSINGTON S
11 KENSINGTON
12 HIGH MELBOURNE ST
13 ARRAN CT
79
B8
1 CLAYTON ST
2 GEORGE ST
3 GORDON TERR
4 STRANTON ST
5 EDEN CT
6 OXFORD TERR
7 BISHOP ST
8 NELSON ST
9 BRAITHWAITE ST
10 THE CLARENCE
67
C8
1 DURHAM CHARE
2 CASTLE CHARE
3 PRINCE'S ST
4 ADELAIDE ST
5 RUNNYMEDE CT
6 SOUTHGATE ST
7 FLINTOFF ST
8 CONWAY HO
9 LAUREL WAY
A
B
C
D
E
F
River Wear
Weardale Way
Auckland Park
Sewell's Wood
Coundongate
King James I Com Coll
Bishop Auckland
Bishop Auckland Cemy
1 LEOPOLD PL
2 OAK TERR
3 LABURNUM RD
4 HAWTHORN RD
5 GENERAL BUCHER CT
6 DIXON ST
7 ST ANDREW'S PL
8 ST ANDREW'S CREST
9 HOLDFORTH CREST
Brack's Farm
The General
Lady Eden
Auckland Park
Hillside
Works
Recn Gd
TA Ctr
St Andrew's Prim Sch
South Church
Cemy
Dene Beck
Caravan Site
Coundon Grange
Wear Valley Bsns Ctr
South Church Ent Pk
BISHOP AUCKLAND
DL14
Eldon Lane Prim Sch
Eldon Lane
THORNCLIFFE GR 1
HILLBECK ST 2
ST CHADS CL 3
PEVERELL ST 4
ST WILFRIDS WLK 5
WEST VIEW 6
BIGLAND TERR 7
KIMBERLEY ST 1
VALLEY GR 2
ST MARK'S CT 3
NEW BROOK TERR 4
ELM TERR 1
BEECH TERR 2
OAK ST 3
REGENT ST 4
LIME TERR 5
OXFORD ST 6
GRAY ST 7
WILSON ST 8
1 TINDALE CRES
2 BRANTWOOD TERR
Romanway Ind Est
Green La
Gallop
Shawbrow Hill
Shildon Tunnel
Shildon Prim Sch
Mast
DL4
Fylands Bridge
SPENCELY ST 1
WESLEY CRES 2
RABY GDNS 3
GARBUTT CL 1
CO-OPERATIVE ST 2
THORNHILL CL 3
Coppy Crooks Farm
Cemy
WEST AUCKLAND RD
ADELAIDE BANK
AUCKLAND TERR
GEORGE ST 1
FREVILLE ST 2
F1
1 RUSKIN AVE
2 DRYBOURNE PK
3 GRANVILLE AVE
4 OSBORNE ST
5 HARKER ST
6 YORK SQ
7 MAUGHAN ST
8 COTTAGE RD
9 LILBURN CL
8
7
29
6
5
28
4
3
27
2
1
26
20
21
22
79
94

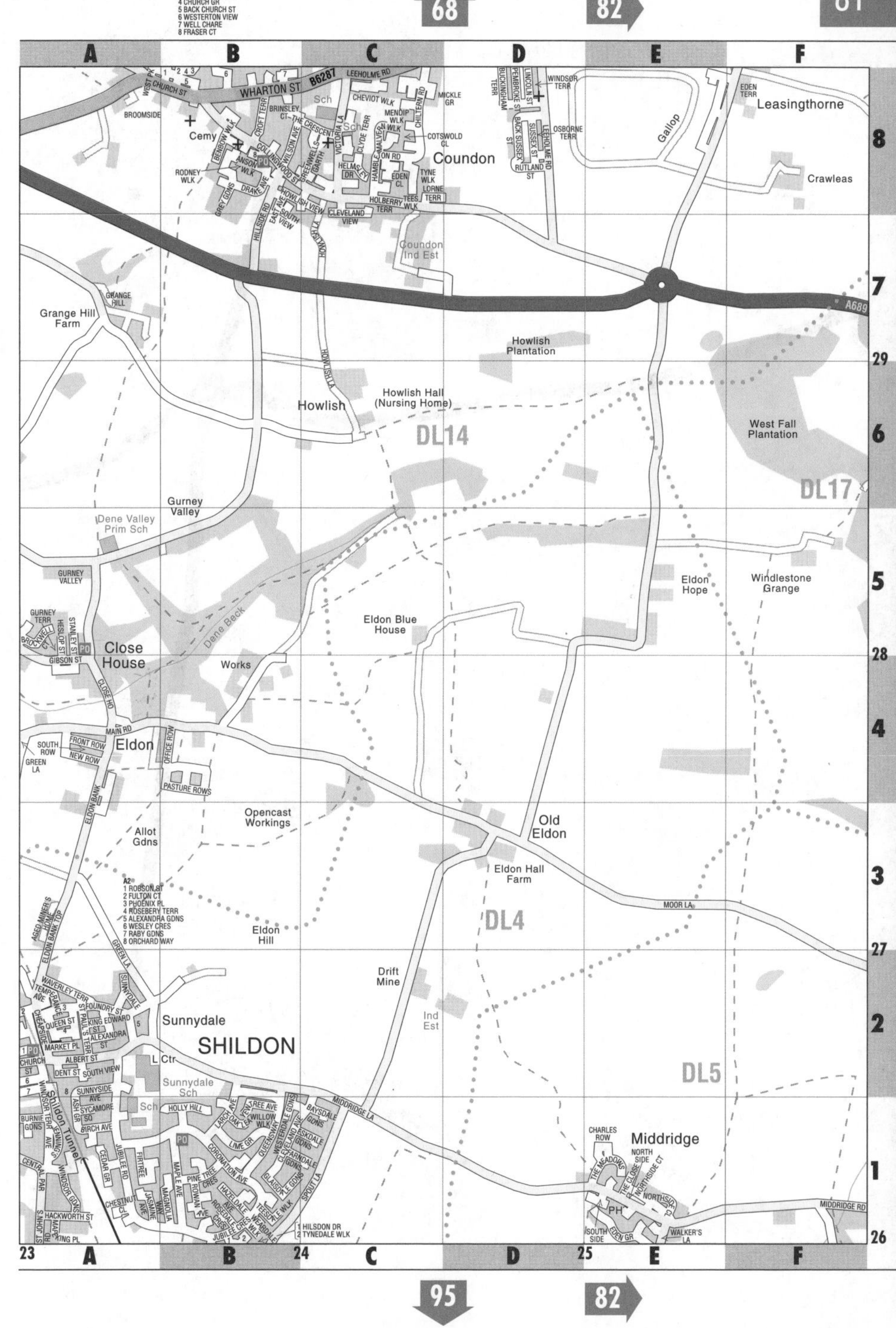

B8
1 FREDERICK ST
2 GURLISH TERR
3 LINGMELL DENE
4 CHURCH GR
5 BACK CHURCH ST
6 WESTERTON VIEW
7 WELL CHARE
8 FRASER CT
68
82
Coundon
Leasingthorne
Crawleas
Gallop
WHARTON ST
B6287
Cemy
Coundon Ind Est
Grange Hill Farm
Howlish Plantation
A689
Howlish
Howlish Hall (Nursing Home)
DL14
West Fall Plantation
DL17
Gurney Valley
Dene Valley Prim Sch
Eldon Hope
Windlestone Grange
Eldon Blue House
Close House
Works
Dene Beck
Eldon
Opencast Workings
Allot Gdns
Old Eldon
Eldon Hall Farm
MOOR LA
DL4
Eldon Hill
A2
1 ROBSON ST
2 FULTON CT
3 PHOENIX PL
4 ROSEBERY TERR
5 ALEXANDRA GDNS
6 WESLEY CRES
7 RABY GDNS
8 ORCHARD WAY
Drift Mine
Sunnydale
SHILDON
Ind Est
DL5
Sunnydale Sch
MIDDRIDGE LA
Middridge
MIDDRIDGE RD
1 HILSDON DR
2 TYNEDALE WLK
95
82

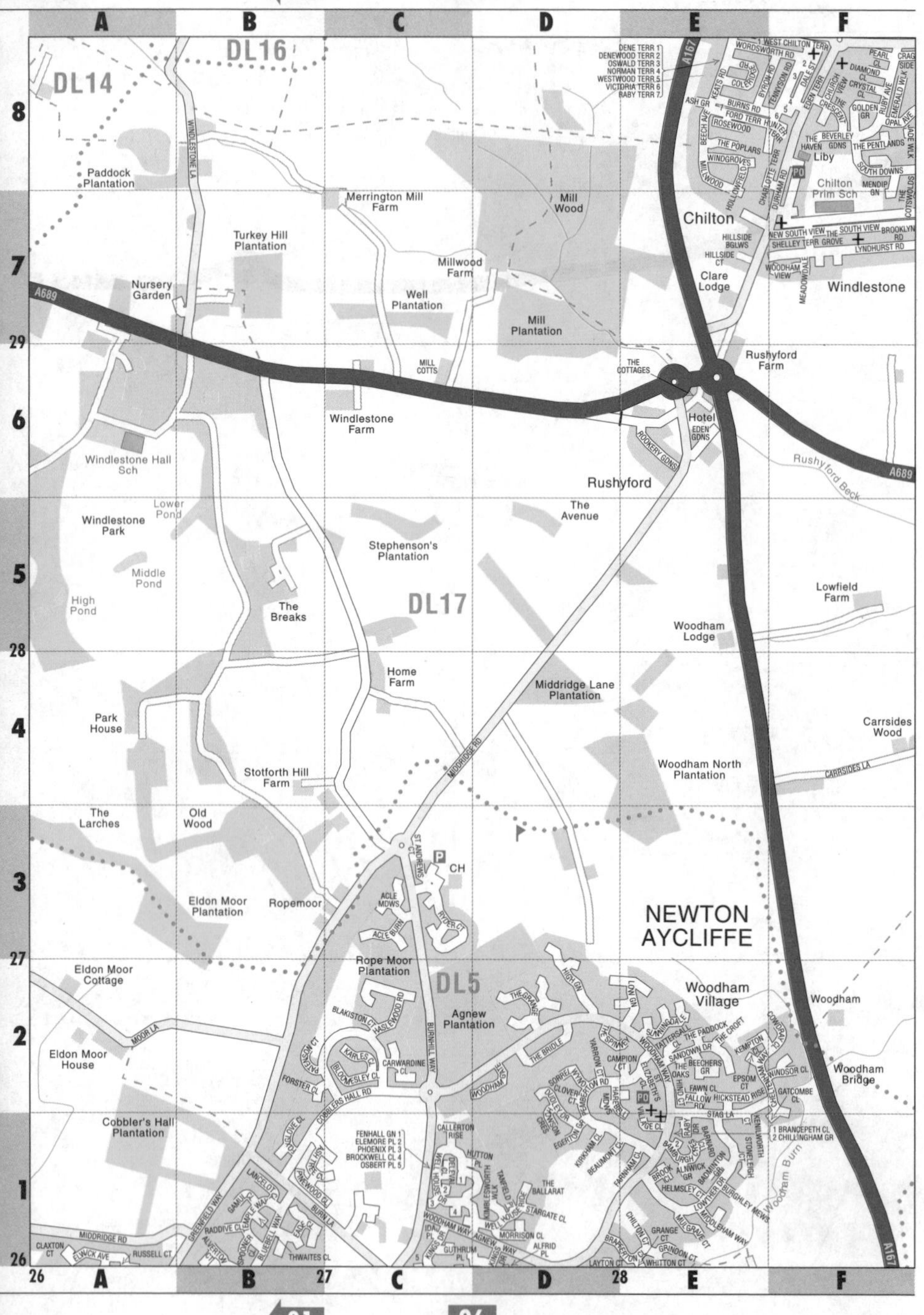

DL16

DL14

8

Paddock
Plantation

Turkey Hill
Plantation

Merrington Mill
Farm

Mill
Wood

7

Nursery
Garden

Well
Plantation

Millwood
Farm

Mill
Plantation

A689

29

MILL
COTTS

Windlestone
Farm

THE
COTTAGES

DENE TERR 1
DENEWOOD TERR 2
OSWALD TERR 3
NORMAN TERR 4
WESTWOOD TERR 5
VICTORIA TERR 6
RABY TERR 7

A167

WORDSWORTH RD

Chilton

Chilton
Prim Sch

Liby

NEW SOUTH VIEW THE SOUTH VIEW
SHELLEY TERR GROVE

HILLSIDE
BGLWS

HILLSIDE
CT

Clare
Lodge

Brooklyn
LYNDHURST RD

Windlestone

Rushyford
Farm

6

Windlestone Hall
Sch

Hotel
EDEN
GDNS

ROOKERY GDNS

Rushyford

A689

Rushyford Beck

Windlestone
Park

Lower
Pond

The
Avenue

5

Middle
Pond

High
Pond

The
Breaks

Stephenson's
Plantation

DL17

Lowfield
Farm

28

Home
Farm

Woodham
Lodge

4

Park
House

Middridge Lane
Plantation

MIDDRIDGE RD

Woodham North
Plantation

CARRSIDES LA

Carrsides
Wood

The
Larches

Old
Wood

Stotforth Hill
Farm

3

Eldon Moor
Plantation

Ropemoor

P
CH

ST ANDREWS

NEWTON
AYCLIFFE

27

Eldon Moor
Cottage

Rope Moor
Plantation

DL5

Agnew
Plantation

Woodham
Village

Woodham

2

Eldon Moor
House

MOOR LA

BLAKISTON CL

CARWARDINE
CL

The
BRIDLE

The PADDOCK
The CROFT

Woodham
Bridge

A167

1

Cobbler's Hall
Plantation

MIDDRIDGE RD

FENHALL GN 1
ELEMORE PL 2
PHOENIX PL 3
BROCKWELL CL 4
OSBERT PL 5

CALLERTON
RISE

HUTTON

The
BALLARAT

STARGATE CL

1 BRANCEPETH CL
2 CHILLINGHAM GR

GRANGE
CT

26

CLAXTON
CT

WICK AVE

RUSSELL CT

THWAITES CL

MORRISON CL
ALFRED

LAYTON CL
WHITTON CL

26 A B 27 C D 28 E F

70
84

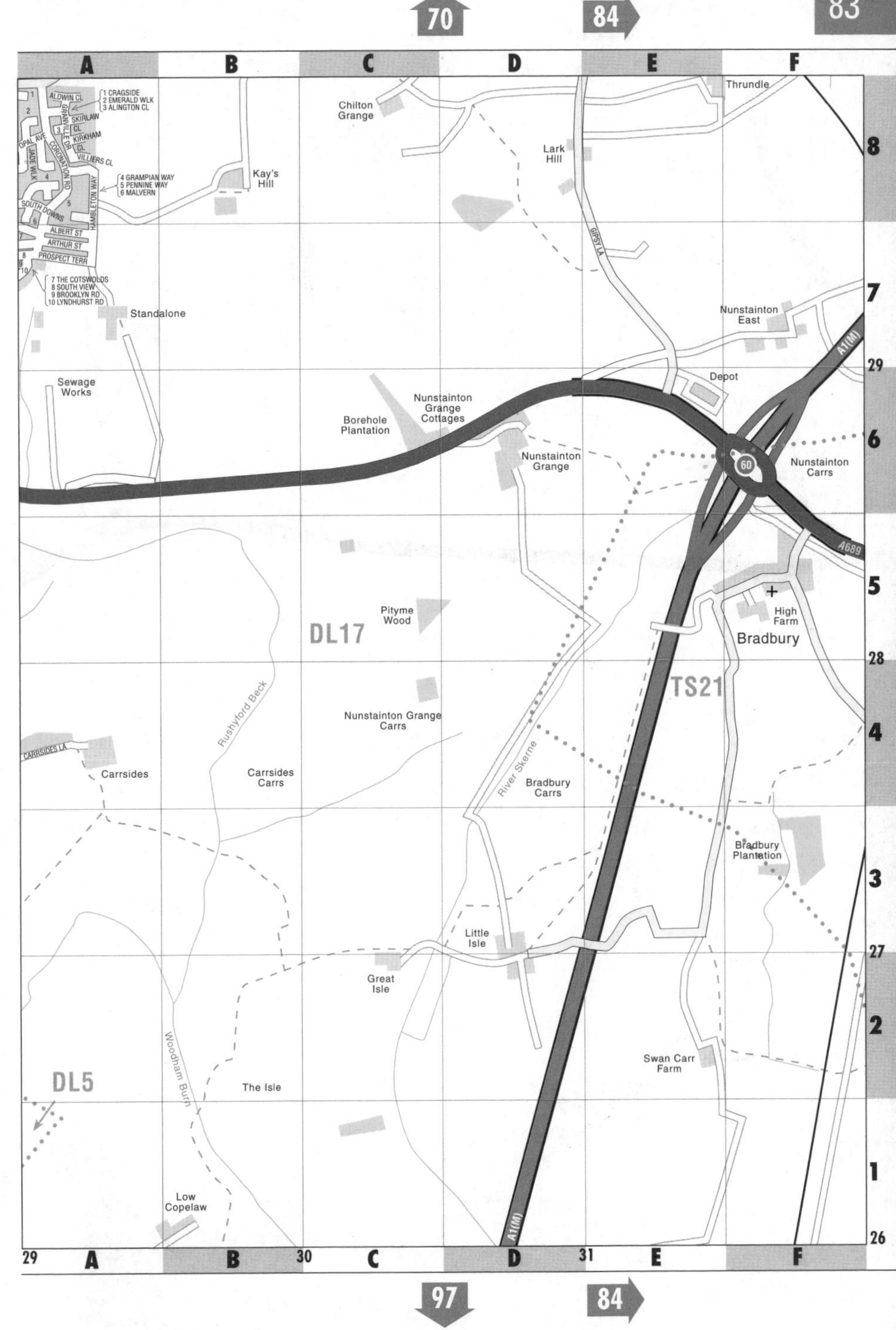
A
B
C
D
E
F
1 CRAGSIDE
2 EMERALD WLK
3 ALINGTON CL
ALDWIN CL
SKIRLAW
CL
KIRKHAM
CL
VILLIERS CL
GRANVILLE DR
CORONATION RD
OPAL AVE
JADE WLK
HAMBLETON WAY
4 GRAMPIAN WAY
5 PENNINE WAY
6 MALVERN
SOUTH DOWNS
ALBERT ST
ARTHUR ST
PROSPECT TERR
7 THE COTSWOLDS
8 SOUTH VIEW
9 BROOKLYN RD
10 LYNDHURST RD
Kay's Hill
Chilton Grange
Lark Hill
Thrundle
GIPSY LA
Standalone
Nunstainton East
Sewage Works
Depot
A1(M)
Nunstainton Grange Cottages
Borehole Plantation
Nunstainton Grange
60
Nunstainton Carrs
A689
Pityme Wood
DL17
High Farm
Bradbury
TS21
Rushyford Beck
Nunstainton Grange Carrs
CARRSIDES LA
Carrsides
Carrsides Carrs
River Skerne
Bradbury Carrs
Bradbury Plantation
Little Isle
Great Isle
Woodham Burn
Swan Carr Farm
DL5
The Isle
Low Copelaw
A1(M)
8
7
29
6
5
28
4
3
27
2
1
26
29
30
31

97
84

A   B   C   D   E   F

8

The Carrs

Green Knowles

Low Hardwick

Brick Kiln Plantation

DL17

7

River Skerne

Tile Shed Plantation

Hardwick Hall Hotel

Hardwick Hall Country Park

A177

29

Black Plantataion

Serpentine Lake

6

Nunstainton Carrs

Brakes Farm

West View

Hardwick Park

CANDY BANK

STATION RD

A689

5

Bath Plantation

West Lodge

East Lodge

A689

A177

Tilery

TS21

Firtree Hill

Sands Hall

Sands Farm

28

Firtree Hill Cottage

Firtree Hill Plantation

Sedgefield Racecourse

4

West Winds

Stables

P

Mordon Moor

3

Mordon Wood

Mordon North Farm

27

Peter's La

2

Harpington Hill

Hopper House

Village Farm

Mordon Carrs

Manor House

Mordon

South Moor Farm

1

Mordon Cottage Farm

Brookfield House

26

32   A   B   33   C   D   34   E   F

86

A B C D E F

8 7 29 6 5 28 4 3 27 2 1 26

35 36 37

South Durham Kennels
B1278
A177
Sedgefield Com
Ind Est
Swallow Hole
Ryall Farm
Todds House Farm
Pinchbeck Farm
Mess Bridge
Redcar Beck
BUTTERWICK RD
Redcar House
Sedgefield Hardwick Prim Sch
Sedgefield Com Coll
WOODLAND MEWS
PINE RIDGE AVE
WALLINGTON DR
NORTH PARK RD
HARDWICK RD
HALL LEA
HAWTHORN RD
MAPLE GROVE
LILAC AVE
THE LANE
THE GARTH
ELM AVE
1 ROSEDALE CL
2 BEECH OVAL
3 OAK TREE CRES
4 HOMEBRYTH HO
Cemy
ST EDMUNDS GN
Green Hill
Sedgefield
Hardwick Hall Country Park
WEST PARK LA
CHURCH VIEW
NORTH END
WHITE HOUSE DR
BOYNSTON GR
EASTWELL CL
BEAUMONT CT
Liby
HIGH ST
THE SQUARE
FRONT ST
RECTORY ROW
CROSS ST
ORCHARD CL
THE ORCHARD
BEACON AVE
Donnewell Farm
BEACON LA
A689
Beacon Hill Farm
PARK VIEW
WEST END
Sedgefield Prim Sch
WYKES CL
NAYLOR RD
THURLOW RD
STOCKTON RD
Cote Nook Farm
STATION RD
DUNELM CT
LAMBTON CRES
THE MEADOWS
1 THURLOW GRANGE
2 LILE GDNS
3 MALTON TERR
4 ST EDMUND'S TERR
5 CRISPIN CT
EDEN DR
HASLEDON GR
CLAREMONT GR
QUEENS DR
HORNBY AVE
CRAGSIDE
THE WILLOWS
THE LEAS
Motel
Manor Farm
Mast
Glower O'er Him
Sewage Works
A177
TS21
Diamond Hall
SPRING LA
Neasless Farm
STOCKTON RD
Layton House
Southfield Farm
Breckon Hill
Neasless Covert
Shotton Beck
West Layton Farm
Heley House
FOXTON LA
New Homer Carr Plantation

99

86

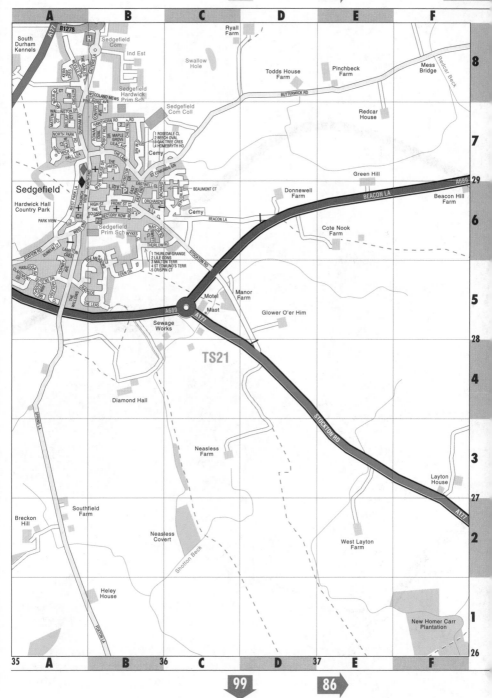

85
73

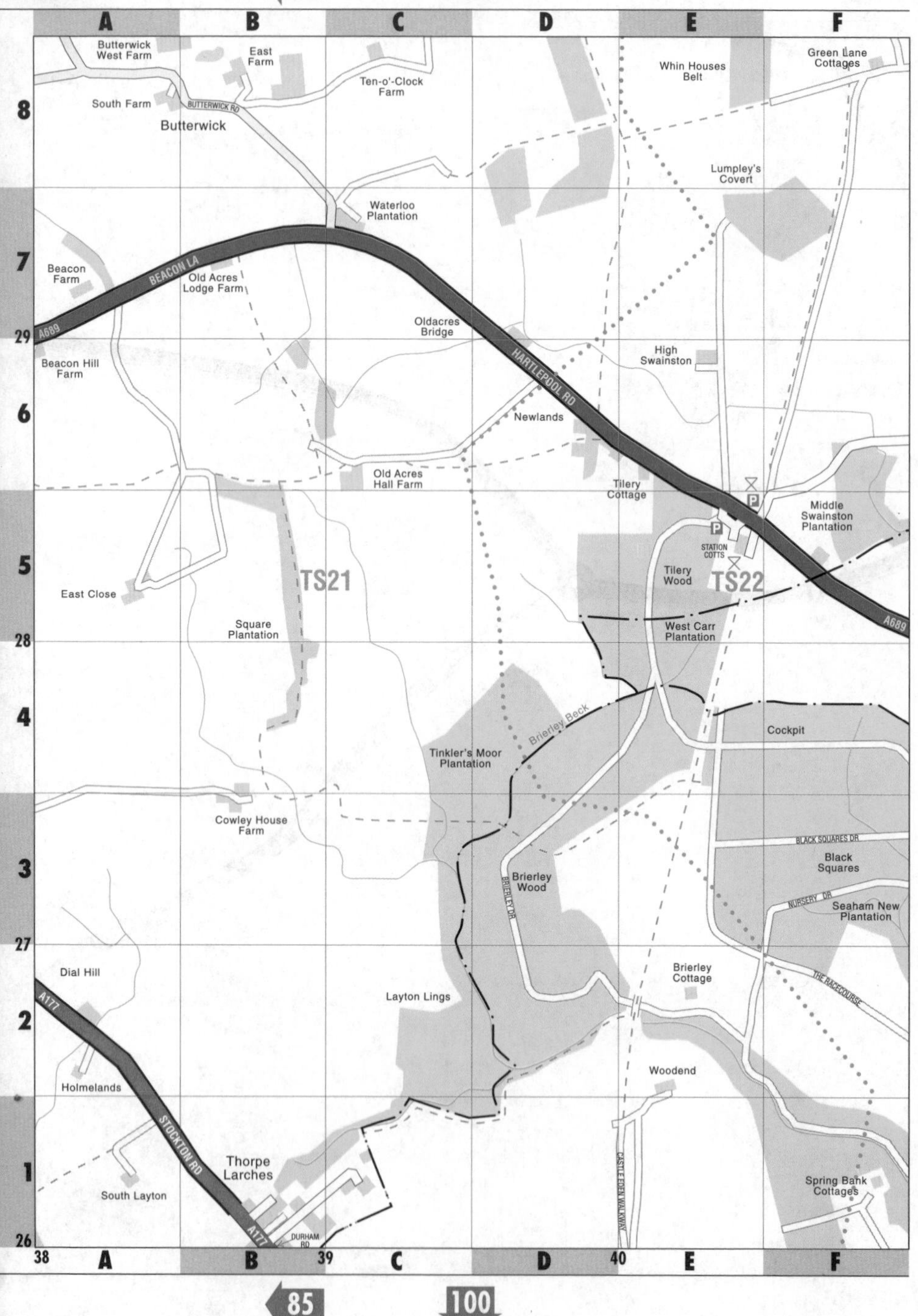
A
B
C
D
E
F
Butterwick West Farm
East Farm
Ten-o'-Clock Farm
Whin Houses Belt
Green Lane Cottages
South Farm
BUTTERWICK RD
Butterwick
8
Lumpley's Covert
Waterloo Plantation
BEACON LA
Beacon Farm
Old Acres Lodge Farm
7
A689
29
Oldacres Bridge
HARTLEPOOL RD
High Swainston
Beacon Hill Farm
6
Newlands
Old Acres Hall Farm
Tilery Cottage
Middle Swainston Plantation
P
STATION COTTS
5
TS21
Tilery Wood
TS22
East Close
Square Plantation
West Carr Plantation
A689
28
4
Brierley Beck
Cockpit
Tinkler's Moor Plantation
Cowley House Farm
BLACK SQUARES DR
Black Squares
3
Brierley Wood
BRIERLEY DR
NURSERY DR
Seaham New Plantation
27
Dial Hill
Brierley Cottage
THE RACECOURSE
A177
Layton Lings
2
Woodend
Holmelands
STOCKTON RD
1
Thorpe Larches
CASTLE EDEN WALKWAY
Spring Bank Cottages
South Layton
A177
DURHAM RD
26
38
39
40

85
100

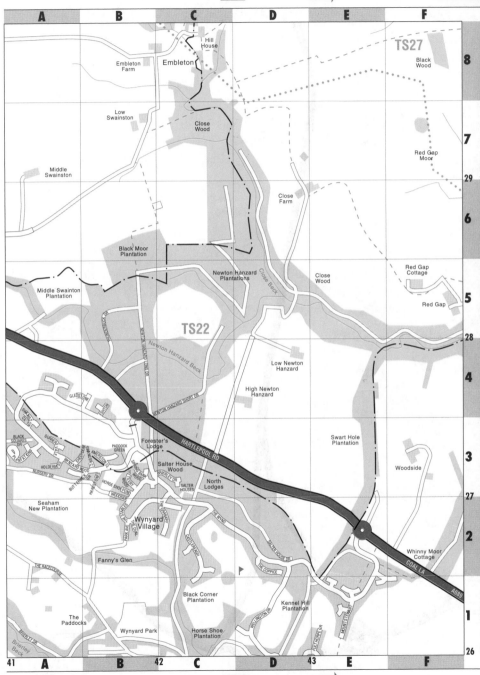

88

A B C D E F

Hill House
Embleton Farm
Embleton
TS27
Black Wood
8
Low Swainston
Close Wood
7
Red Gap Moor
Middle Swainston
29
Close Farm
6
Black Moor Plantation
Newton Hanzard Plantations
Close Beck
Close Wood
Red Gap Cottage
Middle Swainton Plantation
5
Red Gap
TS22
28
Newton Hanzard Beck
NEWTON HANZARD LONG DR
THUNDERBUCK DR
Low Newton Hanzard
4
High Newton Hanzard
GLEDSTONE
ESHTON
NEWTON HANZARD SHORT DR
SWAINSTON CL
BLACK SQUARES DR
GUNNERS VALE
PADDOCK GREEN
Forester's Lodge
HARTLEPOOL RD
Swart Hole Plantation
3
PLANTATIONS
HOLDERNESS
WYNYARD WOOD
SHEEPDENE
SWAINSTON CT
AMERSTON CL
SPRING BANK WOOD
Salter House Wood
BRIERLEY DR
SALTER HOUSES
Woodside
NURSERY DR
BUTTERMERE GR
HARESTONES
HORSE SHOE POND
TILERY WOOD
North Lodges
WOODSIDE
27
Seaham New Plantation
THE STABLES
THE GRANARY
THE WYND
Wynyard Village
PARK AVE
THE OVAL
CASTLEREAGH
2
SALTER HOUSE DR
Whinny Moor Cottage
Fanny's Glen
THE RACECOURSE
THE COPPICE
COAL LA
Black Corner Plantation
A689
Kennel Hill Plantation
1
WELLINGTON DR
The Paddocks
MOUNTSTEWART
FULTHORPE GR
Wynyard Park
Horse Shoe Plantation
BRIERLEY DR
Brierley Beck
26

41 A B 42 C D 43 E F

101
88

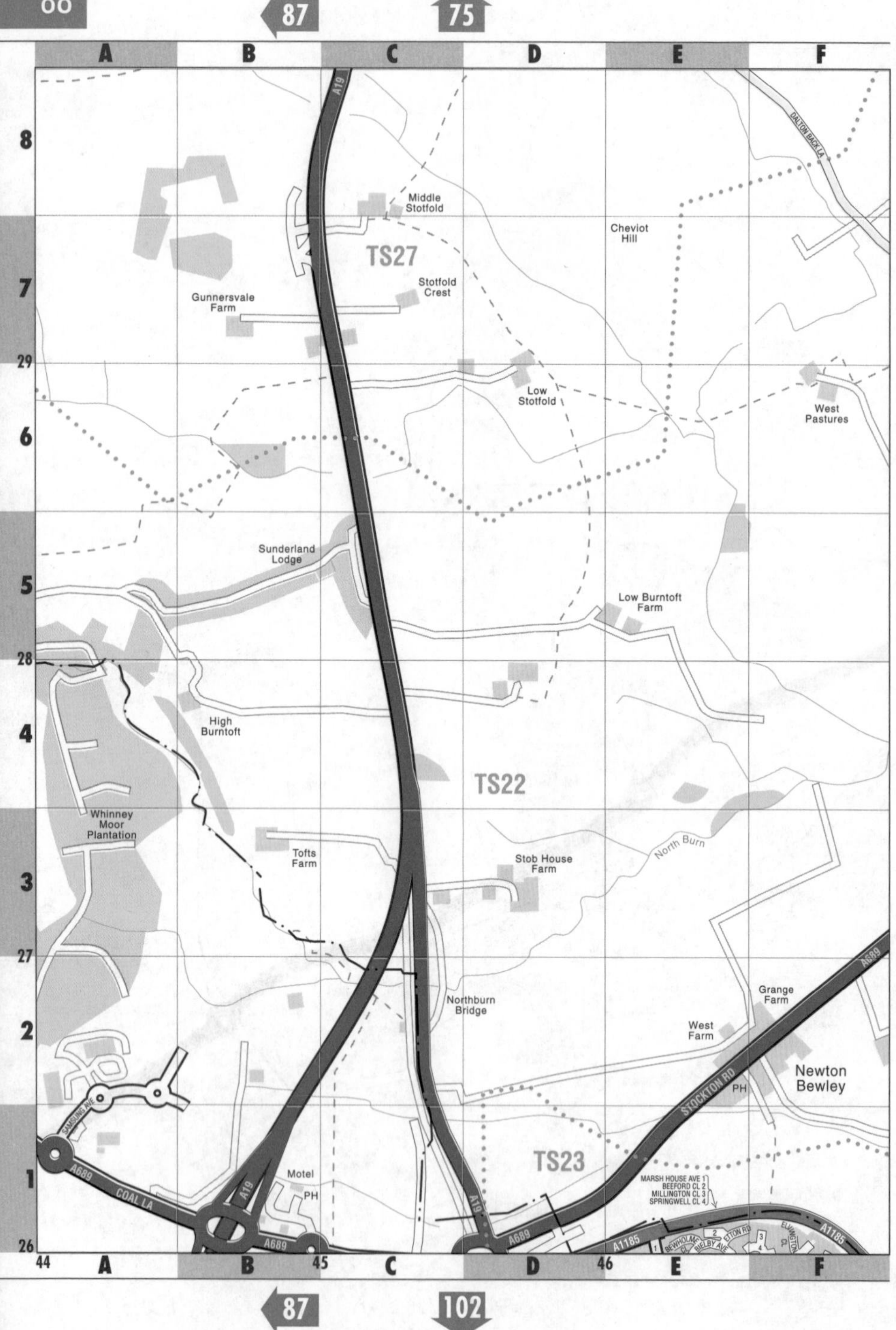

A   B   C   D   E   F

8

7

29

6

5

28

4

3

27

2

1

26

TS27

Middle Stotfold

Gunnersvale Farm

Stotfold Crest

Low Stotfold

Cheviot Hill

West Pastures

Sunderland Lodge

Low Burntoft Farm

High Burntoft

TS22

Whinney Moor Plantation

Tofts Farm

Stob House Farm

North Burn

Northburn Bridge

West Farm

Grange Farm

Newton Bewley

PH

Motel PH

TS23

COAL LA

MARSH HOUSE AVE 1
BEEFORD CL 2
MILLINGTON CL 3
SPRINGWELL CL 4

STOCKTON RD

A689

A19

A689

A1185

44   A   B   45   C   D   46   E   F

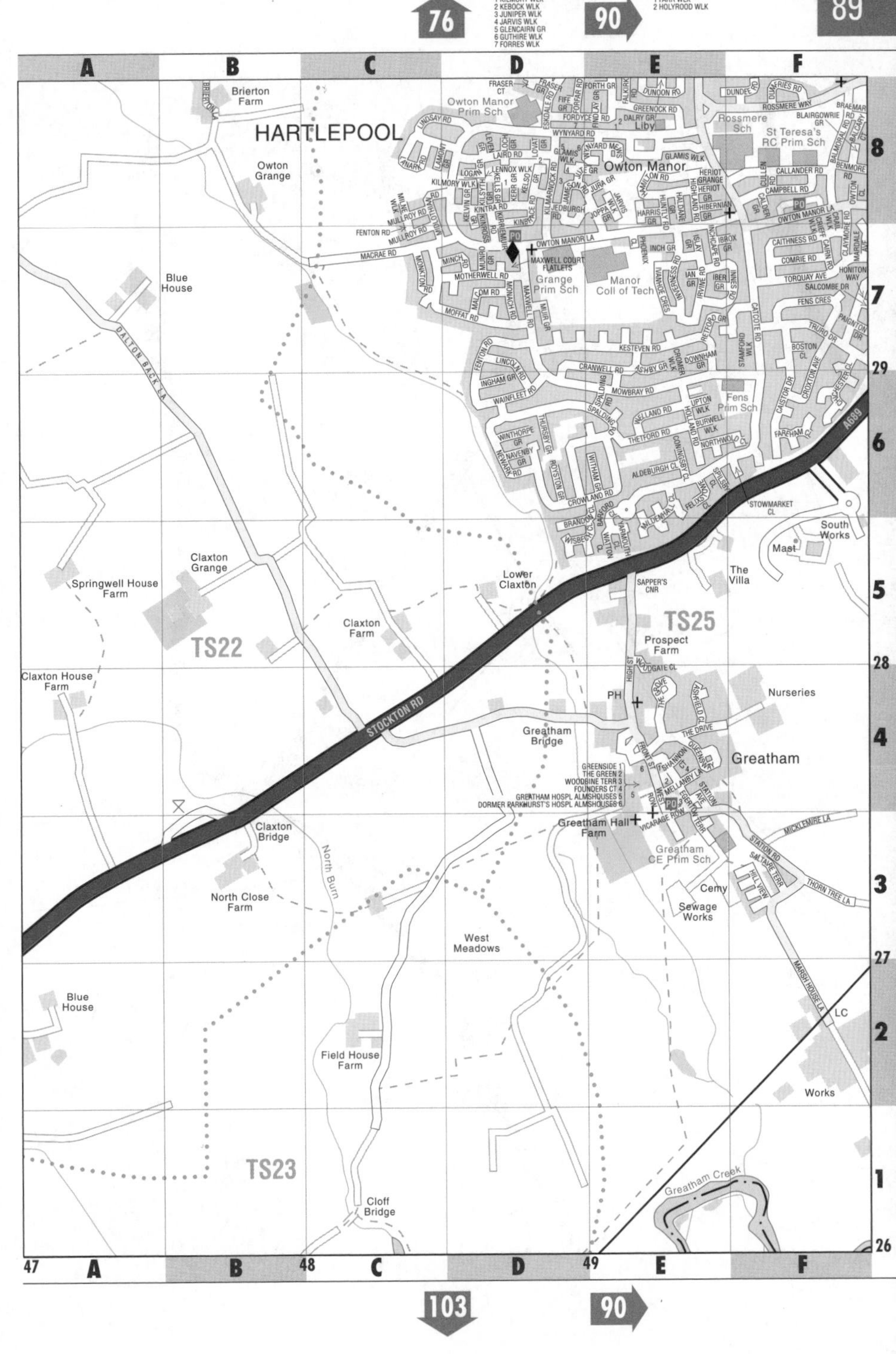

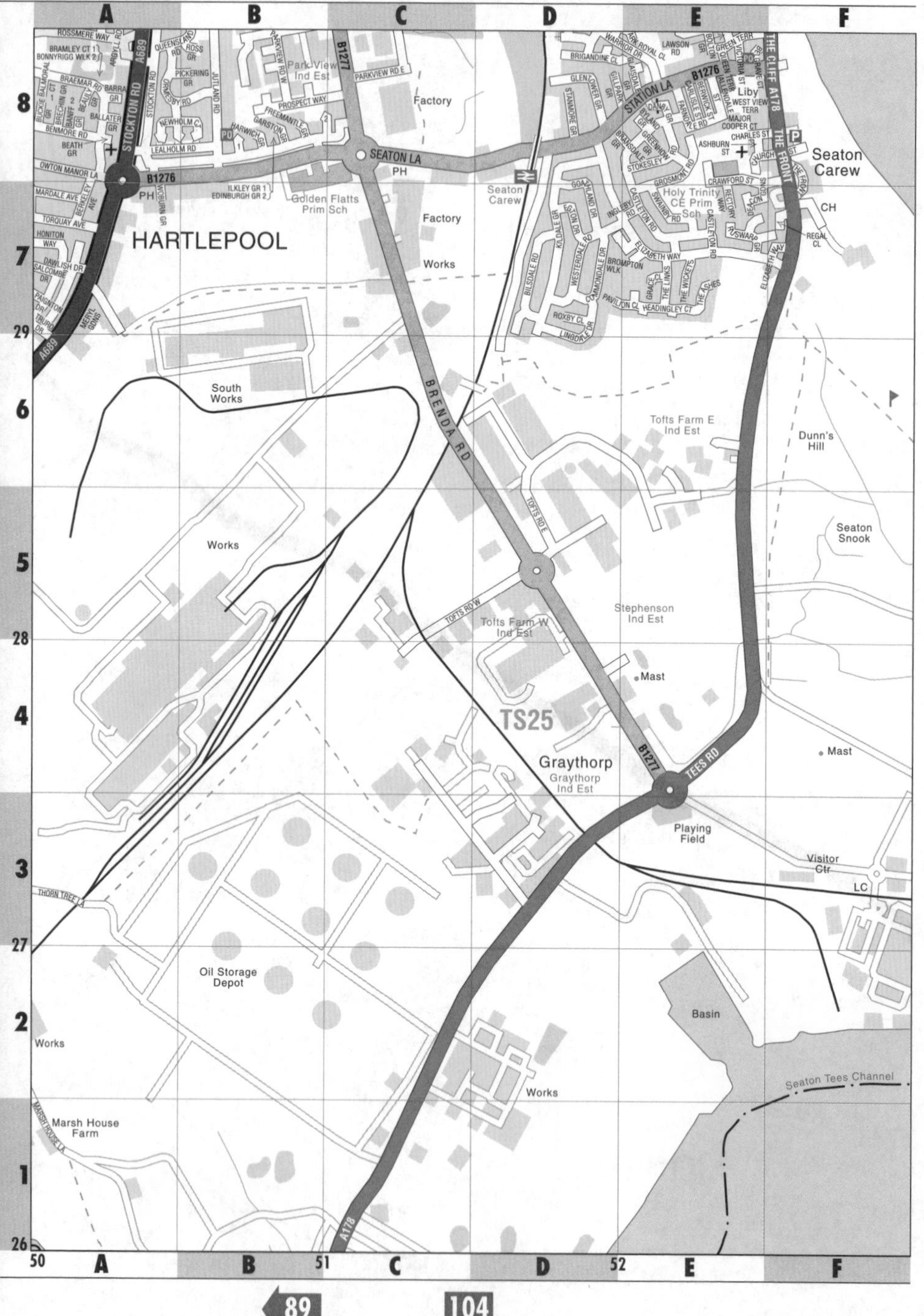

HARTLEPOOL

Seaton Carew

TS25

Graythorp
Graythorp Ind Est

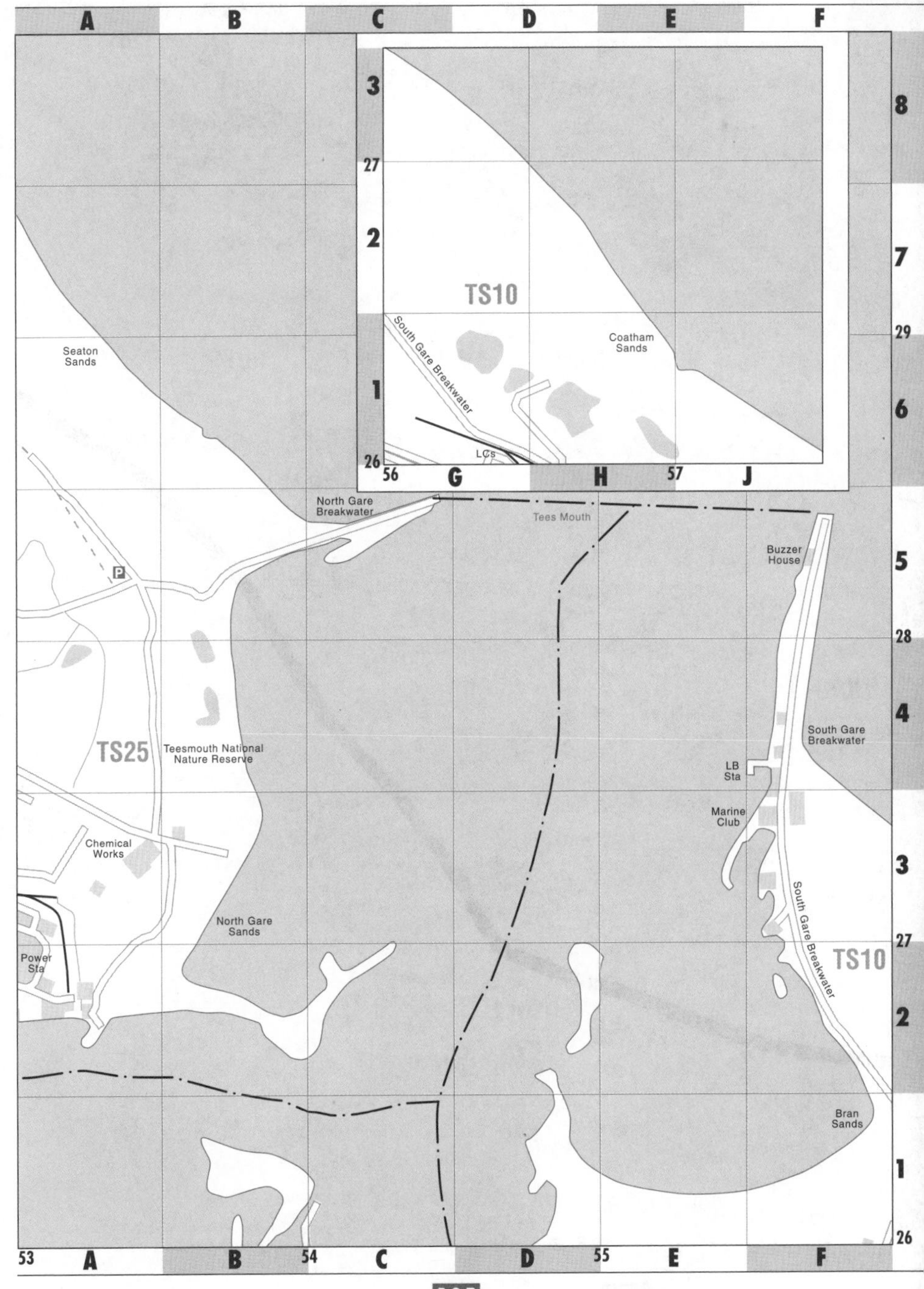

A
B
C
D
E
F
3
27
2
TS10
South Gare Breakwater
Coatham Sands
1
LCs
26
56
G
H
57
J
8
7
29
6
5
28
4
3
27
2
1
26
Seaton Sands
North Gare Breakwater
Tees Mouth
Buzzer House
P
TS25
Teesmouth National Nature Reserve
South Gare Breakwater
LB Sta
Marine Club
Chemical Works
North Gare Sands
South Gare Breakwater
TS10
Power Sta
Bran Sands
53
54
55

105

195
78

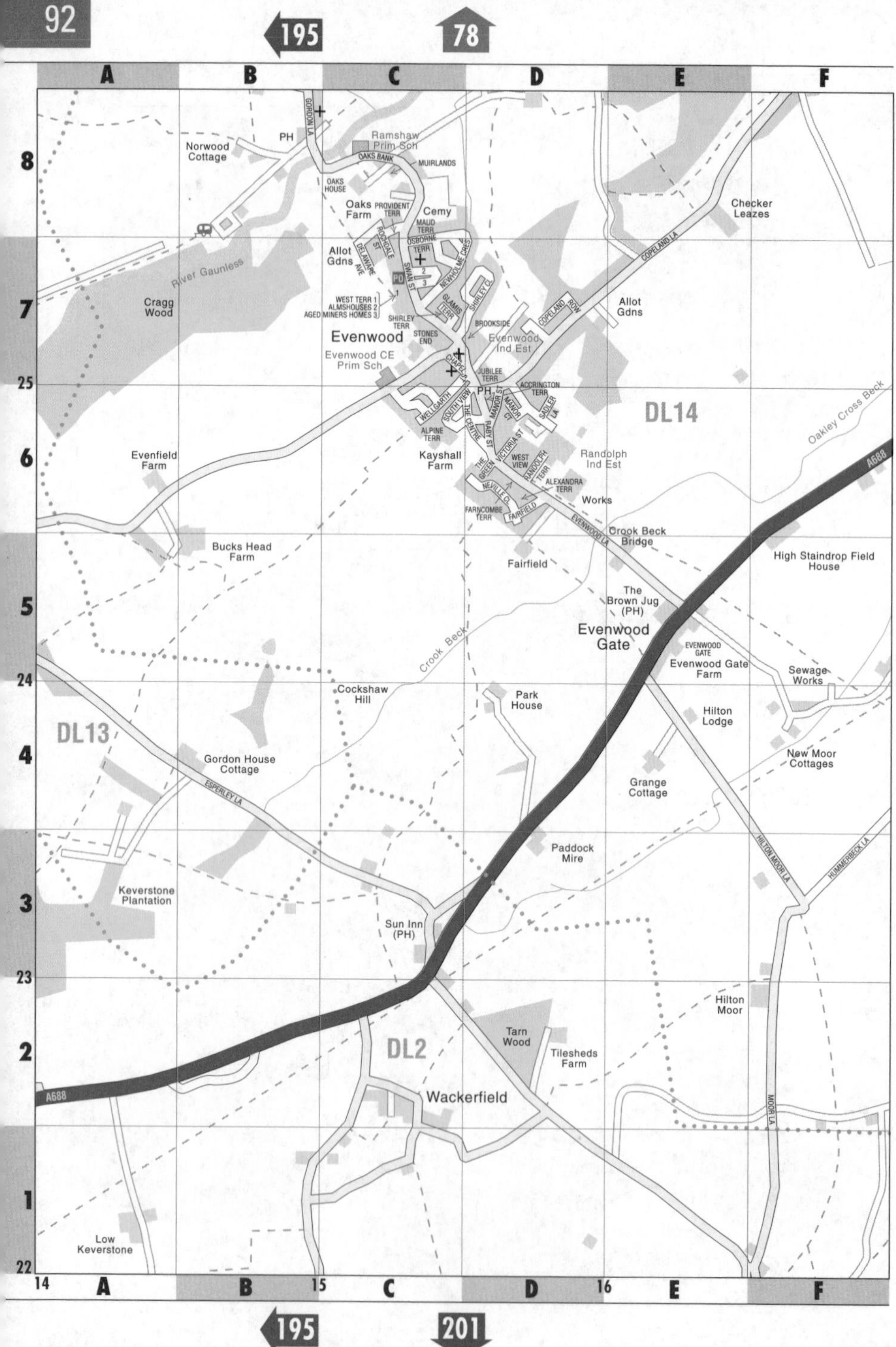
Norwood Cottage
PH
Ramshaw Prim Sch
Oaks Farm
Cemy
Allot Gdns
River Gaunless
Cragg Wood
Evenwood
Evenwood CE Prim Sch
Evenwood Ind Est
Checker Leazes
Allot Gdns
DL14
Oakley Cross Beck
Randolph Ind Est
Kayshall Farm
Evenfield Farm
Works
Crook Beck Bridge
Bucks Head Farm
Fairfield
High Staindrop Field House
The Brown Jug (PH)
Evenwood Gate
Evenwood Gate Farm
Crook Beck
Sewage Works
Cockshaw Hill
Park House
Hilton Lodge
DL13
Gordon House Cottage
New Moor Cottages
Grange Cottage
Paddock Mire
Keverstone Plantation
Sun Inn (PH)
Hilton Moor
Tarn Wood
DL2
Tilesheds Farm
A688
Wackerfield
Low Keverstone

195
201

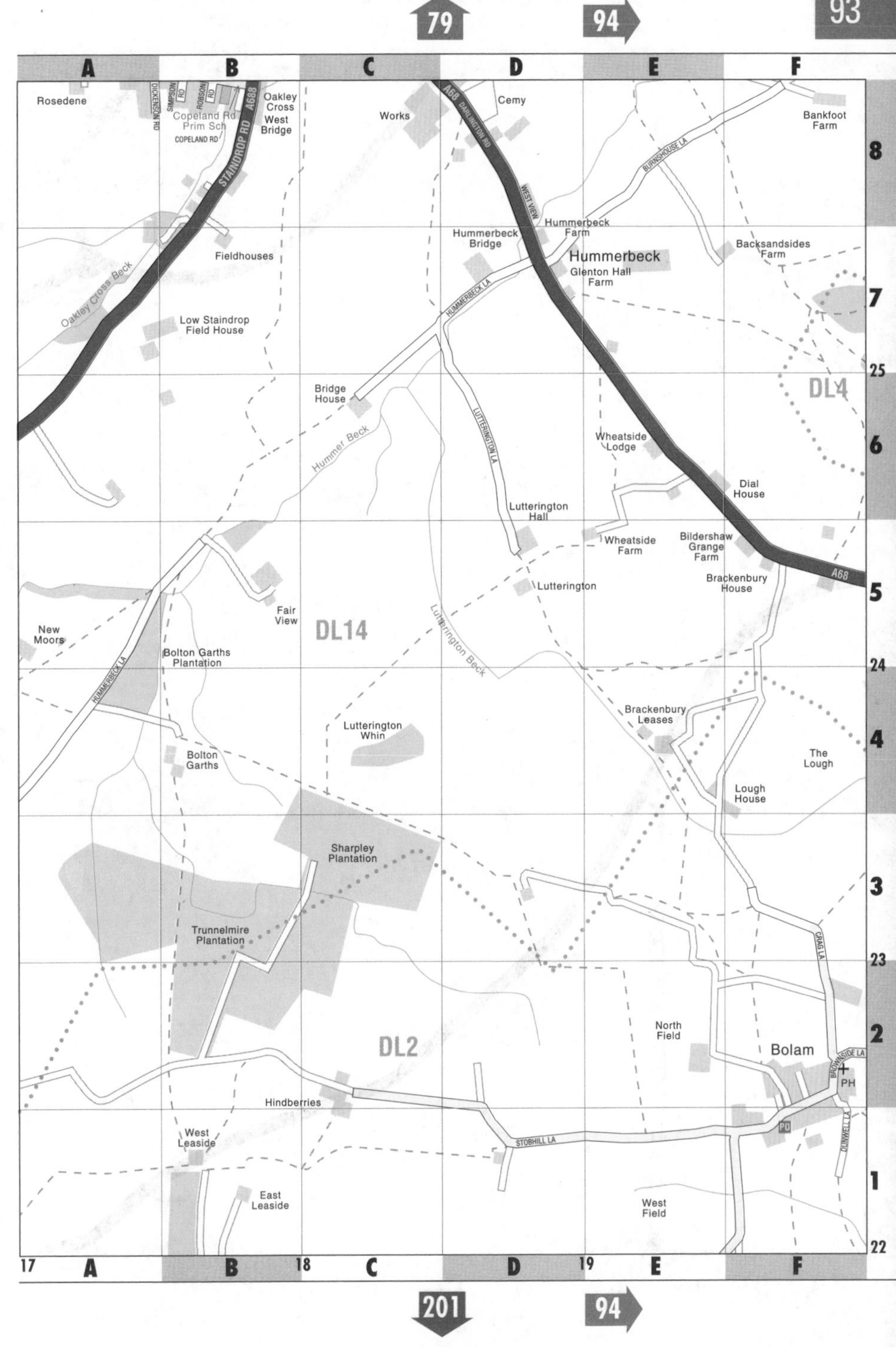
79
94
A
B
C
D
E
F
Rosedene
DICKENSON RD
SIMPSON RD
ROBSON RD
Copeland Rd Prim Sch
COPELAND RD
STAINDROP RD
A688
Oakley Cross
West Bridge
Works
A68
DARLINGTON RD
Cemy
Bankfoot Farm
BURNSHOUSE LA
WEST VIEW
Hummerbeck Farm
Hummerbeck Bridge
Hummerbeck
Glenton Hall Farm
Backsandsides Farm
Fieldhouses
Oakley Cross Beck
Low Staindrop Field House
HUMMERBECK LA
Bridge House
Hummer Beck
LUTTERINGTON LA
Wheatside Lodge
DL4
Dial House
Lutterington Hall
Wheatside Farm
Bildershaw Grange Farm
Brackenbury House
Lutterington
Fair View
New Moors
DL14
Lutterington Beck
Bolton Garths Plantation
HUMMERBECK LA
Brackenbury Leases
Lutterington Whin
The Lough
Bolton Garths
Lough House
Sharpley Plantation
Trunnelmire Plantation
CRAG LA
North Field
DL2
Bolam
BROWNSIDE LA
PH
Hindberries
PO
DUNWELL LA
STOBHILL LA
West Leaside
East Leaside
West Field
8
7
25
6
5
24
4
3
23
2
1
22
17
18
19
201
94

93
80

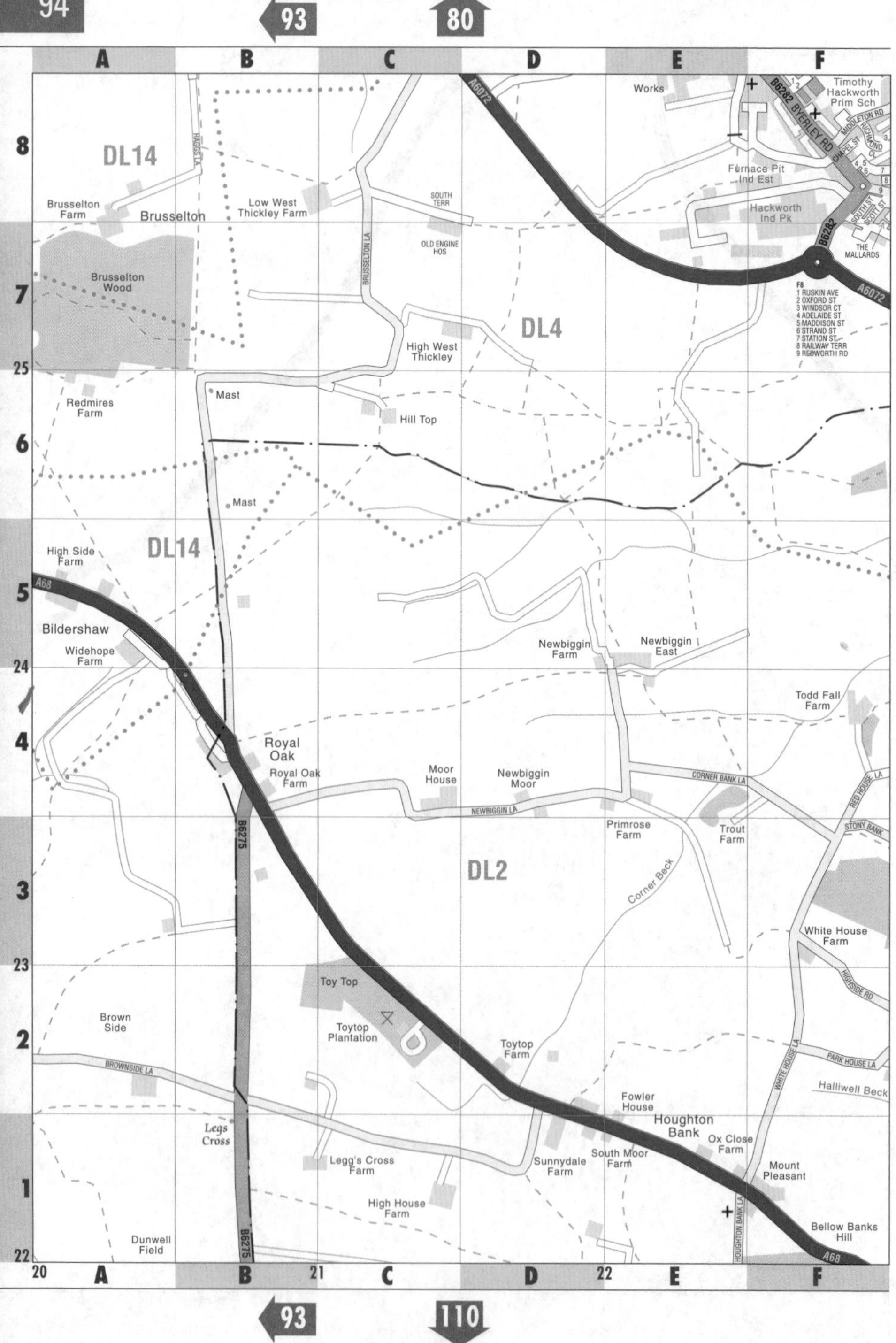
A
B
C
D
E
F
8
7
25
6
5
24
4
3
23
2
1
22
20
21
22
DL14
Works
Timothy
Hackworth
Prim Sch
B6282 BYERLEY RD
MIDDLETON RD
RICHMOND CL
CHAPEL ST
A6072
HAGGS LA
Brusselton
Farm
Brusselton
Low West
Thickley Farm
SOUTH
TERR
Furnace Pit
Ind Est
Hackworth
Ind Pk
SOUTH ST
SCOTT ST
B6282
THE
MALLARDS
OLD ENGINE
HOS
BRUSSELTON LA
Brusselton
Wood
F8
1 RUSKIN AVE
2 OXFORD ST
3 WINDSOR CT
4 ADELAIDE ST
5 MADDISON ST
6 STRAND ST
7 STATION ST
8 RAILWAY TERR
9 REDWORTH RD
DL4
High West
Thickley
Mast
Redmires
Farm
Hill Top
Mast
High Side
Farm
DL14
A68
Bildershaw
Widehope
Farm
Newbiggin
Farm
Newbiggin
East
Todd Fall
Farm
Royal
Oak
Royal Oak
Farm
Moor
House
Newbiggin
Moor
CORNER BANK LA
NEWBIGGIN LA
RED HOUSE LA
STONY BANK
Primrose
Farm
Trout
Farm
B6275
DL2
Corner Beck
White House
Farm
Toy Top
HIGHSIDE RD
Brown
Side
Toytop
Plantation
Toytop
Farm
WHITE HOUSE LA
PARK HOUSE LA
Halliwell Beck
BROWNSIDE LA
Fowler
House
Houghton
Bank
Legs
Cross
Ox Close
Farm
Legg's Cross
Farm
Sunnydale
Farm
South Moor
Farm
Mount
Pleasant
High House
Farm
HOUGHTON BANK LA
Bellow Banks
Hill
Dunwell
Field
B6275
A68

93
110

A8
1 MIDDLETON RD
2 WINDSOR CT
3 SUDBURY HO
4 SHILDON CT
5 MAGNET ST
6 PEARS' TERR
7 TOMLIN ST
8 BLAKE ST

A B C D E F

8 7 25 6 5 24 4 3 23 2 1 22

SHILDON
Locomotion, The NRM at Shildon
New Shildon
Shildon
Dabble Duck Ind Est
Shildon Bsns Ctr
Dale Road Ind Est
Locomotion, The National Railway Mus at Shildon
1 FERENS TERR
2 THICKLEY TERR
All Saints Ind Est
ROYAL GEORGE CL
Factory
Hawthorn House
DL4
George Reynolds Ind Est
New House
East Thickley Grange
Thickley Wood
Middridge Grange
Middridge Grange Mill
Red House Beck
Red House
RED HOUSE LA
SHILDON RD
MILL LA
Redworth Grange
Stobb House Farm
GRANGESIDE
Redworth
MAIN RD
SURTEES RD
HOME FARM CT
STONY BANK
HIGH RD
Redworth Hall Hotel
REDWORTH EST
Redworth Wood
DL2
REDWORTH RD
DL5
Tuft Hill
EDEN GR
MIDDRIDGE FARMS
WALKER'S LA
NEWTON AYCLIFFE
THE MEET 1
HOLDERNESS 2
THE STIRRUP 3
THE CONVERT 4
ZETLAND HUNT 5
THE SADDLERY
BEDALE HUNT
POST HORN
STAINTONDALE
AINSTY HUNT
BRAMHAM CHASE
HURWORTH HILL
HUNTERS GN
WILTON CT
BELFORD WAY
COLWELL CT
MALVERN WAY
GREENFIELD WAY
FEWSTON CL
ALSTON CRES 1
HALLINGTON HEAD 2
STOCKS GN 3
Greenfield Sch Comm & Arts Coll
WILBORE CROFT
THURSBY CL
BURNYNGHILL CL
MENVILLE CL
SHEPPARDS CROFT
ORD NEVILLE DR
FORESTERS PATH
SMYTHSONS CL
HANSARD CL
HASELRIGG CL
EASTFIELDS RD
BINCHESTER CROFT 1
MEATLESBURN CL 2
SPRINGFIELDS 3
JEMISON CL
LOWFIELDS
MIDFIELDS CL
HIGH BARN RD
THE GARTH
WEST FIELDS
HILL FIELDS
School Aycliffe
Water Tower
CHERRYTREE DR
SCHOOL AYCLIFFE LA
NEW LA
Hall Farm
B6444
Heighington
HEIGHINGTON LA
Dormerstiles
Heighington La
Park House
PARK HOUSE LA
HIGHSIDE RD
Hope House Farm
1 THE COTTAGES
2 HOPELANDS CT
3 THE ORCHARD
4 THE COURTINE
Heighington CE Prim Sch
High Side Bank
Halliwell Beck
Halliwell Farm
Twins Burn
Twinsburn Farm
BATT LA
EDEN CL
PINEWOOD CRES
GREENHILL RD
TWINSBURN RD
BURNBECK PL
ST MICHAEL'S CRES
WESTWOOD AVE
JUDITH CL
TWINSBURN CL
SNACKGATE LA
HOPELANDS
HIGHSIDE RD
HALL LA
TUDOR CT
HEIGHINGTON LA
BEECH CRES
STATION RD
CHURCH VIEW
MANOR CT
WATER LA
DARLINGTON RD
MILLBANK
WEST GN
BUCK SQ
EAST GN
VICARAGE CT
SOUTH VIEW
GARTHLANDS
WALWORTH RD
Manor Farm
Nursery
COATSAY MOOR LA
A6072
REDWORTH RD

23 A B 24 C D 25 E F

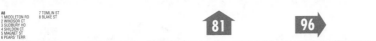

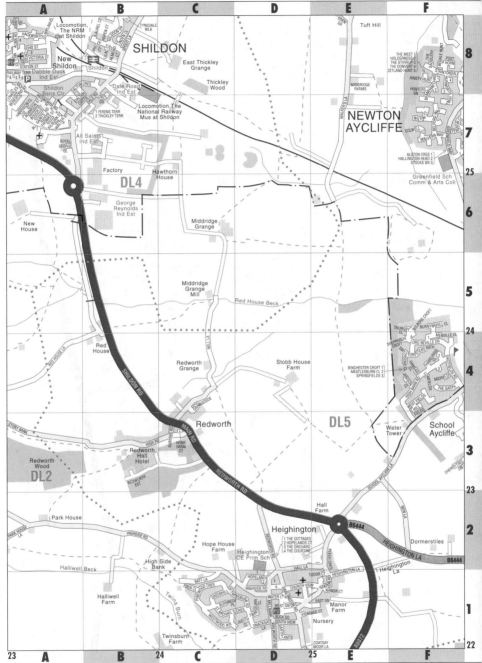

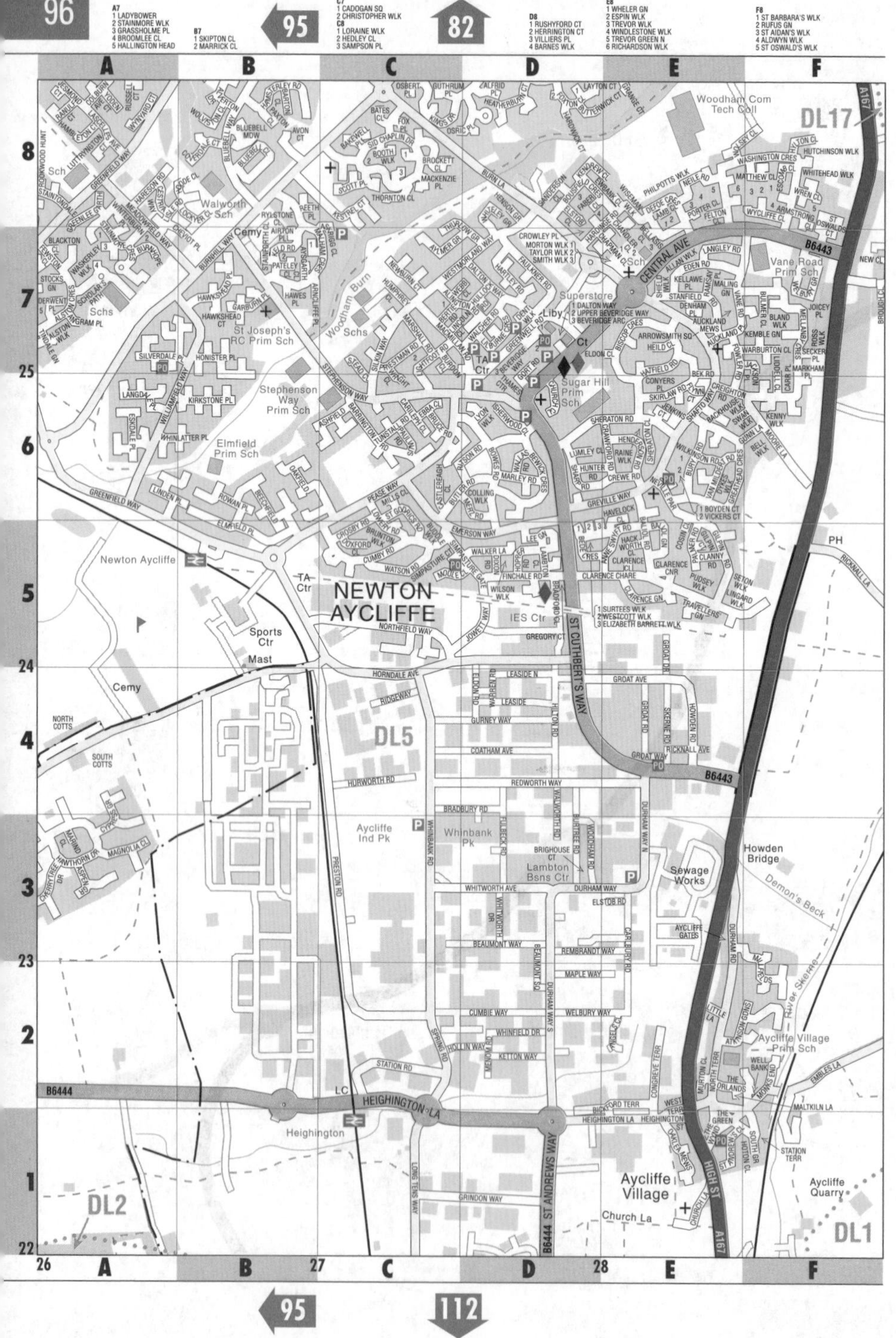
A7
1 LADYBOWER
2 STAINMORE WLK
3 GRASSHOLME PL
4 BROOMLEE CL
5 HALLINGTON HEAD
B7
1 SKIPTON CL
2 MARRICK CL
95
C7
1 CADOGAN SQ
2 CHRISTOPHER WLK
C8
1 LORAINE WLK
2 HEDLEY CL
3 SAMPSON PL
82
D8
1 RUSHYFORD CT
2 HERRINGTON CT
3 VILLIERS PL
4 BARNES WLK
E8
1 WHELER GN
2 ESPIN WLK
3 TREVOR WLK
4 WINDLESTONE WLK
5 TREVOR GREEN N
6 RICHARDSON WLK
F8
1 ST BARBARA'S WLK
2 RUFUS GN
3 ST AIDAN'S WLK
4 ALDWYN WLK
5 ST OSWALD'S WLK
A
B
C
D
E
F
8
7
25
6
5
24
4
3
23
2
1
22
26
27
28
Woodham Com Tech Coll
DL17
A167
Walworth Sch
Cemy
St Joseph's RC Prim Sch
Woodham Burn
Schs
Stephenson Way Prim Sch
Elmfield Prim Sch
Superstore
1 DALTON WAY
2 UPPER BEVERIDGE WAY
3 BEVERIDGE ARC
CROWLEY PL
MORTON WLK 1
TAYLOR WLK 2
SMITH WLK 3
Liby
Ct
Sugar Hill Prim Sch
TA Ctr
CENTRAL AVE
B6443
Vane Road Prim Sch
1 BOYDEN CT
2 VICKERS CT
PH
Newton Aycliffe
NEWTON AYCLIFFE
TA Ctr
Sports Ctr
Mast
IES Ctr
1 SURTEES WLK
2 WESTCOTT WLK
3 ELIZABETH BARRETT WLK
ST CUTHBERT'S WAY
NORTHFIELD WAY
GREGORY CT
HORNDALE AVE
GROAT AVE
Cemy
NORTH COTTS
SOUTH COTTS
DL5
RIDGEWAY
GURNEY WAY
COATHAM AVE
RICKNALL AVE
REDWORTH WAY
HURWORTH RD
BRADBURY RD
Aycliffe Ind Pk
Whinbank Pk
BRIGHOUSE CT
Lambton Bsns Ctr
Howden Bridge
Sewage Works
Demon's Beck
WHITWORTH AVE
DURHAM WAY
AYCLIFFE GATES
BEAUMONT WAY
REMBRANDT WAY
MAPLE WAY
CUMBIE WAY
WELBURY WAY
WHINFIELD DR
HOLLIN WAY
KETTON WAY
STATION RD
River Skerne
Aycliffe Village Prim Sch
B6444
LC
HEIGHINGTON LA
Heighington
BICKFORD TERR
MALTKILN LA
STATION TERR
GRINDON WAY
ST ANDREWS WAY
Aycliffe Village
Church La
Aycliffe Quarry
HIGH ST
DL2
DL1

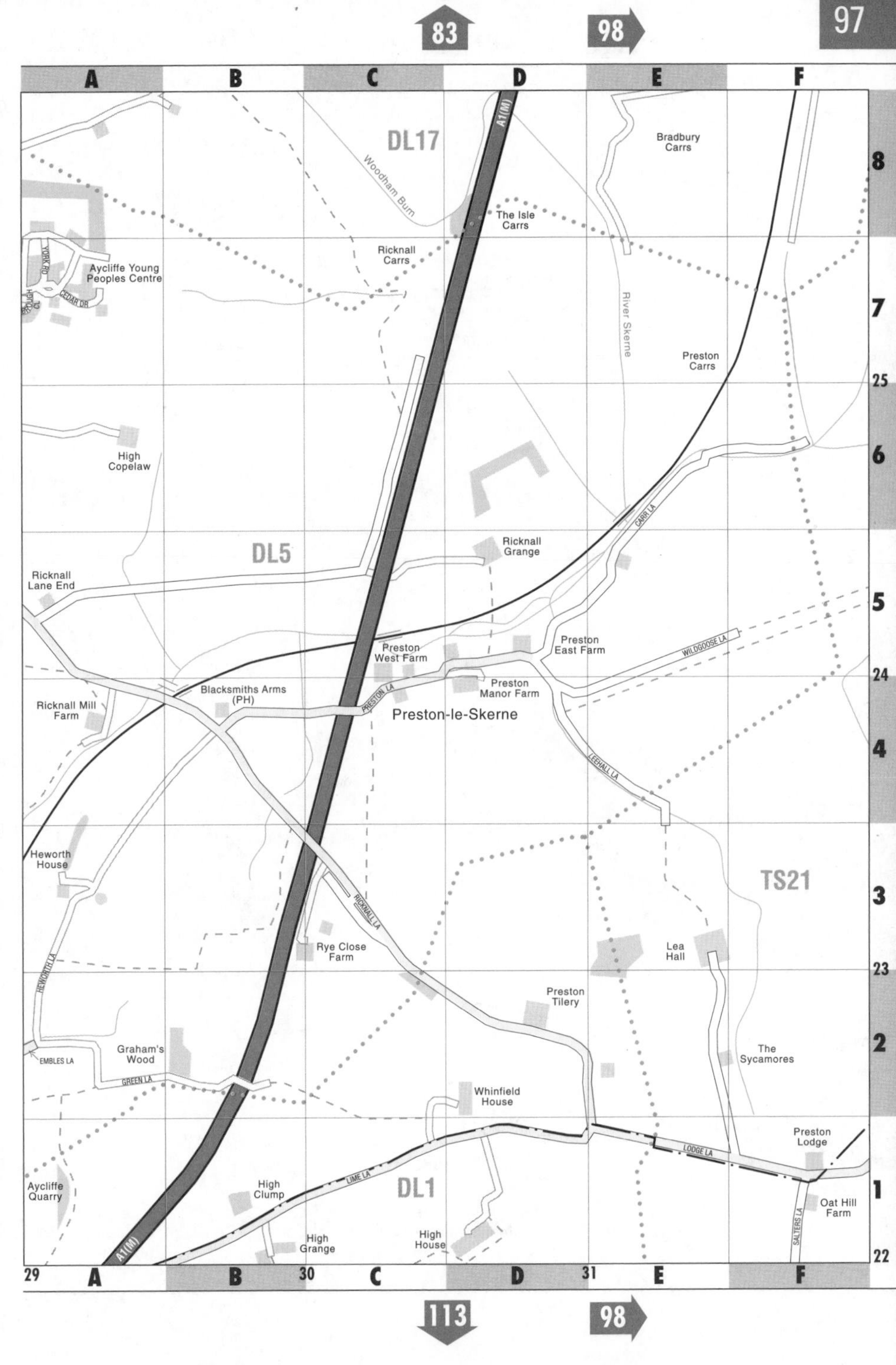
83
98
A
B
C
D
E
F
DL17
A1(M)
Woodham Burn
Bradbury Carrs
The Isle Carrs
Ricknall Carrs
YORK RD
Aycliffe Young Peoples Centre
CEDAR DR
River Skerne
Preston Carrs
High Copelaw
Ricknall Grange
DL5
Ricknall Lane End
CARR LA
Preston West Farm
Preston East Farm
WILDGOOSE LA
Preston Manor Farm
Blacksmiths Arms (PH)
PRESTON LA
Ricknall Mill Farm
Preston-le-Skerne
LEEHALL LA
Heworth House
TS21
RICKNALL LA
Rye Close Farm
Lea Hall
HEWORTH LA
Preston Tilery
Graham's Wood
The Sycamores
EMBLES LA
GREEN LA
Whinfield House
Preston Lodge
LODGE LA
LIME LA
Aycliffe Quarry
High Clump
DL1
Oat Hill Farm
SALTERS LA
High Grange
High House
8
7
25
6
5
24
4
3
23
2
1
22
29
30
31
113
98

97
84

A B C D E F

8

DL17

Mordon Carrs

Mordon Lodge

Croftlands

Boghall Plantation

7

Mordon South Side

LC

Bog Hall Farm

Hope House Farm

25

Howe Hills Plantation

West View

Stillington Beck

6

Stillington Moor

Howe Hills Farm

Merton Grange

5

High Grindon

24

TS21

North Farm

Elstob Beck

Oaklea

4

Elstob La

Elstob

Elstob Hall

Grindon La

3

Elstob Cottage

Elstob Hill Farm

Elstob Hill

23

Grindon Lane Wood

2

Stainton Covert

Lea Close Farm

Stainton Hill House

1

Whinny Hill

Great Stainton

Kings Arms (PH)

Town Farm

22

32 A B 33 C D 34 E F

85
100

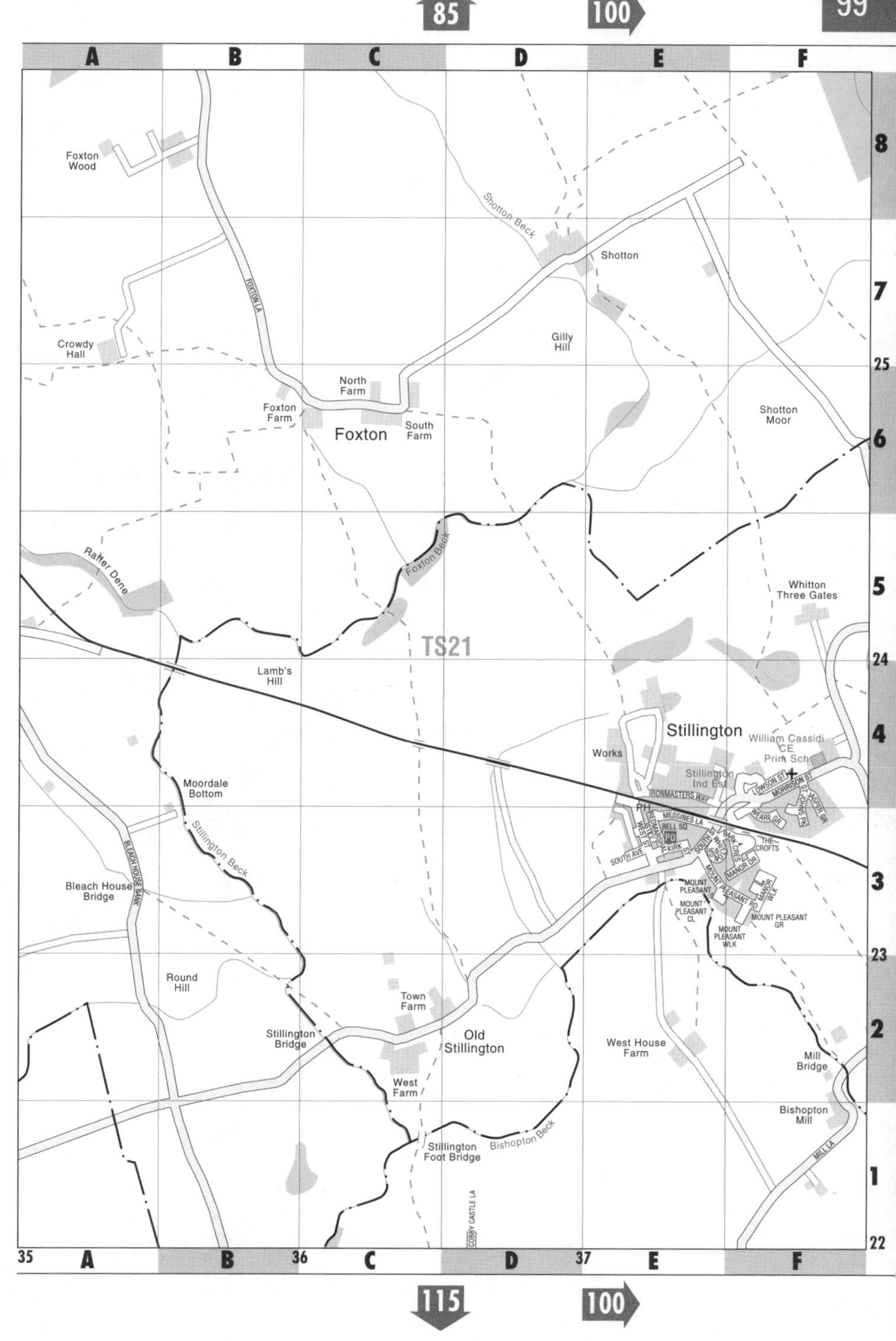
A
B
C
D
E
F
8
7
25
6
5
24
4
3
23
2
1
22
35
36
37
Foxton Wood
Shotton Beck
Shotton
FOXTON LA
Crowdy Hall
Gilly Hill
North Farm
Foxton Farm
Foxton
South Farm
Shotton Moor
Rafter Dene
Foxton Beck
Whitton Three Gates
TS21
Lamb's Hill
Stillington
William Cassidi CE Prim Sch
Works
Stillington Ind Est
Moordale Bottom
IRONMASTERS WAY
LOWSON ST
MORRISON ST
ST JOHNS PK
JASPER GR
WEARE GR
PH
MESSINES LA
BELL SQ
WEST ST
REDMARSHALL ST
PO
KIRK ST
SOUTH AVE
SOUTH ST
PARK CRES
THE CROFTS
MANOR DR
MANOR WLK
Stillington Beck
BLEACH HOUSE BANK
Bleach House Bridge
MOUNT PLEASANT
MOUNT PLEASANT RD
MOUNT PLEASANT CL
MOUNT PLEASANT GR
MOUNT PLEASANT WLK
Round Hill
Town Farm
Old Stillington
Stillington Bridge
West House Farm
Mill Bridge
West Farm
Bishopton Mill
Stillington Foot Bridge
Bishopton Beck
MILL LA
COBBY CASTLE LA

115
100

99
86

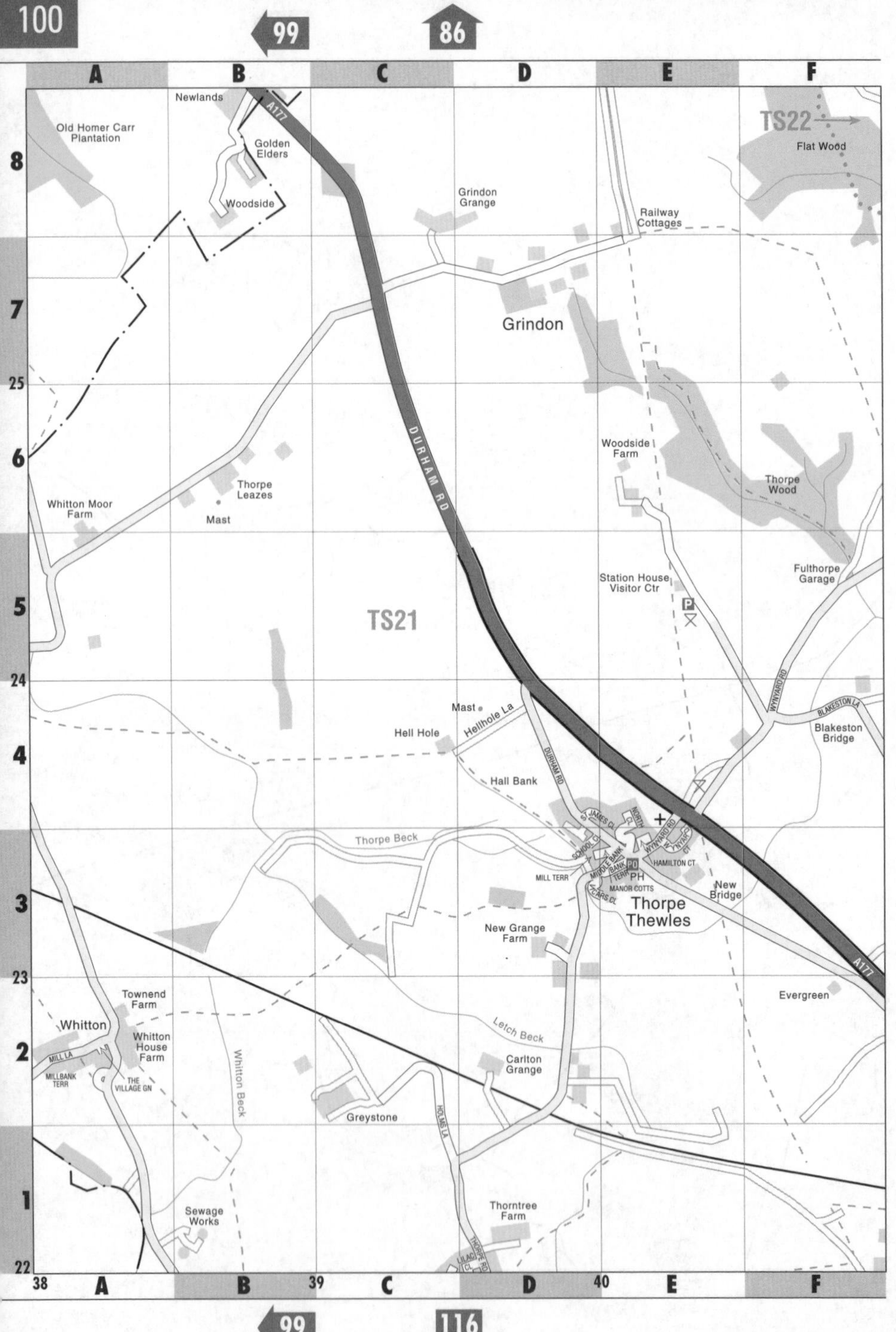
A
B
C
D
E
F
Newlands
Old Homer Carr Plantation
Golden Elders
Woodside
A177
TS22
Flat Wood
Grindon Grange
Railway Cottages
Grindon
DURHAM RD
Woodside Farm
Thorpe Wood
Thorpe Leazes
Mast
Whitton Moor Farm
Fulthorpe Garage
Station House Visitor Ctr
TS21
WYNYARD RD
BLAKESTON LA
Blakeston Bridge
Mast
Hellhole La
Hell Hole
Hall Bank
ST JAMES CL
NORTH CL
SCHOOL CL
WYNYARD RD
WYNYARD CT
Thorpe Beck
MIDDLE BANK
BANK TERR
PO
PH
HAMILTON CT
MILL TERR
MANOR COTTS
CARS CL
New Bridge
Thorpe Thewles
New Grange Farm
Evergreen
Townend Farm
Whitton
Whitton House Farm
Letch Beck
MILL LA
MILLBANK TERR
THE VILLAGE GN
Whitton Beck
Carlton Grange
Greystone
HOLMES LA
Sewage Works
Thorntree Farm
THORPE RD
LILAC CL
8
7
25
6
5
24
4
3
23
2
1
22
38
39
40

99
116

87
102

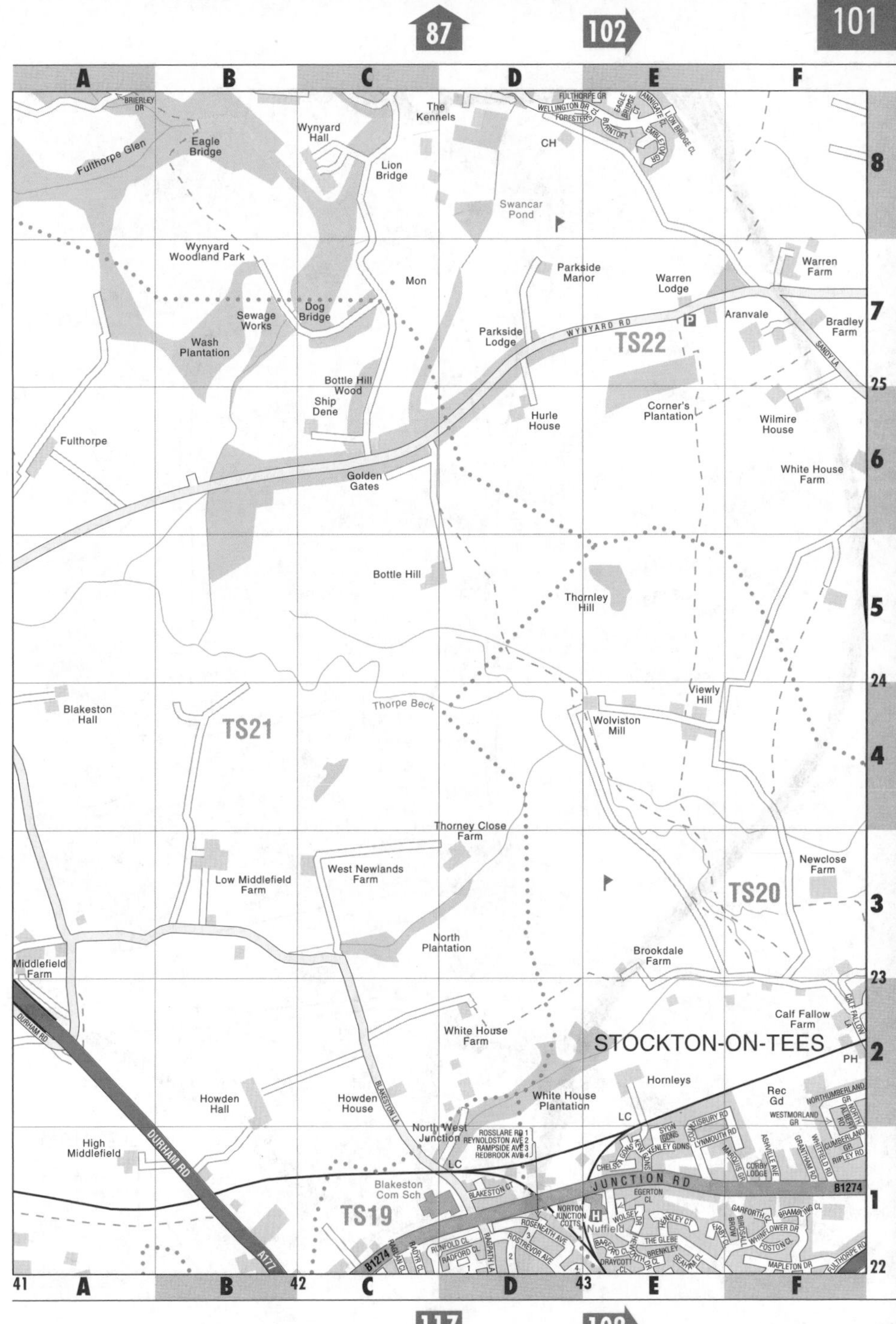
A
B
C
D
E
F
Fulthorpe Glen
Eagle Bridge
Wynyard Hall
The Kennels
Lion Bridge
CH
Swancar Pond
Wynyard Woodland Park
Mon
Parkside Manor
Warren Lodge
Warren Farm
Dog Bridge
Sewage Works
Wash Plantation
Parkside Lodge
WYNYARD RD
TS22
Aranvale
Bradley Farm
SANDY LA
Bottle Hill Wood
Ship Dene
Corner's Plantation
Hurle House
Wilmire House
Fulthorpe
Golden Gates
White House Farm
Bottle Hill
Thornley Hill
Thorpe Beck
Blakeston Hall
TS21
Viewly Hill
Wolviston Mill
Thorney Close Farm
West Newlands Farm
Low Middlefield Farm
Newclose Farm
TS20
North Plantation
Middlefield Farm
Brookdale Farm
Calf Fallow Farm
DURHAM RD
White House Farm
STOCKTON-ON-TEES
PH
Hornleys
Rec Gd
Howden Hall
Howden House
BLAKESTON LA
White House Plantation
LC
High Middlefield
North West Junction
ROSSLARE RD 1
REYNOLDSTON AVE 2
RAMPSIDE AVE 3
REDBROOK AVE 4
LC
JUNCTION RD
B1274
Blakeston Com Sch
BLAKESTON CT
TS19
Nuffield
A177
B1274
8
7
25
6
5
24
4
3
23
2
1
22
41
42
43

117
102

101

88

E8
1 BETJEMAN CL
2 DRYDEN CL
3 LOWELL CL
4 SANDHALL CL
5 WALLINGTON WLK
6 HALTON CT
7 BUTSFIELD WAY
8 NEWBIGGIN RD
9 WESTERTON RD

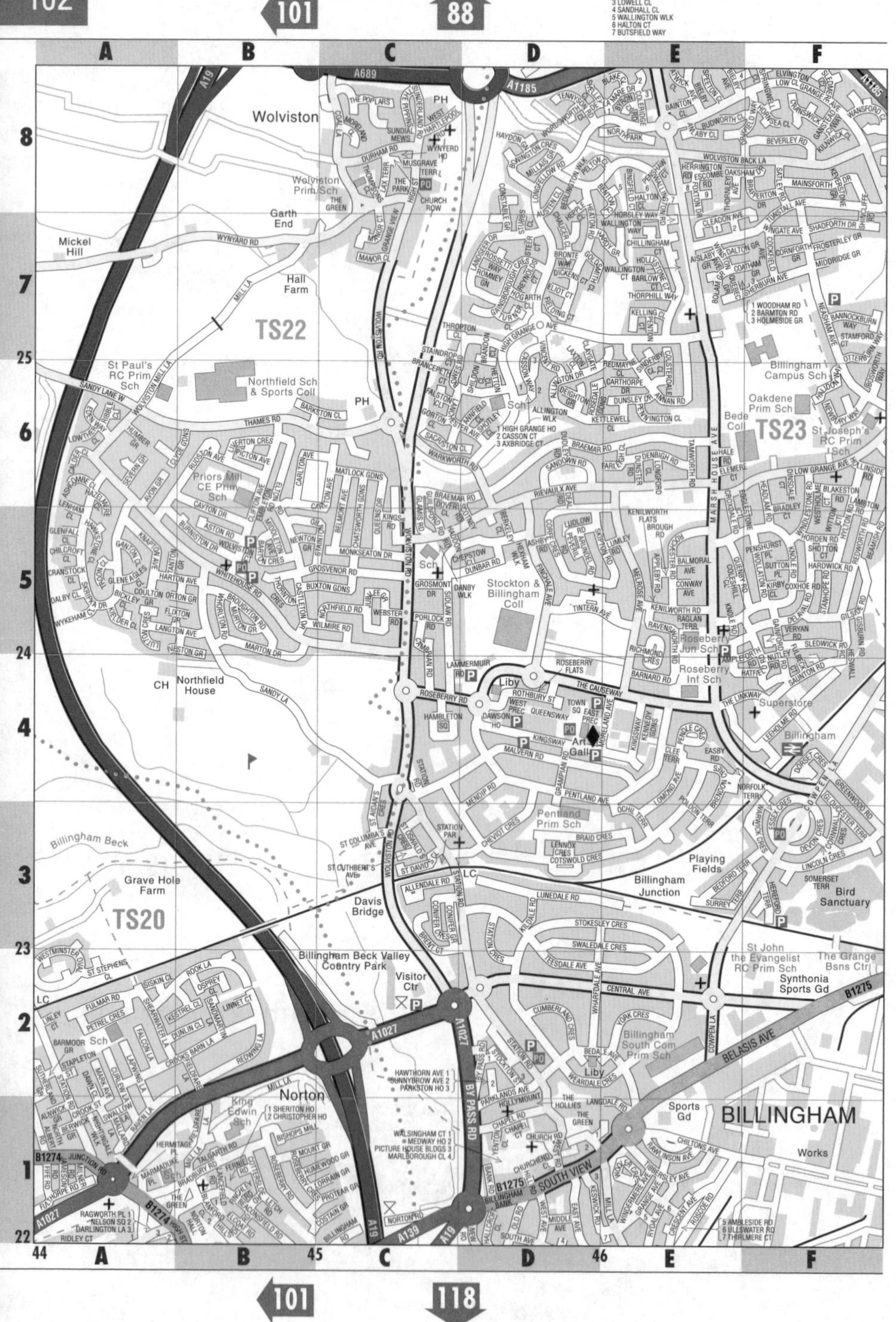

101

118

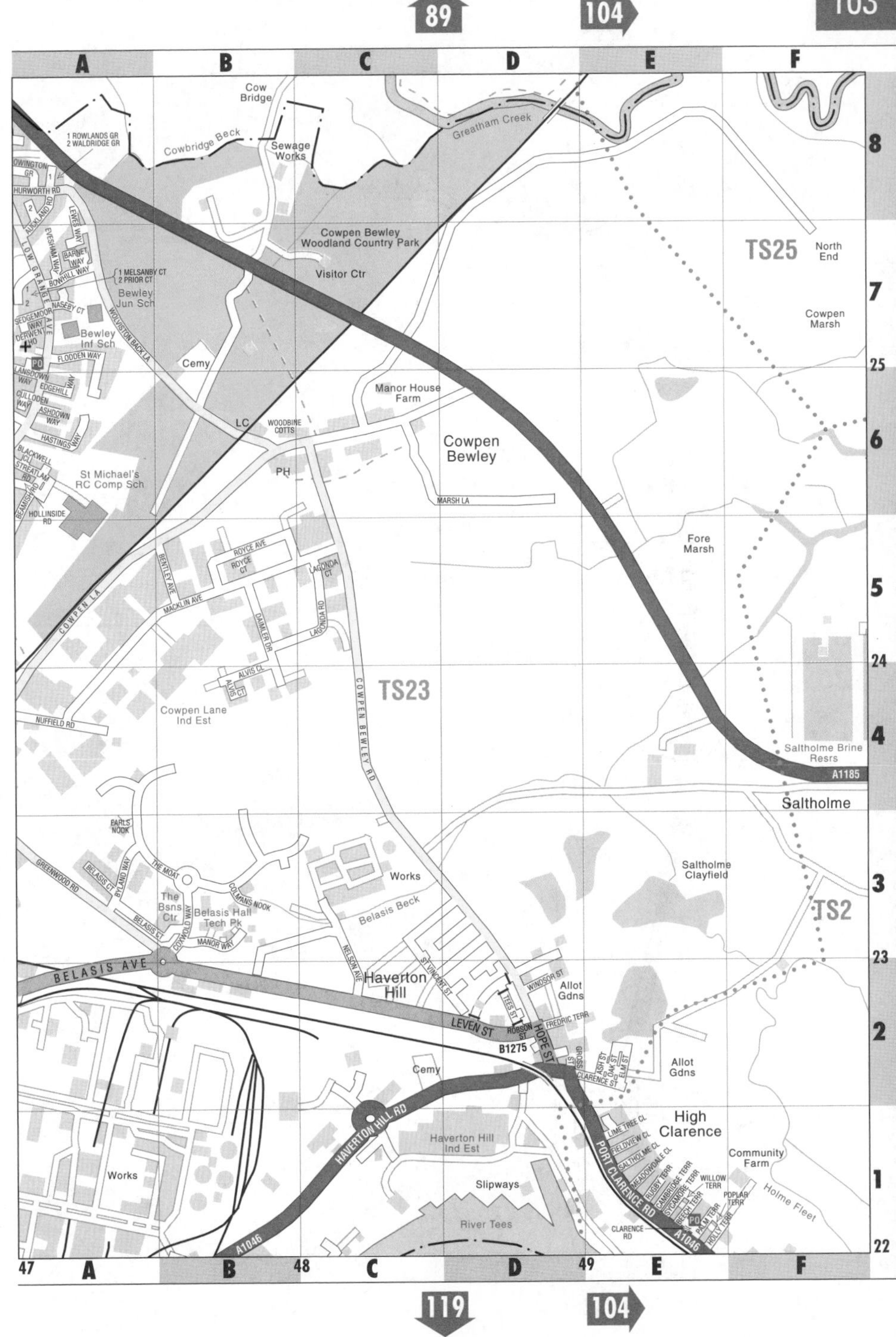

89
104
A
B
C
D
E
F
Cow Bridge
Cowbridge Beck
Sewage Works
Greatham Creek
Cowpen Bewley Woodland Country Park
Visitor Ctr
TS25
North End
Cowpen Marsh
Bewley Jun Sch
Bewley Inf Sch
Cemy
Manor House Farm
LC
WOODBINE COTTS
Cowpen Bewley
PH
St Michael's RC Comp Sch
MARSH LA
Fore Marsh
ROYCE AVE
ROYCE CT
LAGONDA CT
LAGONDA RD
BENTLEY AVE
MACKLIN AVE
DAIMLER DR
COWPEN LA
ALVIS CL
ALVIS CT
TS23
COWPEN BEWLEY RD
Cowpen Lane Ind Est
NUFFIELD RD
Saltholme Brine Resrs
A1185
Saltholme
PARLS NOOK
GREENWOOD RD
BELASIS CT
BYLAND WAY
THE MOAT
COLMANS NOOK
The Bsns Ctr
Belasis Hall Tech Pk
COXWOLD WAY
MANOR WAY
Works
Belasis Beck
Saltholme Clayfield
TS2
BELASIS AVE
NELSON AVE
Haverton Hill
ST VINCENT ST
WINDSOR ST
Allot Gdns
TEES ST
LEVEN ST
ROBSON ST
HOPE ST
FREDRIC TERR
B1275
GROSS ST
ASH ST
OAK ST
ELM ST
CLARENCE ST
Cemy
HAVERTON HILL RD
Haverton Hill Ind Est
LIME TREE CL
FIELDVIEW CL
SALTHOLME CL
MEADOWDALE CL
High Clarence
Community Farm
Works
Slipways
PORT CLARENCE RD
RUGBY TERR
CAMBRIDGE TERR
SYCAMORE TERR
WILLOW TERR
BEECH TERR
POPLAR TERR
PALM TERR
HOLLY TERR
Holme Fleet
River Tees
CLARENCE RD
A1046
8
7
25
6
5
24
4
3
23
2
1
22
47
48
49

103
90

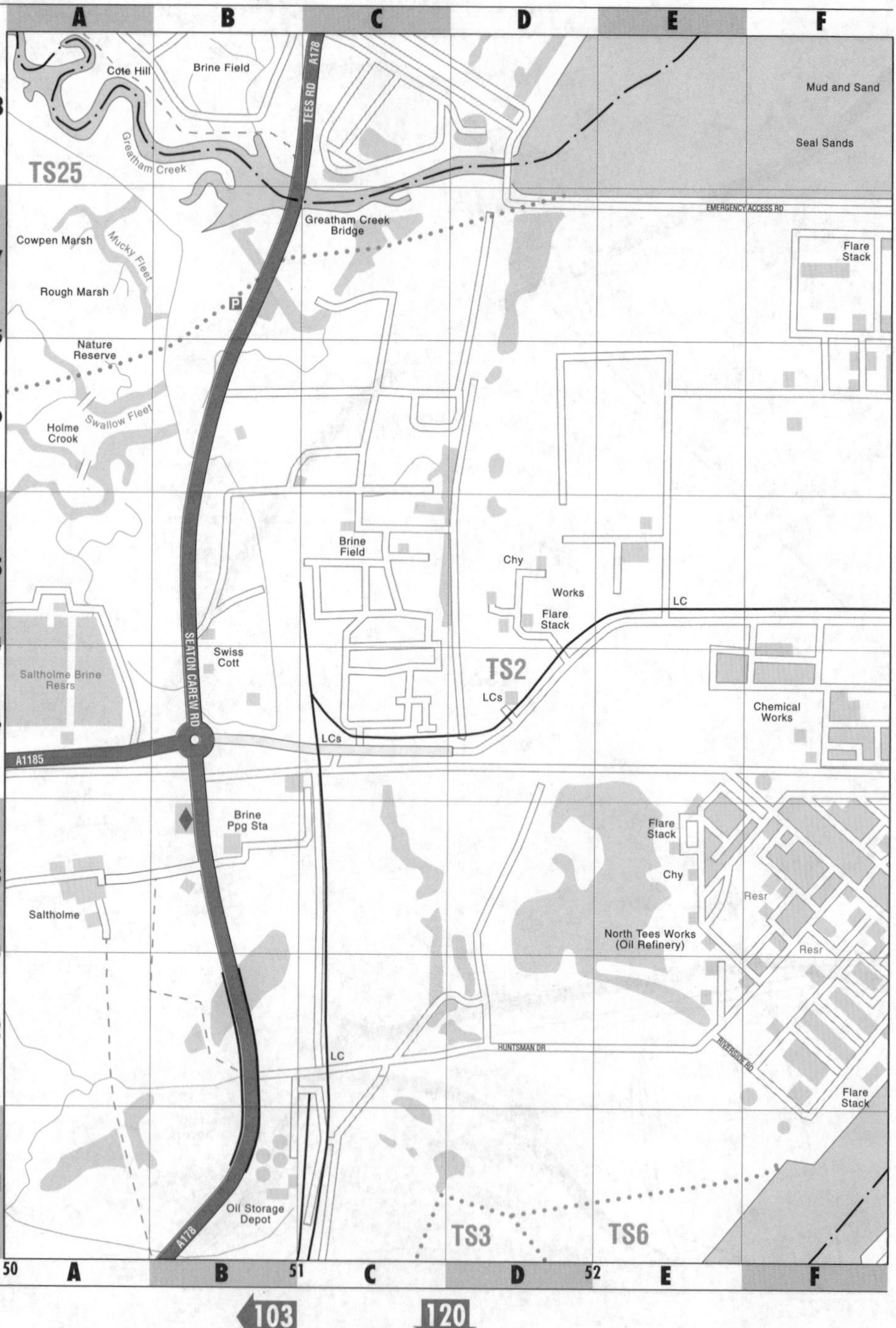

A B C D E F

8

Cote Hill
Brine Field

TEES RD A178

Mud and Sand

Seal Sands

TS25

Greatham Creek

EMERGENCY ACCESS RD

7

Cowpen Marsh

Mucky Fleet

Greatham Creek
Bridge

Flare
Stack

Rough Marsh

P

25

Nature
Reserve

Swallow Fleet

6

Holme
Crook

5

Brine
Field

Chy

Works

Flare
Stack

LC

Saltholme Brine
Resrs

24

Swiss
Cott

TS2

LCs

Chemical
Works

4

A1185

SEATON CAREW RD

LCs

Brine
Ppg Sta

Flare
Stack

3

Chy

Resr

North Tees Works
(Oil Refinery)

Saltholme

23

Resr

2

A178

LC

HUNTSMAN DR

RIVERSIDE RD

Flare
Stack

1

Oil Storage
Depot

22

TS3

TS6

50 A B 51 C D 52 E F

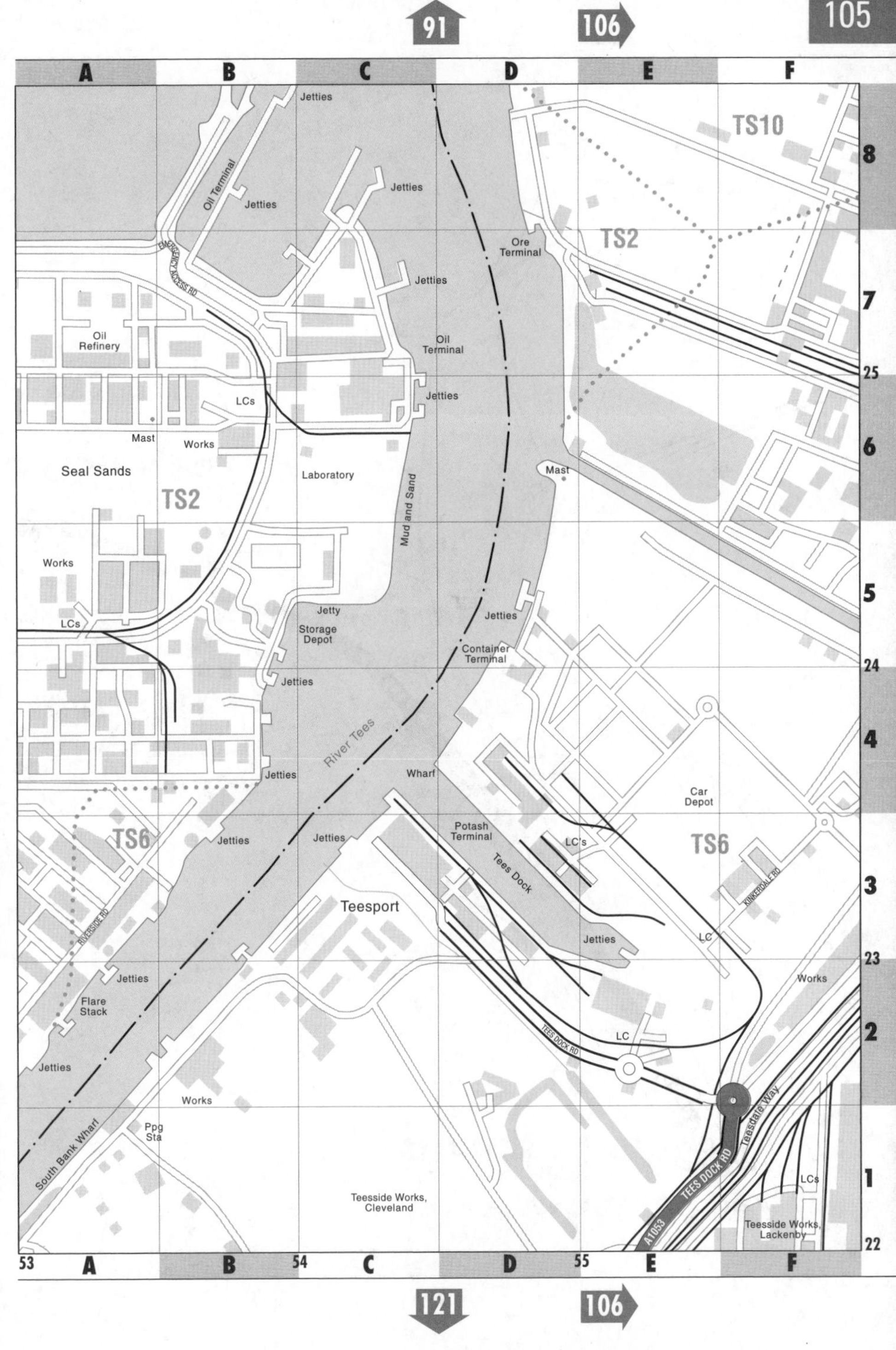
91
106
A
B
C
D
E
F
Jetties
Oil Terminal
Jetties
Jetties
TS10
8
Emergency Access Rd
Ore Terminal
TS2
Jetties
7
Oil Refinery
Oil Terminal
25
Jetties
LCs
Mast
Works
6
Seal Sands
Laboratory
Mast
TS2
Mud and Sand
Works
5
Jetty
Jetties
LCs
Storage Depot
Container Terminal
24
Jetties
River Tees
4
Jetties
Wharf
Car Depot
Potash Terminal
TS6
LC's
TS6
Jetties
Jetties
Tees Dock
Kinkerdale Rd
3
Teesport
Riverside Rd
Jetties
LC
23
Jetties
Works
Flare Stack
2
LC
Tees Dock Rd
Jetties
Works
Teesdale Way
Ppg Sta
South Bank Wharf
Tees Dock Rd
1
A1053
LCs
Teesside Works, Cleveland
Teesside Works, Lackenby
22
53
A
B
54
C
D
55
E
F
121
106

105

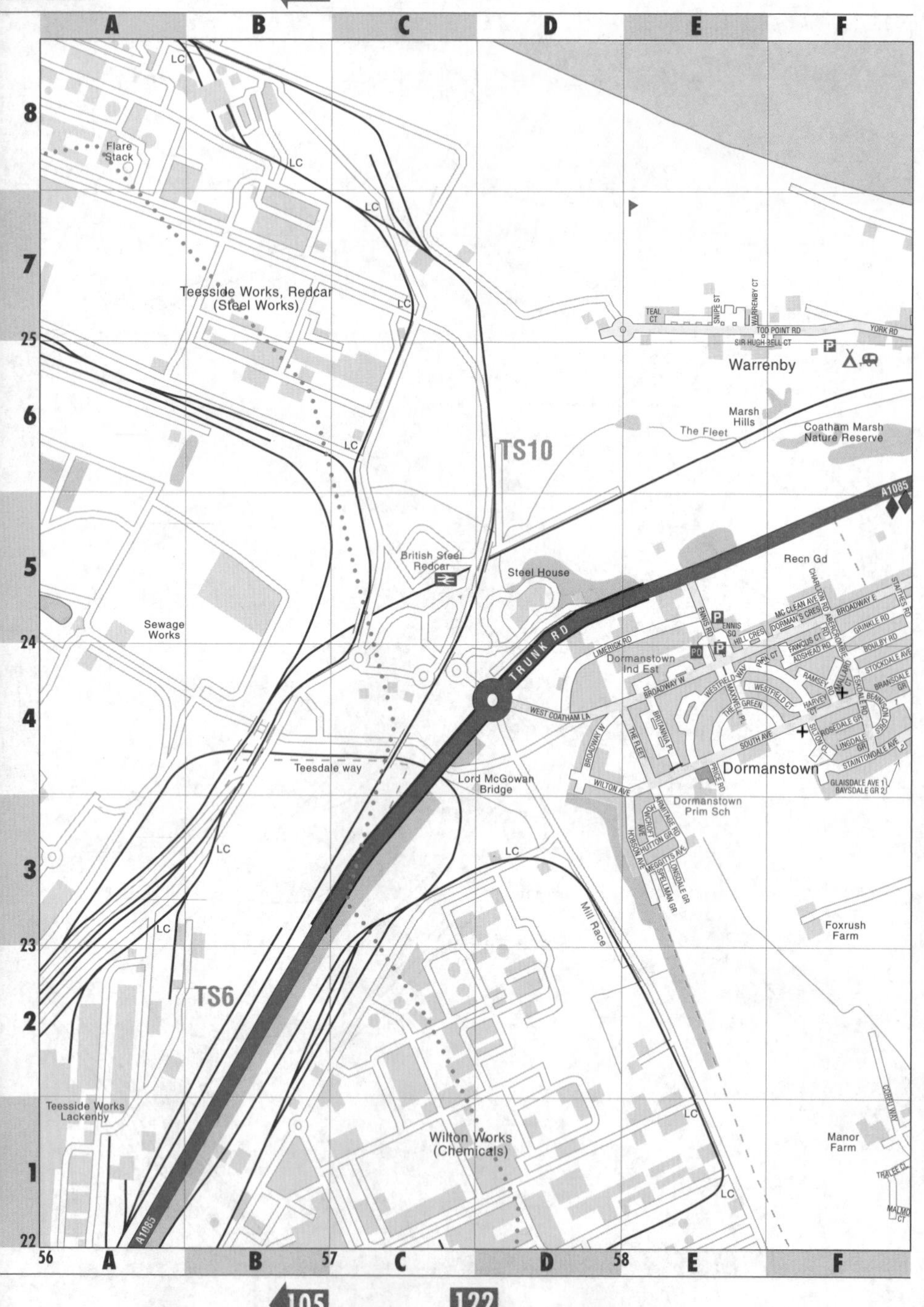
A
B
C
D
E
F
8
7
25
6
5
24
4
3
23
2
1
22
56
57
58
LC
Flare Stack
Teesside Works, Redcar (Steel Works)
TEAL CT
SNIPE ST
WARRENBY CT
TOD POINT RD
YORK RD
SIR HUGH BELL CT
Warrenby
Marsh Hills
The Fleet
Coatham Marsh Nature Reserve
TS10
A1085
British Steel Redcar
Steel House
Recn Gd
Sewage Works
TRUNK RD
LIMERICK RD
ENNIS RD
ENNIS SQ
HILL CRES
MC CLEAN AVE
DORMAN'S CRES
CHARLTON RD
ABERCROMBIE
BROADWAY E
STAITHES RD
GRINKLE RD
FAWCUS CT
ADSHEAD RD
BOULBY RD
STOCKDALE AVE
BRANSDALE GR
RAMSEY RD
MALLARD CT
ESKDALE RD
BENNISON CRES
HARVEY CT
WESTFIELD CT
WESTFIELD WAY
MAXWELL PL
THE GREEN
PARK CT
Dormanstown Ind Est
BROADWAY W
BRITANNIA PL
WEST COATHAM LA
THE FLEET
SOUTH AVE
SILTON CL
ROSEDALE GR
LINGDALE GR
STAINTONDALE AVE
GLAISDALE AVE
BAYSDALE GR
PRICE RD
Dormanstown
WILTON AVE
Dormanstown Prim Sch
ARMITAGE RD
ASHCROFT
HUTTON GR
HOBSON AVE
MEGGITTS AVE
LONSDALE GR
SPELLMAN GR
Teesdale way
Lord McGowan Bridge
Mill Race
Foxrush Farm
TS6
Teesside Works Lackenby
Wilton Works (Chemicals)
Manor Farm
CORPORATION
TRALEE CL
MALMO CT

105
122

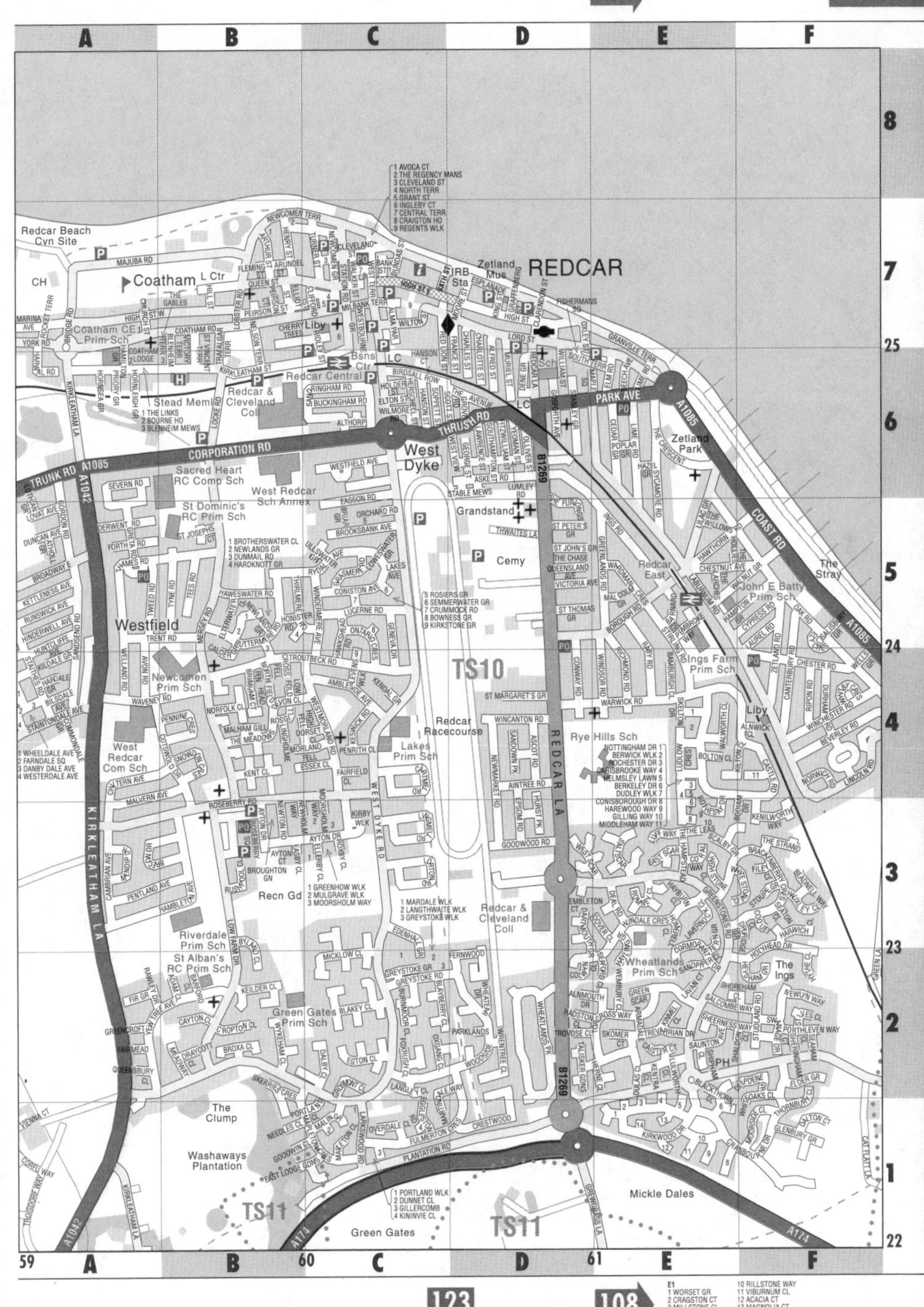

E1
1 WORSET GR
2 CRAGSTON CT
3 MILLSTONE CL
4 JUNIPER CL
5 AZALIA GR
6 FINCHDALE CL
7 BRAMBLE DYKES
8 AMBERLEY CL
9 ABERCORN CL
10 RILLSTONE WAY
11 VIBURNUM CL
12 ACACIA CT
13 MAGNOLIA CT
14 DIDCOT CL

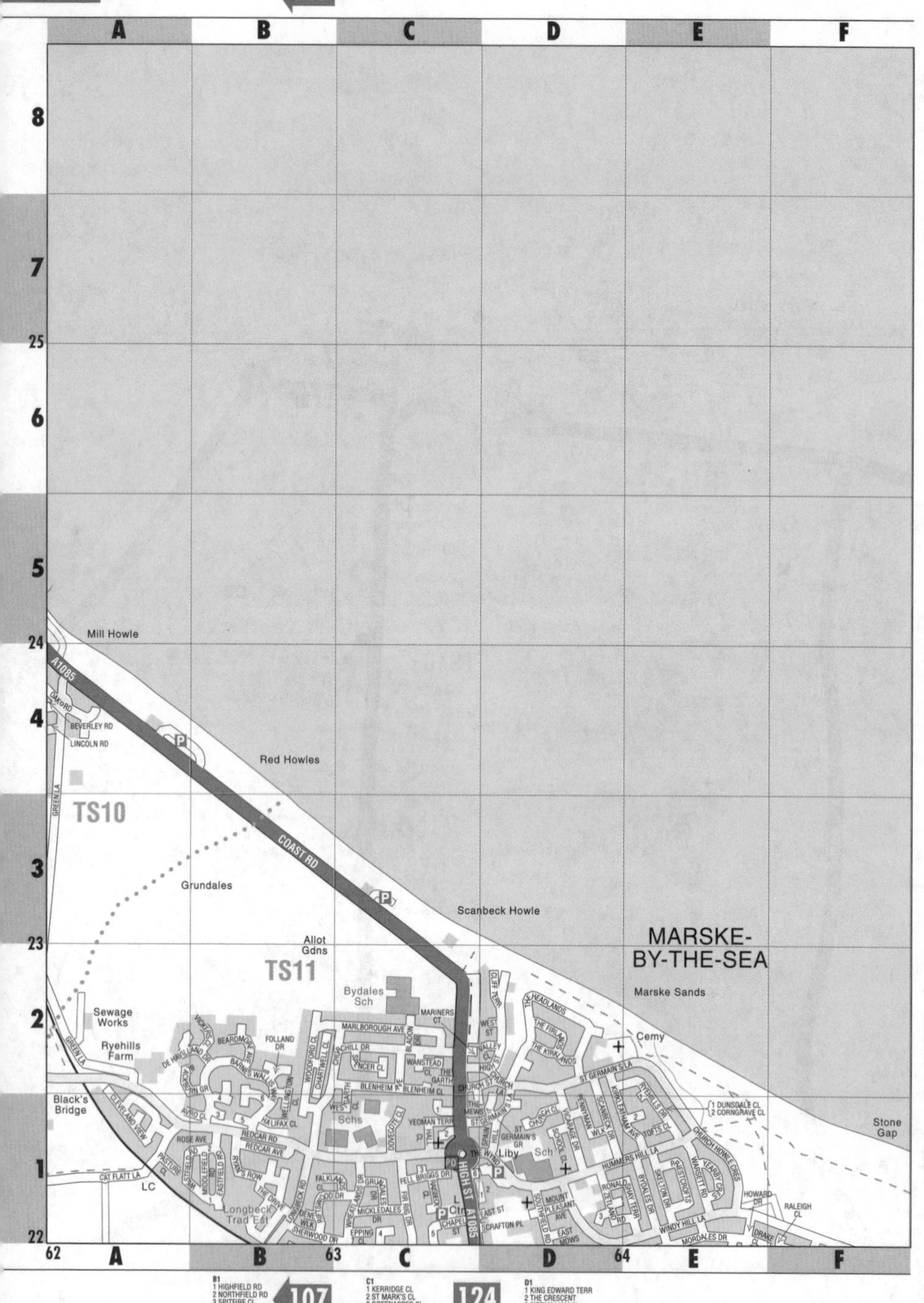

	A	B	C	D	E	F

8

7

25

6

5

24

Mill Howle

A1085

OXFORD

BEVERLEY RD

LINCOLN RD

4

GREEN LA

P

TS10

Red Howles

COAST RD

3

Grundales

P

Scanbeck Howle

MARSKE-BY-THE-SEA

23

Allot Gdns

TS11

Bydales Sch

MARINERS CT

Marske Sands

2

Sewage Works

Ryehills Farm

MARLBOROUGH AVE

FOLLAND DR

CHILL DR

HEADLANDS

THE KIRK-WDS

Cemy

GERMAIN SLA

Black's Bridge

BLENHEIM CL BLENHEIM CL

CHURCH ST CHURCH

WEST

YEOMAN TERR

MEWS

1 DUNSDALE CL
2 CORNGRAVE CL

Stone Gap

1

ROSE AVE

REDCAR RD

REDCAR AVE

West Schs

FALKLAND

GERMAIN'S DR

Liby

Sch

HUMMERSEA

HOWARD DR

RALEIGH CL

CAT FLATT LA

LC

Longbeck Trad Est

SHERWOOD DR

MICKLEDALES DR

EPPING

CHAPEL ST

PO

HIGH ST

EAST ST

SCRAFTON PL

MOUNT PLEASANT AVE

EAST MEWS

WINDY HILL LA

MORDALES DR

DRAKE

22

62	A	B	**63**	C	D	**64**	E	F

107 124

B1
1 HIGHFIELD RD
2 NORTHFIELD RD
3 SPITFIRE CL
4 LANCASTER DR
5 LYSANDER CT
6 BRABAZON DR

C1
1 KERRIDGE CL
2 ST MARK'S CL
3 GREENACRES CL
4 INGLEWOOD AVE
5 CHAPEL CL
6 ADELAIDE PL

D1
1 KING EDWARD TERR
2 THE CRESCENT
3 FITZWILLIAM CL

	A	B	C	D	E	F	

8

7

25

6

5

24

4

3

23

2

1

Saltburn
Sands

TS11

22

65 A   B   66 C   D   67 E   F

201 94

	A	B	C	D	E	F

8

B6275

Blue House Farm

Side Hill

Hillside Farm

Houghton-le-Side

Manor House

Bolam Grange

Kitching's Plantation

7

Houghton Grange

Great Boldearns Hill

Sandforth Moor

21

Houghton Plantation

Ling Plantations

6

Ling Back

Grimshaw Hill

BLIND LA

Covertside

Dobinson's Rush

East Limekiln Banks

Denton Grange Moor

Ling Bridge

HOUGHTON LA

5

Hopper's Plantation

SUMMERHOUSE MASK LA

20

Banks Cottage

Limekiln Banks

DL2

Denton Grange East

4

Denton Grange West

Tenement Beck

Willow Beds

Stripe Plantation

Bow Bridge

Wry Nook Plantation

3

North Farm

Summerhouse

Glebe Farm

PH

PO

B6279

Denton Hall Farm

RABY COTTS

Denton Hall

THE GRANGE

19

The Grange

Denton

DENTON HALL COTTS

Tomtit Wood

2

Summerhouse Beck

DENTON CROSS ROADS

REN LA

Castle Farm

Kilnfield Plantation

1

Ruffley Hill

B6275

B6279

18

20	A	B	21	C	D	22	E	F

201 130

95
112

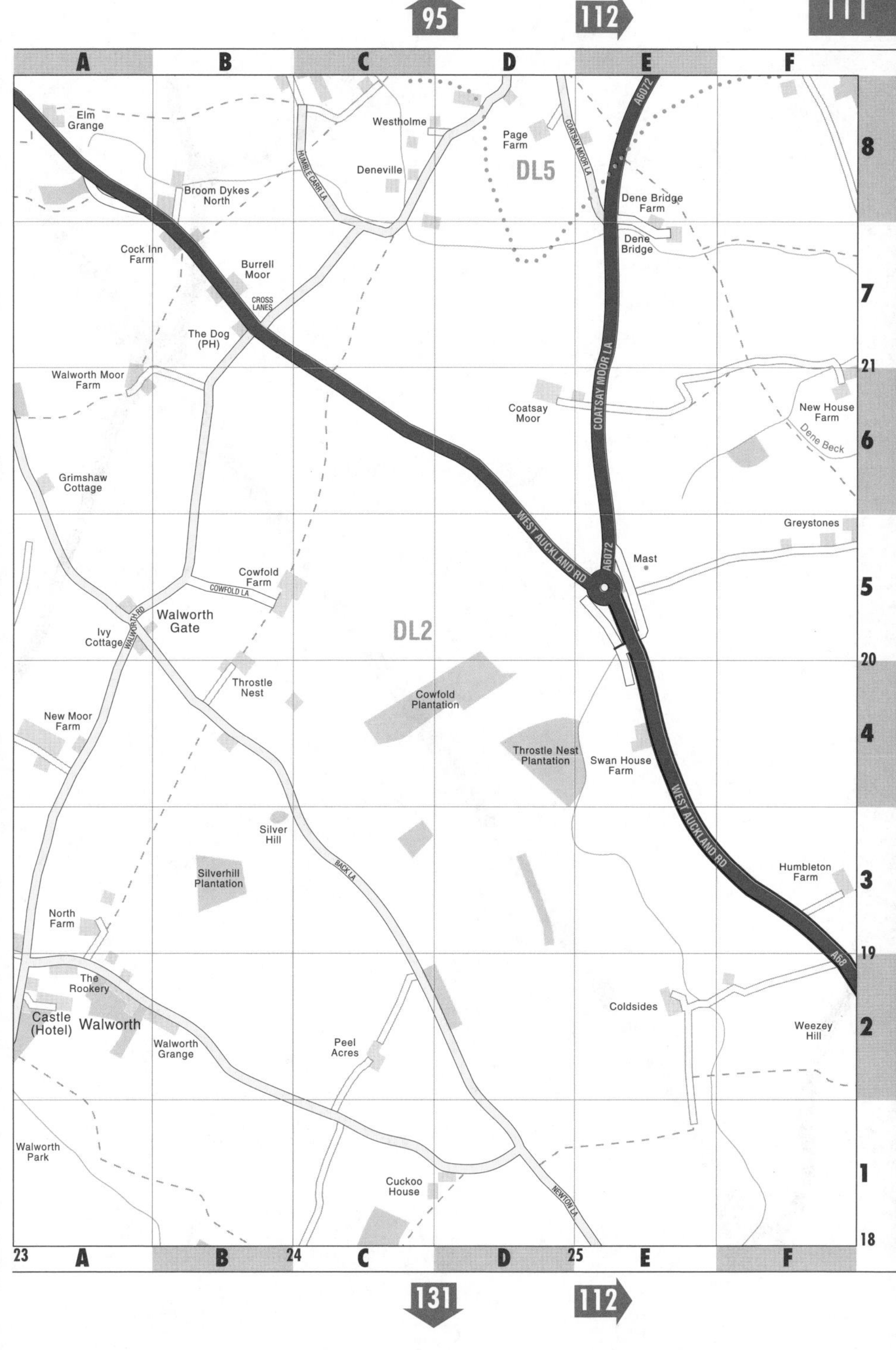
A
B
C
D
E
F
Elm Grange
Westholme
Page Farm
COATSAY MOOR LA
A6072
DL5
8
HUMBLE CARR LA
Deneville
Broom Dykes North
Dene Bridge Farm
Dene Bridge
Cock Inn Farm
Burrell Moor
CROSS LANES
7
The Dog (PH)
21
Walworth Moor Farm
Coatsay Moor
COATSAY MOOR LA
New House Farm
Dene Beck
6
Grimshaw Cottage
WEST AUCKLAND RD
Greystones
A6072
Mast
Cowfold Farm
COWFOLD LA
5
Walworth Gate
WALWORTH RD
Ivy Cottage
DL2
20
Throstle Nest
Cowfold Plantation
New Moor Farm
4
Throstle Nest Plantation
Swan House Farm
WEST AUCKLAND RD
Silver Hill
BACK LA
Silverhill Plantation
Humbleton Farm
3
North Farm
19
A68
The Rookery
Coldsides
Castle (Hotel)
Walworth
Weezey Hill
2
Walworth Grange
Peel Acres
Walworth Park
1
Cuckoo House
NEWTON LA
18
23
24
25

131
112

111
96

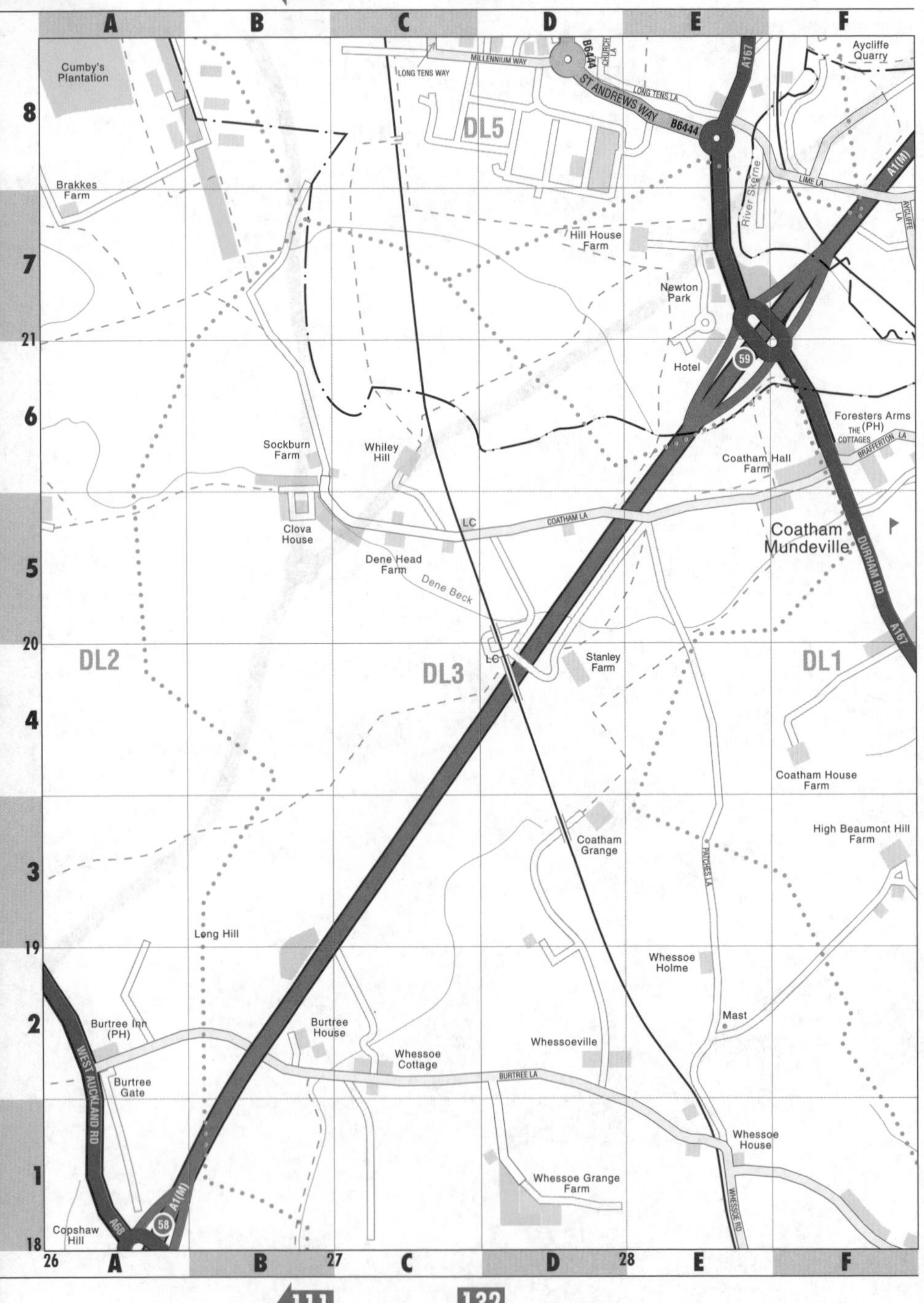
A
B
C
D
E
F
Cumby's Plantation
Brakkes Farm
LONG TENS WAY
MILLENNIUM WAY
B6444
CHURCH LA
ST ANDREWS WAY
LONG TENS LA
B6444
DL5
A167
Aycliffe Quarry
River Skerne
LIME LA
AYCLIFFE LA
A1(M)
Hill House Farm
Newton Park
Hotel
59
Foresters Arms (PH)
THE COTTAGES
BRAFFERTON LA
Sockburn Farm
Whiley Hill
Coatham Hall Farm
Clova House
LC
COATHAM LA
Coatham Mundeville
DURHAM RD
Dene Head Farm
Dene Beck
A167
DL2
LC
Stanley Farm
DL3
DL1
Coatham House Farm
High Beaumont Hill Farm
Coatham Grange
PATCHES LA
Long Hill
Wessoe Holme
Burtree Inn (PH)
Burtree House
Mast
Whessoeville
Whessoe Cottage
WEST AUCKLAND RD
BURTREE LA
Burtree Gate
Whessoe House
A1(M)
Whessoe Grange Farm
WHESSOE RD
A68
Copshaw Hill
58
8
7
21
6
5
20
4
3
19
2
1
18
26
27
28

111
132

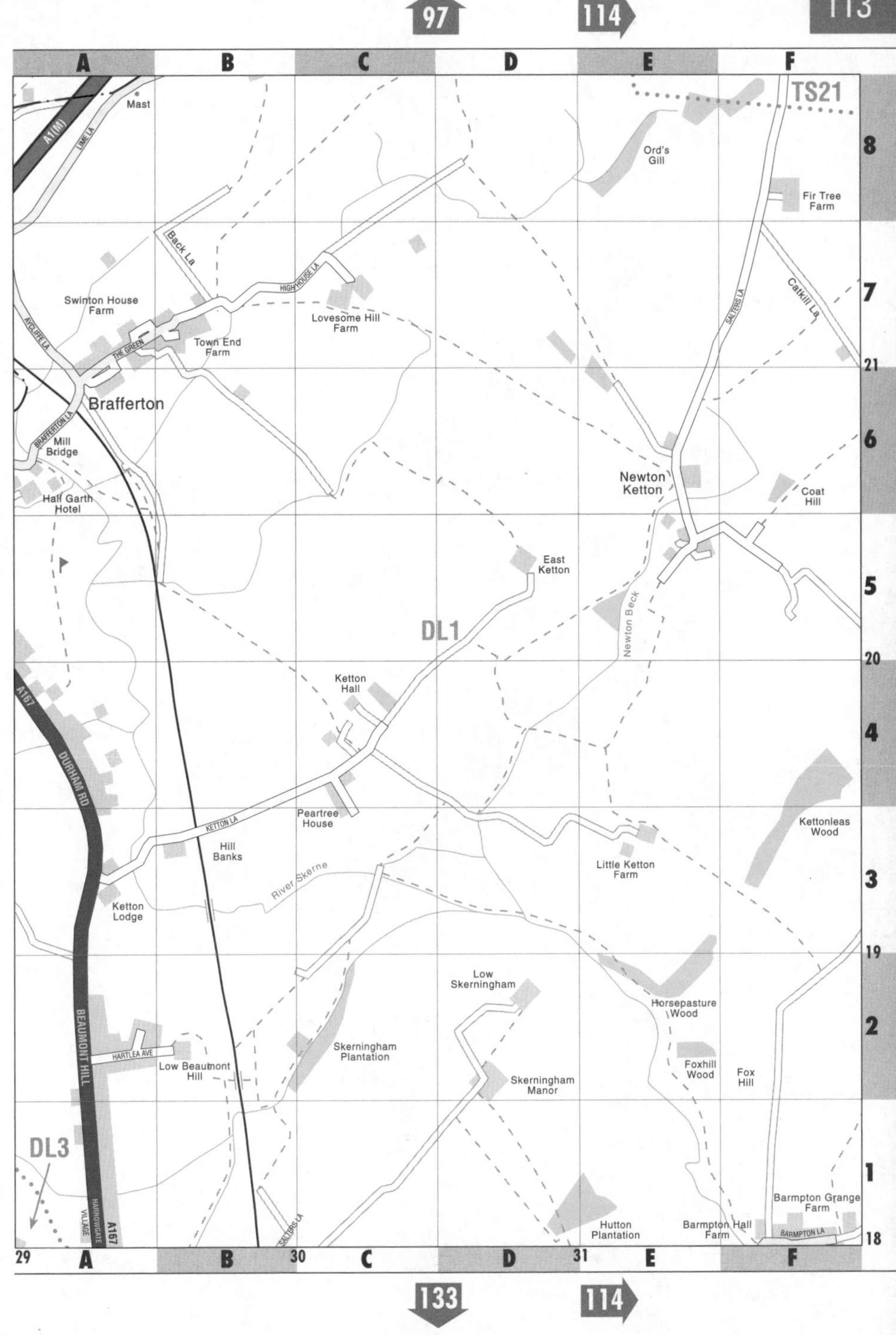
97
114
A
B
C
D
E
F
TS21
Mast
A1(M)
LIME LA
Ord's Gill
Fir Tree Farm
8
Back La
HIGH HOUSE LA
Swinton House Farm
Lovesome Hill Farm
7
Catkill La
SALTERS LA
AYCLIFFE LA
THE GREEN
Town End Farm
21
Brafferton
BRAFFERTON LA
Mill Bridge
6
Newton Ketton
Coat Hill
Hall Garth Hotel
East Ketton
5
Newton Beck
DL1
20
A167
Ketton Hall
4
DURHAM RD
Peartree House
KETTON LA
Hill Banks
Kettonleas Wood
Little Ketton Farm
River Skerne
3
Ketton Lodge
19
Low Skerningham
Horsepasture Wood
2
BEAUMONT HILL
HARTLEA AVE
Skerningham Plantation
Low Beaumont Hill
Foxhill Wood
Fox Hill
Skerningham Manor
DL3
1
Barmpton Grange Farm
HARROWGATE VILLAGE
A167
SALTERS LA
Hutton Plantation
Barmpton Hall Farm
BARMPTON LA
18
29
30
31
133
114

113
98

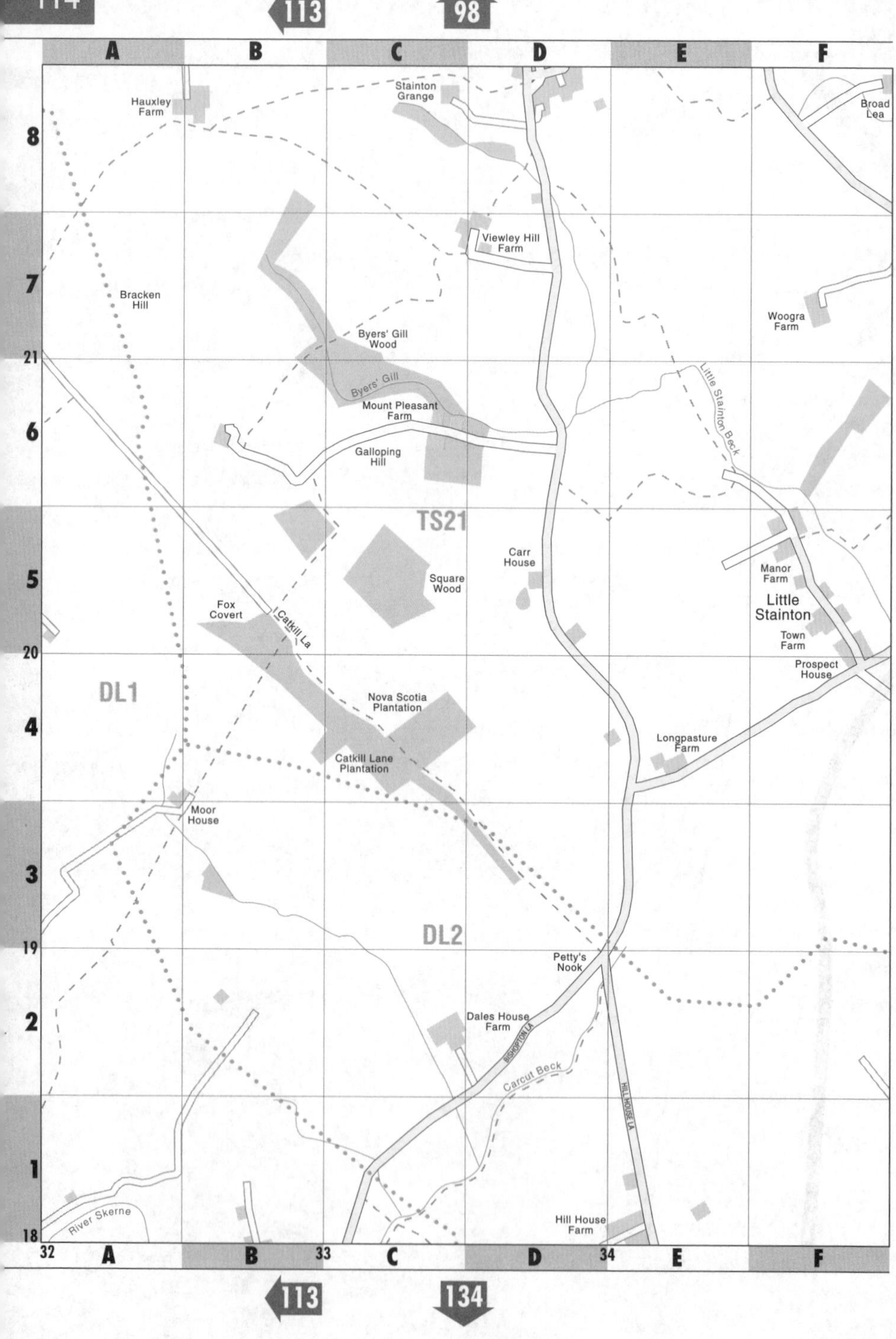
A
B
C
D
E
F
8
7
21
6
5
20
4
3
19
2
1
18
32
33
34
Hauxley Farm
Stainton Grange
Broad Lea
Viewley Hill Farm
Bracken Hill
Byers' Gill Wood
Woogra Farm
Byers' Gill
Mount Pleasant Farm
Little Stainton Beck
Galloping Hill
TS21
Carr House
Manor Farm
Square Wood
Little Stainton
Fox Covert
Catkill La
Town Farm
Prospect House
DL1
Nova Scotia Plantation
Longpasture Farm
Catkill Lane Plantation
Moor House
DL2
Petty's Nook
Dales House Farm
BISHOPTON LA
Carcut Beck
HILL HOUSE LA
River Skerne
Hill House Farm

113
134

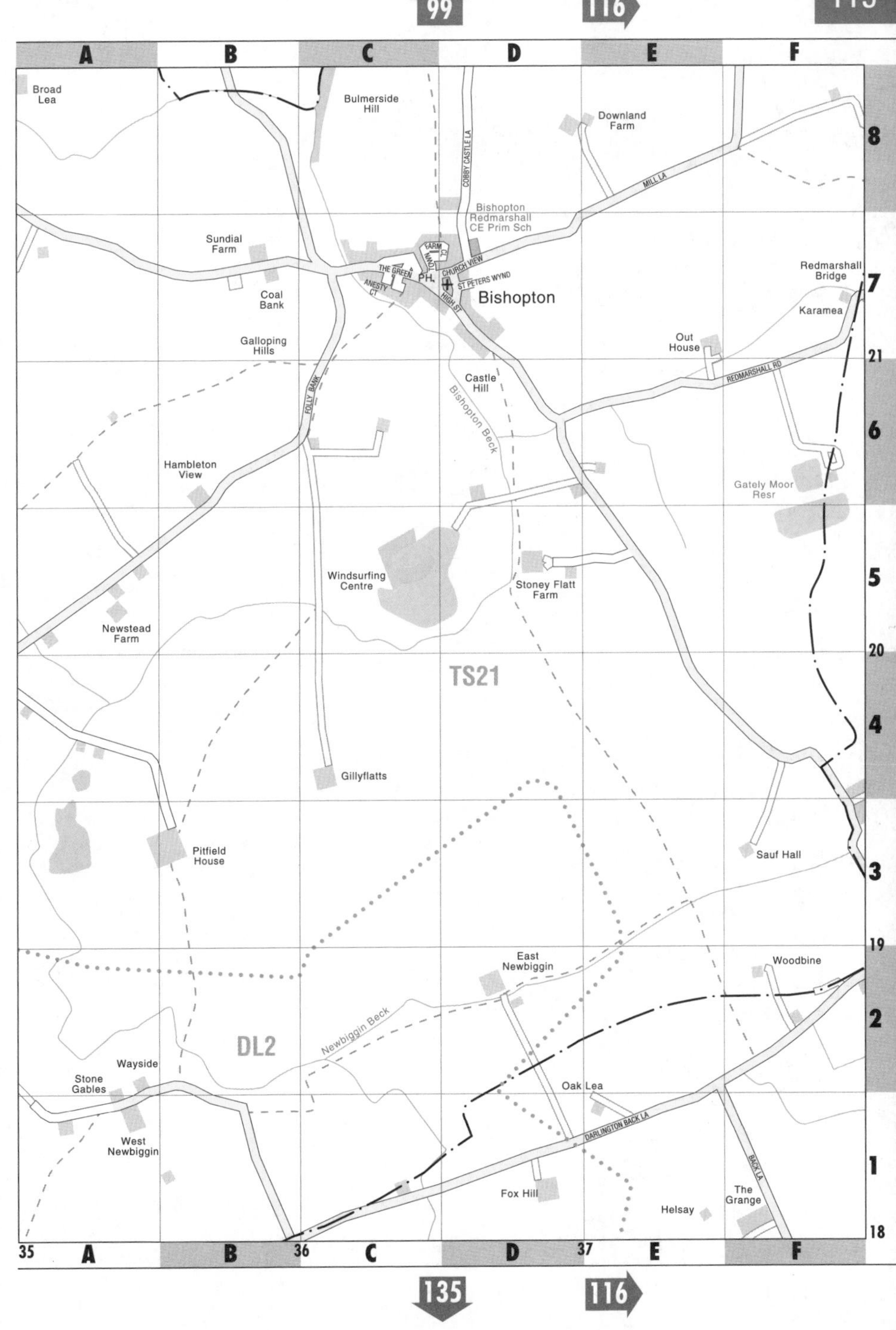
99
116
A
B
C
D
E
F
Broad Lea
Bulmerside Hill
Downland Farm
COBBY CASTLE LA
MILL LA
Bishopton Redmarshall CE Prim Sch
Sundial Farm
FARM CL
TOWN
THE GREEN
CHURCH VIEW
PH
ST PETERS WYND
ANESTY CT
HIGH ST
Bishopton
Coal Bank
Galloping Hills
Redmarshall Bridge
Karamea
Out House
REDMARSHALL RD
FOLLY BANK
Castle Hill
Bishopton Beck
Hambleton View
Gately Moor Resr
Windsurfing Centre
Stoney Flatt Farm
Newstead Farm
TS21
Gillyflatts
Pitfield House
Sauf Hall
East Newbiggin
Woodbine
Newbiggin Beck
DL2
Wayside
Stone Gables
West Newbiggin
Oak Lea
DARLINGTON BACK LA
BACK LA
Fox Hill
The Grange
Helsay
8
7
21
6
5
20
4
3
19
2
1
18
35
36
37
135
116

115 100

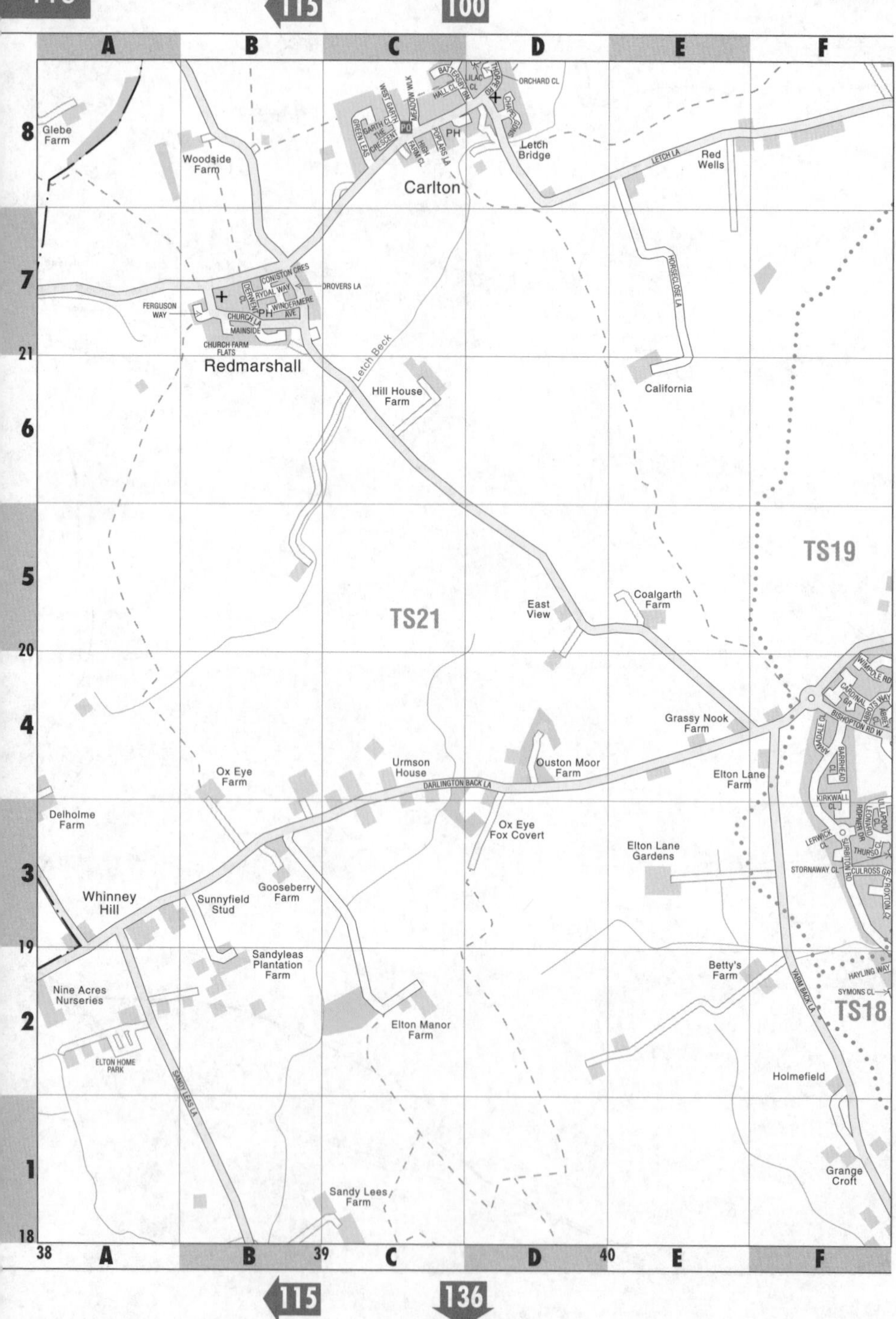
A
B
C
D
E
F
8
7
21
6
5
20
4
3
19
2
1
18
38
39
40
Glebe Farm
Woodside Farm
Carlton
WEST GARTH
MEADOW WALK
GARTH CL
THE CRESCENT
GREEN LEAS
PO
HIGH FARM CL
POPLARS LA
BATTERSBY RD
HALL CL
LILAC CL
THORPE RD
ORCHARD CL
CHAPEL GDNS
PH
Letch Bridge
LETCH LA
Red Wells
CONISTON CRES
RYDAL WAY
DROVERS LA
DERWENT CL
WINDERMERE AVE
FERGUSON WAY
CHURCH LA
MAINSIDE
CHURCH FARM FLATS
Redmarshall
Letch Beck
Hill House Farm
HORSECLOSE LA
California
TS19
TS21
East View
Coalgarth Farm
WIMPOLE RD
CARDINAL GR
ABBOTS WAY
ABBEY
BISHOPTON RD W
Grassy Nook Farm
ARMADALE CL
BARRHEAD CL
Ox Eye Farm
Urmson House
Ouston Moor Farm
Elton Lane Farm
DARLINGTON BACK LA
Delholme Farm
Ox Eye Fox Covert
KIRKWALL CL
ULLAPOOL CL
LEONARD CL
ROPNER DR
LERWICK CL
SURBITON RD
THURSO CL
Elton Lane Gardens
STORNAWAY CL
CULROSS GR
CROXTON CL
Whinney Hill
Gooseberry Farm
Sunnyfield Stud
Sandyleas Plantation Farm
Betty's Farm
HAYLING WAY
YARM BACK LA
SYMONS CL
TS18
Nine Acres Nurseries
Elton Manor Farm
ELTON HOME PARK
Holmefield
SANDY LEAS LA
Grange Croft
Sandy Lees Farm

115 136

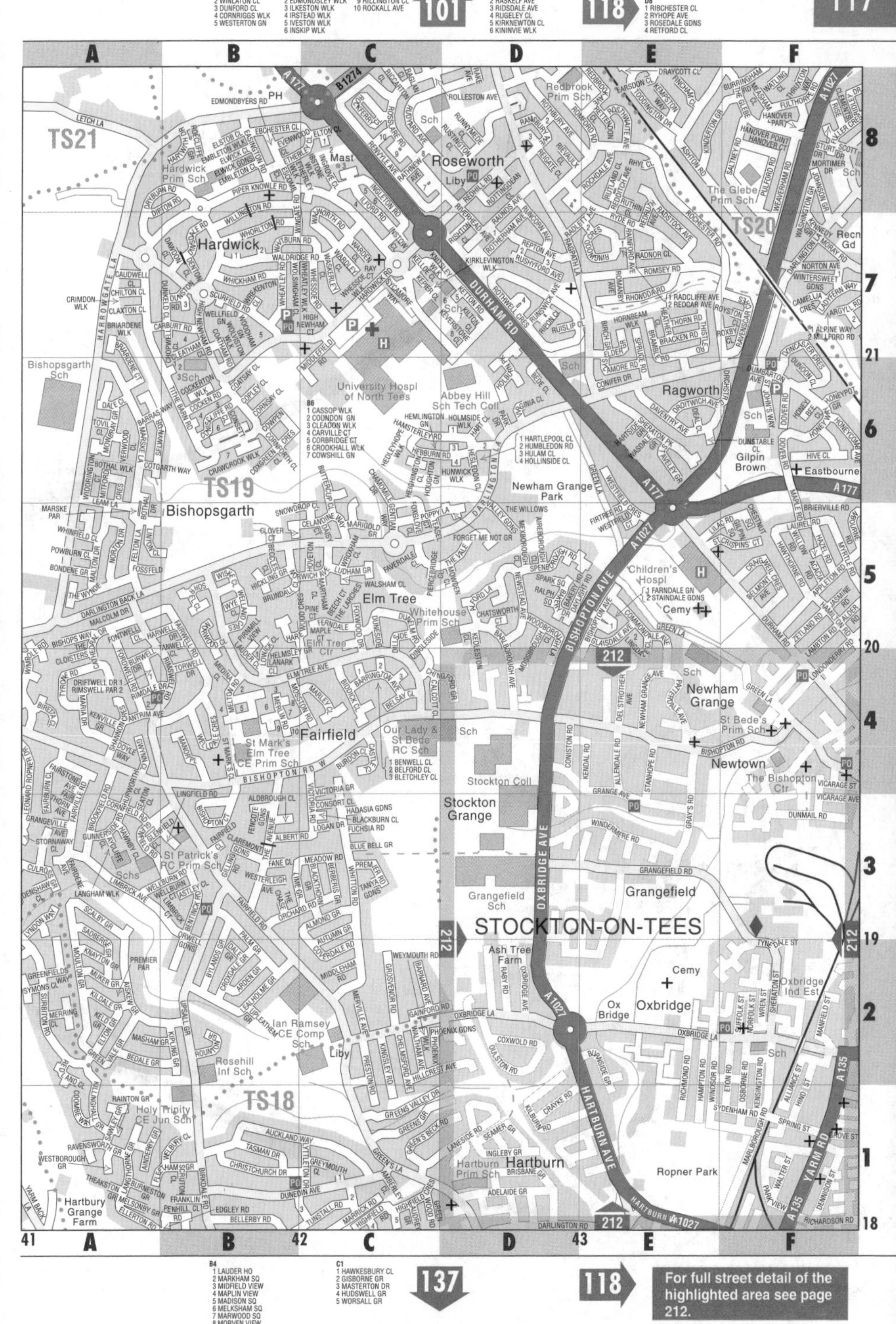

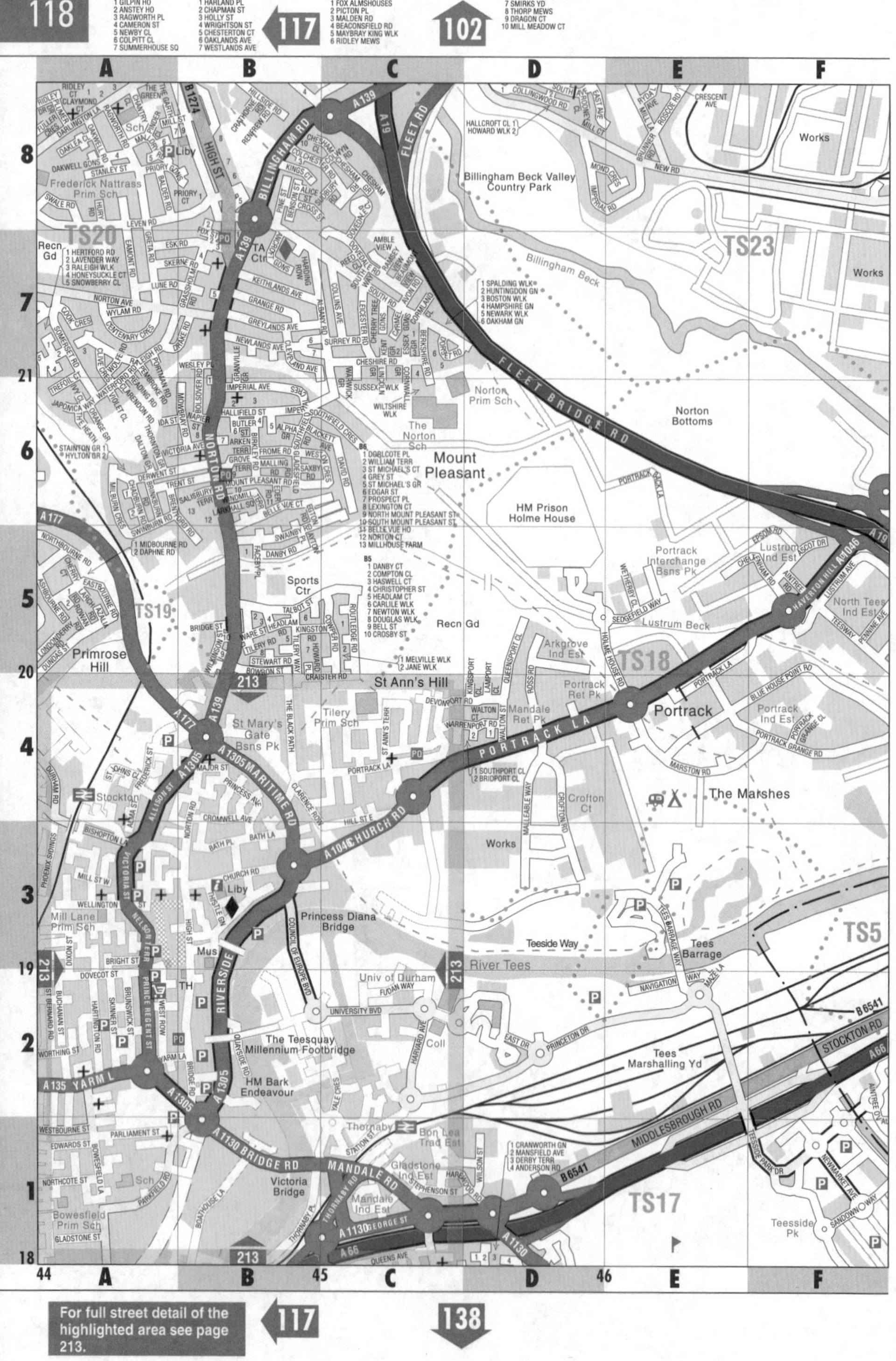

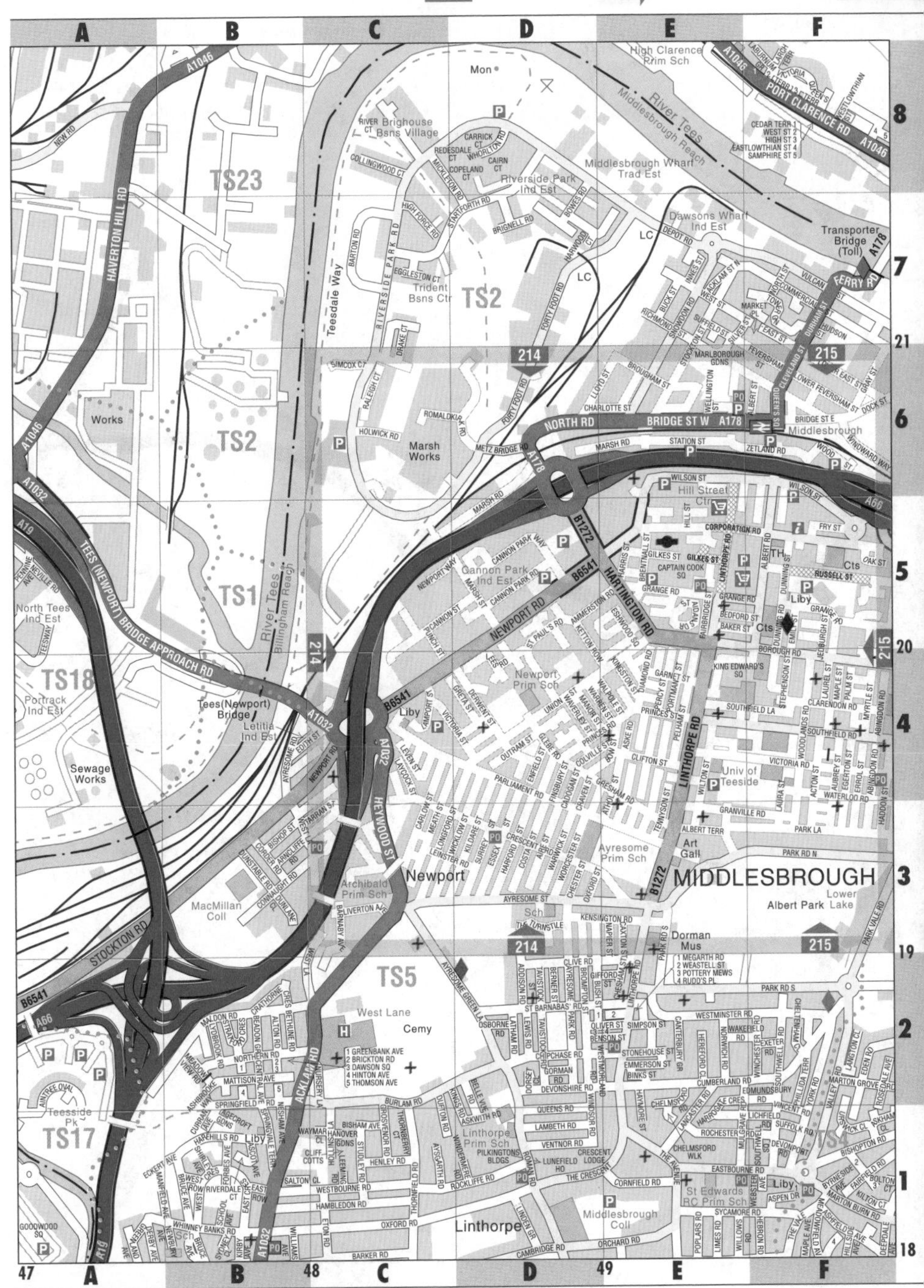

For full street detail of the highlighted area see pages 214 and 215.

F1
1 PALLADIUM BLDGS
2 CROFTON AVE
3 HAWTHORNE AVE
4 ROSECROFT AVE

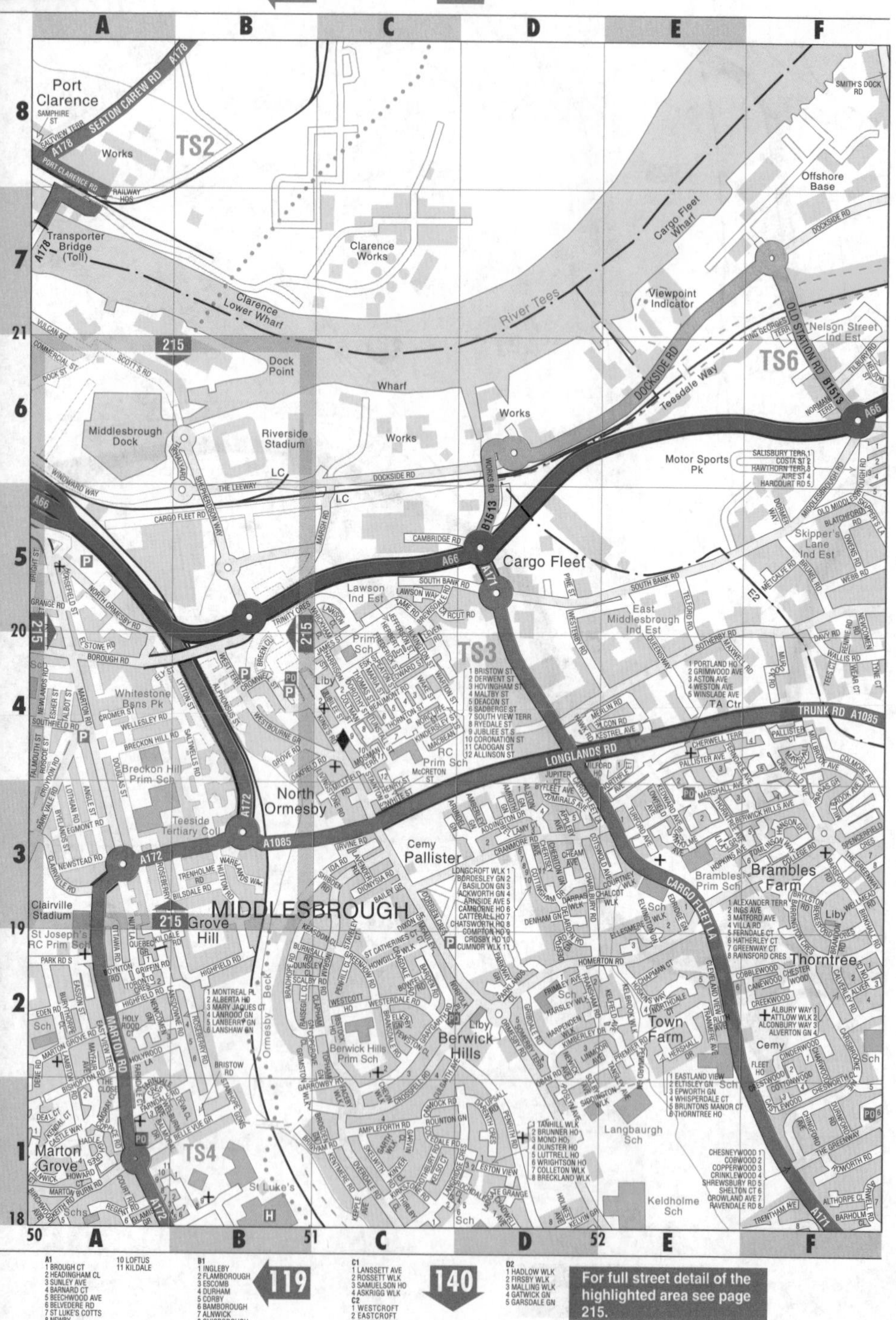

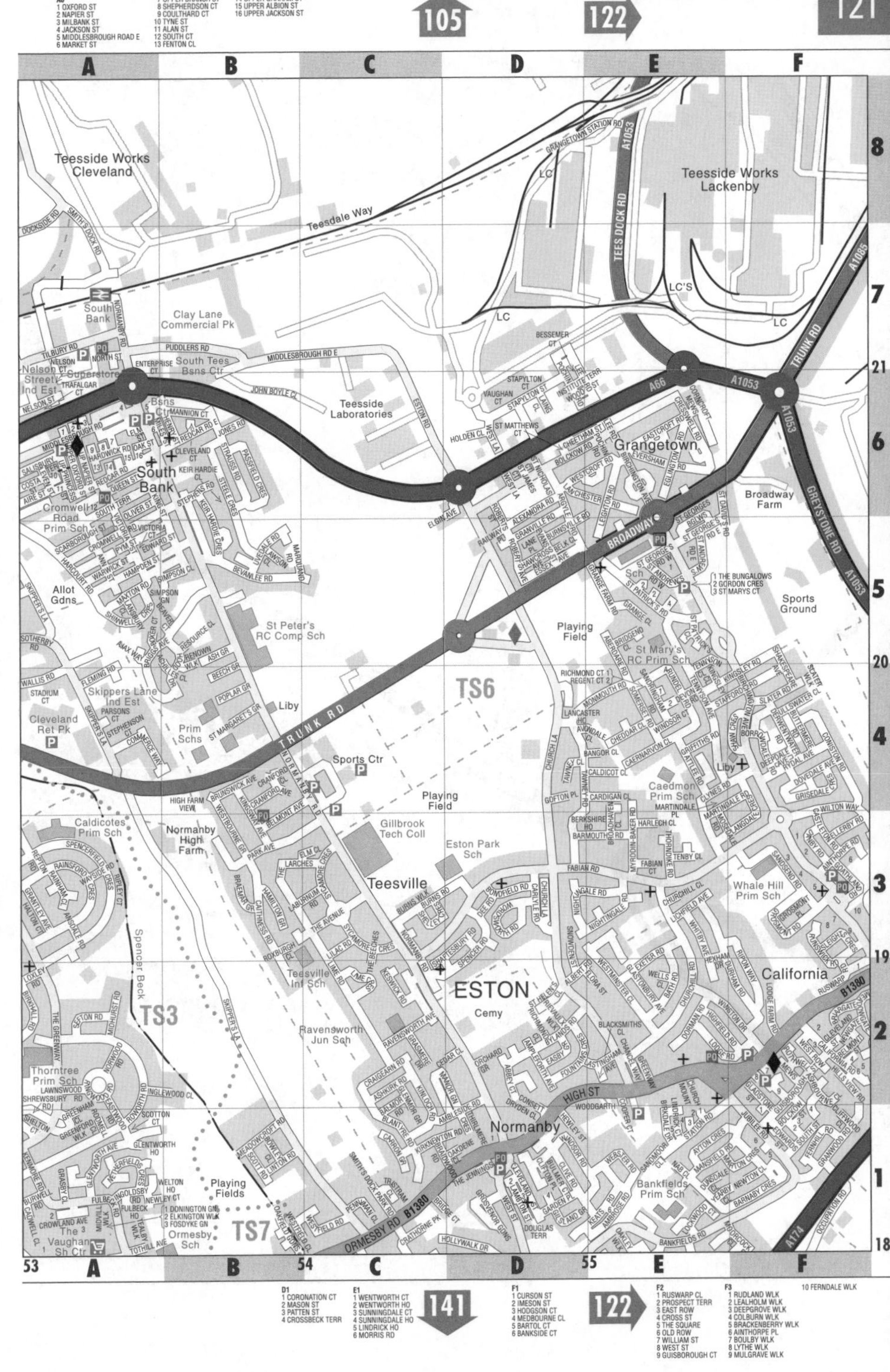
A6
1 OXFORD ST
2 NAPIER ST
3 MILBANK ST
4 JACKSON ST
5 MIDDLESBROUGH ROAD E
6 MARKET ST
7 UPPER BRANCH ST
8 SHEPHERDSON CT
9 COULTHARD CT
10 TYNE ST
11 ALAN ST
12 SOUTH CT
13 FENTON CL
14 UPPER GRAHAM ST
15 UPPER ALBION ST
16 UPPER JACKSON ST
105
122
Teesside Works Cleveland
Teesdale Way
South Bank
Clay Lane Commercial Pk
South Tees Bsns Ctr
Nelson Street Ind Est
Superstore
Teesside Laboratories
Teesside Works Lackenby
GRANGETOWN STATION RD
TEES DOCK RD
A1053
A1085
TRUNK RD
A66
Grangetown
Broadway Farm
BROADWAY
GREYSTONE RD
Sports Ground
Playing Field
St Mary's RC Prim Sch
St Peter's RC Comp Sch
TS6
Skippers Lane Ind Est
Cleveland Ret Pk
Allot Gdns
Cromwell Road Prim Sch
Prim Schs
Liby
Sports Ctr
Playing Field
Gillbrook Tech Coll
Eston Park Sch
Caedmon Prim Sch
Whale Hill Prim Sch
Caldicotes Prim Sch
Normanby High Farm
Teesville
Teesville Inf Sch
Ravensworth Jun Sch
ESTON
Cemy
California
TS3
Spencer Beck
Thorntree Prim Sch
Normanby
HIGH ST
B1380
Playing Fields
TS7
Ormesby Sch
The Vaughan Sh Ctr
Bankfields Prim Sch
A174
ORMESBY RD
1 DONINGTON GN
2 ELKINGTON WLK
3 FOSDYKE GN
1 THE BUNGALOWS
2 GORDON CRES
3 ST MARYS CT
53
54
55
D1
1 CORONATION CT
2 MASON ST
3 PATTEN ST
4 CROSSBECK TERR
E1
1 WENTWORTH CT
2 WENTWORTH HO
3 SUNNINGDALE CT
4 SUNNINGDALE HO
5 LINDRICK HO
6 MORRIS RD
141
F1
1 CURSON ST
2 IMESON ST
3 HODGSON CT
4 MEDBOURNE CL
5 BARTOL CT
6 BANKSIDE CT
122
F2
1 RUSWARP CL
2 PROSPECT TERR
3 EAST ROW
4 CROSS ST
5 THE SQUARE
6 OLD ROW
7 WILLIAM ST
8 WEST ST
9 GUISBOROUGH CT
F3
1 RUDLAND WLK
2 LEALHOLM WLK
3 DEEPGROVE WLK
4 COLBURN WLK
5 BRACKENBERRY WLK
6 AINTHORPE PL
7 BOULBY WLK
8 LYTHE WLK
9 MULGRAVE WLK
10 FERNDALE WLK

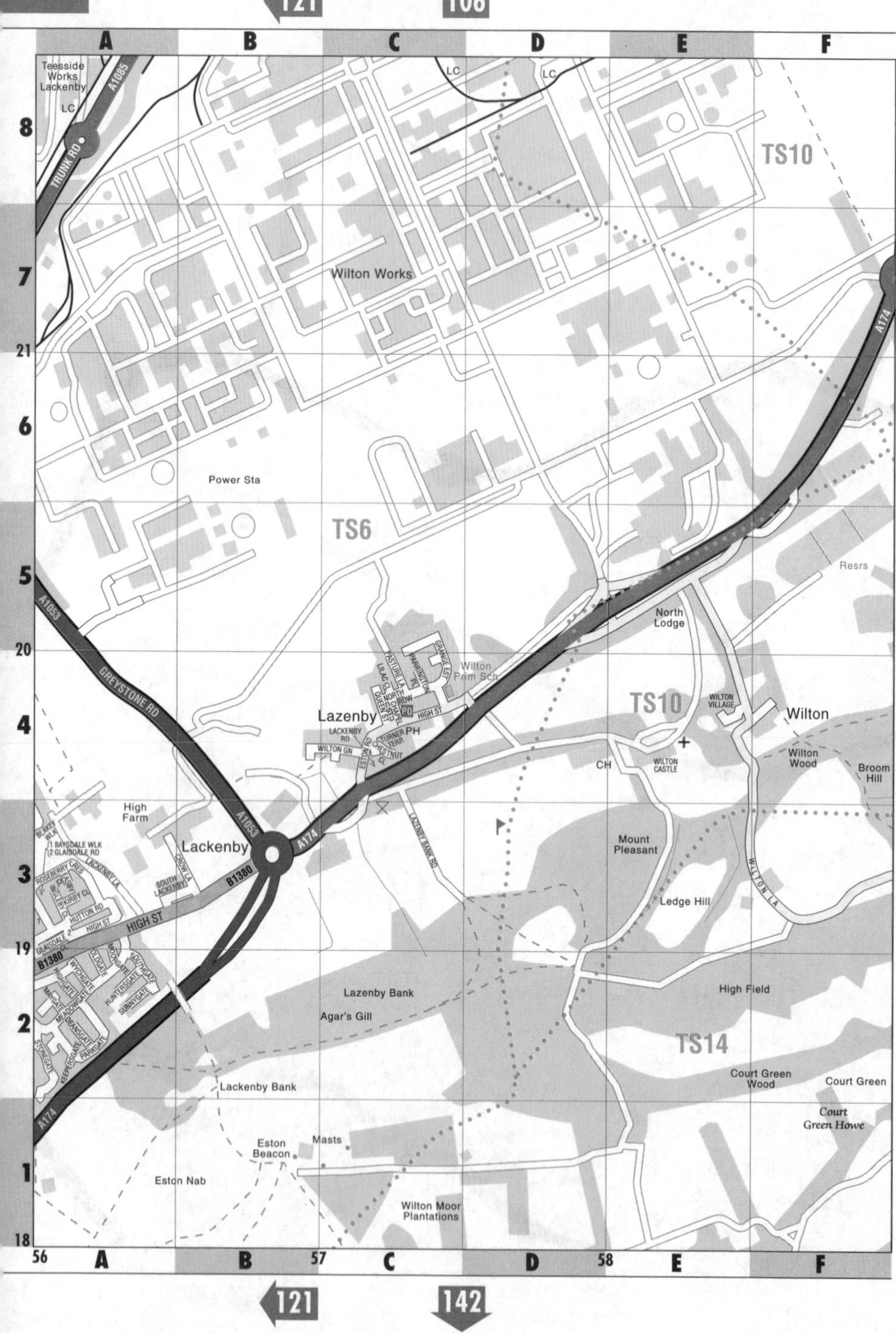

121
106

TS10

Teesside
Works
Lackenby
LC

LC

LC

Wilton Works

21

Power Sta

TS6

Resrs

North
Lodge

Wilton Prim Sch

GREYSTONE RD

Lazenby

LACKENBY
RD
NORTH
TERR
WILTON GN
TURNER PH

TS10

WILTON
VILLAGE

Wilton

Wilton
Wood

Broom
Hill

CH

WILTON
CASTLE

High
Farm

1 BAYDALE WLK
2 GLAISDALE RD

Lackenby

SOUTH
LACKENBY

B1380

HIGH ST

ROSEBERRY CRES

SURREY CL

HUTTON RD

Mount
Pleasant

Ledge Hill

B1380

LACKENBY BANK RD

High Field

TS14

Lazenby Bank

Agar's Gill

Court Green
Wood

Court Green

Lackenby Bank

Court
Green Howe

Eston
Beacon

Masts

1

Eston Nab

Wilton Moor
Plantations

18

56

57

58

121
142

107
124

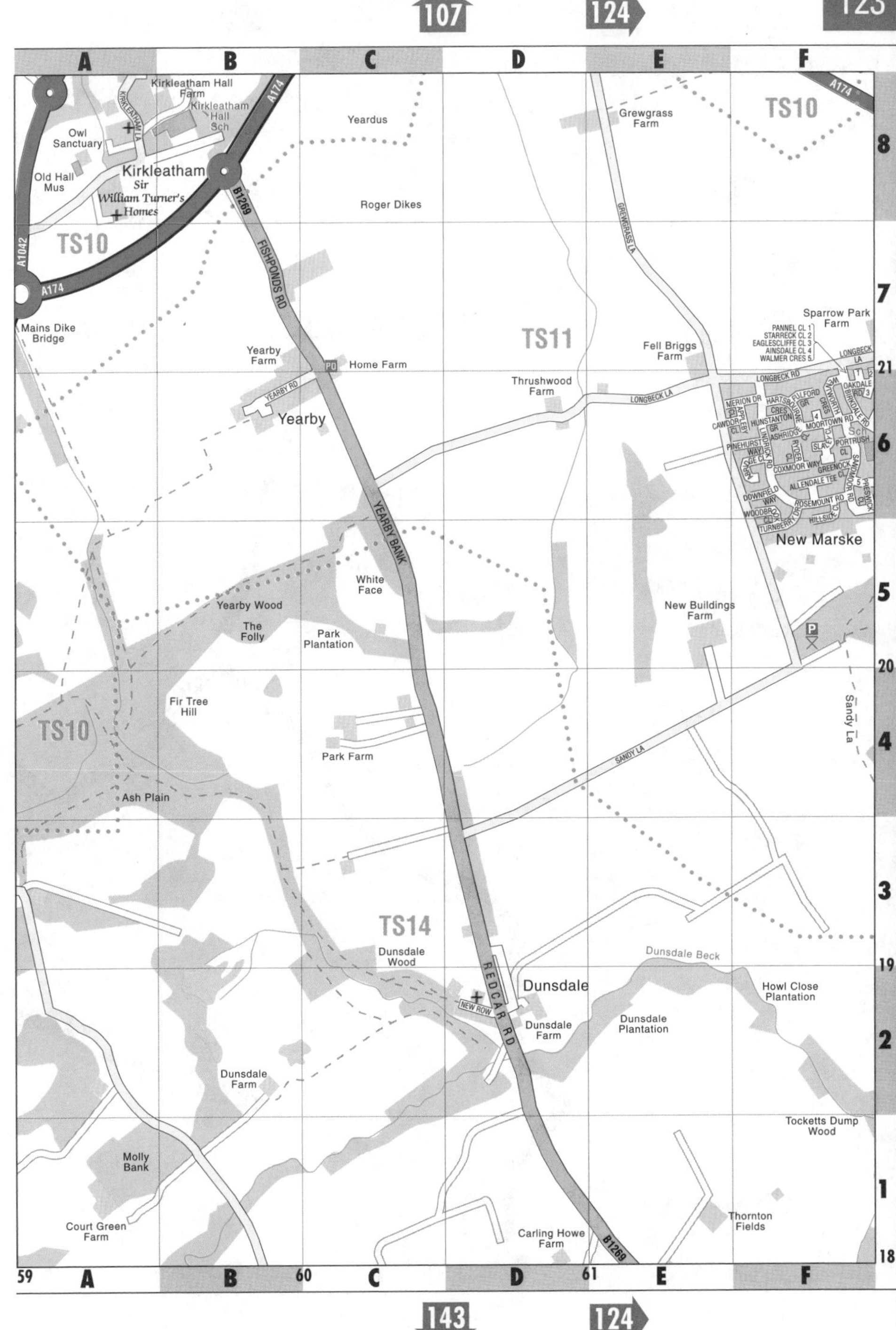
A
B
C
D
E
F
Kirkleatham Hall Farm
Kirkleatham Hall Sch
KIRKLEATHAM LA
A174
Owl Sanctuary
Old Hall Mus
Kirkleatham
Sir William Turner's Homes
TS10
A1042
A174
Yeardus
Roger Dikes
B1269
FISHPONDS RD
Grewgrass Farm
TS10
A174
GREWGRASS LA
Mains Dike Bridge
Yearby Farm
PO
Home Farm
YEARBY RD
Yearby
TS11
Thrushwood Farm
LONGBECK LA
Fell Briggs Farm
Sparrow Park Farm
PANNEL CL 1
STARRECK CL 2
EAGLESCLIFFE CL 3
AINSDALE CL 4
WALMER CRES 5
LONGBECK LA
LONGBECK RD
MERION DR
HARTSBOURNE CRES
FULFORD GR
CRES
WENTWORTH
OAKDALE RD
BIRKDALE RD
CAWDOR CL
APPLEBY CL
HUNSTANTON GR
MOORTOWN RD
ASHRIDGE CL
LINDRICK RD
PINEHURST WAY
RYDER CL
SLALEY CL
PORTRUSH CL
Sch
COXMOOR WAY
GREENOCK CL
SANDMOOR RD
ALLENDALE TEE
PRESWICK CL
DOWNFIELD WAY
ROSEMOUNT RD
WOODBROOK CL
TURNBERRY DR
HILLSIDE CL
New Marske
YEARBY BANK
White Face
Yearby Wood
The Folly
Park Plantation
New Buildings Farm
P
Fir Tree Hill
TS10
Park Farm
SANDY LA
Sandy La
Ash Plain
TS14
Dunsdale Wood
Dunsdale Beck
REDCAR RD
Dunsdale
NEW ROW
Dunsdale Farm
Dunsdale Plantation
Howl Close Plantation
Dunsdale Farm
Tocketts Dump Wood
Molly Bank
Court Green Farm
Carling Howe Farm
B1269
Thornton Fields
8
7
21
6
5
20
4
3
19
2
1
18
59
60
61

143
124

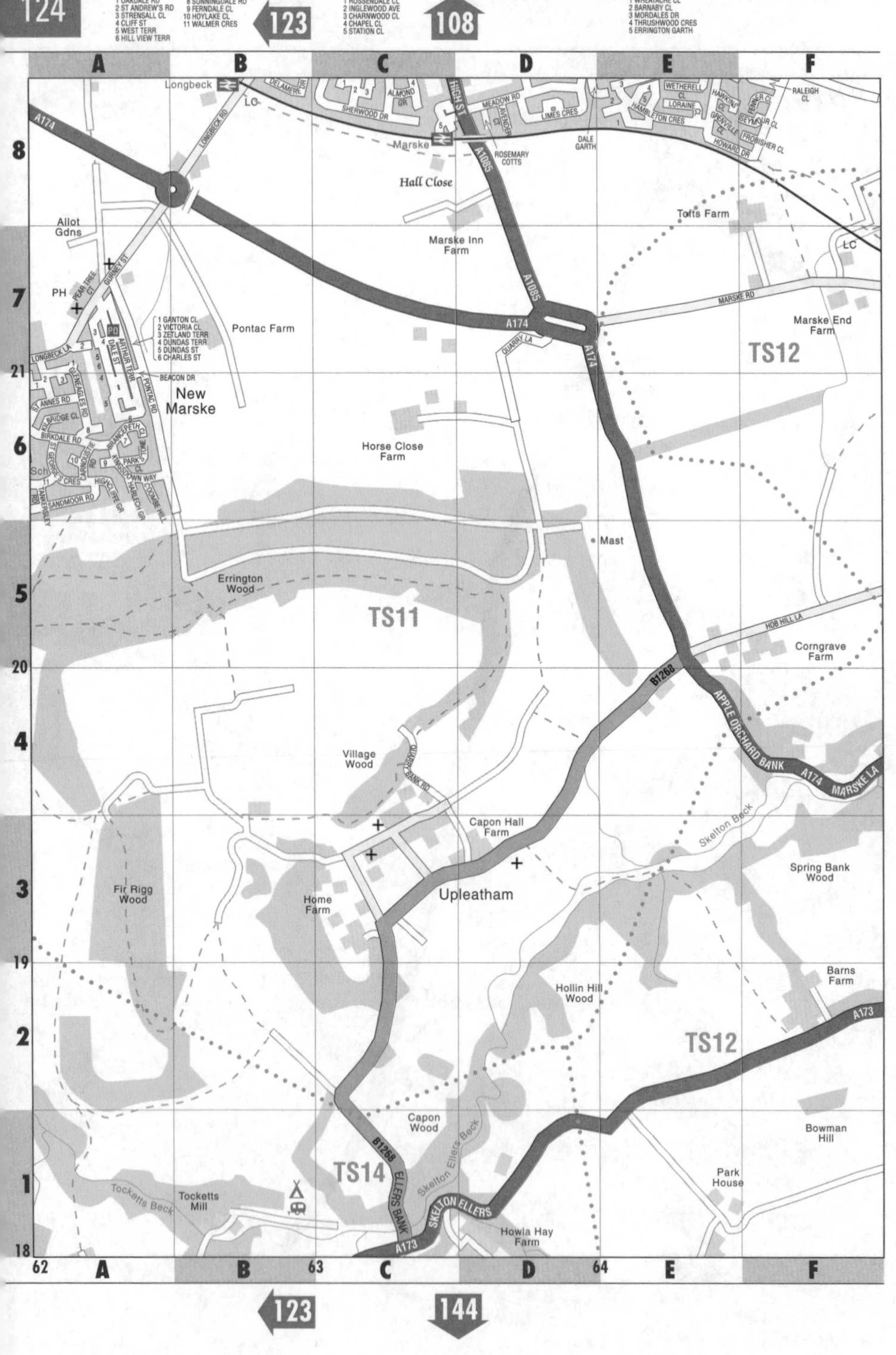

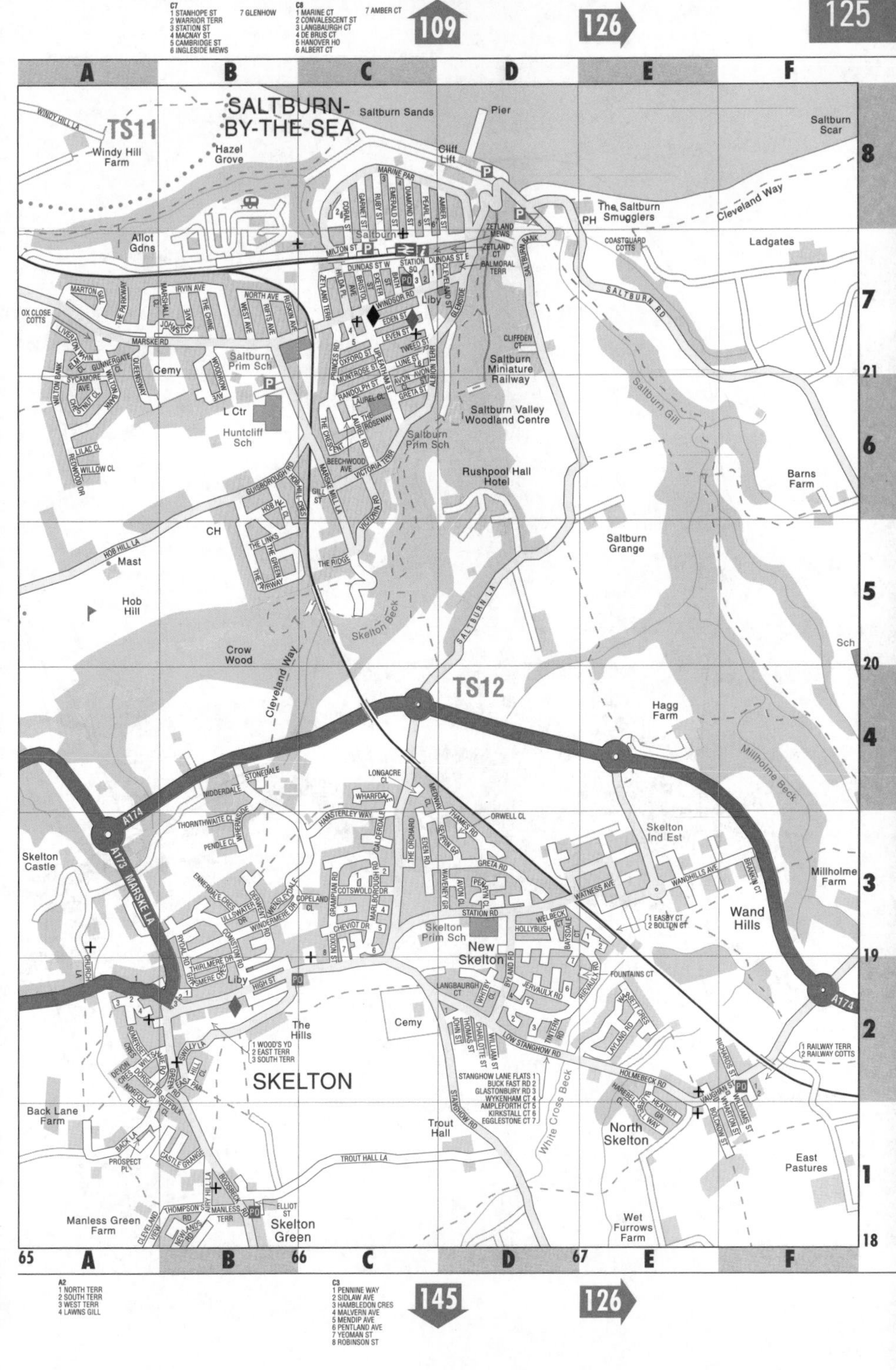

C7
1 STANHOPE ST
2 WARRIOR TERR
3 STATION ST
4 MACNAY ST
5 CAMBRIDGE ST
6 INGLESIDE MEWS
7 GLENHOW
C8
1 MARINE CT
2 CONVALESCENT ST
3 LANGBAURGH CT
4 DE BRUS CT
5 HANOVER HO
6 ALBERT CT
7 AMBER CT
109
126
A
B
C
D
E
F
SALTBURN-BY-THE-SEA
Saltburn Sands
Pier
Saltburn Scar
TS11
Windy Hill Farm
Hazel Grove
Cliff Lift
The Saltburn Smugglers
Cleveland Way
Ladgates
Allot Gdns
Saltburn
COASTGUARD COTTS
SALTBURN RD
MARSKE RD
Saltburn Prim Sch
Cemy
L Ctr
Huntcliff Sch
Saltburn Miniature Railway
Saltburn Valley Woodland Centre
Saltburn Gill
Rushpool Hall Hotel
Barns Farm
CH
HOB HILL LA
Mast
Hob Hill
Saltburn Grange
Skelton Beck
SALTBURN LA
Crow Wood
Sch
TS12
Hagg Farm
Millholme Beck
A174
A173
MARSKE LA
Skelton Castle
Skelton Ind Est
Millholme Farm
Wand Hills
Skelton Prim Sch
New Skelton
Liby
The Hills
Cemy
1 WOOD'S YD
2 EAST TERR
3 SOUTH TERR
SKELTON
STANGHOW LANE FLATS 1
BUCK FAST RD 2
GLASTONBURY RD 3
WYKENHAM CT 4
AMPLEFORTH CT 5
KIRKSTALL CT 6
EGGLESTONE CT 7
1 RAILWAY TERR
2 RAILWAY COTTS
1 EASBY CT
2 BOLTON CT
Back Lane Farm
Trout Hall
TROUT HALL LA
White Cross Beck
North Skelton
East Pastures
Manless Green Farm
Skelton Green
Wet Furrows Farm
8
7
21
6
5
20
4
3
19
2
1
18
65
66
67
A2
1 NORTH TERR
2 SOUTH TERR
3 WEST TERR
4 LAWNS GILL
C3
1 PENNINE WAY
2 SIDLAW AVE
3 HAMBLEDON CRES
4 MALVERN AVE
5 MENDIP AVE
6 PENTLAND AVE
7 YEOMAN ST
8 ROBINSON ST
145
126

125

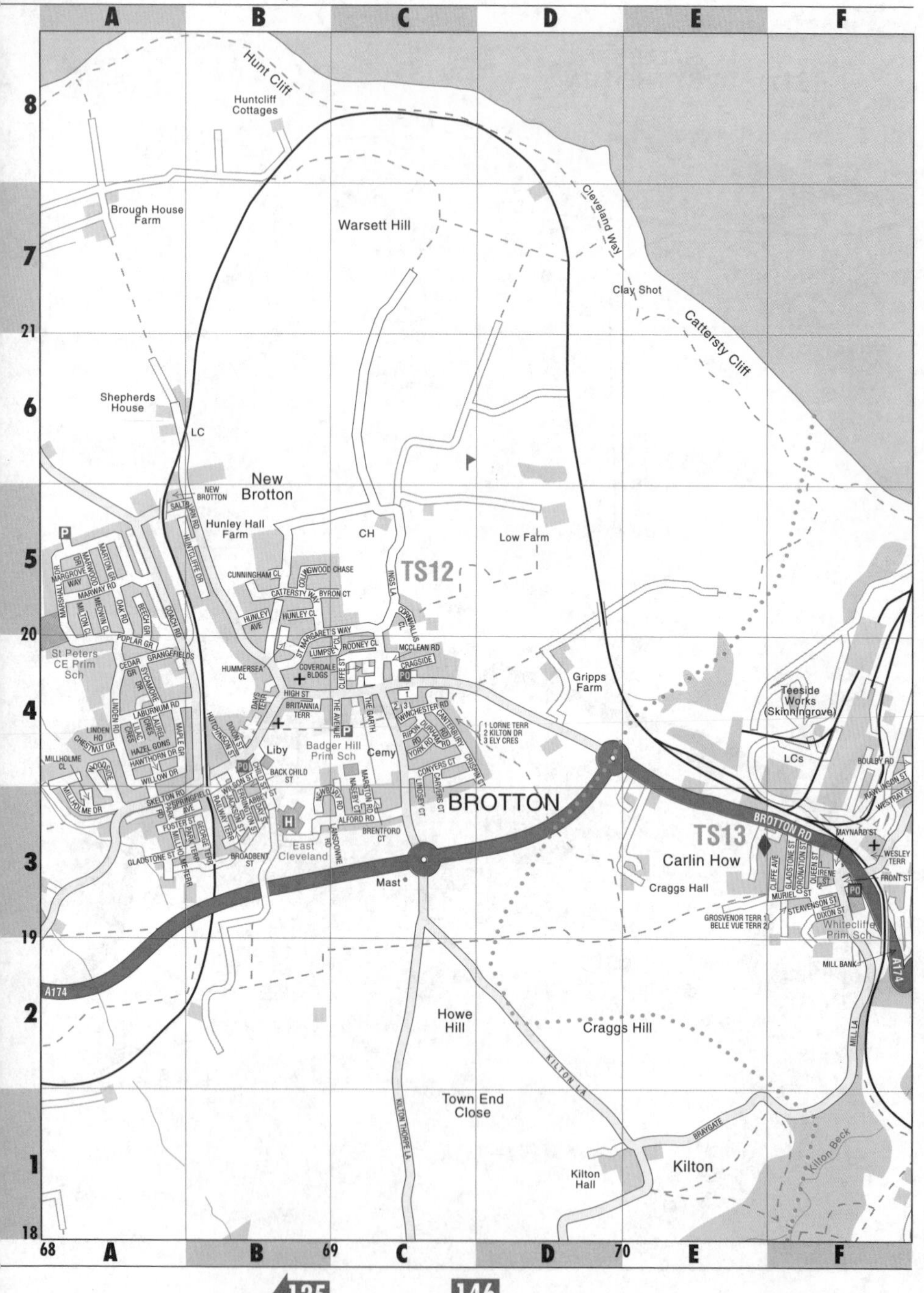
A
B
C
D
E
F
8
7
21
6
5
20
4
3
19
2
1
18
68
69
70
Hunt Cliff
Huntcliff Cottages
Brough House Farm
Warsett Hill
Cleveland Way
Clay Shot
Cattersty Cliff
Shepherds House
LC
New Brotton
Hunley Hall Farm
CH
Low Farm
TS12
St Peters CE Prim Sch
Gripps Farm
Teeside Works (Skinningrove)
LCs
Liby
Badger Hill Prim Sch
Cemy
BROTTON
BROTTON RD
TS13
Carlin How
Craggs Hall
East Cleveland
Mast
Whitecliffe Prim Sch
A174
Howe Hill
Craggs Hill
Town End Close
Kilton Hall
Kilton
Kilton Beck
KILTON LA
KILTON THORPE LA
BRAYGATE
MILL LA
MILL BANK
1 LORNE TERR
2 KILTON DR
3 ELY CRES
GROSVENOR TERR 1
BELLE VUE TERR 2
HIGH ST
BRITANNIA TERR
THE AVENUE
THE GARTH
COVERDALE BLDGS
CUNNINGHAM CL
CATTERSTY WAY
BYRON CT
HUNLEY CL
HUNLEY AVE
ST MARGARET'S WAY
RODNEY CL
LUMPSEY CL
MCCLEAN RD
CRAGSIDE
HUMMERSEA CL
WINCHESTER RD
CANTERBURY RD
RIPON RD
DURHAM RD
YORK RD
CONYERS CT
CARVERS CT
CRISPIN CT
LINDSEY CT
MARSTON RD
NASEBY CL
NEWBURY RD
ALFORD RD
BRENTFORD CT
LANSDOWNE RD
BACK CHILD ST
CHILD ST
HUTCHINSON ST
DIXON ST
SKELTON RD
SPRINGFIELD AVE
FOSTER ST
PARK ST
GEORGE TERR
MILLHOLME TERR
GLADSTONE ST
BROADBENT ST
RAILWAY TERR
ABBEY ST
SALTBURN RD
HUNTCLIFFE DR
COACH RD
MARSHALL DR
MARGROVE WAY
MARTON GR
MARWAY RD
MILTON CL
MEDWIN CL
OAK RD
BEECH GR
POPLAR GR
CEDAR GR
GRANGEFIELDS
SYCAMORE DR
LINDEN RD
LINDEN HO
LABURNUM RD
LILAC CRES
LAUREL CRES
MAPLE GR
HAZEL GDNS
HAWTHORN DR
WILLOW DR
CHESTNUT GR
MILLHOLME CL
MILLHOLME DR
BOULBY RD
RAWLINSON ST
WESTRAY ST
MAYNARD ST
WESLEY TERR
FRONT ST
CLIFFE AVE
GLADSTONE ST
CORONATION ST
QUEEN ST
IRENE ST
MURIEL ST
STEAVENSON ST
DIXON ST
PO
P
H

125

146

A
B
C
D
E
F
8
7
21
6
5
20
4
3
19
2
1
18
71
72
73
Jetty
Hummersea Point
Cleveland Way
Hummersea Bank
The Warren
Warsett Hill
Skinningrove
Skinningrove Farm
Hummersea Farm
Spring House Farm
Mining Mus
TS13
Deepdale Farm
Downdinner Hill
Micklow Hill
Upton Farm
Rose Hill Farm
Grange Farm
LOFTUS
Hummersea Prim Sch
Butter Bank
East Loftus
Harry Dack Inf Sch
Loftus Jun Sch
Liby
Cemy
FAR FOULSYKE
PH
LOFTUS BANK
WEST RD
HIGH ST
ARLINGTON ST
WHITBY RD
A174
B1366
SKINNINGROVE BANK RD
HUMMERSEA LA
MICKLOW LA
CROSS LA
GRANGE LA
UPTON HILL
UPTON COTTS
1 NEW GROVE TERR
2 WILSON TERR
3 NEW COMPANY ROW
1 SEYMOUR HILL TERR
2 ROBINSON TERR
3 PARK TERR
SCARBOROUGH ST 1
CLIFF CRES 2
WHITECLIFF TERR 1
RAILWAY TERR 2
CO-OPERATIVE CL
MARINE TERR
LARVIK CT
ROCKCLIFFE VIEW
ROCKCLIFFE TERR
BOULBY RD
MOUNT PLEASANT
OVERMANS COTTS
PRIMROSE HILL
ANGLING GN
GROVE RD
HUTTON ST
ZETLAND ROW
GROVE HILL
MILL LA
SKINNINGROVE RD
DEEPDALE LA
DEEPDALE RD
NORTH TERR
WESTFIELD WLK
WESTFIELD WAY
ROSEDALE CRES
QUEENS RD
OAK WLK
PINE WLK
ELM WLK
LIME WLK
CEDAR GR
ASH GR
BEECH GR
CORONATION RD
SYCAMORE WLK
HAZEL WLK
ZETLAND TERR
NEWCOMMEN TERR
CLEVELAND ST
EAST ST
GLADSTONE ST
NORTH RD
SOUTH VIEW
ST HILDA'S PL
VICTORIA TERR
MICKLOW TERR
EAST CRES
CHAPEL ROW
ZETLAND RD
STATION RD
DUNDAS ST
WEST PARK AVE
MILL VIEW
NEW LONDON RD
LIVERTON TERR
GRAHAM ST
DOWNE ST
LOW CLEVELAND ST
LIVERTON RD
HIRDS DR
LAUREL RD
GASKELL LA
CO-OPERATIVE TERR
WOOD VIEW
HALL GROUNDS
WATER LA
LINGBERRY GARTH
CHURCH ROW
BOULBY DR
GRENDALE CT
CROMWELL AVE
ROBINSON ST
TEES ST
TYNE ST
TWEED ST
DERWENT PK
HUMBER CL
LOY LA
WREN ST
DAM ST
JOHN ST
SPRING HEAD TERR
ST HILDA'S TERR
HARTINGTON ST
CONSCOTT
KENNEDY CRES
P
PO

147
128

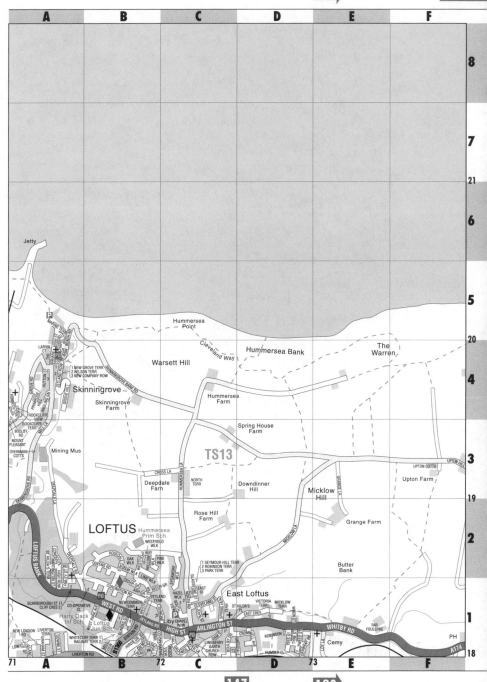

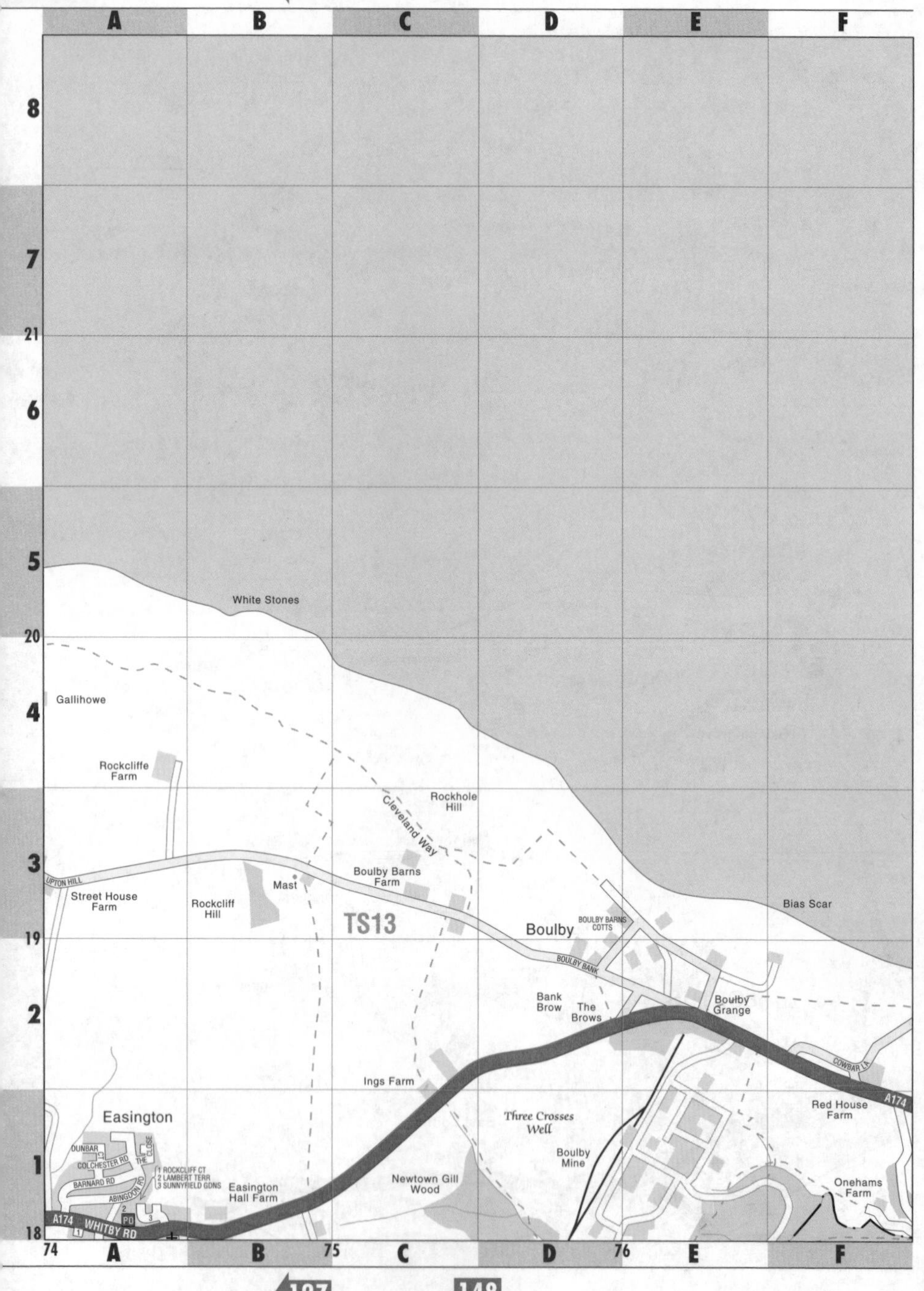

A   B   C   D   E   F

8

7

21

6

5

White Stones

20

4   Gallihowe

Rockcliffe
Farm

Rockhole
Hill

Cleveland Way

3   UPTON HILL

Street House
Farm

Rockcliff
Hill

Mast

Boulby Barns
Farm

TS13

Boulby

BOULBY BARNS
COTTS

Bias Scar

19

BOULBY BANK

2

Bank
Brow   The
Brows

Boulby
Grange

DUNBAR LN

A174

Ings Farm

Red House
Farm

1

Easington

DUNBAR
COLCHESTER RD   THE
BARNARD RD

1 ROCKCLIFF CT
2 LAMBERT TERR
3 SUNNYFIELD GDNS

ABINGDON

Easington
Hall Farm

Three Crosses
Well

Newtown Gill
Wood

Boulby
Mine

Onehams
Farm

18   A174   WHITBY RD   PO

74   A   B   75   C   D   76   E   F

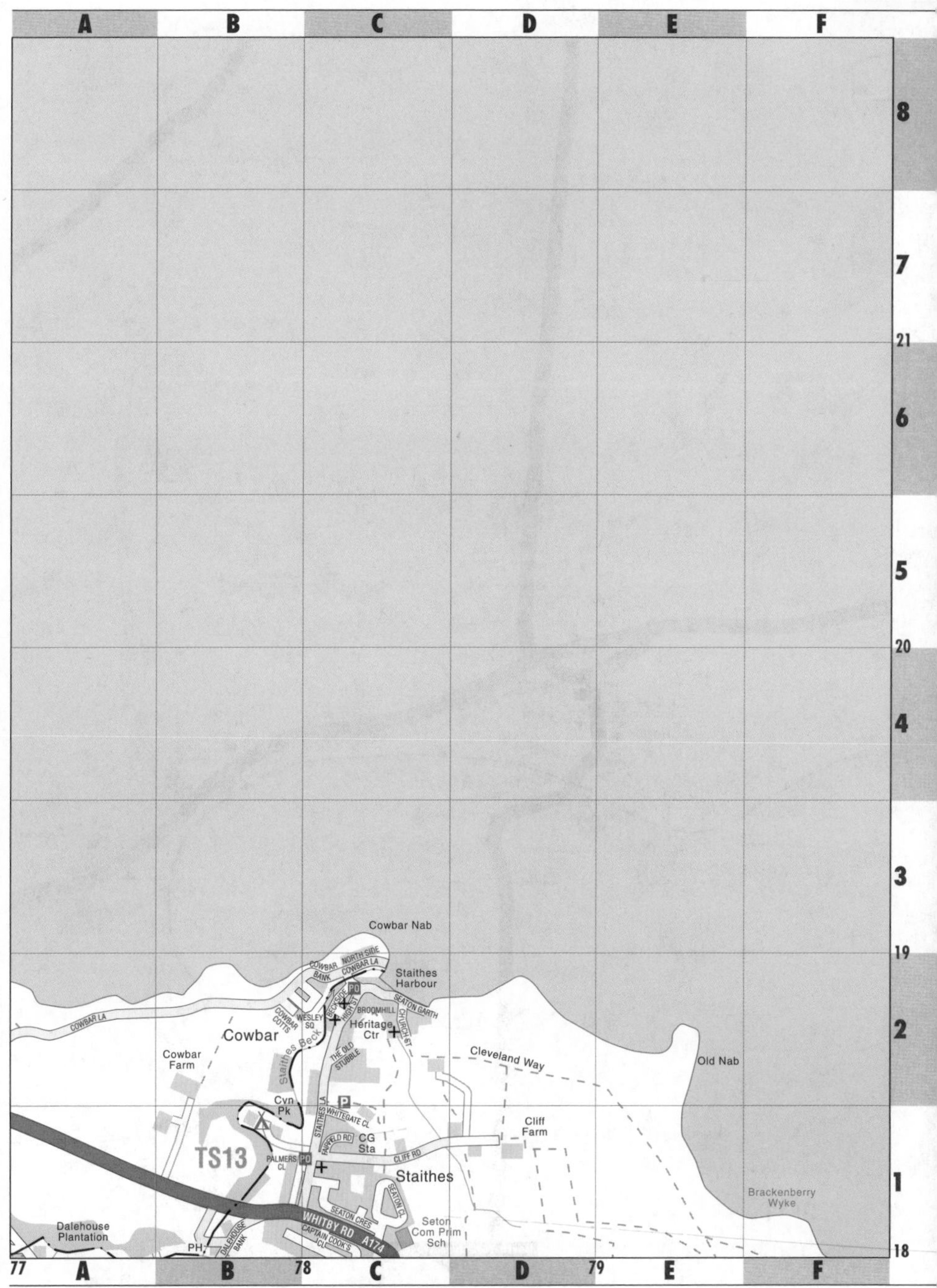
A
B
C
D
E
F
8
7
21
6
5
20
4
3
19
2
1
18
77
78
79
Cowbar Nab
Staithes Harbour
COWBAR BANK
NORTH SIDE
COWBAR LA
COWBAR LA
COWBAR COTTS
WESLEY SQ
BECKSIDE
HIGH ST
BROOMHILL
SEATON GARTH
CHURCH ST
Heritage Ctr
Cowbar
Staithes Beck
THE OLD STUBBLE
Cleveland Way
Old Nab
Cowbar Farm
Cyn Pk
STAITHES LA
WHITEGATE CL
FAIRFIELD RD
CG Sta
Cliff Farm
TS13
PALMERS CL
CLIFF RD
Staithes
SEATON CL
Brackenberry Wyke
SEATON CRES
Seton Com Prim Sch
WHITBY RD A174
CAPTAIN COOK'S CL
Dalehouse Plantation
PH
DALEHOUSE BANK

149

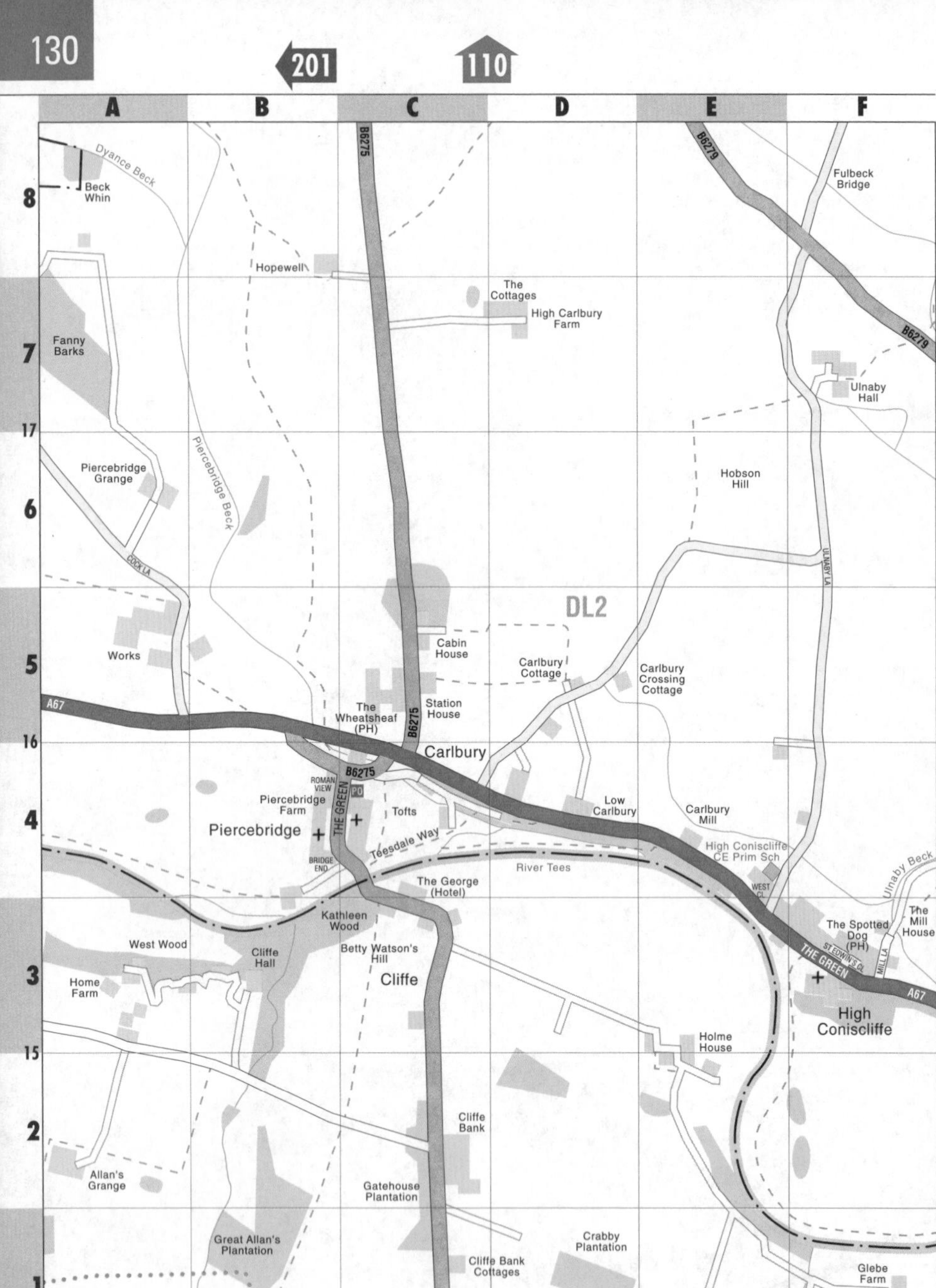

Dyance Beck

Beck Whin

Hopewell

The Cottages

High Carlbury Farm

Fulbeck Bridge

B6279

Fanny Barks

Ulnaby Hall

Piercebridge Grange

Piercebridge Beck

Hobson Hill

DL2

Works

Cabin House

Carlbury Cottage

Carlbury Crossing Cottage

A67

The Wheatsheaf (PH)

Station House

B6275

Carlbury

ROMAN VIEW

Piercebridge Farm

THE GREEN

Tofts

Low Carlbury

Carlbury Mill

Carlbury

Ulnaby Beck

Piercebridge

Teesdale Way

High Coniscliffe CE Prim Sch

BRIDGE END

River Tees

WEST

The George (Hotel)

Kathleen Wood

The Spotted Dog (PH)

The Mill House

West Wood

Cliffe Hall

Betty Watson's Hill

Cliffe

THE GREEN

A67

Home Farm

High Coniscliffe

Holme House

Cliffe Bank

Allan's Grange

Gatehouse Plantation

Crabby Plantation

Great Allan's Plantation

Cliffe Bank Cottages

Glebe Farm

B6275

Manfield Gill

DL11

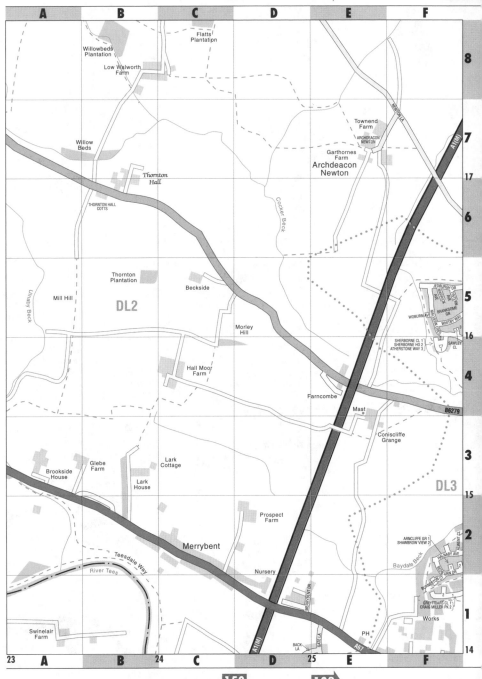

132

A B C D E F

8 7 17 6 5 16 4 3 15 2 1 14

Flatts Plantation
Willowbeds Plantation
Low Walworth Farm
NEWTON LA
Townend Farm
ARCHDEACON NEWTON
Garthornes Farm
Archdeacon Newton
A1(M)
Willow Beds
Thornton Hall
THORNTON HALL COTTS
Cocker Beck
Thornton Plantation
Beckside
Mill Hill
Ulnaby Beck
DL2
JEDBURGH DR
MARRICK AVE
AVE
TINTERN AVE
BRANKSOME GN
WOBURN AVE
MALVERN CRES
WHITBY WAY
Morley Hill
SHERBORNE CL 1
SHERBORNE HO 2
ATHERSTONE WAY 3
SAWLEY CL
D
Hall Moor Farm
Farncombe
Mast
B6279
Conscliffe Grange
Brookside House
Glebe Farm
Lark Cottage
Lark House
DL3
Prospect Farm
ARNCLIFFE GR 1
SHAWBROW VIEW 2
ALWENT CL
HALNABY AVE
Baydale Beck
BEDBURN DR
BURNESTON CT
Merrybent
Teesdale Way
River Tees
Nursery
MERRYBENT DR
GREYFRIARS CL 1
CRAIG MILLER PK 2
Works
Swinelair Farm
BACK LA
GATE LA
PH
A67

23 A B 24 C D 25 E F

150

132

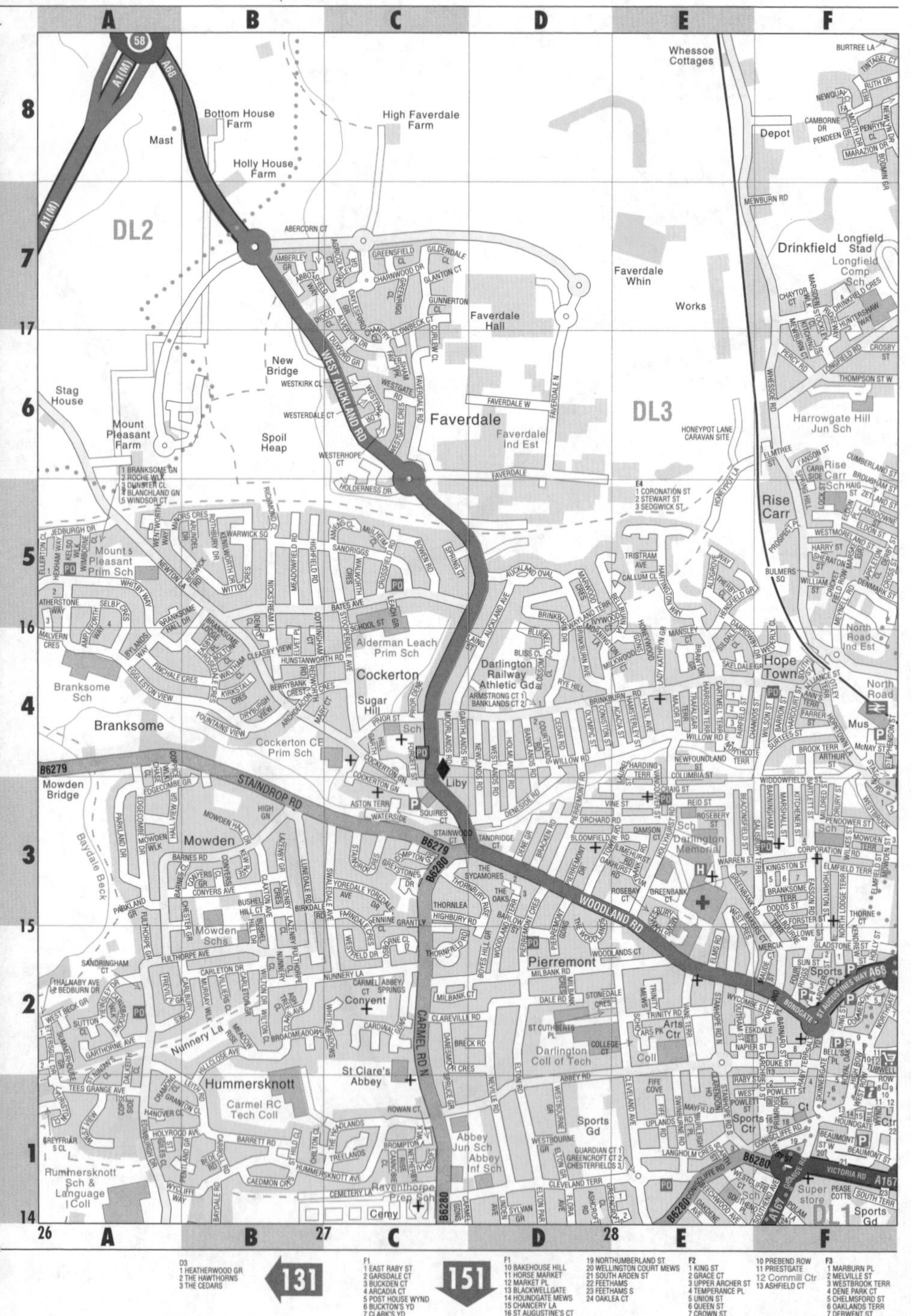

D3
1 HEATHERWOOD GR
2 THE HAWTHORNS
3 THE CEDARS

F1
1 EAST RABY ST
10 HORSE MARKET
11 MARKET PL
12 MARKET PL
13 BLACKWELLGATE
14 HOUNDGATE MEWS
15 CHANCERY LA
16 ST AUGUSTINE'S CT
17 LARCHFIELD HO
18 HOGARTH CT

F1
10 BAKEHOUSE HILL
11 HORSE MARKET
12 MARKET PL
13 BLACKWELLGATE
14 HOUNDGATE MEWS
15 CHANCERY LA
16 ST AUGUSTINE'S CT
17 LARCHFIELD HO
18 HOGARTH CT

2 BUCKDEN CT
3 ARCADIA CT
4 ARCADIA CT
5 POST HOUSE WYND
6 BUCKTON'S YD
7 CLAIRE'S YD
8 EAST ROW
9 CHURCH ROW

19 NORTHUMBERLAND ST
20 WELLINGTON COURT MEWS
21 SOUTH ARDEN ST
22 FEETHAMS
23 FEETHAMS S
24 OAKLEA CT

F2
1 KING ST
2 GRACE CT
3 UPPER ARCHER ST
4 TEMPERANCE PL
5 UNION ST
6 QUEEN ST
7 CROWN ST
8 WINSTON ST
9 PROSPECT PL

10 PREBEND ROW
11 PRIESTGATE
12 Cornmill Ctr
13 ASHFIELD CT

F3
1 MARBURN PL
2 MELVILLE ST
3 WESTBROOK TERR
4 DENE PARK CT
5 CHELMSFORD ST
6 OAKLANDS TERR
7 DERWENT ST

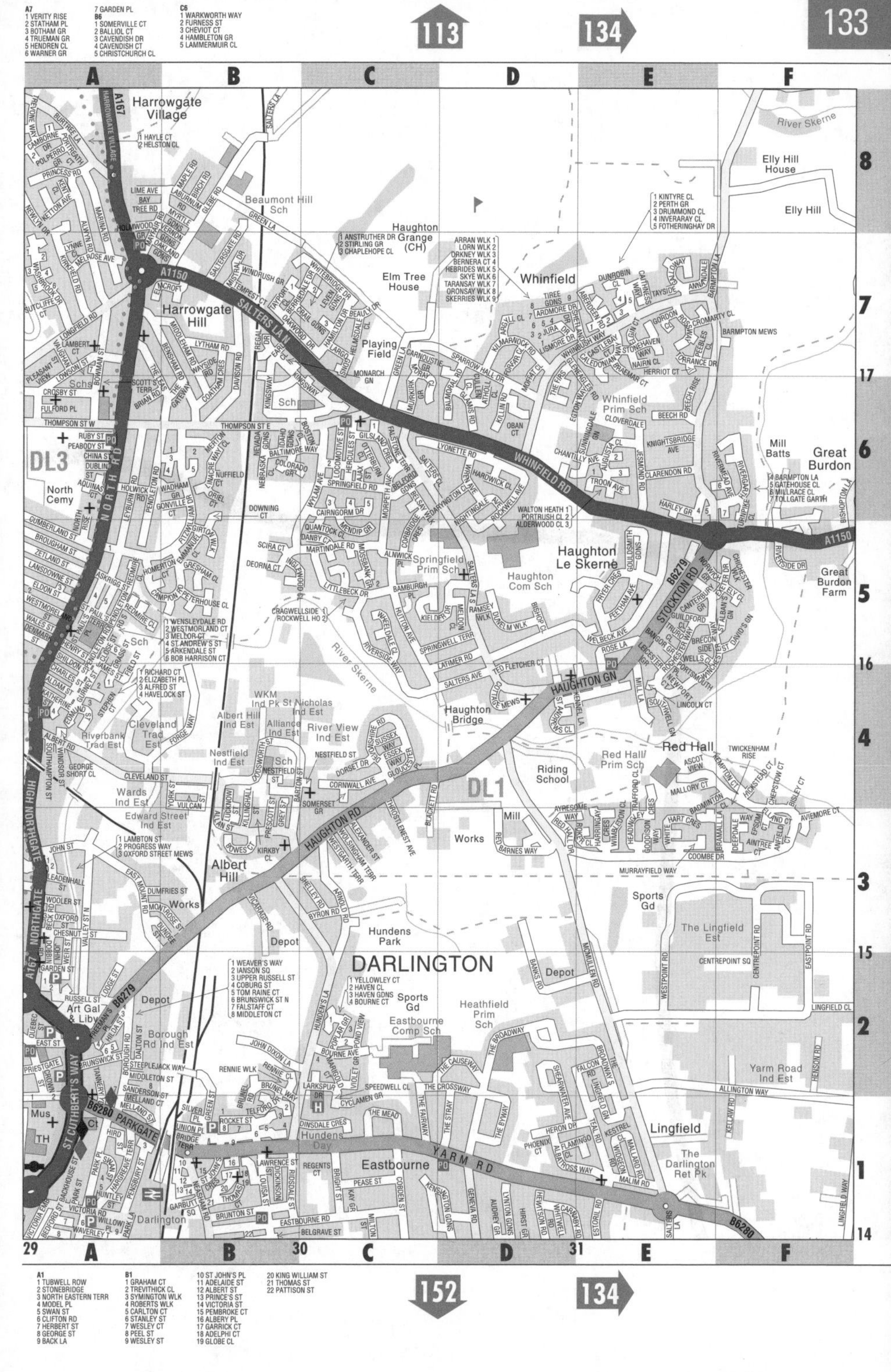

133
113
134
152
A7
1 VERITY RISE
2 STATHAM PL
3 BOTHAM GR
4 TRUEMAN GR
5 HENDREN CL
6 WARNER GR
7 GARDEN PL
B6
1 SOMERVILLE CT
2 BALLIOL CT
3 CAVENDISH DR
4 CAVENDISH CT
5 CHRISTCHURCH CL
C6
1 WARKWORTH WAY
2 FURNESS ST
3 CHEVIOT CT
4 HAMBLETON GR
5 LAMMERMUIR CL
A
B
C
D
E
F
8
7
17
6
5
16
4
3
15
2
1
14
29
30
31
Harrowgate Village
1 HAYLE CT
2 HELSTON CL
Beaumont Hill Sch
River Skerne
Elly Hill House
Elly Hill
1 KINTYRE CL
2 PERTH GR
3 DRUMMOND CL
4 INVERARAY CL
5 FOTHERINGHAY DR
1 ANSTRUTHER DR
2 STIRLING GR
3 CHAPLEHOPE CL
Haughton Grange (CH)
ARRAN WLK 1
LORN WLK 2
ORKNEY WLK 3
BERNERA CT 4
HEBRIDES WLK 5
SKYE WLK 6
TARANSAY WLK 7
ORONSAY WLK 8
SKERRIES WLK 9
Elm Tree House
Whinfield
Harrowgate Hill
A1150
A167
SALTERS LAN
Playing Field
BARRAMPTON MEWS
Whinfield Prim Sch
WHINFIELD RD
DL3
North Cemy
NORTH RD
Mill Batts
Great Burdon
4 BARMPTON LA
5 GATEHOUSE CL
6 MILLRACE CL
7 TOLLGATE GARTH
WALTON HEATH 1
PORTRUSH CL 2
ALDERWOOD CL 3
Springfield Prim Sch
Haughton Com Sch
Haughton Le Skerne
Great Burdon Farm
B6279
STOCKTON RD
CRAGWELLSIDE 1
ROCKWELL HO 2
1 WENSLEYDALE RD
2 WESTMORLAND CT
3 MELLOR CT
4 ST ANDREW'S ST
5 ARKENDALE ST
6 BOB HARRISON CL
1 RICHARD CT
2 ELIZABETH PL
3 ALFRED ST
4 HAVELOCK ST
HAUGHTON GN
WKM Ind Pk
St Nicholas Ind Est
Albert Hill Ind Est
Alliance Ind Est
River View Ind Est
Cleveland Trad Est
Riverbank Trad Est
Haughton Bridge
Red Hall
Red Hall Prim Sch
Riding School
Nestfield Ind Est
Wards Ind Est
Edward Street Ind Est
DL1
Mill
Works
1 LAMBTON ST
2 PROGRESS WAY
3 OXFORD STREET MEWS
HAUGHTON RD
Albert Hill
Works
Sports Gd
The Lingfield Est
HIGH NORTHGATE
Hundens Park
Depot
DARLINGTON
1 WEAVER'S WAY
2 IANSON SQ
3 UPPER RUSSELL ST
4 COBURG ST
5 TOM RAINE CT
6 BRUNSWICK ST N
7 FALSTAFF CT
8 MIDDLETON CT
1 YELLOWLEY CT
2 HAVEN CL
3 HAVEN GDNS
4 BOURNE CT
Depot
Sports Gd
Heathfield Prim Sch
Eastbourne Comp Sch
Art Gal & Liby
Borough Rd Ind Est
Yarm Road Ind Est
B6280 PARKGATE
ST CUTHBERT'S WAY
Mus
TH
Hundens Day
Eastbourne
YARM RD
Lingfield
The Darlington Ret Pk
B6280
Darlington
A1
1 TUBWELL ROW
2 STONEBRIDGE
3 NORTH EASTERN TERR
4 MODEL PL
5 SWAN ST
6 CLIFTON RD
7 HERBERT ST
8 GEORGE ST
9 BACK LA
B1
1 GRAHAM CT
2 TREVITHICK CL
3 SYMINGTON WLK
4 ROBERTS WLK
5 CARLTON CT
6 STANLEY ST
7 WESLEY CT
8 PEEL ST
9 WESLEY ST
10 ST JOHN'S PL
11 ADELAIDE ST
12 ALBERT ST
13 PRINCE'S ST
14 VICTORIA ST
15 PEMBROKE CT
16 ALBERY PL
17 GARRICK CT
18 ADELPHI CT
19 GLOBE CL
20 KING WILLIAM ST
21 THOMAS ST
22 PATTISON ST

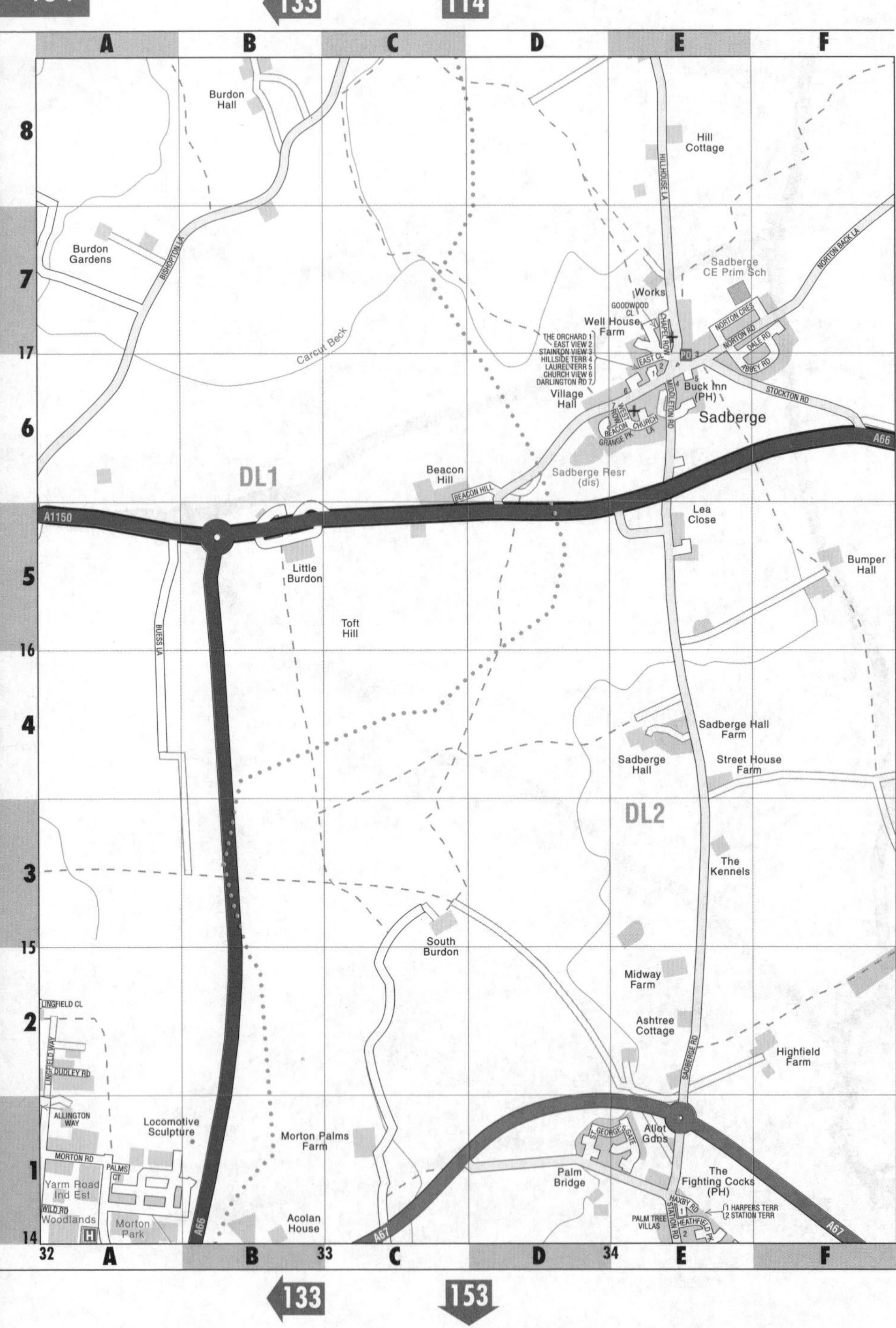
A
B
C
D
E
F
Burdon Hall
Hill Cottage
HILLHOUSE LA
Burdon Gardens
BISHOPTON LA
Sadberge CE Prim Sch
NORTON BACK LA
Works
GOODWOOD CL
Well House Farm
CHAPEL ROW
NORTON CRES
NORTON RD
DALE RD
ABBEY RD
Carcut Beck
THE ORCHARD 1
EAST VIEW 2
STAINTON VIEW 3
HILLSIDE TERR 4
LAUREL TERR 5
CHURCH VIEW 6
DARLINGTON RD 7
EAST CL
PO
Buck Inn (PH)
STOCKTON RD
Village Hall
MIDDLETON RD
WEST ROW
BEACON GRANGE PK
CHURCH LA
Sadberge
A66
DL1
Beacon Hill
BEACON HILL
Sadberge Resr (dis)
A1150
Lea Close
Little Burdon
Bumper Hall
Toft Hill
BUESS LA
Sadberge Hall Farm
Sadberge Hall
Street House Farm
DL2
The Kennels
South Burdon
Midway Farm
LINGFIELD CL
LINGFIELD WAY
Ashtree Cottage
DUDLEY RD
SADBERGE RD
Highfield Farm
ALLINGTON WAY
Locomotive Sculpture
Morton Palms Farm
ST GEORGES GATE
Allot Gdns
MORTON RD
PALMS CT
Yarm Road Ind Est
Palm Bridge
The Fighting Cocks (PH)
WILD RD
Woodlands
Morton Park
A66
Acolan House
A67
HAXBY RD
STATION RD
HEATHFIELD PK
1 HARPERS TERR
2 STATION TERR
PALM TREE VILLAS
A67
8
7
17
6
5
16
4
3
15
2
1
14
32
33
34

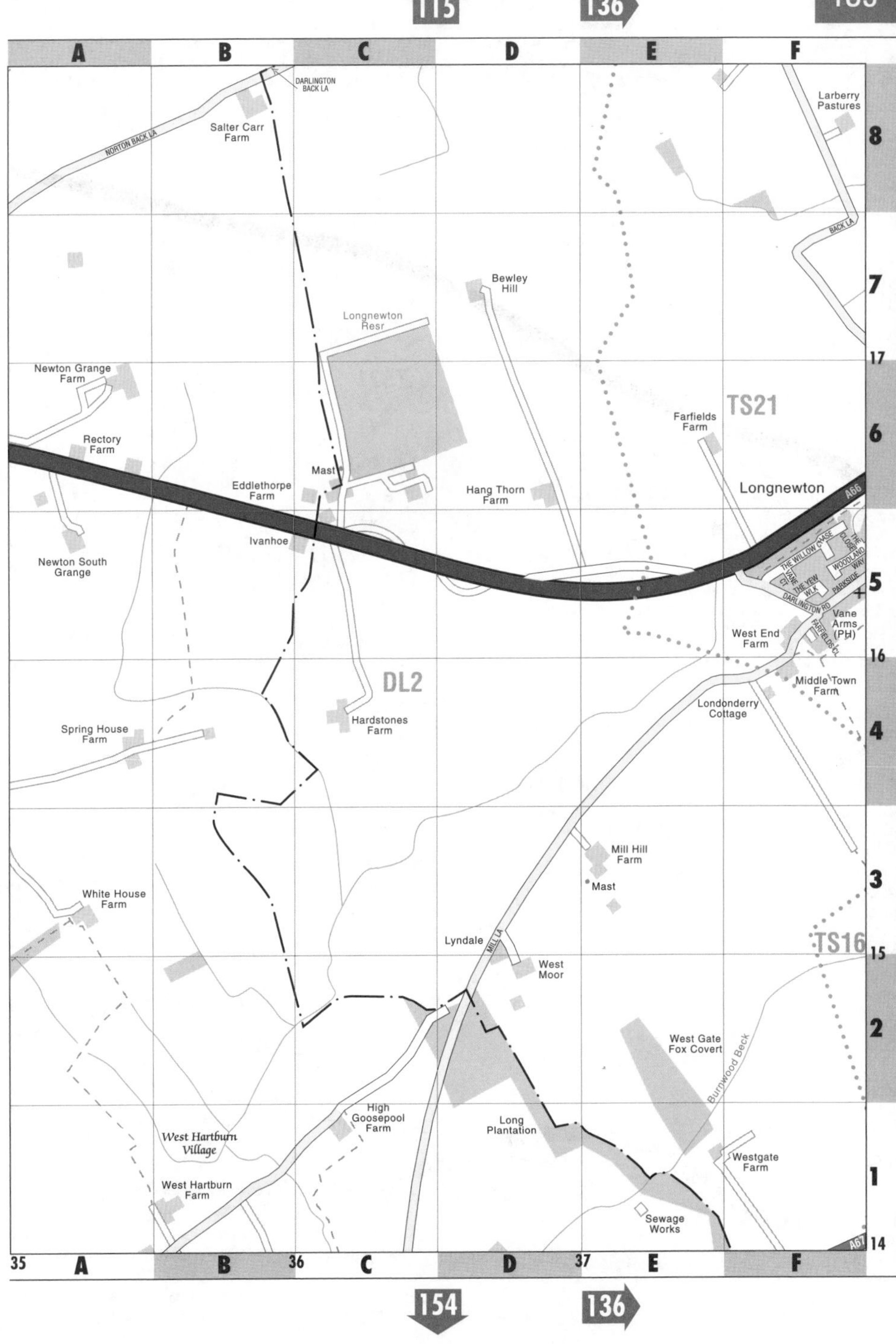

A B C D E F

8

7

17

6

TS21

5

16

4

3

TS16

15

2

1

14

35 A B 36 C D 37 E F 14

NORTON BACK LA

DARLINGTON
BACK LA

Salter Carr
Farm

Longnewton
Resr

Bewley
Hill

Larberry
Pastures

BACK LA

Newton Grange
Farm

Rectory
Farm

Mast

Farfields
Farm

Longnewton

A66

THE WILLOW CLOSE
WOODLAND
PARK
VIEW
THE YEW
THE ELM
PARKSIDE
WOODLAND
WAY

Eddlethorpe
Farm

Hang Thorn
Farm

Ivanhoe

Newton South
Grange

DARLINGTON RD

Vane
Arms
(PH)

West End
Farm

PETER ELM CL

DL2

Hardstones
Farm

Middle Town
Farm

Londonderry
Cottage

Spring House
Farm

White House
Farm

Mill Hill
Farm

Mast

Lyndale

MILL LA

West
Moor

West Gate
Fox Covert

Burnwood Beck

West Hartburn
Village

West Hartburn
Farm

High
Goosepool
Farm

Long
Plantation

Westgate
Farm

Sewage
Works

A67

135
116

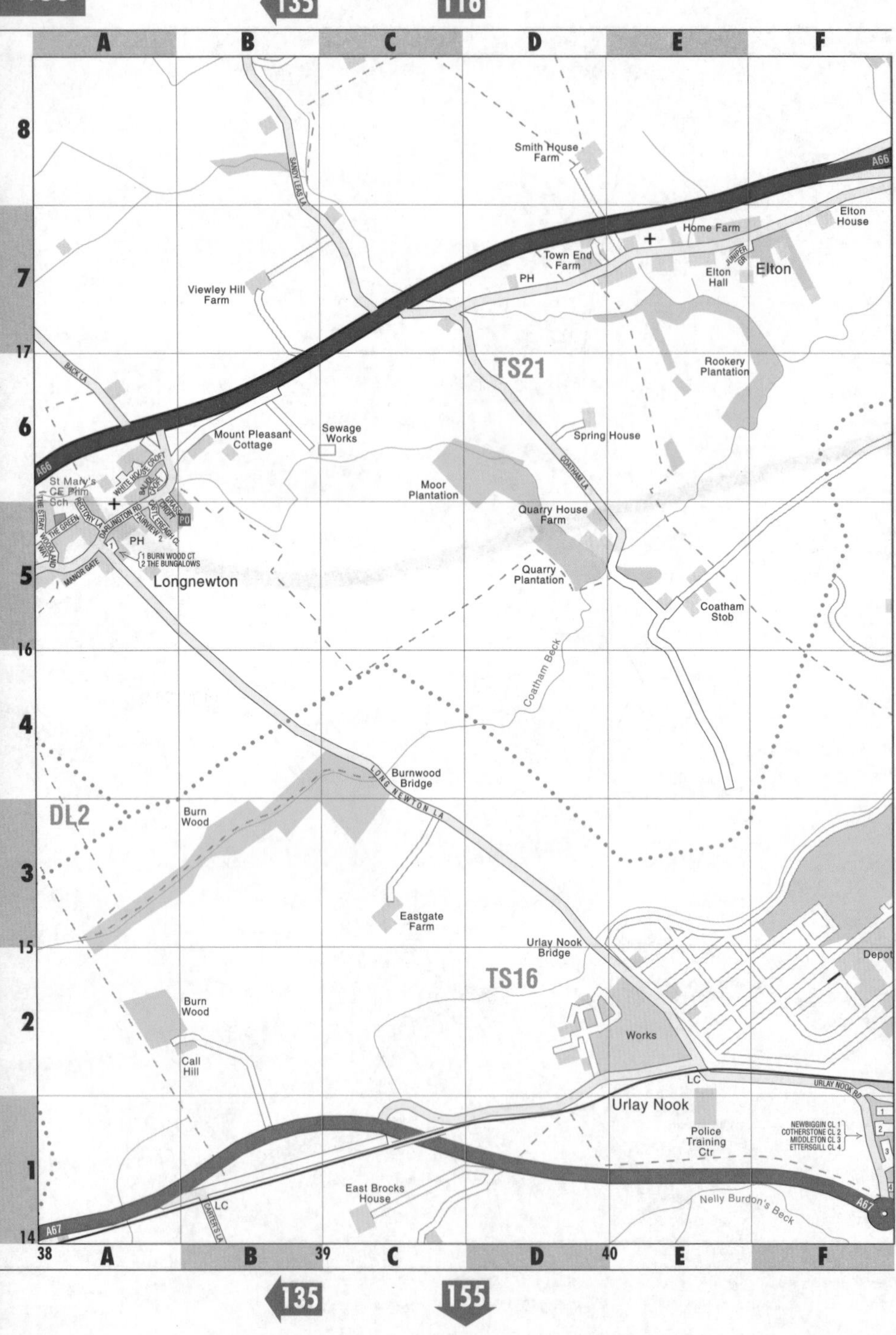
A
B
C
D
E
F
8
7
17
6
5
16
4
3
15
2
1
14
38
39
40
Smith House Farm
A66
Elton House
Home Farm
Town End Farm
Juniper Gr
Elton Hall
Elton
PH
Viewley Hill Farm
Sandy Leas La
Back La
TS21
Rookery Plantation
Mount Pleasant Cottage
Sewage Works
Spring House
Coatham La
White House Croft
Balliol Croft
St Mary's CE Prim Sch
Moor Plantation
Rectory La
Darlington Rd
Grass Croft
Castlereagh Cl
Fairview
PO
The Stray
The Green
Woodland Way
Manor Gate
Quarry House Farm
1 Burn Wood Ct
2 The Bungalows
Longnewton
Quarry Plantation
Coatham Stob
Coatham Beck
Long Newton La
Burnwood Bridge
DL2
Burn Wood
Eastgate Farm
Urlay Nook Bridge
TS16
Depot
Burn Wood
Works
Call Hill
LC
Urlay Nook Rd
Urlay Nook
Police Training Ctr
Newbiggin Cl 1
Cotherstone Cl 2
Middleton Cl 3
Ettersgill Cl 4
East Brocks House
Carter's La
Nelly Burdon's Beck
A67

135
155

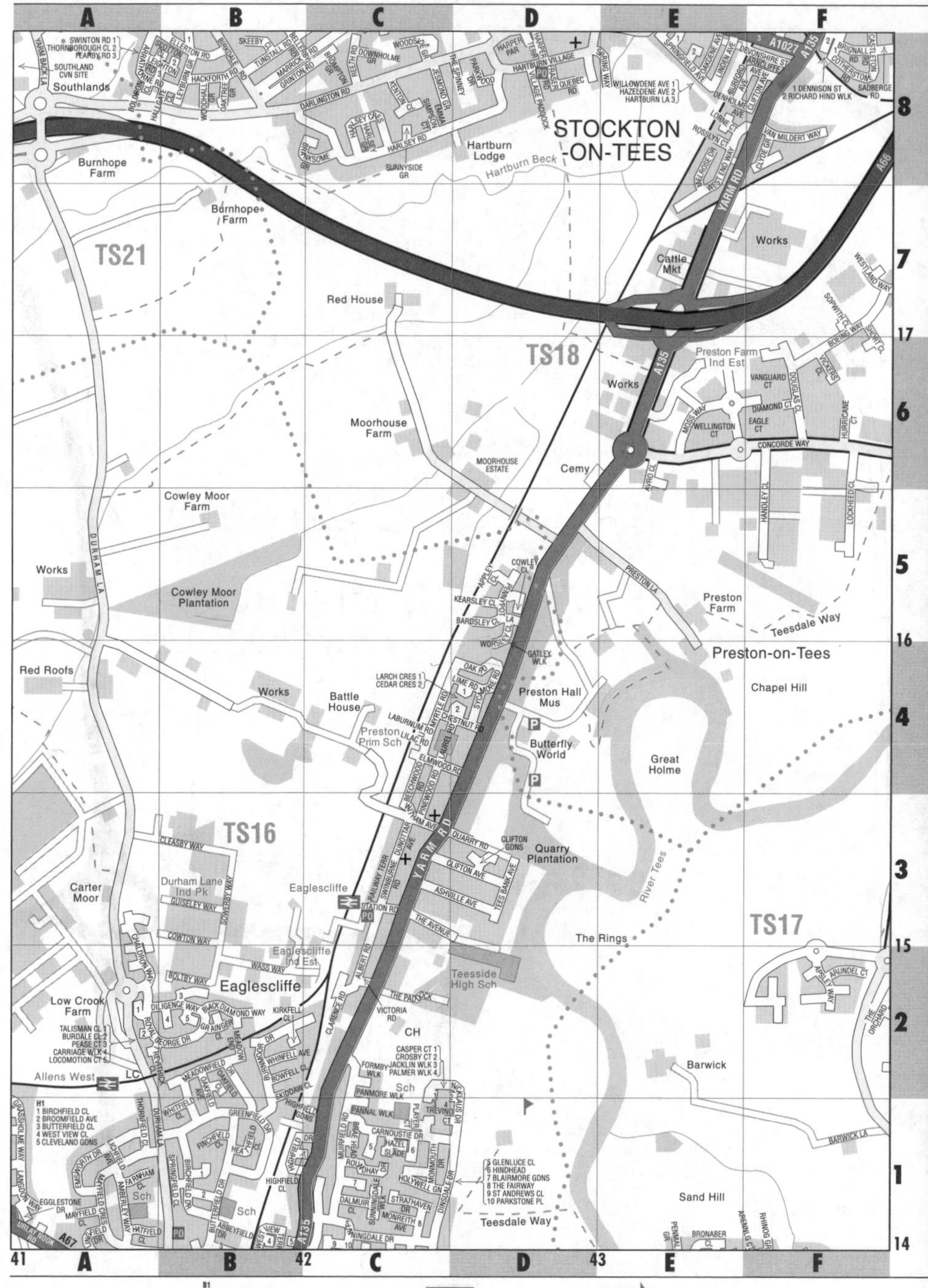
STOCKTON
-ON-TEES
Southlands
Burnhope Farm
TS21
TS18
TS16
TS17
Red House
Moorhouse Farm
Cowley Moor Farm
Cowley Moor Plantation
Works
Red Roofs
Battle House
Preston Prim Sch
Preston Hall Mus
Butterfly World
Great Holme
Preston Farm
Preston-on-Tees
Chapel Hill
Teesdale Way
Quarry Plantation
River Tees
The Rings
Eaglescliffe
Eaglescliffe Ind Est
Durham Lane Ind Pk
Carter Moor
Low Crook Farm
Allens West
Teesside High Sch
Barwick
Sand Hill
Hartburn Lodge
Hartburn Beck
Cattle Mkt
Preston Farm Ind Est
Cemy
YARM RD
DURHAM LA
PRESTON LA
CONCORDE WAY
A1027
A135
A66
A67

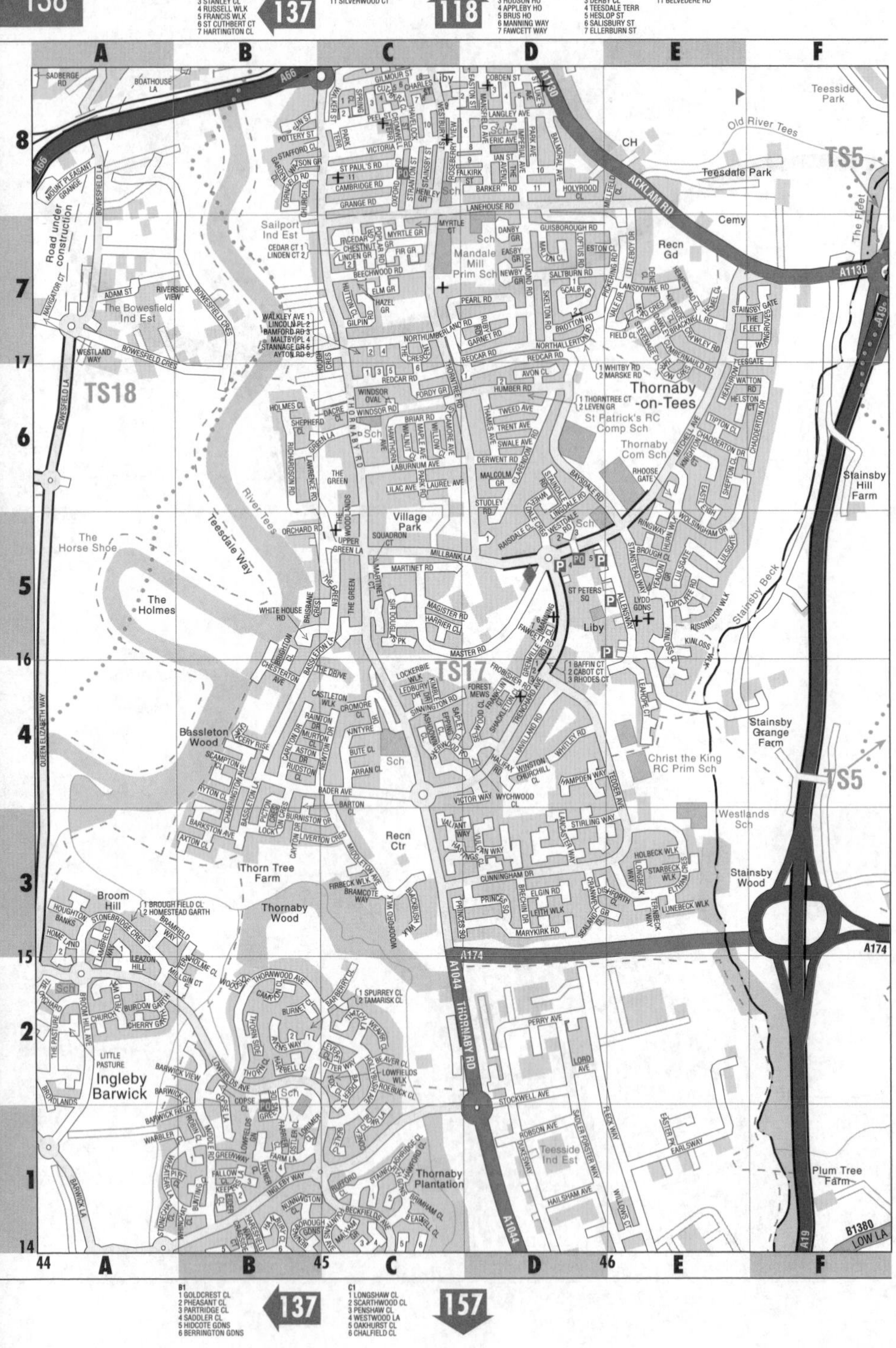

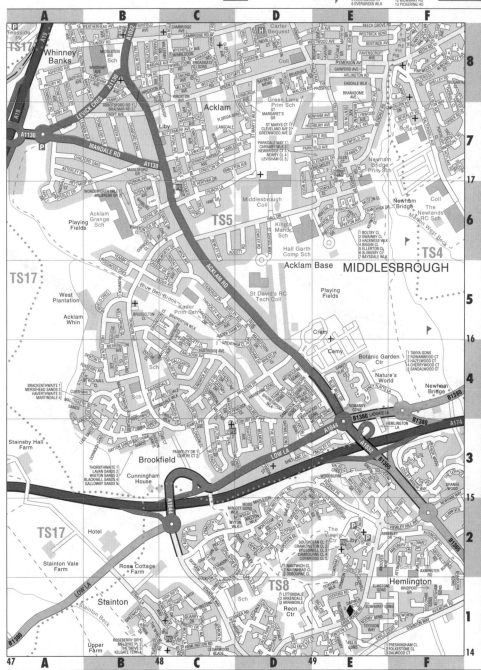

140

F8
1 CROSTHWAITE AVE
2 MULBERRY CT
3 KEITHWOOD CL
4 WHITEBEAM CT
5 ELDERWOOD CT
6 EVERGREEN WLK
7 LIMETREE CT
8 BROOKSIDE AVE
9 HOLLYHURST AVE
10 SWALEDALE HO
11 FROME HO
12 MOWBRAY HO
13 PICKERING HO

A B C D E F

8 7 17 6 5 16 4 3 15 2 1 14

Whinney Banks

Acklam

TS5

TS17

TS4

MIDDLESBROUGH

Acklam Base

Brookfield

TS8

Stainton

Hemlington

ABBOTSFORD RD 1
BRAEMAR RD 2

ST MARYS CT 1
CLEVELAND AVE 2
GREENWOOD AVE 3

PARKDALE WAY 1
CARNABY WLK 2
NEWBRIDGE CT 3
NEWBY CL 4
LEVISHAM CL 5

WORDSWORTH VALE 1
MELBREAK GR 2

1 BOLTBY CL
2 SWAINBY CL
3 HACKNESS WLK
4 BIGGIN CL
5 ELLERTON CL
6 SLINGSBY CL
7 BAYSDALE WLK

1 TANYA GDNS
2 ROWANWOOD CT
3 HAZELWOOD CT
4 CHERRYWOOD CT
5 SANDALWOOD CT

BRACKENTHWAITE 1
MERSEHEAD SANDS 2
HAVERTHWAITE 3
MARTINDALE 4

PAUNTLEY DR 1
CENTRE CT 2

THORNTHWAITE 1
LAVAN SANDS 2
WIGTON SANDS 3
BLACKHALL SANDS 4
GALLOWAY SANDS 5

SOUTHDEAN CL 1
CRAMLINGTON CL 2
CRESSWELL CL 3
CAMBOURNE CL 4
CORBRIDGE CL 5

1 NANTWICH CL
2 NAIRNHEAD CL
3 OSBOURNE CL

1 LITTONDALE
2 ARKENDALE
3 ARRANDALE

ROSEBERRY DR 1
MELDYKE PL 2
THE DRIVE 3
KELGATE TERR 4

1 FRESHINGHAM CL
2 FOLKESTONE CL
3 DALWOOD CT

47 A B 48 C D 49 E F

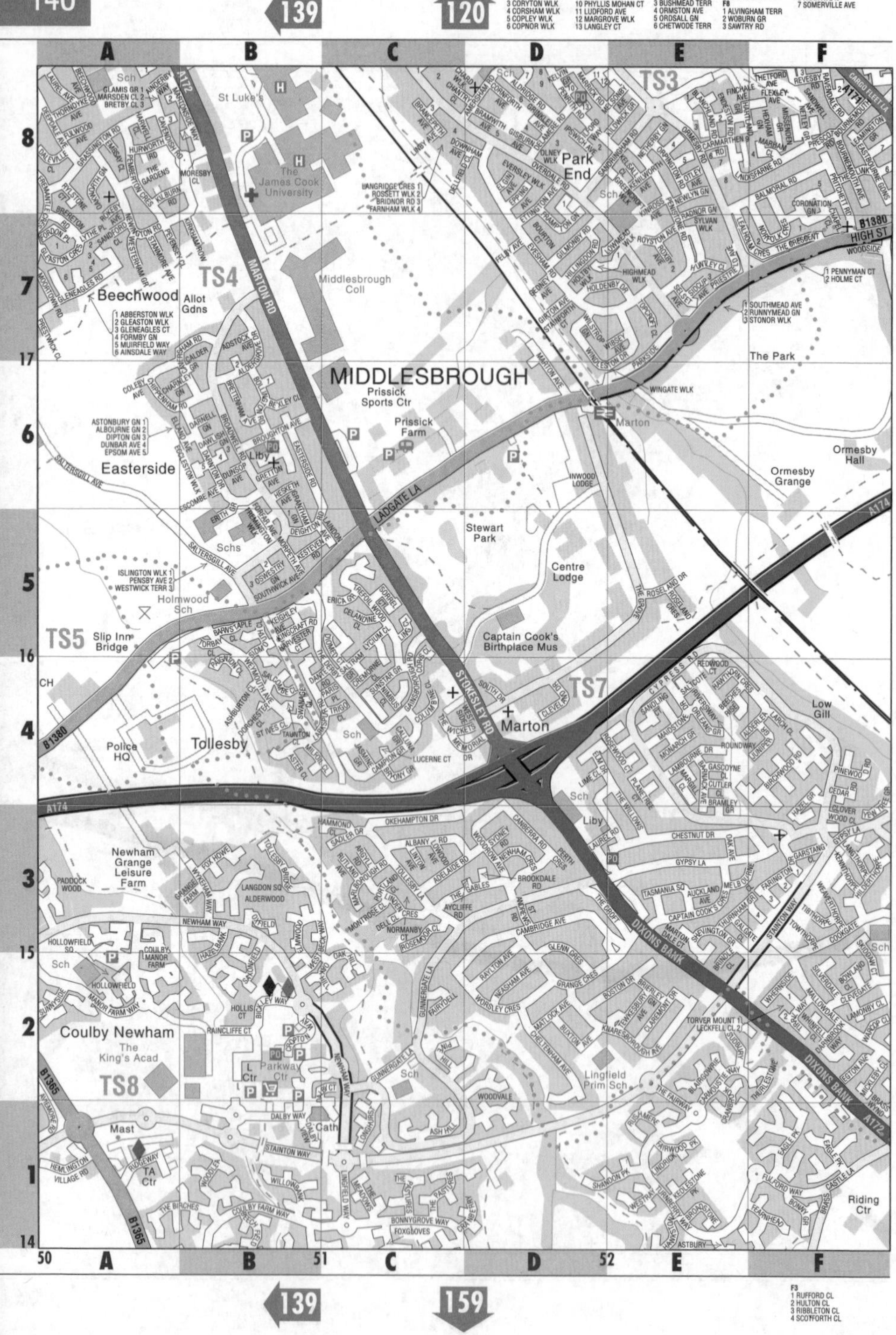

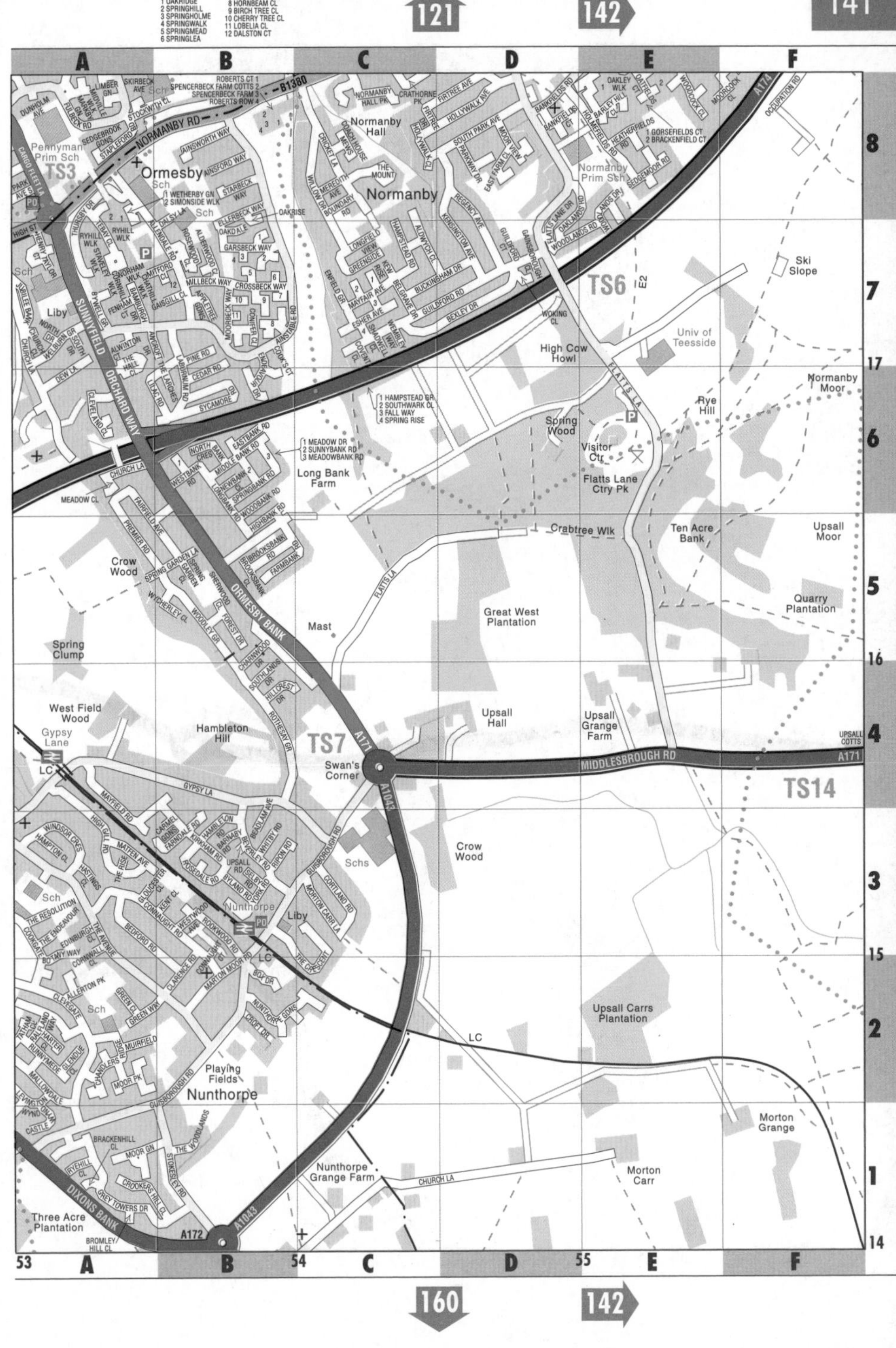

141
121
142
160
142
B7
1 OAKRIDGE
2 SPRINGHILL
3 SPRINGHOLME
4 SPRINGWALK
5 SPRINGMEAD
6 SPRINGLEA
7 ASHWOOD CL
8 HORNBEAM CL
9 BIRCH TREE CL
10 CHERRY TREE CL
11 LOBELIA CL
12 DALSTON CT
A
B
C
D
E
F
8
7
6
5
4
3
2
1
17
16
15
14
53
54
55
Ormesby
Normanby
Normanby Hall
Pennyman Prim Sch
Normanby Prim Sch
TS3
TS6
TS7
TS14
NORMANBY RD
B1380
ROBERTS CT 1
SPENCERBECK FARM COTTS 2
SPENCERBECK FARM 3
ROBERTS ROW 4
1 WETHERBY GN
2 SIMONSIDE WLK
1 GORSEFIELDS CT
2 BRACKENFIELD CT
1 HAMPSTEAD GR
2 SOUTHWARK CL
3 FALL WAY
4 SPRING RISE
1 MEADOW DR
2 SUNNYBANK RD
3 MEADOWBANK RD
SUNNYFIELD
ORCHARD WAY
ORMESBY BANK
A174
A171
A1043
A172
MIDDLESBROUGH RD
DIXONS BANK
Ski Slope
Univ of Teesside
High Cow Howl
Normanby Moor
Rye Hill
Spring Wood
Visitor Ctr
Flatts Lane Ctry Pk
Long Bank Farm
Crabtree Wlk
Ten Acre Bank
Upsall Moor
Crow Wood
Great West Plantation
Quarry Plantation
Mast
Spring Clump
West Field Wood
Gypsy Lane
Hambleton Hill
Upsall Hall
Upsall Grange Farm
UPSALL COTTS
Swan's Corner
Schs
Crow Wood
Nunthorpe
Liby
Upsall Carrs Plantation
LC
Playing Fields
Nunthorpe
Morton Grange
Nunthorpe Grange Farm
CHURCH LA
Morton Carr
Three Acre Plantation
BROMLEY HILL CL

141
122

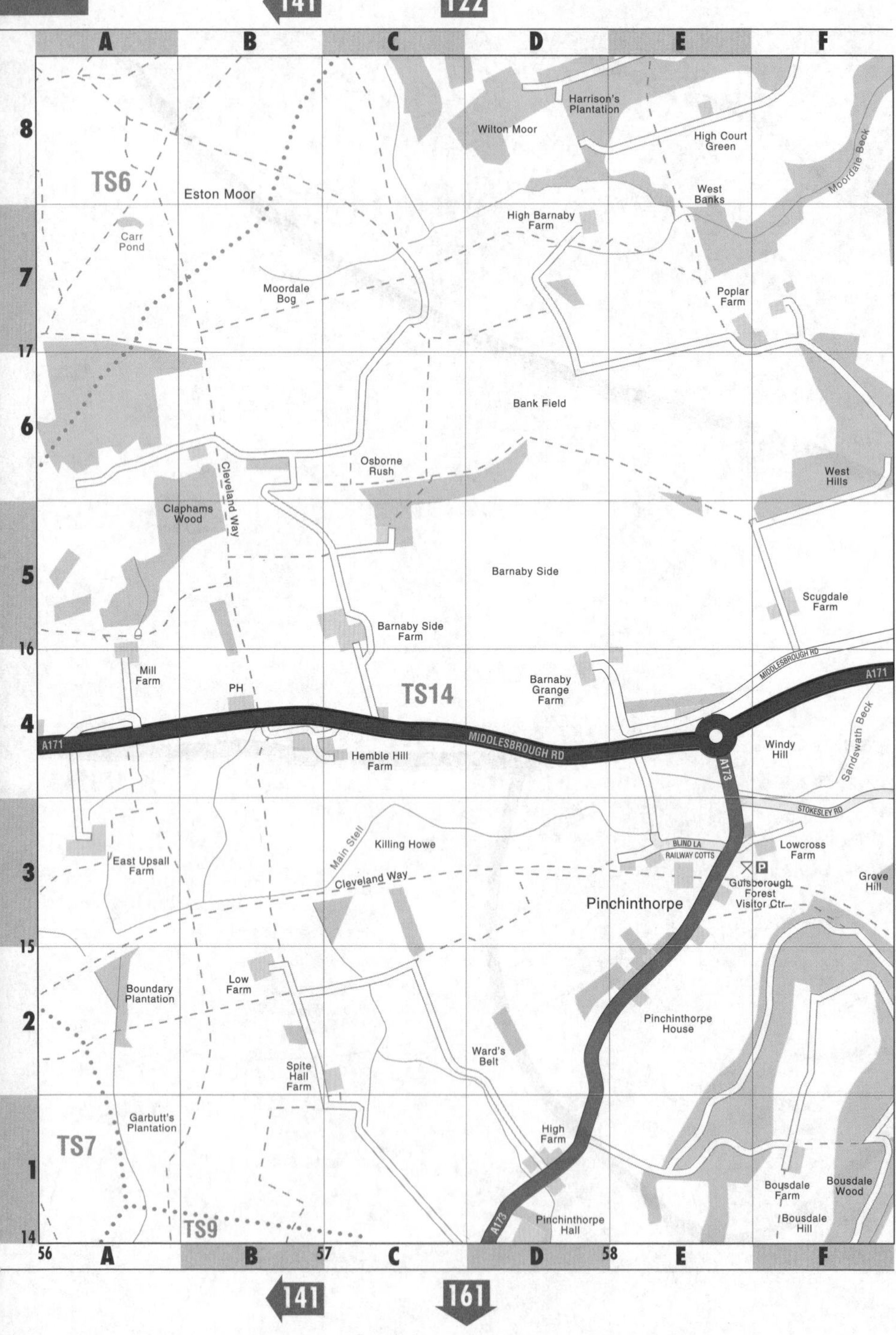
A
B
C
D
E
F
8
7
17
6
5
16
4
3
15
2
1
14
56
57
58
TS6
Eston Moor
Carr Pond
Moordale Bog
Harrison's Plantation
Wilton Moor
High Court Green
Moordale Beck
West Banks
High Barnaby Farm
Poplar Farm
Bank Field
Osborne Rush
West Hills
Claphams Wood
Cleveland Way
Barnaby Side
Scugdale Farm
Barnaby Side Farm
Mill Farm
PH
TS14
Barnaby Grange Farm
MIDDLESBROUGH RD
A171
MIDDLESBROUGH RD
A171
Hemble Hill Farm
A173
Windy Hill
Sandswath Beck
STOKESLEY RD
Main Stell
Killing Howe
BLIND LA
RAILWAY COTTS
Lowcross Farm
East Upsall Farm
Cleveland Way
Guisborough Forest Visitor Ctr
Grove Hill
Pinchinthorpe
Boundary Plantation
Low Farm
Pinchinthorpe House
Ward's Belt
Spite Hall Farm
Garbutt's Plantation
TS7
High Farm
Bousdale Farm
Bousdale Wood
Bousdale Hill
A173
Pinchinthorpe Hall
TS9

141
161

123
144

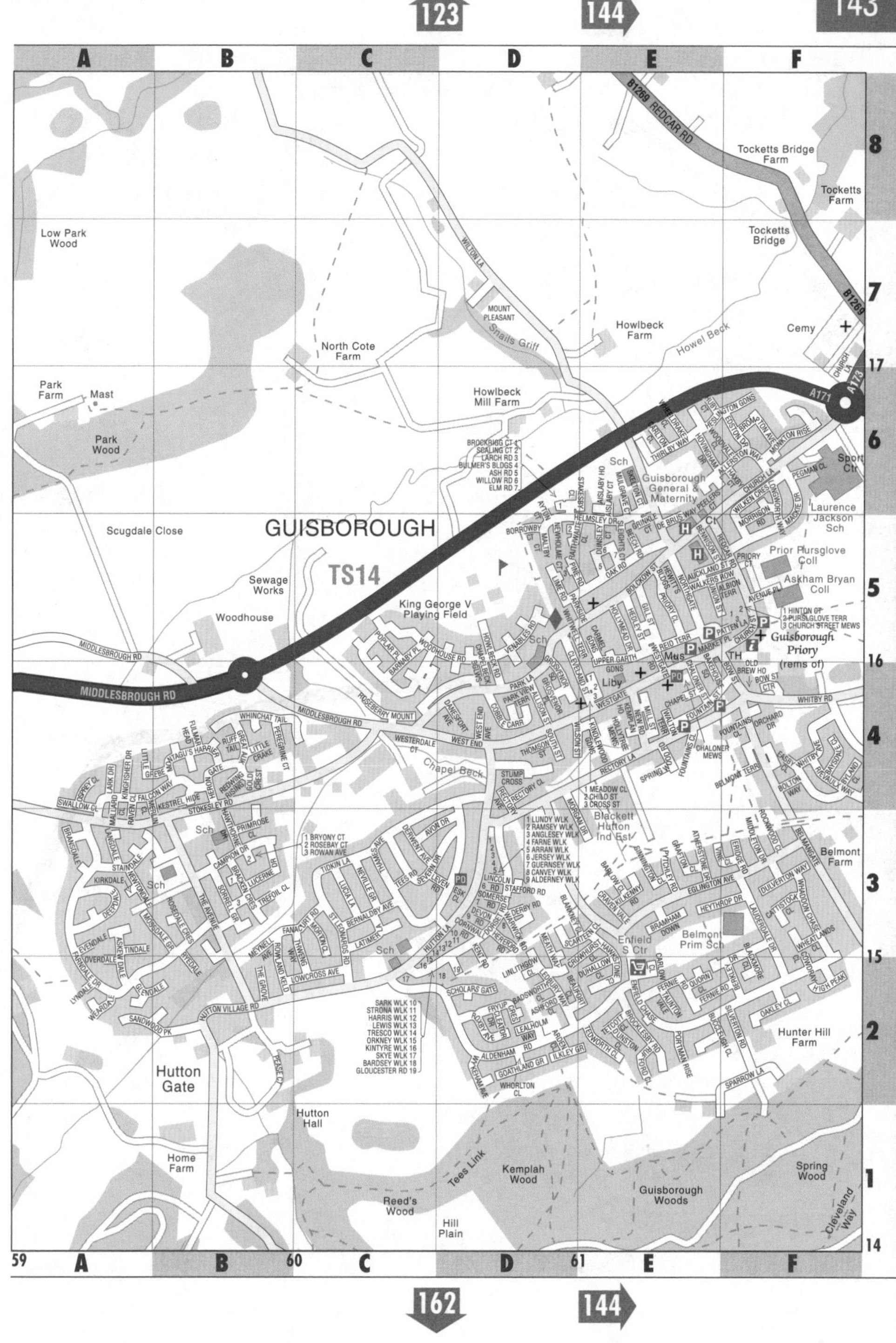
A
B
C
D
E
F
8
7
17
6
5
16
4
3
15
2
1
14
59
60
61
B1269 REDCAR RD
Tocketts Bridge Farm
Tocketts Farm
Tocketts Bridge
B1269
Cemy
CHURCH LA
Low Park Wood
WILTON LA
MOUNT PLEASANT
Snails Griff
North Cote Farm
Howlbeck Farm
Howel Beck
Park Farm
Mast
Park Wood
Howlbeck Mill Farm
A171
A173
BROCKRIGG CT 1
SCALING CT 2
LARCH RD 3
BULMER'S BLDGS 4
ASH RD 5
WILLOW RD 6
ELM RD 7
Sch
Guisborough General & Maternity
Sport Ctr
Laurence Jackson Sch
Scugdale Close
GUISBOROUGH
TS14
Prior Pursglove Coll
Askham Bryan Coll
Sewage Works
King George V Playing Field
Woodhouse
1 HINTON CT
2 PURSGLOVE TERR
3 CHURCH STREET MEWS
Guisborough Priory
(rems of)
MIDDLESBROUGH RD
Mus
TH
Liby
WHITBY RD
WESTGATE
WEST END
Chapel Beck
STUMP CROSS
RECTORY LA
1 MEADOW CL
2 CHILD ST
3 CROSS ST
Blackett Hutton Ind Est
1 LUNDY WLK
2 RAMSEY WLK
3 ANGLESEY WLK
4 FARNE WLK
5 ARRAN WLK
6 JERSEY WLK
7 GUERNSEY WLK
8 CANVEY WLK
9 ALDERNEY WLK
1 BRYONY CT
2 ROSEBAY CT
3 ROWAN AVE
STOKESLEY RD
Belmont Farm
EGLINGTON AVE
Enfield S Ctr
Belmont Prim Sch
SARK WLK 10
STRONA WLK 11
HARRIS WLK 12
LEWIS WLK 13
TRESCO WLK 14
ORKNEY WLK 15
KINTYRE WLK 16
SKYE WLK 17
BARDSEY WLK 18
GLOUCESTER RD 19
HUTTON VILLAGE RD
SANDWOOD PK
Hutton Gate
Hunter Hill Farm
SPARROW LA
WHORLTON CL
Hutton Hall
Home Farm
Tees Link
Kemplah Wood
Guisborough Woods
Spring Wood
Cleveland Way
Reed's Wood
Hill Plain

162
144

143
124

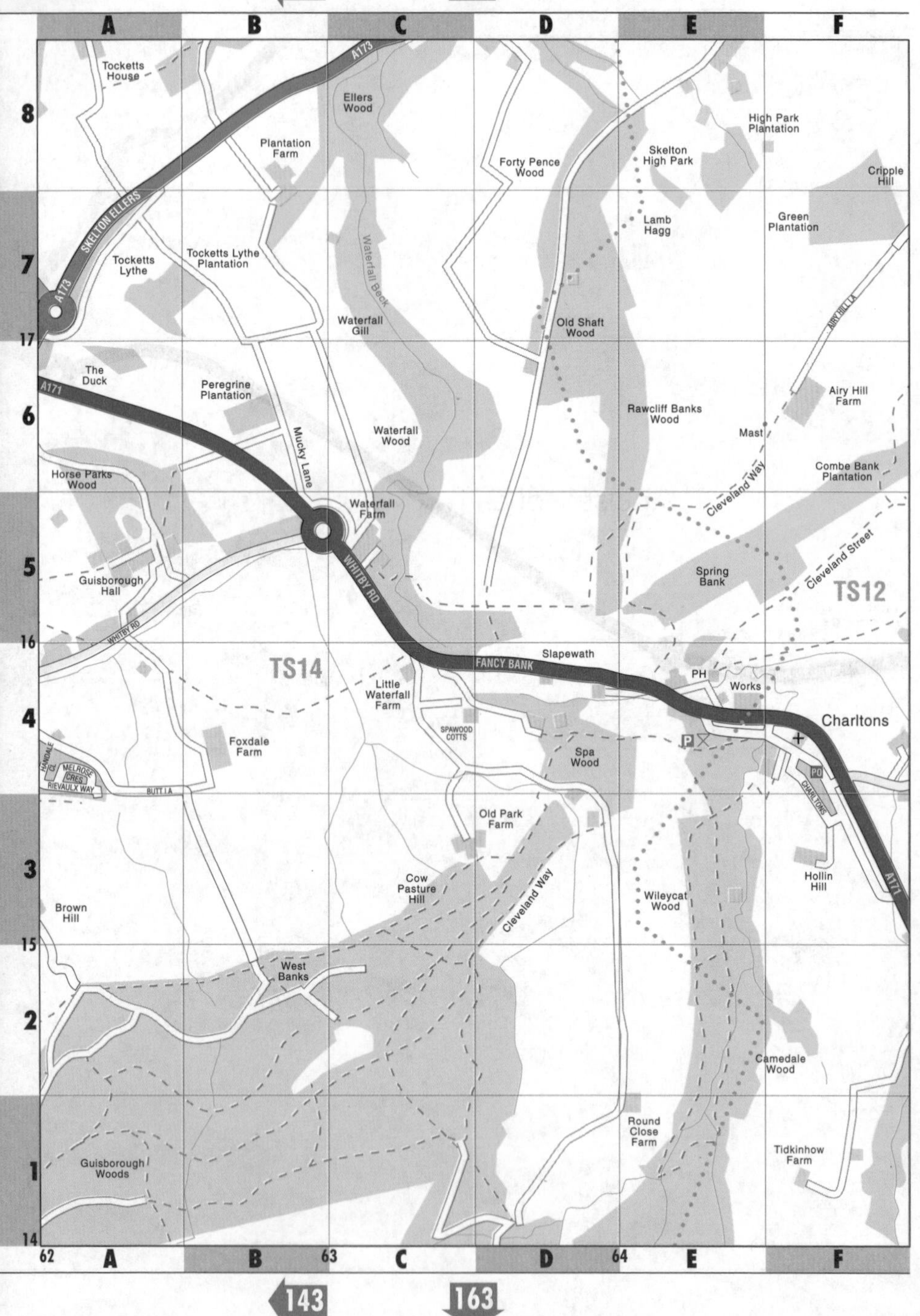
A
B
C
D
E
F
8
7
17
6
5
16
4
3
15
2
1
14
62
63
64
Tocketts House
A173
Ellers Wood
Plantation Farm
High Park Plantation
Skelton High Park
Forty Pence Wood
Cripple Hill
SKELTON ELLERS
Lamb Hagg
Green Plantation
Tocketts Lythe
Tocketts Lythe Plantation
Waterfall Beck
Old Shaft Wood
Waterfall Gill
AIRY HILL LA
The Duck
A171
Peregrine Plantation
Airy Hill Farm
Rawcliff Banks Wood
Mast
Waterfall Wood
Mucky Lane
Horse Parks Wood
Cleveland Way
Combe Bank Plantation
Waterfall Farm
Cleveland Street
Spring Bank
WHITBY RD
Guisborough Hall
TS12
WHITBY RD
Slapewath
TS14
FANCY BANK
PH
Works
Little Waterfall Farm
Charltons
SPAWOOD COTTS
Foxdale Farm
Spa Wood
P
PO
HANDALE CL
MELROSE CRES
RIEVAULX WAY
BUTT LA
CHARLTONS
Old Park Farm
Cow Pasture Hill
Hollin Hill
Cleveland Way
Wileycat Wood
Brown Hill
West Banks
Camedale Wood
Round Close Farm
Tidkinhow Farm
Guisborough Woods

143
163

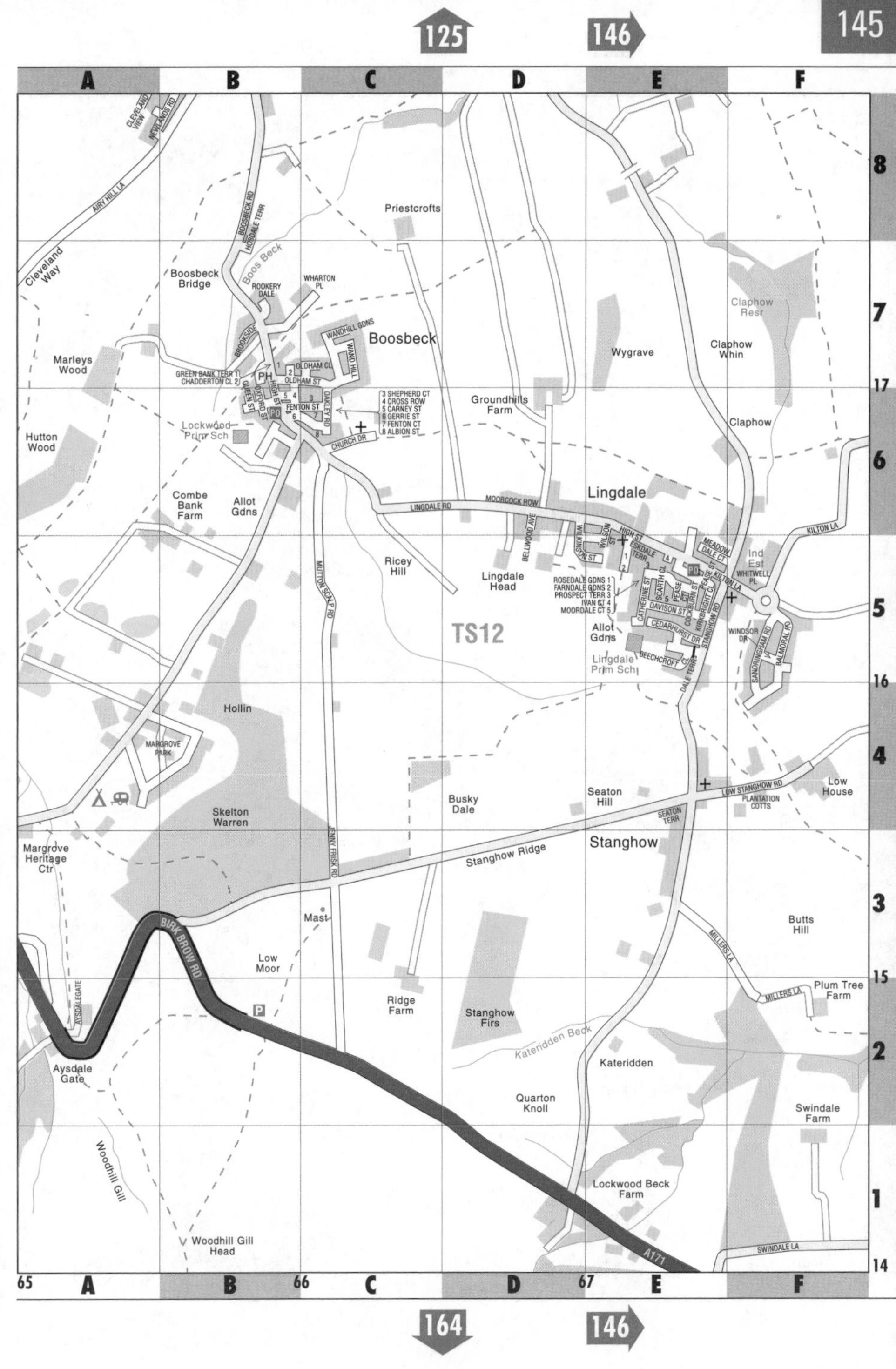
125
146
A
B
C
D
E
F
8
7
17
6
5
16
4
3
15
2
1
14
65
66
67
164
146
CLEVELAND VIEW
NEWLANDS RD
AIRY HILL LA
Cleveland Way
BOOSBECK RD
HOSDALE TERR
Boos Beck
Boosbeck Bridge
ROOKERY DALE
WHARTON PL
Priestcrofts
WANDHILL GDNS
Boosbeck
WAND HILL
BROOKSIDE
OLDHAM CL
OLDHAM ST
GREEN BANK TERR 1
CHADDERTON CL 2
PH
QUEEN ST
OXFORD ST
HIGH ST
FENTON ST
OAKLEY RD
CHURCH DR
3 SHEPHERD CT
4 CROSS ROW
5 CARNEY ST
6 GERRIE ST
7 FENTON CT
8 ALBION ST
PO
Marleys Wood
Lockwood Prim Sch
Hutton Wood
Combe Bank Farm
Allot Gdns
Groundhills Farm
Wygrave
Claphow Resr
Claphow Whin
Claphow
LINGDALE RD
MOORCOCK ROW
Lingdale
BELLWOOD AVE
WILKINSON ST
WILSON ST
HIGH ST
ESKDALE TERR
MEADOW DALE CT
KILTON LA
Ind Est
WHITWELL PL
Ricey Hill
MUTTON SCALP RD
Lingdale Head
ROSEDALE GDNS 1
FARNDALE GDNS 2
PROSPECT TERR 3
IVAN CT 4
MOORDALE CT 5
CATHERINE ST
SCARTH CL
PEASE CT
PEASE ST
COCKBURN ST
KIRKBRIGHT CL
STANGHOW RD
DAVISON ST
CEDARHURST DR
BEECHCROFT CL
DALE TERR
WINDSOR DR
SANDRINGHAM RD
BALMORAL RD
TS12
Allot Gdns
Lingdale Prim Sch
Hollin
MARGROVE PARK
Skelton Warren
JENNY FRISK RD
Busky Dale
Seaton Hill
LOW STANGHOW RD
PLANTATION COTTS
SEATON TERR
Low House
Stanghow
Stanghow Ridge
Margrove Heritage Ctr
Mast
Butts Hill
BIRK BROW RD
MILLERS LA
Low Moor
Ridge Farm
Stanghow Firs
Plum Tree Farm
AYSDALEGATE
P
Kateridden Beck
Kateridden
Aysdale Gate
Quarton Knoll
Swindale Farm
Woodhill Gill
Lockwood Beck Farm
Woodhill Gill Head
A171
SWINDALE LA

145
126

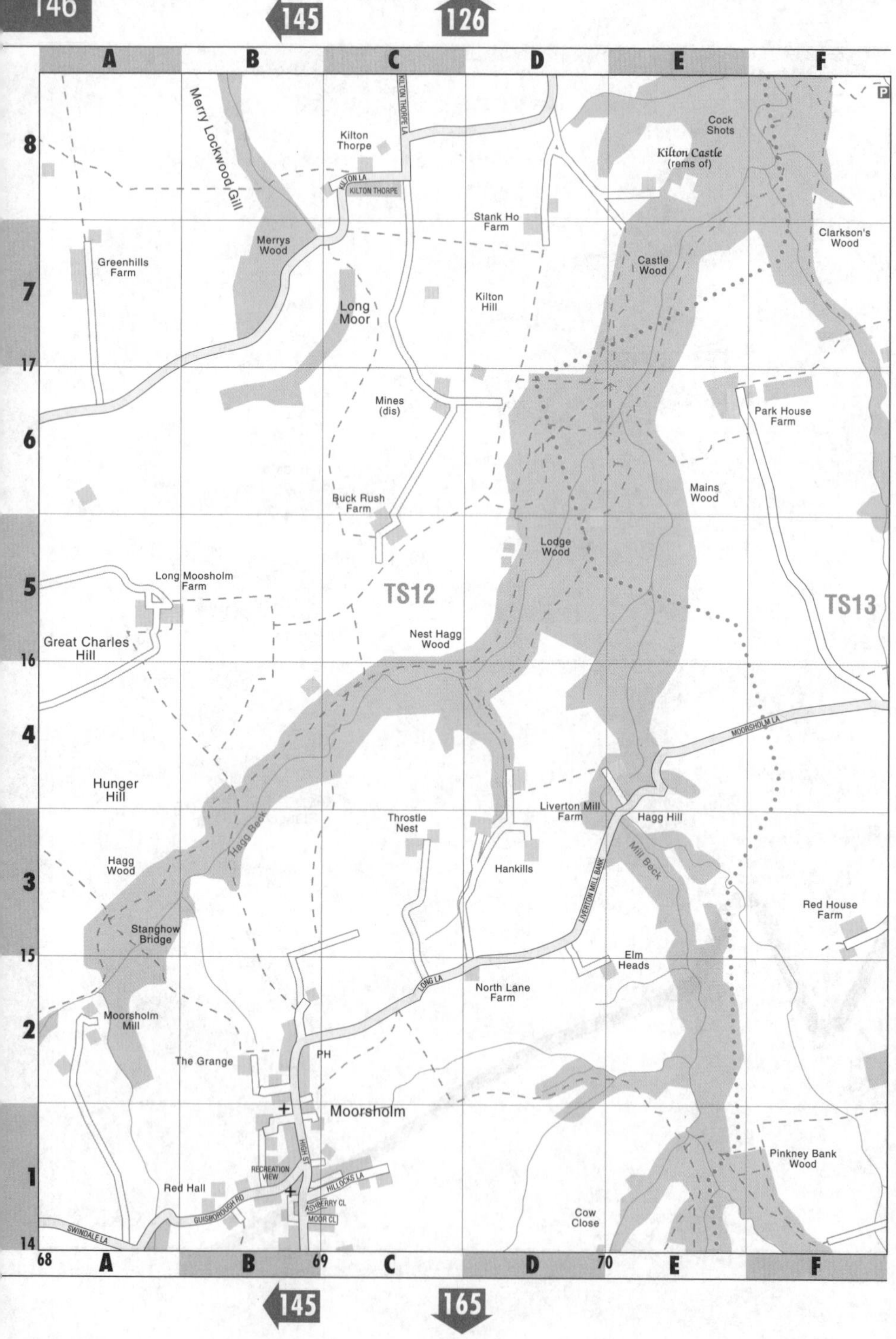
A
B
C
D
E
F
8
7
17
6
5
16
4
3
15
2
1
14
68
69
70
Merry Lockwood Gill
Kilton Thorpe
KILTON THORPE LA
KILTON LA
KILTON THORPE
Cock Shots
Kilton Castle
(rems of)
Stank Ho Farm
Merrys Wood
Greenhills Farm
Long Moor
Kilton Hill
Castle Wood
Clarkson's Wood
Mines (dis)
Park House Farm
Mains Wood
Buck Rush Farm
Lodge Wood
Long Moosholm Farm
TS12
TS13
Great Charles Hill
Nest Hagg Wood
MOORSHOLM LA
Hunger Hill
Hagg Beck
Throstle Nest
Liverton Mill Farm
Hagg Hill
Mill Beck
Hagg Wood
Hankills
LIVERTON MILL BANK
Red House Farm
Stanghow Bridge
LONG LA
Elm Heads
North Lane Farm
Moorsholm Mill
PH
The Grange
Moorsholm
HIGH ST
RECREATION VIEW
HILLOCKS LA
Pinkney Bank Wood
Red Hall
GUISBOROUGH RD
ASHBERRY CL
MOOR CL
Cow Close
SWINDALE LA
P

145
165

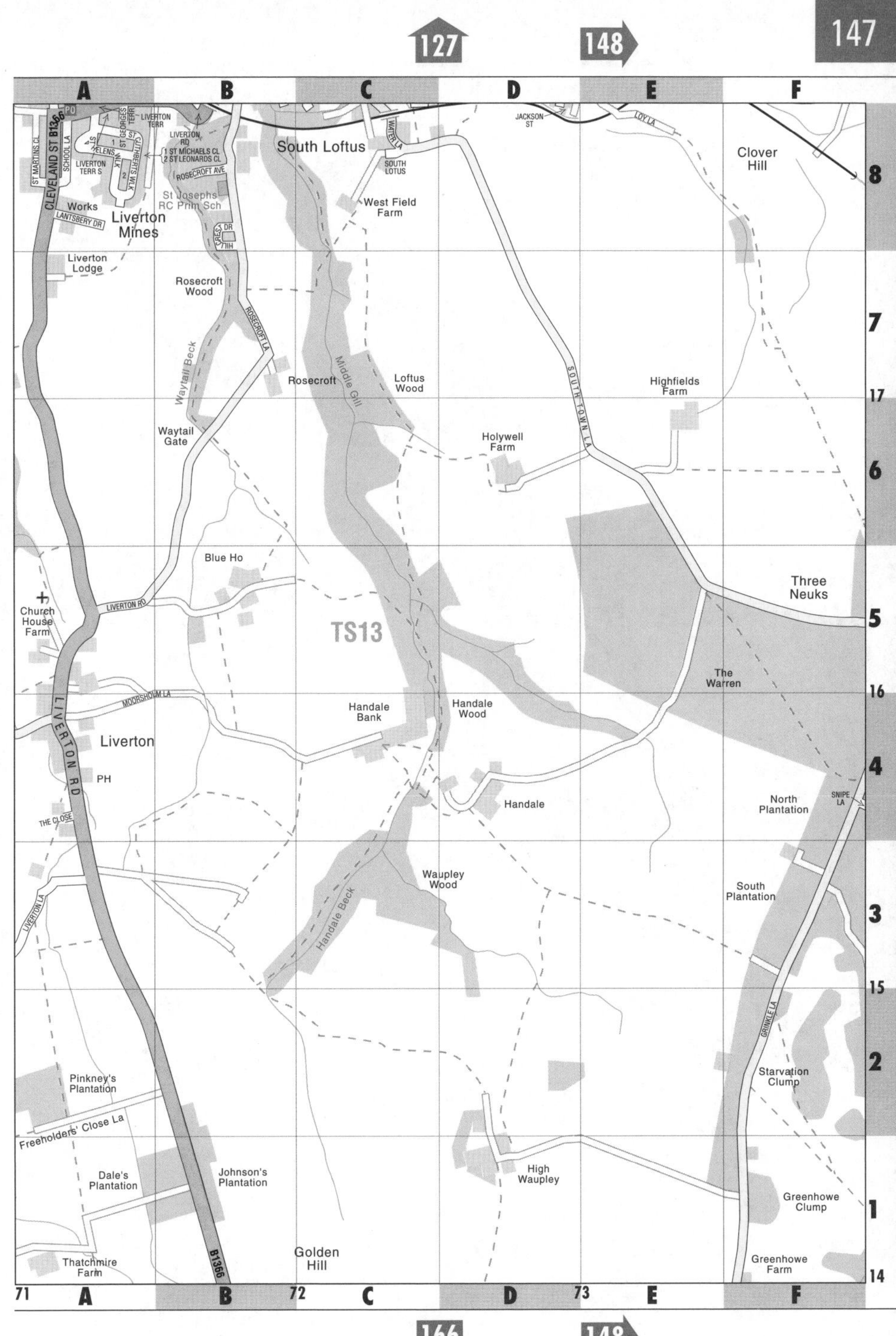
A
B
C
D
E
F
8
7
17
6
5
16
4
3
15
2
1
14
71
72
73
South Loftus
Clover Hill
Liverton Mines
Works
St Josephs RC Prim Sch
West Field Farm
Liverton Lodge
Rosecroft Wood
Rosecroft
Loftus Wood
Middle Gill
Highfields Farm
Waytail Beck
Waytail Gate
Holywell Farm
Blue Ho
Three Neuks
Church House Farm
TS13
The Warren
Handale Bank
Handale Wood
Liverton
PH
Handale
North Plantation
Waupley Wood
South Plantation
Handale Beck
Pinkney's Plantation
Starvation Clump
Freeholders' Close La
Dale's Plantation
Johnson's Plantation
High Waupley
Greenhowe Clump
Golden Hill
Thatchmire Farm
Greenhowe Farm
CLEVELAND ST B1366
LIVERTON RD
ROSECROFT LA
SOUTH TOWN LA
LIVERTON RD
MOORSHOLM LA
LIVERTON LA
THE CLOSE
GRINKLE LA
SNIPE LA
LOY LA
JACKSON ST
WATER LA
SOUTH LOTUS
ROSECROFT AVE
LANTSBERY DR
B1366

147
128

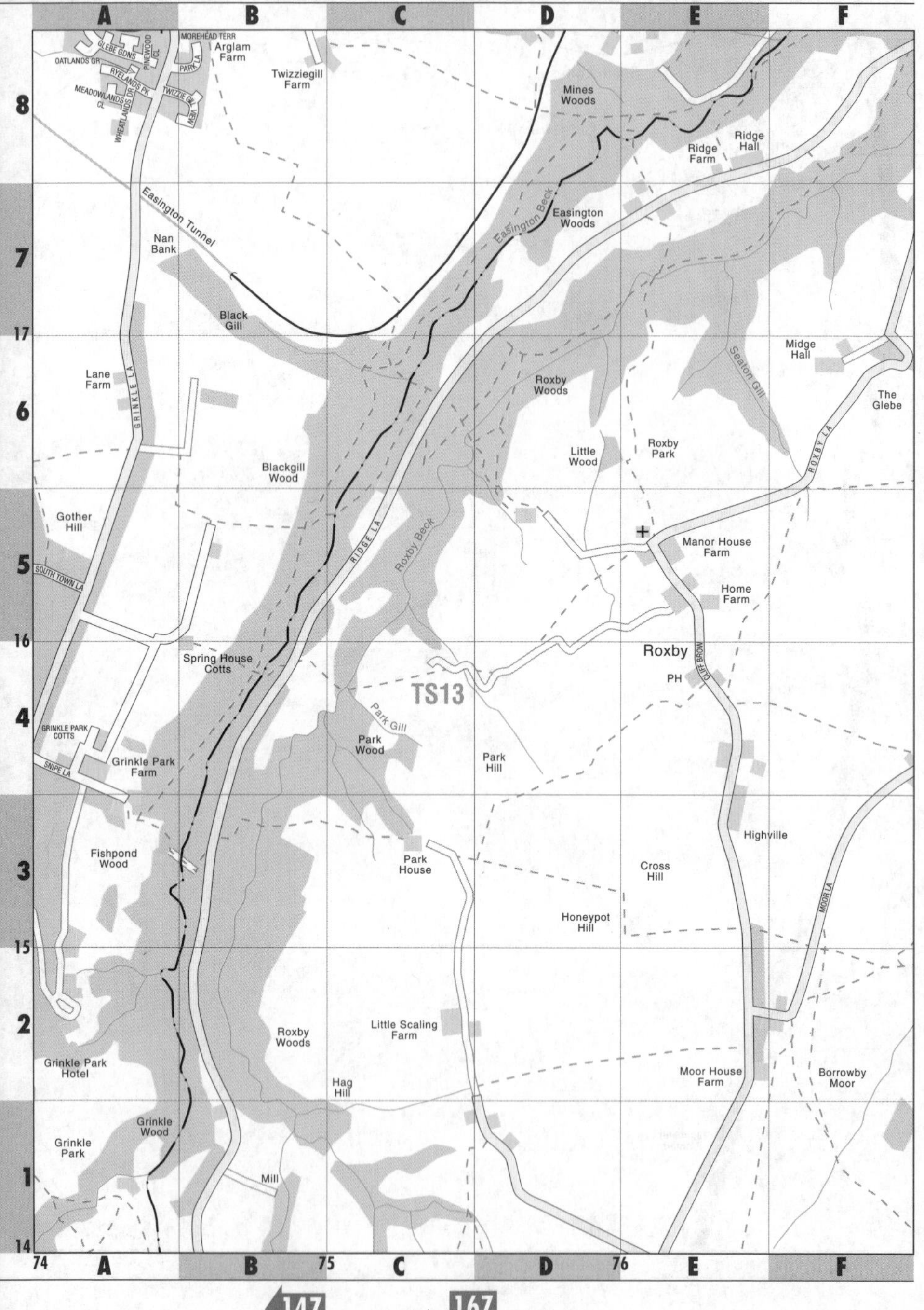
A
B
C
D
E
F
GLEBE GDNS
OATLANDS GR
PINEWOOD CL
RYELANDS PK
MEADOWLANDS CL
WHEATLANDS DR
MOREHEAD TERR
PARK LA
TWIZZIE GILL VIEW
Arglam Farm
Twizziegill Farm
Mines Woods
Ridge Farm
Ridge Hall
8
Easington Tunnel
Easington Beck
Easington Woods
Nan Bank
7
Black Gill
17
Lane Farm
GRINKLE LA
Roxby Woods
Midge Hall
Seaton Gill
The Glebe
6
Little Wood
Roxby Park
ROXBY LA
Blackgill Wood
Gother Hill
Manor House Farm
5
SOUTH TOWN LA
RIDGE LA
Roxby Beck
Home Farm
16
Spring House Cotts
Roxby
CLIFF BROW
PH
TS13
4
GRINKLE PARK COTTS
Park Gill
Park Wood
Park Hill
SNIPE LA
Grinkle Park Farm
Highville
Fishpond Wood
Park House
Cross Hill
3
Honeypot Hill
MOOR LA
15
2
Little Scaling Farm
Roxby Woods
Grinkle Park Hotel
Moor House Farm
Borrowby Moor
Hag Hill
Grinkle Wood
Grinkle Park
1
Mill
14
74
75
76

147
167

129

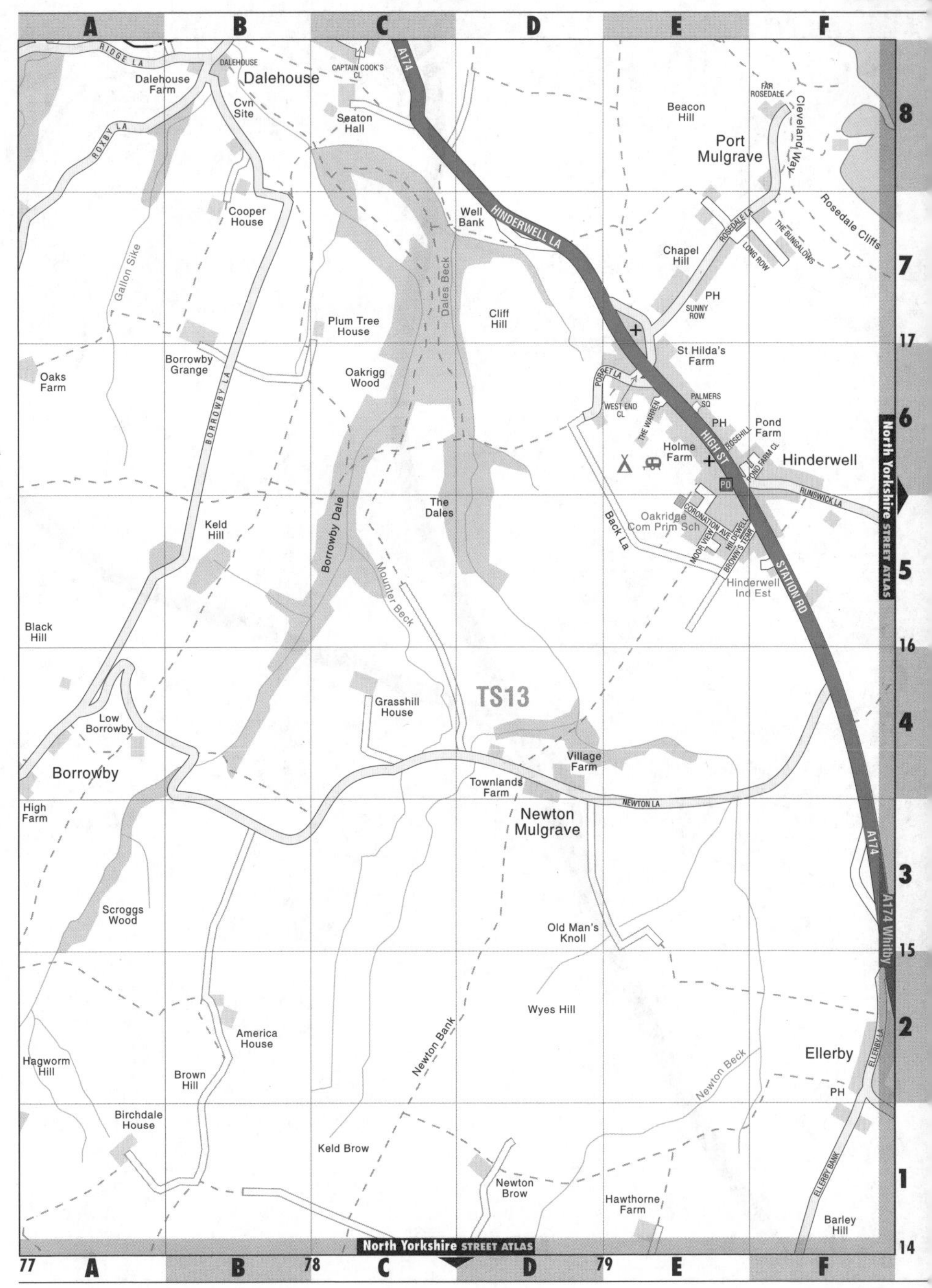

A
B
C
D
E
F
Dalehouse
Dalehouse Farm
Cvn Site
Seaton Hall
Captain Cook's Cl
A174
Beacon Hill
Far Rosedale
Cleveland Way
Port Mulgrave
Rosedale Cliffs
Roxby La
Ridge La
Cooper House
Well Bank
Hinderwell La
Chapel Hill
Rosedale La
Long Row
The Bungalows
Gallon Sike
Dales Beck
PH
Sunny Row
Plum Tree House
Cliff Hill
St Hilda's Farm
Oaks Farm
Borrowby Grange
Oakrigg Wood
Porret La
West End Cl
The Warren
Palmers Sq
Pond Farm
Borrowby La
High St
Rosehill
Holme Farm
Pond Farm Cl
Hinderwell
Runswick La
Keld Hill
The Dales
Back La
Oakridge Com Prim Sch
Coronation Ave
Moor View
Hildewell
Brown's Terr
Borrowby Dale
Mounter Beck
Station Rd
Hinderwell Ind Est
Black Hill
TS13
Grasshill House
Low Borrowby
Village Farm
Borrowby
Townlands Farm
Newton La
High Farm
Newton Mulgrave
Scroggs Wood
Old Man's Knoll
A174 Whitby
Wyes Hill
America House
Newton Bank
Hagworm Hill
Brown Hill
Ellerby
Ellerby La
Newton Beck
Birchdale House
Keld Brow
Newton Brow
Hawthorne Farm
Ellerby Bank
Barley Hill
North Yorkshire STREET ATLAS
8
7
17
6
5
16
4
3
15
2
1
14
77
78
79

131

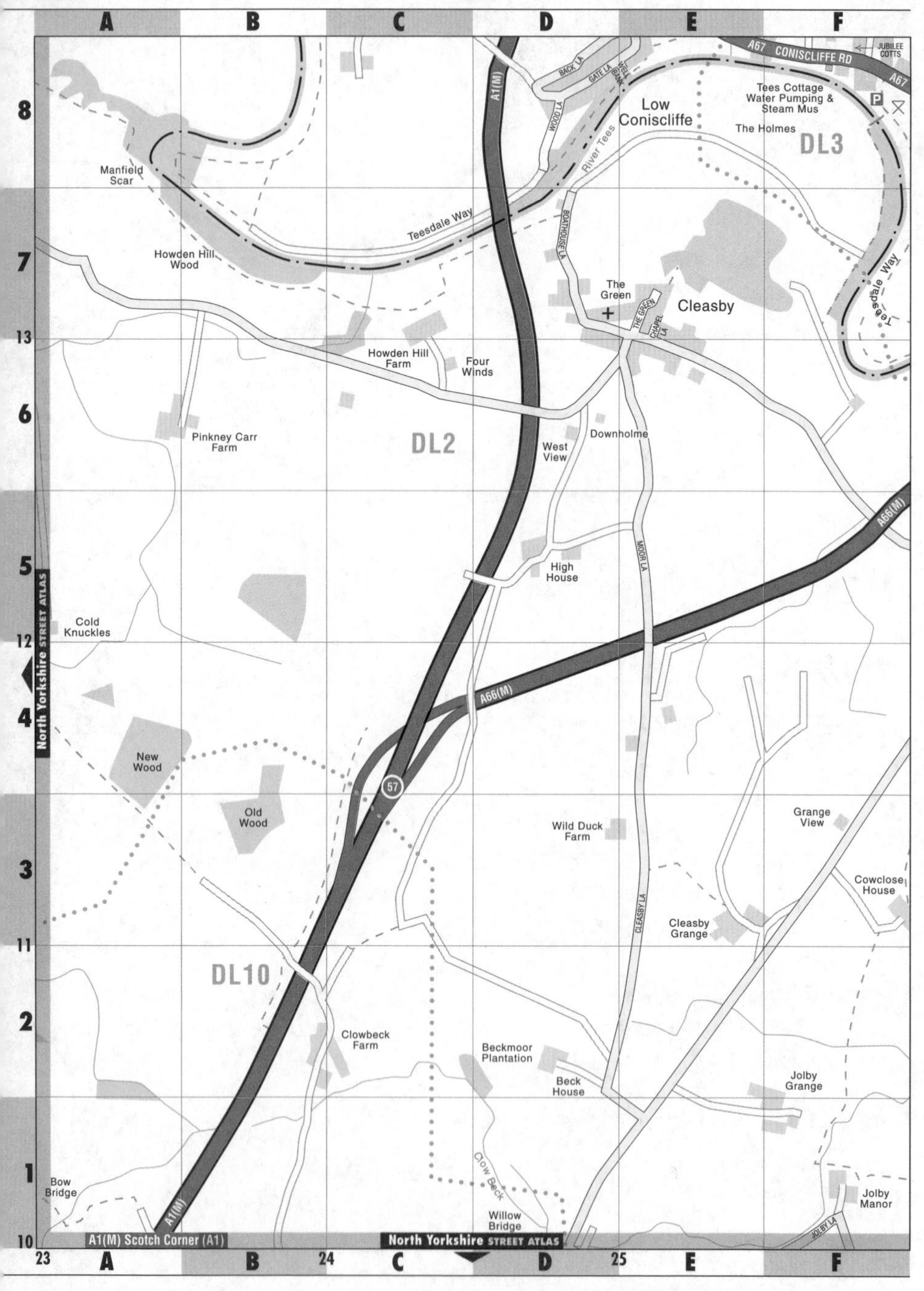
A
B
C
D
E
F
8
7
13
6
5
12
4
3
11
2
1
10
23
24
25
A67
CONISCLIFFE RD
JUBILEE COTTS
A67
BACK LA
GATE LA
WELL BANK
WOOD LA
A1(M)
Low Conisclifffe
Tees Cottage Water Pumping & Steam Mus
The Holmes
DL3
Manfield Scar
River Tees
Teesdale Way
BOATHOUSE LA
Howden Hill Wood
The Green
THE GREEN
CHAPEL LA
Cleasby
Teesdale Way
Howden Hill Farm
Four Winds
Pinkney Carr Farm
DL2
West View
Downholme
A66(M)
MOOR LA
High House
Cold Knuckles
North Yorkshire STREET ATLAS
A66(M)
New Wood
57
Old Wood
Wild Duck Farm
Grange View
Cowclose House
CLEASBY LA
Cleasby Grange
DL10
Clowbeck Farm
Beckmoor Plantation
Beck House
Jolby Grange
Clow Beck
Bow Bridge
Willow Bridge
Jolby Manor
JOLBY LA
A1(M)
A1(M) Scotch Corner (A1)
North Yorkshire STREET ATLAS

132
152

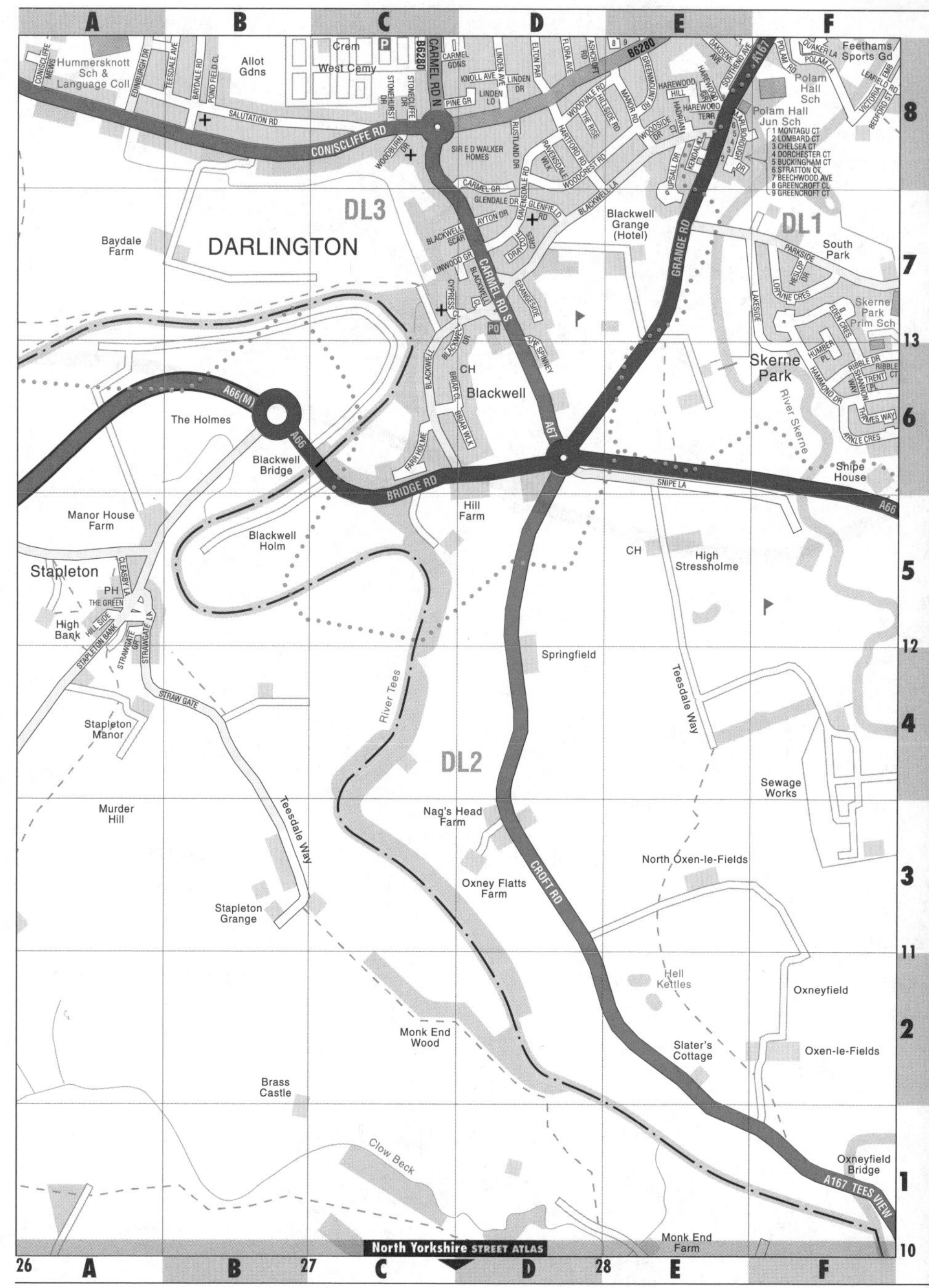
A
B
C
D
E
F
Hummersknott Sch & Language Coll
Allot Gdns
Crem
West Cemy
Feethams Sports Gd
Polam Hall Sch
Polam Hall Jun Sch
1 MONTAGU CT
2 LOMBARD CT
3 CHELSEA CT
4 DORCHESTER CT
5 BUCKINGHAM CT
6 STRATTON CT
7 BEECHWOOD AVE
8 GREENCROFT CL
9 GREENCROFT CT
CONISCLIFFE RD
SALUTATION RD
CARMEL RD N
CARMEL RD S
B6280
A167
SIR E D WALKER HOMES
DL3
DL1
DL2
DARLINGTON
Baydale Farm
Blackwell Grange (Hotel)
South Park
Skerne Park
Skerne Park Prim Sch
GRANGE RD
Blackwell
CH
A66(M)
A66
A67
The Holmes
Blackwell Bridge
BRIDGE RD
SNIPE LA
Snipe House
Hill Farm
Manor House Farm
Blackwell Holm
High Stressholme
Stapleton
PH
High Bank
Springfield
River Tees
River Skerne
Teesdale Way
Stapleton Manor
Sewage Works
Murder Hill
Nag's Head Farm
North Oxen-le-Fields
Oxney Flatts Farm
CROFT RD
Stapleton Grange
Hell Kettles
Oxneyfield
Monk End Wood
Slater's Cottage
Oxen-le-Fields
Brass Castle
Clow Beck
Oxneyfield Bridge
A167 TEES VIEW
Monk End Farm
8
7
6
5
4
3
2
1
13
12
11
10
26
27
28

152

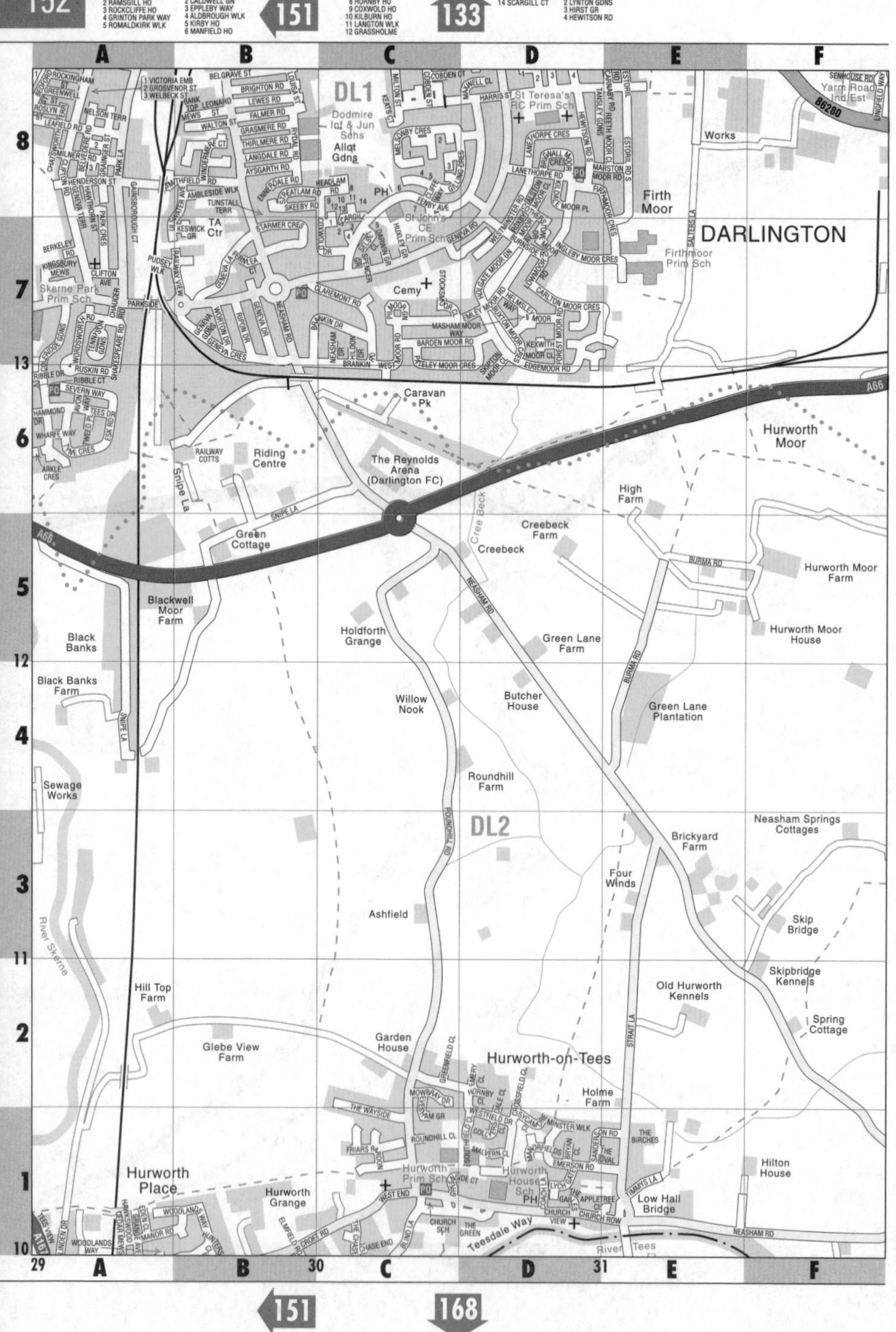

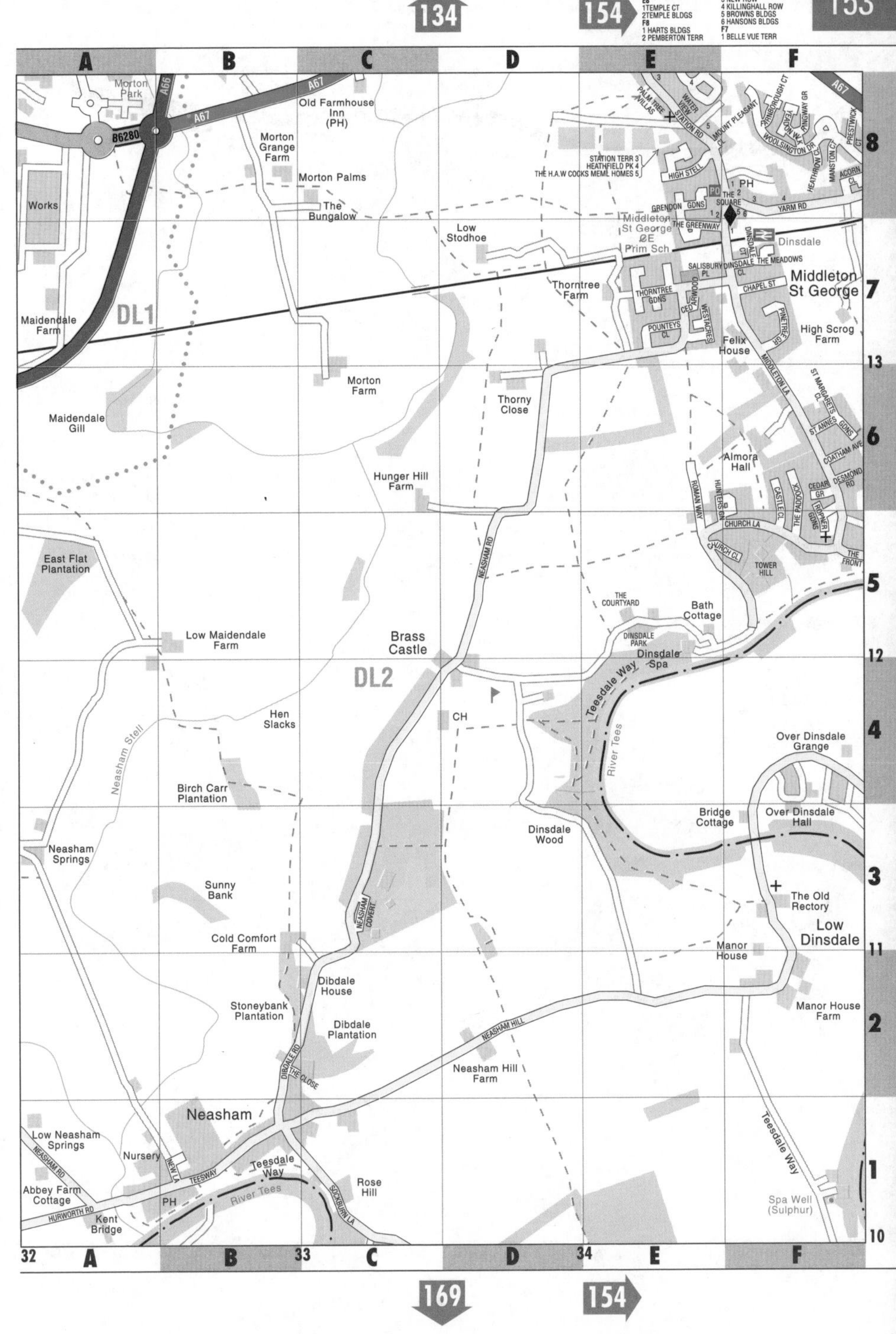
A
B
C
D
E
F
Morton Park
A66
A67
B6280
Old Farmhouse Inn (PH)
Morton Grange Farm
Morton Palms
The Bungalow
Works
Low Stodhoe
Maidendale Farm
DL1
Thorntree Farm
Middleton St George CE Prim Sch
Middleton St George
Dinsdale
High Scrog Farm
Felix House
Morton Farm
Thorny Close
Maidendale Gill
Hunger Hill Farm
Almora Hall
East Flat Plantation
Low Maidendale Farm
Brass Castle
DL2
The Courtyard
Bath Cottage
Dinsdale Park
Dinsdale Spa
Tower Hill
Teesdale Way
River Tees
Hen Slacks
CH
Over Dinsdale Grange
Birch Carr Plantation
Bridge Cottage
Over Dinsdale Hall
Neasham Springs
Dinsdale Wood
Neasham Stell
Sunny Bank
The Old Rectory
Low Dinsdale
Cold Comfort Farm
Manor House
Dibdale House
Stoneybank Plantation
Dibdale Plantation
Manor House Farm
Neasham Hill Farm
Neasham
Low Neasham Springs
Nursery
Abbey Farm Cottage
Kent Bridge
PH
Rose Hill
Spa Well (Sulphur)
NEASHAM RD
NEASHAM COVERT
NEASHAM HILL
DIBDALE RD
THE CLOSE
TEESWAY
SOCKBURN LA
HURWORTH RD
NEW LA
PALM TREE VILLAS
WATER VIEW
STATION RD
MOUNT PLEASANT
STATION TERR 3
HEATHFIELD PK 4
THE H.A.W COCKS MEML HOMES 5
HIGH STELL
GRENDON GDNS
THE GREENWAY
THE SQUARE
YARM RD
DINSDALE CT
THE MEADOWS
SALISBURY PL
DINSDALE CL
CHAPEL ST
THORNTREE GDNS
CEDARWOOD
WESTACRES
POUNTEYS CL
PINETREE GR
MIDDLETON LA
ST MARGARETS CL
ST ANNES GDNS
COATHAM AVE
DESMOND RD
CEDAR GR
ROMAN WAY
HUNTERS GN
CASTLE CL
THE PADDOCK
RAPHAEL GDNS
CHURCH LA
CHURCH CL
THE FRONT
WOOLSINGTON DR
HEATHROW CL
MANSTON CT
ACORN CL
PRESTWICK CT
RINGWAY GR
YEADON WK
FARNBOROUGH CT
PO
8
7
6
5
4
3
2
1
13
12
11
10
32
33
34

153
135

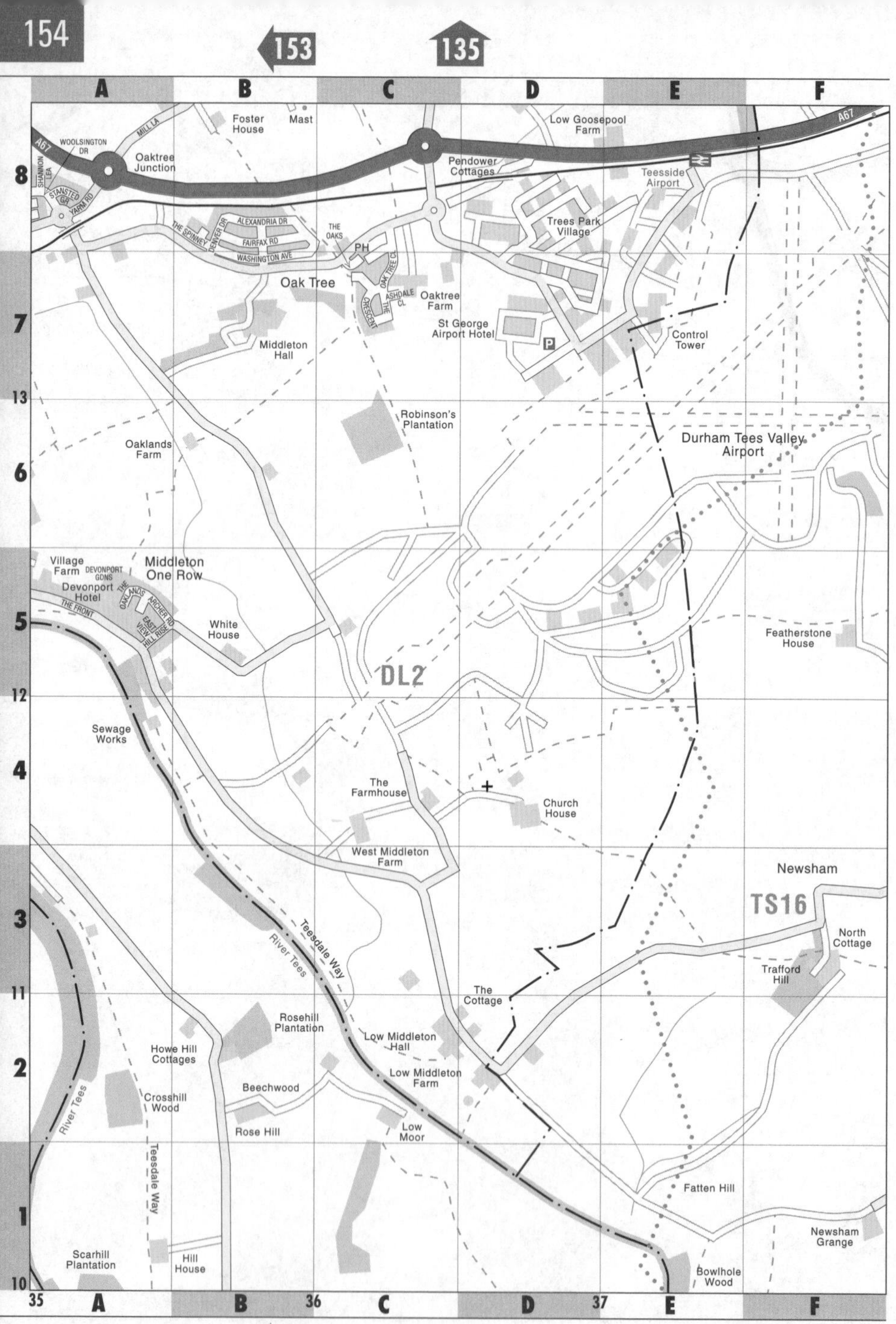
A
B
C
D
E
F
Foster House
Mast
Low Goosepool Farm
A67
Oaktree Junction
Pendower Cottages
Teesside Airport
Trees Park Village
PH
Oak Tree
Oaktree Farm
St George Airport Hotel
Control Tower
Middleton Hall
Robinson's Plantation
Durham Tees Valley Airport
Oaklands Farm
Village Farm
Middleton One Row
Devonport Hotel
White House
Featherstone House
DL2
Sewage Works
The Farmhouse
Church House
West Middleton Farm
Newsham
TS16
Teesdale Way
River Tees
North Cottage
Trafford Hill
The Cottage
Rosehill Plantation
Low Middleton Hall
Howe Hill Cottages
Low Middleton Farm
Beechwood
Crosshill Wood
Rose Hill
Low Moor
Fatten Hill
Newsham Grange
Scarhill Plantation
Hill House
Bowlhole Wood
8
7
13
6
5
12
4
3
11
2
1
10
35
36
37

153
170

136
156

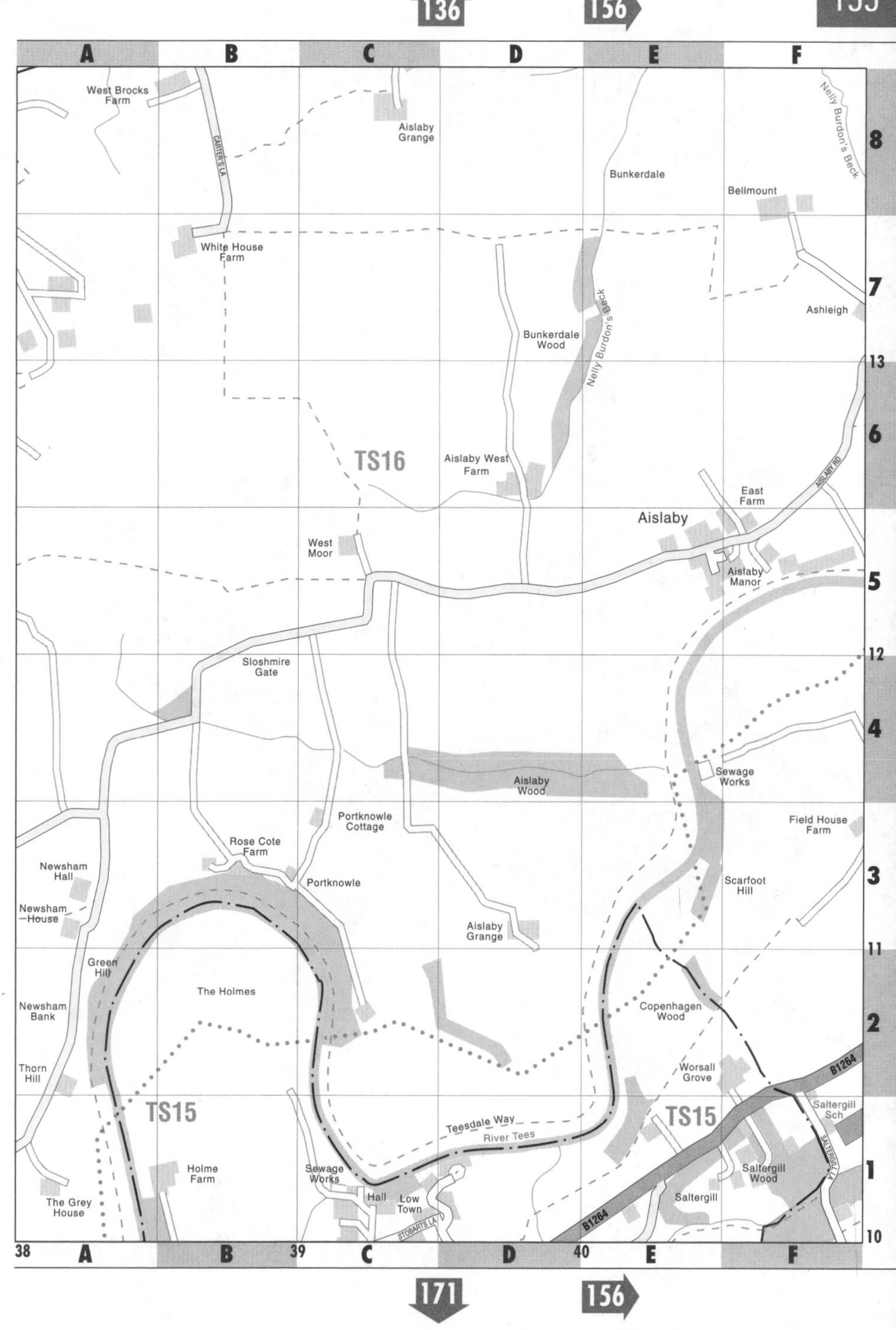
A
B
C
D
E
F
West Brocks Farm
Aislaby Grange
CARTER'S LA
Nelly Burdon's Beck
8
Bunkerdale
Bellmount
White House Farm
7
Ashleigh
Bunkerdale Wood
Nelly Burdon's Beck
13
6
TS16
Aislaby West Farm
AISLABY RD
East Farm
Aislaby
West Moor
Aislaby Manor
5
12
Sloshmire Gate
4
Sewage Works
Aislaby Wood
Portknowle Cottage
Field House Farm
Rose Cote Farm
Newsham Hall
Portknowle
3
Scarfoot Hill
Newsham House
Aislaby Grange
11
Green Hill
The Holmes
Newsham Bank
Copenhagen Wood
2
Thorn Hill
Worsall Grove
B1264
Saltergill Sch
TS15
Teesdale Way
TS15
River Tees
SALTERGILL LA
Holme Farm
Sewage Works
1
Saltergill Wood
Hall
Low Town
The Grey House
Saltergill
STOBARTS LA
B1264
10
38
A
B
39
C
D
40
E
F

171
156

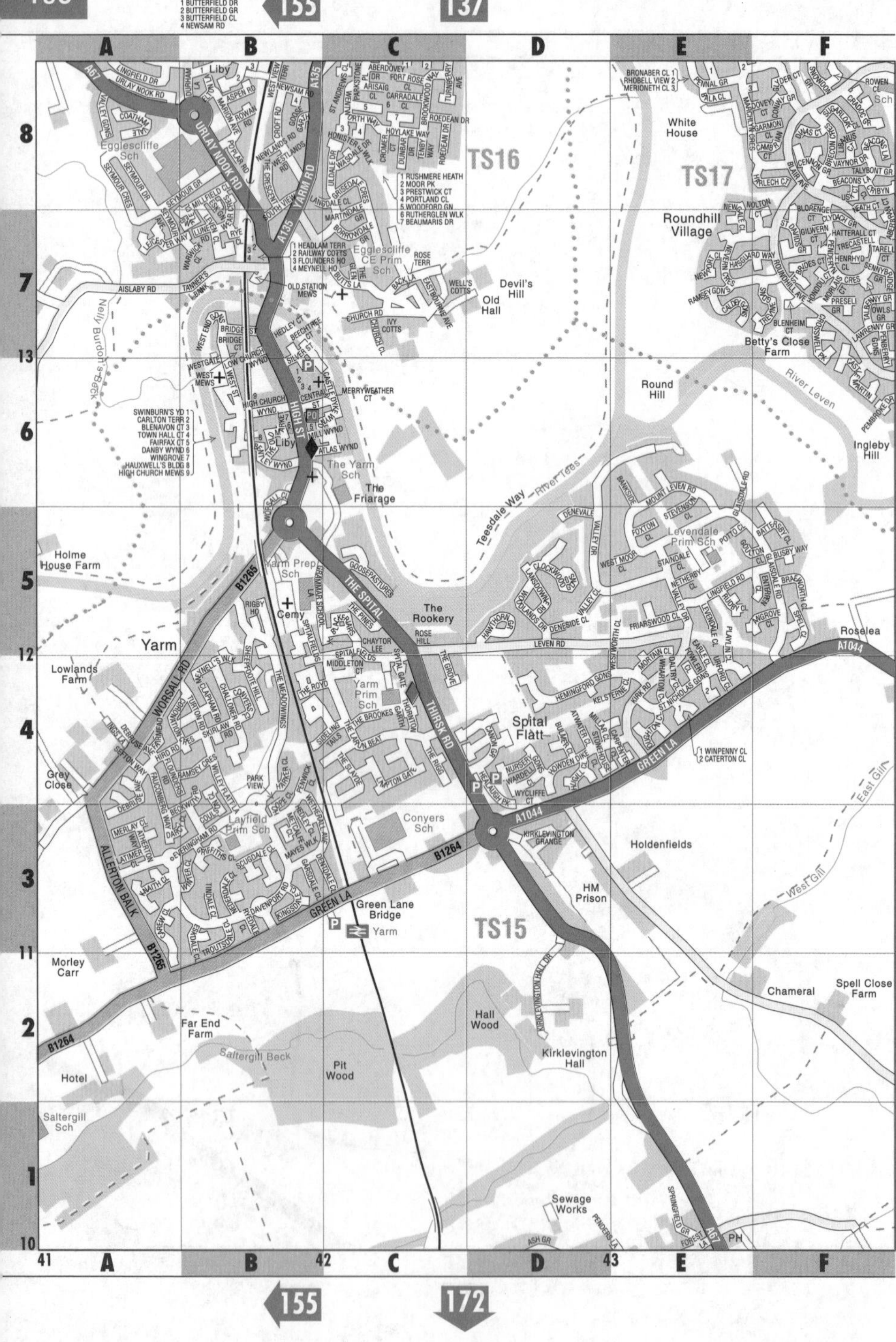
B8
1 BUTTERFIELD DR
2 BUTTERFIELD GR
3 BUTTERFIELD CL
4 NEWSAM RD
155
137
A
B
C
D
E
F
8
7
13
6
5
12
4
3
11
2
1
10
41
42
43
TS16
TS17
TS15
Egglescliffe Sch
Egglescliffe CE Prim Sch
URLAY NOOK RD
YARM RD
A135
A67
White House
Roundhill Village
Devil's Hill
Old Hall
Betty's Close Farm
Round Hill
River Leven
Ingleby Hill
1 RUSHMERE HEATH
2 MOOR PK
3 PRESTWICK CT
4 PORTLAND CL
5 WOODFORD GN
6 RUTHERGLEN WLK
7 BEAUMARIS DR
1 HEADLAM TERR
2 RAILWAY COTTS
3 FLOUNDERS HO
4 MEYNELL HO
BRONABER CL 1
RHOBELL VIEW 2
MERIONETH CL 3
AISLABY RD
Nelly Burdon's Beck
OLD STATION MEWS
HIGH ST
SWINBURN'S YD 1
CARLTON TERR 2
BLENAVON CT 3
TOWN HALL CT 4
FAIRFAX CT 5
DANBY WYND 6
WINGROVE 7
HAUXWELL'S BLDG 8
HIGH CHURCH MEWS 9
The Yarm Sch
The Friarage
River Tees
Teesdale Way
Holme House Farm
Yarm Prep Sch
Cemy
The Rookery
Levendale Prim Sch
LEVEN RD
A1044
Roselea
Yarm
Lowlands Farm
WORSALL RD
B1265
THE SPITAL
THIRSK RD
Yarm Prim Sch
Spital Flatt
GREEN LA
1 WINPENNY CL
2 CATERTON CL
Grey Close
Layfield Prim Sch
Conyers Sch
Holdenfields
B1264
ALLERTON BALK
HM Prison
East Gill
West Gill
Green Lane Bridge
Yarm
Morley Carr
Chameral
Spell Close Farm
Far End Farm
Hall Wood
Saltergill Beck
Pit Wood
Kirklevington Hall
Hotel
Saltergill Sch
Sewage Works
PH
155
172

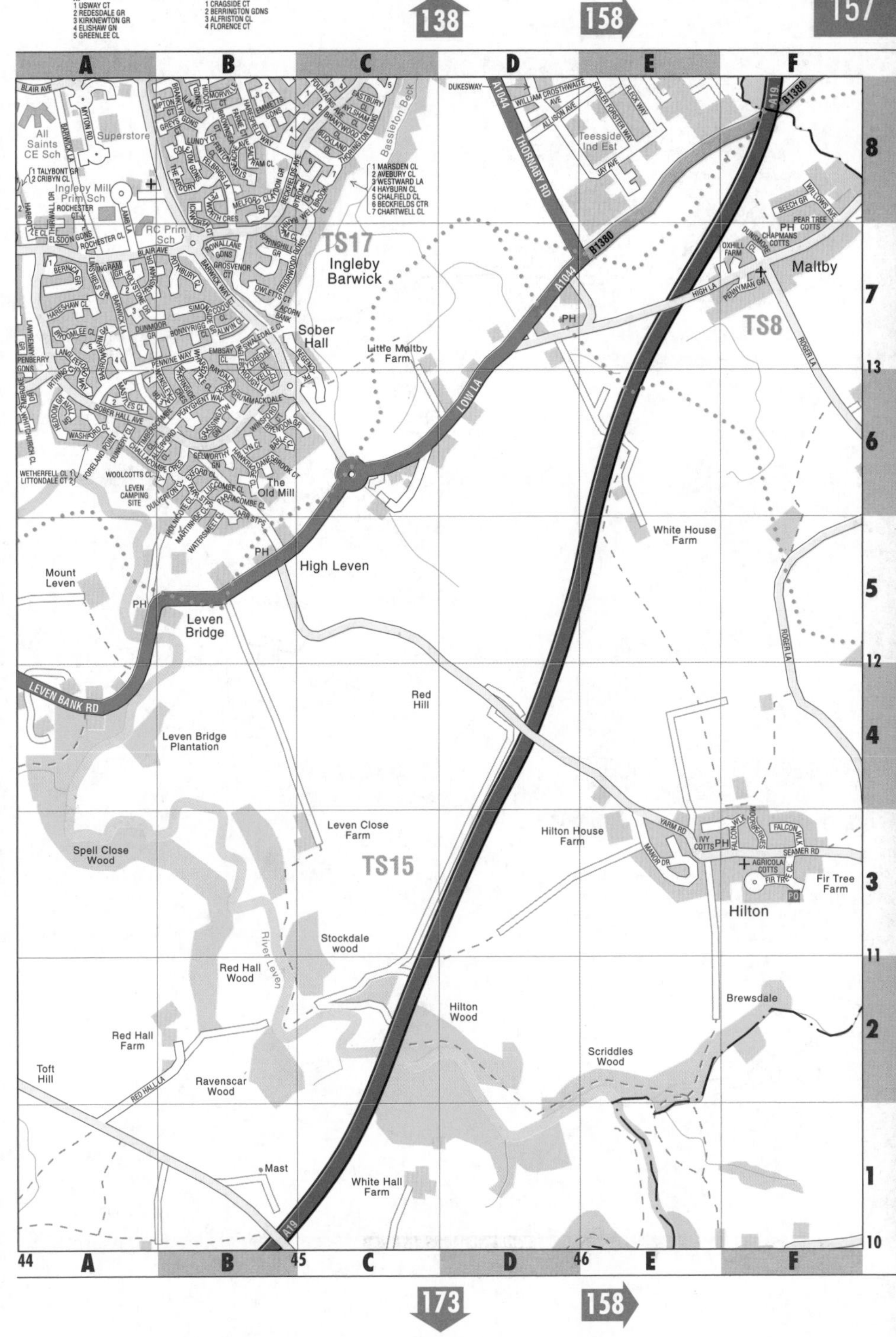

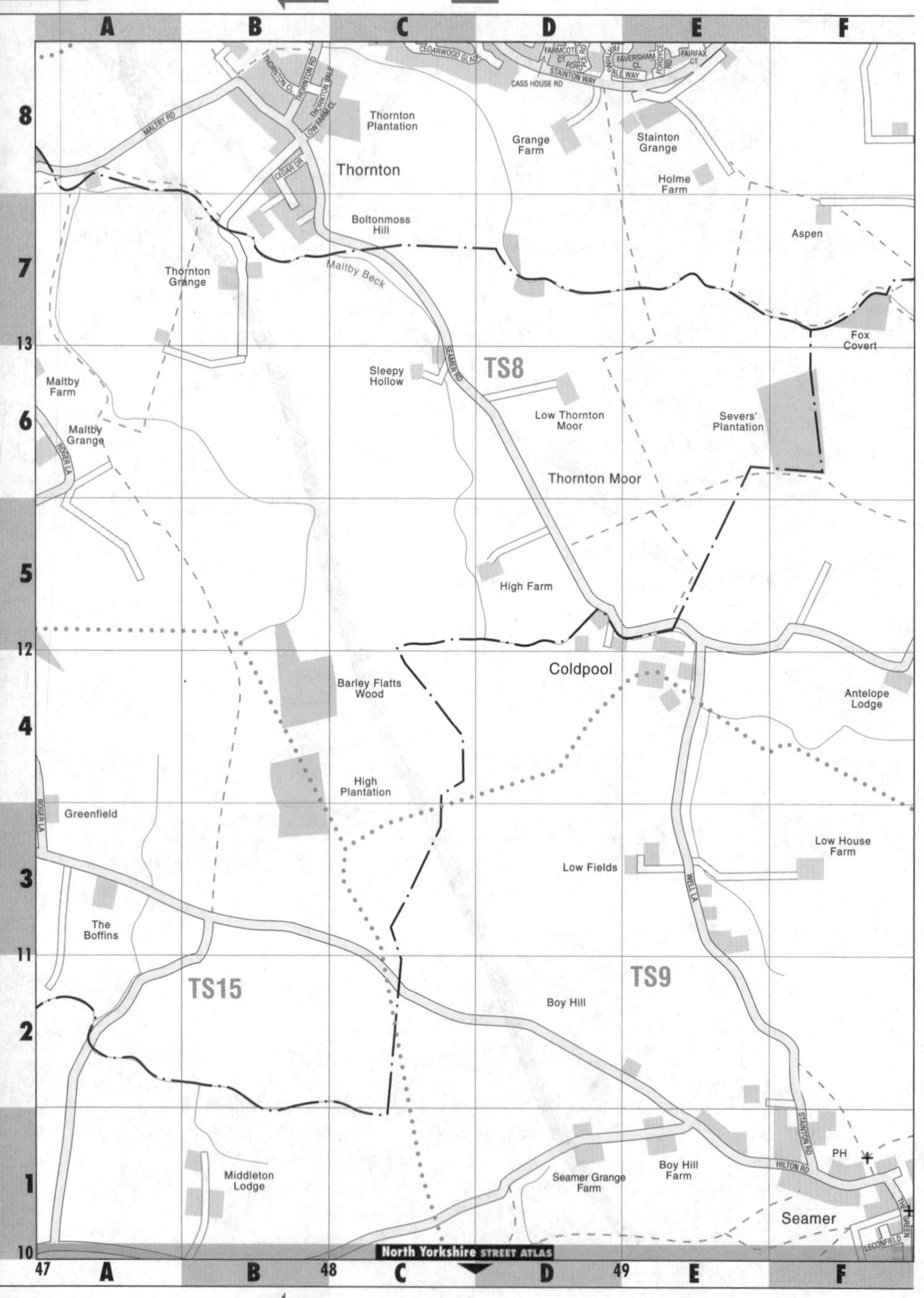

A B C D E F

8

Thornton
Plantation

Grange
Farm

Stainton
Grange

Thornton

CEDARWOOD GLADE
FARMCOTE CT
CASS HOUSE RD
STAINTON WAY
FAVERSHAM CL
DALE WAY
FAIRFAX CT

Holme
Farm

7

Boltonmoss
Hill

Aspen

MALTBY RD
THORNTON CL
THORNTON RD
THORNTON DALE
CEDAR VW

Thornton
Grange

Maltby Beck

13

Sleepy
Hollow

TS8

Fox
Covert

6

Maltby
Farm

Low Thornton
Moor

Severs'
Plantation

Maltby
Grange

RUSSELL LA

BENDER RD

Thornton Moor

5

High Farm

12

Barley Flatts
Wood

Coldpool

Antelope
Lodge

4

High
Plantation

Low House
Farm

3

Greenfield

Low Fields

BELL LA

Low House
Farm

11

The
Boffins

ROSE LA

TS15

TS9

2

Boy Hill

Middleton
Lodge

Seamer Grange
Farm

Boy Hill
Farm

STAINTON RD

HILTON RD

PH

1

Seamer

LECONFIELD

10

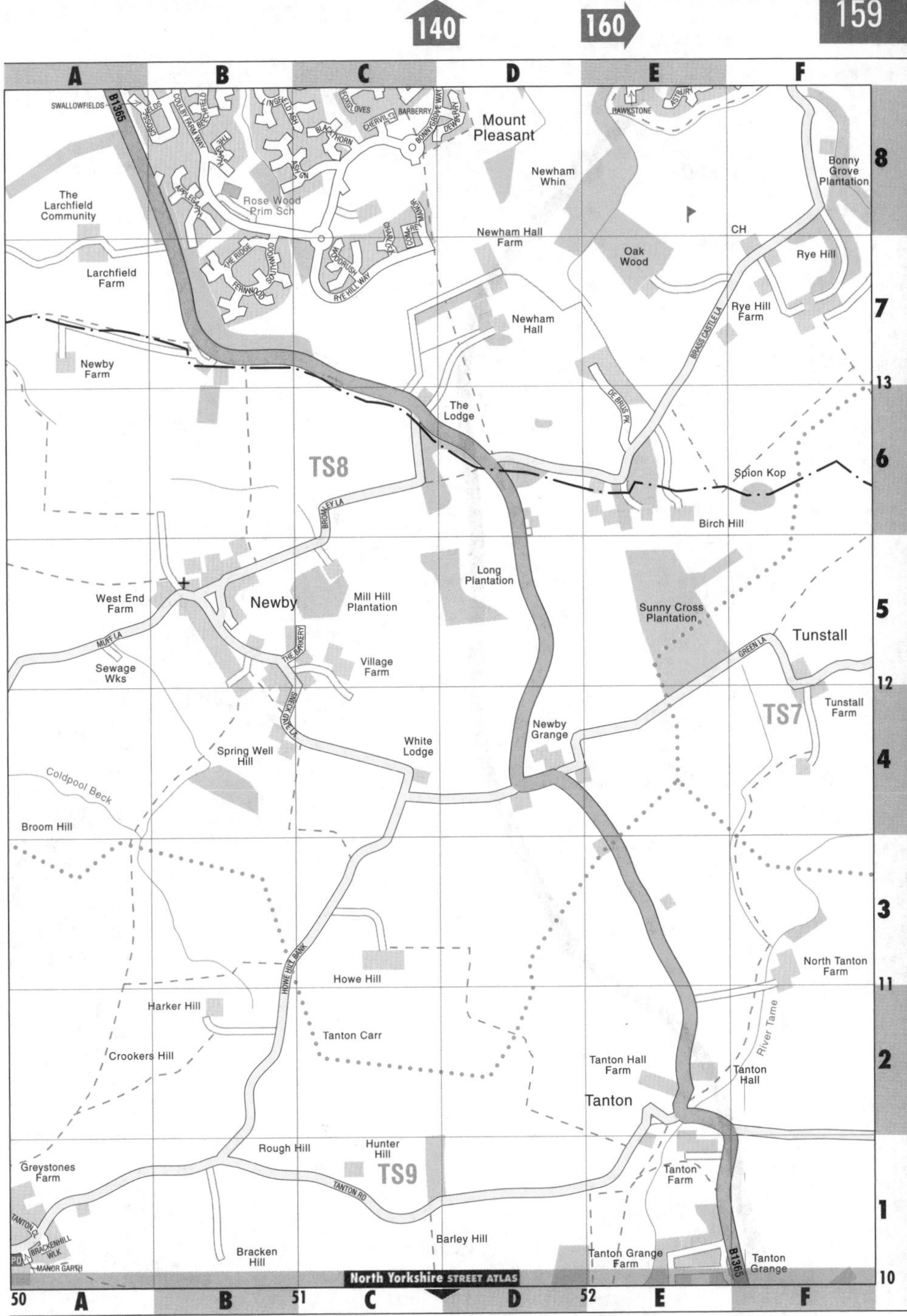

The Larchfield Community

Larchfield Farm

Newby Farm

SWALLOWFIELDS

B1305

Rose Wood Prim Sch

Mount Pleasant

Newham Whin

Newham Hall Farm

HAWKSTONE

CH

Bonny Grove Plantation

Rye Hill

Oak Wood

Rye Hill Farm

Newham Hall

The Lodge

Spion Kop

Birch Hill

TS8

West End Farm

Newby

Mill Hill Plantation

Long Plantation

Sunny Cross Plantation

Tunstall

TS7

Tunstall Farm

Sewage Wks

Village Farm

White Lodge

Newby Grange

Spring Well Hill

Coldpool Beck

Broom Hill

North Tanton Farm

Howe Hill

Harker Hill

Tanton Carr

River Tame

Crookers Hill

Tanton Hall Farm

Tanton Hall

Tanton

Greystones Farm

Rough Hill

Hunter Hill

TS9

TANTON RD

Tanton Farm

Bracken Hill

Barley Hill

Tanton Grange Farm

Tanton Grange

B1305

North Yorkshire STREET ATLAS

159
141

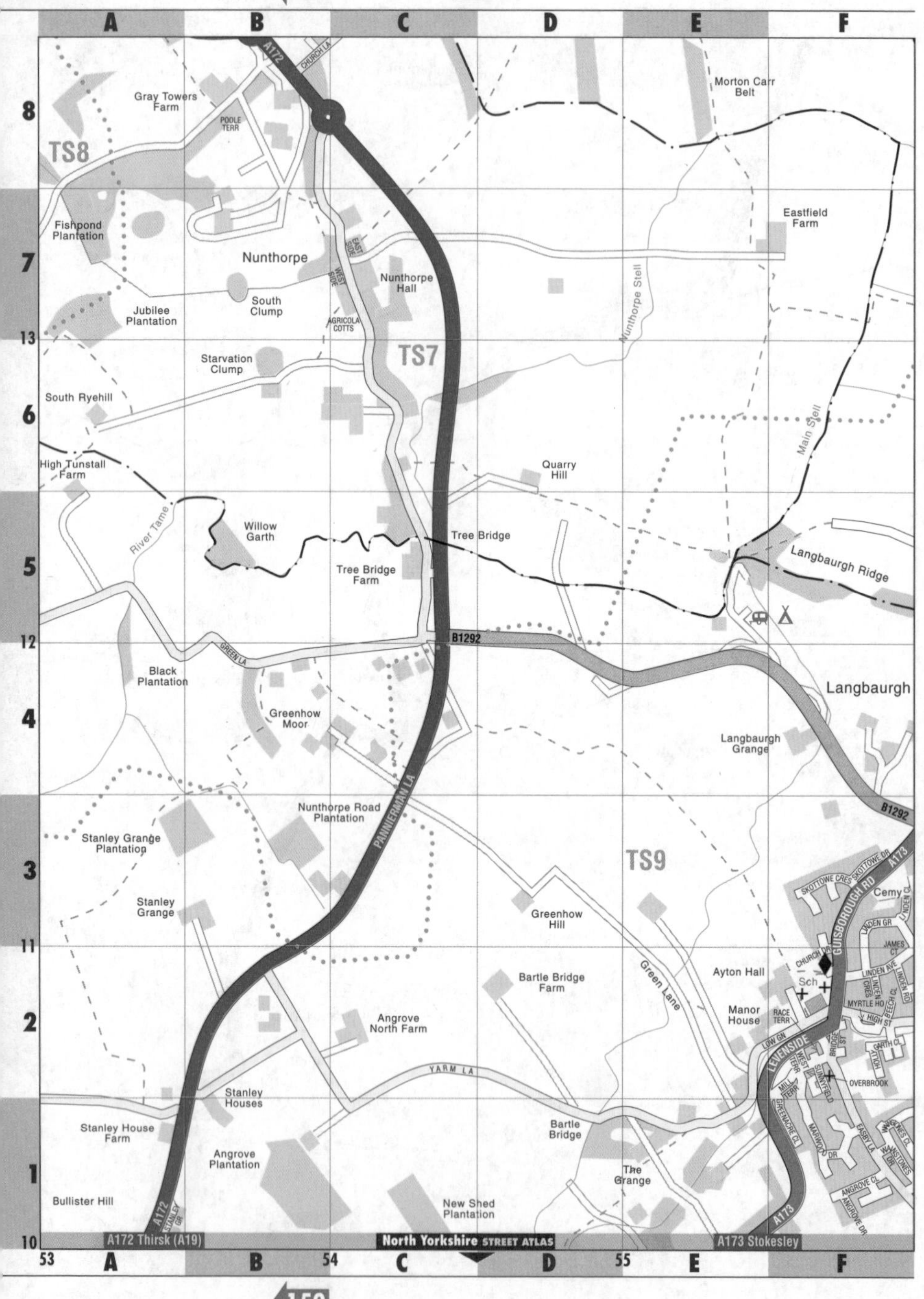

8

TS8

Gray Towers
Farm

POOLE
TERR

A172

CHURCH LA

Morton Carr
Belt

7

Fishpond
Plantation

Nunthorpe

Eastfield
Farm

Jubilee
Plantation

South
Clump

Nunthorpe
Hall

13

AGRICOLA
COTTS

WEST SIDE

TS7

Starvation
Clump

6

South Ryehill

Quarry
Hill

High Tunstall
Farm

Nunthorpe Stell

Main Spill

Willow
Garth

River Tame

Tree Bridge

Langbaurgh Ridge

5

Tree Bridge
Farm

12

B1292

GREEN LA

Langbaurgh

Black
Plantation

4

Greenhow
Moor

Langbaurgh
Grange

B1292

Nunthorpe Road
Plantation

PANNIERMAN LA

TS9

3

Stanley Grange
Plantation

Greenhow
Hill

SPROTONE CRES

SPROTONE DR

GUISBOROUGH RD

A173

Cemy

Stanley
Grange

11

Green Lane

Ayton Hall

CHURCH LA

Sch

JAMES

LINDEN GR

LINDEN RD

Bartle Bridge
Farm

MYRTLE HO

2

Angrove
North Farm

Manor
House

RACE
TERR

Y HIGH

GARTH CL

OVERBROOK

YARM LA

LEVENSIDE

LOW GR

Stanley
Houses

Bartle
Bridge

A173

Stanley House
Farm

1

Angrove
Plantation

The
Grange

A173

Bullister Hill

New Shed
Plantation

A172

North Yorkshire STREET ATLAS

142
162

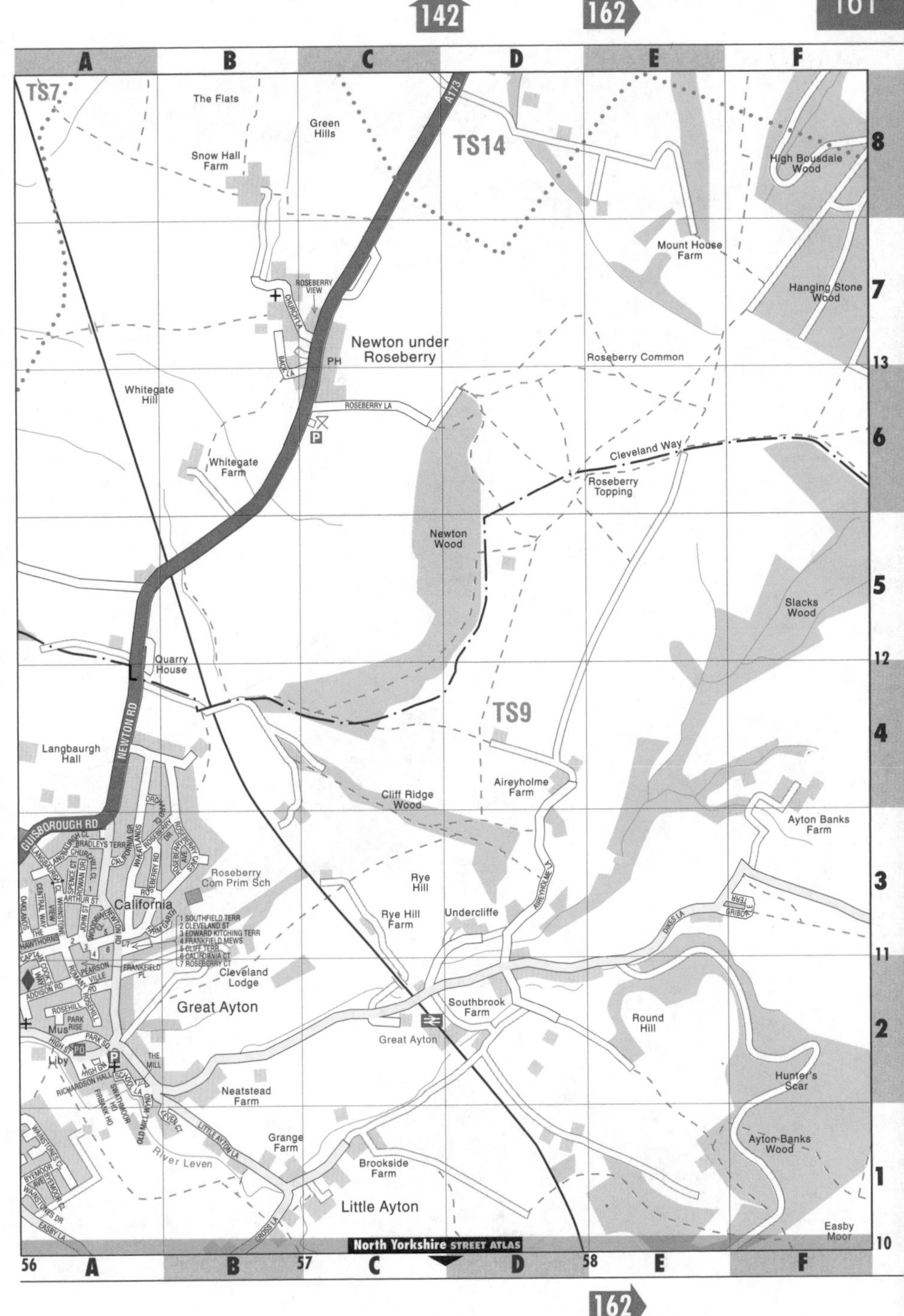
A
B
C
D
E
F
TS7
The Flats
Green Hills
Snow Hall Farm
TS14
A173
High Bousdale Wood
Mount House Farm
Hanging Stone Wood
ROSEBERRY VIEW
CHURCH LA
Newton under Roseberry
PH
BACK LA
Roseberry Common
Whitegate Hill
ROSEBERRY LA
Whitegate Farm
Cleveland Way
Roseberry Topping
Newton Wood
Slacks Wood
Quarry House
TS9
NEWTON RD
Langbaurgh Hall
Aireyholme Farm
Cliff Ridge Wood
GUISBOROUGH RD
Ayton Banks Farm
Roseberry Com Prim Sch
Rye Hill
California
Rye Hill Farm
Undercliffe
AIREYHOLME LA
1 SOUTHFIELD TERR
2 CLEVELAND ST
3 EDWARD KITCHING TERR
4 FRANKFIELD MEWS
5 CLIFF TERR
6 CALIFORNIA CT
7 ROSEBERRY CT
DIKES LA
GRIBDAE TERR
Cleveland Lodge
Great Ayton
Southbrook Farm
Round Hill
Great Ayton
Mus
Liby
Neatstead Farm
Hunter's Scar
River Leven
Grange Farm
Ayton Banks Wood
Brookside Farm
Little Ayton
Easby Moor
8
7
13
6
5
12
4
3
11
2
1
10
56
57
58
North Yorkshire STREET ATLAS

162

Hutton Village

Highcliff Wood

Highcliff Nab

Hutton Lowcross Woods

Blue Lake Wood

Hutton Wood

Bold Venture Gill

Codhill Farm

Cleveland Way

TS14

Hutton Moor

Black Nab

The Race

Codhill Slack

Codhill Heights

Sleddale Beck

Newton Moor

Great Ayton Moor

TS9

Sleddale

High Intake Plantation

Cleveland Way

Nab End

Lonsdale Plantation

Kildale Moor

Oak Tree Farm

YO21

Lonsdale

Lonsdale Beck

Percy Cross Rigg

Cockshaw Hill

Lonsdale Farm

DIKES LA

P

Little Ayton Moor

Coate Moor

The Pale

Pale End

Cleveland Way

Easby Moor

Pale End Plantation

Woodend Farm

NEW ROW

Captain Cook's Monument

Bankside Farm

Quarry Hill

144
164

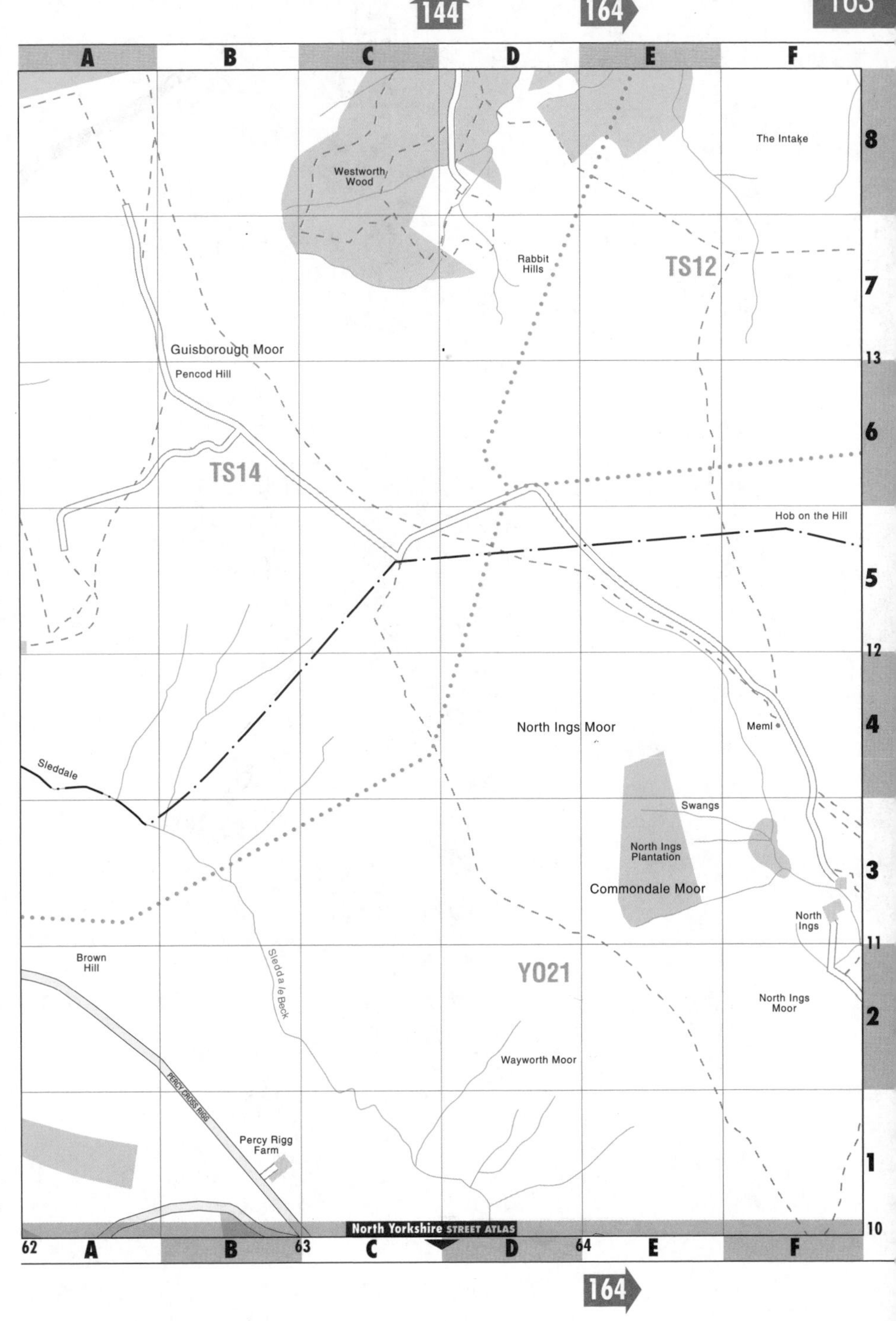
A
B
C
D
E
F
8
7
13
6
5
12
4
3
11
2
1
10
62
63
64
Westworth Wood
The Intake
Rabbit Hills
TS12
Guisborough Moor
Pencod Hill
TS14
Hob on the Hill
North Ings Moor
Meml
Sleddale
Swangs
North Ings Plantation
Commondale Moor
North Ings
Brown Hill
Sleddale Beck
YO21
North Ings Moor
Wayworth Moor
PERCY CROSS RIGG
Percy Rigg Farm

164

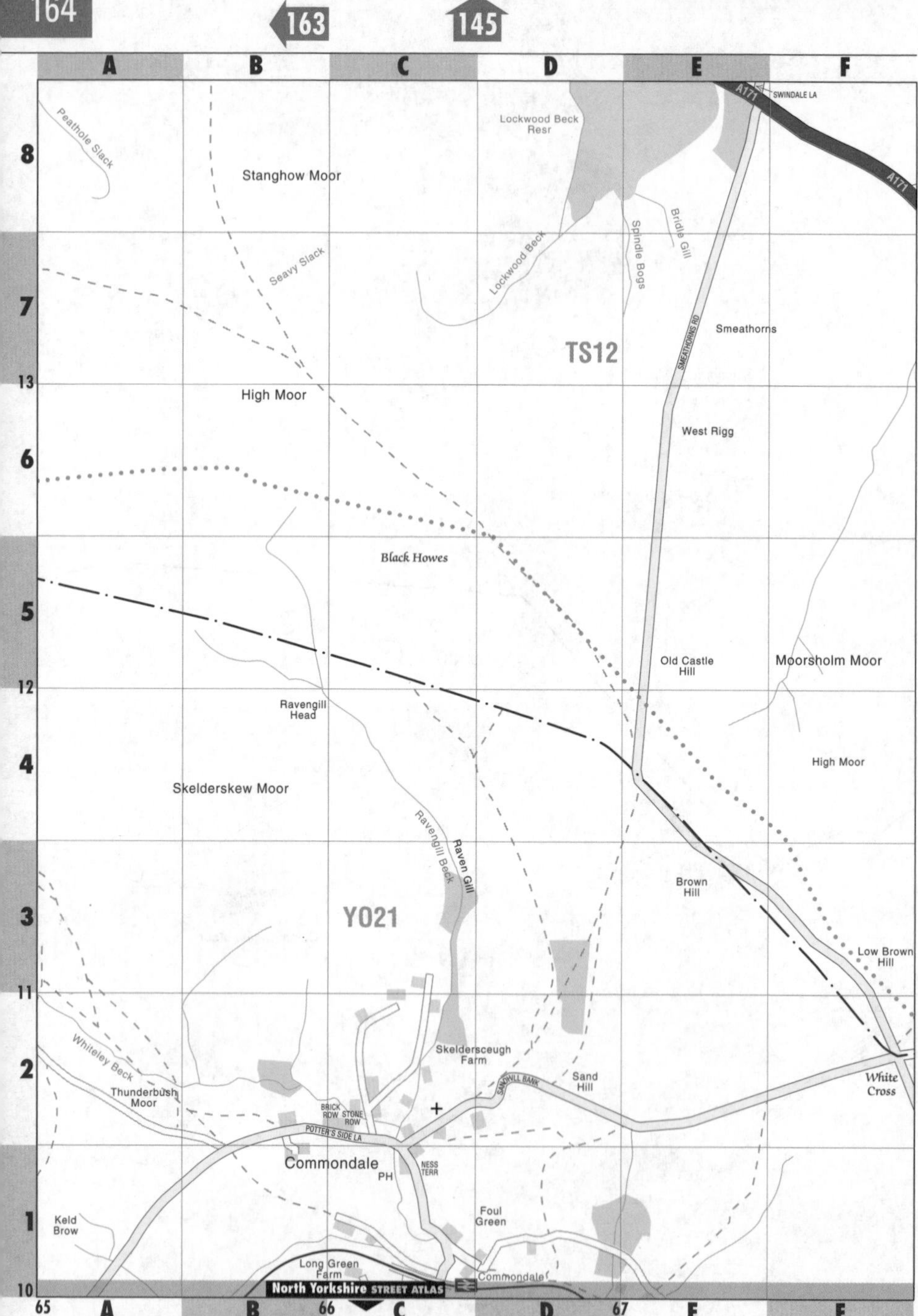

A   B   C   D   E   F

8

Peathole Slack

Stanghow Moor

Lockwood Beck
Resr

SWINDALE LA

A171

A171

7

Seavy Slack

Lockwood Beck

Spindle Bogs

Bridle Gill

GUISBOROUGH RD

TS12

Smeathorns

13

High Moor

West Rigg

6

Black Howes

5

Moorsholm Moor

12

Ravengill
Head

Old Castle
Hill

4

Skelderskew Moor

Ravengill Beck

Raven Gill

High Moor

3

YO21

Brown
Hill

Low Brown
Hill

11

Skeldersceugh
Farm

2

Whiteley Beck

Thunderbush
Moor

BRICK
ROW STONE
ROW

SANDHILL BANK

Sand
Hill

White
Cross

POTTER'S SIDE LA

Commondale

PH

NESS
TERR

1

Keld
Brow

Foul
Green

10

Long Green
Farm

Commondale

65   A   B   66   C   D   67   E   F

146
166

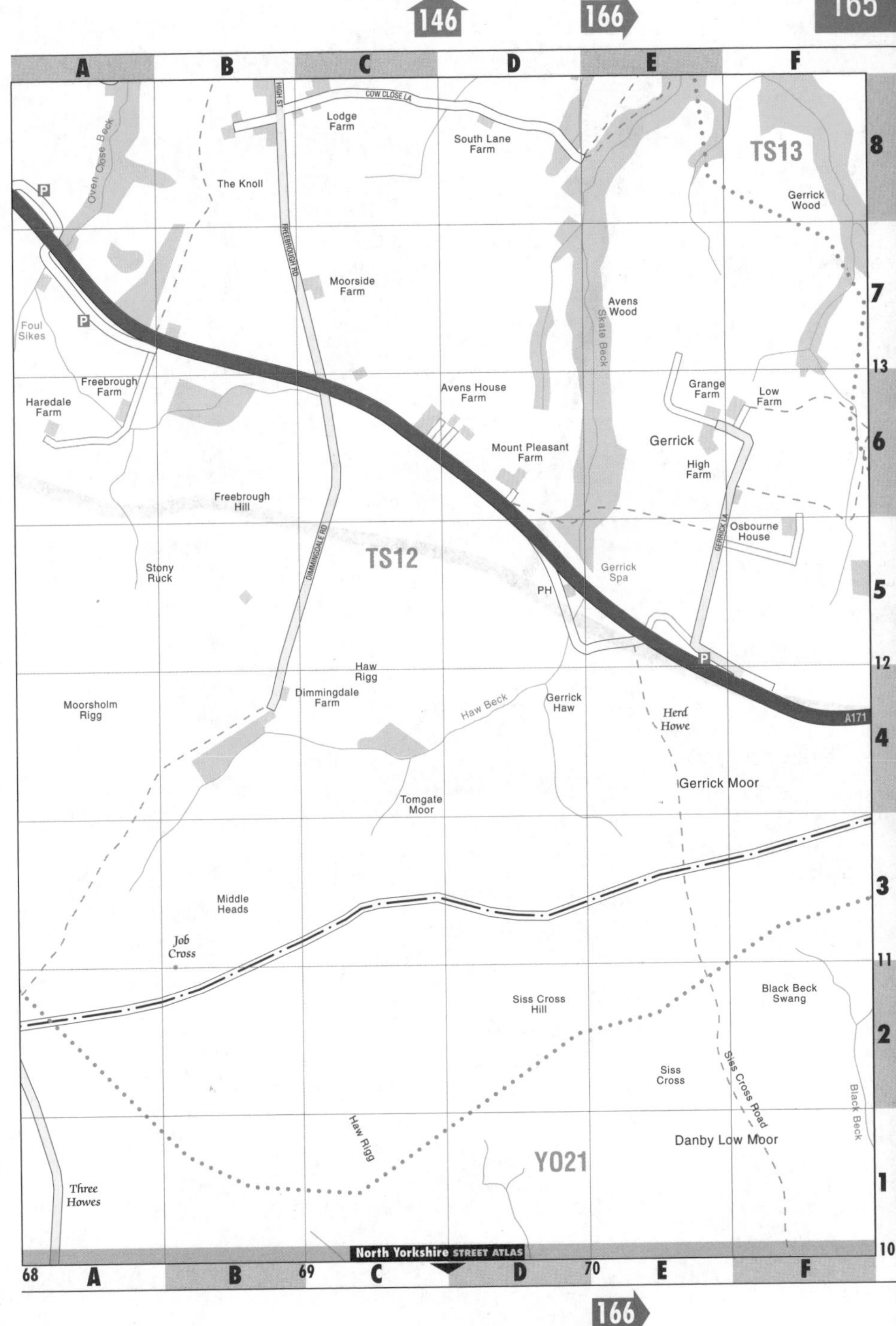
A
B
C
D
E
F
8
7
13
6
5
12
4
3
11
2
1
10
68
69
70
COW CLOSE LA
HIGH ST
Lodge Farm
South Lane Farm
TS13
Oven Close Beck
The Knoll
Gerrick Wood
FREEBROUGH RD
Moorside Farm
Avens Wood
Skate Beck
Foul Sikes
Freebrough Farm
Haredale Farm
Avens House Farm
Grange Farm
Low Farm
Gerrick
Mount Pleasant Farm
High Farm
Freebrough Hill
Osbourne House
GERRICK LA
DIMMINGDALE RD
TS12
Stony Ruck
Gerrick Spa
PH
Haw Rigg
Dimmingdale Farm
Moorsholm Rigg
Haw Beck
Gerrick Haw
Herd Howe
A171
Gerrick Moor
Tomgate Moor
Middle Heads
Job Cross
Siss Cross Hill
Black Beck Swang
Siss Cross
Siss Cross Road
Black Beck
Haw Rigg
Danby Low Moor
YO21
Three Howes

166

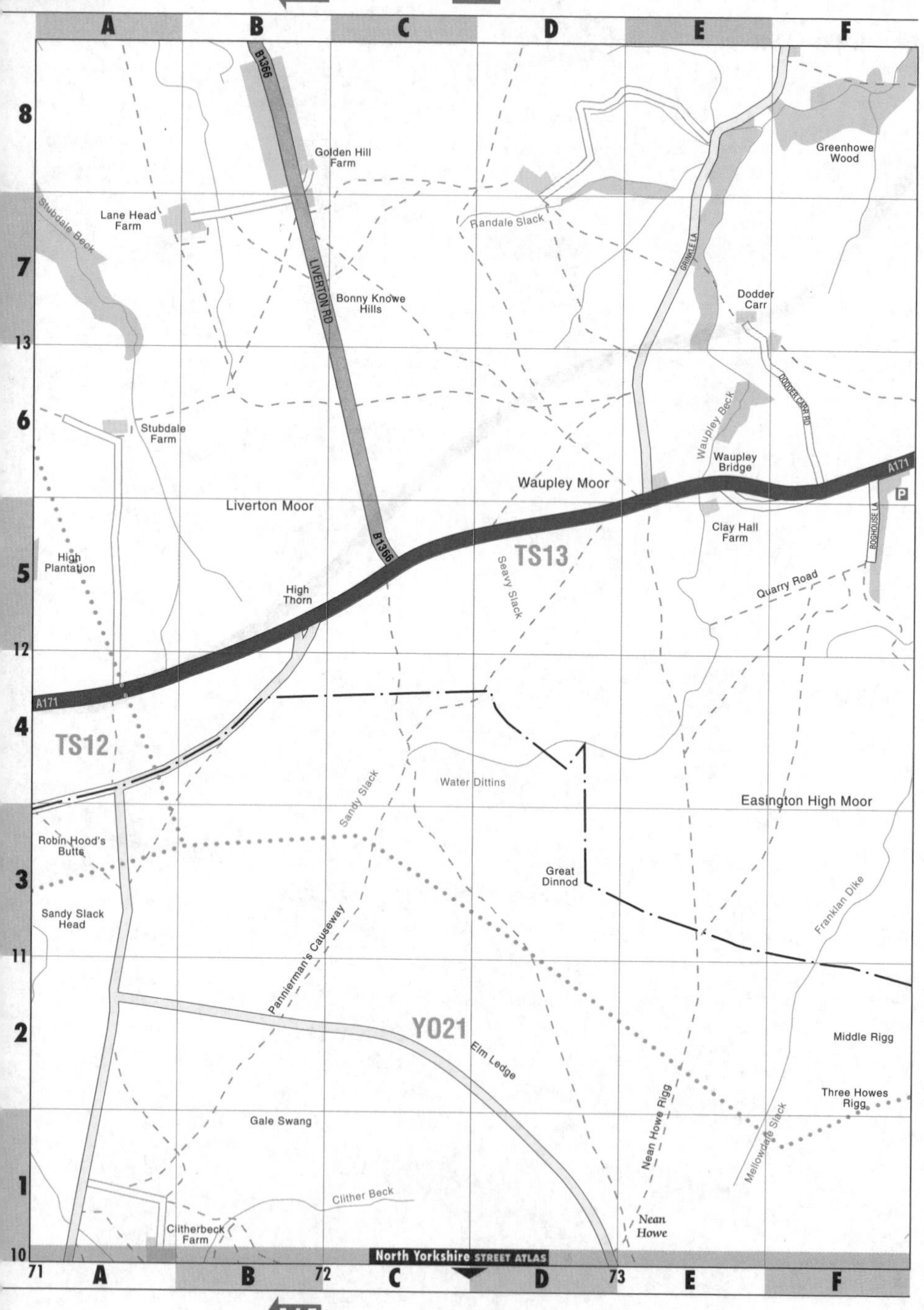

8

A **B** **C** **D** **E** **F**

Golden Hill
Farm

Lane Head
Farm

Stubdale Beck

Randale Slack

Greenhowe
Wood

7

LIVERTON RD.

Bonny Knowe
Hills

BRANT LEA

Dodder
Carr

13

6

Stubdale
Farm

DODDER CARR RD.

Waupley Beck

Waupley
Bridge

Liverton Moor

Waupley Moor

Waupley Moor

A171

P

High
Plantation

B1366

Clay Hall
Farm

5

High
Thorn

Seavy Slack

TS13

Quarry Road

12

A171

BOGHOUSE LA

4

TS12

Sandy Slack

Water Dittins

Easington High Moor

Robin Hood's
Butts

3

Great
Dinnod

Franklan Dike

Sandy Slack
Head

11

Panierman's Causeway

2

YO21

Elm Ledge

Middle Rigg

Nean Howe Rigg

Mallowdale Slack

Three Howes
Rigg

Gale Swang

1

Clither Beck

Nean
Howe

Clitherbeck
Farm

10

71 **A** **B** **72** **C** **D** **73** **E** **F**

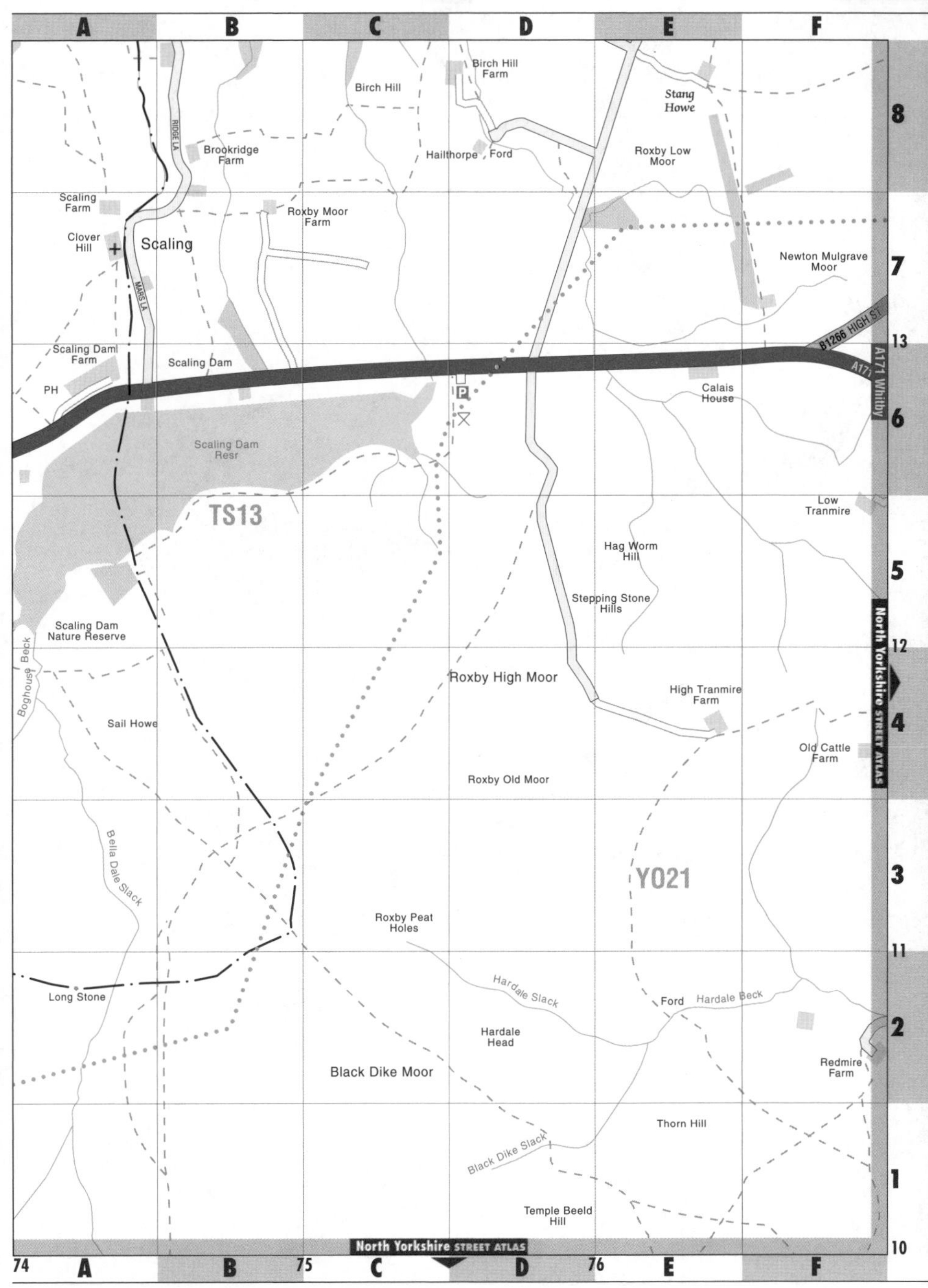
A
B
C
D
E
F
Birch Hill Farm
Birch Hill
Stang Howe
8
RIDGE LA
Brookridge Farm
Hailthorpe
Ford
Roxby Low Moor
Scaling Farm
Roxby Moor Farm
Clover Hill
Scaling
7
Newton Mulgrave Moor
MARS LA
B1266 HIGH ST
13
Scaling Dam Farm
Scaling Dam
A171
A171 Whitby
PH
Calais House
6
Scaling Dam Resr
TS13
Low Tranmire
Hag Worm Hill
5
Stepping Stone Hills
Scaling Dam Nature Reserve
North Yorkshire STREET ATLAS
12
Boghouse Beck
Roxby High Moor
High Tranmire Farm
Sail Howe
4
Old Cattle Farm
Roxby Old Moor
Bella Dale Slack
YO21
3
Roxby Peat Holes
11
Hardale Slack
Long Stone
Ford
Hardale Beck
Hardale Head
2
Redmire Farm
Black Dike Moor
Thorn Hill
Black Dike Slack
1
Temple Beeld Hill
North Yorkshire STREET ATLAS
10
74
75
76

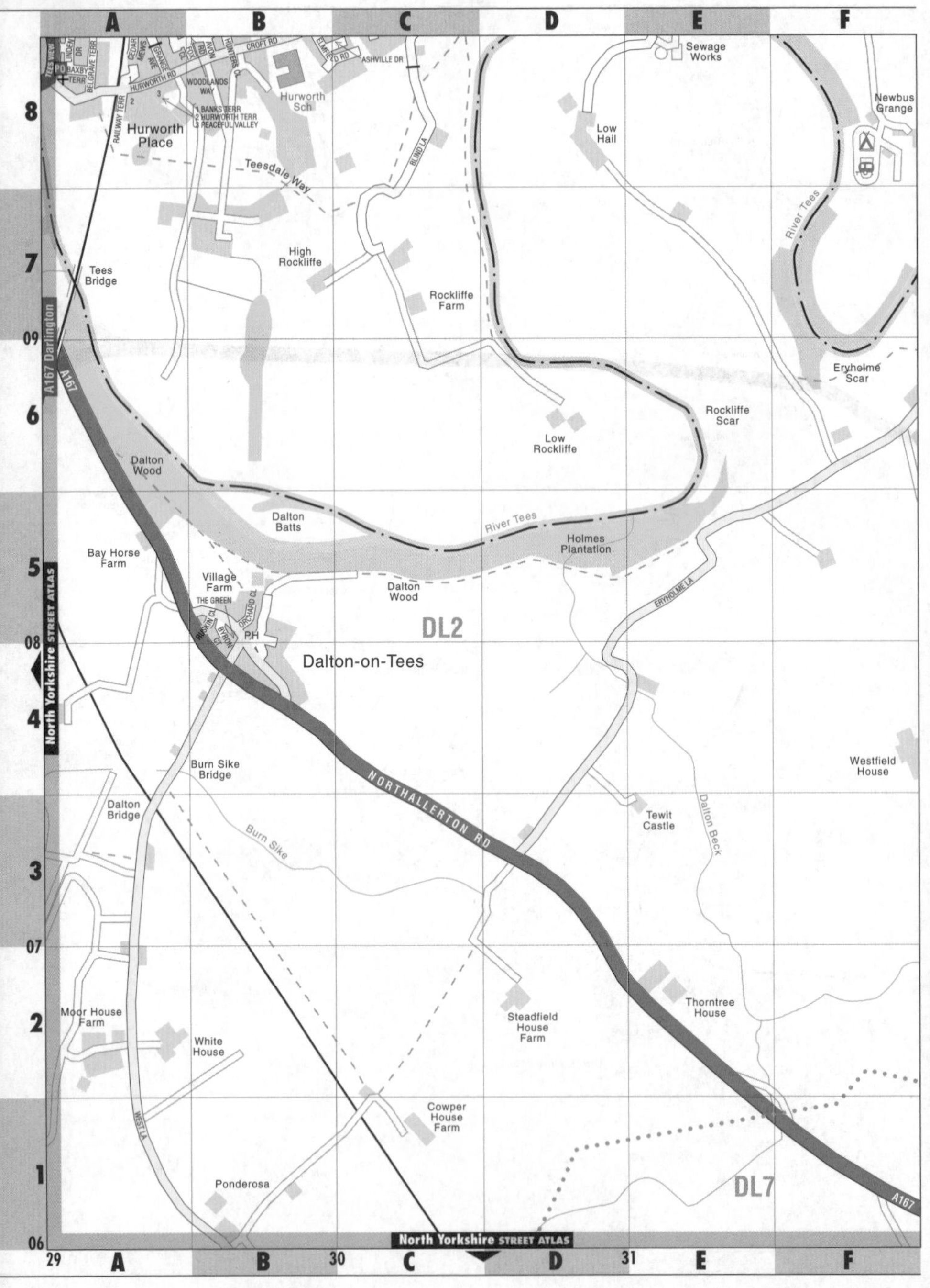

Sewage Works

Newbus Grange

Hurworth Place

Hurworth Sch

Banks Terr
Hurworth Terr
Peaceful Valley

Woodlands Way

ASHVILLE DR

CROFT RD

Low Hall

River Tees

8

Teesdale Way

High Rockliffe

Rockliffe Farm

Eryholme Scar

7

Tees Bridge

09

A167 Darlington

A167

Low Rockliffe

Rockliffe Scar

6

Dalton Wood

Dalton Batts

River Tees

Holmes Plantation

Bay Horse Farm

5

08

North Yorkshire STREET ATLAS

Village Farm

THE GREEN

PH

Dalton Wood

DL2

Dalton-on-Tees

ERYHOLME LA

Westfield House

4

Burn Sike Bridge

NORTHALLERTON RD

Tewit Castle

Dalton Beck

Dalton Bridge

Burn Sike

3

07

Moor House Farm

White House

Steadfield House Farm

Thorntree House

2

Cowper House Farm

MELL LA

DL7

A167

Ponderosa

1

06

29   A   B   30   C   D   31   E   F

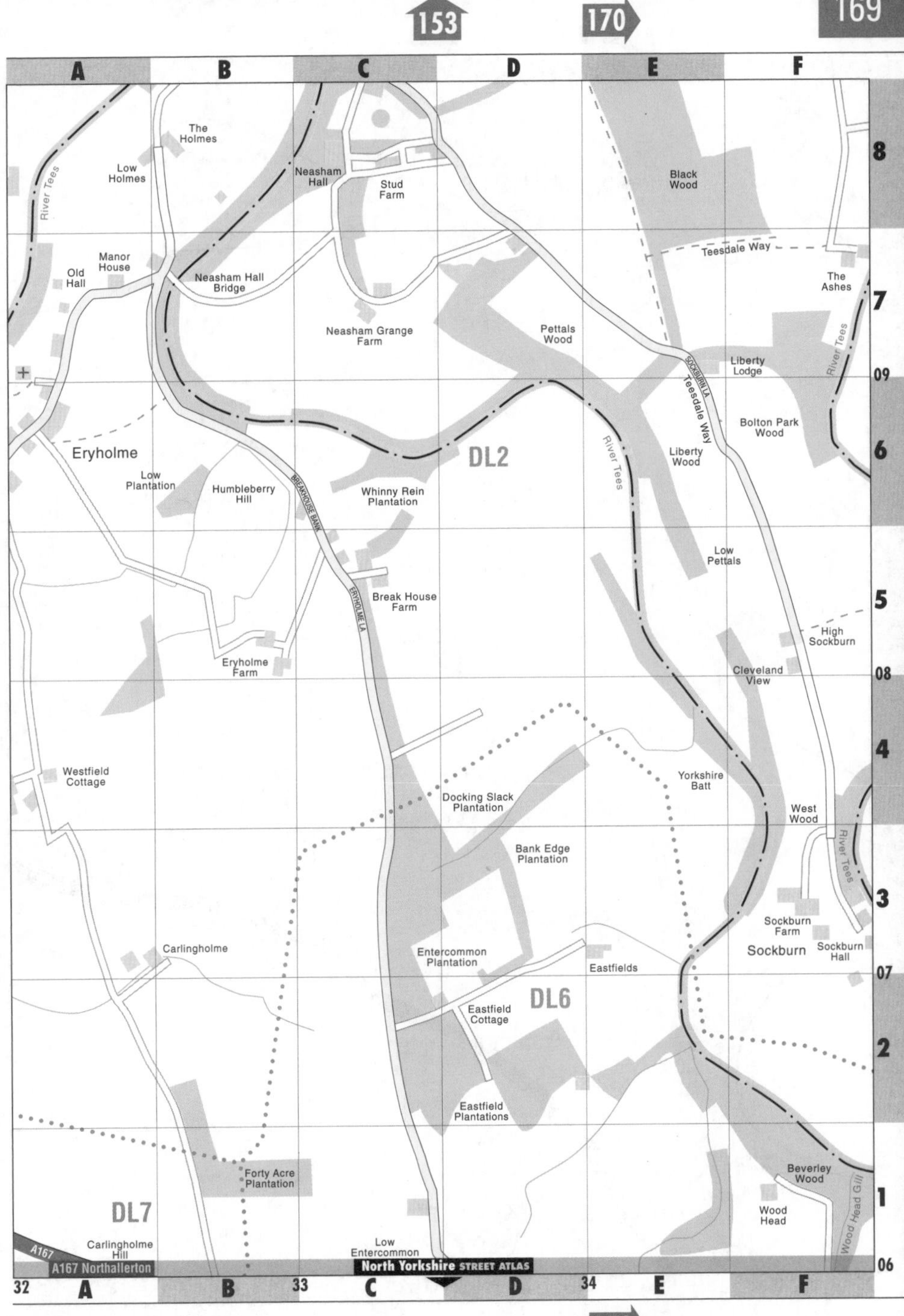
A
B
C
D
E
F
8
7
09
6
5
08
4
3
07
2
1
06
The Holmes
Low Holmes
River Tees
Neasham Hall
Stud Farm
Black Wood
Manor House
Old Hall
Neasham Hall Bridge
Teesdale Way
The Ashes
Neasham Grange Farm
Pettals Wood
Liberty Lodge
SOCKBURN LA
Teesdale Way
Bolton Park Wood
Eryholme
DL2
River Tees
Liberty Wood
Low Plantation
Humbleberry Hill
BREAKHOUSE BANK
Whinny Rein Plantation
Low Pettals
Break House Farm
ERYHOLME LA
High Sockburn
Eryholme Farm
Cleveland View
Westfield Cottage
Yorkshire Batt
Docking Slack Plantation
West Wood
Bank Edge Plantation
River Tees
Sockburn Farm
Carlingholme
Entercommon Plantation
Sockburn
Sockburn Hall
Eastfields
DL6
Eastfield Cottage
Eastfield Plantations
Beverley Wood
Forty Acre Plantation
DL7
Wood Head
Wood Head Gill
Carlingholme Hill
Low Entercommon
A167
A167 Northallerton
North Yorkshire STREET ATLAS
32
33
34

169
154

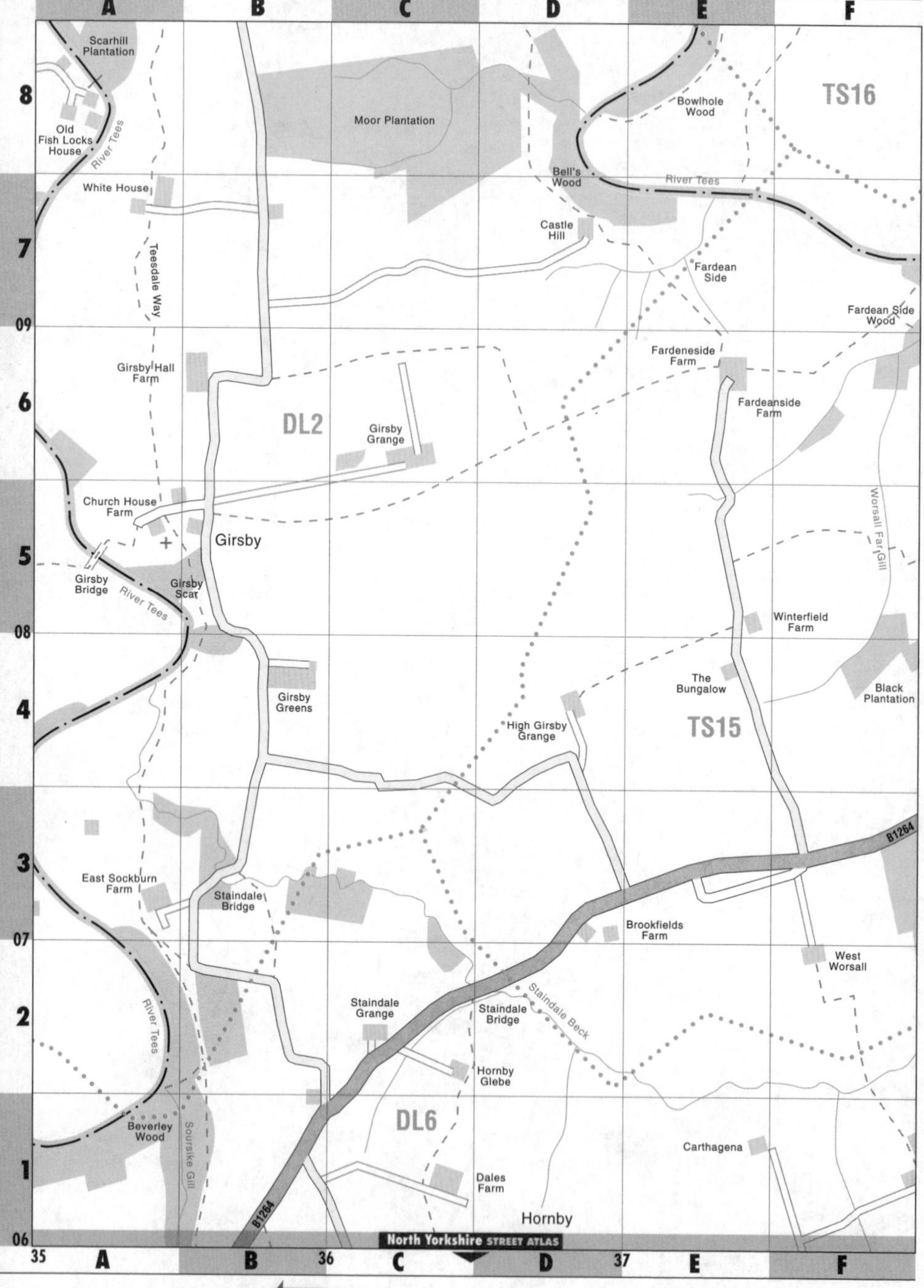
A
B
C
D
E
F
8
7
09
6
5
08
4
3
07
2
1
06
35
36
37
Scarhill Plantation
Old Fish Locks House
River Tees
White House
Teesdale Way
Moor Plantation
Bell's Wood
Castle Hill
Bowlhole Wood
TS16
Fardean Side
Fardean Side Wood
Fardeneside Farm
Fardeanside Farm
Girsby Hall Farm
DL2
Girsby Grange
Church House Farm
Girsby
Girsby Bridge
Girsby Scar
Worsall Far Gill
Winterfield Farm
The Bungalow
Black Plantation
Girsby Greens
High Girsby Grange
TS15
East Sockburn Farm
Staindale Bridge
B1264
Brookfields Farm
West Worsall
Staindale Grange
Staindale Beck
Hornby Glebe
Beverley Wood
Soursike Gill
DL6
Carthagena
Dales Farm
Hornby
North Yorkshire STREET ATLAS

169

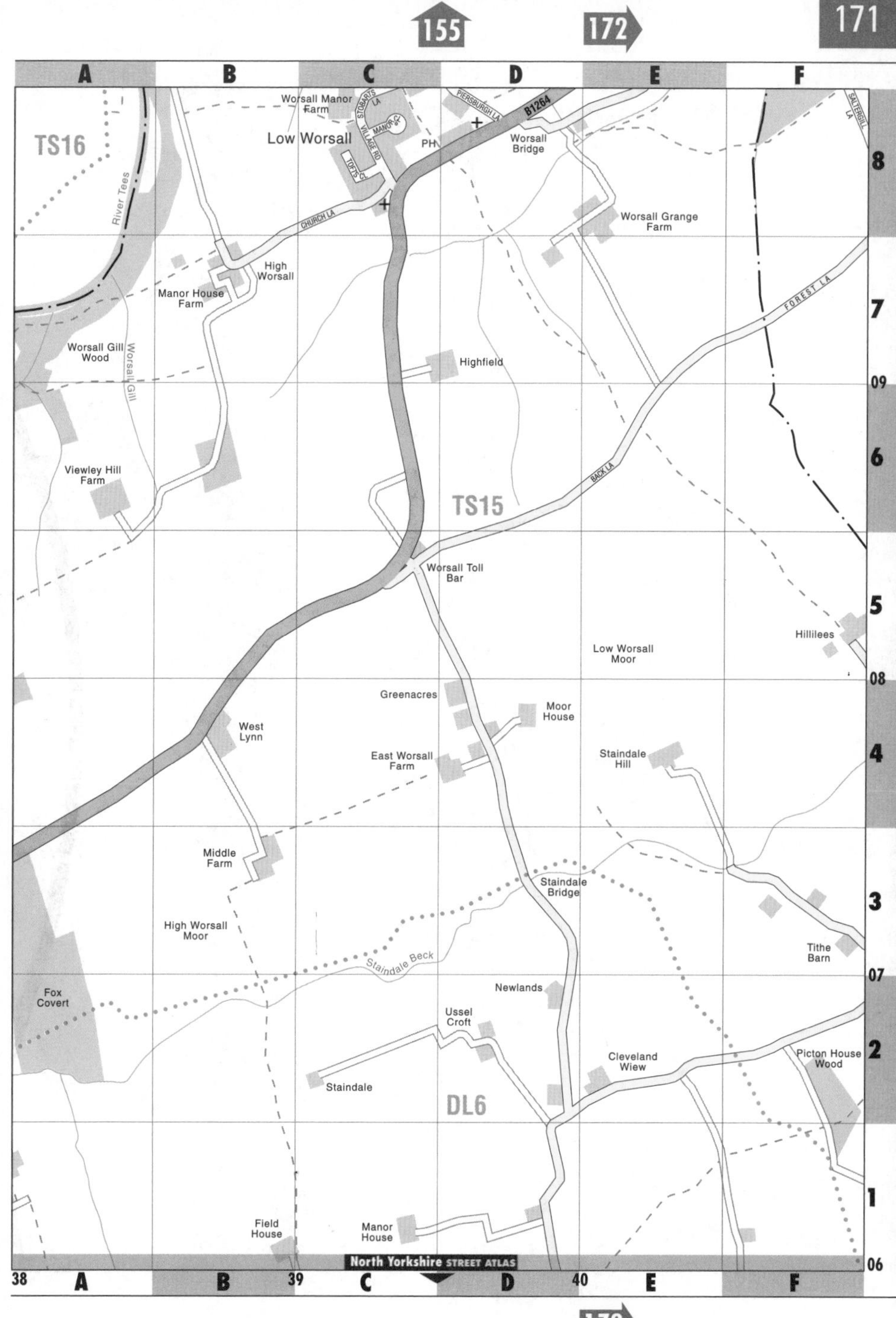

TS16

Low Worsall

Worsall Manor Farm

PH

Worsall Bridge

B1264

Worsall Grange Farm

CHURCH LA

High Worsall

Manor House Farm

FOREST LA

Worsall Gill Wood

Highfield

Viewley Hill Farm

TS15

BACK LA

Worsall Toll Bar

Hillilees

Low Worsall Moor

Greenacres

Moor House

West Lynn

East Worsall Farm

Staindale Hill

Middle Farm

Staindale Bridge

High Worsall Moor

Staindale Beck

Tithe Barn

Fox Covert

Newlands

Ussel Croft

Picton House Wood

Staindale

Cleveland Wiew

DL6

Field House

Manor House

171

156

A
B
C
D
E
F
8
7
09
6
5
08
4
3
07
2
1
06
41
42
43
Low Forest Farm
Grove Platation
Grove Farm
FOREST LA
Manor Farm
SALTERGILL LA
The Forest
High Forest Farm
ASH GR
BIRCH CL
BRACKSIDE LA
PENDERS LA
TOWN END CL
PUMP LA
STRATHMORE DR
THE GREEN
MANOR GARTH
HALL MOOR CL
MOOR CL
ST MARTINS WAY
GROVE BANK
KNOWLES CL
WESTSON
Kirklevington Prim Sch
Kirklevington
Knowles Farm
A67
Fir Tree Farm
Hill House Farm
Moor House Farm
A19
A67
Picton Manor
Hill House
Sand Hills Farm
Grange Plantation
TS15
LONG LA
PH
LC
Grange Farm
Picton House Farm
Picton Stell Bridge
Picton Plantation
Tithe Barn Farm
Glebe Farm
Picton
RAILWAY COTTS
Poplars Farm
BACK LA
YORK ST
Gowsers Plantation
Picton Stell
KAY HOUSE LA
Four Wynds
Kay House
High Grange
New Dales Plantation
Low Flatts Plantation
Corps House Farm
Picton Grange
Lime Bridge
Mount Pleasant Farm
West Moor Farm
HAGGITT HILL LA
Mount Flatts Farm
A19 Thirsk

171

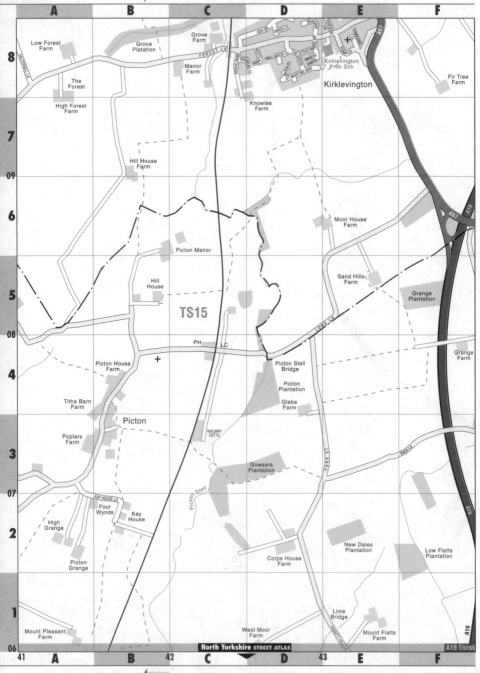

157

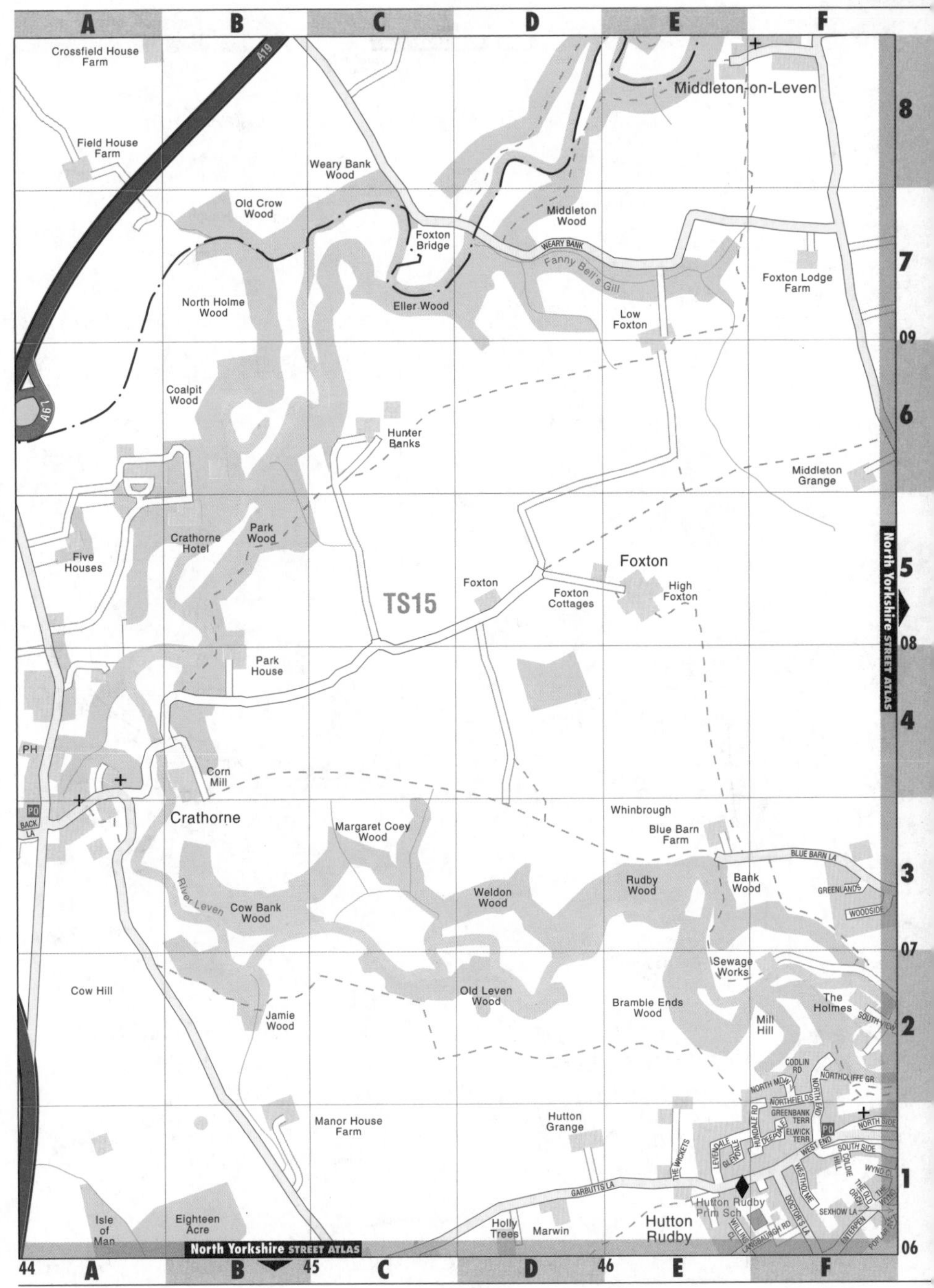

A
B
C
D
E
F
Crossfield House Farm
A19
Middleton-on-Leven
8
Field House Farm
Weary Bank Wood
Old Crow Wood
Middleton Wood
Foxton Bridge
WEARY BANK
Fanny Bell's Gill
7
Foxton Lodge Farm
North Holme Wood
Eller Wood
Low Foxton
09
Coalpit Wood
A61
6
Hunter Banks
Middleton Grange
Five Houses
Crathorne Hotel
Park Wood
Foxton
5
Foxton
Foxton Cottages
High Foxton
TS15
North Yorkshire STREET ATLAS
08
Park House
4
PH
Corn Mill
PO
BACK LA
Crathorne
Whinbrough
Margaret Coey Wood
Blue Barn Farm
BLUE BARN LA
3
Rudby Wood
Bank Wood
GREENLANDS
Weldon Wood
River Leven
Cow Bank Wood
WOODSIDE
07
Sewage Works
Cow Hill
Old Leven Wood
Bramble Ends Wood
The Holmes
SOUTH VIEW
Jamie Wood
Mill Hill
2
CODLIN RD
NORTH MDW
NORTHCLIFFE GR
NORTHFIELDS
NORTH END
GREENBANK TERR
HUNDALE RD
ELWICK TERR
PO
NORTH SIDE
Manor House Farm
Hutton Grange
LEVENDALE
GLENDALE
DEEPDALE
WEST END
SOUTH SIDE
THE WICKETS
WESTHOLME
HILL
COLDIE
WYND CL
1
GARBUTTS LA
THE OLD ORCH
THE WYND
Hutton Rudby Prim Sch
DOCTOR'S LA
SEXHOW LA
Isle of Man
Eighteen Acre
Holly Trees
Marwin
Hutton Rudby
WILLING CL
LANGBAURGH RD
ENTERPEN
POPLAR
06
44
45
46

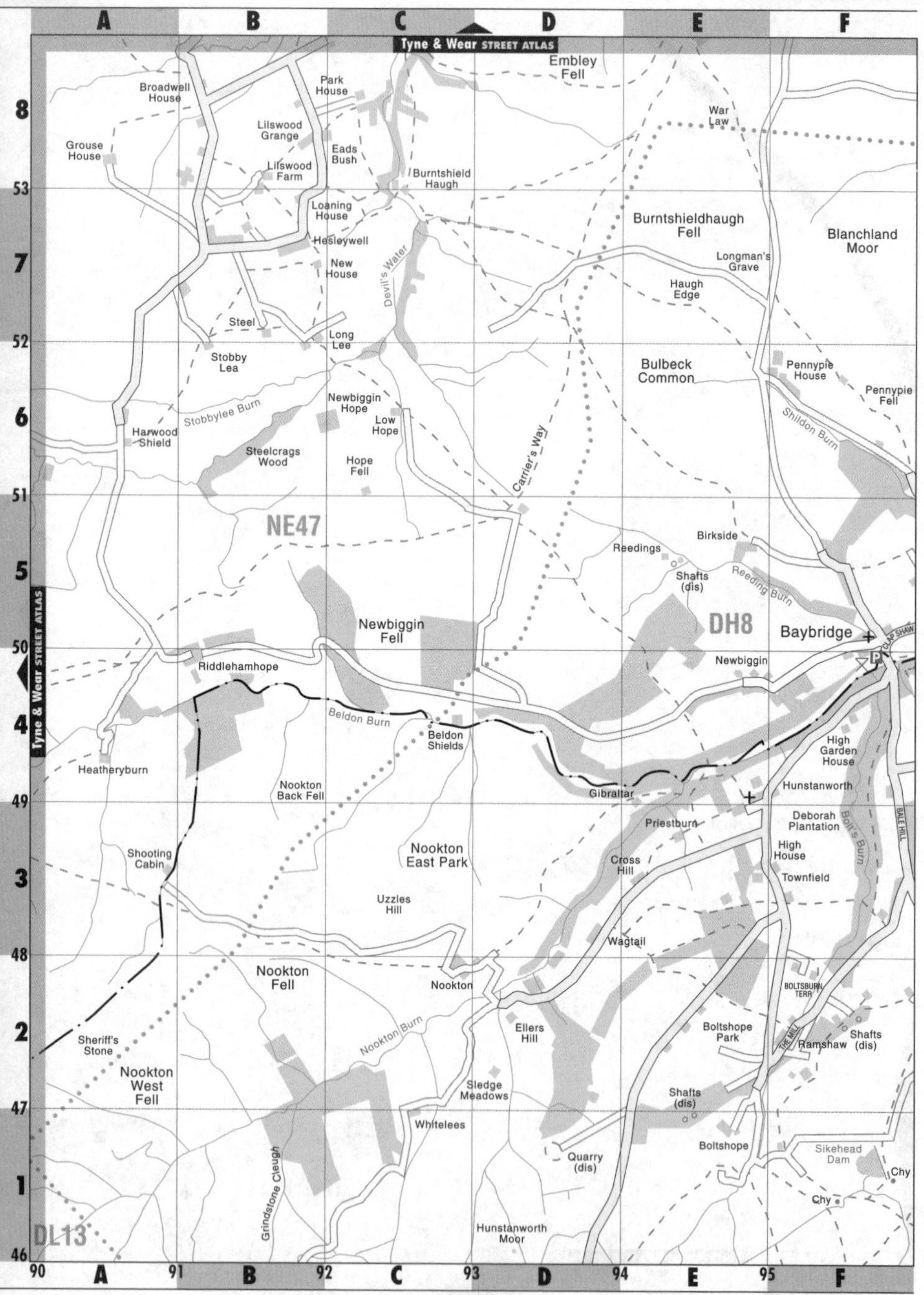

Tyne & Wear STREET ATLAS

Tyne & Wear STREET ATLAS

Embley Fell

War Law

Broadwell House

Park House

Lilswood Grange

Eads Bush

Burntshield Haugh

Burntshieldhaugh Fell

Blanchland Moor

Grouse House

Lilswood Farm

Loaning House

Longman's Grave

Hesleywell

Haugh Edge

New House

Pennypie House

Pennypie Fell

Steel

Long Lee

Bulbeck Common

Stobby Lea

Devil's Water

Shildon Burn

Stobbylee Burn

Newbiggin Hope

Low Hope

NE47

Harwood Shield

Steelcrags Wood

Hope Fell

Carrier's Way

Birkside

Reedings

Shafts (dis)

Reeding Burn

Newbiggin Fell

DH8

Baybridge

Riddlehamhope

Newbiggin

Beldon Burn

Heatheryburn

Beldon Shields

High Garden House

Nookton Back Fell

Gibraltar

Hunstanworth

Shooting Cabin

Priestburn

Deborah Plantation

Nookton East Park

Cross Hill

High House

Uzzles Hill

Townfield

Bolt's Burn

Nookton Fell

Wagtail

Nookton

Boltsburn Terr

Sheriff's Stone

Ellers Hill

Boltshope Park

Ramshaw

Shafts (dis)

Nookton West Fell

Sledge Meadows

Shafts (dis)

Whitelees

Boltshope

Sikehead Dam

Chy

DL13

Grindstone Cleugh

Nookton Burn

Quarry (dis)

Chy

Hunstanworth Moor

180

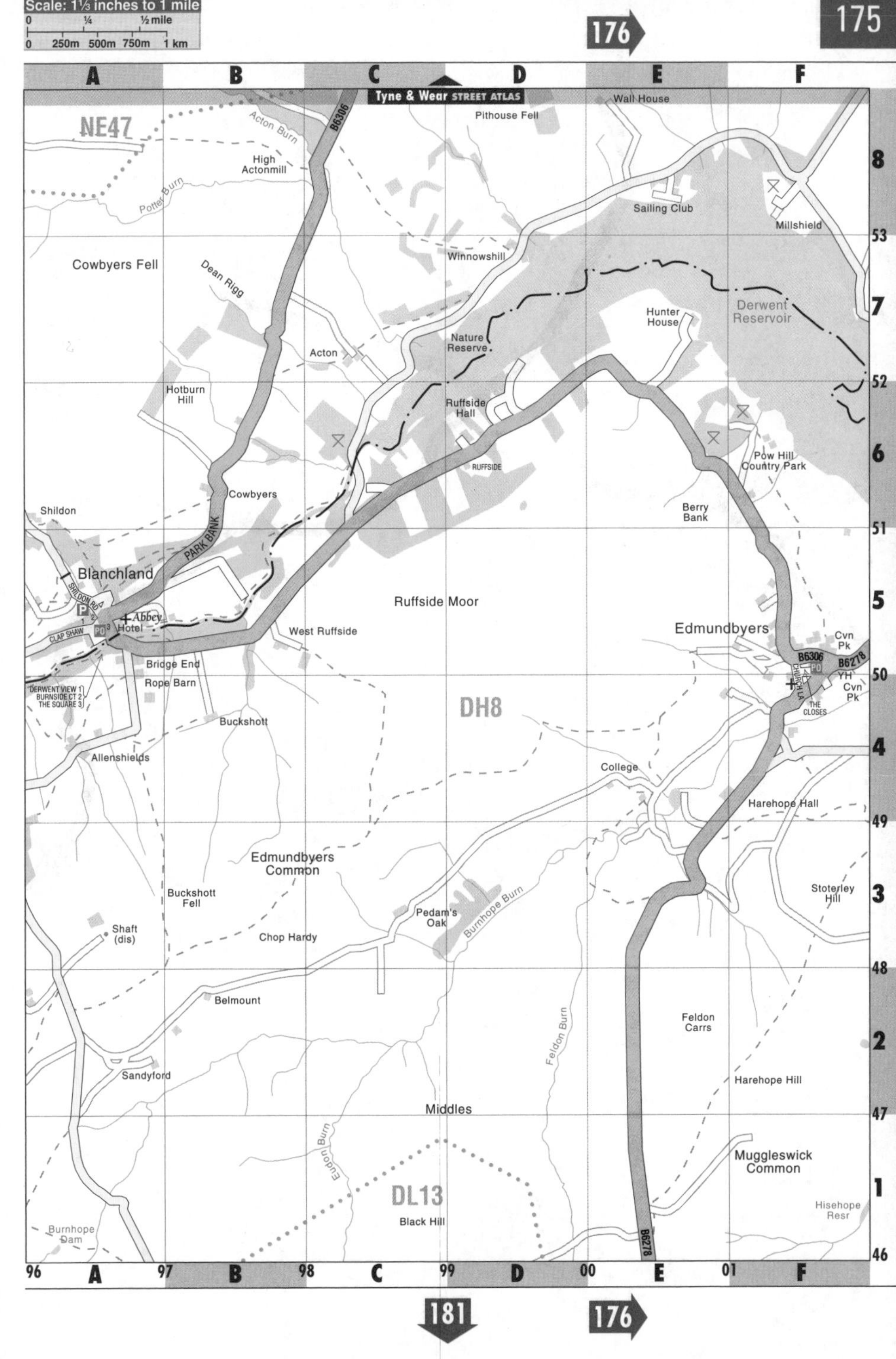
Scale: 1⅓ inches to 1 mile
0 ¼ ½ mile
0 250m 500m 750m 1 km
176
A B C D E F
Tyne & Wear STREET ATLAS
NE47
Acton Burn
B6306
Pithouse Fell
Wall House
High Actonmill
Potter Burn
Sailing Club
Millshield
Winnowshill
Cowbyers Fell
Dean Rigg
Hunter House
Derwent Reservoir
Acton
Nature Reserve
Hotburn Hill
Ruffside Hall
RUFFSIDE
Pow Hill Country Park
Cowbyers
Shildon
Berry Bank
PARK BANK
Blanchland
SHILDON RD
Abbey
Hotel
Ruffside Moor
West Ruffside
Edmundbyers
Cvn Pk
CLAP SHAW
Bridge End
Rope Barn
B6306
B6278
CHURCH LA
YH
DERWENT VIEW 1
BURNSIDE CT 2
THE SQUARE 3
THE CLOSES
DH8
Buckshott
Allenshields
College
Harehope Hall
Edmundbyers Common
Buckshott Fell
Stoterley Hill
Shaft (dis)
Pedam's Oak
Burnhope Burn
Chop Hardy
Belmount
Feldon Carrs
Feldon Burn
Sandyford
Harehope Hill
Middles
Eddon Burn
Muggleswick Common
DL13
Black Hill
Hisehope Resr
Burnhope Dam
B6278
8 53 7 52 6 51 5 50 4 49 3 48 2 47 1 46
96 97 98 99 00 01
181
176

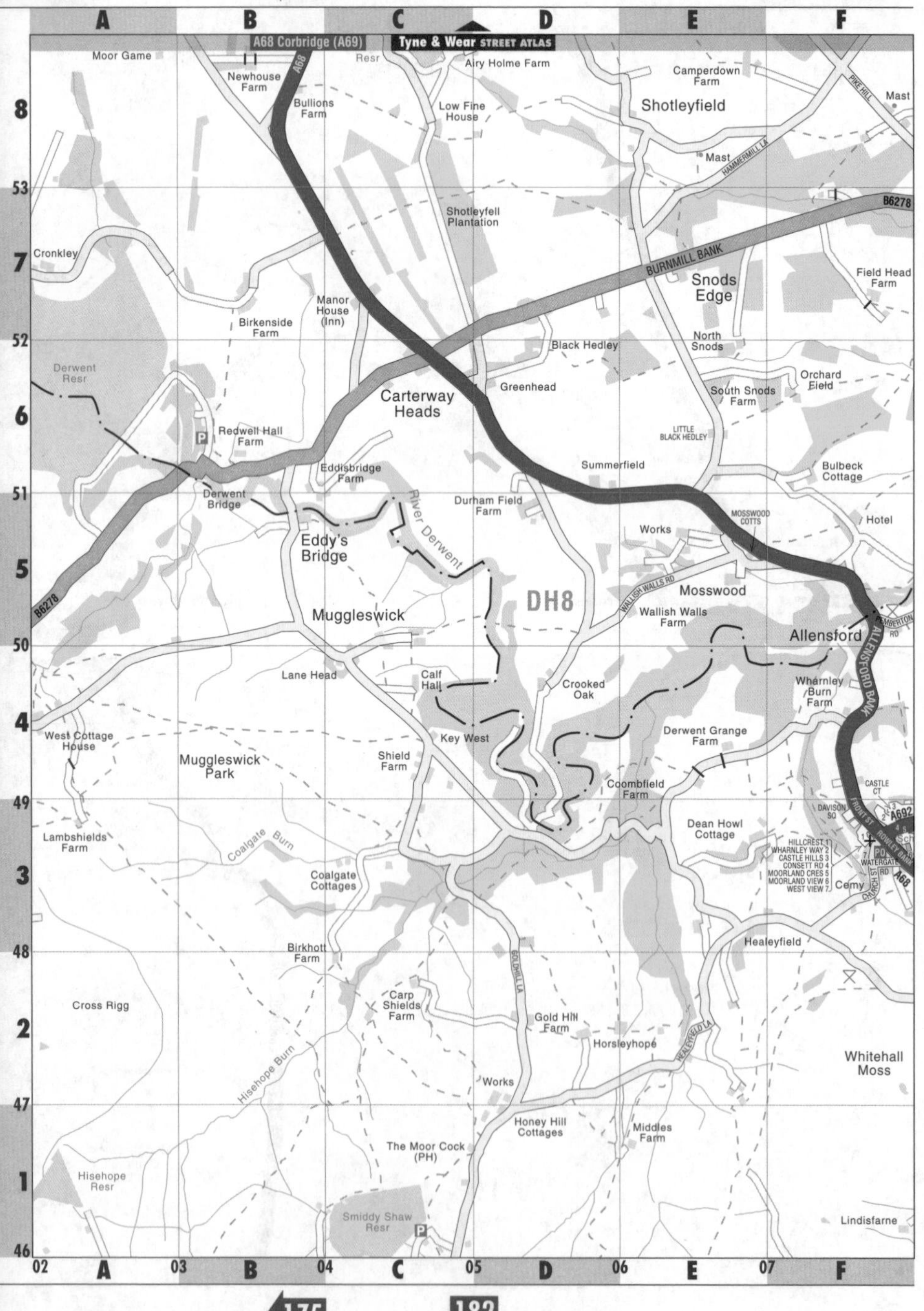

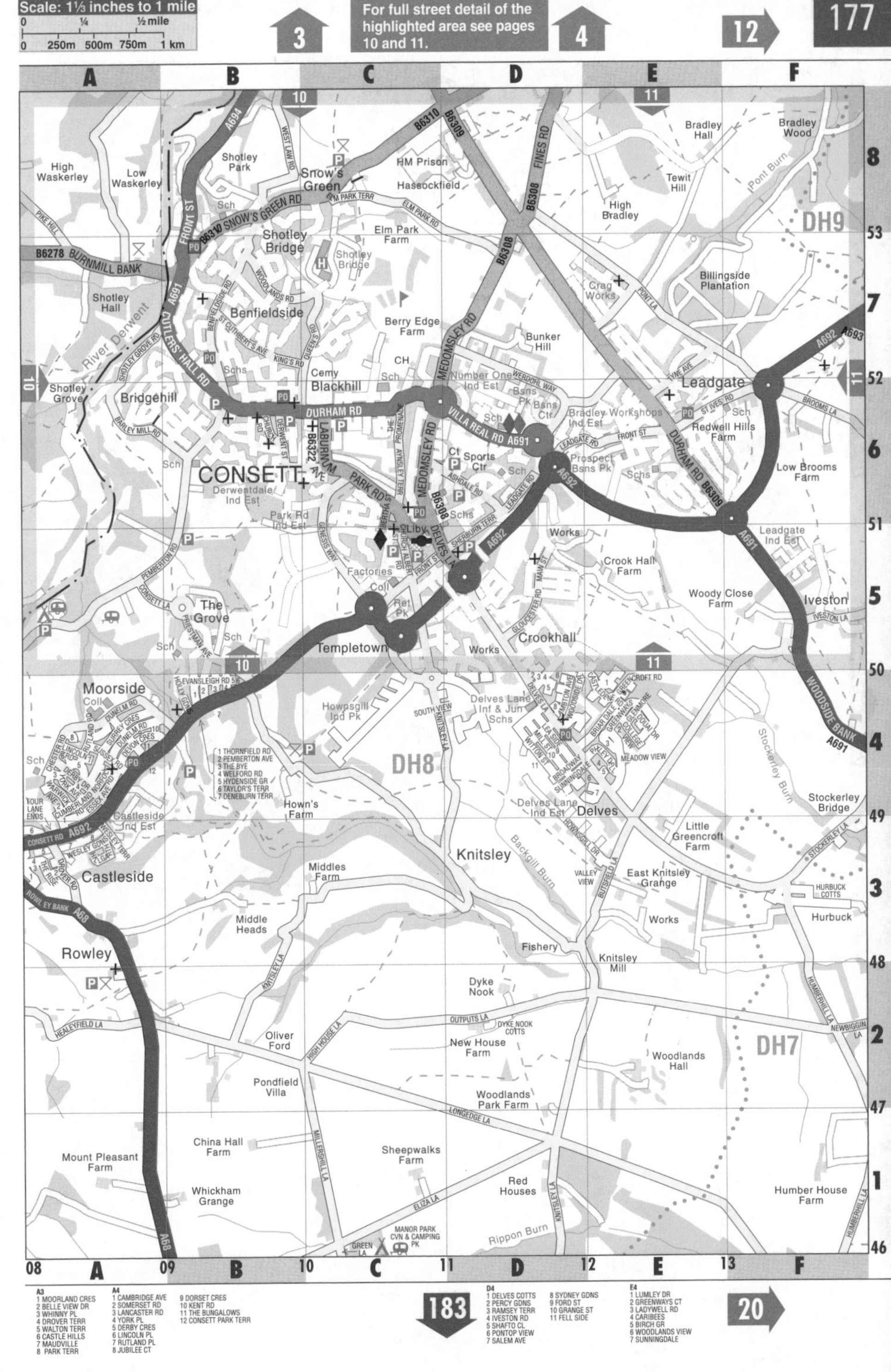

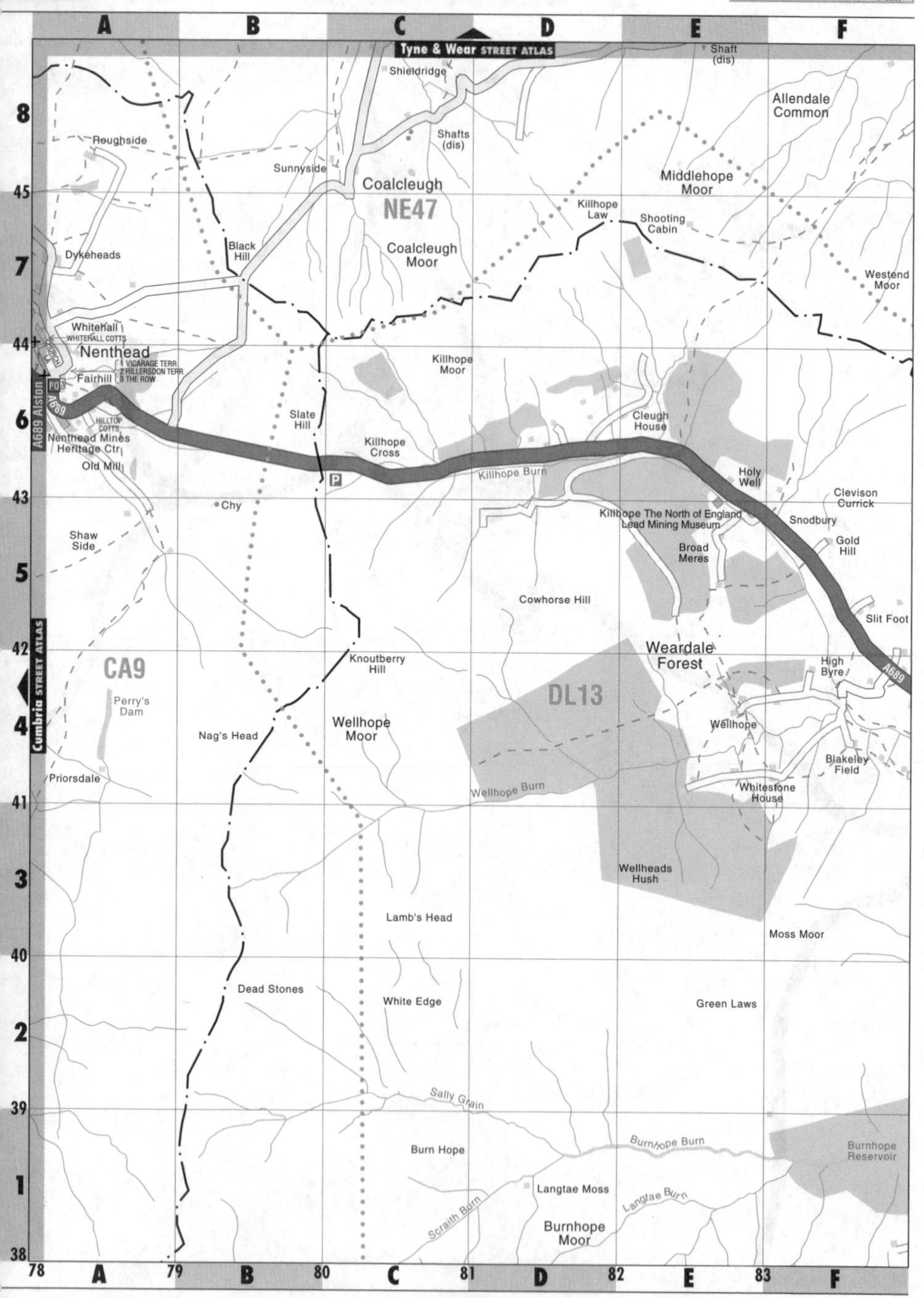

Tyne & Wear STREET ATLAS

Shaft
(dis)

Allendale
Common

Shieldridge

Shafts
(dis)

Middlehope
Moor

Coalcleugh

NE47

Killhope
Law

Shooting
Cabin

Westend
Moor

Coalcleugh
Moor

Roughside

Sunnyside

Black
Hill

Dykeheads

Killhope
Moor

Whitehall
WHITEHALL COTTS
Nenthead
Fairhill

1 VICARAGE TERR
2 HILLERSDON TERR
3 THE ROW

Cleugh
House

Holy
Well

Clevison
Currick

PO

HILLTOP
COTTS

A689 Alston
A689

Slate
Hill

Killhope
Cross

Killhope Burn

Snodbury

Gold
Hill

Nenthead Mines
Heritage Ctr

Old Mill

Chy

Killhope The North of England
Lead Mining Museum

Broad
Meres

Slit Foot

Shaw
Side

Cowhorse Hill

Weardale
Forest

High
Byre

A689

Cumbria STREET ATLAS

CA9

Knoutberry
Hill

DL13

Perry's
Dam

Nag's Head

Wellhope
Moor

Wellhope

Blakeley
Field

Priorsdale

Wellhope Burn

Whitestone
House

Wellheads
Hush

Lamb's Head

Moss Moor

Dead Stones

White Edge

Green Laws

Sally Grain

Burn Hope

Burnhope Burn

Burnhope
Reservoir

Langtae Moss

Scraith Burn

Langtae Burn

Burnhope
Moor

Scale: 1⅓ inches to 1 mile

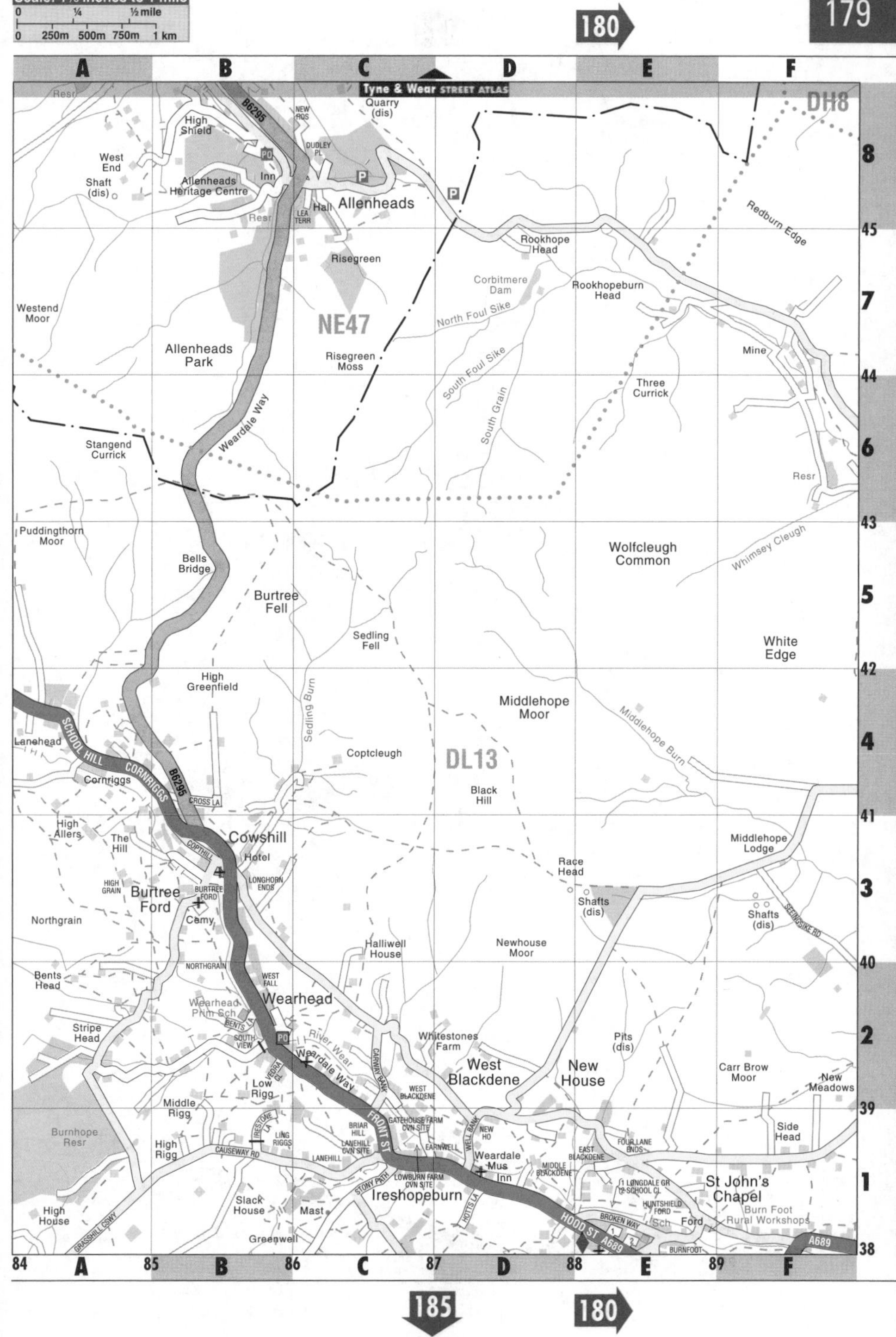

Tyne & Wear STREET ATLAS
DH8
NE47
DL13
Allenheads
Allenheads Heritage Centre
High Shield
West End
Shaft (dis)
Quarry (dis)
Risegreen
Rookhope Head
Corbitmere Dam
Rookhopeburn Head
Redburn Edge
Westend Moor
Allenheads Park
Risegreen Moss
Three Currick
Mine
Stangend Currick
Weardale Way
Resr
Puddingthorn Moor
Wolfcleugh Common
Whimsey Cleugh
Bells Bridge
Burtree Fell
Sedling Fell
White Edge
High Greenfield
Middlehope Moor
Middlehope Burn
Lanehead
Cornriggs
Coptcleugh
Black Hill
Cowshill
High Allers
The Hill
Middlehope Lodge
Race Head
Burtree Ford
Northgrain
Shafts (dis)
Halliwell House
Newhouse Moor
Bents Head
Wearhead
Stripe Head
Whitestones Farm
West Blackdene
New House
Pits (dis)
Carr Brow Moor
New Meadows
Low Rigg
Middle Rigg
Burnhope Resr
High Rigg
Side Head
Weardale Mus
St John's Chapel
Ireshopeburn
Slack House
Mast
High House
Greenwell
Burn Foot Rural Workshops
B6295
A689

180
185
180

179
174
Scale: 1⅓ inches to 1 mile

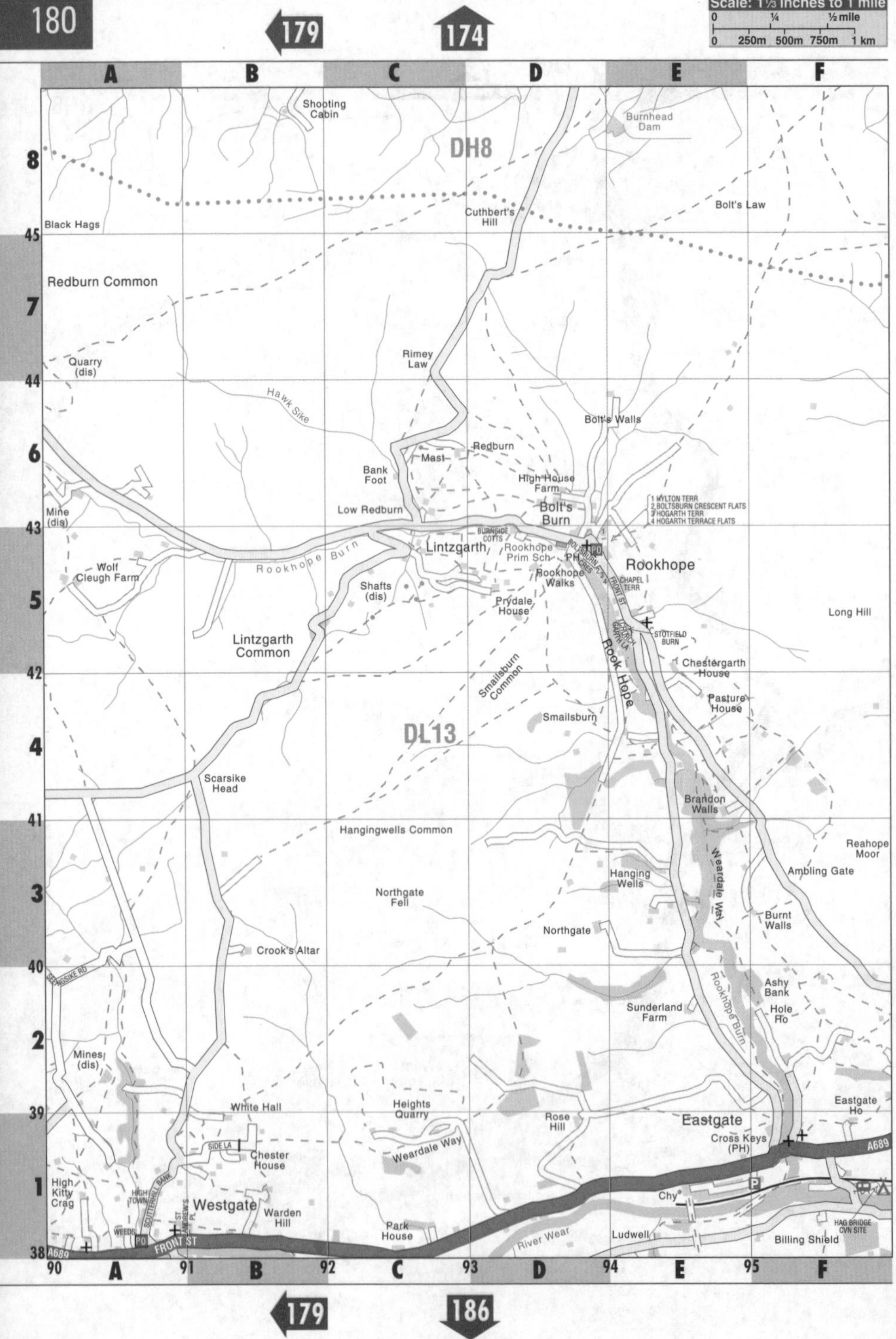
Shooting Cabin
Burnhead Dam
DH8
Black Hags
Cuthbert's Hill
Bolt's Law
Redburn Common
Quarry (dis)
Rimey Law
Hawk Sike
Bolt's Walls
Redburn
Mast
Bank Foot
High House Farm
Mine (dis)
Low Redburn
Bolt's Burn
1 HYLTON TERR
2 BOLTSBURN CRESCENT FLATS
3 HOGARTH TERR
4 HOGARTH TERRACE FLATS
BURNSIDE COTTS
Lintzgarth
Rookhope Prim Sch
PH
PO
Rookhope
Wolf Cleugh Farm
Rookhope Burn
Shafts (dis)
Rookhope Walks
FRONT ST
CHAPEL TERR
Prydale House
Long Hill
Lintzgarth Common
STOTFIELD BURN
Chestergarth House
Smailsburn Common
Rook Hope
Pasture House
Smailsburn
DL13
Scarsike Head
Brandon Walls
Hangingwells Common
Reahope Moor
Ambling Gate
Weardale Way
Hanging Wells
Northgate Fell
Burnt Walls
Northgate
Crook's Altar
Ashy Bank
Sunderland Farm
Rookhope Burn
Hole Ho
Mines (dis)
Heights Quarry
Eastgate Ho
White Hall
Rose Hill
Eastgate
Cross Keys (PH)
A689
SIDE LA
Chester House
Weardale Way
High Kitty Crag
SCUTTERHILL BANK
Westgate
Warden Hill
Chy
Park House
River Wear
Ludwell
Billing Shield
HAG BRIDGE CVN SITE
WEEDS
FRONT ST
A689

179
186

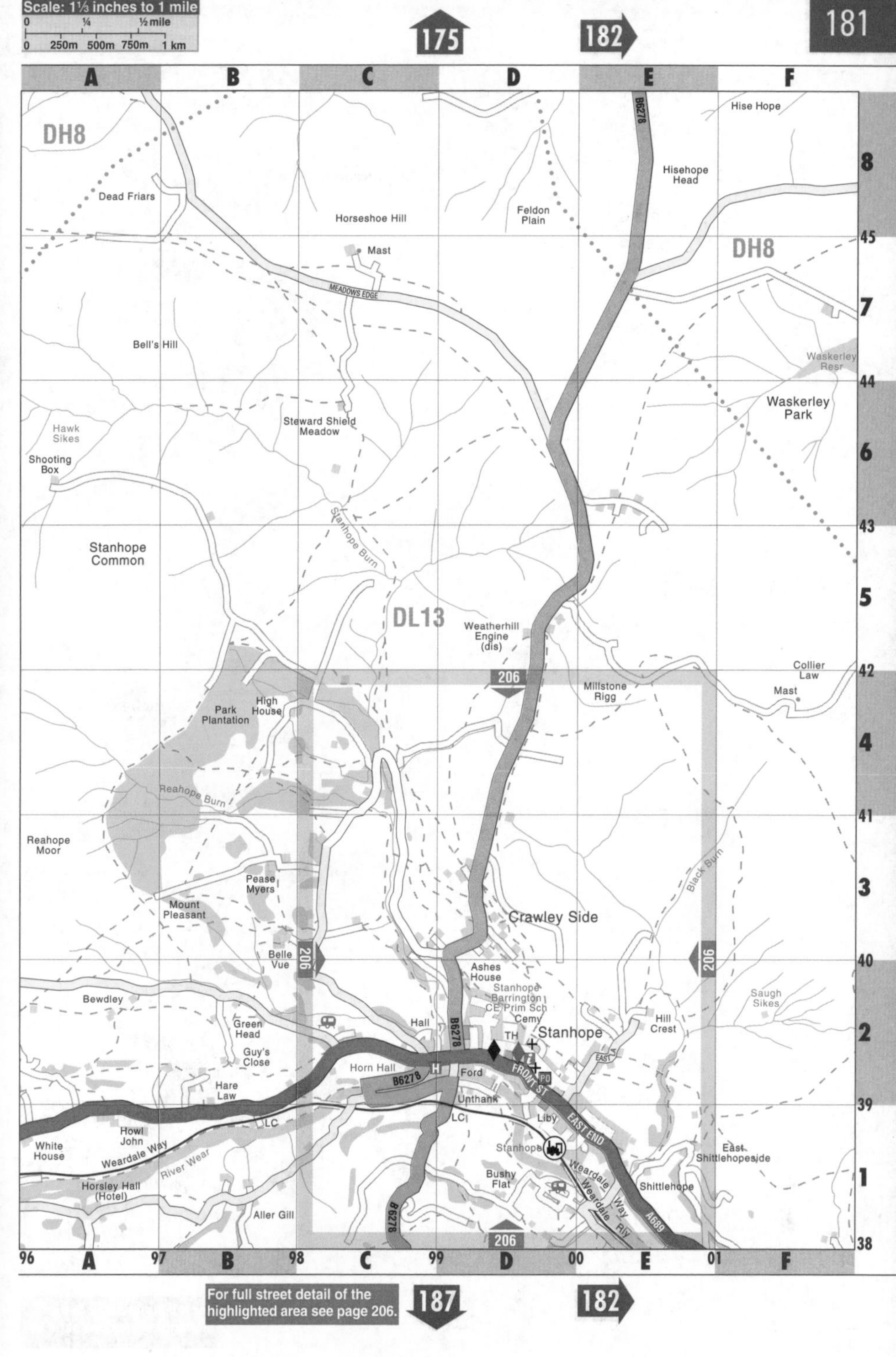

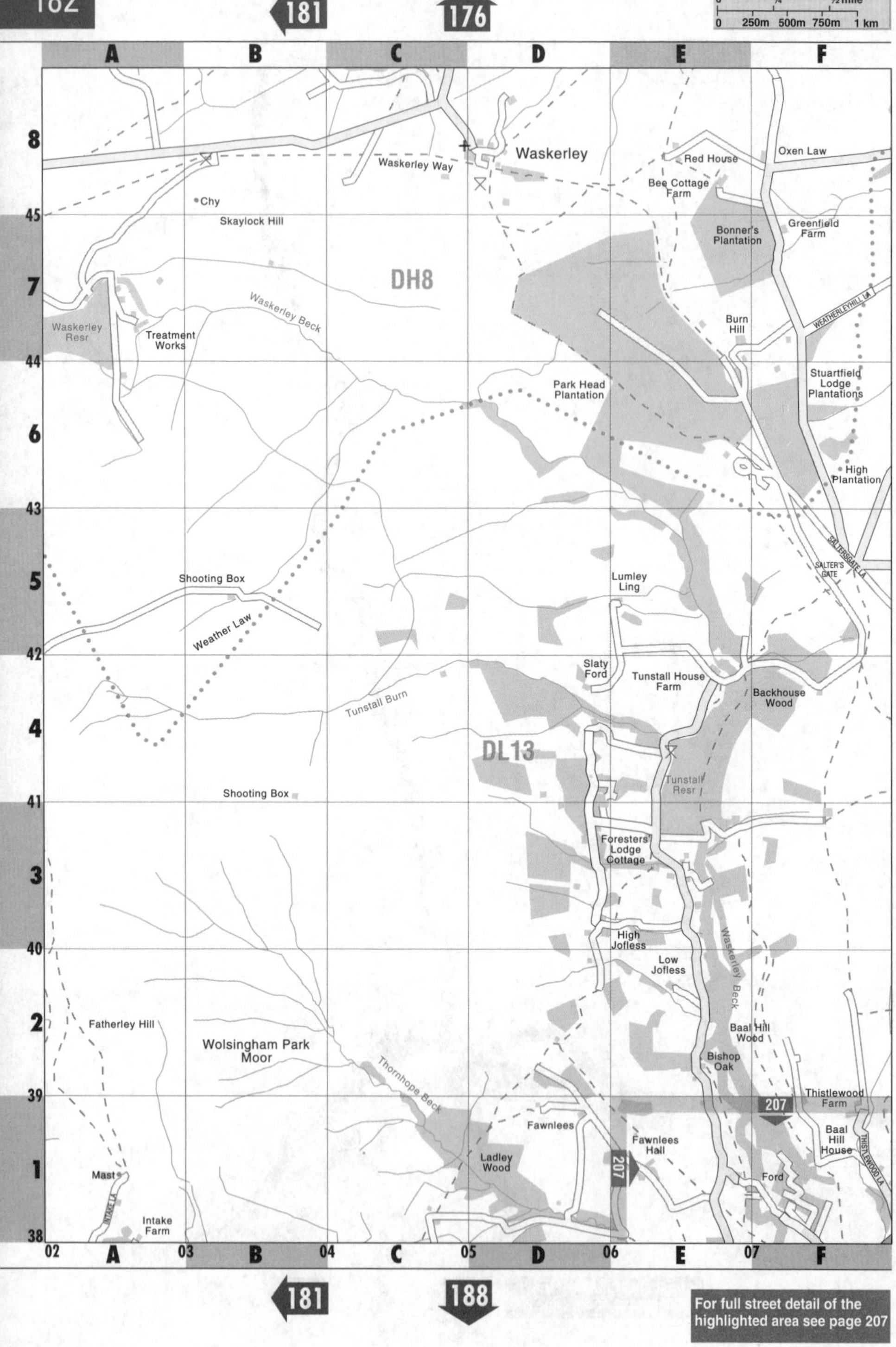

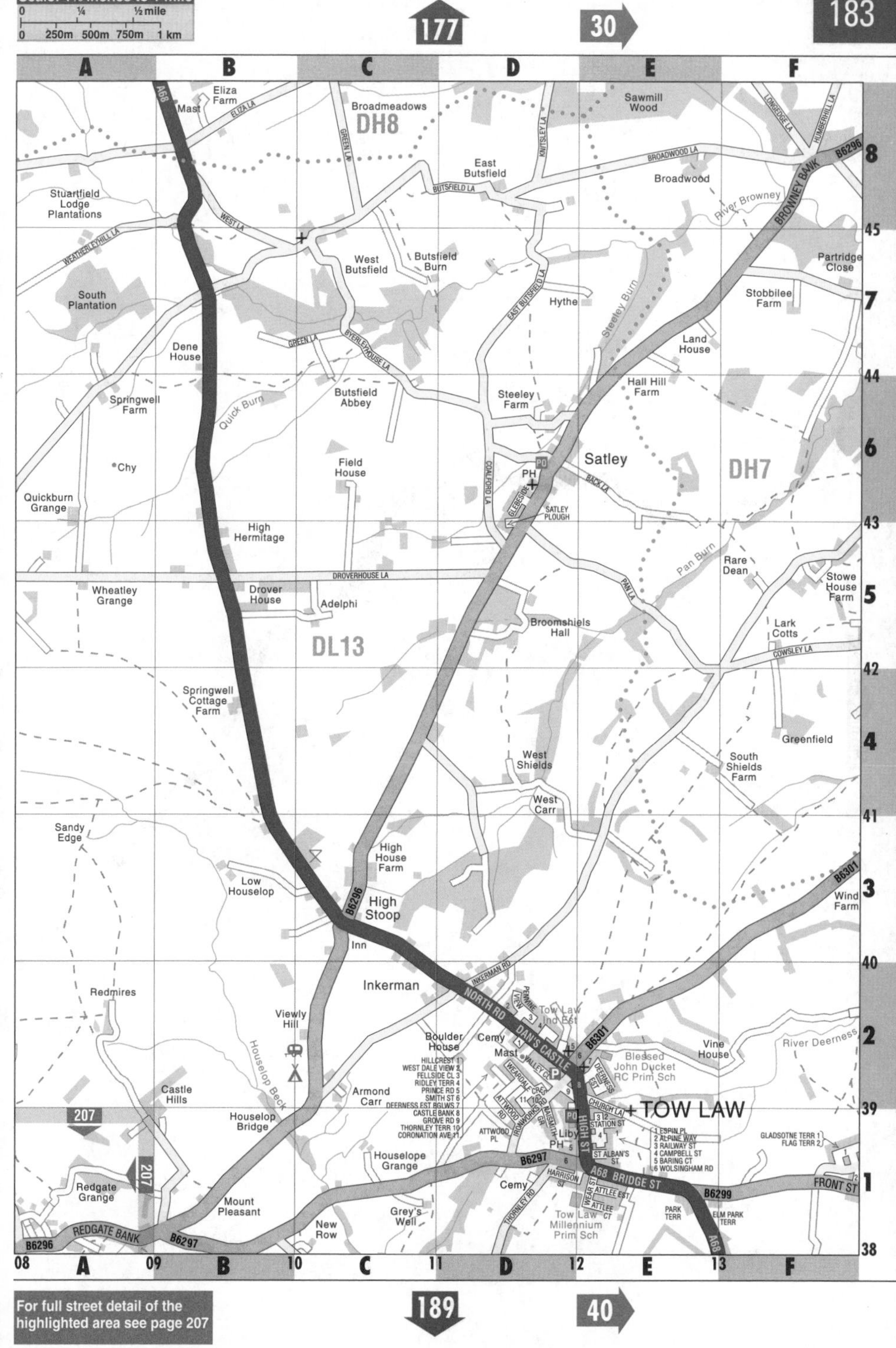
Scale: 1⅓ inches to 1 mile
0 ¼ ½ mile
0 250m 500m 750m 1 km
177
30
A B C D E F
Eliza Farm
Mast
ELIZA LA
Broadmeadows
DH8
GREEN LA
KNITSLEY LA
Sawmill Wood
LONGEDGE LA
HUMBERHILL LA
BROADWOOD LA
B6296
East Butsfield
BUTSFIELD LA
Broadwood
River Browney
BROWNEY BANK
Stuartfield Lodge Plantations
WEST LA
WEATHERLEYHILL LA
West Butsfield
Butsfield Burn
Partridge Close
South Plantation
EAST BUTSFIELD LA
Hythe
Steeley Burn
Stobbilee Farm
GREEN LA
BYERLEYHOUSE LA
Land House
Dene House
Hall Hill Farm
Springwell Farm
Quick Burn
Butsfield Abbey
Steeley Farm
Chy
Field House
PO
PH
Satley
DH7
BACK LA
COALFORD LA
GLEBESIDE
SATLEY PLOUGH
Quickburn Grange
High Hermitage
Pan Burn
Rare Dean
Stowe House Farm
DROVERHOUSE LA
PAN LA
Wheatley Grange
Drover House
Adelphi
Broomshiels Hall
Lark Cotts
DL13
COWSLEY LA
Springwell Cottage Farm
Greenfield
West Shields
South Shields Farm
West Carr
Sandy Edge
High House Farm
Low Houselop
B6296
High Stoop
B6301
Wind Farm
Inn
Redmires
Inkerman
INKERMAN RD
NORTH RD
DAN'S CASTLE
PENNINE VIEW
Tow Law Ind Est
B6301
Viewly Hill
Boulder House
Cemy
Mast
VALLEY CL
Blessed John Ducket RC Prim Sch
Vine House
River Deerness
HILLCREST 1
WEST DALE VIEW 2
FELLSIDE CL 3
RIDLEY TERR 4
PRINCE RD 5
SMITH ST 6
DEERNESS EST BGLWS 7
CASTLE BANK 8
GROVE RD 9
THORNLEY TERR 10
CORONATION AVE 11
WEARDALE CRES
DEERNESS EST
Houselop Beck
Castle Hills
Armond Carr
ATTWOOD RD
IRONWORKS RD
NAISMITH GR
CHURCH LA
TOW LAW
207
Houselop Bridge
ATTWOOD PL
PO
HIGH ST
STATION ST
Liby
PH
1 ESPIN PL
2 ALPINE WAY
3 RAILWAY ST
4 CAMPBELL ST
5 BARING CT
6 WOLSINGHAM RD
GLADSOTNE TERR 1
FLAG TERR 2
Houselope Grange
B6297
ST ALBAN'S ST
207
HARRISON ST
A68 BRIDGE ST
FRONT ST
Redgate Grange
Cemy
THORNLEY RD
WEAR ST
ATTLEE EST
ATTLEE CT
B6299
Mount Pleasant
Grey's Well
Tow Law Millennium Prim Sch
PARK TERR
ELM PARK TERR
REDGATE BANK
New Row
B6296
B6297
A68
45 44 43 42 41 40 39 38
8 7 6 5 4 3 2 1
08 09 10 11 12 13
189
40
For full street detail of the highlighted area see page 207

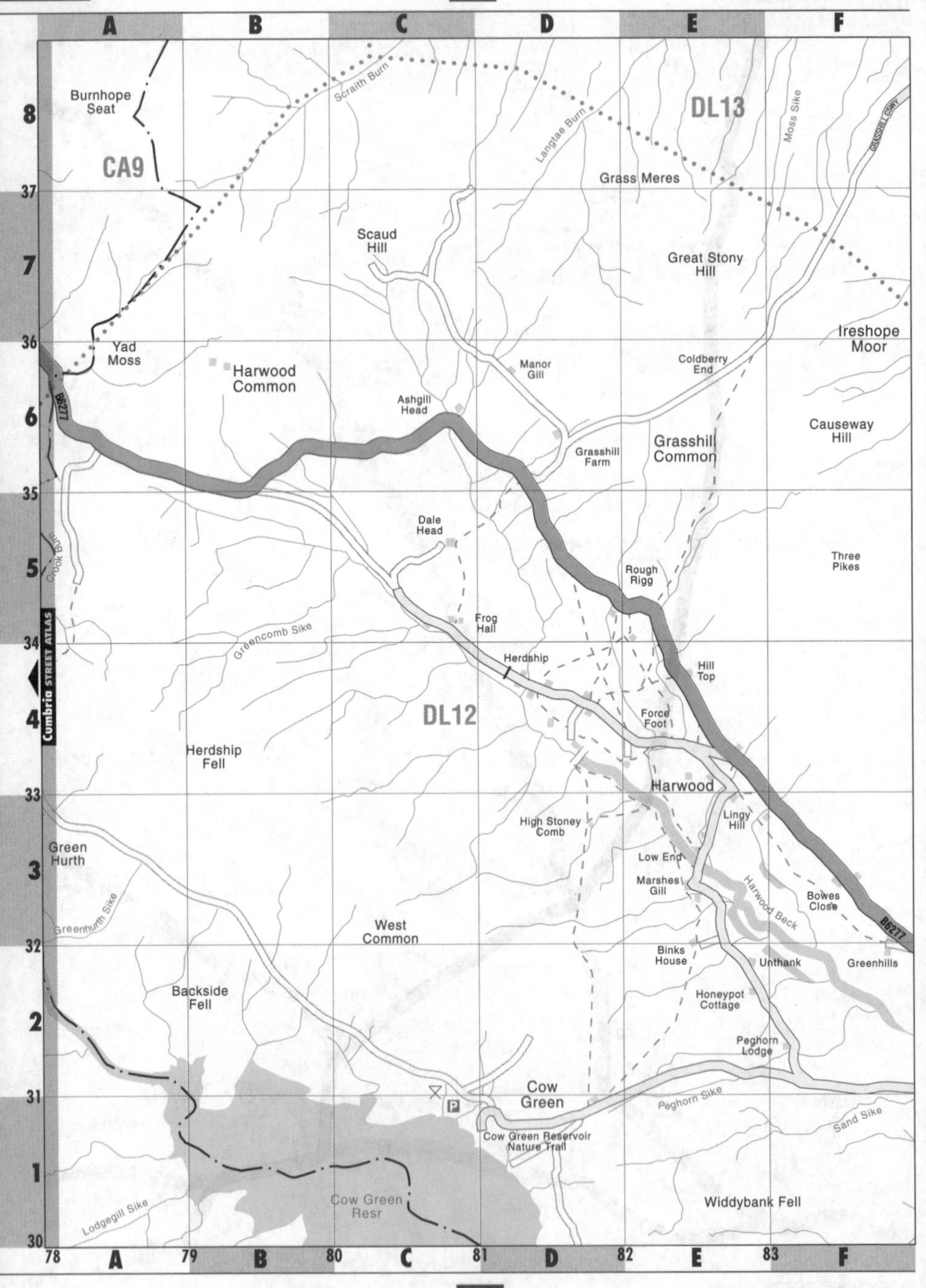

Scale: 1½ inches to 1 mile

0   ¼   ½ mile
0   250m 500m 750m 1 km

| A | B | C | D | E | F |

Burnhope
Seat

CA9

DL13

Scraith Burn

Langlae Burn

Moss Sike

GRASSHILL CWY

8

37

Grass Meres

Scaud
Hill

Great Stony
Hill

7

Ireshope
Moor

36

Yad
Moss

B6277

Harwood
Common

Ashgill
Head

Manor
Gill

Coldberry
End

Causeway
Hill

6

Grasshill
Farm

Grasshill
Common

35

Dale
Head

Rough
Rigg

Three
Pikes

5

Cook Burn

Greencomb Sike

Frog
Hall

Herdship

Hill
Top

34

DL12

Force
Foot

4

Cumbria STREET ATLAS

Herdship
Fell

Harwood

Lingy
Hill

33

High Stoney
Comb

Low End

Bowes
Close

B6277

3

Green
Hurth

Marshes
Gill

Harwood Beck

Greenburn Sike

West
Common

Binks
House

Unthank

Greenhills

32

Backside
Fell

Honeypot
Cottage

Peghorn
Lodge

2

Peghorn Sike

Sand Sike

31

P

Cow
Green

Lodgegill Sike

Cow Green Reservoir
Nature Trail

1

Cow Green
Resr

Widdybank Fell

30

| 78 | A | 79 | B | 80 | C | 81 | D | 82 | E | 83 | F |

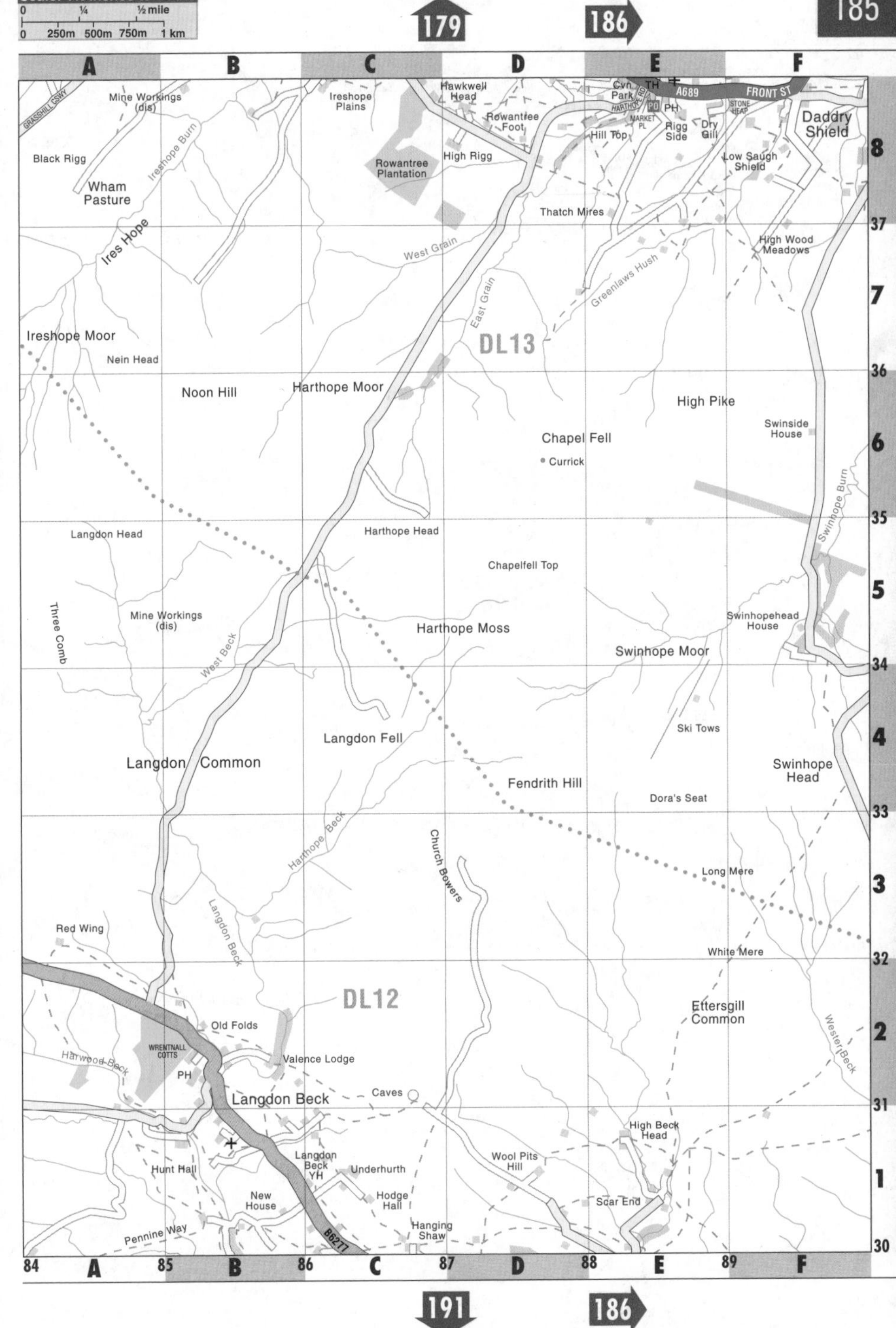
Scale: 1⅓ inches to 1 mile
0 ¼ ½ mile
0 250m 500m 750m 1 km
179
186
A B C D E F
Mine Workings (dis)
Ireshope Plains
Hawkwell Head
Rowantree Foot
Cvn Park
TH
A689
FRONT ST
PH
Rigg Side
Dry Gill
Hill Top
Daddry Shield
Black Rigg
Wham Pasture
Ireshope Burn
Rowantree Plantation
High Rigg
Low Saugh Shield
Thatch Mires
Ires Hope
West Grain
High Wood Meadows
Greenlaws Hush
East Grain
DL13
Ireshope Moor
Nein Head
Noon Hill
Harthope Moor
High Pike
Swinside House
Chapel Fell
Currick
Swinhope Burn
Langdon Head
Harthope Head
Chapelfell Top
Three Comb
Mine Workings (dis)
West Beck
Harthope Moss
Swinhopehead House
Swinhope Moor
Ski Tows
Langdon Fell
Langdon Common
Fendrith Hill
Swinhope Head
Dora's Seat
Church Bowers
Harthope Beck
Long Mere
Red Wing
Langdon Beck
White Mere
DL12
Ettersgill Common
Old Folds
Wester Beck
WRENTNALL COTTS
Harwood Beck
Valence Lodge
PH
Caves
Langdon Beck
High Beck Head
Hunt Hall
Langdon Beck YH
Underhurth
Wool Pits Hill
New House
Hodge Hall
Scar End
Pennine Way
Hanging Shaw
B6277
8
37
7
36
6
35
5
34
4
33
3
32
2
31
1
30
84 85 86 87 88 89
191
186

185
180

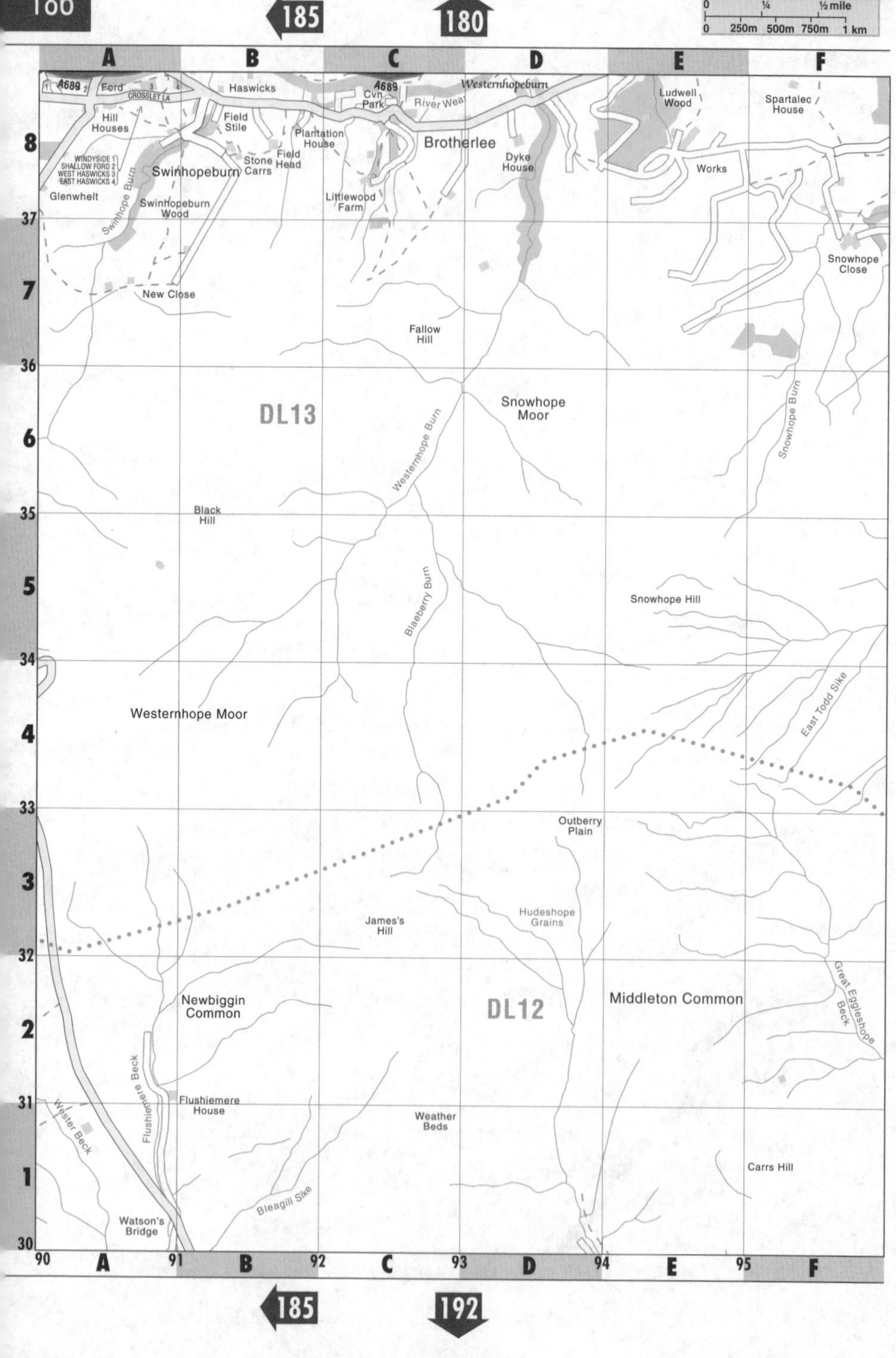
Scale: 1⅓ inches to 1 mile
0 ¼ ½ mile
0 250m 500m 750m 1 km
A B C D E F
8
37
7
36
6
35
5
34
4
33
3
32
2
31
1
30
90 91 92 93 94 95
A689
Ford
CROSSLET LA
Haswicks
Cvn Park
River Wear
Westernhopeburn
Ludwell Wood
Spartalec House
Hill Houses
Field Stile
Plantation House
Brotherlee
WINDYSIDE 1
SHALLOW FORD 2
WEST HASWICKS 3
EAST HASWICKS 4
Swinhopeburn
Stone Carrs
Field Head
Dyke House
Works
Glenwhelt
Swinhope Burn
Swinhopeburn Wood
Littlewood Farm
Snowhope Close
New Close
Fallow Hill
Snowhope Moor
DL13
Westernhope Burn
Snowhope Burn
Black Hill
Blaeberry Burn
Snowhope Hill
Westernhope Moor
East Todd Sike
Outberry Plain
James's Hill
Hudeshope Grains
Newbiggin Common
DL12
Middleton Common
Great Eggleshope Beck
Flushiemere Beck
Flushiemere House
Wester Beck
Weather Beds
Carrs Hill
Bleagill Sike
Watson's Bridge

185
192

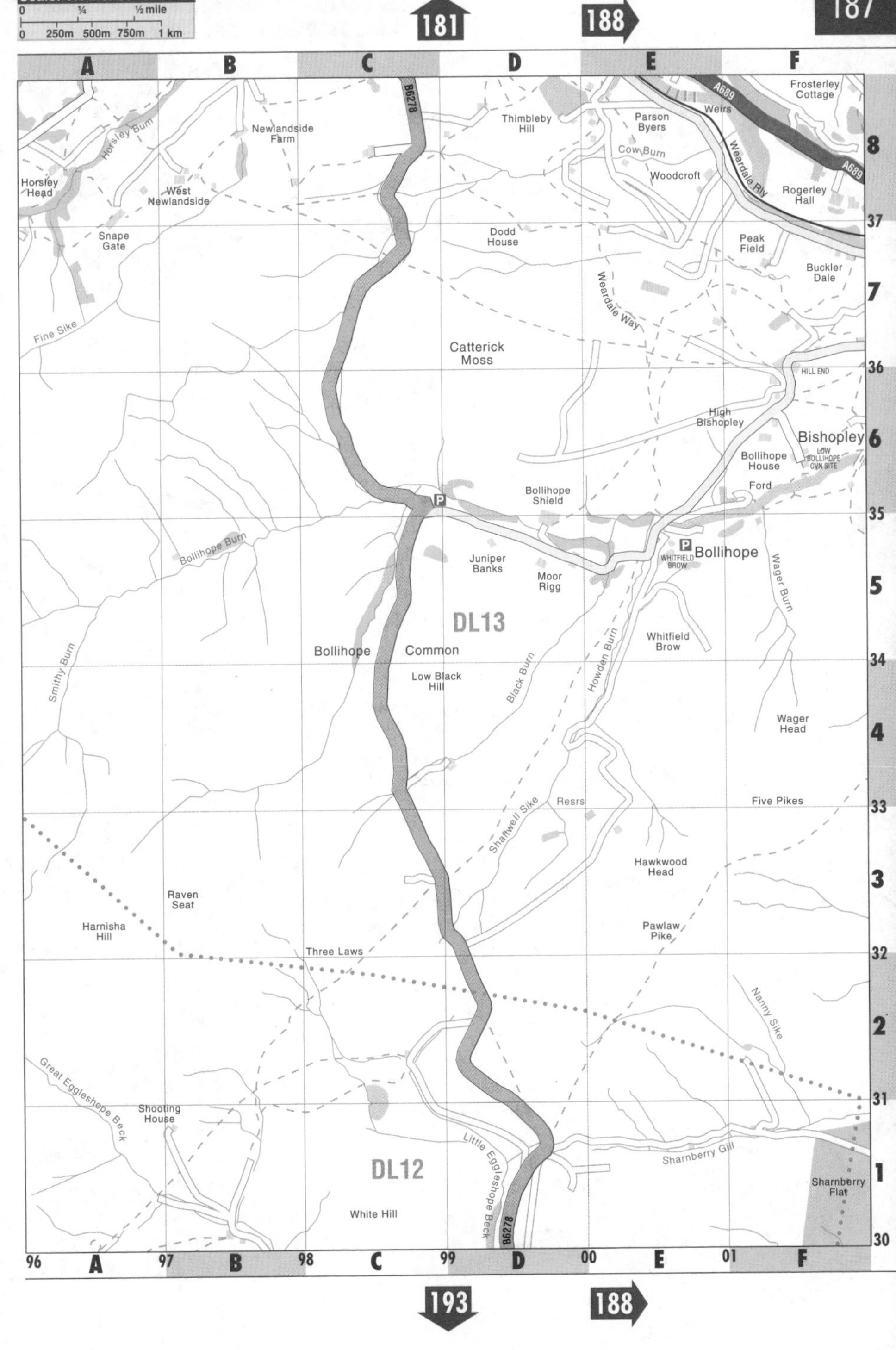

Scale: 1⅓ inches to 1 mile
0
¼
½ mile
0
250m
500m
750m
1 km
181
188
A
B
C
D
E
F
B6278
A689
Frosterley Cottage
Weirs
Thimbleby Hill
Parson Byers
Newlandside Farm
Horsley Burn
Cow Burn
Weardale Rly
Horsley Head
West Newlandside
Woodcroft
Rogerley Hall
Snape Gate
Dodd House
Peak Field
Buckler Dale
Weardale Way
Fine Sike
Catterick Moss
HILL END
High Bishopley
Bishopley
Bollihope House
LOW BOLLIHOPE CVN SITE
Bollihope Shield
Ford
Bollihope Burn
Juniper Banks
WHITFIELD BROW
Bollihope
Moor Rigg
Wager Burn
DL13
Whitfield Brow
Smithy Burn
Bollihope
Common
Low Black Hill
Black Burn
Howden Burn
Wager Head
Shafwell Sike
Resrs
Five Pikes
Hawkwood Head
Raven Seat
Harnisha Hill
Pawlaw Pike
Three Laws
Nanny Sike
Great Eggleshope Beck
Shooting House
Little Eggleshope Beck
Sharnberry Gill
DL12
Sharnberry Flat
White Hill
8
37
7
36
6
35
5
34
4
33
3
32
2
31
1
30
96
97
98
99
00
01

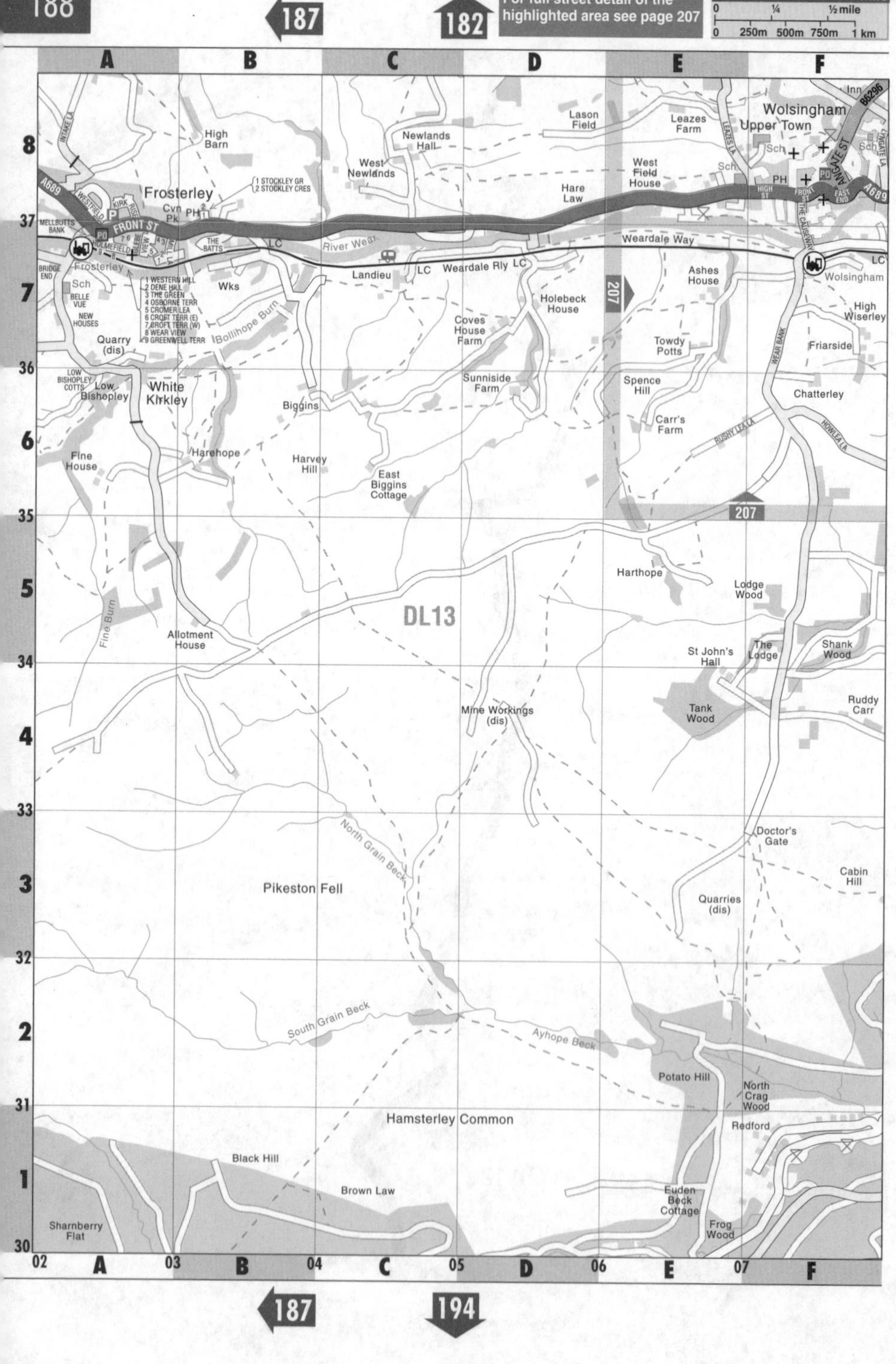

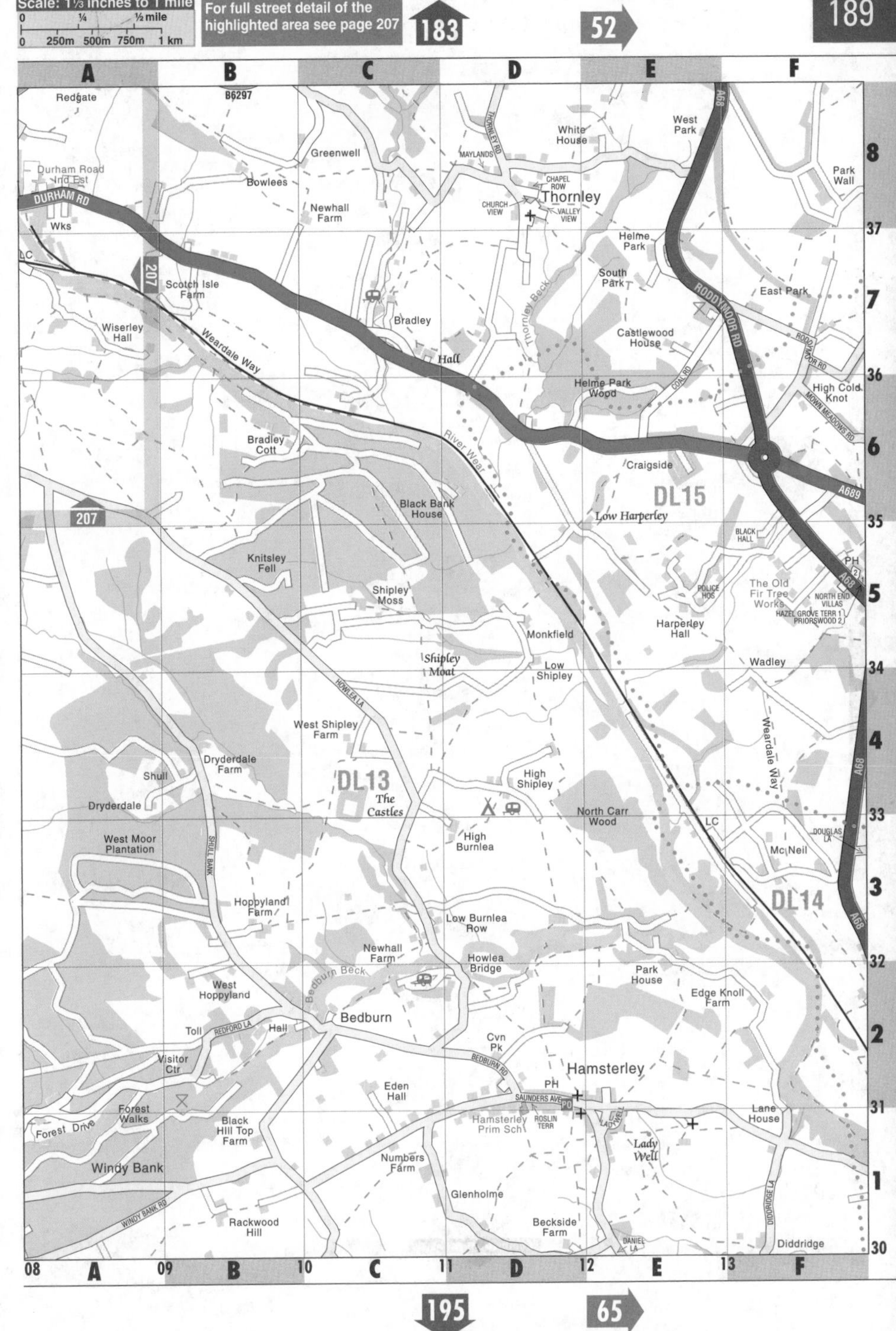

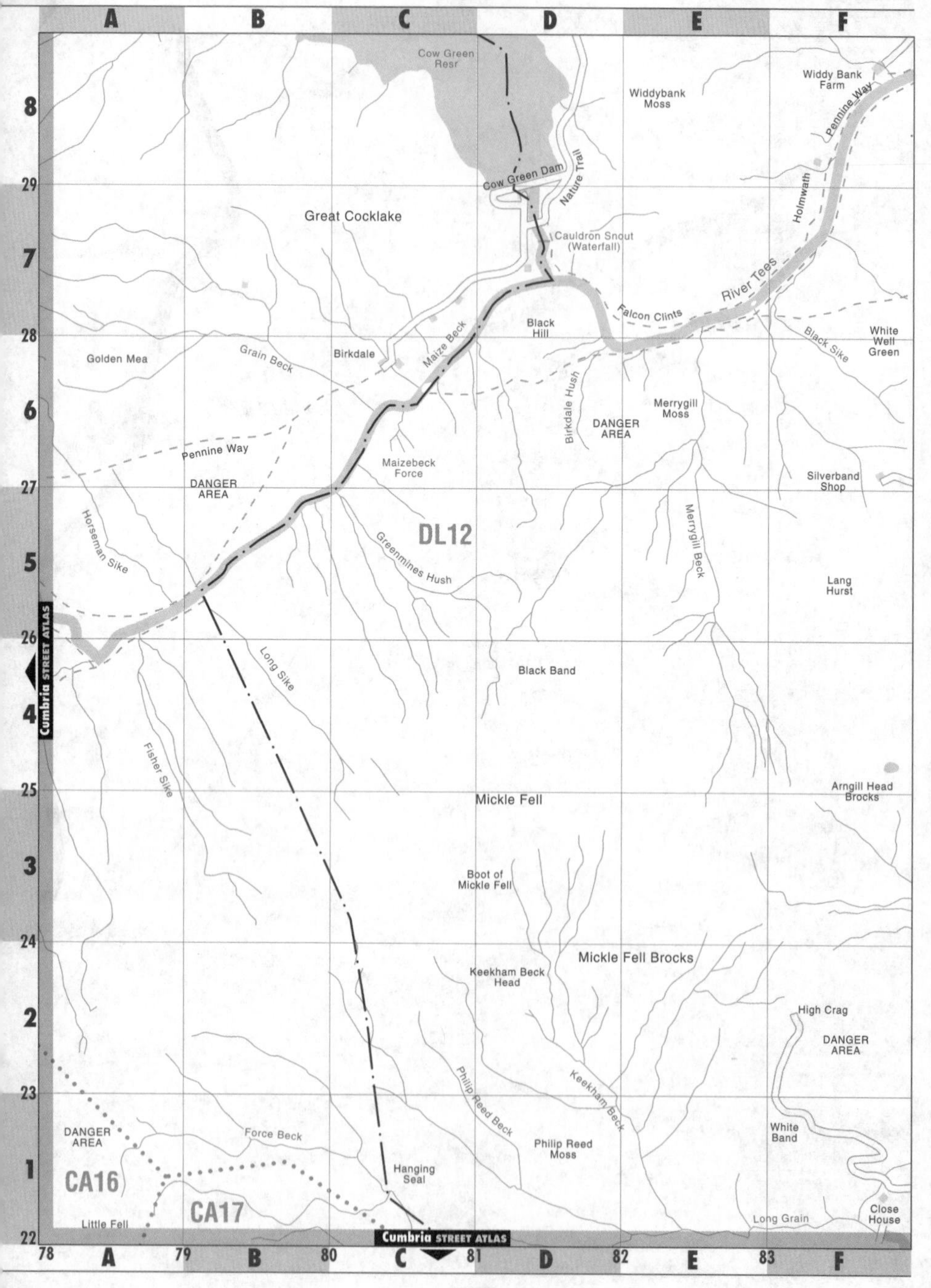

Scale: 1⅓ inches to 1 mile

0   ¼   ½ mile

0   250m 500m 750m 1 km

A   B   C   D   E   F

8

Cow Green Resr

Widdy Bank Farm

Widdybank Moss

Pennine Way

29

Great Cocklake

Cow Green Dam

Holmwath

Nature Trail

7

Cauldron Snout (Waterfall)

Cauldron Snout Clints

River Tees

Black Hill

Falcon Clints

Black Sike

28

Golden Mea

Grain Beck

Birkdale

Maize Beck

White Well Green

6

Pennine Way

Maizebeck Force

Birkdale Hush

DANGER AREA

Merrygill Moss

Silverband Shop

27

DANGER AREA

Horseman Sike

Greenmines Hush

DL12

Merrygill Beck

Lang Hurst

5

26

Long Sike

Black Band

Cumbria STREET ATLAS

4

Fisher Sike

Mickle Fell

Arngill Head Brocks

25

3

Boot of Mickle Fell

Mickle Fell Brocks

24

Keekham Beck Head

High Crag

2

DANGER AREA

Keekham Beck

Philip Reed Beck

23

DANGER AREA

Force Beck

Philip Reed Moss

White Band

1

CA16

Hanging Seal

CA17

Close House

Little Fell

Long Grain

22

Cumbria STREET ATLAS

78   A   79   B   80   C   81   D   82   E   83   F

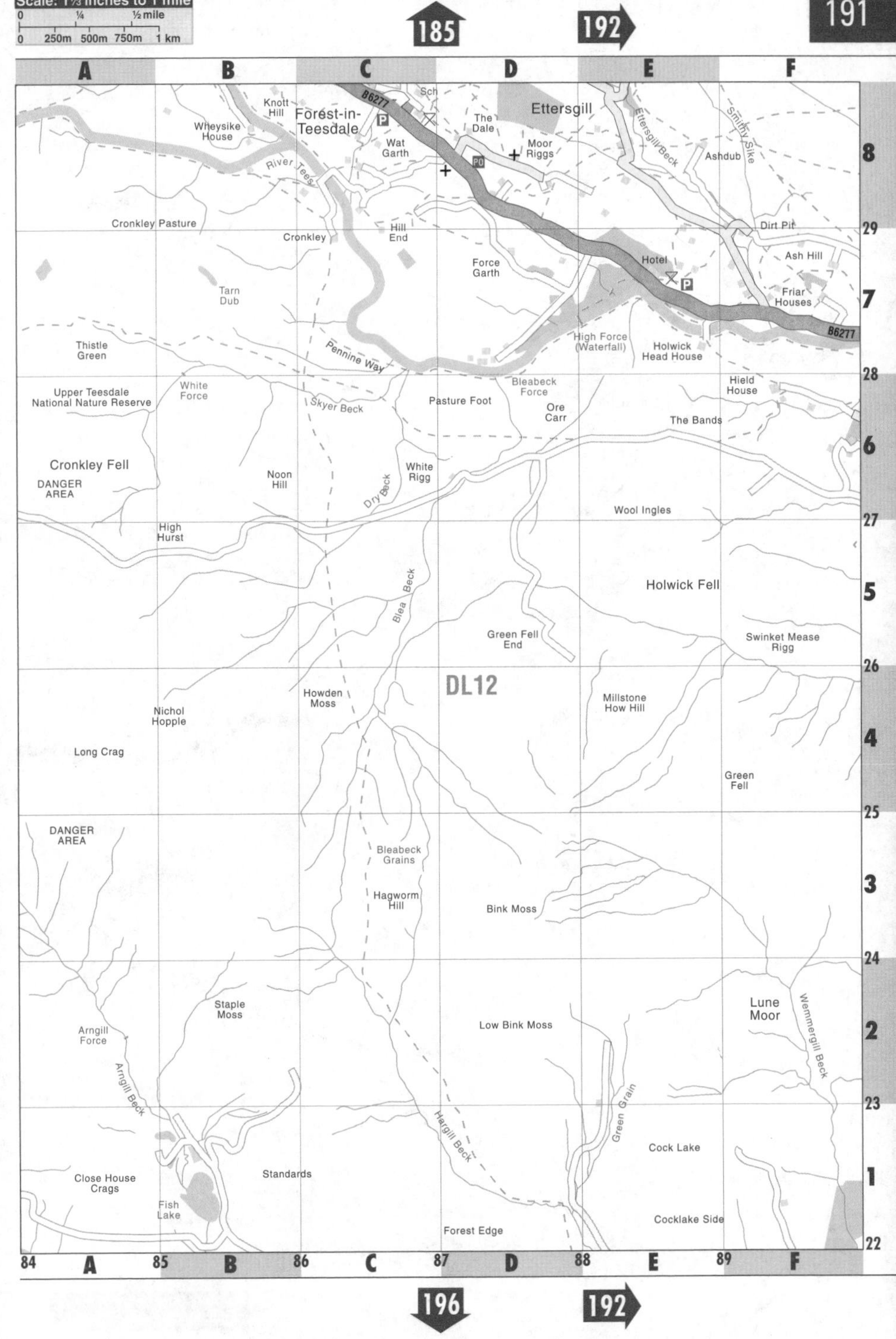

Scale: 1⅓ inches to 1 mile

0	¼	½ mile

0	250m	500m	750m	1 km

185   192

8

Knott Hill
Wheysike House
Forest-in-Teesdale
B6277
P
Wat Garth
Sch
The Dale
Ettersgill
Moor Riggs
Ettersgill Beck
Slight Sike
Ashdub
River Tees
50
+
+
Cronkley Pasture
Hill End
Cronkley
Force Garth
Dirt Pit

29

7

Tarn Dub
Hotel
P
Ash Hill
Friar Houses
B6277

28

Thistle Green
Pennine Way
High Force (Waterfall)
Holwick Head House
Hield House

Upper Teesdale National Nature Reserve
White Force
Skyer Beck
Pasture Foot
Bleabeck Force
Ore Carr
The Bands

6

Cronkley Fell
DANGER AREA
Noon Hill
Dry Beck
White Rigg
Wool Ingles

27

High Hurst
Blea Beck
Holwick Fell

5

Green Fell End
Swinket Mease Rigg

26

Howden Moss
DL12
Millstone How Hill

Nichol Hopple
Long Crag

4

Green Fell

25

DANGER AREA
Bleabeck Grains

3

Hagworm Hill
Bink Moss

24

Staple Moss
Lune Moor

2

Arngill Force
Low Bink Moss
Wemmergill Beck

Arngill Beck

23

Hargill Beck
Green Grain
Cock Lake

Close House Crags
Standards
Cocklake Side

1

Fish Lake
Forest Edge

22

84   85   86   87   88   89

A   B   C   D   E   F

196   192

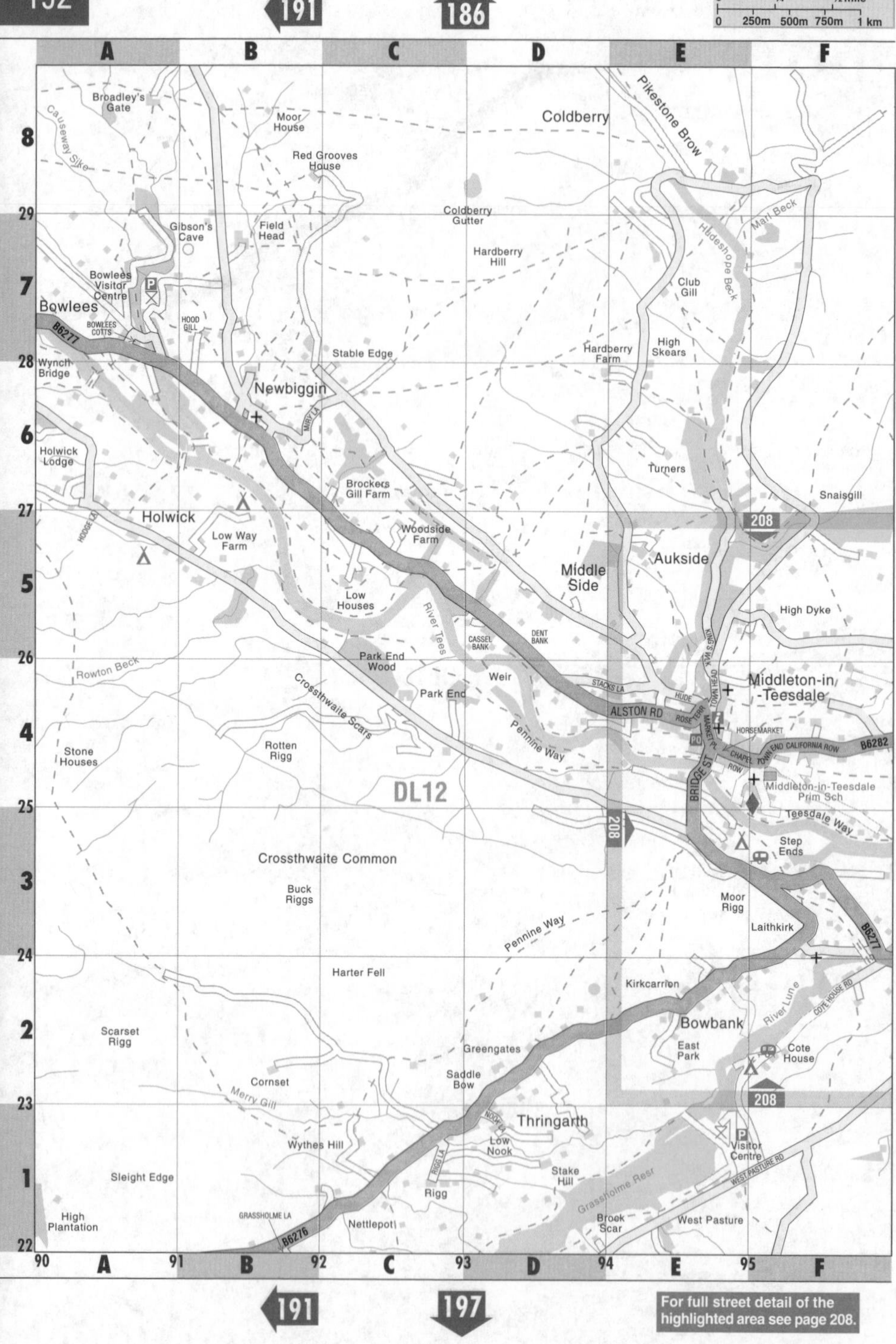

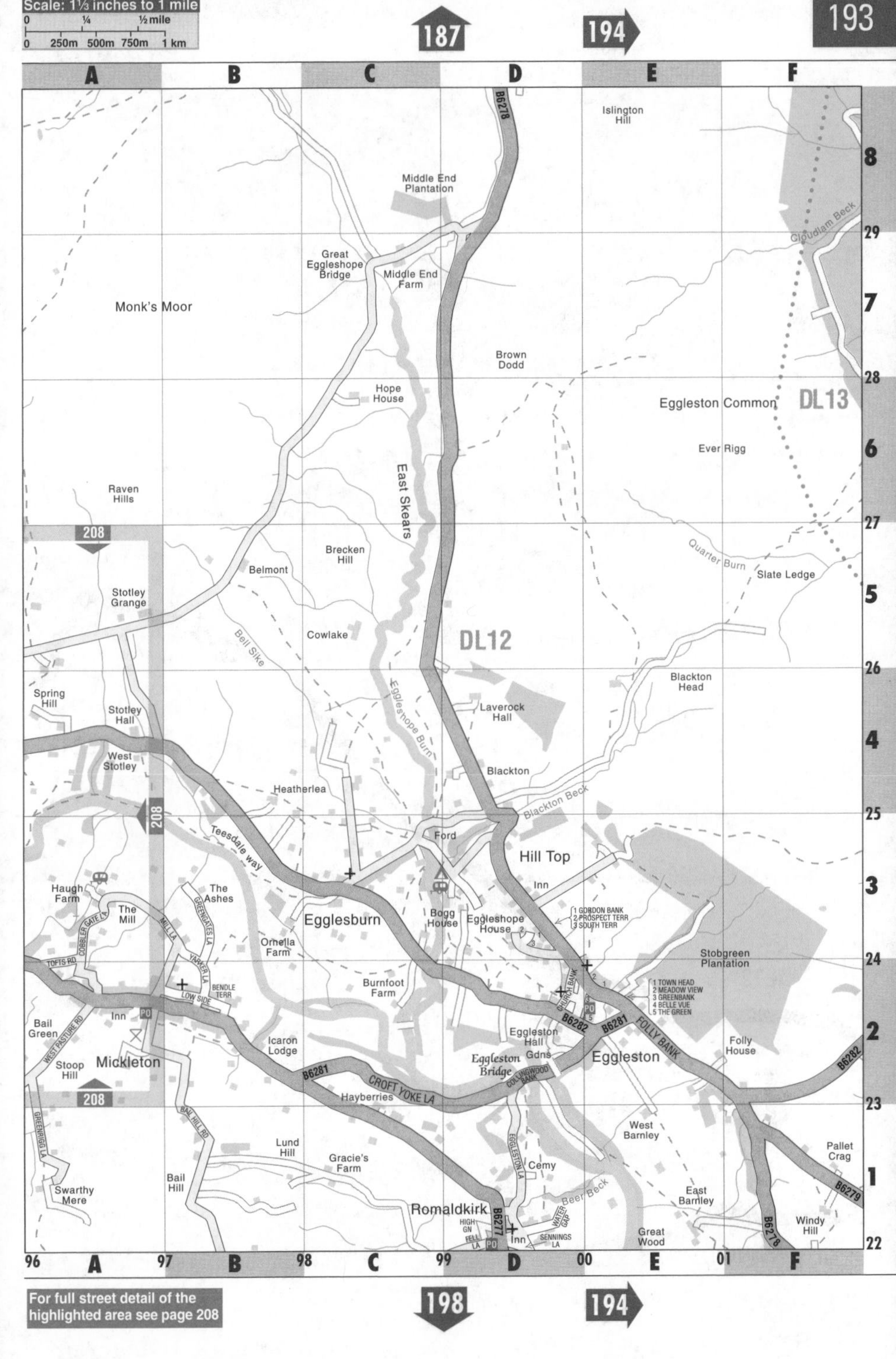

193
188

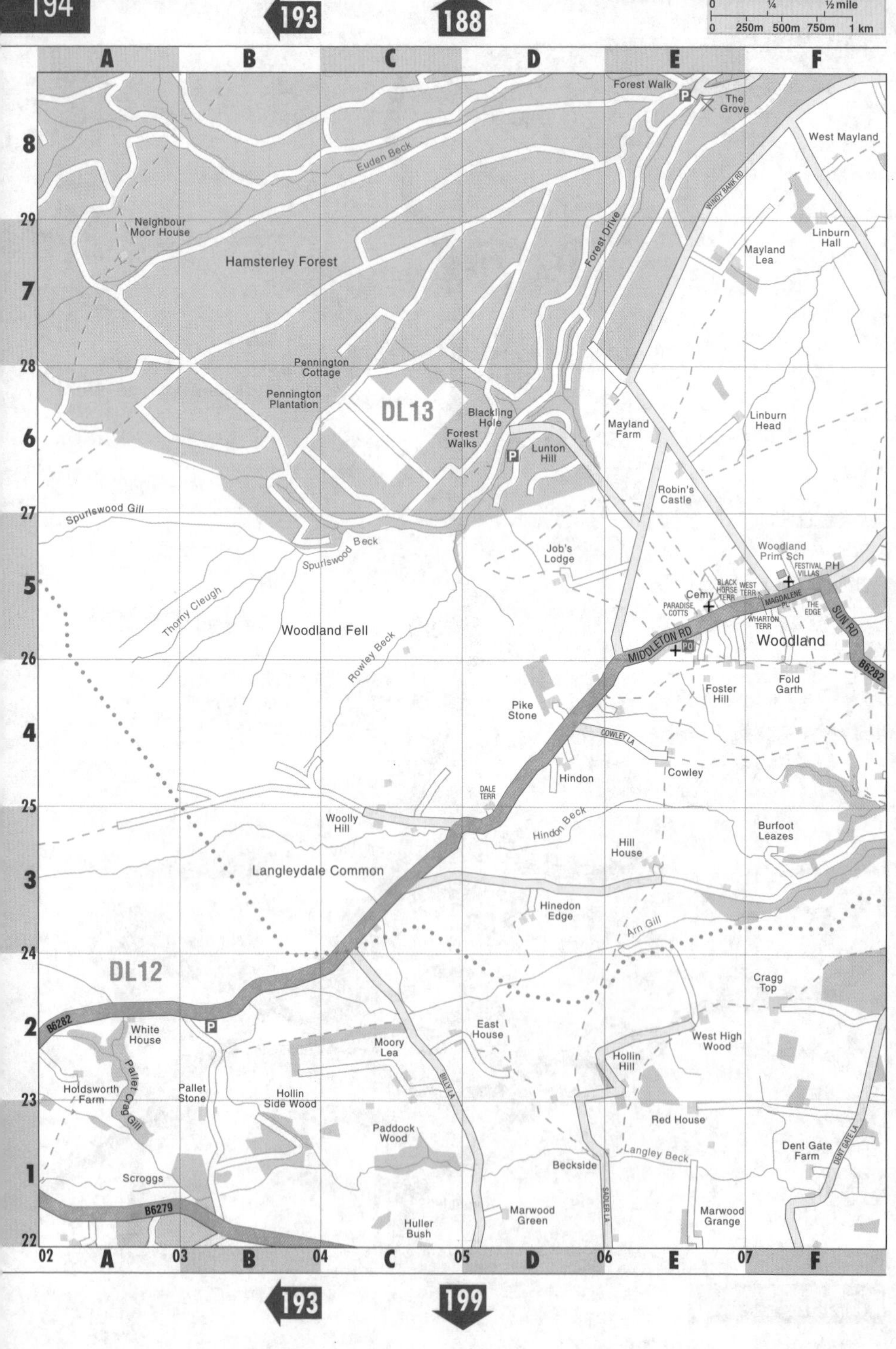
Scale: 1⅓ inches to 1 mile
0 ¼ ½ mile
0 250m 500m 750m 1 km
Forest Walk
The Grove
West Mayland
Euden Beck
Windy Bank Rd
Neighbour Moor House
Hamsterley Forest
Forest Drive
Linburn Hall
Mayland Lea
Pennington Cottage
Pennington Plantation
DL13
Blackling Hole
Forest Walks
Lunton Hill
Mayland Farm
Linburn Head
Robin's Castle
Spurlswood Gill
Spurlswood Beck
Job's Lodge
Woodland Prim Sch
Festival Villas
PH
Black Horse Terr
West Terr
Cemy
Paradise Cotts
Magdalene Pl
The Edge
Wharton Terr
Sun Rd
Thorny Cleugh
Woodland Fell
Middleton Rd
PO
Woodland
Rowley Beck
B6282
Foster Hill
Fold Garth
Pike Stone
Cowley La
Hindon
Cowley
Dale Terr
Woolly Hill
Hindon Beck
Burfoot Leazes
Hill House
Langleydale Common
Hinedon Edge
Arn Gill
DL12
Cragg Top
B6282
White House
East House
Moory Lea
West High Wood
Hollin Hill
Pallet Crag Gill
Billy La
Holdsworth Farm
Pallet Stone
Hollin Side Wood
Red House
Paddock Wood
Dent Gate La
Dent Gate Farm
Langley Beck
Beckside
Scroggs
Sadler La
B6279
Marwood Green
Marwood Grange
Huller Bush
A B C D E F
02 03 04 05 06 07
8 29 7 28 6 27 5 26 4 25 3 24 2 23 1 22

193
199

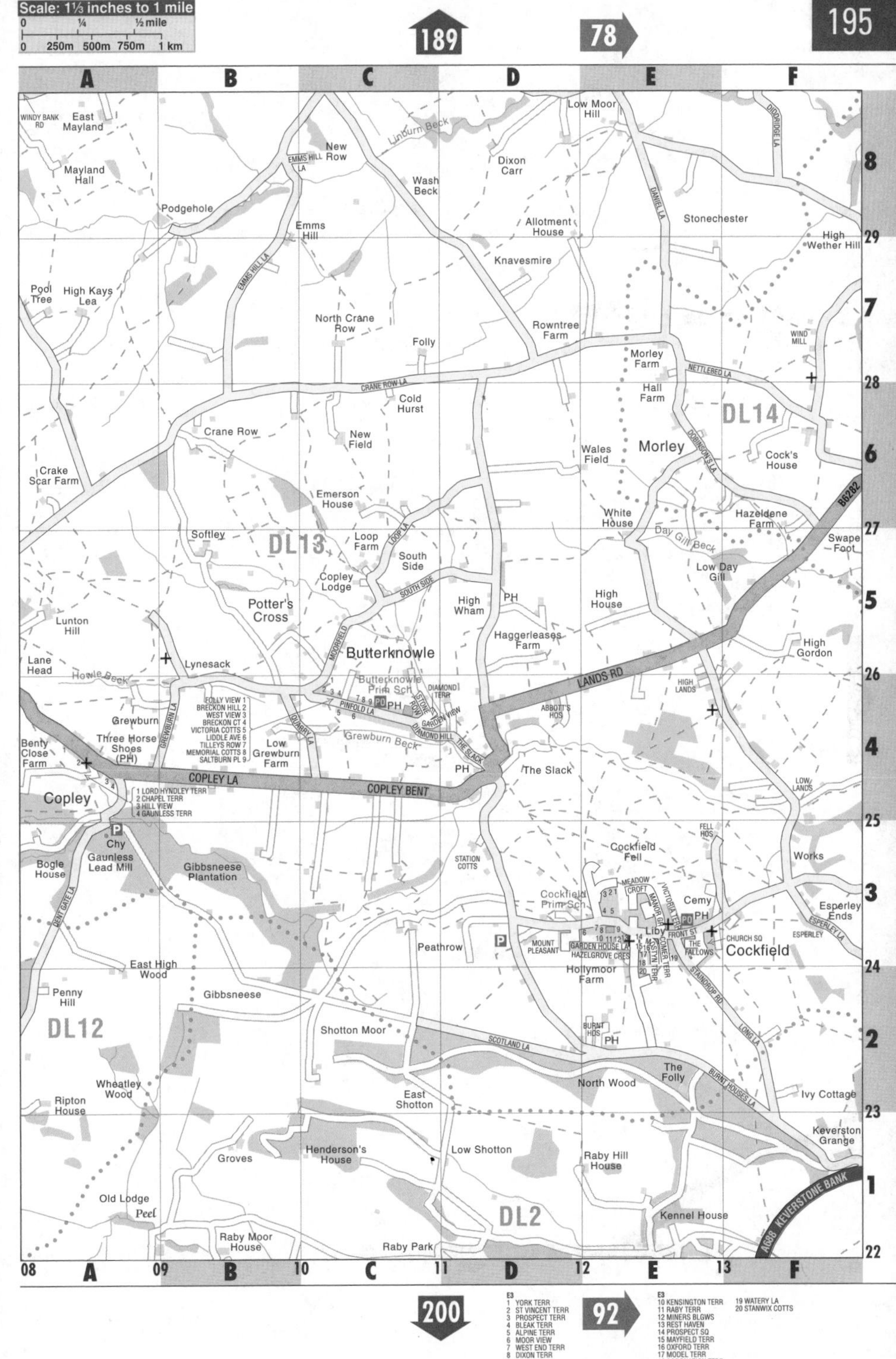

Scale: 1⅓ inches to 1 mile
0 ¼ ½ mile
0 250m 500m 750m 1 km
189
78
East Mayland
Mayland Hall
New Row
Linburn Beck
Low Moor Hill
Dixon Carr
Wash Beck
Podgehole
Emms Hill
Allotment House
Stonechester
High Wether Hill
Knavesmire
Pool Tree
High Kays Lea
North Crane Row
Folly
Rowntree Farm
Morley Farm
Hall Farm
Crane Row
Cold Hurst
New Field
DL14
Morley
Wales Field
Cock's House
Crake Scar Farm
Emerson House
White House
Hazeldene Farm
Day Gill Beck
Softley
DL13
Loop Farm
South Side
Swape Foot
Copley Lodge
Low Day Gill
Lunton Hill
Potter's Cross
High Wham
High House
Haggerleases Farm
High Gordon
Lane Head
Lynesack
Butterknowle
Howle Beck
Butterknowle Prim Sch
LANDS RD
High Lands
Abbott's Hos
Grewburn
Grewburn Beck
Three Horse Shoes (PH)
Low Grewburn Farm
Benty Close Farm
The Slack
COPLEY LA
COPLEY BENT
Low Lands
Copley
1 LORD HYNDLEY TERR
2 CHAPEL TERR
3 HILL VIEW
4 GAUNLESS TERR
FOLLY VIEW 1
BRECKON HILL 2
WEST VIEW 3
BRECKON CT 4
VICTORIA COTTS 5
LIDDLE AVE 6
TILLEYS ROW 7
MEMORIAL COTTS 8
SALTBURN PL 9
Chy
Gaunless Lead Mill
Fell Hos
Cockfield Fell
Bogle House
Gibbsneese Plantation
Station Cotts
Works
Cockfield Prim Sch
Cemy
Esperley Ends
Peathrow
Mount Pleasant
Cockfield
Hollymoor Farm
East High Wood
Penny Hill
Gibbsneese
DL12
Shotton Moor
Burnt Hos
SCOTLAND LA
North Wood
The Folly
Wheatley Wood
Ripton House
East Shotton
Ivy Cottage
Keverston Grange
Henderson's House
Low Shotton
Groves
Raby Hill House
Old Lodge
Peel
DL2
Kennel House
Raby Moor House
Raby Park
A688 KEVERSTONE BANK
200
92
E3
1 YORK TERR
2 ST VINCENT TERR
3 PROSPECT TERR
4 BLEAK TERR
5 ALPINE TERR
6 MOOR VIEW
7 WEST END TERR
8 DIXON TERR
9 VANE TERR
E3
10 KENSINGTON TERR
11 RABY TERR
12 MINERS BLGWS
13 REST HAVEN
14 PROSPECT SQ
15 MAYFIELD TERR
16 OXFORD TERR
17 MODEL TERR
18 CORONATION TERR
19 WATERY LA
20 STANWIX COTTS

191

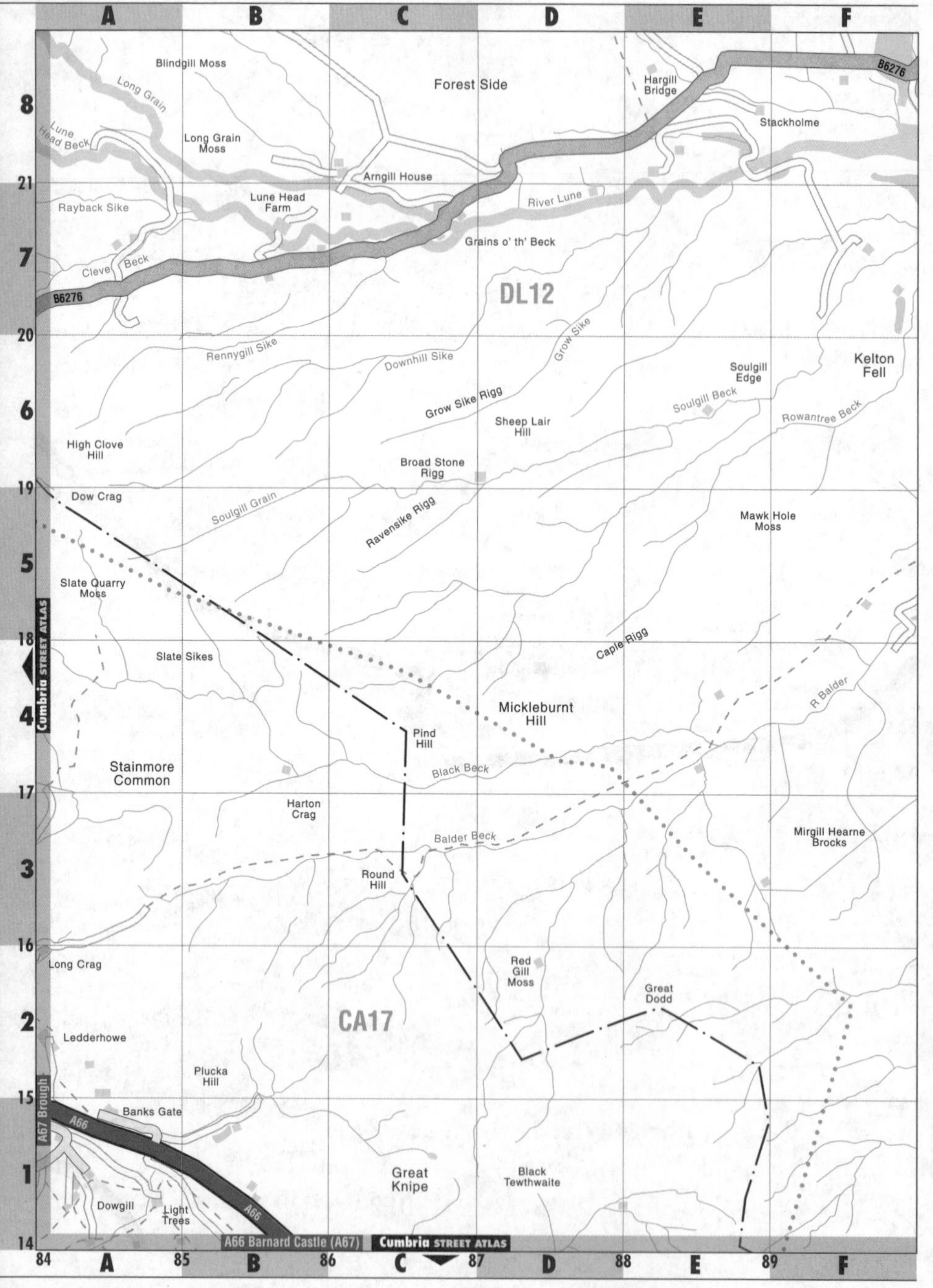

Scale: 1⅓ inches to 1 mile

DL12

CA17

Forest Side
Blindgill Moss
Long Grain
Long Grain Moss
Arngill House
Hargill Bridge
Stackholme
B6276
Lune Head Beck
Rayback Sike
Lune Head Farm
River Lune
Clevel Beck
B6276
Grains o' th' Beck
Rennygill Sike
Downhill Sike
Grow Sike
Kelton Fell
High Clove Hill
Grow Sike Rigg
Sheep Lair Hill
Soulgill Edge
Soulgill Beck
Rowantree Beck
Dow Crag
Broad Stone Rigg
Soulgill Grain
Ravensike Rigg
Mawk Hole Moss
Slate Quarry Moss
Slate Sikes
Caple Rigg
R Balder
Mickleburnt Hill
Pind Hill
Stainmore Common
Harton Crag
Black Beck
Balder Beck
Mirgill Hearne Brocks
Round Hill
Long Crag
Red Gill Moss
Great Dodd
Ledderhowe
Plucka Hill
Banks Gate
A66
A67 Brough
Dowgill
Light Trees
A66
Great Knipe
Black Tewthwaite
A66 Barnard Castle (A67)   Cumbria STREET ATLAS

Cumbria STREET ATLAS

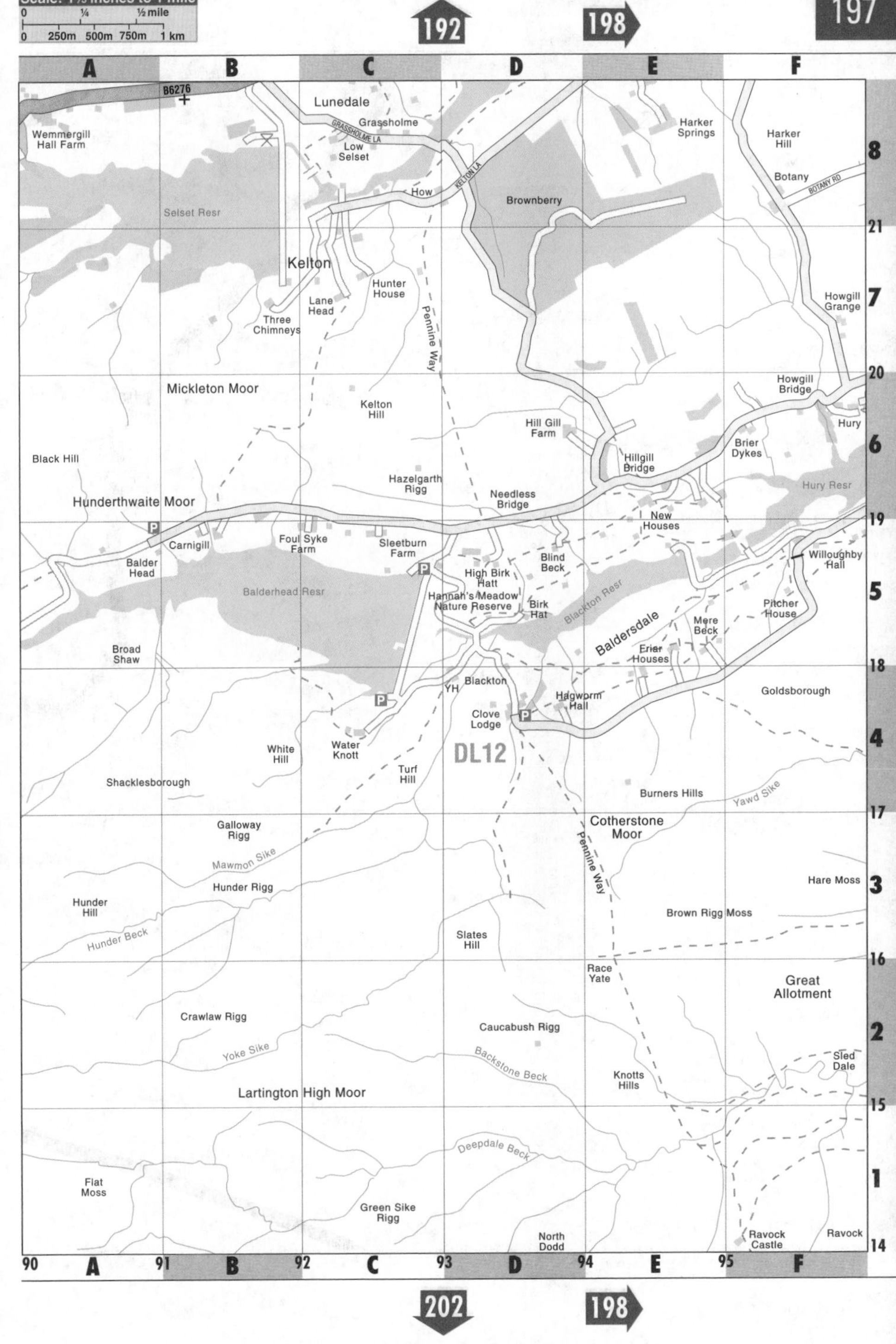

Scale: 1⅓ inches to 1 mile
0 ¼ ½ mile
0 250m 500m 750m 1 km
192
198
A B C D E F
B6276
Wemmergill Hall Farm
Lunedale
Grassholme
GRASSHOLME LA
Low Selset
Harker Springs
Harker Hill
8
Botany
BOTANY RD
KELTON LA
How
Brownberry
Selset Resr
21
Kelton
Hunter House
Lane Head
Three Chimneys
Pennine Way
Howgill Grange
7
20
Mickleton Moor
Kelton Hill
Howgill Bridge
Hill Gill Farm
Hury
Black Hill
6
Hillgill Bridge
Brier Dykes
Hazelgarth Rigg
Hury Resr
Needless Bridge
Hunderthwaite Moor
New Houses
19
Carnigill
Foul Syke Farm
Sleetburn Farm
Balder Head
Blind Beck
Willoughby Hall
High Birk Hatt
Balderhead Resr
Hannah's Meadow Nature Reserve
Birk Hat
Blackton Resr
5
Pitcher House
Mere Beck
Baldersdale
Broad Shaw
Friar Houses
18
Blackton
YH
Goldsborough
Hagworm Hall
Clove Lodge
White Hill
Water Knott
DL12
4
Turf Hill
Shacklesborough
Burners Hills
Yawd Sike
17
Cotherstone Moor
Galloway Rigg
Mawmon Sike
Hunder Rigg
Hare Moss
3
Hunder Hill
Brown Rigg Moss
Hunder Beck
Slates Hill
16
Race Yate
Great Allotment
Crawlaw Rigg
Caucabush Rigg
2
Yoke Sike
Backstone Beck
Sled Dale
Knotts Hills
Lartington High Moor
15
Deepdale Beck
1
Flat Moss
Green Sike Rigg
North Dodd
Ravock Castle
Ravock
14
90 A 91 B 92 C 93 D 94 E 95 F
202
198

197
193

Scale: 1⅓ inches to 1 mile

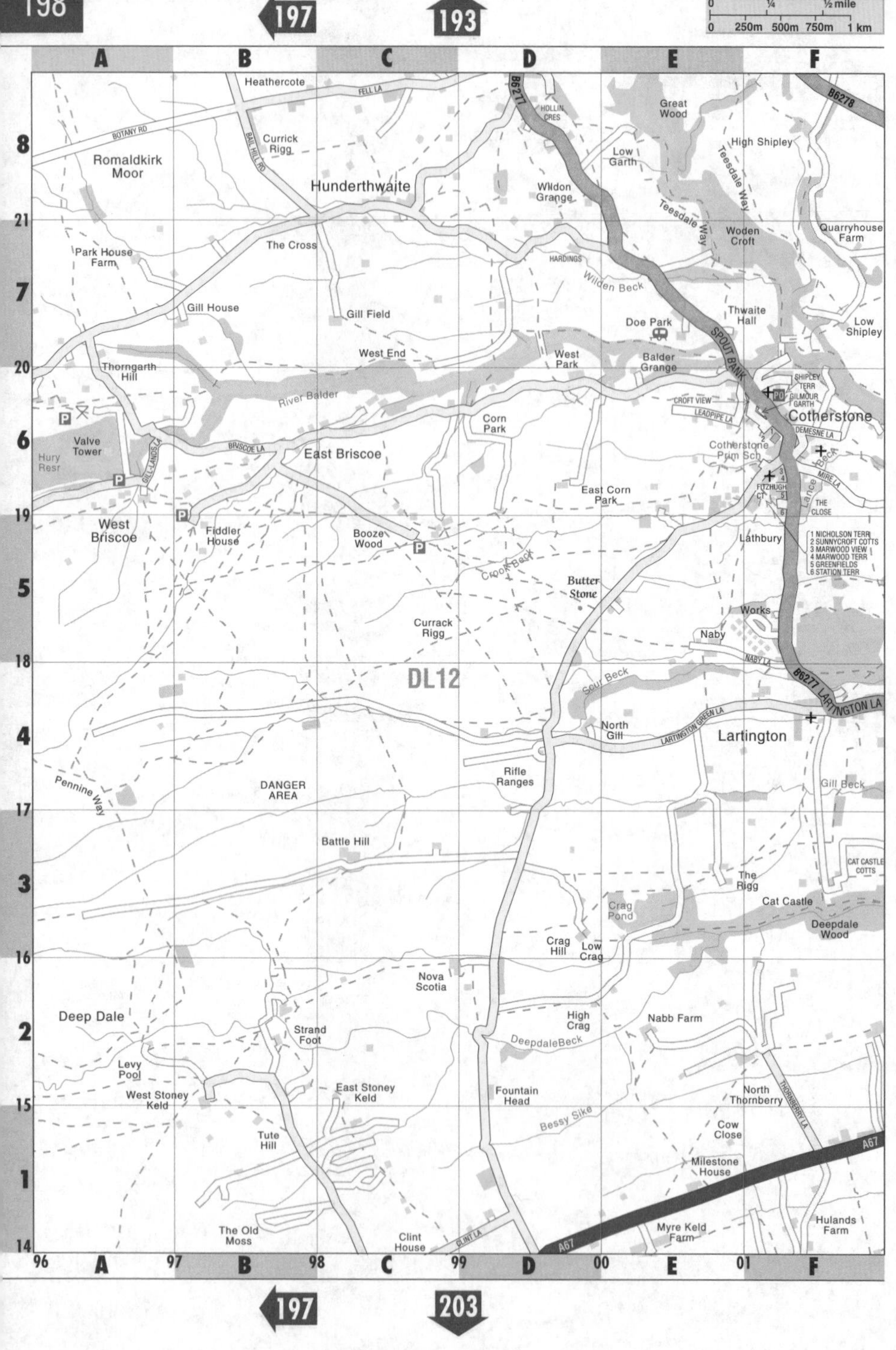
Heathercote
Romaldkirk Moor
Currick Rigg
Hunderthwaite
Wildon Grange
Low Garth
Great Wood
High Shipley
Teesdale Way
Woden Croft
Quarryhouse Farm
Park House Farm
The Cross
Wilden Beck
Gill House
Gill Field
Doe Park
Thwaite Hall
Low Shipley
West End
West Park
Balder Grange
Thorngarth Hill
River Balder
Cotherstone
Valve Tower
Hury Resr
Corn Park
East Briscoe
Cotherstone Prim Sch
West Briscoe
Fiddler House
Booze Wood
East Corn Park
Lathbury
1 NICHOLSON TERR
2 SUNNYCROFT COTTS
3 MARWOOD VIEW
4 MARWOOD TERR
5 GREENFIELDS
6 STATION TERR
Crook Beck
Butter Stone
Works
Currack Rigg
Naby
DL12
Sour Beck
North Gill
Lartington
Pennine Way
DANGER AREA
Rifle Ranges
Gill Beck
Battle Hill
The Rigg
Cat Castle
Crag Pond
Deepdale Wood
Crag Hill
Low Crag
Nova Scotia
Deep Dale
Strand Foot
High Crag
Nabb Farm
DeepdaleBeck
Levy Pool
West Stoney Keld
East Stoney Keld
Fountain Head
North Thornberry
Bessy Sike
Tute Hill
Cow Close
Milestone House
The Old Moss
Clint House
Myre Keld Farm
Hulands Farm

197
203

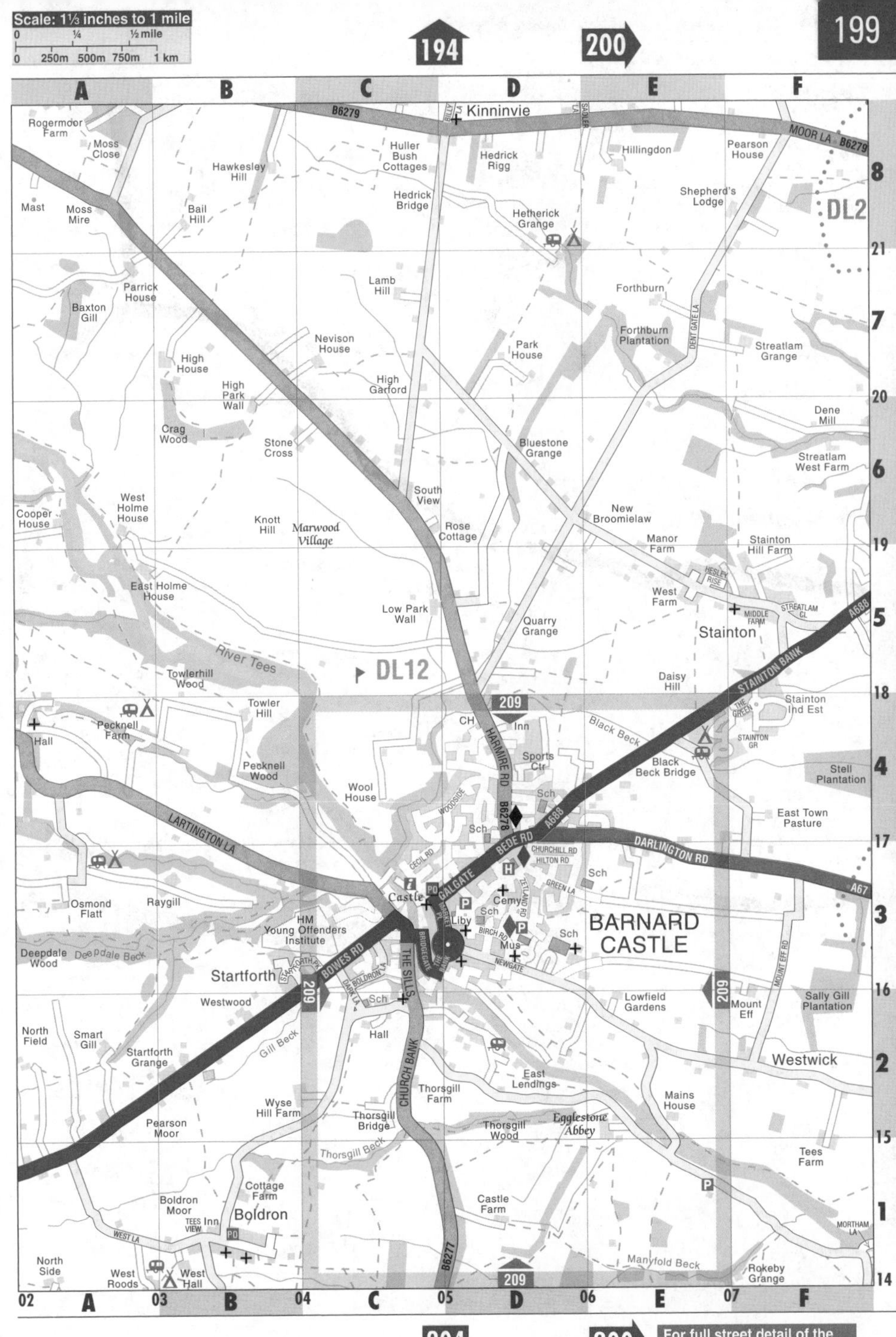

Scale: 1⅓ inches to 1 mile

0   ¼   ½ mile
0   250m 500m 750m 1 km

194
200

A   B   C   D   E   F

8

DL2

21

Rogermoor Farm
Moss Close
Mast
Moss Mire
Hawkesley Hill
Bail Hill
Kinninvie
B6279
Huller Bush Cottages
Hedrick Rigg
Hillingdon
Pearson House
MOOR LA
B6279
Shepherd's Lodge

7

Parrick House
Baxton Gill
High House
High Park Wall
Lamb Hill
Nevison House
Hedrick Bridge
Hetherick Grange
Park House
Forthburn
Forthburn Plantation
DENT GATE LA
Streatlam Grange
High Gatford

20

Crag Wood
Stone Cross
Knott Hill
Marwood Village
Bluestone Grange
New Broomielaw
Manor Farm
Stainton Hill Farm
Dene Mill
Streatlam West Farm

6

Cooper House
West Holme House
East Holme House
Rose Cottage
South View
West Farm
REBEN RIGE
RISE
STREATLAM CL
MIDDLE FARM
STAINTON GR

19

River Tees
Towlerhill Wood
Low Park Wall
Quarry Grange
Daisy Hill
Stainton
STAINTON BANK
A688
Stainton Ind Est
THE GREEN

5

▶ DL12

18

Towler Hill
Peknell Farm
Hall
Pecknell Wood
Wool House
CH
Inn
Sports Ctr
Black Beck
Black Beck Bridge
Stainton

4

LARTINGTON LA
Osmond Flatt
Raygill
Sch
Sch
WOODGATE
ECIL RD
BEDE RD
HARMIRE RD
A688
CHURCHILL RD
HILTON RD
DARLINGTON RD
Sch
East Town Pasture
Stell Plantation
A67

17

Deepdale Wood
Deepdale Beck
HM Young Offenders Institute
Startforth
Castle
GAI GATE
Liby
Cemry
Mus
NEWGATE
GREEN LA
Sch
Sch
Sch
BARNARD CASTLE

3

North Field
Smart Gill
Startforth Grange
Westwood
BOWES RD
THE SILLS
BOLDRON
CHURCH BANK
Hall
Gill Beck
Sch
Lowfield Gardens
Mount Eff
MONKEY EFF RD
Sally Gill Plantation
Westwick

2

16

Pearson Moor
Wyse Hill Farm
Thorsgill Bridge
Thorsgill Farm
Thorsgill Beck
Thorsgill Wood
Egglestone Abbey
East Lendings
Mains House
Tees Farm

15

Cottage Farm
Boldron Moor
TEES INN VIEW
Boldron
WEST LA
B6277
Castle Farm
Manyfold Beck
Rokeby Grange
MORTHAM LA

1

North Side
West Roods
West Hall
14

02   A   03   B   04   C   05   D   06   E   07   F

204
200

For full street detail of the highlighted area see page 209

199
195

Scale: 1⅓ inches to 1 mile

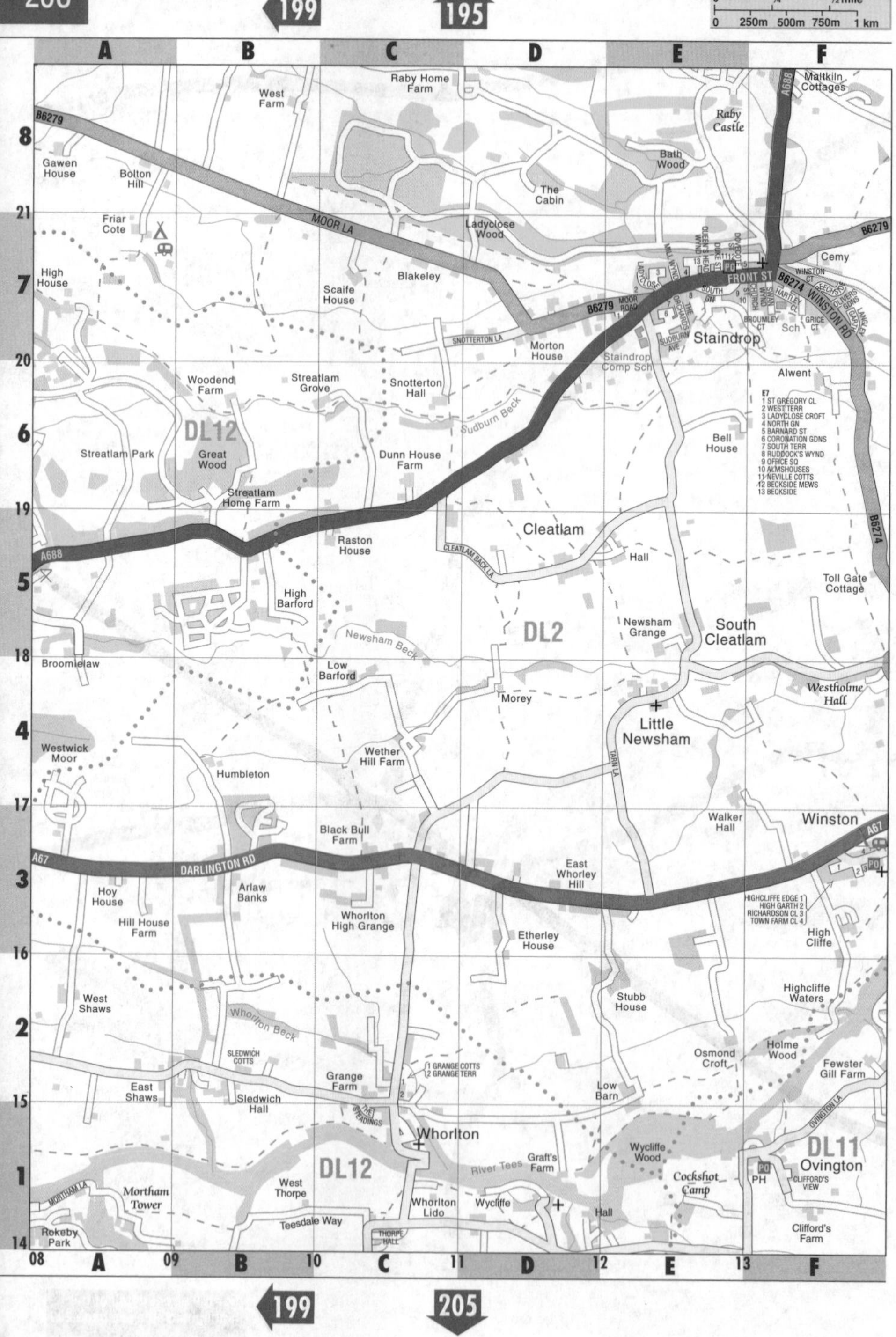
A
B
C
D
E
F
B6279
Gawen House
Bolton Hill
West Farm
Raby Home Farm
Maltkiln Cottages
Raby Castle
Bath Wood
The Cabin
Friar Cote
MOOR LA
Ladyclose Wood
High House
Blakeley
Scaife House
Cemy
FRONT ST
B6274
WINSTON RD
B6279
SNOTTERTON LA
Morton House
Staindrop
Staindrop Comp Sch
Sch
Alwent
Woodend Farm
Streatlam Grove
Snotterton Hall
DL12
Sudburn Beck
Streatlam Park
Great Wood
Dunn House Farm
Bell House
E7
1 ST GREGORY CL
2 WEST TERR
3 LADYCLOSE CROFT
4 NORTH GN
5 BARNARD ST
6 CORONATION GDNS
7 SOUTH TERR
8 RUDDOCK'S WYND
9 OFFICE SQ
10 ALMSHOUSES
11 NEVILLE COTTS
12 BECKSIDE MEWS
13 BECKSIDE
Streatlam Home Farm
Cleatlam
A688
Raston House
CLEATLAM BACK LA
Hall
B6274
Toll Gate Cottage
High Barford
DL2
Newsham Grange
South Cleatlam
Newsham Beck
Broomielaw
Low Barford
Morey
Westholme Hall
Little Newsham
Westwick Moor
Humbleton
Wether Hill Farm
TARN LA
Walker Hall
Winston
Black Bull Farm
A67
DARLINGTON RD
East Whorley Hill
Hoy House
Arlaw Banks
HIGHCLIFFE EDGE 1
HIGH GARTH 2
RICHARDSON CL 3
TOWN FARM CL 4
Hill House Farm
Whorlton High Grange
Etherley House
High Cliffe
West Shaws
Stubb House
Highcliffe Waters
Whorlton Beck
SLEDWICH COTTS
1 GRANGE COTTS
2 GRANGE TERR
Osmond Croft
Holme Wood
Fewster Gill Farm
East Shaws
Sledwich Hall
Grange Farm
Low Barn
THE STEADINGS
Whorlton
OVINGTON LA
DL11
Ovington
Wycliffe Wood
Graft's Farm
River Tees
DL12
Cockshot Camp
PH
CLIFFORD'S VIEW
MORTHAM LA
Mortham Tower
West Thorpe
Whorlton Lido
Wycliffe
Hall
Teesdale Way
Clifford's Farm
Rokeby Park
THORPE HALL
08
09
10
11
12
13
8
21
7
20
6
19
5
18
4
17
3
16
2
15
1
14

199
205

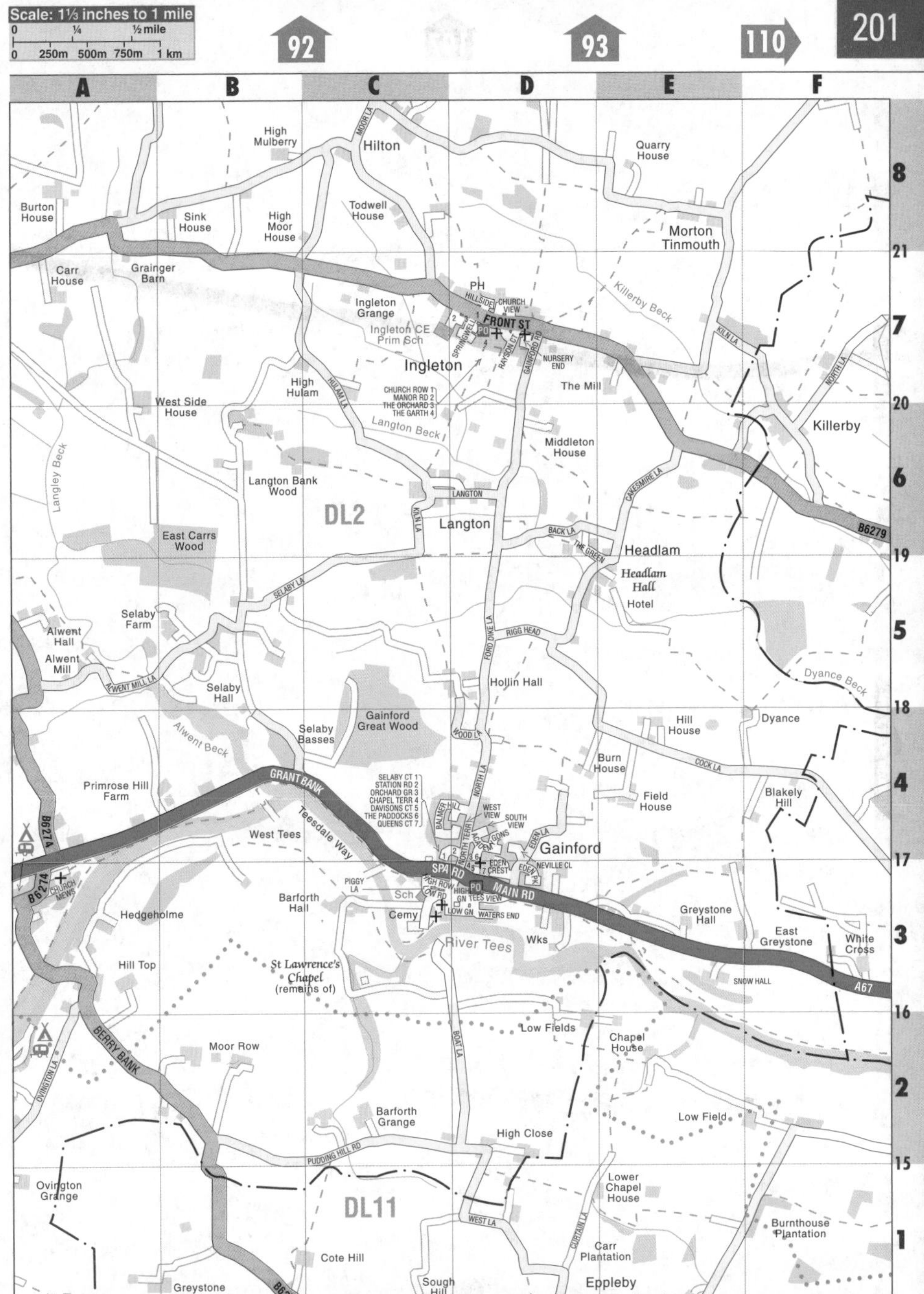

Scale: 1⅓ inches to 1 mile

| 0 | ¼ | ½ mile |

| 0 | 250m | 500m | 750m | 1 km |

Burton House

Carr House

Grainger Barn

Sink House

High Moor House

High Mulberry

Hilton

Todwell House

Ingleton Grange

Ingleton CE Prim Sch

Ingleton

West Side House

High Hulam

Langton Bank Wood

DL2

East Carrs Wood

Langley Beck

Selaby Farm

Alwent Hall

Alwent Mill

EWENT MILL LA

Selaby Hall

Selaby Basses

Gainford Great Wood

GRANT BANK

Teesdale Way

Primrose Hill Farm

West Tees

Alwent Beck

PH

HILLSIDE CHURCH VIEW

FRONT ST

CHURCH ROW 1
MANOR RD 2
THE ORCHARD 3
THE GARTH 4

Langton Beck

Langton

BACK LA

The Mill

NURSERY END

Middleton House

Headlam

Headlam Hall Hotel

CREAMERE LA

Killerby Beck

Morton Tinmouth

Quarry House

Killerby

B6279

Hollin Hall

RIGG HEAD

Dyance Beck

Hill House

Dyance

Burn House

COCK LA

Field House

Blakely Hill

SELABY CT 1
STATION RD 2
ORCHARD GR 3
CHAPEL TERR 4
DAVISONS CT 5
THE PADDOCKS 6
QUEENS CT 7

WEST VIEW

SOUTH VIEW

Gainford

NEVILLE CL

SPA RD

MAIN RD

Greystone Hall

East Greystone

White Cross

A67

SNOW HALL

Barforth Hall

PIGGY LA

Sch

Cemy

LOW GN. WATERS END

Wks

River Tees

Hedgeholme

Hill Top

St Lawrence's Chapel (remains of)

Low Fields

Chapel House

Moor Row

Low Field

Barforth Grange

High Close

PUDDING HILL RD

Lower Chapel House

BERRY BANK

Ovington Grange

DL11

WEST LA

Carr Plantation

Burnthouse Plantation

Cote Hill

Greystone

Sough Hill

Eppleby

Rennison

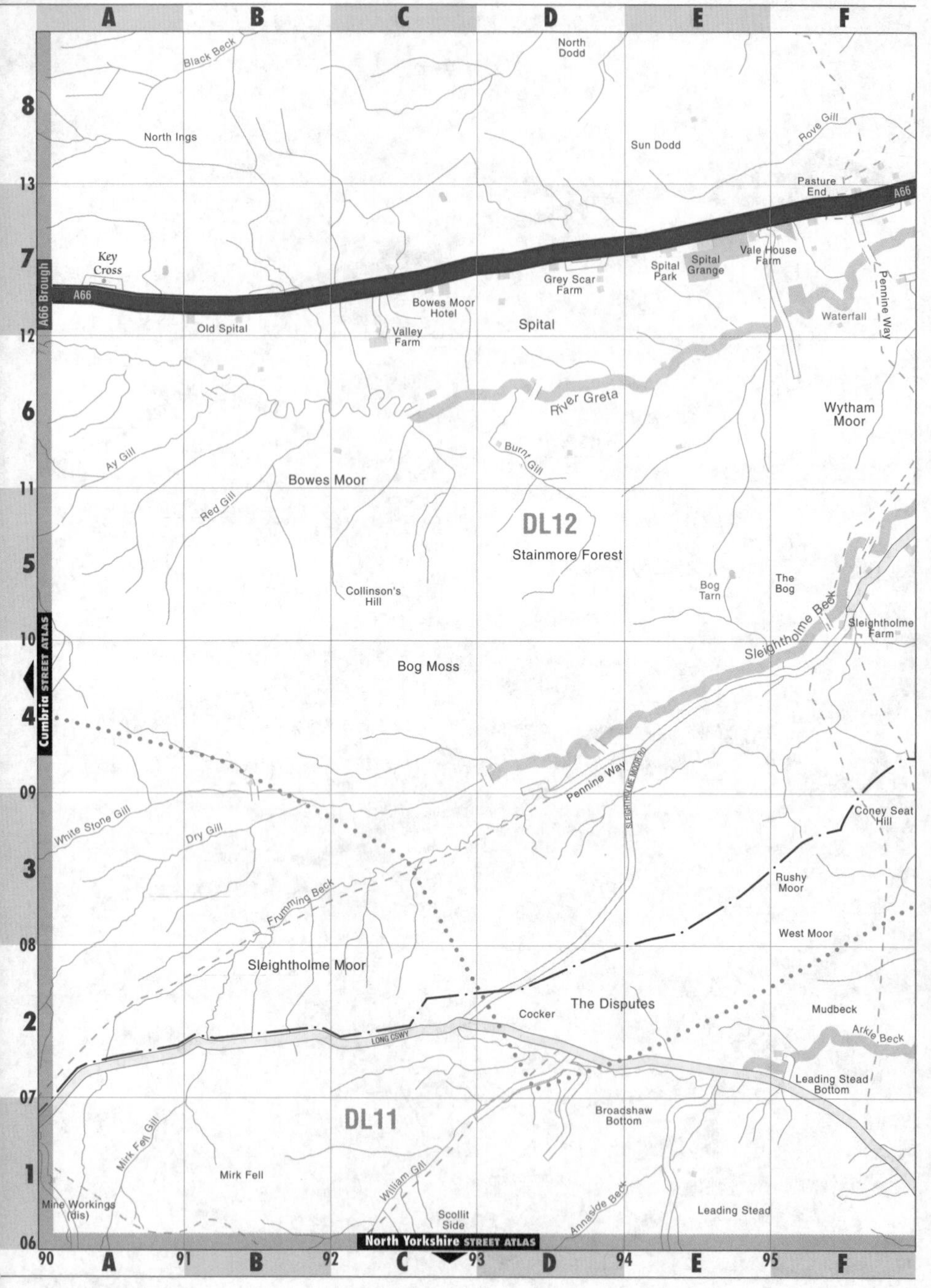

Scale: 1⅓ inches to 1 mile

0   ¼   ½ mile
0   250m 500m 750m 1 km

A B C D E F

8

13

7

12

6

11

5

10

4

09

3

08

2

07

1

06

A66 Brough

Cumbria STREET ATLAS

Black Beck

North Ings

Key
Cross

A66

Old Spital

Ay Gill

Red Gill

Bowes Moor

Collinson's
Hill

Bog Moss

White Stone Gill

Dry Gill

Frumming Beck

Sleightholme Moor

Mirk Fell Gill

Mine Workings
(dis)

Mirk Fell

William Gill

Scollit
Side

North
Dodd

Sun Dodd

Bowes Moor
Hotel

Valley
Farm

Grey Scar
Farm

Spital

Spital
Park

Spital
Grange

Vale House
Farm

Pasture
End

A66

Rove Gill

Waterfall

Pennine Way

Wytham
Moor

River Greta

Burnt Gill

DL12

Stainmore Forest

Bog
Tarn

The
Bog

Sleightholme Beck

Sleightholme
Farm

Pennine Way

SLEIGHTHOLME MOOR

Coney Seat
Hill

Rushy
Moor

West Moor

The Disputes

Cocker

Mudbeck

Arkle Beck

Leading Stead
Bottom

LONG CAUSEY

DL11

Broadshaw
Bottom

Annadale Beck

Leading Stead

90 A 91 B 92 C 93 D 94 E 95 F

Scale: 1⅓ inches to 1 mile

198
204

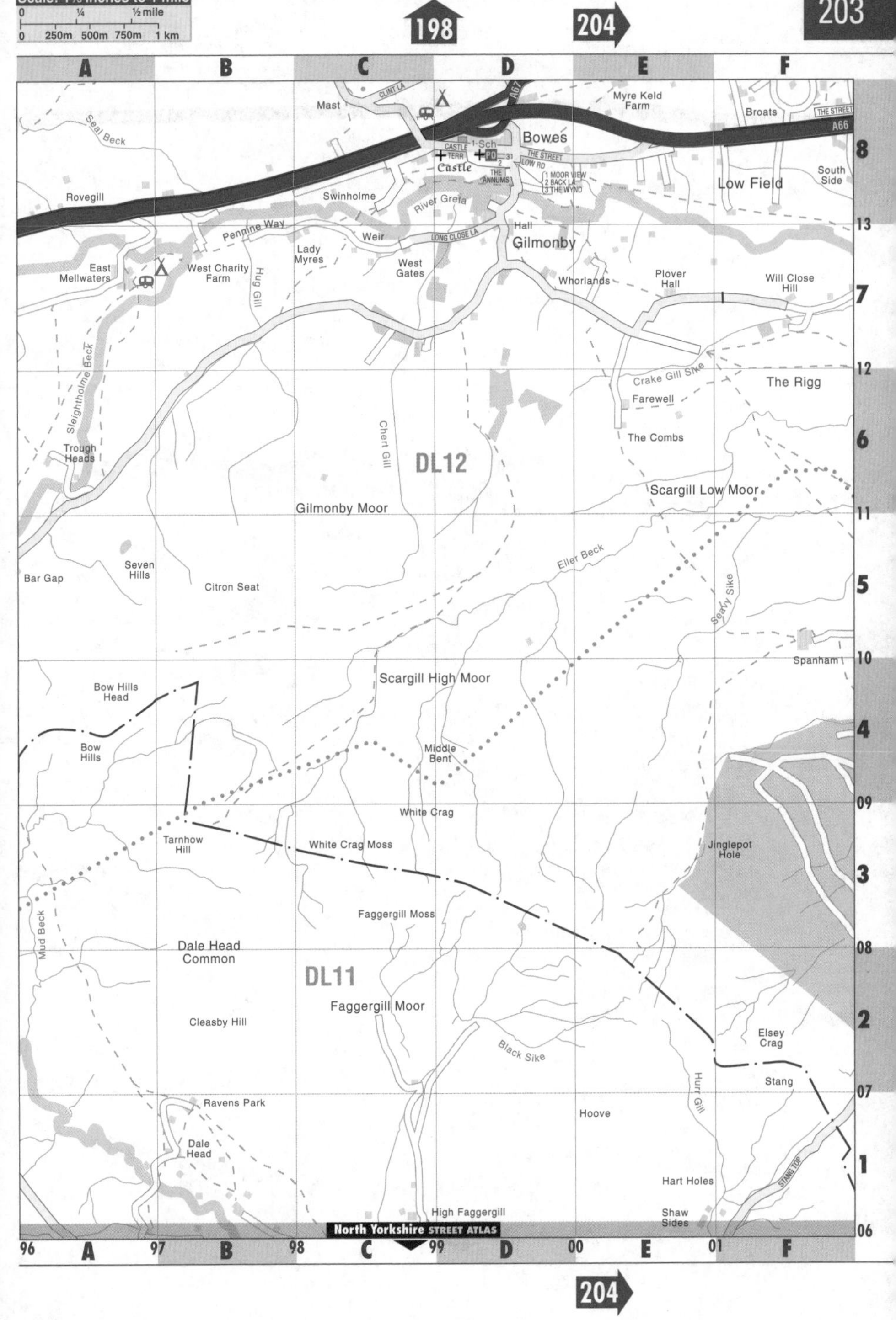

A B C D E F
Mast
CLINT LA
A67
Myre Keld Farm
Broats
THE STREET
A66
Seal Beck
Bowes
Sch
CASTLE TERR
PO
THE STREET
LOW RD
Castle
THE ANNUMS
1 MOOR VIEW
2 BACK LA
3 THE WYND
South Side
Low Field
Rovegill
Swinholme
River Greta
Hall
Pennine Way
Weir
LONG CLOSE LA
Gilmonby
East Mellwaters
West Charity Farm
Hug Gill
Lady Myres
West Gates
Whorlands
Plover Hall
Will Close Hill
Sleightholme Beck
Crake Gill Sike
The Rigg
Farewell
Chert Gill
The Combs
Trough Heads
DL12
Scargill Low Moor
Gilmonby Moor
Eller Beck
Seven Hills
Bar Gap
Citron Seat
Seavy Sike
Spanham
Scargill High Moor
Bow Hills Head
Bow Hills
Middle Bent
White Crag
Tarnhow Hill
White Crag Moss
Jinglepot Hole
Faggergill Moss
Mud Beck
Dale Head Common
DL11
Faggergill Moor
Cleasby Hill
Elsey Crag
Black Sike
Hurr Gill
Stang
Ravens Park
Hoove
Dale Head
STANG TOP
Hart Holes
High Faggergill
Shaw Sides
8 13 7 12 6 11 5 10 4 09 3 08 2 07 1 06
96 97 98 99 00 01

204

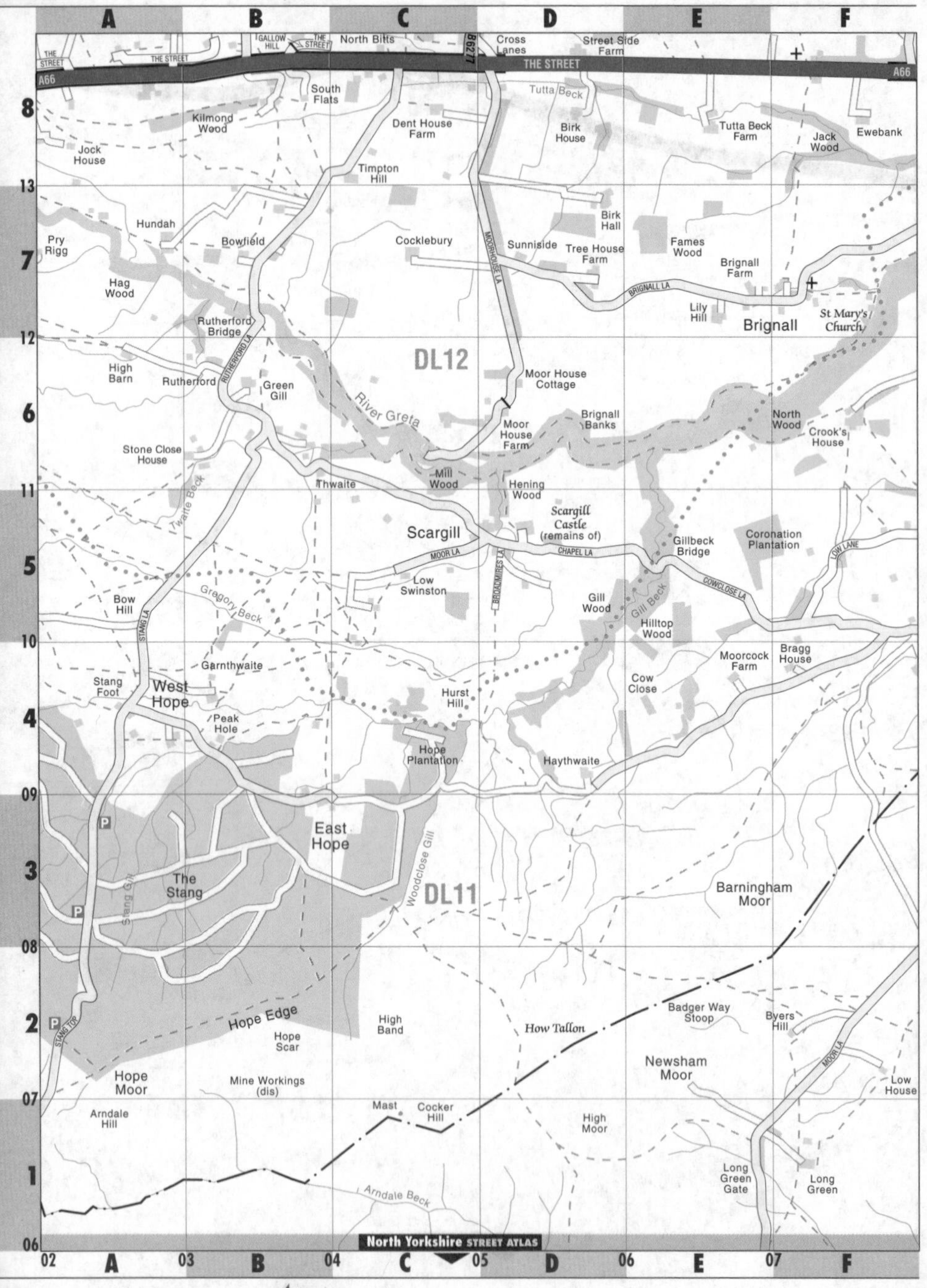

Scale: 1½ inches to 1 mile

0   ¼   ½ mile
0   250m 500m 750m 1 km

A   B   C   D   E   F

THE STREET

GALLOW HILL

THE STREET

North Bitts

Cross Lanes

Street Side Farm

THE STREET

A66

A66

8

South Flats

Kilmond Wood

Dent House Farm

Tutta Beck

Birk House

Tutta Beck Farm

Jack Wood

Ewebank

Jock House

13

Timpton Hill

Birk Hall

Fames Wood

7

Pry Rigg

Hundah

Bowfield

Cocklebury

Sunniside

Tree House Farm

Brignall Farm

Hag Wood

BRIGNALL LA

Lily Hill

Brignall

St Mary's Church

12

Rutherford Bridge

DL12

Moor House Cottage

High Barn

Rutherford

Green Gill

River Greta

Moor House Farm

Brignall Banks

North Wood

Crook's House

6

Stone Close House

Thwaite

Mill Wood

Hening Wood

Scargill Castle (remains of)

Gillbeck Bridge

Coronation Plantation

11

Scargill

MOOR LA.

CHAPEL LA.

Gill Wood

Gill Beck

Hilltop Wood

5

Bow Hill

Gregory Beck

Low Swinston

Gill Wood

Hilltop Wood

Moorcock Farm

Bragg House

10

Stang Foot

West Hope

Garnthwaite

Hurst Hill

Cow Close

4

Peak Hole

Hope Plantation

Haythwaite

09

East Hope

Woodclose Gill

Barningham Moor

3

The Stang

DL11

08

Hope Edge

High Band

How Tallon

Badger Way Stoop

Byers Hill

2

Hope Scar

Newsham Moor

Low House

Hope Moor

Mine Workings (dis)

Mast

Cocker Hill

High Moor

07

Arndale Hill

Long Green Gate

Long Green

1

Arndale Beck

North Yorkshire STREET ATLAS

06

02   A   03   B   04   C   05   D   06   E   07   F

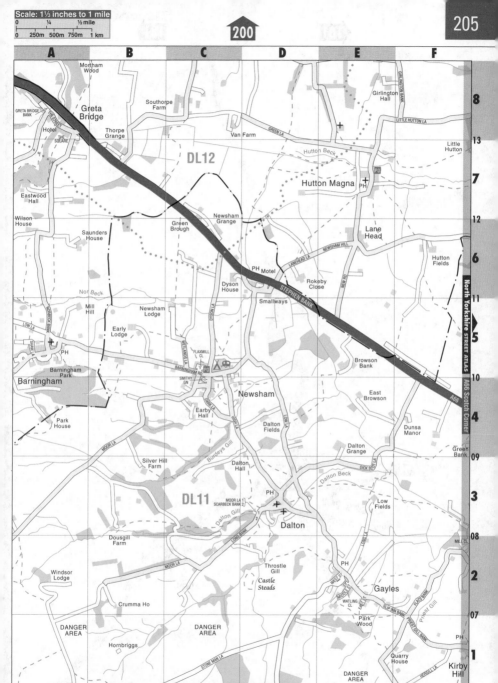
Scale: 1⅓ inches to 1 mile
0 ¼ ½ mile
0 250m 500m 750m 1 km
200
A B C D E F
8 13 7 12 6 11 5 10 4 09 3 08 2 07 1 06
Mortham Wood
Greta Bridge
GRETA BRIDGE BANK
THE STREET
Hotel
THE SQUARE
Southorpe Farm
Thorpe Grange
Van Farm
GREEN LA
GIRLINGTON BANK
Girlington Hall
LITTLE HUTTON LA
Little Hutton
Hutton Beck
DL12
Hutton Magna
PH
Eastwood Hall
Wilson House
Newsham Grange
Green Brough
Lane Head
Saunders House
NEWSHAM HILL
LANEHEAD LA
Hutton Fields
PH Motel
Dyson House
Rokeby Close
NEW RD
Nor Beck
STEPHEN BANK
Smallways
North Yorkshire STREET ATLAS
Mill Hill
Newsham Lodge
NORBECK BANK
LOW LA
DYSON LA
Early Lodge
SHAW LA
PH
WETLANDS LA
FLAXMILL CL
Browson Bank
BARNINGHAM RD
Barningham Park
SMITHY GN
Barningham
A66 Scotch Corner
Newsham
East Browson
DARK LA
A66
Earby Hall
Park House
HIGH LA
Dalton Fields
LOW LA
Dunsa Manor
MOOR LA
Burdeys Gill
Dalton Grange
Green Bank
Silver Hill Farm
Dalton Hall
DICK SCOT LA
Dalton Beck
PH
DL11
MOOR LA 1
SCARBECK BANK 2
Low Fields
Dalton Gill
Dalton
LONG BANK
Dousgill Farm
LONG LA
MILL CL
MOOR LA
Throstle Gill
PH
Windsor Lodge
Castle Steads
WEST ST
MIDDLE ST
Gayles
WATLING CL
EAST ST
FLATS BANK
Crumma Ho
SLIP INN BANK
Priest Gill
Park Wood
PRIEST GILL BANK
DANGER AREA
DANGER AREA
PH
Hornbriggs
Quarry House
STONE MAN LA
Kirby Hill
HERGILL LA
DANGER AREA
North Yorkshire STREET ATLAS
08 A 09 B 10 C 11 D 12 E 13 F

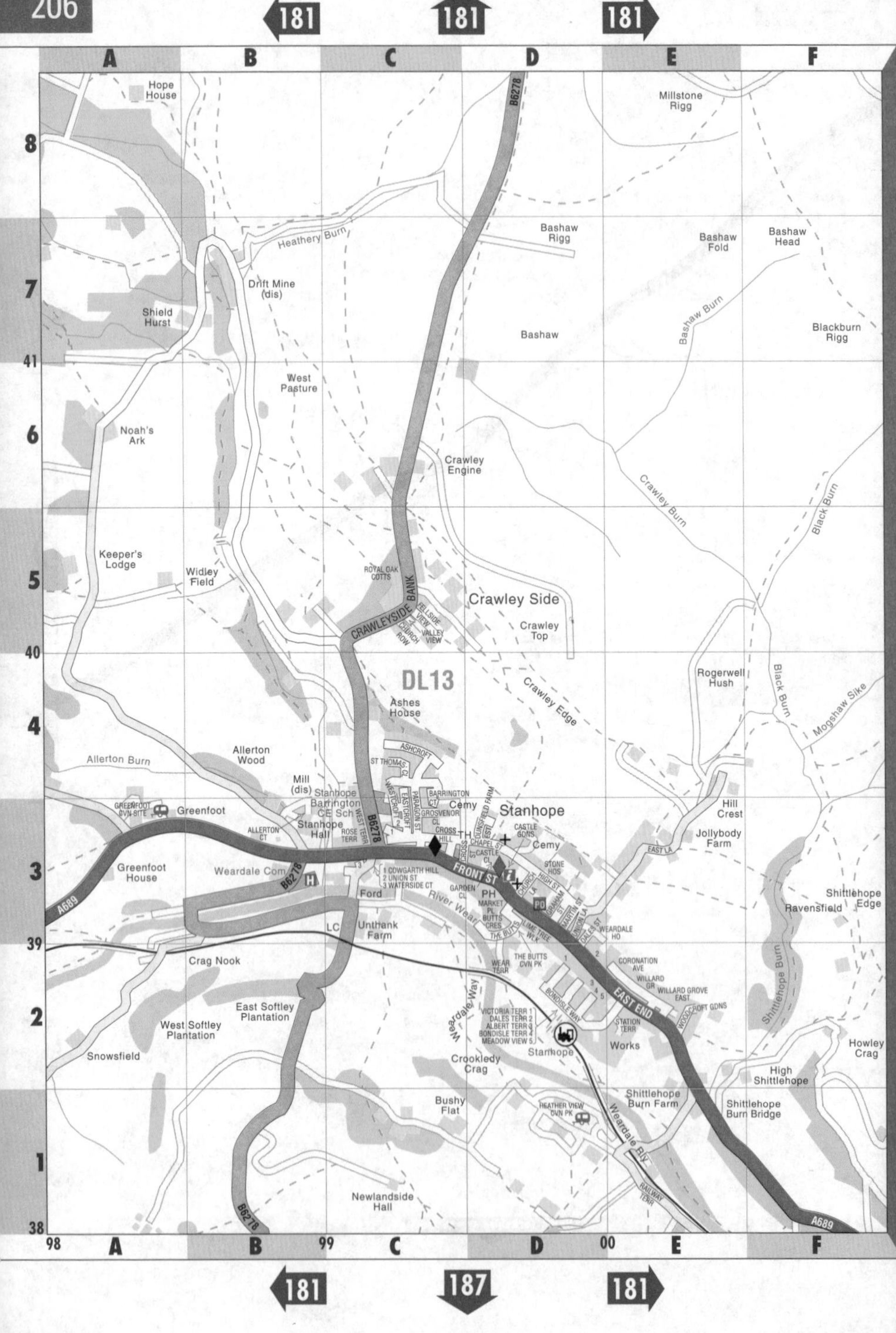
181
181
181
A
B
C
D
E
F
8
7
41
6
5
40
4
3
39
2
1
38
98
99
00
Hope House
Millstone Rigg
B6278
Heathery Burn
Bashaw Rigg
Bashaw Fold
Bashaw Head
Drift Mine (dis)
Shield Hurst
Bashaw
Bashaw Burn
Blackburn Rigg
West Pasture
Noah's Ark
Crawley Engine
Crawley Burn
Black Burn
Keeper's Lodge
Widley Field
ROYAL OAK COTTS
CRAWLEYSIDE BANK
Crawley Side
Crawley Top
DL13
Crawley Edge
Rogerwell Hush
Black Burn
Mogshaw Sike
Ashes House
Allerton Wood
Allerton Burn
Mill (dis)
Stanhope Barrington CE Sch
Stanhope Hall
Greenfoot
GREENFOOT CVN SITE
Stanhope
Cemy
Hill Crest
Jollybody Farm
Greenfoot House
Weardale Com
A689
Ford
River Wear
FRONT ST
EAST END
Unthank Farm
LC
Crag Nook
Shittlehope Edge
Ravensfield
Shittlehope Burn
East Softley Plantation
West Softley Plantation
Weardale Way
Snowsfield
Crookledy Crag
Stanhope
Works
Howley Crag
High Shittlehope
Bushy Flat
Shittlehope Burn Farm
Shittlehope Burn Bridge
HEATHER VIEW CVN PK
Weardale Rly
Newlandside Hall
RAILWAY TERR
A689
B6278
1 COWGARTH HILL
2 UNION ST
3 WATERSIDE CT
VICTORIA TERR 1
DALES TERR 2
ALBERT TERR 3
BONDISLE TERR 4
MEADOW VIEW 5
181
187
181

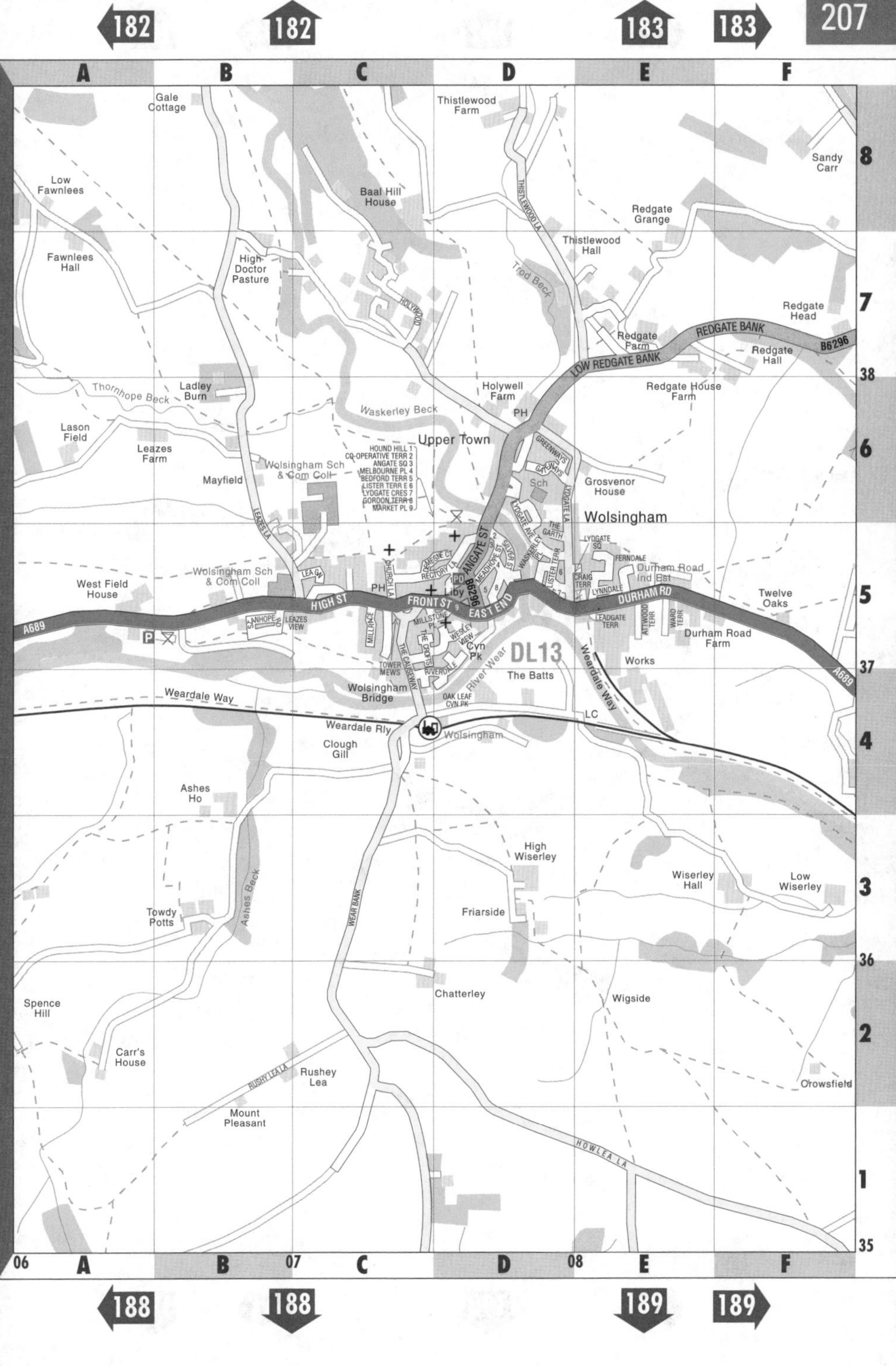
182
182
183
183
A
B
C
D
E
F
Gale Cottage
Thistlewood Farm
Sandy Carr
Low Fawnlees
Baal Hill House
Redgate Grange
Fawnlees Hall
High Doctor Pasture
Thistlewood Hall
THISTLEWOOD LA
Trod Beck
HOLYWOOD
Redgate Head
Redgate Farm
REDGATE BANK
Redgate Hall
B6296
LOW REDGATE BANK
Ladley Burn
Thornhope Beck
Holywell Farm
Redgate House Farm
Waskerley Beck
PH
Lason Field
Leazes Farm
Upper Town
HOUND HILL 1
CO-OPERATIVE TERR 2
ANGATE SQ 3
MELBOURNE PL 4
BEDFORD TERR 5
LISTER TERR E 6
LYDGATE CRES 7
GORDON TERR 8
MARKET PL 9
Wolsingham Sch & Com Coll
Mayfield
GREENWAYS
GALLOWAYS
Sch
Grosvenor House
LYDGATE LA
Wolsingham
LEAZES LA
LYDGATE AVE
THE GARTH
ANGATE ST
LYDGATE SQ
DEMESNE CT
RECTORY LA
MEADHOPE ST
SILVER ST
WASKERLEY
FERNDALE
Durham Road Ind Est
West Field House
Wolsingham Sch & Com Coll
LEA GN
CHURCH LA
PO
Liby
LISTER TERR
CRAIG TERR
LYNNDALE
Twelve Oaks
PH
B6296
DURHAM RD
HIGH ST
FRONT ST
EAST END
A689
NNHOPE
LEAZES VIEW
MILLRACE
MILLSTONE PL
WESLEY VIEW
LEADGATE TERR
ATTWOOD TERR
WARD TERR
Durham Road Farm
P
THE CAUSEWAY
THE CROFTS
Cyn Pk
DL13
Weardale Way
Works
TOWER MEWS
RIVERDALE
River Wear
The Batts
37
A689
Weardale Way
Wolsingham Bridge
OAK LEAF CVN PK
LC
Weardale Rly
Wolsingham
Clough Gill
Ashes Ho
High Wiserley
Ashes Beck
Wiserley Hall
Low Wiserley
Towdy Potts
WEAR BANK
Friarside
Chatterley
Wigside
Spence Hill
Carr's House
RUSHY LEA LA
Rushey Lea
Crowsfield
Mount Pleasant
HOWLEA LA
8
7
38
6
5
4
3
36
2
1
35
06
07
08
188
188
189
189

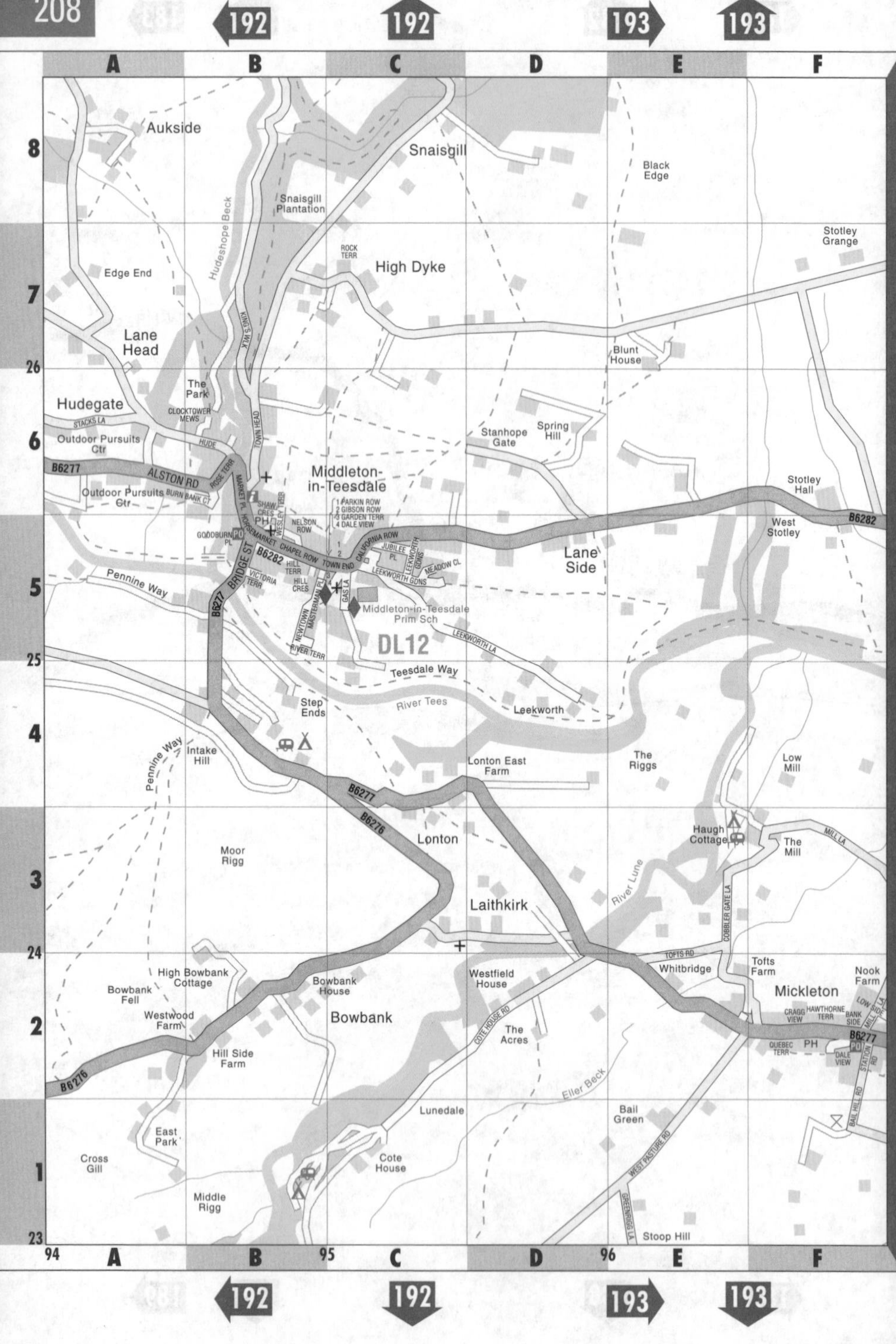

Aukside

Snaisgill

Black
Edge

Stotley
Grange

Snaisgill
Plantation

Edge End

ROCK
TERR

High Dyke

Lane
Head

Blunt
House

Hudegate

The
Park

STACKS LA

CLOCKTOWER
MEWS

Outdoor Pursuits
Ctr

Stanhope
Gate

Spring
Hill

Stotley
Hall

B6277 ALSTON RD

HUDE

Middleton-
in-Teesdale

West
Stotley

B6282

Outdoor Pursuits
Ctr

BURN BANK CT

PH

1 PARKIN ROW
2 GIBSON ROW
3 GARDEN TERR
4 DALE VIEW

CHAPEL ROW

GARDEN
PL

NELSON
ROW

CALIFORNIA ROW

JUBILEE

MEADOW CL

Lane
Side

GODOBURN
PL

B6282

VICTORIA
TERR

HILL
TERR

TOWN END

LEEKWORTH GDNS

Pennine Way

MARKET PL

BRIDGE ST

B6277

NEWTOWN
TERR

MILL
CRES

RIVER TERR

Middleton-in-Teesdale
Prim Sch

LEEKWORTH LA

DL12

Teesdale Way

Step
Ends

River Tees

Leekworth

Pennine Way

Intake
Hill

Lonton East
Farm

The
Riggs

Low
Mill

Moor
Rigg

B6277

B6276

Lonton

Haugh
Cottage

The
Mill

MILL LA

River Lune

Laithkirk

COBBLER GATE LA

High Bowbank
Cottage

Bowbank
House

Westfield
House

Whitbridge

TOFTS RD

Tofts
Farm

Mickleton

Nook
Farm

Bowbank
Fell

Westwood
Farm

Bowbank

The
Acres

COTE HOUSE RD

CRAGG
VIEW

HAWTHORNE
TERR

BANK
SIDE

LOW

QUEBEC
TERR

PH

B6277

DALE
VIEW

B6276

Hill Side
Farm

Cross
Gill

East
Park

Middle
Rigg

Cote
House

Lunedale

Eller Beck

Bail
Green

WEST PASTURE RD

Stoop Hill

VY EBERGREEN

STATION RD

BAIL SIDE RD

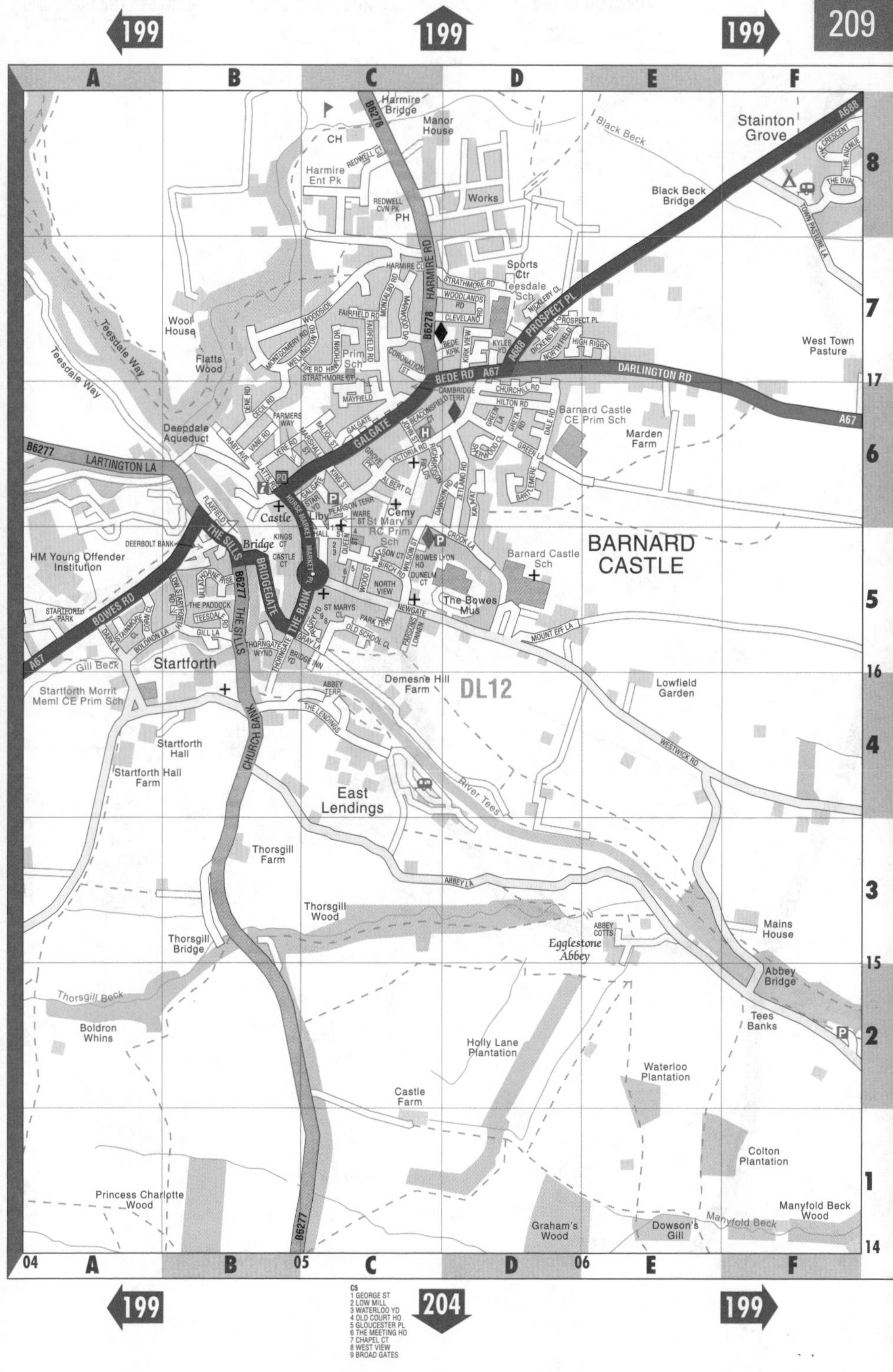

C5
1 GEORGE ST
2 LOW MILL
3 WATERLOO YD
4 OLD COURT HO
5 GLOUCESTER PL
6 THE MEETING HO
7 CHAPEL CT
8 WEST VIEW
9 BROAD GATES

33 34

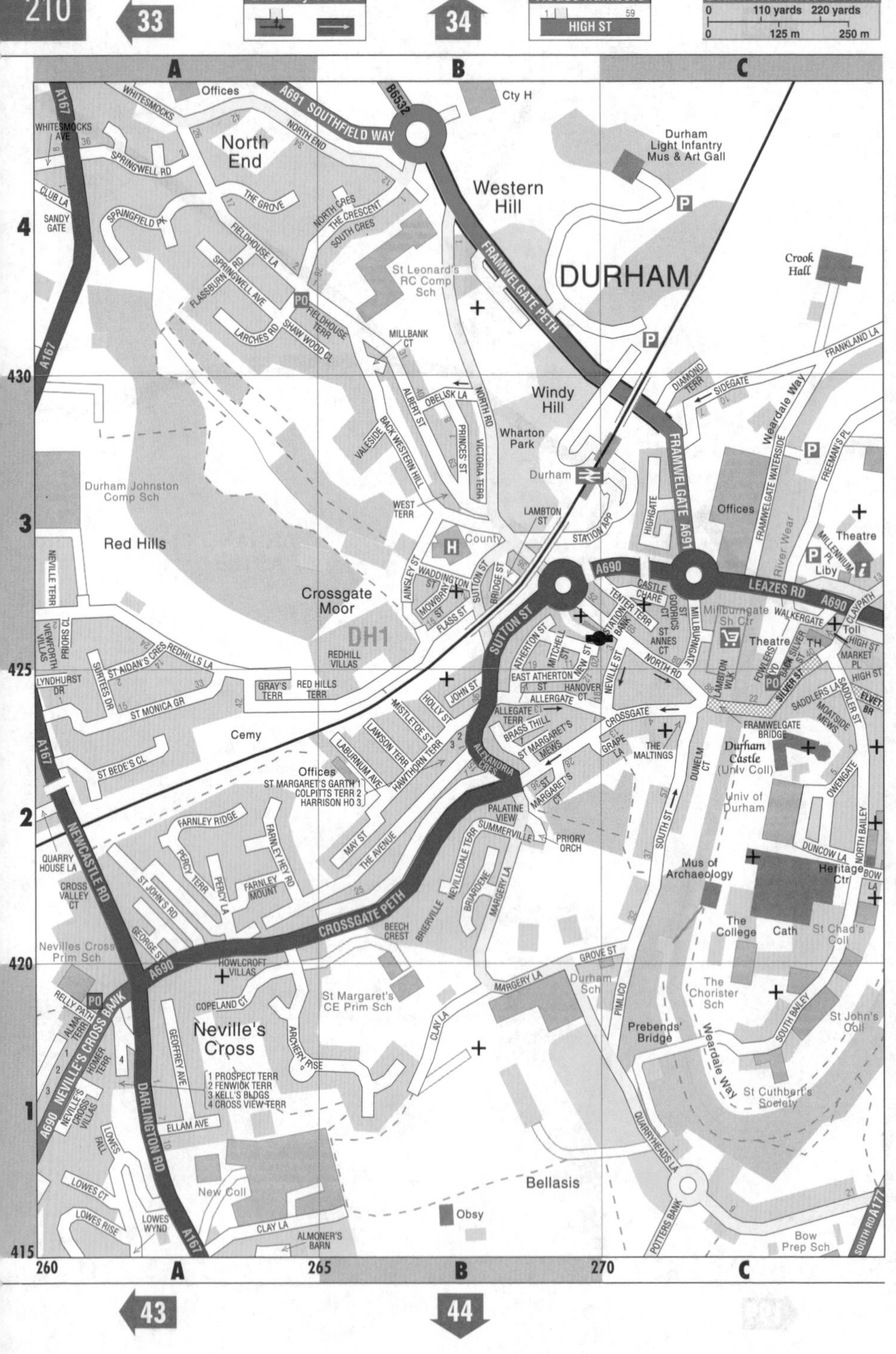
One-way streets
House numbers
1
59
HIGH ST
Scale: 5⅓ inches to 1 mile
0
110 yards
220 yards
125 m
250 m
A
B
C
4
3
2
1
430
425
420
415
260
265
270
DURHAM
North End
Western Hill
Windy Hill
Wharton Park
Red Hills
Crossgate Moor
DH1
Cemy
Neville's Cross
Bellasis
Offices
Cty H
Durham Light Infantry Mus & Art Gall
Crook Hall
St Leonard's RC Comp Sch
Durham Johnston Comp Sch
County
Durham
Theatre
Liby
Millburngate Sh Ctr
Toll
TH
Durham Castle (Univ Coll)
Univ of Durham
Mus of Archaeology
Heritage Ctr
The College
Cath
St Chad's Coll
The Chorister Sch
St John's Coll
Prebends' Bridge
St Cuthbert's Society
Durham Sch
St Margaret's CE Prim Sch
Nevilles Cross Prim Sch
New Coll
Obsy
Bow Prep Sch
The Maltings
Priory Orch
Redhill Villas
A691 SOUTHFIELD WAY
B6532
A167
A690
A691
A177
FRAMWELGATE PETH
FRAMWELGATE
LEAZES RD
SUTTON ST
CROSSGATE PETH
NEWCASTLE RD
NEVILLE'S CROSS BANK
DARLINGTON RD
SOUTH RD
WHITESMOCKS
WHITESMOCKS AVE
NORTH END
SPRINGWELL RD
CLUB LA
SANDY GATE
SPRINGFIELD PK
THE GROVE
FIELDHOUSE LA
SPRINGWELL AVE
FLASSBURN RD
LARCHES RD
SHAW WOOD CL
FIELDHOUSE TERR
NORTH CRES
THE CRESCENT
SOUTH CRES
MILLBANK CT
OBELISK LA
ALBERT ST
NORTH RD
PRINCES ST
VICTORIA TERR
VALESIDE
BACK WESTERN HILL
WEST TERR
LAMBTON ST
STATION APP
HIGHGATE
DIAMOND TERR
SIDEGATE
FRANKLAND LA
Weardale Way
FRAMWELGATE WATERSIDE
River Wear
FREEMAN'S PL
MILLENNIUM PL
CLAYPATH
WALKERGATE
CASTLE CHARE
TENTER TERR
ST GODRICS CT
MILLBURNGATE
ST ANNES CT
STATION BANK
NORTH RD
NEVILLE ST
NEW ST
MITCHELL ST
ATHERTON ST
EAST ATHERTON ST
HANOVER CT
ALLERGATE
ALLEGATE TERR
BRASS THILL
ST MARGARET'S MEWS
CROSSGATE
GRAPE LA
ST MARGARET'S CT
ALEXANDRIA CRES
AINSLEY ST
WADDINGTON ST
MOWBRAY ST
FLASS ST
SUTTON ST
BRIDGE ST
JOHN ST
HOLLY ST
MISTLETOE ST
LAWSON TERR
LABURNUM AVE
HAWTHORN TERR
ST MARGARET'S GARTH 1
COLPITTS TERR 2
HARRISON HO 3
MAY ST
THE AVENUE
PALATINE VIEW
SUMMERVILLE
NEVILLEDALE TERR
BRIARDENE
MARGERY LA
BRIERVILLE
BEECH CREST
LAMBTON WLK
FOWLERS YD
BACK SILVER ST
SILVER ST
HIGH ST
MARKET PL
SADDLERS LA
SADDLER ST
ELVET BR
MOATSIDE MEWS
FRAMWELGATE BRIDGE
OWENGATE
NORTH BAILEY
DUNCOW LA
BOW LA
DUNELM CT
SOUTH ST
GROVE ST
PIMLICO
SOUTH BAILEY
QUARRYHEADS LA
POTTERS BANK
NEVILLE TERR
VIEWFORTH VILLAS
PRIORS CL
LYNDHURST DR
SURTEES DR
ST AIDAN'S CRES
REDHILLS LA
ST MONICA GR
GRAY'S TERR
RED HILLS TERR
ST BEDE'S CL
QUARRY HOUSE LA
CROSS VALLEY CT
FARNLEY RIDGE
PERCY TERR
PERCY LA
FARNLEY HEY RD
FARNLEY MOUNT
ST JOHN'S RD
GEORGE ST
HOWLCROFT VILLAS
COPELAND CT
GEOFFREY AVE
ARCHERY RISE
CLAY LA
1 PROSPECT TERR
2 FENWICK TERR
3 KELL'S BLDGS
4 CROSS VIEW TERR
ELLAM AVE
RELLY PATH
ALMA TERR
HOMER TERR
NEVILLE'S CROSS VILLAS
LOWES FALL
LOWES CT
LOWES RISE
LOWES WYND
ALMONER'S BARN
PO
P
H

43 44

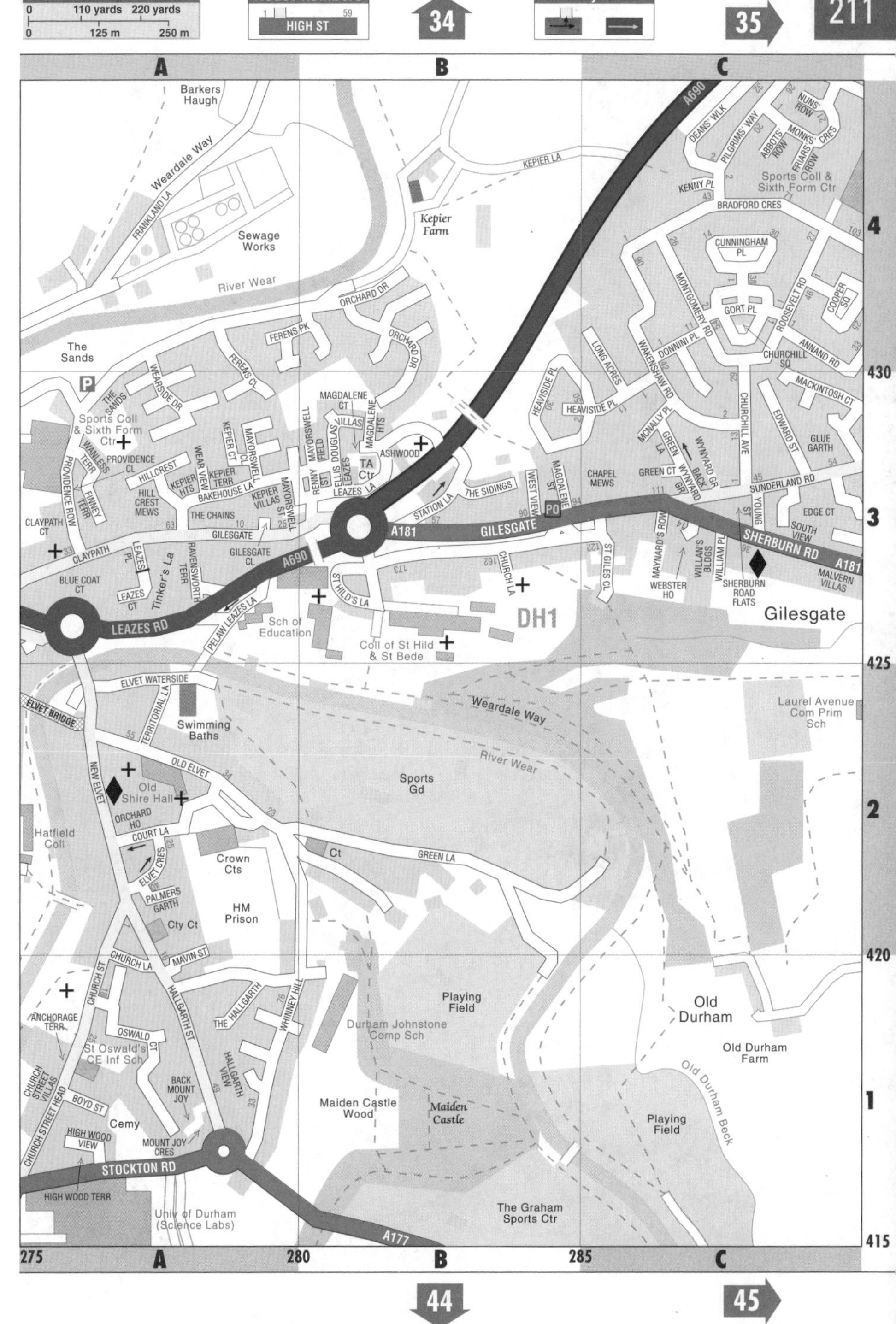

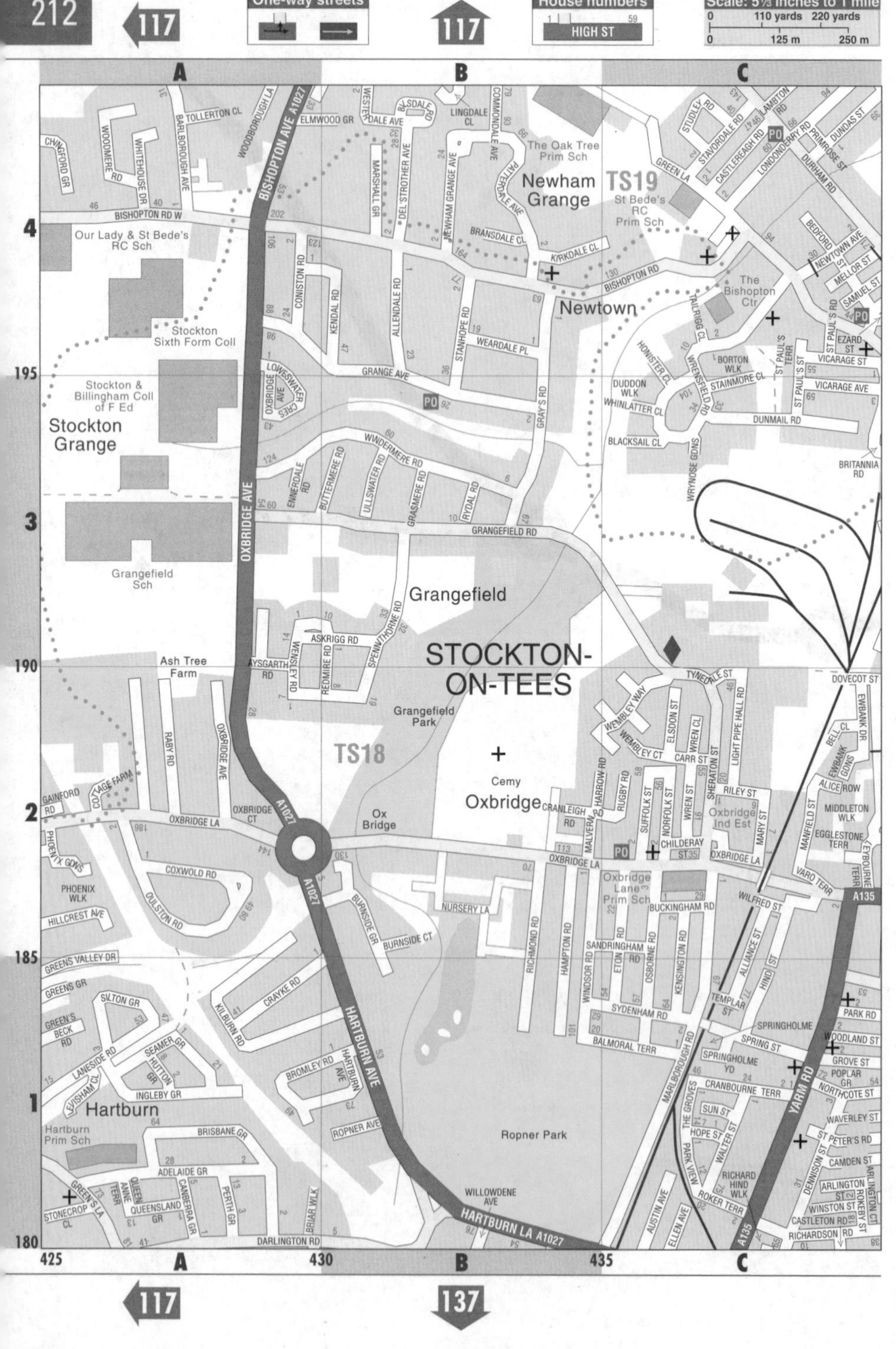

212
117
One-way streets
117
House numbers
HIGH ST
Scale: 5⅓ inches to 1 mile
110 yards
220 yards
125 m
250 m
A
B
C
BISHOPTON AVE A1027
WOODBOROUGH LA
TOLLERTON CL
CHINGFORD GR
WOODMERE RD
WHITEHOUSE DR
BARLBOROUGH AVE
ELMWOOD GR
WESTERDALE AVE
BILSDALE RD
LINGDALE CL
COMMONDALE AVE
MARSHALL GR
DEL STROTHER AVE
NEWHAM GRANGE AVE
PATTERDALE AVE
The Oak Tree Prim Sch
Newham Grange
TS19
St Bede's RC Prim Sch
GREEN LA
STUDLEY RD
STAVORDALE RD
CASTLEREAGH RD
LAMBTON RD
LONDONDERRY RD
PRIMROSE ST
DUNDAS ST
DURHAM RD
BEDFORD ST
NEWTOWN AVE
MELLOR ST
SAMUEL ST
BISHOPTON RD W
Our Lady & St Bede's RC Sch
BRANSDALE CL
KIRKDALE CL
BISHOPTON RD
CONISTON RD
KENDAL RD
ALLENDALE RD
STANHOPE RD
WEARDALE PL
The Bishopton Ctr
Newtown
TAILRIGG CL
ST PAUL'S TERR
ST PAUL'S RD
EZARD ST
VICARAGE ST
Stockton Sixth Form Coll
HONISTER CL
WRENSFIELD RD
BORTON WLK
STAINMORE CL
ST PAUL'S ST
VICARAGE AVE
DUDDON WLK
WHINLATTER CL
DUNMAIL RD
GRANGE AVE
OXBRIDGE AVE
LOWESWATER CRES
GRAY'S RD
PO
Stockton & Billingham Coll of F Ed
Stockton Grange
BLACKSAIL CL
WRYNOSE GDNS
BRITANNIA RD
WINDERMERE RD
ENNERDALE RD
BUTTERMERE RD
ULLSWATER RD
GRASMERE RD
RYDAL RD
OXBRIDGE AVE
GRANGEFIELD RD
Grangefield Sch
Grangefield
SPENNITHORNE RD
ASKRIGG RD
WENSLEY RD
REDMIRE RD
AYSGARTH RD
Ash Tree Farm
STOCKTON-ON-TEES
Grangefield Park
TYNEDALE ST
WEMBLEY WAY
WEMBLEY CT
ELSDON ST
WREN CL
CARR ST
SHERATON ST
LIGHT PIPE HALL RD
DOVECOT ST
EWBANK DR
BELL CL
EWBANK GDNS
ALICE ROW
RABY RD
OXBRIDGE AVE
TS18
Cemy
Oxbridge
HARROW RD
RUGBY RD
SUFFOLK ST
NORFOLK ST
WREN ST
RILEY ST
MIDDLETON WLK
GAINFORD RD
COTTAGE FARM
OXBRIDGE LA
OXBRIDGE CT
A1027
Ox Bridge
CRANLEIGH RD
MALVERN RD
Oxbridge Ind Est
MARY ST
MANFIELD ST
EGGLESTONE TERR
PHOENIX GDNS
COXWOLD RD
CHILDERAY ST
OXBRIDGE LA
LEYBOURNE TERR
VARO TERR
PHOENIX WLK
OULSTON RD
BURNSIDE GR
NURSERY LA
Oxbridge Lane Prim Sch
BUCKINGHAM RD
WILFRED ST
A135
HILLCREST AVE
BURNSIDE CT
RICHMOND RD
HAMPTON RD
WINDSOR RD
SANDRINGHAM RD
ETON RD
OSBORNE RD
KENSINGTON RD
ALLIANCE ST
HIND ST
GREENS VALLEY DR
GREENS GR
CRAYKE RD
SILTON GR
GREEN'S BECK RD
KILBURN RD
SYDENHAM RD
TEMPLAR ST
PARK RD
SPRINGHOLME
HARTBURN AVE
SEAMER GR
LANESIDE RD
HUTTON GR
BROMLEY RD
HARTBURN AVE
BALMORAL TERR
MARLBOROUGH RD
SPRING ST
WOODLAND ST
SPRINGHOLME YD
GROVE ST
LEVISHAM CL
INGLEBY GR
CRANBOURNE TERR
POPLAR GR
NORTHCOTE ST
Hartburn
SUN ST
YARM RD
Hartburn Prim Sch
BRISBANE GR
ROPNER AVE
THE GROVES
HOPE ST
WALTER ST
Ropner Park
WAVERLEY ST
ST PETER'S RD
ADELAIDE GR
PARK VIEW
CAMDEN ST
GREEN'S LA
QUEEN ANNE TERR
CANBERRA GR
PERTH GR
WILLOWDENE AVE
RICHARD HIND WLK
DENNISON ST
ARLINGTON ST
ARLINGTON CT
STONECROP CL
QUEENSLAND GR
BRIAR WLK
AUSTIN AVE
ROKER TERR
WINSTON ST
CASTLETON RD
ROKEBY ST
HARTBURN LA A1027
ELLEN AVE
RICHARDSON RD
DARLINGTON RD
4
195
3
190
2
185
1
180
425
430
435
117
137

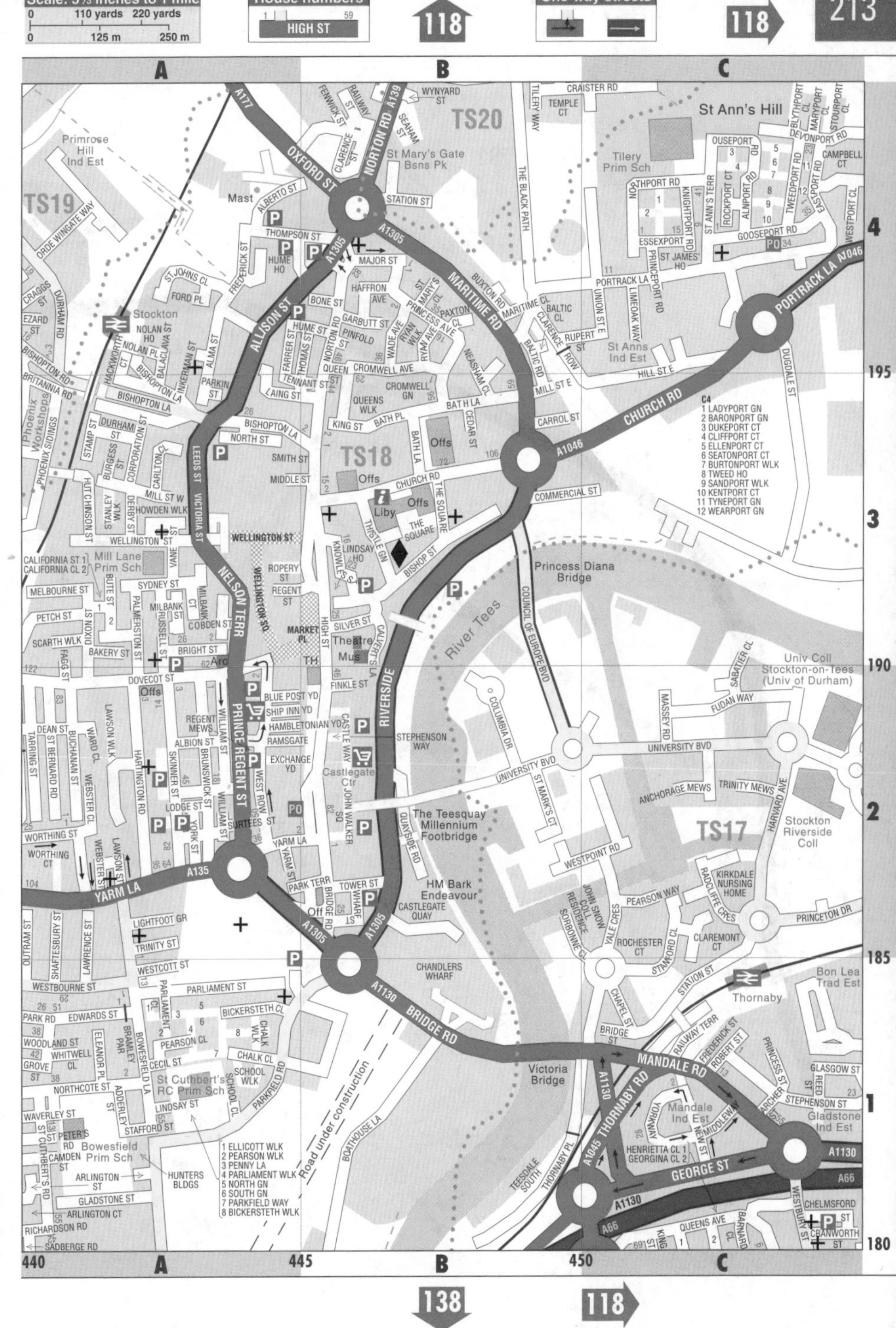

Scale: 5⅓ inches to 1 mile
0 110 yards 220 yards
0 125 m 250 m
House numbers
HIGH ST
One-way streets
118
A
B
C
TS19
TS20
TS18
TS17
Primrose Hill Ind Est
ORDE WINGATE WAY
OXFORD ST
NORTON RD
A139
A177
FENWICK ST
RAILWAY ST
WYNYARD ST
SEAHAM ST
CLARENCE ST
St Mary's Gate Bsns Pk
STATION ST
Mast
ALBERTO ST
THOMPSON ST
HUME HO
MAJOR ST
HAFFRON AVE
A1305
MARITIME RD
BUXTON RD
MARITIME CL
BALTIC CL
CLARENCE ROW
RUPERT ST
BALTIC RD
St Anns Ind Est
HILL ST E
MILL ST E
CARROL ST
CHURCH RD
A1046
PORTRACK LA
DUGDALE ST
CRAISTER RD
TEMPLE CT
TILERY WAY
THE BLACK PATH
Tilery Prim Sch
St Ann's Hill
OUSEPORT RD
NORTHPORT RD
KNIGHTPORT RD
ST ANN'S TERR
ROCKPORT CT
ALNPORT RD
TWEEDPORT RD
EASTPORT RD
WESTPORT CL
BLYTHPORT CL
MARYPORT CL
STOURPORT CL
DEVONPORT RD
CAMPBELL CT
GOOSEPORT RD
ESSEXPORT
ST JAMES' HO
PRINCEPORT RD
UNION ST E
LIMEOAK WAY
Stockton
CRAGGS ST
DURHAM RD
ST JOHNS CL
FORD PL
FREDERICK ST
NOLAN HO
NOLAN PL
HACKWORTH CT
BALACLAVA ST
INKERMAN ST
ALMA ST
BISHOPTON LA
BISHOPTON RD
BRITANNIA RD
PARKIN ST
ALLISON ST
BONE ST
GARBUTT ST
HUME ST
PINFOLD ST
FARRER ST
THOMAS ST
NORTON RD
WADE AVE
RYAN WLK
RYAN AVE
PRINCESS AVE
ST MARY'S CL
PAXTON CL
NEASHAM CL
QUEEN ST
CROMWELL AVE
TENNANT ST
LAING ST
CROMWELL GN
QUEENS WLK
BATH LA
BATH PL
KING ST
CEDAR ST
Offs
Phoenix Workshops
PHOENIX SIDINGS
STAMP ST
DURHAM ST
BURGESS ST
CORPORATION ST
CARLTON CL
NORTH ST
SMITH ST
MIDDLE ST
LEEDS ST
VICTORIA ST
MILL ST W
HOWDEN WLK
HUTCHINSON ST
STANLEY WLK
DERBY ST
WELLINGTON ST
VANE ST
CALIFORNIA ST
CALIFORNIA CL
Mill Lane Prim Sch
MELBOURNE ST
BUTE ST
SYDNEY ST
NELSON TERR
WELLINGTON SQ
ROPERY ST
REGENT ST
CHURCH RD
THE SQUARE
Liby
THISTLE GN
LINDSAY HO
KNOWLES ST
BISHOP ST
COMMERCIAL ST
Princess Diana Bridge
COUNCIL OF EUROPE BVD
River Tees
PETCH ST
DIXON ST
PALMERSTON ST
RUSSELL ST
MILBANK CT
MILBANK ST
COBDEN ST
SCARTH WLK
BAKERY ST
BRIGHT ST
MARKET PL
HIGH ST
SILVER ST
CALVERT'S LA
Theatre
Mus
TH
Arc
FAGG ST
DOVECOT ST
FINKLE ST
BLUE POST YD
SHIP INN YD
HAMBLETONIAN YD
RAMSGATE
EXCHANGE YD
CASTLE WAY
RIVERSIDE
STEPHENSON WAY
Castlegate Ctr
JOHN WALKER SQ
WEST ROW
LAWSON WLK
DEAN ST
TARRING ST
ST BERNARD RD
BUCHANAN ST
WARD CL
WEBSTER CL
REGENT MEWS
ALBION ST
HARTINGTON RD
SKINNER ST
BRUNSWICK ST
WILLIAM ST
PRINCE REGENT ST
LODGE ST
YORK ST
SURTEES ST
YARM LA
YARM ST
WORTHING ST
WORTHING CT
WEBSTER ST
LAWSON ST
A135
QUAYSIDE RD
The Teesquay Millennium Footbridge
HM Bark Endeavour
CASTLEGATE QUAY
PARK TERR
BRIDGE RD
TOWER ST
WHARF ST
Off
OUTRAM ST
SHAFTESBURY ST
LAWRENCE ST
LIGHTFOOT GR
TRINITY ST
WESTCOTT ST
WESTBOURNE ST
PARLIAMENT ST
PARLIAMENT CL
BICKERSTETH CL
PARK RD
EDWARDS ST
WOODLAND ST
WHITWELL CL
ELEANOR PL
BRAMLEY PAR
BOWESFIELD LA
PEARSON CL
CHALK WLK
CHALK CL
CECIL ST
SCHOOL WLK
GROVE ST
NORTHCOTE ST
ADDERLEY ST
St Cuthbert's RC Prim Sch
LINDSAY ST
SCHOOL CL
PARKFIELD RD
WAVERLEY ST
ST PETER'S RD
ST CUTHBERT'S RD
CAMDEN ST
Bowesfield Prim Sch
STAFFORD ST
ARLINGTON ST
HUNTERS BLDGS
GLADSTONE ST
ARLINGTON CT
RICHARDSON RD
SADBERGE RD
1 ELLICOTT WLK
2 PEARSON WLK
3 PENNY LA
4 PARLIAMENT WLK
5 NORTH GN
6 SOUTH GN
7 PARKFIELD WAY
8 BICKERSTETH WLK
Road under construction
BOATHOUSE LA
CHANDLERS WHARF
A1130
BRIDGE RD
Victoria Bridge
TEESDALE SOUTH
THORNABY PL
COLUMBIA DR
UNIVERSITY BVD
ST MARK'S CT
WESTPOINT RD
JOHN SNOW COLL
RESIDENCE
SORBONNE CL
YALE CRES
PEARSON WAY
ROCHESTER CT
STAMFORD CL
CLAREMONT CT
STATION ST
CHAPEL ST
BRIDGE ST
Thornaby
RAILWAY TERR
FREDERICK ST
ROBERT ST
PRINCESS ST
MANDALE RD
A1045 THORNABY RD
YORKWAY
Mandale Ind Est
MIDDLEWAY
NEW ST
HENRIETTA CL 1
GEORGINA CL 2
GEORGE ST
A66
QUEENS AVE
BARNARD CL
KING ST
ARCHER ST
STEPHENSON ST
GLASGOW ST
REED ST
Gladstone Ind Est
WESTBURY ST
CHELMSFORD ST
CRANWORTH ST
Bon Lea Trad Est
Univ Coll Stockton-on-Tees (Univ of Durham)
SABATIER CL
FUDAN WAY
MASSEY RD
ANCHORAGE MEWS
TRINITY MEWS
HARVARD AVE
Stockton Riverside Coll
KIRKDALE NURSING HOME
RADCLIFFE CRES
PRINCETON DR
C4
1 LADYPORT GN
2 BARONPORT GN
3 DUKEPORT CT
4 CLIFFPORT CT
5 ELLENPORT CT
6 SEATONPORT CT
7 BURTONPORT WLK
8 TWEED HO
9 SANDPORT WLK
10 KENTPORT CT
11 TYNEPORT GN
12 WEARPORT GN
4
3
2
1
195
190
185
180
440
445
450
138

119 119

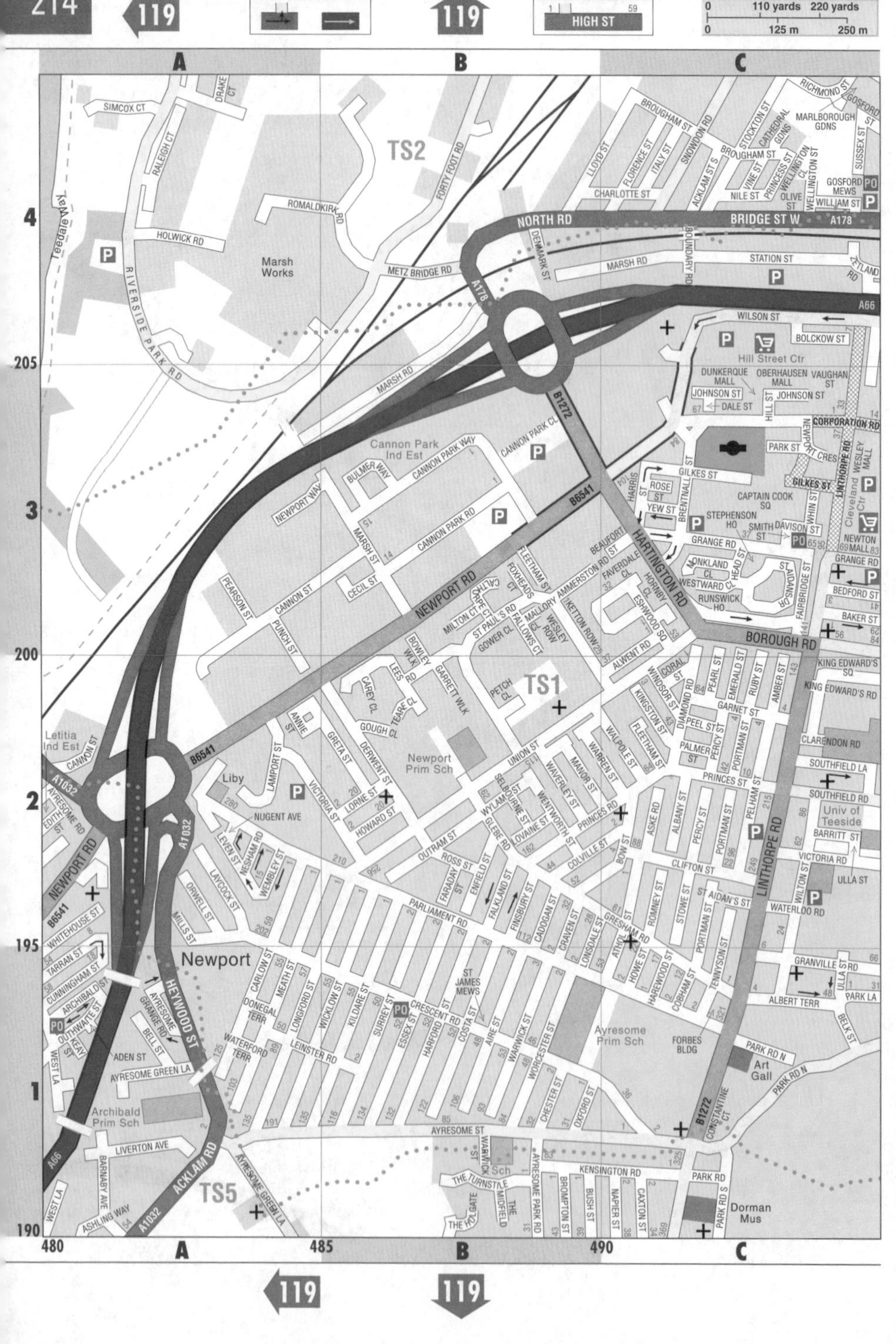
One-way streets
House numbers
1 59
HIGH ST
Scale: 5⅓ inches to 1 mile
0 110 yards 220 yards
0 125 m 250 m
TS2
TS1
TS5
Marsh Works
Cannon Park Ind Est
Newport
Newport Prim Sch
Ayresome Prim Sch
Archibald Prim Sch
Hill Street Ctr
Univ of Teesside
Art Gall
Dorman Mus
NORTH RD
BRIDGE ST W
NEWPORT RD
LINTHORPE RD
BOROUGH RD
HARTINGTON RD
ACKLAM RD
HEYWOOD ST
PARLIAMENT RD
AYRESOME ST
RIVERSIDE PARK RD

119 119

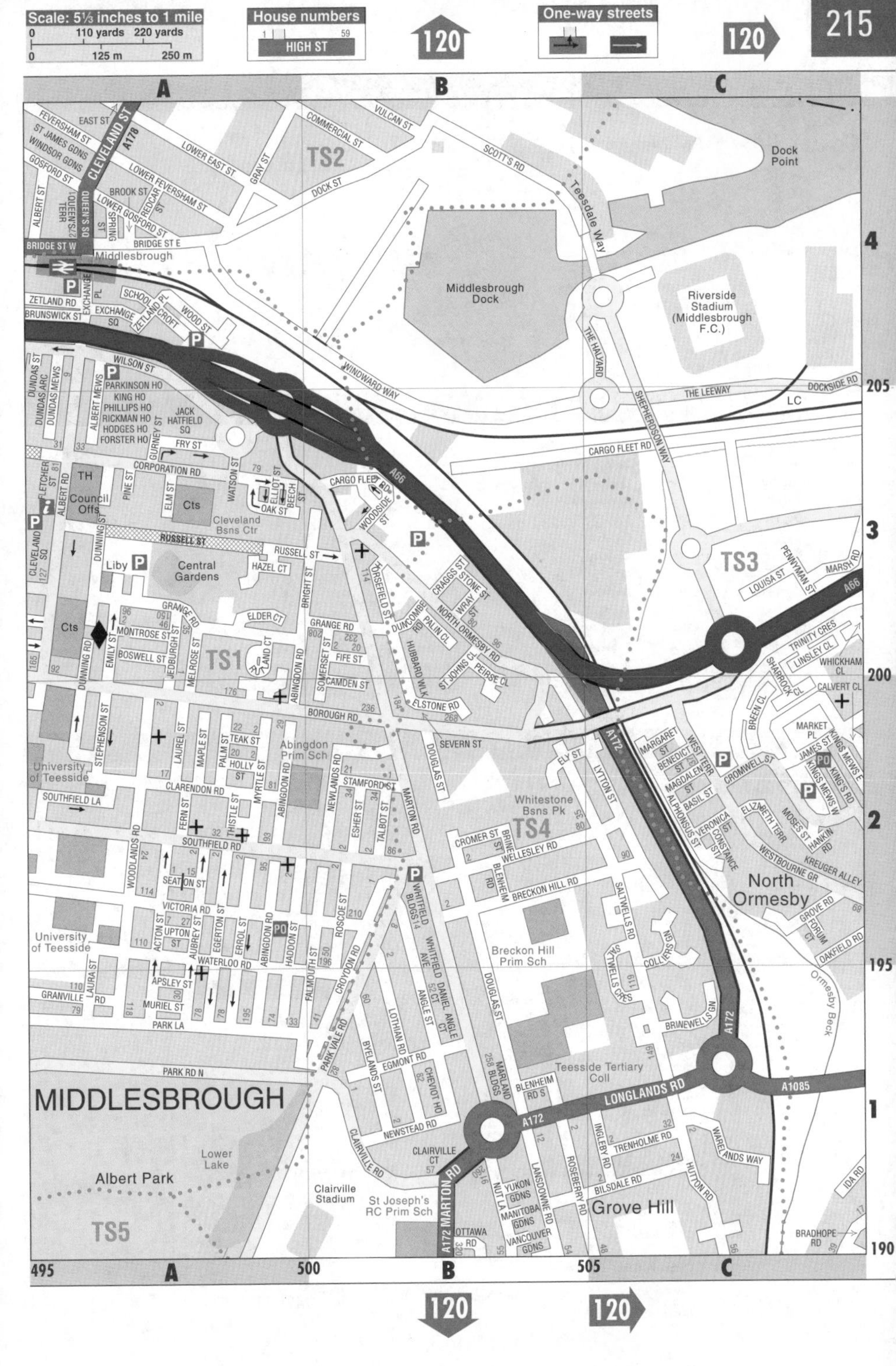
Scale: 5⅓ inches to 1 mile
0
110 yards
220 yards
125 m
250 m
House numbers
1
59
HIGH ST
120
One-way streets
120
A
B
C
TS2
COMMERCIAL ST
VULCAN ST
SCOTT'S RD
DOCK ST
GRAY ST
LOWER EAST ST
EAST ST
FEVERSHAM ST
ST JAMES GDNS
WINDSOR GDNS
GOSFORD ST
CLEVELAND ST
A178
LOWER FEVERSHAM ST
BROOK ST
REDCAR ST
LOWER GOSFORD ST
SPRING ST
QUEEN'S SQ
QUEEN'S TERR
ALBERT ST
BRIDGE ST W
BRIDGE ST E
Middlesbrough
Teesdale Way
Dock Point
Middlesbrough Dock
Riverside Stadium (Middlesbrough F.C.)
4
ZETLAND RD
EXCHANGE PL
SCHOOL CROFT
ZETLAND PL
WOOD ST
BRUNSWICK ST
EXCHANGE SQ
THE HALYARD
WINDWARD WAY
THE LEEWAY
DOCKSIDE RD
LC
205
SHEPHERDSON WAY
WILSON ST
DUNDAS ST
DUNDAS ARC
DUNDAS MEWS
ALBERT MEWS
PARKINSON HO
KING HO
PHILLIPS HO
RICKMAN HO
HODGES HO
FORSTER HO
JACK HATFIELD SQ
GURNEY ST
FRY ST
CARGO FLEET RD
CORPORATION RD
WATSON ST
ELLIOT ST
BEECH ST
OAK ST
A66
CARGO FLEET RD
WOODSIDE ST
FLETCHER ST
ALBERT RD
TH
Council Offs
PINE ST
ELM ST
Cts
Cleveland Bsns Ctr
CLEVELAND SQ
DUNNING ST
RUSSELL ST
3
Liby
Central Gardens
HAZEL CT
RUSSELL ST
TS3
PENNYMAN ST
LOUISA ST
MARSH RD
BRIGHT ST
HORSEFIELD ST
CRAGGS ST
STONE ST
WRAY ST
NORTH ORMESBY RD
GRANGE RD
ELDER CT
GRANGE RD
DUNCOMBE RD
PALIN CL
Cts
MONTROSE ST
EMILY ST
JEDBURGH ST
MELROSE ST
BOSWELL ST
TS1
RYLAND CT
ABINGDON RD
SOMERSET ST
FIFE ST
CAMDEN ST
HUBBARD WLK
ST JOHNS CL
PEIRSE CL
TRINITY CRES
LINSLEY CL
WHICKHAM CL
SHARROCK CL
CALVERT CL
200
DUNNING RD
ELSTONE RD
BOROUGH RD
STEPHENSON ST
LAUREL ST
MAPLE ST
PALM ST
TEAK ST
HOLLY ST
MYRTLE ST
Abingdon Prim Sch
SEVERN ST
DOUGLAS ST
A172
MARGARET ST
BENEDICT ST
MAGDALEN ST
ALPHONSUS ST
BASIL ST
WEST TERR
CROMWELL ST
BREEN CL
MARKET PL
JAMES ST
KINGS MEWS E
KINGS MEWS W
KING'S RD
University of Teesside
CLARENDON RD
SOUTHFIELD LA
FERN ST
THISTLE ST
NEWLANDS RD
STAMFORD ST
ESHER ST
TALBOT ST
MARTON RD
ELY ST
LYTTON ST
Whitestone Bsns Pk
TS4
VERONICA ST
CONSTANCE ST
ELIZABETH TERR
MOSES ST
HANKIN RD
2
WOODLANDS RD
SOUTHFIELD RD
CROMER ST
BRINE ST
WELLESLEY RD
KREUGER ALLEY
WESTBOURNE GR
SEATON ST
BLENHEIM RD
BRECKON HILL RD
SALTWELLS RD
North Ormesby
VICTORIA RD
EGERTON ST
WHITFIELD BLDGS
WHITFIELD AVE
ROSCOE ST
GROVE RD
FORUM CT
ACTON ST
UPTON ST
AUBREY ST
ERROL ST
ABINGDON RD
HADDON ST
DANIEL CT
ANGLE CT
Breckon Hill Prim Sch
SALTWELLS CRES
COLLIERS GN
OAKFIELD RD
University of Teesside
WATERLOO RD
LAURA ST
APSLEY ST
FALMOUTH ST
CROYDON RD
ANGLE ST
195
GRANVILLE RD
MURIEL ST
LOTHIAN RD
DOUGLAS ST
BRINEWELLS GN
Ormesby Beck
PARK LA
PARK VALE RD
BYELANDS ST
EGMONT RD
CHEVIOT HO
MARLAND BLDGS
Teesside Tertiary Coll
PARK RD N
BLENHEIM RD S
LONGLANDS RD
A1085
MIDDLESBROUGH
NEWSTEAD RD
A172
1
Lower Lake
CLAIRVILLE RD
CLAIRVILLE CT
INGLEBY RD
TRENHOLME RD
WARELANDS WAY
Albert Park
Clairville Stadium
St Joseph's RC Prim Sch
MARTON RD
A172
YUKON GDNS
NUT LA
MANITOBA GDNS
LANSDOWNE RD
ROSEBERRY RD
BILSDALE RD
Grove Hill
HUTTON RD
IDA RD
TS5
OTTAWA RD
VANCOUVER GDNS
BRADHOPE RD
190
495
500
505
120
120

Index

Church Rd 6 Beckenham BR2......... **53** C6

Place name
May be abbreviated on the map

Location number
Present when a number indicates the place's position in a crowded area of mapping

Locality, town or village
Shown when more than one place has the same name

Postcode district
District for the indexed place

Page and grid square
Page number and grid reference for the standard mapping

Public and commercial buildings are highlighted in magenta. **Places of interest** are highlighted in blue with a star★

Abbreviations used in the index

Abbreviation	Meaning
Acad	Academy
App	Approach
Arc	Arcade
Ave	Avenue
Bglw	Bungalow
Bldg	Building
Bsns, Bus	Business
Bvd	Boulevard
Cath	Cathedral
Cir	Circus
Cl	Close
Cnr	Corner
Coll	College
Com	Community
Comm	Common
Cott	Cottage
Cres	Crescent
Cswy	Causeway
Ct	Court
Ctr	Centre
Ctry	Country
Cty	County
Dr	Drive
Dro	Drove
Ed	Education
Emb	Embankment
Est	Estate
Ex	Exhibition
Gd	Ground
Gdn	Garden
Gn	Green
Gr	Grove
H	Hall
Ho	House
Hospl	Hospital
HQ	Headquarters
Hts	Heights
Ind	Industrial
Inst	Institute
Int	International
Intc	Interchange
Junc	Junction
L	Leisure
La	Lane
Liby	Library
Mdw	Meadow
Meml	Memorial
Mkt	Market
Mus	Museum
Orch	Orchard
Pal	Palace
Par	Parade
Pas	Passage
Pk	Park
Pl	Place
Prec	Precinct
Prom	Promenade
Rd	Road
Recn	Recreation
Ret	Retail
Sh	Shopping
Sq	Square
St	Street
Sta	Station
Terr	Terrace
TH	Town Hall
Univ	University
Wk, Wlk	Walk
Wr	Water
Yd	Yard

Index of localities, towns and villages

A

Acklam 139 C7
Acklam Base 139 D5
Aislaby 155 E5
Albert Hill 133 B3
Allenheads 179 C8
Allensford 176 F5
Annfield Plain 12 E4
Archdeacon Newton 131 E7
Auckland Park 80 E6
Aukside 208 B8
Aycliffe Village 96 E1
Ayton 9 F2

B

Barley Mow 9 C2
Barlow 1 C6
Barnard Castle 209 E5
Barningham 205 A4
Baybridge 174 F5
Beamish 14 F8
Bearpark 33 B3
Bedburn 189 C2
Beechwood 140 A7
Bellevue 77 C4
Benfieldside 10 C5
Berwick Hills 120 D2
Bildershaw 94 A5
Billingham 102 F1
Billy Row 52 E7
Binchester 68 A5
Birtley 9 C3
Bishop Auckland 80 C4
Bishopgarth 117 B5
Bishop Middleham 71 B4
Bishopton 115 D7
Blackfyne 10 E4
Blackhall Colliery 50 C4
Blackhall Mill 4 B7
Blackhall Rocks 50 E2
Blackhill 10 E4
Blackwell 151 D6
Blanchland 175 A5
Blaydon 2 B7
Bolam 93 F2
Boldron 199 B1
Bollihope 187 E5
Boosbeck 145 C7
Borrowby 149 A4
Boulby 128 D3
Bournmoor 17 D3
Bowbank 208 C2
Bowburn 45 D1
Bowes 203 D8
Bowlees 192 A7
Bradbury 83 F5
Brafferton 113 A6
Brambles Farm 120 F3
Brancepeth 54 E8
Brandon 43 B5
Brandon Village 43 A5
Branksome 132 A4
Brass Castle 153 C5
Brasside 34 F8
Bridgehill 10 C4
Brignall 204 E7
Brookfield 139 B3
Broom Hill Hetton-le-Hole 27 A6
Broom Hill Stanley 13 D7
Broompark 43 C8
Brotherlee 186 C8
Brotton 126 D3
Burdon 18 B3
Burnhope 21 E4
Burnopfield 6 A6
Burtree Ford 179 B3
Butterknowle 195 C5
Butterwick 86 A8
Byermoor 6 D7
Byers Green 54 E1

C

California 121 F2
Canada 16 B4
Cargo Fleet 120 D5
Carlbury 130 C4
Carlin How 126 E3
Carlton 116 C8
Carrville 35 D5
Carterway Heads 176 C6
Cassop 46 F1
Castle Eden 61 C8
Castleside 177 A3
Catchgate 12 E5
Causey 7 B4
Charltons 144 F4
Chester le Street 16 E4
Chester Moor 24 B7
Chilton 82 E7
Chilton Lane 70 C3
Chilton Moor 26 A7
Chopwell 4 B8
Church Kelloe 58 F6
Cleasby 150 E7
Cleatlam 200 D5
Cliffe 130 C3
Close House 81 A5
Clough Dene 6 A3
Coalcleugh 178 C8
Coatham 107 B7
Coatham Mundeville 112 F5
Cockerton 132 C4
Cockfield 195 F3
Cold Hesledon 29 B2
Coldpool 158 D4
Colliery Row 26 B8
Commondale 164 C1
Consett 10 D3
Copley 195 A4
Cornforth 57 E1
Cornsay 30 B4
Cornsay Colliery 31 A3
Cotherstone 198 F6
Coulby Newham 140 A2
Coundon 81 D8
Coundongate 80 F8
Coundon Grange 80 F5
Cowbar 129 B2
Cowpen Bewley 103 D6
Cowshill 179 B3
Coxhoe 58 B4
Craghead 14 D2
Crathorne 173 B3
Crawley Side 206 D5
Croft on Heugh 77 E8
Crook 52 D2
Crookgate Bank 6 C6
Crookhall 11 B2
Crossgate Moor 210 B3
Croxdale 56 B6

D

Daddrey Shield 185 F8
Daisy Hill 23 B6
Dalehouse 149 B8
Dalton 205 D3
Dalton-le-Dale 29 A5
Dalton-on-Tees 168 B4
Dalton Piercy 75 E3
Darlington 133 C2
Dawdon 29 D5
Deaf Hill 60 A5
Dean Bank 69 D5
Delves 177 D4
Deneside 29 A6
Denton 110 D2
Dipton 12 C8
Dormanstown 106 E4
Doxford Park 18 A4
Drinkfield 132 F7
Dunsdale 123 D2
Durham 210 C4

E

Eaglescliffe 137 B2
Easington Loftus 128 A1
Easington Peterlee 39 A4
Easington Colliery 39 E5
Easington Lane 37 D8
Eastbourne Darlington 133 C1
Eastbourne Stockton-on-Tees .117 F6
East Briscoe 198 C6
Easterside 140 A6
Eastgate 180 E1
East Hedleyhope 40 C5
East Hope 204 B3
East Kyo 13 B6
Eastlea 28 F7
East Loftus 127 D1
East Rainton 26 D4
East Stanley 14 A7
Ebchester 3 F3
Eddy's Bridge 176 B5
Eden Vale 61 D7
Edmondsley 23 B6
Edmundbyers 175 E5
Egglesburn 193 C3
Eggleston 193 E2
Eldon 81 A4
Eldon Lane 80 F4
Elemore Vale 37 B8
Ellerby 149 F2
Elm Tree 117 C5
Elstob 98 E4
Elton 136 F7
Elwick 75 D6
Embleton 87 C8
Eppleby 201 D1
Eryholme 169 A6
Escomb 66 D1
Esh 31 F4
Esh Winning 41 E8
Eston 121 D2
Etherley Dene 79 F6
Etherley Grange 79 C6
Ettersgill 191 D8
Evenwood 92 C7
Evenwood Gate 92 D5

F

Fairfield 117 C4
Faverdale 132 C6
Fellside 2 F6
Fence Houses 26 A8
Ferryhill 70 A6
Ferryhill Station 70 D4
Fir Tree 52 A1
Fishburn 72 D4
Fleming Field 48 B7
Flint Hill 5 E1
Foggy Furze 77 C2
Forest-in-Teesdale 191 C8
Foxton Hutton Rudby 173 E5
Foxton Sedgefield 99 C6
Framwellgate 34 B5
Frosterley 188 A8

G

Gainford 201 D4
Gateshead 9 C8
Gayles 205 E2
Gerrick 165 E6
Gilesgate 211 C3
Gilesgate Moor 35 B3
Gilmonby 203 D7
Girsby 170 B5
Grangefield 212 B3
Grangetown 121 E6
Grange Villa 15 A5
Graythorp 90 D4

Great Ayton 161 B2
Great Burdon 133 F6
Great Chilton 70 C1
Greatham 89 F4
Great Lumley 25 B8
Great Stainton 98 C1
Greencroft 12 D3
Greenside 1 B8
Greta Bridge 205 B8
Grindon 100 D7
Grove Hill 215 C1
Guisborough 143 C5

H

Hallgarth 36 B4
Hamsterley Blackhall Mill 4 B5
Hamsterley Morley 189 E2
Hamsterley Mill 5 A5
Hardwick 117 B7
Harelaw 12 E6
Harperley 13 A6
Harrowgate Hill 133 B7
Harrowgate Village 133 A8
Hart 62 F3
Hartburn 212 A1
Hartlepool 77 E4
Hart Station 63 D5
Harwood 184 E4
Haswell 37 F3
Haswell Plough 37 E1
Haughton Le Skerne 133 E5
Haverton Hill 103 C2
Hawthorn 39 B7
Headlam 201 E6
Heighington 95 D2
Helmington Row 53 C3
Hemlington 139 F1
Hesleden 50 A1
Hett 56 E6
Hetton Downs 27 B5
Hetton le Hill 37 A7
Hetton-le-Hole 27 B4
High Beechburn 52 D1
High Clarence 103 E1
High Coniscliffe 130 F3
High Dubmire 26 B8
High Etherley 78 F5
Highfield 1 C2
High Flatts 16 A6
High Forge 7 F1
High Friarside 5 E6
High Handenhold 15 B7
High Haswell 37 D4
High Hesleden 50 C1
High Job's Hill 53 B2
High Leven 157 C5
High Moorsley 36 D8
High Pittington 36 C5
High Shincliffe 45 B5
High Spen 1 A3
High Stoop 183 C3
High Urpeth 8 B1
High Westwood 4 B4
Hill Top Eggleston 193 D2
Hill Top Langley Park 32 D5
Hilton Ingleton 201 C8
Hilton Stockton-on-Tees 157 F3
Hinderwell 149 F6
Hobson 6 A4
Holmside 22 D7
Holwick 192 A5
Hooker Gate 1 A2
Hope Town 132 F4
Horden 49 E7
Hornby 170 D1
Houghall 44 D5
Houghton Bank 94 E1
Houghton-le-Side 110 F8
Houghton-le-Spring 26 C7
Howden-le-Wear 65 E7
Hummerbeck 93 E2
Hummersknott 132 B1
Hunderthwaite 198 C8
Hunwick 66 E6
Hurworth Burn 73 F7
Hurworth-on-Tees 152 D2
Hurworth Place 152 A1
Hutton Gate 143 B2
Hutton Henry 61 C5
Hutton Magna 205 E7
Hutton Rudby 173 E1
Hutton Village 162 C8

I

Ingleby Barwick 138 A2
Ingleton 201 C7
Inkerman 183 C2
Ireshopeburn 179 C1
Iveston 11 F1

K

Kelloe 58 D5
Kelton 197 C7
Kibblesworth 8 D5
Killerby 201 F6
Kilton 126 E1
Kimblesworth 23 F3
Kinninvie 199 D8
Kip Hill 7 A1
Kirby Hill 205 F1
Kirkleatham 123 B8
Kirklevington 172 E8
Kirk Merrington 69 B3
Knitsley 177 D3

L

Lackenby 122 B3
Laithkirk 208 D3
Lanchester 20 F4
Lane Ends 66 E7
Lane Head 205 E6
Langbaurgh 160 F4
Langdon Beck 185 B2
Langley Moor 43 D6
Langley Park 32 C6
Langton 201 D6
Lartington 198 F4
Lazenby 122 C4
Leadgate 11 D4
Leamside 25 E2
Leasingthorne 81 F8
Leazes 5 F6
Leeholme 68 C1
Lendings 209 C4
Leven Bridge 157 B5
Lingdale 145 E6
Lingfield 133 E1
Linthorpe 119 D1
Lintz 5 F5
Lintzford 5 B7
Lintzgarth 180 C5
Little Ayton 161 C1
Little Newsham 200 E4
Little Stainton 114 F5
Little Thorpe 39 C2
Littletown 36 E4
Liverton 147 A4
Liverton Mines 147 A8
Loftus 127 B2
Longnewton 136 B4
Low Coniscliffe 150 E8
Low Dinsdale 153 F3
Low Downs 27 B6
Lowe's Barn 43 F8
Low Etherley 78 F6
Low Job's Hill 53 A4
Low Moorsley 26 F1
Low Pittington 36 B6
Low Spennymoor 69 B8
Low Westwood 4 A5
Low Worsall 171 C8
Ludworth 47 C7
Lyons 27 C2

M

Maiden Law 21 A8
Mainsforth 70 F3
Maltby 157 F7
Malton 21 B1
Marley Hill 7 A8
Marske-by-the-Sea 108 E2
Marton 140 D4
Marton Grove 120 A1
Meadowfield 43 D4
Medomsley 4 C1
Merrington Lane 69 A8
Merrybent 131 C2
Merryoaks 44 A6
Metal Bridge 57 B2
Mickleton 208 F2
Middle Rainton 26 C3
Middlesbrough 215 A1
Middle Side 192 D5
Middlestone 68 E3
Middlestone Moor 68 C6
Middleton 77 D8
Middleton-in-Teesdale 208 C6
Middleton One Row 154 A5
Middleton-on-Leven 173 E8
Middleton St George 153 F7
Middridge 81 E1
Mill Hill 18 B6
Monk Hesleden 62 C7
Moor End 35 C4
Moorsholm 146 C1
Moorside 177 A4
Mordon 84 C1
Morley 195 E6
Morton Tinmouth 201 E8
Mount Pleasant Middlesbrough 159 D8
Mount Pleasant Spennymoor 56 B1
Mount Pleasant Stockton-on-Tees 118 D6
Mowden 132 B3
Murton 28 B2

N

Neasham 153 B1
Nenthead 178 A6
Nettlesworth 23 E4
Neville's Cross 210 A1
Newbiggin Lanchester 20 B4
Newbiggin Middleton-in-Teesdale 192 B6
New Brancepeth 42 E7
New Brotton 126 B5
Newby 159 B5
New Coundon 67 F1
Newfield Pelton 15 C5
Newfield Willington 67 B8
Newham Grange 212 B4
New House 179 D2
New Hunwick 66 D6
New Kyo 13 B4
New Lambton 17 F2
Newlands 3 D3
New Marske 124 B6
Newport 214 A1
Newsham Barnard Castle 205 D4
Newsham Middleton St George 154 F3
New Shildon 95 A8
New Silksworth 18 B8
New Skelton 125 D3
Newton Aycliffe 96 C5
Newton Bewley 88 F2
Newton Hall 34 C6
Newton Ketton 113 E6
Newton Mulgrave 149 D3
Newton under Roseberry 161 C7
Newtown 212 B4
New Town 26 F8
No Place 14 D7
Normanby 141 C8
North Bitchburn 66 A6
North Close 69 A5
North End 210 A4
Northlea 19 B1
North Ormsby 215 C2
North Side 9 D6
North Skelton 125 E1
Norton 102 B1
Nunthorpe Middlesbrough 141 B2
Nunthorpe Middlesbrough 160 B7

O

Oakenshaw 54 A6
Oak Tree 154 B7
Old Cassop 46 D4
Old Eldon 81 D3
Old Quarrington 58 A8
Old Stillington 99 D2
Old Thornley 47 C1
Old Town 77 D5
Ormesby 141 B8
Ornsby Hill 20 F5
Ouston 8 F2
Ovington 200 F1
Owton Manor 89 E6
Oxbridge 212 B2
Oxhill 13 D6

P

Pallister 120 C3
Park End 140 D8
Parkside 29 B5
Pelton 15 E6
Pelton Fell 15 E4
Pelton Lane Ends 15 B6
Penshaw 17 F8
Perkinsville 15 F8
Peterlee 49 B6
Pickering Nook 6 A4
Picktree 16 E7
Picton 172 B3
Piercebridge 130 B4
Pierremont 132 D2
Pinchinthorpe 142 E3
Pity Me 34 B7
Plawsworth 24 B4
Port Clarence 120 A8
Port Mulgrave 149 E8
Portobello 9 E4
Portrack 118 E4
Potter's Cross 195 B5
Preston-le-Skerne 97 C4
Preston-on-Tees 137 E4
Primrose Hill 118 A5

Q

Quaking Houses 13 D2
Quarrington Hill 58 D7
Quebec 31 B4

R

Ragworth 117 E6
Rainton Bridge 26 E6
Rainton Gate 25 F1
Ramshaw 78 B1
Redcar 107 D7
Red Hall 133 E4
Redmarshall 116 B6
Redworth 95 C3
Rickleton 16 E7
Rift House 76 E2
Rise Carr 132 F5
Roddymoor 52 C6
Romaldkirk 193 D1
Rookhope 180 E5
Roseworth 117 D8
Roundhill Village 156 E7
Rowlands Gill 1 E2
Rowley 177 A3
Roxby 148 E4
Royal Oak 94 B4
Running Waters 46 C6
Rushyford 82 E6
Ryehope Colliery 18 E7
Ryhope 18 F6

S

Sacriston 23 C4
Sadberge 134 E6
St Ann's Hill 213 C4
St Helen Auckland 79 E2
St John's Chapel 179 F1
Saltburn-by-the-Sea 125 B8
Saltholme 103 F4
Satley 183 E6
Scaling 167 A7
Scargill 204 C5
School Aycliffe 95 F3
Seaham 29 C6
Seaham Grange 18 F2
Seamer 158 F1
Seaton 28 D8
Seaton Carew 90 F8
Sedgefield 85 A6
Shadforth 46 E7
Sheep Hill 6 B7
Sherburn 36 A1
Sherburn Hill 36 C1
Shield Row 14 A8
Shildon 95 B8
Shincliffe 45 A6
Shiney Row 17 F5
Shotley Bridge 10 D6
Shotleyfield 176 E8
Shotton 49 B3
Shotton Colliery 48 D5
Silksworth 18 A6
Skelton 125 B2
Skelton Green 125 B1
Skerne Park 151 F6
Skinningrove 127 B4
Snaisgill 208 C8
Sniperley Park 33 F5
Snods Edge 176 E7
Snow's Green 10 D7
Sober Hall 157 C7
Sockburn 169 F3
South Bank 121 A6
South Church 80 E5
South Cleatlam 200 E5
South Hetton 38 A7
South Loftus 147 C8
South Moor 13 D4
South Pelaw 16 B6
South Stanley 13 F5
South Wingate 61 B3
Spennymoor 68 C7
Spital Flatt 156 D4
Springwell 9 F8
Staindrop 200 E7
Stainton Barnard Castle 199 F5
Stainton Middlesbrough 139 B1
Stainton Grove 209 F8
Staithes 129 C1
Stanghow 145 E3
Stanhope 206 D3
Stanley 13 E6
Stanley Crook 52 F8
Stapleton 151 A5
Startforth 209 B5
Station Town 60 E5
Stillington 99 E4
Stockton Grange 212 A3
Stockton-on-Tees 212 B3
Stony Heap 12 A3
Summerhouse 110 A3
Sunderland 18 D8
Sunderland Bridge 56 B8
Sunniside Crook 40 A1
Sunniside Stanley 7 A8
Sunnybrow 53 E1
Sunnydale 81 B2

T

Tanfield 6 D3
Tanfield Lea 6 D1
Tan Hills 23 F3
Tantobie 6 A2
Tanton 159 E2
Teesport 105 C3
Teesville 121 C3
Templetown 10 F1
The Grove 10 C1
The Headland 64 G8
The Middles 14 B3
Thinford 56 E1
Thornaby-on-Tees 138 E6
Thornlaw South 47 C3
Thornley Tow Law 189 D8
Thornley Wheatley Hill 47 D4
Thornton 158 C8
Thorntree 120 F2
Thorpe Larches 86 B1
Thorpe Thewles 100 E3
Thringarth 192 D1
Throston 64 D1
Tindale Crescent 79 F3
Toft Hill 78 D5
Tollesby 140 B4
Toronto 66 F2
Tow Law 183 E1
Town Farm 120 E2
Town Kelloe 59 B6
Trimdon 72 E8
Trimdon Colliery 60 A4
Trimdon Grange 59 E3
Tudhoe 56 A3
Tudhoe Colliery 56 A4
Tudhoe Grange 55 F2
Tudhoe Village 55 F4
Tunstall Middlesbrough 159 F5
Tunstall New Silksworth 18 C7
Tursdale 57 C4

U

Upleatham 124 C3
Upper Town 207 D6
Urlay Nook 136 E1
Urpeth 8 E2
Ushaw Moor 32 F2

W

Wackerfield 92 C2
Waldridge 15 E1
Walworth 111 A2
Walworth Gate 111 B5
Warrenby 106 E6
Washington 9 F4
Waskerley 182 D8
Waterhouses 41 B6
Wearhead 179 B2
Wellfield 48 F1
West Auckland 79 C2
West Blackdene 179 D2
West Briscoe 198 A5
West Cornforth 70 E8
West Dyke 107 C6
West End 65 A4
Western Hill 210 B4
Westerton 68 B3
Westfield 107 A5
Westgate 180 B1
West Hope 204 A4
West Kyo 12 F5
Westlea 28 F7
West Park 76 C5
West Pelton 15 A6
West Rainton 26 B2
West View 63 E3
Westwick 199 F2
Wheatley Hill 47 F2
Whickham 2 E6
Whinfield 133 D7
Whinney Banks 139 A8
White Kirkley 188 A6
White-le-Head 6 A1
Whitesmocks 33 F3
Whitton 100 A2
Whorlton 200 C1
Willington 53 E2
Wilton 122 F4
Windlestone 82 F7
Wingate 60 D7
Winlaton Mill 2 C6
Winston 200 F3
Witton Gilbert 33 A8
Witton-le-Wear 65 B3
Witton Park 66 A1
Wolsingham 207 E6
Wolviston 102 B8
Woodham Village 82 E2
Woodhouses 79 D4
Woodland 194 F5
Woodside 79 B8
Woodstone Village 17 D1
Wynyard Village 87 B2

Y

Yarm 156 A5
Yearby 123 B6

A

A J Cook Terr DH6 48 C5
A J Cook's Cotts NE39 1 B2
Abberley Dr TS8 139 F2
Abberston Wlk TS4 140 A7
Abbey Cl TS19 116 F4
Abbey Cotts DL12 209 E3
Abbey Ct TS6 121 D2
Abbey Gdns DL15 54 A3
Abbey Hill Sch Tech Coll TS19 117 D6
Abbey Inf Sch DL3 132 D1
Abbey Jun Sch DL3 132 C1
Abbey La DL12 209 D3
Abbey Mews DH7 23 C2
Abbey Rd
Bishop Auckland DL14 80 B5
Darlington DL3 132 D1
Durham DH1 34 B8
Sadberge DL2 134 F6
Abbey Road Ind Est DH1 34 C8
Abbey Springs DL3 132 C2
Abbey St Brotton TS12 126 B3
Hartlepool TS24 77 F8
Abbey Terr DL12 209 C4
Abbeydale Gdns DH6 38 A6
Abbeyfield Dr TS16 137 B1
Abbeywoods DH1 34 B8
Abbots Gn DL15 54 A3
Abbots Way TS19 116 F4
Abbots Wlk DH9 14 F8
Abbots' Row DH1 211 C4
Abbotsfield Way DL3 132 B7
Abbotsford Rd TS5 139 B8
Abbotside Cl DH2 8 D2
Abbott's Hos DL13 195 D4
Abdale Ave TS5 139 B8
Aberbran Ct TS17 156 F7
Abercorn Cl 9 TS10 107 E1
Abercorn Ct DL3 132 B7
Abercrombie Rd TS10 106 F5
Aberdare Rd TS6 121 E5
Aberdeen DH2 8 F1
Aberdeen Rd
Darlington DL1 133 E7
Hartlepool TS25 77 A1
Aberdovey Dr TS16 156 C8
Aberfalls Rd TS8 139 F2
Aberfoyle DH2 8 F1
Aberfoyle Ct DH9 14 B6
Abernethy DH2 8 F2
Aberwick Dr DH2 23 F8
Abingdon Prim Sch TS1 215 A2
Abingdon Rd TS1 215 A2
Abington DH2 8 F1
Abotts Lea TS27 75 E3
Abraham Ind Est DL14 79 F3
Abridge Cl TS11 123 F6
Acacia Ave SR8 50 B6
Acacia Ct 12 TS10 107 E1
Acacia Gdns DL15 52 D4
Acacia Rd
Bishop Auckland DL14 80 B7
Stockton-on-T TS19 117 F5
Acacia St DL3 132 E4
Academy Gdns DL2 201 D4
Acclom St TS24 77 A7
Accrington Terr DL14 92 D6
Acer Dr DH6 37 F3
Achilles Cl TS6 121 B4
Acklam Grange Sch TS5 139 B6
Acklam Rd
Middlesbrough TS5 139 C5
Thornaby-on-T TS17 138 E8
Acklam St N TS2 119 E7
Acklam St S TS2 214 C4
Acklam Whin Prim Sch TS5 139 B4
Ackworth Gn TS3 120 D3
Acle Burn DL5 82 C3
Acle Mdws DL5 82 C3
Aclet Cl DL14 80 B4
Acorn Bank TS17 157 B7
Acorn Cl
Middleton St George DL2 153 F8
Sacriston DH7 23 B4
Acorn Croft DH7 33 B8
Acorn Dr DL15 54 A6
Acorn Pl Brandon DH7 43 B4
Durham DH1 34 B8
Acorn St DH2 15 B7
Acornclose La DH7 22 F4
Acre Rigg Inf & Jun Schs SR8 49 B8
Acre Rigg Rd SR8 49 B8
Acton Dene DH9 14 C7
Acton Rd DH7 41 E8
Acton St TS1 215 A2
Ada St E SR7 28 D2
Ada St W SR7 28 D2
Adam Cl TS10 107 B2
Adam St 3 Peterlee SR8 50 B6
Stockton-on-T TS18 138 A7
Adam's Bldgs DH9 12 C8
Adams Terr DH8 4 A2
Adamson St DL4 95 A7
Adcott Rd TS5 139 C6
Adderley St TS18 213 A1
Addington Dr TS3 120 D3
Addison Rd Coundon DL14 68 C1
Great Ayton TS9 161 A2
Addison Rd *continued*
Hartlepool TS24 77 B7
Middlesbrough TS5 119 D2
Toronto DL14 66 D3
Addison St
Coundon Grange DL14 80 F5
Crook DL15 52 E4
Adelaide Bank DL14,DL4 80 E3
Adelaide Gr TS18 212 A1
Adelaide Pl 6 TS11 108 C1
Adelaide Rd TS7 140 C3
Adelaide Row 4 SR7 29 D7
Adelaide St
5 Bishop Auckland DL14 80 C8
12 Chester le Street DH3 16 C2
11 Darlington DL1 133 B1
4 Shildon DL4 94 F8
Adelaide Terr DL4 80 E3
Adelphi Ct 18 DL1 133 B1
Aden Ct DH7 33 A4
Aden St TS5 214 A1
Adfrid Pl SR8 49 D7
Admiral Way TS24 77 D6
Admirals Ave TS3 120 D3
Adolphus Pl DH1 35 B2
Adolphus St W SR7 29 D7
Adrian Pl SR8 49 E5
Adshead Rd TS10 106 F4
Adstock Ave TS4 140 B7
Adventure La DH4 25 F2
Agecroft Gdns TS5 119 B1
Aged Miner's Home DL14 81 A3
Aged Miner's Homes
Bearpark DH7 33 A3
Burnopfield NE16 6 A6
Chester le Street DH2 24 B7
Hetton-le-H DH5 27 A2
3 Houghton-le-S DH5 26 F8
Quebec DH7 31 B4
Ryhope SR2 18 E7
Sacriston DH7 23 D3
2 Seaham SR7 18 F1
Aged Miners Homes
Chester le Street DH2 16 C4
Shotton Colliery DH6 48 B7
Wheatley Hill DH6 47 F2
Aged Miners' Homes 5 TS27 50 D3
Aged Miners' Homes
Bournmoor DH4 17 E2
Brandon DH7 43 B5
Brandon, Meadowfield DH7 43 C3
Aged Miners' Homes DH5 26 C4
Aged Miners' Homes DL14 92 C7
Aged Miners' Homes TS21 72 D5
Aged Miners' Homes DH3 17 B1
Aged Miners' Homes DH5 26 F6
Aged Miners' Homes NE39 1 A4
Aged Miners' Homes 5 DH4 26 C8
Aged Miners' Homes NE11 8 C6
Aged Miners' Homes DH2 23 F4
Aged Miners' Homes 8 DH7 32 C6
Aged Miners' Homes SR7 28 B3
Aged Miners' Homes
Pelton DH2 15 C6
Peterlee SR8 49 F7
Quarrington Hill DH6 58 D7
Aged Miners' Homes
Seaham SR7 29 D6
Seaham,Northlea SR7 28 F8
Aged Miners' Homes DH6 36 C1
Aged Miners' Homes DL16 68 C6
Aged Miners' Homes DH9 14 B4
Aged Workers Homes DL15 52 D4
Agnes St DH9 13 F7
Agnew Way DL5 82 D1
Agricola Cotts
Hilton TS15 157 F3
Mount Pleasant TS7 160 C7
Agricola Ct DL3 132 C7
Aidan Cl DH9 14 B7
Aidans Wlk DL17 70 A7
Aiden Way DH5 27 A5
Ainderby Gr TS18 117 A1
Ainderby Way TS4 140 A8
Ainderby Wlk TS24 64 B1
Ainsdale Cl TS11 123 F6
Ainsdale Way TS4 140 A7
Ainsford Way TS7 141 B8
Ainsley Gr DL3 132 C7
Ainsley St Durham DH1 210 B3
Hartlepool TS25 77 D4
Ainstable Rd TS7 141 B7
Ainsty Hunt DL5 95 F8
Ainsworth Way TS7 141 B8
Ainthorpe Cl SR3 18 B7
Ainthorpe Pl 6 TS6 121 F3
Ainthorpe Rd TS6 121 F3
Aintree Ct DL1 133 F3
Aintree Dr DH8 10 D7
Aintree Oval
Middlesbrough TS17 119 A2
Thornaby-on-T TS17 118 F2
Aintree Rd Redcar TS10 107 D4
Aintree Rd *continued*
Stockton-on-T TS18 118 F5
Airdrie Gr TS25 76 F1
Aire St
Middlesbrough TS1 214 B1
South Bank TS6 121 A6
Aireborough Cl TS19 117 D5
Airedale Gdns DH5 26 F2
Aireyholme La TS9 161 D3
Aireys Cl DH4 26 C8
Airton Pl DL5 96 B7
Airville Mount SR3 18 A4
Airy Hill La TS12 145 A8
Aiskew Gr TS19 117 A2
Aislaby Ct TS14 143 E6
Aislaby Gr TS23 102 E7
Aislaby Ho TS14 143 E6
Aislaby Rd TS16 156 A7
Aitken's Bldgs DH9 12 C8
Ajax St DL1 133 C6
Ajax Way TS6 121 A5
Alan St 11 TS6 121 A6
Albany Ct 9 TS26 77 A6
Albany Rd Marton TS7 140 C3
Stockton-on-T TS20 118 C7
Albany St TS1 214 C2
Albatross Way DL1 133 D1
Albert Cl DL12 209 C6
Albert Ct 6 TS12 125 C8
Albert Hill DL14 80 C7
Albert Hill Ind Est DL1 133 B4
Albert Mews TS1 215 A3
Albert Rd Consett DH8 10 F2
Darlington DL1 133 A4
Eaglescliffe TS16 137 C2
Eston TS6 121 D2
Middlesbrough TS1 215 A3
Stockton-on-T TS19 117 B3
Albert St
6 Chester le Street DH3 16 C3
Chilton DL17 83 A7
Crook DL15 52 E4
12 Darlington DL1 133 B1
Durham DH1 210 B3
Esh Winning DH7 41 E8
Hartlepool TS24 77 C5
Middlesbrough TS2 215 A4
Rowlands Gill NE39 1 A1
Seaham SR7 29 E6
Shildon DL4 81 A2
Thornley (nr Wheatley Hill) DH6 47 D4
West Pelton DH2 15 A5
Albert Terr Billy Row DL15 52 E7
Middlesbrough TS1 214 C1
Stanhope DL13 206 D2
Alberta Ho TS4 120 A2
Alberto St TS18 213 A4
Albery Pl 16 DL1 133 B1
Albion Ave DL4 80 F2
Albion Gdns NE16 5 F5
Albion Pl DL15 53 F3
Albion St Boosbeck TS12 145 C6
Spennymoor DL16 68 C6
Stockton-on-T TS18 213 A2
Albion Terr
Bishop Auckland DL14 80 C7
Guisborough TS14 143 F5
Hartlepool TS24 77 F8
Saltburn-by-t-S TS12 125 C7
Witton Park DL14 66 A1
Albourne Gn TS4 140 B6
Albury Way TS3 120 F2
Alconbury Way TS3 120 F2
Alcote Gr DH6 48 D6
Aldam St DL1 133 A4
Aldbrough Cl
11 Ryhope SR2 18 F6
Stockton-on-T TS19 117 B3
Aldbrough Wlk 4 DL1 152 C8
Aldeburgh Cl TS25 89 E6
Aldenham Rd TS14 143 D2
Alder Cl DH5 26 F3
Alder Cres DH9 5 F2
Alder Gr DH8 11 D3
Alder Lea Cl DH1 35 A3
Alder Pk DH7 43 A3
Alder Rd Peterlee SR8 50 B6
Stockton-on-T TS19 117 F5
Alderburgh Way SR7 29 D8
Alderdene DH7 20 E3
Alderdene Cl DH7 33 B1
Aldergrove Dr TS4 140 B7
Alderlea TS7 140 F4
Alderman Leach Prim Sch DL3 132 C5
Alderman Wood Rd DH9 13 E8
Alderney Wlk TS14 143 D3
Alderside Cres DH7 20 E4
Alderson St
4 Bishop Auckland DL14 80 B6
2 Hartlepool TS26 77 A5
Alderwood
Coulby Newham TS8 140 B3
Washington NE38 17 B8
Alderwood Cl
Darlington DL1 133 E6
Hartlepool TS27 63 C4
Ormesby TS7 141 B7
Aldgrove Way DL3 132 E5
Aldhome Ct DH1 34 A6
Aldhun Cl DL14 80 B4
Aldin Grange Hall DH7 33 D2
Aldin Grange Terr DH7 33 C3
Aldin Rise DH7 33 C2
Aldridge Ct DH7 33 B2
Aldridge Rd TS3 140 D8
Aldwark Cl TS5 139 C3
Aldwin Cl DL17 83 A8
Aldwych Cl TS6 141 C7
Aldwyn Wlk 4 DL5 96 F8
Alexander Dr DH5 26 F3
Alexander St DL1 133 C3
Alexander Terr TS3 120 E3
Alexandra Cl DH1 34 A6
Alexandra Gdns 5 DL4 81 A2
Alexandra Rd TS6 121 D6
Alexandra St
11 Consett DH8 10 F2
Pelton DH2 15 C6
Rowlands Gill NE39 1 A1
Shildon DL4 81 A2
Alexandra Terr
Crook DL15 52 F4
Evenwood DL14 92 D6
Haswell DH6 37 F3
Wheatley Hill DH6 47 F3
Alexandria Cres DH1 210 B2
Alexandria Dr DL2 154 B8
Alexandrina St 1 SR7 29 D6
Alford DH2 8 F2
Alford Ct TS25 77 A1
Alford La TS19 117 D5
Alford Rd TS12 126 C3
Alfred St Darlington DL1 133 A4
Hartlepool TS24 64 F1
Redcar TS10 107 D6
Seaham SR7 29 E6
Alfred St E SR7 29 E6
Alfreton Cl DH7 43 A2
Alfrid Pl DL5 96 D8
Alfriston Cl 3 TS17 157 B8
Alhambra Terr TS21 72 C5
Alice Row TS18 212 C2
Alice St TS20 118 B8
Aline St
New Silksworth SR3 18 B7
Seaham SR7 29 E7
Alington Cl DL17 83 A8
Alington Pl 3 DH1 35 A2
Alington Rd DL5 96 C7
Alison Pl TS24 64 F1
All Saints CE Sch TS17 157 A8
All Saints Dr DH5 27 A5
All Saints Ind Est DL4 95 B7
All Saints RC Prim Sch DH7 20 E4
All Saints' Rd DL4 95 A7
Allan St Darlington DL1 133 B3
Easington SR8 39 F5
Allan Wlk DL5 96 E7
Allen St DH3 16 C2
Allendale Rd
Billingham TS23 102 C3
Brandon DH7 43 C4
Ormesby TS7 141 B7
Stockton-on-T TS18 212 B4
Allendale St
Hartlepool TS25 90 E8
Hetton-le-H DH5 27 A2
Allendale Tee TS11 123 F6
Allendale Terr
Annfield Plain DH9 12 F4
Haswell DH6 37 F3
Allenheads Heritage Ctr* NE47 179 B8
Allens West Sta TS16 137 A2
Allensford Bank DH8 176 F4
Allensway TS17 138 E5
Allerford Cl TS17 157 B6
Allergate DH1 210 B2
Allergate Terr DH1 210 B2
Allerston Way TS14 143 F6
Allerton Balk TS15 156 A3
Allerton Cl TS24 77 B8
Allerton Ct DL13 206 B3
Allerton Pk TS7 141 A2
Allerton Pl NE16 2 F5
Alliance Ind Est DL1 133 B4
Alliance St
Darlington DL3 132 F4
Hartlepool TS24 64 F1
Stockton-on-T TS18 212 C2
Allington Dr TS23 102 D6
Allington Way DL1 133 F2
Allington Wlk TS23 102 D6
Allinson St TS3 120 C4
Allison Ave TS17 157 D8
Allison Gdns DH8 10 F4
Allison St Consett DH8 10 F4
Guisborough TS14 143 D4
Stockton-on-T TS18 213 A4
Alloa Gr TS25 77 A1
Alloway Gr TS8 139 F2
Alloy Terr NE39 1 C1
Alma Par TS10 107 C7
Alma Pl DH1 35 B3
Alma Rd DL4 95 A8
Alma St Hartlepool TS26 77 A6
Stockton-on-T TS18 213 A4
Alma Terr Durham DH1 210 A1
Stanley Crook DL15 52 E8
Almond Cl Haswell DH6 37 F3
Spennymoor DL16 68 D7
Almond Ct
Middlesbrough TS4 139 F8
Shildon DL4 95 B8
Almond Gr
Marske-by-t-S TS11 124 C8
Stockton-on-T TS19 117 C3
Almond Terr 5 SR8 50 B6
Almoner's Barn DH1 44 A7
Almshouses
Evenwood DL14 92 C7
10 Staindrop DL2 200 E7
Alness Gr TS25 77 A1
Alnmouth Dr TS10 107 D2
Alnport Rd TS18 213 C4
Alnwick 7 TS4 120 B1
Alnwick Ave TS29 59 E4
Alnwick Cl
Bishop Auckland DL14 80 A6
Chester le Street DH2 16 A1
Ferryhill DL17 70 B5
Hartlepool TS27 63 D3
Redcar TS10 107 F4
Alnwick Ct TS4 120 A1
Alnwick Gr
Newton Aycliffe DL5 82 E1
Stockton-on-T TS20 102 A1
Alnwick Pl DL1 133 C5
Alnwick Rd DH1 34 C7
Alnwick St SR8 49 F8
Alpha Gr TS20 118 B6
Alphonsus St TS3 215 C2
Alpine Cl DH4 17 F5
Alpine Ct DH2 16 C3
Alpine Terr
5 Cockfield DL13 195 E3
Evenwood DL14 92 C6
Alpine Way
Stockton-on-T TS20 117 F7
Tow Law DL13 183 E1
Alston Cres DL5 96 A7
Alston Gn TS3 120 D3
Alston Moor Cl DL1 152 D8
Alston Rd Consett DH8 10 C4
Middleton-In-T DL12 208 A6
Alston St TS26 77 B4
Alston Terr DH8 10 C4
Alston Way DH7 43 C4
Alston Wlk
Newton Aycliffe DL5 96 A7
Peterlee SR8 49 E7
Sherburn DH6 36 A1
Althorp TS10 107 C6
Althorpe Cl TS3 120 F1
Alton Rd TS5 119 B2
Alum Waters DH7 43 A8
Alva Gr TS25 77 A1
Alverstone Ave 3 TS25 77 B3
Alverton Cl TS3 120 F2
Alverton Ct DL5 82 B1
Alverton Dr
Darlington DL3 132 C7
Newton Aycliffe DL5 96 B8
Alverton Gn TS3 120 F2
Alvingham Terr 1 TS3 140 F8
Alvis Cl TS23 103 B4
Alvis Ct TS23 103 B4
Alwent Cl DL3 131 F2
Alwent Mill La DL2 201 A5
Alwent Rd TS1 214 C3
Alwin NE38 9 F1
Alwin Cl TS17 157 B7
Alwinton Ct TS7 141 A7
Alwinton Dr DH2 16 A1
Alwyn Cl DH4 17 E3
Alwyn Gdns DH8 10 F1
Alwyn Rd DL3 133 A7
Amber Ct 7 TS12 125 C8
Amber St
Middlesbrough TS1 214 C2
Saltburn-by-t-S TS12 125 D8
Amberley Cl
Stockton-on-T TS18 117 C1
8 Redcar TS10 107 E1
Amberley Gn TS3 120 D3
Amberley Gr DL3 132 B7
Amberley Way TS16 137 A1
Amberton Rd TS24 77 B8
Amberwood Cl 2 TS27 63 C4
Amble Cl TS26 76 D6
Amble View TS20 118 C7
Ambleside Ave
Redcar TS10 107 C4
Seaham SR7 28 F8
Ambleside Cl SR8 49 E7
Ambleside Gr TS5 139 D7
Ambleside Mews DH8 11 D4
Ambleside Rd
Billingham TS23 102 E1
Eston TS6 121 D1
Ambleside Wlk DL1 152 B8
Ambrose Rd TS6 121 E1
Amersham Cres SR8 49 D7
Amersham Rd TS3 140 D8
Amerston Cl TS22 87 B3
Amesbury Cres TS8 139 F2
Amiens Cl DL3 132 C5
Ammerston Rd TS1 214 B3
Amos Dr DH9 12 F1
Ampleforth Ave TS6 121 D2
Ampleforth Ct TS12 125 D2
Ampleforth Rd
Billingham TS23 102 F5
Middlesbrough TS3 120 C1
Ampleforth Way DL3 132 A5
Amroth Gn TS3 120 D3
Ancaster Rd NE16 2 F6
Anchor Ct TS24 77 F8
Anchor Ho TS24 77 D6
Anchor Ret Pk TS24 77 C7
Anchorage Mews TS17 213 C2
Anchorage Terr DH1 211 A1
Anchorage The DH3 16 D3
Ancroft Dr TS7 141 B7
Ancroft Garth DH1 45 B4
Ancroft Gdns TS20 118 B7
Ancrum Way NE16 2 F5
Anderson Rd TS17 118 D1
Andover Way TS8 139 E2
Andrew St 2 TS24 77 C5
Andrew Terr DH6 47 E1

Andrew's La SR8 39 B2
Andrews House Sta* NE16 7 B7
Anesty Ct TS21 115 C7
Anfield Ct DL1 133 F3
Angate Sq DL13 207 D5
Angate St DL13 207 D5
Angel of the North (Mon)* NE9 9 A8
Angels Cl DL5 96 E2
Angle Ct TS4 215 B1
Angle St TS4 215 B1
Anglesey Ave 1 TS3 140 E8
Anglesey Gr TS26 76 E8
Anglesey Wlk TS14 143 D3
Angling Gn TS13 127 A4
Angrove Cl
Great Ayton TS9 160 F1
Yarm TS15 156 F5
Angrove Dr TS9 160 F1
Angus DH2 8 F2
Angus Sq DH7 43 D5
Angus St Brandon DH7 43 E6
Easington SR8 39 F4
Hartlepool TS26 77 A6
Angus Terr SR8 39 F3
Anlaby Cl TS23 102 E8
Ann Ave DH6 58 D6
Ann Crook Way TS24 64 F1
Ann St 4 Consett DH8 10 F2
South Bank TS6 121 A5
Ann's Pl DH7 43 E6
Ann's Terr DL3 132 F4
Annan Rd TS23 102 E6
Annand Rd DH1 211 C4
Annandale DL1 133 E7
Annandale Cres TS24 63 F2
Annaside Mews DH8 11 D4
Anne Swyft Rd DL5 96 E5
Annfield Cl TS23 102 D6
Annfield Pl DH9 12 E4
Annfield Plain Inf Sch DH9 12 F3
Annfield Plain Jun Sch DH9 13 A3
Annfield Terr DH9 12 E5
Annie St TS1 214 A2
Annigate Cl TS22 101 E8
Annums The DL12 203 D8
Ansdale Rd TS3 121 A3
Anson Ho 2 TS17 138 D5
Anson Wlk DL14 81 B8
Anstey Ho 2 TS20 118 A8
Anstruther Dr DL1 133 B7
Anthony Ct DH9 13 E7
Anthony St Easington SR8 39 F5
Stanley DH9 13 E7
Antliff Terr 3 DH9 12 F4
Antrim Ave TS19 117 A4
Antrim Gdns SR7 29 C8
Anvil Ct DH1 34 A7
Apperley Ave DH1 45 C4
Apple Orchard Bank TS11,TS12 124 F4
Appleby Ave TS3 120 D3
Appleby Cl TS11 123 F6
Appleby Ct
Bournmoor DH4 17 D1
Crook DL15 52 E3
Appleby Gr TS24 77 B8
Appleby Ho 4 TS17 138 D5
Appleby Rd TS23 102 E5
Appleby St DL14 80 D5
Appleby Way SR8 49 A3
Appledore Gdns
Chester le Street DH3 16 D5
Edmondsley DH7 23 B7
Applegarth Coxhoe DH6 58 A3
Mount Pleasant TS8 159 B8
Appleton Cl DL3 132 F5
Appleton Cres DL15 53 F3
Appleton Rd
Middlesbrough TS5 139 B8
Stockton-on-T TS19 117 F5
Appletree Cl DL2 152 D1
Appletree Gdns TS7 141 B7
Applewood Cl TS27 63 B4
Appley Cl TS16 137 D5
Apsley St TS1 215 A1
Apsley Way TS17 137 F2
Aptec Enterprise Pk DL14 79 D1
Aquinas Ct DL3 133 A6
Arabella Cl TS24 64 E1
Arabella St TS24 64 E1
Arbourcourt Ave DH7 41 D8
Arbroath DH2 8 F1
Arbroath Gr TS25 76 F1
Arc (Theatre & Arts Ctr) TS18 213 A3
Arcadia DH2 8 F1
Arcadia Ave DH3 16 C5
Arcadia Ct 4 DL3 132 F1
Arch Ct TS24 64 C1
Archdeacon Cres DL3 132 B4
Archdeacon Newton DL2 131 E7
Archer Ave DL14 80 A4
Archer Rd DH1 154 A5
Archer St Darlington DL3 132 F2
Thornaby-on-T TS17 213 C1
Archery Rise DH1 210 A1
Archibald Prim Sch TS5 214 A1
Archibald St TS5 214 A1
Arden Cl TS14 143 D2
Arden Gr TS19 117 B2
Arden St DH6 48 C7
Ardmore Dr DL1 133 D7
Ardrossan DH2 8 F1
Ardrossan Ct TS25 77 A1
Ardrossan Rd TS25 77 A1
Arena Bsns Pk DH4 26 C7
Argent St SR8 39 F5
Argory The TS17 157 B8
Argyle Ct DH9 7 A1
Argyle Pl DH6 37 F7
Argyle Rd TS6 121 D6
Argyll DH2 8 F1
Argyll Cl DL1 133 D7
Argyll Rd Hartlepool TS25 77 A1
Marton TS7 140 C3
Stockton-on-T TS20 117 F7
Arisaig DH2 8 F1
Arisaig Cl TS16 156 C8
Ark Royal Cl
Hartlepool TS25 90 E8
Seaton Carew TS25 77 D1
Arken Terr TS20 118 B6
Arkendale TS8 139 D1
Arkendale St DL1 133 A5
Arkgrove Ind Est TS18 118 D5
Arkle Cres DL1 151 F6
Arkley Cres TS24 64 A2
Arlington Cl DH4 17 E3
Arlington Ct TS18 213 A1
Arlington Rd TS5 139 E8
Arlington St Loftus TS13 127 C1
Stockton-on-T TS18 212 C1
Stockton-on-T TS18 213 A1
Armadale TS10 107 E2
Armadale Cl TS19 116 F4
Armadale Gr TS25 76 F1
Armitage Rd TS10 106 E3
Armondside Rd NE17 4 C6
Armoury St 5 DL16 55 F1
Armstrong Ave TS28 60 E8
Armstrong Cl DL5 96 F8
Armstrong Ct DL3 132 D4
Armstrong Ind Est NE37 9 F7
Armstrong Rd SR8 49 D8
Arncliffe Ave TS18 137 F8
Arncliffe Gdns TS26 77 A5
Arncliffe Gr DL2 131 F2
Arncliffe Pl DL5 96 B7
Arncliffe Rd TS5 119 B3
Arndale Ho 14 DH3 9 C4
Arnison Ctr The DH1 34 C8
Arnold Ave TS27 50 D4
Arnold Cl DH9 14 A6
Arnold Gr TS25 76 E2
Arnold Rd DL1 133 C3
Arnold St DL14 79 C1
Arnside Ave TS3 120 D3
Arran Cl TS17 138 C4
Arran Ct
13 Bishop Auckland DL14 80 B6
Silksworth SR3 18 A6
Arran Gr TS25 77 A1
Arran Wlk Darlington DL1 133 D7
Guisborough TS14 143 D3
Arrandale TS8 139 D1
Arrathorne Rd TS18 137 A8
Arrowsmith Sq DL5 96 E7
Artemis Ct DH7 43 D4
Arthur Ave SR2 19 A6
Arthur Pit Cotts DL15 52 C7
Arthur St Beamish DH2 15 A7
Chilton DL17 83 A7
Crook DL15 52 F4
Darlington DL3 132 F4
Eldon Lane DL14 80 F4
Great Ayton TS9 161 A3
Redcar TS10 107 B7
Ryhope SR2 19 A6
Ushaw Moor DH7 32 F2
Arthur Terr
Bishop Auckland DL14 80 B5
Ferryhill DL17 70 C4
New Marske TS11 124 A7
Stanley Crook DL15 40 E1
Arun Cl SR8 49 C5
Arundel Cl DL14 80 A6
Arundel Ct TS17 137 F2
Arundel Dr DL3 132 B5
Arundel Gn TS3 120 D3
Arundel Rd
Billingham TS23 102 D5
Eston TS6 121 E4
Arundel St TS10 107 B7
Arundel Way DH7 43 C4
Arundel Wlk DH2 15 F7
Ascot Ave TS5 119 B1
Ascot Ct DL14 68 D1
Ascot Dr TS18 118 F5
Ascot Pl DH2 15 F8
Ascot Rd Consett DH8 10 E7
Redcar TS10 107 D4
Ascot St SR8 39 F4
Ascot View DL1 133 E4
Ash Ave Durham DH1 35 A1
Ushaw Moor DH7 33 A2
Ash Cres Peterlee SR8 50 A6
Seaham SR7 29 C5
Ash Dr DL15 54 C3
Ash Gn TS8 159 C8
Ash Gr Chilton DL17 82 E8
Kirklevington TS15 172 D8
Loftus TS13 127 B2
Shildon DL4 81 A1
South Bank TS6 121 B5
Spennymoor DL16 68 E7
Wingate TS29 60 A5
Ash Hill TS8 140 C1
Ash Mdws NE38 16 E7
Ash Rd TS14 143 E5
Ash St Billingham TS23 103 E2
Consett DH8 10 F2
12 Langley Park DH7 32 C6
Ash Terr
Annfield Plain DH9 12 E5
Bowburn DH6 57 D8
Cornforth DL17 70 E8
Leadgate DH8 11 D4
Murton SR7 28 D3
Tantobie DH9 6 B2
The Middles DH9 14 B3
Ash Tree Cl
Darlington DL3 132 B2
Newton Aycliffe DL5 82 B1
Ash Tree Terr DH7 22 D7
Ash Trees Sch TS23 102 D6
Ashberry Cl TS12 146 B1
Ashbourne Cl TS6 121 F2
Ashbourne Ct DH6 57 F3
Ashbourne Dr DH6 57 F3
Ashbourne Rd TS19 118 A5
Ashbrook Cl DH7 42 F3
Ashbrooke Ct TS27 61 C4
Ashbrooke Est DH6 48 C6
Ashbrooke Way TS5 119 B2
Ashburn St TS25 90 E8
Ashburton Cl TS8 140 B4
Ashby Cres DH8 10 D5
Ashby Gr TS25 89 E7
Ashby La DH8 10 D4
Ashby Rd TS23 102 D5
Ashcombe Cl TS22 102 A6
Ashcroft DL13 206 C4
Ashcroft Gdns DL14 80 C6
Ashcroft Rd DL3 151 D8
Ashdale Hemlington TS8 139 D1
Penshaw DH4 17 E8
Ashdale Cl DL2 154 C7
Ashdale Rd DH8 11 A3
Ashdown Ave DH1 35 B3
Ashdown Cl TS17 138 C4
Ashdown Way TS23 103 A6
Ashes The TS25 90 E7
Ashfield Consett DH8 10 D6
Newton Aycliffe DL5 96 C6
Ashfield Ave TS4 119 F1
Ashfield Cl TS25 89 E4
Ashfield Ct
13 Darlington DL3 132 F2
High Spen NE39 1 A4
Ashfield Terr DH3 16 D2
Ashford Ave TS5 139 A8
Ashford Cl TS14 143 D2
Ashford Dr DH7 23 B4
Ashford Gr DH6 47 E4
Ashgrove DH2 15 F2
Ashgrove Ave TS25 77 B3
Ashgrove Terr DH3 9 B5
Ashkirk Cl DH2 16 A1
Ashkirk Rd TS6 121 C2
Ashleigh DH2 16 A5
Ashleigh Ave DH1 34 B5
Ashleigh Gr DH7 20 E4
Ashley Ct DH9 13 C8
Ashley Gdns TS24 76 F7
Ashley Terr DH3 16 C4
Ashling Way TS5 214 A1
Ashmore Terr DH6 47 F3
Ashridge Cl
Ingleby Barwick TS17 138 C1
New Marske TS11 123 F6
Ashton Ct DL16 56 A3
Ashton Downe 2 DH2 16 C2
Ashton Rd TS20 117 E8
Ashton Rise
Chester le Street DH2 16 C2
Peterlee SR8 49 E7
Ashton St SR8 39 F4
Ashtree Cl NE39 1 F3
Ashtree La NE21,NE39 1 B5
Ashvale Ave NE11 8 C6
Ashvale Homes TS24 63 C5
Ashville Ave
Eaglescliffe TS16 137 D3
Stockton-on-T TS20 101 F1
Ashville Dr DL2 168 C8
Ashwood
Chester le Street DH3 16 D2
Durham DH1 211 B3
South Hetton DH6 38 A6
Ashwood Cl
Hartlepool TS27 63 C4
7 Ormesby TS7 141 B7
Ashwood Grange DH6 47 C3
Ashwood Mdw SR8 49 F7
Aske Rd
Middlesbrough TS1 214 C2
Redcar TS10 107 D6
Askern Dr TS5 139 E6
Askerton Dr SR8 49 A3
Askew Dale TS14 143 A3
Askham Bryan Coll TS14 143 F5
Askham Cl TS4 119 F1
Askrigg Cl
Newton Aycliffe DL5 96 C8
Urpeth DH2 8 E2
Askrigg Rd TS18 212 B3
Askrigg St DL1 133 A5
Askrigg Wlk 4 TS3 120 C1
Askwith Rd TS5 119 D1
Aspatria Ave 4 TS27 50 D3
Aspen Ave 7 SR8 50 B6
Aspen Cl Durham DH1 35 A3
Shiney Row DH4 17 F5
Spennymoor DL16 68 D7
Aspen Ct Consett DH8 10 E4
Great Lumley DH3 25 A7
Aspen Ct *continued*
Shildon DL4 95 B8
Aspen Dr TS5 119 F1
Aspen Gr DL5 96 A3
Aspen Rd TS16 156 B8
Aspley Cl SR3 18 A6
Asquith St DH6 47 E4
Asquith Terr DH9 12 E5
Association St DL4 80 F2
Astbury Marton TS8 140 E1
Mount Pleasant TS8 159 E8
Astbury Cl NE38 17 B8
Aster Cl TS7 140 B4
Asterley Dr TS5 139 A7
Astley Cl TS19 117 B3
Aston Ave TS3 120 E4
Aston Dr TS17 138 B4
Aston Rd TS22 102 B5
Aston Terr DL3 132 C3
Aston Way NE16 2 F5
Astonbury Gn TS4 140 B6
Athelstan Rigg SR2 19 A7
Atherstone Dr TS14 143 E3
Atherstone Way DL3 132 A5
Atherton Cl DL16 68 F7
Atherton Dr DH4 26 A7
Atherton St DH1 210 B3
Atherton Terr DL14 80 E5
Atherton Way TS15 156 A3
Athlone Pl DH3 9 D1
Athol Gdns SR2 19 A6
Athol Gr SR3 18 A7
Athol St TS1 214 C2
Atholl DH2 8 F2
Atholl Cl DL1 133 D6
Atholl Gr Hartlepool TS25 77 A1
Redcar TS10 107 A5
Atkinson Ct TS24 64 A3
Atkinson Gdns DL5 96 E2
Atkinson Gr DH6 48 B7
Atkinson Rd DH3 16 D5
Atlas Wynd TS15 156 C6
Attingham Cl TS8 139 F2
Attlee Ave TS27 50 F1
Attlee Cres DH6 37 E1
Attlee Ct DL13 183 E1
Attlee Est DL13 183 E1
Attlee Gr SR2 18 E8
Attlee Rd TS6 121 E4
Attlee Sq DH6 35 F2
Attlow Wlk TS3 120 F2
Attwood Pl DL13 183 D1
Attwood Rd DL13 183 D2
Attwood Terr
Spennymoor DL16 56 B4
Wolsingham DL13 207 E5
Atwater Cl TS15 156 D4
Atwick Cl TS23 102 E8
Aubrey St TS1 215 A2
Auckland DH2 16 A3
Auckland Ave
Darlington DL3 132 D5
Marton TS7 140 E3
Auckland Castle* DL14 67 C1
Auckland Ct DL15 53 F2
Auckland Mews DL5 96 E7
Auckland Oval DL3 132 D5
Auckland Park Hospl DL14 80 B6
Auckland Pl DL5 96 E7
Auckland Rd
Billingham TS23 103 A8
Bishop Auckland DL14 80 D5
Durham DH1 34 D7
Ferryhill DL17 70 B6
Auckland St TS14 143 E5
Auckland Terr DL4 80 E2
Auckland View DL14 78 F5
Auckland Way
Hartlepool TS26 76 C5
Stockton-on-T TS18 117 B1
Auckland Wynd DL4 80 E2
Audrey Gr Darlington DL1 133 D1
Stockton-on-T TS18 117 C1
Augusta Cl DL1 133 E6
Augustine Cl DH1 34 A6
Austen Cl TS23 102 D8
Austen Pl DH9 14 B4
Austen Way DL15 52 C3
Austin Ave TS18 212 C1
Auton Cl DH7 33 B3
Auton Field DH7 33 C3
Auton Field Terr DH7 33 C3
Auton Stile DH7 33 B3
Autumn Gr TS19 117 C3
Avalon Ct TS8 139 F2
Avebury Cl TS17 157 C8
Avens Way TS17 138 B2
Avenue 1 DL17 69 E1
Avenue 2 DL17 69 E1
Avenue 3 DL17 69 E1
Avenue 4 DL17 69 D1
Avenue Pl TS14 143 F5
Avenue Prim Sch The TS7 141 A3
Avenue Rd TS24 77 B6
Avenue St DH1 45 B4
Avenue The
Annfield Plain DH9 12 E3
Birtley DH3 9 C4
Bournmoor DH3 17 E6
Brotton TS12 126 C4
Burnhope DH7 21 E5
Chester le Street DH2 16 B3
Consett DH8 11 A2
Coxhoe DH6 58 A4
Durham DH1 210 B2
Eaglescliffe TS16 137 C3
Avenue The *continued*
Eston TS6 121 C3
Guisborough TS14 143 B3
Hetton-le-H DH5 27 B4
Middlesbrough TS5 119 E1
Murton SR7 28 D3
Nunthorpe TS7 141 A3
Pelton DH2 15 E7
Pity Me DH1 34 A7
Redcar TS10 107 D6
Rowlands Gill NE39 1 F1
Seaham SR7 29 A7
Stainton Grove DL12 209 F8
Stockton-on-T TS19 117 B3
Thornaby-on-T TS17 138 D8
Wheatley Hill DH6 47 E3
Avenue Vivian DH4 17 F1
Aviemore Ct DL1 133 F3
Aviemore Rd TS8 139 F2
Avill Gr TS17 157 A6
Avoca Ct TS10 107 B7
Avon Cl Rowlands Gill NE39 1 F3
Skelton TS12 125 D3
Thornaby-on-T TS17 138 D6
Avon Cres DH4 26 A8
Avon Ct DL5 96 B8
Avon Dr TS14 143 D3
Avon Gr TS22 102 A6
Avon Rd
Hurworth-on-T DL2 168 B8
Peterlee SR8 49 C5
Redcar TS10 107 A4
Stanley DH9 13 F5
Stockton-on-T TS20 118 C7
Avon St Easington SR8 39 E4
Saltburn-by-t-S TS12 125 C6
Avon Way DL1 152 A6
Avoncroft Cl SR7 28 D8
Avondale Cl TS6 121 D4
Avondale Gdns TS24 77 B8
Avondale Ho DH2 15 F8
Avondale Rd 2 DH8 10 F3
Avondale Terr DH3 16 C3
Avondene Flats 4 TS24 77 C6
Avro Cl
Marske-by-t-S TS11 108 B1
Stockton-on-T TS18 137 E6
Axbridge Ct TS23 102 D7
Axford Terr NE17 4 B6
Axminster Rd TS8 139 F2
Axton Cl TS17 138 B3
Axwell View NE21 2 C8
Aycliffe Cl TS19 117 A3
Aycliffe Gates DL5 96 E3
Aycliffe Ind Pk DL5 96 C3
Aycliffe La
Brafferton DL1 113 A7
Mordon TS21 84 B1
Aycliffe Rd TS7 140 D3
Aycliffe Village Prim Sch DL5 96 E2
Aycliffe Young Peoples Ctr DL5 97 A7
Aykley Ct DH1 34 A4
Aykley Gn DH1 34 A4
Aykley Heads Bsns Ctr DH1 34 B4
Aykley Heads Sports Gd DH1 34 C4
Aykley Rd DH1 34 B6
Aykley Vale DH1 34 B5
Aylesbury Dr SR3 18 A5
Aylmer Gr DL5 96 C7
Aylsham Cl TS17 157 C8
Aylsham Ct SR3 18 A4
Aylton Dr TS5 139 C3
Aylward Pl DH9 14 B5
Aynsley Terr DH8 10 F3
Ayr Gr TS25 77 A1
Ayresome Grange Rd TS5 214 A1
Ayresome Green La TS5 119 D2
Ayresome Park Rd TS5 119 D2
Ayresome Prim Sch TS1 214 B1
Ayresome Rd TS5 119 B4
Ayresome St TS1 214 B1
Ayresome Way DL1 133 D3
Aysdalegate TS12 145 A2
Aysgarth Cl DL5 96 B7
Aysgarth Rd
Darlington DL1 152 B8
Middlesbrough TS5 119 C1
Stockton-on-T TS18 212 A3
Ayton Cres TS6 121 E1
Ayton Ct
Guisborough TS14 143 D6
Redcar TS10 107 B3
Ayton Dr Darlington DL3 151 D7
Redcar TS10 107 C3
Ayton Pl TS20 118 B5
Ayton Prim Sch NE38 9 F3
Ayton Rd
Thornaby-on-T TS17 138 C6
Washington NE38 9 F4
Azalea Ave 6 SR8 50 B6
Azalia Gr 5 TS10 107 E1
Azalia Rd TS19 118 A5

B

Babbacombe Dr DL17 70 C5
Back Child St TS12 126 B4

Back Church St 5 DL14 ..81 B8
Back Coronation Terr
Coxhoe DH6 ...57 F5
Hetton-le-H DH5 ...27 A2
Back East Par DH8 ...11 A2
Back Eldon Terr DL17 ...70 C4
Back La Bowes DL12 ...203 D8
Crathorne TS15 ...172 F3
9 Darlington DL1 ...133 A1
Eaglescliffe TS16 ...156 C7
Great Ayton TS9 ...161 B6
Great Lumley DH3 ...25 A8
Great Stainton TS21 ...98 D1
Headlam DL2 ...201 D6
Leadgate DH8 ...11 F2
Longnewton TS21 ...135 F7
Low Coniscliffe DL2 ...150 D8
Low Worsall TS15 ...171 E6
Satley DL7,DL13 ...183 E6
Skelton TS12 ...125 A1
Walworth DL2 ...111 C3
Back Loud Terr DH9 ...12 D4
Back Mount Joy DH1 ...211 A1
Back North Railway St SR7 ...29 D8
Back North Terr SR7 ...29 D8
Back Palmerston St DH8 ...10 F2
Back Ryhope St SR2 ...18 E7
Back Silver St DH1 ...210 C3
Back South Railway St SR7 ...29 D7
Back Sussex St DL14 ...81 D8
Back Throston St TS24 ...77 F8
Back Victoria Terr DH9 ...12 E5
Back Western Hill DH1 ...210 B3
Back Wynyard Gr DH1 ...211 C3
Backhouse St DL1 ...133 A1
Backhouse Wlk DL5 ...96 E6
Backstone Burn DH8 ...10 C5
Backstone Rd DH8 ...10 C4
Bacon Wlk TS25 ...76 D2
Baden St
Chester le Street DH3 ...16 C2
Hartlepool TS26 ...77 A4
Bader Ave TS17 ...138 C4
Bader Inf Sch TS17 ...138 C4
Bader Prim Sch TS17 ...138 C4
Badger Cl SR3 ...18 A5
Badger Hill Prim Sch TS12 ...126 C4
Badger La TS17 ...138 C2
Badger's Wood DH9 ...7 A1
Badminton Cl DL1 ...133 F4
Badminton Gr DL5 ...82 E1
Badsworth Cl TS14 ...143 D2
Baff St DL16 ...68 F8
Baffin Ct TS17 ...138 D4
Bail Hill Rd DL12 ...193 B1
Bailey Gr TS3 ...120 C3
Bailey Rise SR8 ...49 D8
Bailey St Hartlepool TS26 ...77 B5
Tantobie DH9 ...6 B2
Bailey Way DH5 ...27 B2
Bainbridge Ave DL15 ...54 A3
Bainbridge Ct DL14 ...79 D2
Bainbridge St DH1 ...35 D4
Bainton Cl TS23 ...102 E8
Bakehouse Hill
Bishop Auckland DL14 ...67 C1
10 Darlington DL1 ...132 F1
Bakehouse La DH1 ...211 A3
Bakehouse Sq TS14 ...143 E4
Baker Cl TS27 ...63 D3
Baker St Leadgate DH8 ...11 C4
Middlesbrough TS1 ...214 C3
Bakers Ct DL3 ...132 F2
Bakery Dr TS19 ...117 D5
Bakery Ho TS19 ...117 D5
Bakery St TS18 ...213 A3
Bakewell Pl DL5 ...96 C8
Bala Cl TS17 ...156 E8
Balaclava St TS18 ...213 A4
Balcary Ct TS25 ...89 F8
Balder Rd TS20 ...118 A8
Baldoon Sands TS5 ...139 B4
Baldwin St SR8 ...39 F4
Bale Hill DH8 ...174 F3
Balfour Gdns 4 DH8 ...10 F4
Balfour St DH8 ...10 F4
Balfour Terr Chopwell NE17 ...4 B8
Middlesbrough TS5 ...139 B8
Baliol Croft TS21 ...136 A6
Baliol Gn DL5 ...96 E5
Baliol Rd DL5 ...96 E5
Baliol Sq DH1 ...44 A7
Baliol St DL12 ...209 C6
Ballarat The DL5 ...82 D1
Ballater Cl DH9 ...14 B6
Ballater Gr TS25 ...90 A8
Balliol Cl SR8 ...49 B5
Balliol Ct 2 DL1 ...133 B6
Balmer Hill DL2 ...201 C4
Balmor Rd TS6 ...121 C2
Balmoral DH3 ...25 A8
Balmoral Ave
Billingham TS23 ...102 E5
Thornaby-on-T TS17 ...138 D8
Balmoral Cres DH5 ...26 F7
Balmoral Ct TS25 ...90 A8
Balmoral Dr
Middlesbrough TS4 ...120 A1
Peterlee SR8 ...49 A3
Balmoral Gr
Bishop Auckland DL14 ...80 A6
Consett DH8 ...11 A4
Balmoral Rd
Darlington DL1 ...133 D6
Ferryhill DL17 ...70 B7
Hartlepool TS25 ...89 F8
Lingdale TS12 ...145 F5
Middlesbrough TS3 ...140 F8
Balmoral Terr
Saltburn-by-t-S TS12 ...125 D7
Stockton-on-T TS18 ...212 C1
Trimdon TS29 ...59 D3
Baltic Cl TS18 ...213 B4
Baltic Rd TS18 ...213 B4
Baltic St TS25 ...77 C4
Baltic The DL14 ...79 A8
Baltimore Way DL1 ...133 B6
Bamborough 6 TS4 ...120 B1
Bamburgh Ave
Bishop Auckland DL14 ...80 A6
Peterlee SR8 ...49 F8
Bamburgh Cl TS10 ...107 E4
Bamburgh Cres DL5 ...82 E1
Bamburgh Ct TS27 ...63 D3
Bamburgh Dr TS7 ...141 A7
Bamburgh Par
3 Spennymoor DL16 ...68 F8
Spennymoor DL16 ...69 A8
Bamburgh Pl DL1 ...133 C5
Bamburgh Rd
Durham DH1 ...34 C7
Ferryhill DL17 ...70 B7
Hartlepool TS27 ...63 D3
Bamford Rd TS17 ...138 C6
Banbury Gr TS5 ...139 B6
Banesley La NE11 ...8 A8
Banff Gr TS25 ...90 A8
Bangor Cl TS6 ...121 E4
Bangor Gr DL1 ...133 E5
Bangor St TS26 ...77 A4
Bank Foot Gr DL15 ...52 D5
Bank Rd TS23 ...102 D1
Bank Sands TS5 ...139 B3
Bank Side DL12 ...208 F2
Bank St TS10 ...107 C7
Bank Terr TS21 ...100 E3
Bank The DL12 ...209 C5
Bank Top DL17 ...71 B3
Bank Top Mews DL1 ...152 B8
Bank Top Terr TS29 ...59 D1
Bank Well DL14 ...78 F6
Bankfields Ct TS6 ...141 D8
Bankfields Prim Sch TS6 ...121 E1
Bankfields Rd Eston TS6 ...121 E1
Normanby TS6 ...141 D8
Bankhead Terr DH4 ...26 A8
Banklands Ct DL3 ...132 D4
Banklands Rd DL3 ...132 D4
Banks Holt DH2 ...15 F2
Banks Rd DL1 ...133 D2
Banks Terr DL2 ...168 A8
Bankside TS15 ...156 E6
Bankside Cl SR2 ...18 E7
Bankside Ct 6 TS6 ...121 F1
Bankston Cl TS26 ...76 C7
Bankwell Dr DL14 ...78 F6
Bannerman Terr
Sherburn Hill DH6 ...36 C1
3 Ushaw Moor DH7 ...32 F2
Bannockburn Way TS23 ...102 F7
Baptist St TS24 ...77 F8
Barbara Mann Ct TS26 ...77 B6
Barbary Cl DH2 ...15 E7
Barberry TS8 ...159 C8
Barberry Cl TS17 ...138 C2
Barcusclose La DH9,NE16 ...6 D5
Barden Moor Rd DL1 ...152 C7
Barden Rd TS3 ...120 C2
Bardsey Wlk TS14 ...143 D2
Bardsley Cl TS16 ...137 D5
Barford Cl Hartlepool TS25 ...89 E6
Redcar TS10 ...107 B2
Stockton-on-T TS20 ...101 E1
Barford Dr DH2 ...16 A1
Bargate Bank DH7 ...30 F8
Barholm Cl TS3 ...120 F1
Baring Ct DL13 ...183 D1
Barker Rd
Middlesbrough TS5 ...119 C1
Thornaby-on-T TS17 ...138 D8
Barker's Bldgs DH6 ...57 F3
Barkery The TS8 ...159 C5
Barkston Ave TS17 ...138 B3
Barkston Cl TS22 ...102 C6
Barkwood Rd NE39 ...1 D2
Barlborough Ave TS19 ...212 A4
Barle Cl TS17 ...157 B6
Barley Cl TS26 ...76 E7
Barley Hill Cl TS6 ...141 E8
Barley Mill Cres DH8 ...10 B4
Barley Mill Rd DH8 ...10 B4
Barley Mow DH3 ...16 D8
Barley Mow Prim Sch DH3 ...9 D1
Barlow Cl TS14 ...143 E3
Barlow Cres NE21 ...1 C6
Barlow Ct TS23 ...102 E7
Barlow Fell Rd NE21 ...1 C5
Barlow La NE21 ...1 E7
Barlow Rd NE21 ...1 C6
Barlow St DL3 ...132 D3
Barlowfield Cl NE21 ...2 A8
Barmoor Gr TS20 ...102 A2
Barmouth Rd TS6 ...121 E3
Barmpton La DL1 ...133 E7
Barmpton Mews DL1 ...133 F7
Barmton Rd TS23 ...102 E7
Barn Hill DH9 ...13 E7
Barn Hollows SR7 ...39 C7
Barn The 3 DH2 ...16 B1
Barnaby Ave TS5 ...214 A1
Barnaby Cl 2 TS11 ...124 E8
Barnaby Cres TS6 ...121 F1
Barnaby Pl TS14 ...143 C5
Barnaby Rd TS7 ...141 B3
Barnack Ave TS7 ...140 E4
Barnard Ave
Bishop Auckland DL14 ...80 B6
Ludworth DH6 ...47 C7
Stockton-on-T TS19 ...117 C2
Barnard Castle* DL12 ...209 B6
Barnard Castle CE Prim Sch DL12 ...209 D6
Barnard Castle Sch DL12 ...209 D5
Barnard Cl Durham DH1 ...34 D7
Newton Aycliffe DL5 ...82 E1
Spennymoor DL16 ...56 A2
Thornaby-on-T TS17 ...213 C1
Barnard Ct
Bournmoor DH4 ...17 D1
4 Middlesbrough TS4 ...120 A1
Barnard Gr
Hartlepool TS24 ...63 D4
Redcar TS10 ...107 E5
Barnard Grove Prim Sch TS24 ...63 D4
Barnard Pk DH5 ...27 A4
Barnard Rd
Billingham TS23 ...102 E4
Ferryhill DL17 ...70 B7
Barnard St
Darlington DL3 ...132 F2
5 Staindrop DL2 ...200 E7
Barnard Wynd SR8 ...49 B3
Barnes Cl DL3 ...132 B3
Barnes Ct TS24 ...63 E3
Barnes Rd Darlington DL3 ...132 B3
Murton SR7 ...28 C3
Barnes St DH5 ...27 A4
Barnes Wallis Way TS11 ...108 B2
Barnes Wlk 4 DL5 ...96 D8
Barnet Way TS23 ...103 A7
Barnett Sq DH6 ...37 F2
Barnfield Rd DL16 ...56 A1
Barnfield Way DL15 ...54 B4
Barningham Rd DL11 ...205 C5
Barningham St DL3 ...132 F3
Barns The DH9 ...13 F7
Barnstaple Cl TS8 ...140 B5
Barnstones DH2 ...24 A4
Baronport Gn 2 TS18 ...213 C4
Barr Hills 6 DH8 ...10 F3
Barr House Ave DH8 ...10 F3
Barra Gr TS25 ...90 A8
Barrack Terr NE11 ...8 D6
Barras Gr TS3 ...120 F3
Barras Way TS19 ...117 A6
Barrasford Rd DH1 ...34 D6
Barratt Way DL17 ...57 E2
Barrett Rd DL3 ...132 B1
Barrhead Cl TS19 ...116 F4
Barrington Ave TS19 ...117 C4
Barrington Cres TS3 ...120 F3
Barrington Ct
Hetton-le-H DH5 ...27 A4
Stanhope DL13 ...206 C4
Barrington Mdws DL14 ...79 F6
Barrington Rd DL5 ...96 C6
Barrington St DL14 ...67 A2
Barrington Terr
Ferryhill DL17 ...69 E6
Hetton-le-H DH5 ...27 A5
Barritt St TS1 ...214 C2
Barron St DL3 ...132 F4
Barron's Way DH7 ...21 D5
Barrowburn Gn TS17 ...157 A7
Barsby Gn 4 TS3 ...120 C2
Barsford Rd TS3 ...120 F3
Barsloan Gr SR8 ...49 B8
Bartlemere DL12 ...209 D6
Bartlett St DL3 ...132 F3
Bartol Ct 5 TS6 ...121 F1
Barton Ave TS25 ...77 A3
Barton Cl
Newton Aycliffe DL5 ...96 B8
Thornaby-on-T TS17 ...138 B3
Barton Cres TS22 ...102 B5
Barton Pk SR2 ...18 D7
Barton Rd TS2 ...119 C7
Barton St DL1 ...133 B4
Barwick Cl TS17 ...138 B2
Barwick Fields TS17 ...138 B1
Barwick La TS17 ...157 A7
Barwick St
Cold Hesledon SR7 ...28 E1
Easington SR8 ...39 F4
Barwick View TS17 ...138 B2
Barwick Way TS17 ...157 B7
Basic Cotts DH6 ...57 F5
Basil St TS3 ...215 C2
Basildon Gn TS3 ...120 D3
Basingstoke Rd SR8 ...49 C7
Bassenthwaite TS5 ...139 B4
Bassenthwaite Ave 4 DH2 ...16 B1
Bassenthwaite Gr DL14 ...79 B1
Bassleton La TS17 ...138 B4
Bates Ave DL3 ...132 C5
Bates Cl DL5 ...96 C8
Batey St DH9 ...12 E5
Bath La Consett DH8 ...10 F3
Stockton-on-T TS18 ...213 B3
Bath Pl TS18 ...213 B3
Bath Rd TS6 ...121 E2
Bath St Redcar TS10 ...107 C7
Bath St *continued*
Saltburn-by-t-S TS12 ...125 C7
Bath Terr Hartlepool TS24 ...64 G8
Seaham SR7 ...29 D8
Bathgate Terr 1 TS24 ...77 B4
Batt La DL5 ...95 C1
Battersby Cl TS15 ...156 F5
Battersby Gn TS21 ...116 C8
Battle Gn DH2 ...15 E5
Batts Terr DL14 ...67 C1
Batts The DL13 ...188 B7
Baxby Terr DL2 ...168 A8
Baxton Cotts DH8 ...10 C4
Bay Ave SR8 ...50 B6
Bay Ct DH7 ...33 B1
Bay Tree Rd DL1 ...133 A8
Bayberry Mews TS5 ...139 D8
Baydale Rd DL3 ...151 B8
Baysdale DH4 ...17 E8
Baysdale Cl
Bishop Auckland DL14 ...79 E6
Guisborough TS14 ...143 F4
Baysdale Ct TS12 ...125 D3
Baysdale Gdns DL4 ...81 C1
Baysdale Gr TS10 ...106 F4
Baysdale Rd TS17 ...138 D6
Baysdale Wlk Eston TS6 ...122 A3
Middlesbrough TS5 ...139 E6
Baytree Terr DH2 ...15 B7
Beach Gr SR8 ...50 B6
Beach Rd TS13 ...127 A4
Beachdale Cl TS28 ...60 F5
Beachfield Dr TS25 ...77 A3
Beacon Ave TS21 ...85 C6
Beacon Dr TS11 ...124 A6
Beacon Grange Pk DL2 ...134 E6
Beacon Hill DL1 ...134 D6
Beacon La TS21 ...85 C6
Beacon St TS24 ...64 F1
Beacons La TS17 ...156 F8
Beaconsfield Ct DL12 ...209 C6
Beaconsfield Rd TS20 ...102 B1
Beaconsfield Sq TS24 ...64 F1
Beaconsfield St
2 Consett DH8 ...10 F4
Darlington DL3 ...132 E3
Hartlepool TS24 ...64 F1
Stanley DH9 ...13 F7
Beaconsfield Terr DH3 ...9 B4
Beadlam Ave TS7 ...141 B3
Beadnell Cl Blaydon NE21 ...2 A8
3 Chester le Street DH2 ...16 A1
Ingleby Barwick TS17 ...138 C1
Beadnell Way TS10 ...107 F3
Beadon Gr TS5 ...119 B2
Beagle Sq 6 SR3 ...18 A7
Beal Wlk DH1 ...45 B5
Beale Cl TS17 ...138 C1
Beamish Cl DH7 ...32 B6
Beamish Ct Pelton DH2 ...15 C6
Stanley DH9 ...13 E6
Beamish Hills DH9 ...14 D7
Beamish North of England Open Air Mus* DH9 ...7 D2
Beamish Prim Sch DH9 ...14 D7
Beamish Rd TS23 ...103 A6
Beamish St DH9 ...13 E7
Beamish View Birtley DH3 ...9 E5
Chester le Street DH2 ...15 C3
Stanley DH9 ...14 C7
Beamishburn Rd DH9,NE16 ...7 B3
Beaney La
Kimblesworth DH2 ...24 A6
Waldridge DH2 ...23 F6
Beardmore Ave TS11 ...108 B2
Bearpark Colliery Rd DH7 ...33 C3
Bearpark Prim Sch DH7 ...33 B4
Beath Gr TS25 ...90 A8
Beatrice Terr DH4 ...17 E8
Beaufort Cl TS14 ...143 E2
Beaufort St TS1 ...214 C3
Beauly Dr DL1 ...133 C7
Beauly Gr TS25 ...90 A8
Beaumaris DH4 ...17 D3
Beaumaris Dr TS16 ...156 C8
Beaumont Cl Durham DH1 ...34 A7
Newton Aycliffe DL5 ...82 D1
Beaumont Cres SR8 ...39 E1
Beaumont Ct TS21 ...85 C6
Beaumont Hill DL1 ...113 A2
Beaumont Hill Sch DL1 ...133 B8
Beaumont Pl SR8 ...49 E5
Beaumont Rd TS3 ...120 C4
Beaumont Sq DL5 ...96 D3
Beaumont St
9 Bishop Auckland DL14 ...80 B6
Darlington DL1 ...132 F1
Ferryhill DL17 ...69 E6
Seaham SR7 ...29 D6
Beaumont St W DL1 ...132 F1
Beaumont View TS20 ...118 C7
Beaumont Way DL5 ...96 D3
Beaurepaire DH7 ...33 A3
Beaver Cl Durham DH1 ...34 C8
Ingleby Barwick TS17 ...138 C2
Beaver Ct TS6 ...121 B5
Beccles Cl TS19 ...117 B5
Beck Pl SR8 ...49 D7
Beck Rd DL1 ...133 A3
Beckenham Gdns TS8 ...139 F1
Beckett Cl DL14 ...79 E7
Beckfields Ave TS17 ...157 B8
Beckfields Ctr TS17 ...157 C8
Beckside Mews 12 DL2 ...200 E7
Beckston Cl TS26 ...76 C6
Beckwith Dr TS29 ...59 D1
Beckwith Rd TS15 ...156 B3
Beckwith's La DL16 ...69 A3
Beda Cotts DH9 ...6 A2
Bedale Ave TS23 ...102 E2
Bedale Cl DH1 ...35 D4
Bedale Gr TS19 ...117 A2
Bedale Hunt DL5 ...95 F8
Bedale St DH5 ...27 A2
Bedburn NE38 ...9 F1
Bedburn Cl DL15 ...53 A3
Bedburn Dr
Bishop Auckland DL14 ...79 E5
Darlington DL3 ...131 F2
Bedburn Rd DL13 ...189 D2
Beddow Ct DL14 ...66 A1
Bede Ave DH1 ...35 B1
Bede Cl Escomb DL14 ...66 D1
Stanley DH9 ...14 B7
Stockton-on-T TS19 ...117 D6
Bede Coll TS23 ...102 E6
Bede Cres DL5 ...96 D5
Bede Ct DH3 ...16 C3
Bede Gr Cornforth DL17 ...57 D1
Hartlepool TS25 ...76 F3
Bede Kirk DL12 ...209 D7
Bede Pl DL16 ...69 A3
Bede Rd
Barnard Castle DL12 ...209 D7
Darlington DL3 ...132 B1
Bede St SR8 ...39 F4
Bede Terr Bowburn DH6 ...45 D1
Chester le Street DH2 ...16 B3
1 Ferryhill DL17 ...70 A5
Bede Way Durham DH1 ...34 C6
Peterlee SR8 ...49 D6
Peterlee SR8 ...49 E5
Bedford Ave Birtley DH3 ...9 D1
Chester le Street DH3 ...16 D8
Bedford Pl
Bishop Auckland DL14 ...80 B5
New Silksworth SR3 ...18 A8
Peterlee SR8 ...49 C8
Willington DL15 ...54 A3
Bedford Rd TS7 ...141 A3
Bedford St
Darlington DL1 ...152 A8
Hartlepool TS24 ...77 F8
Hetton-le-H DH5 ...26 F4
Middlesbrough TS1 ...214 C3
Stockton-on-T TS19 ...212 C4
Bedford Terr
Billingham TS23 ...102 E3
Wolsingham DL13 ...207 D5
Bedfordshire Dr DH1 ...35 D3
Bedlington Wlk TS23 ...102 D8
Beech Ave
Blackhall Rocks TS27 ...50 E2
Chilton DL17 ...82 E8
Crook DL15 ...52 E4
4 Houghton-le-S DH4 ...26 D8
Murton SR7 ...28 D3
Redcar TS10 ...107 E6
Spennymoor DL16 ...68 E7
Beech Cl Durham DH1 ...34 E8
Great Ayton TS9 ...160 F2
Beech Cres Ferryhill DL17 ...70 A5
Heighington DL5 ...95 E2
Seaham SR7 ...29 C5
Beech Crest DH1 ...210 B2
Beech Ct Langley Park DH7 ...32 C6
Stockton-on-T TS19 ...117 C5
Beech Field TS8 ...140 B1
Beech Gr Blackhall Mill NE17 ...4 B6
Brotton TS12 ...126 A5
Burnhope DH7 ...21 D4
Dipton DH9 ...12 C7
Ferryhill DL17 ...70 A5
Loftus TS13 ...127 B1
Maltby TS8 ...157 F8
South Bank TS6 ...121 B4
Trimdon TS29 ...59 E3
Ushaw Moor DH7 ...33 B1
Wingate TS29 ...60 A5
Witton-le-W DL14 ...65 B3
Beech Grove Prim Sch TS6 ...121 B4
Beech Grove Rd TS5 ...139 E8
Beech Oval TS21 ...85 B7
Beech Par DL17 ...57 E1
Beech Pk DH7 ...43 A3
Beech Rd
Bishop Auckland DL14 ...80 C7
Darlington DL1 ...133 E6
Durham DH1 ...34 B5
Guisborough TS14 ...143 E5
Leadgate DH8 ...11 D3
Sherburn DH6 ...35 F2
Beech Rise DL1 ...133 E6
Beech St TS1 ...215 A3
Beech Terr
Annfield Plain DH9 ...12 E5
Burnopfield NE16 ...6 C6
Eldon Lane DL14 ...80 F4
Middlesbrough TS2 ...103 E1
4 Peterlee SR8 ...50 A6
Stanley DH9 ...13 E4
The Middles DH9 ...14 B3
Beech View DH1 ...45 D7
Beechbrooke SR2 ...18 F6
Beechburn Pk DL15 ...52 F2
Beechcroft Ave DH7 ...42 F3
Beechcroft Cl
Durham DH1 ...35 A3
Lingdale TS12 ...145 E5
Beechdale Rd
Consett DH8 ...11 A3
Durham DH1 ...35 D4
Beechers Gr DL5 ...82 E2
Beeches Rise TS7 ...140 E4

Beeches The TS6 ....121 C3
Beechfield
Mount Pleasant TS8 ......159 B8
Newton Aycliffe DL5 ......96 B6
Beechfield Rise DH6 ......58 A5
Beechgrove La DH2,DH7 . .14 F2
Beechgrove Terr DH9 .....14 E1
Beechside DL2 ....200 F7
Beechtree Ct TS15 ......156 B7
Beechways DH1 ....33 F3
Beechwood NE39 ....1 A2
Beechwood Ave
Darlington DL3 ....132 E1
Middlesbrough TS4 ....140 A8
Saltburn-by-t-S TS12 ......125 C6
Beechwood Dr DL14 .....80 C5
Beechwood Prim Sch
TS4 ....140 A8
Beechwood Rd
Eaglescliffe TS16 ....137 C4
Fishburn TS21 ....72 C4
Thornaby-on-T TS17 ....138 C7
Beechwoods DH2 ....16 B5
Beeford Cl TS23 ....88 E1
Beeford Dr TS5 ....139 E6
Beehive Workshops DH1 .35 B2
Bek Rd Durham DH1 ....34 C6
Newton Aycliffe DL5 ....96 E7
Belasis Ave TS23 ....103 A2
Belasis Ct TS23 ....103 A3
Belasis Hall Tech Pk
TS23 ....103 B3
Belford Cl TS19 ....117 C4
Belford Gdns DL1 ....133 C6
Belford St SR8 ....39 F1
Belford Way DL5 ....95 F7
Belgrave Ave DH6 ....58 A3
Belgrave Ct Coxhoe DH6 ...58 A3
Hartlepool TS25 ....90 E8
Belgrave Dr TS6 ....141 C7
Belgrave St DL1 ....152 B8
Belgrave Terr DL2 ....168 A8
Belk Cl TS6 ....121 D5
Belk St Hartlepool TS24 ......77 B7
Middlesbrough TS1 ....214 C1
Bell Cl TS18 ....212 C2
Bell Mdw DH7 ....43 A3
Bell Sq TS21 ....99 E3
Bell St
Bishop Auckland DL14 ......80 B6
Cornforth DL17 ....57 D1
Crook DL15 ....52 F3
Middlesbrough TS5 ....214 A1
9 Stockton-on-T TS20 ....118 B5
Bell Wlk DL5 ....96 F6
Bell's Folly DH1 ....44 A7
Bell's Pl DL3 ....132 F2
Bellamy Ct TS3 ....120 D3
Bellasis Cl DL5 ....96 E7
Bellasis Gr TS27 ....63 D3
Bellburn La DL3 ....132 E5
Belle St DH9 ....13 F6
Belle View Dr 2 DH8 .....177 A3
Belle Vue Crook DL15 ......52 F3
Eggleston DL12 ....193 E2
Frosterley DL13 ....188 A7
Quarrington Hill DH6 ....58 D8
Belle Vue Ct Durham DH1 . .35 B3
Stockton-on-T TS20 ....118 B6
Belle Vue Gdns 7 DH8 .....10 F3
Belle Vue Gr TS4 ....120 B1
Belle Vue Ho 11 TS20 ....118 B6
Belle Vue Rd TS5 ....119 D2
Belle Vue St DL16 ....68 E7
Belle Vue Terr
Carlin How TS13 ....126 F3
Durham DH1 ....35 B3
Hunwick DL15 ....66 E6
1 Middleton St George
DL2 ....153 F7
Willington DL15 ....53 F3
Belle Vue Way TS25 ....77 C3
Bellerby Dr DH2 ....8 E2
Bellerby Rd TS18 ....117 B1
Bellister Pk SR8 ....49 E4
Bellows Burn La TS27 ......62 B5
Bells Bldgs 6 DH9 ....12 F5
Bells Pl 4 DH9 ....12 F5
Bells Wood Ct DH8 ....10 D4
Bells' Ville DH1 ....35 A2
Bellwood Ave TS12 ....145 D6
Bellwood Terr DH8 ....11 D3
Belmangate TS14 ....143 F3
Belmont Ave
Billingham TS22 ....102 C5
Eston TS6 ....121 B3
Hawthorn SR7 ....39 B8
Middlesbrough TS5 ....139 D3
Stockton-on-T TS19 ....117 F5
Belmont Bsns Pk DH1 ....35 B4
Belmont CE Jun Sch
DH1 ....35 C3
Belmont Cheveley Park Prim
Sch DH1 ....35 E4
Belmont Comp Sch DH1 . .35 C3
Belmont Gdns TS26 ....77 A5
Belmont Ho DH1 ....35 C3
Belmont Ind Est DH1 .....35 B4
Belmont Inf Sch DH1 .....35 C3
Belmont Prim Sch TS14 .143 F3
Belmont Rise DH5 ....27 A1
Belmont St TS6 ....121 F2
Belmont Terr TS14 ....143 F4
Belmont Villa DH1 ....35 C3
Belmonte Ave TS27 ....50 F2
Belsay NE38 ....9 F4
Belsay Ave SR8 ....49 F8
Belsay Cl Ferryhill DL17 ....70 B6
Belsay Cl *continued*
Stockton-on-T TS19 ....117 C4
Belsay Ct TS21 ....85 A7
Belsay Wlk DL1 ....133 C6
Belton Dr TS5 ....139 E6
Belvedere Rd
Darlington DL1 ....152 A8
6 Middlesbrough TS4 ....120 A1
11 Thornaby-on-T TS17 ...138 D8
Belverdere Gdns DH6 ......48 B7
Belvoir Gr DL14 ....80 A6
Benbow Wlk DL14 ....81 B8
Bendle Terr DL12 ....193 B2
Benedict St TS3 ....215 C2
Benevente St 2 SR7 ....29 D6
Benfield Cl DH8 ....10 D6
Benfieldside Prim Sch
DH8 ....10 C5
Benfieldside Rd DH8 .....10 C6
Beningborough Gdns
TS17 ....138 B1
Benmore Rd TS25 ....90 A8
Bennett Rd TS25 ....76 D3
Bennison Cres TS10 .....106 F4
Bennison St TS14 ....143 E5
Benridge Bank DH4 ....26 A2
Benridge Cl TS5 ....139 B5
Bensham Rd DL1 ....133 B7
Benson St
Chester le Street DH3 ......16 C2
4 Hartlepool TS26 ....77 A5
Middlesbrough TS5 ....119 E2
Stanley DH9 ....13 E7
Stockton-on-T TS20 ....118 B8
Bent House La DH1 ....45 A8
Bentick St TS26 ....77 A6
Bentinck Ave TS5 ....139 E8
Bentinck Rd TS19 ....117 B3
Bentley Ave TS23 ....103 B5
Bentley St 5 TS26 ....77 A5
Bentley Wynd TS15 ....156 B6
Benton Cl TS23 ....102 E8
Benton Rd TS5 ....139 E7
Benton Terr DH9 ....13 F7
Bents La DL13 ....179 B2
Benville Terr DH7 ....42 E8
Benwell Cl TS19 ....117 C4
Berberis Gr TS19 ....117 C3
Beresford Cres TS3 ....120 F3
Beresford St DL4 ....95 A7
Berkeley Ave TS25 ....90 A7
Berkeley Cl TS23 ....102 D5
Berkeley Dr TS10 ....107 E3
Berkeley Gr DL14 ....80 A6
Berkeley Rd DL1 ....152 A7
Berkley Dr TS14 ....143 F2
Berkshire Cl DH1 ....35 C3
Berkshire Ho TS6 ....121 E3
Berkshire Rd Peterlee SR8 .49 C8
Stockton-on-T TS20 ....118 C7
Berksyde DH8 ....11 A1
Bernaldby Ave TS14 ......143 C3
Bernard Gilpin Prim Sch
DH5 ....26 E8
Bernard Shaw St 8 DH4 .26 D8
Bernard St DH4 ....26 D8
Bernard Terr DH2 ....15 E5
Berner St TS5 ....119 D2
Bernera Ct DL1 ....133 D7
Bernica Gr TS17 ....157 A7
Berriedale Dr DL1 ....133 B7
Berrington Gdns 2
TS17 ....157 B8
Berry Ave TS29 ....59 E4
Berry Bank DL11,DL2 .....201 A2
Berry Edge Factories
DH8 ....10 E2
Berry Edge Rd DH8 ....10 F2
Berry Edge View DH8 .....10 E3
Berrybank Crest DL3 ....132 B4
Berryfield Cl SR3 ....18 A5
Bertha St Consett DH8 .....10 F3
Ferryhill DL17 ....70 A5
Hartlepool TS26 ....77 C4
Bertie Rd DL5 ....96 C7
Bertram St 3 DH3 ....9 C4
Berwick NE38 ....9 F4
Berwick Chase SR8 ....49 B3
Berwick Ct TS29 ....59 E4
Berwick Gr TS20 ....102 A1
Berwick Hills Ave TS3 ...120 F3
Berwick Hills Prim Sch
TS3 ....120 C2
Berwick Rd DL3 ....132 B5
Berwick St TS25 ....90 E8
Berwick Wlk TS10 ....107 E4
Bessemer Ct TS6 ....121 D7
Bessemer Rd DH6 ....37 F7
Bessemer St Consett DH8 . .10 E3
Ferryhill DL17 ....69 E5
Best's Yd DH7 ....33 A8
Bethany Gdns DH9 ....12 F5
Bethany Terr 1 DH9 ....12 F5
Bethune Ave SR7 ....29 A7
Bethune Rd TS5 ....119 B2
Betjeman Cl
1 Billingham TS23 ....102 E8
Stanley DH9 ....14 A6
Bevan Ave SR2 ....18 E6
Bevan Cres DH6 ....47 E1
Bevan Gr Durham DH1 ......35 B3
Shotton Colliery DH6 ......48 C6
Bevan Sq SR7 ....28 C4
Bevanlee Rd TS6 ....121 B5
Beveridge Arc DL5 ....96 D7
Beveridge Cl TS21 ....72 C5
Beveridge Way DL5 ....96 D7
Beverley Dr NE21 ....1 F8
Beverley Gdns
Chester le Street DH3 ......16 D2
Chilton DL17 ....82 F8
4 Consett, Blackfyne DH8 . .10 F3
Consett, Blackhill DH8 .....10 D5
Beverley Rd
Billingham TS23 ....102 F8
Middlesbrough TS4 ....139 F7
Nunthorpe TS7 ....141 B3
Redcar TS10 ....107 F4
Beverley Sch TS4 ....139 F7
Beverley Terr
Annfield Plain DH9 ....12 E5
5 Consett DH8 ....10 F3
Beverley Way SR8 ....49 C7
Bevin Gr TS27 ....50 F2
Bevin Sq DH6 ....38 B7
Bewholme Cl TS23 ....88 E1
Bewick Cl DH2 ....24 A8
Bewick Cres DL5 ....96 D6
Bewicke Maine Cvn Site
DH2 ....8 E5
Bewicke View DH3 ....9 D5
Bewley Gr
Middlesbrough TS5 ....139 C6
Peterlee SR8 ....49 A3
Bewley Inf Sch TS23 ....103 A7
Bewley Jun Sch TS23 ...103 A7
Bewley Terr DH7 ....42 E8
Bexley Cl TS4 ....140 B6
Bexley Dr Hartlepool TS25 . .77 B2
Normanby TS6 ....141 D7
Bglws The DL15 ....52 E4
Bickersteth Cl TS18 ......213 A1
Bickersteth Wlk TS18 ...213 A1
Bickford Terr DL5 ....96 E2
Bickley Cl TS22 ....102 A5
Bickley Way TS8 ....140 B2
Biddick Cl TS19 ....117 C4
Biddick La NE38 ....17 D8
Bielby Ave TS23 ....102 E8
Biggin Cl TS5 ....139 E6
Bigland Terr DL14 ....80 D5
Billingham Bank TS23 ...102 D1
Billingham Beck Valley
Country Pk* TS23 .....118 D8
Billingham Beck Valley Ctry
Pk* TS23 ....102 C2
Billingham Beck Valley Ctry
Pk Visitor Ctr* TS23 ...102 C2
Billingham Campus Sch
TS23 ....102 F7
Billingham Halt TS23 ....102 F4
Billingham Rd TS20 ......102 C1
Billingham South Com Prim
Sch TS23 ....102 E2
Billy Hall Farm DL15 ....52 F6
Billy Hill DL15 ....52 E8
Billy La DL12 ....194 C2
Billy Row Gn DL15 ....52 E7
Bilsdale Ave TS10 ....107 A4
Bilsdale Rd
Hartlepool TS25 ....90 D7
Middlesbrough TS4 ....215 C1
Stockton-on-T TS19 ....212 B4
Binchester Croft DL5 ......95 F4
Bingfield Ct TS23 ....102 E8
Binks St TS5 ....119 E2
Birch Ave
Bishop Auckland DL14 ......80 B5
Shildon DL4 ....81 A1
Birch Cl TS15 ....172 D8
Birch Cres NE16 ....6 A6
Birch Dr DL15 ....54 C2
Birch Gr 5 Consett DH8 . .177 E4
Stockton-on-T TS19 ....117 E7
Birch Mdws DL15 ....66 D7
Birch Mews NE16 ....5 F6
Birch Pl DH7 ....41 D8
Birch Rd
Barnard Castle DL12 .....209 C5
Cornforth DL17 ....57 E1
Darlington DL1 ....133 B8
Birch St DH8 ....10 F2
Birch Tree Cl 9 TS7 ......141 B7
Birch Wlk TS24 ....77 A8
Bircham St DH9 ....13 D5
Birches The
Coulby Newham TS8 ......140 A1
Hurworth-on-T DL2 ....152 E1
Stanley DH9 ....13 F8
Birchfield Cl 1 TS16 .....137 B1
Birchfield Dr TS16 ....137 B1
Birchgate Rd TS5 ....139 D8
Birchgrove Ave DH1 ....35 B3
Birchill Gdns TS26 ....76 E7
Birchington Ave TS6 ....121 F4
Birchmere DL16 ....55 E2
Birchwood Ave TS4 ......120 A1
Birchwood Cl DH9 ....14 E8
Birchwood Dr DH6 ....48 F5
Birchwood Rd TS7 ....140 F4
Birdsall Brow TS20 ....101 F1
Birdsall Row TS10 ....107 C6
Biretta Cl TS19 ....117 A4
Birk Brow Rd TS14 ....145 B3
Birkdale Cl 6 TS27 ....63 C4
Birkdale Dr Eston TS6 ....121 E1
Shiney Row DH4 ....17 F4
Birkdale Gdns DH1 ....35 D3
Birkdale Rd
Darlington DL3 ....132 B3
New Marske TS11 ....124 A6
Stockton-on-T TS18 ....117 B1
Birkhall Rd TS3 ....121 A2
Birkhead Cotts NE11 ....7 E6
Birkheads La NE11 ....7 E6
Birkland La DH9,NE11,NE16 .7 E7
Birkley Rd TS20 ....118 B6
Birtley Ave TS5 ....139 C5
Birtley East Com Prim Sch
DH3 ....9 C6
Birtley La DH3 ....9 D3
Birtley Villas 1 DH3 ....9 C5
Biscop Cres DL5 ....96 E7
Bisham Ave TS5 ....119 C1
Bishop Auckland Coll
DL14 ....79 F5
Bishop Cl DL1 ....133 D5
Bishop Ian Ramsey CE Prim
Sch DH8 ....4 C1
Bishop Middleham CE Prim
Sch DL17 ....71 C3
Bishop St
7 Bishop Auckland DL14 . . .80 B8
Middlesbrough TS5 ....119 B3
Stockton-on-T TS18 ....213 B3
Bishop's Cl DL16 ....68 F8
Bishopdale DH4 ....17 E8
Bishopgarth DL17 ....71 B3
Bishops Ct
Bishop Middleham DL17 ....71 C4
High Shincliffe DH1 ....44 F6
Bishops Mill TS20 ....102 B1
Bishops Way Durham DH1 .34 B7
Stockton-on-T TS19 ....117 A5
Bishops Wynd DH5 ....26 E7
Bishopsgarth Sch TS19 .117 A6
Bishopton Ave TS19 .....117 E5
Bishopton Ct TS19 ....117 B3
Bishopton Ctr The TS19 .212 C4
Bishopton La
Bishopton DL1,DL2,TS21 . .114 D2
Stockton-on-T TS18 ....213 A3
Bishopton Rd
Middlesbrough TS4 ....119 F1
Stockton-on-T TS18,TS19 . .212 C4
Bishopton Rd W TS19 ...117 B4
Bishopton Redmarshall CE
Prim Sch TS21 ....115 D7
Bisley Ct DL1 ....133 F4
Black Boy Rd
Fence Houses DH4 ....26 A7
Great Lumley DH4 ....25 E7
Black Diamond Way
TS16 ....137 B2
Black Dr DH3 ....17 B5
Black Hall DL15 ....189 F5
Black Horse Terr DL13 ...194 E5
Black House La DH7 ....22 F8
Black La DH6 ....47 F3
Black Path The TS18,
TS20 ....213 B4
Black Rd Billy Row DL15 . . .52 F7
Brandon DH7 ....43 E6
Ryhope SR2 ....18 F7
Black Squares Dr TS21,
TS22 ....86 F3
Black Thorn Cl DH7 ....43 A3
Blackburn Cl
Bearpark DH7 ....33 A4
Stockton-on-T TS19 ....117 C3
Blackburn Gr TS11 ....108 A2
Blackbush Wlk TS17 ......138 C3
Blackcap Cl NE38 ....9 F3
Blackcliffe Way DH7 ......33 A4
Blackdown Cl SR8 ....49 B5
Blackett Ave TS20 ....118 B6
Blackett Hutton Ind Est
TS14 ....143 E3
Blackett Rd DL1 ....133 C4
Blackett St
Annfield Plain DH9 ....12 E4
Bishop Auckland DL14 ......80 C7
Blackfell Rd NE37 ....9 F6
Blackfriars TS15 ....156 C5
Blackfyne Com Sch DH8 ..10 F4
Blackgate E 6 DH6 ....58 A4
Blackgate W 5 DH6 ....58 A4
Blackhall Colliery Ind Est
TS27 ....50 D4
Blackhall Colliery Prim Sch
TS27 ....50 D4
Blackhall Sands TS5 .....139 B3
Blackhills Rd SR8 ....50 A7
Blackhills Terr SR8 ....50 A7
Blackling Hole* DL13 ....194 D6
Blackmore Cl TS14 ....143 F2
Blackmore Wlk TS25 ......76 D2
Blacksail Cl TS19 ....212 C3
Blacksmiths Cl TS6 ....121 E2
Blackthorn TS8 ....159 C8
Blackthorn Cl TS10 ......107 E2
Blackthorn Gr TS19 ......117 C3
Blackthorne Ave 9 SR8 . .50 B6
Blackton Cl DL5 ....96 A7
Blackton Rd TS26 ....76 C6
Blackwater Ho 7 SR3 .....18 A6
Blackwell DL3 ....151 C6
Blackwell Cl
Billingham TS23 ....103 A6
Darlington DL3 ....151 D7
Blackwell Gr DL3 ....151 C7
Blackwell La DL3 ....151 D7
Blackwell Scar DL3 ....151 C7
Blackwellgate 13 DL1 ....132 F1
Blackwood Cl TS27 ....63 C4
Bladeside DL15 ....52 F3
Bladon Dr TS11 ....108 C2
Blagden Gr DL14 ....79 E5
Blaidwood Dr DH1 ....44 A5
Blair Ave
Ingleby Barwick TS17 .....156 F8
Spennymoor DL16 ....69 A8
Blair Cl DH6 ....35 F1
Blair Ct DH7 ....43 E5
Blair Gr DL14 ....80 B6
Blairgowrie TS8 ....140 E2
Blairgowrie Gr TS25 ......89 F8
Blairmore Gdns TS16 ....137 C1
Blaise Garden Village
TS26 ....76 D6
Blake Cl Billingham TS23 . .102 E8
Stanley DH9 ....14 A6
Blake St Hartlepool TS26 . . .77 A7
8 Shildon DL4 ....95 A8
Blake Wlk 3 TS26 ....77 A7
Blakelock Gdns TS25 ......77 A4
Blakelock Rd TS25 ....76 F3
Blakeston Com Sch
TS19 ....101 C1
Blakeston Ct TS19 ....101 D1
Blakeston La
Stockton-on-T TS19,TS21 . .101 C2
Wynyard Village TS21 .....100 F4
Blakeston Rd TS23 ....102 F6
Blakey Cl TS10 ....107 C2
Blakey Wlk TS6 ....122 A3
Blakiston Ct DL5 ....82 C2
Blanche Gr SR8 ....49 D5
Blanche Terr DH9 ....6 B2
Blanchland Ave DH1 .....34 E6
Blanchland Gn DL3 ....132 A5
Blanchland Rd TS3 ....140 E8
Bland Wlk DL5 ....96 F7
Blandford Pl SR7 ....29 D7
Blandford St DL17 ....69 E5
Blanford Cl TS20 ....102 B1
Blankney Cl TS14 ....143 D3
Blantyre Rd TS6 ....121 C1
Blatchford Rd TS6 ....120 F5
Blaxton Pl NE16 ....2 F5
Blayberry Cl TS10 ....107 C2
Blaykeston Cl SR7 ....18 E1
Bleach House Bank TS21 .99 A3
Bleak Terr 4 DL13 ....195 E3
Blenavon Ct TS15 ....156 B6
Blencathra Cres DL15 .....52 F2
Blencathra Way NE21 ......2 C8
Blenheim Ave TS11 ....108 C2
Blenheim Cl TS11 ....108 C2
Blenheim Ct TS17 ....156 F7
Blenheim Mews TS10 ....107 B6
Blenheim Rd TS4 ....215 B2
Blenheim Rd S TS4 ....215 B1
Blenheim Terr TS10 ....107 B7
Blenkinsopp Ct SR8 ....49 B2
Blessed John Ducket RC
Prim Sch DL13 ....183 E2
Bletchley Cl TS19 ....117 C4
Blind La
Chester le Street DH3 ......16 D6
Easington SR8 ....39 C5
Guisborough TS14 ....142 E3
Hurworth-on-T DL2 ....168 C8
New Silksworth SR3 ....18 B7
Summerhouse DL2 ....110 B6
Blindy La DH5 ....27 C1
Bliss Cl DL3 ....132 D4
Bloemfontein Pl DH9 .....14 B3
Bloemfontein Prim Sch
DH9 ....14 A3
Bloom Ave DH9 ....13 E6
Bloomesley Cl DL5 ....82 C2
Bloomfield Dr DH5 ....26 D3
Bloomfield Rd DL3 ....132 D3
Blorenge Ct TS17 ....156 F7
Blossom Cl DL3 ....132 D4
Blossomfield Way DH6 ....37 F3
Blue Barn La TS15 ....173 F3
Blue Bell Gr
Middlesbrough TS5 ....139 E4
Stockton-on-T TS19 ....117 C3
Blue Coat CE Jun Sch
DH1 ....34 C6
Blue Coat Ct DH1 ....211 A3
Blue House Bldgs DH1 ...35 C4
Blue House Est DL16 ......69 A3
Blue House Point Rd
TS18 ....118 F4
Blue Post Yd TS18 ....213 A2
Bluebell Cl
Bishop Auckland DL14 ......79 E7
Blackhall Colliery TS27 .....50 D3
Darlington DL3 ....132 D4
Leadgate DH8 ....11 C3
Newton Aycliffe DL5 ....96 B8
Bluebell Dr DL16 ....68 D7
Bluebell Mdw DL5 ....96 B8
Bluebell Way
Hartlepool TS26 ....63 D2
Newton Aycliffe DL5 ....96 B8
Skelton TS12 ....125 E1
Bluehouse Bank DH2,DH9 .15 A3
Blumer St DH4 ....26 A8
Blyth Terr DH3 ....9 B4
Blythe Ave DL14 ....79 D3
Blythport Cl TS18 ....213 C4
Blyton Ave SR2 ....18 E6
Boagey Wlk TS24 ....64 A2
Boar La TS17 ....138 C1
Boat La DL11,DL2 ....201 D2
Boathouse La
Cleasby DL2 ....150 D7
Stockton-on-T TS18 ....213 B1
Bob Hardisty Dr DL14 .....80 B7
Bob Harrison Ct DL1 .....133 A5
Bobby Shafto Cvn Pk DH9 .8 A1
Boddy St DL14 ....80 A3
Bodiam Dr TS10 ....107 F3

Bodmin Gr
Darlington DL3 ....132 F8
Hartlepool TS26 ....76 D8
Boeing Way TS18 ....137 F7
Boghouse La TS13 ....166 F5
Bogma Ave DH6 ....57 F3
Bolam NE38 ....9 F4
Bolam Gr TS23 ....102 E7
Bolam St SR8 ....39 F4
Bolam's Bldgs NE16 ....5 A6
Bolckow Rd TS6 ....121 D6
Bolckow St Eston TS6 ....121 F1
Guisborough TS14 ....143 E5
Middlesbrough TS1 ....214 C4
Skelton TS12 ....125 F1
Boldron Cl TS18 ....137 A8
Boldron La DL12 ....209 A5
Bollihope Gr DL14 ....79 E5
Bollington Rd TS4 ....140 B6
Bolsover Rd TS20 ....118 B6
Boltby Cl TS5 ....139 E6
Boltby Way TS16 ....137 B2
Bolton Cl Darlington DL3 ....132 B4
Durham DH1 ....34 C8
Redcar TS10 ....107 E4
Bolton Ct TS4 ....119 F1
Bolton Gr
Bishop Auckland DL14 ....80 A6
Seaton Carew TS25 ....90 E8
Bolton Way TS14 ....143 F4
Bolton's Bglws NE17 ....4 B8
Boltsburn Cres DL13 ....180 D5
Boltsburn Crescent Flats
DL13 ....180 D5
Boltsburn Terr DH8 ....174 F2
Bon Lea Trad Est TS17 ....213 C1
Bond St TS24 ....77 F8
Bondene Gr TS19 ....117 A5
Bondfield Rd TS6 ....121 D3
Bondgate DL3 ....132 F2
Bondisle Terr DL13 ....206 D2
Bondisle Way DL13 ....206 D2
Bone Mill Bank DL14 ....80 E6
Bone St TS18 ....213 B4
Bonemill La
Chester le Street NE38 ....16 F8
Washington NE38 ....17 C8
Bonington Cres TS23 ....102 D8
Bonnie Gr DL16 ....54 E1
Bonny Gr TS8 ....140 F1
Bonnygrove Way
Coulby Newham TS8 ....140 C1
Mount Pleasant TS8 ....159 C8
Bonnyrigg Cl TS17 ....157 B7
Bonnyrigg Wlk TS25 ....90 A8
Boosbeck Rd TS12 ....145 B8
Booth Wlk DL5 ....96 C8
Bordesley Gn TS3 ....120 D3
Borough Rd
Darlington DL1 ....133 A2
Middlesbrough TS1 ....215 B2
Redcar TS10 ....107 E5
Borough Road Ind Est
DL1 ....133 A2
Borrowby Ct TS14 ....143 D5
Borrowby La TS13 ....149 B6
Borrowdale Birtley DH3 ....9 D1
Leadgate DH8 ....11 D4
Borrowdale Cl DH1 ....35 E4
Borrowdale Cres NE21 ....2 B8
Borrowdale Dr DH1 ....35 C4
Borrowdale Gr
Crook DL15 ....52 F2
Eaglescliffe TS16 ....156 C7
Middlesbrough TS5 ....139 C7
Borrowdale Rd TS6 ....121 F4
Borrowdale St
Hartlepool TS25 ....77 B3
Hetton-le-H DH5 ....27 A2
Borton Wlk TS19 ....212 C4
Boscombe Gdns TS8 ....139 F1
Boston Cl Darlington DL1 ....133 C6
Hartlepool TS25 ....89 F7
Boston Dr TS7 ....140 E2
Boston St SR8 ....39 F4
Boston Wlk TS20 ....118 C7
Boswell Gr TS25 ....76 E2
Boswell St TS1 ....215 A3
Bosworth Way TS23 ....102 F6
Botany Rd DL12 ....198 A8
Botany Way TS7 ....141 A2
Bothal Dr TS19 ....117 A5
Bothal Wlk TS19 ....117 A6
Botham Gr 3 DL3 ....133 A7
Bottle Works Rd SR7 ....29 E6
Bouch St DL4 ....95 A7
Boulby Bank TS13 ....128 D2
Boulby Barns Cotts
TS13 ....128 D3
Boulby Cl SR3 ....18 C7
Boulby Dr TS13 ....127 C1
Boulby Rd Redcar TS10 ....106 F5
Skinningrove TS13 ....127 A4
Boulby Wlk 7 TS6 ....121 F3
Boulmer Ct DH2 ....16 C2
Boundary Cl DH7 ....33 A1
Boundary La DH8 ....3 A3
Boundary Rd
Middlesbrough TS1 ....214 C4
Normanby TS6 ....141 C8
Bourne Ave DL1 ....133 C2
Bourne Ct Darlington DL1 ....133 C2
Stanley DH9 ....14 B7
Bourne Ho TS10 ....107 A6
Bourne St SR8 ....39 F4
Bourne Terr 4 DH9 ....12 F4
Bourne Way DL15 ....54 A3
Bournemouth Ave TS3 ....140 F8
Bournemouth Dr
Hartlepool TS24 ....63 D4
Seaham SR7 ....28 F6
Bournemouth Rd TS3 ....140 F8
Bournmoor Prim Sch
DH4 ....17 E3
Bourton Ct TS3 ....140 D7
Bousfield Cres DL5 ....96 D8
Bow La DH1 ....210 C2
Bow Prep Sch DH1 ....210 C1
Bow St Bowburn DH6 ....45 D1
Guisborough TS14 ....143 F4
Middlesbrough TS1 ....214 C2
Thornley (nr Wheatley Hill)
DH6 ....47 D4
Bow St Ctr TS14 ....143 F4
Bowburn Inf Sch DH6 ....57 D8
Bowburn Jun Sch DH6 ....45 D1
Bowburn North Ind Est
DH6 ....45 C1
Bowburn South Ind Est
DH6 ....57 C8
Bowen Rd DL3 ....132 C5
Bowes Ave
Hetton-le-H DH5 ....27 B1
Seaham SR7 ....28 F6
Bowes Castle* DL12 ....203 D8
Bowes Cl DL17 ....70 B6
Bowes Cres NE16 ....6 D8
Bowes Ct Darlington DL1 ....133 B3
Durham DH1 ....34 D7
Bowes Farm Cotts DH3 ....17 D5
Bowes Gn TS24 ....63 D4
Bowes Gr
Bishop Auckland DL14 ....80 A6
Spennymoor DL16 ....56 A2
Bowes Hill DL14 ....78 B3
Bowes Hutchinsons CE Aided
Prim Sch DL12 ....203 D8
Bowes Lea DH4 ....17 F4
Bowes Lyon Cl NE39 ....5 D8
Bowes Lyon Ho DL12 ....209 C5
Bowes Mus The* DL12 ....209 D5
Bowes Rd
Barnard Castle DL12 ....209 A5
Billingham TS23 ....102 C6
Middlesbrough TS2 ....119 D7
Newton Aycliffe DL5 ....96 D6
Bowes Rly* NE9 ....9 E8
Bowes Terr DH9 ....12 D8
Bowesfield Cres TS18 ....138 B7
Bowesfield Ind Est The
TS18 ....138 A7
Bowesfield La TS18 ....138 A8
Bowesfield Prim Sch
TS18 ....213 A1
Bowesville NE16 ....6 B5
Bowfell Cl TS16 ....137 B2
Bowfell Rd TS3 ....120 C2
Bowhill Way TS23 ....103 A7
Bowland Cl TS7 ....140 F2
Bowlees Cotts DL12 ....192 A7
Bowlees Visitor Ctr
DL12 ....192 A7
Bowley Cl TS6 ....121 B1
Bowley Wlk TS1 ....214 B3
Bowline Ho TS24 ....77 C7
Bowman St DL3 ....133 A7
Bowmont Dr DH9 ....13 C8
Bowmont Wlk DH2 ....16 A1
Bowness Cl
Hartlepool TS25 ....77 B2
Peterlee SR8 ....49 E7
Bowness Gr Ferryhill DL17 ....69 F6
Redcar TS10 ....107 C5
Bowood Cl SR2 ....18 D6
Bowron St TS20 ....118 B5
Bowser St TS24 ....77 C5
Box Dr TS7 ....141 B2
Boxer Ct TS6 ....121 A5
Boyd St Consett DH8 ....11 A1
Durham DH1 ....211 A1
Easington SR8 ....39 F4
Boyd Terr DH9 ....13 D5
Boyden Cl DL14 ....79 C2
Boyden Ct DL5 ....96 E6
Boyes Hill Gr DL3 ....132 D2
Boyne Ct Brandon DH7 ....43 D5
Sedgefield TS21 ....85 A7
Boyne St DL15 ....54 A4
Boyne View Trimdon TS29 ....59 E1
Trimdon TS29 ....72 E8
Boynston Gr TS21 ....85 B7
Boynton Rd TS4 ....120 A2
Boyntons DH2 ....23 F4
Brabazon Dr 6 TS11 ....108 B1
Brabourn Gdns TS8 ....139 F1
Brack's Rd DL14 ....80 E7
Bracken Cl DH9 ....13 E6
Bracken Cres TS14 ....143 B3
Bracken Ct DH7 ....33 A2
Bracken Field Rd DH1 ....34 B5
Bracken Hill SR8 ....48 F5
Bracken Hill Ind Pk SR8 ....48 F4
Bracken Hill Rd DL15 ....66 C7
Bracken Rd
Darlington DL3 ....132 D3
Stockton-on-T TS19 ....117 E7
Brackenbeds Cl DH2 ....15 F6
Brackenbeds La DH2 ....15 F7
Brackenberry Cres
TS10 ....107 F3
Brackenberry Wlk 5
TS6 ....121 F3
Brackendale Ct TS28 ....60 F5
Brackendale Rd DH1 ....35 D4
Brackenfield Ct TS6 ....141 E8
Brackenhill Ave DH6 ....48 E6
Brackenhill Cl TS7 ....141 A1
Brackenhill Wlk TS9 ....159 A1
Brackenridge NE16 ....5 E6
Brackenthwaite TS5 ....139 B4
Bracknell Cl SR3 ....18 C8
Bracknell Rd TS17 ....138 E7
Bradbury Cl DH9 ....13 C8
Bradbury Rd
Newton Aycliffe DL5 ....96 D4
Stockton-on-T TS20 ....102 B1
Bradford Cl DL5 ....96 D5
Bradford Cres DH1 ....211 C4
Bradhope Rd TS3 ....120 B2
Bradley Ave DH5 ....26 E6
Bradley Bglws DH8 ....11 C6
Bradley Cl DH2 ....8 E2
Bradley Cotts DH8 ....11 C6
Bradley Ct TS23 ....102 F6
Bradley Lodge Dr DH9 ....12 E8
Bradley St Easington SR8 ....39 F4
Leadgate DH8 ....11 C4
Bradley Terr Dipton DH9 ....12 E7
Easington Lane DH5 ....27 C1
Bradley Workshops Ind Est
DH8 ....11 C4
Bradleys Terr TS9 ....161 A3
Bradman Dr DH3 ....16 E1
Bradshaw Ct TS24 ....63 F2
Brae Head TS16 ....137 C1
Braemar Ct Consett DH8 ....10 C3
Darlington DL1 ....133 E7
Braemar Gr TS6 ....121 B3
Braemar Rd
Billingham TS23 ....102 D6
Hartlepool TS25 ....90 A8
Middlesbrough TS5 ....139 B8
Braemar Terr 1 SR8 ....50 B6
Braeside Burnhope DH7 ....21 D4
Edmondsley DH7 ....23 B7
Kirklevington TS15 ....172 D8
Braeworth Cl TS15 ....156 F5
Brafferton Cl DL5 ....82 E1
Brafferton Dr TS23 ....102 F8
Brafferton La DL1 ....113 A6
Brafferton St 2 TS26 ....76 F6
Brafferton Wlk TS5 ....139 C5
Braid Cres TS23 ....102 D3
Braidwood Rd TS6 ....121 C1
Braithwaite Rd SR8 ....49 F6
Braithwaite St
9 Bishop Auckland DL14 ....80 B8
Shildon DL4 ....80 E1
Brakespeare Pl SR8 ....49 E5
Bramall La DL1 ....133 F3
Bramble Dykes 7 TS10 ....107 E1
Bramble Rd TS19 ....117 E7
Brambles Prim Sch TS3 ....120 E3
Brambles The DH3 ....9 D6
Brambling Cl TS20 ....101 F1
Bramcote Way TS17 ....138 C3
Bramfield Way TS17 ....138 A3
Bramhall Dr NE38 ....17 B8
Bramham Chase DL5 ....95 F8
Bramham Down TS14 ....143 E3
Bramley Ct TS25 ....90 A8
Bramley Gr TS7 ....140 E4
Bramley Par TS18 ....213 A1
Brampton Cl TS8 ....139 E3
Brampton Ct SR8 ....39 B3
Bramwell Terr DH8 ....11 A4
Bramwith Ave TS3 ....140 D8
Brancepath Wlk TS24 ....63 F3
Brancepeth Ave TS3 ....140 C8
Brancepeth Chare SR8 ....49 B3
Brancepeth Cl
Durham DH1 ....34 E6
New Marske TS11 ....124 A6
Newton Aycliffe DL5 ....82 E1
Brancepeth Ct TS22 ....102 C6
Brancepeth Gr DL14 ....80 A6
Brancepeth Rd DL17 ....70 A6
Brancepeth Terr DL15 ....54 A4
Brancepeth View DH7 ....42 F3
Brancpeth Cl DH7 ....33 C1
Brandlings Way SR8 ....49 D6
Brandon Cl
Billingham TS23 ....102 D7
Blaydon NE21 ....2 A8
Chester le Street DH2 ....15 F1
Hartlepool TS25 ....89 D5
Houghton-le-S DH4 ....26 D7
Brandon Jun & Inf Sch
DH7 ....43 C4
Brandon La Brandon DH7 ....43 C5
New Brancepeth DH7,DL15 ....42 B5
Brandon Rd
Esh Winning DH7 ....41 E8
Middlesbrough TS3 ....120 F2
Brandon View DH7 ....43 C8
Brankin Ct TS12 ....125 F3
Brankin Dr DL1 ....152 C7
Brankin Rd DL1 ....152 C7
Branklyn Gdns TS17 ....157 B8
Branksome Ave TS5 ....139 E7
Branksome Gn DL3 ....131 F5
Branksome Gr TS18 ....137 C8
Branksome Hall Dr DL3 ....132 A5
Branksome Lodge DL3 ....132 B5
Branksome Sch DL3 ....132 A4
Branksome Terr DL3 ....132 F3
Bransdale
Guisborough TS14 ....143 A3
Penshaw DH4 ....17 E8
Spennymoor DL16 ....55 E1
Bransdale Cl TS19 ....212 B4
Bransdale Gr
Hartlepool TS25 ....90 E8
Redcar TS10 ....106 F4
Bransdale Rd TS3 ....120 C2
Brantwood DH2 ....15 F2
Brantwood Cl TS17 ....157 C8
Brantwood Terr DL14 ....80 A3
Brass Castle La
Marton TS8 ....140 F1
Mount Pleasant TS8 ....159 E7
Brass Thill DH1 ....210 B2
Brass Wynd TS8 ....140 F1
Braunespath Est DH7 ....42 F8
Brawton Gr DL3 ....132 E4
Braygate TS12 ....126 E1
Breakhouse Bank DL2 ....169 C6
Breamish Dr NE38 ....16 F8
Brechin Dr TS17 ....138 D3
Brechin Gr TS25 ....90 A8
Breck Rd DL3 ....132 D2
Brecken Way DH7 ....43 C4
Breckland Wlk TS3 ....120 D1
Breckon Ct DL13 ....195 C4
Breckon Hill DL13 ....195 C4
Breckon Hill Prim Sch
TS4 ....215 B2
Breckon Hill Rd TS4 ....215 B2
Breckon Terr TS21 ....72 C5
Brecon Cl SR8 ....49 B5
Brecon Cres TS17 ....156 F8
Brecon Dr TS10 ....107 A3
Brecon Pl DH2 ....15 F8
Brecon Rd DH1 ....34 E7
Brecon Side DL1 ....133 E5
Brecongill Cl TS24 ....77 B8
Breen Cl TS3 ....215 C2
Brenda Rd TS25 ....90 C6
Brendon Cres TS23 ....102 E4
Brendon Gr TS17 ....157 B6
Brendon Pl SR8 ....49 B7
Brenkley Cl TS20 ....101 E1
Brent Ct TS23 ....102 C3
Brentford Ct TS12 ....126 C3
Brentford Rd TS20 ....118 B6
Brentnall St TS1 ....214 C3
Brentwood Ct DH9 ....14 C6
Brereton Rd TS4 ....140 A7
Bretby Cl TS4 ....140 A8
Brettenham Ave TS4 ....140 B6
Breward Wlk 2 TS24 ....77 B7
Brewer St DL14 ....80 B6
Brewer Terr SR2 ....19 A6
Brewery Sq DH9 ....13 F7
Brewery St 7 TS24 ....77 B5
Brewsdale Rd TS3 ....120 C5
Brian Rd DL1 ....133 A6
Briar Ave Brandon DH7 ....43 A3
2 Houghton-le-S DH4 ....26 D8
Briar Cl Darlington DL3 ....151 C6
Great Lumley DH4 ....17 E1
Kimblesworth DH2 ....23 F3
Shiney Row DH4 ....17 F4
Spennymoor DL16 ....68 D6
Briar Dale DH8 ....177 E4
Briar Gdns DL15 ....52 D3
Briar Glen SR7 ....28 A3
Briar Gr Redcar TS10 ....107 C5
Trimdon TS29 ....72 D8
Briar Hill DL13 ....179 C1
Briar Lea
Witton Gilbert DH7 ....23 B1
Shiney Row DH4 ....17 F4
Briar Mews DH8 ....10 D5
Briar Rd Durham DH1 ....35 D4
Rowlands Gill NE39 ....1 D2
Thornaby-on-T TS17 ....138 C6
Briar Terr NE16 ....6 C6
Briar Wlk Darlington DL3 ....151 D6
Hartlepool TS26 ....77 A6
Stockton-on-T TS18 ....212 A1
Briardene Burnopfield NE16 ....5 E6
Durham DH1 ....210 B2
Esh Winning DH7 ....31 C1
Lanchester DH7 ....20 E3
Briardene Ave TS5 ....139 E7
Briardene Ct TS19 ....117 A7
Briardene Way SR8 ....39 E4
Briardene Wlk TS19 ....117 A7
Briargate TS6 ....121 F2
Briarhill DH2 ....16 A5
Briarhill Gdns TS26 ....76 E7
Briarside DH8 ....10 D5
Briarsyde Cl NE16 ....2 E5
Briarvale Ave TS5 ....139 D8
Briarwood Ave DH2 ....15 E3
Briarwood St DH4 ....17 E1
Briary Gdns DH8 ....10 C6
Briary The DH8 ....10 D6
Brick Garth DH5 ....27 C1
Brick Row
Commondale YO21 ....164 C2
Ryhope SR2 ....18 E7
Brickton Rd TS5 ....119 B2
Bridge Ct Eston TS6 ....121 C1
Shadforth DH6 ....46 E7
Yarm TS15 ....156 B7
Bridge End Coxhoe DH6 ....57 F5
Frosterley DL13 ....188 A7
Piercebridge DL2 ....130 B4
Willington DL15 ....53 F3
Bridge House Est DL17 ....69 F5
Bridge Inn Yd DL12 ....209 B5
Bridge Island DH8 ....10 B6
Bridge Rd
Bishop Auckland DL14 ....80 A8
Cornforth DL17 ....57 E2
Darlington DL2,DL3 ....151 C6
Redcar TS10 ....107 A7
Bridge Rd *continued*
Shotton Colliery DH6 ....48 D6
Stockton-on-T TS18 ....213 B1
Bridge Rd Bglws DH6 ....48 D5
Bridge St
Bishop Auckland DL14 ....67 B1
Consett DH8 ....10 D3
Durham DH1 ....210 B3
Ferryhill DH6 ....57 B2
Great Ayton TS9 ....160 F2
Hartlepool TS24 ....77 D5
Howden-le-W DL15 ....65 E7
Langley Park DH7 ....32 C7
Middleton-In-T DL12 ....208 B5
Stanley DH9 ....13 E4
Stockton-on-T TS20 ....118 B5
Thornaby-on-T TS17 ....213 C1
Tow Law DL13 ....183 E1
Willington DL15 ....53 E1
Yarm TS15 ....156 B7
Bridge St E TS2 ....215 A4
Bridge St W TS2 ....214 C4
Bridge Terr
Darlington DL1 ....133 B1
Station Town TS28 ....60 F5
Bridge View TS21 ....72 D4
Bridge Way DH7 ....32 D6
Bridgefield Ct DL15 ....65 E7
Bridgegate DL12 ....209 B5
Bridgemere Dr DH1 ....34 A6
Bridgend Cl TS6 ....121 E5
Bridgepool Cl TS24 ....64 C2
Bridle The DL5 ....82 D2
Bridnor Rd TS3 ....140 C8
Bridport Cl TS18 ....118 D4
Bridport Gr TS8 ....139 F1
Brier Ave SR8 ....49 F8
Brierley Dr TS21,TS22 ....86 D3
Brierley Gn TS7 ....140 E2
Brierton Com Sch TS25 ....76 E1
Brierton La TS25 ....76 C1
Brierville DH1 ....210 B2
Brierville Rd TS19 ....117 F5
Brig Open TS24 ....77 F8
Brigandine Cl TS25 ....90 D8
Briggs Ave TS6 ....121 A5
Brigham Rd TS3 ....120 C1
Brighouse Bsns Village
TS2 ....119 C8
Brighouse Ct DL5 ....96 D3
Bright St Consett DH8 ....10 F4
Darlington DL1 ....133 C1
Hartlepool TS26 ....76 F6
Middlesbrough TS1 ....215 B3
Stockton-on-T TS18 ....213 A3
Brightlea DH3 ....9 E5
Brighton Cl TS17 ....138 B4
Brighton Rd DL1 ....152 B8
Brighton Terr DH6 ....36 D1
Brignall Cl DH3 ....25 B7
Brignall La DL12 ....204 E7
Brignall Moor Cres DL1 ....152 D8
Brignall Rd TS18 ....137 F8
Brignell Rd TS2 ....119 D7
Brimham Cl TS17 ....138 C1
Brimham Ct TS10 ....107 B4
Brimston Cl TS26 ....76 D7
Brindle Cl TS7 ....140 E2
Brindley Rd SR8 ....48 F6
Brine St TS4 ....215 B2
Brinewells Gn TS4 ....215 C1
Brinkburn DH2 ....16 A3
Brinkburn Ave DL3 ....132 D4
Brinkburn Cl
Bishop Auckland DL14 ....79 E5
Blaydon NE21 ....2 A8
Brinkburn Ct TS25 ....76 F4
Brinkburn Dr DL3 ....132 D5
Brinkburn Rd
Darlington DL3 ....132 E4
Hartlepool TS25 ....77 A4
Stockton-on-T TS20 ....118 A6
Brinsley Ct DL14 ....81 B8
Briony Cl DL16 ....56 B3
Brisbane Cres TS17 ....138 C5
Brisbane Gr TS18 ....212 A1
Briscoe La DL12 ....198 B6
Briscoe Way TS8 ....139 C1
Bristol Ave TS12 ....125 C7
Bristol Wlk TS26 ....76 E8
Bristow Rd TS4 ....120 B1
Bristow St TS3 ....120 C4
Britain Ave TS5 ....139 C7
Britannia Cl 7 TS24 ....77 C6
Britannia Pl TS10 ....106 E4
Britannia Rd
New Silksworth SR3 ....18 A7
Stockton-on-T TS19 ....212 C3
Britannia Terr
Brotton TS12 ....126 B4
Fence Houses DH4 ....26 A8
British Steel Redcar Halt
TS10 ....106 C5
Britten Cl DH9 ....14 A5
Brixham Cl SR7 ....29 A6
Broad Cl TS8 ....139 B1
Broad Field Rd TS24 ....64 F1
Broad Gates 9 DL12 ....209 C5
Broad Rd TS27 ....50 F2
Broadbent St TS12 ....126 B3
Broadgate Gdns TS5 ....139 C8
Broadgate Rd
Langley Park DH7 ....32 C3
Middlesbrough TS5 ....139 C8
Broadhaven Cl TS6 ....121 E3
Broadlands TS17 ....138 A2
Broadmeadows
Bowburn DH6 ....45 E1

Broadmeadows *continued*
Darlington DL3 ....132 B2
Broadmires La DL12 ....204 D5
Broadmires Terr DH2 .....23 E4
Broadoak Dr DH7 ....20 E3
Broadoaks
Bishop Middleham DL17 ....71 B3
Murton SR7 ....28 A2
Broadstone TS8 ....140 E1
Broadview Villas DH6 ....36 A1
Broadviews DH3 ....25 A7
Broadway
Chester le Street DH3 ......16 D5
Consett DH8 ....177 D4
Eston TS6 ....121 E5
Whickham NE16 ....2 F5
Broadway Ave TS29 ....59 C1
Broadway E TS10 ....106 F5
Broadway S The DL1 ....133 E2
Broadway The
Darlington DL1 ....133 D2
Houghton-le-S DH4 ....26 E8
Broadway W TS10 ....106 E4
Broadwell Rd TS4 ....140 B6
Broadwood La DL7,DL13 .183 E8
Broadwood View
Chester le Street DH3 ......16 D2
Consett DH8 ....10 C5
Brockett Cl DL5 ....96 C8
Brocklesby Rd TS14 .....143 E2
Brockrigg Ct TS14 ......143 D6
Brockwell TS27 ....50 C3
Brockwell Cl
Fishburn TS21 ....72 D4
Newton Aycliffe DL5 ....82 C1
Brockwell Ct
Close House DL14 ....81 A5
Willington DL15 ....54 C3
Brockwell Dr NE39 ....1 E3
Brockwell Rd NE38 ....9 F5
Brogden Gn TS3 ....120 C1
Broken Banks DL14 ....80 B8
Broken Way DL13 ....179 E1
Bromley Cl DH1 ....45 B4
Bromley Hill Cl TS7 .....141 A1
Bromley La TS8 ....159 C6
Bromley Rd TS18 ....212 A1
Brompton Ave TS14 ......143 F6
Brompton Cl DH2 ....8 E2
Brompton Gr TS18 ....137 C8
Brompton Rd TS5 ....119 D2
Brompton St TS5 ....119 D2
Brompton Wlk
Darlington DL3 ....132 C1
Seaton Carew TS25 ....90 D7
Bronaber Cl TS17 ....156 E8
Bronte Ct DL15 ....52 C2
Bronte Pl DH9 ....14 B4
Bronte Way TS23 ....102 D7
Brook Cl DL5 ....82 E1
Brook St
Coundon Grange DL14 ......80 F5
3 Hartlepool TS26 ....77 A6
Middlesbrough TS2 ....215 A4
2 Spennymoor DL16 ....55 F1
Brook Terr
Darlington DL3 ....132 F4
Eldon Lane DL14 ....80 F4
Brook View DH7 ....20 E3
Brookdale DH1 ....35 E4
Brookdale Rd TS7 ....140 D3
Brooke Cl DH9 ....14 A6
Brookes Rise DH7 ....43 D5
Brookes The TS15 ....156 C4
Brookfield Rd TS19 .....117 A3
Brooklands DL14 ....80 B4
Brooklyn Rd DL17 ....82 F7
Brooklyn St SR7 ....28 D2
Brooklyn Terr N SR7 .....28 D2
Brooksbank Ave TS10 ...107 C5
Brooksbank Cl TS7 .....141 B5
Brooksbank Rd TS7 .....141 B5
Brookside Boosbeck TS12 .145 B7
Evenwood DL14 ....92 D7
Houghton-le-S DH5 ....26 D6
Sacriston DH7 ....23 C4
Witton Gilbert DH7 ....33 B8
Brookside Ave Crook DL15 .52 E2
8 Middlesbrough TS4 ....139 F8
Brookside Cotts DL15 ....52 E2
Brookwood Way TS16 ...156 C8
Broom Cl Blaydon NE21 .....2 B8
Stanley DH9 ....14 B7
Broom Cottages Prim Sch
DL17 ....70 A6
Broom Cotts 5 DL17 .....70 A5
Broom Cres DH7 ....33 B1
Broom Ct NE9 ....9 F8
Broom Farm W DH7 ....43 C8
Broom Hall Dr DH7 ....33 C1
Broom Hill Ave TS17 ....138 A2
Broom La DH7 ....43 D8
Broom Rd DL17 ....70 A6
Broom St DL16 ....56 C1
Broom Terr
Burnopfield NE16 ....6 C6
Crook DL15 ....52 E4
Broome Ct DH7 ....43 C8
Broome Rd DH1 ....35 D4
Broomfield Ave 2 TS16 .137 B1
Broomfield Cres NE17 .....4 B8
Broomhill DH9 ....13 E7
Broomhill Est DH5 ....26 F6
Broomhill Gdns TS26 .....76 E7
Broomhill Terr
Hetton-le-H DH5 ....26 F5
Medomsley DH8 ....11 A8
Broomlee Cl
Ingleby Barwick TS17 .....157 A7
4 Newton Aycliffe DL5 ....96 A7
Brooms La DH8 ....11 F4
Brooms The DH2 ....8 F2
Broomside Coundon DL14 ..81 A8
Ferryhill DL17 ....70 A5
Broomside Ct DH1 ....35 D4
Broomside La DH1 ....35 D4
Brotherswater Cl TS10 ..107 B5
Brotton Rd
Carlin How TS13 ....126 F3
Thornaby-on-T TS17 ......138 D7
Brough Cl
Newton Aycliffe DL5 ....97 A7
Thornaby-on-T TS17 ......138 E5
Brough Ct Hartlepool TS27 .63 D3
1 Middlesbrough TS4 ....120 A1
Brough Field Cl TS17 ...138 A2
Brough Gr DL14 ....80 A6
Brough Rd TS23 ....102 E5
Brougham Ct SR8 ....49 B3
Brougham Ent Ctr TS24 ..77 B7
Brougham Prim Sch
TS24 ....77 B7
Brougham St
Darlington DL3 ....133 A5
Middlesbrough TS2 ....214 C4
Brougham Terr TS24 .....77 B7
Broughton Ave TS4 ......140 B6
Broughton Gn TS10 ......107 B3
Broughton Rd TS22 ......102 B5
Broumley Ct DL2 ....200 F7
Browbank DH7 ....23 D2
Brown St DL4 ....80 F2
Brown's Bldgs DH3 ....9 C1
Brown's Terr
Hinderwell TS13 ....149 E5
3 Langley Park DH7 ......32 C6
Browney Bank DH7 ....183 F8
Browney La
Brandon DH6,DH7 ....43 E2
Spennymoor DL16 ....55 F8
Browney Prim Sch DH7 ...43 D3
Browning Ave TS25 ....76 F3
Browning Cl DH9 ....14 A6
Browning Hill DH6 ....58 A4
Browning Pl DL15 ....52 C3
Browning St SR8 ....39 F4
Brownney Ct DH7 ....32 C7
Browns Bldgs Dipton DH9 .12 C8
5 Middleton St George
DL2 ....153 F8
Browns Cl DH6 ....58 A4
Brownsea Ct TS17 ....157 B8
Brownside La DL2 ....94 A2
Broxa Cl TS10 ....107 B2
Bruce Ave TS5 ....119 B1
Bruce Cres
Hartlepool TS24 ....64 A3
Wingate TS28 ....60 D8
Bruce Glasier Terr DH6 ...48 C5
Bruce Kirkup Rd SR8 .....49 F8
Bruce Pl SR8 ....49 C8
Bruce Rd DL5 ....96 C6
Bruce St DH7 ....23 B6
Brundall Cl TS19 ....117 B5
Brunel Cl TS24 ....64 C1
Brunel Rd Darlington DL1 .133 B2
South Bank TS6 ....120 F5
Brunel St DL17 ....69 E6
Brunel Way DL1 ....133 B2
Brunner Ho TS3 ....120 D1
Brunner Rd TS23 ....118 E8
Brunswick Ave TS6 ......121 B4
Brunswick St
Darlington DL1 ....133 A2
1 Hartlepool TS24 ....77 C5
Middlesbrough TS1 ....215 A4
Stockton-on-T TS18 ......213 A2
Brunswick St N DL1 ....133 A2
Bruntoft Ave TS24 ....63 F3
Brunton St DL1 ....133 B1
Brunton Wlk DL5 ....96 C5
Bruntons Manor Ct TS3 .120 E2
Brus Cnr TS24 ....64 A3
Brus Ho 5 TS17 ....138 D5
Brusselton Cl TS5 ......139 C5
Brusselton La DL4 ....94 C7
Brusselton View DL14 ....80 A4
Bryan Cl DL2 ....152 D1
Bryan St DL16 ....56 A1
Bryan's Leap NE16 ....6 A7
Brydon Cres DH6 ....38 B6
Brylston Rd TS3 ....120 F3
Bryony Ct TS14 ....143 B3
Bryony Gr TS7 ....140 C4
Bsns Ctr The TS23 ......103 B3
Buccleugh Cl TS14 ......143 E2
Buchanan St TS18 ....213 A2
Buck Fast Rd TS12 ......125 D2
Buck Sq DL5 ....95 D1
Buck St TS2 ....119 E7
Buckden Ct 3 DL3 ......132 F1
Buckham St DH8 ....10 E4
Buckie Gr TS25 ....90 A8
Buckingham Ave TS27 ....62 F2
Buckingham Ct DL1 .....151 E8
Buckingham Dr TS6 .....141 D7
Buckingham Rd
Peterlee SR8 ....49 B8
Redcar TS10 ....107 C6
Stockton-on-T TS18 ......212 C2
Buckingham Terr DL14 ...81 D8
Buckinghamshire Rd
DH1 ....35 C3
Buckland Cl TS17 ....157 C8
Buckton's Yd 6 DL3 ....132 F1
Buddle Cl SR8 ....49 D8
Buddle St DH8 ....11 A2
Buddle Wlk DL5 ....96 C5
Bude Sq SR7 ....28 D4
Budworth Cl TS23 ....102 E8
Buess La DL1 ....134 A5
Bull Wynd DL1 ....132 F1
Bullfinch Dr NE16 ....2 F7
Bullion La DH2 ....16 B3
Bullion Lane Prim Sch
DH2 ....16 B3
Bulmer Cl
Newton Aycliffe DL5 ....96 F7
Yarm TS15 ....156 D4
Bulmer Ct TS6 ....121 D1
Bulmer Pl TS24 ....63 F2
Bulmer Way TS1 ....214 B3
Bulmer's Bldgs TS14 ....143 D5
Bulmers Sq DL3 ....132 F5
Bungalows The Birtley DH3 .9 B6
11 Consett DH8 ....177 A4
Ebchester DH8 ....3 F4
Eston TS6 ....121 E5
Hesleden TS27 ....50 D1
Hetton-le-H DH5 ....26 F6
Kibblesworth NE11 ....8 E8
Longnewton TS21 ....136 A5
Medomsley NE17 ....4 B4
New Brancepeth DH7 ....42 F8
Peterlee SR8 ....49 C6
Peterlee,Horden SR8 ......49 F8
Port Mulgrave TS13 ......149 F7
South Hetton DH6 ....38 B6
Tanfield Lea DH9 ....13 C8
Thornley (nr Wheatley Hill)
DH6 ....47 C3
Bunting Cl Hartlepool TS26 .63 E1
Ingleby Barwick TS17 .....138 B1
Burbank Ct 11 TS24 ......77 C5
Burbank St TS24 ....77 C5
Burdale Cl TS16 ....137 A2
Burdon Ave DH5 ....27 A8
Burdon Cl
Newton Aycliffe DL5 ....96 C7
Stockton-on-T TS19 ......117 C4
Burdon Cres Ryhope SR2 ..18 E6
Seaham SR7 ....18 F1
Wingate TS28 ....48 E1
Burdon Dr SR8 ....48 E7
Burdon Garth TS17 ......138 A2
Burdon La SR2,SR3 ....18 C5
Burdon Pl SR8 ....49 E6
Burdon Plain NE16 ....7 B7
Burdon Rd Burdon SR3 ....18 B5
New Silksworth SR3 ....18 B6
Burdon Wlk TS27 ....49 A1
Burford Ave TS18 ....137 E8
Burgess St TS18 ....213 A3
Burghley Ct TS8 ....139 F2
Burghley Mews DL5 ....82 E1
Burke Pl TS24 ....64 E1
Burke St DL4 ....80 F1
Burlam Rd TS5 ....119 C2
Burlawn Cl 3 SR2 ....18 F8
Burleigh Pl DL3 ....132 E1
Burma Rd DL2 ....152 E4
Burn Bank Ct DL12 ......208 B6
Burn Crook DH5 ....26 D6
Burn Gdns SR8 ....39 C4
Burn La Hetton-le-H DH5 ..27 A3
Newton Aycliffe DL5 ....96 D8
Burn Oval TS29 ....59 C1
Burn Park Rd DH4 ....26 D8
Burn Pl DL15 ....53 F3
Burn Prom 8 DH4 ....26 E8
Burn Rd TS25 ....77 C4
Burn St DH6 ....45 D1
Burn Terr 11 DL16 ....55 F1
Burn Valley Gdns TS28 ...60 F5
Burn Valley Gr TS25 .....77 A4
Burn Valley Rd TS26 .....77 A4
Burn Wood Ct TS21 ......136 A5
Burn's Cl TS27 ....62 F3
Burn's Terr DH6 ....48 D6
Burnaby Cl TS25 ....77 B2
Burnbeck Pl DL5 ....95 C1
Burnden Gr 2 DH4 ....17 F5
Burnell Rd DH7 ....41 E8
Burneston Ct DL3 ....131 F1
Burneston Gr TS18 ......117 A1
Burnet Cl TS17 ....138 B2
Burnett Cres DH6 ....58 E5
Burneze Pl NE16 ....6 A4
Burnfoot DL13 ....179 E1
Burnfoot Rural Workshops
DL13 ....179 E1
Burnhall Dr SR7 ....19 A1
Burnhill Way DL5 ....96 B7
Burnhills La NE40 ....1 B8
Burnholme Ave TS3 ......120 E3
Burnhope DL5 ....96 A7
Burnhope Cl DL15 ....52 D2
Burnhope Prim Sch DH7 .21 D4
Burnhope Rd TS26 ....76 C6
Burnhope Way SR8 ....49 C6
Burnhopeside Ave DH7 ...21 A3
Burnie Gdns DL4 ....81 A1
Burnigill DH7 ....43 C3
Burnington Dr DL15 ......53 E3
Burnip Rd SR7 ....28 C4
Burniston Dr
Billingham TS22 ....102 B5
Thornaby-on-T TS17 ......138 B3
Burnlea 4 DH4 ....26 C8
Burnmere DL16 ....55 E2
Burnmill Bank DH8 ......176 E7
Burnmoor Cl TS10 ....107 C2
Burnmoor Dr TS16 ....137 B2
Burnop Terr NE39 ....1 A2
Burnopfield Prim Sch
NE16 ....6 A6
Burnopfield Rd NE39 ......1 F1
Burns Ave
Blackhall Colliery TS27 ....50 C4
Hartlepool TS25 ....76 E3
Burns Ave N DH5 ....26 E7
Burns Ave S DH5 ....26 E7
Burns Cl Stanley DH9 .....14 A6
West Rainton DH4 ....26 A2
Burns Rd Chilton DL17 ....82 E8
Eston TS6 ....121 C3
Burns St DH6 ....47 E2
Burns Wlk TS6 ....121 C3
Burnsall Rd TS3 ....120 B2
Burnshouse La DL14 ......93 E8
Burnside Esh Winning DH7 .31 D1
Lanchester DH7 ....20 E4
Peterlee SR8 ....49 D6
Witton Gilbert DH7 ....33 B8
Burnside Ave SR8 ....50 A6
Burnside Cotts DL13 ....180 D5
Burnside Ct
Blanchland DH8 ....175 A5
Stockton-on-T TS18 ......212 B2
Burnside Gr TS18 ....212 B2
Burnside Rd
Darlington DL1 ....152 D7
Rowlands Gill NE39 ....1 D2
Burnston Cl TS26 ....76 D7
Burnsville Rd TS6 ......121 D5
Burnt Hos DL13 ....195 E2
Burnt Houses La DL13,
DL2 ....195 F2
Burnthouse Bank DH2 ....15 F4
Burnthouse Cl NE21 ....2 A8
Burntoft TS22 ....101 E8
Burnway SR7 ....29 A8
Burnynghill Cl DL5 ......95 F5
Burringham Rd TS20 .....117 F8
Burt Cl Haswell DH6 .....37 E3
Peterlee SR8 ....49 D8
Burtonport Wlk 7 TS18 .213 C4
Burtree Ford DL13 ......179 B3
Burtree La DL3 ....112 D2
Burtree Rd DL5 ....96 D3
Burwell Dr TS19 ....117 A4
Burwell Rd TS3 ....120 F1
Burwell Wlk TS25 ....89 E6
Bury Rd DL5 ....96 E6
Burythorpe Cl TS4 ......120 A2
Busby Way TS15 ....156 F5
Bush Blades Mews DH9 ...12 F7
Bush St TS5 ....119 D2
Bushblades La DH9 ....12 F7
Bushel Hill Ct DL3 .....132 B3
Bushel Hill Dr DL3 .....132 B2
Bushmead Terr 3 TS3 ...140 E8
Bushston Cl TS26 ....76 D7
Business Sch (Univ of
Durham) DH1 ....44 B7
Busty Bank NE16,NE39 .....6 A8
Busty Terr DL4 ....80 E3
Butchers Race DL16 ......56 C2
Bute Ave TS25 ....77 A3
Bute Cl TS17 ....138 C4
Bute Ct 3 SR3 ....18 A6
Bute St
Stockton-on-T TS18 ......213 A3
Tantobie DH9 ....6 A2
Butler Rd DL5 ....96 D6
Butler St Easington SR8 ..39 F4
Stockton-on-T TS20 ......118 B6
Butsfield La Consett DH8 .177 E3
Satley DL13 ....183 D8
Butsfield Way 7 TS23 ..102 E8
Butt La TS14 ....144 A4
Buttercup Cl TS19 ......117 C6
Butterfield Cl 3 TS16 ..156 B8
Butterfield Dr TS16 ....137 B1
Butterfield Gr 2 TS16 ..156 B8
Butterfly World* TS16 ..137 D4
Butterknowle Prim Sch
DL13 ....195 C4
Buttermere Peterlee SR8 ..49 A3
Spennymoor DL16 ....55 E2
Buttermere Ave
Easington Lane DH5 ....37 C8
Middlesbrough TS5 ....139 C7
Buttermere Cl DH2 ....16 C2
Buttermere Cres
Blaydon NE21 ....2 B8
South Hetton DH6 ....37 E8
Buttermere Gr
Bishop Auckland DL14 .....79 B1
Crook DL15 ....52 F2
Buttermere Rd
Eston TS6 ....121 F4
Redcar TS10 ....107 B5
Stockton-on-T TS18 ......212 B3
Butterwick Ct DL5 ....96 D8
Butterwick Gr TS22 ......87 B3
Butterwick Rd
Fishburn TS21 ....72 D5
Hartlepool TS24 ....63 E3
Sedgefield TS21 ....72 F2
Button's Bank DH7,DL15 ..41 B5
Butts Cres DL13 ....206 D3
Butts Cvn Pk The DL13 ..206 D3
Butts La Eaglescliffe TS16 .156 C7
Hart TS27 ....62 F3
Butts The DL13 ....206 D3
Buxton Ave TS7 ....140 D2
Buxton Gdns TS22 ....102 C5
Buxton Moor Cres DL1 ..152 D7
Buxton Rd TS18 ....213 B4
By Pass Rd TS23 ....102 D1
Bydales Dr TS11 ....108 E1
Bydales Sch TS11 ....108 C2
Bye The DH8 ....177 B4
Byelands St TS4 ....215 B1
Byemoor Ave TS9 ....161 A1
Byemoor Cl TS9 ....161 A1
Byer Sq DH5 ....27 A6
Byer St DH5 ....27 A6
Byerley Ct DL14 ....80 E1
Byerley Park Prim Sch
DL5 ....96 A8
Byerley Rd DL4 ....94 F8
Byerleyhouse La DL13 ...183 C7
Byers Ct SR3 ....18 B8
Byers Green Prim Sch
DL16 ....54 D1
Byerside Cvn Site NE17 ....4 C5
Byfleet Ave TS3 ....120 D3
Byland Cl
Bishop Auckland DL14 .....79 D2
Guisborough TS14 ....143 F4
Redcar TS10 ....107 B3
Byland Ct DH7 ....33 B3
Byland Gr TS25 ....90 E8
Byland Rd Nunthorpe TS7 .141 B3
Skelton TS12 ....125 D2
Byland Way TS23 ....103 A3
Bylands Gr TS19 ....117 B2
Bylands Rd TS6 ....121 D2
Bylands Way DL3 ....132 A4
Byony Toft SR2 ....19 A7
Byrne Terr W 2 SR3 .....18 B7
Byrneside Ave TS4 ......119 F1
Byron Ave
Bishop Auckland DL14 .....80 B6
Blackhall Colliery TS27 ....50 D4
Chester le Street DH2 .....15 E3
Byron Cl Billingham TS23 ..102 E8
Stanley DH9 ....14 A6
Byron Ct Brotton TS12 ...126 B5
Crook DL15 ....52 C2
Dalton-on-T DL2 ....168 B5
Byron Lodge Est 6 SR7 ...18 E1
Byron Rd Chilton DL17 ....82 E8
Darlington DL1 ....133 C3
Byron St Easington SR8 ...39 F4
Hartlepool TS26 ....76 F6
Ouston DH2 ....8 F1
Wheatley Hill DH6 ....47 F2
Byron Terr
Houghton-le-S DH5 ....26 E7
5 Seaham SR7 ....18 F1
Shotton Colliery DH6 .....48 D6
Byron's Ct SR7 ....19 C2
Byway The DL1 ....133 D1
Bywell Dr SR8 ....49 C3
Bywell Gr TS7 ....141 A7

C

Cabot Ct TS17 ....138 D4
Cadger Bank DH7 ....20 E3
Cadogan Sq 1 DL5 ....96 C7
Cadogan St
Middlesbrough TS1 ....214 B2
Middlesbrough, North Ormesby
TS3 ....120 C4
Cadwell Cl TS3 ....121 A1
Cadwell La SR8 ....39 B4
Caedmon Cres DL3 ....132 B1
Caedmon Prim Sch TS6 .121 E4
Caernarvon Cl TS6 ......121 E4
Caernarvon Gr TS26 ......76 D8
Cain Terr DH6 ....47 E2
Cairn Ct TS2 ....119 D8
Cairn Rd TS25 ....89 F7
Cairngorm Dr DL1 ....133 C6
Cairns Rd SR7 ....28 A3
Cairnston Rd TS26 ....76 C7
Caister Ct TS10 ....107 E2
Caistor Dr TS25 ....89 F6
Caithness Rd Eston TS6 ..121 B3
Hartlepool TS25 ....89 F7
Caithness Way DL1 ......133 E7
Cakesmire La DL2 ....201 E6
Calcott Cl TS19 ....117 C4
Calder Cl Billingham TS22 .102 A6
Bishop Auckland DL14 .....79 E6
Calder Gr Hartlepool TS25 ..89 F8
Middlesbrough TS4 ....140 B6
Redcar TS10 ....107 B4
Calderdale TS12 ....125 C3
Caldermere DL16 ....55 E2
Caldew Ct DH5 ....27 B2
Caldey Gdns TS17 ......156 E7
Caldicot Cl TS6 ....121 E4
Caldicotes Prim Sch
TS3 ....121 A3
Caldwell Cl TS8 ....139 E2
Caldwell Dr DL15 ....52 D4
Caldwell Gn 2 DL1 ......152 C8
Caledonia Blaydon NE21 ....2 B8
Great Lumley DH3 ....25 A8
Caledonian Rd TS25 ......77 A3
Caledonian Way DL1 .....133 E7
Calf Fallow La TS20 .....101 F2
California DL14 ....79 C8
California Cl TS18 .....213 A3
California Ct TS9 ......161 A3
California Gr TS9 ......161 A3
California Rd TS6 ......121 F2
California Row DL12 ....208 C5
California St TS18 .....213 A3
Callaley Ave NE16 ....2 F6

Callander DH2 9 A2
Callander Rd TS25 89 F8
Callerton Pl DH9 14 D2
Callerton Rise DL5 82 C1
Calley Cl SR8 49 C3
Callington Cl DH4 17 E2
Callington Dr SR2 18 F7
Callum Cl DL3 132 E5
Calluna Gr TS7 140 C4
Calow Way NE16 2 F5
Calstock Cl SR7 28 D2
Calthorpe Ct TS1 214 B3
Calverley Rd TS3 120 F2
Calvert Cl TS3 215 C2
Calvert St DL15 52 E4
Calvert Terr SR7 28 C3
Calvert's La TS18 213 B3
Cam Mead SR3 18 A4
Camberley Cl SR3 18 C8
Camberley Dr DH7 42 F3
Camborne Dr DL3 133 A8
Camborne Ho TS3 120 D3
Cambourne Cl TS8 139 E2
Cambrian Ave TS10 107 A3
Cambrian Ct TS17 156 F8
Cambrian Rd TS23 102 C5
Cambridge Ave
1 Consett DH8 177 A4
Marton TS7 140 D3
Middlesbrough TS5 139 C8
Willington DL15 53 F3
Cambridge Dr DH3 25 A6
Cambridge Pl DH3 9 C1
Cambridge Rd
Middlesbrough TS5 139 C8
Middlesbrough, Cargo Fleet TS3 120 C5
New Silksworth SR3 18 A7
Peterlee SR8 49 C8
Thornaby-on-T TS17 138 C8
Cambridge St
Coundon DL14 68 D1
5 Saltburn-by-t-S TS12 125 C7
Spennymoor DL16 68 F8
Cambridge Terr
Barnard Castle DL12 209 C6
Bowburn DH6 57 D8
Middlesbrough TS2 103 E1
Cambridgeshire Dr DH1 35 C2
Camden Sq SR7 29 C6
Camden Square Inf Sch SR7 29 C6
Camden St
Middlesbrough TS1 215 B2
Stockton-on-T TS18 212 C1
Camellia Cres TS20 117 F7
Camelon St 9 TS17 138 D8
Camelot Cl SR7 29 C8
Cameron Rd TS24 77 B7
Cameron St 4 TS20 118 A8
Camp St SR8 39 F4
Campbell Ct TS18 213 C4
Campbell Rd TS25 89 F8
Campbell St
Easington SR8 39 F4
Tow Law DL13 183 E1
Campbell Terr DH5 27 B1
Camperdown Ave DH3 16 D5
Campion Cl TS17 138 B2
Campion Ct DL5 82 E2
Campion Dr
Guisborough TS14 143 B3
Tanfield Lea DH9 13 D8
Campion Gr TS7 140 C4
Campion Pl DL14 79 F7
Campion Rd DL1 133 B5
Campion St 3 TS26 77 A5
Canberra Gr TS18 212 A1
Canberra Rd TS7 140 D3
Candlish Terr SR7 29 E6
Canewood TS3 120 F2
Cann Rd SR8 49 D7
Cann St SR8 39 C4
Canney Hill DL14 80 F8
Cannobie Cl DL3 132 C1
Cannock Rd TS3 120 C1
Cannon Park Cl TS1 214 B3
Cannon Park Ind Est TS1 214 B3
Cannon Park Rd TS1 214 B3
Cannon Park Way TS1 214 B3
Cannon St
Middlesbrough TS1 214 A2
Middlesbrough TS1 214 A3
Canon Gr TS15 156 D4
Canterbury Cl
Great Lumley DH3 25 A6
Spennymoor DL16 55 E3
Canterbury Cres DL15 53 F2
Canterbury Gr
Darlington DL1 133 E5
Middlesbrough TS5 119 E2
Canterbury Rd
Brotton TS12 126 C4
Durham DH1 34 E7
Redcar TS10 107 F4
Canton Gdns TS5 139 D3
Canvey Wlk TS14 143 D3
Capstan Ho TS24 77 D6
Captain Cook Prim Sch TS7 140 D4
Captain Cook Sq TS1 214 C3
Captain Cook's Birthplace Mus* TS7 140 D5
Captain Cook's Cl TS13 149 C8
Captain Cook's Cres TS7 140 E3
Captain Cook's Monument* TS9 162 A1
Captain Cook's Mus* TS9 161 A2
Captain Cook's Way TS9 161 A2
Captain Cooks & Staithes Heritage Ctr* TS13 129 C2
Captains Wlk TS24 77 D6
Caradoc Rd TS28 60 E8
Caragh Rd DH2 16 C1
Carburt Rd TS19 117 B7
Carcut Rd TS3 120 C5
Cardiff St SR8 39 F4
Cardigan Cl TS6 121 E4
Cardigan Gr TS26 63 E1
Cardinal Gdns DL3 132 C2
Cardinal Gr TS19 116 F4
Cardwell Wlk 1 TS17 138 C8
Carew Cl TS15 156 A3
Carey Cl Bowburn DH6 57 D8
Middlesbrough TS1 214 B2
Cargo Fleet La TS3 120 E3
Cargo Fleet Rd
Middlesbrough TS1 215 B3
Middlesbrough TS3 215 C3
Caribbees 4 DH8 177 E4
Carileph Cl DL5 96 C6
Carisbrooke Ave TS3 120 F2
Carisbrooke Cres DL14 79 E6
Carisbrooke Rd TS26 76 D5
Carisbrooke Way TS10 107 E3
Carisbrooke Wlk DL3 132 A2
Carlbury Ave TS5 139 C4
Carlbury Cres DL3 132 B2
Carlbury Rd DL5 96 E3
Carleton Dr DL3 132 B2
Carleton Gr DL3 132 B2
Carlile Hill TS8 139 D1
Carlile Wlk 6 TS20 118 B5
Carlingford Rd DH2 16 B1
Carlisle Gr DL14 80 A6
Carlisle Rd DH1 34 E7
Carlisle St TS25 90 E8
Carlow Cl TS14 143 E2
Carlow St TS1 214 A1
Carlton Ave TS22 102 C6
Carlton Cl
Guisborough TS14 143 E6
Stockton-on-T TS18 213 A3
Urpeth DH2 8 E2
Carlton Ct 5 DL1 133 B1
Carlton Dr TS17 138 B4
Carlton Moor Cres DL1 152 D7
Carlton St Ferryhill DL17 70 C3
Hartlepool TS26 77 A5
Carlton Terr
Easington SR8 39 B3
Yarm TS15 156 B6
Carlyle Cres DH6 48 D6
Carlyle Rd TS6 121 D3
Carmarthen Rd TS3 140 E8
Carmel Ct DL3 132 C2
Carmel Gdns
Darlington DL3 151 C8
Guisborough TS14 143 E5
Middlesbrough TS5 139 D3
Nunthorpe TS7 141 B3
Stockton-on-T TS20 118 C7
Carmel Gr DL3 151 D8
Carmel RC Tech Coll DL3 132 B1
Carmel Rd DH9 13 D6
Carmel Rd N DL3 132 C2
Carmel Rd S DL3 151 D7
Carnaby Rd DL1 133 D1
Carnaby Wlk TS5 139 E7
Carnation Ave DH4 17 E3
Carney St TS12 145 B6
Carnforth Gdns NE39 1 E3
Carnoustie DH2 9 A1
Carnoustie Cl DH8 10 E5
Carnoustie Dr TS16 137 C1
Carnoustie Gr
Darlington DL1 133 C7
Hartlepool TS27 63 C4
Carnoustie Rd TS11 124 A6
Carnoustie Way TS8 140 E2
Carole Dunes DH6 58 D7
Caroline St
Bishop Auckland DL14 80 B6
Hartlepool TS26 77 B4
Hetton-le-H DH5 27 A4
Seaham SR7 29 D7
Carpenter Cl TS15 156 E4
Carr Ave DH7 43 B4
Carr Ho Dr DH1 34 C6
Carr House Dr DH1 34 D7
Carr House Mews DH8 11 B3
Carr La Mordon DL5,TS21 97 E6
Spennymoor DL16 55 E2
Carr Pl DL5 96 F6
Carr Row DH4 25 E3
Carr Side DL3 132 F6
Carr St 5 Hartlepool TS26 77 A7
Spennymoor DL16 55 E1
Stockton-on-T TS18 212 C2
Carr's Terr DL14 65 B3
Carradale Cl TS16 156 C8
Carrhouse La SR7 27 F4
Carriage Wlk TS16 137 B2
Carrick Ct TS2 119 D8
Carrick St TS24 63 F2
Carrmere Rd 1 SR2 18 E8
Carrmyers DH9 12 E6
Carrock Cl SR8 49 D4
Carrol St TS18 213 B3
Carroll Rd DL3 132 B1
Carroll Wlk TS25 76 D2
Carron Gr TS6 121 C1
Carrowmore Rd DH2 16 C1
Carrs The DH1 34 C7
Carrsdale DH1 35 D5
Carrside DH1 34 B6
Carrside Rd TS29 72 D7
Carrsides La DL17 82 F4
Carrsway DH1 35 D5
Carter Bequest Hospl TS5 139 D8
Carter's La
Eaglescliffe TS16 155 B8
Middleton St George TS16 136 B1
Carthorpe Dr TS23 102 E6
Cartington Cl SR8 49 D3
Cartington Rd DH1 34 D5
Cartmel Ct
Chester le Street DH2 16 A2
Spennymoor DL16 55 E3
Cartmel Rd TS10 107 C4
Cartmel Terr DH2 15 B7
Cartmell Terr DL3 132 E4
Carvers Ct TS12 126 C4
Carville Ct 4 TS19 117 B6
Carville Est DL15 53 E4
Carville Terr DL15 53 E4
Carvis Cl DH7 43 A3
Carwardine Cl DL5 82 C2
Carway Bank DL13 179 C2
Casebourne Rd TS25 77 C3
Casper Ct TS16 137 C2
Cass House Rd TS8 139 E1
Cassel Bank DL12 192 D5
Casson Ct TS23 102 D6
Casson Way TS23 102 D6
Cassop Gr TS5 139 B5
Cassop Prim Sch DH6 58 D8
Cassop Wlk 1 TS19 117 B6
Castle Ave DH6 45 C1
Castle Bank DL13 183 E2
Castle Chare
3 Bishop Auckland DL14 80 C8
Durham DH1 210 C3
Castle Cl
Chester le Street DH3 16 D2
Crook DL15 52 E2
Hetton-le-H DH5 27 B2
Middleton St George DL2 153 F6
Spennymoor DL16 56 C3
Stanhope DL13 206 D3
Stockton-on-T TS19 117 C4
Castle Close Ind Est DL15 52 E2
Castle Ct
Annfield Plain DH9 13 A3
Barnard Castle DL12 209 B5
Castleside DH8 176 F3
Castle Dene Gr DH4 26 D8
Castle Dyke Wynd TS15 156 C6
Castle Eden Ctry Pk* TS21 100 F6
Castle Eden Dene (Nature Reserve)* TS27 49 E3
Castle Gdns DL13 206 D3
Castle Grange TS12 125 B1
Castle Hills 6 DH8 177 A3
Castle Howard Cl TS27 63 D3
Castle Rd TS10 107 F4
Castle Riggs DH2 16 B3
Castle St SR8 39 F4
Castle Terr DL12 203 D8
Castle View
Chester le Street DH3 16 C5
Esh Winning DH7 31 D1
Howden-le-W DL15 66 A6
Ushaw Moor DH7 33 C1
Witton-le-W DL14 65 B3
Castle Way
Middlesbrough TS4 120 A1
Stockton-on-T TS18 213 B2
Castle Wynd TS7 141 A1
Castlebay Ct DL1 133 E7
Castledene Rd DH8 11 B1
Castlefields
Bournmoor DH4 17 D3
Esh Winning DH7 31 F1
Castlegarth DL16 68 C5
Castlegate Ctr TS18 213 B2
Castlegate Quay TS18 213 B2
Castlemain Cl DH4 17 D3
Castlemartin TS17 156 F6
Castlereagh TS22 87 C2
Castlereagh Cl
Longnewton TS21 136 A5
Newton Aycliffe DL5 96 C6
Castlereagh Homes The SR7 19 D1
Castlereagh Rd
Seaham SR7 29 D7
Stockton-on-T TS19 212 C4
Castlereagh St SR3 18 A7
Castlereigh Cl DH4 17 D3
Castleside Ind Est DH8 177 A4
Castleside Prim Sch
Castleside DH8 176 F3
Consett, Bridgehill DH8 10 D5
Castleton Ave TS5 139 B8
Castleton Dr TS22 102 B5
Castleton Rd Eston TS6 121 F3
Hartlepool TS25 90 E7
Stockton-on-T TS18 137 F8
Castleton Wlk TS17 138 C4
Castlewood TS3 120 F1
Cat Castle Cotts DL12 198 F3
Cat Flatt La TS11 108 A1
Catchgate Prim Sch DH9 12 E4
Catchwell Rd DH9 12 D8
Catcote Rd TS25 76 E2
Catcote Sch TS25 76 E4
Caterhouse Rd DH1 34 C6
Caterton Cl TS15 156 E4
Cathedral Dr TS19 117 A5
Cathedral Gdns TS2 214 C4
Cathedral View DH7 23 D2
Catherine Cl DL16 69 A8
Catherine Rd TS24 77 D5
Catherine St
Hartlepool TS24 64 G8
Lingdale TS12 145 E5
Catherine Terr
Annfield Plain DH9 13 B4
Stanley DH9 13 F8
Catterall Ho TS3 120 D3
Cattersty Way TS12 126 B5
Cattistock Cl TS14 143 F3
Caudwell Cl TS19 117 A7
Cauldron Snout (Waterfall)* DL12 190 D7
Causeway Rd DL13 179 B1
Causeway The
Billingham TS23 102 D4
Darlington DL1 133 D2
Wolsingham DL13 207 C5
Causey Arch* DH9 7 A4
Causey Arch Sta* NE16 7 A4
Causey Dr DH9 14 A8
Causey Rd DH9,NE16 7 A3
Causey View DH9 14 B7
Causey Way DH9 7 A1
Cavell Pl DH9 14 A5
Cavell Sq SR8 39 D5
Cavendish Ct
Brandon DH7 43 A3
4 Darlington DL1 133 B6
Ferryhill DL17 69 E5
Cavendish Dr 3 DL1 133 B6
Cavendish Pl
Burnopfield NE16 6 A4
2 New Silksworth SR3 18 A7
Cavendish Rd TS4 140 A8
Caversham Rd TS4 140 B7
Cawdor Cl TS11 123 F6
Cawood Dr TS5 139 E6
Cawthorn Cl TS8 139 C2
Cawthorne Terr NE16 6 A4
Caxton Gr TS25 76 E3
Caxton St TS5 214 C1
Caxton Way DH3 16 D8
Cayton Cl TS10 107 B2
Cayton Dr
Billingham TS22 102 B5
Middlesbrough TS5 139 E7
Thornaby-on-T TS17 138 B3
Cecil Cres DH7 20 F3
Cecil Rd DL12 209 B6
Cecil St
Middlesbrough TS1 214 B3
Stockton-on-T TS18 213 A1
Cedar Ave DH2 23 F3
Cedar Cl Durham DH1 35 A3
Eston TS6 121 D2
Cedar Cres
Burnopfield NE16 5 F6
Eaglescliffe TS16 137 D4
Willington DL15 54 C3
Cedar Ct
Annfield Plain DH9 12 E4
Langley Park DH7 32 A6
South Hetton DH6 37 F7
Spennymoor DL16 69 A8
Thornaby-on-T TS17 138 C7
Thornley (nr Wheatley Hill) DH6 47 C3
Cedar Dr Durham DH1 44 B5
Newton Aycliffe DL5 97 A7
Thornton TS8 158 B8
Cedar Gdns Consett DH8 10 C1
Crook DL15 52 D4
Cedar Gr Brotton TS12 126 A4
Loftus TS13 127 B1
Middleton St George DL2 153 F6
Redcar TS10 107 E6
Shildon DL4 81 A1
Thornaby-on-T TS17 138 C7
Cedar Mews DL2 168 A8
Cedar Rd
Bishop Auckland DL14 80 C7
Darlington DL3 132 D4
Marton TS7 140 F4
Ormesby TS7 141 B6
Cedar St Peterlee SR8 50 B6
Stockton-on-T TS18 213 B3
Waldridge DH2 15 E1
Cedar Terr Cornforth DL17 70 E8
7 Fence Houses DH4 26 A8
Middlesbrough TS2 119 F8
Cedar Wlk 3 TS24 77 A8
Cedarhurst Dr TS12 145 E5
Cedars DH2 16 B5
Cedars Cres SR7 28 D3
Cedars The Coxhoe DH6 58 A3
3 Darlington DL3 132 D3
Cedarwood
Great Lumley DH4 17 E1
Middleton St George DL2 153 E7
Cedarwood Glade TS8 158 C8
Celandine Cl TS7 140 C5
Celandine Way TS19 117 C5
Cemetery La DL3 132 C1
Cemetery Rd Stanley DH9 13 F7
Wheatley Hill DH6 47 F2
Witton-le-W DL14 65 B3
Cennon Gr TS17 156 F8
Centenary Cres TS20 118 A7
Central Ave
Billingham TS23 102 D2
Bishop Auckland DL14 79 D3
Brandon DH7 43 C3
Middlesbrough TS5 119 B2
Newton Aycliffe DL5 96 E7
Central Bldgs 2 TS24 77 C6
Central Dr DL16 68 D6
Central Par DL4 81 A1
Central St TS15 156 B6
Central Terr TS10 107 C7
Central Way TS9 161 A3
Centre Ct TS5 139 C3
Centre The DL14 92 D6
Centrepoint Rd DL1 133 F2
Centrepoint Sq DL1 133 F2
Century Terr DH9 12 E5
Cestria Prim Sch DH3 16 D3
Cestria Way DL5 96 A8
Chadburn Gn TS4 139 F7
Chadburn Rd TS20 118 A6
Chadderton Cl TS12 145 B7
Chadderton Dr TS17 138 F6
Chadwell Ave 7 TS3 140 D8
Chaffinch Cl TS26 63 E1
Chains The DH1 211 A3
Chair La DH6,DL16 56 A5
Chalcot Wlk TS3 120 D3
Chaldron Way TS16 137 A2
Chalfield Cl 6 TS17 138 C1
Chalfont Way DH7 43 C4
Chalford Oaks TS5 139 B7
Chalk Cl TS18 213 A1
Chalk Wlk TS18 213 A1
Challacombe Cres TS17 157 A6
Challener Way DL14 79 D2
Challoner Rd
Hartlepool TS24 77 A8
Yarm TS15 156 B4
Challoner Sq 4 TS24 77 A8
Chaloner Mews TS14 143 E4
Chaloner St TS14 143 E4
Chamomile Dr TS19 117 C6
Chancel Way TS6 121 E2
Chancery La 15 DL1 132 F1
Chancery Rise TS17 138 B4
Chandler Cl Durham DH1 35 A1
Newton Aycliffe DL5 96 E8
Chandler Ct SR8 39 F4
Chandlers Cl TS24 77 D6
Chandlers Ford DH4 17 F8
Chandlers Ridge TS7 141 A2
Chandlers Ridge Prim Sch TS7 141 A2
Chandlers Wharf TS18 213 B1
Chandos SR3 18 A4
Chandos St DL3 132 F4
Chantilly Ave DL1 133 E6
Chantry Cl
Middlesbrough TS3 140 C8
Stockton-on-T TS20 118 A8
Darlington DL3 132 C6
Chantry Pl DH4 26 A2
Chapel Ave NE16 6 B6
Chapel Cl
Hamsterley DL13 189 D2
Kibblesworth NE11 8 D6
4 Marske-by-t-S TS11 124 C8
Middlesbrough TS3 140 F8
Chapel Ct
7 Barnard Castle DL12 209 C5
Billingham TS23 102 D1
Sherburn DH6 36 A1
Witton Gilbert DH7 33 A8
Chapel Gdns TS21 116 D8
Chapel Hill Rd SR8 49 F6
Chapel La Cleasby DL2 150 E7
Haswell DH6 37 F3
Scargill DL12 204 D5
Chapel Mews DH1 211 C3
Chapel Rd TS23 102 D1
Chapel Row Birtley DH3 9 E3
Middleton-In-T DL12 208 B5
Sadberge DL2 134 E7
Thornley (nr Tow Law) DL13 189 D8
Chapel St
Bishop Auckland DL14 79 C1
Evenwood DL14 92 C7
Guisborough TS14 143 E4
Hetton-le-H DH5 27 B4
Hunwick DL15 66 D7
Kirk Merrington DL16 69 A3
Lazenby TS6 122 C4
Marske-by-t-S TS11 108 C1
Middleton St George DL2 153 F7
Shildon DL4 94 F8
Skinningrove TS13 127 A4
Stanhope DL13 206 D3
Stanley Crook DL15 52 F8
Tantobie DH9 6 B2
Thornaby-on-T TS17 213 C1
Toronto DL14 66 F2
Willington DL15 53 F3
Wingate TS28 60 E6
Chapel Terr Copley DL13 195 A4
Ferryhill DL17 69 F6
Gainford DL2 201 D3
Rookhope DL13 180 E5
Chapel View
Rowlands Gill NE39 1 E3
West Rainton DH4 25 F1
Chapelbeck Bglws TS14 143 D4
Chapelgarth TS8 139 C1
Chaplehope Cl DL1 133 C7

Chaplin St SR7 29 D5
Chapman Cl DL5 96 E7
Chapman Ct TS3 120 E2
Chapman St 2 TS20 118 B7
Chapmans Cotts TS8 157 F7
Chard Wlk TS3 140 C8
Chare Bank DH8 3 E3
Chare La DH6 46 E7
Chare The SR8 49 D6
Charlaw Cl DH7 23 B4
Charlaw La DH7 22 E4
Charlaw Terr DH7 23 B3
Charlbury Rd TS3 120 D3
Charles Perkins Meml Cottage Homes DH3 9 C3
Charles Row DL5 81 E1
Charles St
Darlington DL1 133 A4
Easington SR8 39 F4
Hartlepool TS24 77 C5
New Marske TS11 124 A7
Redcar TS10 107 D6
Ryhope SR2 19 A6
Seaham SR7 29 D7
Seaton Carew TS25 90 E8
Shildon DL4 95 A8
Spennymoor DL16 68 F8
Stanley DH9 13 E4
Thornaby-on-T TS17 138 C8
Charles Terr DH2 15 E6
Charlock TS8 159 C7
Charlotte St
Hartlepool TS26 77 A4
Middlesbrough TS2 214 C4
Redcar TS10 107 D6
Skelton TS12 125 D2
Stanley DH9 13 E4
Charlotte Terr DL17 82 F8
Charlton Rd TS10 106 F5
Charltons TS12 144 F3
Charnley Gn TS4 140 B6
Charnwood DH9 13 E8
Charnwood Cl 3 TS11 124 C8
Charnwood Dr
Darlington DL3 132 C7
Ormesby TS7 141 B5
Charrington Ave TS17 138 B4
Chart Ho TS24 77 D6
Charterhouse St TS25 77 A3
Charters Cres DH6 38 A6
Chartwell Cl
Ingleby Barwick TS17 157 C8
Marske-by-t-S TS11 108 B2
Chartwell Pl DH8 10 F4
Charwood TS3 120 F2
Chase Cl DL3 132 A4
Chase Ct DH6 36 A1
Chase End DL2 152 C1
Chase The
Hurworth-on-T DL2 152 C1
Redcar TS10 107 D5
Stockton-on-T TS19 117 B3
Washington NE38 9 F1
Chatham Gdns TS24 77 A8
Chatham Rd TS24 77 A8
Chatham Sq 5 TS24 77 A8
Chathill Wlk TS7 141 A7
Chatsworth Ave 7 DL14 80 B6
Chatsworth Ct TS19 117 D5
Chatsworth Gdns TS22 102 C5
Chatsworth Ho TS3 120 D3
Chatsworth Terr DL1 152 A8
Chatton Cl
Chester le Street DH2 16 A1
9 Middlesbrough TS3 140 D8
Chaucer Ave
Blackhall Colliery TS27 50 C4
Hartlepool TS25 76 F3
Chaucer Cl
Billingham TS23 102 D7
Stanley DH9 14 A6
Chaucer Rd DL1 152 A7
Chaucer St 9 DH4 26 D8
Chaytor Ct DL3 132 F7
Chaytor Lee TS15 156 C5
Chaytor Rd DH8 10 C4
Chaytor Terr TS21 72 C4
Chaytor Terr N DH9 14 C3
Chaytor Terr S DH9 14 C3
Cheadle Wlk 8 TS3 140 D8
Cheam Ave TS3 120 D3
Cheapside Shildon DL4 81 A2
2 Spennymoor DL16 68 F8
Cheddar Cl TS6 121 E4
Cheddar Ct DH9 12 F3
Cheesmond Ave DL14 79 F4
Cheetham St TS6 121 D6
Chelker Cl TS26 76 C6
Chelmsford Ave TS18 117 C2
Chelmsford Rd TS5 119 E2
Chelmsford St
5 Darlington DL3 132 F3
5 New Silksworth SR3 18 A8
Thornaby-on-T TS17 213 C1
Chelmsford Wlk TS5 119 E1
Chelsea Ct DL1 151 E8
Chelsea Gdns TS20 101 E1
Chelston Cl TS26 76 C7
Cheltenham Ave
Marton TS7 140 D2
8 Thornaby-on-T TS17 138 D8
Cheltenham Cl TS5 119 F2
Cheltenham Rd TS18 118 F5
Cheltenham Way DL5 82 F2
Chepstow Cl
Billingham TS23 102 D5
Consett DH8 10 D7
Chepstow Ct DL1 133 F4
Chepstow Wlk TS26 76 E8
Cheriton Gn TS3 120 D3
Cherribank SR2 18 E6
Cherry Ave SR8 50 B6
Cherry Banks DH3 16 D5
Cherry Cotts DH9 6 B2
Cherry Ct TS19 118 A5
Cherry Dr DH6 37 F3
Cherry Garth TS17 138 A2
Cherry Gr SR7 29 C6
Cherry Knowle Hospl SR2 18 E4
Cherry Pk DH7 43 A3
Cherry Tree Cl 10 TS7 141 B7
Cherry Tree Dr
Sedgefield TS21 85 B7
Willington DL15 53 E2
Cherry Tree Gdns TS20 118 C7
Cherry Tree Sq 6 SR2 18 E8
Cherry Trees TS10 107 B7
Cherrytree Dr
Langley Park DH7 32 B6
Newton Aycliffe DL5 96 A3
Cherrytree Rd DH2 16 A5
Cherrywood Ct TS5 139 E4
Cherrywood Gdns SR3 18 B7
Chertsey Ave TS3 120 D3
Chervil Ct TS8 159 C8
Cherwell Rd SR8 49 B5
Cherwell Terr TS3 120 E4
Chesham Cl TS20 118 B8
Chesham Gr TS20 118 C8
Chesham Rd TS20 118 C8
Chesham St TS5 119 E2
Cheshire Ave DH3 9 C1
Cheshire Dr DH1 35 C2
Cheshire Pl DL14 80 B5
Cheshire Rd TS20 118 C7
Chesneywood TS3 120 F2
Chesnut St DL1 133 A3
Chester Cres DL17 70 F8
Chester Dr DL15 53 F2
Chester Gdns DH7 23 B1
Chester Gr DL3 132 B3
Chester Pl SR8 49 B7
Chester Rd
Bournmoor DH3,DH4 17 D3
Chester le Street DH3 16 F5
Consett DH8 177 A4
Hartlepool TS26 76 F7
Redcar TS10 107 F4
Stanley DH9 14 A7
Chester Road Est DH9 14 A7
Chester St
Bishop Auckland DL14 80 C7
Middlesbrough TS1 214 B1
Waldridge DH2 15 E1
Chester Terr SR8 39 D4
Chester-le-Street CE Jun Sch DH2 16 B5
Chester-le-Street Com Hospl DH3 16 C2
Chester-le-Street Sta DH3 16 C3
Chesterfields DL3 132 E1
Chesters Dene DH8 3 E3
Chesters The DH8 3 E3
Chesterton Ave TS17 138 B4
Chesterton Ct 5 TS20 118 B7
Chesterton Rd TS25 76 E3
Chesterwood TS3 120 F2
Chestnut Ave
Ferryhill DL17 70 A6
Redcar TS10 107 E5
Spennymoor DL16 68 E7
Chestnut Cl Lazenby TS6 122 C4
Saltburn-by-t-S TS12 125 A6
Shildon DL4 81 A1
Chestnut Ct DL14 78 E5
Chestnut Dr Haswell DH6 38 A3
Marton TS7 140 E3
Chestnut Gr
Billy Row DL15 52 D7
Brotton TS12 126 A4
Thornaby-on-T TS17 138 C7
Ushaw Moor DH7 33 A1
Chestnut Rd
Eaglescliffe TS16 137 D4
Sedgefield TS21 85 B7
Chestnut Sq TS19 117 F5
Chestnut Way SR7 29 C6
Chesworth Cl TS3 120 F1
Chetwode Terr 6 TS3 140 E8
Cheveley Park Sh Ctr DH1 35 D4
Cheveley Wlk DH1 35 D3
Chevin Wlk TS3 120 C1
Cheviot Cl DH2 24 A8
Cheviot Cres TS23 102 D3
Cheviot Ct
Annfield Plain DH9 12 F3
3 Darlington DL1 133 C6
Seaham SR7 29 A8
Cheviot Dr TS12 125 C3
Cheviot Gdns SR7 29 B8
Cheviot Ho TS4 215 B1
Cheviot La SR2 18 E7
Cheviot Pl
Newton Aycliffe DL5 96 B7
Peterlee SR8 49 B6
Cheviot Rd DH2 16 B1
Cheviot Terr DH9 14 A5
Cheviot Wlk DL14 81 C8
Chevychase Ct SR7 18 F2
Cheyne The SR3 18 A5
Chez Nous Ave TS25 77 B3
Chichester Cl TS25 89 F6
Chichester Rd DH1 34 D8
Chichester Wlk DL1 133 F5
Chilcroft Cl TS22 102 A5
Child St Brotton TS12 126 B4
Guisborough TS14 143 E4
Childeray St TS18 212 C2
Chillingham Ct TS23 102 E7
Chillingham Dr DH2 16 A1
Chillingham Gr
Newton Aycliffe DL5 82 E1
Peterlee SR8 49 A3
Chillingham Rd DH1 34 D6
Chiltern Ave
Chester le Street DH2 16 B2
Redcar TS10 107 A4
Chiltern Gdns DH9 14 B5
Chiltern Rd DL14 81 C8
Chilton Cl Darlington DL3 132 B1
Middlesbrough TS5 139 C6
Stockton-on-T TS19 117 A7
Chilton Ct DL5 82 E1
Chilton Garth SR8 49 F5
Chilton Gdns 10 DH4 26 A8
Chilton Ind Est DL17 69 E2
Chilton La DL17 70 C4
Chilton Prim Sch DL17 82 F7
Chilton Way DL17 69 E1
Chiltons Ave TS23 102 E1
China St DL3 133 A6
Chine The TS12 125 B7
Chingford Ave TS3 120 F1
Chingford Gr TS19 212 A4
Chipchase NE38 9 F4
Chipchase Ct
Bournmoor DH4 17 D1
Seaham SR7 18 F2
Chipchase Rd TS5 119 D2
Chippenham Rd TS4 140 A6
Chirnside Terr DH9 12 E3
Chisholm Rd TS29 72 D8
Chopwell Cl TS19 117 B7
Chopwell Rd NE17 4 C6
Chopwell View DH9 12 C7
Chopwell Woods Rd NE39 1 A3
Chorister Sch The DH1 210 C1
Christ Church Art Gal* TS24 77 C6
Christ the King RC Prim Sch TS17 138 E4
Christchurch Cl 5 DL1 133 B6
Christchurch Dr TS18 117 B1
Christchurch Pl SR8 49 C5
Christopher Ho TS20 102 B1
Christopher St
4 Hartlepool TS26 77 A6
4 Stockton-on-T TS20 118 B5
Christopher Wlk 2 DL5 96 C7
Church Bank
Barnard Castle DL12 209 B4
Consett DH8 10 C6
Eggleston DL12 193 D2
Stanley DH9 13 F7
Church Chare DH3 16 D3
Church Cl Bournmoor DH4 17 E4
Eaglescliffe TS16 156 C7
Ebchester DH8 3 E3
Hartlepool TS24 77 F8
Kirk Merrington DL16 69 A3
Marske-by-t-S TS11 108 D1
Middleton St George DL2 153 F5
Newton Aycliffe DL5 96 D6
Ormesby TS7 141 A7
Peterlee SR8 49 E5
Seaham SR7 29 C8
Stainton TS8 139 C1
Thornaby-on-T TS17 138 B8
Church Ct SR7 29 A8
Church Dr
Bishop Auckland DL14 80 D6
Boosbeck TS12 145 C6
Great Ayton TS9 160 F2
Church Farm Flats TS21 116 B7
Church Field Way TS17 138 A2
Church Gn SR7 29 C8
Church Gr 4 DL14 81 B8
Church Hill DL15 52 F4
Church Howle Cres TS11 108 E1
Church La Durham DH1 211 A1
Durham, Gilesgate DH1 211 B3
Edmundbyers DH8 175 F5
Eston TS6 121 D4
Ferryhill DL17 69 F6
Great Ayton TS9 161 B7
Guisborough TS14 143 F7
Hunwick DL15 66 E6
Low Worsall TS15 171 C8
Marske-by-t-S TS11 108 D2
Middlesbrough TS5 139 C6
Middleton St George DL2 153 F5
Murton SR7 28 C2
Nenthead CA9 178 A6
Newton Aycliffe DL5 96 E1
Nunthorpe TS7 141 C1
Ormesby TS7 141 A6
Ormesby TS7 141 A7
Redmarshall TS21 116 B7
Sadberge DL2 134 E6
Shadforth DH6 46 E7
Skelton TS12 125 A2
Stanhope DL13 206 D3
Tow Law DL13 183 E2
Wolsingham DL13 207 C5
Church La N SR7 28 B3
Church Mdws DH7 43 D5
Church Mews DL2 201 A3
Church Mount TS6 121 E2
Church Par DH7 23 B4
Church Pk
Thornley (nr Wheatley Hill) DH6 47 F3
Wheatley Hill DH6 47 F3
Church Rd
Billingham TS23 102 D1
Consett DH8 10 D4
Eaglescliffe TS16 156 C7
Ferryhill DL17 69 F6
Hetton-le-H DH5 27 A5
Pelton DH2 15 D6
Stockton-on-T TS18 213 C3
Trimdon TS29 59 D1
Church Row
Crawley Side DL13 206 C5
9 Darlington DL1 132 F1
Hartlepool TS24 77 B4
Hurworth-on-T DL2 152 E1
Ingleton DL2 201 D7
Loftus TS13 127 C1
Wolviston TS22 102 C8
Church Sch DL2 152 C1
Church Sq Cockfield DL13 195 E3
1 Hartlepool TS24 77 C6
High Etherley DL14 78 F5
Church St
Annfield Plain DH9 12 F4
Birtley DH3 9 C4
Bishop Middleham DL17 71 B3
Byers Green DL16 67 F8
Castleside DH8 176 F3
Consett DH8 10 F2
Coundon DL14 81 B8
1 Coxhoe DH6 58 A4
Crook DL15 52 F4
Durham DH1 211 A1
Ferryhill DL17 70 C3
Guisborough TS14 143 F5
Hartlepool TS24 77 C6
Haswell DH6 37 E3
Hesleden TS27 50 A1
High Etherley DL14 78 F5
8 Houghton-le-S DH4,DH5 26 E8
Howden-le-W DL15 65 E7
1 Langley Park DH7 32 C6
Leadgate DH8 11 C4
Marske-by-t-S TS11 108 D2
Murton SR7 28 D2
1 Quarrington Hill DH6 58 D8
Redcar TS10 107 A7
Sacriston DH7 23 B3
Seaham SR7 29 D7
Seaton Carew TS25 90 F8
Shildon DL4 80 F2
5 Spennymoor DL16 68 F8
Staindrop DL2 200 F7
Stanley DH9 13 F7
Station Town TS28 60 F6
Sunniside NE16 7 A8
Toronto DL14 67 A2
West Rainton DH4 26 A2
Wheatley Hill DH6 48 A3
Willington DL15 53 C3
Church St E DH6 58 A4
Church Street Head DH1 211 A1
Church Street Mews TS14 143 F5
Church Street Villas DH1 211 A1
Church Vale DH6 36 C4
Church View
Bishopton TS21 115 D7
Chilton DL17 82 F8
Consett DH8 10 E2
Durham DH1 35 D4
Haswell DH6 37 E3
Heighington DL5 95 D1
2 High Etherley DL14 78 F5
Hurworth-on-T DL2 152 D1
Ingleton DL2 201 D7
Kimblesworth DH2 24 A3
Lanchester DH7 20 F3
New Silksworth SR3 18 A7
Quebec DH7 31 B4
Sadberge DL2 134 E6
Sedgefield TS21 85 A6
Shotton Colliery DH6 48 C7
Thornley (nr Tow Law) DL13 189 D8
Thornley (nr Wheatley Hill) DH6 47 D4
Willington DL15 54 B3
Church Villas DH6 46 E7
Church Wlk Easington SR8 39 B3
Hartlepool TS24 77 F8
Thornley (nr Wheatley Hill) DH6 47 C4
Church Wynd DH6 35 F1
Churchend Cl TS23 102 D1
Churchgarth La DL13 180 E5
Churchill Ave DH1 211 C3
Churchill Cl Consett DH8 10 C6
Eston TS6 121 E3
Great Ayton TS9 161 A3
Churchill Dr TS11 108 C2
Churchill Rd
Barnard Castle DL12 209 D6
Eston TS6 121 E2
Churchill Sq
Durham DH1 211 C4
Fence Houses DH4 26 B8
Churchill Terr DH6 46 E8
Cinderwood TS3 120 F2
Cirrus Ho 14 SR3 18 A6
Clairville Ct TS4 215 B1
Clairville Rd TS4 215 B1
Clairville Stad TS4 215 B1
Clanny Rd DL5 96 E5
Clap Shaw DH8 175 A5
Clapham Gn TS3 120 B2
Clapham Rd TS15 156 B4
Clappersgate SR8 39 A3
Clara St SR7 29 B8
Clare Ave DL3 132 B2
Clare Rd SR8 49 B5
Claremont Ct TS17 213 C2
Claremont Dr
Hartlepool TS26 76 F5
Marton TS7 140 E2
Claremont Gdns TS19 117 B3
Claremont Gr TS21 85 A5
Claremont Pk TS26 76 F4
Claremont Rd DL1 152 C7
Clarence Chare DL5 96 E5
Clarence Cl DL5 96 E5
Clarence Cnr DL5 96 E5
Clarence Gdns
Bishop Auckland DL14 80 B8
Consett DH8 10 F4
Crook DL15 53 A3
Clarence Gn DL5 96 E5
Clarence Ho 6 DL16 68 F8
Clarence Rd
Eaglescliffe TS16 137 C2
Hartlepool TS24 77 B6
Middlesbrough TS2 103 E1
Nunthorpe TS7 141 B2
Clarence Row TS18 213 B4
Clarence St
Billingham TS23 103 E2
Bishop Auckland DL14 80 B8
Bowburn DH6 57 D8
Coxhoe DH6 57 F6
Hartlepool TS24 64 F1
3 Seaham SR7 29 D7
Spennymoor DL16 68 F8
Stockton-on-T TS18 213 B4
Tantobie DH9 6 B2
Clarence Terr
Chester le Street DH3 16 C3
Willington DL15 53 E3
Clarence The 10 DL14 80 B8
Clarence Villas DH6 57 F6
Clarendon Ho DL3 132 E1
Clarendon Rd
Darlington DL1 133 E6
Middlesbrough TS1 214 C2
Middlesbrough TS1 215 A2
Stockton-on-T TS20 118 A6
Thornaby-on-T TS17 138 D6
Clarendon St
13 Consett DH8 10 F3
Redcar TS10 107 D7
Clareville Rd DL3 132 C2
Clark St TS24 77 C5
Clark Terr Leadgate DH8 11 B6
Stanley DH9 13 F8
Clark's Terr 2 SR7 18 E1
Clark's Yd 7 DL3 132 F1
Clarke Terr SR7 28 C3
Clarkson Ct TS25 76 F1
Claude Ave TS5 139 E8
Claude St DH5 27 A3
Claude Terr SR7 28 D3
Clavering Pl DH9 12 F3
Clavering Prim Sch TS24 63 C3
Clavering Rd TS27 63 D3
Claxton Ave DL3 132 B3
Claxton Cl TS19 117 A7
Claxton Ct DL5 82 A1
Claxton St 5 SR8 50 A7
Clay La Durham DH1 210 A1
Durham DH1 210 B1
Clay Lane Commercial Pk TS6 121 B7
Claydon Gr TS17 157 B8
Claygate TS23 102 D7
Claymond Ct TS20 118 A8
Claymore Rd TS25 89 F7
Claypath DH1 211 A3
Claypath Ct DH1 211 A3
Claypath Rd DH5 27 B2
Claypool Farm Cl TS27 61 D5
Clayton Ct DL14 67 B1
Clayton St 1 DL14 80 B8
Cleadon Ave TS23 102 E7
Cleadon St 8 DH8 10 F3
Cleadon Wlk 3 TS19 117 B6
Clearpool Cl TS24 64 C1
Cleasby La Cleasby DL2 150 E3
Stapleton DL2 151 A5
Cleasby View DL3 132 B4
Cleasby Way TS16 137 B3
Cleatlam Back La DL2 200 C5
Cleatlam Cl TS19 117 B7
Cleator Dr TS14 143 D2
Clee Terr TS23 102 E4
Clements Rise TS20 117 F8
Clemmy Bank DL14 65 B3
Clepstone Ave TS5 139 C8
Clervaux Terr TS21 72 D5
Clevecoat Wlk TS27 62 F2
Clevegate TS7 141 A2
Cleveland Ave
Bishop Auckland DL14 80 B6
Chester le Street DH2 16 B2
Darlington DL3 132 E1
Middlesbrough TS5 139 D8
Shildon DL4 81 B1
Stockton-on-T TS20 118 B7
Trimdon TS29 59 D1
Cleveland Bsns Ctr TS1 215 A3

Cleveland Cl TS7 .... **141** A6
Cleveland Coll of Art & Design TS5 .... **139** D8
Cleveland Ct
Ferryhill DL17 .... **70** C5
South Bank TS6 .... **121** B6
Cleveland Ctr TS1 ...... **214** C3
Cleveland Dr TS7 .... **140** D4
Cleveland Gdns 5 TS16 . **137** B1
Cleveland Nuffield Hospl The TS20 .... **101** E1
Cleveland Pl SR8 .... **49** B6
Cleveland Rd
Barnard Castle DL12 ..... **209** D7
Hartlepool TS24 .... **64** C1
Cleveland Ret Pk TS6 .... **121** A4
Cleveland Sq TS1 .... **215** A3
Cleveland St
Darlington DL1 .... **133** A4
Eston, California TS6 ...... **121** F2
Great Ayton TS9 .... **161** A3
Guisborough TS14 .... **143** D4
Hartlepool TS24 .... **64** F1
Liverton TS13 .... **147** A8
Loftus TS13 .... **127** C1
Middlesbrough TS2 .... **215** A4
Normanby TS6 .... **121** D1
Redcar TS10 .... **107** C7
Saltburn-by-t-S TS12 ...... **125** D7
Cleveland Terr
Darlington DL3 .... **132** D1
Stanley DH9 .... **14** A5
Cleveland Trad Est DL1 .. **133** A4
Cleveland View
Coundon DL14 .... **81** C8
Ferryhill DL17 .... **70** B5
Fishburn TS21 .... **72** C4
Marske-by-t-S TS11 .... **108** A1
Middlesbrough TS3 .... **120** E2
Skelton TS12 .... **125** A1
Cleves Ave DL17 .... **70** C5
Cleves Cl DL17 .... **70** B6
Cleves Cotts 1 DL17 ..... **70** B5
Cleves Cross Grange DL17 .... **70** B6
Cleves Cross Prim Sch DL17 .... **70** B6
Cleves Ct DL17 .... **70** B7
Cliff Brow TS13 .... **148** E4
Cliff Cotts TS5 .... **119** C1
Cliff Rd SR2 .... **19** A6
Cliff St 4 TS11 .... **124** A6
Cliff Terr Easington SR8 .... **39** B4
Great Ayton TS9 .... **161** A3
Hartlepool TS24 .... **64** G8
Marske-by-t-S TS11 .... **108** D2
Ryhope SR2 .... **19** A6
Cliff The Hartlepool TS25 .... **90** F8
Seaton Carew TS25 .... **77** E1
Cliff View SR2 .... **19** A6
Cliffden Ct TS12 .... **125** D7
Cliffe Ave TS13 .... **126** F3
Cliffe Ct TS25 .... **77** E1
Cliffe St TS12 .... **126** C4
Cliffe Way DL1 .... **152** C8
Clifford Ave DL14 .... **80** B5
Clifford Cl TS24 .... **63** F2
Clifford Rd DH9 .... **13** F6
Clifford St
Chester le Street DH3 ...... **16** C1
Langley Park DH7 .... **32** B6
Redcar TS10 .... **107** C7
Clifford Terr DH3 .... **16** C2
Clifford's Bank DH7 .... **31** C3
Clifford's View DL11 ...... **200** F1
Cliffords Gate DH7 .... **31** C1
Cliffport Ct 4 TS18 .... **213** C4
Cliffwood Cl TS6 .... **121** F1
Clifton Ave
Billingham TS22 .... **102** B6
Darlington DL1 .... **152** A7
Eaglescliffe TS16 .... **137** D3
Hartlepool TS26 .... **77** A5
Stockton-on-T TS18 .... **137** F8
Clifton Gdns TS16 .... **137** D3
Clifton Gn DL15 .... **53** E2
Clifton Pl TS6 .... **121** D1
Clifton Rd DL1 .... **152** A8
Clifton Sq SR8 .... **49** D6
Clifton St TS1 .... **214** C2
Clint La DL12 .... **198** D1
Clive Cres TS20 .... **118** A7
Clive Rd Eston TS6 .... **121** D1
Middlesbrough TS5 .... **119** D2
Clive St DL17 .... **70** C4
Clockburn Lonnen NE16 .... **2** E4
Clockburnsyde Cl NE16 ..... **2** E5
Clocktower Mews DL12 .. **208** B6
Clockwood Gdns TS15 ... **156** D5
Cloisters The
Stockton-on-T TS19 .... **117** A4
Wingate TS28 .... **48** E1
Close E The DH2 .... **16** C5
Close Ho DL14 .... **81** A4
Close St DL1 .... **133** A5
Close The Brancepeth DH7 .. **42** E1
Burnopfield NE16 .... **6** C7
Chester le Street DH2 ...... **16** C5
Consett DH8 .... **10** D6
Cotherstone DL12 .... **198** F6
Durham DH1 .... **35** D3
High Etherley DL14 .... **78** F6
Houghton-le-S DH5 .... **26** F8
Lanchester DH7 .... **20** E4
Liverton TS13 .... **147** A4
Close The *continued*
Longnewton TS21 .... **135** F5
Middlesbrough TS4 .... **120** A1
Middridge DL5 .... **81** E1
Neasham DL2 .... **153** B2
Spennymoor DL16 .... **56** A2
Closeburn Sq SR3 .... **18** B6
Closes The DH8 .... **175** F5
Clough Dene Tantobie DH9 .. **6** B2
Tantobie, Clough Dene DH9, NE16 .... **6** A3
Clove Hitch Ho TS24 ...... **77** C7
Clover Ave NE21 .... **2** C6
Clover Ct
Newton Aycliffe DL5 .... **82** D2
Spennymoor DL16 .... **56** B3
Stockton-on-T TS19 .... **117** B5
Clover Dr
Bishop Auckland DL14 ..... **79** F7
Hartlepool TS26 .... **76** E7
Clover Hill Com Prim Sch NE16 .... **2** F4
Clover Ho SR3 .... **18** A4
Clover Laid DH7 .... **43** A3
Clover Wood Cl TS7 ..... **140** F3
Cloverdale DL1 .... **133** E6
Cloverhill DH2 .... **15** F2
Clowbeck Ct DL3 .... **132** C7
Clowes Terr DH9 .... **12** F4
Clowes Wlk DH9 .... **14** B7
Club La DH1 .... **210** A4
Clydach Gr TS17 .... **156** F7
Clyde Gdns TS22 .... **102** B6
Clyde Gr TS18 .... **137** F8
Clyde St DH9 .... **14** B7
Clyde Terr Coundon DL14 ... **81** C8
Spennymoor DL16 .... **68** E7
Clydesdale Garth DH1 .... **34** D8
Clydesdale St DH5 .... **27** A2
Clynes Rd TS6 .... **121** E4
Co-operative Bldgs DH9 .. **12** C8
Co-operative Cl TS13 ... **127** B1
Co-operative St
Chester le Street DH3 ...... **16** C4
Shildon DL4 .... **80** E2
Co-operative Terr
Beamish DH2 .... **15** A7
Burnhope DH7 .... **21** E5
Burnopfield NE16 .... **6** B6
Consett DH8 .... **10** C7
Coxhoe DH6 .... **57** F4
Crook DL15 .... **52** F3
Dipton DH9 .... **12** C8
Hunwick DL15 .... **66** D7
Loftus TS13 .... **127** B1
Medomsley DH8 .... **4** B1
New Brancepeth DH7 .... **42** F8
Stanley Crook DL15 .... **52** F8
Trimdon TS29 .... **59** D5
West Pelton DH2 .... **15** A4
Wolsingham DL13 .... **207** D5
Co-operative Terr E DH9 . **12** D8
Co-operative Terr W DH9 .... **12** C8
Co-operative Villas
Brandon DH7 .... **43** E5
Sherburn Hill DH6 .... **36** D1
Co-operatve Villas DH9 .. **12** C8
Coach House Mews TS6 .... **141** C8
Coach La DL2 .... **152** D1
Coach Rd TS12 .... **126** A5
Coal La Elwick TS27 .... **74** E6
Wolviston TS22 .... **102** C8
Wynyard Village TS22 ...... **87** F2
Coal Rd DL13 .... **189** E6
Coalbank Rd DH5 .... **26** F2
Coalbank Sq DH5 .... **26** F2
Coalford La
High Pittington DH6 .... **36** C4
Satley DL13 .... **183** D6
Coalford Rd DH6 .... **35** F2
Coast Rd
Blackhall Rocks TS27 ...... **50** E2
Marske-by-t-S TS11 .... **108** B3
Peterlee SR8 .... **50** B6
Redcar TS10 .... **107** F5
Coast View TS27 .... **50** F2
Coastguard Cotts TS12 .. **125** E7
Coate Cl TS8 .... **139** D2
Coates Cl DH9 .... **14** A5
Coatham Ave
Middleton St George DL2 .. **153** F6
Newton Aycliffe DL5 .... **96** D4
Coatham CE Prim Sch TS10 .... **107** A6
Coatham Cl TS8 .... **139** E2
Coatham Cres DL1 .... **133** B6
Coatham Dr TS26 .... **76** D5
Coatham Gr TS23 .... **102** E7
Coatham La
Coatham Mundeville DL3 .. **112** D5
Elton TS21 .... **136** D6
Coatham Lodge TS10 .... **107** A7
Coatham Marsh Nature Reserve* TS10 .... **106** F6
Coatham Rd
Redcar TS10 .... **107** B7
Stockton-on-T TS19 .... **117** B6
Coatham Vale TS16 ...... **156** A8
Coatsay Cl TS19 .... **117** B6
Coatsay Moor La DL2, DL5 .... **111** E6
Cobb Wlk TS24 .... **64** E1
Cobble Carr TS14 .... **143** D4
Cobbler Gate La DL12 ... **208** E3
Cobblers Hall Rd DL5 .... **82** C2
Cobblewood TS3 .... **120** F2
Cobby Castle La TS21 ... **115** D8
Cobden Ct DL1 .... **152** C8
Cobden St Consett DH8 .... **11** A3
Darlington DL1 .... **133** C1
Hartlepool TS26 .... **76** F6
Stockton-on-T TS18 .... **213** A3
Thornaby-on-T TS17 ...... **138** D8
Cobey's Carr La DL14, DL15 .... **54** B1
Cobham St TS1 .... **214** C1
Coburg St DL1 .... **133** A2
Cobwood TS3 .... **120** F2
Cochrane Terr
Ferryhill DL17 .... **70** C2
Ushaw Moor DH7 .... **33** A1
Willington DL15 .... **53** E3
Cock La Headlam DL2 .... **201** E4
Piercebridge DL2 .... **130** A6
Cock's Cotts 2 DH7 .... **32** F2
Cockburn St TS12 .... **145** E5
Cocken La DH3 .... **25** B5
Cocken Rd Durham DH1 .... **25** C3
Stockton-on-T TS19 .... **117** B6
West Rainton DH4 .... **25** C3
Cockerton CE Prim Sch DL3 .... **132** C4
Cockerton Gn DL3 .... **132** C4
Cockerton Wlk TS19 ...... **117** B6
Cockfield Ave TS23 ...... **102** F7
Cockfield Prim Sch DL13 .... **195** E3
Cockhouse La DH7 .... **32** E2
Cockshaw Nook DL14 ...... **67** B1
Cockton Hill Inf Sch DL14 .... **80** C6
Cockton Hill Jun Sch DL14 .... **80** C6
Cockton Hill Rd DL14 ..... **80** B6
Codlin Rd TS15 .... **173** F2
Cohort Cl DH8 .... **3** E3
Colburn Ave DL5 .... **96** A8
Colburn Wlk 4 TS6 .... **121** F3
Colchester Rd TS20 ...... **118** B8
Cold Hesledon Ind Est
Cold Hesledon SR7 .... **28** F3
Seaham SR7 .... **29** A2
Coldie Hill TS15 .... **173** F1
Coldingham Ct DH7 .... **23** B3
Coldstream DH2 .... **9** A2
Coldstream Dr NE21 .... **2** A8
Coldwell Cl DH6 .... **37** F7
Colebrooke DH3 .... **9** D2
Coleby Ave TS4 .... **140** A6
Coledale Rd TS3 .... **120** C1
Colenso St TS26 .... **77** A4
Colepike Rd DH7 .... **20** E3
Coleridge Ave
Blackhall Colliery TS27 .... **50** C5
Hartlepool TS25 .... **77** B3
Coleridge Cl DL15 .... **53** F1
Coleridge Gdns
Darlington DL1 .... **152** A7
Dipton DH9 .... **12** D8
Coleridge Pl DH2 .... **15** E3
Coleridge Rd
Billingham TS23 .... **102** E8
Chilton DL17 .... **82** E8
Coleshill Cl TS23 .... **102** E5
Coleton Gdns TS17 .... **157** B8
Colin Terr 7 SR2 .... **18** F6
Coll of St Hild & St Bede (Univ of Durham) DH1 . **211** B3
College Cl TS27 .... **75** E3
College Ct DL3 .... **132** E2
College Rd
Langley Park DH7 .... **32** D4
Middlesbrough TS3 .... **120** F3
College St DL4 .... **80** E2
College View
Bearpark DH7 .... **33** A4
Consett DH8 .... **177** E4
Esh Winning DH7 .... **41** D7
Colleton Wlk TS3 .... **120** D1
Collier Cl DL15 .... **52** D3
Collierley La DH9 .... **5** D1
Collierley Prim Sch DH9 . **12** C8
Colliers Gn TS4 .... **215** C2
Colliery La DH5 .... **27** B2
Collin Ave TS4 .... **139** F7
Colling Ave SR7 .... **29** A7
Colling Wlk DL5 .... **96** D6
Collingdon Gn NE39 .... **1** A4
Collingdon Rd NE39 .... **1** A4
Collingwood Bank DL12 . **193** D2
Collingwood Chase TS12 .... **126** B5
Collingwood Coll (Univ of Durham) DH1 .... **44** C6
Collingwood Ct TS2 ...... **119** C8
Collingwood Rd
Billingham TS23 .... **118** D8
Hartlepool TS26 .... **77** A6
Collingwood St
Coundon DL14 .... **81** B8
Hetton-le-H DH5 .... **27** A6
Collins Ave TS20 .... **118** C7
Collinson Ave TS5 .... **139** A8
Collison St DH8 .... **10** F3
Collyers Cl DL2 .... **152** D1
Colmans Nook TS23 ...... **103** B3
Colmore Ave TS3 .... **120** F4
Colorado Gr DL1 .... **133** B6
Colpitt Cl 6 TS20 .... **118** A8
Colpitts Terr DH1 .... **210** B2
Colsterdale Cl TS23 ..... **102** E6
Colston Rise SR8 .... **49** C7
Colt Pk NE17 .... **4** B5
Coltman St TS3 .... **120** C4
Coltspool NE11 .... **8** D6
Columbia Dr TS17 .... **213** B2
Columbia St DL3 .... **132** E4
Columbine Cl TS7 .... **140** C4
Colville Ct DH9 .... **14** B6
Colville St TS1 .... **214** B2
Colwell Ct DL5 .... **95** F7
Colwyn Cl TS10 .... **107** D2
Colwyn Rd
Hartlepool TS26 .... **77** A4
Stockton-on-T TS20 .... **118** C8
Comer Terr DL13 .... **195** E3
Comet Dr SR8 .... **39** C4
Comet Sq SR3 .... **18** A7
Comfrey Manor TS8 ...... **159** C8
Commerce Way TS6 ..... **121** A4
Commercial Rd E DH6 .... **57** F5
Commercial Rd W DH6 .... **57** F5
Commercial Sq DH7 .... **43** C4
Commercial St
Brandon DH7 .... **43** C5
Crook DL15 .... **52** E4
Darlington DL3 .... **132** F2
East Hedleyhope DL13 ...... **40** D5
Esh Winning DH7 .... **31** A3
Ferryhill DL17 .... **70** C3
Hartlepool TS24 .... **64** F1
Hartlepool, Middleton TS24 . **77** D7
Middlesbrough TS2 .... **119** F7
Stockton-on-T TS18 .... **213** B3
Trimdon TS29 .... **60** A5
Willington DL15 .... **54** A3
Commondale Ave TS19 .. **117** E5
Commondale Dr TS25 .... **90** D7
Commondale Gr TS10 ... **107** A4
Commondale Sta YO21 . **164** C1
Compass Ho TS24 .... **77** D6
Compton Cl 2 TS20 ...... **118** B5
Compton Gr
Bishop Auckland DL14 ..... **80** A6
Darlington DL3 .... **132** C3
Compton Ho TS3 .... **120** D3
Compton Rd TS25 .... **76** D2
Comrie Rd TS25 .... **89** F7
Concorde Sq 5 SR3 .... **18** A7
Concorde Way TS18 ...... **137** F6
Cone Terr DH3 .... **16** D4
Coney Cl TS17 .... **138** C1
Congburn Bank DH7 .... **23** B7
Congreve Terr DL5 .... **96** E2
Conifer Ave TS21 .... **85** B7
Conifer Cl Blaydon NE21 .... **2** B8
Durham DH1 .... **35** A3
Ormesby TS7 .... **141** B7
Conifer Cres TS23 .... **102** C3
Conifer Dr TS19 .... **117** E6
Conifer Gr TS23 .... **102** C3
Coningsby Cl TS25 .... **89** E6
Conisborough Dr TS10 .. **107** E3
Coniscliffe Mews DL3 ... **151** A8
Coniscliffe Rd
Darlington DL3 .... **151** C8
Hartlepool TS26 .... **76** C5
Stanley DH9 .... **13** D6
Stockton-on-T TS19 .... **117** B6
Conishead Terr DH6 .... **37** F8
Coniston DH3 .... **9** D2
Coniston Ave
Bishop Auckland DL14 ..... **79** B1
Easington Lane DH5 .... **37** C8
Redcar TS10 .... **107** C5
Coniston Cl
Chester le Street DH2 ...... **16** C2
Durham DH1 .... **35** E4
Peterlee SR8 .... **49** E6
Coniston Cres
Blaydon NE21 .... **2** B8
Crook DL15 .... **52** F3
Redmarshall TS21 .... **116** B7
Coniston Dr DH7 .... **23** B3
Coniston Gr TS5 .... **139** C7
Coniston Rd Eston TS6 ... **121** F4
Ferryhill DL17 .... **69** F5
Hartlepool TS25 .... **77** C3
Skelton TS12 .... **125** B3
Stockton-on-T TS18 .... **212** A4
Coniston St DL3 .... **132** D4
Coniston Way DH8 .... **11** D4
Connaught Ct TS7 .... **141** B3
Connaught Rd
Middlesbrough TS5 .... **119** B3
Nunthorpe TS7 .... **141** B3
Connolly Terr NE17 .... **4** C6
Conrad Wlk TS25 .... **76** D2
Consett Bsns Pk DH8 ...... **11** B4
Consett Cl TS19 .... **117** B6
Consett Dryden Cl TS6 .. **121** D1
Consett Inf Sch DH8 ...... **11** A3
Consett Jun Sch DH8 ...... **11** A3
Consett La DH8 .... **10** B2
Consett Park Terr 12 DH8 .... **177** A4
Consett Rd
Castleside DH8 .... **176** F3
Lanchester DH7 .... **20** E5
Consett St Pius Xth RC Prim Sch DH8 .... **10** C1
Consett Terr DH7 .... **32** A5
Consort Cl TS19 .... **117** C3
Constable Cl DH9 .... **13** F6
Constable Gr TS23 .... **102** D7
Constables Garth 7 DH3 .... **9** C4
Constance St Consett DH8 . **10** F2
Middlesbrough TS3 .... **215** C2
Pelton DH2 .... **15** E7
Constantine Ct TS1,TS5 . **214** C1
Constantine Rd DL15 ...... **66** A6
Convalescent St 2 TS12 .... **125** C8
Conway Ave TS23 .... **102** E5
Conway Gr DL14 .... **80** B6
Conway Ho 9 DL14 .... **80** C8
Conway Pl DH2 .... **15** F8
Conway Rd TS10 .... **107** D4
Conway Wlk TS26 .... **76** E8
Conwy Gr TS17 .... **156** F8
Conyers DH2 .... **23** F4
Conyers Ave
Chester le Street DH2 ...... **16** B5
Darlington DL3 .... **132** B3
Conyers Cl
Darlington DL3 .... **132** B3
Yarm TS15 .... **156** B4
Conyers Cres SR8 .... **39** E1
Conyers Ct TS12 .... **126** C4
Conyers Gdns DH2 .... **16** B5
Conyers Gr DL3 .... **132** B3
Conyers Pl
Chester le Street DH2 ...... **16** B5
Newton Aycliffe DL5 .... **96** E6
Conyers Rd DH2 .... **16** C5
Conyers Sch TS15 .... **156** C3
Conyers Terr 4 DL17 ..... **70** A5
Cook Ave DH7 .... **33** B3
Cook Cres Murton SR7 ..... **28** B3
Stockton-on-T TS20 .... **118** A7
Cook Gr SR8 .... **39** E1
Cook Way SR8 .... **48** F7
Cook's Ct TS7 .... **141** B7
Cooke's Wood DH7 .... **43** D8
Cookgate TS7 .... **140** F3
Cookshold La DH6 .... **36** B2
Cookson Pl DH9 .... **14** B5
Cookson Terr
Chester le Street DH2 ...... **16** B3
Seaham SR7 .... **28** D2
Coombe Dr DL1 .... **133** E3
Coombe Hill TS11 .... **124** A6
Coombe Way TS18 .... **117** A1
Coop Bldgs 13 DH3 .... **9** C4
Cooper Ct TS6 .... **121** E2
Cooper Sq DH1 .... **211** C4
Cooper's Terr DH6 .... **47** D4
Cooperative Terr
Great Lumley DH4 .... **17** F1
Shotton Colliery DH6 .... **48** D6
Cooperative Workshops DH7 .... **23** C3
Coopers Cl DH6 .... **47** D4
Copeland Cl TS12 .... **125** C3
Copeland Ct
Durham DH1 .... **210** A1
Middlesbrough TS2 .... **119** D8
Copeland La DL14 .... **92** E7
Copeland Rd DL14 .... **79** B1
Copeland Rd Prim Sch DL14 .... **93** B8
Copeland Row DL14 .... **92** D7
Copgrove Cl TS3 .... **120** B2
Copley Bent DL13 .... **195** C4
Copley Cl TS19 .... **117** B6
Copley Ho 13 DL1 .... **152** C8
Copley La DL13 .... **195** B4
Copley Wlk 5 TS3 .... **140** D8
Copnor Wlk 6 TS3 .... **140** D8
Copperfield DH1 .... **44** A7
Copperwood TS3 .... **120** F1
Copperwood Cl 1 TS27 ... **63** C4
Coppice Hill DH7 .... **41** F8
Coppice Rd TS4 .... **120** A1
Coppice The
Coulby Newham TS8 ...... **139** F3
Wynyard Village TS22 ...... **87** D2
Coppice Wlk DL3 .... **132** A4
Coppice Wood DL15 .... **66** D7
Coppy La DH9 .... **7** C4
Copse Cl TS17 .... **138** B2
Copse La TS17 .... **138** B1
Copse Side DL3 .... **132** A1
Copse The
Bishop Auckland DL14 ..... **80** A7
Burnopfield NE16 .... **5** F6
Hartlepool TS24 .... **77** A8
Witton-le-W DL14 .... **65** B3
Copthill DL13 .... **179** B3
Coptleigh DH5 .... **27** A7
Coquet NE38 .... **9** F1
Coquet Cl
Ingleby Barwick TS17 ..... **157** B7
Peterlee SR8 .... **49** C5
Redcar TS10 .... **107** F3
Coquet Dr DH2 .... **15** E8
Coquet Gdns DH9 .... **13** E4
Coral St
Middlesbrough TS1 .... **214** C2
Saltburn-by-t-S TS12 ...... **125** C8
Coral Way TS10 .... **107** E3
Corbett St Easington SR8 .. **39** F4
Seaham SR7 .... **29** B8
Corbridge Cl TS8 .... **139** E2
Corbridge Cres DL1 ...... **133** C5
Corbridge Ct 5 TS19 .... **117** B6
Corbridge Rd DH8 .... **11** A7
Corby 5 TS4 .... **120** B1
Corby Ave TS5 .... **139** A7
Corby Gr SR8 .... **49** A3
Corby Lodge TS20 .... **101** F1
Corcyra St 3 SR7 .... **29** D6
Corder Rd TS5 .... **119** B3
Corfe Cres TS23 .... **102** D5
Corfu Way TS10 .... **106** F1
Coris Cl TS7 .... **140** C4
Cormland Cl TS20 .... **118** C7
Cormorant Cl 4 NE38 .... **9** F3
Cormorant Dr TS10 ..... **107** E2

Corn Cl DL12 209 A5
Corn Mill Dr DH5 26 D6
Cornbank Cl SR3 18 A5
Corncroft Mews TS6 121 E6
Cornelia Cl 7 SR3 18 A7
Cornelia Terr SR7 29 D7
Corner Bank La DL2 94 E4
Cornfield Garth SR8 49 F5
Cornfield Rd
Middlesbrough TS5 119 E1
Stockton-on-T TS19 117 A3
Thornaby-on-T TS17 138 B8
Cornforth Ave TS3 140 D8
Cornforth Cl TS19 117 B6
Cornforth Gr TS23 102 F7
Cornforth La
Cornforth DH6 57 F2
Coxhoe DH6 57 F3
Corngrave Cl TS11 108 E1
Cornhill Wlk TS7 141 A7
Cornmill Ctr 12 DL1 132 F2
Cornmoor DH2 15 F2
Cornriggs DL13 179 A4
Cornriggs Wlk 4 TS19 117 B7
Cornsay Cl
Middlesbrough TS5 139 B6
Stockton-on-T TS19 117 B6
Cornsay La DH7 30 B5
Cornwall Ave DL1 133 C4
Cornwall Cl TS7 141 A3
Cornwall Cres TS23 102 F3
Cornwall Ct SR7 28 D3
Cornwall Gr TS20 118 C7
Cornwall Pl DL14 80 B5
Cornwall Rd TS14 143 D3
Cornwall St Easington SR8 39 F4
Hartlepool TS25 77 A3
Cornwall Wlk DH1 35 D3
Cornwallis Cl TS12 126 C5
Coronation Ave
Blackhall Colliery TS27 50 E3
Durham DH1 35 D4
Fishburn TS21 72 C4
Hinderwell TS13 149 E5
2 Peterlee SR8 50 A6
6 Ryhope SR2 18 F6
Shildon DL4 81 B1
Stanhope DL13 206 E2
Tow Law DL13 183 D2
Coronation Cotts DH6 48 C6
Coronation Cres
High Pittington DH6 36 B6
Yarm TS15 156 A4
Coronation Ct 1 TS6 121 D1
Coronation Dr TS25 77 D3
Coronation Gdns 6 DL2 200 E7
Coronation Gn
Easington Lane DH5 37 D8
Middlesbrough TS3 140 F8
Coronation Homes DH7 41 F8
Coronation Rd
Chilton DL17 83 A8
Loftus TS13 127 B1
Wingate TS28 60 D8
Coronation Sq DH6 38 B7
Coronation St
Barnard Castle DL12 209 C7
Carlin How TS13 126 F3
Chester le Street DH3 16 D1
Crook DL15 52 E4
1 Darlington DL3 132 E4
Middlesbrough TS3 120 C4
Coronation St S SR7 28 D2
Coronation Terr
Annfield Plain DH9 13 B4
Chester le Street DH3 16 C2
18 Cockfield DL13 195 E3
Cornforth DL17 57 D1
Coxhoe DH6 57 F5
Durham DH1 35 C1
Fir Tree DL15 52 A1
Hetton-le-H DH5 27 A2
Hunwick DL15 66 D7
Kibblesworth NE11 8 C6
Kirk Merrington DL16 69 A3
Trimdon TS29 59 E1
West Pelton DH2 15 B4
Willington DL15 53 C3
Wingate TS29 59 F6
Corporation Rd
Darlington DL3 132 F3
Hartlepool TS24 64 E1
Middlesbrough TS1 215 A3
Redcar TS10 107 B6
Corporation Road Com Prim Sch DL3 132 F3
Corporation St TS18 213 A3
Corpus Christi RC Prim Sch TS3 120 E3
Corriedale Cl DH1 34 C8
Corrighan Terr DH5 26 C4
Corry Cl TS27 50 E3
Corsair NE16 2 F6
Corscombe Cl DL17 70 C5
Corsham Wlk 4 TS3 140 D8
Cort St DH8 10 E3
Cortland Rd Consett DH8 10 C4
Nunthorpe TS7 141 C3
Corvan Terr DH9 6 A2
Coryton Wlk 3 TS3 140 D8
Cosgrove Ave DL14 80 A4
Cosin Cl DL5 96 E5
Costa St
Middlesbrough TS1 214 B1
South Bank TS6 121 A6
Costain Gr TS20 102 C1
Cote House Rd DL12 208 D2
Cotgarth Way TS19 117 A6
Cotherstone Cl
2 Consett DH8 10 F1
Egglescliffe TS16 136 F1
Cotherstone Dr TS5 139 C4
Cotherstone Moor Dr DL1 152 D7
Cotherstone Prim Sch DL12 198 F6
Cotherstone Rd
Durham DH1 34 D5
Stockton-on-T TS18 137 F8
Cotsford Cres 3 SR8 50 A6
Cotsford Inf Sch SR8 50 B6
Cotsford Jun Sch SR8 50 B7
Cotsford La SR8 50 B6
Cotsford Park Est SR8 50 B6
Cotswold Ave
Chester le Street DH2 16 B1
Middlesbrough TS3 120 E3
Cotswold Cl DL14 81 C8
Cotswold Cres TS23 102 D3
Cotswold Dr
Redcar TS10 107 B4
Skelton TS12 125 C3
Cotswold Pl SR8 49 B6
Cotswold Terr DH9 14 A5
Cotswolds The DL17 82 F7
Cottage Farm TS19 212 A2
Cottage Mews DL1 133 D4
Cottage Rd 8 DL4 80 F1
Cottages Rd SR7 29 D6
Cottages The Chilton DL17 82 E6
Coatham Mundeville DL1 112 F6
Heighington DL5 95 D1
Cottersloe Rd TS20 102 B1
Cottingham Cl SR8 49 B7
Cottingham Ct DL3 132 B4
Cottingham Dr TS3 120 D3
Cottonwood
Middlesbrough TS3 120 F2
Shiney Row DH4 17 F6
Coulby Farm Way
Coulby Newham TS8 140 B1
Mount Pleasant TS8 159 B8
Coulby Manor Farm TS8 140 A2
Coulby Manor Way TS8 139 F3
Coulby Newham Sch TS8 140 B2
Coulson Cl TS15 156 B3
Coulson St DL16 69 B8
Coulthard Ct 9 TS6 121 A6
Coulton Gr TS22 102 A5
Coulton Terr DL16 69 A3
Council Of Europe Bvd TS17 213 B3
Coundon Gn 2 TS19 117 B6
Coundon Ind Est DL14 81 C7
Coundon Prim Sch DL14 81 C8
Countess Cl SR7 29 C8
Countisbury Rd TS20 101 E2
County Hospl DH1 210 B3
Courageous Cl TS25 77 D1
Court La DH1 211 A2
Court Rd TS4 120 A1
Court St SR8 39 F4
Courtine The DL5 95 D1
Courtlands Rd DL3 132 D4
Courtney Dr
1 New Silksworth SR3 18 A7
Pelton DH2 15 F7
Courtney Wlk TS3 120 E3
Courtyard The
Middleton St George DL2 153 E5
Tanfield Lea DH9 13 C8
Covent Cl TS6 141 C7
Coventry Rd DH1 34 E7
Coverdale TS8 139 D1
Coverdale Bldgs TS12 126 C4
Coverdale Ct DL5 96 B8
Coverdale Rd TS19 117 C2
Coverley DH3 25 A8
Covert The DL5 95 F8
Cow Close La TS12 165 C8
Cow Green Resr Nature Trail* DL12 184 D1
Cowclose La DL11 204 E5
Cowdray Cl
Guisborough TS14 143 F2
Newton Aycliffe DL5 82 F2
Cowell Gr NE39 1 C2
Cowell St SR8 49 F7
Cowen St NE21 2 B8
Cowen Terr NE39 1 F3
Cowfold La DL2 111 B5
Cowgarth Hill DL13 206 C3
Cowley Cl
Egglescliffe TS16 137 D5
Seaton Carew TS25 77 E2
Cowley Cres DH5 26 C4
Cowley La DL13 194 E4
Cowley Rd TS5 139 D6
Cowley St DH6 48 D6
Cowpen Bewley Rd TS23 103 C4
Cowpen Bewley Woodland Ctry Pk* TS23 103 C7
Cowpen Bewley Woodland Ctry Pk Visitor Ctr* TS23 103 C7
Cowpen Cres TS19 117 B6
Cowpen La TS23 103 A5
Cowpen Lane Ind Est TS23 103 B4
Cowper Gr TS25 76 D2
Cowper Rd TS20 118 C5
Cowscote Cres TS13 127 A2
Cowshill Gn 7 TS19 117 B6
Cowsley La DH7 30 A1
Cowton Way TS16 137 B3
Coxgreen Cl TS19 117 B6
Coxhoe Prim Sch DH6 57 F3
Coxhoe Rd TS23 102 F5
Coxmoor Way TS11 123 F6
Coxwold Cl TS5 139 E6
Coxwold Dr DL1 152 C7
Coxwold Ho 9 DL1 152 C8
Coxwold Rd TS18 212 A2
Coxwold Way TS23 103 B3
Craddock St DL16 68 E8
Cradley Dr TS5 139 C3
Cradoc Gr TS17 156 F8
Cradock St DL14 80 C6
Crag La DL2 93 F3
Crag Works DH8 11 C6
Cragdale Gdns DH5 26 F2
Cragdale Rd TS3 120 C2
Cragg View DL12 208 F2
Craggs St
Middlesbrough TS4 215 B3
Stockton-on-T TS19 213 A4
Craggyknowe NE37 9 F6
Craghead La DH9 14 E3
Craghead Rd DH2 15 E4
Cragleas NE16 6 A4
Cragside Brotton TS12 126 C4
Chester le Street DH2 16 A4
Chilton DL17 83 A8
Sedgefield TS21 85 A5
Witton Gilbert DH7 33 B8
Cragside Cl DL16 68 F7
Cragside Ct
Annfield Plain DH9 12 F3
Consett DH8 10 C4
4 Houghton-le-S DH5 26 F8
Ingleby Barwick TS17 138 B1
Cragston Cl TS26 76 D7
Cragston Ct 2 TS10 107 E1
Cragwellside DL1 133 C5
Craig Lea Rd DL15 52 A6
Craig Miller Pk DL3 131 F1
Craig St 2 Birtley DH3 9 C4
Darlington DL3 132 E3
Craig Terr Easington SR8 39 B3
Wolsingham DL13 207 E5
Craigearn Rd TS6 121 C2
Craigland Villas DH7 23 C2
Craigton Ho TS10 107 C7
Craigweil Cres TS19 117 F5
Craigwell Dr SR3 18 A4
Crail Gdns DL1 133 C7
Crail Wlk TS25 89 F8
Craister Rd TS20 213 C4
Crake Way NE38 9 F2
Cramlington Cl TS8 139 E2
Cramond Cl DL3 132 A1
Cranage Cl TS5 139 B8
Cranberry TS8 140 D1
Cranbourne Dr TS10 107 F1
Cranbourne Terr TS18 212 C1
Cranbrook TS8 140 E1
Crane Row La DL13 195 C6
Cranfield Ave TS3 120 F4
Cranford Ave TS6 121 B4
Cranford Cl TS6 121 B4
Cranford Gdns TS5 139 B7
Cranford Terr SR8 39 B4
Cranleigh DH3 25 A7
Cranleigh Rd TS18 212 B2
Cranmore Rd TS3 120 D3
Cranstock Cl TS22 102 A5
Cranston Pl SR2 19 A6
Cranswick Cl TS23 102 F8
Cranswick Dr TS5 139 E6
Cranwell Gr TS17 138 D3
Cranwell Rd TS25 89 E7
Cranworth Gn TS17 118 D1
Cranworth St TS17 213 C1
Craster Cl DH2 15 F1
Crathie DH3 9 C7
Crathorne Cres TS5 119 B2
Crathorne Ct NE16 5 F6
Crathorne Pk Eston TS6 121 C1
Normanby TS6 141 C8
Crathorne Rd TS20 118 B8
Craven St TS1 214 B2
Craven Vale TS14 143 E3
Craven's Bldgs TS28 60 F5
Crawcrook Wlk TS19 117 B6
Crawford Ave SR8 49 D8
Crawford Avenue W SR8 49 C8
Crawford Cl
Bishop Auckland DL14 80 A4
Sherburn DH6 35 F1
Crawford Rd DL5 96 E6
Crawford St TS25 90 E8
Crawlaw Bglws SR8 39 E5
Crawlaw Rd SR8 39 E5
Crawley Rd TS17 138 E7
Crawleyside Bank DL13 206 C5
Crayke Rd TS18 212 A1
Creekwood TS3 120 F2
Creighton Rd DL5 96 E6
Cremorne Cl TS7 140 C4
Crescent Ave TS23 102 E1
Crescent Cl DH6 35 F1
Crescent Lodge TS5 119 D1
Crescent Rd TS1 214 B1
Crescent The
3 Blackhall Colliery TS27 50 D3
Carlton TS21 116 C8
Chester le Street DH2 16 B3
Chilton DL17 82 F8
Consett, Benfieldside DH8 10 C6
Consett, Blackfyne DH8 10 F4
Crescent The *continued*
Consett, Bridgehill DH8 10 C4
Coundon DL14 81 C8
Durham DH1 210 B4
Egglescliffe TS16 156 B8
Easington SR8 39 E5
Hartlepool TS26 76 F6
Hetton-le-H DH5 27 A3
High Etherley DL14 78 F5
Kibblesworth NE11 8 C6
Kimblesworth DH2 23 F4
Langley Park DH7 32 A6
Maiden Law DH7 21 A8
2 Marske-by-t-S TS11 108 D1
Middlesbrough TS5 119 D1
Middleton St George DL2 154 C7
Nunthorpe TS7 141 C2
Ormesby TS7 140 F7
Redcar TS10 107 E6
Rowlands Gill NE39 1 F2
Saltburn-by-t-S TS12 125 C6
Sherburn DH6 35 F1
Stainton Grove DL12 209 F8
Tanfield Lea DH9 13 D8
Thornaby-on-T TS17 138 C7
Waldridge DH2 24 A7
West Rainton DH4 25 F2
Witton Gilbert DH7 23 B1
Cresswell Ave SR8 50 A6
Cresswell Cl Blaydon NE21 2 A8
Hemlington TS8 139 E2
Cresswell Ct TS26 76 D6
Cresswell Dr TS26 76 E6
Cresswell Rd Eston TS6 121 E6
Hartlepool TS26 76 E6
Crest The TS26 76 D6
Crestwood
Middlesbrough TS3 120 F2
Redcar TS10 107 D1
Crewe Ave DH1 35 B1
Crewe Rd DL5 96 E6
Cribyn Cl TS17 156 F8
Crichton Ave DH3 16 D1
Cricket Field Row DL3 132 F5
Cricket La TS6 141 C8
Cricket Terr NE16 6 A6
Crieff Wlk TS25 89 F8
Crimdon Cl TS8 139 E2
Crimdon Gr DH4 26 C7
Crimdon Terr TS27 51 A1
Crimdon Wlk TS19 117 A7
Crime Rigg Bank DH6 46 D8
Crinklewood TS3 120 F1
Crispin Ct Brotton TS12 126 C4
Sedgefield TS21 85 B6
Croft Ave Crook DL15 52 E3
Middlesbrough TS5 139 B7
Croft Ct DH7 20 E4
Croft Dr TS7 141 B2
Croft Gdns DL17 70 C4
Croft Rd Darlington DL2 151 D3
Egglescliffe TS16 156 B8
Hurworth-on-T DL2 152 B1
Croft Rigg DH7 43 A3
Croft Side DL14 79 D6
Croft St Crook DL15 52 E3
Sacriston DH7 23 C3
Croft Terr
Annfield Plain DH9 13 A4
Coundon DL14 81 B8
Hartlepool TS24 77 F8
Croft Terr (E) DL13 188 A7
Croft Terr (W) DL13 188 A7
Croft The
Kirk Merrington DL16 68 F3
Marton TS7 140 E3
Newton Aycliffe DL5 82 E2
Sherburn Hill DH6 36 D1
Croft View
Cotherstone DL12 198 F6
Lanchester DH7 20 E4
Croft Way DL15 54 B4
Croft Yoke La DL12 193 C2
Crofton Ave 2 TS4 119 F1
Crofton Ct TS18 118 D4
Crofton Rd TS18 118 D4
Crofts The Stillington TS21 99 F3
Wolsingham DL13 207 C5
Croftside DH3 9 C5
Cromarty DH2 8 F2
Cromarty Cl DL1 133 E7
Cromer Ct TS16 156 C8
Cromer Lea DL13 188 A7
Cromer St TS4 215 B2
Cromer Wlk TS25 89 E7
Cromore Cl TS17 138 C4
Crompton Ct DL17 69 E5
Cromwell Ave
Loftus TS13 127 D1
Stockton-on-T TS18 213 B4
Cromwell Gn TS18 213 B3
Cromwell Rd TS6 121 A5
Cromwell Road Prim Sch TS6 121 A5
Cromwell St
Hartlepool TS26 77 C4
Middlesbrough TS3 215 C2
Cromwell Terr TS17 138 C8
Cronniewell NE17 4 B5
Crook (Beechburn) Ind Est DL15 52 E2
Crook Bsns Ctr DL15 52 E3
Crook Hall* DH1 210 C4
Crook La DL12 209 D5
Crook Prim Sch DL15 52 E3
Crook St TS20 102 A1
Crookers Hill Cl TS7 141 A1
Crookhall La DH8 11 C3
Crookhall Rd DH8 11 A3
Crookhall Wlk 6 TS19 117 B6
Crooks Barn La TS20 102 B2
Crooksbarn Prim Sch TS20 102 A2
Cropton Cl TS10 107 B2
Cropton Way TS8 140 B2
Crosby Ct TS16 137 D1
Crosby Ho TS3 120 D3
Crosby Rd DL5 96 C5
Crosby St Darlington DL3 133 A6
10 Stockton-on-T TS20 118 B5
Crosby Wlk 8 TS17 138 C8
Cross Fell TS10 107 B4
Cross Hill DL13 206 C3
Cross La Cowshill DL13 179 B4
Great Ayton TS9 161 B1
Loftus TS13 127 C3
Sacriston DH7 23 C4
Cross Lanes DL2 111 B7
Cross Row
Boosbeck TS12 145 B6
Durham DH1 34 C7
Hunwick DL15 66 D5
Cross St
Bishop Auckland DL14 79 D2
Consett DH8 10 D4
Crook DL15 53 B3
Darlington DL3 132 F5
Easington SR8 39 F4
8 Fence Houses DH4 26 A8
Guisborough TS14 143 E4
High Pittington DH6 36 D3
Sedgefield TS21 85 B6
Shildon DL4 95 A8
Stanhope DL13 206 C3
Stockton-on-T TS20 118 B8
Sunderland Bridge DH6 56 B7
4 Eston TS6 121 F2
Cross Terr NE39 1 D1
Cross Valley Ct DH1 210 A2
Cross View Terr DH1 210 A1
Crossbeck Terr 4 TS6 121 D1
Crossbeck Way TS7 141 B7
Crosscliff TS8 139 E2
Crossfell Rd TS3 120 C1
Crossfield DH7 23 C2
Crossfield Cl DL2 152 D1
Crossfield Cres DH6 48 C7
Crossfield Rd DL3 132 C5
Crossfields TS8 159 B8
Crossgate DH1 210 C2
Crossgate Moor Gdns DH1 33 F3
Crossgate Peth DH1 210 B2
Crossgate Rd DH5 27 A2
Crossleas DH7 23 C3
Crosslet La DL13 186 A8
Crossway The DL1 133 D2
Crossways
Langley Park DH7 32 C6
Sacriston DH7 23 C2
Crosswell Pk TS17 156 F7
Crosthwaite Ave 1 TS4 139 F8
Crow La TS6 122 B3
Crow Trees La DH6 57 D8
Crowhurst Cl TS14 143 E3
Crowland Ave
Middlesbrough TS3 120 F1
Middlesbrough TS3 121 A1
Crowland Rd TS25 89 E6
Crowley Pl DL5 96 D7
Crown St
Bishop Auckland DL14 80 D5
Darlington DL1 133 A2
7 Darlington DL3 132 F2
Crowther Ind Est
Birtley NE38 9 F4
Washington NE38 9 F5
Crowther Rd NE38 9 F5
Croxdale Gr
Bishop Auckland DL14 79 E5
Stockton-on-T TS19 117 B2
Croxdale Rd TS23 102 E5
Croxden Gr 7 TS3 140 E8
Croxton Ave TS25 89 F6
Croxton Cl TS19 116 F3
Croydon Rd TS1 215 B1
Crummackdale TS17 157 B6
Crummock Rd TS10 107 C5
Crystal Cl DL17 82 F8
Culgaith Ave TS3 120 C2
Cullen Cl DL1 133 D6
Cullen Rd TS25 89 F8
Culloden Terr SR8 39 F3
Culloden Way TS23 103 A6
Culross Gr TS19 116 F3
Culzean Ct DH8 10 D4
Cumberland Cres TS23 102 D2
Cumberland Gr TS20 101 F1
Cumberland Pl DH3 9 D1
Cumberland Rd
Consett DH8 177 A4
Middlesbrough TS5 119 E2
New Silksworth SR3 18 A8
Cumberland St
Coundon Grange DL14 80 F5
Darlington DL3 133 A5
Cumberland Terr DL15 53 F3
Cumbernauld Rd TS17 138 E7
Cumbie Way DL5 96 D2
Cumbria Pl DH9 14 A7
Cumbria Wlk 11 TS25 77 B4
Cumbrian Ave DH2 16 C2
Cumbrian Way SR8 49 E6

Cumby Rd DL5 96 C5
Cummings Ave DH6 35 F2
Cummings Sq TS28 60 D8
Cumnor Wlk TS3 120 D3
Cundall Rd TS26 76 F6
Cunningham Cl TS12 126 B5
Cunningham Dr TS17 138 D3
Cunningham Pl DH1 211 C4
Cunningham St TS5 214 A1
Curlew Cl DL3 132 C6
Curlew La TS20 102 A2
Curran Ave TS5 119 B1
Curson St [1] TS6 121 F1
Curtain La DL11 201 D1
Curthwaite TS5 139 B4
Cut Throat La NE17,NE39 4 C4
Cuthbert Ave DH1 35 B1
Cuthbert Cl Durham DH1 35 B1
Thornaby-on-T TS17 138 C8
Cuthbert Rd DL17 57 E1
Cuthbert St DL16 56 A2
Cutler Cl TS7 140 E4
Cutler's Ave DH8 10 C5
Cutlers' Hall Rd DH8 10 C5
Cutting St [3] SR7 18 F1
Cyclamen Gr DL1 133 C1
Cypress Cl DL3 151 C7
Cypress Ct DH7 43 B3
Cypress Gr Durham DH1 35 A3
Newton Aycliffe DL5 96 A3
Cypress Pk DH7 41 D8
Cypress Rd Marton TS7 140 E4
Redcar TS10 107 F5
Cypress Sq [12] SR3 18 A8
Cypress View DH6 47 E3
Cyril St DH8 10 F4

D

D'Arcy Sq SR7 28 E4
D'Arcy St DH7 32 C7
Dabble Duck Ind Est DL4 95 A8
Dacre Cl TS17 138 C6
Dacre Gdns DH8 11 A2
Daffodil Ave SR8 49 F7
Daffodil Cl TS27 50 D3
Dahlia Cres SR8 39 D3
Daimler Dr TS23 103 B5
Dairy La DH4 26 C8
Daisy Cotts [10] DH3 9 C4
Daisy Ct TS19 117 C5
Daisy Hill DH8 10 F8
Dalby Cl Billingham TS22 102 A5
Redcar TS10 107 C2
Dalby Ct TS8 140 C2
Dalby View TS8 140 B1
Dalby Way TS8 140 B1
Dalcross Ct TS8 139 E1
Dalden Gr SR7 29 D8
Dale Cl
Hurworth-on-T DL2 152 D1
Stockton-on-T TS19 117 A6
Dale Garth TS11 124 D8
Dale Gr Shildon DL4 95 B7
Stockton-on-T TS19 117 B2
Dale Rd
Barnard Castle DL12 209 D6
Darlington DL3 132 D2
Sadberge DL2 134 F7
Shildon DL4 95 B7
Dale Road Ind Est DL4 95 B8
Dale St
Bishop Auckland DL14 79 E3
Chilton DL17 82 F8
Consett DH8 10 D3
Langley Park DH7 32 C7
Middlesbrough TS1 214 C3
New Marske TS11 124 A7
Ushaw Moor DH7 32 F2
Dale Terr Billy Row DL15 52 D6
Dalton-le-D SR7 29 A5
Lingdale TS12 145 E5
Woodland DL13 194 D4
Dale View Crook DL15 53 A3
High Etherley DL14 78 E6
Mickleton DL12 208 F2
Middleton-In-T DL12 208 C5
Dalehouse TS13 149 B8
Dales Park Rd TS8 139 D1
Dales St DL13 206 D3
Dales Terr DL13 206 D2
Daleside DH7 23 C5
Daleston Ave TS5 139 D8
Daleston Cl TS26 76 C7
Daleville Cl TS4 140 A8
Dalkeith Cl DL3 132 A1
Dalkeith Cres TS8 139 E3
Dalkeith Rd TS25 76 E1
Dallas Ct TS8 139 E1
Dallas Rd TS25 76 E1
Dallymore Dr DH6 45 C2
Dalmuir Cl TS16 137 C1
Dalry Gr TS25 89 E8
Dalston Ct [12] TS7 141 B7
Dalsy La TS7 141 B7
Dalton Ave
Bishop Auckland DL14 79 E3
Seaham SR7 29 B7
Dalton Back La
Dalton Piercy TS27 75 E1
Hartlepool TS22,TS27 89 A7
Dalton Cl DL14 79 E3
Dalton Cotts DL4 95 A7
Dalton Cres DL4 95 A8
Dalton Ct TS10 107 F1
Dalton Gr
Billingham TS23 102 E7
Stockton-on-T TS20 118 A6
Dalton Hts
Dalton Piercy TS27 75 E3
Seaham SR7 28 E6
Dalton Pk SR7 28 E2
Dalton St Darlington DL1 133 A2
Hartlepool TS26 77 A5
Dalton Terr Chopwell NE17 4 B8
Murton SR7 28 D2
Wheatley Hill DH6 47 E1
Dalton Way DL5 96 D7
Daltry Cl TS15 156 E4
Dalwood Ct TS8 139 E1
Dam St TS13 127 C1
Damson Ct DL3 132 E3
Damson Way DH1 35 B2
Dan's Castle DL13 183 D2
Danby Cl
New Silksworth SR3 18 B6
Washington NE38 16 F8
Danby Ct Darlington DL1 133 C5
[1] Stockton-on-T TS20 118 B5
Danby Dale Ave TS10 107 A4
Danby Gr Hartlepool TS25 90 E8
Thornaby-on-T TS17 138 D7
Danby Rd Eston TS6 121 F3
Stockton-on-T TS20 118 B5
Danby Wlk TS23 102 C5
Danby Wynd TS15 156 B6
Danelaw DH3 25 A8
Danesbrook Ct TS17 157 B6
Danesfort Ave TS14 143 D4
Danesmoor Cres DL3 132 C2
Daniel Ct TS4 215 B1
Daniel La DL13,DL14 195 E8
Dante Rd TS7 140 B4
Daphne Cres SR7 29 C5
Daphne Rd TS19 118 A5
Darcy Cl TS15 156 A3
Darenth Cres TS3 120 D1
Dark La
Barnard Castle DL12 209 A5
Newsham DL11 205 C4
Darley Ct DH2 24 A5
Darling Pl DH9 14 B5
Darlington Arts Ctr*
DL3 132 E2
Darlington Ave SR8 49 F7
Darlington Back La
Longnewton DL2,TS21 115 E1
Stockton-on-T TS19,TS21 116 C4
Darlington Coll of Tech
DL3 132 D2
Darlington Golf Course
DL1 133 D8
Darlington La
Stockton-on-T TS20 117 F7
Stockton-on-T, Bishopsgarth
TS19 117 D6
Darlington Locomotive
Sculpture* DL1 134 B1
Darlington Meml Hospl
DL3 132 E3
Darlington Mus* DL1 133 A1
Darlington Railway Athletic
Gd DL3 132 D4
Darlington Railway Ctr &
Mus* DL3 132 F4
Darlington Rd
Barnard Castle DL12 209 E7
Bishop Auckland DL14 79 C1
Durham DH1 210 A1
Ferryhill DL17 69 F5
Heighington DL5 95 D1
Longnewton TS21 136 A5
Sadberge DL2 134 E6
Stockton-on-T TS18 137 C8
Whorlton DL2 200 B3
Darlington Ret Pk The
DL1 133 E1
Darlington St TS24 77 F8
Darlington Sta DL1 133 A1
Darnbrook Way TS7 140 F2
Darnell Gn TS4 140 B6
Darnton Dr TS4 140 B6
Darras Wlk TS3 120 D3
Darrowby Dr DL3 132 E4
Dart Rd SR8 49 C5
Dartmouth Cl SR7 29 A6
Dartmouth Gr TS10 107 D3
Darvel Rd TS25 76 E1
Darwen Ct TS8 139 E1
Darwin Gr Darlington DL1 152 C7
Hartlepool TS25 76 D3
Daryngton Cl DL1 133 D6
Dauntless Cl TS25 77 E1
Davenport Rd TS15 156 B3
Daventry Ave TS19 117 E6
David Rd TS20 118 C6
David Terr Bowburn DH6 45 D2
Eldon Lane DL14 80 E4
Quarrington Hill DH6 58 D7
Davis Ave DL14 79 E3
Davis Cres DH7 32 A7
Davis Terr SR8 39 D4
Davis Wlk SR8 49 E8
Davison Ave SR3 18 B7
Davison Cres SR7 28 B4
Davison Dr TS24 63 F2
Davison Rd DL1 133 B7
Davison Sq DH8 176 F3
Davison St Lingdale TS12 145 E5
Middlesbrough TS1 214 C3
Davison Terr DH7 23 B4
Davisons Ct DL2 201 D3
Davy Dr SR8 48 F8
Davy Rd TS6 120 F5
Davy St DL17 69 E6
Dawdon Cl TS19 117 B7
Dawdon Cres SR7 29 D6
Dawdon Ind Est SR7 29 E4
Dawley Cl TS17 138 E7
Dawlish Cl SR7 28 F6
Dawlish Dr TS25 90 A7
Dawlish Gn TS4 140 B6
Dawn Cl TS20 102 A2
Dawson Ho TS23 102 D4
Dawson Rd
Barnard Castle DL12 209 D6
Wingate TS28 60 E8
Dawson Sq TS5 119 B2
Dawson St DL15 52 F3
Dawsons Wharf Ind Est
TS5 119 E7
Day St TS12 126 B3
Daylesford Gr DL3 132 C7
Daylight Rd TS19 117 E5
Days Terr TS12 126 B4
De Brus Ct [4] TS12 125 C8
De Brus Pk TS8 159 E6
De Brus Way TS14 143 E5
De Havilland Dr TS11 108 B2
De La Mare Dr TS23 102 E8
Deacon Gdns TS25 90 E7
Deacon St TS3 120 C4
Deaf Hill Prim Sch TS29 59 F6
Deaf Hill Terr TS29 59 F6
Deal Cl TS19 117 E6
Deal Ct TS4 120 A1
Deal Rd Billingham TS23 102 D6
Redcar TS10 107 E3
Dean & Chapter Ind Est
DL17 69 E6
Dean Bank Grange DL17 69 E5
Dean Bank Prim Sch
DL17 69 E6
Dean Cl Peterlee SR8 49 F5
Shildon DL4 80 F2
Dean Gdns DL4 80 F2
Dean Pk DL17 70 A5
Dean Rd DL17 70 A5
Dean St Langley Park DH7 32 D8
Shildon DL4 80 F2
Stockton-on-T TS18 213 A2
Deanery Ct DL14 80 F4
Deanery View DH7 20 F4
Deans' Wlk DH1 211 C4
Deansgate TS6 122 A2
Debruse Ave TS15 156 A4
Dee Rd TS6 121 D3
Deepdale
Guisborough TS14 143 A3
Hutton Rudby TS15 173 F1
Deepdale Ave Eston TS6 121 F4
Middlesbrough TS4 119 F1
Middlesbrough, Beechwood
TS4 140 A8
Deepdale Cl NE16 2 F4
Deepdale La TS13 127 A3
Deepdale Rd TS13 127 A1
Deepdale St DH5 27 A2
Deepdale Way DL1 133 F3
Deepdene Gr TS10 107 F2
Deepgrove Wlk [3] TS6 121 F3
Deerbolt Bank DL12 209 B5
Deerness Ct DH7 43 C4
Deerness Est DL13 183 E2
Deerness Estate Bglws
DL13 183 E2
Deerness Gr DH7 31 D2
Deerness Hts DH7 43 B5
Deerness Rd DL14 80 A6
Deerness Valley Comp Sch
DH7 33 A3
Deerness View
East Hedleyhope DL13 40 D5
Ushaw Moor DH7 32 D2
Deerpool Cl TS24 64 C1
Defoe Cres DL5 96 E8
Deighton Gr TS23 102 D6
Deighton Rd TS4 140 B5
Del'strother Ave TS19 212 B4
Delamere Cl NE38 17 B7
Delamere Ct [8] SR3 18 A6
Delamere Dr TS11 124 B8
Delamere Gdns SR8 39 D4
Delamere Rd TS3 140 D8
Delarden Rd TS3 120 D3
Delaval DH2 16 A3
Delaval Rd TS23 102 F5
Delavale Cl SR8 49 F5
Delaware Ave DL14 92 C7
Deleval Cl DL5 82 C1
Delight Bank DH9 12 D7
Delight Ct DH9 12 D8
Delight Row DH9 12 D8
Dell Cl TS7 140 C3
Dell Side DL15 54 B2
Dell The DL14 80 C8
Dellfield Cl TS3 140 D8
Delvedere DH8 11 B1
Delves Cotts DH8 177 D4
Delves La DH8 11 A1
Delves Lane Ind Est
DH8 177 D4
Delves Lane Inf Sch
DH8 177 D4
Delves Lane Jun Sch
DH8 177 D4
Demesne Ct DL13 207 D5
Demesne La DL12 198 F6
Denbigh Rd TS23 102 E6
Dene Ave Easington SR8 39 E6
Dene Ave *continued*
Houghton-le-S DH5 27 A7
Rowlands Gill NE39 1 D1
Shotton Colliery DH6 48 D6
Dene Bank DH7 33 B8
Dene Bank Ave SR8 50 B6
Dene Bridge DL15 65 E8
Dene Bridge Row DL17 69 D1
Dene Cl TS17 138 E7
Dene Com Sch of Tech
SR8 50 A6
Dene Com Tech Sch SR8 49 F5
Dene Cotts DH2 15 D1
Dene Cres
Rowlands Gill NE39 1 D1
Sacriston DH7 23 D3
Shotton Colliery DH6 48 D6
Dene Ct Birtley DH3 9 C7
Hamsterley NE17 4 B6
Shadforth DH6 46 E6
Witton Gilbert DH7 23 B1
Dene Dr DH1 35 D5
Dene Garth TS27 75 E3
Dene Gdns DH5 26 F7
Dene Gr
Bishop Auckland DL14 80 C7
Darlington DL3 132 D3
Redcar TS10 107 D6
Dene Hall Dr DL14 79 F7
Dene Hill DL13 188 A7
Dene House Prim Sch
SR8 49 F5
Dene House Rd SR7 29 C8
Dene Park Ct [4] DL3 132 F3
Dene Pk DH7 41 D8
Dene Rd
Barnard Castle DL12 209 B6
Blackhall Rocks TS27 50 E3
Middlesbrough TS4 120 A2
Rowlands Gill NE39 1 D1
Seaham SR7 29 B5
Dene St Esh DH7 31 D3
Hetton-le-H DH5 27 B6
Peterlee SR8 50 A7
Stanley DH9 13 D5
Dene Terr Chilton DL17 82 E8
Peterlee SR8 50 A6
Seaham SR7 29 D8
Shotton Colliery DH6 48 D6
Dene The
Chester le Street DH2 24 B8
Medomsley DH8 4 A2
West Rainton DH4 26 A2
Dene Valley Prim Sch
DL14 81 A5
Dene View
Burnopfield NE16 6 A6
Cassop DH6 46 F2
Castle Eden TS27 61 D7
Hesleden TS27 50 C1
High Spen NE39 1 A3
Rowlands Gill NE39 1 C2
Stanley DH9 14 C7
Willington DL15 53 E3
Dene Villas
Chester le Street DH3 16 D1
Kirk Merrington DL16 69 C1
Peterlee SR8 50 B6
Dene Way SR7 29 C8
Dene Wlk TS11 108 B1
Deneburn Terr DH8 177 B4
Denecrest DH8 4 A2
Deneholme Terr DH7 22 D7
Deneside
Bishop Auckland DL14 80 C6
Howden-le-W DL15 65 E8
Lanchester DH7 21 A3
Sacriston DH7 23 C4
Spennymoor DL16 55 F1
Witton Gilbert DH7 33 B8
Deneside Cl TS15 156 D5
Deneside Jun & Inf Schs
SR7 29 A6
Deneside Rd DL3 132 D3
Denesyde DH8 4 A2
Denevale TS15 156 D5
Deneway NE39 2 A4
Denewood Cl DL15 53 F3
Denewood Ct DH9 14 B4
Denewood Terr DL17 82 F8
Denham Gn TS3 120 D3
Denham Gr NE21 1 F8
Denham Pl DL5 96 E7
Denholme Ave TS18 137 E8
Denmark St
Darlington DL3 133 A5
Middlesbrough TS2 214 B4
Dennis St DH6 47 F3
Dennison Cres DH3 9 C6
Dennison St TS18 212 C1
Dennison Terr DL17 70 C4
Denshaw Cl TS19 117 A3
Dent Bank DL12 192 D5
Dent Cl DH6 37 E3
Dent Gate La
Barnard Castle DL12 199 E7
Copley DL12,DL13 195 A3
Dent St
Bishop Auckland DL14 80 A3
Hartlepool TS26 77 B6
Shildon DL4 81 A2
Dent Wlk DL5 96 D7
Dent's Villas DL14 79 B8
Dentdale DH4 17 E8
Dentdale Cl TS15 156 C3
Denton Cl Darlington DL3 132 B4
Middlesbrough TS5 139 B4
Stockton-on-T TS19 117 B7
Denton Cross Roads
DL2 110 B2
Denton Hall Cotts DL2 110 D2
Denver Dr DL2 154 B8
Denwick Cl DH2 24 A8
Deorna Ct DL1 133 B5
Depot Rd TS2 119 E7
Derby Ave TS5 139 A8
Derby Cl [3] TS17 138 D8
Derby Cres [5] DH8 177 A4
Derby Dr DH8 177 A4
Derby Rd
Guisborough TS14 143 D3
Stanley DH9 13 E5
Derby St Darlington DL3 132 F5
Hartlepool TS25 77 B3
Stockton-on-T TS18 213 A3
Derby Terr TS17 118 D1
Derby The TS7 140 C4
Derbyshire Dr DH1 35 D2
Dere Ave DL14 80 A3
Dere Pk DH8 11 C4
Dere Rd DH8 11 B1
Derwent Ave
Bishop Auckland DL14 79 B1
Crook DL15 52 F3
Guisborough TS14 143 C3
Rowlands Gill NE39 1 E1
Derwent Cl
Redmarshall TS21 116 B7
Sacriston DH7 23 B3
Seaham SR7 29 C8
Derwent Cote NE17 4 B5
Derwent Cres
Great Lumley DH3 25 B7
Hamsterley NE17 4 B5
Leadgate DH8 11 D5
Derwent Ctr The [14] DH8 10 F2
Derwent Dale DH8 10 C6
Derwent Haven NE17 4 B5
Derwent Ho TS23 103 A7
Derwent Mews DH8 10 D4
Derwent Pk TS13 127 D1
Derwent Pl Consett DH8 10 C6
Newton Aycliffe DL5 96 A7
Derwent Rd Ferryhill DL17 69 F6
Peterlee SR8 49 E7
Redcar TS10 107 A5
Skelton TS12 125 B3
Thornaby-on-T TS17 138 D6
Derwent St
Blackhall Mill NE17 4 C6
Consett DH8 10 D4
[7] Darlington DL3 132 F3
Hartlepool TS26 77 B6
Hetton-le-H DH5 27 B2
Middlesbrough TS1 214 B2
Middlesbrough, North Ormesby
TS3 120 C4
Stockton-on-T TS20 118 A6
Tanfield Lea DH9 13 E8
Derwent Terr
Annfield Plain DH9 12 E4
Burnopfield NE16 6 B7
South Hetton DH6 37 E8
Spennymoor DL16 56 A1
Derwent Valley Cotts
NE39 1 F1
Derwent Valley Villas
NE17 4 A6
Derwent View
Blanchland DH8 175 A5
Burnopfield NE16 6 B6
Dipton DH9 12 C7
Blaydon NE21 2 B8
Derwent View Terr DH9 5 D1
Derwent Walk Cty Pk*
NE16,NE21,NE39 2 C5
Derwentcote Steel Furnace*
NE17 4 E6
Derwentdale Ct DH8 10 D3
Derwentdale Ind Est
DH8 10 D3
Derwentside Bsns Ctr
DH8 11 B4
Derwentside Coll
Consett DH8 10 F2
Lanchester DH7 20 F4
Stanley DH9 13 E6
Derwentwater Ave
[1] Chester le Street DH2 16 B1
Middlesbrough TS5 139 C7
Derwentwater Rd TS6 121 F4
Desford Gn TS3 120 D2
Desmond Rd DL2 153 F6
Deva Cl TS4 120 B1
Devon Cl TS10 107 B4
Devon Cres
Billingham TS23 102 F3
Birtley DH3 9 B6
Consett DH8 177 A4
Skelton TS12 125 A2
Devon Dr
New Silksworth SR3 18 A8
Willington DL15 54 A3
Devon Pl DL14 80 C5
Devon Rd Eston TS6 121 E4
Guisborough TS14 143 D3
Devon St Hartlepool TS25 77 B3
Hetton-le-H DH5 26 F4
Devonport Gdns DL2 154 A5
Devonport Rd
Middlesbrough TS5 119 F1
Stockton-on-T TS18 213 C4
Devonshire Rd
Darlington DL1 133 C4
Durham DH1 35 C2
Middlesbrough TS5 119 D2

Devonshire St TS18 .....137 F8
Dew La TS7 ....141 A6
Dewberry TS8 ....159 D8
Dewberry Cl TS26 ....63 D2
Dewberry Ct DL14 ....79 F7
Deyncourt DH1 ....44 A6
Dial Stob Hill DL14 ....67 C1
Diamond Cl DL17 ....82 F8
Diamond Ct TS18 ....137 F6
Diamond Hill DL13 ......195 C4
Diamond Rd
Middlesbrough TS1 ....214 C2
Thornaby-on-T TS17 ......138 D7
Diamond St
Saltburn-by-t-S TS12 ......125 C8
Shildon DL4 ....80 F1
Diamond Terr
Butterknowle DL13 ....195 C4
Durham DH1 ....210 C3
Dibdale Rd DL2 ....153 B2
Dick Scot La DL11 ......205 E3
Dickens Ct TS23 ....102 D7
Dickens Gr TS25 ....76 F3
Dickens Rd DL12 ....209 D7
Dickens St Hartlepool TS24 .63 F3
Houghton-le-S DH4 ....26 D8
Spennymoor DL16 ....68 F8
Dickens Wynd DH1 ....44 A7
Dickenson Rd DL14 ......93 A8
Dickins Wlk SR8 ....49 E5
Dickinson St DL1 ....133 B1
Didcot Cl Darlington DL3 .132 C7
14 Redcar TS10 ....107 E1
Diddridge La DL13 ......189 F1
Diggerland* DH7 ....32 C7
Dikes La TS9 ....161 E3
Diligence Way TS16 .....137 B2
Dilks St DL14 ....80 A3
Dillon St SR7 ....29 D7
Dillside TS19 ....117 C5
Dilston Cl SR8 ....49 C3
Dilston Rd DH1 ....34 D6
Dimmingdale Rd TS12 ..165 C5
Dinas Ct TS17 ....156 F8
Dingleside TS19 ....117 C4
Dinsdale Ave TS5 ....139 C5
Dinsdale Cl DL2 ....153 F7
Dinsdale Cotts 3 SR2 ....18 F6
Dinsdale Cres DL1 ......133 C1
Dinsdale Ct
Billingham TS23 ....102 F6
Middleton St George DL2 ..153 F7
Dinsdale Dr Durham DH1 ..35 E4
Eaglescliffe TS16 ....137 C1
Dinsdale Pk DL2 ....153 E5
Dinsdale Rd TS19 ....117 B7
Dinsdale St SR2 ....18 F6
Dinsdale St S SR2 ....18 F6
Dinsdale Sta DL2 ....153 F7
Dinsley Dr TS29 ....60 A5
Dinting Cl SR8 ....49 B5
Diomed Ct TS7 ....140 C5
Dionysia Rd TS3 ....120 C3
Dipton Gn TS4 ....140 B6
Dipton Rd TS19 ....117 B8
Dipwood Rd NE39 ....1 E1
Dipwood Way NE39 ....5 D8
Dishforth Cl TS17 ....138 D3
Disraeli St DH4 ....26 B8
Dixon Ave DH8 ....3 F4
Dixon Est DH6 ....48 C5
Dixon Estate Bglws DH6 ..48 C5
Dixon Gr TS3 ....120 C3
Dixon Rd
Houghton-le-S DH5 ....26 D6
Newton Aycliffe DL5 ....96 D5
Dixon Rise SR8 ....50 B6
Dixon St
Bishop Auckland DL14 ......80 C7
Brotton TS12 ....126 B4
Consett DH8 ....10 E4
Skelton TS12 ....125 C3
Stockton-on-T TS18 ....213 A3
Dixon Terr 8 DL13 ......195 E3
Dixons Bank Marton TS7 .140 E3
Nunthorpe TS7 ....141 A1
Dobinson's La DL14 .....195 E6
Dobson Pl TS24 ....63 E3
Dobson Terr Murton SR7 ..28 C3
Wingate TS28 ....48 D1
Dock St TS2 ....215 B4
Dockside Rd
Middlesbrough TS3 ....120 E6
South Bank TS6 ....121 A7
Doctor's La TS15 ....173 F1
Dodd Terr DH9 ....12 F3
Dodder Carr Rd TS13 ...166 F6
Dodds Cl DH6 ....48 A3
Dodds St DL3 ....132 F3
Dodds Terr Birtley DH3 .....9 C6
Wingate TS28 ....48 D1
Dodford Rd TS8 ....139 E1
Dodmire Inf Sch DL1 ....152 C8
Dodmire Jun Sch DL1 ...152 C8
Dodsworth St DL1 ....133 B4
Dodsworth Wlk TS27 .....63 D3
Dolphin Ctr The DL1 .....132 F1
Dominies Cl NE39 ....1 F3
Dominion Rd DH7 ....43 B3
Don Cres DH3 ....25 B7
Donald Ave DH6 ....37 F8
Doncaster Cres TS19 ....117 F7
Donegal Terr TS1 ....214 A1
Donerston Gr SR8 ....49 A3
Donington Gn TS3 ......121 A1
Donkin Rd NE37 ....9 F7
Donnini Pl DH1 ....211 C4
Dorchester Cl
Middlesbrough TS8 ....140 B4
Stockton-on-T TS19 ......117 F6
Dorchester Ct DL1 ......151 E8
Dorchester Dr TS24 ......63 D4
Doreen Ave SR7 ....28 F6
Doric Rd DH7 ....42 F7
Dorlcote Pl 1 TS20 .....118 B6
Dorlonco Villas DH7 ......43 C3
Dorman Mus* TS5 ....214 C1
Dorman Rd TS6 ....121 E2
Dorman's Cres TS10 .....106 F5
Dormand Ct TS28 ....60 F5
Dormand Dr SR8 ....49 D3
Dormand Villa TS28 ....60 F5
Dormanstown Ind Est
TS10 ....106 E4
Dormanstown Prim Sch
TS10 ....106 E4
Dormer Parkhurst's Hospl
Almshouses TS25 ....89 E4
Dormer Way TS6 ....120 F5
Dornoch Sands TS5 .....139 B3
Dorothy St TS3 ....120 C4
Dorothy Terr
Sacriston DH7 ....23 C2
9 Thornaby-on-T TS17 ....138 C8
Dorrien Cres TS3 ....120 C3
Dorset Ave DH3 ....9 D1
Dorset Cl
Middlesbrough TS5 ....119 D2
Redcar TS10 ....107 C4
Dorset Cres
Billingham TS23 ....102 F4
9 Consett DH8 ....177 A4
Dorset Dr Darlington DL1 .133 C4
Willington DL15 ....54 A3
Dorset Pl DL14 ....80 C5
Dorset Rd
Guisborough TS14 ....143 D3
Skelton TS12 ....125 A2
Stockton-on-T TS20 ....118 C7
Dorset St
Easington Lane DH5 ....37 C8
Hartlepool TS25 ....77 B3
Douai Dr DH8 ....177 E4
Douglas Ave SR8 ....49 F7
Douglas Cl TS18 ....137 F6
Douglas Cres DL14 ....80 E6
Douglas Ct DH9 ....12 E3
Douglas Gdns DH1 ....44 A7
Douglas La DL14,DL15 ....65 B6
Douglas St TS4 ....215 B1
Douglas Terr Crook DL15 ..52 E5
Dipton DH9 ....12 A6
Normanby TS6 ....121 D1
Douglas Villas DH1 .....211 B3
Douglas Wlk 8 TS20 .....118 B5
Douthwaite Rd DL14 .....80 A4
Dove Cl DH7 ....43 A4
Dove Ct 10 DH3 ....9 C5
Dovecot Hill DL14 ....80 D4
Dovecot St TS18 ....213 A2
Dovecote Cl TS11 ....108 C1
Dovecote Farm DH2 ......15 F2
Dovecote St DL2 ....200 E7
Dovedale Ave Eston TS6 ..121 F4
Willington DL15 ....53 F2
Dovedale Cl TS20 ....118 C8
Dovedale Rd TS20 ....118 C7
Dover Cl Billingham TS23 .102 C6
Redcar TS10 ....107 E3
Dover Rd TS19 ....117 F6
Dover St TS24 ....77 C6
Dovey Ct TS17 ....156 F8
Down Terr TS29 ....59 E3
Downe St TS13 ....127 A1
Downfield Way TS11 ....123 F6
Downham Ave TS3 ....140 D8
Downham Gr TS25 ....89 E7
Downholme Gr TS18 ....137 C8
Downing Ct DL1 ....133 B5
Downs La DH5 ....27 B5
Downs Pit La DH5 ....27 C5
Downside Rd TS5 ....139 A8
Dowsey Rd DH6 ....35 F2
Dowson Rd TS24 ....63 F3
Dowson Sq SR7 ....28 A3
Doxford Ave DH5 ....26 F6
Doxford Cl DL5 ....96 C5
Doxford Dr SR8 ....48 F6
Doxford Park Way SR3 ....18 A5
Doxford Terr DH5 ....26 F6
Doxford Terr N SR7 ....28 A3
Doxford Terr S SR7 ....28 A3
Doxford Wlk TS8 ....139 E1
Doyle Way TS19 ....117 A4
Doyle Wlk TS25 ....76 D2
Dragon Ct 9 TS20 ....118 B8
Dragon La DH1 ....35 B2
Dragon Ville DH1 ....35 B1
Dragonville Ind Est DH1 ..35 B2
Dragonville Pk DH1 ......35 B2
Drake Ave DL14 ....81 B8
Drake Cl TS11 ....108 E1
Drake Ct TS2 ....119 C7
Drake Rd TS20 ....118 B7
Drake St DL16 ....68 F8
Draycote Cres DL3 ......151 D7
Draycott Ave TS5 ....139 D3
Draycott Cl Redcar TS10 ..107 B2
Stockton-on-T TS20 ....117 E8
Drayton Rd TS25 ....76 D2
Driffield Way TS23 ......102 F8
Driftwell Dr TS19 ....117 A4
Drinkfield Cres DL3 .....132 F7
Drive The Birtley DH3 ....9 D1
Consett DH8 ....10 D6
Drive The *continued*
Greatham TS25 ....89 E4
Marske-by-t-S TS11 ....108 B1
Stainton TS8 ....139 C1
Thornaby-on-T TS17 ......138 C4
Droitwich Ave TS19 ......117 E6
Dronfield Cl 2 DH2 ....16 A1
Drover Rd DH8 ....177 A3
Drover Terr 4 DH8 ......177 A3
Droverhouse La DL13 ...183 C5
Drovers La TS21 ....116 B7
Drum Ind Est DH2 ....16 B7
Drum Rd DH2,DH3 ....16 B8
Drummond Cl DL1 ....133 E7
Druridge Gr TS10 ....107 F3
Drury St DL3 ....132 F3
Drybeck Sq SR3 ....18 B6
Drybourne Ave DL4 ....80 F1
Drybourne Pk 2 DL4 .....80 F1
Dryburgh View DL3 .....132 B4
Dryburn Hill DH1 ....34 A5
Dryburn Pk DH1 ....34 A5
Dryburn Rd Durham DH1 ..34 A5
Stockton-on-T TS19 ......117 A8
Dryburn View DH1 ....34 A5
Dryden Cl
2 Billingham TS23 ....102 E8
Stanley DH9 ....14 A6
Dryden Rd TS25 ....76 E2
Dublin St DL3 ....133 A6
Dubmire Cotts DH4 ....26 A8
Dubmire Ct DH4 ....26 A8
Dubmire Prim Sch DH4 ..26 A8
Duchy Rd TS26 ....76 C5
Duddon Cl SR8 ....49 E6
Duddon Sands TS5 ......139 B3
Duddon Wlk TS19 ....212 C3
Dudley Dr DL5 ....82 D2
Dudley Gr DL14 ....80 A6
Dudley Pl NE47 ....179 C8
Dudley Rd
Billingham TS23 ....102 D6
Darlington DL1 ....134 A2
Dudley Terr DH9 ....13 B4
Dudley Wlk TS10 ....107 E3
Duffy Terr DH9 ....13 A3
Dufton Rd TS5 ....119 C1
Dugdale St TS18 ....213 C4
Duhallow Cl TS14 ....143 E2
Duke St Annfield Plain DH9 .12 F5
Bishop Auckland DL14 .....80 B6
Darlington DL3 ....132 F2
Hartlepool TS26 ....76 F6
Seaham SR7 ....29 B8
Staindrop DL2 ....200 E7
Dukeport Ct 3 TS18 .....213 C4
Dukesway TS17 ....138 D1
Dulas Cl TS10 ....107 E2
Dulverton Cl TS17 ....157 B6
Dulverton Way TS14 .....143 F3
Dumbarton Ave TS19 ....117 F6
Dumfries Rd TS25 ....89 F8
Dumfries St DL1 ....133 A3
Dunbar Ave TS4 ....140 B6
Dunbar Dr TS16 ....156 C8
Dunbar Rd
Billingham TS23 ....102 D5
Hartlepool TS25 ....76 F1
Duncan Ave TS10 ....107 A5
Duncan Pl TS13 ....127 C1
Duncan Rd TS25 ....76 E1
Duncombe Bank DL17 ....70 C5
Duncombe Cl DL16 ....68 D7
Duncombe Cres DH9 .....13 F8
Duncombe Rd TS4 ......215 B3
Duncombe Terr 2 DL17 ..70 B5
Duncow La DH1 ....210 C2
Dundas Arc TS1 ....215 A3
Dundas Mews TS1 ......215 A3
Dundas St
16 Hartlepool TS24 ....77 C5
Loftus TS13 ....127 B1
Middlesbrough TS1 ....215 A4
New Marske TS11 ....124 A7
Redcar TS10 ....107 C7
Spennymoor DL16 ....68 F8
Stockton-on-T TS19 ....118 A5
Dundas St E TS12 ....125 D7
Dundas St W TS12 ....125 C7
Dundas Terr TS11 ....124 A7
Dundee Rd TS25 ....89 F8
Dundee St DL1 ....133 B3
Dunedin Ave TS18 ....117 C1
Dunedin Cl DH9 ....12 F5
Dunelm DH7 ....23 C2
Dunelm Ave DL15 ....54 A3
Dunelm Chare DL14 ....66 E1
Dunelm Cl 6 Birtley DH3 ...9 C4
Leadgate DH8 ....11 D3
Dunelm Ct
Barnard Castle DL12 .....209 C5
Brandon DH7 ....43 A3
Durham DH1 ....210 C2
Sedgefield TS21 ....85 A6
Spennymoor DL16 ....55 E3
Dunelm Dr DH4 ....26 D7
Dunelm Gr DL4 ....80 E2
Dunelm Ind Est DL15 .....54 A4
Dunelm Pl DH6 ....48 D7
Dunelm Rd Consett DH8 ..177 A4
Hetton-le-H DH5 ....26 F4
Stockton-on-T TS19 ....117 C5
Thornley (nr Wheatley Hill)
DH6 ....47 B3
Trimdon TS29 ....59 D1
Dunelm Terr
Dalton-le-D SR7 ....28 F4
4 Ferryhill DL17 ....70 A6
Dunelm Way DH8 ....11 D3
Dunelm Wlk
Darlington DL1 ....133 D5
Leadgate DH8 ....11 D3
Peterlee SR8 ....49 D7
Duneside TS19 ....117 C5
Dunford Cl 3 TS19 ......117 B7
Dunholm Ave TS3 ....141 A8
Dunholm Cl DH5 ....26 E7
Dunholme Cl DH1 ....34 B5
Dunkeld Cl
Shiney Row DH4 ....17 F5
Stockton-on-T TS19 ....117 B7
Dunkerque Mall TS1 ....214 C3
Dunkery Cl TS17 ....157 A6
Dunkirk Ave DH5 ....26 F7
Dunlane Cl TS5 ....119 B3
Dunlin Cl TS20 ....102 B2
Dunlin Dr NE38 ....9 F3
Dunlin Ho TS24 ....77 D6
Dunlin Rd TS26 ....63 E1
Dunmail Rd Redcar TS10 .107 B5
Stockton-on-T TS19 ....212 C3
Dunmoor Ct DH2 ....16 A1
Dunmoor Gr TS17 ....157 A7
Dunmow Ave 2 TS3 .....140 E8
Dunn Rd SR8 ....49 D7
Dunn St DH9 ....12 F4
Dunnet Cl TS10 ....107 C1
Dunning Rd Ferryhill DL17 .69 F6
Middlesbrough TS1 ....215 A3
Dunning St TS1 ....215 A3
Dunnock Dr NE38 ....9 F2
Dunns Yd 7 DH9 ....12 F5
Dunoon Cl TS19 ....117 F6
Dunoon Rd TS25 ....89 E8
Dunottar Ave TS16 ......137 C3
Dunrobin Cl DL1 ....133 E7
Dunsany Terr DH2 ....15 E4
Dunsdale Cl Eston TS6 ...121 E1
Marske-by-t-S TS11 ....108 E1
Dunsfield Farm Est
DL13 ....206 D3
Dunsley Cl TS3 ....120 B2
Dunsley Ct TS14 ....143 E5
Dunsley Dr TS23 ....102 E6
Dunsmore Cl TS8 ....157 F7
Dunsop Ave TS4 ....140 B6
Dunstable Cl TS19 ....117 E6
Dunstable Rd TS5 ....119 B3
Dunstan Cl DH2 ....16 A1
Dunstanburgh Ct DH4 ....17 D1
Dunster Cl DL3 ....132 A5
Dunster Ho TS3 ....120 D1
Dunster Rd TS23 ....102 E6
Dunston Cl TS14 ....143 E2
Dunston Rd
Hartlepool TS26 ....76 D7
Stockton-on-T TS19 ....117 B7
Dunvegan DH3 ....9 E2
Dunvegan Ave DH2 ....16 B1
Dunwell La DL2 ....93 F1
Durham 4 TS4 ....120 B1
Durham Ave SR8 ....49 F8
Durham Castle (Univ
Coll,Univ of Durham)*
DH1 ....210 C2
Durham Cath* DH1 ......210 C2
Durham Chare 2 DL14 ....80 C8
Durham Constabulary HQ
DH1 ....34 B5
Durham Ct DH7 ....23 D2
Durham Cty Cricket Gd
(Riverside)* DH3 ....16 E2
Durham Gdns DH7 ....23 B1
Durham Gilesgate Prim Sch
DH1 ....35 A3
Durham Gilesgate Sports Coll
& Sixth Form Ctr
Durham DH1 ....211 A3
Durham,Gilesgate Moor DH1 35 A3
Durham High Sch for Girls
DH1 ....44 B5
Durham Johnston Comp Sch
Durham DH1 ....211 B1
Durham,Red Hills DH1 ...210 A3
Durham La Easington SR8 ..39 A3
Elton TS16,TS21 ....137 A5
Haswell DH6 ....37 C1
Shadforth DH6 ....46 F8
Shotton Colliery DH6,SR8 ...38 D1
Durham Lane Ind Pk
TS16 ....137 B3
Durham Lane Prim Sch
TS16 ....137 A1
Durham Light Infantry Mus &
Art Gall* DH1 ....210 C4
Durham Moor Cres DH1 ..34 A5
Durham Newton Hall Inf Sch
DH1 ....34 C6
Durham Pl DH3 ....9 D1
Durham Rd
Annfield Plain DH9 ....13 A3
Binchester DL16 ....68 C5
Birtley DH3 ....9 C3
Bowburn DH6 ....57 D8
Brancepeth DH7 ....42 E1
Brotton TS12 ....126 C4
Chester le Street DH3 ......16 C1
Chilton DL17 ....82 F7
Coatham Mundeville DL1 ..113 A4
Consett DH8 ....10 E4
Coundongate DL14 ....80 E8
Crook DL15 ....53 A3
Durham DH1 ....34 A5
East Rainton DH5 ....26 C4
Esh Winning DH7 ....41 E8
Eston TS6 ....121 F2
Durham Rd *continued*
Ferryhill DL17 ....69 F6
Gateshead NE9 ....9 B8
Houghton-le-S DH5 ....26 E7
Lanchester DH7 ....20 F3
Leadgate DH8 ....11 D3
Newton Aycliffe DL5 ....96 E3
Redcar TS10 ....107 F4
Sacriston DH7 ....23 C2
Sedgefield TS21 ....85 A7
Spennymoor DL16 ....56 A2
Stanley DH9 ....14 A4
Stockton-on-T TS19 ......117 D7
Thorpe Thewles TS21 .....100 D4
Ushaw Moor DH7 ....33 A2
Wingate TS28 ....48 D1
Wolsingham DL13 ....207 E5
Wolviston TS22 ....102 C8
Durham Rd W DH6 ....57 D8
Durham Road Ind Est
DL13 ....207 E5
Durham Sch DH1 ....210 B1
Durham St
Bishop Auckland DL14 ......80 B8
Fence Houses DH4 ....26 A8
Hartlepool TS24 ....64 F1
Langley Park DH7 ....32 C7
Middlesbrough TS2 ....119 F7
Seaham SR7 ....29 B8
Spennymoor DL16 ....68 C6
Stockton-on-T TS18 ......213 A3
Durham St Godric's RC Prim
Sch DH1 ....34 C7
Durham Sta DH1 ....210 B3
Durham Tees Valley
Airport DL2 ....154 E6
Durham Terr Durham DH1 .34 A6
2 New Silksworth SR3 ....18 A8
Durham Trinity Sch DH1 ..34 B4
Durham Way
Newton Aycliffe DL5 ....96 D3
Peterlee SR8 ....49 C3
Durham Way N DL5 ......96 E3
Durham Way S DL5 ......96 D2
Durness Gr TS25 ....76 E1
Durnford Rd TS3 ....120 F1
Duxbury Pk NE38 ....17 D8
Duxford Gr DL3 ....132 C6
Dwyer Cres SR2 ....18 F6
Dyke House Comp Sch
TS24 ....77 A8
Dyke Nook Cotts DH7 ...177 D2
Dykes Wlk DL5 ....96 E6
Dyson La DL11 ....205 C5

E

E D Morel Terr NE17 ....4 C8
Eade Cl DL5 ....82 B1
Eagle Bridge Ct TS22 ...101 E8
Eagle Ct TS18 ....137 F6
Eagle Pk TS8 ....140 F1
Eaglescliffe Cl TS11 .....123 F6
Eaglescliffe Ind Est TS16 137 C2
Eaglescliffe Sta TS16 ....137 C3
Eaglesdene DH5 ....27 A4
Eaglesfield Rd TS25 ......76 D1
Eamont Gdns TS26 ....77 A5
Eamont Rd Ferryhill DL17 ..69 F6
Stockton-on-T TS20 ....118 A7
Eardulph Ave DH3 ....16 D3
Earl Cl DL1 ....133 B7
Earl St Annfield Plain DH9 ..12 F5
Hartlepool TS24 ....64 D2
Seaham SR7 ....29 A8
Earl's House Hospl DH1 ..33 E7
Earle Cl TS15 ....156 E4
Earleston Wlk TS25 ....76 D1
Earls Court Rd TS8 ......139 E1
Earls Gn DH5 ....26 D3
Earls Nook TS23 ....103 A3
Earlsdon Ave TS5 ....139 C4
Earlsferry Rd TS25 ....76 D1
Earlsway TS17 ....138 E1
Earn Wlk TS25 ....76 D1
Earnwell DL13 ....179 D1
Earsdon Cl TS20 ....117 E8
Earsdon Rd DH5 ....26 F8
Earsdon Terr 2 SR2 ......18 F6
Easby Ave TS5 ....139 E8
Easby Cl
Bishop Auckland DL14 ......79 E6
Eston TS6 ....122 A3
Guisborough TS14 ....143 F4
Redcar TS10 ....107 B3
Easby Ct DL16 ....55 E3
Easby Gr Eston TS6 ......121 D2
Thornaby-on-T TS17 ......138 D7
Easby La TS9 ....160 F1
Easby Pl DL3 ....132 B4
Easby Rd TS23 ....102 E4
Easdale Wlk TS5 ....139 E8
Easington CE Prim Sch
SR8 ....39 A3
Easington Colliery Prim Sch
SR8 ....39 D4
Easington Colliery Welfare
Gd SR8 ....39 E3
Easington Com Sch SR8 ..39 B3
Easington Lane Prim Sch
DH5 ....37 D8
Easington Rd
Hartlepool TS24,TS27 ......63 D4
Stockton-on-T TS19 ....117 B8

Easington St SR8 39 D4
Easson Rd Darlington DL3 132 F3
Redcar TS10 107 C6
Easson St TS4 120 A2
East Atherton St DH1 210 B2
East Ave Billingham TS23 102 D1
Coundon DL14 81 B8
Waldridge DH2 24 A7
Washington NE38 17 B8
East Blackdene DL13 179 E1
East Block DH7 33 A8
East Bridge St DL15 52 F4
East Butsfield La DL13 183 D7
East Cl DL2 134 E6
East Clere DH7 32 C6
East Cliff Rd SR7 29 F4
East Coronation St SR7 28 D3
East Cres Loftus TS13 127 D1
Middlesbrough TS5 119 B1
East Dr TS17 118 D2
East Durham & Houghall Com Coll
Durham DH1 44 E7
Seaham SR7 29 C8
East Durham & Houghall Com Coll (Burnhope Way Ctr) SR8 49 D6
East Durham & Houghall Com Coll (Howletch Ctr) SR8 49 C7
East Ellen St SR7 28 D2
East End Sedgefield TS21 85 B6
Stanhope DL13 206 E2
Wolsingham DL13 207 D5
East Farm Cl TS6 141 D8
East Gn
Bishop Auckland DL14 79 C1
Heighington DL5 95 E1
Shotton Colliery DH6 48 D6
East Grange Ct SR8 39 B3
East Haswicks DL13 186 A8
East Hetton Aged Workmen's Homes
DH6 58 E5
East La DL13 206 E3
East Law DH8 3 D1
East Lea Blaydon NE21 2 C8
Thornley (nr Wheatley Hill) DH6 47 C5
East Lodge Gdns TS10 107 C1
East Mdws TS11 108 D1
East Middlesbrough Ind Est TS3 120 E5
East Mount Rd DL1 133 A3
East Par
Bishop Auckland DL14 80 B8
Consett DH8 11 A2
Hartlepool TS24 64 D2
Kimblesworth DH2 23 F3
Sedgefield TS21 85 B6
Skelton TS12 125 B2
Stanley DH9 14 A7
East Prec TS23 102 D4
East Raby St 1 DL3 132 F1
East Rainton Prim Sch DH5 26 C4
East Row
8 Darlington DL1 132 F1
3 Eston TS6 121 F2
Middlesbrough TS5 119 B1
East Scar TS10 107 E3
East Side TS7 160 C7
East Side Ave DH7 33 A3
East St
Blackhall Colliery TS27 50 D4
Consett DH8 11 A2
Consett, Crookhall DH8 11 B2
Darlington DL1 133 A2
Gayles DL11 205 E2
Hett DH6 56 E6
Loftus TS13 127 C1
Marske-by-t-S TS11 108 D1
Middlesbrough TS2 119 F7
Sacriston DH7 23 B4
Shotton Colliery DH6 48 D6
Stanley DH9 14 B7
Thornley (nr Wheatley Hill) DH6 47 E4
West Pelton DH2 15 A5
East Stanley Sch DH9 14 A7
East Tanfield Sta* DH9 6 E2
East Terr Billy Row DL15 52 D6
Chopwell NE17 4 C7
Coundon DL14 67 F1
Hesleden TS27 50 A1
Skelton TS12 125 B2
East View
Annfield Plain DH9 12 E6
Brandon DH7 43 C3
Burnopfield NE16 6 A6
Consett DH8 10 F4
Dipton DH9 12 D8
Easington SR8 39 E5
8 Ferryhill DL17 70 A6
Fishburn TS21 72 D5
Kimblesworth DH2 23 F2
Middleton St George DL2 154 A5
Murton SR7 28 D2
1 Peterlee SR8 50 A7
Rowlands Gill NE39 1 C2
Ryhope SR2 18 E6
Sadberge DL2 134 E6
1 Seaham SR7 18 F1
Sherburn Hill DH6 36 D1
Stanley DH9 13 E4
East View *continued*
Thornley (nr Wheatley Hill) DH6 47 C4
Trimdon TS29 59 D3
Wheatley Hill DH6 47 F1
Willington DL15 53 C3
East View Terr
Middlesbrough TS4 120 A2
Seaton Carew TS25 77 E1
Shildon DL4 80 F2
East Villas DH6 37 F4
Eastbank Rd TS7 141 B6
Eastbourne Ave TS16 156 C7
Eastbourne Comp Sch DL1 133 C2
Eastbourne Gdns TS3 140 F8
Eastbourne Rd
Darlington DL1 133 C1
Middlesbrough TS5 119 E1
Stockton-on-T TS19 118 A5
Eastbury Cl TS17 157 C8
Eastcroft
2 Middlesbrough TS3 120 C2
Stanhope DL13 206 C3
Eastcroft Rd TS6 121 E6
Eastdene Rd SR7 28 F7
Eastdene Way SR8 49 F5
Easter Pk TS17 138 D2
Eastern Ave DH7 32 C6
Easterside Prim Sch TS4 140 B5
Easterside Rd TS4 140 B6
Eastfield SR8 49 F5
Eastfield Rd TS11 108 B1
Eastfields DH9 13 E5
Eastfields Rd DL5 95 F4
Eastgate Rd TS5 139 D8
Eastham Sands TS5 139 B3
Eastland Ave TS26 76 F4
Eastland View TS3 120 E3
Eastlands NE38 16 E7
Eastlea Ave DL14 80 C6
Eastlea Cres SR7 29 A7
Eastlea Rd SR7 28 F7
Eastleigh TS17 138 E5
Eastlowthian St TS2 119 F8
Easton St TS17 138 D8
Eastpoint Rd DL1 133 F2
Eastport Rd TS18 213 C4
Eastwell Cl TS21 85 B6
Eastwood DH7 23 C2
Eastwood Rd TS3 121 A1
Eaton Cl NE38 17 B8
Ebba Cl DL5 96 C6
Ebberston Ct DL16 55 E3
Ebchester CE Prim Sch DH8 3 E3
Ebchester Cl TS19 117 B8
Ebchester Hill DH8 3 F2
Ebchester Roman Fort* DH8 3 E4
Eccleston Wlk TS4 140 B6
Eckert Ave TS5 119 A1
Eckford Wlk TS25 76 E1
Eddison Way TS8 139 E1
Eddleston Wlk TS25 76 D1
Eden Ave Burnopfield NE16 6 A6
Leadgate DH8 11 D5
Eden Cl Coundon DL14 81 C8
Heighington DL5 95 C1
Hurworth-on-T DL2 152 A1
Eden Com Prim Sch SR8 49 D7
Eden Cotts Hesleden TS27 50 A1
Leadgate DH8 11 C5
Eden Cres DL1 151 F7
Eden Crest DL2 201 D3
Eden Croft DH9 15 A6
Eden Ct 5 DL14 80 B8
Eden Dr TS21 85 B5
Eden Gdns DL17 82 E6
Eden Gr
Bishop Auckland DL14 79 B1
Middridge DL5 81 E1
Eden La Gainford DL2 201 D4
Peterlee SR8 49 E8
Eden Pk DL2 201 D3
Eden Rd Durham DH1 34 C6
Middlesbrough TS4 119 F2
Newton Aycliffe DL5 96 E7
Skelton TS12 125 C3
Spennymoor DL16 68 F7
Eden St Hartlepool TS24 77 B5
Peterlee SR8 50 A7
Saltburn-by-t-S TS12 125 C7
Spennymoor DL16 68 E7
Eden Terr Chilton DL17 82 F8
Coundon DL14 81 B8
Durham DH1 35 B3
Kirk Merrington DL14 68 F3
Stanley DH9 13 D5
Willington DL15 54 A2
Eden Vale SR8 49 F6
Eden View Coundon DL14 68 E3
Shotton Colliery DH6 48 D6
Eden Way TS22 102 A6
Edendale Cres DL15 65 D7
Edendale Terr SR8 49 F6
Edenfield DH9 15 A7
Edenhall Gr TS10 107 C3
Edenhill Rd SR8 49 E7
Eder Rd TS20 118 B6
Edgar Gr DL14 80 B8
Edgar St Hartlepool TS25 77 B3
6 Stockton-on-T TS20 118 B6
Edge Ct DH1 211 C3
Edge Hill DL14 80 B8
Edge La DH7 21 B6
Edge The DL13 194 F5
Edgecombe Dr DL3 132 A3
Edgecombe Gr DL3 132 A3
Edgehill Way TS23 103 A6
Edgemoor Rd DL1 152 D6
Edgewood Ct DH7 23 B4
Edgeworth Ct TS8 139 F1
Edgley Rd TS18 117 B1
Edgmond Ct SR2 18 E8
Edinburgh Ave TS5 139 D8
Edinburgh Cl TS7 141 A3
Edinburgh Dr DL3 132 A1
Edinburgh Gr TS25 90 B8
Ediscum Garth DL14 79 F6
Edison St SR7 28 D3
Edith St Consett DH8 10 F2
Middlesbrough TS5 119 B4
Seaham SR7 29 E5
Edith Terr DL14 79 B1
Edlingham Ct 6 DH5 26 F8
Edlingham Rd DH1 34 C5
Edmondbyers Rd TS19 117 B8
Edmondsley La DH7 23 B5
Edmondsley Prim Sch DH7 23 B7
Edmondsley Wlk 2 TS19 117 C8
Edmund Ct DH7 33 A4
Edmund St DL1 133 A4
Edmundsbury Rd TS5 119 F2
Edna St DH6 57 D8
Ednam Gr TS25 76 E1
Edridge Gn TS3 120 E3
Edston Dr TS14 143 F6
Edward Ave Bowburn DH6 45 D1
Peterlee SR8 49 F6
Edward Cain Ct 9 SR8 50 A7
Edward Kitching Terr TS9 161 A3
Edward Rd DH3 9 B5
Edward St
Bishop Auckland DL14 80 B8
Burnopfield NE16 6 A6
Chester le Street DH3 16 C3
Craghead DH9 14 C2
Darlington DL1 133 B4
Durham DH1 211 C3
Eldon Lane DL14 80 F4
Esh Winning DH7 41 E8
Hetton-le-H DH5 27 A4
Middlesbrough TS3 120 C4
New Silksworth SR3 18 A7
6 Seaham SR7 29 D6
South Bank TS6 121 A5
Spennymoor DL16 68 E8
Edward Street Ind Est DL1 133 B4
Edward Terr
Annfield Plain DH9 13 B4
New Brancepeth DH7 42 F8
Pelton DH2 15 C6
Edwardia Ct DH8 10 E2
Edwards St Eston TS6 121 F1
Stockton-on-T TS18 213 A1
Edwards Wlk DH7 21 E6
Edwardson Rd DH7 43 D4
Edzell Wlk TS25 76 D1
Egerton Cl TS20 101 E1
Egerton Gr DL5 82 D1
Egerton Rd TS26 76 D5
Egerton St TS1 215 A2
Egerton Terr TS25 89 E4
Egglescliffe CE Prim Sch TS16 156 C7
Egglescliffe Cl 1 TS19 117 C8
Egglescliffe Sch TS16 156 A8
Eggleston Cl Durham DH1 34 E6
Great Lumley DH3 25 B7
Eggleston Ct TS2 119 C7
Eggleston Dr DH8 10 F1
Eggleston Hall Gdns* DL12 193 D2
Eggleston La DL12 193 D1
Eggleston Rd TS10 107 C1
Eggleston View DL3 132 A4
Egglestone Abbey* DL12 209 E3
Egglestone Ct
Billingham TS23 102 E5
Skelton TS12 125 D2
Egglestone Dr
Consett DH8 11 A1
Eaglescliffe TS16 137 A1
Egglestone Terr TS18 212 C2
Egglestone Wlk DL14 79 D2
Eglington Ave TS14 143 E3
Eglington Rd TS6 121 E6
Egmont Rd TS4 215 B1
Egremont Gr SR8 49 A3
Egton Ave TS7 140 F2
Egton Cl TS10 107 C2
Egton Dr TS25 90 D7
Egton Rd TS20 118 B6
Egton Terr DH3 9 C5
Egton Way DL1 133 E6
Eider Cl Hartlepool TS26 76 D8
Ingleby Barwick TS17 138 B1
Eight Houses TS27 61 C5
Eighth Ave DH2 16 B3
Eighth St
Blackhall Colliery TS27 50 D4
Peterlee SR8 50 A7
Elcho St TS26 77 A6
Elcoat Rd TS20 102 B1
Elcoat Terr DL15 53 A2
Elder Cl DH7 33 C1
Elder Ct TS1 215 A3
Elder Gr Redcar TS10 107 F2
Stockton-on-T TS19 117 E7
Elderberry Mews TS21 72 C5
Elderslie Wlk TS25 76 D1
Elderwood Ct 5 TS4 139 F8
Eldon Bank DL4,DL14 81 A3
Eldon Bank Top DL4 81 A3
Eldon Cl Langley Park DH7 32 A6
Newton Aycliffe DL5 96 E7
Eldon Gr TS26 76 F5
Eldon Grove Prim Sch TS26 76 F4
Eldon Lane Prim Sch DL14 80 E4
Eldon Pl DL3 132 F5
Eldon Rd DL5 96 D4
Eldon St Darlington DL3 132 F5
Thornaby-on-T TS17 138 C8
Eldon Terr Ferryhill DL17 70 C4
Fishburn TS21 72 C4
Eldon Wlk 1 TS17 138 D8
Eleanor Pl TS18 213 A1
Elemere Ct TS23 102 E6
Elemore Cl DH7 32 B6
Elemore Hall Sch DH6 37 A5
Elemore La
Easington Lane DH5 37 A7
High Pittington DH6 36 E6
Elemore Pl DL5 82 C1
Elemore St DH6 36 B5
Elemore View DH6 37 F7
Eleventh Ave DH2 16 B3
Eleventh St
Blackhall Colliery TS27 50 C4
Blackhall Colliery TS27 50 D4
8 Peterlee SR8 50 A7
Elgar Cl DH9 14 A5
Elgin Ave Eston TS6 121 D6
Middlesbrough TS3 140 D8
Seaham SR7 28 F7
Elgin Ct DL1 133 E7
Elgin Gr DH9 14 B6
Elgin Pl DH3 9 D2
Elgin Rd Hartlepool TS25 76 E1
Thornaby-on-T TS17 138 D3
Eliot Ct TS23 102 D7
Elisabeth Ave DH3 9 B6
Elishaw Gn 4 TS17 157 A7
Elite Bldgs DH9 13 F7
Eliza La DH8 177 C1
Eliza St DH7 23 B2
Elizabeth Barrett Wlk DL5 96 D5
Elizabeth Ct DH6 36 C5
Elizabeth Pl DL1 133 A4
Elizabeth St
Annfield Plain DH9 13 A4
Blackhall Rocks TS27 50 E2
Seaham SR7 29 C7
2 Thornaby-on-T TS17 138 D8
Elizabeth Terr TS3 215 C2
Elizabeth Way TS25 90 E7
Elkington Wlk TS3 121 A1
Ellam Ave DH1 210 A1
Elland Ave TS4 140 B6
Elland Ct DL1 133 F3
Ellary Wlk TS25 76 D1
Ellen Ave TS18 212 C1
Ellenport Ct 5 TS18 213 C4
Ellerbeck Way TS7 141 B8
Ellerbourne Terr TS28 60 F5
Ellerburne St 7 TS17 138 D8
Ellerby Bank TS13 149 F1
Ellerby Cl TS10 107 C3
Ellerby Gn TS3 120 C2
Ellerby La TS13 149 F2
Ellerby Rd TS6 121 F3
Ellers Bank TS14 124 C1
Ellerton Cl
Darlington DL3 132 A5
Middlesbrough TS5 139 E6
Ellerton Rd TS18 137 B8
Ellesmere
Bournmoor DH3,DH4 17 D3
Spennymoor DL16 55 E2
Ellesmere Dr SR7 28 F7
Ellesmere Wlk TS3 120 E3
Ellett Ct TS24 63 F2
Ellicott Wlk TS18 213 A1
Ellington Cl Ryhope SR2 18 F5
Urpeth DH2 8 E2
Elliot St
Middlesbrough TS1 215 A3
Redcar TS10 107 B7
Skelton TS12 125 B1
Thornley (nr Wheatley Hill) DH6 47 D4
Elliott Rd SR8 49 D7
Elliott St Crook DL15 52 E4
Hartlepool TS26 77 B6
Sacriston DH7 23 C3
Elliott Terr
Annfield Plain DH9 13 A3
Eldon Lane DL14 80 F4
Ellis Gdns TS8 139 E1
Ellis Leazes DH1 211 B3
Ellison Rd SR8 49 E7
Ellison St TS26 77 A4
Elm Ave
Blackhall Rocks TS27 50 F2
Brandon DH7 43 B3
Pelton DH2 15 C6
Sedgefield TS21 85 B7
Elm Cl Eston TS6 121 C3
Saltburn-by-t-S TS12 125 A7
Spennymoor DL16 56 A3
Willington DL15 53 E2
Elm Cres DH2 23 F3
Elm Ct DH7 23 C3
Elm Dr Marton TS7 140 D4
Elm Dr *continued*
Shildon DL4 80 E2
Elm Gdns DL15 52 D7
Elm Gr Burnopfield NE16 5 F6
Hartlepool TS26 76 F6
Thornaby-on-T TS17 138 C7
Ushaw Moor DH7 33 B1
Elm Park Rd DH8 10 F7
Elm Park Terr
Consett DH8 10 E7
Tow Law DL13 183 E1
Elm Rd Cornforth DL17 57 E1
Ferryhill DL17 70 A5
Guisborough TS14 143 E5
Redcar TS10 107 E6
Shildon DL4 80 E2
Elm St Billingham TS23 103 E2
Chester le Street DH3 16 C3
Consett DH8 10 F4
Langley Park DH7 32 C7
Middlesbrough TS1 215 A3
South Bank TS6 121 A6
Stanley DH9 13 D4
Elm Terr
Annfield Plain DH9 12 E5
Birtley DH3 9 B5
Bishop Auckland DL14 80 C6
Eldon Lane DL14 80 F4
Leadgate DH8 11 D4
Peterlee SR8 50 A6
Tantobie DH9 6 B2
The Middles DH9 14 B3
Elm Tree Ave TS19 117 B4
Elm Tree Ctr TS19 117 C5
Elm Wlk TS13 127 B2
Elmcroft DL1 133 B7
Elmdale Rd DH8 11 A3
Elmfield
Houghton-le-S DH5 27 A6
Lanchester DH7 20 E4
Elmfield Ave DH1 35 B3
Elmfield Gdns TS25 76 F1
Elmfield Pl DL5 96 B5
Elmfield Prim Sch DL5 96 B6
Elmfield Rd Consett DH8 10 F4
Hurworth-on-T DL2 168 B8
Elmfield St DL3 132 F3
Elmfield Terr
Darlington DL3 132 F3
Shildon DL4 80 E2
Elmhurst Gdns TS8 139 E1
Elms Rd DL3 132 E2
Elms The Consett DH8 10 E7
Easington Lane DH5 37 D8
Hesleden TS27 50 D1
Elmstone Gdns TS8 139 E1
Elmtree Ct SR7 29 C5
Elmtree Gdns SR8 49 F6
Elmtree St DL3 132 F6
Elmway DH2 16 A5
Elmwood
Chester le Street DH2 15 F2
Coulby Newham TS8 140 B3
Elmwood Gr TS19 212 A4
Elmwood Pl TS26 76 E7
Elmwood Rd
Eaglescliffe TS16 137 C4
Hartlepool TS26 76 E7
Elmwood St DH4 17 E1
Elphin Wlk TS25 76 D1
Elsdon Cl
Chester le Street DH2 15 F1
Peterlee SR8 49 C3
Elsdon Gdns Consett DH8 10 F5
Ingleby Barwick TS17 157 A7
Elsdon Rd DH1 34 D6
Elsdon St TS18 212 C2
Elstob Cl
Newton Aycliffe DL5 96 D8
Stockton-on-T TS19 117 B8
Elstob La TS21 98 C4
Elstob Rd DL5 96 E3
Elstone Rd TS4 215 B2
Elterwater Cl TS10 107 B5
Elterwater Rd DH2 16 B1
Eltham Cres TS17 138 E3
Eltisley Gn TS3 120 E3
Elton Cl TS19 117 C8
Elton Gr Darlington DL3 132 D1
Stockton-on-T TS19 117 A2
Elton Home Pk TS21 116 A2
Elton La TS16 156 B8
Elton Par DL3 151 D8
Elton Rd Billingham TS22 102 B6
Darlington DL3 132 D1
Elton St TS10 107 C6
Eltringham Rd TS26 77 A5
Elvan Gr TS25 76 E1
Elvet Bridge DH1 211 A2
Elvet Cl DL17 57 D1
Elvet Cres DH1 211 A2
Elvet Gn
Chester le Street DH2 16 C2
Hetton-le-H DH5 27 A1
Elvet Hill Rd DH1 44 C7
Elvet Hill,East Asian Studies (Univ of Durham) DH1 44 B7
Elvet Moor DH1 44 A7
Elvet Pl DL3 132 B4
Elvet Waterside DH1 211 A2
Elvington Cl TS23 88 F1
Elvington Gn TS3 120 E2
Elwick Ave
Middlesbrough TS5 139 C6
Newton Aycliffe DL5 82 A1
Elwick Cl TS19 117 B8
Elwick Ct 3 TS26 77 A4
Elwick Gdns TS19 117 B8

Elwick Grange 1 TS26 77 A4
Elwick Hall CE Prim Sch TS27 75 C5
Elwick Rd TS26 76 D5
Elwick Terr TS15 173 F1
Elwick View TS29 72 E8
Elwin Pl DH2 15 E6
Elwin St DH2 15 E7
Ely Cl DL1 133 F5
Ely Cres Brotton TS12 126 C4
Redcar TS10 107 F5
Ely Rd DH1 34 D8
Ely St TS4 215 B2
Ely Terr DH9 13 C5
Embankment Rd
Seaham SR7 29 B8
Seaham, Dawdon SR7 29 E6
Embles La DL5 96 F2
Embleton Ave TS5 139 C7
Embleton Cl Durham DH1 34 D6
Stockton-on-T TS19 117 B8
Embleton Ct TS10 107 D3
Embleton Dr DH2 15 F1
Embleton Gr TS22 101 E8
Embleton Rd TS22 102 B6
Embleton St SR7 29 D5
Embleton Wlk TS19 117 B8
Embsay Cl
Ingleby Barwick TS17 157 B7
Middlesbrough TS4 140 A8
Emerald St
Middlesbrough TS1 214 C2
Saltburn-by-t-S TS12 125 C8
Emerald Wlk DL17 82 F8
Emergency Access Rd TS2 105 B7
Emerson Ave TS5 139 E8
Emerson Ct
Hartlepool TS24 63 F2
4 Peterlee SR8 50 A7
Emerson Rd DL2 152 D1
Emerson Way DL5 96 D5
Emery Cl DL2 152 D2
Emily St TS1 215 A3
Emily St E 2 SR7 29 D7
Emley Moor Rd DL1 152 D7
Emma Simpson Ct TS18 137 C8
Emma St DH8 10 F4
Emmanuel Cl DL1 133 B5
Emmbrook Cl DH5 26 D4
Emmerson Sq DH6 47 C5
Emmerson St Crook DL15 52 F4
Middlesbrough TS5 119 E2
Emmerson Terr W 1 SR3 18 B7
Emmetts Gdns TS17 157 B8
Emms Hill La DL13 195 B7
Empire Bldgs 5 DH1 35 A2
Emsworth Dr TS16 137 A1
Encombe Terr DL17 70 C3
Endeavour Cl TS25 77 E1
Endeavour Dr TS7 141 B6
Endeavour The TS7 141 A3
Enderby Gdns TS8 139 E1
Endeston Rd TS3 140 E8
Endrick Rd TS25 76 D1
Endsleigh Dr TS5 139 A8
Enfield Chase TS14 143 E2
Enfield Gr TS6 141 C7
Enfield Rd SR7 28 F7
Enfield S Ctr TS14 143 E2
Enfield St TS1 214 B2
Engel St NE39 1 B2
Engels Terr DH9 14 A5
Engineman's Terr DL15 65 F4
English Martyrs RC Prim Sch TS19 117 B6
English Martyrs Sch & Sixth Form Coll The TS25 76 E3
Enid Gdns TS27 50 E3
Ennerdale DH3 9 D2
Ennerdale Ave TS5 139 C7
Ennerdale Cl Durham DH1 35 E4
Peterlee SR8 49 D7
Seaham SR7 28 F7
Ennerdale Cres
Blaydon NE21 2 B8
Skelton TS12 125 B3
Ennerdale Dr DL15 52 F3
Ennerdale Gr DL14 79 B1
Ennerdale Pl DH2 16 C1
Ennerdale Rd
Darlington DL1 152 B8
Stockton-on-T TS18 212 A3
Ennerdale St DH5 26 F2
Ennerdale Terr NE17 4 A5
Ennerdale Wlk NE16 2 F5
Ennis Rd TS10 106 E5
Ennis Sq TS10 106 E5
Ensign Ct TS24 77 D6
Enterpen TS15 173 F1
Enterpen Cl TS15 156 F5
Enterprise City DL16 56 D3
Enterprise Ct Seaham SR7 18 F2
South Bank TS6 121 A7
Enterprise Ho TS25 77 C3
Enterprise Way DL16 56 C2
Epping Ave TS3 140 D8
Epping Cl
Marske-by-t-S TS11 108 C1
Seaham SR7 28 F6
Thornaby-on-T TS17 138 C4
Eppleby Way 3 DL1 152 C8
Eppleton Cl DH7 32 B6
Eppleton Hall Cl SR7 28 E8
Eppleton Prim Sch DH5 27 A6
Eppleton Row DH5 27 B4
Eppleton Terr DH2 15 B7
Eppleton Terr E DH5 27 B4
Eppleton Terr W DH5 27 B4
Epsom Ave TS4 140 B6
Epsom Cl DH8 10 E7
Epsom Ct Darlington DL1 133 F3
Newton Aycliffe DL5 82 E2
Epsom Rd Redcar TS10 107 D3
Stockton-on-T TS18 118 F5
Epworth DH9 13 C8
Epworth Gn TS3 120 E2
Eric Ave TS17 138 D8
Erica Gr TS7 140 C5
Eridge Rd TS14 143 F3
Eriskay Wlk TS25 76 D1
Erith Gr TS4 140 B5
Ernest Pl DH1 35 A2
Ernest St Hartlepool TS26 77 A7
Pelton DH2 15 E7
Ernest Terr
Chester le Street DH3 16 C2
Ryhope SR2 19 A6
Stanley DH9 13 F8
Ernest Wlk 2 TS26 77 A7
Errington Bglws DH7 23 B3
Errington Dr DH9 13 C8
Errington Garth 5 TS11 124 E8
Errington Prim Sch TS11 108 D1
Errington St TS12 126 B3
Errington Wood* TS11 124 B5
Errol Pl DH3 9 D2
Errol St Hartlepool TS24 77 B6
Middlesbrough TS1 215 A2
Erskine Rd TS25 76 E1
Eryholme La
Dalton-on-T DL2 168 E5
Eryholme DL2,DL6 169 C5
Escallond Dr SR7 28 F6
Escomb 3 TS4 120 B1
Escomb Cl
Newton Aycliffe DL5 96 F8
Stockton-on-T TS19 117 B8
Escomb Prim Sch DL14 79 D7
Escomb Rd DL14 80 B7
Escombe Ave TS4 140 B6
Escombe Rd TS23 102 E8
Esdale SR2 18 E6
Esh Bank DH7 31 E5
Esh CE Prim Sch DH7 31 F5
Esh Hillside DH7 32 D6
Esh Terr 10 DH7 32 C6
Esh Winning Ind Est DH7 31 E1
Esh Winning Prim Sch DH7 41 D7
Esher Ave TS6 141 C7
Esher St TS1 215 B2
Eshton TS22 87 B4
Eshwood Sq TS1 214 C3
Esk Ave DH3 25 B7
Esk Cl TS14 143 D3
Esk Gdns DL15 52 F2
Esk Gn TS16 156 B8
Esk Gr TS25 76 E1
Esk Rd Darlington DL1 152 A6
Stockton-on-T TS20 118 B7
Esk St TS3 120 C4
Esk Terr 9 DH3 9 C5
Eskdale Birtley DH3 9 E1
Hemlington TS8 139 D1
Eskdale Cl Seaham SR7 28 F7
Yarm TS15 156 B3
Eskdale Ct TS25 76 D1
Eskdale Gdns DL4 81 C1
Eskdale Pl DL5 96 A6
Eskdale Rd
Hartlepool TS25 76 D1
Redcar TS10 106 F4
Eskdale St
Darlington DL3 132 E2
Hetton-le-H DH5 26 F2
Eskdale Terr TS12 145 E5
Eskdale Wlk SR8 49 E6
Esperley DL13 195 F3
Esperley La DL2,DL13 92 B4
Espin Pl DL13 183 E1
Espin Wlk 2 DL5 96 E8
Esplanade TS10 107 D7
Essex Ave Consett DH8 177 A4
Eston TS6 121 D5
Essex Cl TS10 107 C4
Essex Cres
Billingham TS23 102 F3
Seaham SR7 28 F7
Essex Gr
New Silksworth SR3 18 A8
Stockton-on-T TS20 118 C7
Essex Pl Peterlee SR8 49 C8
Willington DL15 54 A3
Essex St Hetton-le-H DH5 26 F4
Middlesbrough TS1 214 B1
Essex Way DL1 133 C4
Essexport Rd TS18 213 C4
Essington Way
Easington SR8 39 C1
Peterlee SR8 49 C7
Estate Hos DH4 17 E4
Esthwaite Ave DH2 16 B1
Esthwaite Gr DL14 79 A1
Eston Cl TS17 138 E7
Eston Park Sch TS6 121 D3
Eston Rd Lazenby TS6 122 C4
South Bank TS6 121 C6
Eston View TS3 120 D1
Estoril Rd DL1 133 E1
Estoril Rd S DL1 152 E8
Ethel Ave SR2 19 A6
Etherley Bank DL14 78 F3
Etherley Cl Durham DH1 34 D6
Stockton-on-T TS19 117 B8
Etherley Grange DL14 79 C6
Etherley La DL14 79 E6
Etherley Lane Prim Sch DL14 80 B7
Etherley Rd DL14 79 B6
Etherley Wlk TS19 117 B8
Eton Rd
Middlesbrough TS5 119 C1
Stockton-on-T TS18 212 C2
Eton St TS25 77 A3
Ettersgill Cl TS16 136 F1
Ettersgill Dr DL3 132 A2
Ettington Ave TS3 140 D8
Etton Rd TS23 88 E1
Ettrick Terr N DH9 14 B3
Ettrick Terr S DH9 14 B3
Ettrick Wlk TS25 76 D1
Evans St TS6 121 D5
Evansleigh Rd DH8 177 B4
Eve St 4 SR8 50 B6
Evelyn Terr DH9 13 E6
Evendale TS14 143 A3
Evenwood CE Prim Sch DL14 92 C7
Evenwood Cl TS19 117 B8
Evenwood Gate DL14 92 E5
Evenwood Gdns TS5 139 D4
Evenwood Ind Est DL14 92 D7
Evenwood La DL14 92 D6
Evenwood Rd DH7 41 E8
Ever Ready Ind Est DH9 6 D2
Everett St TS26 76 F7
Evergreen Wlk 6 TS4 139 F8
Everingham Rd TS15 156 B3
Eversham Rd TS6 121 E6
Eversley Wlk TS3 140 D8
Everton Dr SR7 28 F7
Evesham Gr DL2 152 C2
Evesham Rd
Middlesbrough TS3 140 D7
Seaham SR7 28 F7
Evesham Way TS23 103 A7
Ewbank Cl DL5 96 E8
Ewbank Dr TS18 212 C2
Ewbank Gdns TS18 212 C2
Ewe Hill Cotts DH4 17 F1
Ewe Hill Terr DH4 17 F1
Ewe Hill Terr W DH4 17 F1
Ewehurst Cres DH9 5 E1
Ewehurst Gdns DH9 5 E1
Ewehurst Par DH9 5 E2
Ewehurst Rd DH9 5 E2
Ewehurst Terr DH9 5 E2
Ewesley NE38 17 A8
Exchange Pl TS1 215 A4
Exchange Sq TS1 215 A4
Exchange Yd TS18 213 A2
Exeter Ave SR7 29 B7
Exeter Cl DH3 25 A6
Exeter Dr DL1 133 F5
Exeter Rd Eston TS6 121 E2
Middlesbrough TS5 119 F2
Exeter St Hartlepool TS24 77 C6
Saltburn-by-t-S TS12 125 C7
Exford Cl TS17 157 B6
Exmoor Gr TS26 76 E8
Exmouth Cl SR7 29 A6
Eyre St DH9 13 D5
Ezard St TS19 213 A4

F

Faber Cl DL5 96 D8
Fabian Ct TS6 121 E3
Fabian Rd TS6 121 E3
Faceby Pl TS20 118 B5
Faceby Wlk TS3 120 C1
Factory TS27 49 B1
Fagg St TS18 213 A2
Fair View Burnhope DH7 21 D3
Burnopfield NE16 5 E6
Esh Winning DH7 31 E1
West Rainton DH4 26 A2
Witton Gilbert DH7 23 B1
Fairbairn Rd SR8 49 D8
Fairbridge St TS1 214 C3
Fairburn Ave DH5 26 E6
Fairburn Cl TS19 117 A4
Fairclough Ct SR8 49 B5
Fairdene Ave TS19 117 A3
Fairfalls Terr DH7 42 E8
Fairfax Ct Thornton TS8 158 E8
Yarm TS15 156 B6
Fairfax Rd DL2 154 B8
Fairfield Annfield Plain DH9 12 F5
Consett DH8 11 B1
Evenwood DL14 92 D6
Pelton DH2 15 D7
Fairfield Ave
Middlesbrough TS5 139 B8
Ormesby TS7 141 A5
Fairfield Cl Redcar TS10 107 C4
Stockton-on-T TS19 117 B3
Fairfield Ct DL14 79 F4
Fairfield Inf Sch TS19 117 A3
Fairfield Jun Sch TS19 117 A3
Fairfield Rd
Barnard Castle DL12 209 C7
Middlesbrough TS4 119 F1
Stockton-on-T TS19 117 B3
Fairfield St DL3 132 E4
Fairfield Wlk DL15 53 E1
Fairhills Ave DH9 12 C7
Fairisle DH2 9 A1
Fairlawn Ave DL14 68 C1
Fairlawns Cl TS29 59 F6
Fairmead Redcar TS10 107 A2
Yarm TS15 156 A4
Fairmile Dr SR3 18 A4
Fairport Terr SR8 39 F3
Fairstone Ave TS19 117 A4
Fairthorn Ave TS19 117 A3
Fairview TS21 136 A5
Fairview Dr
Medomsley DH8 11 A8
Spennymoor DL16 69 A8
Fairview Terr DH9 12 E3
Fairville Rd TS19 117 A3
Fairway The
Darlington DL1 133 C1
Eaglescliffe TS16 137 C1
Marton TS8 140 E2
Saltburn-by-t-S TS12 125 B5
Fairways Consett DH8 10 F5
New Silksworth SR3 18 B7
Fairways The
Beamish DH9 15 A7
Quaking Houses DH9 13 E2
Fairwell Rd TS19 117 B5
Fairwood Pk TS8 140 E1
Fairy Cove Wlk TS24 64 F1
Fairy St DH5 27 A4
Fairydell TS7 140 C2
Fakenham Ave TS5 139 B8
Falcon La TS20 102 A2
Falcon Rd Darlington DL1 133 E2
Hartlepool TS26 76 D8
Middlesbrough TS3 120 E4
Falcon Way
Esh Winning DH7 31 C1
Guisborough TS14 143 A4
Falcon Wlk TS15 157 F3
Falkirk Rd TS25 89 E8
Falkirk St TS17 138 D8
Falkland St TS1 214 B2
Falklands Cl TS11 108 C1
Falkous Terr DH7 33 A8
Fall Way TS6 141 C7
Fallow Cl TS17 138 B1
Fallow Rd DL5 82 E2
Fallowfield Terr DH6 38 A7
Fallows Ct TS1 214 B3
Fallows The DL13 195 E3
Fallsway DH1 35 D5
Falmer Rd DL1 152 B8
Falmouth Cl SR7 29 A6
Falmouth Dr DL3 132 F8
Falmouth Gr TS26 76 E8
Falmouth St TS1 215 B1
Falsgrave Pl NE16 2 F5
Falstaff Ct DL1 133 A2
Falston Cl TS23 102 C6
Falstone Dr DH2 15 F1
Falstone Terr DL1 133 C6
Fanacurt Rd TS14 143 C3
Fancy Bank TS14 144 D4
Fane Cl TS19 117 B3
Fane Gr TS5 139 C6
Far Foulsyke TS13 127 E1
Far Rosedale TS13 149 F8
Faraday Rd SR8 49 E8
Faraday St Ferryhill DL17 69 E6
Middlesbrough TS1 214 B2
Murton SR7 28 D3
Faraday Terr DH6 37 E3
Farbridge Cres DH8 3 F3
Fareham Cl TS25 89 F6
Farewell View DH7 43 E6
Farfield Manor TS21 72 A1
Farfield Terr TS29 59 F5
Farfields Cl TS21 135 F5
Farington Dr TS7 140 F3
Farleigh Ct TS23 102 E6
Farley Dr TS5 139 A6
Farm Cl DL14 80 A4
Farm Ct DL15 66 D5
Farm Garth TS9 161 A3
Farm La TS17 138 B1
Farm Rd DH1 44 D5
Farmbank Rd TS7 141 C5
Farmcote Ct TS8 158 D8
Farmer Cres SR7 28 B3
Farmers Way DL12 209 B6
Farnborough Ave TS5 139 C8
Farnborough Ct DL2 153 F8
Farnborough Dr SR3 18 B8
Farncombe Terr DL14 92 D6
Farndale DL16 55 E2
Farndale Cl NE21 1 F8
Farndale Cres
Darlington DL3 132 C3
Middlesbrough TS4 120 A1
Farndale Ct TS4 120 A1
Farndale Dr TS14 143 A2
Farndale Gdns
Lingdale TS12 145 E5
Shildon DL4 81 B1
Farndale Gn TS19 117 E5
Farndale Rd
Hartlepool TS25 90 E8
Middlesbrough TS4 120 A1
Nunthorpe TS7 141 B3
Farndale Sq
Bishop Auckland DL14 79 F4
Redcar TS10 107 A4
Farndale Wlk 10 TS6 121 F3
Farne Ct TS17 157 B8
Farne Wlk TS14 143 D3
Farnell Gr TS25 76 E1
Farnham Cl
Bishop Auckland DL14 80 D6
Durham DH1 34 C5
Eaglescliffe TS16 137 A1
Farnham Cl *continued*
Newton Aycliffe DL5 82 E1
Farnham Rd DH1 34 C5
Farnham Wlk TS3 140 C8
Farnley Hey Rd DH1 210 A2
Farnley Mount DH1 210 A2
Farnley Ridge DH1 210 A2
Farr Holme DL3 151 C6
Farr Wlk 1 TS25 89 E8
Farrer St Darlington DL3 132 F4
Stockton-on-T TS18 213 A4
Farrier Cl Durham DH1 34 A8
Ingleby Barwick TS17 138 B1
Farthingale Way TS8 158 D8
Fastnet Gr 6 TS24 77 C5
Fatherly Terr DH4 26 B8
Fauconberg Way TS15 156 A3
Faulder Wlk TS25 77 B2
Faulkner Rd DL5 96 D7
Faverdale DL3 132 D6
Faverdale Ave TS5 139 B4
Faverdale Cl
Middlesbrough TS1 214 C3
Stockton-on-T TS19 117 C5
Faverdale Ind Est DL3 132 D6
Faverdale N DL3 132 D6
Faverdale Rd DL3 132 C6
Faverdale W DL3 132 D6
Faversham Cl TS8 158 E8
Faversham Pk DL3 132 C6
Fawcett Ave TS8 139 C1
Fawcett Hill Terr DH9 14 C2
Fawcett Rd TS17 138 D5
Fawcett Terr SR2 19 A6
Fawcett Way 7 TS17 138 D5
Fawcus Ct TS10 106 F4
Fawn Cl DL5 82 E2
Faygate Ct TS8 139 D1
Fearby Rd TS18 137 A8
Fearnhead TS8 140 F1
Feather Bed La SR2 19 A6
Featherstone
Great Lumley DH3 25 B8
Washington NE38 9 F5
Featherstone Rd DH1 34 D5
Featherstones DH6 58 A3
Federation Sq SR7 28 D2
Federation Terr DH9 6 B2
Fee Terr SR2 18 E6
Feetham Ave DL1 133 E5
Feethams 22 DL1 132 F1
Feethams S 23 DL1 132 F1
Felbrigg La TS17 157 B8
Felby Ave TS3 140 D7
Felixstowe Cl TS25 89 E6
Fell Bank DH3 9 D4
Fell Briggs Dr TS11 108 C1
Fell Cl DH3 9 E3
Fell Hos DL13 195 E3
Fell La DL12 198 C8
Fell Rd DH2 15 E4
Fell Side 10 DH8 177 D4
Fell Terr NE16 6 B6
Fell View Consett DH8 10 C1
High Spen NE39 1 A3
Fellcross DH3 9 C5
Fellrose Ct DH2 15 E4
Fellside DH3 9 D3
Fellside Cl Stanley DH9 14 B7
Tow Law DL13 183 D2
Fellside Com Prim Sch NE16 2 F6
Fellside Gdns DH1 35 C4
Fellside Rd Byermoor NE16 6 C8
Sunniside NE16 2 F3
Fellside Terr DH9 13 D2
Fellside View DL13 206 C5
Fellston Cl TS26 76 D7
Felltop DH8 10 D3
Felton Cl DL5 96 E8
Felton La TS19 117 A5
Fenby Ave DL1 152 C8
Fence Rd DH3 17 E5
Fencote Gdns TS19 117 B3
Fenhall Gn DL5 82 C1
Fenhall Pk DH7 20 E4
Fenham Ct TS7 141 A7
Fenmoor Cl TS8 139 C2
Fennel Gr SR8 39 B4
Fenner Cl TS11 124 F8
Fens Cres TS25 89 F7
Fens Prim Sch TS25 89 F6
Fens The TS27 63 B3
Fenside Rd SR2 18 F8
Fenton Cl
Chester le Street DH2 16 A2
Ingleby Barwick TS17 157 B8
13 South Bank TS6 121 A6
Fenton Ct TS12 145 C6
Fenton Rd TS25 89 C7
Fenton St TS12 145 C6
Fenton Well La DH3 24 F7
Fenwick Cl DH2 15 F1
Fenwick St
Spennymoor DL16 56 C1
Stockton-on-T TS18 213 B4
Fenwick Terr DH1 210 A1
Ferderick Terr DH6 38 A7
Ferens Cl DH1 211 A4
Ferens Pk DH1 211 B4
Ferens Terr DL4 95 A7
Ferguson Way TS21 116 B7
Fern Ave DH9 13 D5
Fern Cres SR7 29 C4
Fern Gr DL16 68 D6

Fern Rd DH7 .....23 D3
Fern St Consett DH8 .....10 F3
Middlesbrough TS1 .....215 A2
Fern Terr DH9 .....5 F1
Fern Valley DL15 .....52 D2
Ferndale Durham DH1 .....35 D4
Stockton-on-T TS19 .....117 C5
Wolsingham DL13 .....207 E5
Ferndale Ave TS3 .....120 E4
Ferndale Cl
9 New Marske TS11 .....124 A6
Station Town TS28 .....60 F5
Ferndale Ct TS3 .....120 F3
Ferndene Ave DH2 .....15 E3
Fernhill Rd TS6 .....121 F1
Fernie Rd
Guisborough TS14 .....143 E2
Stockton-on-T TS20 .....102 B1
Fernlea Ct DL1 .....152 B7
Fernleigh DH3 .....25 A7
Fernwood
Mount Pleasant TS8 .....159 B7
Redcar TS10 .....107 D2
Sacriston DH7 .....23 B2
Fernwood Ave TS25 .....77 A3
Fernwood Cl SR3 .....18 A5
Fernwood Gr NE39 .....4 F5
Ferrand Dr DH4 .....26 D8
Ferry Rd Hartlepool TS24 .....77 E8
Middlesbrough TS2 .....119 F7
Ferryhill Bus Ent Coll
DL17 .....69 C5
Ferryhill Station Prim Sch
DL17 .....70 C3
Fervesham Terr DL17 .....70 C3
Festival Villas DL13 .....194 F5
Festival Wlk DL16 .....68 F8
Feversham St TS2 .....215 A4
Fewston Cl
Hartlepool TS26 .....76 C6
Middlesbrough TS3 .....120 C2
Newton Aycliffe DL5 .....95 F7
Field Cl TS17 .....138 E7
Field Head TS10 .....107 B4
Field Ho 3 SR3 .....18 A5
Field Hos DH9 .....13 A3
Field House Farm SR7 .....18 F1
Field House Terr DH6 .....37 F3
Field St DL1 .....133 A4
Field View Terr DH7 .....33 B3
Fieldfare Cl 2 NE38 .....9 F3
Fieldfare Ct NE16 .....6 C5
Fieldfare La
Stockton-on-T TS20 .....102 B1
Stockton-on-T TS20 .....102 B2
Fieldfare Rd TS26 .....63 E1
Fieldhouse La DH1 .....210 A4
Fieldhouse Terr DH1 .....210 B4
Fielding Ct
Billingham TS23 .....102 D7
Crook DL15 .....52 C3
Fieldon Dr DL14 .....79 C2
Fieldside East Rainton DH5 .....26 C3
Pelton DH2 .....15 E7
Fieldview Cl TS2 .....103 E1
Fiennes Rd SR8 .....48 F7
Fife Ave DH2 .....16 C3
Fife Cove DL3 .....132 E1
Fife Gr TS25 .....89 D8
Fife Rd
Barnard Castle DL12 .....209 C7
Darlington DL3 .....132 E1
Stockton-on-T TS20 .....102 A1
Fife St Middlesbrough TS1 .....215 B3
Murton SR7 .....28 D2
Fife Terr NE17 .....4 B6
Fifth Ave DH2 .....16 B3
Fifth St
Blackhall Colliery TS27 .....50 D4
Consett DH8 .....11 B2
Peterlee SR8 .....50 A7
Filby Dr DH1 .....35 D5
Filey Cl TS10 .....107 F3
Fillpoke La TS27 .....63 A8
Finchale Ave
Billingham TS23 .....102 D5
Durham DH1 .....34 F8
Middlesbrough TS3 .....140 E8
Finchale Cl DH4 .....26 D8
Finchale Cres DL3 .....132 A4
Finchale Ct DH4 .....25 F2
Finchale Prim Sch DH1 .....34 E7
Finchale Priory* DH1 .....25 B3
Finchale Rd Durham DH1 .....34 D8
Durham, Framwellgate Moor
DH1 .....34 B5
Newton Aycliffe DL5 .....96 D5
Finchale Sq DL14 .....79 D3
Finchale Terr DH4 .....17 E1
Finchale Training Coll
DH1 .....24 D1
Finchale View
Durham DH1 .....34 B7
West Rainton DH4 .....25 E2
Fincham Cl TS20 .....117 E8
Finchdale Cl 6 TS10 .....107 E1
Finchdale Terr 2 DH3 .....16 C3
Finchfield Cl TS16 .....137 B1
Finchley Ct TS5 .....139 E3
Finchley Rd TS20 .....102 B1
Findlay Gr TS25 .....89 E8
Findon Ave Sacriston DH7 .....23 C3
Witton Gilbert DH7 .....23 B1
Findon Hill DH7 .....23 C2
Fine La DH8 .....3 B3
Fines Pk DH9 .....12 F5
Fines Rd DH8 .....4 B1
Fines Terr 5 DH9 .....12 F4
Finings Ave
Langley Park DH7 .....32 A6
Langley Park DH7 .....32 B6
Finings St DH7 .....32 B6
Finkle St
Bishop Auckland DL14 .....67 B1
Stockton-on-T TS18 .....213 B2
Finney Terr DH1 .....211 A3
Finsbury St TS1 .....214 B2
Fir Ave Brandon DH7 .....43 B3
Durham DH1 .....35 A1
Fir Gr Redcar TS10 .....107 A2
Thornaby-on-T TS17 .....138 C7
Fir Pk DH7 .....33 B2
Fir Rigg Dr TS11 .....108 C1
Fir Terr NE16 .....6 B6
Fir Terraces DH7 .....31 D1
Fir Tree Cl Durham DH1 .....35 A3
Hilton TS15 .....157 F3
Firbank Ho TS9 .....161 A2
Firbeck Wlk TS17 .....138 C3
Firby Cl Hartlepool TS24 .....64 C1
Stockton-on-T TS20 .....101 E1
Fire & Rescue Station Cotts
DL15 .....52 E6
Firlands The TS11 .....108 D2
Firs Terr DH7 .....32 D7
Firs The DL1 .....133 D6
Firsby Ct TS8 .....139 E1
Firsby Wlk 2 TS3 .....120 D2
First Ave DH2 .....16 B8
First St
Blackhall Colliery TS27 .....50 D3
Consett DH8 .....11 B2
Leadgate DH8 .....11 C5
Leadgate DH8 .....11 C6
Peterlee SR8 .....50 A7
Wheatley Hill DH6 .....47 F3
Firthmoor Cres DL1 .....152 E8
Firthmoor Prim Sch
DL2 .....152 E7
Firtree DL4 .....81 A1
Firtree Ave TS6 .....141 D8
Firtree Dr
Howden-le-W DL15 .....65 D7
Normanby TS6 .....141 C8
Firtree Rd TS19 .....117 E5
Firtrees DH2 .....16 B5
Firwood Cres NE39 .....1 A3
Firwood Gr DL15 .....66 E6
Firwood Terr DL17 .....70 C2
Fishburn Ind Est TS21 .....72 C5
Fishburn Prim Sch TS21 .....72 D5
Fishburn Terr TS21 .....72 B5
Fishermans Sq TS10 .....107 D6
Fishponds Rd TS10 .....123 B7
Fiske Ct TS5 .....139 C3
Fitzhugh Ct DL12 .....198 F6
Fitzwilliam Cl 3 TS11 .....108 D1
Fitzwilliam Dr DL1 .....133 B6
Fitzwilliam St TS10 .....107 D6
Five Hos DL15 .....52 B3
Flag Terr DL13 .....183 F1
Flambard Ct DL17 .....71 C4
Flambard Dr DL14 .....80 E7
Flambard Rd DH1 .....34 B5
Flamborough 2 TS4 .....120 B1
Flamingo Cl DL1 .....133 E1
Flanders Way DL15 .....52 E4
Flass Ave DH7 .....33 A2
Flass St DH1 .....210 B3
Flass Terr
Esh Winning DH7 .....32 A2
6 Ushaw Moor DH7 .....32 F2
Flassburn Rd DH1 .....210 A4
Flasshall La DH7 .....32 B2
Flats Bank DL11 .....205 F2
Flatts Farm DL14 .....67 B2
Flatts La Eston TS6 .....121 D1
Normanby TS6 .....141 E6
Ormesby TS7 .....141 C5
Flatts Lane Ctry Pk*
TS6 .....141 E6
Flatts Lane Dr TS6 .....141 D7
Flatts Rd DL12 .....209 B6
Flaxfield DL12 .....209 B6
Flaxmill Cl DL11 .....205 C5
Flaxton Ct 2 TS26 .....77 A4
Flaxton St TS26 .....77 A4
Fleck Way TS17 .....138 E1
Fleece Cotts DH7 .....23 B6
Fleece Terr DH7 .....23 B7
Fleet Ave TS24 .....77 D6
Fleet Bridge Rd TS18,
TS20 .....118 D6
Fleet Ho Hartlepool TS24 .....77 D6
Middlesbrough TS3 .....120 F2
Fleet Rd TS18,TS23 .....118 C8
Fleet St DL14 .....80 B6
Fleet The Redcar TS10 .....106 E4
Thornaby-on-T TS17 .....138 F7
Fleetham Cl DH2 .....15 F1
Fleetham Gr TS18 .....117 B1
Fleetham St
Middlesbrough TS1 .....214 B3
Middlesbrough TS1 .....214 C2
Fleming Ct DH6 .....48 B7
Fleming Pl SR8 .....49 D6
Fleming Rd TS6 .....121 A4
Fleming St TS10 .....107 B7
Fletcher St TS1 .....215 A3
Fletcher Wlk TS25 .....76 D2
Flexley Ave TS3 .....140 F8
Flint Hill Bank DH9 .....5 E1
Flint Wlk TS26 .....76 D8
Flintoff St 8 DL14 .....80 C8
Flixton Gr TS22 .....102 B5
Flodden Cl DH2 .....15 F1
Flodden Way TS23 .....103 A7
Flora Ave DL3 .....151 D8
Flora St Eston TS6 .....121 E2
Spennymoor DL16 .....68 E8
Floralia Ave SR2 .....19 A6
Florence Ct 4 TS17 .....157 B8
Florence St TS2 .....214 C4
Florida Gdns TS5 .....139 D7
Flottila Ho TS24 .....77 D6
Flounders Ho TS16 .....156 B7
Flounders Rd TS15 .....156 A4
Flynn Ct DL5 .....96 E6
Fold DH7 .....31 C4
Fold The Burnopfield NE16 .....6 A7
New Silksworth SR3 .....18 B5
Folds The
East Rainton DH5 .....26 D4
Fence Houses DH4 .....26 B8
Folkestone Cl TS8 .....139 E1
Folland Dr TS11 .....108 B2
Folly Bank
Bishopton TS21 .....115 C6
Eggleston DL12 .....193 E2
Folly Terr DH1 .....34 A7
Folly View DL13 .....195 C4
Fondlyset La DH9 .....12 D7
Fonteyn Ct TS8 .....139 E1
Fonteyn Pl DH9 .....14 B5
Fontwell Cl TS19 .....117 A5
Forber Rd TS4 .....139 F7
Forbes Ave TS5 .....119 B1
Forbes Bldg TS1 .....214 C1
Forbes Terr SR2 .....18 E6
Forcett Cl TS5 .....139 C4
Forcett St DL3 .....132 C4
Ford Cres DH7 .....20 F2
Ford Dike La DL2 .....201 D5
Ford Pl TS18 .....213 A4
Ford Rd Durham DH1 .....34 D7
Lanchester DH7 .....20 F2
Ford St 8 Consett DH8 .....177 D4
Lanchester DH7 .....20 F3
Ford Terr DL17 .....82 E8
Ford Way DL14 .....80 A4
Fordham Dr DH7 .....23 B4
Fordham Rd DH1 .....34 C6
Fordon Pl TS4 .....140 A7
Fordwell Rd TS19 .....117 A4
Fordy Gr TS17 .....138 C6
Fordyce Rd
Hartlepool TS25 .....89 E8
Hemlington TS8 .....139 D1
Hemlington TS8 .....139 E1
Fore Bondgate DL14 .....67 B1
Foreland Point TS17 .....157 A6
Forest Dr Ormesby TS7 .....141 B5
Washington NE38 .....16 F8
Forest Gate TS28 .....60 D8
Forest La TS15 .....172 C8
Forest Mews TS17 .....138 D4
Forest Moor Rd DL1 .....152 D7
Forest of Teesdale Prim Sch
DL12 .....191 C8
Forest View DH7 .....42 F3
Forester Cl TS25 .....77 D1
Foresters Cl TS22 .....101 E8
Forfar Ave TS4 .....140 B5
Forfar Cl DL1 .....133 D7
Forfar Rd TS25 .....89 D8
Forge Cl NE17 .....4 B6
Forge La Bournmoor DH3 .....17 B2
Hamsterley Mill NE17 .....4 E5
Forge The DH1 .....34 A8
Forge Way DL1 .....133 B4
Forget Me Not Gr TS19 .....117 D5
Formby Cl 7 TS27 .....63 C4
Formby Gn TS4 .....140 A7
Formby Gr TS27 .....63 D4
Formby Wlk TS16 .....137 C2
Forres Ct DH9 .....14 B6
Forres Wlk 7 TS25 .....89 D8
Forresters Path DL5 .....95 F4
Forster Ave
Cold Hesledon SR7 .....28 E1
Sherburn DH6 .....36 A2
Forster Cl DL5 .....82 B2
Forster Cres DH6 .....38 B6
Forster Ho TS1 .....215 A3
Forster Sq TS28 .....60 D8
Forster St Consett DH8 .....11 A2
Darlington DL3 .....132 F3
Fort Rose Cl TS16 .....156 C8
Forth Cl SR8 .....49 D5
Forth Gr TS25 .....89 E8
Forth Rd TS10 .....107 A5
Forty Foot Rd TS2 .....119 D7
Forum Ct TS3 .....215 C2
Fosdyke Gn TS3 .....121 A1
Foss Way DH8 .....3 E3
Fossfeld TS19 .....117 A5
Foster St TS12 .....126 A3
Foster Terr DH6 .....56 B6
Foston Cl TS20 .....101 F1
Fotheringhay Dr DL1 .....133 E7
Foumarts La DL17 .....71 B3
Foundary TS27 .....61 C7
Founders Ct TS25 .....89 E4
Foundry Fields DL15 .....52 E4
Foundry Rd SR7 .....29 E7
Foundry St DL4 .....81 A2
Fountain St TS14 .....143 E4
Fountains Ave TS17 .....138 C1
Fountains Cl
Guisborough TS14 .....143 E4
Guisborough TS14 .....143 F4
Fountains Cres TS6 .....121 D2
Fountains Ct TS12 .....125 E2
Fountains Dr TS5 .....139 E7
Fountains Sq DL14 .....79 D2
Fountains View DL3 .....132 B4
Four Lane Ends
Consett DH8 .....177 A3
Escomb DL14 .....79 D6
Hetton-le-H DH5 .....27 B2
Houghton-le-S DH5 .....26 D6
St John's Chapel DL13 .....179 E1
Four Riggs DL3 .....132 F2
Four Winds Ct TS26 .....76 D6
Fourth Ave DH2 .....16 B3
Fourth St
Blackhall Colliery TS27 .....50 D4
Consett DH8 .....11 B2
Leadgate DH8 .....11 C5
Leadgate DH8 .....11 C6
Peterlee SR8 .....50 A7
Quaking Houses DH9 .....13 D2
Fourway Ct TS28 .....48 E1
Fowler Cl TS15 .....156 E4
Fowler Rd DL5 .....96 E7
Fowlers Yd DH1 .....210 C3
Fox Almshouses 1
TS20 .....118 B8
Fox Cl Hurworth-on-T DL2 .....168 B8
Ingleby Barwick TS17 .....138 C2
Fox Cover Ct SR7 .....29 C5
Fox Cover Ind Est SR7 .....29 E4
Fox Covert DL16 .....56 C3
Fox Covert Gr DL15 .....65 D8
Fox Hills Cres DH7 .....20 D3
Fox Ho SR3 .....18 A4
Fox Howe TS8 .....140 B3
Fox Pl DL5 .....96 C8
Fox St Seaham SR7 .....29 D6
Stockton-on-T TS20 .....118 B7
Foxberry Ave TS5 .....139 B4
Foxes Row DH7 .....54 E8
Foxglove DH4 .....17 F5
Foxglove Cl
Hartlepool TS26 .....63 D1
Newton Aycliffe DL5 .....82 B1
Stockton-on-T TS19 .....117 C5
Foxglove Dr DL14 .....79 E7
Foxgloves
Coulby Newham TS8 .....140 C1
Mount Pleasant TS8 .....159 C8
Foxgrove DH2 .....15 F2
Foxheads Ct TS1 .....214 B3
Foxhills Covert NE16 .....2 E5
Foxhills The NE16 .....2 E6
Foxlair Cl SR3 .....18 A4
Foxrush Cl TS10 .....107 C2
Foxton Cl
Newton Aycliffe DL5 .....96 D8
Yarm TS15 .....156 E5
Foxton Dr TS23 .....102 E8
Foxton La TS21 .....99 B7
Foxton Way DH1 .....45 B5
Foxwood Dr TS19 .....117 C5
Frampton Gn TS3 .....140 D7
Framwelgate DH1 .....210 C3
Framwelgate Bridge
DH1 .....210 C2
Framwelgate Peth DH1 .....210 B4
Framwelgate Waterside
DH1 .....210 C3
Framwellgate Moor Prim Sch
DH1 .....34 B6
Framwellgate Sch Durham
DH1 .....34 B6
France St TS10 .....107 D7
Frances St 9 SR3 .....18 A7
Frances Terr DL14 .....80 B6
Francis St Beamish DH9 .....7 D1
Stanley Crook DL15 .....52 F8
Francis Wlk 5 TS17 .....138 C8
Frank Ave SR7 .....29 B7
Frank St DH1 .....35 A2
Frankfield Mews TS9 .....161 A3
Frankfield Pl TS9 .....161 A2
Frankland La DH1 .....211 A4
Frankland Rd DH1 .....34 B5
Franklin Cl TS18 .....117 B1
Franklin Ct TS17 .....138 D4
Franklyn Rd SR8 .....49 C7
Fransham Rd TS3 .....120 D2
Fraser Ct 8 Coundon DL14 .....81 B8
Hartlepool TS25 .....89 D8
Fraser Gr TS25 .....89 D8
Fraser Rd TS18 .....137 D8
Fred Peart Sq DH6 .....47 F2
Frederic St TS24 .....64 E1
Frederick Nattrass Prim Sch
TS20 .....118 A8
Frederick St Chopwell NE17 .....4 B8
Coundon DL14 .....68 B1
Middlesbrough TS3 .....120 C4
Seaham SR7 .....29 D7
Stockton-on-T TS18 .....213 A4
Thornaby-on-T TS17 .....213 C1
Frederick St N DH7 .....43 C4
Frederick St S DH7 .....43 D4
Frederick Terr
Hetton-le-H DH5 .....27 B1
South Hetton DH6 .....37 F7
Fredric Terr TS23 .....103 D2
Freebrough Rd TS12 .....165 B7
Freeman's Pl
Darlington DL1 .....133 A2
Durham DH1 .....210 C3
Freemantle Gr TS25 .....90 B8
Fremantle Cres TS4 .....140 A8
Fremington Wlk TS4 .....140 B5
Frensham Dr TS25 .....77 B2
Frensham Way DH7 .....43 C4
Freshingham Cl TS8 .....139 E1
Freville Gr DL3 .....132 A2
Freville St Hartlepool TS24 .....77 C5
Shildon DL4 .....80 E1
Friar St Hartlepool TS24 .....77 F8
Shotton Colliery DH6 .....48 D6
Friar Terr TS24 .....77 F8
Friar's Row NE16 .....5 F5
Friarage Gdns TS24 .....77 F8
Friars Pardon DL2 .....152 C1
Friars' Row DH1 .....211 C4
Friarside DH7 .....33 B8
Friarside Cres NE39 .....5 D8
Friarside Gdns NE16 .....5 F6
Friarswood Cl TS15 .....156 E5
Friendship La TS24 .....77 F8
Frimley Ave TS3 .....120 D2
Frobisher Cl TS11 .....124 F8
Frobisher Rd TS17 .....138 D4
Frome Ho 11 TS4 .....139 F8
Frome Rd TS20 .....118 B6
Front Rd NE39 .....1 A5
Front Row DL14 .....81 A4
Front St Annfield Plain DH9 .....12 F4
5 Annfield Plain DH9 .....12 F5
Bishop Auckland DL14 .....79 C1
Bishop Middleham DL17 .....71 B3
Brandon DH7 .....43 E6
Burnopfield NE16 .....6 B6
Burnopfield, Lintz NE16 .....5 E6
Carlin How TS13 .....126 F3
Castleside DH8 .....176 F3
Chester le Street DH3 .....16 C3
Cockfield DL13 .....195 E3
Consett DH8 .....10 C6
Consett, Templetown DH8 .....10 F2
Coxhoe DH6 .....58 A3
Craghead DH9 .....14 C3
Dipton DH9 .....12 C8
Durham,Gilesgate DH1 .....35 B1
Durham,Pity Me DH1 .....34 A7
Ebchester DH8 .....3 E3
Edmondsley DH7 .....23 B7
Esh DH7 .....31 F5
Fence Houses DH4 .....26 A8
Fishburn TS21 .....72 C5
Frosterley DL13 .....188 A7
Great Lumley DH3 .....25 A7
Greatham TS25 .....89 E4
Hart TS27 .....63 A2
Haswell DH6 .....37 E1
Hesleden TS27 .....50 A1
Hetton-le-H DH5 .....27 A3
Hetton-le-H, Low Moorsley
DH5 .....26 E1
High Pittington DH6 .....36 B6
Hunwick DL15 .....66 D7
Hutton Henry TS27 .....61 C5
Ingleton DL2 .....201 D7
Kelloe DH6 .....58 D5
Kelloe DH6 .....58 E5
Kirk Merrington DL16 .....69 A3
Lanchester DH7 .....20 E4
Langley Park DH7 .....32 B5
Leadgate DH8 .....11 C4
Pelton DH2 .....15 D7
Pelton,Pelton Fell DH2 .....15 D5
Pelton,Perkinsville DH2 .....15 F8
Quarrington Hill DH6 .....58 D8
Quebec DH7 .....31 B4
Rookhope DL13 .....180 E5
Sacriston DH7 .....23 B3
Sedgefield TS21 .....85 B6
Sherburn DH6 .....36 A1
Sherburn Hill DH6 .....36 D1
Shotton Colliery DH6 .....48 D7
South Hetton DH6 .....37 F7
Spennymoor DL16 .....56 B4
Spennymoor, Merrington Lane
DL16 .....69 A8
St John's Chapel DL13 .....185 F8
Staindrop DL2 .....200 E7
Stanhope DL13 .....206 D3
Stanley DH9 .....13 E6
Stanley, East Stanley DH9 .....14 B7
Station Town TS28 .....60 F5
Sunderland Bridge DH6 .....56 B6
Tanfield DH9 .....6 D3
Tantobie DH9 .....6 B2
Tantobie, Pickering Nook
NE16 .....6 A4
Tow Law DL13 .....40 A1
Trimdon TS29 .....59 F5
Ushaw Moor DH7 .....43 C8
Wearhead DL13 .....179 C1
Westgate DL13 .....180 A1
Wheatley Hill DH6 .....47 F3
Willington,Helmington Row
DL15 .....53 C3
Willington,Sunnybrow DL15 .....53 F1
Wingate TS28 .....60 E6
Witton Gilbert DH7 .....33 A8
Wolsingham DL13 .....207 C5
Front St E Coxhoe DH6 .....58 A4
Haswell DH6 .....37 F3
Sunderland Bridge DH6 .....56 B6
Front St N TS29 .....59 E1
Front St S
Quarrington Hill DH6 .....58 D7
Trimdon TS29 .....59 D1
Trimdon TS29 .....59 E1
Front Street Ind Est DH6 .....47 F3
Front The Hartlepool TS25 .....90 F8
Middleton St George DL2 .....154 A5
Frosterley Cl Durham DH1 .....34 D6
Easington Lane DH5 .....37 D8
Great Lumley DH3 .....25 B7

Frosterley Com Sch
DL13 188 A7
Frosterley Gdns DH9 12 F4
Frosterley Gr TS23 102 F7
Frosterley Sta* DL13 188 A7
Fry St TS1 215 A3
Fryer Cres DL1 133 E5
Fryup Cres TS14 143 D2
Fuchsia Rd TS19 117 C3
Fudan Way TS17 213 C2
Fulbeck Cl TS25 76 F1
Fulbeck Ct TS23 102 F4
Fulbeck Ho TS3 121 A1
Fulbeck Rd
Middlesbrough TS3 141 A8
Newton Aycliffe DL5 96 D3
Fulford Gr TS11 123 F6
Fulford Pl DL3 133 A6
Fulford Way TS8 140 F1
Fulforth Cl DH7 33 A4
Fulforth Way DH7 23 B4
Fuller Cres TS20 117 F8
Fulmar Dr NE38 9 F3
Fulmar Head TS14 143 B4
Fulmar Ho TS24 77 D6
Fulmar Rd TS20 102 A2
Fulmerton Cres TS10 107 C1
Fulthorp Ave TS24 63 E3
Fulthorpe Ave DL3 132 B2
Fulthorpe Cl DL3 132 B2
Fulthorpe Gr
Darlington DL3 132 A2
Wynyard Village TS22 101 D8
Fulton Ct DL4 80 F2
Fulwell Rd SR8 49 F5
Fulwood Ave TS4 140 A8
Furlongs The TS10 107 D5
Furnace Pit Ind Est DL4 94 F8
Furness Cl
Bishop Auckland DL14 79 E5
Peterlee SR8 49 B6
Furness St
[2] Darlington DL1 133 C6
Hartlepool TS24 77 B7
Fylingdale Dr SR3 18 C7
Fyndoune DH7 23 C2
Fyndoune Community Coll
DH7 23 C2
Fyndoune Way DH7 23 B1
Fynes Cl SR8 49 D8
Fynway DH7 23 C2

G

Gable Terr DH6 47 F2
Gables The Burnhope DH7 21 D4
Hurworth-on-T DL2 152 D1
Marton TS7 140 D3
Redcar TS10 107 B7
Sedgefield TS21 85 A8
Thornley (nr Wheatley Hill)
DH6 47 C4
Gadwall Rd DH4 26 B6
Gainford DH2 16 A3
Gainford Ave TS5 139 E8
Gainford CE Prim Sch
DL2 201 C3
Gainford Rd
Billingham TS23 102 F5
Ingleton DL2 201 D7
Stockton-on-T TS19 117 C2
Gainford St [4] TS24 77 B5
Gainsborough Cl TS6 141 D7
Gainsborough Cres
Billingham TS23 102 D7
[1] Shiney Row DH4 17 F5
Gainsborough Ct
Bishop Auckland DL14 67 B1
Darlington DL1 152 A8
Gainsborough Rd
Marton TS7 140 C4
Stanley DH9 13 F5
Gair Ct DH2 23 F4
Gairloch Dr DH2 15 F7
Gairsay Cl [5] SR2 18 E8
Gaisgill Cl TS7 141 B7
Gala Cl TS25 77 E2
Galbraith Terr TS29 59 E4
Gale St DH9 13 D5
Galfrid Cl SR7 28 F6
Galgate DL12 209 C6
Galgate Cl TS7 140 E3
Gallagher Cres SR8 49 F6
Galley Hill Prim Sch
TS14 143 B3
Galleys Field Ct TS24 64 F1
Gallow Hill DL12 204 B8
Galloway DL1 133 E7
Galloway Rd SR8 49 D7
Galloway Sands TS5 139 B3
Galsworthy Rd TS25 76 D3
Galt St DH6 47 D4
Gamul Cl DL5 82 B1
Ganstead Way TS23 102 F8
Ganton Cl
Billingham TS22 102 A5
New Marske TS11 124 A7
Garburn Pl DL5 96 B7
Garbutt Cl DL4 80 E2
Garbutt Sq DL1 133 B1
Garbutt St Shildon DL4 80 E2
Stockton-on-T TS18 213 B4
Garbutts La TS15 173 D1
Garden Ave Durham DH1 34 A6
Langley Park DH7 32 B6
Garden Cl [11] Consett DH8 10 F3
Stanhope DL13 206 D3
Garden Cl *continued*
Thornaby-on-T TS17 138 B8
Garden Cres DH8 3 F4
Garden Est DH5 27 B4
Garden House La DL13 195 E3
Garden Pl [12] Consett DH8 10 F3
Crook DL15 52 F4
[7] Darlington DL3 133 A7
Eston TS6 121 D1
Leadgate DH8 11 C4
Garden St Darlington DL1 133 A2
Newfield DL14 67 B7
Garden Terr Coxhoe DH6 57 F3
Leadgate DH8 11 C4
Middleton-In-T DL12 208 C5
Stanley DH9 13 E5
The Middles DH9 14 B3
Thornley (nr Wheatley Hill)
DH6 47 D4
Tow Law DL13 40 A1
Garden View DL13 195 C4
Garden Villas
[3] Annfield Plain DH9 12 F5
Willington DL15 53 F3
Gardens The
Chester le Street DH2 16 B3
Crook DL15 52 F4
Hunwick DL15 66 D5
Middlesbrough TS4 140 A8
Gardiner Cres DH2 15 E4
Gardiner Sq NE11 8 C6
Gardner Ave DL15 53 F2
Gardners Pl DH7 43 D5
Garesfield Gdns
Burnopfield NE16 5 F6
Rowlands Gill NE39 1 E3
Garesfield La NE21,NE39 1 E6
Garforth Cl TS20 101 F1
Garland Terr [6] DH4 26 A8
Garmon Cl TS17 156 F8
Garmondsway Rd DL17 70 F8
Garnet Rd TS17 138 D7
Garnet St
Middlesbrough TS1 214 C2
Saltburn-by-t-S TS12 125 C8
Garrett Wlk TS1 214 B2
Garrick Ct [17] DL1 133 B1
Garrick Gr TS25 76 E2
Garron St SR7 29 D6
Garrowby Rd TS3 120 C1
Garsbeck Way TS7 141 B7
Garsdale DH3 9 E1
Garsdale Cl TS15 156 B3
Garsdale Ct [2] DL3 132 F1
Garsdale Gn [5] TS3 120 D2
Garside Ave DH3 9 C6
Garside Dr TS24 64 A2
Garside Gr SR8 49 B8
Garstang Cl TS7 140 F3
Garston Gr TS25 90 B8
Garth Cl TS21 116 C8
Garth Mdws [1] DL14 78 F5
Garth The Brotton TS12 126 C4
Ferryhill DL17 69 F6
Ingleton DL2 201 D7
Marske-by-t-S TS11 108 C2
Medomsley DH8 4 C2
Mount Pleasant TS8 159 B8
Pelton DH2 15 E7
School Aycliffe DL5 95 F4
Sedgefield TS21 85 B7
Spennymoor DL16 56 B1
Stockton-on-T TS20 118 A8
Wolsingham DL13 207 D5
Garth Wlk TS3 120 C1
Garthlands DL5 95 D1
Garthlands Rd DL3 132 C4
Garthorne Ave DL3 132 A2
Garths The DH7 20 F3
Garvin Cl TS3 120 C1
Gas La DL12 208 C5
Gascoyne Cl TS7 140 E4
Gaskell La TS13 127 B1
Gaskell Way DL15 52 C3
Gatcombe Cl DL5 82 F1
Gate La DL2 150 D8
Gatehouse Cl DL1 133 E6
Gatehouse Factories [13]
DH8 10 F2
Gatehouse Farm Cvn Pk
DL13 179 C1
Gatenby Dr TS5 139 C4
Gatesgarth Cl TS24 64 B1
Gateway The DL1 133 B6
Gateways DL13 207 D6
Gatley Wlk TS16 137 D4
Gatwick Gn [4] TS3 120 D2
Gaunless Lead Mill*
DL13 195 A3
Gaunless Terr
[1] Bishop Auckland DL14 80 C8
Bishop Auckland, South Church
DL14 80 D5
Copley DL13 195 A4
Gayfield Terr SR8 39 F3
Gayhurst Cres SR3 18 B6
Gayton Sands TS5 139 B3
Gedney Ave TS3 140 D7
Gelt Cres DH5 27 B2
Geltsdale TS5 139 C4
General Bucher Ct DL14 80 C7
General Hospl The DL14 80 B6
General's Wood The
NE38 17 B8
Genesis Way DH8 10 E2
Geneva Cres DL1 152 B7
Geneva Dr
Darlington DL1 152 B7
Geneva Dr *continued*
Redcar TS10 107 C5
Geneva Gdns DL1 152 B7
Geneva La DL1 152 B7
Geneva Rd DL1 152 C7
Geneva Terr DL1 152 A8
Gent Rd DL14 80 C6
Gentian Way TS19 117 C5
Geoffrey Ave DH1 210 A1
Geoffrey Terr DH9 13 D5
George Ave SR8 39 E5
George Parkinson Meml
Homes DH6 35 F1
George Pit La DH3,DH4 25 C6
George Reynolds Ind Est
DL4 95 B6
George Short Cl DL1 133 A4
George Sq Shadforth DH6 46 E6
Shotton Colliery DH6 48 D6
George St
[1] Barnard Castle DL12 209 C5
Birtley DH3 9 B4
[2] Bishop Auckland DL14 80 B8
Bishop Auckland,West Auckland
DL14 79 B1
Bowburn DH6 45 D2
Chester le Street DH3 16 D2
Consett DH8 10 F3
Consett, Blackhill DH8 10 D4
Craghead DH9 14 C2
[8] Darlington DL1 133 A1
Dipton DH9 12 D8
Durham DH1 210 A2
Esh Winning DH7 41 E8
Ferryhill DL17 70 C2
Hartlepool TS24 77 C6
Haswell DH6 37 F3
Hetton-le-H DH5 27 A5
Langley Park DH7 32 C7
Murton SR7 28 D2
Redcar TS10 107 D6
Ryhope SR2 19 A6
Seaham SR7 29 D7
Sherburn DH6 36 A1
Sherburn Hill DH6 46 E8
Shildon DL4 80 E1
Thornaby-on-T TS17 213 C1
Trimdon TS29 59 F5
George St E SR3 18 A8
George St W [10] SR3 18 A8
George Street Ind Est
SR7 29 C7
George Terr
Bearpark DH7 33 C3
Brotton TS12 126 B3
Crook DL15 52 F4
Willington DL15 53 E3
Georgia Ct DH8 10 E2
Georgian Theatre TS18 213 B3
Georgiana Cl TS17 213 C1
Gerard St DL16 56 A1
Gerrick La TS12 165 E5
Gerrie St TS12 145 B6
Gervaulx Ct DL16 55 E3
Ghent St DL16 67 E8
Ghyll Field Rd DH1 34 B5
Gib Chare DL14 80 C8
Gibb Sq TS24 64 F1
Gibbon St
Bishop Auckland DL14 80 B8
Spennymoor DL16 68 C5
Gibbs Ct [3] DH2 16 C2
Gibside DH2 16 A3
Gibside Chapel* NE16 2 A1
Gibside Cl DH9 14 B7
Gibside Cres NE16 6 D8
Gibside Ct NE16 6 B6
Gibside Terr NE16 6 B6
Gibside View NE21 2 B8
Gibson Gr TS24 63 D4
Gibson Row DL12 208 C5
Gibson St
Close House DL14 81 A4
Consett DH8 10 F3
Gifford St TS5 119 E2
Gilbert Rd SR8 49 C7
Gilberti Pl TS24 63 F3
Gilderdale DH4 17 E8
Gilderdale Cl DL3 132 C7
Gilesgate DH1 211 B3
Gilesgate Cl DH1 211 A3
Gilesgate Rd DH5 27 B1
Gilkes St TS1 214 C3
Gill Burn NE39 1 E3
Gill Crescent N DH4 17 E1
Gill Crescent S DH4 17 E1
Gill Croft DH2 15 F2
Gill La DL12 209 B5
Gill Side View DH8 10 C5
Gill St Consett DH8 11 A2
Guisborough TS14 143 E5
[5] Hartlepool TS24 77 B5
Saltburn-by-t-S TS12 125 C6
Gill-lands La DL12 198 A6
Gillas La DH5 27 A7
Gillas La E DH5 26 F7
Gillas La W DH5 26 E6
Gillas Lane Prim Sch
DH5 26 F7
Gillbrook Tech Coll TS6 121 C3
Gillercomb TS10 107 C1
Gilliland Cres DH3 9 C6
Gilling Cres
Darlington DL1 152 C8
Spennymoor DL16 69 A8
Gilling Rd TS19 117 B3
Gilling Way TS10 107 E3
Gilling Wlk [3] TS3 120 C2
Gillpark Gr TS25 90 D8
Gilmonby Rd TS3 140 D7
Gilmour Garth DL12 198 F6
Gilmour St TS17 138 C8
Gilpin Ct DL5 96 E5
Gilpin Ho [1] TS20 118 A8
Gilpin Rd
Newton Aycliffe DL5 96 E5
Thornaby-on-T TS17 138 C7
Gilpin Sq TS19 117 F5
Gilpin St DH4 26 D8
Gilside Rd TS23 102 F5
Gilsland Cl TS5 139 B4
Gilsland Cres DL1 133 C6
Gilsland Gr TS6 121 D1
Gilwern Ct TS17 156 F7
Gipsy La DL17 83 E7
Girlington Bank
Hutton Magna DL11 205 F8
Ovington DL11 200 F1
Girrick Cl TS8 139 C1
Girton Ave TS3 140 D7
Girton Cl SR8 49 B5
Girton Wlk DL1 133 B5
Girvan Cl DH9 14 B6
Girvan Terr DH5 27 B1
Girvan Terr W DH5 27 B1
Gisborne Gr [2] TS18 117 C1
Gisburn Ave TS3 140 D8
Gisburn Rd TS23 102 F5
Gladesfield Rd TS20 118 B6
Gladstone Gdns DH8 11 A3
Gladstone Ind Est TS17 213 C1
Gladstone St
Brotton TS12 126 A3
Carlin How TS13 126 F3
Consett DH8 11 A3
Crook DL15 52 E4
Darlington DL3 132 F2
Eston TS6 121 F2
Fence Houses DH4 26 B8
Hartlepool TS24 77 F8
Loftus TS13 127 C1
Stanley DH9 14 D7
Stanley, Oxhill DH9 13 D5
Stockton-on-T TS18 213 A1
Gladstone Terr
Binchester DL14 68 A4
Birtley DH3 9 B4
Coxhoe DH6 57 F3
[9] Ferryhill DL17 70 B5
Penshaw DH4 17 F8
Tow Law DL13 40 A2
Wingate TS28 60 E6
Gladstone Villas DL17 70 B4
Glaisdale DL16 55 E1
Glaisdale Ave
Middlesbrough TS5 139 E7
Redcar TS10 106 F4
Stockton-on-T TS19 117 E5
Glaisdale Cl TS6 122 A3
Glaisdale Gdns DL4 81 B1
Glaisdale Gr TS25 90 E8
Glaisdale Rd Eston TS6 122 A3
Yarm TS15 156 F5
Glamis Cres NE39 2 B4
Glamis Ct DH4 17 D1
Glamis Gr TS4 140 A8
Glamis Rd
Billingham TS23 102 C5
Darlington DL1 133 D6
Glamis Terr DL14 92 C7
Glamis Villas DH3 9 C6
Glamis Wlk TS25 89 D8
Glamorgan Gr TS26 76 D8
Glanton Cl DH2 16 A2
Glanton Ct DL3 132 C7
Glanton Terr [2] SR8 50 B6
Glasgow St TS17 213 C1
Glastonbury Ave TS6 121 E2
Glastonbury Cl DL16 55 E3
Glastonbury Ho [8] TS3 140 E8
Glastonbury Rd TS12 125 D2
Glastonbury Wlk TS26 76 E8
Gleaston Cres TS4 140 A7
Gleaston Ct SR8 49 B3
Gleaston Wlk TS4 140 A7
Glebe Ave SR8 39 D4
Glebe Dr SR7 18 F2
Glebe Est SR7 18 F2
Glebe Gdns Loftus TS13 148 A8
Stainton TS8 139 C1
Glebe Houses DL17 69 F6
Glebe Prim Sch The
TS20 117 F8
Glebe Rd Darlington DL1 133 B8
Great Stainton TS21 98 D1
Middlesbrough TS1 214 B2
Glebe Terr SR8 39 D4
Glebe The TS20 101 E1
Glebe View
Frosterley DL13 188 A7
Murton SR7 28 E4
Glebe Villas DL17 57 E1
Glebeside Satley DL13 183 D6
Witton Gilbert DH7 33 B8
Gledstone TS22 87 A4
Glen Barr DH2 16 B4
Glen Cl NE39 1 E3
Glen Ct TS5 139 E7
Glen Terr DH2 16 A4
Glen The TS16 156 C7
Glen's Flats DH6 36 B5
Glenavon Ave DH2 16 B4
Glenburn Cl NE38 9 F3
Glenbury Gr TS10 107 F1
Glencairn Gr [5] TS25 89 D8
Glencoe Ave DH2 16 B4
Glencoe Rise NE39 1 C1
Glencoe Terr NE39 1 C1
Glencot Gr SR7 39 A7
Glendale
Guisborough TS14 143 A2
Hutton Rudby TS15 173 E1
Glendale Ave TS26 76 F5
Glendale Cl NE21 1 F8
Glendale Dr DL3 151 D7
Glendale Rd TS5 139 E7
Glendene Sch SR8 39 D5
Glendue Cl TS7 141 A2
Gleneagles Cl TS22 102 A5
Gleneagles Ct TS4 140 A7
Gleneagles Rd
Darlington DL1 133 E7
[8] Hartlepool TS27 63 C4
Middlesbrough TS4 140 A7
New Marske TS11 124 A6
Glenfall Cl TS22 102 A5
Glenfield Cl TS19 117 A3
Glenfield Dr TS5 139 E7
Glenfield Rd
Darlington DL3 151 D7
Stockton-on-T TS19 117 A3
Glenholme Cl [7] NE38 9 F3
Glenholme Dr DL15 52 F3
Glenholme Terr TS27 50 E3
Glenhow [7] TS12 125 C7
Glenhurst Cotts SR8 39 D4
Glenhurst Dr NE16 2 F4
Glenhurst Rd SR8 39 D4
Glenhurst Terr SR7 28 D3
Glenluce DH3 9 E3
Glenluce Cl TS16 137 C1
Glenluce Ct DH8 10 C3
Glenmeads DH2 23 F4
Glenmere DL16 55 E2
Glenmor Gr TS6 121 C2
Glenmore DH8 177 E4
Glenmore Ave DH2 16 C4
Glenn Cres TS7 140 D3
Glenroy Gdns DH2 16 B4
Glenside Consett DH8 10 D6
Saltburn-by-t-S TS12 125 D7
Glenside Terr DH2 15 F4
Glenston Cl TS26 76 C7
Glentower Gr TS25 90 D8
Glentworth Ave TS3 121 A1
Glentworth Ho TS3 121 A1
Globe Cl [19] DL1 133 B1
Gloucester Cl
Great Lumley DH3 25 A6
Nunthorpe TS7 141 A3
Gloucester Pl
[5] Barnard Castle DL12 209 C5
Darlington DL1 133 C4
Peterlee SR8 49 B7
Gloucester Rd
Consett DH8 11 B1
Guisborough TS14 143 D2
Gloucester St TS25 77 A3
Gloucester Terr
Billingham TS23 102 F3
Haswell DH6 37 E1
Gloucestershire Dr DH1 35 C3
Glue Garth DH1 211 C3
Glyder Ct TS17 156 F8
Goatbeck Terr DH7 43 D5
Goathland Cl SR3 18 C7
Goathland Dr
Hartlepool TS25 90 D7
New Silksworth SR3 18 B6
Goathland Gr TS14 143 D2
Goathland Rd TS6 121 F3
Gofton Pl TS6 121 D4
Gold Crest TS14 143 B4
Goldcrest Cl
Hartlepool TS26 63 D1
[1] Ingleby Barwick TS17 138 B1
Goldcrest Rd NE38 9 F3
Golden Acre DH8 10 D5
Golden Flatts Prim Sch
TS25 90 B7
Golden Gr DL17 82 F8
Goldfinch Rd TS26 76 D8
Goldhill La DH8 176 D2
Goldsborough Ct TS28 48 E1
Goldsmith Ave TS24 63 E4
Goldsmith Cl TS23 102 D7
Golf Course Rd [3] DH4 17 F5
Gomer Terr DL14 67 B1
Gonville Ct DL1 133 B6
Good Ave TS29 59 E4
Good St DH9 13 E8
Goodburn Pl DL12 208 B5
Goodison Way DL1 133 E3
Goods Sta DL15 52 E3
Goodwell Lea DH7 42 E1
Goodwin Cl TS10 107 B1
Goodwin Wlk [15] TS24 77 C5
Goodwood Cl Consett DH8 10 E6
Sadberge DL2 134 E7
Goodwood Rd TS10 107 D3
Goodwood Sq TS17 119 A1
Goodyear Cres DH1 35 B1
Goose Garth TS16 156 B8
Goosepastures TS15 156 C5
Gooseport Rd TS18 213 C4
Gordon Ave SR8 49 F7
Gordon Bank DL12 193 D3
Gordon Cl DL1 133 E7
Gordon Cres TS6 121 E5
Gordon La DL14 92 B8
Gordon Rd TS10 107 A5

Gordon St 4 TS26 76 F6
Gordon Terr
3 Bishop Auckland DL14 80 B8
Ferryhill DL17 70 A5
Ryhope SR2 19 A6
Stanley DH9 13 F8
Wolsingham DL13 207 D5
Gore Hill Est DH6 47 C4
Gore Sands TS5 139 A3
Gorecock La DH8,DH9 20 B8
Gorleston Way SR3 18 A4
Gorman Rd TS5 119 D2
Gorsedale Gr DH1 35 D3
Gorsefields Ct TS6 141 E8
Gort Pl DH1 211 C4
Gort Rd DL5 96 D7
Gorton Cl TS23 102 C6
Gosford Mews TS2 214 C4
Gosford St TS2 215 A4
Gosforth Ave TS10 107 D6
Goshawk Rd TS26 63 D1
Gough Cl TS1 214 B2
Gouldsmith Gdns DL1 133 E5
Goulton Ct TS15 156 F5
Goundry Ave SR2 19 A6
Gower Cl TS1 214 B3
Gower Wlk TS26 63 E1
Gowland Sq SR7 28 B3
Grace Cl TS25 90 E7
Grace Ct
Annfield Plain DH9 12 E3
2 Darlington DL3 132 F2
Graffenberg St TS10 107 D7
Grafton Cl TS14 143 E3
Graham Ct
1 Darlington DL1 133 B1
Sacriston DH7 23 C3
Graham Sports Ctr The (Univ of Durham) DH1 44 E7
Graham St Hartlepool TS24 64 E1
Liverton TS13 127 A1
Stanhope DL13 206 D3
Graham Terr DH6 36 B5
Graham Way The SR7 29 B6
Grainger Cl TS16 137 B2
Grainger St
Bishop Auckland DL14 67 B1
Darlington DL1 152 A8
Hartlepool TS24 77 B7
Spennymoor DL16 56 B1
Grammar School La TS15 156 B5
Grampian Ave DH2 16 B2
Grampian Ct DH9 12 E3
Grampian Dr SR8 49 B5
Grampian Rd
Billingham TS23 102 D4
Skelton TS12 125 C3
Grampian Way DL17 83 A8
Granaries The DH4 26 B8
Granary Ct DH8 11 B3
Granary The TS22 87 C2
Granby Terr TS28 48 E1
Grand View DH6 45 F8
Grange Ave
Auckland Park DL14 80 E6
Billingham TS23 102 E1
Easington SR8 39 B3
Hartlepool TS26 76 F6
Hurworth-on-T DL2 168 A8
Stockton-on-T TS18 212 B4
Grange Bank DL15 66 A4
Grange Bsns Ctr The TS23 102 F2
Grange Cl Eston TS6 121 E5
Hartlepool TS26 76 E6
Peterlee SR8 49 D8
Grange Cotts DL12 200 C2
Grange Cres Coxhoe DH6 58 A4
Marton TS7 140 D2
Grange Ct
Newton Aycliffe DL5 96 E8
West Pelton DH2 15 B5
Grange Est
Kibblesworth NE11 8 C6
Lazenby TS6 122 C4
Grange Farm TS8 140 B3
Grange Farm Rd TS6 121 E5
Grange Hill DL14 81 A7
Grange La TS13 127 E3
Grange Park Cres DH6 57 E8
Grange Prim Sch TS25 89 D7
Grange Rd
Darlington DL1,DL3 151 E7
Durham DH1 35 C4
Hartlepool TS26 76 F6
Middlesbrough TS1 214 C3
Middlesbrough TS1 215 A3
Stanley DH9 13 D6
Stockton-on-T TS20 118 B7
Thornaby-on-T TS17 138 C8
Grange St
9 Consett DH8 177 D4
Pelton DH2 15 E7
Grange Terr
Chester le Street DH2 15 D4
Kibblesworth NE11 8 C6
Medomsley DH8 4 B1
Shotton Colliery DH6 48 C7
Trimdon TS29 59 D3
Whorlton DL12 200 C2
Grange The
Newton Aycliffe DL5 82 D2
Summerhouse DL2 110 A3
Tanfield Lea DH9 13 C8
Grange View
Billingham TS23 102 C7
Coundongate DL14 80 F8
East Rainton DH5 26 D5
Grange Wood TS8 139 F3
Grangefield Rd TS18 212 B3
Grangefield Sch TS18 212 A3
Grangefields TS12 126 A4
Grangeside
Darlington DL3 151 D7
Redworth DL5 95 C4
Grangetown Prim Sch TS6 121 E5
Grangetown Station Rd TS6 121 E8
Grangeville Ave TS19 117 A3
Grant Bank DL2 201 B4
Grant St Peterlee SR8 50 A7
Redcar TS10 107 C7
Grantham Ave
Hartlepool TS26 77 A5
Seaham SR7 29 B6
Grantham Gn TS4 140 B5
Grantham Rd TS20 101 F1
Grantley Ave TS3 121 A3
Grantly DL3 132 C3
Granton Cl DL3 132 B1
Grants Cres SR7 29 D7
Granville Ave
Annfield Plain DH9 12 F4
Hartlepool TS26 76 F6
3 Shildon DL4 80 F1
Granville Cl DL4 80 F1
Granville Dr DL17 83 A8
Granville Gr TS20 118 B6
Granville Rd
Bishop Auckland DL14 80 A6
Eston TS6 121 D5
Middlesbrough TS1 214 C1
Peterlee SR8 49 F5
Granville Terr
Binchester DL14 67 F5
Redcar TS10 107 E7
Wheatley Hill DH6 47 F3
Granwood Rd TS6 121 F1
Grape La DH1 210 C2
Grasby Cl TS3 121 A1
Grasmere Birtley DH3 9 E2
Spennymoor DL16 55 E2
Grasmere Ave
Bishop Auckland DL14 79 B1
Easington Lane DH5 37 C8
Middlesbrough TS5 139 C6
Grasmere Cres
Blaydon NE21 2 B8
Skelton TS12 125 B2
Grasmere Dr TS6 121 C2
Grasmere Gr DL15 52 F3
Grasmere Rd
Chester le Street DH2 16 B1
Darlington DL1 152 B8
Ferryhill DL17 69 F5
Peterlee SR8 49 E7
Redcar TS10 107 C5
Stockton-on-T TS18 212 B3
Grasmere St 4 TS26 77 A4
Grasmere Terr
Murton SR7 28 D2
South Hetton DH6 38 B7
Stanley DH9 13 D4
Grass Croft TS21 136 A5
Grass St DL1 133 A4
Grassdale DH1 35 D3
Grasshill Cswy DL13 185 A8
Grassholm Rd TS20 118 B7
Grassholme 12 DL1 152 C8
Grassholme Cl DH8 11 A1
Grassholme La DL12 197 C8
Grassholme Pl 3 DL5 96 A7
Grassholme Rd TS26 76 C6
Grassholme Way TS16 137 A1
Grassington Gn TS17 157 B6
Grassington Rd TS4 140 A8
Grasslees NE38 16 F8
Grassmere Mews DH8 11 D4
Gravel Wlks 1 DH5 26 F8
Gray Ave
Chester le Street DH2 16 B2
Durham DH1 34 B5
Murton SR7 28 C3
Sherburn DH6 35 F2
Gray Ct SR8 39 D4
Gray La DL12 209 C5
Gray Sq TS28 60 E8
Gray St Consett DH8 10 E3
Eldon Lane DL14 80 F4
Hartlepool TS24 77 A7
Middlesbrough TS2 215 A4
Gray Terr DH9 13 C5
Gray's Rd TS18 212 B3
Gray's Terr DH1 210 A2
Graygarth Rd TS3 120 C2
Graylands NE38 16 E8
Grayson Rd DL16 68 D6
Graythorp Ind Est TS25 90 D4
Graythwaite DH2 15 F3
Great Auk TS14 143 B4
Great Ayton Sta TS9 161 C2
Great Gates DL14 80 C8
Greatham CE Prim Sch TS25 89 E3
Greatham Cl TS5 139 D4
Greatham Hospl Almshouses TS25 89 E4
Greatham St TS25 77 C3
Greathead Cres DL5 96 E6
Green Bank Terr TS12 145 C7
Green Cl TS7 141 A2
Green Cres DH6 58 A4
Green Ct Durham DH1 211 C3
Esh DH7 31 F4
Green Dragon Mus* TS18 213 B3
Green Gates Prim Sch TS10 107 B2
Green Head DL15 52 B1
Green La
Barnard Castle DL12 209 D6
Bishop Auckland DL14 80 B3
Darlington DL1 133 B8
Darlington DL1 133 C7
Durham DH1 211 B2
Durham,Gilesgate DH1 211 C3
Eldon Lane DL14 80 F4
Haswell DH6 37 D4
Holmside DH7 21 E7
Hunwick DL15 66 B5
Hutton Magna DL12 205 D8
Marske-by-t-S TS11 108 A3
Middlesbrough TS5 139 C8
Newby TS7,TS8 160 B4
Newton Aycliffe DL5 97 A2
Redcar TS10 107 F2
Satley DL13 183 C7
Satley DL8,DL13 183 C8
Seaton SR7 27 F6
Shildon DL4 81 A2
Spennymoor DL16 56 C1
Stockton-on-T TS19 117 E6
Thornaby-on-T TS17 138 C6
Wingate DH6,TS29 59 E8
Yarm TS15 156 C3
Green Lane Cvn Site DL14 80 B3
Green Lane Ind Est DL16 56 C2
Green Lane Prim Sch TS5 139 D8
Green Lea DH7 23 B1
Green Leas TS21 116 C8
Green Rd TS12 125 B2
Green Rise DL16 54 E1
Green Rising DL15 66 D5
Green Scar TS10 107 E2
Green St Consett DH8 10 F3
Consett, Shotley Bridge DH8 10 C7
Darlington DL1 133 B1
Hartlepool TS25 77 C4
Leadgate DH8 11 C4
Seaham SR7 29 D7
Green Terr TS25 90 E8
Green The
Barnard Castle DL12 199 F4
Billingham TS23 102 D1
Bishop Middleham DL17 71 C4
Bishopton TS21 115 C7
Brafferton DL1 113 A7
Chester le Street DH2 16 B3
Chopwell NE17 4 B8
Cleasby DL2 150 E7
Cockfield DL13 195 E3
Cornforth DL17 57 E2
Dalton-on-T DL2 168 B5
Eggleston DL12 193 E2
Elwick TS27 75 D5
Evenwood DL14 92 D6
Frosterley DL13 188 A7
Greatham TS25 89 E4
Hawthorn SR7 39 B7
Headlam DL2 201 D6
Hett DH6 56 E6
High Coniscliffe DL2 130 F3
High Shincliffe DH1 45 B4
2 Houghton-le-S DH5 26 F8
Hurworth-on-T DL2 152 D1
Kimblesworth DH2 23 F4
Kirklevington TS15 172 D8
Longnewton TS21 136 A5
Newton Aycliffe DL5 96 E1
Peterlee SR8 49 A4
Piercebridge DL2 130 B4
Redcar TS10 106 E4
Rowlands Gill NE39 1 C2
Saltburn-by-t-S TS12 125 B5
Seamer TS9 158 F1
Seaton Carew TS25 77 E1
Spennymoor,Tudhoe DL16 56 A3
Spennymoor,Tudhoe Village DL16 55 F4
Stapleton DL2 151 A5
Stockton-on-T TS20 102 B1
Stockton-on-T TS20 118 A8
Thornaby-on-T TS17 138 C5
Thornaby-on-T TS17 138 C6
Trimdon TS29 59 E1
Witton Park DL14 66 A1
Wolviston TS22 102 C8
Green Vale Gr TS19 117 A2
Green Way TS7 141 A2
Green's Bank DH9 15 A7
Green's Beck Rd TS18 117 C1
Green's La TS18 117 C1
Greenacre Cl TS9 160 F1
Greenacres Pelton DH2 15 D7
Stainton TS8 139 B1
Greenacres Cl 3 TS11 108 C1
Greenacres Rd DH8 10 D5
Greenbank DL12 193 E2
Greenbank Ave TS5 119 B2
Greenbank Cl TS29 72 D8
Greenbank Ct
Darlington DL3 132 E3
Hartlepool TS26 76 E6
Greenbank Rd DL3 132 E3
Greenbank St 4 DH3 16 D4
Greenbank Terr TS15 173 F1
Greencroft Redcar TS10 107 A2
South Hetton DH6 38 B7
Greencroft Cl DL3 132 D1
Greencroft Ct DL3 151 E8
Greencroft Ind Est DH9 12 E2
Greencroft Ind Pk DH9 12 E2
Greencroft Parkway DH9 12 F2
Greencroft Rd DH8 177 E4
Greencroft Sch DH9 12 E4
Greencroft Terr DH9 12 E3
Greencroft Wlk TS3 140 E8
Greendale Gdns DH5 26 F2
Greenfield Cl DL2 152 C2
Greenfield Cotts DL15 52 F4
Greenfield Dr TS16 137 B1
Greenfield Sch Comm & Arts Coll DL5 95 F7
Greenfield St DL16 54 E1
Greenfield Terr DH9 12 F4
Greenfield Way DL5 95 F7
Greenfields
Bishop Auckland DL14 79 A4
Cotherstone DL12 198 F6
7 Ferryhill DL17 70 A6
Ouston DH2 9 A2
Greenfields Ind Est DL14 79 F4
Greenfields Rd DL14 79 D5
Greenfields Way TS18 117 A2
Greenfinch Cl
Hartlepool TS26 63 E1
Washington NE38 9 F3
Greenfoot Cvn Site DL13 206 A3
Greenford NE11 8 D6
Greenford La DH2,NE11 8 F6
Greenford Wlk TS3 121 A1
Greengates La DL12 193 B3
Greenham Cl TS3 121 A1
Greenhead Crook DL15 52 E1
Washington NE38 9 F4
Greenhead Cl TS8 139 E3
Greenhill Rd DL5 95 C1
Greenhills DL16 54 E1
Greenhills Est TS28 48 E1
Greenhills Terr DH6 47 F3
Greenhow Cl SR2 18 F5
Greenhow Gr TS25 90 E8
Greenhow Rd TS3 120 C2
Greenhow Wlk TS10 107 C3
Greenland Ave TS5 119 A1
Greenland Jun & Inf Schs DH9 13 D4
Greenland Rd Esh DH7 31 D4
Hartlepool TS24 77 C8
Greenlands
Hutton Rudby TS15 173 F3
Stanley DH9 13 D4
Greenlands Rd TS10 107 E5
Greenlea TS27 75 C5
Greenlea Cl NE39 1 A3
Greenlee Cl 5 TS17 157 A7
Greenlee Garth DL5 96 A8
Greenmount Rd DL3 151 E8
Greenock Cl TS11 123 F6
Greenock Rd TS25 89 E8
Greenrigg Cl DL3 132 C7
Greenrigg La DL12 193 A1
Greens Gr TS18 117 C1
Greens Valley Dr TS18 117 C1
Greensfield Cl DL3 132 C7
Greenshank Cl TS26 63 D1
Greenside Greatham TS25 89 E4
Ingleby Barwick TS17 138 B1
Normanby TS6 141 C7
Greenside Ave SR8 49 F7
Greenside Cl TS21 72 D5
Greenside Ct DL2 152 C1
Greenside Pl DL15 53 A2
Greenstones Rd TS10 107 E3
Greentree La DH9 12 E5
Greenway Eston TS6 121 E2
Ingleby Barwick TS17 138 B1
Greenway Ct TS3 120 F3
Greenway The
Middlesbrough TS3 121 A2
Middleton St George DL2 153 E7
Greenways Consett DH8 177 E4
Willington DL15 53 E2
Wolsingham DL13 207 D6
Greenways Ct 2 DH8 177 E4
Greenwell Rd DL5 96 D7
Greenwell St DL1 152 A8
Greenwell Terr DL13 188 A7
Greenwells Garth DL14 81 C8
Greenwood Ave
Burnhope DH7 21 D4
Houghton-le-S DH4 26 C8
Middlesbrough TS5 139 D8
Greenwood Cl DH6 48 A3
Greenwood Cotts DH6 47 C4
Greenwood Rd
Billingham TS23 103 A3
Hartlepool TS24 77 B7
Stockton-on-T TS18 117 C1
Gregory Ct DL5 96 D5
Gregory Terr
4 Fence Houses DH4 26 A8
10 Ferryhill DL17 70 A6
Gregson St DH7 23 C3
Gregson Terr Seaham SR7 18 F1
South Hetton DH6 38 B6
Grendale Ct TS13 127 D1
Grendon Gdns DL2 153 E8
Grenville Cl TS11 124 E8
Grenville Rd TS17 138 D4
Gresham Cl DL1 133 B5
Gresham Rd TS1 214 C2
Gresley Rd SR8 49 A6
Greta Ave TS25 77 A2
Greta Bridge Bank DL12 205 A8
Greta Pl DH7 20 F3
Greta Rd
Barnard Castle DL12 209 D6
Redcar TS10 107 A5
Skelton TS12 125 D3
Stockton-on-T TS20 118 A7
Greta St
Middlesbrough TS1 214 B2
Saltburn-by-t-S TS12 125 C6
Greta St N DH2 15 C6
Greta St S DH2 15 C6
Gretton Ave TS4 140 B6
Greville Way DL5 96 E6
Grewburn La DL13 195 B4
Grewgrass La
New Marske TS11 123 E7
Redcar TS10 107 E1
Grey Coll (Univ of Durham) DH1 44 C7
Grey Gables DH7 43 C5
Grey Gdns DL14 81 B8
Grey Ridges DH7 43 C4
Grey St
Bishop Auckland DL14 80 B8
Crook DL15 52 F4
Darlington DL1 133 B3
Newfield DL14 67 B7
4 Stockton-on-T TS20 118 B6
Grey Terr 3 Ferryhill DL17 70 B5
10 Ryhope SR2 18 F6
Grey Towers Dr TS7 141 A1
Greyfriars Cl DL3 132 A1
Greylands Ave TS20 118 B7
Greylingstadt Terr DH9 14 A3
Greymouth Cl TS18 117 C1
Greys Ct TS17 157 B8
Greystoke Gr TS10 107 C2
Greystoke Rd TS10 107 C2
Greystoke Wlk TS10 107 C2
Greystone Rd TS6 122 A4
Greystones DH6 47 C7
Greystones Dr DL3 132 C3
Greywood Cl TS27 63 C5
Gribdale Rd TS3 120 D2
Gribdale Terr TS9 161 F3
Grice Ct DL2 200 F7
Griffin Rd TS4 120 A2
Griffiths Cl TS15 156 B3
Griffiths Rd TS6 121 E4
Grimston Wlk TS3 120 B2
Grimwood Ave TS3 120 E4
Grindon Ct DL5 82 E1
Grindon Way DL5 96 D1
Grinkle Ave TS3 140 D8
Grinkle Ct TS14 143 E5
Grinkle La Liverton TS13 147 F2
Loftus TS13 148 A6
Grinkle Park Cotts TS13 148 A4
Grinkle Rd TS10 106 F5
Grinstead Way DH1 35 D5
Grinton Park Way 4 DL1 152 C7
Grinton Rd TS18 137 B8
Grisedale Cl TS5 139 C4
Grisedale Cres
Egglescliffe TS16 156 C8
Eston TS6 121 F4
Grisedale Rd SR8 49 E6
Gritten Sq TS24 64 C2
Groat Ave DL5 96 E4
Groat Dr DL5 96 E5
Groat Rd DL5 96 E4
Groat Way DL5 96 E4
Grosmont DH3 25 A7
Grosmont Cl TS10 107 C2
Grosmont Dr TS23 102 C5
Grosmont Pl TS6 121 F3
Grosmont Rd Eston TS6 121 F3
Hartlepool TS25 90 E8
Gross St TS23 103 D2
Grosvenor Cl DL13 206 C3
Grosvenor Ct TS17 157 B7
Grosvenor Gdns
Eston TS6 121 D1
13 Hartlepool TS26 77 A6
Grosvenor Pl TS14 143 D4
Grosvenor Rd
Billingham TS22 102 C5
Middlesbrough TS5 119 C1
Stockton-on-T TS19 117 C2
Grosvenor Sq TS14 143 D4
Grosvenor St
Darlington DL1 152 A8
5 Hartlepool TS26 77 A6
Grosvenor Terr
Carlin How TS13 126 F3
Consett DH8 11 A3
Trimdon TS29 59 F5
Grove Bank TS15 172 C8
Grove Cl TS26 76 F5
Grove Cotts 9 DH3 9 C4
Grove Ct Hett DH6 56 E5
Shotton Colliery DH6 48 C5
Grove Hill TS13 127 A4
Grove Pk DL12 209 C6
Grove Prim Sch The DH8 10 C1
Grove Rd
Bishop Auckland DL14 80 A7
Brandon DH7 43 A3
Middlesbrough TS3 215 C2
Redcar TS10 107 D6
Skinningrove TS13 127 A4
Tow Law DL13 183 D2
Grove St Durham DH1 210 B2

Grove St *continued*
Stockton-on-T TS18 212 C1
Grove Terr
Brandon DH1,DH7 43 E6
Burnopfield NE16 6 B6
Stockton-on-T TS20 118 B6
Grove The Burnhope DH7 21 D4
Chilton DL17 82 F7
Cornforth DL17 57 E1
Coxhoe DH6 58 A3
Durham DH1 210 A4
Easington SR8 39 A4
Fir Tree DL15 52 A1
Greatham TS25 89 E4
Guisborough TS14 143 B2
Hartlepool TS26 76 F5
Houghton-le-S DH5 26 D6
Marton TS7 140 E5
Middlesbrough TS5 139 D3
Rowlands Gill NE39 1 F1
Ryhope SR2 18 F6
* Woodland DL13 194 E8
Yarm TS15 156 C4
Groves St TS24 77 F8
Groves The TS18 212 C1
Grundales Dr TS11 108 C1
Gudmunsen Ave DL14 80 A4
Guernsey Wlk TS14 143 D3
Guildford Cl DL1 133 E5
Guildford Ct TS6 141 D7
Guildford Rd
Billingham TS23 102 C5
Normanby TS6 141 D7
Guillemot Cl TS26 63 D1
Guisborough 8 TS4 120 B1
Guisborough Ct 9 TS6 121 F2
Guisborough Forest Visitor Ctr* TS14 142 E3
Guisborough General & Maternity Hospl TS14 143 E5
Guisborough Mus* TS14 143 E5
Guisborough Priory* TS14 143 F5
Guisborough Rd
Great Ayton TS9 160 F3
Moorsholm TS12 146 B1
Nunthorpe TS7 141 B2
Saltburn-by-t-S TS12 125 B6
Thornaby-on-T TS17 138 D7
Guisborough Sports Ctr TS14 143 F6
Guisborough St TS6 121 F2
Guiseley Way TS16 137 B3
Gullane Cl DH9 14 B6
Gulliver Rd TS25 76 D2
Gully Rd TS28 60 E8
Gunn La DL5 96 F6
Gunnergate Cl TS12 125 A7
Gunnergate La TS7,TS8 140 C2
Gunners Vale TS22 87 A3
Gunnerside Rd TS19 117 A3
Gunnerton Cl DL3 132 C7
Gurlish Terr DL14 68 B1
Gurney Pease Prim Sch DL1 133 B4
Gurney St Darlington DL1 133 A4
Middlesbrough TS1 215 A3
New Marske TS11 124 A7
Gurney Terr DL14 81 A5
Gurney Valley DL14 81 A5
Gurney Way DL5 96 D4
Guthire Wlk 6 TS25 89 D8
Guthrie Ave TS5 139 A8
Guthrum Pl DL5 82 C1
Gwynn Cl TS19 117 A4
Gypsy La Marton TS7 140 E3
Nunthorpe TS7 141 B4
Gypsy Lane Halt TS7 141 A4

H

Habgood Dr DH1 35 A1
Hackforth Rd TS18 137 B8
Hackness Wlk TS5 139 E6
Hackworth Cl
Ferryhill DL17 69 E5
Newton Aycliffe DL5 96 E5
Shildon DL4 95 A8
Hackworth Ct TS18 213 A4
Hackworth Ind Pk DL4 94 F8
Hackworth Rd
Blackhall Colliery TS27 50 D4
Easington SR8 38 F1
Hackworth St
Ferryhill DL17 69 E5
Shildon DL4 81 A1
Hadasia Gdns TS19 117 C3
Haddon Rd TS23 102 C5
Haddon St TS1 215 A2
Hadleigh Cl TS21 85 A5
Hadleigh Cres TS4 120 A1
Hadlow Wlk 1 TS3 120 D2
Hadnall Cl TS5 139 A6
Hadrian Ave DH3 16 D5
Hadrian Ct
Darlington DL3 151 E8
Station Town TS28 60 E6
Hadrians Way DH8 3 E3
Hadston Cl TS10 107 D2
Haffron Ave TS18 213 B4
Hag Bridge Cvn Site DL13 180 F1
Hagg La Byers Green DL16 55 A1
Byers Green DL14 54 F1
Hagg Rd DL16 67 F8
Haggitt Hill La TS15 172 E1
Haggs La DL14 94 B8
Haig Cres DH1 35 A1
Haig St Darlington DL3 132 F5
Ferryhill DL17 70 C4
Haig Terr DL17 69 E6
Haigh Terr DH1 35 A1
Hailsham Ave TS17 138 D1
Haldane Gr TS25 89 E8
Haldon Pl SR8 49 B5
Hale Rd TS23 102 E6
Hale Rise SR8 49 E6
Half Moon La
Spennymoor DL16 56 C1
Spennymoor DL16 69 B8
Halidon Way TS23 102 F6
Halifax Cl TS11 108 B1
Halifax Pl 9 SR2 18 F6
Halifax Rd TS17 138 D4
Hall Ave DH7 33 A2
Hall Cl Carlton TS21 116 C8
Marske-by-t-S TS11 108 C1
Seaton SR7 18 D1
West Rainton DH4 26 A2
Hall Cl The TS7 141 A7
Hall Cres SR8 39 F1
Hall Dene Way SR7 18 F2
Hall Dr TS5 139 D6
Hall Farm DH1 44 F6
Hall Farm Ct TS29 59 D1
Hall Farm Rd SR3 18 A5
Hall Garth Comp Sch TS5 139 D6
Hall Gdns DH6 36 A1
Hall Grounds TS13 127 C1
Hall Hill Farm* DH7 183 E6
Hall La Haswell DH6 37 F3
Heighington DL5 95 D2
High Shincliffe DH1 44 F5
Houghton-le-S DH5 26 F7
West Rainton DH4 26 A2
Hall Lane Est DL15 53 F2
Hall Lea TS21 85 A7
Hall Moor Cl TS15 172 D8
Hall Rd Consett DH8 10 C2
Esh DH7 31 F4
Hall St DL12 209 C5
Hall Terr DL15 54 A2
Hall View DL15 66 D7
Hall View Gdns DL15 65 D8
Hall View Gr DL3 132 A3
Hall Wlks SR8 39 A3
Hall's Bldgs DH9 14 E1
Hallam Rd SR8 49 D7
Hallcroft Cl TS23 102 D1
Hallfield Cl SR3 18 A5
Hallfield Dr SR8 39 A3
Hallgarth Consett DH8 10 C1
Kirk Merrington DL16 69 A3
Hallgarth Cl TS5 139 C4
Hallgarth La DH6 36 B5
Hallgarth Rd TS29 72 D8
Hallgarth St
Durham DH1 211 A1
Sherburn DH6 35 F1
Hallgarth Terr
Ferryhill DL17 70 A6
Lanchester DH7 20 F3
Hallgarth The DH1 211 A1
Hallgarth View
Durham DH1 211 A1
High Pittington DH6 36 C5
Hallgarth Villas DH6 36 A1
Hallgate Cl TS18 137 B8
Halliday Gr DH7 43 D5
Hallifield St TS20 118 B6
Hallimond Rd DL14 79 D7
Hallington Head DL5 95 F7
Halls Cl TS27 50 D3
Halnaby Ave DL3 131 F2
Halton Cl TS23 102 E8
Halton Ct
6 Billingham TS23 102 E8
Middlesbrough TS3 121 A3
Halton Rd DH1 34 D5
Halyard The TS3 215 C4
Hambledon Ave DH2 16 B2
Hambledon Cres 3 TS12 125 C3
Hambledon Pl SR8 49 A5
Hambledon Rd TS5 119 C1
Hambleton Ave TS10 107 B3
Hambleton Cres TS11 124 E8
Hambleton Ct DL5 96 A8
Hambleton Dr SR7 29 B8
Hambleton Gr 4 DL1 133 C6
Hambleton Rd
Coundon DL14 81 C8
Nunthorpe TS7 141 B3
Hambleton Sq TS23 102 C4
Hambleton Way DL17 83 A8
Hambletonian Yd TS18 213 A2
Hamilton Ct
Shotton Colliery DH6 48 C6
Thorpe Thewles TS21 100 E3
Hamilton Dr DL1 133 C7
Hamilton Gr Eston TS6 121 B3
Redcar TS10 107 A6
Hamilton Rd
Hartlepool TS25 89 E8
Stockton-on-T TS19 117 F5
Hamilton Row DH7 41 B6
Hamilton St SR8 49 F7
Hamilton Terr DH7 23 B6
Hammer Square Bank DH9 7 F1
Hammermill La DH8 176 E8
Hammond Cl TS7 140 C3
Hammond Dr DL1 151 F6
Hampden St TS6 121 A5
Hampden Way TS17 138 D4
Hampshire Gn TS20 118 C7
Hampshire Pl
Bishop Auckland DL14 80 C5
Peterlee SR8 49 B7
Hampshire Rd DH1 35 C3
Hampstead Gdns TS26 76 E6
Hampstead Gr TS6 141 C7
Hampstead Rd TS6 141 C7
Hampstead The TS10 107 E3
Hampton Cl
Annfield Plain DH9 12 E4
Nunthorpe TS7 141 A3
Hampton Ct DH3 16 D7
Hampton Gr TS10 107 F5
Hampton Rd TS18 212 B2
Hamsteels Bank DH7 31 A6
Hamsteels La DH7 31 B6
Hamsteels Prim Sch DH7 31 C1
Hamsterley Cl DH3 25 B7
Hamsterley Cres DH1 34 D6
Hamsterley Ct 6 SR3 18 A6
Hamsterley Dr DL15 52 D3
Hamsterley Forest North Forest Dr* DL13 189 A1
Hamsterley Forest S* DL13 194 D7
Hamsterley Forest Visitor Ctr* DL13 189 B2
Hamsterley Forest, Forest Wlk* DL13 189 A1
Hamsterley Gdns DH9 12 F4
Hamsterley Prim Sch DL13 189 D2
Hamsterley Rd
Newton Aycliffe DL5 96 B8
Stockton-on-T TS19 117 C6
Hamsterley St DL3 132 E4
Hamsterley Way TS12 125 C3
Hanbury Cl TS17 138 B1
Handale Cl TS14 144 A4
Handel Terr DH6 47 E2
Handley Cl TS18 137 F5
Handley Cres DH5 26 C4
Handley Cross DH8 4 C2
Handley St SR8 49 F7
Hangingstone La DH8, DH9 12 C3
Hankin Rd TS3 215 C2
Hannah's Meadow Nature Reserve* DL12 197 D5
Hanover Cl DL3 132 A1
Hanover Ct
Bishop Auckland DL14 80 C6
Durham DH1 210 B2
Stockton-on-T TS20 117 F8
Hanover Gdns
Bishop Auckland DL14 80 C6
Crook DL15 53 A3
Middlesbrough TS5 119 C1
Hanover Ho 5 TS12 125 C8
Hanover Par TS20 117 F8
Hanover Point TS20 117 F8
Hanover Wlk NE21 2 A8
Hansard Cl DL5 95 F4
Hanson Ct TS10 107 C6
Hanson Gr TS3 120 F3
Hanson St TS10 107 C6
Hansons Bldgs 6 DL2 153 F8
Harap Rd
Fishburn TS21,TS29 72 B7
Kelloe DL17 71 E8
Harbinson Cl TS21 72 C5
Harborne Gdns TS5 139 D4
Harbottle Cl TS17 157 A7
Harbour Wlk
Hartlepool TS24 77 C7
Seaham SR7 29 C7
Harcourt Rd TS6 121 A5
Harcourt St
Darlington DL3 132 F4
Hartlepool TS26 76 F6
Hardale Gr TS10 107 A4
Harding Row TS20 118 B7
Harding Terr DL3 132 E4
Hardinge Rd DL5 96 D8
Hardings DL12 198 D7
Hardisty Cres DL14 80 A5
Hardknott Gr TS10 107 B5
Hardwick Ave TS5 139 C7
Hardwick Cl DL1 133 D6
Hardwick Ct
Hartlepool TS26 76 C4
Newton Aycliffe DL5 96 D8
Hardwick Hall Ctry Pk* TS21 84 F7
Hardwick Prim Sch TS19 117 B8
Hardwick Rd
Billingham TS23 102 F5
Sedgefield TS21 85 A7
South Bank TS6 121 A6
Stockton-on-T TS19 117 C7
Hardwick St
Blackhall Colliery TS27 50 C3
Peterlee SR8 50 A6
Hardy Gr TS23 102 D7
Hardy St SR7 29 D7
Hardy Terr
Annfield Plain DH9 13 C4
Crook DL15 52 E4
Hare Law Sch DH9 12 E6
Hare's Bldgs DH2 15 C5
Harebell Cl
Ingleby Barwick TS17 138 B2
Skelton TS12 125 E2
Spennymoor DL16 56 B3
Harebell Mdws DL5 82 D2
Harehills Rd TS5 119 B1
Harelaw DH2 15 D6
Harelaw Gdns DH9 12 E6
Harelaw Ind Est DH9 12 E7
Haresfield Way TS17 157 B8
Hareshaw Cl TS17 157 A7
Hareson Rd DL5 96 A8
Harestones TS22 87 B3
Harewood 9 TS4 120 B1
Harewood Cres TS19 117 B5
Harewood Gr DL3 151 E8
Harewood Hill DL3 151 E8
Harewood Jun Sch TS17 138 D8
Harewood Rd TS17 118 D1
Harewood St TS1 214 C1
Harewood Terr DL3 151 E8
Harewood Way TS10 107 E3
Harford St TS1 214 B1
Hargill Dr NE38 17 A8
Hargill Gr DL15 65 D7
Hargill Haven DL15 65 E7
Hargill Rd DL15 65 D7
Hargreave Terr DL1 133 A1
Harker Cl TS15 156 B4
Harker St 5 DL4 80 F1
Harland Pl 1 TS20 118 B7
Harle St DH7 43 D3
Harlech Cl TS6 121 E3
Harlech Ct TS17 156 F8
Harlech Gr TS11 124 A6
Harlech Wlk TS26 76 E8
Harley Gr DL1 133 E6
Harley Terr DH6 35 F2
Harlow Cres TS17 138 E6
Harlsey Cres TS18 137 C8
Harlsey Gr TS18 137 C8
Harlsey Rd TS18 137 C8
Harmire Cl DL12 209 C7
Harmire Ent Pk DL12 209 C8
Harmire Rd DL12 209 C7
Harold Wilson Dr TS27 49 F1
Harpenden Wlk TS3 120 D2
Harper Bglws DH6 47 E1
Harper Par TS18 137 D8
Harper Terr TS18 137 D8
Harperley Gdns DH9 12 E5
Harperley La DH9 13 B7
Harperley Rd DH9 12 F5
Harperley Terr DL15 52 A1
Harpers Terr DL2 134 E1
Harpington View TS21 84 C1
Harras Bank DH3 9 C3
Harraton Terr
15 Birtley DH3 9 C4
Bournmoor DH3 17 C7
Harrier Cl Hartlepool TS26 76 D8
Thornaby-on-T TS17 138 C5
Harringay Cres DL1 133 E3
Harris Gr TS25 89 E8
Harris St Darlington DL1 152 D8
Middlesbrough TS1 214 C3
Harris Wlk TS14 143 D3
Harrison Cl Peterlee SR8 49 E5
Shildon DL4 95 A7
Harrison Cres DL14 79 F4
Harrison Ct DH3 9 C3
Harrison Garth DH6 35 F2
Harrison Ho DH1 210 B2
Harrison Pl TS24 63 F2
Harrison St
Middlesbrough TS3 120 C4
Tow Law DL13 183 D1
Harrison Terr
Darlington DL3 132 E4
Easington SR8 39 D4
Harrogate Cres TS5 119 E2
Harrogate Terr SR7 28 C3
Harrow Gate Prim Sch TS19 117 C7
Harrow Rd
Middlesbrough TS5 139 D8
Stockton-on-T TS18 212 B2
Harrow St TS25 77 A3
Harrowgate Hill Inf Sch DL3 133 A6
Harrowgate Hill Jun Sch
Darlington DL3 132 F6
Darlington DL3 133 A6
Harrowgate La TS19 117 A7
Harrowgate Village DL1 133 A8
Harry Dack Inf Sch TS13 127 B1
Harry St DL3 132 F5
Harsley Wlk TS3 120 D2
Hart Ave TS26 76 E7
Hart Cl TS19 117 D6
Hart Cres TS27 50 F1
Hart La TS26 76 E7
Hart Lane Cotts TS26 76 F7
Hart Pastures TS27 63 A2
Hart Prim Sch TS27 62 F3
Hart Rd TS27 63 D3
Hart View TS29 72 E8
Hartbrigg La DL14 78 E3
Hartburn Ave TS18 212 B1
Hartburn Ct TS5 139 C5
Hartburn La TS18 212 B1
Hartburn Prim Sch TS18 212 A1
Hartburn Village TS18 137 D8
Hartbushes TS28 61 A4
Harter Cl TS7 141 A2
Hartford Rd DL3 151 D8
Hartforth Ave TS5 139 C4
Harthope Cl NE38 16 F8
Harthope Gr DL14 79 F5
Harthope Rd DL13 185 E8
Hartington Cl TS17 138 C8
Hartington Rd
Middlesbrough TS1 214 C3
Stockton-on-T TS18 213 A2
Hartington St
Consett DH8 11 A3
Loftus TS13 127 A1
7 Thornaby-on-T TS17 138 C8
Hartington Way DL3 132 E5
Hartland Dr DH3 9 D3
Hartland Gr TS3 140 E8
Hartlea Ave DL1 113 A2
Hartlepool TS25 76 F3
Hartlepool Ave SR8 49 F8
Hartlepool Cl TS19 117 D6
Hartlepool Coll of F Ed TS24 77 C5
Hartlepool General Hospl TS24 63 F1
Hartlepool Historic Quay & Heritage Ctr* TS24 77 C7
Hartlepool Ind Est TS24 64 B1
Hartlepool Power Sta Visitor Ctr* TS25 90 F3
Hartlepool Rd
Elwick TS21,TS22 87 C3
Sedgefield TS21 86 D6
Hartlepool Sixth Form Coll TS25 76 F4
Hartlepool St DH6 47 D4
Hartlepool Sta TS24 77 C6
Hartlepool Utd FC (Victoria Pk) TS24 77 B6
Hartlepool-Middleton Grange Sh Ctr TS24 77 B5
Hartley Ave DL14 68 C1
Hartley Cl
11 Hartlepool TS26 77 A6
Staindrop DL2 200 F7
Hartley Rd DL5 96 D7
Hartley St 10 TS26 77 A6
Hartley Terr DL16 56 A1
Harton Ave TS22 102 B5
Harts Bldgs 1 DL2 153 F8
Hartsbourne Cres TS11 123 F6
Hartside Birtley DH3 9 D1
Crook DL15 52 D4
Hartside Cl DL15 52 E4
Hartside Cotts DH9 12 F4
Hartside Cres NE21 2 A8
Hartside Gdns
Easington Lane DH5 27 C1
Hartlepool TS26 76 D7
Hartside Gr TS19 117 E6
Hartside Prim Sch DL15 52 D4
Hartside View
Bearpark DH7 33 A4
Durham DH1 34 A7
Hartville Rd TS24 63 C5
Hartwith Dr TS19 117 B8
Harvard Ave TS17 213 C2
Harvester Cl TS25 77 D2
Harvester Ct TS7 140 B5
Harvey Cl Peterlee SR8 49 D7
Washington NE38 9 F5
Harvey Ct Consett DH8 11 A3
Redcar TS10 106 F4
Willington DL15 54 B4
Harvey Wlk TS25 76 D2
Harwal Rd TS10 107 A6
Harwell Cl TS4 140 A8
Harwell Dr TS19 117 B5
Harwich Cl TS10 107 F3
Harwich Gr TS25 90 B8
Harwick Ct DH9 14 C6
Harwood Ct
Middlesbrough TS2 119 D7
Trimdon TS29 59 E4
Harwood St TS24 77 A7
Haselrigg Cl DL5 95 F4
Hasguard Way TS17 156 E7
Hasledon Gr TS21 85 A5
Haslewood Rd DL5 82 C2
Hastings Ave DH1 44 A7
Hastings Cl
Nunthorpe TS7 141 A3
Thornaby-on-T TS17 138 C3
Hastings Pl TS24 63 F2
Hastings Way TS23 103 A6
Haswell Ave TS25 77 B2
Haswell Ct 3 TS20 118 B5
Haswell Prim Sch DH6 37 E3
Hatfield Ave TS5 139 C7
Hatfield Cl Durham DH1 34 A6
Eaglescliffe TS16 137 A1
Hatfield Coll (Univ of Durham) DH1 211 A2
Hatfield Pl SR8 49 E5
Hatfield Rd
Billingham TS23 102 F4
Newton Aycliffe DL5 96 E7
Hatfield Way DL14 80 D4
Hatherley Ct TS3 120 F3
Hatherley Sq 6 TS27 50 D3
Hatterall Ct TS17 156 F7
Haughton Com Sch DL1 133 D5
Haughton Gn DL1 133 E4
Haughton Rd DL1 133 C3
Hauxley Cl TS10 107 F3
Hauxley Dr DH2 23 F8
Hauxwell's Bldg TS15 156 B6
Havelock Cl DL5 96 E6

Havelock St
Darlington DL1 ....133 A4
Hartlepool TS24 ....77 C5
Thornaby-on-T TS17 ....138 C8
Havelock Terr DH9 ....6 B2
Haven Cl DL1 ....133 C2
Haven Ct DH1 ....34 C8
Haven Gdns DL1 ....133 C2
Haven Ho DH8 ....11 C4
Haven The Burnhope DH7 ...21 D4
Chilton DL17 ....82 F8
Langley Park DH7 ....32 A7
Leadgate DH8 ....11 C4
Haven Wlk TS24 ....64 D2
Haverley Dr SR7 ....28 E8
Haverthwaite TS5 ....139 B4
Haverton Hill Ind Est
TS23 ....103 D1
Haverton Hill Rd
Billingham TS23 ....119 A7
Stockton-on-T TS18 ....118 F5
Havilland Rd TS12 ....118 B5
HAW Cocks Meml Homes The
DL2 ....153 E8
Hawes Ave DH2 ....16 C1
Hawes Cres DL15 ....52 F2
Hawes Pl DL5 ....96 B7
Hawes Rd SR8 ....49 D7
Hawesdale Cres NE21 ....2 B8
Haweswater Gr DL14 ....79 B1
Haweswater Rd TS10 ......107 B8
Hawford Cl TS17 ....138 C1
Hawick Ct DH9 ....14 B6
Hawk Rd TS3 ....120 D4
Hawk Terr DH9 ....9 E2
Hawkesbury Cl ▣ TS18 ...137 C1
Hawkesbury Mews DL3 ...132 E3
Hawkhill Cl DH2 ....24 A8
Hawkhills Terr ◻ DH3 ....9 C5
Hawkins Cl TS11 ....124 E8
Hawkins Rd SR7 ....28 E1
Hawkridge Cl
◻ Hartlepool TS26 ....77 A7
Ingleby Barwick TS17 ......157 B6
Hawkridge St ◻ TS26 ......77 A6
Hawkshead Ct DL5 ....96 B7
Hawkshead Pl DL5 ....96 B7
Hawkshead Rd TS10 ....107 C5
Hawkstone TS8 ....140 E1
Hawkstone Cl
Billingham TS22 ....102 A5
Guisborough TS14 ....143 E2
Hawkswood DL2 ....152 A1
Hawnby Cl TS19 ....117 A3
Hawnby Rd TS5 ....139 E8
Hawsker Cl SR3 ....18 C7
Hawthorn Ave
Billingham TS23 ....102 D2
New Silksworth SR3 ....18 B8
Thornaby-on-T TS17 ....138 C6
Hawthorn Cl DH2 ....23 F3
Hawthorn Cotts
◻ Consett DH8 ....10 D4
South Hetton DH6 ....38 B7
Hawthorn Cres
Durham DH1 ....35 A3
Marton TS7 ....140 E4
Quarrington Hill DH6 ....58 D7
Hawthorn Dr
Barnard Castle DL12 ....209 C7
Brotton TS12 ....126 A4
Newton Aycliffe DL5 ....96 A3
Hawthorn Gr TS15 ....156 D5
Hawthorn Pk DH7 ....43 B4
Hawthorn Rd
Bishop Auckland DL14 ....80 C7
Durham DH1 ....35 D4
Redcar TS10 ....107 E5
Sedgefield TS21 ....85 B7
Spennymoor DL16 ....68 D7
Hawthorn St
◻ Consett DH8 ....10 D4
Darlington DL1 ....152 A8
Easington SR8 ....39 D5
Hawthorn Terr
Annfield Plain DH9 ....13 B4
Bishop Middleham DL17 ....71 C4
Chester le Street DH3 ......16 D2
Consett DH8 ....10 D4
Durham DH1 ....210 B2
New Brancepeth DH7 ....42 E8
South Bank TS6 ....120 F6
Hawthorne Ave
Blackhall Colliery TS27 ......50 E3
◻ Middlesbrough TS4 .....119 F1
Hawthorne Cl
Langley Park DH7 ....32 B6
Murton SR7 ....28 D6
Hawthorne Cres SR8 ....50 A6
Hawthorne Dr TS14 ....143 B3
Hawthorne Rd
Ferryhill DL17 ....70 A6
Stockton-on-T TS19 ....117 F5
Hawthorne Sq SR7 ....29 D8
Hawthorne Terr
Cornforth DL17 ....70 E8
Langley Park DH7 ....32 D8
Mickleton DL12 ....208 F2
Pelton DH2 ....43 B4
Shotton Colliery DH6 ....48 C6
Tanfield DH9 ....6 D3
Hawthorne View DH6 ....47 C3
Hawthorns The
Annfield Plain DH9 ....12 F5
◻ Darlington DL3 ....132 D3
Hawthorns The continued
Great Ayton TS9 ....161 A3
◻ Newton Aycliffe DL5 .....96 C8
Yarm TS15 ....156 B3
Haxby Cl TS5 ....139 E6
Haxby St TS14 ....143 F6
Haxby Rd DL2 ....134 E1
Haxby Wlk TS24 ....64 C1
Hayburn Cl
Ingleby Barwick TS17 ......157 C8
Redcar TS10 ....107 E3
Haydon Gn TS23 ....102 D8
Hayle Ct DL3 ....133 A8
Hayling Gr TS10 ....107 E3
Hayling Way TS18 ....116 F2
Haymore St TS5 ....119 E2
Hayricks The DH9 ....6 D4
Hayston Rd TS6 ....26 E3
Hazard La Hetton-le-H DH5 ...26 E3
West Rainton DH5 ....26 E3
Hazel Ave Brandon DH7 ....43 A3
Darlington DL3 ....132 E4
◻ Houghton-le-S DH4 ......26 C8
Hazel Cres SR8 ....39 D3
Hazel Ct TS1 ....215 A3
Hazel Dr SR27 ....50 A1
Hazel Gdns TS12 ....126 A4
Hazel Gr
Bishop Auckland DL14 ....80 B7
Burnopfield NE16 ....6 C6
Chester le Street DH2 ....16 A5
Hartlepool TS24 ....77 A8
Marton TS7 ....140 F4
Redcar TS10 ....107 E6
Thornaby-on-T TS17 ....138 C7
Hazel Grove Terr DL15 ....189 F5
Hazel Leigh DH3 ....25 A7
Hazel Rd TS19 ....9 E7
Hazel Slade TS16 ....137 C1
Hazel Terr Crook DL15 ......52 D4
Shotton Colliery DH6 ....48 C6
The Middles DH9 ....14 B3
Hazel Wlk TS13 ....127 C1
Hazelbank TS8 ....140 B3
Hazeldale Ave DL4 ....81 B1
Hazeldene Ave TS18 ....137 D8
Hazelgrove Cres DL13 .....195 E3
Hazelhen Cl TS26 ....63 D1
Hazelmere DL16 ....55 E2
Hazelmere Cl TS22 ....102 A6
Hazelwood Ct
Langley Park DH7 ....32 C6
Middlesbrough TS5 ....139 E4
Hazelwood Rise TS24 ......64 E1
Head St TS1 ....214 C3
Headingley Cres DL1 ....133 E3
Headingley Ct TS25 ....90 E7
Headlam Ct ◻ TS20 ....118 B5
Headlam Rd
Billingham TS23 ....102 F6
Darlington DL1 ....152 C8
Stockton-on-T TS20 ....118 B5
Headlam Terr TS16 ....156 B7
Headlands The
Darlington DL3 ....132 C1
Marske-by-t-S TS11 ....108 D2
Healaugh Pk TS15 ....156 D4
Healeyfield La DH8 ....176 E2
Heath Cl Bowburn DH6 .....57 D8
Peterlee SR8 ....49 F5
Heath Rd DL16 ....68 E6
Heath The TS20 ....118 A6
Heather Cl TS19 ....117 E7
Heather Dr
Hetton-le-H DH5 ....27 A5
Middlesbrough TS5 ....139 C6
Heather Gr
Hartlepool TS24 ....63 F1
Skelton TS12 ....125 E1
Spennymoor DL16 ....68 D6
Heather La DL15 ....52 C3
Hetton-le-H DH5 ....27 A5
Middlesbrough TS3 ....120 C3
Redcar TS10 ....107 B7
Seaham SR7 ....29 D8
Henry St N SR7 ....28 D3
Henry St S SR7 ....28 D3
Henry Taylor Ct TS7 ....141 A7
Henry Terr DH4 ....17 F2
Hensfield Gr DL3 ....132 E5
Henshaw Dr TS17 ....157 A7
Hensley Ct TS20 ....101 E1
Henson Cl DL14 ....80 C4
Henson Gr DL5 ....96 D8
Henson Rd DL1 ....133 F2
Heortnesse Rd TS24 ....64 C2
Hepple Cl TS23 ....102 D8
Hepscott Ave TS27 ....50 E3
Hepworth La DL15 ....66 E8
Herbert St ◻ Consett DH8 ...10 D3
◻ Darlington DL1 ....133 A1
Middlesbrough TS3 ....120 C4
Herbert Terr SR7 ....29 D7
Herbert Wlk ◻ TS24 ....77 B7
Hercules St DL1 ....133 C6
Herdinghill NE37 ....9 F6
Hereford Cl TS5 ....119 E2
Hereford Rd TS14 ....143 D3
Hereford St Coundon DL14 ...68 D1
◻ Hartlepool TS25 ....77 B3
Hereford Terr TS23 ....102 F3
Herefordshire Dr DH1 ......35 C3
Hergill La DL11 ....205 F1
Heriot Gr TS25 ....89 E8
Heriot Grange TS25 ....89 E8
Heritage Ctr* DH1 ....210 C2

Hedley Cl
◻ Newton Aycliffe DL5 .....96 C8
Yarm TS15 ....156 B3
Hedley Ct Bearpark DH7 ....33 A4
Yarm TS15 ....156 B7
Hedley Ho DH9 ....13 E4
Hedley La NE11,NE16 ....7 C6
Hedley St TS14 ....143 E5
Hedley Terr Dipton DH9 ....12 A6
Ryhope SR2 ....19 A6
South Hetton DH6 ....37 F7
Hedley's Bldgs DH7 ....33 B8
Hedleyhill La
East Hedleyhope DH7 ....30 E1
East Winning DH7 ....31 A2
Hedleyhill Terr DH7 ....41 A5
Hedlhope Wlk TS19 ....117 C6
Hedworth St DH3 ....16 C3
Heighington CE Prim Sch
DL5 ....95 D2
Heighington Cl TS19 ....117 C6
Heighington La
Heighington DL5 ....95 E1
Newton Aycliffe DL5 ....96 C2
Heighington Rd DL5 ....96 E1
Heighington Sta DL5 ....96 C2
Heights Of Alma DL15 ......52 E8
Heild Cl TS17 ....96 E7
Helena Terr DL14 ....80 B6
Helford Rd SR8 ....49 C4
Hellvellyn Cl DH9 ....12 B7
Helmington Gr DL15 ....53 E1
Helmington Sq DL15 ....66 D7
Helmington Terr DL15 ....66 D7
Helmsdale Cl DL1 ....133 C7
Helmsley Cl Ferryhill DL17 ...70 B5
Middlesbrough TS5 ....139 E7
Helmsley Ct DL5 ....82 E1
Helmsley Dr
Coundon DL14 ....81 C8
Guisborough TS14 ....143 E5
Helmsley Gr TS19 ....117 B4
Helmsley Lawn TS10 ....107 E4
Helmsley Moor Way
DL1 ....152 D7
Helmsley Rd DH1 ....34 D7
Helmsley St TS24 ....77 A7
Helston Cl DL1 ....133 A8
Helston Ct TS17 ....138 F6
Helvellyn Cl NE21 ....2 C8
Hemel Cl TS17 ....138 E7
Hemel St ◻ DH3 ....16 C2
Hemingford Gdns TS15 ....156 D4
Hemlington Cl ◻ SR2 ......118 F6
Hemlington Gn TS19 ....117 C6
Hemlington Hall Prim Sch
TS8 ....139 D1
Hemlington Hall Rd
TS8 ....139 D2
Hemlington La TS8 ....139 E3
Hemlington Rd TS8 ....139 C1
Hemlington Village Rd
TS8 ....140 A1
Hemmel Ct DH7 ....43 C5
Hempstead Ct TS17 ....138 E7
Henderson Ave DH6 ....47 E2
Henderson Gr TS24 ....77 B7
Henderson Rd DL5 ....96 E6
Henderson St DL1 ....152 A8
Hendon St ◻ DL3 ....133 A1
Henley Ave DH7 ....15 E3
Henley Gdns DH8 ....11 A2
Henley Gr TS17 ....138 C8
Henley Rd TS5 ....119 C1
Henrhyd Ct TS17 ....156 F7
Henrietta Cl TS17 ....213 C1
Henrietta St TS24 ....64 E1
Henry Ave DH6 ....47 D2
Henry Smith's Terr TS24 ...64 F1
Henry St Consett DH8 ....10 E3
Darlington DL1 ....133 A5
Hessewelle Cres DH6 ....37 E1
Heswall Rd TS23 ....102 F5
Hett La DH6 ....56 C7
Hett St TS23 ....102 E8
Hetton Lyons Ctry Pk*
DH5 ....27 C4
Hetton Lyons Ind Est
DH5 ....27 B3
Hetton Lyons Prim Sch
DH5 ....27 A2
Hetton Moor Terr DH5 ....27 B2
Hetton Rd DH5 ....26 F3
Hetton Rd DH5 ....26 F3
Hetton Sch DH5 ....26 F3
Heugh Chare TS24 ....64 G8
Heugh Edge DH7 ....23 B5
Heugh Hall Row DH6 ....57 F8
Hever Cl DL14 ....79 E6
Hewitson Rd DL1 ....133 D1
Hewitson Rd S ◻ DL1 ......152 D8
Hewitt Ave SR2 ....18 E8
Hewitt's Bldgs TS14 ....143 E5
Hewley St TS6 ....121 D1
Heworth Dr TS20 ....101 E1
Heworth La DL5 ....97 A3
Hexham NE38 ....9 F4
Hexham Ave SR7 ....29 B6
Hexham Ct DH7 ....23 B3
Hexham Dr
Annfield Plain DH9 ....12 F5
Eston TS6 ....121 D3
Hexham Gn TS3 ....140 F8
Hexham St DL14 ....80 B8
Hexham Way DL3 ....132 A5
Heysham Gr TS10 ....107 F2
Heythrop Dr
Guisborough TS14 ....143 F3
Middlesbrough TS5 ....139 A6
Heywood St TS1,TS5 ....214 A1
Hibernian Gr TS25 ....89 E8
Hickling Gr TS19 ....117 B5
Hickstead Cl DL1 ....133 F4
Hickstead Rise DL5 ....82 E2
Hicksbourne Cl DH7 ....15 E3
Hicksbourne Gdns TS17 ...157 B8
High Barn Rd DL5 ....95 F4
High Barnes DH3 ....25 A7
High Bondgate DL14 ....67 B1
High Carr Cl DH1 ....34 B5
High Carr Rd DH1 ....34 A5
High Chare TS16 ....16 D3
High Church Mews
TS15 ....156 B6
High Church Wynd
TS15 ....156 B6
High Clarence Prim Sch
TS2 ....119 E8
High Coniscliffe CE Prim Sch
DL2 ....130 E4
High Croft DH7 ....43 B5
High Cross St DH6 ....46 F1
High Downs Sq DH5 ....27 A5
High Escomb DL14 ....79 D8
High Farm Cl TS21 ....116 C8
High Farm View TS6 ....121 B4
High Fell TS10 ....107 B4
High Force (Waterfall)*
DL12 ....191 E7
High Force Rd TS2 ....119 C7
High Friarside NE16 ....5 E6
High Garth DL2 ....207 A1
High Gill Rd TS7 ....141 A3
High Gn Darlington DL3 ...132 B3
Gainford DL2 ....201 D3
Great Ayton TS9 ....161 A2
Newton Aycliffe DL5 ....96 C2
Romaldkirk DL12 ....193 D1
High Grange Ave DL5 ....23 C2
High Grange DL14 ....66 A4
High Grange Ave TS23 .....102 D7
High Grange Ho TS23 ....102 D6
High Grange Rd DL16 ....55 F1
High Hamsterley Rd NE39 ...5 A5

Hermiston Ret Pk DH8 ....10 F1
Hermitage Gdns DH2 ....16 B1
Hermitage Pk DH3 ....16 C1
Hermitage Pl TS20 ....102 A1
Hermitage Sch The DH7 ....16 A2
Herne Cl TS10 ....107 E2
Heron Dr DL1 ....133 D1
Heron Gate TS14 ....143 B4
Heronspool Cl TS24 ....64 C1
Herrington Cl DH7 ....32 B6
Herrington Ct ◻ DL5 ....96 D8
Herrington Rd TS23 ....102 E8
Herriot Cl DL1 ....133 E7
Herschell St TS10 ....107 C6
Hershall Dr TS3 ....120 B2
Hertford Cres DH5 ....26 F4
Hertford Pl SR8 ....49 C8
Hertford Rd TS20 ....118 A7
Herton Cl SR8 ....49 C7
Heseldene Terr DL15 ....66 E8
Hesketh Ave TS4 ....140 B6
Hesleden La TS27 ....50 B2
Hesleden Prim Sch TS27 ...50 A1
Hesleden Rd
Blackhall Colliery TS27 ......50 C3
Hesleden TS27 ....50 B2
Hesledon Cl TS19 ....117 D6
Hesley Rise DL12 ....199 E5
Heslington Gdns TS14 .....143 E6
Heslop Dr DL1 ....151 F7
Heslop St
Close House DL14 ....81 A5
◻ Thornley-on-T TS17 ....138 D8
Hessle Rd DL15 ....53 E1
High Shelf DH7 ....43 C5
High Shaws DH7 ....43 C5
High Shincliffe DH1 ....45 B5
Hinderwell TS13 ....149 E6
Howden-le-W DL15 ....65 E7
Lazenby TS6 ....122 C4
Lingdale TS12 ....145 E6
Loftus TS13 ....127 C1
Marske-by-t-S TS11 ....108 C1
Middlesbrough TS7 ....140 F7
Moorsholm TS12 ....146 B1
Newton Aycliffe DL5 ....96 E1
Newton Mulgrave Moor
YO21 ....107 D2
Redcar TS10 ....107 D7
Sedgefield TS21 ....85 B6
Shincliffe DH1 ....45 A6
Skelton TS12 ....125 B2
Skinningrove TS13 ....127 A4
Spennymoor DL16 ....68 F8
Stanhope DL13 ....206 D3
Stanley DH9 ....213 D3
Stockton-on-T TS18 ....213 B3
Stockton-on-T, Norton
TS20 ....118 B8
Thornley (nr Wheatley Hill)
DH6 ....47 C4
Tow Law DL13 ....183 E1
Willington DL15 ....53 F3
Witton-le-W DL14 ....65 E7
Wolsingham DL13 ....207 C5
Wolviston TS22 ....102 C8
Yarm TS15 ....156 B6
High St St S DH7 ....43 E6
High St St N Brandon DH7 ...43 D5
Brandon DH7 ....43 E6
High St St S DH7 ....43 E5
High St W TS10 ....107 A7
High Stell DH1 ....153 E8
High Stone Cl TS10 ....107 E3
High Street South Bk
DH7 ....43 E5
High Terr TS15 ....52 D6
High Town DL13 ....180 A1
High Tunstall Sch TS26 .....76 D6
High View DH7 ....33 A7
High West La SR7 ....33 A7
High West Rd DL15 ....52 E3
High Whitwell Terr DL15 ....52 D4
High Winning Cotts TS27 ...48 F1
High Wood Terr DL14 ....211 A1
High Wood View DH1 ....211 A1
Highbank Rd TS17 ....141 B5
Highbury Ave TS5 ....139 E2
Highbury Rd DL3 ....132 C3
Highclere Dr SR2 ....18 C6
Highcliff Prim Sch
TS14 ....143 C3
Highcliff Rd TS14 ....162 C8
Highcliffe Edge DL2 ....200 F3
Highcliffe Gr TS16 ....124 A6
Highcliffe Terr ◻ DL17 .....70 A6
Highcroft DL1 ....133 F2
Highfield Birtley DH3 ....8 D8
Sacriston DH7 ....23 C3
Highfield Cl TS16 ....137 B1
Highfield Com Prim Sch
NE39 ....1 C2

Highfield Cres
Chester le Street DH3 . . . . . .16 C5
Stockton-on-T TS18 . . . . . . .117 C1
Highfield Day Hospl DH3 .16 C5
Highfield Dr
Eaglescliffe TS16 . . . . .137 B1
Fence Houses DH4 . . . . .26 B7
Highfield Gdns
Chester le Street DH3 . . . . . .16 C5
Eaglescliffe TS16 . . . . .137 C1
Howden-le-W DL15 . . . . . . .65 D7
Highfield Grange DH4 . . . . . .26 B7
Highfield Rd
Darlington DL3 . . . . .132 B5
Eston TS6 . . . . .121 E2
1 Marske-by-t-S TS11 . . . .108 B1
Middlesbrough TS4 . . . . . . .120 A2
Rowlands Gill NE39 . . . . .1 C1
Stockton-on-T TS18 . . . . . . .117 C1
Highfield Rise DH3 . . . . . . .16 C5
Highfield Terr DH7 . . . . . . .32 F1
Highgate Durham DH1 . . .210 C3
Eston TS6 . . . . .122 A2
Highgrove Ct SR8 . . . . .39 C2
Highland Gdns DL4 . . . . . . .80 F2
Highland Rd TS25 . . . . .89 E8
Highland Terr 5 DL17 . . . . .70 A6
Highlight The TS24 . . . . . . .77 C7
Highmead Wlk TS3 . . . . . .140 D7
Highridge Birtley DH3 . . . . . .9 C5
Consett DH8 . . . . .10 C3
Highroad Ave DL17 . . . . . . .71 C4
Highside Rd DL2,DL5 . . . . .95 B2
Highsteads DH8 . . . . .4 B1
Hilda Ave DH1 . . . . .35 A1
Hilda Cl DH1 . . . . .35 B1
Hilda Pk DH2 . . . . .16 B5
Hilda Pl TS12 . . . . .125 C7
Hilda St Annfield Plain DH9 .12 E5
Darlington DL1 . . . . .133 A2
Hilda Terr DH2 . . . . .16 B4
Hilda Wlk TS24 . . . . .77 D5
Hilderthorpe TS7 . . . . . . .140 F3
Hildewell TS13 . . . . .149 E5
Hildon Dr DL1 . . . . .152 C7
Hill Brow SR3 . . . . .18 B6
Hill Cl TS12 . . . . .125 B2
Hill Cres
Middleton-In-T DL12 . . . . . .208 B5
Murton SR7 . . . . .28 C3
Redcar TS10 . . . . .106 E5
Seaham SR7 . . . . .29 E5
Hill Crest Burnhope DH7 . . .21 D4
Burnopfield NE16 . . . . .6 B6
Crook DL15 . . . . .53 B3
Esh DH7 . . . . .31 F4
Sacriston DH7 . . . . .23 D2
Hill Crest Mews DH1 . . . .211 A3
Hill End DL13 . . . . .187 F6
Hill Fields DL5 . . . . .95 F4
Hill Garth DL3 . . . . .132 C4
Hill Mdws DH1 . . . . .45 A5
Hill Rd TS23 . . . . .102 D1
Hill Rise DL2 . . . . .154 A5
Hill Side DL2 . . . . .151 A5
Hill St Middlesbrough TS1 .214 C3
New Silksworth SR3 . . . . . . .18 A7
Redcar TS10 . . . . .107 B7
Seaham SR7 . . . . .29 D6
Hill St Ctr TS1 . . . . .214 C4
Hill St E TS18 . . . . .213 C4
Hill Terr Billy Row DL15 . . . .52 E8
Middleton-In-T DL12 . . . . . .208 B5
Hill Top Birtley DH3 . . . . .9 D4
Stanley DH9 . . . . .14 B7
Hill View Copley DL13 . . . .195 A4
Esh Winning DH7 . . . . .41 E8
Greatham TS25 . . . . .89 F3
Stanley DH9 . . . . .14 D7
Hill View Terr 6 TS11 . . . .124 A6
Hillbeck St DL14 . . . . .80 D5
Hillclose Ave DL3 . . . . . . .132 B2
Hillcrest Castleside DH8 . .176 F3
Durham DH1 . . . . .211 A3
High Shincliffe DH1 . . . . . . .45 B5
Tow Law DL13 . . . . .183 D2
Hillcrest Ave TS18 . . . . . .212 A2
Hillcrest Dr Loftus TS13 . . .147 B8
Nunthorpe TS7 . . . . .141 B4
Hillcrest Gr TS27 . . . . .75 C6
Hillcrest Pl TS27 . . . . .50 A1
Hillcroft 3 Birtley DH3 . . . . .9 C5
Rowlands Gill NE39 . . . . .1 C2
Hillel Wlk TS5 . . . . .139 D4
Hillersdon Terr CA9 . . . . .178 A6
Hillfield DH8 . . . . .10 D3
Hillgarth DH8 . . . . .177 A3
Hillhead La NE16 . . . . .2 D2
Hillhouse Farm 13 TS20 .118 B6
Hillhouse La DL2 . . . . . . .134 E8
Hillingdon Rd TS3 . . . . . .140 D7
Hillmeads DH2 . . . . .23 F4
Hillocks La TS12 . . . . . . .146 C1
Hillrise Cres SR7 . . . . .28 D8
Hills View Rd TS6 . . . . . .121 F2
Hillside Birtley DH3 . . . . .9 D4
Chester le Street DH3 . . . . . .16 C4
Ingleton DL2 . . . . .201 D7
Witton Gilbert DH7 . . . . .23 B1
Hillside Ave TS4 . . . . .139 F8
Hillside Bglws DL17 . . . . . .82 E7
Hillside Cl
Blackhall Rocks TS27 . . . . . .50 E2
New Marske TS11 . . . . .123 F6
Rowlands Gill NE39 . . . . .1 E3
Hillside Ct Chilton DL17 . . . .82 E7
Spennymoor DL16 . . . . .56 B1
Hillside Gdns DH9 . . . . . . .14 A8
Hillside Gr DH6 . . . . .36 B5
Hillside Rd Coundon DL14 . .81 B7
Darlington DL3 . . . . .151 D8
Stockton-on-T TS20 . . . . . . .118 B8
Hillside Terr DL2 . . . . .134 E6
Hillside View DH6 . . . . .35 F2
Hillside Villas SR8 . . . . . . .49 F7
Hillside Way 1 DH4 . . . . . .26 E8
Hillston Cl TS26 . . . . .76 C7
Hillsyde Cres DH6 . . . . . . .47 C4
Hilltop Bglws DH6 . . . . .47 B3
Hilltop Cotts CA9 . . . . . . .178 A6
Hilltop Gdns SR3 . . . . .18 C7
Hilltop Rd DH7 . . . . .33 A4
Hilltop View DH7 . . . . .32 D6
Hillview Gr SR8 . . . . .39 E4
Hilsdon Dr DL4 . . . . .95 B8
Hilton Dr SR8 . . . . .49 D5
Hilton Moor La DL14 . . . . .92 F3
Hilton Rd
Barnard Castle DL12 . . . . .209 D6
Bishop Auckland DL14 . . . . . .80 C6
Newton Aycliffe DL5 . . . . . . .96 D4
Seamer TS9 . . . . .158 F1
Hind Ct DL5 . . . . .82 E2
Hind St TS18 . . . . .212 C2
Hinderwell Ave TS10 . . . . .107 A5
Hinderwell Ind Est TS13 .149 F5
Hinderwell La TS13 . . . . . .149 D7
Hindhead TS16 . . . . .137 C1
Hindpool Cl TS24 . . . . .64 B1
Hinkley Cl SR3 . . . . .18 B6
Hinton Ave TS5 . . . . .119 B2
Hinton Ct TS14 . . . . .143 F5
Hird Rd TS15 . . . . .156 A4
Hird St DL1 . . . . .133 A1
Hirdman Gr TS24 . . . . .63 E4
Hirds Dr TS13 . . . . .127 B1
Hirst Ct DL16 . . . . .68 D6
Hirst Gr 3 DL1 . . . . .152 D8
Hive Cl TS19 . . . . .117 F6
HM Bark Endeavour*
TS18 . . . . .213 B2
HM Prison Durham
DH1 . . . . .211 A2
HM Remand Ctr Low Newton
DH1 . . . . .34 F8
HMS Trincomalee*
TS24 . . . . .77 C7
Hob Hill Cl TS12 . . . . .125 B6
Hob Hill Cres TS12 . . . . . .125 C6
Hob Hill La TS11,TS12 . . . .125 A5
Hobdale Terr TS12 . . . . . .145 B8
Hobson Ave TS10 . . . . . . .106 E3
Hobson Ind Est NE16 . . . . . .6 A5
Hobson's Bldgs DH9 . . . . .12 E5
Hodge La DL12 . . . . .192 A5
Hodges Ho TS1 . . . . .215 A3
Hodgson Ct 3 TS6 . . . . . .121 F1
Hoe The TS24 . . . . .77 D6
Hogarth Cl TS23 . . . . .102 D7
Hogarth Ct 18 DL3 . . . . . .132 F1
Hogarth Terr DL13 . . . . . .180 D5
Hogarth Terrace Flats
DL13 . . . . .180 D5
Holbeck Ave TS5 . . . . .139 D4
Holbeck Wlk TS17 . . . . . . .138 E3
Holberry Terr DL14 . . . . . . .81 C8
Holborn DL16 . . . . .55 F1
Holburn Cl DH7 . . . . .41 E8
Holburn Ct DH7 . . . . .33 B1
Holburn Pk TS19 . . . . .117 D6
Holden Cl TS6 . . . . .121 D6
Holdenby Dr TS3 . . . . .140 D7
Holder St TS10 . . . . .107 C6
Holderness
Newton Aycliffe DL5 . . . . . . .95 F8
Wynyard Village TS22 . . . . . .87 A3
Holderness Dr DL3 . . . . . .132 C5
Holdforth Cl TS24 . . . . .63 F1
Holdforth Crest DL14 . . . . .80 C7
Holdforth Ct TS24 . . . . .64 A1
Holdforth Dr DL14 . . . . .80 C7
Holdforth Rd TS24 . . . . .63 F1
Hole La NE16 . . . . .2 F4
Holehouse La DH7 . . . . .30 A7
Holey Cl TS8 . . . . .139 D2
Holgate Moor Gn DL1 . . . .152 D7
Holgate The TS5 . . . . .214 B1
Holindale DL16 . . . . .68 F7
Holland Rd TS25 . . . . .89 E6
Hollies The
Billingham TS23 . . . . .102 D1
Redcar TS10 . . . . .107 E5
Hollin Cres DL12 . . . . .198 D8
Hollin Way DL5 . . . . .96 D2
Hollingside La DH1 . . . . . . .44 C6
Hollinhill NE39 . . . . .2 A5
Hollinhill La NE39 . . . . .1 F4
Hollins La TS5 . . . . .119 C1
Hollinside Cl TS19 . . . . . .117 D6
Hollinside Rd TS23 . . . . . .102 F6
Hollinside Terr
Lanchester DH7 . . . . .20 C1
Rowlands Gill NE39 . . . . .1 D2
Hollis Ct TS8 . . . . .140 B2
Hollow The DL15 . . . . .52 E1
Hollowdene Crook DL15 . . . .52 E2
Hetton-le-H DH5 . . . . .27 A3
Hollowdene Garth DL15 . . .52 E2
Hollowfield Chilton DL17 . . .82 E8
Coulby Newham TS8 . . . . . .140 A2
Hollowfield Sq TS8 . . . . . .140 A2
Holly Ave
Houghton-le-S DH5 . . . . .26 F8
New Silksworth SR3 . . . . . . .18 B8
Winlaton Mill NE21 . . . . .2 C6
Holly Cres DH7 . . . . .23 D2
Holly Garth Cl TS9 . . . . . .160 F2
Holly Gdns DH8 . . . . .177 B4
Holly Haven DH5 . . . . .26 D4
Holly Hill DL4 . . . . .81 B1
Holly Hill Gdns DH9 . . . . . .13 F5
Holly Hill Gdns E DH9 . . . . .14 A5
Holly Hill Gdns W DH9 . . . .13 F4
Holly La TS8 . . . . .139 C1
Holly Pk Brandon DH7 . . . . . .43 B4
Ushaw Moor DH7 . . . . .33 A2
Holly St Darlington DL3 . . .132 F2
Durham DH1 . . . . .210 B2
Middlesbrough TS1 . . . . . . .215 A2
3 Stockton-on-T TS20 . . . . .118 B7
Holly Terr
Annfield Plain DH9 . . . . .12 E5
Burnopfield NE16 . . . . .6 C5
Crook DL15 . . . . .52 D4
Howden-le-W DL15 . . . . .65 E8
Middlesbrough TS2 . . . . . . .103 E1
Stanley DH9 . . . . .13 D5
Hollybush TS12 . . . . .125 D3
Hollybush Ave TS17 . . . . .138 C2
Hollycarrside Rd SR2 . . . . .18 E8
Hollycrest DH2 . . . . .16 B5
Hollydene
Kibblesworth NE11 . . . . .8 D6
Rowlands Gill NE39 . . . . .1 F2
Hollyhock Terr DH6 . . . . . . .57 E6
Hollyhurst Ave 9 TS4 . . . .139 F8
Hollyhurst Rd
Cornforth DL17 . . . . .57 D1
Darlington DL3 . . . . .132 E3
Hollymead Dr TS14 . . . . . .143 E5
Hollymount
Billingham TS23 . . . . .102 D1
Hartlepool TS26 . . . . .76 E6
Hollys The DH3 . . . . .9 B7
Hollyside Cl DH7 . . . . .33 A4
Hollystone Ct TS23 . . . . . .102 E7
Hollytree Mews TS14 . . . .143 E4
Hollywalk Ave TS6 . . . . . . .141 D8
Hollywalk Cl TS6 . . . . .141 C8
Hollywalk Dr TS6 . . . . .121 D1
Hollywell Ct DH7 . . . . .33 B1
Hollywell Gr DL14 . . . . .79 E5
Holme Ct TS3 . . . . .140 F7
Holme Dene DL15 . . . . .66 D5
Holme House Rd TS18 . . . .118 E5
Holme Lea Terr TS29 . . . . . .60 A5
Holmebeck Rd TS12 . . . . .125 E2
Holmefield DL13 . . . . .188 A7
Holmefields Rd TS6 . . . . . .141 E8
Holmes Cl TS17 . . . . .138 B6
Holmeside Gr TS23 . . . . . .102 F7
Holmesland Villas DH7 . . . .23 C2
Holmewood Dr NE39 . . . . . . .5 D8
Holmfield Villas DH6 . . . . . .57 E6
Holmhill La
Chester le Street DH2,DH3 . .24 C7
Easington SR8 . . . . .39 D5
Holmlands Cres DH1 . . . . . .34 A5
Holmlands Pk DH3 . . . . . . .16 D2
Holmlands Rd DL3 . . . . . .132 D4
Holmlea DH7 . . . . .21 D4
Holms La TS21 . . . . .100 C2
Holmside Ave
Lanchester DH7 . . . . .20 F3
Trimdon TS29 . . . . .59 E3
Holmside Hall Rd DH7 . . . .22 B7
Holmside La
Burnhope DH7 . . . . .21 D4
Holmside DH7 . . . . .22 C6
Holmside Terr DH9 . . . . . . .14 C2
Holmside Wlk TS19 . . . . . .117 D6
Holmwood Ave TS4 . . . . . .139 F8
Holmwood Gr DL1 . . . . . . .133 A8
Holmwood Sch
Middlesbrough TS4 . . . . . . .139 F7
Middlesbrough, Easterside
TS4 . . . . .140 B5
Holnest Ave TS3 . . . . .120 D1
Holnicote Cl TS17 . . . . . . .157 B6
Holt St TS24 . . . . .77 B4
Holt The TS8 . . . . .139 F3
Holtby Wlk TS3 . . . . .140 D7
Holwick Cl DH8 . . . . .11 A1
Holwick Rd
Darlington DL1 . . . . .133 A6
Middlesbrough TS2 . . . . . . .214 A4
Holy Family RC Prim Sch
DL3 . . . . .132 C4
Holy Rood Ct TS4 . . . . . . .120 A2
Holy Trinity CE Jun Sch
TS19 . . . . .117 B1
Holy Trinity CE Prim Sch
TS25 . . . . .90 E8
Holy Well La DL15 . . . . .53 B2
Holyhead Dr TS10 . . . . . . .107 F3
Holyoake Gdns DH3 . . . . . . .9 C4
Holyoake St Ferryhill DL17 .69 E6
Pelton DH2 . . . . .15 C6
Holyoake Terr DH9 . . . . . . .13 E4
Holyrood DH3 . . . . .25 A8
Holyrood Ave DL3 . . . . . . .132 A1
Holyrood Cl TS17 . . . . . . .138 D8
Holyrood Cres TS27 . . . . . . .62 F2
Holyrood La TS4 . . . . .120 A2
Holyrood Wlk 2 TS25 . . . . .89 E8
Holystone Dr TS17 . . . . . .157 A7
Holywell Gn TS16 . . . . . . .137 C1
Holywood DL13 . . . . .207 C7
Home Farm Ct DL5 . . . . . . .95 C3
Home Land TS17 . . . . .138 A3
Homebryth Ho TS21 . . . . . .85 B7
Homelands Hospl DL15 . . . .53 B2
Homer Gr TS25 . . . . .76 E2
Homer Terr DH1 . . . . .210 A1
Homerell Cl TS10 . . . . . . .107 E3
Homerton Ct DL1 . . . . . . .133 B5
Homerton Rd TS3 . . . . . . .120 E2
Homestall TS21 . . . . .72 A1
Homestead Garth TS17 . .138 A3
Honddu Ct TS17 . . . . .156 F7
Honey Bee Cl TS19 . . . . . .117 F6
Honey Way TS19 . . . . .117 F6
Honeycomb Ave TS19 . . . .117 F6
Honeypot Gr TS19 . . . . . . .117 F6
Honeypot La DL3 . . . . . . .132 E5
Honeypot Lane Caravan Site
DL3 . . . . .132 E6
Honeysuckle Cl SR3 . . . . . .18 A5
Honeysuckle Ct TS20 . . . .118 A7
Honeywood Gdns DL3 . . .132 E4
Honister Cl TS19 . . . . .212 C4
Honister Gr TS5 . . . . .139 B6
Honister Pl DL5 . . . . .96 B7
Honister Rd TS10 . . . . . . .107 B5
Honister Sq DL15 . . . . .52 F2
Honister Wlk TS16 . . . . . .156 C8
Honiton Way TS25 . . . . . . .90 A7
Hood Cl TS24 . . . . .63 E4
Hood Dr TS6 . . . . .121 B5
Hood Gill DL12 . . . . .192 B7
Hood St DL13 . . . . .179 E1
Hoode Cl DL5 . . . . .96 B8
Hookergate La NE39 . . . . . . .1 A2
Hookergate Sch NE39 . . . . . .1 B3
Hoope Cl TS15 . . . . .156 B3
Hope Cl TS29 . . . . .72 D8
Hope Shield NE38 . . . . .9 F1
Hope St Billingham TS23 . .103 D2
Consett DH8 . . . . .10 E4
Crook DL15 . . . . .52 E4
Hartlepool TS24 . . . . .77 C6
Sherburn DH6 . . . . .35 F1
Stockton-on-T TS18 . . . . . . .212 C1
Hope View SR2 . . . . .18 F7
Hopelands DL5 . . . . .95 D1
Hopelands Ct DL5 . . . . .95 D1
Hopetown La DL3 . . . . . . .132 F4
Hopgarth Ct DH3 . . . . .16 D4
Hopgarth Gdns DH3 . . . . . .16 D4
Hopkins Ave TS3 . . . . .120 E3
Hopkinson Pl DL16 . . . . . . .69 A3
Hopper Pl DH1 . . . . .34 C5
Hopper Rd DL5 . . . . .96 D5
Hopper St SR8 . . . . .39 C4
Hopper Terr
Shotton Colliery DH6 . . . . . .48 C6
Trimdon TS29 . . . . .59 E3
Hopps St 4 TS26 . . . . .77 A7
Horden Rd TS23 . . . . .102 F5
Hornbeam DH4 . . . . .17 F5
Hornbeam Cl 8 TS7 . . . . .141 B7
Hornbeam Wlk TS19 . . . . .117 E7
Hornby Ave TS21 . . . . .85 A5
Hornby Cl
Hurworth-on-T DL2 . . . . . . .152 D2
Middlesbrough TS1 . . . . . . .214 C3
Seaton Carew TS25 . . . . .77 E2
Hornby Ho 8 DL1 . . . . . . .152 C8
Horndale Ave DL5 . . . . .96 C4
Horndale Inf Sch DL5 . . . . .96 A7
Hornleigh Gr TS10 . . . . . .107 A6
Hornsea Cl TS23 . . . . .102 F8
Hornsea Gr TS10 . . . . .107 A6
Hornsea Rd TS8 . . . . .139 D1
Hornsey Cres DH5 . . . . .27 B1
Hornsey Terr DH5 . . . . .27 B1
Horse Close La TS29 . . . . .59 F2
Horse Market
Barnard Castle DL12 . . . . .209 B6
11 Darlington DL1 . . . . .132 F1
Horse Shoe Pond TS22 . . .87 B3
Horseclose La TS19 . . . . . .116 E7
Horsefield St TS1 . . . . . . .215 B3
Horsemarket DL12 . . . . . .208 B5
Horsley Gr DL14 . . . . .79 F5
Horsley Pl TS24 . . . . .63 F2
Horsley Way TS23 . . . . . . .102 E8
Horton Cres DH6 . . . . .45 D2
Hoskins Way TS3 . . . . .120 E2
Hospital Rd DH7 . . . . .32 B6
Hoton Cl DL5 . . . . .96 F1
Hotts La DL13 . . . . .179 D1
Hough Cres TS17 . . . . . . .138 C7
Houghall Gdns* DH1 . . . . . .44 E7
Houghton Bank La DL2 . . . .94 E1
Houghton Banks TS17 . . . .138 A3
Houghton Ent Ctr DH5 . . . .26 E8
Houghton Enterprise Ctr
DH5 . . . . .26 E8
Houghton Gate DH3 . . . . . .17 B3
Houghton Gn TS19 . . . . . .117 C6
Houghton Kepier Sch
DH4 . . . . .26 D8
Houghton La DL2 . . . . .110 E5
Houghton Rd DH5 . . . . .27 A4
Houghton Rd W DH5 . . . . .27 A4
Houghton St TS24 . . . . .77 B4
Houghwell Gdns DH9 . . . . .13 D8
Houlsyke Cl SR3 . . . . .18 C7
Hound Hill DL13 . . . . .207 D5
Houndgate DL1 . . . . .132 F1
Houndgate Mews 14
DL1 . . . . .132 F1
Hoveton Cl TS19 . . . . .117 C5
Hovingham Cl SR8 . . . . . . .49 E5
Hovingham Dr TS14 . . . . . .143 E6
Hovingham St TS3 . . . . . . .120 C4
Howard Cl DL14 . . . . .80 A5
Howard Ct TS4 . . . . .120 A1
Howard Dr TS11 . . . . .124 E8
Howard Pl TS20 . . . . .118 B5
Howard St
Hartlepool TS24 . . . . .64 D2
Middlesbrough TS1 . . . . . . .214 B2
Howard St Ind Est DL1 . .133 B4
Howard Wlk TS23 . . . . . . .118 D8
Howarth Terr DH6 . . . . .37 F3
Howbeck La TS24 . . . . .64 A1
Howcroft Ave TS10 . . . . . .106 E3
Howden DH8 . . . . .10 D3
Howden Bank DH7 . . . . .20 F6
Howden Dike TS15 . . . . . .156 D4
Howden Gdns TS28 . . . . . . .60 E8
Howden Rd
Hartlepool TS24 . . . . .63 E4
Newton Aycliffe DL5 . . . . . . .96 E4
Howden Sq DL15 . . . . .65 E7
Howden Wlk TS18 . . . . . . .213 A3
Howden-le-Wear Prim Sch
DL15 . . . . .65 E7
Howe Hill Bank TS8,TS9 . .159 B3
Howe St TS1 . . . . .214 C1
Howe Terr DL15 . . . . .52 F3
Howgill Wlk TS3 . . . . .120 C2
Howlbeck Rd TS14 . . . . . .143 D5
Howlcroft Villas DH1 . . . .210 A2
Howlea La
Hamsterley DL13 . . . . .189 C4
Wolsingham DL13 . . . . .207 E1
Howletch La SR8 . . . . .49 C6
Howletch Lane Prim Sch
SR8 . . . . .49 B6
Howlish La DL14 . . . . .81 C7
Howlish View DL14 . . . . . . .81 C8
Hownsgill Dr DH8 . . . . . . .177 D3
Hownsgill Ind Pk DH8 . . . .177 C4
Howson Cres DL5 . . . . .82 D1
Hoy Cres SR7 . . . . .18 F1
Hoylake Cl 10 TS11 . . . . . .124 A6
Hoylake Rd TS4 . . . . .139 F7
Hoylake Way TS16 . . . . . . .156 C8
Hoyle Fold SR3 . . . . .18 A4
Hubbard Wlk TS4 . . . . . . .215 B3
Huby Ct TS14 . . . . .143 E6
Huckelhoven Ct 5 TS24 . . .77 C5
Huckelhoven Way TS24 . . .77 C5
Huddart Terr 2 DH3 . . . . . . .9 C5
Hude DL12 . . . . .208 B6
Hudson Ave SR8 . . . . .49 F7
Hudson Ho 3 TS17 . . . . . .138 D5
Hudson St Ferryhill DL17 . . .69 F6
Middlesbrough TS2 . . . . . . .119 F7
Hudspeth Cres DH1 . . . . . . .34 A7
Hudswell Gr 4 TS18 . . . . .117 C1
Hugar Rd NE39 . . . . .1 A3
Hugill Cl TS15 . . . . .156 D4
Hulam Cl TS19 . . . . .117 D6
Hulam La DL2 . . . . .201 C7
Hullock Rd DL5 . . . . .96 D7
Hulme Ct SR8 . . . . .49 C5
Hulton Cl 2 TS7 . . . . .140 F3
Humber Cl TS13 . . . . .127 D1
Humber Gr TS22 . . . . .102 A6
Humber Hill DH9 . . . . .14 A5
Humber Pl DL1 . . . . .151 F6
Humber Rd TS17 . . . . .138 D6
Humber View DH9 . . . . .12 D2
Humberhill Dr DH7 . . . . . . .20 E3
Humberhill La DH7 . . . . . .177 F2
Humble Carr La DL2 . . . . .111 C8
Humbleburn La DH7 . . . . . .14 E1
Humbledon Rd TS19 . . . . .117 D6
Hume Ho TS18 . . . . .213 A4
Hume St TS18 . . . . .213 B4
Humewood Gr TS20 . . . . . .102 B1
Hummerbeck DL14 . . . . . . .93 D7
Hummerbeck La
Bolam DL14 . . . . .93 D7
Evenwood DL14 . . . . .93 A4
Hummers Hill La TS11 . . .108 E1
Hummersea Cl TS12 . . . . .126 B4
Hummersea La TS13 . . . . .127 C3
Hummersea Prim Sch
TS13 . . . . .127 B2
Hummersknott Ave DL3 . .132 C1
Hummersknott Sch &
Language Coll DL3 . . . .132 A1
Humphrey Cl DL5 . . . . .96 C7
Hundale Cres TS10 . . . . . .107 E3
Hundale Rd TS15 . . . . .173 F1
Hunden's La DL1 . . . . .133 C2
Hundens Day Hospl
DL1 . . . . .133 C1
Hunley Ave TS12 . . . . .126 B5
Hunley Cl TS12 . . . . .126 B5
Hunstanton Gr TS11 . . . . .123 F6
Hunstanworth Rd DL3 . . .132 B4
Hunt Lea NE16 . . . . .2 E5
Huntcliff Sch TS12 . . . . . .125 B6
Huntcliffe Ave TS10 . . . . .107 A5
Huntcliffe Dr TS12 . . . . . .126 B5
Hunter Ave DH7 . . . . .33 A2
Hunter Pl SR8 . . . . .39 E4
Hunter Rd
Newton Aycliffe DL5 . . . . . . .96 D6
Shotton Colliery SR8 . . . . . . .49 A5
Hunter St 12 TS26 . . . . . . .77 A6
Hunter Terr DL17 . . . . .82 F8
Hunters Bldgs TS18 . . . . .213 A1
Hunters Cl
Hurworth-on-T DL2 . . . . . . .152 B1
Medomsley DH8 . . . . .4 C1
Hunters Gn
Middleton St George DL2 . .153 E5
Newton Aycliffe DL5 . . . . . . .95 F8
Huntersgate TS6 . . . . .122 A2

Huntershaw Way DL3 ...132 F7
Huntingdon Gn TS20 ...118 C7
Huntingdon Rd SR8 ...49 C8
Huntingdonshire Dr DH1 ...35 D3
Huntley Ave SR7 ...28 B3
Huntley Cl TS3 ...140 E7
Huntley Cres NE21 ...2 A8
Huntley St DL1 ...133 A1
Huntley Terr [4] SR2 ...18 F6
Huntly Rd TS25 ...89 E8
Huntsgarth DL15 ...53 E1
Huntshield Ford DL13 ...179 E1
Huntsman Dr TS2 ...104 D2
Hunwick Cl TS5 ...139 B5
Hunwick La DL15 ...53 D2
Hunwick Prim Sch DL15 ...66 E6
Hunwick Wlk TS19 ...117 D6
Hurbuck Cotts DH7 ...177 F3
Hurn Wlk TS17 ...138 E5
Hurricane Ct TS18 ...137 F6
Hurst Pk TS10 ...107 D3
Hurworth Burn Rd
Hutton Henry TS28 ...74 A7
Trimdon TS27,TS28,TS29 ...73 D7
Hurworth Cl
Stockton-on-T TS19 ...117 A3
Trimdon TS29 ...72 D8
Hurworth House Sch
DL2 ...152 D1
Hurworth Hunt DL5 ...95 F8
Hurworth Prim Sch DL2 ...152 C1
Hurworth Rd
Billingham TS23 ...103 A8
Hurworth-on-T DL2 ...168 A8
Middlesbrough TS4 ...140 A8
Neasham DL2 ...153 A1
Newton Aycliffe DL5 ...96 C4
Hurworth Sch DL2 ...168 B8
Hurworth St
[3] Bishop Auckland DL14 ...80 B6
Hartlepool TS24 ...77 A7
Hurworth Terr DL2 ...168 A8
Hury Rd TS20 ...118 A8
Hustledown Gdns DH9 ...13 F4
Hustledown Rd DH9 ...13 E4
Hustler Rd TS5 ...139 C3
Hutchinson Ave [3] DH8 ...10 F3
Hutchinson St
Bishop Auckland DL14 ...80 B7
Brotton TS12 ...126 B4
Stockton-on-T TS18 ...213 A3
Hutchinson Wlk DL5 ...96 F8
Hutone Pl TS24 ...63 E4
Hutton Ave
Darlington DL1 ...133 C5
Hartlepool TS26 ...77 A5
Hutton Cl
Bishop Auckland DL14 ...80 C4
Chester le Street DH3 ...16 E1
Fishburn TS21 ...72 D4
Houghton-le-S DH4 ...26 C8
Thornaby-on-T TS17 ...138 C7
Washington NE38 ...9 F5
Hutton Cres TS27 ...61 C5
Hutton Ct
[9] Annfield Plain DH9 ...12 F4
[14] Hartlepool TS26 ...77 A6
Hutton Gr Redcar TS10 ...106 E3
Stockton-on-T TS18 ...212 A1
Hutton Henry CE Prim Sch
TS27 ...61 C5
Hutton La TS14 ...143 C3
Hutton Pl DL5 ...82 D1
Hutton Rd Eston TS6 ...122 A3
Middlesbrough TS4 ...215 C1
Hutton Rudby Prim Sch
TS15 ...173 F1
Hutton St Hartlepool TS24 ...64 C2
Skinningrove TS13 ...127 A4
Hutton Terr DL15 ...53 F3
Hutton Village TS14 ...162 C8
Hutton Village Rd TS14 ...143 B2
Huxley Gr DL1 ...152 C7
Huxley Wlk TS25 ...76 E2
Hybrid Cl DH4 ...17 F5
Hydenside Gr DH8 ...177 B4
Hylton Cl Langley Park DH7 ...32 B6
Newton Aycliffe DL5 ...96 F8
Hylton Ct DH1 ...34 D6
Hylton Gr TS20 ...118 A6
Hylton Rd
Billingham TS23 ...102 F5
Durham DH1 ...34 D6
Ferryhill DL17 ...70 B6
Hartlepool TS26 ...76 D5
Hylton Terr Pelton DH2 ...15 E7
Rookhope DL13 ...180 D5
Ryhope SR2 ...18 E6
Hysehope Terr DH8 ...11 A2
Hythe Cl TS10 ...107 F2

I

I'Anson St DL3 ...132 F6
Ian Gr TS25 ...89 E7
Ian Ramsey CE Comp Sch
TS18,TS19 ...117 C2
Ian St TS17 ...138 D8
Ianson Sq DL1 ...133 A2
Ibbetson St TS24 ...64 F1
Iber Gr TS25 ...89 E7
Ibrox Gr TS25 ...89 E7
Ibstock Ho TS3 ...120 C2
Ibstone Wlk TS19 ...117 C8
Ickworth Ct TS17 ...157 B8
Ida Pl DL5 ...82 C1
Ida Rd TS3 ...120 C3
Ida St TS20 ...118 A6
Idaho Gdns DL1 ...133 B6
IES Ctr DL5 ...96 D5
Ilam Ct TS17 ...157 B8
Ilchester St SR7 ...29 D6
Ilford Rd TS19 ...117 C8
Ilford Way TS3 ...140 D8
Ilkeston Wlk [3] TS19 ...117 C8
Ilkley Gr
Guisborough TS14 ...143 D2
Hartlepool TS25 ...90 B8
Ilston Gn [2] TS3 ...140 D8
Imeson St [2] TS6 ...121 F1
Imex Bsns Ctr DH3 ...9 B4
Imperial Ave
Stockton-on-T TS20 ...118 B6
Thornaby-on-T TS17 ...138 D8
Imperial Bldgs [10] DH4 ...26 E8
Imperial Cres TS20 ...118 B6
Imperial Rd TS23 ...118 D8
Inch Gr TS25 ...89 E7
Inchcape Rd TS25 ...89 E7
Inchcape Terr SR8 ...39 F3
Industrial St DH2 ...15 C6
Ingham Gr TS25 ...89 D6
Ingleborough La TS17 ...157 B6
Ingleby [1] TS4 ...120 B1
Ingleby Cl TS6 ...122 A3
Ingleby Ct TS10 ...107 C7
Ingleby Gr TS18 ...212 A1
Ingleby Mill Prim Sch
TS17 ...157 A8
Ingleby Moor Cres DL1 ...152 D7
Ingleby Rd
Hartlepool TS25 ...90 E7
Middlesbrough TS4 ...215 C1
Ingleby Way TS17 ...138 B1
Inglenook Cl DL15 ...52 E2
Inglesgarth Ct DL16 ...68 E7
Ingleside NE16 ...2 F6
Ingleside Mews [6] TS12 ...125 C7
Ingleton CE Prim Sch
DL2 ...201 C7
Ingleton Rd TS19 ...117 C8
Inglewood Ave [2] TS11 ...124 C8
Inglewood Cl
Darlington DL1 ...133 B5
Middlesbrough TS3 ...121 A2
Ingoldsby Rd TS3 ...121 A1
Ingram Cl DH2 ...16 A1
Ingram Gr TS17 ...157 A7
Ingram Rd TS3 ...120 C2
Ingram Way TS28 ...48 E1
Ingrove Cl TS19 ...117 C8
Ings Ave TS3 ...120 E3
Ings Farm Prim Sch
TS10 ...107 E5
Ings La Brotton TS12 ...126 C5
Yarm TS15 ...156 A4
Ings Rd TS10 ...107 E5
Inkerman Rd DL13 ...183 D2
Inkerman St TS18 ...213 A3
Innes Rd TS25 ...89 F7
Innes St TS2 ...119 E7
Inskip Wlk [6] TS19 ...117 C8
Inst for Middle Eastern &
Islamic Studies (Univ of
Durham) DH1 ...44 B7
Institute St
Byers Green DL16 ...54 E1
Willington DL15 ...54 A6
Institute Terr
Bearpark DH7 ...33 C3
Billy Row DL15 ...52 E7
Eston TS6 ...121 D6
Fir Tree DL15 ...52 A1
Newfield DL14 ...67 B7
Toronto DL14 ...66 F2
Institute Terr E DH2 ...15 F8
Institute Terr W DH2 ...15 F8
Instow Cl TS19 ...117 C7
Insula Cotts DL17 ...71 C4
Intake La DL13 ...188 A8
Intrepid Cl TS25 ...77 D2
Inveraray Cl DL1 ...133 E7
Inverness Rd TS25 ...89 E7
Inwood Lodge TS7 ...140 D6
Ipswich Ave TS3 ...140 D8
Irene St TS13 ...126 F3
Irene Terr DH7 ...32 C6
Irestone La DL13 ...179 B1
Iris Cres DH2 ...8 F2
Iris Terr DH4 ...17 E3
Ironmasters Way TS21 ...99 E4
Ironworks Rd DL13 ...183 D1
Irstead Wlk [4] TS19 ...117 C8
Irthing Cl TS17 ...157 A6
Irvin Ave
Bishop Auckland DL14 ...80 A5
Saltburn-by-t-S TS12 ...125 B7
Irvine Rd Hartlepool TS25 ...89 E7
Middlesbrough TS3 ...120 C3
Isherwood Cl DL5 ...96 D6
Isis Rd SR8 ...49 C5
Islay Gr TS25 ...89 E7
Islay Ho [9] SR3 ...18 A6
Islington Wlk TS4 ...140 B5
Italy St TS2 ...214 C4
Ivan Ct TS12 ...145 E5
Ivanhoe Cres TS25 ...89 E7
Ivanhoe Terr
[11] Chester le Street DH3 ...16 C2
Dipton DH9 ...5 E1
Ivesley Cotts DH7 ...41 B6
Ivesley La DH7 ...41 A7
Iveson Terr DH7 ...23 C3
Iveston Gr TS22 ...102 B5
Iveston La DH8 ...12 A1
Iveston Rd DH8 ...11 B1
Iveston Terr DH9 ...13 F7
Iveston Wlk [5] TS19 ...117 C8
Ivy Ave SR7 ...29 B6
Ivy Cl Spennymoor DL16 ...68 F7
Stockton-on-T TS20 ...118 A6
Ivy Cotts
Bishop Middleham DL17 ...71 B4
Eaglescliffe TS16 ...156 C7
Hilton TS15 ...157 E3
Ivy Cres DL15 ...52 D7
Ivy Gr TS24 ...76 F8
Ivy Pl DH9 ...6 C3
Ivy Terr Langley Park DH7 ...32 C6
Stanley DH9 ...13 D4
The Middles DH9 ...14 B3
Ivyway DH2 ...15 E7
Ivywood Ct DL3 ...132 E5

J

Jack Hatfield Sq TS1 ...215 A3
Jack Lawson Terr DH6 ...47 E2
Jacklin Wlk TS16 ...137 C1
Jackson Pl DL5 ...96 F7
Jackson St Brotton TS12 ...126 B3
Coundon Grange DL14 ...80 F5
Hartlepool TS25 ...77 A3
Loftus TS13 ...147 D8
[4] South Bank TS6 ...121 A6
Spennymoor DL16 ...68 F8
Jackson Terr SR8 ...39 A4
Jacksons Landing TS24 ...77 C7
Jacques Ct TS24 ...64 G8
Jacques Terr DH2 ...16 B4
Jade Wlk DL17 ...83 A8
James Cook University The
TS4 ...140 B8
James Ct TS9 ...160 F3
James St
Annfield Plain DH9 ...13 A4
Bishop Auckland DL14 ...80 B6
Darlington DL1 ...133 A4
Dipton DH9 ...12 B7
Easington SR8 ...39 D5
Hartlepool TS24 ...77 D5
Middlesbrough TS3 ...120 C4
Seaham SR7 ...29 D6
Spennymoor DL16 ...68 F8
Tanfield Lea DH9 ...6 F1
James St N SR7 ...28 D3
James St S SR7 ...28 D3
James Terr
Easington Lane DH5 ...37 B8
Eldon Lane DL14 ...80 E4
Fence Houses DH4 ...26 A8
Jameson Rd
Hartlepool TS25 ...89 D8
Stockton-on-T TS20 ...102 A1
Jameson St [1] DH8 ...10 F3
Jamieson Terr DH6 ...38 B6
Jane St Hetton-le-H DH5 ...27 A6
Stanley DH9 ...13 D4
Jane Wlk TS20 ...118 C5
Japonica Way TS20 ...118 A6
Jarsling Ho TS24 ...77 C7
Jarvis Rd SR8 ...49 D8
Jarvis Wlk [4] TS25 ...89 D8
Jasmine Ave DL4 ...81 A1
Jasmine Cres
Seaham SR7 ...29 C5
Trimdon TS29 ...72 D8
Jasmine Gr TS7 ...140 C4
Jasmine Rd TS19 ...117 F5
Jasmine Terr DH3 ...9 D4
Jasper Ave SR7 ...29 B6
Jasper Gr TS21 ...99 F4
Jay Ave TS17 ...157 E8
Jaywood Cl TS27 ...63 C4
Jedburgh Cl SR7 ...28 A2
Jedburgh Dr DL3 ...132 A5
Jedburgh Rd TS25 ...89 D8
Jedburgh St TS1 ...215 A3
Jefferson St TS3 ...120 C4
Jenison Cl DL5 ...95 F4
Jenkins Ct DL5 ...96 E6
Jenkins Dr DL14 ...80 B4
Jenning's Ave DL4 ...81 A1
Jennings The TS6 ...121 D1
Jenny Frisk Rd TS12 ...145 C3
Jersey St [6] TS24 ...77 C6
Jersey Wlk TS14 ...143 D3
Jervaulx Rd TS12 ...125 D2
Jesmond Ave TS5 ...139 C8
Jesmond Ct DL5 ...96 A8
Jesmond Est [1] TS24 ...77 A8
Jesmond Gdns TS24 ...76 F8
Jesmond Gr TS18 ...137 C8
Jesmond Mews TS26 ...77 A7
Jesmond Rd
Darlington DL1 ...133 E6
Hartlepool TS26 ...76 F7
Jesmond Road Prim Sch
TS26 ...76 F7
Jesmond Sq TS24 ...76 F8
Job's Hill Bank DL15 ...53 A3
Jobson St [7] TS26 ...77 A7
Jobson Terr DL15 ...52 F8
John Boyle Cl TS6 ...121 B6
John Dixon La DL1 ...133 B2
John Dobbin Rd DL1 ...133 A3
John E Batty Prim Sch
TS10 ...107 E5
John Howe Gdns TS24 ...63 E2
John Snow Coll Residence
TS17 ...213 C2
John St
Barnard Castle DL12 ...209 C6
Consett DH8 ...10 F3
Consett, Blackhill DH8 ...10 D4
Craghead DH9 ...14 C2
Darlington DL1 ...133 A3
Durham DH1 ...210 B2
Easington SR8 ...39 E5
Eldon Lane DL14 ...80 F4
Fence Houses DH4 ...26 A8
Great Ayton TS9 ...161 A3
Hartlepool TS24 ...77 C6
Hetton-le-H DH5 ...27 A3
Houghton-le-S DH5 ...26 F8
Loftus TS13 ...127 C1
Ryhope SR2 ...19 A6
Sacriston DH7 ...23 C3
Shildon DL4 ...80 F2
Skelton TS12 ...125 D2
Stanley DH9 ...14 D7
Stanley, South Moor DH9 ...13 D4
John St N DH7 ...43 D4
John St S DH7 ...43 D4
John Street Sq [1] DH8 ...10 F2
John Terr DL14 ...80 E4
John Walker Sq TS18 ...213 B2
John Wilson Ct SR8 ...50 A7
Johnson Cl SR8 ...49 D8
Johnson Est DH6 ...47 F2
Johnson Gr TS20 ...117 F8
Johnson St
Eldon Lane DL14 ...80 F4
[2] Hartlepool TS26 ...77 B5
Middlesbrough TS1 ...214 C3
Johnson Terr
Annfield Plain DH9 ...13 A3
Sunderland Bridge DH6 ...56 B7
Johnson's Bldgs DH8 ...11 E1
Johnson's St TS28 ...60 E6
Johnston Ave TS12 ...125 B7
Joicey Ct TS26 ...77 B6
Joicey Gdns DH9 ...13 F7
Joicey Pl DL5 ...96 F7
Joicey Terr DH9 ...13 D8
Jolby La DL2 ...150 F1
Jolliffe St DH3 ...16 D1
Jones Ct DH6 ...45 D1
Jones Rd Hartlepool TS24 ...63 F2
South Bank TS6 ...121 B6
Jones St [4] DH3 ...9 C4
Joppa Gr TS25 ...89 E8
Joseph Hopper Aged
Miners' Homes DH3 ...9 C7
Joseph Hopper Terr
DL17 ...57 E1
Joseph Patterson Cres The
DL17 ...69 D5
Joseph St DH9 ...13 E5
Jowett Way DL5 ...96 D5
Jowitt Rd TS24 ...63 F2
Jowsey Pl DL16 ...69 A3
Joyce Gr SR8 ...49 A3
Joyce Rd TS24 ...63 E3
Joyce Terr DH7 ...32 B2
Jubilee Ave SR7 ...28 F6
Jubilee Bank TS7 ...141 A7
Jubilee Cl
Edmondsley DH7 ...23 B7
Spennymoor DL16 ...68 E8
Jubilee Cotts
Houghton-le-S DH4 ...26 D8
Low Coniscliffe DL3 ...150 F8
Jubilee Cres
Sherburn Hill DH6 ...36 D1
Shildon DL4 ...81 B1
Jubilee Ct [8] DH8 ...177 A4
Jubilee Gr TS22 ...102 C5
Jubilee Ho
Easington Lane DH5 ...27 C1
[3] Hartlepool TS26 ...77 B5
Jubilee Pl
High Shincliffe DH1 ...44 F6
Middleton-In-T DL12 ...208 C5
Shotton Colliery DH6 ...48 C7
Jubilee Rd Eston TS6 ...121 F1
Shildon DL4 ...81 A1
Jubilee Sq
Easington Lane DH5 ...27 C1
South Hetton DH6 ...37 F7
Jubilee St
Middlesbrough TS3 ...120 C4
Toronto DL14 ...66 F2
Jubilee Terr
Annfield Plain DH9 ...13 B4
Evenwood DL14 ...92 D7
Tantobie DH9 ...6 A2
Willington DL15 ...54 A2
Jubliee St S TS3 ...120 C4
Jude Pl SR8 ...49 C8
Jude St SR8 ...39 C4
Judith Cl DL5 ...95 D1
Judson Rd SR8 ...48 F7
Junction Farm Prim Sch
TS16 ...137 B1
Junction Rd TS19,TS20 ...101 E1
June Ave NE21 ...2 C6
Juniper Cl [4] TS10 ...107 E1
Juniper Gr Elton TS21 ...136 E7
Marton TS7 ...140 F4
Juniper Wlk [3] TS25 ...89 D8
Jupiter Ct Easington SR8 ...39 C4
Middlesbrough TS3 ...120 D4
Jura Dr DL1 ...133 D7
Jura Gr TS25 ...89 E8
Jute Gr TS25 ...89 D8
Jutland Rd TS25 ...90 B8
Jutland Terr DH9 ...13 D8

K

Kader Ave TS5 ...139 C5
Kader Farm Rd TS5 ...139 D5
Kader Prim Sch TS5 ...139 C5
Kalafat DL12 ...209 D6
Karles Cl DL5 ...82 C2
Kate's Cl DL15 ...66 E6
Kateregina DH3 ...9 D4
Katherine St DL1 ...133 A4
Kathleen St TS25 ...77 B3
Katrine Cl DH2 ...16 B1
Katrine Ct SR3 ...18 A5
Katrine Wlk DL14 ...79 B1
Kay Gr DL1 ...133 C1
Kay House La TS15 ...172 B2
Kay St DH9 ...13 F7
Kearsley Cl TS16 ...137 D5
Keating Cl TS27 ...50 D3
Keats Cl DH9 ...14 A6
Keats Ct DL1 ...152 C8
Keats Rd Chilton DL17 ...82 E8
Eston TS6 ...121 E1
Keay St TS5 ...214 A1
Kebock Wlk [2] TS25 ...89 D8
Kedleston Cl TS19 ...117 D5
Kedlestone Pk TS8 ...140 E1
Kedward Ave TS3 ...120 E3
Keepers La TS17 ...138 B1
Keepersgate TS6 ...122 A2
Keighley Ave TS7 ...140 B5
Keilder Cl TS10 ...107 B2
Keilder Rise TS8 ...139 F2
Keir Hardie Ave DH9 ...13 F5
Keir Hardie Cl TS6 ...121 B6
Keir Hardie Cres TS6 ...121 B5
Keir Hardie St
Fence Houses DH4 ...26 B8
Highfield NE39 ...1 B2
Keir Hardie Terr DH6 ...48 C5
Keith Rd TS4 ...139 F8
Keithlands Ave TS20 ...118 B7
Keithwood Cl [3] TS4 ...139 F8
Kelbrook Wlk TS3 ...120 E2
Keld Cl TS17 ...157 B6
Keld Gr TS19 ...117 A2
Keld Rd DL5 ...96 B7
Keldholme Sch TS3 ...120 E1
Keldmere DL16 ...55 E2
Kelfield Ave TS3 ...120 E2
Kelgate Terr TS8 ...139 C1
Kell Cres DH6 ...36 C1
Kell Rd SR8 ...49 F6
Kell's Bldgs DH1 ...210 A1
Kell's Way NE39 ...1 E1
Kellaw Rd DL1 ...133 F1
Kellawe Pl DL5 ...96 E7
Kelleher Ct [5] DH8 ...10 D4
Kellet Sq DL15 ...52 E4
Kelling Cl TS23 ...102 E7
Kelloe Cl TS19 ...117 C7
Kelloe Prim Sch DH6 ...58 E5
Kells Gr TS25 ...89 D8
Kelly Cl DH8 ...10 D4
Kelsall Cl TS3 ...140 E8
Kelso Ct TS3 ...120 C1
Kelso Gr TS25 ...89 D8
Kelso Wlk DL3 ...132 A5
Kelsterne Cl TS15 ...156 E4
Kelton La DL12 ...197 C8
Kelvin Gdns [7] DH8 ...10 F2
Kelvin Gr Hartlepool TS25 ...89 D8
Middlesbrough TS3 ...120 D1
Kelvin St DL17 ...69 E6
Kemble Gn DL5 ...96 F7
Kemp Rd SR8 ...49 C7
Kemplah Ho TS14 ...143 E4
Kempston Way TS20 ...117 E8
Kempton Cl Consett DH8 ...10 D7
Newton Aycliffe DL5 ...82 E2
Kempton Ct DL1 ...133 F4
Kenber Dr TS27 ...50 D3
Kendal DH3 ...9 E2
Kendal Cl Darlington DL1 ...151 E8
Peterlee SR8 ...49 A3
Kendal Ct TS4 ...120 A1
Kendal Gr TS10 ...107 C4
Kendal Rd Hartlepool TS25 ...77 B3
Stockton-on-T TS18 ...212 B4
Kendrew Cl DL5 ...96 D8
Kendrew St DL3 ...132 F2
Kenilworth DH3 ...25 A8
Kenilworth Ave
Bishop Auckland DL14 ...79 F6
Middlesbrough TS3 ...140 E8
Kenilworth Ct DL5 ...82 E1
Kenilworth Dr DL3 ...132 B5
Kenilworth Flats TS23 ...102 E5
Kenilworth Rd TS23 ...102 E5
Kenilworth Way TS10 ...107 F3
Kenley Gdns TS20 ...101 E1
Kenmir Ct DL16 ...69 A8
Kenmir's Bldgs DH6 ...57 F3
Kenmore Rd TS3 ...121 A1
Kennedy Cres TS13 ...127 A4
Kennedy Gdns TS23 ...102 E4
Kennedy Gr TS20 ...117 F7
Kennel La DL1 ...133 D4
Kennthorpe TS7 ...140 F3
Kenny Pl DH1 ...211 C4
Kenny Wlk DL5 ...96 F6
Kensington [11] DL14 ...80 B6
Kensington Ave TS6 ...141 D7
Kensington Ct TS24 ...63 F1

Kensington Gdns
Darlington DL1 133 D1
Ferryhill DL17 69 F6
Kensington Rd
Middlesbrough TS5 214 C1
Stockton-on-T TS18 212 C1
Kensington S 10 DL14 80 B6
Kensington Terr
10 Cockfield DL13 195 E3
Willington DL15 53 F3
Kensington Villas DL15 53 F3
Kent Ave TS25 77 B3
Kent Cl Darlington DL3 133 A8
Nunthorpe TS7 141 B3
Redcar TS10 107 B4
Kent Gdns DH5 26 F4
Kent Gr TS20 118 C7
Kent Rd 10 Consett DH8 177 A4
Guisborough TS14 143 D3
Kent St DL14 68 C1
Kent Terr DH6 37 E1
Kent Wlk SR8 49 C8
Kentmere Birtley DH3 9 E1
Spennymoor DL16 55 E2
Kentmere Pl SR8 49 E6
Kentmere Rd TS3 120 C1
Kenton Cl TS18 137 C8
Kenton Cres DH6 47 C3
Kentport Ct 10 TS18 213 C4
Kentra Cl TS10 107 E2
Kenville Gr TS19 117 A4
Kepier Cl TS19 117 C7
Kepier Cres DH1 35 A3
Kepier Ct DH1 211 A3
Kepier Hts DH1 211 A3
Kepier La DH1 211 B4
Kepier Terr DH1 211 A3
Kepier Villas DH1 211 A3
Kepple Ave TS3 120 C1
Kepwick Cl TS5 139 E6
Kerr Cres TS21 85 A8
Kerr Gr TS25 89 D8
Kerridge Cl 1 TS11 108 C1
Keryhill Dr DH1 34 C8
Kesteven Rd
Hartlepool TS25 89 E7
Middlesbrough TS4 140 B5
Kestrel Ave TS3 120 E4
Kestrel Cl Darlington DL1 133 E1
Hartlepool TS26 63 C1
Stockton-on-T TS20 102 B2
Kestrel Ct 16 Birtley DH3 9 C4
Newton Aycliffe DL5 96 C8
Kestrel Hide TS14 143 B4
Kestrel Way DH6 37 F3
Keswick Dr DL16 56 B1
Keswick Gr
Darlington DL1 152 B7
Middlesbrough TS5 139 C6
Keswick Rd
Billingham TS23 102 D1
Eston TS6 121 C2
Peterlee SR8 49 E7
Redcar TS10 107 C4
Stanley DH9 13 D4
Keswick St TS26 77 A4
Keswick Terr DH6 37 E8
Kettleness Ave TS10 107 A5
Kettlewell Cl TS23 102 E6
Ketton Ave DL3 133 A8
Ketton La DL1 113 B3
Ketton Rd TS19 117 D7
Ketton Row TS1 214 B3
Ketton Way DL5 96 D2
Keverstone Bank DL2 195 F1
Keverstone Cl TS19 117 D7
Keverstone Gr TS23 102 F8
Kew Gdns TS20 101 E1
Kew Rise Darlington DL3 132 B3
Normanby TS6 141 C7
Kexwith Moor Cl DL1 152 D7
Keynsham Ave 9 TS3 140 E8
Kibblesworth Bank NE11 8 B6
Kibblesworth Prim Sch
NE11 8 D6
Kidd Ave DH6 35 F2
Kielder NE38 9 F4
Kielder Cl TS22 102 A5
Kielder Dr
Darlington DL1 133 D5
Trimdon TS29 59 E4
Kielder Rd TS26 76 C6
Kilbride Cl TS17 138 E7
Kilbridge Cl TS11 124 A6
Kilburn Cl SR2 19 A6
Kilburn Dr Peterlee SR8 39 F1
Peterlee SR8 50 A8
Kilburn Ho 10 DL1 152 C8
Kilburn Rd
Middlesbrough TS4 140 A8
Stockton-on-T TS18 212 A1
Kilburn St DL4 95 A7
Kilchurn DH8 10 D3
Kildale
11 Middlesbrough TS4 120 A1
Penshaw DH4 17 E8
Kildale Gr Hartlepool TS25 90 D7
Redcar TS10 107 A4
Stockton-on-T TS19 117 A2
Kildale Moor Pl DL1 152 D8
Kildale Rd
Billingham TS23 102 D3
Middlesbrough TS4 120 A2
Kildare St TS1 214 B1
Kildwick Gr TS3 140 E8
Kilkenny Rd TS14 143 E3
Killerby Cl 7 TS19 117 D7
Killhope Gr DL14 79 E5
Killhope The North of England Lead Mining Mus*
DL13 178 E5
Killin Rd DL1 133 D6
Killinghall Gr TS18 117 A1
Killinghall Row 4 DL2 153 F8
Killinghall St DL1 133 B3
Kilmarnock Rd
Darlington DL1 133 D7
Hartlepool TS25 89 D8
Kilmory Wlk 1 TS25 89 D8
Kiln Cres DL17 71 B4
Kiln La Ingleton DL2 201 E7
Langton DL2 201 C6
Kilnhill Wlk SR8 49 E6
Kilnwick Cl TS23 102 F8
Kilsyth Gr TS25 89 D8
Kilton Cl Redcar TS10 107 F4
Stockton-on-T TS19 117 D7
Kilton Ct TS4 119 F1
Kilton Dro TS12 126 C4
Kilton La Brotton TS12 146 C8
Lingdale TS12 145 F6
Kilton Thorpe TS12 146 C8
Kilton Thorpe La TS12 126 C1
Kilwick St TS24 77 B4
Kimberley Dr TS3 120 D2
Kimberley Gdns DH9 14 C3
Kimberley St
Coundon Grange DL14 80 F5
Hartlepool TS26 77 A4
Kimble Dr TS17 138 C4
Kimblesworth Wlk
Newton Aycliffe DL5 82 D1
8 Stockton-on-T TS19 117 D7
Kimmerton Ave TS5 139 C5
Kinbrace Rd TS25 89 D8
Kindersley St TS3 120 C4
Kinderton Gr TS20 117 E8
Kindlewood Gdns TS14 143 E4
King Albert Pl DL15 52 F4
King Edward Rd SR7 29 D6
King Edward St
Shildon DL4 81 A2
Tanfield Lea DH9 6 C1
King Edward Terr 1
TS11 108 D1
King Edward VIII Terr
DH9 14 A8
King Edward's Rd TS1 214 C2
King Edward's Sq TS1 214 C2
King Edwin Sch TS20 102 B1
King Georges Terr TS6 120 F7
King Ho TS1 215 A3
King James I Com Coll
DL14 80 C8
King James St 7 DL16 55 F1
King Oswy Dr TS24 63 D4
King St Annfield Plain DH9 12 F5
Barnard Castle DL12 209 C6
Birtley DH3 9 B4
1 Darlington DL3 132 F2
Hartlepool TS25 77 C3
Redcar TS10 107 D7
Sherburn DH6 35 F1
Shotton Colliery DH6 48 D6
South Bank TS6 121 A6
Spennymoor DL16 55 F1
Stockton-on-T TS18 213 B3
Thornaby-on-T TS17 213 C1
King St Prim Sch DL16 55 F1
King Terr DH9 13 D5
King William Ct 10 DL16 55 F1
King William Grange 11
DL16 55 F1
King William St
20 Darlington DL1 133 B1
6 Spennymoor DL16 55 F1
King's Acad The TS8 140 A2
King's La DH2 15 D7
King's Manor Sch TS5 139 D6
King's Rd Consett DH8 10 D5
Middlesbrough TS3 120 C4
Wingate TS28 60 D8
King's Wlk DL12 208 B7
Kingcraft Rd TS7 140 B5
Kingfisher TS26 63 D1
Kingfisher Dr TS14 143 A4
Kingfisher Ho TS24 77 D6
Kings Ct
Barnard Castle DL12 209 B5
Stockton-on-T TS20 118 B8
Kings Dr DL5 96 C8
Kings Gr DH1 44 A6
Kings Lodge DL14 67 C1
Kings Mews E TS3 215 C2
Kings Mews W TS3 215 C2
Kings Rd Billingham TS22 102 C5
Middlesbrough TS5 119 D2
Kingsbury Mews DL1 152 A7
Kingsdale Cl TS15 156 B3
Kingsdown Way TS11 124 A6
Kingsley Ave TS25 76 F2
Kingsley Cl Eston TS6 121 E4
Stanley DH9 14 B7
Kingsley Dr DL15 52 C3
Kingsley Prim Sch TS25 76 F2
Kingsley Rd Eston TS6 121 F4
Stockton-on-T TS18 117 C2
Kingsmead DL15 54 B2
Kingsmere DH3 16 C7
Kingsport Cl TS18 118 D4
Kingston Ave
Bearpark DH7 33 B3
Middlesbrough TS5 139 D8
Seaham SR7 29 B6
Kingston Cres DH6 37 E3
Kingston Rd TS20 118 B5
Kingston St
Darlington DL3 132 F3
Middlesbrough TS1 214 C2
Kingsway
Billingham TS23 102 D4
Bishop Auckland DL14 80 C8
Darlington DL1 133 B6
Houghton-le-S DH5 26 F8
Langley Park DH7 32 C6
Kingsway Ave TS6 121 B3
Kingsway Villas DH2 15 D7
Kingswood DH7 32 B6
Kininvie Cl TS10 107 C1
Kininvie Wlk 6 TS19 117 D7
Kinkerdale Rd TS6 105 F3
Kinley Rd DH1 35 D5
Kinloch Ct DH2 16 B1
Kinloch Rd TS6 121 C2
Kinloss Cl TS17 138 E5
Kinloss Wlk TS17 138 E5
Kinmel Cl TS10 107 E2
Kinnock Cl DH6 36 A1
Kinross Ave TS3 140 E8
Kinross Cl DH3 9 D2
Kinross Dr DH9 14 B6
Kinross Gr TS25 89 D8
Kinterbury Cl TS25 77 D2
Kintra Rd TS25 89 D8
Kintyre Cl DL1 133 E7
Kintyre Dr TS17 138 C4
Kintyre Wlk TS14 143 C2
Kinver Cl TS3 120 C1
Kiphill Ct DH9 14 A8
Kipling Ave TS27 50 C5
Kipling Cl DH9 14 A6
Kipling Gr TS19 117 B2
Kipling Rd TS25 76 E3
Kipling's Terr DH1 43 F7
Kira Dr DH1 34 C8
Kirby Ave Durham DH1 34 B5
Middlesbrough TS5 119 B1
Kirby Cl Billingham TS23 102 F5
Eston TS6 122 A3
Kirby Ho 5 DL1 152 C8
Kirby Wlk TS10 107 C3
Kirby's Dr DH6 45 D1
Kirk Merrington Prim Sch
DL16 69 A3
Kirk Rd TS15 156 E4
Kirk Rise DL13 188 A8
Kirk St Consett DH8 10 E3
Stillington TS21 99 E3
Kirk View DL12 209 D7
Kirkbright Cl TS12 145 E5
Kirkby Cl DL1 133 B3
Kirkdale
Guisborough TS14 143 A3
Spennymoor DL16 55 E1
Kirkdale Cl TS19 212 B4
Kirkdale Nursing Home
TS17 213 C2
Kirkdale St DH5 26 F2
Kirkdale Way TS5 139 E6
Kirkfell Cl TS16 137 B2
Kirkfield Gdns DH9 12 E5
Kirkfield Rd DL3 133 A7
Kirkgate Rd TS5 139 C8
Kirkham Cl Chilton DL17 83 A8
Newton Aycliffe DL5 82 D1
Kirkham Rd Durham DH1 34 D6
Nunthorpe TS7 141 B3
Kirkham Row TS4 140 B7
Kirkham Way DL14 80 E6
Kirkland Hill SR8 49 E7
Kirkland Wlk 1 TS3 140 D8
Kirklands The TS11 108 D2
Kirklea Rd DH5 26 F8
Kirkleatham Ave TS11 108 D1
Kirkleatham Hall Sch
TS10 123 B8
Kirkleatham La TS10 107 A3
Kirkleatham St TS10 107 B6
Kirklevington Grange
TS15 156 D3
Kirklevington Hall Dr
TS15 156 D2
Kirklevington Prim Sch
TS15 172 E8
Kirklevington Wlk TS19 117 C7
Kirknewton Cl
7 Houghton-le-S DH5 26 F8
5 Stockton-on-T TS19 117 D7
Kirknewton Gr 3 TS17 157 A7
Kirknewton Rd TS6 121 C1
Kirkstall Ave 4 TS3 140 F8
Kirkstall Cres DL3 132 B4
Kirkstall Ct TS12 125 D2
Kirkstall Wlk DL14 79 D2
Kirkstone DH3 9 D2
Kirkstone Ave SR8 49 E6
Kirkstone Cl Blaydon NE21 2 C8
8 Houghton-le-S DH5 26 F8
Kirk Merrington DL16 69 A3
Kirkstone Ct TS24 64 A1
Kirkstone Dr DH1 35 D5
Kirkstone Gr
Hartlepool TS24 64 A1
Redcar TS10 107 C4
Kirkstone Pl DL5 96 B6
Kirkstone Rd TS3 120 C1
Kirkwall Cl TS19 116 F4
Kirkwood DH7 23 B3
Kirkwood Dr TS10 107 E1
Kirriemuir Rd TS25 89 D7
Kirtley Terr DL17 71 C4
Kitchen Ave DL14 80 A5
Kitchener St DL3 132 F3
Kitchener Terr DL17 70 A5
Kitching Gr DL3 132 F6
Kitching Rd SR8 38 F1
Kitswell Rd DH7 20 C5
Kittiwake Cl TS26 76 D8
Kittiwake Dr NE38 9 F3
Knaith Cl TS15 156 A3
Knapton Ave TS22 102 A5
Knaresborough Ave
TS7 140 E2
Knaresborough Cl TS27 63 D3
Knaresborough Rd SR7 28 C3
Knaresdale DH3 9 D1
Knayton Gr TS19 117 A2
Kneller Cl DH9 13 F6
Knighton Ct TS17 138 E6
Knightport Rd TS18 213 C4
Knightsbridge Ave DL1 133 E6
Knightsbridge Gdns
TS26 76 E6
Knitsley Gdns DH8 10 F1
Knitsley La
Castleside DH8 177 B2
Castleside DH8 177 D1
Consett DH8 177 C4
Consett DH8 10 F1
Knitsley Wlk TS19 117 C7
Knobbyends La NE21 1 F8
Knole Rd TS23 102 F5
Knoll Ave DL3 151 D8
Knoulberry Rd NE37 9 F6
Knowles Cl TS15 172 C8
Knowles St TS18 213 B3
Knox La DH7 31 A3
Kreuger Alley TS3 215 C2
Kyle Ave TS25 77 A3
Kyles Yd DL12 209 D7
Kyo Heugh Rd DH9 13 A6
Kyo La DH9 13 B5
Kyo Rd DH9 12 F5

L

L'Arbre Cres NE16 2 F7
Laburnum Pk DH7 42 F3
Laburnham Ct DH7 33 B1
Laburnum Ave
Consett DH8 10 E4
Crook DL15 52 D4
Durham DH1 210 B2
Thornaby-on-T TS17 138 C6
Laburnum Cres
Easington SR8 39 C4
Kibblesworth NE11 8 C6
Seaham SR7 29 C4
Wingate TS29 60 B5
Laburnum Ct DH7 23 B3
Laburnum Gdns DL15 54 C3
Laburnum Gr TS2 119 F8
Laburnum Rd
Bishop Auckland DL14 80 C7
Brotton TS12 126 A4
Chilton DL17 70 C2
Cornforth DL17 70 E8
Darlington DL1 133 B8
Egglescliffe TS16 137 C4
Eston TS6 121 C3
Ormesby TS7 141 B6
Redcar TS10 107 E5
Laburnum Sq TS29 60 B5
Laburnum St 6 TS26 77 A6
Laburnum Terr
Annfield Plain DH9 12 E5
Shotton Colliery DH6 48 C6
Lacebark DH4 17 F6
Lacey Gr TS26 76 F7
Lackenby La TS6 122 A3
Lackenby Rd TS6 122 C4
Ladgate Grange TS3 120 D1
Ladgate La TS8 140 C6
Ladock Cl SR2 19 A8
Lady Anne Rd DH6 35 F2
Lady Durham Cl DH6 35 F1
Lady Eden Hospl DL14 80 B7
Lady Kathryn Gr DL3 132 E4
Lady St DH5 27 A5
Lady's Piece La DH6 36 A5
Ladybower 1 DL5 96 A7
Ladyclose DL2 200 E7
Ladyclose Croft 3 DL2 200 E7
Ladyfern Way TS20 117 F7
Ladyport Gn 1 TS18 213 C4
Ladysmith Ct DH9 14 A5
Ladysmith St
Bishop Auckland DL14 80 B8
Hartlepool TS25 77 C3
Ladysmith Terr DH7 32 F2
Ladysmock Cl DL16 68 F8
Ladywell DL13 189 E1
Ladywell Rd 3 DH8 177 E4
Ladywood Pk DH4 17 F8
Lagonda Ct TS23 103 C5
Lagonda Rd TS23 103 C5
Laidler Cl TS27 50 D3
Laindon Ave TS4 140 C5
Laing Cl TS6 121 D6
Laing Sq TS28 48 D1
Laing St Consett DH8 10 F4
Darlington DL3 132 D4
Stockton-on-T TS18 213 A3
Laird Rd TS25 89 D8
Lake Bank Terr TS28 60 E6
Lake Ct SR3 18 A6
Lake Rd DH5 26 E8
Lake View TS28 60 E6
Lakeland Dr SR8 49 E7
Lakemore SR8 49 C5
Lakes Ave TS10 107 C5
Lakes Prim Sch TS10 107 C4
Lakeside DL1 151 F7
Lakeside Ct DL16 56 B1
Lakeston Cl TS26 76 D7
Lamb Cl DL5 96 E8
Lamb La TS17 157 A7
Lamb's Pl DH6 57 D8
Lamberd Rd TS24 63 F3
Lambert Ct DL3 133 A7
Lambert Rd NE37 9 F7
Lambeth Rd TS5 119 D1
Lambfield Way TS17 138 A3
Lambourne Cl DH4 17 E3
Lambourne Dr TS7 140 E4
Lambton Ave DH8 177 D4
Lambton Bsns Ctr DL5 96 D3
Lambton Cl DL5 96 D5
Lambton Cres TS21 85 A6
Lambton Ct Peterlee SR8 49 C3
Washington NE38 16 E8
Lambton Dr
Bishop Auckland DL14 80 A6
Hetton-le-H DH5 27 A1
Lambton Gdns NE16 5 E5
Lambton Rd
Billingham TS23 102 F5
Ferryhill DL17 70 B5
Middlesbrough TS4 120 A2
Stockton-on-T TS19 117 F5
Lambton St
Chester le Street DH3 16 D2
Darlington DL1 133 A3
Durham DH1 210 B3
Eston TS6 121 D1
9 Hartlepool TS24 77 C5
Langley Park DH7 32 B7
Shildon DL4 80 E1
Lambton Terr
Craghead DH9 14 D2
Penshaw DH4 17 F8
Lambton Wlk DH1 210 C2
Lammermuir Cl 5 DL1 133 C6
Lammermuir Rd TS23 102 C4
Lamonby Cl TS7 140 F2
Lamont Gr TS25 89 C8
Lamport Cl TS18 118 D4
Lamport St TS1 214 A2
Lanark Cl TS19 117 B4
Lanark Rd TS25 89 C8
Lanark Terr DL17 70 A6
Lanberry Gn TS4 120 B2
Lancashire Dr DH1 35 D3
Lancaster Cl DL14 79 E6
Lancaster Ct TS24 77 B8
Lancaster Dr 4 TS11 108 B1
Lancaster Hill SR8 49 B8
Lancaster Ho TS6 121 D4
Lancaster Rd
3 Consett DH8 177 A4
Hartlepool TS24 77 B8
Middlesbrough TS5 119 E1
Lancaster Rd N TS24 64 B1
Lancaster Terr DH3 16 D2
Lancaster Way TS17 138 D3
Lancefield Rd TS20 102 B1
Lancelot Cl DL5 82 B1
Lancelot St TS26 76 F7
Lanchester Ave TS23 102 C6
Lanchester Endowed Parochial Prim Sch
DH7 20 E4
Lanchester Rd Eston TS6 121 E6
Maiden Law DH7,DH9 21 A8
Landreth Gr TS29 59 E1
Lands Rd DL13 195 E4
Landsdowne Cres DH6 57 E8
Landsdowne Rd DH6 57 F4
Landseer Cl DH9 13 F6
Landseer Dr TS23 102 D7
Landswood Terr NE21 2 D7
Lane Pl TS6 121 D5
Lane The TS21 85 B7
Lanehead La DL11 205 D6
Lanehill DL13 179 C1
Lanehill Cvn Site DL13 179 C1
Lanehouse Rd TS17 138 D8
Laneside Rd TS18 212 A1
Lanethorpe Cres DL1 152 D8
Lanethorpe Rd DL1 152 D8
Langbaurgh Cl TS9 161 A3
Langbaurgh Ct
3 Saltburn-by-t-S TS12 125 C8
Skelton TS12 125 D2
Langbaurgh Rd TS15 173 E1
Langbaurgh Sch TS3 120 E1
Langdale Birtley DH3 9 E1
Guisborough TS14 143 A3
Langdale Ave DL15 52 F3
Langdale Cl
Egglescliffe TS16 156 C8
Leadgate DH8 11 D4
Langdale Cres
Blaydon NE21 2 B8
Durham DH1 35 C5
Eston TS6 121 F3
Langdale Gr TS5 139 D7
Langdale Oval TS29 60 A4
Langdale Pl
Newton Aycliffe DL5 96 A6
Peterlee SR8 49 E6
Langdale Rd
Billingham TS23 102 E1
Darlington DL1 152 B8
Langdale St DH5 27 A2
Langdale Terr NE17 4 A5

Langdale Wlk DL14 ... 79 F4
Langdon Gdns DH9 ... 12 E5
Langdon Sq TS8 ... 140 B3
Langdon Way TS16 ... 137 A1
Langham Wlk TS19 ... 117 A3
Langholm Cres DL3 ... 132 E1
Langhurst SR2 ... 18 E8
Langleeford Way TS17 ... 157 A7
Langley Ave
Burnhope DH7 ... 21 D4
Thornaby-on-T TS17 ... 138 D8
Langley Cl TS10 ... 107 C2
Langley Cres DH7 ... 43 D5
Langley Ct 13 TS3 ... 140 D8
Langley Garth DL2 ... 200 F7
Langley Gr
Bishop Auckland DL14 ... 80 A6
Peterlee SR8 ... 49 A4
Langley La DH7 ... 22 B2
Langley Moor Ind Est DH7 ... 43 E5
Langley Moor Prim Sch DH7 ... 43 E6
Langley Park Ind Est DH7 ... 32 C8
Langley Park Prim Sch DH7 ... 32 C6
Langley Rd Durham DH1 ... 34 C6
Newton Aycliffe DL5 ... 96 E7
Langley St DH7 ... 32 C7
Langley Terr
Annfield Plain DH9 ... 13 A4
Burnhope DH7 ... 21 D5
Langley View DH9 ... 13 C3
Langmere DL16 ... 55 E2
Langridge Cres TS3 ... 120 D1
Langsett Ave 1 TS3 ... 120 C1
Langthorne Ave 10 SR8 ... 50 B6
Langthorne Gr TS18 ... 117 A1
Langthorpe TS7 ... 140 F3
Langthwaite Wlk TS10 ... 107 C2
Langton DL2 ... 201 D6
Langton Ave TS22 ... 102 B5
Langton Cl TS4 ... 119 F2
Langton Lea DH1 ... 45 C5
Langton Terr DH4 ... 17 E2
Langton Wlk 11 DL1 ... 152 C8
Lanivet Cl 4 SR2 ... 18 F8
Lanrood Gn TS4 ... 120 B2
Lansbury Cl Birtley DH3 ... 9 B6
South Bank TS6 ... 121 A5
Lansbury Dr Birtley DH3 ... 9 B5
Murton SR7 ... 28 C3
Lansbury Gr TS24 ... 77 B7
Lansdown Way
Billingham TS23 ... 103 A6
Willington DL15 ... 53 E1
Lansdowne SR2 ... 18 E7
Lansdowne Rd
Brotton TS12 ... 126 C3
Hartlepool TS26 ... 77 A5
Middlesbrough TS4 ... 120 B2
Thornaby-on-T TS17 ... 138 E7
Yarm TS15 ... 156 D5
Lansdowne St DL3 ... 133 A5
Lanshaw Gn TS4 ... 120 B2
Lantsbery Dr TS13 ... 147 A8
Lanyard The TS24 ... 77 C6
Lapwing Cl NE38 ... 9 F3
Lapwing Ct NE16 ... 6 C5
Lapwing La TS20 ... 102 A2
Lapwing Rd TS26 ... 76 D8
Larch Ave
2 Houghton-le-S DH4 ... 26 C8
Shildon DL4 ... 81 B1
Larch Cl TS7 ... 140 F4
Larch Cres TS16 ... 137 D4
Larch Gr TS24 ... 64 A1
Larch Rd
Guisborough TS14 ... 143 D5
Stockton-on-T TS19 ... 118 A5
Larch St DH8 ... 10 F3
Larch Terr
Billingham TS2 ... 119 F8
Tantobie DH9 ... 6 A1
The Middles DH9 ... 14 B3
13 Langley Park DH7 ... 32 C6
Larches Rd DH1 ... 210 A4
Larches The
Burnopfield NE16 ... 6 B7
Esh Winning DH7 ... 41 D8
Eston TS6 ... 121 B3
Ormesby TS7 ... 141 B6
Redcar TS10 ... 107 E5
Stockton-on-T TS19 ... 117 C5
Larchfield Gdns DL15 ... 52 D4
Larchfield Ho 17 DL3 ... 132 F1
Larchfield St DL3 ... 132 F1
Largo Gdns DL1 ... 133 C7
Lark Dr TS14 ... 143 A4
Larkhall Sq TS20 ... 118 B6
Larkhill SR2 ... 18 F7
Larkspur Cl
Hartlepool TS26 ... 63 D2
Tanfield Lea DH9 ... 13 D8
Larkspur Ct DL14 ... 79 F6
Larkspur Dr DL1 ... 133 C2
Larkspur Rd TS7 ... 140 C4
Larkswood Rd TS10 ... 107 C1
Lartington Ct DH3 ... 25 B6
Lartington Green La DL12 ... 198 E4
Lartington La DL12 ... 199 B4
Larun Beat The TS15 ... 156 C4
Larvik Ct TS13 ... 127 A4
Larwood Ct
Annfield Plain DH9 ... 12 E3
Chester le Street DH3 ... 16 E1
Lascelles Ave DL5 ... 96 A8
Lastingham Ave TS6 ... 121 E2
Latham Rd TS5 ... 119 D2
Latimer Cl TS15 ... 156 A3
Latimer La TS14 ... 143 C3
Latimer Rd DL1 ... 133 D5
Laude Bank DH7 ... 31 D4
Lauder Cl TS19 ... 117 B4
Lauder Ho 1 TS19 ... 117 B4
Lauder St TS24 ... 77 B6
Lauderdale Dr TS14 ... 143 F3
Launceston DH3 ... 25 A7
Laura St
Middlesbrough TS1 ... 215 A1
Seaham SR7 ... 29 D6
Laurel Ave Durham DH1 ... 35 A1
Middlesbrough TS4 ... 140 A8
Seaham SR7 ... 29 B7
Thornaby-on-T TS17 ... 138 C6
Laurel Avenue Com Prim Sch DH1 ... 211 C2
Laurel Cl TS12 ... 125 C6
Laurel Cres Beamish DH2 ... 15 B7
Brotton TS12 ... 126 A4
Thornley (nr Wheatley Hill) DH6 ... 47 C3
Trimdon TS29 ... 59 F5
Laurel Ct
Chester le Street DH2 ... 16 B5
Shildon DL4 ... 95 B8
Laurel Dr DH8 ... 11 D3
Laurel Gdns DL15 ... 52 D4
Laurel Pk TS13 ... 127 B1
Laurel Rd Chilton DL17 ... 70 C2
Egglescliffe TS16 ... 137 C4
Marton TS7 ... 140 D3
Redcar TS10 ... 107 F5
Saltburn-by-t-S TS12 ... 125 C6
Stockton-on-T TS19 ... 117 F5
Laurel St Darlington DL3 ... 132 E3
Middlesbrough TS1 ... 215 A2
Laurel Terr
Burnopfield NE16 ... 5 F6
Langley Park DH7 ... 32 D6
Sadberge DL2 ... 134 E6
Laurel Way 10 DL14 ... 80 C8
Laurels The 13 SR3 ... 18 A8
Lauren Ct SR8 ... 39 C4
Laurence Jackson Sch TS14 ... 143 F6
Lauriston Cl DL3 ... 132 A1
Lavan Ct TS10 ... 107 E2
Lavan Sands TS5 ... 139 B3
Lavender Ct TS11 ... 124 D8
Lavender Dr DL14 ... 79 E7
Lavender Gdns DH7 ... 23 D3
Lavender Rd TS3 ... 120 C3
Lavender Way TS20 ... 118 A7
Laverick Terr DH9 ... 13 A3
Lavernock Cl TS10 ... 107 E3
Lavers Rd DH3 ... 9 C5
Lawnhead Sq SR3 ... 18 B6
Lawns Gill 4 TS12 ... 125 A2
Lawns The
Easington Lane DH5 ... 27 C1
Hartlepool TS24 ... 77 F8
Seaham SR7 ... 29 A6
Lawnswood DH5 ... 26 F7
Lawnswood Rd TS3 ... 121 A2
Lawrence Rd TS17 ... 138 B6
Lawrence St
Darlington DL1 ... 133 B1
Redcar TS10 ... 107 D6
Stockton-on-T TS18 ... 213 A2
Lawrenny Gr TS17 ... 156 F7
Lawson Cl
Middlesbrough TS3 ... 120 C5
South Bank TS6 ... 121 B5
Lawson Ct 6 DH2 ... 16 C2
Lawson Ind Est TS3 ... 120 C5
Lawson Rd Bowburn DH6 ... 45 D1
Seaton Carew TS25 ... 77 E1
Lawson St TS18 ... 213 A2
Lawson Terr
Durham DH1 ... 210 B2
Hetton-le-H DH5 ... 27 B1
Lawson Way TS3 ... 120 C5
Lawson Wlk TS18 ... 213 A2
Lawson's St TS29 ... 60 A4
Lax Terr Crook DL15 ... 52 D3
Wolviston TS22 ... 102 C8
Laxford DH3 ... 9 D2
Laxford Ct SR3 ... 18 A5
Laxton Cl TS23 ... 102 D6
Layburn Pl SR8 ... 49 C7
Laycock St TS1 ... 214 A2
Layfield Prim Sch TS15 ... 156 B3
Layland Rd TS12 ... 125 E2
Layton Ct DL5 ... 82 D1
Lazenby Bank* TS6 ... 122 C2
Lazenby Bank Rd TS6 ... 122 C3
Lazenby Cl DL3 ... 132 B3
Lazenby Cres DL3 ... 132 B3
Lazenby Gr DL3 ... 132 B3
Lazenby Rd TS24 ... 63 E4
Lea Gn Birtley DH3 ... 9 E1
Wolsingham DL13 ... 207 C5
Lea La SR8 ... 39 B6
Lea Riggs DH4 ... 26 A2
Lea Side DH8 ... 177 D4
Lea Terr NE47 ... 179 C8
Leach Gr DL3 ... 132 C5
Lead La DH8 ... 3 C6
Leadenhall St DL1 ... 133 A3
Leadgate Com Jun Sch DH8 ... 11 D3
Leadgate Ind Est DH8 ... 11 E2
Leadgate Inf Sch DH8 ... 11 C3
Leadgate Rd Consett DH8 ... 11 B4
Leadgate DH8 ... 11 B4
Leadgate Terr DL13 ... 207 E5
Leadpipe La DL12 ... 198 E6
Leafield Cl DH3 ... 9 D6
Leafield Rd DL1 ... 152 A8
Leaholme Terr TS27 ... 50 E2
Leahope Ct TS17 ... 138 E4
Lealholm Cres TS3 ... 140 E7
Lealholm Rd TS25 ... 90 A8
Lealholm Way TS14 ... 143 D2
Lealholm Wlk 2 TS6 ... 121 F3
Lealholme Gr TS19 ... 117 B2
Leam La TS19 ... 117 A5
Leamington Dr 2 TS25 ... 77 B3
Leamington Gr TS3 ... 140 F8
Leamington Par TS25 ... 77 B3
Leander Ave DH3 ... 16 D7
Leas Gr TS24 ... 64 D2
Leas The Darlington DL1 ... 133 A6
Redcar TS10 ... 107 E3
Sedgefield TS21 ... 85 B5
Leas Wlk TS24 ... 64 D2
Leases The DH6 ... 57 D8
Leaside DL5 ... 96 D4
Leaside N DL5 ... 96 D4
Leasyde Wlk NE16 ... 2 F5
Leatham SR2 ... 18 E8
Leazes Ct DH1 ... 211 A3
Leazes La
Bishop Auckland DL14 ... 79 C3
Durham DH1 ... 211 B3
Wolsingham DL13 ... 207 B5
Leazes Pl DH1 ... 211 A3
Leazes Rd DH1 ... 211 A3
Leazes Rise SR8 ... 49 F5
Leazes The NE16 ... 5 F6
Leazes View
Rowlands Gill NE39 ... 1 D2
Wolsingham DL13 ... 207 B5
Leazes Villas NE16 ... 6 A6
Leazon Hill TS17 ... 138 A2
Leckfell Cl TS7 ... 140 F2
Leconfield TS9 ... 158 F1
Ledbury Dr
Middlesbrough TS5 ... 139 D3
Thornaby-on-T TS17 ... 138 C4
Ledbury Way TS14 ... 143 D2
Lee Gn DL5 ... 96 D5
Lee Hill Ct DH7 ... 20 E3
Lee Rd TS6 ... 121 E6
Lee Terr Easington SR8 ... 39 C4
Hetton-le-H DH5 ... 27 B2
Shotton Colliery DH6 ... 48 C6
Leech Ct SR8 ... 39 F4
Leechmere Cres SR7 ... 18 F1
Leechmere Ind Est SR2 ... 18 F8
Leechmere View 5 SR2 ... 18 F8
Leechmere Way SR2 ... 18 F8
Leechmire Terr TS27 ... 61 C5
Leeds St TS18 ... 213 A3
Leehall La DL5,TS21 ... 97 E4
Leeholme DH5 ... 26 F7
Leeholme Ct DH9 ... 13 A3
Leeholme Rd
Billingham TS23 ... 102 F4
Coundon DL14 ... 81 D8
Leekworth Gdns DL12 ... 208 C5
Leekworth La DL12 ... 208 C5
Leeman's La DH6 ... 56 F5
Leeming Rd TS5 ... 119 C1
Lees Rd TS1 ... 214 B2
Lees St DH9 ... 13 F7
Leesfield Dr DH7 ... 43 C3
Leesfield Gdns DH7 ... 43 C3
Leesfield Rd DH7 ... 43 C3
Leeway The TS3 ... 215 C3
Leicester Gr DL1 ... 133 E5
Leicester Rd TS20 ... 118 C7
Leicester Way TS16 ... 156 A7
Leicester Wlk SR8 ... 49 C8
Leicestershire Dr DH1 ... 35 D3
Leighton Rd Eston TS6 ... 121 E6
Stockton-on-T TS18 ... 137 A8
Leighton Terr Birtley DH3 ... 9 B5
Hartlepool TS27 ... 63 D3
Leinster Rd TS1 ... 214 A1
Leith Gdns DH9 ... 6 D1
Leith Rd DL3 ... 132 B1
Leith Wlk TS17 ... 138 D3
Lendings The DL12 ... 209 C4
Lenham Cl TS22 ... 102 A5
Lenin Terr Chopwell NE17 ... 4 C8
Stanley DH9 ... 13 F5
Lennox Cres TS23 ... 102 D3
Lennox Wlk TS25 ... 89 D8
Leonard Ropner Dr TS19 ... 117 A4
Leonard St DL1 ... 152 B8
Leopold Pl DL14 ... 80 C7
Lerwick Cl TS19 ... 116 F3
Lesbury Cl DH2 ... 15 F1
Lesbury Terr NE17 ... 4 B8
Leslie St DL14 ... 79 D2
Leslie Villas DH6 ... 58 A4
Letch Ave SR7 ... 39 B8
Letch La Carlton TS21 ... 116 E8
Stockton-on-T TS21 ... 117 A8
Letch Rd TS20 ... 102 B1
Letitia Ind Est TS5 ... 119 B4
Leuchars Ct DH3 ... 9 C3
Leven Ave DH2 ... 16 B1
Leven Bank Rd TS15 ... 157 A4
Leven Camping Site TS17 ... 157 A6
Leven Cl TS16 ... 156 B7
Leven Ct TS9 ... 161 B1
Leven Gdns DL1 ... 133 C7
Leven Gr Hartlepool TS25 ... 89 D8
Thornaby-on-T TS17 ... 138 D6
Leven Ho 10 SR3 ... 18 A6
Leven Rd
Bishop Auckland DL14 ... 79 B1
Guisborough TS14 ... 143 D3
Middlesbrough TS3 ... 120 C4
Stockton-on-T TS20 ... 118 A8
Yarm TS15 ... 156 D5
Leven St Billingham TS23 ... 103 D2
Middlesbrough TS1 ... 214 A2
Saltburn-by-t-S TS12 ... 125 C7
South Bank TS6 ... 121 A6
Leven Wlk SR8 ... 49 C4
Levendale TS15 ... 173 E1
Levendale Cl TS15 ... 156 E5
Levendale Prim Sch TS15 ... 156 E5
Levens Wlk TS10 ... 107 C4
Levenside TS9 ... 160 F2
Leveret Cl TS17 ... 138 C2
Levick Cres TS5 ... 139 B7
Levington Wynd TS7 ... 141 A2
Levisham Cl
Middlesbrough TS5 ... 139 E7
New Silksworth SR3 ... 18 C7
Stockton-on-T TS18 ... 212 A1
Lewes Rd DL1 ... 152 B8
Lewes Way TS23 ... 103 A7
Lewis Gr TS25 ... 76 D2
Lewis Rd TS5 ... 119 D2
Lewis Wlk TS14 ... 143 D3
Lexden Ave TS5 ... 139 B7
Lexington Ct Brandon DH7 ... 43 A2
8 Stockton-on-T TS20 ... 118 B6
Leybourne Hold DH3 ... 9 C6
Leybourne Terr TS18 ... 212 C2
Leyburn Cl DH2 ... 8 D1
Leyburn Gr TS18 ... 137 B8
Leyburn Pl DH3 ... 9 B6
Leyburn Rd DL1 ... 133 A6
Leyburn St TS26 ... 77 A4
Leyfield Cl SR3 ... 18 B5
Leyland Cl DH6 ... 45 E2
Libanus Ct TS17 ... 156 F8
Liberty Terr DH9 ... 6 B2
Library Terr DH9 ... 12 F4
Library Wlk DH9 ... 12 F4
Lichfield Ave
Egglescliffe TS16 ... 137 A1
Eston TS6 ... 121 E3
Lichfield Cl DH3 ... 25 A6
Lichfield Rd
Cornforth DL17 ... 70 F8
Middlesbrough TS5 ... 119 F1
Lidcombe Cl SR3 ... 18 C7
Liddel Ct TS25 ... 64 A2
Liddell Cl DL5 ... 96 F6
Liddell Terr NE11 ... 8 C6
Liddle Ave
Butterknowle DL13 ... 195 C4
Sherburn DH6 ... 35 F1
Liddle Cl SR8 ... 49 B8
Lidell Terr DH6 ... 47 E1
Light Pipe Hall Rd TS18 ... 212 C2
Lightfoot Cres TS24 ... 63 F2
Lightfoot Gr TS18 ... 213 A2
Lightfoot Rd DL5 ... 96 C7
Lightfoot Terr DL17 ... 69 E5
Lilac Ave
Blackhall Rocks TS27 ... 50 F2
Durham DH1 ... 34 B5
12 Houghton-le-S DH5 ... 26 E8
New Silksworth SR3 ... 18 B8
Sacriston DH7 ... 23 C3
Sedgefield TS21 ... 85 B7
Thornaby-on-T TS17 ... 138 C6
Lilac Cl Carlton TS21 ... 100 D1
Lazenby TS6 ... 122 C4
Saltburn-by-t-S TS12 ... 125 A6
Spennymoor DL16 ... 68 D7
Lilac Cres Brotton TS12 ... 126 A4
Burnopfield NE16 ... 6 A6
Wingate TS29 ... 60 B5
Lilac Ct DL4 ... 95 B8
Lilac Gdns Beamish DH2 ... 15 B7
Crook DL15 ... 52 D3
Lilac Gr
Chester le Street DH2 ... 16 A5
Middlesbrough TS3 ... 120 E3
Redcar TS10 ... 107 E5
Trimdon TS29 ... 59 D1
Lilac Pk DH7 ... 33 A1
Lilac Pl DH8 ... 11 D3
Lilac Rd Chilton DL17 ... 70 C2
Egglescliffe TS16 ... 137 C4
Eston TS6 ... 121 C3
Ormesby TS7 ... 141 B6
Stockton-on-T TS19 ... 117 F5
Lilac Sq DH4 ... 17 E3
Lilac Terr
Annfield Plain DH9 ... 12 E5
Shotton Colliery DH6 ... 48 C6
Lilac Way DL14 ... 78 E5
Lilburn Cl
Chester le Street DH2 ... 24 A8
9 Shildon DL4 ... 80 F1
Lilburne Cres DL5 ... 96 D7
Lile Gdns TS21 ... 85 B6
Lilian Ave SR2 ... 18 E8
Lilian Terr 4 DH7 ... 32 C6
Lilley Terr NE39 ... 1 F3
Lilleycroft NE39 ... 1 F2
Lillie Terr TS29 ... 59 D3
Lily Bglws DH9 ... 12 E8
Lily Gdns DH9 ... 12 E8
Lilywhite Terr DH5 ... 27 B1
Limber Gn TS3 ... 141 A8
Limbrick Ave TS19 ... 117 A3
Limbrick Ct TS19 ... 117 B3
Lime Ave
Blackhall Rocks TS27 ... 50 E3
Darlington DL1 ... 133 A8
Houghton-le-S DH4 ... 26 C8
Lime Cl TS7 ... 140 D4
Lime Cres Eston TS6 ... 121 C2
Hartlepool TS24 ... 77 A8
Lime Gr
Bishop Auckland DL14 ... 80 B4
Shildon DL4 ... 81 B1
Stockton-on-T TS19 ... 117 B3
Lime La Mordon DL1 ... 97 C1
Newton Aycliffe DL5 ... 112 F8
Lime Pk DH7 ... 43 B4
Lime Rd Eaglescliffe TS16 ... 137 D4
Eston TS6 ... 121 C2
Ferryhill DL17 ... 69 F6
Guisborough TS14 ... 143 D5
Redcar TS10 ... 107 E6
Lime St Stanley DH9 ... 13 D4
Waldridge DH2 ... 15 E1
Lime Terr Eldon Lane DL14 ... 80 F4
Langley Park DH7 ... 32 D6
Lime Tree Cl TS2 ... 103 E1
Lime Tree Wlk DL13 ... 206 D3
Lime Wlk TS13 ... 127 B2
Limecragg Ave DH1 ... 35 B3
Limehurst Rd DL3 ... 132 E3
Limeoak Way TS18 ... 213 C4
Limerick Rd TS10 ... 106 D4
Limes Cres TS11 ... 124 D8
Limes Rd TS5 ... 119 E1
Limetree Ct 7 TS4 ... 139 F8
Limpton Gate TS15 ... 156 C4
Linacre Ct SR8 ... 49 B5
Linacre Way DL1 ... 133 B6
Linburn NE38 ... 17 B8
Linburn Dr DL14 ... 79 F5
Linby Ave TS3 ... 140 C8
Lincoln Ave SR3 ... 18 A8
Lincoln Cl DL5 ... 96 C7
Lincoln Cres
Billingham TS23 ... 102 F3
Hetton-le-H DH5 ... 26 F4
Lincoln Ct DL1 ... 133 E4
Lincoln Dr DL15 ... 53 F2
Lincoln Gr TS20 ... 118 C7
Lincoln Pl
6 Consett DH8 ... 177 A4
Thornaby-on-T TS17 ... 138 C7
Lincoln Rd Consett DH8 ... 177 A4
Durham DH1 ... 34 D7
Guisborough TS14 ... 143 D3
Hartlepool TS25 ... 89 D7
Redcar TS10 ... 107 F4
Lincoln St DL14 ... 81 D8
Lincoln Wlk
Great Lumley DH3 ... 25 A7
Peterlee SR8 ... 49 C8
Lincolnshire Cl DH1 ... 35 C3
Lincombe Dr TS5 ... 139 D3
Linden Ave
Darlington DL3 ... 151 D8
Great Ayton TS9 ... 160 F2
Stockton-on-T TS18 ... 137 E8
Linden Cl
Great Ayton TS9 ... 160 F3
Shildon DL4 ... 95 B8
Linden Cres
Great Ayton TS9 ... 160 F2
Marton TS7 ... 140 C3
Linden Ct
Spennymoor DL16 ... 69 A8
Thornaby-on-T TS17 ... 138 C7
Linden Dr Darlington DL3 ... 151 D8
Hurworth-on-T DL2 ... 168 A8
Linden Gr Coxhoe DH6 ... 57 F4
Great Ayton TS9 ... 160 F3
Hartlepool TS26 ... 76 F5
Houghton-le-S DH4 ... 26 D8
Leadgate DH8 ... 11 D3
Middlesbrough TS5 ... 119 D1
Thornaby-on-T TS17 ... 138 C7
Linden Ho TS12 ... 126 A4
Linden Lo DL3 ... 151 D8
Linden Mews DH7 ... 32 C6
Linden Pk DH7 ... 43 B4
Linden Pl DL5 ... 96 A6
Linden Rd Bearpark DH7 ... 33 B3
Bishop Auckland DL14 ... 80 C6
Brotton TS12 ... 126 A4
Cornforth DL17 ... 70 E8
Ferryhill DL17 ... 70 B5
Great Ayton TS9 ... 160 F2
Linden Terr Coxhoe DH6 ... 57 F4
Ferryhill DL17 ... 70 C3
Linden Way DH8 ... 10 E4
Lindisfarne
High Shincliffe DH1 ... 45 B5
Peterlee SR8 ... 49 D4
Ryhope SR2 ... 18 E6
Lindisfarne Ave DH3 ... 16 D3
Lindisfarne Cl
Bishop Auckland DL14 ... 79 E6
Chester le Street DH2 ... 16 A1
Hartlepool TS27 ... 63 D3
Lindisfarne Rd
Durham DH1 ... 34 D5
Middlesbrough TS3 ... 140 F8
Lindom Ave DH3 ... 16 D3
Lindon Rd DH9 ... 13 E5

Lindrick TS8 . . . . .140 E1
Lindrick Ct TS6 . . . . .121 E1
Lindrick Dr TS27 . . . . .63 C4
Lindrick Ho 5 TS6 . . . . . .121 E1
Lindrick Rd TS11 . . . . .123 F6
Lindsay Ho TS18 . . . . .213 B3
Lindsay Rd TS25 . . . . .89 C8
Lindsay St
Bishop Auckland DL14 . . . . .80 B7
Hetton-le-H DH5 . . . . .27 B5
Stockton-on-T TS18 . . . . . . .213 A1
Lindsey Ct TS12 . . . . .126 C4
Linfield SR2 . . . . .18 E7
Ling Cl TS7 . . . . .140 C5
Ling Riggs DL13 . . . . .179 B1
Lingard Wlk DL5 . . . . .96 E5
Lingdale DH1 . . . . .35 D3
Lingdale Cl TS19 . . . . . . .212 B4
Lingdale Dr TS25 . . . . .90 D6
Lingdale Gr TS10 . . . . . . .106 F4
Lingdale Prim Sch TS12 .145 E5
Lingdale Rd
Lingdale TS12 . . . . .145 C6
Thornaby-on-T TS17 . . . . . .138 D6
Lingey Cl DH7 . . . . .23 B4
Lingfield DH5 . . . . .26 F7
Lingfield Ash TS8 . . . . . . .159 B8
Lingfield Cl DL1 . . . . .133 F2
Lingfield Dr TS16 . . . . . . .156 A8
Lingfield Est The DL1 . . . .133 E3
Lingfield Gn DL1 . . . . .133 E1
Lingfield Prim Sch TS7 .140 D2
Lingfield Rd Consett DH8 . .10 E3
Stockton-on-T TS19 . . . . . . .117 B3
Yarm TS15 . . . . .156 E5
Lingfield Way
Coulby Newham TS8 . . . . . .140 C1
Darlington DL1 . . . . .133 F1
Lingholme
Chester le Street DH2 . . . . . .16 A4
Redcar TS10 . . . . .107 B4
Lingmell Dene DL14 . . . . . .68 B1
Lingmell Rd TS10 . . . . . . .107 C3
Link The TS3 . . . . .140 F8
Links Dr DH8 . . . . .10 E5
Links Prim Sch The
TS16 . . . . .137 C1
Links The Durham DH1 . . . .35 D3
Redcar TS10 . . . . .107 A7
Saltburn-by-t-S TS12 . . . . . .125 B5
Seaton Carew TS25 . . . . .90 E7
Linkway The TS23 . . . . . . .102 E4
Linley Ct TS20 . . . . .102 A2
Linley Hill NE16 . . . . .2 E4
Linlithgow Cl TS14 . . . . . .143 D2
Linmoor Ave TS3 . . . . .120 E2
Linnet Ct TS20 . . . . .102 B2
Linnet Rd TS26 . . . . .63 E1
Linshiels Gr TS17 . . . . . . .157 A7
Linskell SR2 . . . . .18 E8
Linsley Cl TS3 . . . . .215 C3
Lintfort NE38 . . . . .16 E7
Linthorpe Prim Sch
TS5 . . . . .119 D1
Linthorpe Rd TS5 . . . . . . .119 E2
Linton Ave TS7 . . . . .140 C3
Linton Cl TS19 . . . . .117 A5
Linton Rd TS6 . . . . .121 B1
Linton Terr DL15 . . . . .52 F4
Lintz Green La NE16,NE39 . .5 C6
Lintz La NE16 . . . . .5 E4
Lintz Terr
Annfield Plain DH9 . . . . .13 C5
Burnopfield NE16 . . . . .5 F6
Lintzford Gdns NE39 . . . . . .5 D8
Lintzford La NE39 . . . . .1 B1
Lintzford Rd
Hamsterley Mill NE39 . . . . . . .5 C7
Rowlands Gill NE39 . . . . .5 C7
Linwood Gr DL3 . . . . .151 D7
Lion Bridge Cl TS22 . . . . .101 E8
Lishman Ave DL15 . . . . .52 E4
Lisle Rd DL5 . . . . .96 A8
Lismore Dr DL1 . . . . .133 D7
Lister Cl DH5 . . . . .26 D6
Lister Rd SR8 . . . . .49 A8
Lister St TS26 . . . . .77 B5
Lister Terr Crook DL15 . . . . .52 E5
Wolsingham DL13 . . . . .207 D5
Lister Terr E DL13 . . . . . . .207 D5
Litchfield Rd DH1 . . . . .34 D8
Lithgo Cl TS25 . . . . .77 E2
Little Ayton La TS9 . . . . . .161 B1
Little Black Hedley DH8 .176 E6
Little Crake TS14 . . . . . . .143 B4
Little Eden SR8 . . . . .49 D7
Little Grebe TS14 . . . . . . .143 A4
Little Hutton La DL11 . . .205 F8
Little La DL5 . . . . .96 E2
Little Pasture TS17 . . . . .138 A2
Little Thornton TS21 . . . . .72 B5
Littlebeck Dr DL1 . . . . . . .133 C5
Littleboy Dr TS17 . . . . . . .138 E7
Littlebridge Ct DH1 . . . . . .34 A7
Littleburn Bsns Ctr DH7 . .43 E5
Littleburn Ind Est DH7 . . . .43 F4
Littleburn La DH7 . . . . .43 E5
Littleburn Rd DH7 . . . . .43 E4
Littletown La DH6 . . . . . . .36 D3
Littondale TS8 . . . . .139 D1
Littondale Ct TS17 . . . . . .157 A6
Liverton Ave TS5 . . . . . . .214 A1
Liverton Cres
Billingham TS22 . . . . .102 B6
Thornaby-on-T TS17 . . . . . .138 C3
Liverton La TS13 . . . . .147 A3
Liverton Mill Bank
TS12 . . . . .146 D3
Liverton Rd
Liverton TS13 . . . . .147 A4
Loftus TS13 . . . . .127 B1
Liverton Terr TS13 . . . . . .147 A8
Liverton Terr S TS13 . . . .147 A8
Liverton Whin TS12 . . . . .125 A7
Livingstone Rd TS3 . . . . .120 C3
Livingstone St 17 DH8 . . . .10 F3
Lizard Gr TS24 . . . . .77 C5
Lizard Wlk 12 TS24 . . . . . . .77 C5
Lloyd Ave DH5 . . . . .26 C4
Lloyd St TS2 . . . . .214 B4
Lloyds Terr 5 DH7 . . . . . . .32 C6
Lobelia Cl 11 TS7 . . . . . . .141 B7
Lobley Hill Rd DH7 . . . . . .43 D4
Lobleyhill Rd NE16 . . . . . . .6 D8
Lobster Rd TS10 . . . . .107 B7
Local Ave DH6 . . . . .36 C1
Loch Gr TS25 . . . . .89 D8
Lochfield Gdns NE11 . . . . . .8 E8
Lock St DL3 . . . . .132 F5
Locke Rd TS10 . . . . .107 B6
Lockerbie Wlk TS17 . . . . .138 C4
Lockhaugh Rd NE39 . . . . . . .2 A4
Lockheed Cl TS18 . . . . . . .137 F5
Lockton Cl TS8 . . . . .139 C1
Lockton Cres TS17 . . . . . .138 B3
Lockwood Ct TS6 . . . . . . .121 E1
Lockwood Prim Sch
TS12 . . . . .145 B6
Lockyer Cl DL5 . . . . .96 B8
Locomotion Ct TS16 . . . . .137 B2
Locomotion, The National
Railway Mus at Shildon*
Shildon DL4 . . . . .95 A8
* Shildon DL4 . . . . .95 B7
Locomotive St DL1 . . . . . .133 C6
Lodge Cl NE39 . . . . .5 A5
Lodge Farm Rd TS6 . . . . . .121 F2
Lodge La DL1,TS21 . . . . . . .97 E1
Lodge Rd TS6 . . . . .121 E2
Lodge St Byers Green DL16 .54 E1
Darlington DL1 . . . . .133 A2
Stockton-on-T TS18 . . . . . . .213 A2
Lodgeside Mdw SR3 . . . . . .18 B5
Lodore Gr TS5 . . . . .139 B6
Loefield DH3 . . . . .25 A8
Loftus 10 TS4 . . . . .120 A1
Loftus Bank TS13 . . . . . . .127 A1
Loftus Jun Sch TS13 . . . .127 B1
Loftus Rd TS17 . . . . .138 D7
Logan Dr TS19 . . . . .117 C3
Logan Gr TS25 . . . . .89 D8
Logan St Hetton-le-H DH5 . .27 A3
Langley Park DH7 . . . . .32 C7
Logan Terr DH6 . . . . .37 E8
Lombard Ct DL1 . . . . .151 E8
Lombard Dr DH3 . . . . .16 D7
Lomond Ave TS23 . . . . . . .102 E4
Lomond Ct 11 SR3 . . . . .18 A6
Lomond Pl DH2 . . . . .16 B1
Lomond Wlk DL14 . . . . .79 C1
Londonderry Bglws SR8 . .39 D5
Londonderry Ct SR7 . . . . .29 D8
Londonderry Rd TS19 . . . .212 C4
Londonderry St
Hartlepool TS24 . . . . .77 F8
New Silksworth SR3 . . . . . . .18 A7
Seaham SR7 . . . . .29 E5
Londonderry Terr
Easington SR8 . . . . .39 D5
New Silksworth SR3 . . . . . . .18 B7
Long Acres DH1 . . . . .211 C4
Long Bank Birtley DH3 . . . . .9 C7
Dalton DL11 . . . . .205 C2
Long Burn Dr DH2 . . . . .15 F2
Long Close La DL12 . . . . . .203 D7
Long Close Rd NE39 . . . . . . .4 F5
Long Cswy DL11 . . . . .202 C2
Long Dale DH2 . . . . .15 F2
Long Edge DH7 . . . . .22 C4
Long Gair NE21 . . . . .2 A8
Long Garth DH1 . . . . .33 F4
Long La
Cockfield DL13,DL2 . . . . . . .195 F2
Crathorne TS15 . . . . .172 E5
Gayles DL11 . . . . .205 E2
Moorsholm TS12 . . . . .146 C2
Newfield DL14 . . . . .67 D7
Long Newton La TS16,
TS21 . . . . .136 C4
Long Row
Howden-le-W DL15 . . . . .66 A6
Port Mulgrave TS13 . . . . . . .149 F7
Long Tens La DL5 . . . . . . .112 E8
Long Tens Way DL5 . . . . . . .96 C1
Longacre DH4 . . . . .26 C8
Longacre Cl TS12 . . . . . . .125 C4
Longbank Rd TS7 . . . . . . .141 B6
Longbeck La TS11 . . . . . . .124 A7
Longbeck Rd
Marske-by-t-S TS11 . . . . . . .124 B8
New Marske TS11 . . . . .123 F6
Longbeck Sta TS11 . . . . . .124 B8
Longbeck Trad Est
TS11 . . . . .108 B1
Longbeck Way TS17 . . . . .138 E3
Longclose Bank DH8,DH9,
NE17,NE39 . . . . .4 E3
Longcroft Wlk TS3 . . . . . . .120 D3
Longdale Gr DL13 . . . . . . .179 E1
Longdean Pk DH3 . . . . .16 D6
Longedge La DH7,DH8 . . . .177 D1
Longfellow Ct DL15 . . . . . . .52 C2
Longfellow Rd TS23 . . . . .102 D8
Longfellow St DH5 . . . . . . .26 E7
Longfellow Wlk TS25 . . . . .76 D1
Longfield Comp Sch
DL3 . . . . .132 F7
Longfield Rd
Bishop Auckland DL14 . . . . .80 D5
Darlington DL3 . . . . .132 F6
Longfield Stad DL3 . . . . .132 F7
Longfield View TS6 . . . . . .141 C7
Longford Cl TS23 . . . . . . .102 E6
Longford St TS1 . . . . .214 A1
Longhill Ind Est TS25 . . . . .77 C3
Longhorn Ends DL13 . . . .179 B3
Longhurst TS8 . . . . .140 C1
Longlands Dr DH5 . . . . . . .26 E7
Longlands Rd TS3 . . . . . .120 D4
Longnewton St SR7 . . . . . .29 D5
Longscar Wlk 13 TS24 . . . .77 C5
Longshank La DH3 . . . . .9 A6
Longshaw Cl 1 TS17 . . . .138 C1
Longworth Way TS14 . . . .143 F6
Lonsdale DH3 . . . . .9 E1
Lonsdale Ave TS29 . . . . . . .59 E4
Lonsdale Ct
Hamsterley NE17 . . . . .4 B4
5 Hartlepool TS25 . . . . .77 B4
Lonsdale Gr TS10 . . . . . . .106 E3
Lonsdale St TS1 . . . . .214 B2
Loop La DL13 . . . . .195 C5
Loraine Cl TS11 . . . . .124 E8
Loraine Cres DL1 . . . . . . .151 F7
Loraine Wlk 1 DL5 . . . . . . .96 C8
Lord Ave TS17 . . . . .138 D2
Lord Byrons Wlk SR7 . . . . .19 B1
Lord Hyndley Terr DL13 .195 A4
Lord Lawson of Beamish Com
Sch DH3 . . . . .9 D3
Lord Nelson Cl TS25 . . . . .77 D1
Lord Neville Dr DL5 . . . . .95 F4
Lord St New Silksworth SR3 .18 B7
Redcar TS10 . . . . .107 D7
Seaham SR7 . . . . .29 D7
Lorimer Cl TS17 . . . . .138 B1
Lorimers Cl SR8 . . . . .49 B4
Lorn Wlk DL1 . . . . .133 D7
Lorne Ct TS18 . . . . .137 E8
Lorne St
Easington Lane DH5 . . . . . . .37 B8
Middlesbrough TS1 . . . . . . .214 B2
Lorne Terr DL14 . . . . .81 C8
Lorrain Gr TS20 . . . . .102 C1
Lorton Rd TS10 . . . . .107 C3
Lothian Cl Birtley DH3 . . . . .9 D1
Spennymoor DL16 . . . . .68 E7
Lothian Gr TS10 . . . . .107 A5
Lothian Rd TS4 . . . . .215 B1
Loud Terr DH9 . . . . .12 D4
Loud View Terr DH9 . . . . . .12 E3
Lough House Bank DL17 . .70 D4
Louisa St Darlington DL1 . .133 B1
Middlesbrough TS3 . . . . . . .215 C3
Louisa Terr
Bishop Auckland DL14 . . . . . .79 E3
Stanley DH9 . . . . .13 E6
Witton Gilbert DH7 . . . . .33 B8
Louise Terr DH3 . . . . .16 C3
Louvain Terr Crook DL15 . . .52 D3
Hetton-le-H DH5 . . . . .27 A5
Louvain Terr W DH5 . . . . . .27 A5
Lovaine St
Middlesbrough TS1 . . . . . . .214 B2
Pelton DH2 . . . . .15 C6
Lovaine Terr 8 DL17 . . . . .70 B5
Lovat Ave TS10 . . . . .107 A5
Lovat Gr TS25 . . . . .89 D8
Low Albert Terr DL15 . . . . .52 D7
Low Barn Nature Reserve*
DL14 . . . . .65 D3
Low Barn Visitor Ctr*
DL14 . . . . .65 E3
Low Bishopley Cotts
DL13 . . . . .188 A6
Low Bollihope Cvn Site
DL13 . . . . .187 F6
Low Bowes Cl DL14 . . . . . .78 B1
Low Carrs Pk DH1 . . . . . . .34 C7
Low Chare DH3 . . . . .16 D3
Low Church St DH9 . . . . . .12 F5
Low Church Wynd TS15 .156 B7
Low Cleveland St TS13 . . .127 A1
Low Dowfold DL15 . . . . . . .53 A5
Low Downs Rd DH5 . . . . . .27 A6
Low Dyke St TS29 . . . . .60 A4
Low Etherley DL14 . . . . . . .78 F6
Low Farm Cl TS8 . . . . . . .158 B8
Low Farm Dr TS10 . . . . . .107 B3
Low Flatts Rd DH3 . . . . . . .16 C6
Low Fold TS10 . . . . .107 B4
Low Gn Gainford DL2 . . . . .201 D3
Great Ayton TS9 . . . . .160 F2
High Shincliffe DH1 . . . . . . .44 F6
Mordon TS21 . . . . .84 B2
Newton Aycliffe DL5 . . . . . . .82 E2
Low Graham St DH7 . . . . . .23 C3
Low Grange Ave TS23 . . .103 A7
Low Grange Rd DL16 . . . . .56 A1
Low Greenfields DL14 . . . .79 B4
Low Hogg St TS29 . . . . . . .60 A4
Low La Barningham DL11 . .204 F5
High Leven TS8,TS15,TS17 .157 D6
Middlesbrough TS5 . . . . . . .139 D3
Newsham DL11 . . . . .205 D4
Stainton TS17 . . . . .138 F1
Thornaby-on-T TS17 . . . . . .139 A1
Witton-le-W DL14,DL15 . . . .65 D4
Low Lands DL13 . . . . .195 F4
Low Melbourne St DL14 . . .80 B5
Low Mill 2 DL12 . . . . .209 C5
Low Moor Cotts DH1 . . . . .24 D1
Low Moor Rd
Lanchester DH7 . . . . .31 E6
Langley Park DH7 . . . . .32 B6
Low Queen St DL14 . . . . . .66 A1
Low Rd Bowes DL12 . . . . . .203 D8
Coundon DL14 . . . . .68 E3
Gainford DL2 . . . . .201 C3
High Shincliffe DH1 . . . . . . .44 F6
Low Redgate Bank
DL13 . . . . .207 E7
Low Row SR8 . . . . .39 B3
Low Side DL12 . . . . .193 B2
Low Stanghow Rd
Lingdale TS12 . . . . .145 F4
Skelton TS12 . . . . .125 D2
Low Startforth Rd DL12 .209 B5
Low Station Rd DH4 . . . . . .25 E2
Low West Ave NE39 . . . . . . .1 D1
Low Willington DL15 . . . . .54 B2
Low Willington Ind Est
DL15 . . . . .54 C3
Low Yd DL15 . . . . .53 C3
Lowburn Farm Cvn Site
DL13 . . . . .179 C1
Lowcross Ave TS14 . . . . . .143 C2
Lowdale La TS24 . . . . .63 C4
Lowe St DL3 . . . . .132 F2
Lowe's Barn Bank DH1 . . .44 A7
Lowell Cl 3 TS23 . . . . . . .102 E8
Lower Bridge St DL14 . . . .67 B1
Lower East St TS2 . . . . . .215 A4
Lower Feversham St
TS2 . . . . .215 A4
Lower Gosford St TS2 . . .215 A4
Lowery La DH7,DH9 . . . . . .14 D1
Lowery Rd DL5 . . . . .96 C5
Lowes Ct DH1 . . . . .210 A1
Lowes Fall DH1 . . . . .210 A1
Lowes Rise DH1 . . . . .210 A1
Lowes Wynd DH1 . . . . . . .210 A1
Loweswater Ave
Chester le Street DH2 . . . . . .16 B1
Easington Lane DH5 . . . . . . .37 C8
Loweswater Cres TS18 . .212 A3
Loweswater Gr
Bishop Auckland DL14 . . . . .79 B1
Redcar TS10 . . . . .107 C5
Lowfield Ave TS3 . . . . . . .120 E3
Lowfields DL5 . . . . .95 F4
Lowfields Ave TS17 . . . . .138 B2
Lowfields Gn TS17 . . . . . .138 B1
Lowfields Wlk TS17 . . . . .138 B1
Lowhills Rd SR8 . . . . .49 B8
Lowick Cl Birtley DH3 . . . . . .9 D1
Stockton-on-T TS19 . . . . . . .117 B4
Lowland Cl SR3 . . . . .18 A5
Lowland Rd DH7 . . . . .43 B4
Lowmead Wlk TS3 . . . . . .140 E7
Lowmoor Rd DL1 . . . . . . .152 D7
Lowood Ave TS7 . . . . .140 C3
Lowson St
Darlington DL3 . . . . .133 A7
Stillington TS21 . . . . .99 F4
Lowther Ave DH2 . . . . .16 B2
Lowther Cl
Billingham TS22 . . . . .102 A6
Peterlee SR8 . . . . .49 D7
Lowther Ct SR8 . . . . .49 B2
Lowther Dr DL5 . . . . .82 E1
Lowther Rd DL14 . . . . .80 A4
Lowthian Rd TS24,TS26 . . .77 B6
Loxley Rd TS3 . . . . .121 A2
Loy La TS13 . . . . .127 E1
Loyalty Cl TS25 . . . . .77 B2
Loyalty Ct TS25 . . . . .77 B2
Loyalty Rd TS25 . . . . .77 B2
Lucan St TS24 . . . . .77 B6
Luccombe Cl TS17 . . . . . .157 B6
Luce Sands TS5 . . . . .139 B3
Lucerne Ct TS7 . . . . .140 C4
Lucerne Dr TS14 . . . . .143 B3
Lucerne Rd TS10 . . . . .107 C5
Lucia La TS14 . . . . .143 C3
Lucknow St DL1 . . . . .133 B4
Lucombe Cl DH4 . . . . .17 F5
Lucy St 4 DH3 . . . . .16 C4
Ludford Ave 11 TS3 . . . . . .140 D8
Ludham Gr TS19 . . . . .117 C5
Ludlow Cres TS10 . . . . . . .107 E4
Ludlow Rd TS23 . . . . .102 D5
Ludworth Prim Sch DH6 . .47 B7
Luff Way TS10 . . . . .107 E3
Luke Ave DH6 . . . . .46 E1
Luke Cres SR7 . . . . .28 B3
Luke St TS29 . . . . .59 F5
Luke Terr DH6 . . . . .47 E2
Lulsgate TS17 . . . . .138 E5
Lulworth Cl TS10 . . . . .107 E2
Lulworth Gr TS24 . . . . .63 D4
Lumley Cl
Chester le Street DH2 . . . . . .16 B3
Newton Aycliffe DL5 . . . . . . .96 D6
Spennymoor DL16 . . . . .56 A2
Lumley Cres DL17 . . . . .70 B5
Lumley Dr
1 Consett DH8 . . . . .177 E4
Peterlee SR8 . . . . .49 D3
Lumley Gdns NE16 . . . . .5 E5
Lumley Gr DL14 . . . . .80 A6
Lumley Jun Sch DH3 . . . . .25 B7
Lumley Medway Inf Sch
DH3 .25 A8
Lumley New Rd DH3,DH4 . .17 C1
Lumley Rd
Billingham TS23 . . . . .102 E5
Durham DH1 . . . . .34 C7
Redcar TS10 . . . . .107 D6
Lumley Sq TS24 . . . . .77 F8
Lumley St TS13 . . . . .127 A1
Lumley Terr
Chester le Street DH3 . . . . . .16 D2
Coxhoe DH6 . . . . .57 F3
1 Ryhope SR2 . . . . .18 F6
Lumley Thicks DH4 . . . . . . .17 C1
Lumpsey Cl TS12 . . . . . . .126 C4
Lumsden Sq SR7 . . . . .28 B3
Lumsden Terr DH9 . . . . . . .12 E5
Lund Ave DH1 . . . . .34 B6
Lund Ct DH1 . . . . .34 B6
Lund's La DH8 . . . . .12 A1
Lundale Dr DH3 . . . . .25 B6
Lundy Ct TS17 . . . . .157 B8
Lundy Wlk TS14 . . . . .143 D3
Lune Rd Eaglescliffe TS16 .156 B7
Stockton-on-T TS20 . . . . . . .118 A7
Lune St TS12 . . . . .125 C7
Lunebeck Wlk TS17 . . . . .138 E3
Lunedale Ave TS5 . . . . . . .139 E7
Lunedale Rd
Billingham TS23 . . . . .102 D3
Darlington DL3 . . . . .132 B3
Lunefield Ho TS5 . . . . . . .119 D1
Lunesdale St DH5 . . . . .27 A2
Lupin Cl DL14 . . . . .79 F7
Lusby Cres DL14 . . . . .79 F4
Lustrum Ave TS18 . . . . . . .118 F5
Lustrum Ind Est TS18 . . .118 F5
Lutterington La DL14 . . . . .93 D6
Lutton Cres TS22 . . . . . . .102 A5
Luttrell Ho TS3 . . . . .120 D1
Luttryngton Ct DL5 . . . . . . .96 A8
Luxmoore Ave DL15 . . . . . .53 F3
Lych Gate DL2 . . . . .152 D1
Lycium Cl TS7 . . . . .140 C5
Lydbrook Rd TS5 . . . . . . .119 B2
Lydd Gdns TS17 . . . . .138 E5
Lydford Way DH3 . . . . .9 D3
Lydgate Ave DL13 . . . . . . .207 D6
Lydgate Cres DL13 . . . . . .207 D5
Lydgate La DL13 . . . . .207 D6
Lydgate Sq DL13 . . . . .207 E5
Lydia St DL15 . . . . .53 F3
Lydia Terr DL14 . . . . .67 B8
Lyn Cl TS17 . . . . .157 B6
Lyncroft DL3 . . . . .132 C1
Lyndale TS14 . . . . .143 A2
Lynden Rd SR2 . . . . .18 F8
Lyndhurst Ave DH3 . . . . . . .16 C6
Lyndhurst Cl NE21 . . . . .2 A8
Lyndhurst Dr DH1 . . . . . . .210 A2
Lyndhurst Rd Chilton DL17 .82 F7
Stanley DH9 . . . . .13 D6
Lyndon Way TS18 . . . . . . .117 A3
Lyne Cl DH2 . . . . .15 F8
Lyne Rd DL16 . . . . .68 D6
Lyne's Dr DH7 . . . . .43 D5
Lyngrove SR2 . . . . .18 F8
Lynmouth Cl TS8 . . . . . . .139 C2
Lynmouth Rd TS20 . . . . . .101 E1
Lynmouth Wlk TS26 . . . . . .76 E8
Lynn Cres DH6 . . . . .46 F1
Lynn Park Cres DH6 . . . . . .57 F3
Lynn St
13 Chester le Street DH3 . . .16 C2
Hartlepool TS24 . . . . .77 C6
Lynn St S TS24 . . . . .77 D5
Lynn Terr DH6 . . . . .48 A4
Lynndale DL13 . . . . .207 E5
Lynne Cl DL3 . . . . .133 A7
Lynnfield Prim Sch TS26 .77 A6
Lynnfield Rd 6 TS26 . . . . .77 B7
Lynthorpe SR2 . . . . .18 F8
Lynton Ct TS26 . . . . .76 E8
Lynton Gdns DL1 . . . . . . .133 D1
Lynwood Ave TS5 . . . . . . .139 E7
Lyon Wlk DL5 . . . . .96 D6
Lyonette Rd DL1 . . . . .133 D6
Lyons Ave DH5 . . . . .27 B2
Lyons Cotts DH5 . . . . .27 B2
Lyons La DH5 . . . . .27 C1
Lyons The DH5 . . . . .27 B2
Lysander Ct 5 TS11 . . . . .108 B1
Lyster Cl SR7 . . . . .18 E1
Lytham Cl DH8 . . . . .10 E5
Lytham Rd DL1 . . . . .133 B7
Lythe Pl TS4 . . . . .140 A7
Lythe Wlk 8 TS6 . . . . .121 F3
Lyttleton Dr TS18 . . . . . . .117 C1
Lytton St TS4 . . . . .215 C2

M

Maben Ave DL14 . . . . .79 D3
Macaulay Rd TS25 . . . . . . .76 E2
MacBean St TS3 . . . . .120 C4
Macbeth Wlk SR8 . . . . .50 B6
Macdonald Ind Est DL15 . .52 E2
Mackays Ct 15 DH8 . . . . . . .10 F2
Mackays Mews DH9 . . . . . . .13 E7
Mackenzie Pl DL5 . . . . .96 C8
Mackie Dr TS14 . . . . .143 F5
Mackintosh Ct DH1 . . . . . .211 C3
Macklin Ave TS23 . . . . . . .103 B5
Macmillan Coll TS5 . . . . .119 B3
Macmillan Rd DL5 . . . . .96 C7
Macnay St 4 TS12 . . . . . . .125 C7
Macrae Rd TS25 . . . . .89 C7
Maddison St 5 DL4 . . . . . . .94 F8
Madison Sq 5 TS19 . . . . . .117 B4
Madrona Cl DH4 . . . . .17 F5
Mafeking Pl DL4 . . . . .81 A1
Mafeking Terr DH7 . . . . . . .23 B2

Magdalen St TS3 215 C2
Magdalene Ave DH1 35 D4
Magdalene Ct DH1 211 B3
Magdalene Dr TS27 62 F3
Magdalene Hts DH1 211 B3
Magdalene Pl
7 Ferryhill DL17 70 B5
Woodland DL13 194 F5
Magdalene St DH1 211 B3
Magister Rd TS17 138 C5
Maglona St SR7 29 D6
Magnet St 5 DL4 95 A8
Magnolia Cl DL5 96 A3
Magnolia Ct 13 TS10 107 E1
Magnolia Gr NE16 6 B6
Magnolia Way DL4 81 B1
Mahogany Row DH9 7 D1
Maiden Castle* DH1 211 B1
Maiden Law DH4 26 A7
Maidenhair DH4 17 F5
Maidstone Dr TS7 140 E4
Main Rd Eldon DL14 81 A4
Gainford DL2 201 D3
Redworth DL5 95 C3
Main St
Bishop Auckland DL14 80 D5
Consett DH8 11 B2
Ferryhill DL17 69 F6
Shildon DL4 80 F1
Witton Park DL14 79 B8
Mains Ct DH1 34 A5
Mains Park Rd DH3 16 D3
Mainsforth Dr
Billingham TS23 102 F8
Middlesbrough TS5 139 D4
Mainsforth Flats TS24 77 D5
Mainsforth Ind Est DL17 70 D4
Mainsforth Rd DL17 70 D4
Mainsforth Rise DL17 70 C3
Mainsforth Terr TS24 77 D5
Mainside TS21 116 B7
Major Cooper Ct TS25 90 E8
Major St Darlington DL3 132 E4
Stockton-on-T TS18 213 B4
Majuba Rd TS10 107 A7
Malcolm Ave DH6 58 D7
Malcolm Dr TS19 117 A5
Malcolm Gr Redcar TS10 107 E5
Thornaby-on-T TS17 138 D6
Malcolm St 5 SR7 29 D6
Malcom Rd TS25 89 D7
Malden Rd 3 TS20 118 B8
Maldon Rd TS5 119 B2
Malham Cres DL5 96 C7
Malham Gill TS10 107 B4
Malham Gr TS17 138 C1
Malim Rd DL1 133 E1
Malin Gr TS10 107 C1
Maling Gn DL5 96 E7
Mallaig View 10 TS19 117 B4
Mallard Cl
Guisborough TS14 143 A3
Washington NE38 9 F4
Mallard Ct TS10 106 F4
Mallard La TS20 102 A1
Mallard Rd DL1 133 E1
Mallard Way DH4 26 B7
Mallards The DL4 94 F8
Malleable Way TS18 118 D4
Malling Rd TS20 118 B6
Malling Wlk 3 TS3 120 D2
Mallory Cl TS1 214 B3
Mallory Ct DL1 133 E4
Mallory Rd TS20 118 A8
Mallowdale TS7 140 F2
Malltraeth Sands TS5 139 A4
Malmo Ct TS10 106 F1
Malone Gdns DH3 9 D6
Malt Cres SR8 49 F7
Maltby 9 TS4 120 A1
Maltby Cl DL14 80 E6
Maltby Ct TS14 143 D5
Maltby Pl TS17 138 C7
Maltby Rd TS8 158 A8
Maltby St TS3 120 C4
Maltings The
Durham DH1 210 C2
7 Hartlepool TS25 77 B4
New Silksworth SR3 18 C7
Wingate TS28 48 E1
Maltkiln La DL5 96 E2
Malton Cl TS17 138 D7
Malton Dr TS19 117 A5
Malton Terr TS21 85 B6
Malvern DL17 83 A8
Malvern Ave
Chester le Street DH2 16 B2
Redcar TS10 107 A4
4 Skelton TS12 125 C3
Malvern Cl
Hurworth-on-T DL2 152 D1
Peterlee SR8 49 B5
Malvern Cres
Darlington DL3 131 F5
Seaham SR7 29 A7
Wingate TS29 60 A5
Malvern Dr TS5 139 D4
Malvern Rd
Billingham TS23 102 D4
Stockton-on-T TS18 212 B2
Malvern Terr DH9 14 A5
Malvern Villas DH1 211 C3
Malvern Way DL5 95 F7
Malvern Wlk DL14 81 C8
Mandale Ind Est TS17 213 C1
Mandale Mill Prim Sch
TS17 138 C7
Mandale Rd
Middlesbrough TS5 139 B7
Thornaby-on-T TS17 213 C1
Mandale Ret Pk TS18 118 D4
Mandela Cl DH9 13 D5
Manfield Ave TS5 119 A1
Manfield Ho 6 DL1 152 C8
Manfield St TS18 212 C2
Manisty Terr SR8 39 D4
Manitoba Gdns TS4 215 B1
Manless Terr TS12 125 B1
Mann Cres SR7 28 D4
Manners St TS24 77 F8
Manning Cl TS17 138 D5
Manning Way 6 TS17 138 D5
Mannion Ct TS6 121 B6
Manor Cl Consett DH8 10 C1
Elwick TS27 75 D5
Low Worsall TS15 171 C8
Trimdon TS29 72 D8
Wolviston TS22 102 C7
Manor Cl The DH1 45 A6
Manor College of Tech
TS25 89 E7
Manor Cotts TS21 100 E3
Manor Ct Evenwood DL14 92 D6
Ferryhill DL17 70 A6
Heighington DL5 95 E1
Wolviston TS22 102 C7
Manor Dr
Annfield Plain DH9 12 F5
Hilton TS15 157 E3
Stillington TS21 99 F3
Manor Farm Way TS8 140 A2
Manor Field TS27 75 E3
Manor Garth
Kirklevington TS15 172 D8
Seamer TS9 159 A1
Manor Gate TS21 136 A5
Manor Gn TS6 121 D2
Manor Gr DL13 195 E3
Manor Grange DH7 21 A3
Manor Hall Cl SR7 28 E8
Manor House Est
Hutton Henry TS27 61 C5
Hutton Henry TS27 61 D6
**Manor Park Cvn & Camping
Pk** DH8 177 C1
Manor Pl TS19 117 B4
Manor Rd
Bishop Auckland DL14 79 D2
Darlington DL3 151 E8
Hartlepool TS26 76 D6
Hurworth-on-T DL2 152 A1
Ingleton DL2 201 D7
Medomsley DH8 4 C1
Stanley DH9 13 F7
Willington DL15 54 B3
Willington DL15 54 A3
Manor St Evenwood DL14 92 D6
Middlesbrough TS1 214 B2
Manor Terr NE21 2 C7
Manor View
3 Ferryhill DL17 70 A6
High Pittington DH6 36 B4
Manor Way
Billingham TS23 103 B3
Peterlee SR8 49 E5
Manor Wlk TS21 99 F3
Manor Wood TS8 139 F3
Manorfields DL2 152 D1
Manse St DH8 10 E4
Mansell Cres SR8 49 E7
Mansepool Cl TS24 64 B2
Mansfield Ave TS17 138 D8
Mansfield Rd TS6 121 E1
Mansley Ct DL3 132 E4
Manston Ct DL2 153 F8
Manton Ave TS5 139 B8
Maple Ave Durham DH1 35 A2
Middlesbrough TS4 139 F8
New Silksworth SR3 18 B8
Shildon DL4 81 B1
Thornaby-on-T TS17 138 C6
Maple Cl DL15 53 E2
Maple Cres Crook DL15 52 D4
Seaham SR7 29 C4
Maple Ct Brandon DH7 42 F3
High Etherley DL14 78 E5
Stockton-on-T TS19 117 C5
Maple Gdns Consett DH8 10 C4
Stanley DH9 13 E4
Maple Gr Brotton TS12 126 A4
Cornforth DL17 57 E1
Sedgefield TS21 85 B7
Stanley DH9 13 D4
Maple Pk DH7 33 B1
Maple Rd Darlington DL1 133 B8
Stockton-on-T TS19 117 F5
Maple Sq TS10 107 E6
Maple St 18 Consett DH8 10 F3
Middlesbrough TS1 215 A2
Stanley DH9 13 D4
Maple Terr
Annfield Plain DH9 12 E5
Burnopfield NE16 5 F6
Maple Way DL5 96 D2
Mapleton Cl TS10 107 C1
Mapleton Cres TS10 107 C1
Mapleton Dr
Hemlington TS8 139 D2
Stockton-on-T TS20 101 F1
Mapleton Rd
1 Hartlepool TS24 77 B7
Hartlepool TS24 77 B8
Maplewood DH2 16 B4
Maplewood Ct DH7 32 B6
Maplewood Dr DH6 37 F3
Maplewood St DH4 17 E1
Maplin View 4 TS19 117 B4
Marazion Dr DL3 132 F8
Marburn Pl 1 DL3 132 F3
Marchlyn Cres TS17 156 E8
Marcia Ave DH6 48 C7
Mardale TS8 139 D1
Mardale Ave TS25 90 A7
Mardale St DH5 27 A2
Mardale Wlk TS10 107 C2
Margaret Ct DH6 45 D1
Margaret St Ludworth DH6 47 C7
Middlesbrough TS3 215 C2
7 Seaham SR7 29 D6
Margaret Terr
Eldon Lane DL14 80 E4
Rowlands Gill NE39 1 C1
Tanfield Lea DH9 6 C1
Wingate TS29 60 A5
Margate St SR3 18 A8
Margery La DH1 210 B2
Margill Cl TS7 140 E4
Margrove Heritage Ctr*
TS14 145 A3
Margrove Pk TS12 145 B4
Margrove Way TS12 126 A5
Margrove Wlk 12 TS3 140 D8
Marham Cl TS3 140 F8
Maria Dr TS19 117 A4
Maria St
Middlesbrough TS3 120 C4
New Silksworth SR3 18 A7
10 Seaham SR7 29 D7
Marigold Cres DH4 17 E3
Marigold Ct DL1 133 C2
Marigold Gr TS19 117 C5
Marina Ave TS10 107 A7
Marina Rd DL3 133 A8
Marina Terr 8 SR2 18 F6
Marina Way TS24 77 C7
Marine Cres
Blackhall Rocks TS27 50 E2
Hartlepool TS24 77 F8
Marine Ct 1 TS12 125 C8
Marine Dr Hartlepool TS24 64 E2
Sunderland SR2 19 A8
Marine Par TS12 125 C8
Marine Terr TS13 127 A5
Mariners Ct TS11 108 C2
Mariners Point TS24 77 D7
Marion Ave
Eaglescliffe TS16 156 B8
Middlesbrough TS5 139 C8
Maritime Ave TS24 77 C6
Maritime Cl
Hartlepool TS24 77 D6
Stockton-on-T TS18 213 B4
Maritime Cres SR8 39 F3
Maritime Rd TS18 213 B4
Mariville E SR2 19 A5
Mariville W SR2 19 A5
Mark Ave TS20 102 A2
Mark Rise DH5 27 A5
Mark's La DH4 25 F4
Markby Gn TS3 141 A8
Market Cres TS28 60 E6
Market Pl
Barnard Castle DL12 209 C5
Bishop Auckland DL14 67 C1
12 Darlington DL1 132 F1
Durham DH1 210 C3
Esh Winning DH7 41 E8
Guisborough TS14 143 E5
Houghton-le-S DH5 26 F8
Middlesbrough TS2 119 F7
Middlesbrough, North Ormesby
TS3 215 C2
Middleton-In-T DL12 208 B6
Shildon DL4 81 A2
St John's Chapel DL13 185 E8
Stanhope DL13 206 D3
Stockton-on-T TS18 213 A3
Wolsingham DL13 207 D5
Market Place Ind Est
DH5 26 F8
Market St Consett DH8 10 D4
Ferryhill DL17 69 F6
Hetton-le-H DH5 27 B4
6 South Bank TS6 121 A6
Markham Pl DL5 96 F7
Markham Sq 2 TS19 117 B4
Markington Dr SR2 18 F5
Markle Gr DH5 26 D5
Marland Bldgs TS4 215 B1
Marlborough 1 SR7 29 D7
Marlborough Ave TS11 108 C2
Marlborough Cl TS23 102 D1
Marlborough Ct DH5 26 E6
Marlborough Dr DL1 151 E8
Marlborough Gdns TS2 214 C4
Marlborough Rd
Marton TS7 140 C3
Skelton TS12 125 C3
Stockton-on-T TS18 212 C1
Marlborough St TS25 77 A3
Marlbrough Cres 8 SR8 50 B6
Marlene Ave DH6 45 D2
Marley Cl TS19 117 C4
Marley Hill Com Prim Sch
NE16 7 A8
Marley Hill Sta* NE16 7 B7
Marley Rd DL5 96 D6
Marley Wlk TS27 63 D3
Marley's Cotts DH7 31 B4
Marlow Way NE16 2 F5
Marlowe Pl DH5 26 F7
Marlowe Rd TS25 76 E2
Marlsford Gr TS5 139 B7
Marmaduke Pl TS20 102 A1
Marmaduke St DL16 56 A1
Marmion Cl TS25 77 C2
Marquand Rd TS6 121 B5
Marquis Gr TS20 101 F1
Marquis St TS24 77 F8
Marrick Ave DL3 131 F5
Marrick Cl 2 DL5 96 B7
Marrick Rd
Middlesbrough TS3 140 D8
Stockton-on-T TS18 137 B8
Mars La TS13 167 A7
Marsden Cl
Houghton-le-S DH4 26 C8
Ingleby Barwick TS17 157 C8
Middlesbrough TS4 140 A8
Marsden Wlk DL3 132 F7
Marsh House Ave TS23 102 E6
Marsh House La TS25 89 F2
Marsh La TS23 103 D6
Marsh Rd
Middlesbrough TS1 214 B3
Middlesbrough TS1 214 C4
Middlesbrough,Cargo Fleet
TS3 120 C5
Marsh St TS1 214 B3
Marshall Ave TS3 120 E3
Marshall Cl
Hartlepool TS24 63 E3
Saltburn-by-t-S TS12 125 B7
Marshall Ct TS3 120 F4
Marshall Dr TS12 126 A5
Marshall Gr TS18 212 B4
Marshall Rd DL5 96 C7
Marshall St
Barnard Castle DL12 209 C6
Darlington DL3 132 F3
Marshall Terr
Durham DH1 35 A2
Durham DH1 35 B3
Marske Gr DL3 132 F5
Marske La Skelton TS12 125 A3
Stockton-on-T TS19 117 A6
Marske Mill La TS12 125 C6
Marske Par TS19 117 A5
Marske Rd
Saltburn-by-t-S TS12 125 A7
Thornaby-on-T TS17 138 D7
Marske St TS25 77 B4
Marske Sta TS11 124 C8
Marston Gdns TS24 77 A8
Marston Moor Rd DL1 152 E8
Marston Rd Brotton TS12 126 C3
Stockton-on-T TS18 118 E4
Marston Wlk NE16 2 F5
Martha St DH9 6 B2
Martham Cl TS19 117 C5
Martin Ct NE38 9 F2
Martin Gr TS25 76 F3
Martin St DL13 206 D3
Martindale TS5 139 B4
Martindale Cl TS27 75 D6
Martindale Gr TS16 156 C7
Martindale Pk DH5 26 E8
Martindale Pl TS6 121 E4
Martindale Rd
Darlington DL1 133 C5
Eston TS6 121 E4
Martindale Way TS10 107 C2
Martindale Wlk TS28 48 E1
Martinet Ct TS17 138 C5
Martinet Rd TS17 138 C5
Martinhoe Cl TS17 157 B6
Marton Ave TS4 140 D6
Marton Burn Rd TS4 120 A1
Marton Cres TS6 121 F1
Marton Dale Ct TS7 140 E3
Marton Dr TS22 102 B5
Marton Gill TS12 125 A7
Marton Gr TS12 126 A5
Marton Grove Prim Sch
TS4 120 A2
Marton Grove Rd TS4 120 A2
Marton Manor Prim Sch
TS7 140 C4
Marton Moor Rd TS7 141 B2
Marton Rd TS4 120 A2
Marton St TS24 77 A7
Marton Sta TS4 140 E6
Martonside Way TS4 140 B8
Marway Rd TS12 126 A5
Marwood CE Inf Sch
TS9 160 F2
Marwood Cres DL3 132 D5
Marwood Dr
Barnard Castle DL12 209 C7
Brotton TS12 126 A5
Great Ayton TS9 160 F1
Marwood Gr SR8 49 C3
Marwood Sq 7 TS19 117 B4
Marwood Terr DL12 198 F6
Marwood View DL12 198 F6
Marx Cres DH9 13 F5
Marx Terr NE17 4 C8
Mary Ave DH3 9 B6
Mary Cres DH6 58 E6
Mary Ct DL3 132 B4
Mary Jaques Ct TS4 120 A2
Mary Rose Cl TS25 77 D1
Mary St Annfield Plain DH9 13 A4
Hartlepool TS26 77 A6
New Silksworth SR3 18 A8
Seaham SR7 29 E7
Stanley DH9 13 E6
Stockton-on-T TS18 212 C2
Mary Terr Bowburn DH6 45 C1
Mary Terr *continued*
Eldon Lane DL14 80 E4
Marykirk Rd TS17 138 D3
Maryport Cl TS18 213 C4
Masefield Cl DH9 14 B7
Masefield Cres DL15 53 F1
Masefield Rd TS25 76 D3
Masefields DH2 15 E3
Masham Gr TS19 117 A2
Masham Moor Way DL1 152 D7
Maslin Gr SR8 49 A3
Mason Cres SR8 49 F6
Mason St Consett DH8 10 F2
2 Eston TS6 121 D1
Mason Wlk 3 TS24 77 B7
Massey Rd TS17 213 C2
Master Rd TS17 138 D5
Masterman Pl DL12 208 B5
Masterton Dr 3 TS18 117 C1
Mastiles Cl TS17 157 A6
Matfen Ave TS7 141 A3
Matfen Ct
Chester le Street DH2 16 A3
Sedgefield TS21 85 A7
Matford Ave TS3 120 E3
Matlock Ave TS7 140 D2
Matlock Gdns TS22 102 C6
Matterdale Rd SR8 49 F6
Matthew Cl DL5 96 F8
Matthews Cres DH6 38 B6
Matthews Rd SR7 28 E1
Mattison Ave TS5 119 B2
Maud Terr Evenwood DL14 92 C8
Tanfield DH9 6 D3
Maude St DL3 132 F2
Maude Terr DL14 79 E3
Maudlin St DH5 27 B6
Maudville 7 DH8 177 A3
Maughan Cl DL17 57 D1
Maughan St 7 DL4 80 F1
Maughan Terr TS21 72 C4
Maureen Ave TS27 50 E2
Maureen Terr
Durham DH1 35 C6
Seaham SR7 29 C7
Mavin St DH1 211 A1
Maxton Rd TS6 121 A5
Maxwell Cl DL1 152 D8
Maxwell Court Flatlets
TS25 89 D7
Maxwell Pl TS10 106 E4
Maxwell Rd
Hartlepool TS25 89 D7
Middlesbrough TS3 120 E4
May Ave NE21 2 C7
May Cres TS29 60 B5
May Lea DH7 23 B1
May St Birtley DH3 9 C4
Bishop Auckland DL14 80 B8
Durham DH1 210 B2
Hartlepool TS24 77 B8
May Terr DH7 32 C6
Mayberry Gr TS5 139 E8
Maybray King Wlk 5
TS20 118 B8
Mayes Wlk TS15 156 B3
Mayfair Ave
Middlesbrough TS4 120 A2
Normanby TS6 141 C7
Mayfair Rd DL1 133 A8
Mayfair St TS26 77 A6
Mayfield
Barnard Castle DL12 209 C6
Darlington DL3 132 E1
Mayfield Cl
Eaglescliffe TS16 137 A1
Hartlepool TS26 76 E6
Mayfield Cres TS16 137 A1
Mayfield Rd TS7 141 A4
Mayfield Terr 15 DL13 195 E3
Mayfield Wlk DL14 79 D2
Mayflower Cl TS24 77 D6
Maygate TS6 122 A2
Maylands DL13 189 D8
Maynard St TS13 126 F3
Maynard's Row DH1 211 C3
Maynes Way DH9 14 B7
Mayorswell Cl DH1 211 A3
Mayorswell Field DH1 211 B3
Mayorswell St DH1 211 A3
Maythorne Dr DH6 38 B6
Maze La TS17 118 E2
Mazine Terr DH6 37 E2
McAteer Ct DH6 37 E1
Mcauley Ct TS3 120 C2
McClean Ave TS10 106 F5
MCclean Rd TS12 126 C4
McCreton St TS3 120 D4
McCullagh Gdns DL14 80 C6
McCutcheon St 7 SR7 18 E1
McDonald Pl TS24 64 G8
McGuinness Ave SR8 39 E1
McIntyre Terr DL14 80 B6
McMillan Dr DL15 52 D3
McMullen Rd DL1 133 E2
McNally Pl DH1 211 C3
McNay St DL3 132 F4
Mead Cres TS17 138 E7
Mead The DL1 133 C1
Meadfoot Dr TS5 139 C4
Meadhope St DL13 207 D5
Meadow Ave TS27 50 E2
Meadow Cl Coxhoe DH6 57 F4
Guisborough TS14 143 E4
Houghton-le-S DH5 26 F7
Middleton-In-T DL12 208 C5
Ormesby TS7 141 A6
Meadow Croft DL13 195 E3

Meadow Dale Ct TS12 ...145 E5
Meadow Dr
Chester le Street DH2 ...15 F2
Hartlepool TS26 ...76 D5
Ormesby TS7 ...141 B6
Meadow End TS16 ...137 B2
Meadow Gn DL16 ...56 C3
Meadow Grange DH4 ...17 E2
Meadow Hill TS21 ...72 A1
Meadow Ho 4 SR3 ...18 A5
Meadow Rd
Marske-by-t-S TS11 ...124 D8
Stockton-on-T TS19 ...117 C3
Trimdon TS29 ...72 D7
Meadow Rise Consett DH8 .11 A3
Darlington DL3 ...132 B2
Meadow St DH5 ...26 C3
Meadow The TS25 ...77 A2
Meadow View
Bishop Auckland DL14 ...79 C2
Consett DH8 ...177 E4
Coxhoe DH6 ...57 F3
Dipton DH9 ...5 E1
Eggleston DL12 ...193 E2
Sacriston DH7 ...23 C3
Stanhope DL13 ...206 D2
Meadow View Rd TS5 ...119 B2
Meadow Way DH7 ...20 E3
Meadow Wlk TS21 ...116 C8
Meadowbank DH7 ...32 B6
Meadowbank Rd TS7 ...141 B6
Meadowcroft Rd TS6 ...121 B1
Meadowdale DL17 ...82 F7
Meadowdale Cl TS2 ...103 E1
Meadowfield DH8 ...10 D3
Meadowfield Ave
Middlesbrough TS4 ...139 F8
Spennymoor DL16 ...56 D2
Meadowfield Dr TS16 ...137 B2
Meadowfield Ind Est
DH7 ...43 D3
Meadowfield Rd DL3 ...132 B5
Meadowfield Way
Newton Aycliffe DL5 ...96 A8
Tanfield Lea DH9 ...13 C8
Meadowgate TS6 ...122 A2
Meadowgate Dr TS26 ...76 E7
Meadowings The TS15 ...156 B4
Meadowlands Cl TS13 ...148 A8
Meadows Edge DL13 ...181 C7
Meadows La DH4,DH5 ...26 B3
Meadows The
Bournmoor DH4 ...17 D3
Burnopfield NE16 ...6 A4
Coulby Newham TS8 ...140 C1
Middleton St George DL2 ..153 F7
Middridge DL5 ...81 E1
Redcar TS10 ...107 B4
Sedgefield TS21 ...85 B6
West Rainton DH4 ...26 A3
Meadowsweet Cl DH8 ...11 A2
Meadway TS10 ...107 B2
Measham Cl TS20 ...117 F8
Meath St TS1 ...214 A1
Meath Way TS14 ...143 D3
Meatlesburn Cl DL5 ...95 F4
Medbourne Cl 4 TS6 ...121 F1
Medbourne Gdns TS5 ...139 D4
Medina Cl TS19 ...117 B4
Medina Gdns TS5 ...139 E4
Medlar Cl DH4 ...17 F6
Medomsley Cross Rds
DH8 ...11 A8
Medomsley Rd DH8 ...10 F4
Medway DH3 ...25 A7
Medway Cl Peterlee SR8 ...49 C4
Skelton TS12 ...125 C4
Medway Gdns DH9 ...13 E4
Medway Ho TS23 ...102 D1
Medwin Cl TS12 ...126 A5
Medwyn Cl DH4 ...17 E3
Meet The DL5 ...95 F8
Meeting Ho The 6
DL12 ...209 C5
Megarth Rd TS5 ...119 D2
Meggitts Ave TS10 ...106 E3
Melbeck Dr DH2 ...8 E2
Melbourne Cl TS7 ...140 E3
Melbourne Pl DL13 ...207 D5
Melbourne St TS18 ...213 A3
Melbourne Terr DH7 ...23 B5
Melbreak Gr TS5 ...139 B6
Melbury St SR7 ...29 E5
Meldon Ave DH6 ...36 A1
Meldon Cl DL1 ...133 D5
Meldon Way
Annfield Plain DH9 ...13 B4
Blaydon NE21 ...1 F8
High Shincliffe DH1 ...45 B5
Meldrum Sq 9 TS19 ...117 B4
Meldyke La TS8 ...139 C1
Meldyke Pl TS8 ...139 C1
Melford Gr TS17 ...157 B8
Melgrove Way TS21 ...85 A5
Melksham Sq 6 TS19 ...117 B4
Mellanby Cres DL5 ...96 F7
Mellanby La TS25 ...89 E4
Melland Ct DL1 ...133 A1
Melland St DL1 ...133 A1
Mellbutts Bank DL13 ...188 A7
Mellor Ct DL3 ...133 A5
Mellor St TS19 ...212 C4
Melrose Ave
Billingham TS23 ...102 E5
Darlington DL3 ...133 A7
Middlesbrough TS5 ...139 C8
Murton SR7 ...28 A3
Melrose Cres
Guisborough TS14 ...144 A4
Seaham SR7 ...28 F8
Melrose Ct DH8 ...10 C4
Melrose Dr
Bishop Auckland DL14 ...79 D3
Stockton-on-T TS18 ...137 E8
Melrose St
Hartlepool TS25 ...77 A3
Middlesbrough TS1 ...215 A3
Melsanby Ct TS23 ...103 A7
Melsonby Ave TS3 ...140 E8
Melsonby Cres DL1 ...152 C8
Melsonby Gr TS18 ...117 A1
Melton Rd TS19 ...117 B4
Melton Wlk TS8 ...139 D2
Melville St
Chester le Street DH3 ...16 C2
2 Darlington DL1 ...132 F3
Melville Wlk TS20 ...118 C5
Memorial Ave SR8 ...39 E4
Memorial Cotts DL13 ...195 C4
Memorial Dr TS7 ...140 D4
Memorial Homes DH9 ...13 D8
Menceforth Cotts DH2 ...16 B4
Mendip Ave
Chester le Street DH2 ...16 C2
5 Skelton TS12 ...125 C3
Mendip Cl SR8 ...49 B6
Mendip Dr TS10 ...107 A3
Mendip Gn DL17 ...82 F8
Mendip Gr DL1 ...133 C5
Mendip Rd TS23 ...102 D4
Mendip Terr DH9 ...14 A5
Mendip Wlk DL14 ...81 C8
Menom Rd DL5 ...96 D2
Menville Cl DL5 ...95 F4
Mercantile Rd DH4 ...26 C7
Merchant Ho TS24 ...77 D6
Mercia Ct DL3 ...132 F2
Mercia Ret Pk DH1 ...34 C8
Mere Dr DH1 ...34 B7
Meredith Ave TS6 ...141 C8
Mereston Cl TS26 ...76 C7
Merganser Rd TS26 ...63 D1
Merion Dr TS11 ...123 F6
Merioneth Cl TS17 ...156 E8
Merlay Cl TS15 ...156 A3
Merlin Cl
Guisborough TS14 ...143 A4
Seaham SR7 ...29 C8
Merlin Ct DH7 ...41 C8
Merlin Dr DH3 ...16 D7
Merlin Rd
Middlesbrough TS3 ...120 E4
Stockton-on-T TS19 ...117 B4
Merlin Way TS26 ...63 D1
Merriman Gn TS24 ...63 D3
Merring Cl TS18 ...117 A2
Merrington Ave TS5 ...139 B4
Merrington Cl DL16 ...69 A3
Merrington Hts DL16 ...68 F3
Merrington Lane Ind Est
DL16 ...69 B7
Merrington Rd
Ferryhill DL16,DL17 ...69 C5
Kirk Merrington DL17 ...69 C5
Merrington View DL16 ...69 A8
Merrybent DL2 ...131 C2
Merrybent Dr DL2 ...131 D1
Merryweather Ct TS15 ...156 C6
Mersehead Sands TS5 ...139 B4
Mersey Rd TS10 ...107 B5
Mersey St DH8 ...11 D5
Merton Cl DL1 ...133 B6
Merville Ave TS19 ...117 C2
Meryl Gdns TS25 ...90 A7
Merz Rd DL5 ...96 D6
Messenger Bank DH8 ...10 C6
Messines La TS21 ...99 E3
Metcalfe Cl TS15 ...156 B3
Metcalfe Cres SR7 ...28 B3
Metcalfe Rd Consett DH8 ...11 B1
South Bank TS6 ...120 F5
Methold Hos DH9 ...14 E8
Metz Bridge Rd TS2 ...214 B4
Mewburn Ct DL3 ...132 F7
Mewburn Rd DL3 ...132 F7
Mews Ct DH5 ...26 E8
Mews The
Fence Houses DH4 ...26 A7
High Shincliffe DH1 ...44 F6
Kimblesworth DH2 ...24 A4
Marske-by-t-S TS11 ...108 C1
Mexborough Cl TS19 ...117 D5
Meynell Ave TS14 ...143 B3
Meynell Ho TS16 ...156 B7
Meynell Rd DL3 ...132 F5
Meynell's Wlk TS15 ...156 B4
Michael Terr DL16 ...67 E7
Mickle Gr DL14 ...81 C8
Mickle Hill Rd TS27 ...50 D1
Mickleby Cl TS7 ...140 F2
Mickledales Dr TS11 ...108 C1
Micklemire La TS25 ...89 F3
Mickleton Cl Consett DH8 ...10 F1
Great Lumley DH3 ...25 B7
Mickleton Cl CL DH8 ...10 F1
Mickleton Rd TS2 ...119 C8
Micklow Cl TS10 ...107 C2
Micklow La TS13 ...127 D2
Micklow Terr TS13 ...127 D1
Midbourne Rd TS19 ...118 A5
Middle Ave TS23 ...102 D1
Middle Bank TS21 ...100 E3
Middle Bank Rd TS7 ...141 B6
Middle Blackdene DL13 ...179 E1
Middle Chare DH3 ...16 D3
Middle Farm DL12 ...199 F5
Middle Gr DH7 ...43 A3
Middle Rd TS17 ...138 B1
Middle Row DH4 ...17 E1
Middle St
Blackhall Colliery TS27 ...50 D4
Consett DH8 ...10 F2
Gayles DL11 ...205 E2
Stockton-on-T TS18 ...213 A3
Middlefield DH2 ...15 E7
Middlefield Rd
Marske-by-t-S TS11 ...108 B1
Stockton-on-T TS19 ...117 C6
Middlefield Terr DH7 ...32 F1
Middlegate TS24 ...77 F8
Middleham Cl DH2 ...8 E1
Middleham Rd
Cornforth DL17 ...57 E1
Darlington DL1 ...133 B7
Durham DH1 ...34 D7
Stockton-on-T TS19 ...117 C2
Middleham Way
Newton Aycliffe DL5 ...82 E1
Redcar TS10 ...107 F4
Middleham Wk DL16 ...55 F1
Middleham Wlk DL16 ...56 A2
Middlehope Gr DL14 ...79 E5
Middles Rd DH9 ...14 B3
Middlesbrough Coll
Middlesbrough, Acklam
TS5 ...139 D6
Middlesbrough,Beechwood
TS4 ...140 C7
Middlesbrough,Linthorpe
TS5 ...119 D1
Middlesbrough Rd
Guisborough TS7, TS14 ...142 D4
South Bank TS6 ...120 F6
South Bank TS6 ...121 A6
Thornaby-on-T TS17 ...118 E1
Middlesbrough Rd E
TS6 ...121 B7
Middlesbrough Road E 5
TS6 ...121 A6
Middlesbrough Sta TS1 .215 A4
Middlesbrough Wharf Trad
Est TS2 ...119 E8
Middlestone Moor Prim Sch
DL16 ...68 E7
Middleton Ave
Billingham TS22 ...102 B5
Middlesbrough TS5 ...139 B8
Rowlands Gill NE39 ...1 F1
Thornaby-on-T TS17 ...138 C3
Middleton Cl Consett DH8 .11 A1
Egglescliffe TS16 ...136 F1
Seaham SR7 ...18 E1
Middleton Ct
Darlington DL1 ...133 A2
Yarm TS15 ...156 C4
Middleton Dr TS14 ...143 F3
Middleton Grange La 2
TS24 ...77 B6
Middleton La DL2 ...153 F6
Middleton Rd
Hartlepool TS24 ...77 B7
Sadberge DL2 ...134 E6
Shildon DL4 ...94 F8
Woodland DL13 ...194 E5
Middleton St DL1 ...133 A2
Middleton St George CE Prim
Sch DL2 ...153 E7
Middleton Wlk TS18 ...212 C2
Middleton-in-Teesdale Prim
Sch DL12 ...208 C5
Middleway TS17 ...213 C1
Middlewood DH7 ...33 A2
Middlewood Ave DL14 ...79 D2
Middlewood Cl 3 TS27 ...63 C4
Middlewood Rd DH7 ...20 E3
Middridge Farms DL5 ...95 E8
Middridge Gr TS23 ...102 F7
Middridge La DL4,DL5 ...81 C1
Middridge Rd
Langley Park DH7 ...32 B6
Middridge DL5 ...82 A1
Newton Aycliffe DL17,DL5 ...82 C4
Midfield The TS5 ...214 B1
Midfield View 3 TS19 ...117 B4
Midfields DL5 ...95 F4
Midhill Cl Brandon DH7 ...43 B5
7 Langley Park DH7 ...32 C6
Midhurst Rd TS3 ...121 A2
Midlothian Rd TS25 ...89 C8
Midvill Wlk TS3 ...121 A1
Midville Wlk TS3 ...141 A8
Miers Ave TS24 ...64 A2
Milbank Cres DL3 ...132 D2
Milbank Ct
Darlington DL3 ...132 C2
Stockton-on-T TS18 ...213 A3
Milbank Rd
Darlington DL3 ...132 D2
Hartlepool TS24 ...77 B8
Milbank St
3 South Bank TS6 ...121 A6
Stockton-on-T TS18 ...213 A3
Milbank Terr
Redcar TS10 ...107 C7
Shotton Colliery DH6 ...48 D6
Station Town TS28 ...60 F5
Milbanke Cl DH2 ...8 F1
Milbanke St DH2 ...8 F1
Milbourne Ct TS21 ...85 A8
Milburn Cl DH3 ...16 E2
Milburn Cres TS20 ...118 A6
Milburn St DL15 ...52 E4
Milburn Way DL15 ...65 E7
Mildenhall Cl TS25 ...89 E6
Mildred St
Darlington DL3 ...132 F3
Hartlepool TS26 ...77 A7
Miles St TS6 ...121 A6
Milfoil Cl TS7 ...140 B4
Milford Ho TS3 ...120 D4
Milford Mdw DL14 ...80 D4
Milford Terr 9 DL17 ...70 A6
Milkwood Ct DL3 ...132 E4
Mill Bank TS13 ...126 F2
Mill Cl DL11 ...205 F2
Mill Cotts DL17 ...82 C6
Mill Ct Billingham TS23 ...118 D8
Bournmoor DH4 ...17 E2
Hamsterley NE17 ...4 B6
Mill Farm Rd NE39 ...5 A5
Mill Hill Easington SR8 ...39 A1
Houghton-le-S DH5 ...26 D6
Peterlee SR8 ...49 A8
Mill Hill Prim Sch SR3 ...18 A5
Mill Hill Rd SR3 ...18 A6
Mill House Ct DH1 ...35 A2
Mill La Billingham TS23 ...102 E1
Bishop Auckland DL14 ...80 D5
Bishopton TS21 ...115 E8
Carlin How TS13 ...126 F2
Darlington DL1 ...133 E4
Durham DH1 ...35 A2
Ebchester DH8 ...3 E4
Frosterley DL13 ...188 A7
High Coniscliffe DL2 ...130 F3
Kimblesworth DH2,DH3 ...24 B4
Longnewton DL2,TS21 ...135 D3
Mickleton DL12 ...193 B3
New Brancepeth DH7 ...43 A8
Redworth DL4,DL5 ...95 C4
Sherburn DH6 ...36 A1
Shincliffe DH1 ...45 A7
Skinningrove TS13 ...127 A3
Spennymoor DL16 ...55 E4
Stockton-on-T TS20 ...102 B1
Urpeth DH2 ...8 D1
Winlaton Mill NE21 ...2 B7
Wolviston TS22 ...102 B7
Mill Lane Prim Sch
TS18 ...213 A3
Mill Meadow Ct 10
TS20 ...118 B8
Mill Race Cl NE17 ...4 B6
Mill Rd Brandon DH7 ...43 E5
Chopwell NE17 ...4 B8
Seaham SR7 ...28 F8
Mill St Consett DH8 ...177 D4
Crook DL15 ...52 F4
Guisborough TS14 ...143 E4
Shildon DL4 ...95 A8
Stockton-on-T TS20 ...118 A8
Willington DL15 ...53 F3
Mill St E TS18 ...213 B3
Mill St W TS18 ...213 A3
Mill Terr Easington SR8 ...39 A4
Great Ayton TS9 ...160 F2
Houghton-le-S DH5 ...26 D6
Thorpe Thewles TS21 ...100 D3
Mill The Blanchland DH8 ...174 F2
Great Ayton TS9 ...161 A2
Mill View TS13 ...127 B1
Mill Wynd Staindrop DL2 .200 E7
Yarm TS15 ...156 B6
Millais Gr TS23 ...102 D8
Millbank DL5 ...95 D1
Millbank Cl
Bishop Auckland DL14 ...79 C1
Hart TS27 ...63 A3
Millbank Ct DH1 ...210 B4
Millbank La TS17 ...138 C5
Millbank Terr
Eldon Lane DL14 ...80 F4
Stillington TS21 ...100 A2
Millbeck Gr DH5 ...26 D6
Millbeck Way TS7 ...141 B7
Millbrook Ave TS3 ...120 F4
Millburngate DH1 ...210 C3
Millburngate Sh Ctr
DH1 ...210 C3
Millclose Wlk TS21 ...72 B1
Milldale SR7 ...28 F8
Millennium Pl DH1 ...210 C3
Millennium Way DL5 ...112 D8
Miller Cl TS15 ...156 D4
Miller Cres TS24 ...63 D3
Miller Gdns DH2 ...15 D4
Miller Terr SR3 ...18 A8
Millers La TS12 ...145 E3
Millershill La DH8 ...177 C1
Millfield DH7 ...20 E4
Millfield Cl
Chester le Street DH2 ...16 A1
Egglescliffe TS16 ...156 B8
Thornaby-on-T TS17 ...138 E8
Millfield Ct DH8 ...10 C3
Millfield Gr DL15 ...52 E4
Millfield Rd Fishburn TS21 .72 D4
Middlesbrough TS3 ...120 C3
Millfield Road W TS21 ...72 D4
Millfields DL5 ...96 F2
Millford Rd TS20 ...117 F7
Millford Way DH6 ...45 E1
Millgin Ct TS17 ...138 A2
Millhill La DH1 ...44 B7
Millholme Cl TS12 ...126 A3
Millholme Dr TS12 ...126 A3
Millholme Terr TS12 ...126 A3
Millington Cl TS23 ...88 F1
Millom Ct SR8 ...49 A3
Millpool Cl TS24 ...64 C2
Millrace DL13 ...207 C5
Millrace Cl DL1 ...133 F6
Mills Bldgs DL17 ...70 C4
Mills Cl DL5 ...96 C6
Mills St TS1 ...214 A2
Millston Cl TS26 ...76 C8
Millstone Cl 3 TS10 ...107 E1
Millstone Pl DL13 ...207 D5
Millwood DL17 ...82 E8
Milne Wlk TS25 ...89 C8
Milner Gr TS24 ...77 B7
Milner Rd Darlington DL1 .152 A8
Stockton-on-T TS20 ...102 A1
Milton Ave
Bishop Auckland DL14 ...80 B6
Blackhall Colliery TS27 ...50 C5
Houghton-le-S DH5 ...26 F7
Milton Cl Brotton TS12 ...126 A5
Seaham SR7 ...29 B7
Stanley DH9 ...14 B6
Milton Ct TS1 ...214 B3
Milton Gr DH6 ...48 D6
Milton La SR8 ...39 C4
Milton Rd TS26 ...77 A6
Milton St Crook DL15 ...52 E5
Darlington DL1 ...152 C8
Saltburn-by-t-S TS12 ...125 C7
Milton Terr DH2 ...15 E3
Minch Rd TS25 ...89 D7
Minehead Gdns 9 SR3 ...18 A8
Miners Homes DL14 ...79 E3
Miners' Bglws 12 DL13 ...195 E3
Miners' Homes DL15 ...54 A2
Mingarry DH3 ...9 E2
Mingary Cl DH5 ...26 C4
Miniott Wlk TS8 ...139 D2
Minors Cres DL3 ...132 B5
Minstarley DH3 ...25 A7
Minster Ct Durham DH1 ...35 C3
Willington DL15 ...54 A3
Minster Wlk DL2 ...152 D1
Minsterley Dr TS5 ...139 A6
Mire La DL12 ...198 F6
Miry La DL12 ...192 B6
Missenden Gr TS3 ...140 F8
Mission Pl DL16 ...69 A3
Mistletoe St DH1 ...210 B2
Mistral Dr DL1 ...133 B7
Mitchell Ave TS17 ...138 E6
Mitchell Cl SR8 ...49 B8
Mitchell St
Annfield Plain DH9 ...13 A4
Birtley DH3 ...9 C4
Durham DH1 ...210 B3
1 Hartlepool TS26 ...77 A5
Stanley DH9 ...13 D4
Mitchell Terr DH9 ...6 B2
Mitford Cl
Chester le Street DH3 ...16 D8
High Shincliffe DH1 ...45 B5
Ormesby TS7 ...141 B7
Mitford Cres TS19 ...117 A6
Mitford Ct Peterlee SR8 ...49 D4
Sedgefield TS21 ...85 A8
Mitford Dr DH6 ...36 A2
Moat The TS23 ...103 B3
Moatside Mews DH1 ...210 C2
Model Pl 4 DL1 ...133 A1
Model Terr 17 DL13 ...195 E3
Moffat Cl DL1 ...133 D7
Moffat Rd TS25 ...89 D7
Moir Terr SR2 ...19 A6
Mona St DH9 ...13 F7
Monach Rd TS25 ...89 D7
Monarch Gn DL1 ...133 B7
Monarch Gr TS7 ...140 E4
Moncreiff Terr SR8 ...39 D4
Mond Cres TS23 ...118 D8
Mond Ho TS3 ...120 D1
Money Slack DH1 ...44 B5
Monk Ct SR8 ...49 B3
Monkland Cl TS1 ...214 C3
Monks End DL5 ...96 F2
Monks' Cres DH1 ...211 C4
Monkseaton Dr TS22 ...102 C5
Monkswood Sq SR3 ...18 B6
Monkton Rd TS25 ...89 C7
Monkton Rise TS14 ...143 F6
Monmouth Dr TS16 ...137 C1
Monmouth Gr TS26 ...63 E1
Monmouth Rd TS6 ...121 E4
Monreith Ave TS16 ...137 C1
Montagu Ct DL1 ...151 E8
Montagu's Harrier TS14 .143 B4
Montague Ho 2 DH1 ...35 A2
Montague St TS24 ...64 F1
Montalbo Prim Sch
DL12 ...209 C7
Montalbo Rd DL12 ...209 C7
Monteith Cl DL14 ...79 C1
Montfalcon Cl SR8 ...49 C6
Montgomery Gr TS26 ...76 E8
Montgomery Rd
Barnard Castle DL12 ...209 B7
Durham DH1 ...211 C4
Montreal Pl TS4 ...120 A2
Montrose Cl TS7 ...140 C3
Montrose St
Darlington DL1 ...133 B3
Middlesbrough TS1 ...215 A3
Saltburn-by-t-S TS12 ...125 C7
Monument Terr 11 DH3 ...9 C4
Moor Cl
Kirklevington TS15 ...172 D8
Moorsholm TS12 ...146 B1
Moor Cres Durham DH1 ...35 B3

Moor Cres *continued*
Ludworth DH6 47 C7
Moor Ct DH4 17 E3
Moor Edge Brandon DH7 43 B3
Durham DH1 33 F2
Moor End Terr DH1 35 C4
Moor Farm Est DL16 68 E6
Moor Gn TS7 141 A1
Moor Houses DL15 40 E1
Moor La Borrowby TS13 148 F3
Cleasby DL2 150 E5
Dalton DL11 205 C2
Dalton DL11 205 D3
Ingleton DL2,DL14 92 F2
Middridge DL4,DL5 81 E3
Newsham DL11 205 B4
Scargill DL12 204 C5
Staindrop DL2 200 C7
Wingate TS28 60 E7
Moor Par TS24 64 F1
Moor Pk
Eaglescliffe TS16 156 C8
Nunthorpe TS7 141 A2
Moor Rd DL2 200 E7
Moor Terr TS24 64 G8
Moor View Bowes DL12 203 D8
6 Cockfield DL13 195 E3
High Pittington DH6 36 D4
Hinderwell TS13 149 E5
Normanby TS6 141 D8
Thornley (nr Wheatley Hill) DH6 47 E4
Wheatley Hill DH6 47 F3
Moor View Terr DH9 12 E3
Moorbeck Way TS7 141 B7
Moorberries TS15 157 F3
Moorcock Cl Eston TS6 121 F1
Normanby TS6 141 F8
Moorcock Row TS12 145 D6
Moordale Ct TS12 145 E5
Moore Cres DH3 9 C6
Moore Cres N DH5 26 E7
Moore Cres S DH5 26 E7
Moore La DL5 96 F6
Moore Sq TS28 48 D1
Moore St Eldon Lane DL14 80 F4
Hartlepool TS24 77 A8
Redcar TS10 107 D7
Stanley DH9 13 E4
Wheatley Hill DH6 47 F2
Moore Terr DH6 48 D5
Moorfield DL13 195 C5
Moorfoot Ave DH2 16 C2
Moorgate TS6 122 A2
Moorhen Rd TS26 63 D1
Moorhouse Est TS18 137 D6
Moorhouse Gdns DH5 27 B2
Moorhouse La DL12 204 D7
Moorland Cl DL15 53 E1
Moorland Cres 1 DH8 177 A3
Moorland View
Castleside DH8 176 F3
Chopwell NE17 4 B8
Moorlands Consett DH8 10 D5
Dipton DH9 5 E1
Moorlands Cres DH8 10 D4
Moorlands Rd DL3 132 C4
Moorlands The DH1 35 A2
Moormill NE11 8 D6
Moormill La NE11 8 E6
Moors Cl DH4 26 B8
Moorsfield DH4 26 B8
Moorsholm La TS12, TS13 147 A4
Moorsholm Way TS10 107 C3
Moorside DL16 68 D6
Moorside Cl TS10 107 F1
Moorside Com Coll DH8 177 A4
Moorside Cres TS21 72 D4
Moorside Prim Sch DH8 177 A4
Moorsley Rd DH5 26 F2
Moorston Cl TS26 76 C7
Moortown Rd
Middlesbrough TS4 140 A7
New Marske TS11 123 F6
Moorview DH8 10 E4
Moraine Cres NE17 4 B6
Moravian St DL15 52 E4
Moray Cl Birtley DH3 9 D1
Darlington DL1 133 C7
Middlesbrough TS4 120 A1
Peterlee SR8 49 C5
Moray Rd TS20 117 F7
Mordales Dr TS11 108 E1
Mordue Terr DH9 13 A3
Morehead Terr TS13 148 B8
Moreland Ave TS23 102 E4
Moreland Cl TS22 102 C8
Moreland St TS24 77 C5
Moresby Cl TS4 140 B8
Morgan Dr TS14 143 E3
Morinda Cl 4 DH4 17 F5
Morison Gdns TS24 64 F1
Morlais Ct TS17 156 F7
Morland Fell TS10 107 C4
Morland St DL14 80 B5
Morley Cres DH6 58 E6
Morley Gdns 3 DH8 10 F4
Morley La DH7 42 E3
Morley Terr 3 DH4 26 A8
Morningside
Sacriston DH7 23 C4
Washington NE38 16 E8
Morningside Ct 5 DH3 16 C4
Mornington La DL3 132 D4
Morpeth Ave
Darlington DL1 133 C6
Middlesbrough TS4 140 B5
Morpeth Cl Ferryhill DL17 70 B6
Washington NE38 9 F4
Morpeth Gr DL14 80 A6
Morpeth St SR8 49 F8
Morris Cres DH6 47 C4
Morris Rd 6 TS6 121 E1
Morris Sq SR8 39 C3
Morris St DH3 9 C4
Morrison Cl DL5 82 D1
Morrison Rd TS14 143 F5
Morrison Road North Ind Est DH9 13 A3
Morrison St TS21 99 F4
Morrison Terr DL17 70 D4
Morriss Terr DH5 26 F7
Morson Ave DL15 52 E2
Mortain Cl TS15 156 E4
Mortham La DL12 200 A1
Mortimer Dr TS20 117 F8
Mortimer St DH8 10 D3
Morton Carr La TS7 141 C3
Morton Cl TS14 143 C3
Morton Cres DH4 17 F1
Morton Grange Terr DH4 17 E1
Morton Pk DL1 134 A1
Morton Rd DL1 134 A1
Morton Sq SR8 49 C7
Morton St 8 TS26 77 A6
Morton Wlk DL5 96 E7
Morven View 8 TS19 117 B4
Morville Ct TS17 157 B8
Mosedale Rd TS6 121 E3
Moses St TS3 215 C2
Mosman Terr TS3 120 C4
Moss Gdns TS8 139 D2
Moss Way TS18 137 E6
Mossbank Gr DL1 133 C5
Mossbrough Cl TS19 117 D5
Mossdale DH1 35 E4
Mossdale Gr TS14 143 B3
Mossmere DL16 55 E2
Mosston Rd TS19 117 C4
Mossway DH2 15 D7
Mosswood Cotts DH8 176 E5
Mosswood Cres TS5 139 B5
Mostyn Terr DL13 195 E3
Motherwell Rd TS25 89 D7
Moule Cl DL5 96 C5
Moulton Gr TS19 117 A2
Moulton Way 1 DL1 152 C8
Mount Ct DH3 9 D5
Mount Eff La DL12 209 D5
Mount Eff Rd DL12 199 F3
Mount Gr TS20 102 B1
Mount Joy Cres DH1 211 A1
Mount La NE9 9 E8
Mount Leven Rd TS15 156 E6
Mount Lonnen NE9 9 E8
Mount Park Dr DH7 20 E4
Mount Pleasant
Birtley DH3 9 C5
Burnhope DH7 21 D4
Cockfield DL13 195 D3
Dipton DH9 5 E1
Guisborough TS14 143 D7
Houghton-le-S DH5 26 F8
Lanchester DH7 20 E4
Skinningrove TS13 127 A3
Stanley Crook DL15 52 F8
Stillington TS21 99 E3
Mount Pleasant Ave TS11 108 D1
Mount Pleasant Bglws 4 DH3 9 C5
Mount Pleasant Cl
Middleton St George DL2 153 E8
Spennymoor DL16 56 B1
Stillington TS21 99 E3
Mount Pleasant Ct DL16 56 B1
Mount Pleasant Gr TS21 99 F3
Mount Pleasant Grange TS18 138 A8
Mount Pleasant Prim Sch DL3 132 A5
Mount Pleasant Rd
Stillington TS21 99 F3
Stockton-on-T TS20 118 B6
Mount Pleasant View DL16 56 B1
Mount Pleasant Wlk TS21 99 E3
Mount Rd Birtley DH3 9 D5
Gateshead NE9 9 E8
Mount Stewart St SR7 29 D5
Mount The Consett DH8 10 D6
Normanby TS6 141 C8
Mount View DH7 20 E4
Mountbatten Cl TS24 64 C1
Mountside DH8 10 D6
Mountstewart TS22 87 E1
Mountston Cl TS26 76 D7
Moutter Cl SR8 49 E8
Mowbray Dr
Hemlington TS8 139 D2
Hurworth-on-T DL2 152 C2
Mowbray Gr TS19 117 A6
Mowbray Ho 12 TS4 139 F8
Mowbray Rd
Hartlepool TS25 89 E6
Stockton-on-T TS20 118 B6
Mowbray St DH1 210 B3
Mowden Cl TS19 117 D5
Mowden Hall Dr DL3 132 B3
Mowden Inf Sch DL3 132 B2
Mowden Jun Sch DL3 132 B3
Mowden St DL3 132 F3
Mowden Terr DL3 132 F3
Mowden Wlk DL3 132 A3
Mowlam Dr DH9 14 B6
Mown Meadows Rd DL15 189 F6
Moyle Terr NE16 6 A4
Moyne Gdns 4 TS25 77 B4
Muff La TS8 159 A5
Muir Gr TS25 89 D7
Muirfield TS7 141 A2
Muirfield Cl Consett DH8 10 E5
Hartlepool TS27 63 C4
7 New Marske TS11 124 A6
Muirfield Rd TS16 137 C1
Muirfield Way TS4 140 A7
Muirfield Wlk TS27 63 C4
Muirkirk Gr DL1 133 C6
Muirlands DL14 92 C8
Muker Gr TS19 117 A2
Mulberry DH6 58 A4
Mulberry Ct 2 TS4 139 F8
Mulberry Gr NE16 6 A4
Mulberry Terr DH9 13 B4
Mulgrave Ct
Guisborough TS14 143 E6
Newton Aycliffe DL5 82 E1
Mulgrave Rd
Hartlepool TS26 76 F6
Middlesbrough TS5 119 E1
Mulgrave Wlk
9 Eston TS6 121 F3
Redcar TS10 107 C3
Mulheim Cl DL3 132 C5
Mullin Cl Bearpark DH7 33 B3
Willington DL15 54 A6
Mullroy Rd TS25 89 C7
Muncaster Mews SR8 49 A3
Mundell St DH9 13 E4
Mundle Ave NE21 2 C6
Munro Gr TS25 89 D7
Murdock Rd TS3 120 F4
Muriel St
Carlin How TS13 126 F3
Middlesbrough TS1 215 A1
Quaking Houses DH9 13 E3
Redcar TS10 107 D6
Murphy Cres DL14 80 A5
Murphy Gr SR2 18 E7
Murray Ave DL14 80 A5
Murray Ct
Chester le Street DH2 16 B3
Consett DH8 10 D5
Murray Pl DH2 16 C3
Murray Rd DH2,DH3 16 C3
Murray St Hartlepool TS26 77 A6
Peterlee SR8 50 A6
Murray Terr DH9 12 D8
Murray Wlk DL3 132 B2
Murrayfield Dr DH7 43 A3
Murrayfield Way DL1 133 E3
Murton Cl
Newton Aycliffe DL5 96 E2
Thornaby-on-T TS17 138 B4
Murton Gr TS22 102 B5
Murton Jubilee Prim Sch SR7 28 C3
Murton La DH5 27 D1
Murton Prim Sch SR7 28 C3
Mus of Hartlepool & Gray Art Gal* TS24 77 C7
Museum Rd TS24 77 B6
Musgrave Gdns DH1 35 A2
Musgrave St
Bishop Auckland DL14 79 E3
Hartlepool TS24 77 D5
Musgrave Terr TS22 102 C8
Musgrave Wlk 10 TS24 77 C5
Muston Cl TS5 139 E6
Mutton Scalp Rd TS12 145 C5
Myra Ave TS27 50 A1
Myrddin-Baker Rd TS6 121 E3
Myre Hall 9 DH5 26 E8
Myrtle Ct TS17 138 C7
Myrtle Gdns DL1 133 B8
Myrtle Gr Billy Row DL15 52 D7
Burnopfield NE16 5 F6
Thornaby-on-T TS17 138 C7
Trimdon TS29 59 D1
Myrtle Ho TS9 160 F2
Myrtle Rd
Eaglescliffe TS16 137 C4
Stockton-on-T TS19 117 F5
Myrtle St TS1 215 A2
Myrtles DH2 16 B5
Myton Park Prim Sch TS17 156 F8
Myton Rd TS17 157 A8
Myton Wlk TS8 139 D2

N

Nab Cl TS6 121 E1
Naby La DL12 198 F5
Nairn Cl Birtley DH3 9 D2
Darlington DL1 133 E7
Nairnhead Cl TS8 139 D2
Naisbitt Ave SR8 49 E8
Naismith Gr DL13 183 D1
Nanny Pop Lonnen DL16 68 E5
Nansen St DH8 11 A3
Nantwich Cl TS8 139 D2
Napier Cl DH3 16 D8
Napier Ct DL17 69 E5
Napier Rd SR7 29 A8
Napier St Darlington DL3 132 E2
Middlesbrough TS5 214 C1
2 South Bank TS6 121 A6
Stockton-on-T TS20 118 B6
Napoleon Cl SR2 18 F7
Naseby Ct
Billingham TS23 103 A7
Brotton TS12 126 C3
Nash Gr TS25 76 E2
Nattress Terr
Wingate TS28 60 D8
Wingate, Deaf Hill TS29 60 B5
Nature's World* TS5 139 E4
Navenby Cl SR7 19 A1
Navenby Gr TS25 89 D6
Navigation Point TS24 77 D7
Navigation Way TS17 118 E2
Navigator Ct TS18 138 A7
Naworth Ct SR8 49 B3
Naylor Ave NE21 2 C6
Naylor Bldgs NE21 2 C6
Naylor Rd TS21 85 B6
Neale St
Annfield Plain DH9 13 A4
Ferryhill DL17 69 E5
Tantobie DH9 6 B2
Neale Terr 1 DH3 9 C4
Neasham Ave
Billingham TS23 102 F7
Marton TS7 140 D2
Neasham Cl TS18 213 B3
Neasham Covert DL2 153 C3
Neasham Dr DL1 152 C7
Neasham Hill DL2 153 D2
Neasham Rd
Darlington DL1,DL2 152 D5
Middleton St George DL2 153 D5
Neasham DL2 153 A1
Seaham SR7 19 A1
Hurworth-on-T DL2 152 F1
Neath Ct TS17 156 F8
Nebraska Cl DL1 133 B6
Nederdale Cl TS15 156 B3
Needles Cl TS10 107 B1
Neil Cres DH6 58 D7
Neil St DH5 27 C1
Neile Rd DL5 96 E8
Nell Terr NE39 1 C1
Nelson Ave TS23 103 C2
Nelson Cl SR8 50 A7
Nelson Ct TS6 121 A6
Nelson Row DL12 208 B5
Nelson Sq TS20 102 A1
Nelson St
8 Bishop Auckland DL14 80 B8
Chester le Street DH3 16 C2
Consett DH8 10 F2
Crook DL15 52 E4
Ferryhill DL17 70 C4
Hetton-le-H DH5 27 A3
Leadgate DH8 11 C4
Ryhope SR2 18 F7
Seaham SR7 29 B8
South Bank TS6 120 F6
Nelson St Ind Est TS6 120 F6
Nelson Street Ind Est TS6 121 A6
Nelson Terr
Darlington DL1 152 A8
Redcar TS10 107 B7
Sherburn DH6 36 A1
Stockton-on-T TS18 213 A3
Nenthead Cl DH3 25 B7
Nenthead Mines Heritage Ctr* CA9 178 A6
Neptune Cl TS25 77 D2
Neptune Way SR8 39 C4
Nesbit Rd SR8 49 E5
Nesbyt Rd TS24 63 F3
Nesham Ave TS5 119 B1
Nesham Pl DH5 26 F8
Nesham Rd
Hartlepool TS24 64 F1
Middlesbrough TS1 214 A2
Ness Terr YO21 164 C1
Nestfield Ind Est DL1 133 B4
Nestfield St
Darlington DL1 133 B4
Darlington DL1 133 C4
Netherby Cl TS15 156 E5
Netherby Gate TS26 76 E7
Netherby Gn TS3 140 E8
Netherby Rise DL3 132 C1
Netherfields Cres TS3 121 A1
Netherton Cl
Chester le Street DH2 15 F2
Langley Park DH7 32 B6
Netley Gr TS3 140 F8
Nettlebed La DL14 195 E7
Nettles La SR3 18 B6
Nettlesworth Prim Sch DH2 23 F4
Nevada Gdns DL1 133 B6
Nevern Cres TS17 156 E7
Neville Cl Evenwood DL14 92 D6
Gainford DL2 201 D4
Spennymoor DL16 56 B1
Neville Cotts 11 DL2 200 E7
Neville Cres DH3 9 C6
Neville Dene DH1 33 F1
Neville Dr TS21 85 A8
Neville Gr TS14 143 C3
Neville Par DL5 96 E6
Neville Rd
Darlington DL3 132 D1
Peterlee SR8 49 C6
Stockton-on-T TS18 119 A5
Neville Sq DH1 44 A7
Neville St DH1 210 C2
Neville Terr Bowburn DH6 57 E8
Durham DH1 210 A3
Neville's Cross Bank DH1 210 A1
Neville's Cross Villas DH1 210 A1
Neville's Ct TS5 139 D8
Nevilledale Terr DH1 210 B2
Nevilles Cross Prim Sch DH1 210 A1
New Acres DH7 33 A2
New Blackett St DH9 12 E5
New Brancepeth Prim Sch DH7 42 F7
New Brook Terr DL14 80 F5
New Brotton TS12 126 A5
New Cl DL5 96 F7
New Coll (Neville's Cross Campus) DH1 210 A1
New Coll Durham DH1 34 A5
New Company Row TS13 127 A4
New Cross Row TS28 60 E8
New Dr SR7 29 C8
New Durham Rd DH9 13 A3
New Elvet DH1 211 A2
New Front St DH9 6 D1
New Grange Terr DH2 15 D4
New Grove Terr TS13 127 A4
New Ho DL13 179 D1
New Hos NE47 179 C8
New Houses DL13 188 A7
New La Denton DL2 110 D2
Heighington DL5 95 F2
Neasham DL2 153 B1
New London Rd TS13 127 A1
New Marske Prim Sch TS11 123 F6
New Pk DL14 67 A8
New Rd Beamish DH2,DH9 15 A7
Billingham TS23 118 E8
Burnopfield NE16 6 B7
Crook DL15 52 E2
Guisborough TS14 143 E4
Hutton Magna DL11 205 E6
Washington NE38 17 C8
Witton Park DL14 66 A1
New Row Brancepeth DL16 55 A4
Dunsdale TS14 123 D2
Eldon DL14 81 A4
Great Ayton YO21 162 F1
3 Middleton St George DL2 153 F8
Willington DL15 54 A7
New Seaham Prim Sch SR7 18 F1
New Silksworth Inf Sch SR3 18 B7
New Silksworth Jun Sch SR3 18 B7
New South Terr DH3 9 D4
New South View DL17 82 F7
New St Durham DH1 210 B3
Sherburn DH6 36 A1
Thornaby-on-T TS17 213 C1
New Strangford Rd SR7 29 C7
New Watling St DH8 11 D4
Newacres Rd DH9 13 E1
Newark Ave DL14 79 E6
Newark Cl SR8 49 C7
Newark Cres SR7 29 B8
Newark Rd TS25 89 D6
Newark Wlk TS20 118 C7
Newbank Cl TS7 141 B6
Newbiggin Cl TS16 136 F1
Newbiggin La
Heighington DL2 94 D4
Lanchester DH7 20 C4
Newbiggin Rd 8 TS23 102 E8
Newbottle La DH4 25 F7
Newbottle St 4 DH4 26 E8
Newbridge Bank DH3 16 F5
Newbridge Banks DH2 15 A4
Newbridge Ct TS5 139 E7
Newburgh Ct DL16 55 E3
Newburn Ave DH6 45 D1
Newburn Bridge Ind Est TS25 77 D4
Newburn Ct DL5 96 C7
Newburn Rd DH9 14 A8
Newbury Ave TS5 119 B1
Newbury Dr DH8 10 E7
Newbury Rd TS12 126 C3
Newbury Way TS23 102 F6
Newby 8 TS4 120 A1
Newby Cl
Middlesbrough TS5 139 E7
5 Stockton-on-T TS20 118 A8
Newby Gr TS17 138 D7
Newby La DH6 36 C5
Newcastle Ave SR8 49 F8
Newcastle Bank DH3 9 B7
Newcastle Rd Birtley DH3 9 C6
Chester le Street DH3 16 C5
Durham DH1 210 A2
Newcastle Terr DH1 34 A6
Newcomen Gn TS4 120 A2
Newcomen Gr TS10 107 C7
Newcomen Prim Sch TS10 107 B4
Newcomen Rd TS6 120 F5
Newcomen St DL17 69 E6
Newcomen Terr TS10 107 B7
Newcommen Terr TS13 127 B1
Newfield Cres TS5 139 B5
Newfield Terr DH2 15 C5
Newfoundland St DL3 132 E4

Newgale Cl TS17 ...156 E7
Newgate
Barnard Castle DL12 ...209 C5
Eston TS6 ...121 F2
Newgate St DL14 ...80 C8
Newham Ave TS5 ...139 E7
Newham Bridge Prim Sch TS5 ...139 E7
Newham Cres TS7 ...140 D3
Newham Grange Ave TS19 ...212 B4
Newham Grange Leisure Farm* TS8 ...140 A3
Newham Way TS8 ...140 B3
Newhaven Cl TS8 ...139 D2
Newhaven Ct 3 TS24 ...77 C5
Newholm Ct TS25 ...90 A8
Newholm Way TS10 ...107 C3
Newholme Cres DL14 ...92 C7
Newholme Ct TS14 ...143 D5
Newholme Est TS28 ...60 F5
Newhouse Ave DH7 ...31 D1
Newhouse Rd DH7 ...41 E8
Newick Ave TS3 ...120 D2
Newington Rd TS4 ...140 A7
Newker Prim Sch DH2 ...16 B2
Newlands DH8 ...10 D4
Newlands Ave
Bishop Auckland DL14 ...80 B6
Hartlepool TS26 ...76 F5
Stockton-on-T TS20 ...118 B7
Newlands Gr TS10 ...107 B5
Newlands RC Sch The TS4 ...139 F6
Newlands Rd
Darlington DL3 ...132 D4
Durham DH1 ...35 C4
Eaglescliffe TS16 ...156 B8
Middlesbrough TS1 ...215 B2
Skelton TS12 ...145 B8
Trimdon TS29 ...72 D8
Newlands Rd E SR7 ...29 B8
Newlands Rd W SR7 ...29 A8
Newlands View DL15 ...52 F2
Newley Ct TS3 ...121 A1
Newlyn Dr DL3 ...132 F8
Newlyn Gn TS3 ...140 E8
Newlyn Way TS10 ...107 F2
Newmarket Ave TS17 ...118 F1
Newmarket Rd TS10 ...107 D4
Newmarket St DH8 ...10 F3
Newmin Way NE16 ...2 F5
Newport Cl TS17 ...156 E7
Newport Cres TS1 ...214 C3
Newport Ct DL1 ...133 E4
Newport Gr 6 SR3 ...18 A8
Newport Prim Sch TS1 ...214 B2
Newport Rd TS1, TS5 ...214 B3
Newport Way TS1 ...214 A3
Newquay Cl
Darlington DL3 ...132 F8
Hartlepool TS26 ...76 E7
Hemlington TS8 ...139 D2
Newsam Cres 4 TS16 ...156 B8
Newsam Rd TS16 ...156 B8
Newsham Hill DL11 ...205 E6
Newstead Ave TS19 ...117 D5
Newstead Rd TS4 ...215 B1
Newstead Rise DH8 ...10 C5
Newstead Sq SR3 ...18 A6
Newton Aycliffe Sta DL5 ...96 B5
Newton Cap Bank DL14 ...67 B1
Newton Cl TS6 ...121 F1
Newton Dr Durham DH1 ...34 B6
Thornaby-on-T TS17 ...138 C4
Newton Gr TS22 ...102 B5
Newton Hanzard Long Dr TS22 ...87 B4
Newton Hanzard Short Dr TS22 ...87 C4
Newton La
Darlington DL2, DL3 ...132 A5
Newton Mulgrave TS13 ...149 E3
Walworth DL2 ...131 F7
Newton Mall TS1 ...214 C3
Newton Rd
Great Ayton TS9 ...161 A4
Redcar TS10 ...107 B3
Newton St Ferryhill DL17 ...69 E6
Witton Gilbert DH7 ...33 A8
Newton Villas DH6 ...57 E6
Newton Wlk 7 TS20 ...118 B5
Newtondale TS14 ...143 A3
Newtown DL12 ...208 B5
Newtown Ave TS19 ...212 C4
Newtown Ind Est DH3 ...9 C2
Newtown Villas DH7 ...23 C3
Nicholas St DH5 ...27 B5
Nicholson Terr DL12 ...198 F6
Nicholson Way TS24 ...63 E3
Nicholson's Terr DH9 ...14 F8
Nicklaus Dr TS16 ...137 D1
Nickleby Chare DH1 ...44 B7
Nickleby Cl DL12 ...209 D7
Nickstream La DL3 ...132 B5
Nidderdale TS12 ...125 B4
Nidderdale Ave DH5 ...26 F2
Nightingale Ave DL1 ...133 D6
Nightingale Cl TS26 ...63 C1
Nightingale Pl DH9 ...14 B5
Nightingale Rd TS6 ...121 E3
Nightingale Wlk TS20 ...102 A1
Nile St Consett DH8 ...10 F2
Middlesbrough TS2 ...214 C4
Nimbus Cl TS7 ...140 C4
Nimbus Ct 13 SR3 ...18 A6
Nine Acres TS27 ...62 E2
Nine Lands DH4 ...26 C8
Ninefields DL14 ...80 B8
Ninian Terr DH9 ...12 C7
Ninth Ave DH2 ...16 B3
Ninth St
Blackhall Colliery TS27 ...50 D4
6 Peterlee SR8 ...50 A7
Noble St SR8 ...39 E5
Noel Ave NE21 ...2 C6
Noel St DH9 ...14 B7
Noel Terr NE21 ...2 D7
Nolan Ho TS18 ...213 A4
Nolan Pl TS18 ...213 A4
Nolton Ct TS17 ...156 F7
Nook La DL12 ...192 D1
Nookston Cl TS26 ...76 D8
Norbeck Bank DL11 ...205 A5
Norburn La DH7 ...22 F2
Norburn Pk DH7 ...23 A1
Norcliffe St TS3 ...120 C4
Norfolk Ave Birtley DH3 ...9 D1
8 New Silksworth SR3 ...18 A8
Norfolk Cl Hartlepool TS25 ...77 B3
Redcar TS10 ...107 B4
Seaham SR7 ...19 A1
Skelton TS12 ...125 A2
Norfolk Cres TS3 ...140 F7
Norfolk Pl Birtley DH3 ...9 D1
Bishop Auckland DL14 ...80 C5
Middlesbrough TS3 ...120 D2
Norfolk Rd DH8 ...177 A4
Norfolk St Hetton-le-H DH5 ...26 F4
Stockton-on-T TS18 ...212 C2
Norfolk Terr TS23 ...102 F3
Norfolk Wlk SR8 ...49 C8
Norham Ct DH4 ...17 D1
Norham Dr SR8 ...49 C3
Norham Rd DH1 ...34 D7
Norham Wlk TS7 ...141 A7
Norhurst NE16 ...2 E5
Norman Ave SR3 ...18 B7
Norman Rd NE39 ...1 F1
Norman Terr Chilton DL17 ...82 F8
Consett DH8 ...10 E3
High Pittington DH6 ...36 C5
South Bank TS6 ...120 F6
Norman's Bldgs DL15 ...66 D7
Normanby Cl SR7 ...19 A1
Normanby Ct TS7 ...140 C3
Normanby Hall Pk TS6 ...141 C8
Normanby Prim Sch TS6 ...141 D8
Normanby Rd Eston TS6 ...121 B4
Ormesby TS7 ...141 B8
Normandy Cres DH5 ...26 F8
North Albert Rd TS20 ...102 A1
North App DH2 ...16 B4
North Ave Peterlee SR8 ...49 F7
Saltburn-by-t-S TS12 ...125 B7
North Bailey DH1 ...210 C2
North Bank Cres TS7 ...141 B6
North Bitchburn Bank DL15 ...65 F7
North Bitchburn Terr DL15 ...66 A6
North Bondgate DL14 ...67 B1
North Brancepeth Cl DH7 ...43 E6
North Burns DH3 ...16 C4
North Cl Elwick TS27 ...75 C5
Thorpe Thewles TS21 ...100 E4
North Close Rd
Kirk Merrington DL16 ...69 A4
Spennymoor DL16 ...68 F5
North Coronation St SR7 ...28 D3
North Cotts DL5 ...96 A4
North Cres Durham DH1 ...210 B4
Easington SR8 ...39 C3
North Cross St DH8 ...11 C4
North Dene DH3 ...9 C7
North Dr
Chester le Street NE38 ...16 E7
Hartlepool TS26 ...76 E6
Ormesby TS7 ...141 A7
Spennymoor DL16 ...68 D6
North East Ind Est SR8 ...39 D1
North Eastern Terr 3 DL1 ...133 A1
North End Brandon DH7 ...43 A5
Durham DH1 ...210 A4
Hutton Rudby TS15 ...173 F2
Sedgefield TS21 ...85 B7
North End Gdns DL14 ...80 D6
North End Villas DL15 ...189 F5
North Fen TS10 ...107 B4
North Field DL12 ...209 D7
North Gn
4 Staindrop DL2 ...200 E7
Stockton-on-T TS18 ...213 A1
North Haven SR7 ...29 B8
North Holm DH8 ...11 C4
North La Elwick TS27 ...75 C6
Gainford DL2 ...201 D4
Hetton-le-H DH5 ...27 E5
Killerby DL2 ...201 F7
Tow Law DL13, DL15 ...40 C1
Willington DL15 ...53 C6
North Leigh DH9 ...6 D1
North Lodge DH3 ...16 D7
North Lodge Terr DL3 ...132 F3
North Magdalene DH8 ...4 B1
North Mdw TS15 ...173 F2
North Moor Ave TS29 ...59 F4
North Mount Pleasant St 9 TS20 ...118 B6
North Ormesby Prim Sch TS3 ...120 C4
North Ormesby Rd TS1, TS4 ...215 B3
North Park Prim Sch DL16 ...56 A1
North Park Rd TS21 ...85 A7
North Railway St SR7 ...29 D7
North Rd
Annfield Plain DH9 ...12 E6
Chester le Street DH3 ...16 C7
Darlington DL1 ...133 A6
Durham DH1 ...210 B3
Hetton-le-H DH5 ...26 E4
Houghton-le-S DH5 ...26 E4
Loftus TS13 ...127 C1
Middlesbrough TS2 ...214 B4
Seaham SR7 ...29 D8
Seaton Carew TS25 ...77 E1
Spennymoor DL16 ...56 B1
Tow Law DL13 ...183 D2
Wingate TS28 ...60 E8
North Rd E TS28 ...60 E8
North Rd W TS28 ...60 E7
North Rise DL3 ...133 A5
North Road Ind Est DL3 ...132 F4
North Road Prim Sch DL1 ...133 A5
North Road Sta DL3 ...132 F4
North Row TS6 ...122 C4
North Side
Hutton Rudby TS15 ...173 F1
Middridge DL5 ...81 E1
Shadforth DH6 ...46 E7
North St Birtley DH3 ...9 E3
Blackhall Colliery TS27 ...50 D3
Byers Green DL16 ...54 E1
Consett DH8 ...11 B2
East Rainton DH5 ...26 D4
Ferryhill DL17 ...69 F6
Hett DH6 ...56 E6
Middlesbrough TS2 ...119 F7
New Silksworth SR3 ...18 A8
South Bank TS6 ...121 A7
Spennymoor DL16 ...68 F8
Stockton-on-T TS18 ...213 A3
West Rainton DH4 ...26 A2
North Stead Dr DH8 ...10 C5
North Tees Ind Est
Middlesbrough TS18 ...119 A5
Stockton-on-T TS18 ...118 F5
North Terr
Annfield Plain DH9 ...13 C5
Crook DL15 ...52 F4
Durham DH1 ...34 A6
Easington SR8 ...39 B4
Gainford DL2 ...201 D4
Loftus TS13 ...127 C3
11 New Silksworth SR3 ...18 A8
Newton Aycliffe DL5 ...96 E2
Redcar TS10 ...107 C7
Seaham SR7 ...29 D8
1 Skelton TS12 ...125 A2
Willington DL15 ...54 A2
Witton Gilbert DH7 ...33 A8
North Thorn DH9 ...13 F7
North View
Barnard Castle DL12 ...209 C5
Bearpark DH7 ...33 A3
Bishop Middleham DL17 ...71 C4
Bournmoor DH4 ...17 E2
Brandon DH7 ...43 C3
Castle Eden TS27 ...49 B1
Consett DH8 ...10 D4
Dalton Piercy TS27 ...75 F3
1 Durham DH1 ...35 A2
Easington SR8 ...39 E5
Easington Lane DH5 ...27 C1
Haswell DH6 ...37 E1
Hunwick DL15 ...66 D5
Langley Park DH7 ...32 B6
Ludworth DH6 ...47 C7
Medomsley DH8 ...4 B1
Murton SR7 ...28 D2
Ouston DH2 ...8 F1
Pelton DH2 ...15 D5
Rowlands Gill NE39 ...1 C2
Sherburn Hill DH6 ...36 D1
The Middles DH9 ...14 B3
North View Terr DH4 ...26 B8
North View W NE39 ...1 C2
North West Ind Est
Easington SR8 ...39 A1
Peterlee SR8 ...49 A8
Shotton Colliery SR8 ...48 F7
North Wood TS5 ...139 D6
Northallerton Rd
Dalton-on-T DL2 ...168 C3
Thornaby-on-T TS17 ...138 D7
Northampton Rd SR8 ...49 C8
Northampton Wlk 9 TS25 ...77 B4
Northamptonshire Dr DH1 ...35 D3
Northbourne Rd TS19 ...117 F5
Northbrook Ct TS26 ...76 E5
Northburn Gr DL15 ...65 D8
Northcliffe Gr TS15 ...173 F2
Northcote St TS18 ...213 A1
Northcote Terr DL3 ...132 E4
Northdale Ct TS3 ...120 E2
Northdene Ave SR7 ...29 D8
Northern Rd TS5 ...119 B2
Northfield Cl NE16 ...2 F5
Northfield Rd
Billingham TS22 ...102 C5
2 Marske-by-t-S TS11 ...108 B1
Northfield Sch & Sports Coll TS22 ...102 B6
Northfield View DH8 ...11 A3
Northfield Way DL5 ...96 C5
Northfields TS15 ...173 F2
Northfleet Ave TS3 ...120 E4
Northgate
Annfield Plain DH9 ...12 F3
Darlington DL1 ...133 A3
Guisborough TS14 ...143 E5
Hartlepool TS24 ...64 E1
Northgate Jun Sch TS14 ...143 E6
Northgate Rd TS5 ...139 D8
Northgrain DL13 ...179 B2
Northiam Cl TS8 ...139 D2
Northland Ave TS26 ...76 F5
Northlands DH3 ...16 C5
Northlands Pk TS29 ...59 E4
Northlea Rd SR7 ...29 A8
Northleach Dr TS8 ...139 D2
Northpark TS23 ...102 E8
Northport Rd TS18 ...213 C4
Northrop Cl DL15 ...53 E2
Northside Birtley DH3 ...9 D6
Trimdon TS29 ...59 E3
Northside Cl DL5 ...81 E1
Northside Ct DL5 ...81 E1
Northside Terr TS29 ...59 E3
Northumberland Ave
Bishop Auckland DL14 ...80 B6
Willington DL15 ...54 A3
Northumberland Gr
12 Hartlepool TS25 ...77 B4
Stockton-on-T TS20 ...101 F2
Northumberland Pl
Birtley DH3 ...9 D1
Peterlee SR8 ...49 B8
Northumberland Rd TS17 ...138 C7
Northumberland St
19 Darlington DL3 ...132 F1
Peterlee SR8 ...49 F8
Northumberland Wlk 13 TS25 ...77 B4
Northumbria Pl DH9 ...14 B7
Northwold Cl TS25 ...89 E6
Northwood Rd SR7 ...29 B8
Norton Ave Bowburn DH6 ...45 D1
Seaham SR7 ...19 A1
Stockton-on-T TS20 ...118 A7
Norton Back La DL2 ...135 A8
Norton Cl
Auckland Park DL14 ...80 F6
Chester le Street DH2 ...15 F1
Norton Cres DL2 ...134 E7
Norton Ct 12 TS20 ...118 B6
Norton Dr TS19 ...117 A5
Norton Hall TS20 ...102 B1
Norton Junction Cotts TS20 ...101 D1
Norton Prim Sch TS20 ...118 C6
Norton Rd
Billingham TS20, TS23 ...102 C1
Sadberge DL2 ...134 E7
Stockton-on-T TS20 ...118 B6
Norton Sch The TS20 ...118 C6
Norwich Ave TS19 ...117 C5
Norwich Cl DH3 ...25 B7
Norwich Gdns DL15 ...53 F2
Norwich Gr DL1 ...133 E5
Norwich Rd Durham DH1 ...34 D7
Middlesbrough TS5 ...119 E2
Redcar TS10 ...107 F4
Norwood Cl TS19 ...117 B5
Norwood Cres NE39 ...1 F2
Norwood Rd TS3 ...121 A2
Nottingham Dr TS10 ...107 E4
Nottingham Pl SR8 ...49 B8
Nottingham St DL14 ...68 C1
Nottingham Wlk 10 TS25 ...77 B4
Nottinghamshire Rd DH1 ...35 C3
Nuffield Ct DL1 ...133 B6
Nuffield Rd TS23 ...103 A4
Nugent Ave TS1 ...214 A2
Number One Ind Est DH8 ...11 A4
Nuneaton Dr TS8 ...139 D2
Nunnery Cl DL3 ...132 B2
Nunnery La DL3 ...132 C2
Nunnington Cl TS17 ...138 B1
Nuns Cl DL14 ...80 D5
Nuns St TS24 ...77 F8
Nuns' Row DH1 ...211 C4
Nunthorpe Gdns TS7 ...141 B2
Nunthorpe Prim Sch TS7 ...141 C3
Nunthorpe Sch TS7 ...141 C3
Nunthorpe Sta TS7 ...141 B3
Nursery Ct NE17 ...4 B6
Nursery Dr TS21, TS22 ...86 F3
Nursery End DL2 ...201 D7
Nursery Gdns
Easington SR8 ...39 B3
Yarm TS15 ...156 D4
Nursery La
Middlesbrough TS5 ...119 C2
Stockton-on-T TS18 ...212 B2
Nursery The DL14 ...79 C1
Nut La TS4 ...120 A2
Nutfield Cl TS8 ...139 D2
Nuthatch Cl TS26 ...76 D8
Nutley Rd TS23 ...102 F5

O

O' Hanlan St 4 DL16 ...55 F1
O'Neil Dr SR8 ...49 E5
Oak Ave
Blackhall Rocks TS27 ...50 E3
Durham DH1 ...35 A1
5 Houghton-le-S DH4 ...26 D8
Marton TS7 ...140 E3
Oak Ave *continued*
Willington DL15 ...54 B2
Oak Cres DH2 ...24 A3
Oak Ct DH7 ...23 C3
Oak Gdns DL15 ...52 D6
Oak Gr TS24 ...76 F8
Oak Hill TS8 ...140 C2
Oak La DH8 ...10 C7
Oak Lea Shildon DL4 ...81 B1
Witton Gilbert DH7 ...23 B1
Oak Leaf Cvn Pk DL13 ...207 D4
Oak Rd Brotton TS12 ...126 A5
Eaglescliffe TS16 ...137 D4
Easington SR8 ...39 D3
Guisborough TS14 ...143 E5
Redcar TS10 ...107 F5
Oak St Billingham TS23 ...103 E2
10 Consett DH8 ...10 F2
Eldon Lane DL14 ...80 F4
Great Lumley DH4 ...17 E1
Langley Park DH7 ...32 C7
Middlesbrough TS1 ...215 A3
South Bank TS6 ...121 A6
Waldridge DH2 ...15 E1
Oak Terr
Annfield Plain DH9 ...12 E5
Bishop Auckland DL14 ...80 C7
Burnopfield NE16 ...6 C6
Cornforth DL17 ...70 E8
Holmside DH7 ...22 D7
Leadgate DH8 ...11 D4
Murton SR7 ...28 D2
Pelton DH2 ...15 C7
Peterlee SR8 ...50 A6
Spennymoor DL16 ...68 E8
Tantobie DH9 ...6 B2
The Middles DH9 ...14 B3
Oak Tree Cl DL2 ...154 C7
Oak Tree Cres TS21 ...85 B7
Oak Tree Prim Sch The TS19 ...212 B4
Oak Wlk TS13 ...127 B2
Oakdale TS7 ...141 B7
Oakdale Rd Consett DH8 ...11 A3
New Marske TS11 ...123 F6
Oakdale Terr DH3 ...16 C2
Oakdene Ave
Darlington DL3 ...151 E8
Stockton-on-T TS18 ...137 E8
Oakdene Cl TS6 ...121 D1
Oakdene Prim Sch TS23 ...102 F6
Oakdene Rd TS21 ...72 D4
Oakdene Terr DL16 ...68 C5
Oakenshaw Dr TS5 ...139 C5
Oakenshaw Wildlife Reserve* DL15 ...54 B7
Oakerside Dr SR8 ...49 C4
Oakesway TS24 ...64 B1
Oakeys Rd DH9 ...13 F8
Oakfield
Chester le Street DH2 ...15 F2
Newton Aycliffe DL5 ...96 B6
Oakfield Ave TS16 ...137 B2
Oakfield Cl TS16 ...137 B2
Oakfield Cres DH6 ...45 E1
Oakfield Gdns TS7 ...121 B1
Oakfield La DH8 ...10 C1
Oakfield Rd
Middlesbrough TS3 ...215 C2
Whickham NE16 ...2 F5
Oakfields Burnopfield NE16 ...6 B7
Hunwick DL15 ...66 D7
Oakgreen Flats DH7 ...43 B4
Oakham Ave NE16 ...2 F6
Oakham Dr DH1 ...35 D5
Oakham Gn TS20 ...118 C7
Oakhurst Cl 5 TS17 ...138 C1
Oakhurst Rd DL3 ...132 E3
Oakland Ave TS25 ...77 A2
Oakland Gdns DL1 ...133 B7
Oaklands TS9 ...161 A3
Oaklands Ave 6 TS20 ...118 B7
Oaklands Rd TS6 ...141 E8
Oaklands Terr 6 DL3 ...132 F3
Oaklands The DL2 ...154 A5
Oaklea
Chester le Street DH2 ...16 A5
Shiney Row DH4 ...17 F4
Oaklea Cl TS20 ...118 A8
Oaklea Ct 24 DL1 ...132 F1
Oaklea Mews DL5 ...96 E1
Oaklea Terr 2 DL14 ...80 B6
Oakley Cl
Guisborough TS14 ...143 F2
Hemlington TS8 ...139 D2
Oakley Cross Prim Sch DL14 ...79 C1
Oakley Gdns TS24 ...77 A7
Oakley Gn DL14 ...79 D1
Oakley Rd TS12 ...145 C6
Oakley Wlk Eston TS6 ...121 E1
Normanby TS6 ...141 E8
Oakridge
1 Ormesby TS7 ...141 B7
Whickham NE16 ...2 F6
Oakridge Com Prim Sch TS13 ...149 E5
Oakridge Rd DH7 ...33 A1
Oakrise TS7 ...141 B7
Oaks Bank DL14 ...92 C8
Oaks Ho DL14 ...92 C8
Oaks The Cornforth DL17 ...57 D1
Darlington DL3 ...132 D3
Esh Winning DH7 ...41 D7
Hemlington TS8 ...139 D2

Oaks The continued
High Spen NE39 . . . . .1 A3
Hutton Henry TS27 . . . . .61 C5
Middleton St George DL2 . .154 C7
Newton Aycliffe DL5 . . . . . . .82 E2
Oaksham Dr TS23 . . . . .102 F8
Oakstead TS25 . . . . .77 C1
Oaktree Gr TS18 . . . . .137 B8
Oakway Cl DH7 . . . . .43 C4
Oakwell Ct NE17 . . . . .4 C5
Oakwell Gdns TS20 . . . . . . .118 A8
Oakwell Rd TS20 . . . . .118 A8
Oakwood
Annfield Plain DH9 . . . . .12 C4
Coxhoe DH6 . . . . .58 A3
Lanchester DH7 . . . . .21 A2
South Hetton DH6 . . . . .38 B6
Oakwood Cl
Hartlepool TS27 . . . . .63 C4
Sacriston DH7 . . . . .23 C3
Oakwood Ct DH9 . . . . .12 E4
Oakwood Dr DL1 . . . . .133 B7
Oakworth Gn TS4 . . . . .140 A8
Oatfields Ct TS6 . . . . .141 E8
Oatlands Gr TS13 . . . . .148 A8
Oatlands Way DH1 . . . . .34 C8
Oban Ave TS25 . . . . .77 A3
Oban Cl DL1 . . . . .133 D6
Oban Rd TS3 . . . . .120 D2
Obelisk La DH1 . . . . .210 B3
Oberhausen Mall TS1 . . . . .214 C2
Occupation Rd
Eston TS6 . . . . .121 F1
Normanby TS6 . . . . .141 F8
Ocean Rd TS24 . . . . .63 C5
Ocean View
Blackhall Rocks TS27 . . . . . . .50 E2
Hesleden SR7 . . . . .50 A7
Sunderland SR2 . . . . .158 C8
Ochil Terr TS23 . . . . .102 E3
Offerton Dr TS8 . . . . .139 E2
Office Pl DH5 . . . . .27 A3
Office Row DL14 . . . . .81 B4
Office Sq DL2 . . . . .200 E7
Office St Easington SR8 . . . .39 F4
Wheatley Hill DH6 . . . . .48 B3
Official Terr DH7 . . . . .21 B1
Okehampton Dr TS2 . . . . . .140 C3
Old Blackett St DH9 . . . . . . .12 E5
Old Brew Ho TS14 . . . . .143 F4
Old Brewery The DH4 . . . . .26 E8
Old Cemetery Rd TS24 . . . .64 C2
Old Court Ho DL12 . . . . . . .209 C5
Old Elvet DH1 . . . . .211 A2
Old Engine Hos DL4 . . . . . . .94 C7
Old Fir Tree Works The
DL15 . . . . .189 F5
Old Forge The DH7 . . . . . . .42 E1
Old Fulling Mill, Mus of
Archaeology* DH1 . . . . .210 C2
Old Gdns DH7 . . . . .43 C4
Old Hall Farm Rd DL14 . . . .79 D2
Old Hall Mus TS13 . . . . . . .120 A8
Old Hall Rd DH8 . . . . .11 B1
Old Market The TS6 . . . . . .156 B6
Old Middlesbrough Rd
TS6 . . . . .120 F5
Old Mill La DH4 . . . . .24 F6
Old Mill Wynd TS9 . . . . . . .161 A2
Old Orch The TS15 . . . . . . .173 F1
Old Park Terr DL16 . . . . . . .68 A7
Old Pit Terr DH1 . . . . .34 C7
Old Rd TS23 . . . . .102 D1
Old Rectory Cl DH9 . . . . .6 D4
Old Row 6 TS6 . . . . .121 F2
Old School Cl DL12 . . . . . . .209 C5
Old Shire Hall (Univ of
Durham) DH1 . . . . .211 A2
Old Station Mews TS16 . . .156 B7
Old Station Rd TS16 . . . . . .156 C7
Oldbury Gr TS8 . . . . .139 E2
Oldford Cres TS5 . . . . .139 C6
Oldgate TS6 . . . . .122 A2
Oldham Cl TS12 . . . . .145 C7
Oldham St TS12 . . . . .145 C6
Oldstead Ct TS8 . . . . .139 D2
Oley Mdws DH8 . . . . .10 C7
Olga Terr NE39 . . . . .5 C1
Olive St Hartlepool TS24 . . .77 F8
Middlesbrough TS2 . . . . .214 C4
Waldridge DH2 . . . . .9 C1
Oliver Cres Birtley DH3 . . . . .9 C6
Shadforth DH6 . . . . .46 E6
Oliver Pl DH1 . . . . .44 A7
Oliver St
Cold Hesledon SR7 . . . . .28 E1
Middlesbrough TS6 . . . . .119 E2
Seaham SR7 . . . . .29 B8
South Bank TS6 . . . . .121 A6
Stanley DH9 . . . . .13 E4
Olivers Gdns DL2 . . . . .200 F7
Olliver St TS10 . . . . .107 D6
Olney Wlk TS3 . . . . .140 D8
Olympic Cl DL3 . . . . .132 D4
Onslow Terr DH7 . . . . .43 E5
Ontario Cres TS10 . . . . . . .107 C5
Onyx Cl TS25 . . . . .77 C2
Opal Ave DL17 . . . . .82 F8
Orange Gr TS20 . . . . .118 A6
Orchard Ave NE39 . . . . .1 D1
Orchard Cl Carlton TS21 . .116 D8
Crook DL15 . . . . .52 E3
Dalton-on-T DL2 . . . . .168 B5
Great Ayton TS9 . . . . .161 A4
Rowlands Gill NE39 . . . . .5 D8

Orchard Cl continued
Sedgefield TS21 . . . . .85 B6
West Pelton DH9 . . . . .15 A6
Orchard Ct DL14 . . . . .80 C6
Orchard Dene NE39 . . . . .1 D1
Orchard Dr Durham DH1 . .211 B6
Guisborough TS14 . . . . .143 F4
Orchard Gdns DH3 . . . . .16 C1
Orchard Gr Eston TS6 . . . . .121 D2
Gainford DL2 . . . . .201 D4
Orchard Ho DH1 . . . . .211 A2
Orchard Pk 8 DH3 . . . . .9 C4
Orchard Rd
Darlington DL1 . . . . .132 D3
Middlesbrough TS5 . . . . .119 E1
Redcar TS10 . . . . .107 C5
Rowlands Gill NE39 . . . . .1 D1
Stockton-on-T TS17 . . . . . . .117 C3
Thornaby-on-T TS17 . . . . . . .138 B5
Orchard St Birtley DH3 . . . . .9 C4
Pelton DH2 . . . . .15 E7
Orchard Terr
Chester le Street DH3 . . . . . .16 C1
Rowlands Gill NE39 . . . . .5 D8
Orchard The
Chester le Street DH3 . . . . . .16 D4
Durham DH1 . . . . .34 B7
Heighington DL5 . . . . .95 D1
Ingleby Barwick TS17 . . . . . .138 A2
Ingleton DL2 . . . . .201 D7
Sadberge DL2 . . . . .134 E6
Sedgefield TS21 . . . . .85 B6
Skelton TS12 . . . . .125 C3
Orchard Way
Ormesby TS7 . . . . .141 A6
3 Shildon DL4 . . . . .81 A2
Orchards The DL2 . . . . . . .200 E7
Orchid Ct TS27 . . . . .50 D3
Orde Wingate Way
TS19 . . . . .213 A4
Ordsall Gn 8 TS3 . . . . .140 E8
Oriel Cl TS3 . . . . .139 D8
Orkney Ct DL1 . . . . .133 B6
Orkney Dr SR2 . . . . .18 D8
Orkney Wlk
Darlington DL1 . . . . .133 D7
Guisborough TS14 . . . . .143 C2
Orlands The DL5 . . . . .96 E2
Orleans Gr TS7 . . . . .140 E4
Ormesby Bank TS7 . . . . . . .141 B5
Ormesby Hall* TS7 . . . . .141 D4
Ormesby Prim Sch TS7 . . .141 A7
Ormesby Rd Eston TS6 . . . .121 C1
Hartlepool TS25 . . . . .90 A8
Middlesbrough TS3 . . . . .120 D2
Ormesby Sch Eston TS3 . . .121 B1
Ormesby TS7 . . . . .141 B8
Ormston Ave 4 TS3 . . . . . .140 E8
Ornsby Hill DH7 . . . . .20 C6
Oronsay Wlk DL1 . . . . .133 D7
Orpington Rd TS3 . . . . .140 E8
Orr Ave SR8 . . . . .18 B6
Orton Gr TS22 . . . . .102 B5
Orwell Cl Peterlee SR8 . . . . .49 B4
Skelton TS12 . . . . .125 D3
Orwell Gdns Stanley DH9 . . .13 F4
Stockton-on-T TS18 . . . . . . .117 B2
Orwell St TS1 . . . . .214 A2
Orwell Wlk TS25 . . . . .76 E2
Osbert Pl DL5 . . . . .96 C8
Osborne Bldgs DH9 . . . . . . .13 D4
Osborne Cl DL3 . . . . .132 C2
Osborne Gdns DL15 . . . . . . .52 F4
Osborne Rd
Chester le Street DH3 . . . . . .16 C3
Hartlepool TS26 . . . . .77 A5
Middlesbrough TS5 . . . . .119 D2
Stockton-on-T TS18 . . . . . . .212 C2
Osborne St 4 DL4 . . . . .80 F1
Osborne Terr
Coundon DL14 . . . . .81 D8
Easington SR8 . . . . .39 B3
Evenwood DL14 . . . . .92 C7
8 Ferryhill DL17 . . . . .70 B5
Frosterley DL13 . . . . .188 A7
Osborne Villas DH9 . . . . . . .13 E8
Osbourne Cl TS8 . . . . .139 D2
Osprey Cl
Esh Winning DH7 . . . . .41 C8
Guisborough TS14 . . . . .143 A4
Stockton-on-T TS20 . . . . . . .102 B2
Osprey Ho TS24 . . . . .77 D6
Osric Pl DL5 . . . . .96 D8
Ostler Cl TS17 . . . . .138 B1
Oswald Cl Cornforth DL17 . .57 F1
Durham DH1 . . . . .35 A1
Oswald Ct DH1 . . . . .211 A1
Oswald Pl DL17 . . . . .69 F6
Oswald Rd DH5 . . . . .27 A5
Oswald St
Bishop Auckland DL14 . . . . . .79 D2
Craghead DH9 . . . . .12 F5
Oswald Terr Chilton DL17 . . .82 F8
Easington SR8 . . . . .39 D4
Quaking Houses DH9 . . . . . . .13 E3
Oswestry Gn TS4 . . . . .140 B5
Otley Ave TS3 . . . . .140 E8
Otley Terr DL3 . . . . .132 F4
Ottawa Rd TS4 . . . . .120 A2
Otter Way TS17 . . . . .138 C2
Otterburn Cl DL1 . . . . .133 C6
Otterburn Gdns DL14 . . . .139 D4
Otterburn Way TS23 . . . . .102 F7
Otterhill Ct TS8 . . . . .19 D2
Otterington Cl TS27 . . . . . . .63 A3
Otterpool Cl TS24 . . . . .77 C7
Oughton Cl TS15 . . . . .156 E4

Oulston Rd TS18 . . . . .212 A2
TS19 . . . . .212 A2
Our Lady & St Bede's RC Sch
. . . . .212 A2
Our Lady & St Joseph's RC
Prim Sch DH4 . . . . .11 D4
Our Lady & St Thomas RC
Prim Sch DL15 . . . . .53 F3
Our Lady of Lourdes RC Prim
Sch DH4 . . . . .48 B7
Our Lady of the Most Holy
Rosary RC Prim Sch
TS23 . . . . .102 C5
Our Lady of the Rosary RC
Prim Sch SR8 . . . . .49 C6
Our Lady Of The Star RC
Prim Sch SR8 . . . . .39 F1
Our Lady Queen of Martyrs
RC Prim Sch DH7 . . . . .41 A8
Ouse Cres DH3 . . . . .25 B7
Ouseburn Cl SR2 . . . . .18 F8
Ouselaw NE11 . . . . .8 D6
Ouseport Rd TS18 . . . . . . .213 C4
Ouslaw La NE11 . . . . .8 B6
Ousterley Terr DH9 . . . . . . .14 C2
Ouston Inf Sch DH2 . . . . . . .9 A1
Ouston Jun Sch DH2 . . . . . . .8 F1
Ouston La DH2 . . . . .8 F1
Ouston St TS24 . . . . .77 B5
Outhwaite St TS5 . . . . .214 A1
Outputs La DH4 . . . . .177 D2
Outram St Darlington DL3 .132 E2
Middlesbrough TS1 . . . . .214 B2
Stockton-on-T TS18 . . . . . . .213 A2
Ouzel Cl TS26 . . . . .63 D1
Oval Grange TS26 . . . . .76 E6
Oval Pk DL16 . . . . .56 B3
Oval The
Bishop Auckland DL14 . . . . . .79 E3
Chester le Street DH2 . . . . . .24 B7
Cornforth DL17 . . . . .70 F8
Hartlepool TS26 . . . . .76 F5
Houghton-le-S DH4 . . . . .26 D8
Hurworth-on-T DL2 . . . . . . .152 D1
Ouston DH2 . . . . .8 F2
Shildon DL4 . . . . .80 F2
Stainton Grove DL12 . . . . . .209 F8
Wynyard Village TS22 . . . . . .87 B2
Overbrook TS9 . . . . .160 F2
Overdale TS14 . . . . .143 A2
Overdale Cl TS10 . . . . .107 C1
Overdale Rd TS3 . . . . .140 D8
Overdene SR7 . . . . .28 F5
Overfields Prim Sch
TS7 . . . . .141 B8
Overman St DH1 . . . . .45 B4
Overmans Cotts TS13 . . . . .127 A3
Ovington La DL11, DL2 . . . .201 A2
Owen Ct TS17 . . . . .69 F6
Owen Terr Chopwell NE17 . . .4 C8
Tantobie DH9 . . . . .6 B2
Owengate DH1 . . . . .210 C2
Owens Rd TS6 . . . . .120 F5
Owington Gr TS23 . . . . . . .103 A8
Owlet Grange NE39 . . . . .4 E5
Owletts Ct TS17 . . . . .157 B7
Owls Gr TS17 . . . . .156 F7
Owton Cl TS25 . . . . .89 F8
Owton Manor La TS25 . . . .89 D7
Owton Manor Prim Sch
TS25 . . . . .89 D8
Ox Close Cotts TS12 . . . . . .125 A7
Ox Close Cres DL16 . . . . . . .55 F1
Ox Close Prim Sch DL16 . . .55 F1
Oxbridge Ave
Stockton-on-T TS18 . . . . . . .212 A2
Stockton-on-T TS18 . . . . . . .212 A3
Oxbridge Ct TS18 . . . . .212 A2
Oxbridge Ind Est TS18 . . .212 C2
Oxbridge La Stockton-on-T
TS18 . . . . .212 B2
Oxbridge Lane Prim Sch
TS18 . . . . .212 C2
Oxfield TS8 . . . . .140 B3
Oxford Cres DH5 . . . . .26 F4
Oxford Pl DH3 . . . . .9 C1
Oxford Rd Hartlepool TS25 . .77 A3
Middlesbrough TS5 . . . . .119 C1
Spennymoor DL16 . . . . .55 F1
Thornaby-on-T TS17 . . . . . . .138 C8
Oxford St
Annfield Plain DH9 . . . . .12 F5
Boosbeck TS12 . . . . .145 B6
Darlington DL1 . . . . .133 A3
Eldon Lane DL14 . . . . .80 F4
Hartlepool TS25 . . . . .77 B3
Hartlepool TS25 . . . . .77 C4
Hunwick DL15 . . . . .66 D7
Middlesbrough TS1 . . . . .214 B1
Saltburn-by-S TS12 . . . . . . .125 E2
Seaham SR7 . . . . .29 A7
2 Shildon DL4 . . . . .94 F8
1 South Bank TS6 . . . . .121 A6
Stockton-on-T TS18 . . . . . . .213 A4
Oxford Street Mews
DL1 . . . . .133 A3
Oxford Terr
6 Bishop Auckland DL14 . . .80 B8
Bowburn DH6 . . . . .57 D8
10 Cockfield DL13 . . . . .195 E3
Oxfordshire Dr DH1 . . . . .35 C3
Oxgang Cl TS10 . . . . .107 C2
Oxhill Farm TS8 . . . . .157 F7
Oxhill Villas DH9 . . . . .13 B5
Oxley St Consett DH8 . . . . .10 D4
Redcar TS10 . . . . .107 D7
Oxley Terr DH1 . . . . .34 A7
Oysterman Ho TS24 . . . . . . .77 C7

P

Pacific Hall Cl SR7 . . . . .28 E8
Paddock Cl DH4 . . . . .17 F5
Paddock Gn TS22 . . . . .87 B3
Paddock La SR3 . . . . .18 C7
Paddock The
Barnard Castle DL12 . . . . . .209 B5
Coxhoe DH6 . . . . .58 A3
Eaglescliffe TS16 . . . . .137 C2
Elwick TS27 . . . . .75 C5
Esh Winning DH7 . . . . .41 C6
Lanchester DH7 . . . . .20 E3
Middleton St George DL2 . .153 F6
Newton Aycliffe DL5 . . . . . . .82 E2
Spennymoor DL16 . . . . .55 F4
Tanfield Lea DH9 . . . . .13 C8
Willington DL15 . . . . .54 B2
Paddock Wood TS8 . . . . . .140 A3
Paddocks The DL2 . . . . . . .201 D4
Padstow Cl
Hartlepool TS26 . . . . .76 D7
2 Sunderland SR2 . . . . .18 F8
Page Gr DL16 . . . . .68 D7
Paignton Cl TS8 . . . . .140 B4
Paignton Dr TS25 . . . . .89 F7
Palace Row TS27 . . . . .62 F2
Palatine View
Durham DH1 . . . . .210 B2
Sherburn Hill DH6 . . . . .36 C1
Palin Cl TS4 . . . . .215 B3
Palladium Bldgs 1 TS4 . . .119 F1
Pallister Ave TS3 . . . . .120 E4
Pallister Ct TS3 . . . . .120 E4
Pallister Park Prim Sch
TS3 . . . . .120 D2
Palm Gr TS19 . . . . .117 B2
Palm Lea DH7 . . . . .43 A4
Palm Rd DL17 . . . . .57 E1
Palm St 18 Consett DH8 . . .10 F3
Langley Park DH7 . . . . .32 D8
Middlesbrough TS1 . . . . .215 A2
Palm Terr
Middlesbrough TS3 . . . . .103 E1
Tantobie DH9 . . . . .6 C3
The Middles DH9 . . . . .14 B3
Palm Tree Villas DL2 . . . . .153 E8
Palmer Rd Dipton DH9 . . . . . .5 E1
Newton Aycliffe DL5 . . . . . . .96 E5
Shotton Colliery SR8 . . . . . . .49 A5
Palmer St
Middlesbrough TS1 . . . . .214 C2
South Hetton DH6 . . . . .38 B6
Stanley DH9 . . . . .13 D5
Palmer Wlk TS16 . . . . .137 C1
Palmers Garth DH1 . . . . . . .211 A2
Palmers Sq SR13 . . . . .149 E6
Palmers Terr DL17 . . . . .71 B3
Palmerston Ct 2 TS17 . . . .138 C3
Palmerston St
Consett DH8 . . . . .10 F2
Stockton-on-T TS18 . . . . . . .213 A3
Palms Ct DL1 . . . . .134 A1
Pan La DL7,DL2 . . . . .183 E5
Panfield Terr DH4 . . . . .17 E2
Pankhurst Pl DH9 . . . . .14 B5
Panmore Wlk TS16 . . . . . . .137 C2
Pannal Wlk TS16 . . . . .137 C2
Pannel Cl TS11 . . . . .123 F6
Pannell Ave TS5 . . . . .139 B8
Pannell Cl 6 TS5 . . . . .63 C4
Pannell Pl 4 TS27 . . . . .63 C4
Pannierman La TS7,TS9 . . .160 C3
Parade The
Chester le Street DH3 . . . . . .16 D1
Hartlepool TS26 . . . . .76 E6
Pelton DH2 . . . . .15 E7
Paradise Cotts DL13 . . . . .194 E5
Paradise Cres SR8 . . . . .39 D4
Paradise La SR8 . . . . .39 D4
Paradise St SR8 . . . . .50 B6
Paragon Sq DL13 . . . . .206 C3
Paris Pl TS7 . . . . .140 E4
Park Ave
2 Blackhall Colliery TS27 . . .50 D3
Bowburn DH6 . . . . .57 F8
Consett DH8 . . . . .11 A3
Coundongate DL14 . . . . .80 F8
Crook DL15 . . . . .52 E4
Eston TS6 . . . . .121 B3
Hartlepool TS26 . . . . .76 E5
New Silksworth SR3 . . . . . . .18 B7
Redcar TS10 . . . . .107 E6
Stanley DH9 . . . . .13 F7
Thornaby-on-T TS17 . . . . . . .138 D8
Wynyard Village TS22 . . . . . .87 B2
Park Ave N 6 TS3 . . . . .140 F8
Park Ave S TS3 . . . . .140 F8
Park Avenue Cl DL15 . . . . . .52 E4
Park Bank DH8 . . . . .175 B6
Park Cl Annfield Plain DH9 . .13 A3
Langley Park DH7 . . . . .32 D6
Park Cotts NE17 . . . . .4 B6
Park Cres Darlington DL1 . .132 F3
Stillington TS21 . . . . .99 F3
Park Ct TS10 . . . . .106 E4
Park Dr Hartlepool TS26 . . . .76 D6
Langley Park DH7 . . . . .32 D6
Stockton-on-T TS18 . . . . . . .117 D6
Park End Prim Sch TS3 . . .140 E8
Park Hill DH6 . . . . .57 E6
Park House Cl DH6 . . . . .35 F2
Park House Gdns DH6 . . . . .35 F2
Park House La DL2 . . . . .94 F2
Park House Rd DH1 . . . . .44 A7
Park La Blaydon NE21 . . . . . .2 B8
Darlington DL1 . . . . .152 A8

Park La continued
Guisborough TS14 . . . . .143 D4
Loftus TS13 . . . . .148 B8
Middlesbrough TS1 . . . . .215 A1
Murton SR7 . . . . .28 A8
Peterlee SR8 . . . . .50 A7
Park Lane Inf Sch TS14 . . .143 D5
Park Lea 10 E3
Park Mews TS26 . . . . .76 E6
Park Par 1 DL16 . . . . .68 F8
Park Pl
Chester le Street DH3 . . . . . .16 D5
Darlington DL1 . . . . .133 A1
Park Rd Brotton TS12 . . . . .126 A3
Consett DH8 . . . . .10 E3
Hartlepool TS26 . . . . .77 A5
Middlesbrough TS5 . . . . .214 C1
Peterlee SR8 . . . . .49 F8
Rowlands Gill NE39 . . . . .35 F2
Stanley DH9 . . . . .13 D5
Stockton-on-T TS18 . . . . . . .212 C1
Thornaby-on-T TS17 . . . . . . .138 C6
Trimdon TS29 . . . . .60 A4
Witton Park DL14 . . . . .79 A8
Park Rd Ind Est DH8 . . . . . .10 E3
Park Rd N
Chester le Street DH3 . . . . . .16 D4
Middlesbrough TS1 . . . . .215 A1
Park Rd N Ind Est DH8 . . . .10 D3
Park Rd S
Chester le Street DH3 . . . . . .16 D1
Middlesbrough TS5 . . . . .119 F2
Park Rise TS9 . . . . .161 A2
Park Road Central 16 D3
Park Sq Great Ayton TS9 . .161 A2
Hartlepool TS26 . . . . .76 F7
Park St
Bishop Auckland DL14 . . . . . .80 C8
Consett DH8 . . . . .11 A3
Darlington DL1 . . . . .133 A1
Middlesbrough TS1 . . . . .214 C3
Seaham SR7 . . . . .29 D6
Willington DL15 . . . . .54 A4
Park Terr
Barnard Castle DL12 . . . . . .209 C5
Brotton TS12 . . . . .126 B3
Burnopfield NE16 . . . . .6 B5
8 Consett DH8 . . . . .177 A3
Howden-le-W DL15 . . . . .65 F7
Leadgate DH8 . . . . .11 A3
Loftus TS13 . . . . .127 C1
Peterlee SR8 . . . . .50 A6
Stockton-on-T TS18 . . . . . . .213 B2
Thornaby-on-T TS17 . . . . . . .138 C8
Tow Law DL13 . . . . .183 E1
Willington DL15 . . . . .54 A3
Park The
Bishop Middleham DL17 . . . .71 B3
Wolviston TS22 . . . . .103 E1
Park Vale Rd TS4 . . . . .215 B1
Park View Blaydon NE21 . . . .2 C8
Bournmoor DH3 . . . . .17 D4
Burnopfield NE16 . . . . .6 B6
Chester le Street DH3 . . . . . .16 B5
Consett DH8 . . . . .11 A3
Fishburn TS21 . . . . .72 D5
Hetton-le-H DH5 . . . . .27 A3
Kimblesworth DH2 . . . . .23 F4
Pelton DH2 . . . . .15 E5
Peterlee SR8 . . . . .50 A7
Sedgefield TS21 . . . . .85 A6
Shildon DL4 . . . . .80 F1
Stockton-on-T TS18 . . . . . . .212 C1
Willington DL15 . . . . .54 A5
Witton Gilbert DH7 . . . . .32 F8
Yarm TS15 . . . . .156 B4
Park View Com Sch DH3 . .16 C1
Park View Com Sch (Lower)
DH3 . . . . .16 D7
Park View Ind Est TS25 . . .90 B8
Park View Terr
Brandon DH7 . . . . .43 E6
Coundon DL14 . . . . .67 F1
Guisborough TS14 . . . . .143 C4
Park Wood Ave DH7 . . . . . . .33 A3
Parkdale 55 E2
Parkdale Rise NE16 . . . . .7 A2
Parkdale Way TS5 . . . . . . .139 E2
Parker Terr DL17 . . . . .69 F6
Parker's Bldgs DH8 . . . . . . .11 E1
Parkfield TS6 . . . . .57 E6
Parkfield Ave TS5 . . . . .139 E2
Parkfield Rd DL1 . . . . .213 A1
Parkfield Terr DH9 . . . . .12 E6
Parkfield Way TS18 . . . . . .213 A1
Parkgate Darlington DL1 . .133 A1
Eston TS6 . . . . .122 A2
Parkgate La NE21 . . . . .2 B8
Parkhead DH9 . . . . .12 B8
Parkhead Com Prim Sch
NE21 . . . . .2 C8
Parkhead Gdns NE21 . . . . . .2 B8
Parkin Row DL12 . . . . .208 C5
Parkin St TS18 . . . . .213 A3
Parkinson Ho TS1 . . . . .215 A4
Parkland Ct SR7 . . . . .29 B8
Parkland Dr DL3 . . . . .132 A3
Parkland Gr DL3 . . . . .132 A3
Parkland Terr SR7 . . . . .29 B8
Parklands
Hamsterley Mill NE39 . . . . . . .4 F5
Redcar TS10 . . . . .107 D2

Parklands Ave TS23 102 D2
Parklands Cl TS3 120 D2
Parklands Gr DH6 38 B6
Parklands Way TS26 76 C5
Parks The DH3 16 E1
Parkside Burnhope DH7 21 E5
Consett DH8 10 E3
Darlington DL1 152 A7
Guisborough TS14 143 E5
Howden-le-W DL15 65 E8
Longnewton TS21 135 F5
Middlesbrough TS3 140 E7
Sacriston DH7 23 C3
Spennymoor DL16 55 E1
Tanfield Lea DH9 6 C1
Parkside Comp Sch DL15 54 A2
Parkside Cotts DH9 6 C1
Parkside Cres SR7 29 C6
Parkside Inf Sch SR7 29 C5
Parkston Ho TS23 102 D2
Parkstone Cl TS11 124 A6
Parkstone Gr TS24 63 D4
Parkstone Pl TS16 156 C8
Parkview Rd E TS25 90 C8
Parkview Rd W TS25 90 B8
Parkway NE16 2 E6
Parkway Ctr TS8 140 B2
Parkway Dr TS6 141 D8
Parkway Gr TS3 120 D2
Parkway The TS12 125 A7
Parkwood Dr TS18 137 D8
Parliament Cl TS18 213 A1
Parliament Rd TS1 214 B2
Parliament St
Consett DH8 10 F2
Stockton-on-T TS18 213 A1
Parliament Wlk TS18 213 A1
Parmeter St DH9 13 E4
Parnaby St DH8 10 F2
Parnell St DH4 26 B8
Parracombe Cl TS17 157 B6
Parrington Pl TS6 122 C4
Parsons Ct Ferryhill DL17 69 E5
South Bank TS6 121 A4
Parsons Lonnen DL12 209 C5
Parsons Rd SR8 39 D1
Partnership Ct SR7 18 E2
Parton St TS24 77 B8
Partridge Ave TS5 139 C4
Partridge Cl
3 Ingleby Barwick TS17 138 B1
Washington NE38 9 F4
Partridge Terr TS28 60 E8
Passfield Cres TS6 121 B6
Passfield Sq
Easington SR8 39 C3
Thornley (nr Wheatley Hill) DH6 47 D4
Passfield Way SR8 49 B4
Pasteur Rd DH6 37 F7
Pasture Cl TS11 108 A1
Pasture Field TS21 72 B1
Pasture La TS6 122 C4
Pasture Rows DL14 81 B4
Pasture The TS17 138 A2
Pastures The TS8 140 C1
Patches La DL3 112 E3
Pateley Moor Cres DL1 152 C7
Patenson Ct DL5 82 B2
Patrick Cres DH6 37 E8
Patten La TS14 143 E5
Patten St 3 TS6 121 D1
Patterdale Ave
Middlesbrough TS5 139 C7
Stockton-on-T TS19 212 B4
Patterdale Cl Crook DL15 52 F2
Durham DH1 35 E4
Patterdale Mews DH8 11 D4
Patterdale St
Hartlepool TS25 77 B3
Hetton-le-H DH5 27 A2
Pattison Cres TS27 50 F2
Pattison Gdns TS27 50 F2
Pattison St 22 DL1 133 B1
Patton Wlk DH6 48 A3
Paulinus Rd DL5 96 C6
Pauls Gn DH5 27 A6
Pauntley Dr TS5 139 C3
Pavilion Cl TS25 90 E7
Pavilion Terr DH7 21 D5
Pawston Rd NE21,NE39 1 B5
Paxton Cl
Newton Aycliffe DL5 96 B8
Stockton-on-T TS18 213 B4
Paxton St DL17 69 D5
Pea Flatts La DH3 25 C7
Pea Rd DH9 13 D6
Peabody St DL3 133 A6
Peace Haven 4 DL17 70 B5
Peaceful Valley DL2 168 A8
Peakston Cl TS26 76 D7
Pear Lea DH7 43 A4
Pear Tree Cotts TS8 157 F7
Pear Tree Ct TS11 124 A7
Pear Tree Terr
Chopwell NE17 4 B8
Great Lumley DH3 17 B1
Peareth Terr DH3 9 C3
Pearl Cl DL17 82 F8
Pearl Rd TS17 138 D7
Pearl St
Middlesbrough TS1 214 C2
Saltburn-by-t-S TS12 125 C8
Shildon DL4 80 F1
Pears' Terr 6 DL4 95 A8
Pearson Cl TS18 213 A1
Pearson St
Middlesbrough TS1 214 A3
Pearson St *continued*
Spennymoor DL16 69 C8
Stanley DH9 13 F8
Pearson Terr DL12 209 C6
Pearson Ville TS9 161 A2
Pearson Way TS17 213 C2
Pearson Wlk TS18 213 A1
Peart Cl DH6 36 A1
Peartree Bglws NE17 4 C6
Peartree Ct NE17 4 C6
Peartree Terr DH7 22 B6
Pease Cotts DL1 132 F1
Pease Ct
Eaglescliffe TS16 137 B2
Guisborough TS14 143 B2
Lingdale TS12 145 E5
Pease Rd SR8 48 F8
Pease St Darlington DL1 133 C1
Lingdale TS12 145 E5
Pease Way DL5 96 C6
Peaseholm Bglws DL15 52 D4
Peases Row DL14 79 F3
Peases W DL15 52 E7
Peases West Prim Sch DL15 52 D7
Peaton St TS3 120 C4
Peebles Ave TS25 77 A3
Peebles Cl DL1 133 E7
Peel Ave Durham DH1 35 B3
Trimdon TS29 59 E4
Peel Pl DL14 66 F2
Peel St Binchester DL14 68 A5
Bishop Auckland DL14 80 C7
8 Darlington DL1 133 B1
Middlesbrough TS1 214 C2
Thornaby-on-T TS17 138 C8
Peelers Ct TS14 143 E6
Peggy's Wicket DH9 14 F8
Pegman Cl TS14 143 F6
Peile Ct DH8 10 C6
Peile Pk DH8 10 C6
Peirse Cl TS4 215 B3
Peirson Ct TS10 107 B7
Peirson St TS10 107 B7
Pelaw Ave
Chester le Street DH2 16 C5
Stanley DH9 14 A8
Pelaw Bank DH3 16 C4
Pelaw Cres DH2 16 B5
Pelaw Grange Ct DH3 16 C8
Pelaw Leazes La DH1 211 A3
Pelaw Pl DH2 16 C5
Pelaw Rd DH2 16 C5
Pelaw Sq DH2 16 B5
Pelham Ct DH6 58 A3
Pelham St Hartlepool TS24 77 A8
Middlesbrough TS1 214 C2
Pelton Cl TS23 102 D8
Pelton Com Prim Sch DH2 15 F7
Pelton Fell Rd DH2 16 B4
Pelton House Farm Est DH2 15 E6
Pelton La
Chester le Street DH2 16 B5
Pelton DH2 15 C5
Pelton Mews DH2 15 C6
Pemberton Ave DH8 177 B4
Pemberton Bank DH5 27 C1
Pemberton Cres TS4 140 A8
Pemberton Rd
Consett DH8 10 B2
Newton Aycliffe DL5 82 D2
Pemberton St DH5 27 A4
Pemberton Terr 2 DL2 153 F8
Pemberton Terr N DH9 14 B3
Pemberton Terr S DH9 14 B3
Pembroke Ave Birtley DH3 9 D1
New Silksworth SR3 18 A6
Pembroke Ct 15 DL1 133 B1
Pembroke Dr TS17 157 A6
Pembroke Gr TS26 63 E1
Pembroke Pl SR8 49 B8
Pembroke Rd TS20 118 A7
Pembroke St DL14 81 D8
Pembroke Way TS10 107 E5
Penarth Wlk TS26 76 D8
Penberry Gdns TS17 156 F7
Pendeen Gr DL3 132 F8
Penders La TS15 172 E8
Penderyn Cres TS17 156 F7
Pendle Cl Peterlee SR8 49 B5
Skelton TS12 125 B3
Pendle Cres TS23 102 E4
Pendleton Rd
Darlington DL1 133 A5
Darlington DL1 133 A6
Pendleton Rd S DL1 133 A5
Pendock Cl TS5 139 D4
Pendower St DL3 132 F3
Pendragon DH3 25 A8
Penhale Dr SR2 18 F7
Penhill Cl
Middlesbrough TS3 120 C2
Urpeth DH2 8 F1
Penhill Rd TS18 117 B1
Penistone Rd TS3 140 E7
Penllyn Way TS8 139 E3
Pennal Gr TS17 156 E8
Pennard Gn TS3 120 E2
Pennine Ave
Chester le Street DH2 16 B2
Stockton-on-T TS18 118 F5
Pennine Cl DL3 132 C3
Pennine Cres TS10 107 B4
Pennine Ct
Annfield Plain DH9 12 F3
Fir Tree DL15 52 A2
Pennine Dr SR8 49 A5
Pennine Gdns DH9 14 A5
Pennine View
Chopwell NE17 4 B8
Tow Law DL13 183 D2
Pennine Way Chilton DL17 83 A8
Ingleby Barwick TS17 157 B7
1 Skelton TS12 125 C3
Pennington Cl TS23 102 E6
Penny La TS18 213 A1
Pennyman Cl TS6 121 C1
Pennyman Ct TS3 140 F7
Pennyman Gn TS8 157 F7
Pennyman Prim Sch TS3 141 A8
Pennyman St TS3 215 C3
Pennyman Way TS8 139 C1
Pennyman Wlk TS11 108 D1
Pennypot La TS16 137 D5
Penrhyn St TS26 77 B4
Penrith Cl TS10 107 C4
Penrith Rd TS3 120 D1
Penrith St TS24 64 D2
Penryn Ave SR7 28 D3
Penryn Cl Darlington DL3 132 F8
Skelton TS12 125 D3
Penryn Way DH7 43 C4
Pensbury St DL1 133 A1
Pensby Ave TS4 140 B5
Penshaw Cl
3 Ingleby Barwick TS17 138 C1
Langley Park DH7 32 B6
Penshaw Ct TS23 102 E8
Penshaw Gdns DH9 14 B7
Penshaw View Birtley DH3 9 E3
Sacriston DH7 23 D2
Penshaw Way DH3 9 E4
Penshurst Pl TS23 102 F5
Pentilly St TS24 64 F1
Pentland Ave
Billingham TS23 102 D4
Redcar TS10 107 A3
6 Skelton TS12 125 C3
Pentland Cl SR8 49 A5
Pentland Ct 5 DH2 16 C2
Pentland Gr DL3 132 B1
Pentland Prim Sch TS23 102 D3
Pentlands Terr DH9 14 A5
Pentlands The DL17 82 F8
Penton Ct TS23 102 E7
Penwick Cl TS15 156 B4
Penyghent Way TS17 157 B6
Penzance Ct SR7 28 D4
Peppermires DH7 43 A1
Percy Ave DH9 12 E5
Percy Cres DH7 20 F3
Percy Cross Rigg YO21 162 E3
Percy Gdns Consett DH8 11 B1
1 Consett DH8 177 D4
Percy La DH1 210 A2
Percy Rd DL3 132 F6
Percy Sq DH1 44 A7
Percy St
Bishop Auckland DL14 80 B5
Crook DL15 52 E5
Hartlepool TS26 76 F7
Hetton-le-H DH5 27 B4
Middlesbrough TS1 214 C2
Stanley DH9 13 D5
Thornley (nr Wheatley Hill) DH6 47 D4
Wheatley Hill DH6 47 F3
Percy Terr
Annfield Plain DH9 13 B4
Consett DH8 11 B1
Durham DH1 210 A2
Peregrine Ct TS14 143 B4
Perm Terr DL17 71 C4
Perry Ave TS17 138 D2
Perrycrofts SR3 18 A4
Pert Rd TS24 63 E4
Perth Cres TS7 140 D3
Perth Gr Darlington DL1 133 E7
Stockton-on-T TS18 212 A1
Perth St TS24 77 A7
Pesspool Ave DH6 37 F3
Pesspool Bglws DH6 37 F3
Pesspool La
Easington DH6,SR8 38 C4
Haswell DH6 37 F3
Pesspool Terr DH6 37 F3
Petch Cl TS1 214 B2
Petch St TS18 213 A3
Peter Lee Cotts DH6 47 E2
Peter's Bank DH9 13 A7
Peterborough Rd DH1 34 E7
Peterhouse Cl DL1 133 B5
Peterlee Cl SR8 49 C7
Peterlee Com Hospl SR8 49 E5
Peth Gn DH5 27 B1
Peth La DH7 21 B4
Pethside DH7 21 A3
Petrel Cres TS20 102 A2
Petterson Dale DH6 58 A4
Petwell Cres SR8 39 C4
Petwell La SR8 39 C5
Petworth Cres TS17 157 B8
Pevensey Cl TS4 140 A7
Peverell St DL14 80 D5
Peveril Rd TS23 102 D5
Pexton Cl TS8 139 C2
Phalp St DH6 38 B6
Pheasant Cl 2 TS17 138 B1
Pheonix Ct DH8 10 C3
Philip Ave DH6 45 D2
Phillida Terr TS5 119 F2
Phillips Ave TS5 139 E8
Phillips Cl DH6 37 E3
Phillips Ho TS1 215 A3
Philpotts Wlk DL5 96 E8
Phoenix Cl
Hartlepool TS25 89 E7
Langley Park DH7 32 B6
Phoenix Ct DL1 133 D1
Phoenix Gdns TS18 212 A2
Phoenix Pk TS8 139 E3
Phoenix Pl
Newton Aycliffe DL5 82 C1
3 Shildon DL4 81 A2
Phoenix Rd NE38 9 E6
Phoenix Row DL14 78 F7
Phoenix Sidings TS19 213 A3
Phoenix Way DH4 26 C7
Phoenix Wlk TS18 212 A2
Phoenix Workshops TS19 213 A3
Phyllis Mohan Ct 10 TS3 140 D8
Pickard Cl SR8 49 E7
Pickering Gr TS25 90 A8
Pickering Ho 13 TS4 139 F8
Pickering Rd TS17 138 E7
Pickering St TS28 60 D6
Picktree Cotts 2 DH3 16 D4
Picktree Cotts E 3 DH3 16 D4
Picktree Farm Cotts NE38 16 E7
Picktree Gdns TS25 76 F1
Picktree La
Chester le Street DH3 16 D4
Chester le Street,Rickleton DH3,NE38 16 E7
Picktree Lodge Birtley DH3 9 E1
Chester le Street DH3 16 D8
Picktree Mews DH3 16 D4
Picktree Terr 1 DH3 16 D4
Pickwick Cl DH1 44 B7
Pickwick Ind Est DL14 79 C2
Picton Ave
Billingham TS22 102 B6
Middlesbrough TS5 139 B8
Picton Cres TS17 138 B4
Picton Pl 2 TS20 118 B8
Picture House Bldgs TS23 102 D1
Piercebridge Cl TS19 117 C5
Pierremont Cres DL3 132 D3
Pierremont Dr DL3 132 D3
Pierremont Gdns DL3 132 D2
Pierremont Rd DL3 132 D3
Piersburgh La TS15 171 D8
Piggy La DL2 201 C3
Pike Hill DH8 176 F8
Pikeston Cl TS26 76 D7
Pikesyde DH9 12 B7
Pilgrim St TS24 77 C5
Pilgrims' Way DH1 211 C4
Pilkington St TS3 120 C4
Pilkington Way DL14 80 E6
Pilkingtons Bldgs TS5 119 D1
Pilmoor Gn DL1 152 C7
Pilot Ho TS24 77 D6
Pimlico DH1 210 C1
Pimlico Rd DH5 27 B1
Pinder Cl TS20 118 A8
Pinders Way DH6 36 D1
Pine Ave Burnopfield NE16 5 F6
Durham DH1 35 A1
3 Houghton-le-S DH4 26 D8
Pine Ct TS19 117 C5
Pine Gr Darlington DL3 151 C8
Hartlepool TS24 76 F8
Pine Hill TS8 140 C2
Pine Lea DH7 43 A4
Pine Pk DH7 33 B1
Pine Rd Ferryhill DL17 57 B1
Guisborough TS14 143 E5
Ormesby TS7 141 B7
Pine Ridge Ave TS21 85 B8
Pine St Beamish DH2 15 B7
Birtley DH3 9 C5
4 Chester le Street DH3 16 C3
Langley Park DH7 32 D7
Middlesbrough TS1 215 A3
Middlesbrough, Cargo Fleet TS3 120 D5
Stanley DH9 13 D4
Stockton-on-T TS20 118 B8
Waldridge DH2 15 E1
West Pelton DH2 15 A5
Pine Terr DH9 12 E5
Pine Tree Cres DL4 81 B1
Pine View DH9 13 D4
Pine View Villas DH7 41 F8
Pine Wlk TS13 127 B2
Pineda Cl TS5 139 D3
Pinedale Dr DH6 37 F7
Pinehurst Way TS11 123 F6
Pinero Gr TS25 76 D2
Pines The TS15 156 C5
Pinetree DH7 41 D8
Pinetree Gdns DL15 52 D3
Pinetree Gr DL2 153 F7
Pinewood Ave TS4 139 F8
Pinewood Cl
Hartlepool TS27 63 C4
Loftus TS13 148 A8
Newton Aycliffe DL5 82 B1
Pinewood Cres DL5 95 C1
Pinewood Rd
Eaglescliffe TS16 137 C4
Marton TS7 140 F4
Pinewood St DH4 17 E1
Pinfold La DL13 195 C4
Pinfold St TS18 213 B4
Pintail Cl TS26 76 D8
Piper Knowle Rd TS19 117 B8
Pipershaw NE37 9 F6
Pipit Cl TS17 138 A1
Pippins The TS22 102 C8
Pirbright Gr TS8 139 E2
Pirnmill View TS19 117 B5
Pit La Brandon DH7 42 E5
Durham DH1 34 C7
Pithouse La
Medomsley DH8 11 B8
West Rainton DH4 25 E3
Pitt St Binchester DL14 68 A4
Consett DH8 10 F2
Pittington La DH1,DH6 35 F5
Pittington Prim Sch DH6 36 B5
Pittington Rd DH5,DH6 36 A7
Pixley Dell DH8 177 E4
Plane St DH8 11 A2
Planetree Ct TS7 140 E4
Plantagenet Ave DH3 16 D2
Plantation Ave DH6 36 E3
Plantation Cotts TS12 145 F4
Plantation Rd TS10 107 C1
Plantation St DH8 11 D4
Plantation Terr
Fir Tree DL15 52 A1
Howden-le-W DL15 65 E8
Plantation View
Howden-le-W DL15 65 E8
West Pelton DH9 14 F6
Plantation Wlk DH6 37 F7
Plantations TS22 87 A3
Plawsworth Rd DH7 23 C3
Plawsworth Road Inf Sch DH7 23 C3
Player Ct TS16 137 C1
Playlin Cl TS15 156 E4
Pleasant Pl 5 DH3 9 C5
Pleasant View
Burnhope DH7 21 D4
Consett DH8 10 B4
Darlington DL3 133 A6
Leadgate DH8 11 B6
Plover Cl 5 NE38 9 F3
Plover Dr NE16 6 C5
Plover Lodge DH3 9 C6
Plumer Dr TS20 118 A8
Plunkett Rd DH9 5 E1
Plunkett Terr DH2 15 D4
Plymouth Cl SR7 28 F6
Plymouth Gr TS26 76 E8
Plymouth Wlk TS26 76 E8
Pochin Rd Eston TS6 121 D6
Eston TS6 121 E6
Polam Hall Jun Sch DL1 151 E8
Polam Hall Sch DL1 151 F8
Polam La DL1 151 F8
Polam Rd DL1 151 F8
Polden Cl SR8 49 A5
Poldon Terr TS23 102 E3
Polemarch St 4 SR7 29 D6
Police Hos DL15 189 E5
Police Houses SR8 49 C6
Pollard's Dr DL14 80 A7
Polpero Cl DH3 9 D3
Polperro Cl 6 SR2 18 F8
Polperro Gr DL3 133 A8
Pond Farm Cl TS13 149 F6
Pond Field Cl DL3 151 B8
Pond St DH1 45 B4
Pond View DL1 133 C2
Ponds Court Bsns Pk DH8 10 E2
Ponds Ct DH8 10 E2
Pont Bglws DH8 11 B6
Pont La DH8 11 C6
Pont Rd DH8 11 D5
Pont Terr DH8 11 C4
Pont View DH8 11 B5
Pontac Rd TS11 124 A6
Ponteland Cl NE38 9 F4
Ponthaugh NE39 1 F3
Ponthead Mews DH8 11 D4
Pontop Ct 8 DH9 12 F4
Pontop Pike La DH9 12 C6
Pontop St DH5 26 C4
Pontop Terr DH9 12 E3
Pontop View Consett DH8 11 B1
Dipton DH9 12 B7
Rowlands Gill NE39 1 D2
Pontopsyde DH9 12 C7
Poole Terr TS7 160 B8
Pope Gr TS25 76 D3
Poplar Ave
Burnopfield NE16 5 F6
1 Houghton-le-S DH4 26 D8
Hutton Rudby TS15 173 F1
Poplar Cres Birtley DH3 9 B5
Fishburn TS21 72 D5
Poplar Dr Durham DH1 35 A3
Spennymoor DL16 68 F7
Poplar Gr Brotton TS12 126 A4
Darlington DL1 133 C2
Dipton DH9 12 E8
Redcar TS10 107 E6
South Bank TS6 121 B4
Stockton-on-T TS18 212 C1
7 Sunderland SR2 18 E8
Poplar Lea DH7 43 A4
Poplar Pl TS14 143 C5
Poplar Rd Durham DH1 35 D4
Eaglescliffe TS16 156 B8
Thornaby-on-T TS17 138 C7

Poplar St Beamish DH2 ....15 B7
3 Chester le Street DH3 ....16 C3
Sacriston DH7 ....23 C3
Stanley DH9 ....13 D4
Waldridge DH2 ....15 E1
Poplar Terr
Billy Row DL15 ....52 D7
Chester le Street DH3 ....16 D4
Cornforth DL17 ....70 E8
Middlesbrough TS2 ....103 E1
Poplars La TS21 ....116 C8
Poplars Rd TS5 ....119 E1
Poplars The Chilton DL17 ..82 E8
Easington Lane DH5 ....27 C1
Wolviston TS22 ....102 C8
Poppy La TS19 ....117 C5
Poppyfields DH2 ....15 F2
Popular Ave TS27 ....50 E2
Popular Ct 1 DH3 ....16 C3
Porlock Rd TS23 ....102 C5
Porret La TS13 ....149 E6
Porrett Cl TS24 ....63 E4
Port Clarence Rd
Billingham TS2 ....119 F8
Middlesbrough TS2 ....103 E1
Porter Cl DL5 ....96 E8
Porter Terr SR7 ....28 C3
Porthleven Way TS10 ....107 F2
Portland Ave SR7 ....29 A7
Portland Cl
Chester le Street DH2 ....16 A1
Eaglescliffe TS16 ....156 C8
Marton TS7 ....140 C3
Redcar TS10 ....107 C1
Portland Gr TS24 ....63 D4
Portland Ho TS3 ....120 E4
Portland Pl DL3 ....132 F2
Portland Wlk TS10 ....107 C1
Portmadoc Wlk TS26 ....76 D8
Portman Rd TS20 ....118 A7
Portman Rise TS14 ....143 E2
Portman St TS1 ....214 C2
Portmeads Rd DH3 ....9 D4
Portmeads Rise DH3 ....9 D4
Portobello Ind Est DH3 ....9 E4
Portobello Prim Sch DH3 ..9 D2
Portobello Terr DH3 ....9 E2
Portobello Way DH3 ....9 D4
Portrack Back La TS18 ..118 E6
Portrack Grange Cl
TS18 ....118 F4
Portrack Grange Rd
TS18 ....118 F4
Portrack Ind Est TS18 ..118 F4
Portrack Interchange Bsns Pk TS18 ....118 E5
Portrack La TS18 ....118 D4
Portrack Ret Pk TS18 ..118 D4
Portreath Ct DL3 ....133 A8
Portree Cl DH3 ....9 D1
Portrush Cl
Darlington DL1 ....133 E6
Middlesbrough TS4 ....139 F7
New Marske TS11 ....123 F6
Portsmouth Pl DL1 ....133 E5
Post Horn DL5 ....95 F8
Post House Wynd 5
DL3 ....132 F1
Post Office Row DH7 ....30 B3
Post Office St DL14 ....65 B3
Potter Pl DH9 ....14 B5
Potter Wlk 4 TS24 ....77 B7
Potter's Side La YO21 ....164 C2
Potterhouse La DH1 ....33 F8
Potterhouse Terr DH1 ....34 A8
Potters Bank DH1 ....44 B7
Potters Cl DH1 ....44 A7
Pottery Mews TS5 ....119 D2
Pottery St TS17 ....138 B8
Pottery Yd 3 DH4 ....26 E8
Potto Cl TS15 ....156 E5
Potto St DH6 ....48 D6
Potts Rd DL14 ....68 C1
Poulton Cl NE38 ....17 B8
Pounder Pl TS24 ....63 F2
Pounteys Cl DL2 ....153 E7
Pow Hill Ctry Pk* DH8 ..175 F6
Powburn Cl
Chester le Street DH2 ....16 A1
Stockton-on-T TS19 ....117 A5
Powell St TS26 ....77 A4
Powlett Rd TS24 ....64 B1
Powlett St DL3 ....132 F1
Prebend Row
10 Darlington DL1 ....132 F2
Pelton DH2 ....15 D7
Prebends Field DH1 ....35 A4
Preen Dr TS5 ....139 B7
Premier Par TS19 ....117 A2
Premier Rd
Middlesbrough TS3 ....120 E2
Ormesby TS7 ....141 A5
Stockton-on-T TS19 ....117 C3
Prendwick Cl DH2 ....24 A8
Prescot Rd TS3 ....140 F8
Prescott St DL1 ....133 B3
Preseli Gr TS17 ....156 F7
Preston Farm Ind Est
TS18 ....137 E6
Preston Hall Mus*
TS16 ....137 D4
Preston La Mordon DL5 ....97 C4
Stockton-on-T TS18 ....137 E5
Preston Prim Sch TS16 .137 C4
Preston Rd
Newton Aycliffe DL5 ....96 C3
Stockton-on-T TS18 ....117 C2
Preston St 1 TS26 ....77 A7
Prestwick Cl TS4 ....140 A7
Prestwick Ct
Eaglescliffe TS16 ....156 C8
Middleton St George DL2 ..153 F8
Preswick Cl TS11 ....123 F6
Price Ave
Bishop Auckland DL14 ....80 A4
Middlesbrough TS5 ....139 B8
Price Rd TS10 ....106 E4
Priest Gill Bank DL11 ...205 F1
Priestburn Cl DH7 ....31 D1
Priestcrofts TS11 ....108 E1
Priestfield Ave TS3 ....140 E7
Priestfield Gdns NE16 ....5 F6
Priestgate DL1 ....133 A2
Priestman Ave DH8 ....10 C1
Priestman Rd DL5 ....96 C7
Primitive St DL4 ....80 F2
Primrose Ave SR8 ....49 F7
Primrose Cl
Guisborough TS14 ....143 B3
Spennymoor DL16 ....68 D7
Primrose Cres DH4 ....17 E3
Primrose Ct TS27 ....50 D3
Primrose Gdns DH2 ....8 F2
Primrose Hill
Newfield DL14 ....67 B8
Skinningrove TS13 ....127 A4
Primrose Hill Ind Est
TS18,TS19 ....213 A4
Primrose St
Darlington DL3 ....132 F1
Stockton-on-T TS19 ....212 C4
Primrose Terr DH3 ....9 D4
Prince Charles Ave DH6 ..45 D1
Prince Rd DL13 ....183 D2
Prince Regent St TS18 ..213 A2
Prince's St DH9 ....12 F5
Prince's St
Bishop Auckland DL14 ....80 B8
13 Darlington DL1 ....133 B1
Princeton Rd TS18 ....213 C4
Princes Rd
Middlesbrough TS1 ....214 B2
Saltburn-by-t-S TS12 ....125 C7
Princes Sq TS17 ....138 D3
Princes St
Middlesbrough TS1 ....214 C2
Shildon DL4 ....80 E1
Princes' St DH1 ....210 B3
Princess Ave Consett DH8 .10 D5
Stockton-on-T TS18 ....213 B4
Princess Cl TS27 ....50 E2
Princess Ct DL16 ....68 E8
Princess Gdns DH5 ....27 A5
Princess Rd
Darlington DL3 ....133 A8
Seaham SR7 ....29 D6
Princess Road Jun Sch
SR7 ....29 C7
Princess St
Hartlepool TS24 ....64 G8
Middlesbrough TS2 ....214 C4
Spennymoor DL16 ....68 E8
Thornaby-on-T TS17 ....213 C1
Princeton Dr TS17 ....118 D2
Pringle Cl DH7 ....42 E7
Pringle Gr DH7 ....42 F7
Pringle Pl DH7 ....42 F7
Prior Ct TS23 ....103 A7
Prior Dene DL3 ....132 C4
Prior Pursglove Coll
TS14 ....143 F5
Prior St DL3 ....132 C4
Priors Cl DH1 ....210 A3
Priors Grange DH6 ....36 B5
Priors Mill CE Prim Sch
TS22 ....102 B6
Priors Path DL17 ....70 A7
Priorswood DL15 ....189 F5
Priorwood Gdns TS17 ....157 B7
Priory Cl Consett DH8 ....10 C5
Guisborough TS14 ....143 E5
Priory Ct
Guisborough TS14 ....143 F5
Hartlepool TS24 ....77 F8
Sacriston DH7 ....23 C2
Stockton-on-T TS20 ....118 B8
Priory Dr TS8 ....139 C1
Priory Gdns
Stockton-on-T TS20 ....118 A8
Willington DL15 ....54 A3
Priory Gr TS10 ....107 A6
Priory Orch DH1 ....210 B2
Priory Rd Durham DH1 ....34 B6
Middlesbrough TS5 ....139 A8
Priory Road Flats DH1 ....34 B5
Priory Yd DL12 ....209 C5
Prissick St TS24 ....64 G8
Pritchett Rd TS3 ....140 F8
Progress Way DL1 ....133 A3
Promenade SR7 ....19 D1
Promenade The DH8 ....10 F4
Prospect Bsns Pk DH8 ....11 C3
Prospect Cres DH5 ....37 C8
Prospect Pl
Barnard Castle DL12 ....209 D7
9 Consett DH8 ....10 F3
9 Darlington DL3 ....132 F2
Darlington, Rise Carr DL3 ..132 F5
New Brancepeth DH7 ....42 E8
Skelton TS12 ....125 A1
7 Stockton-on-T TS20 ....118 B6
Willington DL15 ....53 F1
Prospect Pl *continued*
Wingate TS29 ....59 F5
Prospect Rd DL15 ....52 E2
Prospect Sq 14 DL13 ....195 E3
Prospect St
2 Chester le Street DH3 ...16 C4
10 Consett DH8 ....10 F3
Prospect Terr
Annfield Plain DH9 ....13 B4
Burnopfield NE16 ....6 A4
1 Chester le Street DH3 ...16 C4
Chilton DL17 ....83 A7
3 Cockfield DL13 ....195 E3
Durham DH1 ....210 A1
Ebchester DH8 ....3 F4
Eggleston DL12 ....193 D3
2 Eston TS6 ....121 F2
Kibblesworth NE11 ....8 C6
Lanchester DH7 ....20 E3
Lingdale TS12 ....145 E5
New Brancepeth DH7 ....42 F8
Shincliffe DH1 ....45 A6
Willington DL15 ....53 F3
Prospect The TS5 ....139 E8
Prospect View DH4 ....25 F2
Prospect Way TS25 ....90 B8
Protear Gr TS20 ....102 C1
Proudfoot Dr DL14 ....80 A5
Providence Cl DH1 ....211 A3
Providence Pl DH1 ....35 B3
Providence Row DH1 ....211 A3
Providence Terr 7 DH9 ...12 F4
Provident St DH2 ....15 C6
Provident Terr
Craghead DH9 ....14 D3
Evenwood DL14 ....92 C8
Prudhoe Ave TS21 ....72 C4
Pudding Hill Rd DL11 ...201 C2
Puddlers Rd TS6 ....121 B7
Pudsey Ct DH1 ....34 C6
Pudsey Wlk
Darlington DL1 ....152 A7
Newton Aycliffe DL5 ....96 E5
Pulford Rd TS20 ....117 F8
Pump La TS15 ....172 E8
Punch St TS1 ....214 A3
Purslglove Terr TS14 ....143 F5
Purves Pl TS24 ....64 A2
Purvis Terr TS29 ....60 B5
Pym St TS6 ....121 A5
Pytchley Rd TS14 ....143 E3

Q

Quaker La DL1 ....151 F8
Quality St DH1 ....45 B5
Quantock Ave DH2 ....16 A2
Quantock Cl TS18 ....133 C5
Quantock Pl SR8 ....49 A6
Quarrington Hill Ind Est
DH6 ....58 D7
Quarry Bank Rd TS11 ....124 C4
Quarry Cres DH7 ....33 A3
Quarry Dr TS8 ....139 C1
Quarry Farm Cl DL15 ....66 D6
Quarry House Gdns DH5 .26 C4
Quarry House La
Durham DH1 ....33 F1
East Rainton DH5 ....26 D4
Quarry Houses DL14 ....68 B3
Quarry La
Butterknowle DL13 ....195 C4
Marske-by-t-S TS11 ....124 D7
Quarry Rd
Eaglescliffe TS16 ....137 D3
New Silksworth SR3 ....18 B7
Stanley DH9 ....13 F7
Quarry Sq DH9 ....6 B2
Quarry St
New Silksworth SR3 ....18 A7
Shildon DL4 ....80 F1
Quarryburn La DL15 ....66 B8
Quarryheads La DH1 ....210 C1
Quay The DH5 ....27 A3
Quayside Rd TS18 ....213 B2
Quebec Gr
Billingham TS23 ....102 E7
Middlesbrough TS4 ....120 A2
Quebec Rd TS18 ....137 D8
Quebec St
Darlington DL1 ....133 A2
2 Langley Park DH7 ....32 C6
Quebec Terr DL12 ....208 F2
Queen Alexandra Rd SR7 .29 D5
Queen Anne Terr TS18 ..212 A1
Queen Elizabeth Dr DH5 .37 D8
Queen Elizabeth Sixth Form
Coll DL3 ....132 E2

Q

queen Elizabeth Way
TS17,TS18 ....138 A4

Q

Queen St
Barnard Castle DL12 ....209 C5
Birtley DH3 ....9 B4
Boosbeck TS6 ....145 B6
Carlin How TS13 ....126 F3
Consett DH8 ....10 F2
Crook DL15 ....52 E3
6 Darlington DL3 ....132 F2
Hartlepool, Middleton TS24 .77 D7
Queen St *continued*
Hartlepool, The Headland
TS24 ....64 G8
Hetton-le-H DH5 ....27 A5
Lazenby TS6 ....122 C4
Redcar TS10 ....107 B7
Seaham SR7 ....29 C7
Seaton Carew TS25 ....77 E1
Shildon DL4 ....81 A2
South Bank TS6 ....121 A6
Stockton-on-T TS18 ....213 B4
Sunderland SR2 ....18 F8
West Pelton DH2 ....15 A5
Queen Terr TS25 ....90 E8
Queen's Ave SR7 ....28 F6
Queen's Pk DH3 ....16 D2
Queen's Rd
Bishop Auckland DL14 ....80 C7
Consett DH8 ....10 E5
Wingate TS28 ....60 D8
Queen's Sq TS2 ....215 A4
Queen's Terr TS2 ....119 F8
Queen's Terr TS2 ....215 A4
Queens Ave TS17 ....213 C1
Queens Ct DL2 ....201 D3
Queens Dr
Billingham TS22 ....102 C5
Sedgefield TS21 ....85 A5
Queens Garth DH6 ....56 B7
Queens Gr DH1 ....44 A7
Queens Head Wynd
DL2 ....200 E7
Queens Par DH9 ....12 F4
Queens Rd Loftus TS13 ...127 B2
Middlesbrough TS5 ....119 D1
Queens Way DH8 ....10 C5
Queens Wlk TS18 ....213 B3
Queensberry Ave TS26 ....76 F5
Queensbury Cl TS10 ....107 A2
Queensbury Rd SR7 ....29 A7
Queensland Ave TS10 ....107 D5
Queensland Gr TS18 ....212 A1
Queensland Rd TS25 ....77 B1
Queensmere DH3 ....16 C7
Queensport Cl TS18 ....118 D5
Queensway
Billingham TS23 ....102 D4
Greatham TS25 ....89 E4
Houghton-le-S DH5 ....26 F8
Middlesbrough TS3 ....120 E4
Saltburn-by-t-S TS12 ....125 A6
Shildon DL4 ....81 B1
Willington DL15 ....54 B2
Quenby Rd TS23 ....102 E5
Quetlaw Rd DH6 ....47 E2
Quigley Terr DH3 ....9 B6
Quilstyle Rd DH6 ....47 E2
Quin Cres TS28 ....60 D8
Quin Sq DH6 ....38 A7
Quinn Cl SR8 ....49 D5
Quorn Cl TS14 ....143 E2

R

Raby Ave
Barnard Castle DL12 ....209 B6
Easington SR8 ....39 E5
Raby Castle* DL2 ....200 E8
Raby Cotts DL2 ....110 D2
Raby Dr DL5 ....82 E1
Raby Gdns
Bishop Auckland DL14 ....80 B6
Burnopfield NE16 ....5 E6
Hartlepool TS24 ....77 A8
7 Shildon DL4 ....81 A2
Raby Rd Durham DH1 ....34 C7
Ferryhill DL17 ....70 A6
Hartlepool TS24,TS26 ....77 B7
Redcar TS10 ....107 E4
Stockton-on-T TS18 ....212 A2
Raby Sq 6 TS24 ....77 A8
Raby St Darlington DL3 ...132 E1
Evenwood DL14 ....92 D6
Hartlepool TS24 ....77 F8
Raby Terr
Bishop Auckland DL14 ....79 B1
Chilton DL17 ....82 E8
11 Cockfield DL13 ....195 E3
Darlington DL3 ....132 F2
Willington DL15 ....53 E3
Race Terr TS9 ....160 F2
Racecourse The TS21,
TS22 ....86 F2
Rachel Cl SR2 ....18 C7
Radcliffe Ave TS19 ....117 E7
Radcliffe Cres TS17 ....213 C2
Radcliffe St DH3 ....9 C3
Radcliffe Terr TS24 ....64 G8
Raddive Cl DL5 ....82 B1
Radford Cl TS19 ....101 D1
Radlett Ave TS19 ....117 D7
Radnor Cl TS19 ....117 E7
Radnor Gn TS3 ....140 E8
Radnor Gr TS26 ....76 D8
Radstock Ave TS19 ....117 E7
Radyr Cl TS19 ....101 C1
Raeburn St 3 TS26 ....76 F6
Rafton Dr TS27 ....63 D3
Raglan Cl TS19 ....101 C1
Raglan Pl NE16 ....6 B6
Raglan St DH8 ....10 F2
Raglan Terr TS23 ....102 E5
Ragpath La Cornsay DH7 ..30 C6
Stockton-on-T TS19 ....117 D7
Ragworth Pl 3 TS20 ....118 A8
Ragworth Rd TS20 ....118 A8
Railway Cl DH6 ....35 F1
Railway Cotts Birtley DH3 ...9 B4
Blackhall Rocks TS27 ....50 F2
Darlington DL2 ....152 B6
Durham DH1 ....33 F1
Eaglescliffe TS16 ....156 B7
Great Lumley DH4 ....25 F8
Guisborough TS14 ....142 E3
Kirklevington TS15 ....172 C3
Skelton TS12 ....125 F2
Wingate TS27 ....48 F1
Witton-le-W DL15 ....65 F4
Railway Gdns DH9 ....12 F4
Railway Hos TS2 ....120 A7
Railway Houses DL14 ....80 F4
Railway Pl Consett DH8 ...10 D3
Eston TS6 ....121 D5
Railway St
Annfield Plain DH9 ....13 A3
Bishop Auckland DL14 ....80 C7
Consett DH8 ....11 A2
Craghead DH9 ....14 C2
Hetton-le-H DH5 ....27 A4
Howden-le-W DL15 ....65 E7
Lanchester DH7 ....20 F3
Langley Park DH7 ....32 C7
Leadgate DH8 ....11 D4
Stockton-on-T TS18 ....213 B4
Tow Law DL13 ....183 E1
Railway Terr
Brotton TS12 ....126 B3
Cornforth DL17 ....57 E2
Eaglescliffe TS16 ....137 C3
Hunwick DL15 ....66 F6
Hurworth-on-T DL2 ....168 A8
Loftus TS13 ....127 B1
Shildon DL4 ....95 A8
Skelton TS12 ....125 F2
Stanhope DL13 ....206 E1
Stanley Crook DL15 ....52 F7
Thornaby-on-T TS17 ....213 C1
Willington DL15 ....54 A3
Witton-le-W DL14 ....65 C3
Railway View DL1 ....152 B7
Raincliffe Ct TS8 ....140 B2
Raine St DL14 ....80 B8
Raine Wlk DL5 ....96 E6
Rainford Ave TS19 ....117 E7
Rainham Cl
Ingleby Barwick TS17 ....157 B7
Middlesbrough TS3 ....121 A3
Rainsford Cres TS3 ....121 A3
Rainton Ave TS5 ....139 C5
Rainton Bridge Ind Est
DH4 ....26 C7
Rainton Dr TS17 ....138 B4
Rainton Gr
Houghton-le-S DH5 ....26 E6
Stockton-on-T TS18 ....117 A1
Rainton Meadows (Nature Reserve)* DH4 ....26 B6
Rainton St SR7 ....29 D6
Rainton View DH4 ....25 F2
Raisbeck Cl TS11 ....108 C1
Raisby Cl TS5 ....139 B4
Raisby Terr DL17 ....57 E1
Raisdale Cl TS17 ....138 D5
Raisegill Cl TS3 ....120 B2
Raithwaite Cl TS14 ....143 D5
Rake Ave TS19 ....117 D8
Raleigh Cl TS11 ....124 F8
Raleigh Ct TS2 ....214 A4
Raleigh Rd TS20 ....118 A7
Raleigh Wlk TS20 ....118 A7
Ralfland Way TS7 ....141 A2
Ralph Ave SR2 ....18 E8
Ralph Sq TS19 ....117 D5
Ramilies SR2 ....18 D6
Ramona Ave DH6 ....58 C5
Rampside Ave TS19 ....101 D1
Ramsay Pl DL5 ....96 E7
Ramsay St Bowburn DH6 ...57 C4
High Spen NE39 ....1 A5
Ramsay Terr 2 DH8 ....177 D4
Ramsbury Ave TS19 ....117 D8
Ramsey Cl
4 Durham DH1 ....35 A2
Peterlee SR8 ....49 D8
Ramsey Cres
Bishop Auckland DL14 ....79 F4
Yarm TS15 ....156 B4
Ramsey Dr DL17 ....69 E5
Ramsey Gdns TS17 ....156 E7
Ramsey Rd TS10 ....106 F4
Ramsey St DH3 ....16 C2
Ramsey View TS20 ....118 C7
Ramsey Wlk
Darlington DL1 ....133 D5
Guisborough TS14 ....143 D3
Ramsgate TS18 ....213 A2
Ramsgill 1 DL1 ....152 C7
Ramsgill Ho 2 DL1 ....152 C7
Ramshaw Cl DH7 ....32 A6
Ramshaw La DL14 ....78 C2
Ramshaw Prim Sch DL14 .92 C8
Ramshaw Terr DL16 ....69 A3
Ramside View DH1 ....35 D5
Randolph St
Coundon Grange DL14 ....80 F5
Saltburn-by-t-S TS12 ....125 C6
Randolph Terr DL14 ....92 D6
Ranksborough St SR7 ....29 B8
Rannoch Ave DH2 ....16 B1
Ranulf Ct DL5 ....96 A8
Raskelf Ave 2 TS19 ....117 D7
Rathnew Ave TS19 ....117 C8
Raunds Ave TS19 ....117 D7
Raven Cl TS14 ....143 A3
Raven Ct DH7 ....41 C8

Raven La TS20 ....102 A1
Raven Terr 7 DH3 ....9 C5
Ravendale Rd TS3 ....120 F1
Ravenscar Cl NE16 ....2 F5
Ravenscar Cres TS19 ....117 F7
Ravenscroft Ave TS5 ....139 E8
Ravensdale TS5 ....139 B4
Ravensdale Rd DL3 ....151 D7
Ravensdale Wlk DL3 ....151 D8
Ravenside Terr DH8 ....10 D4
Ravensworth SR2 ....18 D6
Ravensworth Ave
8 Bishop Auckland DL14 ....80 B6
Eston TS6 ....121 C2
Ravensworth Cres
Byermoor NE16 ....6 D8
Hartlepool TS24 ....63 D5
Ravensworth Ct
Crook DL15 ....53 A3
South Hetton DH6 ....37 F7
Ravensworth Gr TS18 ....117 A1
Ravensworth Jun Sch
TS6 ....121 C2
Ravensworth Rd
Billingham TS23 ....102 E5
Birtley DH3 ....9 B5
Ferryhill DL17 ....70 B6
Ravensworth Terr DH1 ....211 A3
Ravensworth Terrace Prim Sch DH3 ....9 C4
Raventhorpe Prep Sch DL3 ....132 C1
Ravenwood Cl TS27 ....63 B4
Rawcliffe Ave TS5 ....139 C3
Rawley Dr TS10 ....107 A2
Rawlings Ct TS24 ....64 A2
Rawlinson Ave TS23 ....102 E1
Rawlinson St TS13 ....126 F4
Ray Ct TS19 ....117 C7
Raydale TS8 ....139 D1
Raydale Beck TS17 ....157 B6
Raylton Ave TS7 ....140 D2
Rayson Ct DL2 ....201 D7
Reading Rd TS20 ....118 A6
Reading St DL17 ....57 D1
Reay Ct 4 DH2 ....16 C2
Rectory Ave TS14 ....143 D4
Rectory Cl TS14 ....143 D4
Rectory Gdns DL15 ....54 B3
Rectory La Blaydon NE21 ....2 B8
Ebchester DH8 ....3 E3
Guisborough TS14 ....143 E4
Longnewton TS21 ....136 A5
Wolsingham DL13 ....207 D5
Rectory Rd DH5 ....27 A3
Rectory Row TS21 ....85 B6
Rectory Terr DH1 ....45 A6
Rectory View DH6 ....46 E7
Rectory Way TS25 ....90 E7
Red Banks DH2 ....15 F2
Red Barnes Way DL1 ....133 D3
Red Briar Wlk DH1 ....34 A7
Red Cts DH7 ....43 C4
Red Firs DH7 ....43 B4
Red Hall Dr DL1 ....133 D3
Red Hall La TS15 ....157 A2
Red Hall Prim Sch DL1 ....133 E4
Red Hills Terr DH1 ....210 B2
Red House La DL2,DL5 ....95 A4
Red House Sch TS20 ....102 A1
Red Houses DL14 ....78 E5
Red Lion St TS10 ....107 C7
Red Ridges DH7 ....43 C4
Red Rose Prim Sch DH3 ....16 D1
Red Rose Terr DH3 ....16 D2
Redbrook Ave TS19 ....117 E8
Redbrook Prim Sch
TS19 ....117 D8
Redburn Cl DH4 ....26 C8
Redcar & Cleveland Coll
Redcar TS10 ....107 B6
Redcar TS10 ....107 D3
Redcar Ave
Marske-by-t-S TS11 ....108 B1
Stockton-on-T TS19 ....117 E7
Redcar Beach Cvn Site
TS10 ....107 A7
Redcar Central Sta
TS10 ....107 C6
Redcar Cl TS25 ....77 A4
Redcar East Sta TS10 ....107 E5
Redcar La TS10 ....107 D4
Redcar Rd
Dunsdale TS14 ....123 D2
Guisborough TS14 ....143 F5
Marske-by-t-S TS11 ....108 B1
South Bank TS6 ....121 A6
Thornaby-on-T TS17 ....138 C6
Thornaby-on-T TS17 ....138 D7
Redcar Rd E TS6 ....121 B6
Redcar St TS2 ....215 A4
Redcar Sta Bsns Ctr
TS10 ....107 C6
Redditch Ave TS19 ....117 E8
Redesdale Ave NE21 ....1 F8
Redesdale Ct
Middlesbrough TS2 ....119 D8
Trimdon TS29 ....59 E4
Redesdale Gr 2 TS17 ....157 A7
Redesdale Rd DH2 ....16 A1
Redford La DL13 ....189 B2
Redgate Bank DL13 ....207 F7
Redhill Dr NE16 ....2 E4
Redhill Rd TS19 ....117 D8
Redhill Villas DH1 ....210 B3
Redhills La DH1 ....210 A3
Redhills Way DH5 ....27 A2
Redhouse Cl DH7 ....23 D2
Redland Cl TS18 ....117 A2
Redmarshall Rd TS21 ....115 F6
Redmarshall St TS21 ....99 E3
Redmayne Cl TS23 ....102 E6
Redmire Cl DL1 ....133 A5
Redmire Rd TS18 ....212 B3
Redmires Cl DH2 ....8 E1
Redruth Ave TS19 ....117 E7
Redruth Dr DL3 ....132 F8
Redshank Cl
Hartlepool TS26 ....63 D1
Washington NE38 ....9 F2
Redstart Cl TS26 ....63 E1
Redstart Ct NE39 ....1 D2
Redwell Ct DL12 ....209 C8
Redwell Cvn Pk DL12 ....209 C8
Redwing Cl NE38 ....9 F3
Redwing La TS20 ....102 B2
Redwing Rising TS14 ....143 B4
Redwood Brandon DH7 ....43 B4
Esh Winning DH7 ....41 D7
Seaham SR7 ....29 C6
Redwood Cl
Hartlepool TS27 ....63 C5
Hetton-le-H DH5 ....26 F4
Redwood Ct Consett DH8 ....10 E4
Marton TS7 ....140 E4
Redwood Dr TS12 ....125 A6
Redwood Gr SR3 ....18 B7
Redworth Est DL5 ....95 B3
Redworth Gr DL14 ....80 E7
Redworth Rd
Billingham TS23 ....102 F5
Darlington DL3 ....132 B4
Heighington DL5 ....95 D2
Shildon DL4 ....95 A7
Redworth St TS24 ....77 C5
Redworth Way DL5 ....96 D4
Reed Ave DL15 ....54 A6
Reed Cl TS20 ....118 C7
Reed St Hartlepool TS24 ....77 C5
Thornaby-on-T TS17 ....213 C1
Reedston Rd TS26 ....76 C7
Reef Ho TS24 ....77 C7
Reepham Cl 7 TS19 ....117 C8
Reeth Moor Cl DL1 ....152 E8
Reeth Pl DL5 ....96 B8
Reeth Rd
Middlesbrough TS5 ....139 C8
Stockton-on-T TS18 ....137 C8
Regal Cl TS25 ....90 F7
Regal Dr DL1 ....133 B7
Regency Ave TS6 ....141 D8
Regency Ct SR7 ....29 D7
Regency Dr
Hartlepool TS25 ....77 B1
New Silksworth SR3 ....18 B8
Whickham NE16 ....2 F6
Regency Mans The
TS10 ....107 B7
Regency Pk TS17 ....157 C7
Regency West Mall
TS18 ....213 A2
Regent Ct TS6 ....121 E4
Regent Dr NE16 ....2 F4
Regent Mews TS18 ....213 A2
Regent Rd
Middlesbrough TS4 ....120 A1
Ryhope SR2 ....19 A5
Regent Sq TS24 ....77 F8
Regent St
Annfield Plain DH9 ....12 F5
Bishop Auckland DL14 ....80 C8
Eldon Lane DL14 ....80 F4
Hartlepool TS24 ....77 F8
Hetton-le-H DH5 ....27 A5
Shildon DL4 ....80 F1
Stockton-on-T TS18 ....213 A3
Regent Terr TS21 ....72 C4
Regents Ct DL1 ....133 C1
Regents Wlk TS10 ....107 C7
Reid St DL3 ....132 E3
Reid Street Prim Sch
DL3 ....132 E3
Reid Terr TS14 ....143 E5
Reigate Ave TS5 ....139 E8
Reigate Cl TS19 ....117 D8
Relley Cl DH7 ....33 B1
Relley Garth DH7 ....43 D5
Relly Path DH1 ....210 A1
Relton Cl DH4 ....26 A7
Relton Terr DH3 ....16 C2
Relton Way TS26 ....76 E5
Rembrandt Way DL5 ....96 D3
Renfrew Pl DH3 ....9 D2
Renfrew Rd TS20 ....118 B8
Rennie Cl DL1 ....133 B2
Rennie Rd TS6 ....120 F4
Rennie St DL17 ....69 E6
Rennie Wlk DL1 ....133 B2
Renny St DH1 ....211 B3
Renny's La DH1 ....35 B2
Renown Wlk TS6 ....121 B5
Renvyle Ave TS19 ....117 C8
Repton Ave TS19 ....117 D7
Repton Rd TS3 ....121 A3
Rescue Station Cotts
DH5 ....26 F6
Reservoir Terr DL15 ....52 F7
Resolution The TS7 ....141 A3
Resource Cl TS6 ....121 B5
Rest Haven 13 DL13 ....195 E3
Retford Cl 4 TS19 ....117 D8
Retford Gr TS25 ....89 E7
Rettendon Cl TS19 ....117 E8
Revesby Rd TS3 ....140 F8
Reynolds Arena (Darlington FC) The* DL1 ....152 C6
Reynolds Cl DH9 ....13 F6
Reynolds Ct
Billingham TS23 ....102 D7
Peterlee SR8 ....50 B6
Reynoldston Ave TS19 ....101 D1
Rhinog Gr TS17 ....137 F1
Rhobell View TS17 ....156 E8
Rhodes Ct TS17 ....138 D4
Rhodes' Terr DH1 ....43 F8
Rhondda Rd TS19 ....117 E7
Rhoose Gate TS17 ....138 E6
Rhyl Cl TS19 ....117 E8
Ribble Cl TS22 ....102 A6
Ribble Ct DL1 ....151 F6
Ribble Dr DL1 ....151 F6
Ribbleton Cl 3 TS7 ....140 F3
Ribchester Cl 1 TS19 ....117 D8
Riccarton Cl TS19 ....117 C8
Richard Ct
Darlington DL1 ....133 A4
Hartlepool TS26 ....77 A5
Richard Hind Wlk TS18 ....137 F8
Richard St DH5 ....27 A3
Richard Terr DL14 ....80 E4
Richards St TS12 ....125 F2
Richardson Ave DL14 ....79 F4
Richardson Cl DL2 ....200 F3
Richardson Ct DL15 ....53 F2
Richardson Fields DL12 ....209 C6
Richardson Hall TS9 ....161 A2
Richardson Pl
Kirk Merrington DL16 ....68 F3
Kirk Merrington DL16 ....69 A3
Richardson Rd
Stockton-on-T TS18 ....212 C1
Thornaby-on-T TS17 ....138 B6
Richardson St 6 TS26 ....77 A7
Richardson Terr SR2 ....19 A6
Richardson Wlk 6 DL5 ....96 E8
Richmond SR2 ....18 D7
Richmond Ave DL14 ....80 A6
Richmond Cl
Darlington DL3 ....132 B5
Eston TS6 ....121 D2
Ferryhill DL17 ....70 B5
Shildon DL4 ....94 F8
Richmond Cres TS23 ....102 E4
Richmond Ct Durham DH1 ....34 D7
Eston TS6 ....121 E4
Sacriston DH7 ....23 B4
Richmond Dr DH4 ....17 D1
Richmond Rd
Durham DH1 ....34 D7
Redcar TS10 ....107 E4
Stockton-on-T TS18 ....212 B2
Richmond St
Byers Green DL16 ....67 F8
Hartlepool TS25 ....77 B3
Middlesbrough TS2 ....119 E7
Richmond Terr DH6 ....37 F3
Rickleton Ave DH3 ....16 D5
Rickleton Prim Sch NE38 ....16 F8
Rickleton Village Ctr
NE38 ....16 F8
Rickleton Way NE38 ....17 A8
Rickman Ho TS1 ....215 A3
Ricknall Ave DL5 ....96 E4
Ricknall Cl TS5 ....139 B4
Ricknall La DL1,DL5 ....97 C3
Riddell Ct 7 DH2 ....16 C2
Ridding Ct DH7 ....41 D8
Ridding Rd DH7 ....41 D8
Ridge La Dalehouse TS13 ....148 C5
Liverton TS13 ....167 B8
Ridge The
Mount Pleasant TS8 ....159 B7
Saltburn-by-t-S TS12 ....125 C5
Ridgeside DL16 ....69 A5
Ridgeway Birtley DH3 ....9 C6
Coulby Newham TS8 ....140 A1
Darlington DL3 ....132 F7
Lanchester DH7 ....20 E4
Newton Aycliffe DL5 ....96 C4
Ryhope SR2 ....18 C6
Riding Hill DH3 ....25 A7
Riding Hill Rd DH9 ....13 A5
Riding La DH9,NE11 ....8 B4
Ridley Ave
Chester le Street DH2 ....16 B2
Middlesbrough TS5 ....139 C7
Sunderland SR2 ....18 F7
Ridley Ct
9 Hartlepool TS26 ....77 A7
Stockton-on-T TS20 ....118 A8
Ridley Dr TS20 ....117 F8
Ridley Mews 6 TS20 ....118 B8
Ridley St Redcar TS10 ....107 C7
Stanley DH9 ....13 F7
Ridley Terr Leadgate DH8 ....11 D3
Tow Law DL13 ....183 D2
Ridlington Way TS24 ....63 E4
Ridsdale Ave 3 TS19 ....117 D7
Ridsdale St DL1 ....133 B1
Rievaulx Ave TS23 ....102 D6
Rievaulx Cl TS19 ....117 D8
Rievaulx Ct DL16 ....55 E3
Rievaulx Dr TS5 ....139 E7
Rievaulx Rd TS12 ....125 E2
Rievaulx Way TS14 ....143 F4
Rievaulx Wlk TS6 ....121 D2
Rift House Prim Sch
TS25 ....76 E3
Rifts Ave TS12 ....125 B7
Riftswood Dr TS11 ....108 B1
Rigby Ho TS15 ....156 B5
Rigg Head DL2 ....201 D5
Rigg La DL12 ....192 C1
Rigg The TS15 ....156 C4
Riggs The Brandon DH7 ....43 C5
Houghton-le-S DH5 ....26 F8
Hunwick DL15 ....66 D5
Riggston Pl TS26 ....76 D7
Riley St TS18 ....212 C2
Rillington Cl 9 TS19 ....117 C8
Rillston Cl TS26 ....76 D7
Rillstone Way 10 TS10 ....107 E1
Rimdale Dr TS19 ....117 A4
Rimswell Par TS19 ....117 A4
Rimswell Rd TS19 ....117 B4
Ringway TS17 ....138 E5
Ringway Gr DL2 ....153 F8
Ringwood Cres TS19 ....117 E7
Ringwood Rd TS3 ....121 A2
Ripley Ct
Middlesbrough TS3 ....121 A3
Sacriston DH7 ....23 C3
Ripley Rd TS20 ....101 F1
Ripon Cl TS19 ....117 D7
Ripon Ct DH7 ....23 B3
Ripon Dr Darlington DL1 ....152 B7
Willington DL15 ....53 F2
Ripon Rd Brotton TS12 ....126 C4
Durham DH1 ....34 D8
Nunthorpe TS7 ....141 B3
Redcar TS10 ....107 F4
Ripon St DH3 ....16 C1
Ripon Terr
Kimblesworth DH2 ....24 A3
Murton SR7 ....28 C3
Ripon Way TS6 ....121 F2
Rise Carr Prim Sch DL3 ....132 F5
Rise The Consett DH8 ....177 A3
Darlington DL3 ....151 D8
Nunthorpe TS7 ....141 A3
Rishton Cl TS19 ....117 D7
Rissington Wlk TS17 ....138 E5
Ritson Ave DH7 ....33 B3
Ritson Rd DL5 ....96 D6
Ritson St Consett DH8 ....10 D4
Stanley DH9 ....13 F6
Ritson's Rd DH8 ....10 D4
Rium Terr TS24 ....77 B6
River Ct TS2 ....119 C8
River Terr
5 Chester le Street DH3 ....16 D4
Middleton-In-T DL12 ....208 B5
River View
Blackhall Mill NE17 ....4 B6
Willington DL15 ....54 B2
River View Ind Est DL1 ....133 C4
River Wlk DL14 ....79 C2
Riverbank Trad Est DL1 ....133 A4
Riverdale DL13 ....207 D4
Riverdale Ct TS5 ....119 B1
Riverdale Prim Sch
TS10 ....107 B3
Rivergarth DL1 ....133 F6
Riverhead Ave TS19 ....117 D7
Rivermead Ave DL1 ....133 F6
Riversdale Cl NE17 ....4 B6
Riverside
Bishop Auckland DL14 ....80 D6
Consett DH8 ....10 C6
Stockton-on-T TS18 ....213 B2
Riverside Dr DL1 ....133 F5
Riverside Ind Est DH7 ....32 C7
Riverside Park Ind Est
TS2 ....119 D8
Riverside Park Rd TS2 ....119 C7
Riverside Rd TS2 ....104 E2
Riverside Stadium (Middlesbrough FC)
TS3 ....215 C4
Riverside View TS17 ....138 B7
Riverside Way
Darlington DL1 ....133 C5
Rowlands Gill NE39 ....1 D1
Riverston Cl TS26 ....76 C7
Riversway TS7 ....140 E4
Roast Calf La DL17 ....71 C4
Robert Ave TS6 ....121 D5
Robert Sq SR7 ....29 E6
Robert St
New Silksworth SR3 ....18 B7
Seaham SR7 ....29 E6
Spennymoor DL16 ....68 E7
Thornaby-on-T TS17 ....213 C1
Robert Terr Bowburn DH6 ....45 D2
Stanley DH9 ....13 F8
Roberts Ct TS7 ....141 B8
Roberts Row TS7 ....141 B8
Roberts Sq DL17 ....57 D1
Roberts St TS6 ....121 D5
Roberts Wlk 4 DL1 ....133 B1
Robertson Ct 14 DH3 ....16 C2
Robin Cl TS17 ....138 B1
Robin Ct DH5 ....26 C3
Robin La
East Rainton DH4,DH5 ....26 C2
West Rainton DH4,DH5 ....26 C2
Robinson St Consett DH8 ....10 E4
Loftus TS13 ....127 D1
8 Skelton TS12 ....125 C3
Robinson Terr
Burnopfield NE16 ....6 A4
Byers Green DL16 ....54 E1
Loftus TS13 ....127 C1
Robson Ave
Ingleby Barwick TS17 ....138 D1
Peterlee SR8 ....49 D7
Robson Cres DH6 ....45 D2
Robson Ct TS24 ....64 A1
Robson Pl SR2 ....19 A6
Robson Rd DL14 ....93 B8
Robson St
Billingham TS23 ....103 D2
Robson St *continued*
Consett DH8 ....11 A3
1 Shildon DL4 ....81 A2
Robson Terr
High Shincliffe DH1 ....44 F6
High Spen NE39 ....1 B3
Tantobie DH9 ....5 F1
Rochdale Ave TS19 ....117 E8
Rochdale Cl TS3 ....120 D1
Rochdale St
Evenwood DL14 ....92 C7
Hetton-le-H DH5 ....27 A2
Roche Wlk DL3 ....132 A5
Rochester Cl
Bishop Auckland DL14 ....79 E6
Ingleby Barwick TS17 ....157 A7
Rochester Ct
Ingleby Barwick TS17 ....157 A7
Thornaby-on-T TS17 ....213 C2
Rochester Dr TS10 ....107 E4
Rochester Rd
Billingham TS23 ....102 E5
Durham DH1 ....34 D7
Middlesbrough TS5 ....119 E1
Stockton-on-T TS19 ....117 E7
Rochester Way DL1 ....133 E5
Rock Rd DL16 ....68 E6
Rock Terr
Middleton-In-T DL12 ....208 C7
New Brancepeth DH7 ....42 F8
Rockall Ave 10 TS19 ....117 C8
Rockcliffe Ho 3 DL1 ....152 C7
Rockcliffe Terr
Kirk Merrington DL16 ....69 A3
Skinningrove TS13 ....127 A4
Rockcliffe View TS13 ....127 A4
Rocket St DL1 ....133 B1
Rocket Terr TS10 ....107 A7
Rockferry Cl TS19 ....117 C8
Rockingham Cl SR7 ....19 D1
Rockingham Dr DL14 ....79 E6
Rockingham Rd DL15 ....53 F1
Rockingham St DL1 ....152 A8
Rockliffe Rd TS5 ....119 D1
Rockpool Cl TS24 ....64 B2
Rockport Ct TS18 ....213 C4
Rockwell Ave DL1 ....133 D6
Rockwell Ho DL1 ....133 C5
Rockwood Cl TS14 ....143 F3
Roddymoor Ct DL15 ....52 D7
Roddymoor Rd
Billy Row DL15 ....52 D7
Thornley DL15 ....52 B5
Thornley (nr Tow Law)
DL13 ....189 E7
Rodham Terr DH9 ....13 F8
Rodmell Cl TS3 ....121 A1
Rodney Cl
Billingham TS23 ....118 D8
Brotton TS12 ....126 C4
Ryhope SR2 ....18 C6
Rodney St TS26 ....77 A6
Rodney Wlk DL14 ....81 B8
Rodridge Pk TS28 ....60 F6
Rodwell St TS29 ....59 F5
Roebuck Cl TS17 ....138 C2
Roecliffe Gr TS19 ....117 B8
Roedean Dr TS16 ....156 C8
Roger La TS8,TS15 ....158 A6
Roger St DH8 ....10 E3
Rogeri Pl TS24 ....63 F3
Rogerley Terr DH9 ....12 E5
Rogers Cl 1 SR8 ....50 A6
Rogerson Cl DH6 ....56 B7
Rogerson Terr DH6 ....56 B7
Rogues La NE39 ....1 A5
Rokeby Ave TS4 ....140 A8
Rokeby Pk* DL12 ....200 A1
Rokeby Sq DH1 ....44 A7
Rokeby St Hartlepool TS24 ....64 C2
Stockton-on-T TS18 ....212 C1
Rokeby Terr DL15 ....66 E6
Roker Cl DL1 ....133 E3
Roker St TS24 ....77 B5
Roker Terr TS18 ....212 C1
Roland Burn Way NE39 ....1 E2
Rolleston Ave TS19 ....117 C8
Romaine Pk TS24 ....64 C2
Romaine Sq DH6 ....45 C1
Romaldkirk Cl 1 DH8 ....10 F1
Romaldkirk Rd TS2 ....214 B4
Romaldkirk Wlk 5 DL1 ....152 C7
Roman Ave DH3 ....16 D3
Roman Rd TS5 ....119 D1
Roman View DL2 ....130 B4
Roman Way DL2 ....153 E6
Romanby Ave TS19 ....117 E7
Romanby Cl TS24 ....64 C2
Romanby Gdns TS5 ....139 E3
Romanway Ind Est DL14 ....80 A3
Romany Dr DH8 ....10 E2
Romany Rd TS9 ....161 A2
Romford Rd TS19 ....117 E8
Romney Cl TS10 ....107 E3
Romney Dr DH1 ....35 D5
Romney Gn TS23 ....102 D7
Romney St TS1 ....214 C2
Romsey Rd TS19 ....117 E7
Ronaldsay Cl 4 SR2 ....18 E8
Ronaldshay Terr TS11 ....108 E1
Ronan Mews DH4 ....26 A2
Rook La TS20 ....102 B2
Rookery Dale TS12 ....145 B7
Rookery Gdns DL17 ....82 E6
Rookery La NE16 ....2 E4

Rookery The NE16 ....5 F6
Rookhope NE38 ....16 F8
Rookhope Gr DL14 ....79 E5
Rookhope Prim Sch
DL13 ....180 D5
Rookhope Walks*
DL13 ....180 D5
Rookswood Gdns NE39 ....1 E3
Rookwood Hunt DL5 ....96 A8
Rookwood Rd TS7 ....141 B3
Roosevelt Rd DH1 ....211 C4
Roper's Terr TS29 ....59 D3
Ropery La Bournmoor DH3 ....16 F3
Chester le Street DH3 ....16 D2
Ropery Rd TS24 ....64 C2
Ropery St TS18 ....213 A3
Ropery Walk Prim Sch
SR7 ....29 E6
Ropery Wlk SR7 ....29 E6
Ropner Ave TS18 ....212 B1
Ropner Gdns DL2 ....153 F5
Rosa St DL16 ....68 E8
Rosa Street Prim Sch
DL16 ....68 E8
Roscoe Rd TS23 ....102 E1
Roscoe St TS1 ....215 B2
Rose Acre DH1 ....45 A6
Rose Ave
Marske-by-t-S TS11 ....108 A1
Stanley DH9 ....13 D5
Rose Cotts Burnopfield NE16 ....5 E5
Shotton Colliery SR8 ....48 E7
South Hetton DH6 ....38 A7
Rose Cres Bournmoor DH4 ....17 D3
Sacriston DH7 ....23 D3
Rose Ct Esh Winning DH7 ....31 C2
Peterlee SR8 ....49 B3
Rose Gdns NE11 ....8 C6
Rose Hill TS15 ....156 C5
Rose La DL1 ....133 E5
Rose Lea DH7 ....23 B1
Rose St
7 Houghton-le-S DH4 ....26 D8
Middlesbrough TS1 ....214 C3
Trimdon TS29 ....59 E4
Rose Terr
Eaglescliffe TS16 ....156 C7
East Hedleyhope DH7 ....40 E6
6 Langley Park DH7 ....32 C6
Middleton-In-T DL12 ....208 B6
Pelton DH2 ....15 E5
Stanhope DL13 ....206 C3
Rose Wood Prim Sch
TS8 ....159 B8
Rosebank TS26 ....76 F4
Rosebank Cl SR2 ....18 E8
Rosebank Sch DL17 ....70 A5
Rosebay Ct
Darlington DL3 ....132 E3
Guisborough TS14 ....143 B3
Rosebay Rd DH7 ....43 E4
Roseberry Ave TS9 ....161 B3
Roseberry Com Prim Sch
TS9 ....161 B3
Roseberry Cres
Crook DL15 ....52 D4
Eston TS6 ....122 A3
Great Ayton TS9 ....161 B3
Stockton-on-T TS20 ....102 B1
Thornley (nr Wheatley Hill)
DH6 ....47 C4
Roseberry Ct TS9 ....161 A3
Roseberry Dr
Great Ayton TS9 ....161 A3
Stainton TS8 ....139 C1
Roseberry Flats TS23 ....102 D4
Roseberry Inf Sch TS23 ....102 E4
Roseberry Jun Sch
TS23 ....102 E5
Roseberry La TS9 ....161 C6
Roseberry Mews 1 TS26 ....76 F6
Roseberry Mount TS14 ....143 C4
Roseberry Prim Sch DH2 ....15 C5
Roseberry Rd
Billingham TS23 ....102 C4
Great Ayton TS9 ....161 A3
Middlesbrough TS4 ....120 B2
Middlesbrough TS4 ....215 B1
Redcar TS10 ....107 B3
Stockton-on-T TS20 ....102 B1
Trimdon TS29 ....72 D8
Roseberry Sports & Com Coll
DH2 ....15 C6
Roseberry Sq TS10 ....107 B3
Roseberry St DH9 ....14 D7
Roseberry View
Great Ayton TS9 ....161 C7
Thornaby-on-T TS17 ....138 C8
Roseberry Villas DH2 ....15 C5
Rosebery Rd TS26 ....76 F6
Rosebery St DL3 ....132 E3
Rosebery Terr
6 Consett DH8 ....10 F2
4 Shildon DL4 ....81 A2
Roseby Rd SR8 ....49 F6
Rosecroft Ave
Loftus TS13 ....147 B8
4 Middlesbrough TS4 ....119 F1
Rosecroft La TS13 ....147 B7
Rosedale DL16 ....55 E1
Rosedale Ave
Consett DH8 ....10 D5
Hartlepool TS26 ....76 F5
Middlesbrough TS4 ....119 F2
Rosedale Cl TS21 ....85 B7
Rosedale Cres
Darlington DL3 ....132 B4
Guisborough TS14 ....143 B3
Loftus TS13 ....127 B2
Shildon DL4 ....81 B1
Rosedale Gdns
Billingham TS23 ....102 D6
Edmondsley DH7 ....23 B7
Lingdale TS12 ....145 E5
3 Stockton-on-T TS19 ....117 D8
Rosedale Gr TS10 ....106 F4
Rosedale La TS13 ....149 E7
Rosedale Rd Durham DH1 ....35 D4
Nunthorpe TS7 ....141 B3
Rosedale St DH5 ....26 E1
Rosedale Terr
Peterlee SR8 ....49 F7
Willington DL15 ....54 A3
Rosehill Great Ayton TS9 ....161 A2
Hinderwell TS13 ....149 E6
Rosehill Inf Sch TS19 ....117 B2
Roseland Cres TS7 ....140 E5
Roseland Dr TS7 ....140 E5
Roselea Ave SR2 ....18 F7
Rosemary Cotts TS11 ....124 D8
Rosemary Ct 7 DL1 ....152 C8
Rosemary La SR8 ....39 B4
Rosemead Ave DL15 ....54 A3
Rosemoor Cl TS7 ....140 C3
Rosemount Beamish DH9 ....15 A7
Durham DH1 ....34 D8
Rosemount Ct DL14 ....80 D5
Rosemount Rd
Bishop Auckland DL14 ....80 D5
New Marske TS11 ....123 F6
Rosemount Terr DL15 ....52 E4
Roseneath Ave TS19 ....101 D1
Rosetown Ave SR8 ....50 A6
Roseway The TS12 ....125 C6
Rosewood DL17 ....82 E8
Rosewood Cl
Ormesby TS7 ....141 B7
Sacriston DH7 ....23 C3
Rosewood Ct TS7 ....140 E4
Rosewood Gdns DH2 ....16 B5
Rosewood Terr DH3 ....9 B5
Roseworth Prim Sch
TS19 ....117 C8
Rosgill TS10 ....107 B4
Rosiere Gr TS10 ....107 C5
Roslin Terr DL13 ....189 D2
Roslyn Ave TS3 ....120 D1
Roslyn St DL1 ....152 A8
Ross DH2 ....9 A1
Ross Gr TS25 ....90 B8
Ross St
Middlesbrough TS1 ....214 B2
11 Seaham SR7 ....29 D7
Ross Terr 3 DL17 ....70 A5
Ross Wlk DL5 ....96 F7
Rossall St TS25 ....77 A3
Rossendale Cl 1 TS11 ....124 C8
Rossett Wlk
2 Middlesbrough TS3 ....120 C1
Middlesbrough TS3 ....140 C8
Rossetti Way TS23 ....102 D7
Rosslare Rd TS19 ....117 C8
Rosslyn Ave SR2 ....18 F7
Rosslyn Ct TS18 ....137 E8
Rosslyn Pl DH3 ....9 D2
Rossmere DL16 ....55 E2
Rossmere Prim Sch TS25 ....89 F8
Rossmere Way TS25 ....89 F8
Rossway DL1 ....133 E7
Rosthwaite TS5 ....139 B4
Rosthwaite Ave TS19 ....117 E8
Rosthwaite Cl TS24 ....64 B1
Rostrevor Ave TS19 ....101 D1
Rothbury SR2 ....18 D6
Rothbury Ave
Peterlee SR8 ....49 F8
Stockton-on-T TS19 ....117 D8
Rothbury Cl
Chester le Street DH2 ....16 A1
Ingleby Barwick TS17 ....157 B7
Trimdon TS29 ....59 E4
Rothbury Dr DL3 ....132 B5
Rothbury Rd Durham DH1 ....34 D7
Middlesbrough TS3 ....120 C1
Rothbury St TS23 ....102 D4
Rotherham Ave TS19 ....117 D7
Rotherham Cl DH5 ....26 D6
Rothesay DH2 ....8 F1
Rothesay Dr TS10 ....107 E3
Rothesay Gr TS7 ....141 B4
Rothley Ave SR8 ....49 F8
Rothley Terr DH8 ....4 B1
Rothman Cl DL16 ....56 B3
Rothwell Cres TS19 ....117 D7
Rothwell Mews TS6 ....121 F2
Rottingdean Cl TS19 ....117 D8
Rough Lea Colliery DL15 ....66 E8
Rough Lea La DL15 ....66 E7
Rough Lea Terr DL15 ....66 D7
Roundhay Dr TS16 ....137 C1
Roundhill Ave TS17 ....156 F7
Roundhill Cl
Hartlepool TS26 ....76 C6
Hurworth-on-T DL2 ....152 C1
Roundhill Rd DL2 ....152 C3
Roundhill Way DL15 ....54 B4
Roundway TS7 ....140 E4
Rounton Gn TS3 ....120 C1
Rounton Gr TS19 ....117 B2
Routledge Ct TS24 ....64 A1
Routledge Rd TS20 ....118 C5
Row The CA9 ....178 A6
Rowallane Gdns TS17 ....157 B7
Rowan Ave
Guisborough TS14 ....143 B3
Shildon DL4 ....81 B1
Rowan Ct Burnopfield NE16 ....6 B6
Darlington DL3 ....132 C1
Esh Winning DH7 ....41 C7
Spennymoor DL16 ....69 A8
Rowan Dr Durham DH1 ....34 E8
Great Ayton TS9 ....161 A3
Hetton-le-H DH5 ....26 F4
Rowan Gr TS8 ....139 B1
Rowan Lea DH7 ....43 B4
Rowan Oval TS21 ....85 B7
Rowan Pl DL5 ....96 B6
Rowan Rd
Eaglescliffe TS16 ....156 B8
Stockton-on-T TS19 ....118 A5
Rowan Tree Ave DH1 ....35 A4
Rowanwood Ct TS5 ....139 E4
Rowell Cl SR2 ....18 C6
Rowell St TS24 ....64 G8
Rowen Cl TS17 ....156 F8
Rowland Cres TS27 ....49 A1
Rowland Keld TS14 ....143 B2
Rowlands Gill Inf Sch
NE39 ....1 F3
Rowlands Gill Jun Sch
NE39 ....1 F3
Rowlands Gr TS23 ....103 A8
Rowlands Terr TS28 ....60 E6
Rowlandson Terr 5
DL17 ....70 B5
Rowley Bank DH8 ....176 F3
Rowley Cl DH7 ....42 E7
Rowley Cres DH7 ....31 D1
Rowley Dr DH7 ....33 B1
Rowley Link DH7 ....31 D1
Roworth Rd TS3 ....121 A1
Roxburgh Cl Blaydon NE21 ....2 A8
Eston TS6 ....121 B3
Roxby Ave
Guisborough TS14 ....143 D2
Middlesbrough TS3 ....140 E7
Roxby Cl Hartlepool TS25 ....90 D7
Redcar TS10 ....107 C3
Stockton-on-T TS19 ....117 F7
Roxby La TS13 ....148 F6
Roxby Moor Ave DL1 ....152 D7
Roxby Wynd TS28 ....48 E1
Royal George Cl DL4 ....95 A7
Royal George Dr TS16 ....137 B2
Royal Gr DL15 ....52 E4
Royal Oak Cotts DL13 ....206 C5
Royal Oak Yd DL3 ....132 F2
Royal Rd DH9 ....13 F7
Royal Yd DL13 ....195 E3
Royce Ave TS23 ....103 B5
Royce Ct TS23 ....103 B5
Royd The TS15 ....156 B4
Royston Ave TS3 ....140 E7
Royston Cl TS19 ....117 F7
Royston Gr TS25 ....89 D6
Ruberry Ave 8 TS19 ....117 C8
Ruby Ave DL17 ....82 F8
Ruby Rd TS17 ....138 D7
Ruby St Darlington DL3 ....133 A6
Middlesbrough TS1 ....214 C2
Saltburn-by-t-S TS12 ....125 C8
Shildon DL4 ....80 F1
Rudby Cl TS15 ....156 E5
Rudd's Pl TS5 ....119 E2
Ruddock Ave DL14 ....80 A5
Ruddock's Wynd 8 DL2 ....200 E7
Rudds Hill DL17 ....70 C5
Rudland Way DL14 ....78 F6
Rudland Wlk 1 TS6 ....121 F3
Rudston Ave TS22 ....102 B6
Rudston Cl TS17 ....138 B4
Rudyard Ave TS19 ....117 C8
Ruff Tail TS14 ....143 B4
Rufford Cl
Guisborough TS14 ....143 E2
Ingleby Barwick TS17 ....138 C1
1 Marton TS7 ....140 F3
Ruffside DH8 ....175 D6
Rufus Gn 2 DL5 ....96 F8
Rugby Rd TS18 ....212 C2
Rugby St TS25 ....77 A3
Rugby Terr TS2 ....103 E1
Rugeley Cl 4 TS19 ....117 D7
Ruislip Cl TS19 ....117 D7
Rumby Hill DL15 ....52 F1
Rumby Hill Bank DL15 ....65 F8
Rumby Hill La DL15 ....53 A2
Runcie Rd DH6 ....57 D8
Runciman Rd TS24 ....63 F2
Runcorn SR2 ....18 C7
Runcorn Ave TS19 ....117 D7
Runfold Cl TS19 ....101 D1
Runnymead Gn TS3 ....140 E7
Runnymede
Great Lumley DH3 ....25 A8
Nunthorpe TS7 ....141 A2
Ryhope SR2 ....18 D7
Runnymede Cl TS19 ....117 D8
Runnymede Ct 6 DL14 ....80 C8
Runnymede Gdns NE17 ....4 B7
Runswick Ave
Middlesbrough TS5 ....139 C4
Redcar TS10 ....107 A5
Stockton-on-T TS19 ....117 D7
Runswick Cl SR3 ....18 C7
Runswick Dr SR7 ....19 D1
Runswick Ho TS1 ....214 C3
Runswick La TS13 ....149 F5
Runswick Rd TS6 ....121 F2
Rupert St TS18 ....213 B4
Rush Pk DL14 ....79 E6
Rushey Gill DH7 ....43 A4
Rushford SR2 ....18 D6
Rushleigh Ave TS5 ....139 B6
Rushmere TS8 ....140 E1
Rushmere Heath TS16 ....156 C8
Rushmoor DL16 ....69 B8
Rushpool Cl TS10 ....107 B3
Rushsyde Cl NE16 ....2 E5
Rushy Lea La DL13 ....207 B2
Rushyford Ave TS19 ....117 D7
Rushyford Ct 1 DL5 ....96 D8
Ruskin Ave
Chester le Street DH2 ....15 E3
Easington Lane DH5 ....37 D8
Middlesbrough TS5 ....139 B7
Saltburn-by-t-S TS12 ....125 B7
1 Shildon DL4 ....80 F1
Ruskin Cl
Dalton-on-T DL2 ....168 B5
Stanley DH9 ....14 B7
Ruskin Cres DH6 ....47 C4
Ruskin Gr TS25 ....76 F3
Ruskin Rd Birtley DH3 ....9 C4
Darlington DL1 ....152 A6
Russ St DL15 ....53 C3
Russell Cl DH8 ....11 A3
Russell Cres TS29 ....60 B5
Russell Ct DL5 ....96 A8
Russell Pl DL15 ....54 A3
Russell St
Bishop Auckland DL14 ....80 B8
Darlington DL1 ....133 A2
Esh Winning DH7 ....41 C6
Hartlepool TS24 ....64 F1
Middlesbrough TS1 ....215 A3
Stockton-on-T TS18 ....213 A3
Russell Terr DH3 ....9 B6
Russell Wlk
8 Hartlepool TS25 ....77 B4
4 Thornaby-on-T TS17 ....138 C8
Russell's Yd DL15 ....53 F3
Rustington Cl TS19 ....117 D8
Rustland Dr DL3 ....151 D8
Ruswarp Ave 1 TS19 ....117 D7
Ruswarp Cl 1 TS6 ....121 F2
Ruswarp Dr SR3 ....18 B6
Ruswarp Gr TS25 ....90 E7
Ruswarp Rd TS6 ....121 F2
Ruth Ave TS3 ....120 E2
Rutherford Ave SR7 ....28 F8
Rutherford Ct DH7 ....32 B7
Rutherford Ho SR8 ....39 D4
Rutherford La DL12 ....204 B6
Rutherford Terr 2 DL17 ....70 A5
Rutherglen Wlk TS16 ....156 C8
Ruthin Cl TS19 ....117 E8
Rutland Ave
Bishop Auckland DL14 ....80 B6
Marton TS7 ....140 C3
3 New Silksworth SR3 ....18 A7
Rutland Cl TS19 ....117 E8
Rutland Ct TS1 ....215 A3
Rutland Dr DL15 ....54 A3
Rutland Pl 7 DH8 ....177 A4
Rutland Rd DH8 ....177 A4
Rutland Sq DH3 ....9 B5
Rutland St Coundon DL14 ....81 D8
Hetton-le-H DH5 ....26 F4
Seaham SR7 ....29 B8
Rutland Terr DH6 ....37 E1
Rutland Wlk SR8 ....49 C8
Rutter St DH7 ....43 E5
Ryan Ave TS18 ....213 B4
Ryan Terr DH6 ....47 E1
Ryan Wlk TS18 ....213 B4
Ryan's Row TS11 ....108 B1
Rydal Ave
Billingham TS23 ....102 E1
Easington Lane DH5 ....37 C8
Eston TS6 ....121 F4
Middlesbrough TS5 ....139 C7
Redcar TS10 ....107 C5
Stanley DH9 ....13 D4
Rydal Cl DH7 ....23 B3
Rydal Cres Blaydon NE21 ....2 B8
Peterlee SR8 ....49 E6
Rydal Dr DL15 ....53 A3
Rydal Gr DL14 ....79 A1
Rydal Mews DH8 ....11 D4
Rydal Mount SR8 ....39 D4
Rydal Rd
Chester le Street DH2 ....16 C1
Darlington DL1 ....152 B8
Ferryhill DL17 ....69 F5
Skelton TS12 ....125 B3
Stockton-on-T TS18 ....212 B3
Rydal St TS26 ....77 A4
Rydal Way TS21 ....116 B7
Rydale Ct TS29 ....60 A5
Ryde Rd TS19 ....117 E7
Ryde Terr DH9 ....12 F5
Ryde Terrace Bglws 8
DH9 ....12 F5
Ryder Cl TS11 ....123 F6
Ryder Ct DL5 ....82 C3
Rye Cl TS16 ....156 B7
Rye Hill DL3 ....132 D4
Rye Hill Way TS8 ....159 C7
Rye Hills Sch TS10 ....107 D4
Rye View SR2 ....18 F7
Ryedale Durham DH1 ....35 D3
Guisborough TS14 ....143 B2
Ryedale Cl TS15 ....156 B3
Ryedale St TS3 ....120 C4
Ryehill Cl TS7 ....141 A1
Ryehill Gdns TS26 ....76 E7
Ryehill View DH5 ....26 C5
Ryehills Dr TS11 ....108 E1
Ryelands Pk TS13 ....148 A8
Ryelands Way DH1 ....34 C8
Ryemount Rd SR2 ....18 D7
Ryhill Wlk TS7 ....141 A7
Ryhope Ave 2 TS19 ....117 D8
Ryhope Engine Mus*
SR2 ....18 E5
Ryhope General Hospl
SR2 ....18 F5
Ryhope Inf Sch SR2 ....18 E7
Ryhope Jun Sch SR2 ....18 E7
Ryhope Rd SR2 ....19 A8
Ryhope St
Houghton-le-S DH5 ....26 F8
Ryhope SR2 ....18 E7
Ryhope St S SR2 ....18 F7
Ryhope Village CE Prim Sch
SR2 ....18 F6
Rylstone Cl DL5 ....96 B8
Rylstone Ct TS4 ....140 A8
Rymers Cl SR8 ....39 A3
Ryton Cl TS17 ....138 B4
Ryton Cres Seaham SR7 ....29 A7
Stanley DH9 ....14 A8

S

Sabatier Cl TS17 ....213 C2
Sabin Terr DH9 ....13 B4
Sacred Heart RC Comp Sch
TS10 ....107 B6
Sacred Heart RC Prim Sch
Byermoor NE16 ....6 D7
Hartlepool TS26 ....76 F7
Middlesbrough TS1 ....214 B1
Sacriston Cl TS23 ....102 C6
Sacriston Ind Est DH7 ....23 C3
Sacriston Jun & Inf Schs
DH7 ....23 C2
Sacriston La DH7 ....23 B1
Sadberge CE Prim Sch
DL2 ....134 E7
Sadberge Gr TS19 ....117 A2
Sadberge Rd
Middleton St George DL2 ....134 E2
Stockton-on-T TS18 ....138 A8
Sadberge St TS3 ....120 C4
Saddler Cl 4 TS17 ....138 B1
Saddler St
Bishop Auckland DL14 ....80 B8
Durham DH1 ....210 C2
Ferryhill DL17 ....69 F6
Saddlers La DH1 ....210 C2
Saddlery The DL5 ....95 F8
Saddleston Cl TS26 ....76 D7
Sadler Dr TS7 ....140 C3
Sadler Forster Way
TS17 ....138 D1
Sadler La Evenwood DL14 ....92 D6
Kinninvie DL12 ....194 E1
Saffron Wlk TS25 ....77 E1
Sailport Ind Est TS17 ....138 B7
Saint Ct SR3 ....18 A5
St Abbs Wlk 7 TS24 ....77 C5
St Adens Way SR8 ....49 D5
St Agathas Cl DH7 ....43 C5
St Aidan Cres DH6 ....47 C3
St Aidan's Ave DH1 ....34 B5
St Aidan's CE Meml Prim Sch
TS25 ....77 B2
St Aidan's Coll (Univ of
Durham) DH1 ....44 B7
St Aidan's Cres
Billingham TS22 ....102 C3
Durham DH1 ....210 A3
St Aidan's Pl DH8 ....10 E4
St Aidan's St Consett DH8 ....10 E4
1 Hartlepool TS25 ....77 B3
Middlesbrough TS1 ....214 C2
St Aidan's Terr TS29 ....59 F6
St Aidan's Wlk
Bishop Auckland DL14 ....80 C5
3 Newton Aycliffe DL5 ....96 F8
St Aidans Cres DH9 ....13 A3
St Aidans Dr TS1 ....214 C3
St Alban's Cl DH3 ....25 B6
St Alban's Gn DL1 ....133 F5
St Alban's RC Prim Sch
TS10 ....107 B2
St Alban's St DL13 ....183 E1
St Alban's Terr TS29 ....59 E3
St Aldwyn Rd SR7 ....29 B8
St Alphonsus' RC Prim Sch
TS3 ....120 C4
St Andrew's Cl
Consett DH8 ....10 D4
Newton Aycliffe DL5 ....96 E1
St Andrew's Cres DH8 ....10 D4
St Andrew's Crest DL14 ....80 C7
St Andrew's Gdns DH8 ....10 D4
St Andrew's La DL16 ....56 A1
St Andrew's Pl
Bishop Auckland DL14 ....80 C7
Westgate DL13 ....180 A1
St Andrew's Prim Sch
DL14 ....80 C5
St Andrew's RC Prim Sch
TS6 ....121 B4
St Andrew's Rd
Bishop Auckland DL14 ....80 C5
Bishop Auckland DL14 ....80 D5
Consett DH8 ....10 D4
2 New Marske TS11 ....124 A6
Spennymoor DL16 ....56 A1
Tanfield Lea DH9 ....6 F1
St Andrew's Rd E TS6 ....121 E5
St Andrew's Rd W TS6 ....121 E5

St Andrew's Sq SR7 ... 28 E4
St Andrew's St DL1 ... 133 A5
St Andrew's Terr DL14 ... 80 C6
St Andrews DH4 ... 26 B8
St Andrews Cl
Darlington DL1 ... 133 D4
Egglescliffe TS16 ... 156 C8
St Andrews Ct DL5 ... 82 C3
St Andrews Gr TS27 ... 63 D4
St Andrews Rd TS7 ... 140 D3
St Andrews Way DL5 ... 112 D8
St Ann's Ct TS24 ... 77 D5
St Ann's Terr TS18 ... 213 C4
St Anne's CE Prim Sch DL14 ... 80 A6
St Annes Ct DH1 ... 210 C3
St Annes Gdns DL2 ... 153 F6
St Annes Rd TS11 ... 124 A6
St Anns Ind Est TS18 ... 213 C4
St Antony's RC Sec Sch TS3 ... 120 E2
St Arreck Cl TS11 ... 123 F6
St Aubyn's Way DH9 ... 14 B7
St Augustine's Ct 16 DL3 ... 132 F1
St Augustine's RC Prim Sch
Darlington DL3 ... 132 E1
Marton TS7 ... 140 C2
St Augustines Way DL1, DL3 ... 132 F2
St Austell Cl TS8 ... 139 C2
St Barbara's Wlk 1 DL5 ... 96 F8
St Barnabas DH4 ... 17 D3
St Barnabas' Rd TS5 ... 119 D2
St Bede Ave TS21 ... 72 C5
St Bede Cres DH6 ... 47 C3
St Bede's Cl Durham DH1 210 A2
Hetton-le-H DH5 ... 27 A4
St Bede's Ct DH7 ... 20 E5
St Bede's RC Comp Sch DH7 ... 20 E5
St Bede's RC Comp Sch SR8 ... 49 C5
St Bede's RC Prim Sch
Darlington DL1 ... 133 C6
Marske-by-t-S TS11 ... 108 C1
St Bede's RC Prim Sch TS19 ... 212 C4
St Bedes RC Prim Sch DH7 ... 23 B3
St Bedes Way DH7 ... 43 E5
St Bees Wlk 8 TS24 ... 77 C5
St Bega's RC Prim Sch TS24 ... 64 E2
St Benet's RC Prim Sch DH2 ... 8 F1
St Bernadette's RC Prim Sch TS7 ... 140 F3
St Bernard Rd TS18 ... 213 A2
St Brandon's Gr DH7 ... 43 A4
St Brelades Way DH9 ... 14 B7
St Brides Ct TS17 ... 156 F7
St Catherine Cl TS21 ... 72 C5
St Catherine's Ct TS24 ... 77 D5
St Catherines Ct TS3 ... 120 C2
St Chad Sq DH6 ... 47 C3
St Chad's Coll (Univ of Durham) DH1 ... 210 C2
St Chad's RC Prim Sch DL14 ... 79 A8
St Chads Cl DL14 ... 80 D5
St Charles Rd DL16 ... 56 A3
St Charles' RC Prim Sch DL16 ... 56 A2
St Clare's Abbey DL3 ... 132 C2
St Clare's RC Prim Sch TS5 ... 139 B4
St Columba's Ave TS22 ... 102 C3
St Crispins' Ct TS19 ... 117 F5
St Cuthbert Ave DH3 ... 16 D3
St Cuthbert Ct 6 TS17 ... 138 C8
St Cuthbert Rd DH6 ... 47 C3
St Cuthbert St TS24 ... 64 E1
St Cuthbert's Ave
Billingham TS23 ... 102 C3
Consett DH8 ... 10 D5
High Etherley DL14 ... 78 F5
St Cuthbert's Cl DH5 ... 27 A4
St Cuthbert's Cres TS29 ... 59 D1
St Cuthbert's Ct SR7 ... 28 F8
St Cuthbert's RC Prim Sch
Chester le Street DH3 ... 16 D2
Crook DL15 ... 52 F4
Hartlepool TS25 ... 77 B3
Seaham SR7 ... 28 F8
St Cuthbert's RC Prim Sch TS18 ... 213 A1
St Cuthbert's Rd
Peterlee SR8 ... 49 D5
Stockton-on-T TS18 ... 213 A1
Sunniside NE16 ... 7 B7
St Cuthbert's Society (Univ of Durham) DH1 ... 210 C1
St Cuthbert's Terr SR7 ... 28 F5
St Cuthbert's Terr DL17 ... 69 E6
St Cuthbert's Way
Cornforth DL17 ... 57 E1
Darlington DL1 ... 133 A1
Newton Aycliffe DL5 ... 96 D5
St Cuthbert's Wlk DL14 ... 80 C6
St Cuthbert's Wlk DH3 ... 16 C3
St Cuthberts Ave DH1 ... 34 A5
St Cuthberts Dr DH7 ... 23 B3
St Cuthberts Pk NE16 ... 7 A8
St Cuthberts Pl DL3 ... 132 D2
St Cuthberts Way DH6 ... 35 F1
St Cuthberts Wlk
Brandon DH7 ... 43 E5
St Cuthberts Wlk *continued*
Loftus TS13 ... 147 A8
St David's Cl
Billingham TS23 ... 102 C3
Spennymoor DL16 ... 56 B3
St David's Gn DL1 ... 133 F5
St David's RC Tech Coll TS5 ... 139 D5
St David's Rd TS6 ... 121 E6
St David's Wlk TS26 ... 76 D8
St Davids Gr TS17 ... 156 F7
St Davids Way TS5 ... 139 D6
St Dominic's RC Prim Sch TS10 ... 107 B5
St Ebba's Way DH8 ... 3 E3
St Edmund's Terr
Dipton DH9 ... 12 C7
Sedgefield TS21 ... 85 B6
St Edmunds Gn TS21 ... 85 B7
St Edwards RC Prim Sch TS5 ... 119 E1
St Edwin's Cl DL2 ... 130 F3
St Elizabeth's Cl DL5 ... 82 E2
St Francis CE Jun Sch DL5 ... 96 A7
St Francis Gate TS25 ... 77 B2
St Francis of Assisi CE Sch TS17 ... 138 A2
St Francis RC Prim Sch TS5 ... 119 B1
St Gabriel's RC Prim Sch TS3 ... 141 A8
St George's Cres TS11 ... 124 A6
St George's Est NE38 ... 17 C8
St George's Gate DL2 ... 134 D1
St George's Pl DH8 ... 10 E3
St George's Rd E TS6 ... 121 E5
St George's Rd W TS6 ... 121 E5
St Georges Bglws TS6 ... 121 E6
St Georges Terr TS13 ... 147 A8
St Gerards RC Prim Sch TS8 ... 139 F2
St Germain's Gr TS11 ... 108 D1
St Germain's La TS11 ... 108 D2
St Giles Cl
Darlington DL3 ... 132 A1
Durham DH1 ... 211 C3
St Godric's Cl DH1 ... 34 C6
St Godric's Dr DH4 ... 26 A2
St Godric's RC Prim Sch DH6 ... 47 E3
St Godrics Ct DH1 ... 210 C3
St Godrics Rd DL5 ... 96 C6
St Gregory Cl 1 DL2 ... 200 E7
St Gregorys RC Prim Sch TS19 ... 117 D6
St Helen Auckland Com Prim Sch DL14 ... 79 D2
St Helen's Cl TS6 ... 121 D2
St Helen's Cres DH6 ... 58 D7
St Helens Prim Sch TS24 64 E1
St Helen's St TS24 ... 64 E1
St Helens Ind Est DL14 ... 79 E2
St Helens Wlk TS13 ... 147 A8
St Heliers Way DH9 ... 14 B7
St Hild Cl DL3 ... 132 B1
St Hild's CE Sch TS24 ... 63 E3
St Hild's Coll CE Prim Sch, Durham DH1 ... 35 A2
St Hild's La DH1 ... 211 B3
St Hilda Chare TS24 ... 64 G8
St Hilda's Pl TS13 ... 127 C1
St Hilda's Terr TS13 ... 127 A2
St Hilds Ct DH1 ... 35 A2
St Ives Cl
Middlesbrough TS8 ... 140 B4
Redcar TS10 ... 107 F2
St Ives Pl SR7 ... 28 D4
St Ives' Rd DH8 ... 11 D4
St James Cl TS21 ... 100 D4
St James Ct TS6 ... 121 D6
St James Gdns
Middlesbrough TS2 ... 215 A4
Witton-le-W DL14 ... 65 B4
St James Gr TS27 ... 62 F2
St James Mews TS1 ... 214 B1
St James' Fields TS27 ... 61 C8
St James' Ho TS18 ... 213 C4
St Joan's Gr TS25 ... 77 B2
St John the Baptist CE Prim Sch TS19 ... 117 F6
St John the Evangelist RC Prim Sch TS23 ... 102 E2
St John Vianney RC Prim Sch TS24 ... 63 F3
St John's CE Prim Sch
Darlington DL1 ... 152 C7
Shildon DL4 ... 81 A1
St John's Chapel Prim Sch DL13 ... 179 E1
St John's Coll (Univ of Durham) DH1 ... 210 C1
St John's Cres
Bowburn DH6 ... 45 C1
Darlington DL1 ... 133 B1
St John's Ct
Kirk Merrington DL16 ... 69 A3
Sacriston DH7 ... 23 B3
St John's Gdns DL15 ... 53 D2
St John's Gr TS10 ... 107 D5
St John's Pl Birtley DH3 ... 9 C4
10 Darlington DL1 ... 133 B1
St John's RC Comp Sch DL14 ... 79 F5
St John's Rd Brandon DH7 ... 43 E3
Durham DH1 ... 210 A2
St John's Rd DH6 ... 36 B5
St John's Sq 8 SR7 ... 29 D7
St John's Terr DH9 ... 12 C7
St John's Terr 3 SR7 ... 18 E1
St John's Way
6 Annfield Plain DH9 ... 12 F4
Stockton-on-T TS19 ... 117 F6
St John's Wlk DL14 ... 66 D1
St Johns Cl
Middlesbrough TS4 ... 215 B3
Stockton-on-T TS18 ... 213 A4
St Johns Mews DH7 ... 21 E6
St Johns Pk TS21 ... 99 F4
St Joseph's Cl DH1 ... 35 A2
St Joseph's Ct
8 Birtley DH3 ... 9 C5
15 Hartlepool TS26 ... 77 A6
St Joseph's RC Inf Sch DH3 ... 9 C5
St Joseph's RC Jun Sch DH3 ... 9 C4
St Joseph's RC Prim Sch TS23 ... 102 F6
St Joseph's RC Prim Sch
Blackhall Colliery TS27 ... 50 D3
Coundon DL14 ... 81 C8
Hartlepool TS24 ... 77 C5
St Joseph's RC Prim Sch NE39 ... 1 B2
St Joseph's RC Prim Sch
Middlesbrough TS4 ... 215 B1
Murton SR7 ... 28 C2
Newton Aycliffe DL5 ... 96 B7
Stanley DH9 ... 13 F7
St Joseph's RC Prim Sch TS20 ... 118 A8
St Joseph's RC Prim Sch DH7 ... 33 A2
St Joseph's RC Prim Sch, Durham DH1 ... 35 A2
St Josephs Ct
Redcar TS10 ... 107 B5
Stanley DH9 ... 13 F6
St Josephs RC Prim Sch TS13 ... 147 B8
St Lawrence Cl DH6 ... 36 C5
St Lawrence Rd DH6 ... 36 B5
St Leonard's RC Comp Sch DH1 ... 210 B4
St Leonard's RC Prim Sch SR3 ... 18 B7
St Leonards Cl
Loftus TS13 ... 147 A8
Peterlee SR8 ... 49 B5
St Leonards Rd TS14 ... 143 C3
St Luke's TS4 ... 140 B8
St Luke's Ave TS17 ... 138 D8
St Luke's Cl DL14 ... 79 F4
St Luke's Cotts 7 TS4 ... 120 A1
St Lukes Cres TS21 ... 72 A1
St Lukes Ct TS26 ... 76 F7
St Margaret's CE Prim Sch DH1 ... 210 B1
St Margaret's Ct DH1 ... 210 B2
St Margaret's Dr DH9 ... 6 D4
St Margaret's Garth DH1 ... 210 B2
St Margaret's Gr
Hartlepool TS25 ... 77 B2
Middlesbrough TS5 ... 139 D7
Redcar TS10 ... 107 D4
South Bank TS6 ... 121 B4
St Margaret's Mews DH1 ... 210 B2
St Margaret's Way TS12 ... 126 B5
St Margarets Cl DL2 ... 153 F6
St Margarets Gr 1 TS17 ... 138 D5
St Mark's Cl
2 Marske-by-t-S TS11 ... 108 C1
Stockton-on-T TS19 ... 117 B4
St Mark's Ct
Coundon Grange DL14 ... 80 F5
Thornaby-on-T TS17 ... 213 B2
St Mark's Elm Tree CE Prim Sch TS19 ... 117 B4
St Marks Rd TS21 ... 72 C5
St Martins Cl TS13 ... 147 A8
St Martins Way TS15 ... 172 D8
St Mary Magdalen's RC Prim Sch SR7 ... 29 C8
St Mary St TS24 ... 77 F8
St Mary's Ave DL15 ... 52 E4
St Mary's Cath TS8 ... 140 B1
St Mary's CE Prim Sch TS21 ... 136 A5
St Mary's Cl
Bishop Auckland DL14 ... 80 A5
Consett DH8 ... 10 D4
Easington SR8 ... 39 A3
High Shincliffe DH1 ... 44 F6
Stockton-on-T TS18 ... 213 B4
St Mary's Coll TS4 ... 139 F6
St Mary's Coll (Univ of Durham) DH1 ... 44 C7
St Mary's Cres DH8 ... 10 D4
St Mary's Ct TS24 ... 77 F8
St Mary's Dr Sherburn DH6 ... 35 F1
West Rainton DH4 ... 26 A2
St Mary's Gate Bsns Pk TS20 ... 213 B4
St Mary's Gr DL16 ... 56 A3
St Mary's RC Prim Sch DL12 ... 209 C5
St Mary's RC Prim Sch DH8 ... 10 C3
St Mary's RC Prim Sch TS6 ... 121 E5
St Mary's RC Prim Sch
Newton Aycliffe DL5 ... 96 E7
St Mary's RC Prim Sch *continued*
Wingate TS28 ... 60 D6
St Mary's Rd DH1 ... 35 C4
St Mary's St DH8 ... 10 D4
St Mary's Terr DH6 ... 57 E6
St Mary's Wlk TS5 ... 139 D7
St Marys Cl
Barnard Castle DL12 ... 209 C5
Chester le Street DH2 ... 16 B1
St Marys Ct Eston TS6 ... 121 E5
Middlesbrough TS5 ... 139 D8
St Marys RC Prim Sch DH9 ... 13 F4
St Matthews Ct TS6 ... 121 D6
St Matthews View SR3 ... 18 A7
St Mawes Cl TS26 ... 76 D7
St Michael's Cres DL5 ... 95 C1
St Michael's Ct 3 TS20 ... 118 B6
St Michael's Gr 5 TS20 ... 118 B6
St Michael's RC Comp Sch TS23 ... 103 A6
St Michael's RC Prim Sch
Esh DH7 ... 31 F4
Houghton-le-S DH5 ... 26 D7
St Michaels DH4 ... 26 B8
St Michaels Cl TS13 ... 147 A8
St Monica Gr DH1 ... 210 A2
St Nicholas Ct TS6 ... 121 D6
St Nicholas Dr DH1 ... 33 F4
St Nicholas Gdns TS15 ... 156 E4
St Nicholas Ind Est DL1 ... 133 B4
St Nicholas Terr SR8 ... 39 D4
St Ninian's Cl DL3 ... 132 A1
St Oswald Sq DH1 ... 34 A7
St Oswald's CE Inf Sch DH1 ... 211 A1
St Oswald's Cres TS22 ... 102 C3
St Oswald's Dr DH1 ... 44 A5
St Oswald's St TS24 ... 77 A7
St Oswald's Wlk 5 DL5 ... 96 F8
St Oswalds Cl DL14 ... 80 D6
St Oswalds Ct DL5 ... 96 F8
St Oswalds Wlk DL5 ... 96 F7
St Oswin's Pl 8 DH8 ... 10 D4
St Patrick's Cl TS6 ... 121 E5
St Patrick's RC Comp Sch TS17 ... 138 D6
St Patrick's RC Prim Sch
Brandon DH7 ... 43 E5
Consett DH8 ... 10 F3
Dipton DH9 ... 12 E8
Ryhope SR2 ... 18 F6
St Patrick's RC Prim Sch TS19 ... 117 B3
St Patrick's RC Prim Sch TS17 ... 138 C8
St Patrick's Rd TS6 ... 121 E5
St Patrick's Terr SR2 ... 18 F6
St Paul's CE Prim Sch SR2 ... 18 F6
St Paul's Cl DL16 ... 68 E8
St Paul's Gdns DL16 ... 68 E8
St Paul's Gdns DL14 ... 79 A8
St Paul's Pl DL1 ... 133 A5
St Paul's RC Prim Sch TS22 ... 102 A6
St Paul's Rd
Hartlepool TS26 ... 77 A5
Middlesbrough TS1 ... 214 B3
Stockton-on-T TS19 ... 212 C4
Thornaby-on-T TS17 ... 138 C8
Wingate TS29 ... 60 A5
St Paul's St
Spennymoor DL16 ... 68 E8
Stockton-on-T TS19 ... 212 C3
St Paul's Terr
Darlington DL1 ... 133 A5
5 Ryhope SR2 ... 18 F6
Shildon DL4 ... 81 A2
St Paul's Terr
Stockton-on-T TS19 ... 212 C4
West Pelton DH9 ... 15 A6
St Paul's Way DL15 ... 66 D5
St Paulinus RC Prim Sch TS14 ... 143 B3
St Pauls Ct DL16 ... 68 E7
St Pauls Dr DH4 ... 17 E8
St Peter's Gr TS10 ... 107 D5
St Peter's RC Comp Sch TS6 ... 121 B5
St Peter's RC Prim Sch TS6 ... 121 B4
St Peter's Rd TS18 ... 212 C1
St Peters CE Prim Sch TS12 ... 126 A4
St Peters Sq TS17 ... 138 D5
St Peters Wynd TS21 ... 115 D7
St Pius X RC Prim Sch TS3 ... 140 D8
St Stephen's Cl DL15 ... 54 A3
St Stephens Cl TS20 ... 102 A2
St Stevens Cl DH4 ... 17 E8
St Teresa's RC Prim Sch DL1 ... 152 D8
St Therese of Lisieux RC Prim Sch TS17 ... 157 A7
St Thomas Cl SR8 ... 39 A3
St Thomas Gr TS10 ... 107 D5
St Thomas More RC Prim Sch
Durham DH1 ... 35 D3
Middlesbrough TS4 ... 140 B5
St Thomas' Cl
Stanhope DL13 ... 206 C4
Willington DL15 ... 53 F3
St Vincent St TS23 ... 103 C2
St Vincent Terr
2 Cockfield DL13 ... 195 E3
Redcar TS10 ... 107 B6
St Wilfrid's RC Prim Sch DL14 ... 80 A5
St Wilfrids Wlk DL14 ... 80 D5
St William's RC Prim Sch TS29 ... 72 E7
Salcombe Cl
Middlesbrough TS8 ... 140 B4
Seaham SR7 ... 29 A6
Salcombe Dr TS25 ... 90 A7
Salcombe Way TS10 ... 107 E2
Salem Ave 6 DH8 ... 177 D4
Salisbury Ave 10 DH3 ... 16 C2
Salisbury Cl Consett DH8 ... 10 E7
Great Lumley DH3 ... 25 A6
Salisbury Cres DL17 ... 70 F8
Salisbury Gr TS10 ... 107 F5
Salisbury Pl
Bishop Auckland DL14 ... 80 C7
Hartlepool TS26 ... 76 F8
Middleton St George DL2 ... 153 E7
Salisbury Rd DH1 ... 34 E8
Salisbury St Consett DH8 ... 11 A3
Stanley DH9 ... 13 D5
6 Thornaby-on-T TS17 ... 138 D8
Willington DL15 ... 54 A2
Salisbury Terr
Darlington DL3 ... 132 F3
Shildon DL4 ... 80 F1
South Bank TS6 ... 121 A6
Stockton-on-T TS20 ... 118 B6
Salt Yd DL3 ... 132 F2
Saltaire Terr TS25 ... 89 F3
Saltburn Bank TS12 ... 125 D7
Saltburn La TS12 ... 125 D5
Saltburn Miniature Rly* TS12 ... 125 D7
Saltburn Pl DL13 ... 195 C4
Saltburn Prim Sch
Saltburn-by-t-S TS12 ... 125 B7
Saltburn-by-t-S TS12 ... 125 C6
Saltburn Rd
Brotton TS12 ... 126 B5
Saltburn-by-t-S TS12 ... 125 E7
Thornaby-on-T TS17 ... 138 D7
Saltburn Smugglers The* TS12 ... 125 E8
Saltburn Sta TS12 ... 125 C7
Saltburn Valley Woodland Ctr* TS12 ... 125 D6
Saltcote TS7 ... 140 E4
Salter House Dr TS22 ... 87 D2
Salter Houses TS22 ... 87 C3
Salter Wlk TS24 ... 64 E1
Salter's Dr TS21 ... 72 C5
Salter's Gate DL13 ... 182 F5
Salter's La Fishburn TS21 ... 73 A4
Fishburn TS21,TS29 ... 72 C4
Haswell DH6 ... 37 E6
Hetton-le-H SR7 ... 27 F6
Seaton DH5,SR7 ... 27 F6
Shotton Colliery DH6,TS28 ... 48 C5
Trimdon TS29 ... 59 D3
Salter's La TS28 ... 60 E8
Salterfen La SR2 ... 19 A8
Salterfen Rd SR2 ... 19 A8
Saltergill La TS15 ... 155 F1
Saltergill Sch TS15 ... 155 F1
Salters Ave DL1 ... 133 D4
Salters Cl DL1 ... 133 C6
Salters La Brafferton DL1 ... 113 F7
Darlington DL1 ... 133 B8
Darlington, Firth Moor DL1 ... 152 E7
Salters La N DL1 ... 133 B7
Salters La S DL1 ... 133 D5
Saltersgate La DL13 ... 182 F5
Saltersgate Rd DL1 ... 133 B7
Saltersgill Ave
Middlesbrough, Beechwood TS4 ... 139 F7
Middlesbrough, Easterside TS4 ... 140 B5
Saltersgill Cl TS4 ... 139 F8
Saltholme Cl TS2 ... 103 E1
Saltney Rd TS20 ... 117 F8
Salton Cl TS5 ... 119 B1
Saltram Cl TS17 ... 157 B8
Saltram Gr TS7 ... 140 C4
Saltscar TS10 ... 107 E3
Saltview Terr TS2 ... 120 A8
Saltwells Cres TS4 ... 215 C1
Saltwells Rd TS4 ... 215 C2
Salutation Rd DL3 ... 151 B8
Salvin St Spennymoor DL16 ... 56 B1
Sunderland Bridge DH6 ... 56 B6
Salvin Terr TS21 ... 72 B5
Samaria Gdns TS5 ... 139 E4
Sambrook Gdns TS5 ... 139 D4
Samphire St TS2 ... 119 F8
Sampson Pl 3 DL5 ... 96 C8
Samsung Ave TS22 ... 88 A1
Samuel St TS19 ... 212 C4
Samuelson Ho 3 TS3 ... 120 C1
Sancroft Dr DH5 ... 26 E7
Sand St DH9 ... 14 A7
Sandalwood Ct TS5 ... 139 E4
Sandbach DH3 ... 25 A8
Sandbanks Dr TS24 ... 63 D4
Sanders Gdns DH3 ... 9 C5
Sanders' Meml Homes DH2 ... 16 C3
Sanderson Cl DL5 ... 96 D8
Sanderson Rd DL2 ... 152 D1

Sanderson St
3 Coxhoe DH6 .....58 A4
Darlington DL1 .....133 A2
Sandford Cl TS4 .....140 A7
Sandford Rd DH8 .....10 B4
Sandgate DH9 .....13 B4
Sandgate Ind Est TS25 ...77 D4
Sandhall Cl 4 TS23 .....102 E8
Sandhill Bank YO21 .....164 D2
Sandlewood Wlk DH9 ....14 A7
Sandling Ct TS7 .....140 E4
Sandmartin La TS20 .....102 B2
Sandmoor Cl TS6 .....121 E1
Sandmoor Rd TS11 .....123 F6
Sandown Dr DL5 .....82 E2
Sandown Pk TS10 .....107 D4
Sandown Rd TS23 .....102 D6
Sandown Way TS17 .....118 F1
Sandpiper Cl
Redcar TS10 .....107 E2
Washington NE38 .....9 F2
Sandport Wlk 9 TS18 ...213 C4
Sandray Cl DH3 .....9 D1
Sandriggs DL3 .....132 C5
Sandringham Cres 11
SR8 .....50 B6
Sandringham Ct DL3 .....132 A2
Sandringham Dr 2 DH9 ..12 F5
Sandringham Rd
Crook DL15 .....52 F4
Eston TS6 .....121 E4
Hartlepool TS26 .....77 A6
Lingdale TS12 .....145 F5
Middlesbrough TS3 .....140 E8
Redcar TS10 .....107 C6
Stockton-on-T TS18 .....212 C2
10 Thornaby-on-T TS17 .....138 D8
Sandringham Terr DL14 ..68 D1
Sands The DH1 .....211 A3
Sandsay Cl SR2 .....18 D8
Sandsend Rd Eston TS6 ..121 F3
Redcar TS10 .....107 A5
Sandwell Ave TS3 .....140 F8
Sandwell Chare TS24 .....77 F8
Sandwell Dr DH4 .....17 F8
Sandwich Gr TS27 .....63 D4
Sandwick Terr DH6 .....47 E1
Sandwood Pk TS14 .....143 B2
Sandy Bank TS21 .....84 D5
Sandy Flatts Ct TS5 .....139 E4
Sandy Flatts La TS5 .....139 E4
Sandy Gate DH1 .....210 A4
Sandy La Billingham TS22 .102 B4
New Marske TS11,TS14 ..123 E4
Wynyard Village TS22 .....101 F7
Sandy Lane W TS22 .....102 A6
Sandy Leas La TS21 .....116 B2
Sandy Lonnen DL15 .....41 C3
Sandyford DH2 .....15 E7
Sandyford Pl DH2 .....15 E7
Sandypath La NE16 .....6 A7
Sapley Cl TS17 .....138 C4
Sapper's Cnr TS25 .....89 E5
Sarah St TS25 .....77 C3
Sark Wlk TS14 .....143 D3
Satley Cl DL15 .....52 D3
Satley Plough DL13 .....183 D5
Satley Rd TS23 .....102 F8
Saturn Cl SR8 .....39 C4
Saturn St SR7 .....29 A7
Saunders Ave DL13 .....189 D2
Saunton Ave TS10 .....107 E2
Saunton Rd TS23 .....102 F4
Sawley Cl DL3 .....131 F5
Sawley Gr TS18 .....117 A1
Sawmill Ave TS27 .....63 B8
Sawmill Cotts DH9 .....5 E1
Sawmill La DH7 .....43 B4
Sawtry Rd 3 TS3 .....140 F8
Saxby Dr DL15 .....53 E1
Saxby Rd TS20 .....118 B6
Saxon Gn DL14 .....66 D1
Saxon Terr DH8 .....10 E3
Saxonfield TS8 .....140 B2
Sayer Wlk SR8 .....49 E5
Scafell DH3 .....9 D1
Scafell Cl SR8 .....49 E6
Scafell Ct DH9 .....12 E3
Scafell Gdns DL15 .....52 F2
Scalby Gr Redcar TS10 ..107 E3
Stockton-on-T TS19 .....117 A3
Scalby Rd TS3 .....120 B2
Scalby Sq TS17 .....138 D7
Scaling Ct TS14 .....143 D5
Scampton Cl TS17 .....138 B4
Scanbeck Dr TS11 .....108 D1
Scarbeck Bank DL11 .....205 D3
Scarborough St
5 Hartlepool TS24 .....77 C6
Loftus TS13 .....127 A1
South Bank TS6 .....121 A5
10 Thornaby-on-T TS17 .....138 C8
Scardale Way DH1 .....35 E4
Scargill DL1 .....152 C8
Scargill Ct 14 DL1 .....152 C8
Scargill Dr DL16 .....55 F2
Scarteen Cl TS14 .....143 D3
Scarth Cl TS12 .....145 E5
Scarth St DL3 .....132 E1
Scarth Wlk TS18 .....213 A3
Scarthwood Cl 2 TS17 ..138 C1
Scawfell Gr TS25 .....77 B3
Sch of Education (Univ of Durham) DH1 .....211 A3
Scholar's Path DL5 .....96 A7
Scholars Gate TS14 .....143 D2
School Ave
1 Blackhall Colliery TS27 ..50 D3
Coxhoe DH6 .....57 F3
Kelloe DH6 .....58 E6
Middlesbrough TS5 .....119 B1
West Rainton DH4 .....25 F2
School Aycliffe La DL5 ....95 E3
School Cl
Marske-by-t-S TS11 .....108 D1
Spennymoor DL16 .....56 B1
St John's Chapel DL13 ....179 E1
Stockton-on-T TS18 .....213 A1
Thorpe Thewles TS21 .....100 D3
School Croft TS1 .....215 A4
School Ct DH6 .....35 F1
School Gn DH6 .....47 D4
School Hill DL13 .....179 A4
School Hos NE39 .....5 B8
School La
Great Ayton TS9 .....161 A2
High Spen NE39 .....1 A3
Liverton TS13 .....147 A8
Stanley DH9 .....13 D5
School Rd DH5 .....26 C4
School Row DL15 .....54 A6
School St Bowburn DH6 ...57 C4
Darlington DL3 .....132 C4
Easington SR8 .....39 E4
Howden-le-W DL15 .....65 E7
Seaham SR7 .....29 D5
Witton-le-W DL14 .....65 B3
School Terr
Great Lumley DH4 .....17 E1
Stanley DH9 .....13 D5
School View Dipton DH9 ...12 C8
Easington Lane DH5 .....37 D8
West Rainton DH4 .....25 F1
School Wlk TS18 .....213 A1
Schoolhouse La NE16 .....6 E7
Schooner Ct TS24 .....77 D6
Scira Ct DL1 .....133 B5
Scorer's La DH3 .....25 B8
Scotforth Cl 4 TS7 .....140 F3
Scotland Head NE21 .....2 A8
Scotland La DL13 .....195 D2
Scotland St SR2 .....19 A6
Scotney Rd TS23 .....102 D5
Scott Ct DH3 .....25 A7
Scott Dr TS20 .....117 F8
Scott Gr TS25 .....76 D2
Scott Pl DL5 .....96 C8
Scott Rd
Bishop Auckland DL14 .....80 B4
Eston TS6 .....121 B1
Scott St
6 Houghton-le-S DH4 .....26 E8
Redcar TS10 .....107 D6
Shildon DL4 .....94 F8
Stanley DH9 .....13 E6
Scott's Rd TS2 .....215 B4
Scott's Terr
Darlington DL3 .....133 A6
Hetton-le-H DH5 .....27 A4
Scotton Cl TS18 .....137 A8
Scotton Ct TS3 .....121 A1
Scrafton Pl TS11 .....108 D1
Scripton Gill DH7 .....43 A4
Scripton Gill Rd DH7 .....42 F3
Scripton La DH7 .....55 C7
Scruton Cl TS18 .....117 B1
Scugdale Cl TS15 .....156 B3
Scurfield Rd TS19 .....117 B7
Scutterhill Bank DL13 ...180 A1
Sea View
Blackhall Rocks TS27 .....50 F2
Easington SR8 .....39 B3
Ryhope SR2 .....19 A6
Sea View Cotts TS27 .....49 F1
Sea View Gdns SR8 .....50 A8
Sea View Ind Est SR8 .....39 F1
Sea View Terr TS24 .....64 F1
Sea View Wlk SR7 .....28 E4
Seaburn Dr 1 DH4 .....26 C8
Seaford Cl TS10 .....107 E2
Seaham Cl Redcar TS10 ..107 F2
Stockton-on-T TS20 .....101 E1
Seaham Grange Ind Est SR7 .....18 E2
Seaham Kingfisher Ind Est SR7 .....29 A8
Seaham Rd
Houghton-le-S DH5 .....27 A8
Ryhope SR2 .....19 A6
Seaham Sch of Technology SR7 .....19 A1
Seaham St
New Silksworth SR3 .....18 A7
Seaham SR7 .....29 E5
Stockton-on-T TS20 .....213 B4
Seaham Sta SR7 .....29 C8
Sealand Cl TS17 .....138 D3
Seamer Cl TS5 .....139 E7
Seamer Gr TS18 .....212 A1
Seamer Rd Hilton TS15 ....157 F3
Thornton TS8 .....158 C6
Seaside La SR8 .....39 D4
Seaside La S SR8 .....39 E4
Seathwaite TS5 .....139 B3
Seaton Ave DH5 .....27 A7
Seaton Carew Rd TS2 ....104 B4
Seaton Carew Sta TS25 ...90 D8
Seaton Cl Redcar TS10 ..107 F3
Stockton-on-T TS19 .....117 A3
Seaton Cres SR7 .....18 E1
Seaton Gr SR7 .....28 D8
Seaton Holme Discovery Ctr* SR8 .....39 A4
Seaton La Hartlepool TS25 .90 C8
Seaham SR7 .....18 E1
Seaton Pk SR7 .....28 F8
Seaton St TS1 .....215 A2
Seaton Terr TS12 .....145 E4
Seatonport Ct 6 TS18 ..213 C4
Secker Pl DL5 .....96 F7
Second Ave
Chester le Street DH2 .....16 B2
Chester le Street,South Pelaw DH2 .....16 B8
Second St
Blackhall Colliery TS27 .....50 D3
Consett DH8 .....11 B2
Leadgate DH8 .....11 C5
Leadgate DH8 .....11 C6
Peterlee SR8 .....50 A7
Quaking Houses DH9 .....13 D2
Sedgebrook Gdns TS3 ..141 A8
Sedgefield Com Coll TS21 .....85 B7
Sedgefield Com Hospl TS21 .....85 B8
Sedgefield Enterprise Ctr DL16 .....56 D2
Sedgefield Hardwick Prim Sch TS21 .....85 B7
Sedgefield Prim Sch TS21 .....85 B6
Sedgefield Racecourse* TS21 .....84 E5
Sedgefield Rd TS5 .....139 C4
Sedgefield Terr TS21 .....72 B5
Sedgefield Way TS18 ....118 E5
Sedgeletch Rd 5 DH4 .....26 A8
Sedgemoor Rd TS6 .....141 E8
Sedgemoor Way TS23 ...103 A7
Sedgewick Cl TS24 .....64 A3
Sedgwick St 3 DL3 .....132 E4
Seeingsike Rd DL13 .....179 F3
Sefton Rd TS3 .....121 A2
Sefton Way TS15 .....156 A4
Selaby Cl DL2 .....201 C4
Selaby La DL2 .....201 B5
Selborne Gdns DH8 .....10 E6
Selbourne St TS1 .....214 B2
Selbourne Terr DL3 .....132 F3
Selby Cl DL14 .....79 D2
Selby Cres DL3 .....132 A5
Selby Gdns DH8 .....10 C1
Selby Gr TS25 .....77 B1
Selby Rd TS7 .....141 B3
Selby's Grave NE21 .....1 F8
Selkirk Cl TS4 .....139 F7
Selkirk Cres DH3 .....9 C6
Selset Ave TS3 .....140 E7
Selset Cl Darlington DL1 ..152 C7
Hartlepool TS26 .....76 C6
Selwood Cl TS17 .....138 D4
Selworthy Gn TS17 .....157 B6
Selwyn Dr TS19 .....117 A6
Semmerwater Gr TS10 ..107 C5
Senhouse Rd DL1 .....152 F8
Sennings La DL12 .....193 D1
Sennybridge Gr TS17 .....156 F7
Serpentine Gdns TS26 ...76 E7
Serpentine Rd
Hartlepool TS26 .....76 E6
Hartlepool TS26 .....76 E7
Seton Com Prim Sch TS13 .....129 C1
Seton Wlk DL5 .....96 E5
Setting Stones NE38 .....17 A8
Seven Hills Ct DL16 .....56 B2
Sevenacres DH3 .....25 B7
Seventh Ave DH2 .....16 B4
Seventh St
Blackhall Colliery TS27 .....50 D4
Peterlee SR8 .....50 A6
Peterlee SR8 .....50 A7
Severn Cl SR8 .....49 C4
Severn Cres DH9 .....13 E5
Severn Dr TS14 .....143 C3
Severn Gr
Billingham TS22 .....102 A6
Skelton TS12 .....125 D3
Severn Rd TS10 .....107 A6
Severn St TS1 .....215 B2
Severn Way DL1 .....152 A6
Severs Dr TS8 .....139 C1
Sexhow La TS15 .....173 F1
Seymour Ave TS16 .....156 A7
Seymour Cl TS11 .....124 F8
Seymour Cres TS16 .....156 A8
Seymour Dr TS16 .....156 A8
Seymour Gr TS16 .....156 B8
Seymour Hill Terr TS13 ..127 C1
Seymour St
Bishop Auckland DL14 .....80 B6
Consett DH8 .....11 A2
Peterlee SR8 .....50 B6
Seymour Terr DH5 .....27 B1
Shackleton Cl TS17 .....138 D4
Shadforth Cl SR8 .....49 A4
Shadforth Dr TS23 .....102 F7
Shadon Way DH3 .....9 E3
Shadwell Cl TS6 .....141 C7
Shaftesbury Ave
Blackhall Colliery TS27 .....50 D4
Ryhope SR2 .....18 E7
Shaftesbury Cres TS27 ...50 C4
Shaftesbury Rd
Blackhall Colliery TS27 .....50 C5
Eston TS6 .....121 D3
Shaftesbury St TS18 .....213 A2
Shafto Cl 4 DH8 .....177 D4
Shafto St
Byers Green DL16 .....54 E1
Shafto St *continued*
Spennymoor DL16 .....68 F7
Shafto Terr Craghead DH9 .14 D2
Stanley DH9 .....13 F8
Shafto Way DL5 .....96 E6
Shaftsbury Dr DH7 .....43 A2
Shakespeare Ave
Blackhall Colliery TS27 .....50 C5
Eston TS6 .....121 F4
Hartlepool TS25 .....77 A3
Shakespeare Cl DH9 .....14 B7
Shakespeare Rd DL1 .....152 A7
Shakespeare St
Houghton-le-S DH5 .....26 E7
9 Seaham SR7 .....29 D7
Thornley (nr Wheatley Hill) DH6 .....47 F2
Shakespeare Terr
Chester le Street DH2 .....15 E3
Easington SR8 .....39 C4
Shalcombe Cl SR3 .....18 A6
Shaldon Cl TS10 .....107 F2
Shallow Ford DL13 .....186 A8
Shandon Pk TS8 .....140 E1
Shannon Cres TS19 .....117 A4
Shannon Ct TS25 .....89 E4
Shannon Lea DL2 .....154 A8
Shannon Way DL1 .....151 F6
Sharon Ave DH6 .....58 D5
Sharp Cres Durham DH1 ...35 A3
Hartlepool TS24 .....64 A2
Sharp Rd DL5 .....96 D6
Sharpley Dr SR7 .....28 E8
Sharrock Cl TS3 .....215 C2
Shaw Cres Eston TS6 .....121 F4
Middleton-In-T DL12 .....208 B6
Shaw Gr TS25 .....76 D2
Shaw La
Barningham DL11 .....205 A5
Ebchester DH8,NE17 .....3 F4
Shaw St Seaham SR7 .....29 D7
Spennymoor DL16 .....68 F8
Shaw Wood Cl DH1 .....210 A4
Shawbrow View
Bishop Auckland DL14 .....80 B4
Darlington DL3 .....131 F2
Shawcross Ave TS6 .....121 D5
Shearwater Ave DL1 .....133 D2
Shearwater La TS20 .....102 A2
Sheelin Ave DH2 .....16 C1
Sheen Cl DH4 .....26 A2
Sheep Hill NE16 .....6 B6
Sheepdene TS22 .....87 A3
Sheepfoote Hill TS15 .....156 B4
Sheerness Gr TS24 .....77 C5
Sheerness Way TS10 .....107 E2
Shellbark DH4 .....17 F6
Shelley Ave DH5 .....37 D8
Shelley Cl
Billingham TS23 .....102 D8
Crook DL15 .....52 C2
Stanley DH9 .....14 A6
Shelley Cres TS6 .....121 C3
Shelley Ct DH2 .....15 E3
Shelley Gdns DH2 .....15 E3
Shelley Gr TS25 .....76 F3
Shelley Rd
Darlington DL1 .....133 C3
Middlesbrough TS4 .....139 F8
Shelley Sq SR8 .....39 C3
Shelley St SR7 .....29 D7
Shelley Terr DL17 .....82 F7
Shelton Ct TS3 .....121 A1
Shepherd Cl TS17 .....138 B6
Shepherd Ct TS12 .....145 C6
Shepherdson Ct 8 TS6 ..121 A6
Shepherdson Way TS3 ..215 C3
Sheppards Croft DL5 .....95 F4
Sheppey Ct SR3 .....18 A6
Shepton Cl TS17 .....138 E6
Sheraton Bank TS27 .....61 F3
Sheraton Cl DL5 .....96 E6
Sheraton Hall Est TS27 ...61 F3
Sheraton Pk TS19 .....117 E6
Sheraton Rd DL5 .....96 E6
Sheraton St
Darlington DL3 .....132 F5
Stockton-on-T TS18 .....212 C2
Sherborne DH3 .....25 B8
Sherborne Cl DL3 .....131 F4
Sherborne Ho DL3 .....131 F4
Sherburn Ave TS23 .....102 F7
Sherburn Cl TS5 .....139 C4
Sherburn Gn NE39 .....1 F3
Sherburn Hill Prim Sch DH6 .....36 D1
Sherburn Park Dr NE39 ....1 F3
Sherburn Rd Durham DH1 .35 A2
Durham DH1 .....211 C3
Sherburn Road Flats DH1 .....211 C3
Sherburn Sta DH6 .....35 E1
Sherburn Terr
Consett DH8 .....11 A2
Hamsterley NE17 .....3 F5
Sherburn Village Prim Sch DH6 .....36 A2
Sherburn Villas 19 DH8 ...10 F3
Sheridan Dr Crook DL15 ...52 C2
Stanley DH9 .....14 B6
Sheridan Gr TS25 .....76 F3
Sheriff St TS26 .....77 A6
Sheriff's Moor Ave DH5 ..37 C8
Sheringham Cl SR3 .....18 A4
Sheringham Ct TS10 .....107 F2
Sheriton Ho TS20 .....102 B1
Sherwood Cl
Barnard Castle DL12 .....209 D6
Sherwood Cl *continued*
Consett DH8 .....10 E7
Ormesby TS7 .....141 B5
Sherwood Ct
5 Silksworth SR3 .....18 A6
Toronto DL14 .....66 F2
Sherwood Dr TS11 .....124 C8
Sherwood Rd TS17 .....138 C4
Shetland Cl TS5 .....139 D3
Shetland Ct 1 SR3 .....18 A6
Shetland Dr DL1 .....133 D7
Shevington Gr TS7 .....140 E3
Shibden Rd TS3 .....120 C3
Shield Row Gdns DH9 ....13 F8
Shield Row Prim Sch DH9 .....14 A8
Shield Wlk DL5 .....96 E7
Shieldrow La
Annfield Plain DH9 .....13 A3
Annfield Plain, New Kyo DH9 .....13 B4
Shields Rd DH3 .....16 D5
Shields Terr TS24 .....64 C2
Shildon Bsns Ctr DL4 .....95 A8
Shildon Cl TS23 .....102 D6
Shildon Ct 4 DL4 .....95 A8
Shildon Prim Sch DL4 ....80 E2
Shildon Rd
Blanchland DH8 .....175 A5
Redworth DL5 .....95 B4
Shildon St DL1 .....133 A5
Shildon Sta DL4 .....95 B8
Shillmoor Cl DH2 .....15 F1
Shincliffe CE Prim Sch DH1 .....45 B5
Shincliffe La Cassop DH1 ..45 C7
High Shincliffe DH1 .....45 C7
Sherburn DH1 .....45 D7
Shincliffe Rd TS23 .....102 F7
Shinwell Cres
South Bank TS6 .....121 A5
Thornley (nr Wheatley Hill) DH6 .....47 C4
Shinwell Terr Murton SR7 ..28 B3
Wheatley Hill DH6 .....47 E2
Ship Inn Yd TS18 .....213 A2
Shipham Cl TS10 .....107 E2
Shipley Gr DL14 .....79 F5
Shipley Terr
Cotherstone DL12 .....198 F6
Crook DL15 .....53 A3
Shire Chase DH1 .....34 D8
Shirley Ave TS5 .....119 B1
Shirley Cl DL14 .....92 D7
Shirley Terr DL14 .....92 C7
Shoreham Cl TS10 .....107 F2
Shoreswood Dr 3 SR3 ...18 B7
Shoreswood Wlk TS5 .....139 D4
Short Cl TS18 .....137 F7
Short Gr SR7 .....28 A3
Short St DL14 .....80 B5
Shotley Bridge Hospl DH8 .....10 E6
Shotley Bridge Inf Sch DH8 .....10 D6
Shotley Bridge Jun Sch DH8 .....10 C7
Shotley Cl TS23 .....102 D6
Shotley Grove Rd DH8 ....10 B5
Shotton Bank SR8 .....48 F3
Shotton Colliery Ind Est DH6 .....48 D7
Shotton Ct TS23 .....102 F5
Shotton Hall Inf Sch SR8 .49 B4
Shotton Hall Jun Sch SR8 .....49 B4
Shotton Hall Sch SR8 .....49 B4
Shotton La DH6,SR8 .....48 E5
Shotton Prim Sch DH6 ...48 C7
Shotton Rd Peterlee SR8 ...49 A7
Shotton Colliery DH6,SR8 ...48 E7
Shrewsbury Cl SR8 .....49 B5
Shrewsbury Rd TS3 .....121 A1
Shrewsbury St
Hartlepool TS25 .....77 A3
Seaham SR7 .....29 D5
Shrigley Cl NE38 .....17 B8
Shropshire Dr DH1 .....35 C2
Shropshire Wlk 15 TS25 ..77 B4
Shull Bank DL13 .....189 B3
Shummard Cl DH4 .....17 F5
Sid Chaplin Dr DL5 .....96 C8
Sidcup Ave TS3 .....140 E7
Siddington Wlk TS3 .....120 D1
Sidegate DH1 .....210 C3
Sideling Tails TS15 .....156 C4
Sidings The DH1 .....211 B3
Sidlaw Ave
Chester le Street DH2 .....16 A2
2 Skelton TS12 .....125 C3
Sidlaw Rd TS23 .....102 C5
Sidmouth Cl
Middlesbrough TS8 .....140 B5
Seaham SR7 .....28 F6
Sidney Cl DH9 .....14 B6
Sidney Terr DH9 .....13 D8
Siemans St DL17 .....69 E6
Sildale Cl DL3 .....132 E4
Silent Bank DH6 .....46 E4
Silkin Way DL5 .....96 C7
Silkstun Ct 8 SR3 .....18 A7
Silksworth Rd SR3 .....18 A7
Silksworth Terr SR3 .....18 A7
Silkworth La 1 SR3 .....18 A8
Sills The DL12 .....209 B5
Silton Cl TS10 .....106 F4
Silton Gr TS18 .....212 A1
Silver Cts DH7 .....43 B4

Silver Pl DL1 .....133 B1
Silver St
Bishop Auckland DL14 .....67 C1
Consett DH8 .....10 D4
Durham DH1 .....210 C2
Hartlepool TS24 .....77 B5
Middlesbrough TS2 .....119 E7
4 Spennymoor DL16 .....68 F8
Stockton-on-T TS18 .....213 B3
Wolsingham DL13 .....207 D5
Yarm TS15 .....156 B6
Silverdale Nunthorpe TS7 .140 F2
Silksworth SR3 .....18 A4
Silverdale Dr NE21 .....2 A8
Silverdale Pl DL5 .....96 A7
Silverdale Way NE16 .....2 F4
Silverton Rd TS14 .....143 F2
Silverwood Cl TS27 .....63 C4
Silverwood Ct 11 TS17 ..138 C8
Simcox Ct TS2 .....214 A4
Simonburn NE38 .....9 F4
Simonside Gr TS17 .....157 B7
Simonside Wlk TS3 .....141 A8
Simpasture Ct DL5 .....96 C5
Simpasture Gate DL5 .....96 D5
Simpson Ave DL14 .....79 E3
Simpson Cl TS6 .....121 B5
Simpson Gn TS6 .....121 A5
Simpson Rd DL14 .....93 B8
Simpson St
Middlesbrough TS5 .....119 E2
Stanley DH9 .....13 F7
Sinclair Dr DH3 .....16 D8
Sinclair Rd TS25 .....76 D2
Sinderby Cl TS23 .....102 E6
Sinnington Cl TS14 .....143 E3
Sinnington Rd TS17 .....138 C4
Sir Douglas Pk TS17 .....138 C5
Sir E D Walker Homes
DL3 .....151 D8
Sir Hugh Bell Ct TS10 ...106 E7
Sir William Turner's Homes
TS10 .....123 A8
Siskin Cl Hartlepool TS26 ..76 D8
Stockton-on-T TS20 .....102 A2
Sitwell Wlk TS25 .....76 E2
Sixth Ave DH2 .....16 B3
Sixth St
Blackhall Colliery TS27 .....50 D4
Consett DH8 .....11 B2
Peterlee SR8 .....50 A7
Skeeby Cl TS18 .....137 B8
Skeeby Rd DL1 .....152 B8
Skel ton Ct TS14 .....143 E6
Skeldale Gr DL3 .....132 E4
Skelton Dr
Marske-by-t-S TS11 .....108 E1
Redcar TS10 .....107 E4
Skelton Ellers TS14 .....144 A7
Skelton Ind Est TS12 .....125 E3
Skelton Prim Sch TS12 .....125 D3
Skelton Rd Brotton TS12 ..126 A3
Thornaby-on-T TS17 .....138 D7
Skelton St TS24 .....63 F3
Skelwith Rd TS3 .....120 C1
Skerne Ave TS29 .....59 C1
Skerne Cl SR8 .....49 C4
Skerne Gr DH8 .....11 D5
Skerne Park Prim Sch
DL1 .....152 A7
Skerne Rd Hartlepool TS24 .64 A2
Newton Aycliffe DL5 .....96 E4
Stockton-on-T TS20 .....118 B7
Skerries Cres TS10 .....107 B2
Skerries Wlk DL1 .....133 D7
Skiddaw Cl
Eaglescliffe TS16 .....137 B2
Peterlee SR8 .....49 E6
Skiddaw Ct
Annfield Plain DH9 .....12 F3
Nunthorpe TS7 .....140 F2
Skinner St TS18 .....213 A2
Skinnergate DL3 .....132 F1
Skinningrove Bank Rd
TS13 .....127 B4
Skinningrove Rd TS13 ..127 A2
Skiplam Cl TS8 .....139 C2
Skipper's La Eston TS6 ...121 B2
South Bank TS6 .....121 A4
Skipper's La Ind Est
TS6 .....121 A4
Skipper's Lane Ind Est
TS6 .....120 F5
Skippers Mdw DH7 .....33 B1
Skipsea View SR2 .....18 D7
Skipton Cl Ferryhill DL17 ..70 B5
1 Newton Aycliffe DL5 .....96 B7
Skipton Gr DL14 .....80 A6
Skipton Moor Cl DL1 .....152 D7
Skipton Rd TS23 .....102 E5
Skirbeck Ave TS3 .....141 A8
Skirlaw Cl DL17 .....83 A8
Skirlaw Rd
Newton Aycliffe DL5 .....96 E6
Yarm TS15 .....156 B4
Skomer Ct TS10 .....107 E2
Skottowe Cres TS9 .....160 F3
Skottowe Dr TS9 .....160 F3
Skripka Dr TS22 .....102 A5
Skye Ct 2 SR3 .....18 A6
Skye Wlk Darlington DL1 .133 D7
Guisborough TS14 .....143 C2
Skylark Cl TS26 .....63 E1
Slack The DL13 .....195 D4
Slaidburn Rd DH9 .....13 F7
Slake Terr Hartlepool TS24 .77 D6
Hartlepool, Middleton TS24 .77 D7
Slaley Cl TS11 .....123 F6
Slaley Ct 4 SR3 .....18 A6
Slater Pl DH6 .....57 D8
Slater Rd TS6 .....121 F4
Slater St 1 TS26 .....77 A6
Slater Wlk TS6 .....121 F4
Slayde The TS15 .....156 C4
Sledmere Cl
Billingham TS23 .....102 F8
Peterlee SR8 .....49 D8
Sledmere Dr TS5 .....139 E7
Sledwich Cotts DL12 .....200 B2
Sledwick Rd TS23 .....102 F5
Sleightholme Moor Rd
DL11,DL12 .....202 E3
Sleights Cres TS6 .....121 F3
Sleights Ct TS14 .....143 E5
Slingley Cl SR7 .....28 E8
Slingsby Cl TS5 .....139 E6
Slip Inn Bank DL11 .....205 E2
Sloshes La DL14 .....78 C7
Smailes La NE39 .....1 C2
Smailes St DH9 .....13 E5
Smallhope Dr DH7 .....20 F3
Smeathorns Rd TS12 .....164 E7
Smillie Cl SR8 .....49 D7
Smillie Rd SR8 .....39 E1
Smirks Yd 7 TS20 .....118 B8
Smith Cl DH6 .....35 F1
Smith Gr SR2 .....18 E6
Smith St
Middlesbrough TS1 .....214 C3
Ryhope SR2 .....18 F6
Stockton-on-T TS18 .....213 A3
Tow Law DL13 .....183 E2
Smith St S SR2 .....18 F6
Smith Wlk DL5 .....96 E7
Smith's Dock Park Rd
TS6 .....121 C1
Smith's Dock Rd TS6 ...121 A7
Smith's Terr DH5 .....27 B1
Smithfield DH1 .....34 B8
Smithfield Rd DL1 .....152 B8
Smithy Gn DL11 .....205 C4
Smithy La NE11 .....8 E8
Smyth Pl TS24 .....64 A3
Smythsons Cl DL5 .....95 F4
Snackgate La DL5 .....95 D1
Snaith Terr TS28 .....60 D8
Sneck Gate La TS8 .....159 B4
Snipe La Darlington DL2 ..152 B6
Darlington, Blackwell DL2 ..151 E6
Hurworth-on-T DL2 .....152 A4
Loftus TS13 .....148 A4
Snipe St TS10 .....106 E7
Sniperley Gr DH1 .....33 F5
Snipes Dene NE39 .....1 E3
Snotterton La DL2 .....200 D7
Snow Hall DL2 .....201 E3
Snow's Green Rd DH8 .....10 C7
Snowball Cl DL15 .....52 D3
Snowberry Cl TS20 .....118 A7
Snowden St TS6 .....121 D2
Snowden Terr DL15 .....54 A2
Snowdon Cres TS10 .....107 B4
Snowdon Ct DH9 .....12 E3
Snowdon Gr
Hartlepool TS24 .....63 D4
Ingleby Barwick TS17 .....156 F8
Snowdon Pl SR8 .....49 A5
Snowdon Rd TS2 .....119 E7
Snowdrop Ave SR8 .....49 F7
Snowdrop Cl TS19 .....117 C5
Snowdrop Way DL14 .....79 F6
Sober Hall Ave TS17 .....157 A6
Sockburn La DL2 .....169 E7
Soho St DL4 .....95 A8
Somerby Terr TS3 .....120 D2
Somersby Cl TS24 .....64 C2
Somerset Cotts 4 SR3 ...18 A8
Somerset Cres TS12 .....125 A2
Somerset Gr DL1 .....133 C4
Somerset Rd
2 Consett DH8 .....177 A4
Eston TS6 .....121 E4
Guisborough TS14 .....143 D3
Stockton-on-T TS20 .....118 A7
Somerset St
Middlesbrough TS1 .....215 B3
New Silksworth SR3 .....18 A8
Somerset Terr TS23 .....102 F3
Somerville Ave 7 TS3 ...140 F8
Somerville Ct 1 DL1 .....133 B6
Sophia SR7 .....29 D7
Sophia St SR7 .....29 D7
Soppett St TS10 .....107 C6
Sopwith Cl TS18 .....137 F7
Sorbonne Cl TS17 .....213 B2
Sorrel Cl TS19 .....117 B5
Sorrel Ct TS7 .....140 C5
Sorrel Wynd DL5 .....82 D2
Sorrell Gr TS14 .....143 B3
Sotherby Rd
Middlesbrough TS3 .....120 E4
South Bank TS6 .....121 A5
South Acre DL15 .....54 A6
South App DH2 .....16 C2
South Arden St 21 DL1 ..132 F1
South Ave
Billingham TS23 .....118 D8
Redcar TS10 .....106 E4
Shadforth DH6 .....46 E7
Stillington TS21 .....99 E3
South Bailey DH1 .....210 C1
South Bank Bsns Ctr
TS6 .....121 A6
South Bank Rd TS3 .....120 E5
South Bank Sta TS6 .....121 A7
South Burns DH3 .....16 C4
South Church Ent Pk
DL14 .....80 C4
South Church Rd DL14 ...80 C7
South Cl DH5 .....37 D8
South Cleatlam DL2 .....200 E5
South Cotts DL5 .....96 A4
South Cres Durham DH1 .210 B4
Great Lumley DH4 .....17 F1
Hartlepool TS24 .....64 G8
Peterlee SR8 .....39 E1
Seaham SR7 .....29 E7
Washington NE38 .....17 B8
South Cross St DH8 .....11 C4
South Ct
12 South Bank TS6 .....121 A6
Spennymoor DL16 .....68 D5
South Downs DL17 .....82 F8
South Dr Hartlepool TS26 ..76 F6
Marton TS7 .....140 D4
Ormesby TS7 .....141 A7
South End DH6 .....36 C5
South End Villas DL15 .....52 E3
South Farm SR2 .....19 A6
South Fields DH9 .....13 E4
South Gn Hett DH6 .....56 E5
Staindrop DL2 .....200 E7
Stockton-on-T TS18 .....213 A1
South Gr DL5 .....96 F1
South Grange Pk SR7 .....18 F2
South Hetton Ind Est
DH6 .....37 F7
South Hetton Prim Sch
DH6 .....37 F7
South Hetton Rd DH5,
DH6 .....37 D8
South Lackenby TS6 .....122 A3
South Lea DH7 .....23 B1
South Leigh DH9 .....6 D1
South Lotus TS13 .....147 C8
South Magdalene DH8 .....4 B1
South Market St DH5 .....27 B4
South Mdws DH9 .....12 D8
South Moor Hospl
Stanley DH9 .....13 F4
The Middles DH9 .....14 A4
South Moor Rd DH9 .....13 E3
South Mount Pleasant St 10
TS20 .....118 B6
South Par Hartlepool TS25 .77 B3
Thornley (nr Wheatley Hill)
DH6 .....47 D4
South Park Ave TS6 .....141 D8
South Pelaw Inf Sch DH2 .16 B5
South Railway St SR7 .....29 D7
South Rd Durham DH1 .....44 C6
Hartlepool TS24 .....77 B5
High Etherley DL14 .....78 F4
Stockton-on-T TS20 .....118 C7
South Row DL14 .....81 A4
South Sherburn NE39 .....1 E1
South Side
Butterknowle DL13 .....195 C5
Easington SR8 .....39 B3
Hutton Rudby TS15 .....173 F1
Middridge DL5 .....81 E1
Shadforth DH6 .....46 E6
South Side (Dean Rd)
DL17 .....69 F5
South St
Chester le Street DH2 .....16 B4
Consett DH8 .....11 B2
Crook DL15 .....52 E3
Darlington DL3 .....132 F4
Durham DH1 .....210 C2
East Rainton DH5 .....26 C4
Eston TS6 .....121 F1
9 Fence Houses DH4 .....26 A8
Guisborough TS14 .....143 D4
Sherburn DH6 .....36 A1
Shildon DL4 .....94 F8
Spennymoor DL16 .....68 F8
Stillington TS21 .....99 E3
West Rainton DH4 .....26 A2
Willington DL15 .....53 F3
Willington,Sunnybrow DL15 .53 F1
South Stanley Inf Sch
DH9 .....13 E5
South Stanley Jun Sch
DH9 .....13 E5
South Tees Bsns Ctr
TS6 .....121 B7
South Terr
Bishop Auckland DL14 .....80 C8
Chopwell NE17 .....4 B8
Crook DL15 .....53 A4
Darlington DL1 .....132 F1
Durham DH1 .....34 A5
Eggleston DL12 .....193 D3
Esh Winning DH7 .....31 F1
Esh Winning, Cornsay Colliery
DH7 .....31 A2
Peterlee SR8 .....50 A7
Redcar TS10 .....107 E6
Seaham SR7 .....29 E7
Shildon DL4 .....94 C8
2 Skelton TS12 .....125 A2
Skelton TS12 .....125 B2
South Bank TS6 .....121 A6
Spennymoor DL16 .....56 A1
7 Staindrop DL2 .....200 E7
South Thorn DH9 .....13 F8
South Town La TS13 .....147 E6
South View
Annfield Plain DH9 .....13 A3
Beamish DH2 .....15 A7
Billingham TS23 .....102 D1
Birtley DH3 .....9 D4
Bishop Auckland DL14 .....80 C7
South View continued
Bishop Auckland, St Helen
Auckland DL14 .....79 D2
Bishop Middleham DL17 .....71 C4
Brandon DH7 .....43 C3
Burnhope DH7 .....21 D5
Castle Eden TS27 .....49 B1
Chilton DL17 .....82 F7
Chopwell NE17 .....4 A8
Consett DH8 .....177 C4
Consett, Bridgehill DH8 .....10 C4
Coundon DL14 .....81 B7
Durham DH1 .....211 C3
Eaglescliffe TS16 .....156 B8
Easington Lane DH5 .....37 D8
Evenwood DL14 .....92 C6
1 Ferryhill DL17 .....70 A6
Fishburn TS21 .....72 C5
Gainford DL2 .....201 D4
Hart TS27 .....62 F2
Heighington DL5 .....95 D1
Hett DH6 .....56 E6
Hunwick DL15 .....66 D5
Hutton Rudby TS15 .....173 F1
Kimblesworth DH2 .....23 F3
Kirk Merrington DL16 .....69 A3
Langley Park DH7 .....32 C6
Murton SR7 .....28 D2
Newfield DL14 .....67 A7
Pelton DH2 .....15 E7
Pelton,Newfield DH2 .....15 C5
Sacriston DH7 .....23 B4
Seaham SR7 .....28 F5
Sherburn Hill DH6 .....36 D1
Shildon DL4 .....81 A2
Spennymoor DL16 .....68 D6
Tantobie DH9 .....6 B2
The Middles DH9 .....14 B3
Trimdon TS29 .....59 E3
Wearhead DL13 .....179 B2
Wheatley Hill DH6 .....47 E1
South View E NE39 .....1 C2
South View Gdns DH9 .....13 A3
South View Terr
Bearpark DH7 .....33 B3
Fence Houses DH4 .....26 B8
Middlesbrough TS3 .....120 C4
South View W NE39 .....1 C2
South Way TS20 .....118 C7
South West Ind Est SR8 ..48 F6
Southampton St
Darlington DL1 .....133 A4
Redcar TS10 .....107 D6
Southbrooke Ave TS25 .....76 F2
Southburn Cl DH4 .....26 C8
Southburn Gr DL15 .....65 D7
Southburn Terr TS25 .....77 B4
Southdean Cl TS8 .....139 E2
Southdean Dr TS8 .....139 F3
Southdowns DH2 .....16 C2
Southend Ave DL1 .....151 E8
Southend Pl DL3 .....132 F1
Southfield DH2 .....15 E7
Southfield Cl DL2 .....152 D1
Southfield Cres TS20 .....118 C6
Southfield Dr DL14 .....78 E5
Southfield La
Middlesbrough TS1 .....214 C2
Middlesbrough TS1 .....215 A2
Southfield Rd
Marske-by-t-S TS11 .....108 D1
Middlesbrough TS1 .....215 A2
Stockton-on-T TS20 .....118 B6
Southfield Terr TS9 .....161 A3
Southfield Way DH1 .....34 A4
Southgate Eston TS6 .....122 A2
Hartlepool TS24 .....77 F8
Southgate St 7 DL14 .....80 C7
Southland Ave TS26 .....76 F5
Southland Cvn Site
TS21 .....137 A8
Southlands DH6 .....57 E7
Southlands Cvn Site*
TS21 .....137 A8
Southlands Dr TS7 .....141 B4
Southlands Gdns DL4 .....80 F2
Southmead Ave TS3 .....140 E7
Southport Cl TS18 .....118 D4
Southwark Cl TS6 .....141 C7
Southway Lanchester DH7 .20 E4
Peterlee SR8 .....49 C5
Southwell Gn DL1 .....133 E4
Southwell Rd TS5 .....119 F2
Southwell Sq TS5 .....119 F1
Southwick Ave TS4 .....140 B5
Southwood TS8 .....159 B7
Southwood Cres NE39 .....1 F2
Sowerby St DH7 .....23 B2
Sowerby Way TS16 .....137 B3
Spa Dr DH8 .....10 C7
Spa Rd DL2 .....201 C3
Spa Well Cl NE21 .....2 B8
Spa Well Turn NE21 .....2 E7
Spain Hill TS11 .....108 D1
Spalding Rd TS25 .....89 E6
Spalding Wlk TS20 .....118 C7
Spark Sq TS19 .....117 D5
Sparrow Hall Dr DL1 .....133 D7
Sparrow La TS14 .....143 F2
Spaunton Cl TS8 .....139 C2
Spawood Cotts TS14 .....144 C4
Spearman Wlk TS27 .....63 D3
Speeding Dr TS24 .....63 E4
Speedwell Cl DL1 .....133 C1
Speeton Ave TS5 .....139 E6
Speeton Cl TS23 .....102 E8
Spell Cl TS15 .....156 F5
Spellman Gr TS10 .....106 E3
Spen Burn NE39 .....1 A4
Spen La NE39 .....1 B3
Spen St DH9 .....13 E5
Spenborough Rd TS19 .....117 D5
Spence Ct TS9 .....161 A3
Spencely St DL4 .....80 F2
Spencer Cl
Marske-by-t-S TS11 .....108 C2
Stanley DH9 .....14 B6
Spencer Gr DL1 .....152 C7
Spencer Rd TS6 .....121 D3
Spencer St Consett DH8 ...10 F3
Eldon Lane DL14 .....80 F4
Spencerbeck Farm TS7 .141 B8
Spencerbeck Farm Cotts
TS7 .....141 B8
Spencerfield Cres TS3 ..121 A3
Spennithorne Rd TS18 ..212 B3
Spennymoor Comp Sch
DL16 .....68 E7
Spenser Gr TS25 .....76 F3
Spilsby Cl TS25 .....89 E6
Spinnaker Ho TS24 .....77 D6
Spinney The
Darlington DL3 .....151 D6
Easington SR8 .....39 A4
Hartlepool TS26 .....76 C5
Middleton St George DL2 ..154 B8
Newton Aycliffe DL5 .....82 D2
Spennymoor DL16 .....56 C1
Stockton-on-T TS18 .....137 D8
Spire Hollin SR8 .....49 C6
Spital Gate TS15 .....156 C4
Spital The TS15 .....156 C5
Spitalfields TS15 .....156 C5
Spitfire Cl 3 TS11 .....108 B1
Spooner Cl DL5 .....82 B1
Spout Bank DL12 .....198 E7
Spout La DL4 .....81 C1
Spring Bank Wood TS22 ..87 B3
Spring Cl
Annfield Plain DH9 .....13 A3
Ebchester DH8 .....3 E2
Thornaby-on-T TS17 .....138 C8
Spring Ct DL3 .....132 C5
Spring Garden Cl TS7 ...141 B5
Spring Garden La TS7 ...141 B5
Spring Garden Rd TS25 ..77 B3
Spring Gdns DL14 .....79 A2
Spring Head Terr TS13 ..127 C1
Spring Hill DL3 .....132 F6
Spring La TS21 .....85 A3
Spring Rd DL5 .....96 C2
Spring Rise TS6 .....141 C7
Spring St
Middlesbrough TS2 .....215 A4
Stockton-on-T TS18 .....212 C1
Spring Way TS18 .....137 E8
Spring Wood Rd TS14 ...143 E4
Springbank Rd
Newfield DL14 .....67 B7
Ormesby TS7 .....141 B6
Springdale Ave TS29 .....60 B5
Springfell DH3 .....9 D3
Springfield Ave
Brotton TS12 .....126 B3
Stockton-on-T TS18 .....137 E8
Springfield Cl TS16 .....137 B1
Springfield Cres SR7 .....29 C7
Springfield Gdns DH3 .....16 C5
Springfield Gr TS15 .....156 E1
Springfield Pk DH1 .....210 A4
Springfield Prim Sch
DL1 .....133 C5
Springfield Rd
Darlington DL1 .....133 C6
Fishburn TS21 .....72 C4
Middlesbrough TS5 .....119 B2
Springfield Terr
Pelton DH2 .....15 E5
Peterlee SR8 .....39 F3
Willington DL15 .....53 E3
Springfields DL5 .....95 F4
Springhill 2 TS7 .....141 B7
Springhill Gr TS17 .....157 B7
Springholme
3 Ormesby TS7 .....141 B7
Stockton-on-T TS18 .....212 C1
Springholme Yd TS18 ...212 C1
Springhouse La DH8 .....3 E2
Springlea 6 TS7 .....141 B7
Springmead 5 TS7 .....141 B7
Springs The DH3 .....9 E3
Springside DH7 .....23 C3
Springston Rd TS26 .....76 D7
Springsyde Cl NE16 .....2 E5
Springvale Terr TS5 .....119 B1
Springwalk 4 TS7 .....141 B7
Springwell DL2 .....201 D7
Springwell Ave
Durham DH1 .....210 A4
Langley Park DH7 .....32 C6
Trimdon TS29 .....59 E1
Springwell Cl
Billingham TS23 .....102 F8
9 Langley Park DH7 .....32 C6
Springwell Flatlets TS26 .76 E8
Springwell Rd
Durham DH1 .....210 A4
Springwell NE9 .....9 F8
Springwell Sch TS26 .....76 E8
Springwell Terr
Darlington DL1 .....133 D5
Hetton-le-H DH5 .....27 A2
Spruce Ct Shildon DL4 .....95 B8

Spruce Ct *continued*
Spennymoor DL16 68 F7
Spruce Gr DL3 132 C1
Spruce Rd TS19 117 E7
Spurn Wlk 14 TS24 77 C5
Spurrey Cl TS17 138 B2
Squadron Ct TS17 138 C5
Square The
Bishop Auckland DL14 79 D2
Blanchland DH8 175 A5
5 Eston TS6 121 F2
Greta Bridge DL12 205 A8
Lanchester DH7 20 F3
Middleton St George DL2 153 F8
Sedgefield TS21 85 B6
Skinningrove TS13 127 A4
Stockton-on-T TS18 213 B3
Squires Ct DL3 132 C3
St Teresa's RC Prim Sch
TS25 89 F8
Stable Mews TS10 107 D6
Stables The TS22 87 B2
Stack Garth DH7 43 C5
Stacks La DL12 208 A6
Stadium Ct TS6 121 A4
Stafford Cl TS17 138 B8
Stafford Gr SR2 18 E6
Stafford Pl SR8 49 B7
Stafford Rd Eston TS6 121 F4
Guisborough TS14 143 D3
Stafford St
Hetton-le-H DH5 26 F4
Stockton-on-T TS18 213 A1
Staffordshire Dr DH1 35 D3
Stag La DL5 82 E1
Staincliffe Rd TS25 77 E1
Staindale TS14 143 A3
Staindale Cl TS15 156 E5
Staindale Gdns TS19 117 E5
Staindale Pl TS25 76 F2
Staindale Rd TS17 138 D6
Staindrop CE Prim Sch
DL2 200 F7
Staindrop Comp Sch
DL2 200 E7
Staindrop Cres DL3 132 C3
Staindrop Ct TS23 102 C7
Staindrop Dr TS5 139 C5
Staindrop Rd
Bishop Auckland DL14 79 B1
Cockfield DL13 195 E3
Darlington DL3 132 B3
Durham DH1 34 D6
Staindrop St TS24 77 C5
Staindrop Terr DH9 12 F4
Stainemore Terr DL14 68 C1
Stainforth Cl DL5 96 B7
Stainforth Ct TS3 140 D7
Stainforth Gdns TS17 138 C1
Stainmore Cl
Barnard Castle DL12 209 A5
Stockton-on-T TS19 212 C3
Stainmore Cres DL5 96 A7
Stainmore Dr DH3 25 B7
Stainmore Wlk 2 DL5 96 A7
Stainsby Gate TS17 138 F7
Stainsby Rd TS5 139 B8
Stainsby St TS17 138 C8
Stainton Bank DL12 199 F5
Stainton Gr
Barnard Castle DL12 199 F4
Stockton-on-T TS20 118 A6
Stainton Ind Est DL12 199 F4
Stainton Rd
Billingham TS22 102 C5
Seamer TS9 158 F1
Stainton St TS3 120 C3
Stainton View DL2 134 E6
Stainton Way
Coulby Newham TS8 140 B1
Nunthorpe TS7 140 F3
Peterlee SR8 49 C6
Stainton TS8 139 C1
Staintondale DL5 95 F8
Staintondale Ave TS10 106 F4
Stainwood Ct DL3 132 C3
Staithes Ct TS24 77 D5
Staithes Rd TS10 107 A4
Stakesby Cl TS14 143 D6
Stamford Ct TS23 102 F7
Stamford St TS1 215 B2
Stamford Wlk TS25 89 F7
Stamp St TS18 213 A3
Stampley Cl NE21 2 A8
Standerton Terr DH9 14 B3
Standish St DH9 13 D5
Stanelaw Way DH9 6 F1
Stanfield Rd DL5 96 E7
Stanford Cl TS17 213 C1
Stang La DL11,DL12 204 A5
Stang Top DL11 204 A2
Stanghow Lane Flats
TS12 125 D2
Stanghow Rd
Lingdale TS12 145 E5
Skelton TS12 125 D1
Stanhope NE38 9 F5
Stanhope Ave TS26 77 A5
Stanhope Barrington CE Sch
DL13 206 C3
Stanhope Cl Brandon DH7 43 C4
Durham DH1 34 D6
Ferryhill DL17 70 B6
Houghton-le-S DH4 26 D7
Spennymoor DL16 56 A2
Stanhope Gdns
Annfield Plain DH9 13 A4
Middlesbrough TS4 120 B1
Stanhope Gr TS5 139 D7
Stanhope Rd
Billingham TS23 102 F5
Stockton-on-T TS18 212 B4
Wolsingham DL13 207 B5
Stanhope Rd N DL3 132 E2
Stanhope Rd S DL3 132 E1
Stanhope St 1 TS12 125 C7
Stanhope Sta* DL13 206 D2
Stanhope Terr DL15 52 F4
Stank La DH2 24 A1
Stanley (Crook) Prim Sch
DL15 40 F1
Stanley Burn Ct DH9 13 B4
Stanley Burnside Prim Sch
DH9 14 B5
Stanley Cl Sherburn DH6 35 F1
3 Thornaby-on-T TS17 138 C8
Stanley Ct DH9 14 A6
Stanley Gdns DH8 11 A3
Stanley Gr
Great Ayton TS9 160 A1
Redcar TS10 107 D6
Stanley Rd TS25 77 B2
Stanley Sch of Tech DH9 13 E5
Stanley St
Close House DL14 81 A5
14 Consett DH8 10 F3
6 Darlington DL1 133 B1
Seaham SR7 29 B8
Stockton-on-T TS20 118 A8
Stanley Terr
Chester le Street DH3 16 D2
Stanley Crook DL15 40 F1
Thornley (nr Wheatley Hill)
DH6 47 C4
Stanley Way DL15 52 E7
Stanley Wlk TS18 213 A3
Stanmore Ave TS4 140 A7
Stanmore Gr TS25 90 D8
Stannage Gr TS17 138 C6
Stanner's La DL16 55 A3
Stanstead Way TS17 138 E5
Stansted Gr DL2 154 A8
Stanwix Cotts 20 DL13 195 E3
Stapleford Rd TS3 141 A8
Stapleton Bank DL2 151 A4
Stapleton St TS20 102 A2
Stapylton Ct TS6 121 D6
Stapylton St TS6 121 D6
Star Yd DL12 209 C6
Starbeck Way TS7 141 B8
Starbeck Wlk TS17 138 E3
Stargate Cl
Langley Park DH7 32 B6
Newton Aycliffe DL5 82 D1
Starmer Cres DL1 152 B7
Startforth Cl DH3 25 B7
Startforth Morrit Meml CE
Prim Sch DL12 209 A4
Startforth Pk DL12 199 B3
Startforth Rd TS2 119 D7
Statham Pl 2 DL3 133 A7
Station App Durham DH1 210 B3
3 Hartlepool TS24 77 C6
Station Ave Brandon DH7 43 C4
Esh Winning DH7 41 E8
Greatham TS25 89 E4
Hetton-le-H DH5 27 A3
Station Ave N
Fence Houses DH4 17 F1
2 Fence Houses DH4 26 A8
Station Ave S
Fence Houses DH4 17 F1
1 Fence Houses DH4 26 A8
Station Bank DH1 210 C3
Station Cl 5 TS11 124 C8
Station Cotts
Beamish DH9 14 E8
Burnopfield NE39 5 C6
Cockfield DL13 195 D3
Peterlee SR8 50 C6
Sedgefield TS22 86 E5
Station Cres
Billingham TS23 102 D3
Seaham SR7 29 B8
Station Est E SR7 28 A3
Station Est N SR7 28 A3
Station Est S SR7 28 A3
Station Field Rd DH9 6 F1
Station Hos DH2 15 E5
Station House Visitor Ctr*
TS21 100 E5
Station La Birtley DH2,DH3 9 B4
Durham DH1 211 B3
Hartlepool TS25 90 E8
Pelton DH2 15 E6
Station Town TS28 60 E6
Station Lane Ind Est DH3 9 B4
Station Par TS22 102 C3
Station Rd
Annfield Plain DH9 13 A3
Beamish DH9 14 F8
Billingham TS23 102 C3
Bishop Auckland DL14 79 C2
Blackhall Rocks TS27 50 F2
Brandon DH7 43 C3
Chester le Street DH3 16 C3
Consett DH8 11 A2
Cornforth DL17 57 D1
Coxhoe DH6 58 B2
Darlington DL3 132 F4
Eaglescliffe TS16 137 C3
Easington SR8 39 F4
Eston TS6 121 E1
Station Rd *continued*
Gainford DL2 201 D4
Great Ayton TS9 161 B2
Greatham TS25 89 F3
Heighington DL5 95 E1
Hesleden TS27 50 A1
Hetton-le-H DH5 27 A2
High Pittington DH6 36 A6
Hinderwell TS13 149 F5
Howden-le-W DL15 65 E7
Hunwick DL15 66 F5
Lanchester DH7 20 F3
Loftus TS13 127 B1
Mickleton DL12 208 F2
Middleton St George DL2 153 E8
Murton SR7 28 A3
Newton Aycliffe DL5 96 C2
Penshaw DH4 17 E8
Redcar TS10 107 C7
Rowlands Gill NE39 1 F1
Ryhope SR2 19 A6
Seaham SR7 29 A8
Sedgefield TS21 85 A6
Shotton Colliery DH6 48 C7
Skelton TS12 125 D3
Stanley DH9 13 F7
Station Town TS28 60 E6
Stockton-on-T TS20 102 A2
Ushaw Moor DH7 32 F1
West Rainton DH4 25 F1
Wingate TS29 59 F5
Witton-le-W DL14 65 B3
Station Rd N
Hetton-le-H DH5 27 A3
Murton SR7 28 A3
Station Rd S SR7 28 A3
Station Sq TS12 125 C7
Station St
Esh Winning DH7 41 C6
Haswell DH6 37 F3
Middlesbrough TS1 214 C4
3 Saltburn-by-t-S TS12 125 C7
Shildon DL4 95 A8
Stockton-on-T TS20 213 B4
Thornaby-on-T TS17 213 C1
Tow Law DL13 183 E1
Station Terr Consett DH8 11 A2
Cotherstone DL12 198 F6
Evenwood DL14 78 C1
Fence Houses DH4 17 F1
Middleton St George DL2 134 E1
Newton Aycliffe DL5 96 F1
Stanhope DL13 206 E2
Station View
Bishop Auckland DL14 79 C2
Esh Winning DH7 41 E8
Hetton-le-H DH5 27 A3
Witton Park DL14 66 B1
Station Villas DH9 13 F8
Staveley Ct TS3 120 C2
Staveley Gr TS19 117 E6
Staveley Rd SR8 49 E6
Staveley Wlk TS7 141 A7
Stavordale Rd TS19 212 C4
Stavordale St SR7 29 D6
Stavordale St W SR7 29 D5
Stead Cl DL5 96 C7
Stead Meml Hospl TS10 107 B6
Steadings The
Durham DH1 44 A7
Whorlton DL12 200 C1
Steadman's La DH7 31 A4
Steavenson St DH6 57 D8
Steel St DH8 10 F3
Steele Cres TS6 121 B6
Steelhaven 12 DH8 10 F2
Steels Hos DL15 52 C4
Steeplejack Way DL1 133 A2
Steer Ct TS23 102 D7
Steetley Terr DH6 58 C7
Stella Gill Ind Est DH2 15 F5
Stenhouse Ct DL14 80 E7
Stephen Bank DL11 205 D5
Stephen Ct DL1 133 A4
Stephen St Consett DH8 10 F3
Hartlepool TS26 76 F7
Stephen's Terr DH6 47 F3
Stephens Rd Murton SR7 28 B3
South Bank TS6 121 B6
Stephenson Cl DH5 27 B4
Stephenson Ct TS6 121 A4
Stephenson Ho TS1 214 C3
Stephenson Ind Est TS25 90 E5
Stephenson Rd SR8 39 D1
Stephenson Sq SR8 39 B3
Stephenson St
Darlington DL3 132 F4
Ferryhill DL17 69 E6
Middlesbrough TS1 215 A2
Murton SR7 28 C3
Thornaby-on-T TS17 213 C1
Stephenson Way
Blaydon NE21 2 B8
Newton Aycliffe DL5 96 C6
Stockton-on-T TS18 213 B2
Stephenson Way Prim Sch
DL5 96 B7
Stevenage Cl TS17 138 E7
Stevenson Cl TS15 156 E5
Stevenson St DH4 26 D8
Steward Dr DL15 52 D3
Stewart Ave SR2 18 E6
Stewart Dr TS28 48 E1
Stewart Rd TS20 118 B5
Stewart St
2 Darlington DL3 132 E4
Easington SR8 39 D4
New Silksworth SR3 18 A7
Stewart St *continued*
Seaham SR7 29 E6
Stewart St E SR7 29 E6
Stewart's Bldgs DL15 66 D5
Stewartsfield NE39 1 D1
Stileston Cl TS26 76 D7
Stillington Cl SR2 18 F5
Stillington Ind Est TS21 99 E4
Stirling Ave NE39 1 E1
Stirling Cl DL14 79 E6
Stirling Gr DL1 133 C7
Stirling La NE39 1 F1
Stirling Rd TS10 107 E5
Stirling St TS25 77 B3
Stirling Way TS17 138 D3
Stirrup The DL5 95 F8
Stobart St DH7 23 B7
Stobart Terr TS21 72 B5
Stobarts Ct DL14 78 E6
Stobarts La TS15 155 C1
Stobb Cross La DL17 71 B8
Stobb Cross Rd DL17 70 E8
Stobb Cross Villas DL17 70 E8
Stobb House View DH7 43 A5
Stobhill La DL2 93 D1
Stockdale Ave TS10 106 F4
Stockerley La DH7,DH8 177 F3
Stockerley Rd DH8 11 B1
Stockley Cl DL3 132 F7
Stockley Cres DL13 188 B8
Stockley Ct DH7 33 C1
Stockley Gr
Brancepeth DH7 54 E7
Frosterley DL13 188 B8
Stockley House Farm
DL15 54 C7
Stockley La DL15 53 D7
Stocks Gn DL5 96 A7
Stocksmoor Cl DL1 152 C7
Stockton & Billingham Coll
TS23 102 D5
Stockton & Billingham Coll
of F Ed TS18 212 A3
Stockton Ave SR8 49 F8
Stockton Rd
Darlington DL1 133 E5
Durham DH1 211 A1
Easington SR8 39 A2
Greatham TS22,TS23,TS25 89 C4
Hartlepool TS25 77 B2
Hartlepool TS25 77 B4
Hawthorn SR7 39 B7
Middlesbrough TS5 119 A3
Ryhope SR2,SR7 18 F2
Sadberge DL2 134 F6
Sedgefield TS21 85 C6
Thornaby-on-T TS17 118 F2
Stockton Riverside Coll
TS17 213 C2
Stockton Sixth Form Coll
TS19 212 A4
Stockton St
Billingham TS23 102 D2
Hartlepool TS24 77 B5
Middlesbrough TS2 119 E7
Seaham SR7 29 B8
Stockton Sta TS18 213 A4
Stockwell Ave TS17 138 D2
Stockwith Cl TS3 141 A8
Stoker Cres DH6 47 E1
Stoker Terr NE39 1 A3
Stokesley Cres TS23 102 D3
Stokesley Rd
Guisborough TS14 143 A3
Hartlepool TS25 90 E8
Marton TS7 140 D4
Nunthorpe TS7 141 B1
Stokoe St DH8 10 E4
Stone Cross TS21 72 D4
Stone Heap DL13 185 F8
Stone Hos DL13 206 D3
Stone Man La DL11 205 C1
Stone Row
Butterknowle DL13 195 C4
Commondale YO21 164 C2
Skinningrove TS13 127 A4
West Pelton DH2 15 A5
Stone St TS4 215 B3
Stoneacre Ave TS17 157 B8
Stonebank Terr DL14 67 B8
Stonebridge 2 DL1 133 A1
Stonebridge Cres TS17 138 A3
Stonechat Cl
Hartlepool TS26 63 F1
Ingleby Barwick TS17 138 A1
3 Washington NE38 9 F3
Stonecliffe Dr DL3 151 C8
Stonecrop Cl TS18 212 A1
Stonedale TS12 125 B4
Stonedale Cres DL3 132 D2
Stonedale Wlk TS5 139 C4
Stonegate TS6 122 A2
Stonehaven Way DL1 133 E7
Stonehouse Cl TS15 156 D4
Stonehouse St TS5 119 E2
Stonehurst Dr DL3 151 C8
Stoneleigh Ave TS5 139 B7
Stoneleigh Ct DL5 82 E1
Stones End DL14 92 C7
Stonesdale DH4 17 E8
Stonethwaite Cl TS24 64 B1
Stoneybeck DL17 71 C4
Stoneycroft Way SR7 29 C8
Stoneyhurst Ave TS5 139 A8
Stonor Wlk TS3 140 E7
Stony Bank Redworth DL2 95 A3
Willington DL15 54 B2
Stony La DH9 15 A8
Stony Path DL13 179 C1
Stonybeck La DL17 71 E4
Stonyheap La
Annfield Plain DH8,DH9 12 B4
Iveston DH8 12 B2
Stooperdale Ave DL3 132 C4
Store Cotts DH7 23 B6
Store St DH8 10 F3
Store Terr DH5 27 B1
Stornaway Cl TS19 117 A3
Stotfield Burn DL13 180 E5
Stotfold Cl SR7 28 E8
Stotfold St 1 TS26 77 B5
Stotfold Wlk TS5 139 B4
Stoupe Gr TS10 107 F3
Stourport Cl TS18 213 C4
Stowe St TS1 214 C2
Stowmarket Cl TS25 89 F6
Strait La
Hurworth-on-T DL2 152 E2
Stainton TS8 139 B1
Straker St 7 TS26 77 A6
Strand St 6 DL4 94 F8
Strand The TS10 107 F3
Strangford Ave 2 DH2 16 B1
Strangford Rd SR7 29 C7
Strangways St SR7 29 D6
Stranton TS25 77 B4
Stranton Prim Sch TS25 77 B4
Stranton St
4 Bishop Auckland DL14 80 B8
Thornaby-on-T TS17 138 C8
Stratford Cres TS5 119 B2
Stratford Gdns
1 Consett DH8 10 F4
2 Ferryhill DL17 70 A6
Stratford Rd TS25 77 B3
Strathaven Dr TS16 137 C1
Strathmore DH3 25 A8
Strathmore Ave NE39 1 E1
Strathmore Cl DH9 14 B7
Strathmore Cres NE16 6 D8
Strathmore Ct DL12 209 C6
Strathmore Dr TS15 172 D8
Strathmore Rd
Barnard Castle DL12 209 D7
Rowlands Gill NE39 1 E1
Stratton Cl SR2 19 A8
Stratton Ct DL1 151 E8
Stratton St DL16 68 F8
Stratus Ct 12 SR3 18 A6
Strauss Rd TS6 121 B6
Straw Gate DL2 151 B4
Strawberry La
Ferryhill DL17 70 A7
High Shincliffe DH1 45 A4
Strawgate Gr DL2 151 A5
Strawgate La DL2 151 A5
Stray The Darlington DL1 133 D1
Longnewton TS21 136 A5
Streatlam Cl DL12 199 F5
Streatlam Rd
Billingham TS23 103 A6
Darlington DL1 152 B8
Street The Boldron DL12 204 D8
Bowes DL12 203 D8
Greta Bridge DL12 205 A8
Strensall Cl 3 TS11 124 A6
Stretton Cl DH4 26 A7
Stringer Terr DH7 32 A6
Strome Cl TS17 157 C8
Strona Wlk TS14 143 D3
Stronsay Cl 2 SR2 18 E8
Stuart Cl TS27 50 D3
Stuart St 7 TS24 77 B7
Stubbs Cl TS23 102 D7
Studland Dr TS24 63 D4
Studland Rd TS10 107 F2
Studley Rd
Hartlepool TS25 77 B4
Middlesbrough TS5 119 C1
Stockton-on-T TS19 212 C4
Thornaby-on-T TS17 138 D6
Stump Cross TS14 143 D4
Sturt Dr TS20 117 F8
Sudburn Ave DL2 200 E7
Sudbury TS8 140 E2
Sudbury Ho 3 DL4 95 A8
Sudbury Rd TS20 118 C8
Suffield St TS2 119 E7
Suffolk Cl Hartlepool TS25 77 B3
Skelton TS12 125 B1
Suffolk Pl Birtley DH3 9 D1
Bishop Auckland DL14 80 B5
Suffolk Rd TS5 119 F1
Suffolk St Hetton-le-H DH5 26 F4
Stockton-on-T TS18 212 C2
Suffolk Way DH1 34 D8
Suffolk Wlk SR8 49 C8
Sugar Hill Prim Sch DL5 96 D6
Sugar Loaf Cl TS17 156 F8
Suggitt St TS26 76 F6
Sulby Ave TS3 120 D1
Summerdale DH8 10 D7
Summerfield DH9 15 A6
Summerfield Terr NE17 4 A5
Summerfields DH2 15 F2
Summerhill DH8 10 E7
Summerhill Ctry Pk*
TS25 76 C3
Summerhill Visitor Ctr*
TS25 76 D4
Summerhouse Back La
DL2 110 A5
Summerhouse Farm
DH5 26 D5
Summerhouse Gr DL3 132 A2
Summerhouse Sq TS20 118 A8

Summerson St DH5 27 B4
Summerville DH1 210 B2
Sun Rd DL13 194 F5
Sun St
Bishop Auckland DL14 80 C7
Darlington DL3 132 F2
Stockton-on-T TS18 212 C1
Thornaby-on-T TS17 138 B8
Sunderland Ave SR8 49 F8
Sunderland Highway NE38 9 F6
Sunderland Rd
Durham DH1 211 C3
Easington SR7,SR8 39 B5
Peterlee SR8 39 F2
Wolviston TS22 102 C8
Sunderland St
2 Houghton-le-S DH4 26 E8
Leadgate DH8 11 D4
Sundial Mews TS22 102 C8
Sunley Ave 3 TS4 120 A1
Sunnidale NE16 2 E5
Sunningdale
Consett DH8 177 D4
7 Consett DH8 177 E4
Newton Aycliffe DL5 82 E2
Sunningdale Ct 3 TS6 121 E1
Sunningdale Dr TS16 137 C1
Sunningdale Gn DL1 133 E6
Sunningdale Gr TS27 63 D3
Sunningdale Ho 4 TS6 121 E1
Sunningdale Rd
Middlesbrough TS4 139 F7
8 New Marske TS11 124 A6
Sunningdale Wlk TS16 137 C1
Sunniside TS24 77 F8
Sunny Blunts SR8 49 C4
Sunny Row TS13 149 E7
Sunny Terr Dipton DH9 12 C7
Stanley DH9 13 E7
Sunnybank Rd TS7 141 B6
Sunnybanks DH7 20 E4
Sunnybrow 7 SR3 18 A8
Sunnybrow Ave TS23 102 D2
Sunnybrow Prim Sch DL15 53 D2
Sunnycroft Cotts DL12 198 F6
Sunnydale DL4 81 A2
Sunnydale Sch DL4 81 A2
Sunnyfield
Great Ayton TS9 160 F2
Ormesby TS7 141 A7
Sunnygate TS6 122 A2
Sunnyside TS8 140 A2
Sunnyside Ave
Middlesbrough TS4 139 F8
Shildon DL4 81 A2
Sunnyside Gr TS18 137 C8
Sunnyside Prim Sch TS8 140 A2
Sunnyside Terr TS29 59 E3
Sunstar Gr TS7 140 C4
Surbiton Rd TS19 116 F3
Surgery La TS24 64 A2
Surrey Ave SR3 18 A6
Surrey Cres DH8 177 A4
Surrey Pl
Bishop Auckland DL14 80 B5
Willington DL15 54 A3
Surrey Rd TS20 118 C7
Surrey St Hetton-le-H DH5 26 F4
Middlesbrough TS1 214 B1
Surrey Terr
Billingham TS23 102 E3
Birtley DH3 9 C1
Surtees Ave DH6 45 D1
Surtees Dr DH1 210 A2
Surtees Pl DH8 10 C5
Surtees Rd Peterlee SR8 49 E6
Redworth DL5 95 C3
Surtees St
Bishop Auckland DL14 80 B8
Darlington DL3 132 F4
Hartlepool TS24 77 C5
Stockton-on-T TS18 213 A2
Surtees Terr
Craghead DH9 14 D2
Ferryhill DL17 70 C2
Surtees Wlk DL5 96 D5
Sussex Rd DH8 177 A4
Sussex St Coundon DL14 81 D8
Hartlepool TS25 77 B3
Middlesbrough TS2 214 C4
3 New Silksworth SR3 18 A8
Sussex Way DL1 133 C4
Sussex Wlk TS20 118 C6
Sutcliffe Ct DL3 133 A7
Sutherland Gr
Shotton Colliery DH6 48 C7
Stockton-on-T TS20 102 A2
Sutherland Pl DH1 35 A1
Sutherland St SR7 29 B8
Sutton Cl DL3 132 A2
Sutton Pl TS23 102 F5
Sutton St DH1 210 B3
Sutton Way TS4 139 F7
Swainby Cl TS5 139 E6
Swainby Rd
Hartlepool TS25 90 E7
Stockton-on-T TS20 118 B5
Trimdon TS29 72 E8
Swainson Pl 3 TS26 77 B6
Swainson St TS24 77 B6
Swainston Cl
Middlesbrough TS5 139 B5
Wynyard Village TS22 87 A3
Swale Ave TS17 138 D6
Swale Cl TS16 156 B7
Swale Cres DH3 25 B7
Swale Rd TS20 118 A8
Swalebrooke Ave TS25 76 E2
Swaledale Ave DL3 132 C3
Swaledale Cl
Hetton-le-H DH5 26 F1
Ingleby Barwick TS17 157 B7
Swaledale Cres TS23 102 D3
Swaledale Ho 10 TS4 139 F8
Swallow Cl
Esh Winning DH7 31 C1
Guisborough TS14 143 A4
Hartlepool TS26 63 D1
Swallow La TS20 102 A1
Swallow St SR7 29 B8
Swallowfields TS8 159 A8
Swan Rd SR8 49 A5
Swan St Annfield Plain DH9 12 E5
5 Darlington DL1 133 A1
Evenwood DL14 92 C7
Swan Wlk DL5 96 F6
Swan Wynd DL2 200 F7
Swanage Cl TS8 140 B4
Swanage Dr TS10 107 F2
Swanage Gr TS24 63 D4
Swancer Ct TS22 87 B3
Swaniby Rd TS29 59 E1
Swathmoor Ho TS9 161 A2
Swift Gr TS25 76 E2
Swilly La TS12 125 B2
Swinburn Rd TS20 118 A6
Swinburn's Yd TS15 156 B6
Swinburne Pl DH3 9 C3
Swinburne Rd
Darlington DL3 132 E1
Eaglescliffe TS16 137 C3
Hartlepool TS25 76 E2
Swinburne Terr DH9 12 B7
Swindale Cl NE21 2 C8
Swindale La
Lingdale TS12 145 F1
Moorsholm TS12 146 A1
Swingfield Cl DL15 52 D5
Swinhope NE38 17 A8
Swinside Dr DH1 35 C4
Swinton Rd TS18 137 B8
Swyfte Cl TS21 85 B6
Sycamore DH2 16 A5
Sycamore Ave
Blackhall Rocks TS27 50 E3
Saltburn-by-t-S TS12 125 A6
Thornaby-on-T TS17 138 C6
Sycamore Cl
Hurworth-on-T DL2 152 D1
South Hetton DH6 37 F7
Sycamore Cres
Eston TS6 121 C3
Wingate TS29 60 B5
Sycamore Ct DL16 69 A8
Sycamore Dr
Brotton TS12 126 A4
Hesleden TS27 49 F1
Sycamore Gdns DL15 52 D3
Sycamore Gr
Bishop Auckland DL14 79 C1
Willington DL15 54 B3
Sycamore Pk DH7 43 B5
Sycamore Rd
Cornforth DL17 57 E1
Eaglescliffe TS16 137 D4
Fishburn TS21 72 C4
Kimblesworth DH2 23 F3
Middlesbrough TS5 119 E1
Ormesby TS7 141 B6
Redcar TS10 107 E6
Stockton-on-T TS19 117 E6
Sycamore Sq
Easington SR8 39 C3
Shildon DL4 81 A1
Sycamore Terr
Annfield Plain DH9 13 B4
Haswell DH6 37 F3
Middlesbrough TS2 103 E1
Sycamore Way TS19 117 C7
Sycamore Wlk TS13 127 C2
Sycamores The
Burnopfield NE16 6 C5
Darlington DL3 132 D3
Hartlepool TS25 76 F2
Sydenham Rd
Hartlepool TS25 77 B3
Hartlepool TS25 77 C3
Stockton-on-T TS18 212 C1
Sydney Cl TS5 119 B1
Sydney Gdns 7 DH8 177 D4
Sydney Rd TS7 140 D3
Sydney St Beamish DH2 15 A7
Bournmoor DH4 17 E2
Stockton-on-T TS18 213 A3
Syke Rd NE16 5 F5
Syke View 1 DH9 12 F4
Sylvan Gr DL3 132 D1
Sylvan Wlk TS3 140 E7
Sylvia Terr DH9 13 F8
Symington Wlk 3 DL1 133 B1
Symon Terr NE17 4 B8
Symons Cl TS18 117 A2
Syon Gdns TS20 101 E1
Syron NE16 2 F7
Syston Cl DH4 26 A7

T

Tail-upon-End La DH6 45 D2
Tailrigg Cl TS19 212 C4
Talbenny Gr TS17 156 F7
Talbot Cotts DH3 9 C4
Talbot Ct DL14 80 D6
Talbot Pl SR7 29 D7
Talbot St
Middlesbrough TS1 215 B2
Stockton-on-T TS20 118 B5
Talbot Terr 12 DH3 9 C4
Talgarth Rd TS20 102 B1
Talisker Gdns TS10 107 D2
Talisman Cl
Eaglescliffe TS16 137 A2
Sherburn DH6 35 F1
Talland Cl TS27 63 C3
Talybont Gr TS17 156 F8
Tamar Cl SR8 49 C5
Tamar St DH5 37 C8
Tamarind Cl DL5 96 A3
Tamarisk Cl TS17 138 B2
Tame Rd TS3 120 C5
Tamerton Dr DH3 9 D2
Tamworth Cl DL14 79 E6
Tamworth Rd TS23 102 E6
Tanbark DH4 17 F6
Tandridge Ct DL3 132 D3
Tanfield Comp Sch DH9 13 D8
Tanfield Lea Ind Est DH9 6 D2
Tanfield Lea Ind Est N DH9 6 D1
Tanfield Lea Inf Sch DH9 6 C1
Tanfield Lea Jun Sch DH9 6 C1
Tanfield Lea South Ind Est DH9 6 F1
Tanfield Pl DL5 82 D1
Tanfield Rd TS25 77 A2
Tanfield Rly* NE16 7 B7
Tangmere DL16 55 E2
Tanhill Wlk TS3 120 D1
Tankersley Rd TS11 124 A6
Tankerville St TS26 77 A6
Tanmeads DH2 23 F4
Tanner Cl TS17 138 B1
Tanner's Bank TS16 156 B7
Tannery Yd DL1 133 A2
Tansley Ave TS3 120 E2
Tansley Gdns DL1 152 D8
Tantallon DH3 9 D2
Tantallon Ct DH4 17 D1
Tanton Cl TS9 159 A1
Tanton Gr TS22 102 A5
Tanton Rd TS9 159 C1
Tanwell Cl TS19 117 B5
Tanya Gdns
Middlesbrough TS5 139 E4
Stockton-on-T TS19 117 C3
Taransay Wlk DL1 133 D7
Tarell Ct TS17 156 F7
Tarn Cl SR8 49 E6
Tarn Dr SR2 18 F8
Tarn La DL2 200 E4
Tarnston Rd TS26 76 D7
Tarr Stps TS17 157 B6
Tarran St TS5 214 A1
Tarring St TS18 213 A2
Tasman Dr TS18 117 B1
Tasmania Sq TS7 140 E3
Tate Ave DH6 58 D5
Tatham Cl TS7 141 A2
Tattersall Cl DL5 82 E2
Taunton Cl TS8 140 B4
Taunton Gr TS26 76 E8
Taunton Vale TS14 143 E2
Tavistock Cl TS27 63 C3
Tavistock Rd TS5 119 D2
Tavistock Sq SR3 18 A8
Tavistock St TS5 119 D2
Tawney Cl TS6 121 D4
Tawney Rd TS6 121 D4
Tay St DH5 37 D8
Taybrooke Ave TS25 76 F3
Taylor Ave Bearpark DH7 33 B3
Rowlands Gill NE39 1 F1
Trimdon TS29 59 D3
Taylor Ct DL15 53 F3
Taylor Gr TS28 48 D1
Taylor Rd DL14 80 C6
Taylor Sq DL14 80 A5
Taylor St
Annfield Plain DH9 12 E5
Consett DH8 10 F2
Taylor Wlk DL5 96 E7
Taylor's Terr DH8 10 C1
Tayport Cl DL1 133 B7
Tayside DL1 133 E7
Teak St TS1 215 A2
Teal Cl 8 NE38 9 F3
Teal Ct TS10 106 E7
Teal Rd DL1 133 E1
Tealby Wlk TS3 121 A1
Teare Cl TS1 214 B2
Teasdale St DH8 11 A3
Teasdale Terr DH1 35 B2
Teasel Ct TS19 117 C5
Tebay Cl TS7 141 A7
Ted Fletcher Ct DL1 133 D4
Tedder Ave TS17 138 E4
Tedder Avenue Prim Sch TS17 138 E4
Tedworth Cl TS14 143 E2
Tees (Newport) Bridge Approach Rd TS18 119 A5
Tees Bank Ave TS16 137 D3
Tees Barrage* TS17 118 E3
Tees Barrage Way TS17 118 E3
Tees Bay Ret Pk TS25 77 C1
Tees Cl SR8 49 C4
Tees Cottage Water Pumping & Steam Mus* DL3 150 F8
Tees Cres
Spennymoor DL16 55 F1
Stanley DH9 13 F5
Tees Ct TS6 120 F4
Tees Dock Rd Eston TS6 121 E7
Middlesbrough TS6 105 E1
Tees Dr DL1 152 A6
Tees Gr DH8 11 D5
Tees Grange Ave DL3 132 A1
Tees Rd
Guisborough TS14 143 C3
Hartlepool TS25 90 E4
Redcar TS10 107 B5
Tees St Billingham TS23 103 D2
Easington Lane DH5 37 D8
1 Hartlepool TS24 77 B6
Loftus TS13 127 D1
Peterlee SR8 50 A7
Seaham SR7 29 D7
Tees View
Barnard Castle DL12 199 B1
Gainford DL2 201 D3
Hurworth-on-T DL2 168 A8
Trimdon TS29 59 D1
Tees Wlk DL14 81 C8
Teesbrooke Ave TS25 76 F2
Teesdale Airport Sta DL2 154 E8
Teesdale Ave
Billingham TS23 102 D2
Darlington DL3 151 B8
Hartlepool TS26 76 F5
Teesdale Rd DL12 209 B5
Teesdale S TS17 213 B1
Teesdale Sch DL12 209 D7
Teesdale Terr
Annfield Plain DH9 13 A4
4 Thornaby-on-T TS17 138 D8
Teesdale Wlk
Bishop Auckland DL14 79 F5
Shildon DL4 81 B1
Teesgate TS17 138 F7
Teesmouth National Nature Reserve* TS25 91 B4
Teesquay Millennium Footbridge The TS18 213 B2
Teesside High Sch TS16 137 D2
Teesside Ind Est TS17 138 D1
Teesside Park Dr TS17 118 F1
Teesside Pk
Middlesbrough TS17 119 A2
Thornaby-on-T TS17 118 F1
Teesside Tertiary Coll TS4 215 B1
Teesville Inf Sch TS6 121 B3
Teesway Neasham DL2 153 B1
Stockton-on-T TS18 118 F5
Teign Cl SR8 49 C5
Teignmouth Cl TS27 63 C3
Teikyo Univ of Japan DH1 44 C7
Telford Cl Hartlepool TS24 64 C1
High Shincliffe DH1 45 B4
Telford Dr DL1 133 B1
Telford Rd TS3 120 E5
Temperance Ave DL4 81 A2
Temperance Pl 4 DL3 132 F2
Temperance Terr
Billy Row DL15 52 E6
Ushaw Moor DH7 32 F2
Tempest Ct DL1 133 B7
Tempest Rd
Hartlepool TS24 63 E3
Seaham SR7 29 D8
Tempest St 10 SR3 18 A7
Templar St
1 Consett DH8 10 D4
Stockton-on-T TS18 212 C1
Temple Bldgs 2 DL2 153 E8
Temple Ct
1 Middleton St George DL2 153 E8
Stockton-on-T TS20 213 B4
Temple Gdns DH8 10 F1
Temple Way DL5 82 B1
Templeton Cl TS27 63 C3
Tenby Cl TS6 121 E3
Tenby Way TS16 156 C8
Tenby Wlk TS26 63 E1
Tennant St TS18 213 A3
Tennyson Ave
Blackhall Colliery TS27 50 C5
Eston TS6 121 E4
Hartlepool TS25 76 F3
Tennyson Cl TS6 121 E4
Tennyson Gdns
Darlington DL1 152 A7
Dipton DH9 12 C7
Tennyson Rd
Billingham TS23 102 D8
Chester le Street DH2 15 E3
Chilton DL17 82 F8
Easington SR8 39 D4
Tennyson St TS1 214 C1
Tennyson Terr DL15 52 D5
Tenter Terr DH1 210 C3
Tenters St DL14 80 B8
Tenth Ave DH2 16 B3
Tenth St
Blackhall Colliery TS27 50 D4
7 Peterlee SR8 50 A7
Tern Gr TS10 107 E3
Ternbeck Way TS17 138 E3
Ternholme Cl TS17 138 B2
Terr The DH7 43 D4
Terrace The
Consett DH8 10 C6
Dalton Piercy TS27 75 F3
Elwick TS27 75 C5
Terrace The *continued*
Shotton Colliery DH6 48 D7
Territorial La DH1 211 A2
Tetcott Cl TS14 143 E2
Teviot St DH5 37 C8
Tewkesbury Ave TS7 140 E2
Thackeray Gr TS5 139 E8
Thackeray Rd TS25 76 D3
Thackeray St DH4 26 D8
Thames Ave
Guisborough TS14 143 C3
Hartlepool TS24 64 A1
Thornaby-on-T TS17 138 D6
Thames Cres
Fence Houses DH4 26 A8
Stanley DH9 13 F4
Thames Ctr DL5 96 D6
Thames Rd
Billingham TS22 102 B6
Peterlee SR8 49 D5
Redcar TS10 107 A5
Skelton TS12 125 D3
Thames St DH5 37 C8
Thames Way DL1 151 F6
Thatch La TS17 138 C2
Theakston Gr TS18 117 A1
Therby Cl DL3 132 E5
Theresa St SR7 29 E5
Thetford Ave TS3 140 F8
Thetford Rd TS25 89 E6
Thickley Terr DL4 95 A7
Thinford Gdns TS5 139 D4
Thinford La DH6 56 F2
Thinford Rd DH6 57 E3
Thinford St DH6 57 B2
Third Ave
Chester le S, Perkinsville DH2 16 B7
Chester le Street DH2 16 B3
Third St
Blackhall Colliery TS27 50 D3
Consett DH8 11 B2
Leadgate DH8 11 C5
Leadgate DH8 11 C6
Peterlee SR8 50 A7
Quaking Houses DH9 13 D2
Thirlby Cl TS3 120 C1
Thirlby Way TS14 143 E6
Thirlmere Birtley DH3 9 E2
Spennymoor DL16 55 E2
Thirlmere Ave
Chester le Street DH2 16 B1
Easington Lane DH5 37 C8
Middlesbrough TS5 139 C7
Thirlmere Cres
Blaydon NE21 2 B8
Eston TS6 121 D1
Thirlmere Ct TS23 102 E1
Thirlmere Dr TS12 125 B2
Thirlmere Gr DL14 79 A1
Thirlmere Rd
Darlington DL1 152 B8
Ferryhill DL17 69 F5
Peterlee SR8 49 E7
Redcar TS10 107 B5
Thirlmere St TS26 77 A4
Thirsk Gr TS25 77 B1
Thirsk Rd TS15 156 C4
Thirteenth St SR8 49 F7
Thirwall Dr TS17 157 A7
Thistle Cl DL16 68 D7
Thistle Gn TS18 213 B3
Thistle Ho 1 SR3 18 A5
Thistle Rd Brandon DH7 43 F4
Stockton-on-T TS19 117 E7
Thistle Rise TS8 139 F3
Thistle St TS1 215 A2
Thistlecroft DH5 26 E7
Thistledon Ave NE16 2 F6
Thistleflat Rd DL15 52 C2
Thistlewood La DL13 207 D8
Thomas Ct DL1 133 B1
Thomas St
Annfield Plain DH9 13 A4
9 Chester le Street DH3 16 C2
2 Consett DH8 10 F2
Consett, Blackhill DH8 10 D4
Craghead DH9 14 D3
21 Darlington DL1 133 B1
Easington SR8 39 E5
Hetton-le-H DH5 27 B5
11 Langley Park DH7 32 C6
Middlesbrough TS3 120 C4
Ryhope SR2 18 F6
Sacriston DH7 23 B2
Shildon DL4 95 A7
Skelton TS12 125 D2
Stockton-on-T TS18 213 B4
Thomas St S SR2 18 F6
Thomlinson Rd TS25 77 C3
Thompson Gr TS24 64 A1
Thompson Rd DL14 80 C6
Thompson St
2 Hartlepool TS24 77 B4
Peterlee SR8 50 A8
3 Spennymoor DL16 55 F1
Stockton-on-T TS18 213 A4
Thompson St E DL1 133 B6
Thompson St W DL3 133 A6
Thompson Terr SR2 19 A6
Thompson's Rd TS12 125 B1
Thompsons Cl TS22 102 C8
Thomson Ave TS5 119 B2
Thomson St TS14 143 D4
Thorgill Cl TS4 139 F8

Thorington Gdns TS17 . . 157 C8
Thorn Cl
Ingleby Barwick TS17 . . . . . 138 B2
Spennymoor DL16 . . . . 68 D6
Thorn Ho [2] SR3 . . . . 18 A5
Thorn Rd TS19 . . . . 117 E7
Thorn Side TS17 . . . . 138 B2
Thorn Tree La TS25 . . . . 89 F3
Thornaby Com Sch
TS17 . . . . 138 E6
Thornaby Harewood Cty Inf
Sch TS17 . . . . 138 D7
Thornaby Pl TS17 . . . . . . 213 B1
Thornaby Rd TS17 . . . . . . 138 C6
Thornaby Sta TS17 . . . . . . 213 C1
Thornaby Village Sch
TS17 . . . . 138 C6
Thornaby-on-Tees CE Prim
Sch TS17 . . . . 138 D5
Thornbank Cl SR3 . . . . 18 A4
Thornberry Ct TS5 . . . . . . 119 C1
Thornberry La DL12 . . . . . 198 F2
Thornbrough Cl TS18 . . . 137 B8
Thornbury Cl
Hartlepool TS27 . . . . 63 C4
Redcar TS10 . . . . 107 F1
Thornbury Rise DL3 . . . . 132 D3
Thorncliffe Gr DL14 . . . . . . 80 D5
Thorndale Rd DH1 . . . . 35 D3
Thorndike Rd TS6 . . . . . . 121 E3
Thorndyke Ave TS4 . . . . . 140 A8
Thorne Ct DL3 . . . . 132 F2
Thornes Cl SR8 . . . . 49 F5
Thorneyholme Terr DH9 . . 13 F6
Thornfield Cl TS16 . . . . . . 137 A1
Thornfield Gr TS5 . . . . . . 139 C8
Thornfield Pl NE39 . . . . 1 E3
Thornfield Rd
Consett DH8 . . . . 177 B4
Darlington DL3 . . . . 132 C2
Middlesbrough TS5 . . . . . . 119 C1
Thorngate DL12 . . . . 209 B5
Thorngate Wynd DL12 . . . 209 B5
Thornhaugh Ave NE16 . . . . . 2 F6
Thornhill Cl DL4 . . . . 80 F2
Thornhill Gdns
Burnopfield NE16 . . . . 5 F5
Hartlepool TS26 . . . . 76 E7
Shildon DL4 . . . . 80 F2
Thornhill Pl TS26 . . . . 76 F7
Thornhill Rd DH6 . . . . 48 C6
Thornhill Reach SR7 . . . . . 29 B8
Thornhill St DH4 . . . . 26 D8
Thornlaw N DH6 . . . . 47 B4
Thornlea DL3 . . . . 132 C3
Thornlea Gr DH7 . . . . 20 E4
Thornley Ave TS23 . . . . . . 102 E8
Thornley Cl DH7 . . . . 33 B1
Thornley La NE21,NE39 . . . . 2 A6
Thornley Prim Sch DH6 . . 47 C4
Thornley Rd
Tow Law DL13 . . . . 183 D1
Wheatley Hill DH6 . . . . 47 F3
Thornley Station Ind Est
DH6 . . . . 48 D4
Thornley Terr DL13 . . . . . 183 D2
Thornley View NE39 . . . . 1 F2
Thornley Wood* NE21 . . . . . 2 B6
Thornthwaite TS5 . . . . . . 139 B3
Thornthwaite Cl TS12 . . . 125 B3
Thornton Cl Ludworth DH6 . 47 C7
Newton Aycliffe DL5 . . . . . . 96 C8
Thornton TS8 . . . . 158 B8
Thornton Cres TS22 . . . . . 102 B5
Thornton Garth TS15 . . . . 156 C4
Thornton Gr TS20 . . . . . . 118 A6
Thornton Hall Cotts
DL2 . . . . 131 B6
Thornton Lea DH2 . . . . 15 D7
Thornton Rd
Stainton TS8 . . . . 139 B1
Thornton TS8 . . . . 158 B8
Thornton St
Darlington DL3 . . . . 132 F3
Hartlepool TS26 . . . . 77 A5
Middlesbrough TS3 . . . . . . 120 C4
Thornton Terr TS27 . . . . . . 50 E3
Thornton Vale TS8 . . . . . . 158 B8
Thorntons Cl DH2 . . . . 15 D7
Thorntree Ave TS3 . . . . . . 120 E3
Thorntree Ct TS17 . . . . . . 138 D6
Thorntree Gdns DL2 . . . . 153 E7
Thorntree Gill SR8 . . . . 50 A5
Thorntree Ho TS3 . . . . 120 E2
Thorntree Prim Sch
TS3 . . . . 121 A2
Thorntree Rd TS17 . . . . . 138 C6
Thorntree Terr DH9 . . . . . . 14 B7
Thornville Rd TS26 . . . . 77 A6
Thornwood Ave TS17 . . . 138 B2
Thorpe Cres SR8 . . . . 39 F1
Thorpe Hall DL12 . . . . 200 C1
Thorpe Mews [3] TS20 . . . 118 B8
Thorpe Rd Carlton TS21 . . 116 D8
Easington SR8 . . . . 39 C2
Peterlee SR8 . . . . 39 F1
Thorpe St Easington SR8 . . 39 E5
Hartlepool TS24 . . . . 64 E1
[3] Peterlee SR8 . . . . 50 A7
Thorphill Way TS23 . . . . . 102 E7
Three Lane Ends DL14 . . . . 79 D7
Thrislington Cl DL17 . . . . . 57 D1
Thrislington Ind Est
DL17 . . . . 70 D8
Throckley Ave TS5 . . . . . 139 C5
Thropton Cl
Billingham TS23 . . . . 102 C7
Chester le Street DH2 . . . . . 16 A1
High Shincliffe DH1 . . . . 45 B5
Throstlenest Ave DL1 . . . 133 C4
Throston Cl TS26 . . . . 63 F1
Throston Grange La
TS26 . . . . 63 E1
Throston Prim Sch TS26 . . 76 E8
Throston St TS26 . . . . 77 F8
Thrunton Ct [5] DH5 . . . . . . 26 F8
Thrush Rd TS10 . . . . 107 D6
Thrushcross Pl DH1 . . . . . . 35 B3
Thrushwood Cres [4]
TS11 . . . . 124 E8
Thruxton Way TS20 . . . . . 117 F8
Thunderbuck Dr TS22 . . . . 87 B5
Thurlestone TS8 . . . . 140 F2
Thurlow Gdns DL14 . . . . . . 80 E7
Thurlow Gr DL5 . . . . 96 D8
Thurlow Grange TS21 . . . . 85 B6
Thurlow Rd TS21 . . . . 85 B6
Thurlow Way DH5 . . . . 26 D6
Thurnham Gr TS7 . . . . 140 E3
Thursby DH3 . . . . 9 E2
Thursby Cl DL5 . . . . 95 F5
Thursby Dr TS7 . . . . 141 A8
Thursby Gr TS25 . . . . 89 D6
Thurso Cl TS19 . . . . 116 F3
Thwaites Cl DL5 . . . . 82 B1
Thwaites La TS10 . . . . 107 D5
Thweng Way TS14 . . . . . . 143 C2
Tibbersley Ave TS23 . . . . 102 E1
Tibthorpe TS7 . . . . 140 F3
Tidkin La TS14 . . . . 143 C3
Tilbeck Sq SR3 . . . . 18 A5
Tilbury Rd TS6 . . . . 121 A7
Tilery Prim Sch TS18 . . . . 213 C4
Tilery Rd TS20 . . . . 118 B5
Tilery Way TS20 . . . . 118 B5
Tilery Wood TS22 . . . . 87 B3
Tilley Rd NE38 . . . . 9 F5
Tilleys Row DL13 . . . . 195 C4
Timber Rd SR8 . . . . 51 C1
Timberscombe Cl TS17 . . 157 A6
Timmys La DL2 . . . . 152 E1
Timothy Hackworth Prim Sch
DL4 . . . . 94 F8
Timothy Terr DL16 . . . . 68 F7
Tindale TS14 . . . . 143 A3
Tindale Ave DH1 . . . . 34 A5
Tindale Cl TS15 . . . . 156 B3
Tindale Cres DL14 . . . . 80 A3
Tindale Gn DL5 . . . . 96 A7
Tindale St DH8 . . . . 11 C4
Tindale Wlk TS5 . . . . 139 C4
Tindle St DH8 . . . . 10 E4
Tinkler Terr DH3 . . . . 17 B1
Tinmill Pl DH8 . . . . 10 D3
Tintagel DH3 . . . . 25 B8
Tintagel Cl TS27 . . . . 63 C3
Tintagel Ct DL3 . . . . 132 F8
Tintagel Dr SR7 . . . . 29 C8
Tintern Ave
Billingham TS23 . . . . 102 D5
Darlington DL3 . . . . 131 F5
Tintern Rd
Bishop Auckland DL14 . . . . . 79 D2
Skelton TS12 . . . . 125 D2
Tipton Cl TS17 . . . . 138 E6
Tiree Cl DH7 . . . . 43 C5
Tiree Ct SR3 . . . . 18 A6
Tiree Gdns DL1 . . . . 133 D7
Tirril Way TS7 . . . . 140 F2
Tithe Barn Rd TS19 . . . . . 117 B6
Tiverton Gr TS26 . . . . 76 E8
Tivoli Pl [5] DL14 . . . . 80 B6
Toadpool DL14 . . . . 79 B1
Tobin St TS29 . . . . 59 F6
Tocketts Mill* TS14 . . . . . 124 B1
Tod Point Rd TS10 . . . . . . 106 F7
Todd St DL16 . . . . 68 E8
Toddington Dr TS20 . . . . . 117 E8
Toft Cres SR7 . . . . 28 C3
Toft Hill DL14 . . . . 78 D5
Toft Hill La DL14 . . . . 78 B4
Toft Hill Prim Sch DL14 . . . 78 E5
Tofts Cl
Low Worsall TS15 . . . . 171 C8
Marske-by-t-S TS11 . . . . . 108 E1
Tofts Farm E Ind Est
TS25 . . . . 90 E6
Tofts Farm W Ind Est
TS25 . . . . 90 D5
Tofts Rd DL12 . . . . 208 E2
Tofts Rd E TS25 . . . . 90 D5
Tofts Rd W TS25 . . . . 90 C5
Toll Bar Ho SR2 . . . . 19 A8
Toll Bar Rd SR2 . . . . 18 E8
Toll House Rd DH1 . . . . . . 33 F2
Tollerton Cl TS19 . . . . 212 A4
Tollesby Bridge TS8 . . . . 140 B3
Tollesby La TS7 . . . . 140 C3
Tollesby Rd TS5 . . . . 139 E7
Tollesby Sch TS4 . . . . 139 F7
Tollgate Bglws DH9 . . . . . . 12 E5
Tollgate Fields DH4 . . . . . . 25 F1
Tollgate Garth DL1 . . . . . 133 F6
Tollgate Rd NE39 . . . . 4 F5
Tollgate Terr DH9 . . . . 12 E5
Tom Leonard Mining Mus*
TS13 . . . . 127 A3
Tom Raine Ct DL1 . . . . . . 133 A2
Tomlinson Way TS3 . . . . 120 F3
Topaz St SR7 . . . . 29 A7
Topcliffe Dr TS5 . . . . 139 C4
Topcliffe Rd TS17 . . . . . . 138 E5
Topcliffe St TS26 . . . . 76 F6
Topcroft Cl TS3 . . . . 140 E7
Topham Gn TS3 . . . . 120 C2
Topping Cl TS24 . . . . 64 D2
Torbay Cl TS8 . . . . 140 B5
Torbay Gr TS26 . . . . 76 E8
Torbay Wlk TS26 . . . . 76 E8
Torcross Cl TS27 . . . . 63 C3
Torcross Way TS10 . . . . . 107 E2
Toronto Cres TS4 . . . . . . 120 A2
Torquay Ave TS25 . . . . 89 F7
Torrance Dr DL1 . . . . 133 E7
Torver Cl SR8 . . . . 49 E6
Torver Mount TS7 . . . . . . 140 F2
Torwell Dr TS19 . . . . 117 B4
Tothill Ave TS3 . . . . 121 A1
Totnes Cl TS27 . . . . 63 C3
Tovil Cl TS19 . . . . 117 A6
Tow Law Ind Est DL13 . . . 183 D2
Tow Law Millennium Prim
Sch DL13 . . . . 183 E1
Tower Bank DH7 . . . . 20 E8
Tower Ct DH5 . . . . 27 C1
Tower Gn TS2 . . . . 119 F7
Tower Hill DL2 . . . . 153 F5
Tower Mews DL13 . . . . . . 207 C5
Tower Rd
Annfield Plain DH9 . . . . 12 E1
Darlington DL3 . . . . 132 D3
Tower Road Cvn Site
DH9 . . . . 12 F1
Tower St Hartlepool TS24 . . 77 C5
Stockton-on-T TS18 . . . . . 213 B2
Town End DL12 . . . . 208 C5
Town End Cl TS15 . . . . . . 172 E8
Town Farm Cl
Bishopton TS21 . . . . 115 C7
Winston DL2 . . . . 200 F3
Town Hall Ct TS15 . . . . . . 156 B6
Town Head
Eggleston DL12 . . . . 193 E2
Middleton-In-T DL12 . . . . 208 B6
Town Pasture La DL12 . . . 209 F8
Town Sq TS23 . . . . 102 D4
Town Wall TS24 . . . . 77 F8
Towneley Ct DH9 . . . . 13 E5
Townend Ct TS28 . . . . 60 F5
Towngate Bsns Ctr DH7 . . 43 E5
Townley Fields NE39 . . . . . . 1 F2
Townley Rd NE39 . . . . 1 D2
Towthorpe TS7 . . . . 140 F3
Trafalgar Ct TS6 . . . . 121 A6
Trafalgar St Consett DH8 . . 10 F2
Ferryhill DL17 . . . . 70 C4
Trafalgar Terr
Darlington DL3 . . . . 132 E4
Redcar TS10 . . . . 107 B7
Trafford Cl DL1 . . . . 133 E4
Tralee Cl TS10 . . . . 106 F1
Tranmere Ave TS3 . . . . . . 120 E2
Tranter Rd TS4 . . . . 139 F7
Travellers Gate TS25 . . . . . 77 B1
Travellers' Gn DL5 . . . . 96 E5
Traynor Way DH6 . . . . 48 E6
Trecastell TS17 . . . . 156 F7
Tredegar Wlk TS26 . . . . . . 76 D8
Treecone Cl SR3 . . . . 18 A5
Treelands DL3 . . . . 132 C1
Treen Cres SR7 . . . . 28 D3
Trefoil Cl TS14 . . . . 143 B3
Trefoil Ct TS20 . . . . 118 A6
Trefoil Rd DH9 . . . . 13 D8
Trefoil Wood TS7 . . . . . . 140 C5
Tregarth Cl TS4 . . . . 139 F8
Tregoney Ave SR7 . . . . 28 D4
Tremaine Cl TS27 . . . . 63 C3
Trenchard Ave TS17 . . . . 138 D4
Trenholme Rd TS4 . . . . . . 215 C1
Trent Ave TS17 . . . . 138 D6
Trent Cres DH3 . . . . 25 B7
Trent Dale DH8 . . . . 11 D5
Trent Pl DL1 . . . . 151 F6
Trent Rd TS10 . . . . 107 B5
Trent St
Easington Lane DH5 . . . . . . 37 C8
Stockton-on-T TS20 . . . . . 118 B6
Trentbrooke Ave TS25 . . . . 76 F2
Trentham Ave TS3 . . . . . . 120 F1
Tresco Wlk TS14 . . . . 143 D3
Trevarren Dr SR2 . . . . 18 F7
Trevarrian Dr TS10 . . . . . 107 E2
Trevelyan Coll (Univ of
Durham) DH1 . . . . 44 C7
Trevelyan Pl Crook DL15 . . 52 C3
Peterlee SR8 . . . . 49 B5
Trevine Gdns TS17 . . . . . 156 F7
Trevino Ct TS16 . . . . 137 D1
Trevithick Cl
[2] Darlington DL1 . . . . . . 133 B1
Eaglescliffe TS16 . . . . 137 A2
Trevone Sq SR7 . . . . 28 D3
Trevone Way DL3 . . . . . . 133 A8
Trevor Green N [5] DL5 . . . . 96 E8
Trevor Wlk [3] DL5 . . . . 96 E8
Trevose Cl TS10 . . . . 107 D2
Trident Bsns Ctr TS2 . . . 119 C7
Trident Cl TS24 . . . . 77 D6
Trident Rd SR3 . . . . 18 A7
Trigo Cl TS7 . . . . 140 C4
Trimdon Ave TS5 . . . . 139 B5
Trimdon Grange Inf Sch
TS29 . . . . 59 D3
Trimdon Jun Sch TS29 . . . 72 E8
Trimdon Village Inf Sch
TS29 . . . . 72 D8
Trinity Cres TS3 . . . . 215 C3
Trinity Gdns DL15 . . . . 54 A3
Trinity Mews
Darlington DL3 . . . . 132 E2
Trinity Mews *continued*
Thornaby-on-T TS17 . . . . . 213 C2
Trinity Rd DL3 . . . . 132 E2
Trinity St Hartlepool TS24 . . 64 F1
Stockton-on-T TS18 . . . . . 213 A2
Tristram Ave
Darlington DL3 . . . . 132 E5
Hartlepool TS25 . . . . 76 F3
Tristram Cl TS6 . . . . 121 C1
Troisdorf Way TS10 . . . . . 107 A1
Trool Ct SR3 . . . . 18 A5
Troon Ave DL1 . . . . 133 E6
Troon Cl Billingham TS22 . . 102 A5
Consett DH8 . . . . 10 E5
Middlesbrough TS4 . . . . . . 139 F7
Trotter Terr Ryhope SR2 . . . 18 F6
Shotton Colliery DH6 . . . . . . 48 C6
Trout Hall La TS12 . . . . . . 125 C1
Trout's La DH1 . . . . 33 D7
Trout's Lane Sch DH1 . . . . 33 E7
Troutbeck Cl DL16 . . . . 55 E2
Troutbeck Rd TS10 . . . . . 107 C4
Troutbeck Way SR8 . . . . . . 49 E7
Troutpool Cl TS24 . . . . 64 C1
Troutsdale Cl TS15 . . . . . 156 B3
Trowsdale St DH9 . . . . 12 E5
Trueman Gr [4] DL3 . . . . . 133 A7
Trunk Rd
Eston, Grangetown TS6 . . . 122 A8
Eston, Teesville TS6 . . . . . 121 C4
Redcar TS10 . . . . 106 D4
Truro Ave SR7 . . . . 28 D4
Truro Cl DL1 . . . . 133 E5
Truro Dr TS25 . . . . 89 F7
Tuart St DH3 . . . . 16 C3
Tubwell Row DL1 . . . . 132 F1
Tudhoe Colliery Prim Sch
DL16 . . . . 56 B4
Tudhoe Grange Comp Sch
Spennymoor DL16 . . . . 56 A1
Spennymoor DL16 . . . . 56 A2
Tudhoe Hall Farm Ct
DL16 . . . . 55 F4
Tudhoe Ind Est DL16 . . . . . 56 B4
Tudhoe La DL16 . . . . 56 A3
Tudhoe Moor DL16 . . . . 56 C1
Tudhoe Park Villas DL16 . . 56 A2
Tudor Ct Heighington DL5 . . 95 E1
Shotton Colliery DH6 . . . . . . 48 D7
Tudor Dr DH9 . . . . 6 D3
Tudor Grange SR8 . . . . 39 A3
Tudor Rd DH3 . . . . 16 D5
Tudor Terr DH8 . . . . 10 E3
Tummel Ct SR3 . . . . 18 A6
Tunstall Ave
Billingham TS23 . . . . 102 F8
Bowburn DH6 . . . . 45 D1
Hartlepool TS26 . . . . 76 F6
Tunstall Bank SR2,SR3 . . . . 18 D7
Tunstall Gr
Bishop Auckland DL14 . . . . . 79 F5
Hartlepool TS26 . . . . 76 E7
Leadgate DH8 . . . . 11 D4
Tunstall Hope Rd SR3 . . . . 18 C8
Tunstall Rd
Newton Aycliffe DL5 . . . . . . 96 C6
Stockton-on-T TS18 . . . . . 137 B8
Tunstall St TS3 . . . . 120 C4
Tunstall Terr
Darlington DL2 . . . . 152 B8
New Silksworth SR3 . . . . . . 18 B7
Ryhope SR2 . . . . 18 D7
Tunstall View SR3 . . . . 18 B8
Tunstall Village Gn SR3 . . . 18 C7
Tunstall Village Rd SR3 . . . 18 B7
Tunstall Villas SR3 . . . . 18 B7
Turford Ave TS3 . . . . 120 E3
Turnberry DH2 . . . . 8 F2
Turnberry Ave TS16 . . . . . 156 C8
Turnberry Cl DH8 . . . . 10 E5
Turnberry Dr TS11 . . . . . . 123 F5
Turnberry Gr TS27 . . . . 63 C4
Turnberry Way TS8 . . . . . 140 E1
Turnbull Cl DH1 . . . . 35 A2
Turnbull Cres SR7 . . . . 28 C3
Turnbull St TS24 . . . . 77 B7
Turner Cl TS23 . . . . 102 D7
Turner St Consett DH8 . . . . 10 D4
Redcar TS10 . . . . 107 C7
Turner Terr TS6 . . . . 122 C4
Turner Wlk TS25 . . . . 76 D2
Turnpike Cl DL1 . . . . 133 F6
Turnpike Wlk TS21 . . . . 72 A1
Turnstile The TS5 . . . . . . 214 B1
Turnstone Dr NE38 . . . . 9 F3
Tursdale Aged Mine Workers
War Meml Homes DH6 . . 57 C3
Tursdale Bsns Pk DH6 . . . . 57 C4
Turton Rd TS15 . . . . 156 B4
Tuscan Cl DH7 . . . . 42 E8
Tuson Wlk TS24 . . . . 77 B7
Tweddle Cres TS27 . . . . . . 50 F2
Tweddle Terr DH6 . . . . 45 C1
Tweed Ave Leadgate DH8 . . 11 D5
Thornaby-on-T TS17 . . . . . 138 D6
Tweed Cl Pelton DH2 . . . . . 15 F8
Peterlee SR8 . . . . 49 D5
Sunderland SR2 . . . . 18 F8
Tweed Ho [8] TS18 . . . . . . 213 C4
Tweed Pl DL1 . . . . 152 A6
Tweed Rd Redcar TS10 . . . 107 A5
Spennymoor DL16 . . . . 56 B3
Tweed St
Easington Lane DH5 . . . . . . 37 C8
Loftus TS13 . . . . 127 D1
Saltburn-by-t-S TS12 . . . . 125 C7
Tweed Terr DH9 . . . . 13 F5
Tweed Wlk TS24 . . . . 77 A7
Tweedport Rd TS18 . . . . . 213 C4
Twelfth Ave DH2 . . . . 16 B4
Twelfth St SR8 . . . . 49 F7
Twickenham Rise DL1 . . . 133 F4
Twinsburn Cl DL5 . . . . 95 D1
Twinsburn Rd DL5 . . . . 95 D1
Twizell La DH9 . . . . 14 F5
Twizzie Gill View TS13 . . . 148 B8
Tyne Ave DH8 . . . . 11 D5
Tyne Cres Darlington DL1 . 152 A6
Spennymoor DL16 . . . . 55 F1
Tyne Ct TS6 . . . . 120 F4
Tyne Rd Redcar TS10 . . . . 107 B5
Stanley DH9 . . . . 13 E5
Tyne Rd E DH9 . . . . 13 F5
Tyne St Consett DH8 . . . . . . 11 A2
Easington Lane DH5 . . . . . . 37 C8
Loftus TS13 . . . . 127 D1
[5] Seaham SR7 . . . . 29 D7
[10] South Bank TS6 . . . . . 121 A6
Tyne Terr SR8 . . . . 39 D4
Tyne Wlk DL14 . . . . 81 C8
Tynebrooke Ave TS25 . . . . 76 F2
Tynedale St
Hetton-le-H DH5 . . . . 26 E1
Stockton-on-T TS18 . . . . . 212 C2
Tynedale Terr DH9 . . . . 13 A4
Tynedale Wlk DL4 . . . . 95 B8
Tyneport Gn [11] TS18 . . . 213 C4
Tyrone Rd TS19 . . . . 117 A4
Tyzack St DH7 . . . . 23 B7

U

Ugly La DH2 . . . . 23 F4
Uldale Dr TS16 . . . . 156 C8
Ulla St
Middlesbrough TS1 . . . . . . 214 C1
Middlesbrough TS1 . . . . . . 214 C2
Ullapool Cl TS19 . . . . 116 F3
Ullathorne Rise DL12 . . . 209 B5
Ullerdale Cl DH1 . . . . 35 E4
Ullswater Ave
Easington Lane DH5 . . . . . . 37 C8
Evenwood DL14 . . . . 79 A1
Middlesbrough TS5 . . . . . . 139 C7
Ullswater Cl Eston TS6 . . . 121 F4
Spennymoor DL16 . . . . 56 B1
Ullswater Cres
Blaydon NE21 . . . . 2 B8
Crook DL15 . . . . 52 F2
Ullswater Dr TS12 . . . . . . 125 B3
Ullswater Gr TS10 . . . . . . 107 C5
Ullswater Rd
Billingham TS23 . . . . 102 E1
Chester le Street DH2 . . . . . 16 B1
Ferryhill DL17 . . . . 69 F5
Hartlepool TS25 . . . . 77 C3
Stockton-on-T TS18 . . . . . 212 B3
Ullswater Terr DH6 . . . . . . 37 E8
Ulnaby La DL2 . . . . 130 F6
Ulswater Ave DL1 . . . . 152 B8
Union La
Chester le Street DH2 . . . . . 24 B7
Stanhope DL13 . . . . 206 D3
Union Pl DL1 . . . . 133 B1
Union Rd TS24 . . . . 64 C2
Union St
Bishop Auckland DL14 . . . . . 80 C7
[5] Darlington DL3 . . . . . . 132 F2
Guisborough TS14 . . . . . . 143 E5
Hartlepool TS24 . . . . 77 F8
Hetton-le-H DH5 . . . . 27 A4
Middlesbrough TS1 . . . . . . 214 B2
Seaham SR7 . . . . 29 D6
Stanhope DL13 . . . . 206 C3
Union St E TS18 . . . . 213 C4
Unity Terr
Annfield Plain DH9 . . . . 13 B4
Dipton DH9 . . . . 12 E7
Tantobie DH9 . . . . 6 B2
Univ Coll Stockton-on-Tees
(Univ of Durham)
TS17 . . . . 213 C2
Univ Coll, Univ of Durham
DH1 . . . . 210 C2
Univ Hospl of North Durham
DH1 . . . . 34 A4
Univ of Durham DH1 . . . . 210 C2
Univ of Durham (Dept of
Psychology & Biological
Sciences) DH1 . . . . 44 D7
Univ of Durham (Science
Labs) DH1 . . . . 211 A1
Univ of Durham Botanical
Gdns* DH1 . . . . 44 C6
Univ of Durham Oriental
Mus* DH1 . . . . 44 B7
Univ of Teesside
Middlesbrough TS1 . . . . . . 215 A2
Normanby TS6 . . . . 141 E7
University Bvd TS17 . . . . 213 C2
University Hospl of North
Tees TS19 . . . . 117 C6
Unshaw Moor Inf Sch
DH7 . . . . 32 F2
Unsworth Gdns [9] DH8 . . . 10 F2
Unsworth St [8] DH8 . . . . . . 10 F2
Uphill Dr DH7 . . . . 23 D3
Uplands Cl DL15 . . . . 52 D5
Uplands Rd DL3 . . . . 132 E1
Uplands The DH3 . . . . 9 D5
Upleatham St TS12 . . . . . 125 C7
Upleathem Gr TS19 . . . . . 117 B2
Upper Albion St [15] TS6 . 121 A6
Upper Archer St [3] DL3 . . 132 F2
Upper Branch St [7] TS6 . . 121 A6

Upper Chare SR8 ... 49 D6
Upper Church St
5 Hartlepool TS24 ... 77 B6
Spennymoor DL16 ... 56 B1
Upper Garth Gdns TS14 ... 143 E5
Upper Graham St 14
TS6 ... 121 A6
Upper Green La TS17 ... 138 C5
Upper Jackson St 16
TS6 ... 121 A6
Upper Napier St TS6 ... 121 A6
Upper Oxford St TS6 ... 121 A6
Upper Princess St TS6 ... 121 A6
Upper Russell St DL1 ... 133 A2
Upper Teesdale National Nature Reserve*
DL12 ... 191 A6
Upper Yoden Way SR8 ... 49 E6
Uppingham St TS25 ... 77 A3
Upsall Cotts TS14 ... 141 F4
Upsall Dr DL3 ... 151 E8
Upsall Gr TS19 ... 117 B2
Upsall Rd
Middlesbrough TS3 ... 120 D1
Nunthorpe TS7 ... 141 B3
Upton Cotts TS13 ... 127 F3
Upton Ct TS17 ... 157 B8
Upton Hill TS13 ... 127 F3
Upton St TS1 ... 215 A2
Upton Wlk TS25 ... 89 E6
Urford Cl TS15 ... 156 E4
Urlay Gr TS5 ... 139 D5
Urlay Nook Rd TS16 ... 156 B8
Urpeth Terr DH2 ... 15 A7
Urpeth Villas DH9 ... 14 F7
Urswick Cl TS4 ... 119 F1
Urwin St DH5 ... 27 B3
Ushaw Coll DH7 ... 32 D4
Ushaw Moor Jun Sch
DH7 ... 33 A2
Ushaw Terr DH7 ... 32 F2
Ushaw Villas DH7 ... 32 F1
Usher Ave DH6 ... 35 F2
Usk Ct TS17 ... 156 F8
Usway Ct 1 TS17 ... 157 A7
Usworth Rd TS25 ... 77 B1
Usworth Road Ind Est
TS25 ... 77 B1
Uvedale Rd TS6 ... 121 B5

V

Vale Dr TS17 ... 138 E7
Vale St DH5 ... 37 B8
Vale The Hartlepool TS26 ... 76 D5
Middlesbrough TS4 ... 119 F1
Stockton-on-T TS19 ... 117 D5
Vale View DH7 ... 21 E5
Valeside DH1 ... 210 B3
Valiant Way TS17 ... 138 C3
Valley Cl Hartlepool TS26 ... 76 C5
Marske-by-t-S TS11 ... 108 D2
Tow Law DL13 ... 183 D2
Yarm TS15 ... 156 D5
Valley Dene NE17 ... 4 B7
Valley Dr Esh Winning DH7 ... 31 C1
Hartlepool TS26 ... 76 C5
Yarm TS15 ... 156 E5
Valley Garth DH7 ... 31 C2
Valley Gdns Consett DH8 ... 10 C4
Eaglescliffe TS16 ... 156 A8
Stockton-on-T TS19 ... 117 D5
Valley Gr
Coundon Grange DL14 ... 80 F5
Lanchester DH7 ... 20 F3
Valley Rd
Chester le Street DH2 ... 15 E3
Middlesbrough TS4 ... 119 F2
Valley St N DL1 ... 133 A3
Valley Terr DL15 ... 65 F7
Valley The DL13 ... 40 D5
Valley View
Annfield Plain DH9 ... 12 F5
Birtley DH3 ... 9 B6
Burnopfield NE16 ... 5 F7
Consett DH8 ... 177 E3
Consett, Bridgehill DH8 ... 10 B5
Crawley Side DL13 ... 206 C5
Hetton-le-H DH5 ... 26 D1
Leadgate DH8 ... 11 C3
Rowlands Gill NE39 ... 1 D2
Sacriston DH7 ... 23 B2
Sunderland Bridge DH6 ... 56 B6
Thornley (nr Tow Law)
DL13 ... 189 D8
Ushaw Moor DH7 ... 33 B1
Valley View Ct DL14 ... 80 E3
Van Mildert Cl
Coundongate DL14 ... 80 E7
Peterlee SR8 ... 49 B4
Van Mildert Coll (Univ of Durham) DH1 ... 44 B6
Van Mildert Rd DL5 ... 96 E6
Van Mildert Way TS18 ... 137 F8
Vancouver Gdns TS4 ... 215 B1
Vancouver St DL3 ... 132 E3
Vane Ct TS21 ... 135 F5
Vane Rd
Barnard Castle DL12 ... 209 B6
Newton Aycliffe DL5 ... 96 E7
Vane Road Prim Sch DL5 ... 96 F7
Vane St Easington SR8 ... 39 E4
Hartlepool TS24 ... 64 E1
11 New Silksworth SR3 ... 18 A7
New Silksworth SR3 ... 18 A7
Stockton-on-T TS18 ... 213 A3
Vane Terr
9 Cockfield DL13 ... 195 E3
Darlington DL3 ... 132 E2
Seaham SR7 ... 29 D8
Vane Villas DH1 ... 35 B1
Vanguard Ct TS18 ... 137 F6
Varo Terr TS18 ... 212 C2
Vart Rd DL14 ... 80 B5
Vaughan Ct TS6 ... 121 D6
Vaughan Sh Ctr The
TS3 ... 121 A1
Vaughan St
Darlington DL3 ... 133 A7
Middlesbrough TS1 ... 214 C3
Shildon DL4 ... 80 E1
Skelton TS12 ... 125 F2
Vaynor Dr TS17 ... 156 F8
Vedra Cl DL13 ... 179 B2
Venables Rd TS14 ... 143 D5
Venerable Bede CE Sec Sch
SR2 ... 18 C7
Ventnor Ave TS25 ... 77 A2
Ventnor Rd TS5 ... 119 D1
Verdun Terr DL17 ... 57 D1
Vere Rd DL12 ... 209 B6
Verity Rise 1 DL3 ... 133 A7
Verner Cl TS24 ... 63 C5
Verner Rd TS24 ... 63 C5
Vernon Ct TS8 ... 139 C1
Vernon Gdns DL1 ... 133 B8
Veronica St TS3 ... 215 C2
Verwood Cl TS19 ... 117 A6
Veryan Rd TS23 ... 102 F5
Viador DH3 ... 16 C4
Viburnum Cl 11 TS10 ... 107 E1
Vicarage Ave TS19 ... 212 C3
Vicarage Cl
Howden-le-W DL15 ... 65 D7
Pelton DH2 ... 15 E7
South Hetton DH6 ... 38 B6
Vicarage Ct
6 Hartlepool TS25 ... 77 B4
Heighington DL5 ... 95 D1
Vicarage Dr
Marske-by-t-S TS11 ... 108 D1
Trimdon TS29 ... 59 E1
Vicarage Est TS28 ... 60 E8
Vicarage Farm Cl DL14 ... 79 D8
Vicarage Flats DH7 ... 43 B4
Vicarage Gdns DL15 ... 54 A3
Vicarage Rd
Cornforth DL17 ... 57 E1
Darlington DL1 ... 133 B3
New Silksworth SR3 ... 18 A7
Vicarage Row TS25 ... 89 E4
Vicarage St TS19 ... 212 C4
Vicarage Terr
Coxhoe DH6 ... 58 A3
Murton SR7 ... 28 C2
Nenthead CA9 ... 178 A6
Vicars Cl TS21 ... 100 D3
Viceroy St SR7 ... 29 D7
Vickers Cl
Marske-by-t-S TS11 ... 108 B2
Stockton-on-T TS18 ... 137 F6
Vickers Ct DL5 ... 96 E6
Vickers St DL14 ... 80 B8
Victor St 5 DH3 ... 16 C3
Victor Terr DH7 ... 33 B3
Victor Way TS17 ... 138 D4
Victoria Ave
Bishop Auckland DL14 ... 80 C8
Brandon DH7 ... 43 C4
Crook DL15 ... 52 F3
Redcar TS10 ... 107 D5
Stockton-on-T TS20 ... 118 B6
Victoria Cl TS11 ... 124 A7
Victoria Cotts DL13 ... 195 C4
Victoria Ct 3 Consett DH8 ... 10 F2
South Bank TS6 ... 121 A5
Ushaw Moor DH7 ... 33 A2
Victoria Emb DL1 ... 151 F8
Victoria Gdns
5 Middlesbrough TS3 ... 140 F8
Spennymoor DL16 ... 68 E7
Victoria Gr TS19 ... 117 C4
Victoria Homes TS25 ... 77 A4
Victoria La DL14 ... 81 C8
Victoria Mews SR8 ... 39 B3
Victoria Pl
15 Chester le Street DH3 ... 16 C2
Hartlepool TS24 ... 77 F8
Victoria Rd
Barnard Castle DL12 ... 209 C6
Consett DH8 ... 10 F2
Darlington DL1 ... 132 F1
Eaglescliffe TS16 ... 137 C2
Hartlepool TS24,TS26 ... 77 B6
Middlesbrough TS1 ... 215 A2
Saltburn-by-t-S TS12 ... 125 C6
Stockton-on-T TS19 ... 117 C3
Thornaby-on-T TS17 ... 138 C8
Victoria St Consett DH8 ... 10 E3
Crook DL15 ... 52 E4
14 Darlington DL1 ... 133 B1
Evenwood DL14 ... 92 D6
Hartlepool TS24 ... 77 F8
Hetton-le-H DH5 ... 27 A4
Lanchester DH7 ... 20 E4
Middlesbrough TS1 ... 214 B2
Sacriston DH7 ... 23 C3
Seaham SR7 ... 29 C7
Seaton Carew TS25 ... 90 E8
Shildon DL4 ... 95 A8
Shotton Colliery DH6 ... 48 D6
South Bank TS6 ... 121 A5
Spennymoor DL16 ... 68 E7
Stockton-on-T TS18 ... 213 A3
Victoria St *continued*
Willington DL15 ... 54 A4
Victoria Terr
Annfield Plain DH9 ... 12 F4
Beamish DH2 ... 15 A7
Billingham TS2 ... 119 F8
Chilton DL17 ... 82 F8
Cockfield DL13 ... 195 E3
Coxhoe DH6 ... 57 F3
Durham DH1 ... 210 B3
Hamsterley NE17 ... 4 B6
Hartlepool TS24 ... 77 C6
Lanchester DH7 ... 20 E4
Loftus TS13 ... 127 D1
Middleton-In-T DL12 ... 208 B5
Murton SR7 ... 28 D2
Pelton DH2 ... 15 C6
Rowlands Gill NE39 ... 1 C1
Saltburn-by-t-S TS12 ... 125 C6
Stanhope DL13 ... 206 D2
Trimdon TS29 ... 59 F5
Victory St E DH5 ... 27 B4
Victory St W DH5 ... 27 B4
Victory Terr TS10 ... 107 B7
Vienna Ct TS10 ... 107 A1
View La DH9 ... 13 F7
View Tops DH9 ... 14 F8
Viewforth Rd SR2 ... 18 F5
Viewforth Villas DH1 ... 210 A3
Viewley Centre Rd TS8 ... 139 E2
Viewley Hill Ave TS8 ... 139 F2
Viewley Hill Prim Sch
TS8 ... 139 E2
Viewly Ctr The TS8 ... 139 E2
Vigo La DH3 ... 16 D8
Vigodale DH3 ... 9 E1
Villa Rd TS3 ... 120 F3
Villa Real Bglws DH8 ... 11 B4
Villa Real Ct DH8 ... 11 A4
Villa Real Est DH8 ... 11 A4
Villa Real Rd DH8 ... 11 A4
Villa Real Sch DH8 ... 11 B4
Villa St DL16 ... 68 E7
Village Cl DL5 ... 82 E1
Village Gn The TS21 ... 100 A2
Village Paddock TS18 ... 137 D8
Village Rd TS15 ... 171 C8
Village The
Brancepeth DH7 ... 54 E8
Castle Eden TS27 ... 49 D1
Ryhope SR2 ... 19 A6
Villas The
Annfield Plain,Greencroft
DH9 ... 12 E3
Annfield Plain,Harelaw DH9 ... 12 E6
Burnhope DH7 ... 21 D5
Ferryhill DL17 ... 69 E5
Thornley (nr Wheatley Hill)
DH6 ... 47 C4
Villiers Cl Chilton DL17 ... 83 A8
Darlington DL3 ... 132 B2
Villiers Pl
3 Chester le Street DH3 ... 16 C4
3 Newton Aycliffe DL5 ... 96 D8
Villiers Rd DL16 ... 55 F1
Villiers St Hartlepool TS24 ... 77 B5
Spennymoor DL16 ... 68 F8
Vincent Rd
Billingham TS23 ... 102 D7
Middlesbrough TS5 ... 119 F1
Vincent St Easington SR8 ... 39 E4
Hartlepool TS24 ... 64 C2
Seaham SR7 ... 29 D6
Vincent Terr DH9 ... 13 A3
Vindomora Rd DH8,NE17 ... 3 E4
Vindomora Villas DH8 ... 3 E4
Vine Cl TS14 ... 143 F3
Vine Pl 7 DH4 ... 26 E8
Vine St Byers Green DL16 ... 54 E1
Darlington DL3 ... 132 E3
Middlesbrough TS2 ... 214 C4
Spennymoor DL16 ... 55 F1
Viola Cres Ouston DH2 ... 8 F2
Sacriston DH7 ... 23 D3
Violet Cl TS20 ... 118 A6
Violet Gr DL1 ... 133 C2
Violet St 6 DH4 ... 26 D8
Violet Terr DH4 ... 17 D3
Virginia Cl TS19 ... 117 D6
Virginia Gdns TS5 ... 139 D4
Viscount Rd 4 SR3 ... 18 A7
Vivian Cres 1 DH2 ... 16 C2
Vollum Rise TS24 ... 64 E1
Voltigeur Dr TS27 ... 63 A3
Vulcan St Darlington DL1 ... 133 B4
Middlesbrough TS2 ... 119 F7
Vulcan Way TS17 ... 138 D3
Vyner St DL16 ... 68 E8
Vyners Cl DL16 ... 69 A6

W

Wackerfield DL2 ... 92 C2
Waddington St
1 Bishop Auckland DL14 ... 80 B6
Durham DH1 ... 210 B3
Wade Ave TS18 ... 213 B4
Wadham Cl SR8 ... 49 B5
Wadham Gr DL1 ... 133 B6
Wagtail Cl NE21 ... 2 C8
Wagtail La Craghead DH9 ... 14 A1
Quaking Houses DH9 ... 13 F1
Wagtail Terr DH9 ... 14 C2
Waine Cres DL14 ... 80 B5
Wainfleet Rd TS25 ... 89 D6
Wainstones Cl TS9 ... 161 A1
Wainstones Dr TS9 ... 160 F1
Wainwright Cl TS25 ... 77 E2
Wainwright Wlk TS25 ... 77 E2
Wake St TS3 ... 120 C4
Wakefield Rd TS5 ... 119 E2
Wakenshaw Rd DH1 ... 211 C4
Walcher Rd DL5 ... 96 D7
Walden Cl DH2 ... 8 D2
Walden Terr TS21 ... 72 C4
Waldon St TS24 ... 77 B5
Waldridge Fell Country Park
Nature Trail* DH2 ... 23 E8
Waldridge Gr TS23 ... 103 A8
Waldridge La
Chester le Street DH2 ... 15 F2
Chester le Street DH2 ... 16 A2
Waldridge DH2 ... 23 E7
Waldridge Rd
Chester le Street DH2,DH3 ... 16 B2
Stockton-on-T TS19 ... 117 B7
Waldron St DL14 ... 80 B8
Wales St DL3 ... 133 A5
Walk The TS27 ... 75 C5
Walker Dr DL14 ... 80 A4
Walker La DL5 ... 96 D5
Walker St Bowburn DH6 ... 57 D8
Redcar TS10 ... 107 C7
Thornaby-on-T TS17 ... 138 C8
Walker Terr DL17 ... 70 C5
Walker's La DL5 ... 95 E7
Walkergate DH1 ... 210 C3
Walkers Row TS14 ... 143 E5
Walkley Ave TS17 ... 138 C6
Walkworth La DL16 ... 56 A2
Wallace St DH4 ... 26 D8
Wallas Rd DL5 ... 96 D6
Waller Ct TS24 ... 64 A2
Waller St DH5 ... 26 E7
Wallflower Ave SR8 ... 49 F7
Wallington Ct TS23 ... 102 F7
Wallington Dr TS21 ... 85 A7
Wallington Rd TS23 ... 102 E8
Wallington Way TS23 ... 102 E7
Wallington Wlk 5 TS23 ... 102 E8
Wallis Rd TS6 ... 120 F4
Wallish Walls Rd DH8 ... 176 E5
Wallnook La DH7 ... 32 D7
Walmer Ave DL14 ... 80 B6
Walmer Cres 11 TS11 ... 124 A6
Walnut Cl TS17 ... 138 C6
Walnut Gr TS10 ... 107 F5
Walpole Cl SR7 ... 28 F6
Walpole Rd TS25 ... 76 E3
Walpole St TS1 ... 214 C2
Walsham Cl TS19 ... 117 C5
Walsingham Ct TS23 ... 102 D1
Walter St Shildon DL4 ... 95 A7
Stockton-on-T TS18 ... 212 C1
Walter Terr DH5 ... 27 B1
Waltham Ave TS18 ... 117 C2
Waltham Cl DL3 ... 132 B4
Walton Ave
Middlesbrough TS5 ... 139 D8
Seaham SR7 ... 28 F6
Walton Cl DH9 ... 14 A5
Walton Ct TS18 ... 118 D4
Walton Heath DL1 ... 133 E6
Walton St Darlington DL1 ... 152 B8
Stockton-on-T TS18 ... 118 D4
Walton Terr Consett DH8 ... 11 A4
5 Consett,Castleside
DH8 ... 177 A3
Ebchester DH8 ... 3 E4
Guisborough TS14 ... 143 E4
Wingate TS28 ... 48 D1
Walton's Bldgs 1 DH7 ... 32 F2
Waltons Terr DH7 ... 42 F8
Walworth Cl TS10 ... 107 E4
Walworth Cres DL3 ... 132 C5
Walworth Gr TS5 ... 139 C6
Walworth Rd
Ferryhill DL17 ... 70 A7
Heighington DL2 ... 111 A5
Newton Aycliffe DL5 ... 96 D4
Stockton-on-T TS19 ... 117 C7
Walworth Sch DL5 ... 96 B8
Wand Hill TS12 ... 145 C7
Wandhill Gdns TS12 ... 145 C7
Wandhills Ave TS12 ... 125 E3
Wanless Terr DH1 ... 211 A3
Wansbeck Ave DH9 ... 13 F5
Wansbeck Cl Pelton DH2 ... 15 F7
Spennymoor DL16 ... 55 E2
Wansbeck Ct SR8 ... 49 C4
Wansbeck Gdns TS26 ... 77 A5
Wansbeck Gr DH8 ... 11 D5
Wansford Cl TS23 ... 102 F8
Wansford Way NE16 ... 2 F5
Wanstead Cl TS11 ... 108 C2
Wantage Rd DH1 ... 35 D5
Warbler Cl TS17 ... 138 A1
Warburton Cl DL5 ... 96 F7
Warcop Cl TS7 ... 140 F2
Ward Cl TS18 ... 213 A2
Ward Jackson Prim Sch
TS24 ... 77 C5
Ward Terr DL13 ... 207 E5
Wardale Ave TS5 ... 139 C4
Wardell Cl TS15 ... 156 D4
Warden Cl TS19 ... 117 C7
Warden Gr DH5 ... 26 F7
Wardle St DH9 ... 13 E3
Wardley Cl TS19 ... 117 C7
Wardman Cres TS10 ... 107 E5
Wards Ind Est DL1 ... 133 A4
Ware St
Barnard Castle DL12 ... 209 C6
Stockton-on-T TS20 ... 118 B5
Wareham Way DL15 ... 53 F1
Warelands Way TS4 ... 215 C1
Waring Terr SR7 ... 28 F6
Wark St DH3 ... 16 C1
Warkworth Ave
Bishop Auckland DL14 ... 80 A6
Peterlee SR8 ... 49 F8
Warkworth Cres SR7 ... 28 E7
Warkworth Dr
Chester le Street DH2 ... 24 A8
Hartlepool TS26 ... 76 D6
Warkworth Rd
Billingham TS23 ... 102 C6
Durham DH1 ... 34 C7
Warkworth Way 1 DL1 ... 133 C6
Warnbrook Ave SR7 ... 28 D2
Warnbrook Cres TS27 ... 50 F2
Warner Gr 6 DL3 ... 133 A7
Warren Cl TS24 ... 63 F1
Warren Ct TS24 ... 64 A1
Warren Rd
Hartlepool TS24 ... 64 A2
Newton Aycliffe DL5 ... 96 D4
Warren St Darlington DL3 ... 132 E3
Hartlepool TS24 ... 64 E1
Middlesbrough TS1 ... 214 B2
Peterlee SR8 ... 50 A7
Warren The TS13 ... 149 E6
Warrenby Ct TS10 ... 106 E7
Warrenport Rd TS18 ... 118 D4
Warrior Dr TS25 ... 77 D1
Warrior Terr 2 TS12 ... 125 C7
Warsett Cres TS12 ... 125 E2
Warsett Rd TS11 ... 108 E1
Warton St TS3 ... 120 C4
Warwick Ave DH8 ... 177 A4
Warwick Cl
Eaglescliffe TS16 ... 156 B7
Spennymoor DL16 ... 56 A2
Warwick Cres TS23 ... 102 F3
Warwick Ct DH1 ... 44 A7
Warwick Dr DH5 ... 26 E7
Warwick Gr
Hartlepool TS26 ... 76 F5
Stockton-on-T TS20 ... 118 C7
Warwick Pl
Hartlepool TS24 ... 77 C5
Peterlee SR8 ... 49 B7
Willington DL15 ... 54 A3
Warwick Rd
Bishop Auckland DL14 ... 80 A6
Guisborough TS14 ... 143 D3
Redcar TS10 ... 107 E4
Warwick Road Sch DL14 ... 80 A6
Warwick Sq DL3 ... 132 B5
Warwick St
Middlesbrough TS1 ... 214 B1
South Bank TS6 ... 121 A5
Warwick Terr SR3 ... 18 A8
Warwick Terr W SR3 ... 18 A8
Warwickshire Dr DH1 ... 35 D2
Wasdale Cl
Hartlepool TS24 ... 64 B1
Peterlee SR8 ... 49 E6
Wasdale Dr TS16 ... 156 C8
Wasdale Gr TS19 ... 117 E6
Washbrook Dr DL3 ... 133 A7
Washford Cl TS17 ... 157 A6
Washington Ave DL2 ... 154 B7
Washington Birtley Service
Area DH3 ... 9 E3
Washington Cres DL5 ... 96 F8
Washington Gr TS20 ... 117 F8
Washington Highway
DH4,NE38 ... 17 E8
Washington Hospl NE38 ... 16 E8
Washington Sq SR8 ... 39 B3
Washington St TS2 ... 214 C4
Waskdale Cres NE21 ... 2 B8
Waskerley Cl TS19 ... 117 C7
Waskerley Dr DH6 ... 48 B7
Waskerley Gr DL14 ... 79 F5
Waskerley Pl DL13 ... 207 D5
Waskerley Wlk DL5 ... 96 A7
Wass Way TS16 ... 137 B2
Water Gap DL12 ... 193 D1
Water House Rd DL15 ... 41 E4
Water La Heighington DL5 ... 95 D1
Loftus TS13 ... 147 C8
Water St DH7 ... 23 C3
Water View DL2 ... 153 E8
Waterford Cl DH5 ... 26 D4
Waterford Rd TS20 ... 118 A6
Waterford Terr TS1 ... 214 A1
Watergate La DL15 ... 52 F1
Watergate Rd DH8 ... 176 F3
Waterloo Cl DL15 ... 52 E4
Waterloo Rd
Middlesbrough TS1 ... 214 C2
Middlesbrough TS1 ... 215 A2
Waterloo Terr DL4 ... 80 E2
Waterloo Yd 3 DL12 ... 209 C5
Waters End DL2 ... 201 D3
Waterside DL3 ... 132 C3
Waterside Cotts DL14 ... 66 F1
Waterside Ct DL13 ... 206 C3
Waterside Way TS26 ... 76 C8
Watersmeet Cl TS17 ... 157 B5
Waterson Cres DH7 ... 23 B1
Waterworks The SR2 ... 18 E5
Watery La 19 DL13 ... 195 E3
Watkin Cres SR7 ... 28 C3
Watling Ave SR7 ... 28 F6
Watling Cl Gayles DL11 ... 205 E2
Stockton-on-T TS20 ... 117 F8
Watling Rd DL14 ... 80 B4

Watling St DH8 .... 11 D4
Watling Street Bglws
DH8 .... 11 C5
Watling Terr DL15 .... 53 E4
Watling Way DH7 .... 20 E3
Watness Ave TS12 .... 125 E3
Watson Cl Seaham SR7 .... 28 F6
Wheatley Hill DH6 .... 48 A3
Watson Cres TS29 .... 60 B5
Watson Ct DL12 .... 209 C5
Watson Gr TS17 .... 138 B8
Watson Rd DL5 .... 96 C5
Watson St Burnopfield NE16 .6 B6
Consett DH8 .... 10 E4
High Spen NE39 .... 1 A5
Middlesbrough TS1 .... 215 A3
Spennymoor DL16 .... 68 C5
Stanley DH9 .... 13 F8
Watson's Bldgs DH7 .... 23 B7
Watt St DL17 .... 69 E6
Watton Cl TS25 .... 89 E5
Watton Rd TS17 .... 138 F6
Watts St SR7 .... 28 C3
Waveney Gdns DH9 .... 13 E4
Waveney Gr TS12 .... 125 D3
Waveney Rd Peterlee SR8 .. 49 B4
Redcar TS10 .... 107 A4
Waverley Cl Blaydon NE21 .. 1 F8
Shotton Colliery DH6 .... 48 B7
Waverley St
Middlesbrough TS1 .... 214 B2
Stockton-on-T TS18 .... 212 C1
Waverley Terr
Darlington DL1 .... 133 A1
Dipton DH9 .... 5 E1
Hartlepool TS25 .... 76 F3
Shildon DL4 .... 81 A2
Wayland Terr DL3 .... 132 D5
Waymar Cl TS5 .... 119 C1
Wayside DH6 .... 56 B6
Wayside Ct DH7 .... 33 B3
Wayside Rd
Darlington DL1 .... 133 B7
Middlesbrough TS3 .... 121 A3
Wayside The DL2 .... 152 C1
Wear Ave DH8 .... 11 D5
Wear Bank DL13 .... 207 C3
Wear Chare DL14 .... 67 C1
Wear Cres
Eaglescliffe TS16 .... 156 B7
Great Lumley DH3 .... 25 B7
Wear Ct TS6 .... 120 F4
Wear Lodge DH3 .... 16 C7
Wear Rd Byers Green DL16 .54 E2
Stanley DH9 .... 13 F5
Wear St
Chester le Street DH3 .... 16 D2
Consett DH8 .... 11 A2
Fence Houses DH4 .... 26 A7
Hetton-le-H DH5 .... 27 A3
6 Seaham SR7 .... 29 D7
Spennymoor DL16 .... 68 F8
Tow Law DL13 .... 183 E1
Wear Terr
Bishop Auckland DL14 .... 67 C1
Easington SR8 .... 39 D4
Stanhope DL13 .... 206 D2
Witton-le-W DL14 .... 65 D4
Wear Valley Bsns Ctr
DL14 .... 80 C5
Wear View
Byers Green DL16 .... 54 E1
Durham DH1 .... 211 A3
Frosterley DL13 .... 188 A7
Hunwick DL15 .... 66 E7
Toronto DL14 .... 66 F2
Weardale TS14 .... 143 A2
Weardale Com Hospl
DL13 .... 206 B3
Weardale Cres
Billingham TS23 .... 102 D2
Tow Law DL13 .... 183 D2
Weardale Ct DL15 .... 65 D7
Weardale Dr DL14 .... 79 F4
Weardale Gr TS5 .... 139 E8
Weardale Ho DL13 .... 206 D3
Weardale Mus* DL13 .... 179 D1
Weardale Pk DH6 .... 48 A3
Weardale Pl TS18 .... 212 B4
Weardale Rly* DL13 .... 187 F8
Weardale St
Hetton-le-H DH5 .... 26 E1
Spennymoor DL16 .... 56 B1
Weardale Terr
Annfield Plain DH9 .... 13 A4
Chester le Street DH3 .... 16 D2
Weardale Wlk DL4 .... 81 B1
Weare Gr TS21 .... 99 F3
Wearhead Prim Sch
DL13 .... 179 B2
Wearport Gn 12 TS18 .... 213 C4
Wearside Dr DH1 .... 211 A3
Weary Bank TS15 .... 173 D7
Weastell St TS5 .... 119 E2
Weatherhead Ave TS5 .... 139 B8
Weatherleyhill La DL13 .... 183 A7
Weaver Cl TS17 .... 138 C2
Weaver's Way DL1 .... 133 A2
Weaverham Rd TS20 .... 117 F8
Weaverthorpe TS7 .... 140 F3
Webb Ave Murton SR7 .... 28 C3
Seaham SR7 .... 28 F7
Webb Cl DL5 .... 96 C7
Webb Rd TS6 .... 120 F5
Webb Sq SR8 .... 39 E1
Webster Ave TS5 .... 119 F1
Webster Cl TS18 .... 213 A2
Webster Ho DH1 .... 211 C3
Webster Rd
Billingham TS22 .... 102 C5
Eston TS6 .... 121 E1
Webster St TS18 .... 213 A2
Wederly Cl DL3 .... 132 F4
Wedgwood Rd SR7 .... 28 F6
Weeds DL13 .... 180 A1
Weir St DL1 .... 133 A2
Welbeck Ave DL1 .... 133 E5
Welbeck Ct TS12 .... 125 D3
Welbeck St DL1 .... 152 A8
Welburn Ave TS4 .... 120 A1
Welburn Cl DH6 .... 48 B7
Welburn Gr TS7 .... 141 A7
Welbury Cl TS18 .... 117 B1
Welbury Gr DL5 .... 96 F7
Welbury Way DL5 .... 96 D2
Welby Dr DH7 .... 32 F2
Weldon Cl DH6 .... 48 B7
Weldon Terr DH3 .... 16 D2
Welfare Cl SR8 .... 39 E4
Welfare Cres
Blackhall Colliery TS27 .... 50 C3
South Hetton DH6 .... 38 D6
Welfare Rd DH5 .... 27 A4
Welfare Terr DH6 .... 57 F4
Welford Rd DH8 .... 177 B4
Well Bank Billy Row DL15 .. 52 E8
Low Coniscliffe DL2 .... 150 E8
Newton Aycliffe DL5 .... 96 F2
St John's Chapel DL13 .... 179 D1
Well Chare 7 DL14 .... 81 B8
Well House Dr DL5 .... 82 C1
Well House Ride DL5 .... 82 D1
Well La TS8,TS9 .... 158 E3
Well's Cotts TS16 .... 156 C7
Welland Cl
Middlesbrough TS5 .... 139 C4
Peterlee SR8 .... 49 C4
Welland Cres TS19 .... 117 B5
Welland Rd
Hartlepool TS25 .... 89 E6
Redcar TS10 .... 107 A4
Wellbrook Cl TS17 .... 157 C8
Wellburn Ct TS19 .... 117 B3
Wellburn Rd TS19 .... 117 B3
Welldale Cres TS19 .... 117 B4
Welldeck Gdns TS26 .... 76 F6
Welldeck Rd TS26 .... 76 F6
Wellesley Rd TS4 .... 215 B2
Wellfield Com Sch TS28 .... 60 E8
Wellfield Gn TS19 .... 117 B7
Wellfield Mews SR2 .... 18 E5
Wellfield Rd Murton SR7 .... 28 B3
Rowlands Gill NE39 .... 1 C2
Wingate TS27,TS28 .... 48 E1
Wellfield Rd N TS28 .... 48 E1
Wellfield Rd S TS28 .... 48 E1
Wellfield Terr Ryhope SR2 .18 E5
Wingate TS27 .... 48 F1
Wellgarth DL14 .... 92 C6
Wellgarth Ct DL15 .... 66 A6
Wellgarth Mews TS21 .... 72 A1
Wellhope NE38 .... 16 F8
Wellington Cl
Marske-by-t-S TS11 .... 108 B1
Middlesbrough TS2 .... 214 C4
Wellington Court Mews 20
DL1 .... 132 F1
Wellington Ct TS18 .... 137 E6
Wellington Dr TS22 .... 87 D1
Wellington Rd DL12 .... 209 C7
Wellington Sq TS18 .... 213 A3
Wellington St
High Pittington DH6 .... 36 B5
Middlesbrough TS2 .... 214 C4
Stockton-on-T TS18 .... 213 A3
Wellington Terr DH7 .... 23 A7
Wellmead Rd TS3 .... 120 F3
Wells Ave TS24 .... 64 A2
Wells Cl Darlington DL1 .... 133 E5
Eston TS6 .... 121 E2
Wells Cres SR7 .... 28 F7
Wells Gr Redcar TS10 .... 107 F4
Willington DL15 .... 53 F2
Wells St TS24 .... 64 F1
Wellspring Cl TS5 .... 139 B5
Wellsprings Bsns Ctr
DH6 .... 57 D8
Welsh Terr DH9 .... 13 A3
Welton Ho TS3 .... 121 A1
Wembley Ct TS18 .... 212 C2
Wembley St TS1 .... 214 A2
Wembley Way
Normanby TS6 .... 141 C7
Stockton-on-T TS18 .... 212 C2
Wembury Cl TS10 .... 107 E2
Wensley Cl DH2 .... 8 E1
Wensley Rd TS18 .... 212 A3
Wensley Terr DL17 .... 70 C3
Wensleydale TS12 .... 125 B3
Wensleydale Gr TS17 .... 157 B6
Wensleydale Rd DL1 .... 133 A5
Wensleydale Sq DL14 .... 79 F5
Wensleydale St TS25 .... 77 B3
Wentworth Cres TS11 .... 123 F6
Wentworth Ct 1 TS6 .... 121 E1
Wentworth Gr TS27 .... 63 D3
Wentworth Ho 2 TS6 .... 121 E1
Wentworth St TS1 .... 214 B2
Wentworth Way
Darlington DL3 .... 132 A5
Eaglescliffe TS16 .... 156 C8
Werdohl Way DH8 .... 11 B4
Wesley Cl DH9 .... 14 B7
Wesley Cres 6 DL4 .... 81 A2
Wesley Ct
2 Annfield Plain DH9 .... 12 F4
7 Darlington DL1 .... 133 B1
Wesley Gdns DH8 .... 177 A3
Wesley Gr DL14 .... 80 B7
Wesley Mall TS1 .... 214 C3
Wesley Pl TS20 .... 118 B7
Wesley Row TS1 .... 214 B3
Wesley Sq 4 TS24 .... 77 B6
Wesley St Consett DH8 .... 10 F2
Consett, Blackhill DH8 .... 10 D4
Coundon Grange DL14 .... 80 F5
Crook DL15 .... 52 E4
9 Darlington DL1 .... 133 B1
Willington DL15 .... 54 A3
Wesley Terr
Annfield Plain DH9 .... 12 F4
Chester le Street DH3 .... 16 C3
Consett DH8 .... 177 A3
Dipton DH9 .... 5 D1
Middleton-In-T DL12 .... 208 B5
Sherburn Hill DH6 .... 36 C1
Skinningrove TS13 .... 126 F3
Wesley View DL13 .... 207 D5
Wesley Way SR7 .... 28 F7
Wesleyan Rd DL16 .... 68 F8
West Acre DH8 .... 10 C5
West Auckland Rd
Darlington DL2,DL3 .... 132 C6
Shildon DL14,DL4 .... 80 C1
Walworth DL2 .... 111 D5
West Ave
Billingham TS23 .... 102 D1
Easington SR8 .... 39 E5
Murton SR7 .... 28 C3
Rowlands Gill NE39 .... 1 D1
Saltburn-by-t-S TS12 .... 125 B7
Waldridge DH2 .... 24 A7
Washington NE38 .... 17 B8
West Beck Gr DL3 .... 132 A2
West Beck Way TS8 .... 140 C3
West Blackdene DL13 .... 179 C2
West Block DH7 .... 33 A8
West Brandon Rd DL15 .... 41 E3
West Bridge St
Crook DL15 .... 52 F4
Penshaw DH4 .... 17 E8
West Chilton Terr DL17 .... 69 E1
West Cl Chilton DL17 .... 69 F3
High Coniscliffe DL2 .... 130 E4
Shildon DL4 .... 80 E1
West Coatham La TS10 .. 106 D4
West Cornforth Prim Sch
DL17 .... 57 E1
West Coronation St SR7 .. 28 D3
West Cres Chopwell NE17 .... 4 B7
Darlington DL3 .... 132 E3
Easington SR8 .... 39 D4
Middlesbrough TS5 .... 119 B1
West Dale View DL13 .... 183 D2
West Dr
Chester le Street DH2 .... 15 F2
Lanchester DH7 .... 20 E3
West Dyke Rd TS10 .... 107 C3
West Ellen St SR7 .... 28 D2
West End
Guisborough TS14 .... 143 D4
Hunwick DL15 .... 66 D7
Hurworth-on-T DL2 .... 152 C1
Hutton Rudby TS15 .... 173 F1
Sedgefield TS21 .... 85 A6
West End Ave TS14 .... 143 D4
West End Cl TS13 .... 149 E6
West End Gdns TS15 .... 156 B7
West End Terr
7 Cockfield DL13 .... 195 E3
Willington DL15 .... 53 E3
West End Villas DL15 .... 52 D4
West End Way TS18 .... 137 E8
West Fall DL13 .... 179 B2
West Farm Burdon SR3 .... 18 B3
Medomsley DH8 .... 4 C2
West Farm Ct DH7 .... 43 C8
West Farm La DH8 .... 4 C2
West Fields DL5 .... 95 F4
West Garth TS21 .... 116 C8
West Gn DL5 .... 95 D1
West Gr Seaham SR7 .... 28 F7
Trimdon TS29 .... 59 D1
West Hartlepool Rd
TS22 .... 102 C8
West Haswicks DL13 .... 186 A8
West Haven DH8 .... 10 E3
West High Horse Cl NE39 .. 2 A4
West La
Bishop Auckland DL14 .... 79 F4
Blaydon NE21 .... 2 A8
Boldron DL12 .... 199 A1
Byermoor NE16 .... 2 C1
Chester le Street DH3 .... 16 C2
Dalton-on-T DL2 .... 168 A1
Eston TS6 .... 121 D6
Gainford DL11 .... 201 D1
Medomsley NE17 .... 4 B4
Middlesbrough TS5 .... 119 B2
Middlesbrough TS5 .... 119 C2
Satley DL13 .... 183 B8
South Hetton DH6,SR7 .... 38 D6
Trimdon TS29 .... 59 B1
West Lane Hospl TS5 .... 119 C2
West Law Rd DH8 .... 10 D8
West Lea Blaydon NE21 .... 2 C8
Witton Gilbert DH7 .... 33 B8
West Leigh DH9 .... 13 D8
West Mews TS15 .... 156 B6
West Moor Cl TS15 .... 156 E5
West Moor Rd DL1 .... 152 C7
West Ousterley Rd DH9 .... 13 F3
West Par Consett DH8 .... 11 A2
Coxhoe DH6 .... 57 F5
Leadgate DH8 .... 11 C4
West Park Ave TS13 .... 127 B1
West Park La TS21 .... 85 A6
West Park Prim Sch
TS26 .... 76 C5
West Pasture Rd DL12 .... 192 F1
West Pelton Prim Sch
DH9 .... 14 F6
West Pk Coundon DL14 .... 68 A1
Hartlepool TS26 .... 76 D6
West Powlett St DL3 .... 132 E1
West Prec TS23 .... 102 D4
West Rainton Prim Sch
DH4 .... 25 F1
West Rd Annfield Plain DH9 .12 F3
Billingham TS23 .... 102 D1
Bishop Auckland DL14 .... 80 B8
Consett DH8 .... 10 C4
Crook DL15 .... 52 D3
Loftus TS13 .... 127 B1
Shildon DL4 .... 80 E1
Tantobie DH9 .... 6 A1
Willington DL15 .... 53 E3
West Redcar Com Sch
TS10 .... 107 A4
West Redcar Comp Sch
Annexe TS10 .... 107 B6
West Row Birtley DH3 .... 9 E3
Darlington DL1 .... 132 F1
Eston TS6 .... 121 F2
Greatham TS25 .... 89 E4
Middlesbrough TS5 .... 119 B1
Sadberge DL2 .... 134 E6
Stockton-on-T TS18 .... 213 A2
West Scar TS10 .... 107 D3
West Shield Row Villas
DH9 .... 13 E8
West Side Marton TS7 .... 140 D4
Mount Pleasant TS7 .... 160 C7
West Springs DL15 .... 52 E3
West St Billingham TS2 .... 119 F8
5 Birtley DH3 .... 9 C4
Blackhall Colliery TS27 .... 50 D3
Cornforth DL17 .... 57 D1
Darlington DL3 .... 132 F1
Eston, Normanby TS6 .... 121 D1
8 Eston,California TS6 .... 121 F2
Ferryhill DL17 .... 69 F6
Gayles DL11 .... 205 E2
Hett DH6 .... 56 E6
Leadgate DH8 .... 11 C4
Middlesbrough TS2 .... 119 E7
New Silksworth SR3 .... 18 A8
Seaham SR7 .... 29 D7
Shotton Colliery DH6 .... 48 C6
Stillington TS21 .... 99 E3
Tanfield Lea DH9 .... 13 D8
West Pelton DH2 .... 15 A5
Yarm TS15 .... 156 B6
West St Cotts TS27 .... 50 C3
West Terr Billy Row DL15 .... 52 E7
Burnhope DH7 .... 21 D5
Coxhoe DH6 .... 57 F5
Durham DH1 .... 210 B3
Evenwood DL14 .... 92 C7
Fishburn TS21 .... 72 B5
Great Ayton TS9 .... 160 F2
Middlesbrough TS3 .... 215 C2
5 New Marske TS11 .... 124 A6
Newton Aycliffe DL5 .... 96 E2
Redcar TS10 .... 107 C7
3 Skelton TS12 .... 125 A2
Spennymoor DL16 .... 68 D7
2 Staindrop DL2 .... 200 E7
Stanhope DL13 .... 206 C3
Woodland DL13 .... 194 F5
West View
8 Barnard Castle DL12 .. 209 C5
Bishop Auckland, South Church
DL14 .... 80 D5
Bishop Auckland, Tindale Crescent
DL14 .... 79 F3
Bishop Middleham DL17 .... 71 C4
Bournmoor DH4 .... 17 E3
Brandon DH7 .... 43 C3
Burnopfield NE16 .... 6 A6
Butterknowle DL13 .... 195 C4
Castleside DH8 .... 176 F3
Chester le Street DH3 .... 16 C4
Consett DH8 .... 10 D5
Cornforth DL17 .... 57 E1
Crook DL15 .... 53 A3
Darlington DL3 .... 132 A1
Durham DH1 .... 211 B3
Easington SR8 .... 39 B3
East Hedleyhope DL13 .... 40 D5
Esh Winning DH7 .... 41 E7
Esh Winning DH7 .... 41 E8
Evenwood DL14 .... 92 D6
11 Ferryhill DL17 .... 70 A6
Gainford DL2 .... 201 D4
Hunwick DL15 .... 66 D7
Kibblesworth NE11 .... 8 D6
Kirk Merrington DL16 .... 68 F3
Lanchester DH7 .... 20 F3
Medomsley DH8 .... 11 A8
Murton SR7 .... 28 C2
Newfield DL14 .... 67 B7
2 Peterlee SR8 .... 50 A7
Redcar TS10 .... 107 D6
Ryhope SR2 .... 18 E6
Sacriston DH7 .... 23 B3
Sherburn Hill DH6 .... 36 C1
Shildon DL14 .... 93 D8
West View Cl 4 TS16 .... 137 B1
West View Gdns DH9 .... 13 E7
West View Prim Sch
TS24 .... 63 F2
West View Rd TS24 .... 64 A3
West View Terr
Eaglescliffe TS16 .... 137 B1
Seaton Carew TS25 .... 90 E8
Shildon DL4 .... 80 E3
West Villas DH9 .... 15 A6
Westacres DL2 .... 153 E7
Westbank Rd TS7 .... 141 B6
Westbeck Gdns TS5 .... 139 E8
Westborough Gr TS18 .... 117 A1
Westbourne Gr
Darlington DL3 .... 132 D1
Eston TS6 .... 121 B3
Middlesbrough TS3 .... 215 C2
Redcar TS10 .... 107 C7
Westbourne Rd
Hartlepool TS25 .... 77 A4
Middlesbrough TS5 .... 119 C1
Westbourne St TS18 .... 213 A1
Westbrook DL3 .... 132 F3
Westbrook Terr 3 DL3 .... 132 F3
Westbrooke Ave TS25 .... 77 A2
Westbrooke Gr TS25 .... 77 A2
Westbury St TS17 .... 138 C8
Westcliff Cl SR8 .... 39 A3
Westcliffe Ct DL3 .... 132 E1
Westcott Dr
Auckland Park DL14 .... 80 E6
Durham DH1 .... 34 A5
Westcott Ho TS3 .... 120 C2
Westcott Rd SR8 .... 49 D7
Westcott St TS18 .... 213 A1
Westcott Terr DL17 .... 69 E5
Westcott Wlk DL5 .... 96 D5
Westcroft
1 Middlesbrough TS3 .... 120 C2
Stanhope DL13 .... 206 C3
Westcroft Rd TS6 .... 121 E6
Westdale Rd TS17 .... 138 D5
Westerby Rd TS3 .... 120 D5
Westerdale Penshaw DH4 .. 17 E8
Spennymoor DL16 .... 55 E1
Westerdale Ave
Redcar TS10 .... 107 A4
Stockton-on-T TS19 .... 212 B4
Westerdale Ct
Darlington DL3 .... 132 C6
Guisborough TS14 .... 143 D4
Westerdale Gdns DL4 .... 81 B1
Westerdale Rd
Hartlepool TS25 .... 90 D7
Middlesbrough TS3 .... 120 C2
Westerham Gr TS4 .... 140 A7
Westerhope Ct DL3 .... 132 C6
Westerleigh Ave TS19 .... 117 B3
Western Ave DH7 .... 31 D1
Western Hill Consett DH8 .. 10 C5
Frosterley DL13 .... 188 A7
Ryhope SR2 .... 18 E7
Western Lodge Cotts
DH1 .... 34 A4
Western Terr N SR7 .... 28 D3
Western Terr S SR7 .... 28 D3
Westernmoor NE37 .... 9 F6
Westerton Cl DL14 .... 68 B5
Westerton Gn 5 TS19 .... 117 B7
Westerton Rd
9 Billingham TS23 .... 102 E8
Coundon DL14 .... 68 C1
Westerton View 6 DL14 .. 81 B8
Westfield DL13 .... 188 A8
Westfield Ave TS10 .... 107 C6
Westfield Cl TS6 .... 121 B1
Westfield Cres TS19 .... 117 E6
Westfield Ct
Redcar TS10 .... 106 E4
Stockton-on-T TS19 .... 117 E5
Westfield Dr Crook DL15 .... 52 C3
Darlington DL3 .... 132 C2
Hurworth-on-T DL2 .... 152 D1
Westfield Rd
Bishop Auckland DL14 .... 80 B6
Eston TS6 .... 121 C1
Marske-by-t-S TS11 .... 108 A1
Westfield Terr
Bishop Middleham DL17 .... 71 B4
Loftus TS13 .... 127 B1
Westfield Way
Loftus TS13 .... 127 B2
Redcar TS10 .... 106 E4
Westfield Wlk TS13 .... 127 B2
Westfields
Spennymoor DL16 .... 55 E1
Stanley DH9 .... 13 E5
Westgarth Cl TS11 .... 108 C1
Westgarth Gr DH6 .... 48 C7
Westgarth Prim Sch
TS11 .... 108 C1
Westgarth Terr DL1 .... 133 C3
Westgate
Guisborough TS14 .... 143 E4
Yarm TS15 .... 156 B6
Westgate Ave SR3 .... 18 A8
Westgate Cres DL3 .... 132 C6
Westgate Gr SR3 .... 18 A8
Westgate Rd
Bishop Auckland DL14 .... 80 B8
Darlington DL3 .... 132 C6
Guisborough TS14 .... 143 E4
Middlesbrough TS5 .... 139 C8
Westhills DH9 .... 6 A2
Westhills Cl DH7 .... 23 B5
Westholme TS15 .... 173 F1
Westholme Ct TS23 .... 102 F6
Westkirk Cl DL3 .... 132 C6

Westland Ave TS26 76 F4
Westland Way TS18 138 A7
Westlands Bowburn DH6 57 E6
Kirklevington TS15 172 D8
Westlands Ave 7 TS20 118 B7
Westlands Rd
Darlington DL3 132 D4
Egglescliffe TS16 156 B8
Westlands Sch TS17 138 E3
Westlea Ave DL14 80 C6
Westlea Prim Sch SR7 28 F8
Westlea Rd SR7 28 F7
Westline Ind Est DH2 9 B2
Westlowthian St TS2 119 F8
Westminster Cl TS6 121 E2
Westminster Oval TS20 102 A2
Westminster Rd
Darlington DL1 152 D7
Middlesbrough TS5 119 E2
Westmoor Cl DL16 68 D7
Westmoreland St
Darlington DL3 132 F5
3 Hartlepool TS25 77 B4
Westmoreland Wlk 14
TS25 77 B4
Westmorland Cl DL16 56 B2
Westmorland Ct DL3 133 A5
Westmorland Gr TS20 101 F2
Westmorland Pl DL15 54 A3
Westmorland Rd
Middlesbrough TS5 119 D2
Redcar TS10 107 C4
Westmorland Rise SR8 49 B8
Westmorland Way DL5 96 D7
Weston Ave
Middlesbrough TS3 120 F4
Whickham NE16 2 F5
Weston Cres TS20 118 C6
Weston View SR8 49 C7
Westpark Dr DL3 132 C6
Westpoint Rd
Darlington DL1 133 E2
Thornaby-on-T TS17 213 C2
Westport Cl TS18 213 C4
Westray
Chester le Street DH2 16 B1
Marton TS8 140 E1
Westray Cl 3 SR2 18 E8
Westray St TS13 126 F3
Westview Terr DH9 12 E3
Westward Cl TS1 214 C3
Westward Pl NE38 17 B8
Westway SR8 49 C5
Westwick Rd DL12 209 E4
Westwick Terr TS4 140 B5
Westwood Ave
Heighington DL5 95 C1
Middlesbrough TS5 139 E8
Nunthorpe TS7 141 B3
Westwood Cl NE16 6 B7
Westwood La TS17 157 C8
Westwood Terr DL17 82 F8
Westwood View
Chester le Street DH3 16 C1
Sacriston DH7 23 B2
Westwood Way TS27 63 C3
Westworth Cl TS15 156 E4
Wetherall Ave TS15 156 B3
Wetherburn Ave SR7 28 B3
Wetherby Cl Consett DH8 10 D7
Stockton-on-T TS18 118 E5
Wetherby Gn TS3 141 A8
Wetherell Cl TS11 124 E8
Wetherfell Cl TS17 157 A6
Wetlands La DL11 205 C5
Weymouth Ave TS8 140 B4
Weymouth Dr
Hartlepool TS24 63 D4
Seaham SR7 29 A6
Shiney Row DH4 17 F5
Weymouth Rd TS18 117 C2
Whaddon Chase TS14 143 F3
Whale Hill Prim Sch
TS6 121 F3
Whalton Cl DH6 36 A1
Wharf St TS18 213 B2
Wharfdale TS12 125 C4
Wharfdale Ave TS23 102 D2
Wharfe Way DL1 152 A6
Wharfedale Cl TS17 157 B7
Wharnley Way DH8 176 F3
Wharrier Sq DH6 47 E1
Wharton Cl
East Rainton DH5 26 D4
Yarm TS15 156 E4
Wharton Pl TS12 145 C7
Wharton St Coundon DL14 81 B8
Hartlepool TS24 77 B6
Skelton TS12 125 F1
Wharton Terr
Hartlepool TS24 77 B8
Woodland DL13 194 F5
Wheat Cl DH8 10 E7
Wheatacre Cl 1 TS11 124 E8
Wheatbottom DL15 53 A3
Wheatear Cl 1 NE38 9 F3
Wheatear Dr TS10 107 D2
Wheatear La TS17 138 A1
Wheatfield Gdns DL15 53 A3
Wheatlands TS9 161 A3
Wheatlands Cl TS14 143 F3
Wheatlands Dr
Loftus TS13 148 A8
Marske-by-t-S TS11 108 C1
Wheatlands Pk TS10 107 D2
Wheatlands Prim Sch
TS10 107 E3
Wheatley Cl TS5 139 D4
Wheatley Green La DH7 22 D8
Wheatley Hill Prim Sch
DH6 47 E2
Wheatley Rd TS19 117 B7
Wheatley Terr DH6 47 E2
Wheatley Wlk TS19 117 C7
Wheatleywell La DH2,
DH3 24 B5
Wheeldale Ave TS10 107 A4
Wheeldale Cl DL1 133 C5
Wheeldale Cres TS17 138 D5
Wheeldrake Cl TS14 143 E6
Wheldon Terr DH2 15 E7
Wheler Gn 1 DL5 96 E8
Whernside
Nunthorpe TS7 140 F2
Skelton TS12 125 B3
Whernside Cres TS17 157 B7
Whessoe Rd
Darlington DL3 132 F6
Stockton-on-T TS19 117 C7
Whessoe Wlk TS19 117 C7
Whickham Cl
Houghton-le-S DH4 26 C8
Middlesbrough TS3 120 C5
Whickham Ind Est NE16 2 F8
Whickham Parochial CE Prim
Sch NE16 2 F5
Whickham Rd TS19 117 B7
Whickham St SR8 39 D4
Whin Mdws TS24 63 E3
Whin St TS1 214 C3
Whinbank Pk DL5 96 D3
Whinbank Rd DL5 96 C3
Whinbush Way DL1 133 E7
Whinchat Cl
Hartlepool TS26 63 E1
Ingleby Barwick TS17 138 B1
Whinchat Tail TS14 143 B4
Whindyke TS27 50 C3
Whinfell Ave TS16 137 B2
Whinfell Cl TS7 140 F2
Whinfield Ave DH6 48 C6
Whinfield Cl TS19 117 A5
Whinfield Dr DL5 96 D2
Whinfield Ind Est NE39 1 C1
Whinfield Prim Sch
DL1 133 E6
Whinfield Rd DL1 133 D6
Whinfield Terr NE39 1 D2
Whinfield Way NE39 1 C1
Whinflower Dr TS20 101 F1
Whingroves TS17 138 F7
Whinlatter Cl TS19 212 C3
Whinlatter Pl DL5 96 A6
Whinney Banks Prim Sch
TS5 139 B8
Whinney Banks Rd TS5 119 B1
Whinney Cl NE21 2 A8
Whinney Hill DH1 211 A1
Whinny La DH8 3 E1
Whinny Pl 3 DH8 177 A3
Whinside DH9 13 D7
Whinston Cl TS26 76 C7
Whinstone Dr TS8 139 C1
Whinstone Prim Sch
TS17 138 B2
Whinstone View TS9 161 A3
Whisperdale Ct TS3 120 E2
Whitburn Cl DH7 32 B6
Whitburn Rd TS19 117 B7
Whitburn St TS24 77 B4
Whitby Ave Eston TS6 121 E3
Guisborough TS14 143 F4
Whitby Cl
Bishop Auckland DL14 79 E6
Skelton TS12 125 D2
Whitby Cres TS10 107 F4
Whitby Gr 4 TS24 77 C5
Whitby Rd
Guisborough TS14 144 C5
Loftus TS13 127 E1
Nunthorpe TS7 141 B3
Thornaby-on-T TS17 138 D7
Whitby St Hartlepool TS24 77 C5
Hartlepool TS26 77 C4
Whitby Way DL3 132 A5
Whitby Wlk TS24 77 C5
Whitchurch Cl TS17 157 A6
White Cedars DH7 43 A3
White Cres TS27 50 A1
White Gates Dr DH5 27 B2
White Hart Cres DL1 133 E3
White Hart Ct TS27 62 F2
White Hill Rd DH5 37 C8
White House Ave 4 DH7 32 F2
White House Croft
TS21 136 A6
White House Dr TS21 85 B7
White House La DL2 94 F2
White House Rd TS17 138 B5
White Kirkley DL13 188 A6
White Lea Cl SR8 49 F5
White Lea Rd DL15 52 C8
White St TS3 120 C3
White Stone Cl TS10 107 F3
White-le-Head Gdns DH9 6 A1
Whitebeam Ct 4 TS4 139 F8
Whitebridge Dr DL1 133 C7
Whitecliff Terr TS13 127 B1
Whitecliffe Prim Sch
TS13 126 E3
Whitegates Rd DH6 35 F2
Whitehall Cotts CA9 178 A7
Whitehall La DH8 11 F1
Whitehead Wlk DL5 96 F8
Whitehill Cres DH2 15 E4
Whitehill Hall Gdns DH2 16 A4
Whitehouse Ave DH7 21 D4
Whitehouse Cres DH6 48 F6
Whitehouse Ct
Easington SR8 39 B3
Peterlee SR8 49 B8
Ushaw Moor DH7 33 A2
Whitehouse Dr TS19 212 A4
Whitehouse Ind Pk DH6 48 E6
Whitehouse La DH7 32 F2
Whitehouse Prim Sch
TS19 117 D5
Whitehouse Rd
Billingham TS22 102 B5
Spennymoor DL16 68 F7
Whitehouse St TS5 214 A2
Whitehouse Terr DH7 21 D5
Whitehouse Way SR8 48 F6
Whiteley Gr DL5 96 D8
Whitemeadows DL3 132 C2
Whiteoak Ave DH1 35 B3
Whiteoaks Cl TS10 107 F2
Whitesmocks DH1 34 A4
Whitesmocks Ave DH1 210 A4
Whitestone Bsns Pk
TS4 215 B2
Whitethroat Cl 6 NE38 9 F3
Whitfield Ave TS4 215 B2
Whitfield Bldgs TS4 215 B2
Whitfield Brow DL13 187 E5
Whitfield Cl TS16 137 B1
Whitfield Dr TS25 77 B2
Whitfield Rd TS20 101 F1
Whitfield St Consett DH8 11 A3
Crook DL15 52 E4
Whithorn Gr TS8 139 E3
Whitley Rd TS17 138 D4
Whitrout Rd TS24 63 E3
Whitton Cl TS5 139 B6
Whitton Ct DL5 82 E1
Whitton Gr TS21 99 E3
Whitton Rd TS19 117 C3
Whitwell Acres DH1 45 C4
Whitwell Cl TS18 213 A1
Whitwell Ct DH1 35 A3
Whitwell Pl TS12 145 F5
Whitwell Rd DL1 133 D1
Whitwell Terr Crook DL15 52 D5
Guisborough TS14 143 E5
Whitworth Ave DL5 96 D3
Whitworth Cl DL16 68 D7
Whitworth Dr DL5 96 D3
Whitworth Gdns TS25 76 F1
Whitworth Hall Ctry Pk*
DL16 55 B2
Whitworth La DH7,DL16 54 F6
Whitworth Mdws DL16 68 C5
Whitworth Rd
Shotton Colliery SR8 48 F6
Spennymoor DL16 68 D8
Washington NE37 9 F7
Whitworth Sch DL16 68 E6
Whitworth Terr DL16 68 E8
Whorlton Cl TS14 143 D2
Whorlton Lido* DL12 200 C1
Whorlton Rd
Billingham TS22 102 B5
Middlesbrough TS2 119 D8
Stockton-on-T TS19 117 B7
Wibsey Ave TS3 140 E7
Wickets The
Hutton Rudby TS15 173 E1
Marton TS7 140 C4
Seaton Carew TS25 90 E7
Wicklow St TS1 214 B1
Widdowfield St DL3 132 F3
Widdrington Ct TS19 117 A6
Widecombe Wlk DL17 70 C5
Widgeon Rd DL1 133 E1
Wigdan Walls Rd DL14 79 D6
Wigeon Cl NE38 9 F2
Wigham Terr NE16 6 A4
Wigton Sands TS5 139 B3
Wilbore Croft DL5 95 F5
Wild Rd DL1 134 A1
Wilder Gr TS25 76 D3
Wildgoose La DL1 97 E5
Wilfred St
Chester le Street DH3 16 C2
Stockton-on-T TS18 212 C2
Wilfrid St DH3 9 C3
Wilk's Hill DH7 31 A4
Wilken Cres TS14 143 F6
Wilkes St DL3 132 F3
Wilkinson Rd
Newton Aycliffe DL5 96 E6
Peterlee SR8 39 E1
Wilkinson St
Byers Green DL16 67 E8
Lingdale TS12 145 D5
Stockton-on-T TS20 118 B5
Wilkinson Terr SR2 18 E6
Willan's Bldgs DH1 211 C3
Willard Gr DL13 206 E2
Willard Grove E DL13 206 E2
Willerby Gn TS5 139 C8
Willerby Gr SR8 49 B7
Willey Flatt La TS15 156 B4
William Cassidi CE Prim Sch
TS21 99 F4
William Crosthwaite Ave
TS17 157 D8
William Johnson St SR7 28 D2
William Keers Cres The
DL17 69 D5
William Morris Ave NE39 1 B2
William Morris Terr DH6 48 C5
William Pl DH1 211 C3
William Russell Homes
DH7 42 E1
William St
Annfield Plain DH9 13 A3
Auckland Park DL14 80 F6
Bowburn DH6 45 D1
Chester le Street DH3 16 C3
Craghead DH9 14 C2
Darlington DL3 132 F5
7 Eston TS6 121 F2
Ferryhill DL17 70 D2
Hartlepool TS24 77 C5
Middlesbrough TS2 214 C4
Pelton DH2 15 C5
Redcar TS10 107 D6
Skelton TS12 125 D2
Stanley DH9 13 D4
Stockton-on-T TS18 213 A2
William Terr 2 TS20 118 B6
Williamfield Way DL5 96 A6
Williams Ave TS5 119 B1
Williams Cl DH9 14 A5
Williams Rd SR7 28 C3
Williams St TS12 125 F1
Williams Terr SR2 18 E6
Williamson Sq TS28 60 D8
Willington CE Prim Sch
DL15 54 A2
Willington Prim Sch
DL15 53 F3
Willington Rd TS19 117 B8
Willins Cl TS15 173 E1
Willis St DH5 27 A5
Willow Ave DL15 52 D4
Willow Chase The TS21 135 F5
Willow Cl Brandon DH7 43 B3
Saltburn-by-t-S TS12 125 A6
Thornaby-on-T TS17 138 C6
Willow Cres
Easington Lane DH5 27 D1
Leadgate DH8 11 D3
Willow Ct Coxhoe DH6 57 F4
High Etherley DL14 78 E5
Willow Dr Brotton TS12 126 A4
Normanby TS6 141 C8
Trimdon TS29 72 E8
Willow Gr Hartlepool TS24 77 A8
Peterlee SR8 50 B5
Willow Pk DH7 32 A6
Willow Pl DL1 133 A1
Willow Rd
Darlington DL3 132 D4
Esh Winning DH7 31 D1
Ferryhill DL17 70 A6
Guisborough TS14 143 E5
Houghton-le-S DH4 26 C8
Spennymoor DL16 68 C6
Stockton-on-T TS19 117 F5
Willow Rd E DL3 132 E4
Willow Terr TS2 103 E1
Willow Tree Ave
Durham DH1 35 A3
Shincliffe DH1 45 A6
Willow View NE16 6 A6
Willow Wlk
2 Hartlepool TS24 77 A8
Loftus TS13 127 B2
Shildon DL4 81 B1
Willowbank TS8 140 B1
Willowdene Ave TS18 137 E8
Willows Ave TS8 157 F8
Willows Ct TS17 138 E1
Willows Rd TS5 119 E1
Willows The
Bishop Auckland DL14 80 C8
Durham DH1 35 D5
Marton TS7 140 E4
Redcar TS10 107 E5
Sedgefield TS21 85 A5
Stockton-on-T TS19 117 D5
Willowvale DH2 16 A5
Wilmire Rd TS22 102 C5
Wilmore Rd TS10 107 C6
Wilson Ave Birtley DH3 9 C5
Coundon DL14 81 B8
Wilson Cres DH1 35 A3
Wilson Pl SR8 49 D8
Wilson St
Barnard Castle DL12 209 C5
Brotton TS12 126 B4
Crook DL15 52 E4
Darlington DL3 132 F4
Eldon Lane DL14 80 F4
Guisborough TS14 143 D4
Hartlepool TS26 76 F6
Lingdale TS12 145 E6
Middlesbrough TS1 214 C4
Stanley Crook DL15 52 F8
Thornaby-on-T TS17 118 D1
Wilson Terr
New Silksworth SR3 18 A8
Skinningrove TS13 127 A4
Wilson Wlk DL5 96 D5
Wilstrop Gn TS3 140 D7
Wilton Ave
Hartlepool TS26 76 F5
Redcar TS10 106 D4
Wilton Bank TS12 125 A6
Wilton Castle TS10 122 E4
Wilton Cl DL3 132 B2
Wilton Ct DL5 95 F7
Wilton Dr DL3 132 B2
Wilton Gn TS6 122 C4
Wilton La
Guisborough TS14 143 D7
Redcar TS10,TS14 122 F3
Wilton Prim Sch TS6 122 C4
Wilton Rd TS26 77 A5
Wilton St
Middlesbrough TS1 214 C2
Redcar TS10 107 C7
Wilton Village TS10 122 E4
Wilton Way TS6 121 F4
Wiltshire Cl DH1 35 C3
Wiltshire Rd TS12 125 A2
Wiltshire Way TS26 76 E8
Wiltshire Wlk TS20 118 C6
Wimbledon Cl DL1 133 E3
Wimbledon Ct TS5 139 C8
Wimbledon Rd TS5 139 C8
Wimborne Cl DL3 132 A5
Wimpole Rd TS19 117 A4
Wincanton Rd TS10 107 D4
Winchester Cl DH3 25 A7
Winchester Ct DL16 55 E3
Winchester Dr
Brandon DH7 43 A2
Shotton Colliery SR8 48 F5
Winchester Rd
Brotton TS12 126 C4
Durham DH1 34 E7
Middlesbrough TS5 119 F2
Redcar TS10 107 F4
Winchester Way DL1 133 F5
Winchester Wlk TS26 76 E8
Wind Mill DL14 195 F7
Windermere Birtley DH3 9 D2
Spennymoor DL16 55 E2
Windermere Ave
Billingham TS23 102 E1
Chester le Street DH2 16 C1
Easington Lane DH5 37 C8
Redcar TS10 107 C5
Redmarshall TS21 116 B7
Windermere Cres NE21 2 B8
Windermere Ct DL1 152 B8
Windermere Dr
Bishop Auckland DL14 79 B1
Skelton TS12 125 B3
Windermere Gdns DL15 52 F2
Windermere Rd
Ferryhill DL17 69 F5
Hartlepool TS25 77 B2
Hartlepool TS25 77 C2
Middlesbrough TS5 119 D1
Seaham SR7 28 E7
South Hetton DH6,SR7 38 B7
Stockton-on-T TS18 212 B3
Windermere Terr DH9 13 D5
Windgroves DL17 82 E8
Windleston Cl 1 TS19 117 B7
Windleston Dr TS3 140 D6
Windlestone Hall Sch
DL17 82 A6
Windlestone La DL16,
DL17 82 B8
Windlestone Rd TS23 102 F6
Windlestone Wlk 4 DL5 96 E8
Windmill Hill DH1 44 B7
Windmill Terr TS20 118 B6
Windrush Gr DL1 133 B7
Winds La SR7 28 B3
Winds Lonnen Est SR7 28 A3
Windsor Ave
Ferryhill DL17 70 A6
Spennymoor DL16 68 E7
Windsor Cl DL5 82 F2
Windsor Cres
Houghton-le-S DH5 26 F8
Nunthorpe TS7 141 A3
Windsor Ct
Bishop Auckland DL14 80 B8
Chester le Street DH3 16 D2
Darlington DL3 132 A5
Eston TS6 121 E4
Peterlee SR8 39 A3
Rowlands Gill NE39 1 F2
2 Shildon DL4 95 A8
Sunderland Bridge DH6 56 B7
Windsor Dr
Annfield Plain DH9 12 F5
Houghton-le-S DH5 26 E6
Lingdale TS12 145 F5
New Silksworth SR3 18 A7
South Hetton DH6 37 F8
Windsor Gdns
Consett DH8 11 A2
Middlesbrough TS2 215 A4
Shildon DL4 81 A1
Wingate TS29 59 F5
Windsor Oval TS17 138 C6
Windsor Pl DH6 48 D6
Windsor Rd Birtley DH3 9 B6
Eston TS6 121 D1
Middlesbrough TS5 119 D1
Redcar TS10 107 E4
Saltburn-by-t-S TS12 125 C7
Seaham SR7 28 F7
Stockton-on-T TS18 212 B2
Thornaby-on-T TS17 138 C6
Windsor Sq TS29 72 D8
Windsor St
Billingham TS23 103 D2
Darlington DL1 133 A4
Hartlepool TS26 77 B5
Middlesbrough TS1 214 C2
Wingate TS29 59 F5
Windsor Terr
Annfield Plain DH9 13 B4
Cornforth DL17 57 E1
Coundon DL14 81 D8
Crook DL15 52 F4
Dipton DH9 12 B7

Windsor Terr *continued*
Great Lumley DH3 25 B7
Haswell DH6 37 F2
Leadgate DH8 11 D4
Murton SR7 28 D2
Peterlee SR8 50 B6
Shildon DL4 81 A1
Windsor Terr S SR7 28 D2
Windward Way TS1,TS2, TS3 215 B4
Windy Bank Rd DL13 194 E8
Windy Hill La TS11 108 E1
Windyside DL13 186 A8
Wingate Ave TS23 102 F7
Wingate Cl DH4 26 D8
Wingate Grange Ind Est TS28 60 D7
Wingate Inf Sch TS28 60 E7
Wingate Jun Sch TS28 60 E7
Wingate La DH6 47 E1
Wingate Rd
Stockton-on-T TS19 117 B7
Wingate TS29 60 A5
Wingate Wlk TS4 140 E6
Wingrove
Rowlands Gill NE39 1 D1
Yarm TS15 156 B6
Wingrove Cl TS28 48 E1
Wingrove Terr DH8 11 D4
Winlaton Care Village NE21 1 F6
Winlaton Cl [2] TS19 117 B7
Winlaton West Lane Com Prim Sch NE21 2 A8
Winpenny Cl TS15 156 E4
Winsford Ct TS17 157 B6
Winslade Ave TS3 120 F4
Winslade Cl SR3 18 B8
Winslow Cres SR7 28 E7
Winster NE38 16 F8
Winston Ave TS23 102 E7
Winston Churchill Cl TS17 138 D4
Winston Ct DL2 200 F7
Winston Dr TS6 121 F2
Winston Gn DH4 17 F8
Winston Rd DL2 200 F7
Winston St
[8] Darlington DL3 132 F2
Stockton-on-T TS18 212 C1
Winter Cl Hartlepool TS25 77 B2
Yarm TS15 156 B3
Winterbottom Ave TS24 64 A2
Winterburn Pl DL5 96 A8
Wintersweet Gdns TS20 117 F7
Winterton Ave TS21 72 B1
Winterton Cotts
Sedgefield TS21 72 B1
Sedgefield TS21 72 B2
Winthorpe Gr TS25 89 D6
Winton Ct NE21 2 C8
Wisbech Cl TS25 89 D5
Wiseman Wlk DL5 96 E8
Wiske Cl TS19 117 B5
Witbank Rd DL3 132 E3
Witham Ave TS16 137 C3
Witham Gr TS25 89 E6
Withernsea Gr SR2 18 D7
Witton Ave DH7 23 C3
Witton Castle* DL14 65 C1
Witton Castle Cvn Pk DL14 65 C1
Witton Cres DL3 132 B5
Witton Ct TS23 102 F5
Witton Dr DL16 56 A2
Witton Garth SR8 49 C3
Witton Gilbert Prim Sch DH7 33 A8
Witton Gr Durham DH1 33 F5
Houghton-le-S DH4 26 C7
Witton Rd Ferryhill DL17 70 B7
Sacriston DH7 23 B2
Witton St DH8 177 D4
Witton Tower Gdns DL14 65 A3
Witton Way DL14 78 E6
Witton-le-Wear Prim Sch DL14 65 B3
WKM Ind Pk DL1 133 B4
Woburn Ave DL3 131 F5
Woburn Dr SR3 18 A6
Woburn Gr
Hartlepool TS25 90 A7
[2] Middlesbrough TS3 140 F8
Woking Cl TS6 141 D7
Wolfe Rd TS20 118 A7
Wollaton Rd TS23 102 F5
Wolseley Cl DH6 57 D8
Wolseley St DL17 70 C4
Wolsey Cl DL5 96 E8
Wolsey Dr TS20 101 E1
Wolsey Rd Seaham SR7 28 E6
Spennymoor DL16 56 B3
Wolsingham Cl TS19 117 B7
Wolsingham Dr
Durham DH1 34 D6
Middlesbrough TS5 139 D4
Thornaby-on-T TS17 138 E5
Wolsingham Prim Sch DL13 207 D6
Wolsingham Rd
Brancepeth DH7,DL15 42 C2
Esh Winning DH7 41 B5
Stanley Crook DL15 40 E1
Tow Law DL13 183 D1
Wolsingham Sch & Com Coll DL13 207 C6
Wolsingham Sta* DL13 207 D4
Wolsingham Terr
Annfield Plain DH9 12 F4
Darlington DL1 133 C3
Wolviston Back La
Billingham TS23 102 F8
Billingham TS23 103 A7
Wolviston Cl DL5 96 B8
Wolviston Ct TS22 102 B5
Wolviston Mill La TS22 102 A6
Wolviston Prim Sch TS22 102 C8
Wolviston Rd
Billingham TS23 102 C5
Hartlepool TS25 77 A3
Wolviston Wlk TS19 117 B7
Wood La Ferryhill DL17 70 A7
Gainford DL2 201 D4
Low Coniscliffe DL2 150 D8
Wood Lea DH5 27 A7
Wood Sq DL14 80 A5
Wood St
Barnard Castle DL12 209 C5
Burnopfield NE16 6 A6
Consett DH8 10 C6
Eston TS6 121 D6
Hartlepool TS24 64 G8
Middlesbrough TS1 215 A4
Pelton DH2 15 E7
Spennymoor DL16 68 C5
Wood Terr NE39 1 A2
Wood View
Esh Winning DH7 31 E1
High Shincliffe DH1 44 F6
Langley Park DH7 32 C7
Loftus TS13 127 C1
Sunderland Bridge DH6 56 B6
Willington DL15 54 A7
Wingate TS29 60 B5
Wood Vue DL16 55 F2
Wood's Terr SR7 28 D3
Wood's Terr E SR7 28 D3
Wood's Terr N SR7 28 D3
Wood's Yd TS12 125 B2
Woodbank Rd TS7 141 B6
Woodbine Ave SR8 49 F8
Woodbine Cl TS9 161 A3
Woodbine Cotts TS23 103 B6
Woodbine Rd DH1 34 A7
Woodbine Terr
Annfield Plain DH9 13 B4
Birtley DH3 9 D4
Greatham TS25 89 E4
New Brancepeth DH7 42 E8
Woodborough La TS19 117 D5
Woodbrook Cl TS11 123 F6
Woodburn DH9 13 C8
Woodburn Cl Blaydon NE21 2 A8
Hemlington TS8 139 E3
Woodburn Dr DL3 151 C8
Woodcock Cl TS6 141 E8
Woodcrest Rd DL3 151 D8
Woodcroft Gdns DL13 206 E2
Woodfield SR8 49 C6
Woodford Cl TS11 108 B2
Woodford Gn TS16 156 C8
Woodford Wlk TS17 138 C3
Woodgarth TS6 121 E2
Woodgate Cl TS25 89 E5
Woodhall Cl DH2 8 E2
Woodhall Gr TS18 137 B8
Woodham Burn Inf Sch DL5 96 C7
Woodham Burn Jun Sch DL5 96 C7
Woodham Com Tech Coll DL5 96 E8
Woodham Ct DH7 20 E4
Woodham Gate DL5 82 D2
Woodham Gn TS19 117 B7
Woodham Rd
Billingham TS23 102 E7
Newton Aycliffe DL5 96 D3
Woodham View DL17 82 F7
Woodham Way DL5 82 C1
Woodhay Ave TS5 139 B8
Woodhouse Close Inf Sch DL14 80 A4
Woodhouse Close Jun Sch DL14 80 A4
Woodhouse La
Bishop Auckland DL14 80 A5
Bishop Auckland, St Helen Auckland DL14 79 D3
Woodhouse Rd TS14 143 C5
Woodhouses DL14 79 D5
Woodhouses La NE16 2 E6
Woodifield Hill DL15 52 C3
Woodland Ave SR8 50 A6
Woodland Cl
Bearpark DH7 33 A3
Trimdon TS29 72 D8
Woodland Cres DH6 58 D5
Woodland Ct DH8 10 D6
Woodland Grange DH4 17 F1
Woodland Mews TS21 85 B8
Woodland Pl DH7 41 E7
Woodland Prim Sch DL13 194 F5
Woodland Rd DL3 132 E3
Woodland St TS18 212 C1
Woodland Terr
Bearpark DH7 33 A3
Darlington DL3 132 D2
Esh Winning DH7 41 E7
Kimblesworth DH2 23 E4
Woodland View
West Rainton DH4 25 F1
West Rainton DH4 26 A1
Wingate TS28 60 D8
Woodland Way TS21 136 A5
Woodlands
Chester le Street DH3 16 C4
Great Lumley DH4 17 F1
Lanchester DH7 20 F3
Seaham SR7 19 A1
Washington NE38 16 E8
Burnopfield NE16 6 B6
Woodlands Ave DH6 47 F2
Woodlands Cl NE39 1 A3
Woodlands Cres DH8 10 D6
Woodlands Ct Crook DL15 53 A3
Darlington DL3 132 D2
Kibblesworth NE11 8 D6
Woodlands Dr
Normanby TS6 141 E8
Yarm TS15 156 D5
Woodlands Gr TS26 76 D6
Woodlands Hospl DL1 134 A1
Woodlands Rd
Barnard Castle DL12 209 D7
Bishop Auckland DL14 80 C7
Consett DH8 10 D6
Esh Winning DH7 41 D8
Middlesbrough TS1 215 A2
Normanby TS6 141 D7
Rowlands Gill NE39 1 D2
Woodlands Terr DH9 12 C7
Woodlands The
Darlington DL3 132 D2
Kibblesworth NE11 8 D6
Nunthorpe TS7 141 B1
Thornaby-on-T TS17 138 C5
Woodlands View [6] DH8 177 E4
Woodlands Way DL2 152 A1
Woodlea
Coulby Newham TS8 140 B1
Lanchester DH7 20 E3
Woodlea Cl DH5 27 A4
Woodlea Prim Sch DH4 17 E1
Woodlea Rd NE39 1 B2
Woodley Gr TS7 141 B5
Woodmans Way NE16 2 F4
Woodmansey Cl SR8 49 B7
Woodmere Rd TS19 212 A4
Woodpack Ave NE16 2 F6
Woodrow Ave
Marton TS7 140 D3
Saltburn-by-t-S TS12 125 B6
Woodrush TS8 159 C7
Woodside
Barnard Castle DL12 209 C7
Beamish DH9 14 F8
Brotton TS12 126 A4
Hutton Rudby TS15 173 F3
Ingleby Barwick TS17 138 B2
Ormesby TS7 140 F7
Redcar TS10 107 D2
Sacriston DH7 23 B2
Shadforth DH6 46 E8
Witton Park DL14 79 B8
Wynyard Village TS22 87 B3
Woodside Ave DH7 33 A3
Woodside Bank DH8 177 F4
Woodside Dr
Consett DH8 177 D4
Darlington DL3 151 E8
Woodside Gdns DH9 14 C3
Woodside Gr
Stockton-on-T TS18 137 C8
Tantobie DH9 6 C3
Woodside La DH4 25 E1
Woodside St TS1 215 B3
Woodside Terr
Chopwell NE17 4 B8
Quaking Houses DH9 13 D2
Woodside View DH7 23 B6
Woodside Wlk NE39 1 C1
Woodstock Terr DL17 71 B4
Woodstock Way TS27 63 C4
Woodstone Terr DH4 17 D1
Woodvale TS8 140 D2
Woodvale Cl TS14 143 F6
Woodvale Rd DL3 151 D8
Woodville Ave TS4 139 F8
Woody Cl DH8 11 C1
Woolcotts Cl TS17 157 B6
Wooler Cres TS23 102 E1
Wooler Rd TS26 76 E6
Wooler St DL1 133 A3
Wooley Dr DH7 33 C1
Wooley Terr DL15 52 F8
Woolsington Dr DL2 153 F8
Worcester Cl DH3 25 A6
Worcester Gdns [5] TS25 77 B3
Worcester Pl DL14 80 B5
Worcester Rd DH1 34 D7
Worcester St TS1 214 B1
Wordsworth Ave
[6] Bishop Auckland DL14 80 B6
Blackhall Colliery TS27 50 C5
Chester le Street DH2 15 E3
Easington Lane DH5 37 D8
Hartlepool TS25 77 A3
Seaham SR7 28 E7
Wheatley Hill DH6 47 F2
Wordsworth Ave E DH5 26 E7
Wordsworth Ave W DH5 26 E7
Wordsworth Cl TS23 102 D8
Wordsworth Ct DL15 52 D8
Wordsworth Gdns DH9 12 D8
Wordsworth Rd
Chilton DL17 82 F8
Wordsworth Rd *continued*
Darlington DL1 152 A7
Easington SR8 39 C4
Eston TS6 121 D3
Wordsworth Vale TS5 139 B6
Works Rd
Middlesbrough TS3 120 D6
Spennymoor DL16 56 B1
Worley Terr DH9 6 A1
Worsall Cl TS15 156 B6
Worsall Gr [5] TS18 117 C1
Worsall Rd TS15 156 B4
Worset Gr [1] TS10 107 E1
Worset La TS26,TS27 76 B8
Worsley Cl TS16 137 D5
Worsley Cres TS7 140 D2
Worthing Ct TS18 213 A2
Worthing St TS18 213 A2
Worthington Cl DL15 52 F3
Worton Cl DH6 48 C7
Worton Dr DL1 152 B7
Wraith Terr Peterlee SR8 49 F8
Ryhope SR2 18 E6
Wray St TS4 215 B3
Wrekenton Cl TS19 117 B7
Wren Ave DL1 133 D6
Wren Cl
Newton Aycliffe DL5 96 F8
Stockton-on-T TS18 212 C2
[9] Washington NE38 9 F3
Wren St Loftus TS13 127 D1
Stockton-on-T TS18 212 C2
Wrensfield Rd TS19 212 C3
Wrentnall Cotts DL13 185 B2
Wrentree Cl TS10 107 D2
Wright Cl DL5 96 C6
Wrightson Ho TS3 120 D1
Wrightson St [4] TS20 118 B7
Wroxham Cl TS19 117 C5
Wroxton Ave TS5 139 C8
Wroxton Cl TS5 139 B8
Wrynose Gdns TS19 212 C3
Wycherley Ave TS5 139 C8
Wycherley Cl TS7 141 B5
Wychgate TS6 122 A2
Wychwood Cl TS17 138 D4
Wycliffe Cl DL5 96 F8
Wycliffe Ct TS15 156 D4
Wycliffe Rd SR7 28 F7
Wycliffe Way DL3 132 A1
Wycombe St DL3 132 F2
Wye Cl TS19 117 B5
Wykeham Ave TS14 143 D2
Wykeham Cl
Billingham TS22 102 A5
Redcar TS10 107 B2
Wykeham Way TS8 140 B3
Wykenham Ct TS12 125 D2
Wykes Cl TS21 85 B6
Wylam Ave DL1 133 C6
Wylam Cl DL4 95 A8
Wylam Rd Stanley DH9 14 A8
Stockton-on-T TS20 118 A7
Wylam St Bowburn DH6 57 D8
Craghead DH9 14 C2
Middlesbrough TS1 214 B2
Wylam Terr Bowburn DH6 57 E6
Stanley DH9 13 F8
Wynd Cl TS15 173 F1
Wynd The Bowes DL12 203 D8
Hutton Rudby TS15 173 F1
Marske-by-t-S TS11 108 D1
Newton Aycliffe DL5 96 E1
Pelton DH2 15 E6
Stainton TS8 139 B1
Wynyard Village TS22 87 C2
Wynde The TS19 117 A5
Wyndley Cl NE16 2 F5
Wynds The DH7 41 D8
Wyndways Dr DH9 5 E1
Wynnstay Gdns TS24 77 A7
Wynyard DH2 16 A3
Wynyard Ct
Newton Aycliffe DL5 96 A8
Thorpe Thewles TS21 100 E3
Wynyard Gr
Coundongate DL14 80 E7
Durham DH1 211 C3
Wynyard Mews TS25 89 E8
Wynyard Rd
Hartlepool TS25 89 D8
Thorpe Thewles TS21 100 E3
Thorpe Thewles TS21 100 F4
Trimdon TS29 72 D8
Wynyard Village TS22 101 E7
Wynyard St
Fence Houses DH4 26 A8
New Silksworth SR3 18 A7
Seaham SR7 29 D5
Stockton-on-T TS20 213 B4
Wynyard Wood TS22 87 A3
Wynyard Woodland Pk TS22 101 B7
Wynyerd Ho TS22 102 C8
Wyverne Ct TS25 77 A1

Y

Yale Cres TS17 213 C2
Yarker La DL12 193 B2
Yarm Back La TS19,TS21 116 F2
Yarm Cl TS25 77 A2
Yarm La Great Ayton TS9 160 C2
Stockton-on-T TS18 213 A2
Yarm Prep Sch TS15 156 B5
Yarm Prim Sch TS15 156 C4
Yarm Rd Darlington DL1 133 D1
Yarm Rd *continued*
Eaglescliffe TS16 137 C3
Hilton TS15 157 E3
Middleton St George DL2 153 F8
Stockton-on-T TS18 137 E7
Yarm Road Ind Est DL1 133 F2
Yarm Sch TS15 156 C6
Yarm St TS18 213 A2
Yarm Sta TS15 156 C3
Yarmouth Cl
Hartlepool TS25 89 E5
Seaham SR7 29 A6
Yarrow Ct DL5 82 D2
Yeadon Gr TS17 138 E5
Yeadon Wlk DL2 153 F8
Yearby Bank TS11,TS14 123 C5
Yearby Cl Eston TS6 121 E1
Middlesbrough TS5 139 B6
Yearby Cres TS11 108 E1
Yearby Rd TS11 123 B6
Yeckhouse La DH7 20 B3
Yellowley Ct DL1 133 C2
Yenton Cl TS23 102 D1
Yeoman St Redcar TS10 107 D6
[7] Skelton TS12 125 C3
Yeoman Terr TS11 108 C1
Yeovil Wlk TS26 76 E8
Yetholm Ave DH2 16 B2
Yew Cl DL16 68 E7
Yew St TS1 214 C3
Yew Tree Ave TS10 107 A2
Yew Tree Gr TS7 140 F4
Yew Wlk The TS21 135 F5
Yewbank Ave DH1 35 B3
Yewtree Ave DL4 81 B1
Yiewsley Dr DL3 132 A2
Yoden Ave SR8 49 F7
Yoden Cres SR8 49 F8
Yoden Ct DL5 96 A8
Yoden Rd SR8 49 D7
Yoden Way Peterlee SR8 49 D6
Peterlee SR8 49 F6
Yohden Prim Sch SR8 50 B6
Yoredale Ave DL3 132 C3
Yoredale Cl TS17 157 B7
Yoredale Dr DL3 132 C3
York Ave Consett DH8 177 A4
Peterlee SR8 49 F7
York Cl DL14 68 C1
York Cres
Billingham TS23 102 E2
Durham DH1 34 E8
Hetton-le-H DH5 26 F4
York Ct
Chester le Street DH3 16 D2
Witton Park DL14 66 A1
York Flatlets [6] TS24 77 B5
York Hill Cres DL16 56 B3
York Hill Rd DL16 56 B3
York Pl [4] Consett DH8 177 A4
Hartlepool TS24 77 F7
York Rd Birtley DH3 9 C1
Brotton TS12 126 C4
Consett DH8 10 C5
Hartlepool TS26 77 B5
Middlesbrough TS5 119 F2
Newton Aycliffe DL5 97 A7
Nunthorpe TS7 141 B3
Peterlee SR8 49 C8
Redcar TS10 106 F7
York Sq [6] DL4 80 F1
York St Annfield Plain DH9 12 F5
Crathorne TS15 172 E3
Darlington DL1 133 B4
Hetton-le-H DH5 26 E1
New Silksworth SR3 18 A8
Stockton-on-T TS18 213 A2
York Terr
Chester le Street DH3 16 D2
[1] Cockfield DL13 195 E3
Willington DL15 53 E3
York Villas DL16 56 B3
Yorkshire Dr DH1 35 D3
Yorkshire Pl DL14 80 B5
Yorkway TS17 213 C1
Young St Durham DH1 211 C3
Hartlepool TS26 77 B6
Yukon Gdns TS4 215 B1

Z

Zetland Ct TS12 125 D7
Zetland Hunt DL5 95 F8
Zetland Mews TS12 125 D7
Zetland Mus* TS10 107 D7
Zetland Pl TS1 215 A4
Zetland Prim Sch TS10 107 D6
Zetland Rd
Barnard Castle DL12 209 D6
Hartlepool TS26 76 F6
Loftus TS13 127 B1
Marske-by-t-S TS11 108 D1
Middlesbrough TS1 215 A4
Redcar TS10 107 F4
Stockton-on-T TS19 117 F5
Zetland Row TS13 127 A4
Zetland St DL3 133 A5
Zetland Terr Loftus TS13 127 B1
New Marske TS11 124 A7
Saltburn-by-t-S TS12 125 C7

Name and Address	Telephone	Page	Grid reference

Addresses

Name and Address	Telephone	Page	Grid reference

NG	NH	NJ	NK
NM	NN	NO	NP
NR	NS	NT	NU
NX	NY	NZ	
SC	SD	SE	TA
SH	SJ	SK	TF TG
SM SN	SO	SP	TL TM
SR SS	ST	SU	TQ TR
SW SX	SY	SZ	TV

Any feature in this atlas can be given a unique reference to help you find the same feature on other Ordnance Survey maps of the area, or to help someone else locate you if they do not have a Street Atlas.

The grid squares in this atlas match the Ordnance Survey National Grid and are at 500 metre intervals. The small figures at the bottom and sides of every other grid line are the National Grid kilometre values (**00** to **99** km) and are repeated across the country every 100 km (see left).

To give a unique National Grid reference you need to locate where in the country you are. The country is divided into 100 km squares with each square given a unique two-letter reference. Use the administrative map to determine in which 100 km square a particular page of this atlas falls.

The bold letters and numbers between each grid line (**A** to **F**, **1** to **8**) are for use within a specific Street Atlas only, and when used with the page number, are a convenient way of referencing these grid squares.

Example   The railway bridge over DARLEY GREEN RD in grid square B1

Step 1: Identify the two-letter reference, in this example the page is in **SP**

Step 2: Identify the 1 km square in which the railway bridge falls. Use the figures in the southwest corner of this square: Eastings **17**, Northings **74**. This gives a unique reference: **SP 17 74**, accurate to 1 km.

Step 3: To give a more precise reference accurate to 100 m you need to estimate how many tenths along and how many tenths up this 1 km square the feature is (to help with this the 1 km square is divided into four 500 m squares). This makes the bridge about **8** tenths along and about **1** tenth up from the southwest corner.

This gives a unique reference: **SP 178 741**, accurate to 100 m.

Eastings (read from left to right along the bottom) come before Northings (read from bottom to top). If you have trouble remembering say to yourself "Along the hall, THEN up the stairs"!

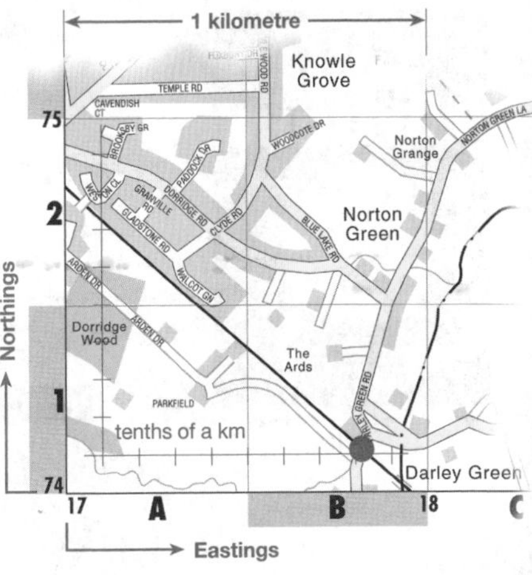